INTERNATIONAL ACCOUNTING STANDARDS

A GUIDE TO PREPARING ACCOUNTS

Third Edition

First Edition 1998
Second Edition 2000

ISBN 1 84140 196 X

British Library Cataloguing-in-Publication Data
A catalogue record for this book is available from the British Library

Typeset by Type Study, Scarborough, North Yorkshire
Printed in Great Britain by William Clowes, Beccles, Suffolk

INTERNATIONAL ACCOUNTING STANDARDS

A GUIDE TO PREPARING ACCOUNTS

Third Edition

Bruce Mackenzie
Senior Editor
and
Andy Simmonds
Assistant Editor
Deloitte & Touche

Deloitte & Touche

www.deloitte.co.uk

ABG Professional Information
40 Bernard Street
London
WC1N 1LD
Tel: 020 7920 8991
Fax: 020 7920 8992
Website: www.abgweb.com

CONTENTS

CHAPTER 4

General requirements for financial statements

CHAPTER 5

Income statement: format and components

CHAPTER 6

Income statement: revenue recognition

CHAPTER 7

Income statement: earnings per share

CHAPTER 8

Equity statement

CHAPTER 9

Balance sheet format

CHAPTER 10

Balance sheet assets

CHAPTER 11

Balance sheet: equity and liabilities

CHAPTER 12

Balance sheet: financial instruments

CHAPTER 13

Cash flow statements

CHAPTER 14

Disclosure: notes to the financial statements

CHAPTER 15

Events after the balance sheet date

CHAPTER 16

Disclosure: segment reporting

CHAPTER 17

Related party disclosures

CHAPTER 18

Consolidated financial statements: business combinations

CHAPTER 19

Consolidated financial statements: subsidiaries

CHAPTER 20

Consolidated financial statements: associates

CHAPTER 21

Consolidated financial statements: joint ventures

CHAPTER 22

Foreign currency

CHAPTER 23

Taxes

CHAPTER 24

Accounting for leases

CHAPTER 25

Employee benefits

CHAPTER 26

Government grants

CHAPTER 27

Construction contracts

CHAPTER 28

Hyperinflationary economies

CHAPTER 29

Interim financial reporting

APPENDIX I

APPENDIX II

Foreword

It has always been difficult to justify the fact that certain transactions are accounted for in totally different ways throughout the world. With the new structure of the International Accounting Standards Board in place, accounting for preparers of IAS financial statements enters a new era. The Board's aim is to ensure that the accounting is the same whether the transaction takes place in Singapore, Sydney, Seattle or Southampton. To achieve this, we face many challenges as we pursue our aim of producing a single set of high quality, global standards.

Throughout the world, standard setters in various jurisdictions are attempting to harmonise national accounting standards with International Standards. The key national players in national accounting standard setting are working closely with the IASB, to achieve high quality standards for cross-border listings. With international standards becoming mandatory for all listed companies within the European Union by 2005, preparers who have never before used IAS will need to take an interest in developments at the IASB.

Whether your financial reports are already prepared under international standards, if you intend to adopt them in the future, or are simply getting ready for future change, this book will bring you up-to-date with all the latest developments in financial accounting. It discusses the restructuring of the International Accounting Standards Board, the EU adoption of the Board's standards, the IOSCO endorsement and the projects to be addressed by the new Board. I think many readers will find the set of model financial statements based on international standards and the financial statement disclosure checklist particularly helpful. These are included as appendices III and IV to the book.

As the IASB faces its new challenges, so too do the people for whom the standards are provided. For current and future preparers and users of international standards, this book is an invaluable guide in preparing financial statements. I warmly recommend it as a useful tool in a complex world.

Sir David Tweedie
Chairman, International Accounting Standards Board

Acknowledgements

The associate authors who have contributed to this book are Phil Barden, Sarah Bate, Elizabeth Buckley, Elizabeth Chrispin, Lisa Crow, Sasha Dorofeyev, Richard Gillin, Tracy Gordon, Chris Griffin, Hugh Harrison, Bruce Mackenzie, Veronica Poole, Claire Richards, Andy Simmonds, Henrietta Thompson, Parizan Trewin and Ken Wild.

The authors would also like to extend their thanks to the technical departments of the following Deloitte Touche Tohmatsu offices for their contributions: Stephen Taylor, Norma Hall and Paul Pacter from Hong Kong; Graeme Berry, Trevor Derwin and Glynnis Carthy from South Africa; Martin Faarborg from Denmark; and Laurence Rivat and Melissa Perry from France.

CHAPTER 1

Introduction

1.1 Purpose

The purpose of the book is to clarify the requirements of International Accounting Standards (IASs) in order to assist preparers, users and auditors of financial statements prepared in accordance with IASs. Comparisons with Generally Accepted Accounting Principles in the UK (UK GAAP) and Generally Accepted Accounting Principles in the US (US GAAP) are made in order to assist in the clarification of the IASs by providing a point of reference rather than to indicate a superior or preferred treatment. These comparisons are high level and not intended to be definitive in establishing all the differences between the relevant reporting frameworks.

1.2 How to use the book

The format of the book has been designed so that a user may look up a topic and find a discussion of all the related IAS guidance and literature in one chapter. Each chapter begins with a brief summary of the requirements and a review of the development of the requirements. The recognition, measurement and disclosure requirements related to the topic are then explained. Illustrative examples and excerpts from published accounts are also included in most chapters to clarify key points.

Matters of interpretation have been specifically identified and are highlighted as shown below:

Although the Framework is much more concise than the UK SOP or the US Concept Statements, it may be referred to more frequently by preparers of financial statements given the less prescriptive nature of IASs in general and the range of topics on which IASs are silent. In such cases, it is appropriate to look to the Framework for guidance.

Where no specific guidance is contained in IAS literature the interpretations represent the opinion of Deloitte & Touche. These interpretations do not necessarily reflect the views of the IASB and therefore are subject to change and interpretation by the IASB or the Standing Interpretations Committee (SIC).

1.3 Contents of this edition

This edition contains explanation and guidance for all International Accounting Standards and Interpretations of the Standing Interpretations Committee issued as of 31 July 2001.

At the time of writing, the new IASB was still in its start-up phase (see Chapter 2). Therefore, there were no outstanding exposure drafts issued by the board at that time. There were, however, draft interpretations outstanding that had been issued by the SIC. These have been referred to in the relevant chapters, and summaries of the outstanding draft interpretations can be found in Appendix I.

IAS also includes three Standards that deal with industry-specific issues. These are:

- IAS 26, *Accounting and Reporting by Retirement Benefit Plans*;
- IAS 30, *Disclosures in the Financial Statements of Banks and Similar Financial Institutions*; and
- IAS 41, *Agriculture.*

Given the specialised nature of these Standards and the limited number of enterprises to which they apply, a summary of their requirements has been presented in Appendix II since further discussion is beyond the scope of this book.

Appendix III contains a set of IAS compliant Model Financial Statements, and Appendix IV contains an IAS Disclosure Checklist.

1.4 References and abbreviations used

References to accounting standards are indicated as follows:

IAS 8 (r1993).14	International Accounting Standard 8 (revised 1993), paragraph 14
IFRS	International Financial Reporting Standard
SIC-2	Standing Interpretations Committee Interpretation No. 2

SIC-D4	Draft Standing Interpretations Committee Interpretation No. 4
Framework.14	Framework for the Preparation and Presentation of Financial Statements, paragraph 14
Insight, Dec.96, p.14	IASC *Insight*, December 1996 edition, page 14
ASB	UK Accounting Standards Board
FRS 8.14	UK Financial Reporting Standard 8, paragraph 14
SSAP 8.14	UK Statement of Standard Accounting Practice 8, paragraph 14
FASB	US Financial Accounting Standards Board
SFAS 8.14	US Statement of Financial Accounting Standards No. 8, paragraph 14
APB 8.14	US Accounting Principles Board Opinion No. 8, paragraph 14

1.5 Items to note about International Accounting Standards

1.5.1 Standard paragraphs

International Accounting Standards currently contain standard paragraphs which are indicated by italic, bold type in the actual Standards and guidance paragraphs which are indicated by normal type. Although the standard paragraphs use the verb, 'should,' the use of this word should not be interpreted as making compliance optional. The standard paragraphs are required to be followed in order for an enterprise to be in compliance with that particular IAS. The guidance paragraphs explain the intention of the standard paragraphs and provide the interpretation of the IASC Board of those paragraphs. These paragraphs form part of the Standards and therefore have the same authority as standard paragraphs. This format is currently under review (see **2.2**).

1.5.2 Use of the word enterprise

International Accounting Standards refer to enterprises. The IASC Framework for the Preparation and Presentation of Financial Statements defines a reporting enterprise as one for which there are users who rely on the financial statements as their major source of financial information about the enterprise. Thus, the term enterprise is very broad and may encompasses both the public and private sector and many forms of legal enterprise.

1.5.3 Benchmark and allowed alternative treatments

During the Improvements project in the late 1980s and early 1990s (see Chapter **2**), when an IAS allowed a choice of accounting treatments for similar transactions, the IASC Board began designating one accounting treatment as the benchmark treatment and the other treatment as the allowed alternative treatment. The Board's intention in making this distinction was not to identify a preferred treatment but merely to identify a point of reference when making its choice between alternatives. An enterprise which complies with the allowed alternative treatment is in compliance with International Accounting Standards, and no reconciliation between amounts calculated under the allowed alternative treatment is required to amounts calculated in accordance with the benchmark treatment. However, particular IASs may require disclosure of the effect of the benchmark treatment if the allowed alternative treatment is chosen. The IASB has established a new improvements project (see **2.5.8**). One of the aims of this project is to evaluate and eliminate the choices in IAS to aid comparability between IAS reporting enterprises.

1.5.4 Reformatting

At the conclusion of the Improvements project, in November 1994, the IASC Board approved reformatted versions of the 18 existing IASs which were not dealt with as part of the project. The reformatting did not involve any substantive changes to the IASs, although the Board did bring certain terminology into line with current IASC practice and update all cross references to the revised IASs.

1.5.5 Materiality

As noted in the Preface to Statements of International Accounting Standards, International Accounting Standards are not intended to apply to immaterial items.

1.5.6 Further advice

Deloitte & Touche would be pleased to advise readers on how to apply the principles set out in this book to their specific circumstances. We recommend that professional advice be obtained, as this book has been written in general terms and therefore cannot be relied on to cover specific situations; application of the principles set out will depend upon the particular circumstances involved.

For IAS news, standard summaries and other helpful information, please consult the Deloitte & Touche IAS website at www.iasplus.com.

1.6 List of IASs, SICs and draft SICs at 31 July 2001

International Accounting Standards

IAS 1 (revised 1997)	Presentation of Financial Statements
IAS 2 (revised 1993)	Inventories
IAS 3	No longer effective (Superseded by IAS 27 and 28).
IAS 4	No longer effective (Superseded by IAS 16, IAS 22 and IAS 38)
IAS 5	No longer effective (Superseded by IAS 1)
IAS 6	No longer effective (Superseded by IAS 15)
IAS 7 (revised 1992)	Cash Flow Statements
IAS 8 (revised 1993)	Net Profit or Loss for the Period, Fundamental Errors and Changes in Accounting Policies
IAS 9	No longer effective (Superseded by IAS 38)
IAS 10 (revised 1999)	Events After the Balance Sheet Date (Effective 1 January 2000)
IAS 11 (revised 1993)	Construction Contracts
IAS 12 (revised 2000)	Income Taxes
IAS 13	No longer effective (Superseded by IAS 1)
IAS 14 (revised 1997)	Segment Reporting
IAS 15	Information Reflecting the Effects of Changing Prices
IAS 16 (revised 1998)	Property, Plant and Equipment
IAS 17 (revised 1997)	Accounting for Leases
IAS 18 (revised 1993)	Revenue
IAS 19 (revised 2000)	Employee Benefit Costs
IAS 20	Accounting for Government Grants and Disclosure of Government Assistance
IAS 21 (revised 1993)	The Effects of Changes in Foreign Exchange Rates
IAS 22 (revised 1998)	Business Combinations

IAS 23 (revised 1993)	Borrowing Costs
IAS 24	Related Party Disclosures
IAS 25	No longer effective (Superseded by IAS 39 and IAS 40)
IAS 26	Accounting and Reporting by Retirement Benefit Plans
IAS 27	Consolidated Financial Statements and Accounting for Investments in Subsidiaries
IAS 28 (revised 2000)	Accounting for Investments in Associates
IAS 29	Financial Reporting in Hyperinflationary Economies
IAS 30	Disclosures in the Financial Statements of Banks and Similar Financial Institutions
IAS 31(revised 2000)	Financial Reporting of Interests in Joint Ventures
IAS 32 (revised 1998)	Financial Instruments: Disclosure and Presentation
IAS 33	Earnings per share
IAS 34	Interim Financial Reporting
IAS 35	Discontinuing Operations
IAS 36	Impairment of Assets
IAS 37	Provisions, Contingent Liabilities and Contingent Assets
IAS 38	Intangible Assets
IAS 39 (revised 2000)	Financial Instruments: Recognition and Measurement (Effective 1 January 2001)
IAS 40	Investment Properties (Effective 1 January 2001)
IAS 41	Agriculture (Effective 1 January 2003)

Interpretations of the Standing Interpretation Committee

SIC-1	Consistency – Different Cost Formulas for Inventories (IAS 2)
SIC-2	Consistency – Capitalisation of Borrowing Costs (IAS 23)
SIC-3	Elimination of Unrealised Profits and Losses on Transactions with Associates (IAS 28)
SIC-5	Classification of Financial Instruments – Contingent Settlement Provisions (IAS 32)
SIC-6	Costs of Modifying Existing Software (Framework)
SIC-7	Introduction of the Euro (IAS 21)
SIC-8	First-Time Application of IASs as the Primary Basis of Accounting (IAS 1)
SIC-9	Business Combinations – Classification either as Acquisitions or Uniting of Interests (IAS 22)
SIC-10	Government Assistance – No Specific Relation to Operating Activities (IAS 20)
SIC-11	Foreign Exchange – Capitalisation of Losses Resulting from Severe Currency Devaluations (IAS 21)
SIC-12	Consolidation – Special Purpose Entities (IAS 27)
SIC-13	Jointly Controlled Entities – Non-Monetary Contributions by Venturers (IAS 31)
SIC-14	Property, Plant and Equipment – Compensation for the Impairment or Loss of Items (IAS 16)
SIC-15	Operating Leases – Incentives (IAS 17)
SIC-16	Share Capital – Reacquired Own Equity Instruments (Treasury Shares) (IAS 32)
SIC-17	Equity – Costs of an Equity Transaction (IAS 32)
SIC-18	Consistency – Alternative Methods (IAS 1)

SIC-19	Reporting Currency – Measurement and Presentation of Financial Statements Under IAS 21 and IAS 29 (IAS 21 and IAS 29)
SIC-20	Equity Accounting Method – Recognition of Losses (IAS 27)
SIC-21	Income Taxes – Recovery of Revalued Non-Depreciable Assets (IAS 12)
SIC-22	Business Combinations – Subsequent Adjustment of Fair Values and Goodwill Initially Reported (IAS 22)
SIC-23	Property, Plant and Equipment – Major Inspection or Overhaul Costs (IAS 16)
SIC-24	Earnings Per Share – Financial Instruments and Other Contracts that May be Settled in Shares (IAS 33)
SIC-25	Income Taxes – Changes in the Tax Status of an Enterprise or its Shareholders (IAS 12)

Draft Interpretations of the Standing Interpretation Committee

SIC-D26	Property, Plant and Equipment – Results of Incidental Operations
SIC-D27	Transactions in the Legal Form of a Lease and Leaseback
SIC-D28	Business Combinations – Measurement of Shares Issued as Purchase Consideration
SIC-D29	Disclosure – Service Concession Arrangements
SIC-D30	Reporting Currency – Translation from Measurement Currency to Presentation Currency
SIC-D31	Revenue – Barter Transactions Involving Advertising Services
SIC-D32	Intangible Assets – Web Site Costs

CHAPTER 2

The International Accounting Standards Board

2.1 Brief history

In 1973, the professional accountancy bodies of Australia, Canada, France, Germany, Japan, Mexico, the Netherlands, the United Kingdom and Ireland and the United States of America founded the International Accounting Standards Committee ('IASC'). According to the Constitution of the IASC, its Objectives were:

> '(a) to formulate and publish in the public interest accounting standards to be observed in the presentation of financial statements and to promote their world-wide acceptance and observance; and
>
> (b) to work generally for the improvement and harmonisation of regulations, accounting standards and procedures relating to the presentation of financial statements.'
>
> – *IASC Constitution*

All of the professional accountancy bodies that are members of the International Federation of Accountants ('IFAC') are members of IASC.

2.1.1 *Restructuring*

In 1997, the IASC Board appointed a Strategy Working Party to assess the objectives of the IASC and the most appropriate structure of the IASC to enable it to meet those objectives. In December 1998, the Strategy Working Party issued a discussion paper entitled *Shaping IASC for the Future.* In November 1999, after extensive consultation, the IASC Board unanimously approved a resolution supporting a proposed new structure. The new structure would establish an independent organisation such as a foundation. This new organisation would have the following main bodies: the Trustees, the Board, the Standing Interpretations Committee and the Standards Advisory Council. Each of these structures is discussed in **2.3** below. The Trustees would appoint the Board members, exercise oversight and raise the funds needed, whereas the Board would have sole responsibility for setting accounting standards.

In 2000, the IASC approved a new constitution that allowed for the changes recommended by the Strategic Working Party. In the same year the IASC Member Bodies approved the restructuring of the Board and the new constitution. Under the new IASB Constitution, the objectives of IASB are:

> '(a) to develop, in the public interest, a single set of high quality, understandable and enforceable global accounting standards that require high quality, transparent and comparable information in financial statements and other financial reporting to help participants in the world's capital markets and other users make economic decisions;
> (b) to promote the use and rigorous application of those Standards; and
> (c) to bring about convergence of national accounting standards and International Accounting Standards to high quality solutions.'
>
> *(New IASB Constitution)*

The Trustees elected Sir David Tweedie as the first chairman of the new restructured IASC Board in June 2000.

In 2001, the Trustees announced the new members of the International Accounting Standards Board (IASB). The Board members, and their backgrounds, are listed in section **2.3.2** below.

From April 2001, the new IASB structure took effect and the first official meeting of the Board was held in London on 18 April 2001.

2.2 Current status of International Accounting Standards

IASs are used by companies, governments, accountancy bodies and Stock Exchanges for a wide range of purposes including company accounts, Stock Exchange listings and national accounting requirements or as a benchmark for development of such requirements. At the first meeting of the IASB in April 2001, the IASB passed a resolution adopting all existing Standards and Interpretations, making clear that the existing pronouncements continue to be applicable unless and until they are amended or withdrawn after formal due process. It was also decided that all new Standards passed by the IASB would be named 'International Financial Reporting Standards'. Existing and amended IAS Standards will not be renamed.

One of the first issues that the new IASB addressed was the Preface to the Standards. The IASB established a project to look at the Preface and make recommendations for changes. At the IASB meeting in July 2001, the Board approved an Exposure Draft which will be published for public comment. This exposure will address, amongst other things, the following points:

- new IASB Standards will be called International Financial Reporting Standards (as detailed above);
- IFRS will apply to general purpose financial statements of profit-oriented entities;
- all paragraphs in the Standards are of equal authority (no more black-letter and grey-letter – see below);
- an objective of the IASB is to reconsider allowed alternatives currently in IASs;
- due process for Interpretations will include negative clearance of Drafts by the IASB as well as approval of final interpretations (at least eight votes required);
- due process for Standards will normally include an advisory group, a discussion document, an exposure draft (at least 8 votes required), and approval of a final Standard (again at least eight votes required);
- both Exposure Drafts and final Standards will include dissenting views of IASB members and a basis for conclusions.

A key issue in the revised Preface will be the relative status of 'grey-letter' paragraphs. At its meetings in April and May 2001, the IASB agreed that paragraphs in bold italic type and plain type have equal authority. Those in bold italic type indicate the main principles while those in plain type explain those main principles or their application in a particular situation. There should be no distinction between the 'black' and 'grey' letter paragraphs in new IASB Standards.

2.2.1 Companies

Many companies, particularly in Europe, are now starting to comply with IASs in their annual financial statements. The growing number of companies across the world who choose to implement IASs illustrates the increasing acceptance of IASs as an appropriate benchmark for comparison of company accounts across national boundaries. By using IAS as their basis of preparation, companies are enhancing their comparability.

2.2.2 Governments

In developing countries, IASs, with some minor modifications to suit local needs, are often adopted as national accounting requirements by the government or appropriate accountancy body. Other countries allow IASs as either the primary or alternative framework under which local companies may prepare accounts.

2.2.3 European Union

By 1 January 2005, all companies listed on Stock Exchanges within the European Union will be required to prepare consolidated accounts using accounting standards issued by the IASB. This change in EU policy will herald a new era of financial reporting within Europe as companies will begin to prepare financial statements using the same accounting framework and underlying accounting standards.

History of EU developments

In June 2000, the European Commission ('EC') communicated its recommendations on the implementation of International Accounting Standards to the Council and the European Parliament. In its recommendations document, titled 'EU Financial Reporting Strategy: the Way Forward', the Commission stated its intention to submit legislation to the European Parliament that would make it mandatory for all EU listed enterprises (including banks and insurers) to prepare consolidated financial statements in accordance with International Accounting Standards (IASs). Individual Members States will be allowed to extend the requirement to unlisted enterprises and separate financial statements. Implementation of the strategy, including the new accounting requirements, is expected to be effective, at the latest, from 1 January 2005. However, the Commission encourages earlier application of IASs. This Regulation was proposed by the European Commission in February 2001.

The EC announcement said:

> 'The Regulation would help eliminate barriers to cross-border trading in securities by ensuring that company accounts throughout the EU are more transparent and can be more easily compared. This would in turn increase market efficiency and reduce the cost of raising capital for companies. The proposal is a priority measure under the Financial Services Action Plan, endorsed by the Lisbon European Council as a key element of the creation of an integrated financial services market. It is also in line with the strategy outlined in the Commission's June 2000 Communication on the future of financial reporting in Europe.'

There has been no directive on unlisted companies, and national standard setters will be free to choose the accounting framework for these companies.

European Financial Reporting Advisory Group (EFRAG)

The EC Regulation proposed to establish a new EU mechanism to:

> 'assess IAS and give them legal endorsement for use within the EU. This mechanism will use an Accounting Regulatory Committee set up under the proposal that will operate at the political level under established EU rules on decision-making by regulatory committees. The Accounting Regulatory Committee, chaired by the Commission and composed of representatives of the Member States, will adopt or reject IAS on the basis of a proposal made by the Commission.'

In March 2001, a large group of organisations representing the European accounting profession, preparers, users, and national standard setters proposed to organise a private-sector structure that would:

(a) provide input to the IASB; and
(b) assess IAS and SIC Interpretations.

The Proposal describes the latter process as 'endorsement'. The structure would be known as EFRAG: the European Financial Reporting Advisory Group. The proposal envisages a two-tier structure:

(1) An accounting technical committee of 'highly-qualified technical experts' drawn from national standard setters, the accountancy profession, preparers and users, limited in size; and
(2) A Supervisory Board of European Organisations 'to guarantee representation of the full European interest and to enhance the legitimacy and credibility of EFRAG.

In June 2001, the European Financial Reporting Advisory Group appointed the Technical Expert Group and the Supervisory Board to serve as Europe's 'IAS Endorsement Mechanism'. The EFRAG Supervisory Board will monitor the work of the Technical Expert Group and ascertain that the individual members work in the European interest. EFRAG will operate independently of each of the European organisations involved. EFRAG was operational from September 2001.

The four main functions of the Technical Expert Group are as follows:

- Proactive contribution to the work of the IASC: proactive coordination of European standard setters, the accounting profession, users and preparers so as to contribute to and influence the IASB standard-setting process efficiently. The mechanism should normally provide the IASB with submissions on any discussion paper or exposure draft issued by the IASB or SIC (Standing Interpretations Committee). It would also contribute to the development of technical and conceptual papers on emerging topics that would be brought to the attention of the IASB.
- Initiating changes to the EU Accounting Directives: to help the Commission in their assessment of possible non-conformity of an IAS or SIC with EU Accounting Directives and recommending appropriate changes to the Directives.
- Technical assessment of the IASC Standards and Interpretations: confirming or conversely rejecting a Standard or Interpretation for application in the EU.
- Implementation guidance: identifying issues for which the IASB general interpretation guidance (i.e., SIC Interpretations) is not sufficient to

ensure consistent application of a given Standard in the EU. The mechanism would communicate such situations to the IASB and urge it to identify appropriate solutions. Also, in cooperation with European securities markets supervisors, the mechanism would develop implementation guidance specifically relevant to EU listed companies.

2.2.4 Accountancy bodies

In many countries, national standard setting-bodies promulgate national accounting standards. During the 1990s, the IASC strengthened its ties with these standard setters. With increasing frequency, IASC is undertaking joint projects with standard setters in Australia, Canada, New Zealand, the United Kingdom and the United States (known, for historical reasons dating back to before New Zealand joined the group, as the G4+1 Group of standard setters) with the aim of increasing harmonisation in areas that both the IASC and the national standard setters are considering. In addition, when national standard setters are developing new national standards, they are considering the analogous IASs and have become less inclined to adopt approaches that are vastly different from those of the IASC. At its meeting in London in January 2001, the G4+1 group of standard setters agreed that as the new IASB was ready to start its activities, the G4+1 group would disband and cancel its planned future activities. The projects that the groups were busy with have been submitted to the IASB as potential projects.

Even though the G4+1 has disbanded, the national standard setters will still play an active role in the IASB. Seven leading national accounting standard setters have an IASB member resident in their jurisdiction. The IASB constitution envisages a 'partnership' between the IASB and these national bodies. At the May IASB meeting, the Board met with the chairs of those national accounting standard setters having an IASB liaison member in residence.

In addition, all IASB members have contact responsibilities with national standard setters not having a liaison member resident in their jurisdiction, and many of those countries are represented on the Standards Advisory Council (see **2.3.4**).

2.2.5 Stock Exchanges and securities regulators

Currently, Stock Exchanges in London, Frankfurt, Zurich, Luxembourg, Thailand, Johannesburg, Hong Kong, Amsterdam and Rome and EASDAQ all accept, in certain circumstances, financial statements for foreign registrants prepared in accordance with IASs. The large Stock Exchanges that currently do not accept IASs without reconciliation for foreign registrants are those in Canada, Japan and the USA. However, Stock Exchanges in these countries, as well as many others, are members of the International Organisation of Securities Commissions (IOSCO).

IOSCO endorsement

The IASC has worked closely with the IOSCO in the past. In 1995, the IASC Board and the IOSCO Technical Committee announced a work programme based around a set of 'core standards' and agreed that once IASC completed the work programme, the IOSCO Technical Committee would consider recommending that its members accept financial statements prepared in accordance with IAS in documents used for cross-border filings and listings. In March 1999, the IASC substantially completed the 'core standards' and the Technical Committee of IOSCO began its assessment. This assessment was focused on whether the core standards were of sufficiently high quality to warrant permitting foreign issuers to use them to access a country's capital markets as an alternative to domestic standards. In March 2000, they concluded their work and recommended to the IOSCO Technical Committee that IOSCO endorse IASC Standards for the purpose of multinational offerings and cross-border listings. The Technical Committee approved that recommendation in May 2000 and submitted it to the IOSCO President's Committee for adoption.

The President's Committee recommended that IOSCO members permit incoming multinational issuers to use the 30 IASC 2000 Standards to prepare their financial statements for cross-border offerings and listings, as supplemented in the manner described below in the 'supplemental treatments' where necessary to address outstanding substantive issues at a national or regional level.

The supplemental treatments are:

- reconciliation: requiring reconciliation of certain items to show the effect of applying a different accounting method, in contrast with the method applied under IASC standards;
- disclosure: requiring additional disclosures, either in the presentation of the financial statements or in the footnotes; and
- interpretation: specifying use of a particular alternative provided in an IASC standard, or a particular interpretation in cases where the IASC standard is unclear or silent.

In addition, as part of national or regional specific requirements, waivers may be envisaged of particular aspects of an IASC standard, without requiring that the effect of the accounting method used be reconciled to the effect of applying the IASC method. The use of waivers should be restricted to exceptional circumstances such as issues identified by a domestic regulator when a specific IASC standard is contrary to domestic or regional regulation. The concerns identified and the expected supplemental treatments are described in the Assessment Report.

US SEC and Canadian CSA

In February 2000, the US Securities and Exchange Commission (SEC) issued a concept release titled *International Accounting Standards.* The release primarily addressed the acceptability of the IOSCO endorsed IASC Core Standards for US listings. The SEC received 93 responses to its request for comments on the paper. The majority of US respondents supported the current requirement of reconciliation to US GAAP, while the majority of non-US respondents supported the elimination of the reconciliation and the acceptance of IAS as a basis for preparing accounts for US exchanges.

The SEC is still evaluating the responses and will thereafter develop a way forward.

A similar discussion paper has been released by the Canadian Securities Administration (CSA). Currently Canadian companies are required to prepare accounts under Canadian GAAP. Foreign-based companies are required to provide a reconciliation of their national GAAP to Canadian GAAP. The paper proposes allowing companies, both local and foreign, to prepare accounts using Canadian GAAP, US GAAP, IAS or any other proposed GAAPs, with no requirement for reconciliation.

2.3 Organisation

2.3.1 Trustees

In May 2000, the first Nominating Committee of the IASC appointed the first Trustees of the new IASC structure. The Trustees comprise 19 individuals with six from North America, six from Europe, four from the Asia Pacific region and three from other areas. The aim of the mix was to establish a geographical balance of all interested parties.

The Trustees are responsible for appointing the members of the International Accounting Standards Board (IASB), the Standing Interpretations Committee and the Standards Advisory Council. The Trustees are also responsible for, amongst other things, the IASC budget, promotion of IASs, establishing and amending operating procedures, amendments to the constitution, and reviewing the strategy and effectiveness of the IASC. The full responsibilities of the Trustees are set out in the IASC constitution.

2.3.2 IASB

The IASB is made up of 14 Board members, each with one vote. The Trustees are responsible for the appointment of the Board members. The IASB constitution provides that:

> 'The foremost qualification for membership of the Board shall be technical expertise. The Trustees should select members of the Board so that the Board will comprise a group of people representing, within that group, the best available combination of technical skills and background experience of relevant international business and market conditions in order to contribute to the development of high quality, global accounting standards.'
>
> *(New IASB Constitution para 24)*

The Board is made up of 12 full-time and two part-time members. In order to achieve balance on the Board, the new constitution provides the Board should be made up of five auditors, three preparers of financial statements and at least one academic. There are no requirements in the new constitution for the remaining two Board members.

In terms of the new constitution, the Board shall:

> '(a) have complete responsibility for all IASC technical matters including the preparation and issuing of International Accounting Standards and Exposure Drafts, both of which shall include any dissenting opinions, and final approval of Interpretations by the Standing Interpretations Committee;
>
> (b) publish an Exposure Draft on all projects and normally publish a Draft Statement of Principles or other discussion document for public comment on major projects;
>
> (c) have full discretion over the technical agenda of IASC and over project assignments on technical matters. In organising the conduct of its work, the Board may outsource detailed research or other work to national standard setters or other organisations;
>
> (d) *(i)* establish procedures for reviewing comments made within a reasonable period on documents published for comment, *(ii)* normally form Steering Committees or other types of specialist advisory groups to give advice on major projects, *(iii)* consult the Standards Advisory Council on major projects, agenda decisions and work priorities and *(iv)* normally issue bases for conclusions with International Accounting Standards and Exposure Drafts;
>
> (e) consider holding public hearings to discuss proposed standards, although there is no requirement to hold public hearings for every project; and
>
> (f) consider undertaking field tests (both in developed countries and in emerging markets) to ensure that proposed standards are practical and workable in all environments, although there is no requirement to undertake field tests for every project.'
>
> *(New IASB Constitution para 36)*

The first Board under the new structure was announced by the Trustees in January 2001 and comprises:

- *Sir David Tweedie, Chairman*
  Sir David Tweedie served as the first full-time Chairman of the UK Accounting Standards Board, with a term from 1990 to 2000. He has worked on international standards setting issues both as the first Chairman of the G4+1, a cooperative group among leading standard setters, and as a member of the previous IASC Board.

- *Thomas E Jones, Vice-Chairman*
  Former Principal Financial Officer of Citicorp and Chairman of the IASC Board.
- *Mary Barth*
  As a part-time Board member, Mary Barth will retain her position as a Professor of Accounting at the Graduate School of Business at Stanford University.
- *Hans-Georg Bruns – Liaison to German Standard Setter*
  Hans-Georg Bruns has served as the Chief Accounting Officer for DaimlerChrysler and has been head of a principal working group of his home country's German Accounting Standards Committee.
- *Anthony T Cope*
  Tony Cope joined the US Financial Accounting Standards Board in 1993. Prior to that engagement, Mr Cope, worked as a financial analyst in the USA for 30 years, ultimately becoming Director of Fixed Income Research, Wellington Management Co. in Boston.
- *Robert P Garnett*
  Robert Garnett is the Executive Vice-President of Finance for Anglo American plc, a South African company, listed on the London Stock Exchange.
- *Gilbert Gelard – Liaison to French Standard Setter*
  Gilbert Gelard has extensive experience with French industry. He served as a Deputy CFO with Groupe Hachette from 1973 to 1982 and Deputy Group Comptroller with Elf Aquitaine from 1982 to 1987.
- *Robert H Herz*
  Robert Herz, as a part-time member of the Board, will continue to be a partner at PricewaterhouseCoopers where he has been in charge technical and professional matters in the USA and in the Americas.
- *James J Leisenring – Liaison to the US Standard Setter*
  Jim Leisenring has worked on issues related to accounting standards setting over the last three decades, as the Vice-Chairman and most recently as Director of International Activities of the US Financial Accounting Standards Board (FASB) in his home country.
- *Warren McGregor – Liaison to Australian and New Zealand Standard Setters*
  Warren McGregor developed an intimate knowledge of standard-setting issues with his work over 20 years at the Australian Accounting Research Foundation, where he ultimately became the Chief Executive Officer.
- *Patricia O'Malley – Liaison to Canadian Standard Setter*
  Patricia O'Malley currently serves as Chair of the Accounting Standards Board of Canada.
- *Harry K Schmid*
  Harry Schmid brings over 40 years of experience as a preparer of financial statements for Nestlé, ultimately becoming Senior Vice-President at its headquarters, responsible for corporate reporting.

- *Geoffrey Whittington – Liaison to UK Standard Setter*
  Geoffrey Whittington is the PricewaterhouseCoopers Professor of Financial Accounting at Cambridge University and formerly served as a member of the UK Monopolies and Merger Commission. He has served as a member of the UK Accounting Standards Board in his native England.
- *Tatsumi Yamada – Liaison to Japanese Standard Setter*
  Mr Yamada brings extensive experience with international standard setting as a Japanese member of the previous IASC board between 1996 and 2000, of which he became an Executive Committee member in 2000.

2.3.3 Standing Interpretations Committee

In 1997, the Standing Interpretations Committee ('SIC') was formed to consider, on a timely basis, accounting issues that are likely to receive divergent or unacceptable treatment in the absence of authoritative guidance. (SIC Operating Procedures) The Committee reviews such issues in light of existing IASs and the Framework for the Preparation and Presentation of Financial Statements ('the Framework') and concentrates on issues of broad importance to users and preparers of financial statements as opposed to very specific issues which affect a relatively small number of companies. It reviews areas where current practice is considered inappropriate as well as new or emerging issues that may not have been considered when existing standards were formulated.

The Committee is comprised of 12 members with representatives of IOSCO and the EC acting as observers. In addition, some Board members are appointed as Board liaison members and attend SIC meetings as observers. In the spirit of harmonisation, the Committee works with other, similar national bodies such as the US Emerging Issues Task Force and the UK Urgent Issues Task Force to ensure that differences in interpretation will be minimised where possible.

At its meeting with its Standards Advisory Council on 23 July, the IASB presented a paper that proposed major changes to the structure of the Standing Interpretations Committee (SIC). These were:

(1) **Name of Committee and output**: It is proposed to change the Committee name to emphasise the changes occurring within the IASC and the relationship of the Committee with the IFRS. The new Committee will be known as the International Financial Reporting Issues Committee (IFRIC). The proposal also plans to extend the mandate of the IFRIC (see below).

    It is also proposed to change the output from 'Interpretations' to 'Abstracts'. It is believed that this too will reflect the change in the mandate. This change is in line with other standard setters' 'interpretative' committees, and will aid in convergence. The US EITF and UK UITF both release 'Abstracts'.

(2) **Mandate**: It has been proposed that the scope of the IFRIC's activities be broadened to allow the IFRIC to address issues beyond interpretations of existing standards. This will allow IFRIC to answer questions that would otherwise be answered by external parties, and could result in divergent practices. SAC members raised concerns that there would be conflicts between the IASB and the IFRIC agendas. SAC members also expressed concerns that the new IFRIC would be setting new 'mini standards' with the same status as IFRS. These would all be fed back into the project.

(3) **Members and Chairman**: It is proposed that the new IFRIC will have 12 members and a non-voting chairman. It is proposed that the Chairman be non-voting in order that the 12 members of IFRIC can concentrate on the technical issues, and the Chairman can deal with the running of the meeting. The Chairman will be either an IASB liaison member, senior IASB staff member or outside party. It is most likely to be a senior member of the IASB staff. SAC members expressed concerns over a non-voting Chairman. It was also proposed that the Big Five firms should all have a permanent seat on IFRIC as they see the practical issues daily. These comments will be fed into the proposal Committee to be presented to the Trustees.

(4) **Procedures**: An Agenda Committee will be formed to consider and make recommendations on proposed IFRIC agenda items. This will increase IFRIC efficiency and work as a screening process for issues submitted by the public to IFRIC. Sources of questions posed to the committee will remain confidential. The Agenda Committee will make recommendations on an agenda, but the final decision will be with the IFRIC.

The proposal introduces a review process by the IASB of Draft Abstracts. These will take the form of negative clearance. It is felt that this is important, as it is futile to issue a draft abstract that the IASB is opposed to at an early stage. Final approval of an Abstract will be given in a public meeting of the IASB by voting.

Other recommendations set out in the draft paper are as follows:

- there should be a principle-based approach to the guidance to be issued;
- the proposed IFRIC structure will also have the ability to reconsider a member's membership should they not attend meetings regularly;
- the proposal makes provision for meeting electronically; these must still be public meetings;
- issues where consensus is not reached within three meetings will be automatically referred to the Board;

- regular IFRIC review of the mandate and operating procedures;
- the IFRIC will meet every two months.

2.3.4 Standards Advisory Council

The Standards Advisory Council (SAC) is composed of 43 regional representative members and five international organisation members. It will provide a forum for organisations and individuals with an interest in international financial reporting to participate in the standard setting process. The SAC will normally meet three times each year (at meetings open to the public) to:

- advise the Board on priorities in the Board's work;
- inform the Board of the implications of proposed standards for users and preparers of financial statements; and
- give other advice to the Board or to the Trustees.

Key criteria for selecting SAC members are geographic diversity, diversity of professional backgrounds, representation of key interests at stake, and the ability to provide advice to the Board on technical standard-setting issues. Standards Advisory Council members are not paid, and they will normally be expected to be associated with organisations that will meet the costs of their participation in meetings, although exceptions may be made for certain individuals. The Constitution mandates that the IASB Chairman serves as the Chairman of the Standards Advisory Council. The Deputy Chairman of SAC will chair the meetings of the SAC and coordinate its agenda. Peter Wilmot, Chairman of the South African Accounting Practices Board, was appointed Deputy Chairman of the SAC at the first meeting of the SAC in July 2001.

On 25 June 2001, the IASC Trustees announced the appointment of 49 persons to the SAC. The 49 members include chief financial and accounting officers from some of the world's largest corporations and international organisations, leading financial analysts and academics, regulators, accounting standard setters and partners from leading accounting firms. They come from six continents, 29 countries and five international organisations. Additionally, the European Commission, the US Securities and Exchange Commission, and the Financial Services Agency of Japan will participate as observers.

On 23 July 2001, the SAC met for the first time in London. The two day meeting allowed SAC members to make introductory comments and discuss the SIC (see **2.3.3**), the preface (see **2.2**) and the IASB agenda (see **2.5**).

2.3.5 IASB staff

The IASB staff is based in London and includes Jim Saloman, Technical Director (Kevin M Stevenson has been appointed Director of Technical

Activities and will take over those responsibilities from Jim Saloman from the beginning of 2002), Wayne S Upton, Director of Research, and 15 technical staff. There are also supporting administration staff and a publications department.

2.4 Due process

The following make up the steps in the IASB's due process.

Step 1:	Agenda Decision The IASB meets with the SAC and national standard setters and appoints a project to the IASB Technical Agenda.
Step 2:	Advisory Group and Project Staff The Board may appoint an Advisory Group to aid in the project. This Group may include industry representatives and specialists with a vested interest in the development of a specific Standard. Project management is assigned to the IASB Staff.
Step 3:	Discussion Document The staff, along with the Advisory Group if one is appointed, may draft a discussion document for the Board. This document may be published by the Board for public comment, but this is not mandated.
Step 4:	Exposure Draft An Exposure Draft is prepared by the Staff and submitted to the Board for approval. An Exposure Draft requires eight of the 14 Board members' approval before it is released for public comment. Exposure Drafts are generally published with a comment period of 90 days.
Step 5:	Comments Received Comments are received and analysed by the staff, and submitted to the Board for discussion. Changes to the Exposure Draft are considered and a draft Standard submitted to the Board.
Step 6:	International Financial Reporting Standard The draft Standard is discussed by the Board and voted on section by section, and finally in its entirety. A Standard requires approval by eight of the 14 Board members before it is published as a final IFRS.

2.5 IASB Agenda

After consultation with the Standards Advisory Council, national accounting standard setters, regulators, and other interested parties, the IASB announced its Technical Agenda. The projects that the IASB aims to address are divided as follows.

The first set of projects are where the IASB aims to provide leadership and promote convergence, and include:

- accounting for insurance contracts;
- business combinations;
- performance reporting;
- accounting for share-based payments.

The second set of projects aims to provide easier adoption and application of IFRS. These projects are important especially in light of the adoption of IAS across EU member countries by 2005. They include:

- guidance on first-time application of International Financial Reporting Standards;
- activities of financial institutions: disclosure and presentation.

The third set of projects aims to improve existing IAS/IFRS and include:

- preface to International Financial Reporting Standards;
- improvements to existing International Financial Reporting Standards;
- amendments to IAS 39 (r2000), *Financial Instruments: Recognition and Measurement.*

These projects are the main projects that the new Board will address. Each of these is summarised below.

In addition to these projects, the IASB has identified 16 other issues which it aims to address. These will be covered in conjunction with national standard setting bodies around the world. These projects are:

- accounting measurement;
- accounting for extractive industries;
- accounting for financial instruments: a comprehensive project;
- accounting for leases;
- accounting for small and medium entities and in emerging economies;
- accounting for taxes on income;
- business combinations: phase two;

- consolidation policy;
- definitions of elements of financial statements;
- derecognition issues: other than those addressed in IAS 39 (r2000);
- employee benefits;
- impairment of assets;
- intangible assets;
- liabilities and revenue recognition;
- management's discussion and analysis;
- revaluation of certain assets.

Information on the progress of these projects can be found at www.iasplus.com (maintained by Deloitte Touche Tohmatsu).

2.5.1 Accounting for Insurance Contracts

The project focuses on accounting for insurance contracts rather than all aspects of accounting by insurance companies. An issues paper was published in December 1999. The Insurance Steering Committee is developing a Draft Statement of Principles (DSOP) (a kind of pre-exposure draft) that will take into account the views expressed in the responses to the issues paper.

The IASB has asked the Steering Committee to complete its work on the Draft Statement of Principles.

Among the most important factors affecting the direction of the insurance project is that the deliberations and resolution of the Financial Instruments Project is viewed by the IASB as a long-term project. Prior to this view, the Insurance Steering Committee's tentative conclusions on accounting for insurance contracts were all in the assumed context of a future Standard that would require full fair value for financial instruments.

What does this mean for the insurance project? The Steering Committee is urging the IASB to continue focusing on the insurance project in light of the European Commission's proposal that listed companies follow International Accounting Standards by 2005. Therefore, the Steering Committee has decided to propose to the IASB a 'non-fair value' version of the asset/liability model for accounting for insurance contracts. This model includes measuring insurance liabilities on a prospective basis and is referred to as the 'entity-specific value' (representing the value of an insurance liability to the enterprise that holds it – which may reflect factors that are not available (or not relevant) to other market participants). The Steering Committee further recommends that fair value of insurance contracts be considered as the IASB contemplates full fair value for financial instruments.

The Steering Committee aims to finalise the DSOP by October 2001 and report to the IASB, which will then decide how to progress the project. The

IASB staff, with the support of Steering Committee members, will continue work on finalising the draft DSOP (including especially the sections on participating contracts, presentation and disclosure). The Steering Committee Chairman has asked the IASB to authorise field visits to a number of insurers late in 2001. These field visits have been approved by the Board at its September 2001 meeting in London.

2.5.2 Business combinations

Business combination accounting is an area of considerable divergence across jurisdictions. The IASB has identified four aspects of a project on business combinations that need to be addressed. These are:

(a) **Scope of the project**
Issues likely to be included in the project are:
  (i) the method, or methods, of accounting for business combinations;
  (ii) definitions of such terms as business combination, joint ventures and transactions among entities under common control;
  (iii) acquired intangible assets other than goodwill;
  (iv) goodwill. Amortisation and impairment testing;
  (v) negative goodwill. Definition, recognition, and amortisation;
  (vi) acquisition provisions;
  (vii) in-process research and development. Ascertaining if it a recognisable intangible asset and, if not, whether it should be charged as an expense at acquisition or included in goodwill;
  (viii) improvements. There are some business combinations issues under consideration in the improvements project. These could be addressed in this project;
  (ix) disclosures and transition.

(b) **Definitions**
The reason that definitions of the term's business combinations, joint ventures, and transactions among entities under common control are important is because those definitions determine whether particular transactions do or do not come under the scope of IAS 22 (r1998).

(c) **Methods of accounting for business combinations**
Three methods under consideration are:
  (i) purchase method;
  (ii) pooling of interests method; and
  (iii) fresh start method.

The Board discussed these methods and tentatively agreed that they should not introduce a new method, but should firstly look at the methods currently in IAS 22 (r1998), *Business Combinations.* The board also tentatively agreed that the only method that should be allowed is the purchase method.

(d) **Acquired intangible assets**
This aspect of the project would focus on intangible assets other than goodwill acquired in a business acquisition. At its July meeting, the IASB tentatively agreed that an intangible asset that either exists as a result of contractual or legal right, or is separable from the business, should be recognised as an intangible asset when determining the fair value of acquired assets in a business combination. This intangible would be separate asset and not included as part of goodwill.

2.5.3 Performance reporting

The IASB project on reporting financial performance is considering whether to move in a similar direction, or perhaps even more in the direction of a recent G4+1 study which recommended that financial performance should be presented in one financial statement rather than two or more statements. The G4+1 study. also recommended that:

- recycling should not generally be permitted (note the word 'generally');
- the category of extraordinary items should be abolished;
- abnormal or exceptional items should not be reported as a separate category of revenue or expenses;
- results of continuing and discontinued operations should be segregated; and
- changes in accounting policy should be reported by retrospectively applying the new policy with restatement of prior periods.

A Steering Committee is developing a Draft Statement of Principles. The following are some of the tentative decisions made by them:

- There should be a single statement of 'recognised income and expenses' which should report all increases or decreases in net assets of the enterprise, other than those increases or decreases arising from transactions with owners in their capacity as owners.
- No recycling between the 'new' statement and the statement of shareholders' equity.
- The statement would comprise three sections: business activities, financing activities and investing activities. The aim is to align these categories with those of the cash flow statement.
- Items recognised under accrual accounting conventions and those representing fair value adjustments would be differentiated.
- Income taxes, discontinuing operations and the cumulative foreign exchange translation account will be reported separately.
- Capital transactions will be reported in a separate statement of shareholders' equity.
- IAS 8 (r1993), *Net Profit or Loss for the Period, Fundamental Errors and Changes in Accounting Policies*, would be revised to require retrospective

restatement in prior periods for all errors and changes in accounting policy. Extraordinary items will be abolished.

2.5.4 *Accounting for share-based payments*

This project would seek to develop a Standard on all aspects of accounting for share-based payments to employees (including employee stock options), suppliers, creditors and others. This project would result in a new Standard providing guidance in this area. There is no existing IAS addressing recognition and measurement. IAS 19 (r2000), *Employee Benefits*, requires some disclosures.

The IASB has identified two fundamental issues that the project would need to address:

- Should a transaction paid for in shares be accounted for the same way as a transaction paid for in cash?
- If so, how should it be measured?

A paper will be presented and discussed with the SAC at its next meeting. The IASB are analysing the responses received by the national standard setters around the world who exposed the G4+1 paper as well as the comments received by the IASC. This project provides the IASB with an opportunity to provide leadership and a basis for convergence. At the IASB meeting in September 2001, the Board decided to re-issue the G4+1 discussion paper with an extended deadline for comments to be submitted.

2.5.5 *Guidance on first-time application of International Financial Reporting Standards*

In SIC-8, *First-Time Application of IASs as the Primary Basis of Accounting*, the Standing Interpretations Committee concluded:

> 'In the period when IASs are applied in full for the first time as the primary accounting basis, the financial statements of an enterprise should be prepared and presented as if the financial statements had always been prepared in accordance with the Standards and Interpretations effective for the period of first-time application. Therefore, the Standards and Interpretations effective for the period of first-time application should be applied retrospectively, except when:
> (a) individual Standards or Interpretations require or permit a different transitional treatment; or
> (b) the amount of the adjustment relating to prior periods cannot be reasonably determined.'

Concerns have been raised about that interpretation and other issues related to first-time application of International Accounting Standards, particularly because of the European Commission proposal that all EU listed enterprises apply IAS by 2005. At its May 2001 meeting, the IASB considered a paper that identified a number of issues relating to the first-time application of IAS. Some of the issues identified were interpretive, while others were problems that had arisen in practice where compliance with the requirements of IAS as directed by SIC-8 resulted in significant costs, perhaps beyond that contemplated by the SIC and IASC when they approved SIC-8.

In theory, SIC-8 achieves complete comparability between enterprises, both between first-time adopters of IAS and those entities already applying IAS, and across all entities using IAS. However, the degree of comparability is subject, in part, to the availability of alternatives in some Standards and to determinations made about exemptions written into individual Standards and the overall exemption in SIC 8.3(b) that retrospective application is not required when 'the amount of the adjustment relating to prior periods cannot be reasonably determined'. In the context of some of the practical application problems raised in the May Board paper, different enterprises converting to IAS might make very different interpretations of what is practicable or reasonably determinable, especially where the costs of compliance are very high.

IASB will address this significant and urgent issue in a separate project and will develop a separate Standard which is intended to provide easier application of IFRS, while retaining a conceptually sound solution when adopting IAS for the first time.

2.5.6 Activities of financial institutions: disclosure and presentation

This project is considering possible revisions to the presentation and disclosure requirements of IAS 30, *Disclosures in the Financial Statements of Banks and Similar Financial Institutions*, particularly in light of developments in the industry and the issuance of IAS 1 (revised 1997), *Presentation of Financial Statements*, and IAS 39 (r2000), *Financial Instruments: Recognition and Measurement.*

Entities likely to be included in this project include:

- banks and other financial institutions that take deposits, grant credit, provide other lending or financing services, and provide investment services;
- consolidated financial statements that include at least one subsidiary that is a bank or similar financial institution, even if the parent company is not a bank or similar financial institution.

This project will address the issues raised by the Steering Committee considering the changes to IAS 30. The project aims to update existing disclosure requirements relating to the business activities of banks, and extend the scope of the new/revised Standard to include other institutions whose business is to take deposits, grant credits or provide other financing or investment services. Both the Basle Committee and various financial institutions are supporting the project. The Steering Committee will continue its work and draft an Exposure Draft for the Board. While this Standard will supersede the existing IAS 30, it is likely that the presentation and disclosure provisions of IAS 32 (r1998) and IAS 39 (r2000) would generally continue to apply to banks and similar financial institutions. Since this project does not address recognition and measurement issues, IAS 39 (r2000) would continue to apply in that area.

2.5.7 Preface to International Financial Reporting Standards

The existing Preface to Statements of International Accounting Standards sets out, among other things:

- the objectives of IFRS;
- the definition of financial statements;
- the definition of accounting standards;
- the scope of accounting standards;
- IASB operating procedures (including advisory groups, discussion documents, Exposure Drafts and Standards, and voting);
- the authority of IFRS.

Unfortunately, the Preface is out of date in light of the IASB's structure and operating procedures under the new Constitution. At its July 2001 Board meeting the IASB approved an Exposure Draft of a revised Preface to IASB Standards for a public comment period of 90 days. Among other things, the proposal will suggest that:

- new IASB Standards will be called International Financial Reporting Standards;
- IFRS will apply to general purpose financial statements of profit-oriented entities;
- all paragraphs in the Standards are of equal authority (no more black-letter and grey-letter);
- an objective of the IASB is to reconsider allowed alternatives;
- due process for interpretations will include negative clearance of Drafts by the IASB as well as approval of final interpretations (at least eight votes required);
- due process for Standards will normally include an advisory group, a discussion document, an exposure draft (at least eight votes required), and approval of a final Standard (again at least eight votes required);
- both EDs and final Standards will include dissenting views of IASB members and a basis for conclusions.

2.5.8 Improvements to existing International Accounting Standards

In the late 1980s the IASC undertook a project to improve existing IASs and to reduce the number of alternative treatments permitted for like transactions. The Standards amended were IAS 2, 8, 9, 11, 16, 18, 19, 21, 22, and 23 and they became effective for financial statements covering periods beginning on or after 1 January 1995. The project became known as the comparability and/or improvements project. It was during this project that the old IASC Board began designating benchmark and allowed alternative treatments.

Under the new IASB, it has been proposed that the existing IASC Standards will undergo another round of improvements. This project covers a variety of issues related to identifying problems with implementing existing IASC Standards. The issues addressed are those that have been identified by various sources as narrow issues of substance whose resolution could improve the quality of the IASC Standards and/or increase convergence of national and international standards. Also included are issues for which an IASC standard allows explicit or implicit alternative treatments. The issues could be addressed in a large single project or a group of sub-projects. Sources of improvements issues include IOSCO, national standard setters, international accounting firms and the SIC/IFRIC.

Potential topics for improvements fall broadly into six categories:

(1) elimination of choices (explicit or implicit);
(2) elimination of conceptual inconsistencies between IASs;
(3) additional guidance;
(4) additional disclosure;
(5) drafting improvements;
(6) improvements in the structure.

The IASB has received over 40 responses to its request for ideas for possible improvements to IASs totalling over 1,000 pages. The IASB has appointed a subcommittee of IASB members (Robert Herz, Gilbert Gelard, James Leisenring and Warren McGregor) to consider all proposed improvements.

2.5.9 Amendments to IAS 39, Financial Instruments: Recognition and Measurement

This project would consider limited revisions to IAS 39 (r2000), *Financial Instruments: Recognition and Measurement,* based on issues identified by IASB constituents and the IAS 39 Implementation Guidance Committee. This would be a limited-scope project; it would not address derecognition issues, which the IASB may deal with in a separate future project.

2.6 Communication with the IASB

For additional information related to the IASB, the IASB website is updated regularly and is an excellent source of information. The relevant addresses are as follows:

Internet:	www.iasb.org.uk
E-mail:	iasb@iasb.org.uk
Address:	International Accounting Standards Board First Floor, 30 Cannon Street London EC4M 6XH United Kingdom
	IASB Publications Department 166 Fleet Street London EC4A 2DY United Kingdom

CHAPTER 3

The Framework

3.1 Sources

The Framework for the Preparation and Presentation of Financial Statements.

IAS 1 (r1997) *Presentation of Financial Statements.*

3.2 Evolution of the Framework

In 1989, the IASC issued the Framework for the Preparation and Presentation of Financial Statements ('the Framework'). The Framework establishes the broad set of accounting principles on which future IASs and any revisions to existing IASs will be based. The concept of the Framework as a foundation on which to build future accounting standards is similar to the purpose envisaged for the US FASB Statements of Financial Accounting Concepts ('US Concepts Statements') and the UK ASB Statement of Principles for Financial Reporting ('UK SOP'). The FASB issued six US Concepts Statements in the late 1970s and early 1980s with an additional Concepts Statement issued in February 2000. Since the Framework was developed subsequent to the majority of the US Concepts Statements, the IASC Board was able to 'build' on them by addressing many of the same topics included in the US Concepts Statements but adapting the discussion for the international environment.

Similarly, the ASB added the Statement of Principles project to its agenda subsequent to the issuance of the majority of the US Concepts Statements and the Framework. Thus, the UK SOP builds on the Framework and the US Concepts Statements by covering similar topics adapted to the UK environment but also by adding new topics such as the remeasurement of assets or liabilities, derecognition principles, presentation of financial information and the reporting entity.

3.3 Purpose

According to the Framework, its purposes are to:

'(a) assist the Board of IASC in the development of future International Accounting Standards and in its review of existing International Accounting Standards;
(b) assist the Board of IASC in promoting harmonisation of regulations, accounting standards and procedures relating to the presentation of financial statements by providing a basis for reducing the number of alternative accounting treatments permitted by International Accounting Standards;
(c) assist national standard-setting bodies in developing national standards;
(d) assist preparers of financial statements in applying International Accounting Standards and in dealing with topics that have yet to form the subject of an International Accounting Standard;
(e) assist auditors in forming an opinion as to whether financial statements conform with International Accounting Standards;
(f) assist users of financial statements in interpreting the information contained in financial statements prepared in conformity with International Accounting Standards; and
(g) provide those who are interested in the work of IASC with information about its approach to the formulation of International Accounting Standards.'

(Framework.1)

3.4 Status

Similar to the UK SOP and the US Concepts Statements, the Framework does not have the status of an accounting standard and does not override any IAS where conflicts may arise. As the IASB continues to reduce the number of alternative accounting treatments permitted under IASs, the number of conflicts between IASs and the Framework is expected to decrease.

Although the Framework is much more concise than the UK SOP and the US Concepts Statements, it may be referred to more frequently by preparers of financial statements given the less prescriptive nature of IASs in general and the range of topics on which IASs are silent. In such cases, it is appropriate to look to the Framework for guidance.

3.5 Scope

The Framework applies to the general purpose financial statements of both public and private enterprises. A full set of financial statements prepared in accordance with the Framework generally contains a balance sheet, an income statement, a statement of changes in financial position (since the revision of IAS 7, referred to as a cash flow statement) and any notes or schedules which form an integral part of the financial statements.

Note that IAS 1 (r1997) requires an additional primary financial statement, the statement of changes in equity, which presents the gains and losses not currently presented in the income statement. See Chapter **8** for further discussion of this primary statement. Any additional information provided with the accounts such as reports of the directors or remuneration committee are not within the scope of the Framework.

3.5.1 Comparison with UK GAAP

The UK SOP identifies similar primary statements as those identified in the Framework, but in addition, requires a statement of total recognised gains and losses which may be similar to the statement of changes in equity required by IAS 1 (r1997).

Following the ASB's discussion paper *Reporting Financial Performance: Proposals for Change*, FRED 22 *Reporting Financial Performance* was issued for comment in December 2000. FRED 22 makes suggestions for amendments to FRS 3, *Reporting Financial Performance.* The most significant proposal is that financial performance should be reported in a single statement – effectively combining the profit and loss account with the statement of total recognised gains and losses (STRGL).

FRED 22 proposes a single statement for reporting financial performance which would present all changes in equity, other than those arising from transactions with shareholders as owners, and divide items into three main components of financial performance:

(a) the results of operating (or trading) activities;
(b) the results of financing and other treasury activities; and
(c) other gains and losses.

In general, the first two components correspond to the profit and loss account, while the third largely comprises items currently reported in the statement of total recognised gains and losses.

3.5.2 Comparison with US GAAP

While not listing specific statements which make up the financial statements, US Concepts Statement No. 5, *Recognition and Measurement in Financial Statements of Business Enterprises*, ('US Concepts Statement 5') essentially identifies the same three primary statements as the Framework as well as a reconciliation of stockholders' equity and a statement of comprehensive income. While US Concepts Statement 5 states that a full set of financial statements should show comprehensive income, US Concepts Statements are not accounting standards and until recently, no requirement existed for the disclosure of comprehensive income. In June 1997, the FASB issued SFAS 130, *Reporting Comprehensive Income*, which establishes standards for the reporting and display of comprehensive income and its components.

3.6 Users of financial statements

The Framework and the UK SOP both identify the following users of financial statements: investors, employees, lenders, suppliers and other trade creditors, customers, governments and their agencies and the public. Neither document indicates that the needs of one set of users are paramount but both explain that financial statements that meet the needs of investors will generally meet the needs of other users as well.

3.7 Topics covered

It is beyond the scope of this book to give full details and discussion of each topic covered in the Framework. The following sections summarise briefly the topics included in the Framework and draw comparisons with the analogous parts of the UK SOP and the US Concepts Statements.

3.8 Objective of financial statements

The Framework states that, 'the objective of financial statements is to provide information about the financial position, performance and changes in financial position of an enterprise that is useful to a wide range of users in making economic decisions.' (Framework.12)

3.8.1 Comparison with UK GAAP

This objective is very similar to that in the UK SOP except that the UK SOP adds the objective that information should be useful in assessing the stewardship of management.

The Framework acknowledges that financial statements do show the results of the stewardship of management but concludes that users who assess this stewardship are doing so in order to make economic decisions about the enterprise rather than as an end in itself. Thus, while this objective is not stated explicitly in the Framework as it is in the UK SOP, it is encompassed in the objectives set by the Framework.

The objective also refers to providing information about changes in financial position, whilst that in the UK SOP does not. However, it is clear from both documents that it is expected that such information will be provided.

3.8.2 Comparison with US GAAP

US Concepts Statement No. 1, *Objectives of Financial Reporting by Business Enterprises* ('US Concepts Statement 1'), defines similar objectives to those of the Framework but, in addition, states that financial reporting should provide information to help present and potential investors and creditors and other users in assessing the amounts, timing, and uncertainty of future cash flows. (CON 1.37) IAS 1 (r1997) revisits the objectives of financial statements and increases the emphasis on helping the users of financial statements in predicting the enterprise's future cash flows and the timing and certainty of those cash flows.

3.9 Underlying assumptions

The two underlying assumptions of financial statements prepared under IASs are that they are prepared on a going concern basis and under the accruals basis of accounting. The going concern basis assumes that an enterprise will be in operation 'for the foreseeable future' rather than for a specific period of time. The Framework does not prohibit a basis other than that of going concern but notes that where the going concern assumption is inappropriate, the alternate basis of accounting adopted must be disclosed.

Consistent with the Framework, IAS 1 (r1997) requires management to make an assessment when financial statements are being prepared of an enterprise's ability to continue as a going concern. The guidance in IAS 1 (r1997) indicates that management should consider all available information for the foreseeable future, which should be at least, but is not limited to, twelve months from the balance sheet date. (IAS 1 (r1997).24) See **4.7.3** and **4.7.4** for further discussion of the going concern and accruals concepts.

3.9.1 Comparison with UK GAAP and US GAAP

Similarly, in the UK, FRS 18, *Accounting Policies*, requires the use of the accruals basis of accounting and, except in specified circumstances, the going concern assumption and disclosure of the circumstances surrounding any departure from the latter. In the US, US Concepts Statement 1 states that the accruals basis of accounting and the going concern assumption are generally the most relevant bases for most financial statements and financial statement users.

3.10 Qualitative characteristics of financial statements

'Qualitative characteristics are the attributes that make the information provided in financial statements useful to users.' (Framework.24) The Framework identifies the four primary qualitative characteristics of financial statements as understandability, relevance, reliability and comparability. It also defines and explains the relationships between the primary qualitative characteristics and secondary characteristics including the relationships between relevance and materiality; and reliability and faithful representation, substance over form, neutrality, prudence and completeness.

3.10.1 Comparison with UK GAAP

The UK SOP identifies the same four primary characteristics as the Framework.

The concept of a true and fair view, which is fundamental to UK GAAP, is not directly dealt with in the Framework. However, the Framework does note that if the qualitative characteristics and IASs are applied properly, a true and fair view of the information presented should result. As discussed more fully in the next chapter, IAS 1 (r1997) has built on this concept and only permits departures from IASs in extremely rare circumstances.

3.10.2 Comparison with US GAAP

US Concepts Statement No. 2, *Qualitative Characteristics of Accounting Information*, sets out a hierarchy of qualities with usefulness for decision making as the primary quality.

3.11 Elements of financial statements

The Framework provides definitions of the elements of financial statements. These definitions should be applied in conjunction with the recognition criteria set out later in the Framework and not in isolation as the definitions may encompass items which fail to meet the recognition criteria and thus should not be recognised in the financial statements. The following definitions are included in the Framework:

Asset	'a resource controlled by the enterprise as a result of past events and from which future economic benefits are expected to flow to the enterprise.'
Liability	'a present obligation of the enterprise arising from past events, the settlement of which is expected to result in an outflow from the enterprise of resources embodying economic benefits.'

Equity 'the residual interest in the assets of the enterprise after deducting all its liabilities.'

Income 'increases in economic benefits during the accounting period in the form of inflows or enhancements of assets or decreases of liabilities that result in increases in equity, other than those relating to contributions from equity participants.'*

Expenses 'decreases in economic benefits during the accounting period in the form of outflows or depletions of assets or incurrences of liabilities that result in decreases in equity, other than those relating to distributions to equity participants.'*

(Framework.49 & 70)

*Revaluations or restatements of assets and liabilities may meet the definitions of income or expenses. However, they are not included in the income statement and the Framework states that such items are included in equity as capital maintenance adjustments or revaluation reserves.

3.11.1 Comparison with UK GAAP

The definitions above are broadly similar to those in the UK SOP although the UK SOP uses the terms ownership interest, gains and losses rather than equity, income and expenses. It is important to note that the definitions of income and expenses and gains and losses in both the Framework and the UK SOP are very wide and encompass both revenue and expenses arising in the normal course of operations and other types of gains and losses.

3.11.2 Comparison with US GAAP

US Concepts Statement No. 6, *Elements of Financial Statements*, ('US Concepts Statement 6') defines assets, liabilities and equity in similar terms to those used above. However, unlike the Framework and the UK SOP, US Concepts Statement 6 provides separate definitions of comprehensive income and its components, revenues, expenses, gains and losses.

3.12 Recognition of the elements of financial statements

Recognition is the process whereby an item is incorporated into the financial statements. The Framework identifies the following two criteria which must be met for an item which meets the definition of an element to be recognised:

(a) it is probable that any future economic benefit associated with the item will flow to or from the enterprise; and
(b) the item has a cost or value that can be measured with reliability.

(Framework.83)

However, an item which does not meet the recognition criteria but is relevant to the financial statements may still need to be disclosed. For example, if the amount of a contingent liability that exists at the balance sheet date cannot be reliably measured, the existence and nature of the liability, the information relevant to a user of the financial statements, would need to be disclosed as required by IAS 10 (r1999), *Events After the Balance Sheet Date* (see Chapter **15**).

The Framework identifies the matching principle as appropriate for the recognition of expenses. Thus, when economic benefits arise over a period of time, the related expenses are systematically recognised over the same period of time. However, expenses are recognised immediately if no future benefit exists.

In addition, application of the matching concept does not allow the recognition of items in the balance sheet which do not meet the definition of assets and liabilities. This recognition issue is addressed and clarified in IAS 37, *Provisions, Contingent Liabilities and Contingent Assets*, in respect of provisions and contingent liabilities.

3.12.1 Comparison with UK GAAP

The initial recognition criteria set out in the UK SOP are substantially the same as those set out in the Framework. Additionally, the UK SOP distinguishes between two different stages of recognition: initial recognition and remeasurement. The remeasurement of assets is covered in various IASs and is discussed in Chapter **10**.

3.12.2 Comparison with US GAAP

Similar to the Framework, US Concepts Statement 5 includes in its recognition criteria reliable measurement but also adds the criteria of relevance and reliability. While the inflow or outflow of future economic benefit is not a specific criterion in US Concepts Statement 5, this concept is included in the US definitions of each element of the financial statements.

3.13 Measurement of the elements of financial statements

Measurement is the process whereby the monetary amount at which items will be recognised in the income statement or carried in the balance sheet is determined. (Framework.99) The Framework distinguishes four measurement bases which are often used in financial reporting: historical cost, current cost, realisable (settlement) value and present value. IASs do not require that one measurement basis is chosen. In fact, the Framework recognises that the most widely adopted approach to financial reporting is a combination of historical cost with other bases.

The IASB currently has a project on Measurement on its agenda. This project will be all embracing as it has an effect not only on measurement of assets and liabilities but also on performance reporting (where changes in value are of a capital or income nature). This project will most likely result in a change to the Framework.

3.13.1 Comparison with UK GAAP and US GAAP

Similarly, the UK SOP concludes that no one basis of measurement can fulfill all the needs of the users of financial statements and that the use of a combination of bases is appropriate. US Concepts Statement 5 also anticipates that the use of a variety of measurement bases is likely to continue.

In recent years, the use of discounting when measuring assets and liabilities has become more frequently prescribed in individual accounting standards issued by IASC, the ASB and the FASB. In order to establish basic principles around discounting methodology for use in future standards, each standard setter has added a project on discounting to its agenda. In April 1997, the ASB published a Working Paper, *Discounting in Financial Reporting*, and in June 1997, the FASB published a proposed Concepts Statement, *Using Cash Flow Information in Accounting Measurement.* Based on comments received, the FASB revised its proposals, issued a further exposure draft in March 1999 and issued US Concepts Statement 7, *Using Cash Flow Information and Present Value in Accounting Measurements* in February 2000. The IASC adopted a project on discounting in April 1998 and its successor, the IASB, is expected continue the work started by the IASC.

3.14 Concepts of capital and capital maintenance

The Framework distinguishes between the financial and physical concepts of capital but does not indicate a preference for either.

CHAPTER 4

General requirements for financial statements

4.1 Source

The Framework for the Preparation and Presentation of Financial Statements.

IAS 1 (r1997)	*Presentation of Financial Statements.*
SIC-8	*First-Time Application of IASs as the Primary Basis of Accounting.*
SIC-18	*Consistency – Alternative Methods.*
SIC-19	*Reporting Currency – Measurement and Presentation of Financial Statements Under IAS 21 and IAS 29 (effective 1 January 2001).*

4.2 Brief summary of requirements

IAS 1 (r1997) prescribes the basis for presentation of general purpose financial statements in order to ensure comparability both with the enterprise's own financial statements of previous periods and with the financial statements of other enterprises.

It sets out overall considerations for the presentation of financial statements, guidelines for their structure and minimum requirements for the content of financial statements. The presentation requirements of specific financial statements are discussed in this book in Chapters **5**, **8**, **9**, **13** and **14**.

SIC-8 requires compliance with all effective Standards and Interpretations when an enterprise adopts IASs as the primary basis of reporting for the first time. It requires transitional adjustments to be recorded in the opening balance of retained earnings of the earliest period presented, and prescribes how to apply the transitional provisions of individual Standards in the period of first-time application of IASs.

SIC-18 requires consistent application of chosen accounting policies where a choice is permitted by the relevant IAS.

SIC-19 requires an enterprise to determine a currency for measuring items in its financial statements (the 'measurement currency'). It also states that an enterprise may choose to present its financial statements in a different currency (the 'presentation currency').

4.3 Development of requirements

The Presentation project was one of the projects identified by IOSCO as part of the core standards required in order to recommend IASs for acceptance by stock exchanges for cross-border listings (see Chapter **2**). Prior to IAS 1 (r1997), presentation was addressed in several IASs including, among others, IAS 1, IAS 5, IAS 13, and IAS 7 (r1992). However, these standards, excepting IAS 7 (r1992), *Cash Flow Statements*, did not dictate one format for financial statements to follow. They, along with other IASs, focused on the accounting information to be disclosed within financial statements rather than on the format of the statements. IAS 1 (r1997) replaced IAS 1, IAS 5 and IAS 13.

In July 1998 the Standing Interpretations Committee issued Interpretation No. 8 (SIC-8) which contains guidance for enterprises that apply IASs for the first time. SIC-8 became effective on 1 August 1998.

In January 2000, the Standing Interpretations Committee issued Interpretation No. 18 (SIC-18) which requires consistent application of chosen accounting policies where IASs permit such a choice. SIC-18 is effective for financial periods beginning on or after 1 July 2000.

In November 2000, the Standing Interpretations Committee issued Interpretation No. 19 (SIC-19) which requires an enterprise to determine a currency for measuring items in its financial statements (the 'measurement currency'). It also states that an enterprise may choose to present its financial statements in a different currency (the 'presentation currency'). SIC-19 is effective for periods beginning on or after 1 January 2001.

In April 1997, the IASC agreed in principle to undertake a review of the way in which performance is measured and reported. In July 1999, this project was added to the Board's agenda. It will be based on a Position Paper developed by the G4+1 group of accounting standard setters (since disbanded) of which the IASC was a member. The most significant proposal of the G4+1 Position Paper, *Reporting Financial Performance: Proposals for Change*, is that financial performance should be reported in a single statement – effectively combining the profit and loss account with the statement showing changes in equity. The statement would divide items into three main components:

- the results of operating (or trading) activities;
- the results of financing and other treasury activities; and
- other gains and losses.

The IASB staff is preparing a report on this subject in the form of a Draft Statement of Principles for consideration by the IASB, and the requirements included in IAS 1 (r1997) relating to the components of financial statements may change in due course.

4.4 Scope

IAS 1(r1997) applies to all reporting enterprises. However:

- for enterprises falling under the scope of IAS 30, *Disclosures in the Financial Statements of Banks and Similar Financial Institutions*, the additional presentation requirements of that IAS apply; and
- for enterprises without a profit objective, such as charities, some of the line item descriptions or the titles of the statements presented may need to be modified.

IAS 1 (r1997) applies to the presentation of all general purpose financial statements prepared in accordance with IASs, including statements presented in annual reports and prospectuses. It does not apply to interim condensed financial statements.

The requirements of IAS 1 (r1997) apply equally to financial statements of consolidated and individual enterprises. However, IAS 1 (r1997) 'does not preclude the presentation of consolidated financial statements complying with International Accounting Standards and financial statements of the parent company under national requirements within the same document, as long as the basis of preparation of each is clearly disclosed in the statement of accounting policies.' (IAS 1 (r1997).2) This practice is followed in several countries in continental Europe.

4.5 Responsibility for financial statements

> 'The board of directors and/or other governing body of an enterprise is responsible for the preparation and presentation of its financial statements.'
>
> (IAS 1 (r1997).6)

However, IAS 1 (r1997) does not contain a requirement for a statement of this fact in the financial statements.

In certain countries, directors are required to disclose the fact that they take responsibility for the financial statements as part of their corporate governance disclosures. Even though these disclosures do not form part of the relevant accounting standards, corporate governance disclosures are required by the relevant securities exchanges.

An enterprise is required to disclose the date when the financial statements were authorised for issue and who gave that authorisation. It is important for users to know when the financial statements were authorised for issue, as the financial statements do not reflect events after that date. If the enterprise's owners or others have the power to amend the financial statements after issuance, that fact is also disclosed. (IAS 10 (r1999) *Events After the Balance Sheet Date*, para 16-17)

4.6 Components of financial statements

A full set of financial statements prepared in accordance with IASs includes the following components:

(a) a balance sheet;
(b) an income statement;
(c) a statement showing either:
  (i) all changes in equity; or
  (ii) changes in equity other than those arising from capital transactions with owners and distributions to owners;
(d) a cash flow statement; and
(e) accounting policies and explanatory notes.

(IAS 1 (r1997).7)

Although at present International Accounting Standards only cover information included within the financial statements, enterprises are encouraged to present additional information about the enterprise outside of the financial statements.

The IASB has added a potential project to its research agenda on Management Discussion and Analysis (MD&A). Although it will probably be a long-term project it indicates the new IASB's intention to extend its reach to matters beyond the traditional financial statements.

4.7 Overall considerations

4.7.1 Fair presentation and compliance with International Accounting Standards

Over the past several years, as more companies have adopted IASs, a practice has emerged of companies either stating compliance with IASs when a brief examination of such financial statements reveals departures, or stating compliance with IASs with exceptions for particular IASs. Due to a lack of enforcement powers, these violations are difficult for the IASB to address. In addition, it is not the role of IASB to enforce correct use of IASs.

However, with the rise of cross-border listings in recent years, regulatory bodies of the major international stock exchanges are becoming increasingly concerned with such misleading assertions. In the US, representatives of the Securities and Exchange Commission have stated that foreign 'registrants preparing financial statements in accordance with home-country GAAP, and in its footnotes asserting that the financial statements 'comply in all material respects, with' or 'are consistent' with IASs will be challenged by the Staff, when the Staff believes the assertion to be untrue. Where the assertion cannot be sustained, the Staff will require either the statement to be removed, or include the necessary adjustments to the financial statements to make the statement factually supportable.'[1]

The views of the IASB about such practices are clearly evident in IAS 1 (r1997). IAS 1 (r1997) requires that in order for an enterprise to present fairly its financial statements in accordance with IASs, it must comply with *all* IASs. An enterprise is permitted not to follow a particular IAS only in the extremely rare circumstances when compliance would be misleading. To emphasise the importance of these requirements, they have been reproduced below:

> 'Financial statements should present fairly the financial position, financial performance and cash flows of an enterprise. The appropriate application of International Accounting Standards, with additional disclosure when necessary, results, in virtually all circumstances, in financial statements that achieve a fair presentation.'
>
> (IAS 1 (r1997).10)
>
> 'A fair presentation requires:
>
> (a) selecting and applying accounting policies in accordance with paragraph 20 (see **4.7.2**);
>
> (b) presenting information, including accounting policies, in a manner which provides relevant, reliable, comparable and understandable information; and

[1] Taken from a case study presented by an SEC staff member, Donald J. Gannon, at the AICPA Annual National Conference on Current SEC Developments on 8–9 December 1998.

(c) providing additional disclosures when the requirements in International Accounting Standards are insufficient to enable users to understand the impact of particular transactions or events on the enterprise's financial position and financial performance.'

(IAS 1 (r1997).15)

'An enterprise whose financial statements comply with International Accounting Standards should disclose that fact. Financial statements should not be described as complying with International Accounting Standards unless they comply with *all* the requirements of each applicable Standard and each applicable Interpretation of the Standing Interpretations Committee.'

(IAS 1 (r1997).11) [emphasis added]

As referred to above, an enterprise is required to disclose compliance with IASs (when this is the case). Although the placement of the statement is not prescribed, such disclosure would naturally fit in the accounting policies section of the financial statements.

'Inappropriate accounting treatments are not rectified either by disclosure of the accounting policies used or by notes or explanatory material.'

(IAS 1 (r1997).12)

'In the extremely rare circumstances when management concludes that compliance with a requirement in a Standard would be misleading, and therefore that departure from a requirement is necessary to achieve a fair presentation, an enterprise should disclose:

(a) that management has concluded that the financial statements fairly present the enterprise's financial position, financial performance and cash flows;
(b) that it has complied in all material respects with applicable International Accounting Standards except that it has departed from a Standard in order to achieve a fair presentation;
(c) the Standard from which the enterprise has departed, the nature of the departure, including the treatment that the Standard would require, the reason why that treatment would be misleading in the circumstances and the treatment adopted; and
(d) the financial impact of the departure on the enterprise's net profit or loss, assets, liabilities, equity and cash flows for each period presented.'

(IAS 1 (r1997).13)

'The existence of conflicting national requirements is not, in itself, sufficient to justify a departure in financial statements prepared using International Accounting Standards.'

(IAS 1 (r1997).14)

'Departure is not appropriate simply because another treatment would also give a fair presentation.'

(IAS 1 (r1997).16)

'When assessing whether a departure from a specific requirement in International Accounting Standards is necessary, consideration is given to:

(a) the objective of the requirement and why that objective is not achieved or is not relevant in the particular circumstances; and
(b) the way in which the enterprise's circumstances differ from those of other enterprises which follow the requirement.'

(IAS 1 (r1997).17)

Comparison with UK GAAP

Under UK GAAP, the concept of a true and fair override is similar to the concept outlined above under which departures from IASs are permitted only in the extremely rare circumstances in which it would be misleading for an enterprise to follow the requirements of a particular IASs.

Comparison with US GAAP

Under US GAAP, no option for an override of the requirements of accounting pronouncements exists.

4.7.2 Accounting policies

Management selects and applies the accounting policies of an enterprise so that the financial statements comply with all the requirements of each applicable International Accounting Standard and interpretation of the Standing Interpretations Committee. However, given the limited number of IASs, situations will inevitably arise when no IAS exists in a particular area. Where this is the case, management adopts accounting policies which provide information that is:

> '(a) relevant to the decision-making needs of users; and
> (b) reliable in that they:
>   (i) represent faithfully the results and financial position of the enterprise;
>   (ii) reflect the economic substance of events and transactions and not merely the legal form;
>   (iii) are neutral, that is free from bias;
>   (iv) are prudent; and
>   (v) are complete in all material respects.'
>
> (IAS 1 (r1997).20)

Essentially, this standard requires that accounting policies be selected that meet the four primary qualitative characteristics of financial statements established in the Framework (see Chapter **3**). This requirement appears appropriate as logically, if management follows guidance in the Framework in an area where no IAS exists, it will be following a similar method to that used by the IASB if it were addressing the issue.

In addition to the primary qualitative characteristics, management considers:

> '(a) the requirements and guidance in International Accounting Standards dealing with similar and related issues;
> (b) the definitions, recognition and measurement criteria for assets, liabilities, income and expenses set out in the IASC Framework; and
> (c) pronouncements of other standard setting bodies and accepted industry practices to the extent, but only to the extent, that these are consistent with (a) and (b) of this paragraph.'
>
> (IAS 1 (r1997).22)

Examples, where the use of pronouncements of other standard setting bodies or accepted industry practises may be appropriate, include specific accounting policies used in insurance, extractive/mining, oil and gas, and other industries which are currently not covered by IASs. At the moment, the only three industry specific Standards within IASs are IAS 26 on accounting and reporting by retirement benefit plans, IAS 30 which deals with disclosures in the financial statements of banks and other financial institutions and IAS 41 dealing with agriculture.

When, in accordance with specific provisions in that Standard, an International Accounting Standard is applied before its effective date, that fact is required to be disclosed. (IAS 1 (r1997).19)

4.7.3 Going concern

Financial statements are normally prepared on the going concern basis. However, management has a responsibility when preparing financial statements to make an assessment of an enterprise's ability to continue as a going concern to ensure that this basis is appropriate. In general, the going concern assumption is appropriate unless management either intends to liquidate the enterprise or to cease trading, or has no realistic alternative but to do so. (IAS 1 (r1997).23)

When making its assessment management considers budgeted profitability, debt repayment schedules, potential replacement financing, etc. Such information should cover a period of not less than twelve months from the reporting date.

> 'When management is aware, in making its assessment, of material uncertainties related to events or conditions which may cast significant doubt upon the enterprise's ability to continue as a going concern, those uncertainties should be disclosed. When the financial statements are not prepared on a going concern basis, that fact should be disclosed, together with the basis on which the financial statements are prepared and the reason why the enterprise is not considered to be a going concern.'
>
> (IAS 1 (r1997).23)

However, conformity with the going concern assumption does not need to be disclosed. The assumption is that the company prepares the accounts under the going concern basis unless otherwise indicated. Events after the balance sheet date form an important part of the evidence which management considers when making the assessment of an enterprise's ability to continue as a going concern. These events may indicate whether the whole or part of the enterprise is no longer a going concern.

IAS 10 (r1999), *Events After the Balance Sheet Date*, advises that deterioration in operating results and financial position after the balance sheet date may indicate a need to consider whether the going concern assumption is still appropriate. If that assumption is no longer appropriate that Standard requires a fundamental change in the basis of accounting, rather than an adjustment to the amounts recognised within the original basis of accounting. See Chapter **15** for further discussion.

An example of financial statements prepared on a basis other than going concern is financial statements of a company in liquidation where it may be more appropriate to measure long-term assets at the net realisable value or liquidation value rather than historical cost or revalued amounts.

4.7.4 *Accruals basis of accounting*

IAS 1 (r1997) requires that all financial statements, except the cash flow statement, be prepared on the accruals basis. (IAS 1 (r1997).25) However, a caveat is included that the application of the matching principle does not allow the recognition of items in the balance sheet which do not meet the definition of assets or liabilities. Thus, amounts may not be recognised as assets unless *future* economic benefits are expected to flow to the enterprise and amounts may not be recognised as liabilities unless a *present* obligation of the enterprise exists at the balance sheet date.

4.7.5 *Materiality and aggregation*

The Framework establishes the concept of materiality by explaining that information is material if its omission or misstatement could influence the economic decisions of users taken on the basis of the financial statements. Thus, materiality is not necessarily based on size alone but on the size of an item judged in the particular circumstances of its omission.

Whether an amount is or is not material should be judged by reference to the needs of the users of the financial statements and in cases of doubt it should be treated as material. What must be decided is whether the item or matter is of significance to the user of the financial statements in relation to the specific provision of IASs under consideration. No arbitrary percentage yardstick can be applied in judging whether an amount or other disclosure is not material. Qualitative factors must also be considered. In this respect disclosure of an item, such as tax expense, cannot be considered immaterial regardless of its size in relation to other costs shown in the income statement.

IASs do not apply to immaterial items. Thus, if following the disclosure requirements of specific IASs would lead to the disclosure of immaterial information in the financial statements, these disclosures do not need to be made. (IAS 1 (r1997).32)

The concept of materiality also helps preparers to determine the level of precision of information which is presented in the financial statements. Thus, rounding to the nearest thousand, million or other figure as appropriate, is acceptable if it improves the understandability of the financial information presented and the level of precision used does not prevent the disclosure of material information.

When preparing financial statements, many small transactions of a similar nature are aggregated into line items on the face of the financial statements or in the notes thereto to provide understandable information to users. However, information that is material either individually or in the aggregate may not be aggregated with other information. Thus, material items should be disclosed individually and not hidden by grouping them with other similar or nonsimilar items. In addition, the fact that items are not material enough to warrant disclosure on the face of a financial statement does not necessarily lead to the conclusion that separate disclosure in the notes to the financial statements is not required.

4.7.6 Offsetting

When assets and liabilities, such as receivables and payables, are with the same party, a temptation may exist to offset such amounts in the balance sheet. Similarly, when items of income and expense arise from one transaction, a preparer may wish to disclose the net amount in the income statement. However, offsetting generally impairs the ability of the user to understand the nature of the transactions of the enterprise. Thus, to enhance comparability between companies, offsetting is only permitted in a limited number of situations under IAS 1 (r1997).

Specifically, 'assets and liabilities should not be offset except when offsetting is required or permitted by another International Accounting Standard'. (IAS 1 (r1997).33)

> 'Items of income and expense should be offset when, and only when:
>
> (a) an International Accounting Standard requires or permits it; or
> (b) gains, losses and related expenses arising from the same or similar transactions and events are not material. Such amounts should be aggregated in accordance with paragraph 29' (as described in the previous section).
>
> (IAS 1 (r1997).34)

When offsetting best reflects the substance of the transaction, certain gains and losses may be presented net of the related immaterial expenses. Generally, these types of gains and losses are incidental to the revenue generating purpose of the enterprise. For example:

> '(a) gains and losses on the disposal of non-current assets, including investments and operating assets, are reported by deducting from the proceeds on disposal the carrying amount of the asset and related selling expenses;

(b) expenditure that is reimbursed under a contractual arrangement with a third party (a sub-letting agreement for example), is netted against the related reimbursement; and
(c) extraordinary items may be presented net of related taxation and minority interest with the gross amounts shown in the notes.'

(IAS 1 (r1997).36)

Also, gains and losses arising from a group of similar transactions, such as from the sale of financial instruments held for trading purposes, may be offset if none of them is material individually.

A financial asset and a financial liability, as defined by IAS 32 (r1998), *Financial Instruments: Disclosure and Presentation,* should be offset and the net amount reported in the balance sheet only when an enterprise has a legal right and intent to settle on a net basis or to realise the asset and settle the liability simultaneously. As long as both legal right and intent are present, offsetting is required, although the arrangement may take various forms and involve more than one financial asset and liability. (IAS 32 (r1998).33) See Chapter **12** for further discussion of the offsetting of financial assets and financial liabilities.

Presenting assets net of valuation allowances such as allowances for doubtful accounts or for stock obsolescence is not considered offsetting and as such is neither required nor prohibited by IAS 1 (r1997).

4.7.7 Comparative information and consistency of presentation

IAS 1 (r1997) requires that comparative information be disclosed for all numerical information in the financial statements unless an IAS provides a specific exemption from disclosing comparative information. For example, in July 1997, the Board approved an amendment to IAS 16 to permit the omission of comparative numbers relating to property, plant and equipment when a reconciliation table is provided. In its more recently issued standards, the Board has provided similar exemptions in respect of reconciliation of movement in provisions and intangible assets. (IAS 37.84, and IAS 38.107) Comparative information should be included in narrative and descriptive information when it is relevant to an understanding of the current period's financial statements. (IAS 1 (r1997).38)

'The presentation and classification of items in the financial statements should be retained from one period to the next unless:

(a) a significant change in the nature of the operations of the enterprise or a review of its financial statement presentation demonstrates that the change will result in a more appropriate presentation of events or transactions; or
(b) a change in presentation is required by an International Accounting Standard or an Interpretation of the Standing Interpretations Committee.'

(IAS 1 (r1997).27)

Consistency of presentation is essential to the comparability of financial statements from year to year. In those rare circumstances described above, an enterprise may choose, or be required, to alter the presentation of items in its financial statements. When such a change in presentation takes place, prior year comparative information is required to be restated to be consistent with the current year presentation, unless such restatement is impracticable. In addition, the nature, amount of and reason for any reclassification is required to be disclosed. When it is impracticable to reclassify comparative amounts, an enterprise is required to disclose the reason for not reclassifying and the nature of the changes that would have been made if amounts were reclassified. (IAS 1 (r1997).40)

IAS 1 (r1997) permits a change in presentation to comply with national requirements as long as the revised presentation is consistent with the requirements of IAS 1 (r1997). (IAS 1 (r1997).28)

4.7.8 Consistency of application of accounting policies

The consistency requirement in IAS 1 (r1997) applies only to presentation. However, the Framework paragraph 39 and the Standing Interpretations Committee make it clear that the principle also applies to recognition and measurement. For example, under SIC-1, an enterprise must use the same cost formula for all inventories having similar nature and use to the enterprise, but the choice of cost method may be made for each separate classification of inventories. SIC-2 requires consistent application of the chosen policy of whether to capitalise or expense borrowing costs which meet specified conditions.

In May 1999 the Standing Interpretations Committee issued SIC-18 that extends these requirements to all circumstances where a choice of accounting policy is allowed by the relevant IAS. SIC-18 states that if one or more alternative accounting policies are available under an IAS or Interpretation, an enterprise should choose and apply consistently one of those policies unless the Standard or Interpretation specifically requires or permits categorisation of items (transactions, events, balances, or amounts) for which different policies may be appropriate. If a Standard requires or permits separate categorisation of items, the most appropriate accounting policy should be selected and applied consistently to each category.

Examples where IASs permit a choice of accounting policy, and once selected such policy would be required to apply to all items, include recognition of changes in the fair value of available for sale financial assets in accordance with IAS 39 (r2000), *Financial Instruments: Recognition and Measurement*, and the treatment of changes of accounting policy and fundamental errors in accordance with IAS 8 (r1993), *Net Profit or Loss for the Period, Fundamental Errors and Changes in Accounting Policies.*

An example where an enterprise is given a choice of accounting policy in respect of different categories of items is that of cost formulas for inventories in accordance with IAS 2, *Inventories*. Although, an enterprise has a choice of using the first-in, first-out (FIFO)/weighted average cost formulas or using the last-in, last-out (LIFO) formula, application of the chosen policy should be consistent for all current inventory of the same category.

The appendix to SIC-18 provides examples of other situations where IASs give a choice of accounting policy for recognition and measurement of items and methods of presentation and classification.

4.7.9 First-time application of IASs

SIC-8 requires that when an enterprise wishes to describe its financial statements for the first time as complying with IASs, it should prepare these financial statements as if they had always been prepared in accordance with the IASs and SICs effective for the period of first-time application. Retrospective application of Standards and Interpretations is required in all cases, except when:

- individual IASs or SICs require or permit a different transitional treatment; or
- the amount of the adjustment relating to prior periods cannot be reasonably determined.

(SIC-8.3)

Comparative information is also required to be prepared in accordance with IASs. (SIC-8.4) Where it is impracticable to provide such comparative information, that fact should be disclosed. (SIC-8.7(b))

Any adjustment resulting from the transition to IASs should be treated as an adjustment to the opening balance of retained earnings of the earliest period presented in accordance with the benchmark treatment in IAS 8 (r1993). (SIC-8.5) The SIC concluded that it is inappropriate to use the allowed alternative treatment in IAS 8 (r1993).54 to recognise the cumulative effect of changes resulting from the transition from national GAAP to IASs in the income statement as this would not result in useful information about the enterprise's performance in the transition period. (SIC-8.11)

On the first-time applications of IASs, an enterprise should apply the transitional provisions of the effective IASs and SICs only for periods ending on the date prescribed in the respective IASs and SICs. (SIC-8.6)

This provision means that all enterprises applying IASs are treated equally, regardless of whether or not they applied IASs in previous periods. Enterprises applying IASs for the first time may, for example, either write off balances of goodwill that arose in periods beginning prior to 1 January 1995 directly against equity or capitalise and amortise them (IAS 22 (r1998).101), regardless of the previous treatment under national GAAP. This transitional treatment, however, is not appropriate for goodwill purchased in periods beginning on or after 1 January 1995. (SIC-8.6 and SIC-8.12)

For each International Accounting Standard that permits a choice of transitional accounting policies, the policy selected should be disclosed. (SIC-8.7)

In some cases, the amount of the adjustment of the opening balance of retained earnings relating to prior periods cannot be reasonably determined or restatement of comparative information is not practical. In these circumstances SIC-8 allows financial statements to be still described as complying with IASs, provided that the appropriate disclosure is made. (SIC-8.13)

Concerns have been raised about that interpretation and other issues related to first-time application of International Accounting Standards. At its May 2001 meeting, the IASB considered a paper that identified a number of issues relating to the first-time application of IAS. Some of the issues identified were interpretative, while others were problems that had arisen in practice where compliance with the requirements of IAS as directed by SIC-8 resulted in significant costs, perhaps beyond that contemplated by the SIC and the IASC when they approved SIC-8.

In theory, SIC-8 achieves complete comparability between enterprises, both between first-time adopters of IAS and those entities already applying IAS, and across all entities using IAS. However, the degree of comparability is subject, in part, to the availability of alternatives in some standards and to determinations made about exemptions written into individual standards (e.g., IAS 8.49 notes that 'comparative information should be restated unless it is impracticable to do so') and the overall exemption in SIC-8.3(b) that retrospective application is not required when 'the amount of the adjustment relating to prior periods cannot be reasonably determined'. In the context of some of the practical application problems raised in the May Board paper, different enterprises converting to IAS might make very different interpretations of what is practicable or reasonably determinable, especially where the costs of compliance are very high.

This project has been adopted as a priority project by the new IASB. The project is seen as one of the more urgent issues facing the new board with the adoption of IAS across the EC by 2005 (see Chapter **2**).

4.7.10 Reporting currency

IAS 21 (r1993), *The Effects of Changes in Foreign Exchange Rates*, whilst not specifying the currency in which an enterprise presents its financial statements, defines the term 'reporting currency' as the currency used in presenting the financial statements. The reporting currency used by an enterprise also has implications for accounting measurement in the financial statements.

In November 2000, the Standing Interpretations Committee issued SIC-19, which discusses the appropriate determination of both the currency used by an enterprise for measuring items in its financial statements (the 'measurement currency'), and the currency used for presenting its financial statements (the 'presentation currency').

SIC-19 states that the measurement currency should provide information about the enterprise that is useful and reflects the economic substance of the underlying events and circumstances relevant to that enterprise. The measurement currency will generally be the currency of the country in which the enterprise is domiciled. However, there may be instances where another currency is appropriate. For example, if an enterprise uses a particular currency to a significant extent within its operations, rather than the local currency, it may be appropriate to use this as the measurement currency. When such a situation occurs the reason for using that currency must be disclosed in the financial statements.

Once the measurement currency has been selected it should be used consistently unless there has been a change in the underlying events and circumstances relevant to the enterprise. The reason for any such change would need to be disclosed.

Where the selected measurement currency is a currency of a hyperinflationary economy then SIC-19 requires that:

> '(a) the enterprise's own financial statements should be restated under IAS 29, *Financial Reporting in Hyperinflationary Economies*; and
> (b) when the enterprise is a foreign entity as defined in IAS 21 and is included in the financial statements of another reporting enterprise, its financial statements should be restated under IAS 29 before being translated into the reporting currency of the other reporting enterprise.'
>
> (SIC-19.7)

Normally, an enterprise will present its financial statements in the same currency as the measurement currency, and for groups, the measurement currency of the parent. However, IAS 21.4 does not specify the currency to be used in the presentation of financial statements. SIC-19 states that an enterprise may choose to present its financial statements in a different currency to the measurement currency. The reason for this choice would need to be disclosed within the financial statements, along with the measurement currency, and a description of the translation process.

The method of translating the financial statements from the measurement currency to the presentation currency is not specified under International Accounting Standards. However, in order for the financial statements to be presented fairly, it would be necessary to use a method that would not lead to reporting in a manner that is inconsistent with the measurement of items using the measurement currency.

There should be consistent use of the presentation currency, and disclosure of the reason for any change in the currency used.

4.8 Structure and content

4.8.1 Identification of financial statements

Information included in the financial statements must be separately identifiable from other information that may be provided in the same document. This is generally achieved by meeting the requirements that each component of the financial statements be clearly identified and that the following information be displayed, preferably on each page of the financial statements:

> '(a) the name of the reporting enterprise or other means of identification;
> (b) whether the financial statements cover the individual enterprise or a group of enterprises;
> (c) the balance sheet date or the period covered by the financial statements, whichever is appropriate to the related component of the financial statements;
> (d) the reporting currency; and
> (e) the level of precision used in the presentation of figures in the financial statements.'
>
> (IAS 1 (r1997).46)

Item (e) refers to the practice of rounding in financial statements. This practice is not prohibited as, indeed, in many cases it enhances the clarity of the financial statements. However, it is necessary to indicate frequently the level of rounding which has taken place, for example, € million or €'000, etc. The above information is generally displayed in page headings and/or column headings.

Although not required, a change in the company's name during the period or since the end of the period might usefully be disclosed by mentioning the former name in the heading on each page of the financial statements.

4.8.2 Reporting period

> 'Financial statements should be presented at least annually. When, in exceptional circumstances, an enterprise's balance sheet date changes and annual financial statements are presented for a period longer or shorter than one year, an enterprise should disclose, in addition to the period covered by the financial statements:
>
> (a) the reason for a period other than one year being used; and
> (b) the fact that comparative amounts for the income statement, changes in equity, cash flows and related notes are not comparable.'
>
> (IAS 1 (r1997).49)

Some enterprises, particularly in the retail industry, may wish to report periods of 52 weeks rather than one year. As long as the results are not materially different from results which would be given for a one year period, this is not prohibited.

Many enterprises report more frequently than once a year. In 1998 the IASC issued IAS 34 on interim reporting (see Chapter **29**).

4.8.3 Timeliness

IAS 1 (r1997) suggests that an enterprise should be in a position to issue its financial statements within six months of the balance sheet date. (IAS 1 (r1997).52) However, in practice, domestic laws and requirements of regulators will determine deadlines for the issuance of financial statements.

4.9 Future developments

The SIC has published a draft interpretation of IAS 1 (r1997). SIC D-29, *Disclosure – Service Concession Arrangements*, considers the information that should be disclosed in the notes to the financial statements by both parties to a service concession arrangement.

A service concession arrangement exists when an enterprise (the Concession Operator) agrees with another enterprise (the Concession Provider) to provide services that are normally considered public services. Examples of service concession arrangements involve water treatment and supply facilities, motorways, car parks, tunnels, bridges, airports and telecommunication networks. Examples of arrangements that are not service concession arrangements include an enterprise outsourcing the operations of its internal services (e.g., employee cafeteria and accounting or information technology functions).

The draft interpretation proposes the following disclosures:

- description of the arrangement;
- significant terms such as the period of the concession, contractual

repricing dates, and the basis upon which repricing or renegotiation is determined;

- the nature and extent (quantity, time period, or amount as appropriate) of the following:
  - transferred rights to use specified assets;
  - obligations to provide or rights to expect provision of services;
  - obligations to acquire or build items of property, plant and equipment;
  - obligations to deliver or rights to receive specified assets at the end of the concession period;
  - renewal options;
  - other rights and obligations (e.g., major overhauls); and
- changes in the arrangement occurring during the period.

The draft was issued for public comment on 9 July 2001. The comment deadline is 10 September 2001.

CHAPTER 5

Income statement: format and components

5.1 Sources

IAS 1 (r1997)	*Presentation of Financial Statements.*
IAS 8 (r1993)	*Net Profit or Loss for the Period, Fundamental Errors and Changes in Accounting Policies.*
IAS 12 (r2000)	*Income Taxes.*
IAS 27	*Consolidated Financial Statements and Accounting for Investments in Subsidiaries.*
IAS 32 (r1998)	*Financial Instruments: Disclosure and Presentation.*
IAS 33	*Earnings Per Share.*
IAS 35	*Discontinuing Operations.*

5.2 Brief summary of the requirements

IAS 1 (r1997) allows a choice between two methods of income statement presentation: the nature of expenditure method; and the function of expenditure method. The function of expenditure method, also referred to as the cost of sales method, is likely to be the more familiar of the two formats to UK and US financial statement preparers. However, both formats are acceptable under UK GAAP and the UK Companies Act 1985.

5.3 Development of the requirements

Prior to the issuance of IAS 1 (r1997) in September 1997, IASs did not prescribe a standard format for the income statement. Various IASs required the disclosure of certain items in the financial statements but no specific format was adopted. IAS 1 (r1997) has greatly enhanced the ease with which a user can compare the income statements of different enterprises reporting under IASs.

IAS 1 (r1997) replaced IAS 1, *Disclosure of Accounting Policies*, IAS 5, *Information to be Disclosed in Financial Statements*, and IAS 13, *Presentation of Current Assets and Current Liabilities.*

In June 1998 IAS 35 was issued. The new Standard superseded paragraphs 19–22 of IAS 8 (r1993). IAS 35 deals with presentation and disclosure of discontinuing operations. It considerably expands the guidance section of the definition of discontinuing operations, provides illustrations of presentation and disclosure, and links its requirements with other standards such as IAS 36 on impairments and IAS 37 on provisions.

The G4+1 group of accounting standard setters of which IASC was a member issued a Position Paper *Reporting Financial Performance* in January 1998 and a further paper in June 1999. Along with participating national standard setters the old IASC Board added this project to its agenda. The paper proposed that financial performance, including both 'traditional' income statement items and items recognised directly in equity, should be presented in one statement, and discusses the structure and composition of such statement. Other proposals include: reporting of profits and losses currently shown after operating profits within the 'operating' or 'other' sections of the statement, and abolition of the distinction between the treatment of 'fundamental errors' and other material errors. The new IASB has added this project to its agenda. The project, reporting recognised income and expenses, has been included as one of the leadership projects that the IASB aims to address first (see Chapter **2**).

5.4 Items required to be presented on the face of the income statement

The following items are required by particular IASs to be presented on the face of the income statement.

Line item	**Standard which requires its presentation**
Revenue	IAS 1 (r1997)*
Results of operating activities	IAS 1 (r1997)*
Finance costs	IAS 1 (r1997)*
Share of profits or losses of associates and joint ventures accounted for under the equity method	IAS 28 (r2000) and IAS 1 (r1997)
Pre-tax gain or loss on the disposal of assets or settlement of liabilities attributable to a discontinuing operation	IAS 35
Tax expense	IAS 12 (r2000) and IAS 1 (r1997)

Profit or loss from ordinary activities	IAS 8 (r1993) and IAS 1 (r1997)
Extraordinary items	IAS 8 (r1993) and IAS 1 (r1997)
Minority interest	IAS 1 (r1997)*
Net profit or loss for the period	IAS 1 (r1997)*
Basic earnings per share	IAS 33
Diluted earnings per share	IAS 33

* IAS 1 (r1997) does not require that these exact captions are used but only that 'line items which present' these items are included on the face of the income statement. (IAS 1 (r1997).75)

Additional headings and subtotals are permitted when it adds to the understandability of the financial statements. Additional line items are required to be included if:

- an IAS requires them;
- they are required to present fairly the enterprise's performance; or
- they add to the understandability of the financial statements.

For example, the allowed alternative treatment of IAS 8 (r1993) requires the effect of a change in accounting policy to be disclosed. Generally, an item of this type would be considered material due to its amount and the fact that by its nature, it is different from the normal operating activities of the enterprise. As such, it would be disclosed on the face of the income statement even though IAS 8 (r1993) does not explicitly require this presentation. In addition, it is considered best practice to present items on the face of the income statement when an IAS encourages but does not require such presentation as is the case with the components of the results of operating activities as discussed below.

5.5 Revenue and the results of operating activities

As shown in **5.4**, revenue and the results of operating activities are the only line items relating to operating activities required to be presented on the face of the income statement. However, IAS 1 (r1997) encourages the components of the results of operating activities to be presented on the face of the income statement. If such information is not presented on the face of the income statement, it must be given in the notes to the financial statements.

As well as allowing a choice of the placement of operating activity information, IAS 1 (r1997) allows a choice between two presentation methods for the components of the results of operating activities: the nature of expenditure method (see *Example 5.1*) and the function of expenditure method (see *Example 5.2*), also referred to as the cost of sales method.

The nature of expenditure method is similar to the Format 2 presentation permitted by Schedule 4 of the British Companies Act 1985 and the function of expenditure method is similar to the Format 1 presentation of Schedule 4. The function of expenditure or cost of sales method is widely adopted in the UK and will probably look more familiar to UK preparers and users of financial statements with its disclosure of revenue, cost of sales and gross profit. The nature of expenditure method may be less familiar but is, in fact, an easier presentation from a preparer's point of view as it does not require an allocation of costs between cost of sales and administrative expenses. However, if the function of expenditure method is used, disclosure of the items shown under the nature of expenditure is required in the notes to the financial statements, but not vice versa.

Given the relative simplicity of the nature of expenditure method, it is well suited to small enterprises who may not have intricate costing systems in place to produce the information required under the function of expenditure method. This method also appears to have a high degree of objectivity as the judgmental allocations of expenses necessary in the function of expenditure presentation are not required. However, the function of expenditure presentation may provide more relevant information to users of financial statements since a gross profit figure is shown and thus may be preferred by enterprises with a more sophisticated user base. As noted above, a choice between these two methods of presentation is permitted.

Once one method of presentation is chosen it should be applied consistently in accordance with IAS 1 (r1997).27.

5.5.1 Pro forma IAS income statements and UK profit and loss account

The following examples are provided to illustrate the two presentation methods introduced above and discussed in more detail below and to clarify differences between presentations under IAS and under UK GAAP. The examples are for illustrative purposes only and should not be considered to be complete or appropriate for all circumstances. The IAS examples are expanded versions of the examples of the minimum requirements for income statements included in the appendix to IAS 1 (r1997). For a full set of IAS Model Financial Statements, see Appendix III.

Example 5.1

Enterprise name

Income statement

For the year ended 31 December 20X2
(IAS nature of expenditure method)

	Note	*20X2*	*20X1*
		£'000	*£'000*
Revenue		200	150
Other operating income		20	15
Changes in inventories of finished goods and work in progress		(50)	10
Work performed by the enterprise and capitalised		140	100
Raw material and consumables used		(185)	(180)
Staff costs		(50)	(40)
Depreciation and amortisation expense		(25)	(20)
Other operating expenses		(10)	(5)
Profit from operations		40	30
Finance cost		(25)	(20)
Income from associates		20	20
Income from other investments		20	15
Amounts written off investments		–	(30)
Profit on sale of items of property, plant and equipment in continuing operations		30	25
Loss on assets in discontinuing operation		(20)	(20)
Profit before tax		65	20
Income tax expense		(20)	(6)
Profit after tax		45	14
Minority interest		(15)	(5)
Net profit or loss from ordinary activities		30	9
Extraordinary items (net of tax and minority interest)		–	–
Net profit for the period		30	9
Basic earnings per share		30p	9p
Diluted earnings per share		15p	5p

Example 5.2

Enterprise name

Income statement

For the year ended 31 December 20X2
(IAS nature of expenditure method)

	Note	*20X2* *£'000*	*20X1* *£'000*
Revenue		200	150
Cost of sales		(100)	(75)
Gross profit		100	75
Other operating income		20	15
Distribution costs		(40)	(30)
Administrative expenses		(20)	(15)
Other operating expenses		(20)	(15)
Profit from operations	1	40	30
Finance cost		(25)	(20)
Income from associates		20	20
Income from other investments		20	15
Amounts written off investments		–	(30)
Profit on sale of items of property, plant and equipment in continuing operations		30	25
Loss on assets in discontinuing operation		(20)	(20)
Profit before tax		65	20
Income tax expense		(20)	(6)
Profit after tax		45	14
Minority interest		(15)	(5)
Net profit or loss from ordinary activities		30	9
Extraordinary items (net of tax and minority interest)		–	–
Net profit for the period		30	9
Basic earnings per share		30p	9p
Diluted earnings per share		15p	5p

The following information would be included in a note to the financial statements:

1. Operating expenses	*20X2* *£'000*	*20X1* *£'000*
Operating profit is stated after charging:		
Total staff costs	50	40
Depreciation and amortisation expense	25	20

Example 5.3

Enterprise name
Profit and loss account
For the year ended 31 December 20X2
(UK Format 1)

	Note	*20X2* *£'000*	*20X2* *£'000*	*20X1* *£'000*
TURNOVER				
Continuing operations		120		100
Acquisitions		60		
		180		
Discontinued operations		20		50
Total turnover			200	150
Cost of sales			(100)	(75)
Gross profit			100	75
Net operating expenses			(60)	(35)
OPERATING PROFIT				
Continuing operations		40		40
Acquisitions		20		
		60		
Discontinued operations		(30)		(20)
less utilisation of prior year provisions		10		10
Group operating profit			40	30
Share of operating profits of associates			20	20
			60	50
Profit on sale of fixed assets in continuing operations			30	25
Provision for loss on operations to be discontinued			–	(15)
Loss on disposal of discontinued operations			(60)	(50)
less utilisation of prior year provisions			40	30
PROFIT ON ORDINARY ACTIVITIES BEFORE INTEREST			70	40
Investment income			20	15
Amounts written off investments			–	(30)
Interest payable and similar charges			(25)	(20)
PROFIT ON ORDINARY ACTIVITIES BEFORE TAXATION			65	5
Tax on profit on ordinary activities			(20)	(2)
PROFIT ON ORDINARY ACTIVITIES AFTER TAXATION			45	3
Equity minority interests			(14)	–
Non-equity minority interests			(1)	(1)
PROFIT FOR THE FINANCIAL YEAR			30	2
Dividends paid and proposed – including amounts in respect of non-equity shares			(5)	(1)
Retained profit for the financial year			25	10
Earnings per ordinary share			30p	2p
Diluted earnings per share			15p	1p

5.5.2 *Nature of expenditure method*

Under the nature of expenditure method (see *Example 5.1*), revenue and expense line items are determined by their own nature rather than allocated and classified according to the function or purpose they serve in the operations of the enterprise. For example, the line items 'revenue' and 'other operating revenue' (if any and material) are shown together at the top of the income statement since they are of a similar nature (i.e. revenue). The components of operating expenses including depreciation and amortisation expense, staff costs, raw materials and consumables used and other operating expenses are required to be disclosed as separate line items either on the face of the income statement, which is encouraged, or in the notes to the financial statements. Other line items are required to be included if they are necessary for a fair presentation of the income statement.

5.5.3 *Function of expenditure method (cost of sales method)*

Under the function of expenditure method (see *Example 5.2*), expenses are classified according to their function within the enterprise into the following suggested categories: cost of sales, distribution costs, administrative expenses and other operating expenses. These line items may be disclosed either on the face of the income statement, which is encouraged, or in the notes to the financial statements. If the items are presented on the face of the income statement, the cost of sales line item follows revenue to give a gross profit subtotal. Other operating income, if material, is shown below this subtotal as its function is outside that of the main revenue producing operations of the business. Distribution costs, administrative expenses and other operating expenses are then disclosed to arrive at operating profit or loss. Other line items may be included, if they are necessary, for a fair presentation of the income statement.

The allocation of expenses between cost of sales, distribution costs, administrative expenses and other operating expenses is made by management based on the function or purpose of the expense within the enterprise.

Items in the cost of sales category may include, among other things, direct labour and materials, fixed and variable production overheads (including depreciation expense or an allocation thereof) and variances from standard cost when a standard costing system is used. (For further discussion of costs capitalised as inventory, see **10.9.6**).

Generally, distribution costs include all costs to deliver products to customers including, among other things, transportation expense, advertising expense, salaries and related employment taxes of sales people and depreciation and maintenance of delivery vehicles.

Administrative expenses normally include, among other things, salaries and related employment taxes of administrative staff, professional fees, depreciation and amortisation expense, rent, bad debt expense and insurance. Depending on the particular circumstances, research and development costs may be included in administrative expenses or other operating expenses. In some cases, development costs may be required to be capitalised in accordance with IAS 38, *Intangible Assets* (see **10.7.8**).

As noted above, if an enterprise classifies expenses by function it should disclose additional information on the nature of expenses, including depreciation and amortisation expense and staff costs. (IAS 1 (r1997).83)

IASs do not specify where on the income statement amortisation of goodwill and intangible assets is to be shown. However, both IAS 22 (r1998), *Business Combinations*, and IAS 38, *Intangible Assets*, require disclosure of line item(s) in which amortisation charge is included. Therefore, it appears that it may be included either before or after operating profit and may be split between two or more items on the income statement as long as it is disclosed where the amount has been charged. See **10.5.6** and **10.7.12** for a further discussion.

5.6 Finance costs

Finance costs include net interest income or expense and other items that generally would be considered interest income or expense, such as the amortisation of bond premiums or discounts, etc. Income and expense, including interest income and expense, may only be offset for presentation on the face of the income statement when an IAS requires or permits it or when they are immaterial. (IAS 1 (r1997).34) (For a further discussion of offsetting see **4.7.6**)

In the rare case when financial instruments of the enterprise, such as redeemable preference shares, are classified as financial liabilities rather than equity, in accordance with IAS 32 (r1998), related dividend payments are recognised in the income statement rather than directly in equity. (IAS 32 (r1998).30) IAS 32 (r1998) states that such dividend payments may be presented either with other finance costs or as a separate item. (IAS 32 (r98).32) Separate presentation may be desirable based on materiality or differing tax deductibility of such dividends from normal interest payments. (See **11.4** for a discussion of the distinction between financial liabilities and equity and Chapter **8** for a discussion of the treatment of dividends paid relating to equity instruments.)

If the components of finance costs are material, they are required to be disclosed separately either on the face of the income statement or in a note to the financial statements. See **5.6.1** for an example of such a note.

5.6.1 *Examples from published financial statements*

Note that the excerpts given do not always comply in full with all aspects of IAS and as such are not necessarily examples of best practice but merely of current practice.

Example 5.4

8. Financial income and expenses

	Year ended December 31	
	2000	*1999*
	€m	*€m*
Income from long-term investments		
Dividend income	**70**	6
Interest income	**2**	2
Other interest and financial income		
Interest income from short-term investments	**210**	194
Other financial income	**17**	5
Exchange gains and losses	**−1**	−5
Interest expenses and other financial expenses		
Interest expenses	**−115**	−254
Other financial income	**−81**	−6
Total	**102**	−58

Nokia
Finland
31 December 2000
International Accounting Standards

Example 5.5

21. Financial result

Financial result consists of the following:

(€'000)	*2000*	*1999*
Interest income	12,612	7,284
Interest expense	(108,517)	(84,933)
Interest expense, net	**(95,905)**	**(77,649)**
Income from investments	474	441
Write up of investments	3,126	–
Option premiums regarding discontinued currency options	1	(2,096)
Other-net, primarily net exchange gains	(1,650)	(4,567)
Financial result	**(93,954)**	**(83,871)**

ADIDAS-Salomon
Germany
31 December 2000
International Accounting Standards

5.6.2 Comparison with UK GAAP

Most items included as finance costs under IAS 1 (r1997) would be considered interest income or expense under UK GAAP. The main difference is the treatment of dividends.

In the UK, dividends paid on equity instruments as well as dividends paid on non-equity instruments are deducted from the net profit or loss for the period on the face of the profit and loss account, to arrive at the retained profit or loss for the period. Under IAS 32 (r1998), dividends paid related to equity instruments (for example, ordinary shares) are required to be debited to equity and recognised in the statement of changes in equity, while dividends paid on redeemable preference shares and other financial instruments classified as financial liabilities (which would generally be classified as non-equity instruments under UK GAAP) are included in arriving at net income or loss for the period and presented either with other finance costs or as a separate item on the face of the income statement.

5.6.3 Comparison with US GAAP

Most items included as finance costs under IAS 1 (r1997) would be considered interest income or expense under US GAAP. Under a US presentation, dividends paid are generally recognised in the statement of stockholders' equity. This includes dividends paid related to redeemable preference shares which are not classified as equity. Under IAS 32 (r1998), dividends paid related to redeemable preference shares would be included in the income statement, although dividends paid related to equity instruments are included in the statement of changes in equity.

5.7 Share of profits of associates and joint ventures accounted for by the equity method

As indicated by IAS 1 (r1997), items included here are the enterprise's share of the income or loss from associates and joint ventures accounted for under the equity method (see Chapters **20** and **21**).

5.8 Tax expense

IAS 12 (r2000) requires the tax expense on income related to profit or loss from ordinary activities to be disclosed on the face of the income statement. (IAS 12 (r2000).77) Numerous other tax related disclosures are required to be made in the notes to the financial statements (see Chapter **23**).

5.9 Minority interest

Minority interest on the income statement represents the amount of profit after tax attributable to interests which are not owned, directly or indirectly through subsidiaries, by the parent enterprise. (IAS 27.6) It is normally calculated by multiplying the profit after tax of consolidated subsidiaries which are not 100 per cent owned by the enterprise (directly or indirectly) by the percentage of ownership interest which is not owned, directly or indirectly, by the enterprise.

5.10 Profit or loss from ordinary activities

'Ordinary activities are any activities which are undertaken by an enterprise as part of its business and such related activities in which the enterprise engages in furtherance of, incidental to, or arising from these activities.' (IAS 8 (r1993).6) IAS 8 (r1993) defines ordinary activities very broadly with the intended result that very few items of income or expense are beyond the scope of the ordinary activities of an enterprise. If an item is outside of the scope of ordinary activities, it is an extraordinary item which is discussed in **5.11**.

However, 'when items of income or expense within profit or loss from ordinary activities of an enterprise are of such size, nature or incidence that their disclosure is relevant to explain the performance of the enterprise for the period, the nature and amount of such items should be disclosed separately.' (IAS 8 (r1993).16)

This disclosure is usually made in the notes to the financial statements. IAS 8 (r1993) does not refer to a specific name for such items of income or expense but in UK terms, for example, such items are generally referred to as exceptional items (see **5.10.1**). IAS 8 (r1993) gives the following examples of circumstances which may give rise to such items:

- 'the write-down of inventories to net realisable value or property, plant and equipment to recoverable amount, as well as the reversal of such write-downs;
- a restructuring of the activities of an enterprise and the reversal of any provisions for the costs of restructuring;
- disposals of items of property, plant and equipment;
- disposals of long-term investments;
- discontinued operations;
- litigation settlements; and
- other reversals of provisions.'

(IAS 8 (r1993).18)

If an enterprise determines that the item is material enough to warrant disclosure on the face of the income statement, IAS 8 (r1993) and IAS 1 (r1997) are silent on the issue of where on the income statement such items are disclosed. In practice, the item may be disclosed as part of the normal expense to which it is most closely related or as a separate line item. In either case, by definition, these items are included within profit from ordinary activities. For example, a disposal of a long-term investment in securities by an enterprise which is not in the business of making such investments may give rise to a material gain or loss which would appropriately be disclosed by adding a separate line item under finance costs on the face of the income statement. As no specific rules exist in this regard, in order to achieve a fair presentation, management will need to consider the substance of such transactions on an individual basis to determine where the item fits by its nature on the face of the income statement.

5.10.1 Comparison with UK GAAP

FRS 3, *Reporting Financial Performance,* defines exceptional items in broadly the same terms as IAS 8 (r1993) refers to the unnamed items which are of such size, nature or incidence that their disclosure is relevant to explain the performance of the enterprise. However, one should not assume that the two types of items are identical. For example, given the more limited nature of extraordinary items under UK GAAP as discussed in **5.11.1**, most items which are considered to be extraordinary under IAS 8 (r1993) would be considered exceptional under FRS 3.

Also, FRS 3 is more prescriptive than IAS 8 (r1993) in that it states that with the exception of three specific exceptional items, which must be shown immediately below operating profit or loss, exceptional items should be recognised in the statutory format heading to which they relate. The three exceptions are: profits or losses on the sale or termination of an operation; costs of a fundamental restructuring having a material effect on the nature and focus of the reporting entity's operations; and profits or losses on the disposal of fixed assets. As discussed previously, IASs do not provide guidance on the positioning of similar items.

5.10.2 Comparison with US GAAP

Under US GAAP, items which are of such size, nature or incidence that their disclosure is relevant to explain the performance of the enterprise as described in IAS 8 (r1993) generally would be included in operating profit or loss. For example, profits or losses arising from a restructuring are explicitly required to be included in operating activities. While these explicit requirements do not apply directly to non-listed companies, they are considered best practice. The required inclusion in operating profit or loss under US GAAP is more prescriptive than IAS 8 (r1993) which merely requires disclosure within profit or loss from ordinary activities.

5.10.3 Examples of disclosure of items which are of such size, nature or incidence that their disclosure is relevant to explain the performance of the enterprise for the period

Note that the excerpts given do not always comply in full with all aspects of IAS and as such are not necessarily examples of best practice but merely of current practice.

Example 5.6

5. Other operating income and expenses, net (extracts)

	1997 *€ million*	*1998* *€ million*	*1999* *€ million*
Restructuring and workforce adjustments costs and provisions	**(235)**	(244)	(681)
Gains and losses on sale of tangible and intangible fixed assets (except vehicle sales)	**(49)**	(62)	(41)
Gains and losses on transactions on investments in operating subsidiaries and affiliates	**41**	22	7
Amorisation of goodwill on acquisition of consolidated companies	**10**	–	(4)
Items of an unusual nature or abnormally high amount	**(21)**	16	(2)
Total	**(254)**	**(268)**	**(721)**

Renault
France
31 December 1999
French GAAP/International Accounting Standards (with certain exceptions)

Example 5.7

Income Statements (extract)

	Note	*2000 (CHF million)*	*1999 (CHF million)*
Earnings before interest and taxes (EBIT) before equity-accounted investments		**603**	674
Profit/(loss) from associated undertakings	6	(777)	(381)
Exceptional income	7	296	350
Exceptional costs	8	(2,714)	0
Profit/(loss) from operating investments		**(3,195)**	(31)

Notes (extract)

7. Exceptional income	*2000 (CHF million)*	*1999 (CHF million)*
Singapore Airlines		47
Delta Airlines	100	
Equant	28	124
Galileo	171	
Austrian Airlines	(28)	
Other	25	29
Subtotal	**296**	**200**
Release of provisions		150
Total	**296**	**350**

The investments in Equant, Galileo and Austrian Airlines were reclassified from 'shareholdings in other companies' (note 15) to 'Securities' (note 11) and marked to market rather than cost. The difference between these two amounts was taken directly to the profit and loss account. The group plans to dispose of these investments, which are no longer of strategic importance, at the best possible opportunity.

CHF 150 million of the CHF 300 million provision established for restructuring activities required in response to market liberalisation was released in 1999.

8. Exceptional costs		*2000 (CHF million)*	*1999 (CHF million)*
Movement in provisions		(2,208)	
Value adjustments to loans receivable from associated undertakings	(355)		
Value adjustments to loans receivable from other companies	(151)	(506)	
Total		**(2,714)**	**0**

Provisions totalling CHF 2,208 million were effected in the 2000 business year for restructuring costs, impairment of assets and other liabilities. Provisions have not been established for the group's share of its associated undertakings' expected future operating losses (see Note 18).

The value adjustment to loans to associated undertakings and other companies were established taking into due consideration these companies' negative equity positions (see Note 15).

SAir Group
Switzerland
30 December 2000
International Accounting Standards

Example 5.8

Income Statements (extract)

	Notes	*Group* 2000 R'm	*Group* 1999 R'm	*Company* 2000 R'm	*Company* 1999 R'm
Profit before exceptional items		**1,087**	738	**525**	157
Exceptional items	8	**668**	951	**(28)**	131
Profit before taxation		**1,755**	1,689	**497**	288

Notes (extract)

8. Exceptional Items

During the year the group disposed of its remaining interest in Comparex Holdings Limited, including an in specie distribution of Dimension Data shares.

	Group 2000	Group 1999	Company 2000	Company 1999
Proceeds on disposal	**936**	1,378		
Carrying value of shares	**238**	335		
Net profit on disposal	**698**	1,043		
Profit/(loss) on sale of property and non-current assets	**29**	(6)	–	190
Impairment losses	**(59)**	(86)	**(28)**	(59)
	668	951	**(28)**	131
Attributable exceptional items of associate	–	1		
	668	952	**(28)**	131
Taxation – current	**(2)**	1		
– deferred	**1**	3		
	667	956	**(28)**	131
Minority interest	**3**	3		
Attributable to ordinary shareholders	**670**	959	**(28)**	131

Barloworld Limited
South Africa
30 September 2000
International Accounting Standards

5.11 Extraordinary items

'Extraordinary items are income or expenses that arise from events or transactions that are clearly distinct from the ordinary activities of the enterprise and therefore are not expected to recur frequently or regularly.' (IAS 8 (r1993).6) IAS 8 (r1993) explains that the occurrence of an extraordinary item is extremely rare because 'virtually all' items of income or expense arise in the course of the ordinary activities of the enterprise. (IAS 8 (r1993).12) However, IAS 8 (r1993) does provide two examples of circumstances which may lead to extraordinary items: the expropriation of assets, and earthquakes or other natural disasters (unless the enterprise insures against such disasters).

The total of all extraordinary items is required to be disclosed on the face of the income statement. (IAS 8 (r1993).10) IASs do not state exactly where on the income statement extraordinary items should be disclosed. In the example income statements in the appendix to IAS 1 (r1997), extraordinary items are shown after income tax expense and minority interest. If this order of presentation is adopted, the extraordinary item would be shown net of tax and minority interest.

The nature, amount and the related tax expense of each extraordinary item is required to be disclosed either on the face of the income statement or in the notes to the financial statements. (IAS 8 (r1993).11 and IAS 12 (r2000).81(b))

5.11.1 Comparison with UK GAAP

The provision of examples of extraordinary items in IAS 8 (r1993) may lead some to believe that IAS 8 (r1993) is more permissive of extraordinary items than FRS 3, *Reporting Financial Performance*, which has all but outlawed them and provides no examples of extraordinary items. While this may be the case, the intent of IAS 8 (r1993) is certainly that extraordinary items will be rare. A review of the breadth of items which IAS 8 (r1993) gives as examples of items which would be disclosed due to their size, nature or incidence, but not as extraordinary items, illustrates the intent of the IASC that most items of an unusual nature be included in profit or loss from the ordinary activities of the enterprise.

5.11.2 Comparison with US GAAP

APB 30, *Reporting the Results of Operations – Reporting the Effects of Disposal of a Segment of a Business, and Extraordinary, Unusual and Infrequently Occurring Events and Transactions,* states that to be considered an extraordinary item, an event or transaction must be both unusual in nature and infrequent in occurrence. Events or transactions which meet one but not both of these criteria are considered unusual items and are included as a separate component in income from continuing operations. (APB 30.26) In practice, extraordinary items are rare and include items which have been explicitly permitted or required to be treated as extraordinary such as gains or losses resulting from the expropriation of assets, a major casualty (for example, an earthquake), a prohibition under a newly enacted law or regulation, a restructuring of payables, the extinguishment of debt, or the disposal of a significant part of the assets or a separable segment of previously separate companies within two years of a business combination.

5.12 Net profit or loss for the period

> 'All items of income and expense recognised in a period should be included in the determination of the net profit or loss for the period unless an International Accounting Standard requires or permits otherwise.'
>
> (IAS 8 (r1993).7)

IAS 8 (r1993) does not define the terms 'income' and 'expense'. However, as defined in the Framework, these elements of the financial statements include all changes in net assets of the enterprise, with the exception of those resulting from contributions from or distributions to equity participants and certain other specific items (capital maintenance adjustments and revaluation surpluses or deficits which may meet the definition of income and expenses, but are specifically excluded and treated as changes in equity). The term 'equity participant' includes persons, such as warrant holders, who do not at present have a residual ownership interest in the enterprise. Thus, inflows of resources from the issue of warrants are not included in the net profit or loss for the period.

In summary, only contributions, including subscriptions to equity instruments from, and distributions to, equity participants are excluded from income and expense. Other transactions with equity participants are included.

Examples of items required by specific International Accounting Standards to be excluded from income and recognised directly in equity include:

- the correction of fundamental errors in accordance with the benchmark treatment (IAS 8 (r1993));
- changes in accounting policies in accordance with the benchmark treatment (IAS 8 (r1993));
- current and deferred tax which relates to items that are charged or credited directly to equity, including amounts arising on initial recognition of the equity component of a compound financial instrument (IAS 12 (r2000));
- certain revaluation surpluses and deficits arising on items of property, plant and equipment (IAS 16 (r1998));
- gains and losses arising on the translation of the financial statements of a foreign entity (IAS 21 (r1993));
- depending on a choice of accounting policy, gains and losses on remeasurement to fair value of available-for-sale financial assets until such assets are disposed of or become impaired (IAS 39 (r2000), *Financial Instruments: Recognition and Measurement*); and

- in respect of cash flow hedges and hedges of investments in a foreign entity, the portion of the gain or loss on the hedging instrument that is determined to be an effective hedge and, in limited circumstances, the ineffective portion of the hedge (IAS 39 (r2000)).

See Chapter **8** for a discussion of the manner of presentation of these items.

5.13 Earnings per share and other per share amounts

IAS 33 requires disclosure on the face of the income statement of basic earnings per share and diluted earnings per share for each class of ordinary shares that has a different right to share in the net profit for the period. See Chapter 7 for a discussion of the calculation of these and other per share figures.

5.14 Discontinuing operations

Previous requirements relating to the presentation and disclosure of discontinuing[1] operations included in IAS 8 (r1993) were very limited with little guidance as to the definition of a discontinuing operation, or the timing and display of required disclosures. Moreover, in the absence of standards covering recognition and measurement in such circumstances, various inconsistent practices developed among enterprises reporting under IASs.

IAS 35 supersedes these earlier requirements. While still allowing a certain amount of choice in presentation, the Standard provides more guidance in the application of the definition of discontinuing operations and specifies and illustrates disclosure requirements at various stages of discontinuance. The volume of detailed disclosure in respect of each discontinuing operation has also been expanded.

5.14.1 Definition

'A discontinuing operation is a component of an enterprise:

(a) that the enterprise, pursuant to a single plan, is:
   (i) disposing of substantially in its entirety, such as by selling the component in a single transaction, by de-merger or spin-off of ownership of the component to the enterprise's shareholders;

[1] IAS 35 uses the term 'discontinuing' operation instead of 'discontinued' operation to reflect the fact that it requires recognition of a discontinuance when a detailed formal plan is adopted and announced, and not only at or near the end of the process of discontinuing the operation as was the case prior to introduction of the new regime. (IAS 35.4)

(ii) disposing of piecemeal, such as by selling off the component's assets and settling its liabilities individually; or

(iii) terminating through abandonment;

(b) that represents a separate major line of business or geographical area of operations; and

(c) that can be distinguished operationally and for financial reporting purposes.'

(IAS 35.2)

A single plan

As stated in criterion (a) above, discontinuance may take different forms but a critical element which differentiates it from other kinds of business transactions involving closure of facilities, abandonment of product lines and disposals of related assets and liabilities is the existence of an overall co-ordinated plan. (IAS 35.3)

For example, 'instead of disposing of a major component in its entirety, an enterprise may discontinue and dispose of the component by selling its assets and settling its liabilities piecemeal (individually or in small groups)'. These individual disposals may result in a gain or loss, and may occur over a period of months or even longer, sometimes, straddling different accounting periods. However, as mentioned above, to qualify as a discontinuing operation, the disposals must be pursuant to a single plan. (IAS 35.5)

IAS 35 does not give a definition of a 'single plan'. However, the Standard states that a discontinuing operation is a special case of a 'restructuring' as this term is defined in IAS 37, *Provisions, Contingent Liabilities and Contingent Assets.* (IAS 35.20) Therefore, definitions of and guidance on what constitutes a 'detailed, formal plan for discontinuance' and 'announcement of the plan' given in that Standard are relevant in determining whether a particular disposal or termination of an operation meets the definition above (see **11.9**).

IAS 35 does not discuss any restriction for the time over which the plan is to be implemented. However, the length of the period of implementation may impact an enterprise's ability to recognise a restructuring provision in respect of the discontinuing operation. This is further discussed in **5.14.2**.

> 'An enterprise may terminate an operation by abandonment without substantial sales of assets. An abandoned operation would be a discontinuing operation if it satisfies the criteria in the definition. However, changing the scope of an operation or the manner in which it is conducted is not an abandonment because that operation, although changed, is continuing.'
>
> (IAS 35.6)

Some activities do not necessarily satisfy criterion (a) of the definition, but might do so in combination with other circumstances. For example:

- ‘• gradual or evolutionary phasing out of a product line or class of service;
- discontinuing, even if relatively abruptly, several products within an ongoing line of business;
- shifting of some production or marketing activities for a particular line of business from one location to another;
- closing of a facility to achieve productivity improvements or other cost savings; and
- selling a subsidiary whose activities are similar to those of the parent or other subsidiaries.’

(IAS 35.8)

A separate major line of business or geographical area of operation
Sale, termination or abandonment of a reportable business segment or geographical segment as defined in IAS 14 (r1997), *Segment Reporting*, would normally satisfy criterion (b) in the definition above. However, a part of a segment may also satisfy that criterion. This is illustrated by the fact that even if the enterprise operates in a single business or geographical segment and therefore does not report segment information, a major product or service line may also satisfy the criteria of the definition. (IAS 35.9) This allows some flexibility and also acknowledges the fact that while the risk profile of a particular component of the business may be not unique enough to warrant separate disclosure under IAS 14 (r1997) on a continuing basis, it may still be beneficial to the users of financial statements to have early access to that information, when such a segment is being discontinued.

Operational and financial distinguishability
To draw the line, an enterprise needs to decide whether a component can be distinguished both operationally and for financial reporting purposes (criterion (c) of the definition). To make this assessment, an enterprise must be able to attribute directly to the component:

- operating assets and liabilities;
- income or gross revenue; and
- at least a majority of operating expenses.

(IAS 35.11)

Items of the financial statements are ‘directly attributable to a component if they would be eliminated when the component is sold, abandoned or otherwise disposed of. Interest and other financing cost is attributed to a discontinuing operation only if the related debt is similarly attributed’. (IAS 35.12)

Further guidance for attributing different elements of financial statements to a component of the business can be found in IAS 14 (r1997) (see **16.9**).

When deciding whether the discontinuance of a component requires disclosure in accordance with IAS 35, the Standard stresses the ability of an enterprise to distinguish such a component operationally. In practice, the level of sophistication of an enterprise's financial reporting system may be a significant factor in management's ability to distinguish a particular component of the business and to attribute to it all elements of the financial statements that are required to be disclosed.

While every sale or disposal of a component of a business will not qualify as a discontinuing operation, additional disclosure may still be required by another IAS. For example, an abandonment of a component may form part of a restructuring and thus be covered by IAS 37 (see **11.9**). Alternatively, the component may be material enough to require separate disclosure under IAS 8 (r1993) as an item akin to the UK exceptional item (see **5.10.1**).

However, the Standard restricts the use of the term 'discontinuing operation' to those events that meet the definition above. (IAS 35.43)

5.14.2 Recognition and measurement

IAS 35 does not establish any new principles for deciding when and how to recognise and measure items resulting from a discontinuing operation. Instead, it requires that enterprises follow the recognition and measurement principles in other IASs, specifically:

- IAS 36, *Impairment of Assets*, in respect of any impairment losses (or reversals) related to the assets to be discontinued (see **10.12**);
- IAS 37, *Provisions, Contingent Liabilities and Contingent Assets*, in respect of any provisions required to be made (see **11.9**);
- IAS 19 (r2000), *Employee Benefits*, in respect of any termination benefits paid to affected employees, and the effect of any curtailment of defined benefit pension plans, etc (see Chapter **25**);
- IAS 16 (r1998), *Property, Plant and Equipment*, in respect of disposals of tangible fixed assets (see **10.3.11**).

Provisions

IAS 35 specifically states that a discontinuing operation will also be a 'restructuring' as it is defined in IAS 37. Therefore, when considering which items related to a discontinuing operation qualify for recognition as a provision and the timing for recognition, the rules related to restructuring provisions, as set out in IAS 37, should be followed (see **11.9**).

For example, on the basis of principles in IAS 37 provision cannot be made for future operating losses which relate to a discontinuing operation. (IAS 37.82)

As was noted in **5.14.1** IAS 35 does not require that a discontinuance is completed within a specified period. However, as for other types of restructuring provisions, for the recognition criteria to be met IAS 37 requires that a restructuring 'needs to be planned to begin as soon as possible and to be completed in a timeframe that makes significant changes to the plan unlikely'. (IAS 37.74)

Impairment of assets

IAS 35 does provide some additional guidance for the recognition and measurement of impairment losses in relation to the assets that are part of a discontinuing operation. In this context, the approval and announcement of a plan for discontinuance is deemed to be an 'indication that the assets attributable to the discontinuing operation may be impaired or that an impairment loss previously recognised for those assets should be increased or reversed.' (IAS 35.22) According to IAS 36, management then has an obligation to test for impairment all assets attributable to this discontinuing operation.

Whether the recoverable amount of an asset included within a discontinuing operation is assessed for the individual asset or for the asset's cash generating unit is determined as follows:

- where the operation is being sold in a single transaction, recoverable amount is determined for the operation as a whole and then allocated to individual assets in accordance with IAS 36;
- where the operation is disposed of through a piecemeal sale, recoverable amount is determined for individual assets or groups of assets;
- where the operation is abandoned, recoverable amount is determined for individual assets.

(IAS 35.23)

The carrying amount (recoverable amount) of a discontinuing operation would include the carrying amount (recoverable amount) of any goodwill that can be allocated to that discontinuing operation on a reasonable and consistent basis. (IAS 35.26) The residual amount of any goodwill allocated to the discontinuing operation will be included in the calculation of the resulting net gain or loss on discontinuance.

Subsequent to announcement of the plan, negotiation with potential purchasers or other events may indicate that the assets of a discontinuing operation are either further impaired or their recoverable amount has increased. When such events occur, an enterprise re-estimates the recoverable amount of the assets and recognises an additional impairment loss or reversal as appropriate. (IAS 35.24)

5.14.3 Disclosure

The disclosures required in respect of discontinuing operations should be made separately for each discontinuing operation. (IAS 35.38)

On and after the initial disclosure event

The 'initial disclosure event' is the earlier of the following two occurrences:

- the enterprise entering into a binding sale agreement for substantially all of the assets attributable to the discontinuing operation; or
- the enterprise's board of directors or similar governing body both approving and announcing a detailed, formal plan for the discontinuance.

(IAS 35.16)

The announcement by the Board of its intentions to discontinue an operation should be such that it creates an expectation in the minds of those affected by the decision that the operation will be discontinued. For example, an employee should have the expectation created that his/her job will be made redundant. Parties affected by such an announcement include landlords, suppliers, customers and employees.

When the initial disclosure event occurs, either during an accounting period or after the period end but before the financial statements are authorised for issue, the following disclosures are required to be included in those financial statements:

- a description of the discontinuing operation;
- the business or geographical segment(s) in which it is reported in accordance with IAS 14 (r1997), *Segment Reporting* (see Chapter **16**);
- the date and the nature of the initial disclosure event;
- the date or period in which the discontinuance is expected to be completed if known or determinable;
- the carrying amounts, as of the balance sheet date, of the total assets and the total liabilities to be disposed of;
- the amounts of revenue, expenses, and pre-tax profit or loss from ordinary activities attributable to the discontinuing operation during the current financial reporting period, and the income tax expense relating thereto as required by paragraph 81(h) of IAS 12 (r2000) , *Income Taxes*; and
- the amounts of net cash flows attributable to the operating, investing, and financing activities of the discontinuing operation during the current financial reporting period.

(IAS 35.27 and 29)

When considering which items should be included in this disclosure, the test is whether or not the item will be disposed of, settled, reduced or eliminated when the discontinuance is complete. Only those items which will cease or be significantly reduced after the discontinuance qualify for inclusion in the disclosure.

The requirement to give the disclosures when the initial disclosure event occurs after the period end but before the financial statements are authorised for issue is consistent with the requirements of IAS 10 (r1999), *Events After the Balance Sheet Date*, in respect of events occurring after the balance sheet date.

Other disclosures

In the period when an enterprise disposes of individual assets or settles individual liabilities attributable to a discontinuing operation or enters into binding agreements for the sale of such assets or settlement of such liabilities (which may be in the period of initial disclosure event or in a later period) disclosures are required of:

- ‘the amount of the pre-tax gain or loss and
- income tax expense relating to the gain or loss, as required by paragraph 81(h) of IAS 12 (r2000)’.

(IAS 35.31)

The disclosure of the amount of pre-tax gain or loss from the sale of or settlement of assets and liabilities is the only disclosure in IAS 35 that is *required* to be presented on the face of the income statement.

Additionally, in relation to the assets to be disposed of the enterprise discloses:

- ‘the net selling price or range of prices (which is after deducting the expected disposal costs) of those net assets for which the enterprise has entered into binding sale agreements;
- the expected timing of receipt of those cash flows; and
- the carrying amount of those net assets.’

(IAS 35.31)

If assets are either sold, or subject to a binding sale agreement entered into, after the period end but before the financial statements are approved for issue, the above disclosures should be included in the financial statements if non-disclosure would affect the ability of the financial statement users to make proper evaluations and decisions. (IAS 35.32)

Subsequent to the period of initial disclosure, an enterprise will need to include in its financial statements ‘a description of any significant changes in the amount or timing of cash flows relating to the assets and liabilities to be disposed of or settled and the events causing those changes.’ (IAS 35.33)

All of the above disclosures 'should continue in financial statements for periods up to and including the period in which the discontinuance is completed.' (IAS 35.35)

'If an enterprise abandons or withdraws from a plan that was previously reported as a discontinuing operation, that fact and its effect should be disclosed.' (IAS 35.36) This means the reversal of any impairment loss or provision previously recognised in respect of that discontinuing operation and disclosure of the effect of this reversal on the financial statements of current and prior periods.

Interim reports

IAS 35 requires disclosure in the notes to an interim financial report of 'any significant activities or events since the end of the most recent annual reporting period relating to a discontinuing operation and any significant changes in the amount or timing of cash flows relating to the assets and liabilities to be disposed of or settled'. (IAS 35.47)

5.14.4 Presentation

IAS 35 allows a choice of presentation for the required numerical disclosures; they can be presented either on the face of the financial statements or in the notes thereto except that the disclosure of any pre-tax gain or loss recognised on the disposal of assets or settlement of liabilities should be shown on the face of the income statement. However, it encourages presentation of the elements of income and expense and the elements of the cash flows on the face of the relevant statements. (IAS 35.39) Appendix I to the Standard gives an illustrative example of two types of income statement presentation:

- a columnar format, where additional columns are provided to segregate the elements of income and expense relating to discontinuing operations and continuing operations with a total column; and
- a vertical format, effectively consisting of two income statements (one for continuing operations, and one for discontinuing operation) where only totals of profit or loss from ordinary activities are shown for the whole enterprise.

Whether an enterprise chooses to present a segregated income statement and cash flow statement or chooses to disclose the analysis in the notes to the financial statements, comparative figures presented in financial statements prepared after the initial disclosure event should be restated to segregate continuing and discontinuing operations in a manner consistent with the current year. (IAS 35.45)

Where prior period figures have been restated, it is good practice to indicate this in the heading to the comparative figures on each page of the financial statements, together with a reference to the note explaining the restatement.

Example 5.9

	2000	*1999 as restated (see note 2)*
	£'000	*£'000*
Turnover	2,543	2,487

The Standard explicitly disallows presenting a discontinuing operation as an extraordinary item. This means that the results of a discontinuing operation are included in results of ordinary activities of an enterprise. The guidance note explains that the two examples of extraordinary items cited in IAS 8 (r1993) (closure of operations due to expropriation of assets and natural disasters) do not fall within the scope of discontinuing operations, as defined by IAS 35, as such events are not within the control of the management of the enterprise. (IAS 35.41 and IAS 35.42) Disclosure requirements in respect of such extraordinary items are discussed in **5.11**.

5.14.5 Comparison with UK GAAP

Under FRS 3, *Reporting Financial Performance*, to qualify as a ***discontinued operation*** (as opposed to ***discontinuing operation*** under IASs), among other things, a sale or termination must be completed either by the end of the reporting period or the earlier of three months into the new reporting period and the date on which the financial statements are approved. IAS 35 does not set a time limit for the completion of the discontinuance. In the UK the ASB is developing a new standard to replace FRS 3. The exposure draft, FRED 22, *Revision of FRS 3 'Reporting Financial Performance'*, proposes a move away from FRS 3's discontinued operations and suggests adopting IAS 35's definition of discontinuing operations and adopting an amended version of IAS 35's definition of initial disclosure event.

FRS 3 requires that, at a minimum, turnover and operating profit be analysed between continuing and discontinued operations on the face of the income statement. In addition, it requires disclosure on the face of the income statement or in the notes of each of the statutory format headings between turnover and operating profit analysed between continuing and discontinued operations. This approach is retained in FRED 22 and expanded to include an analysis of the financing and treasury section and other gains and losses section of the proposed performance statement. IAS 35 requires disclosure of all material amounts of revenue and expenses as well as pre-tax profit or loss from ordinary activities attributable to a discontinuing operation. But unlike FRS 3, it allows a choice between presentation of this information on the face of the income statement and in the notes thereto. In addition to continuing and discontinued operations, the analysis required under UK GAAP includes acquisitions, as a component of continuing operations.

In contrast to IAS 35, UK GAAP does not require disclosure of the elements of cash flows relating to discontinued operations. However, FRS 1 (revised), *Cash Flow Statements*, encourages disclosure of a division of cash flows from operating activities into those relating to continuing and to discontinued operations when it is useful to users of the financial statements.

There are no equivalent requirements in UK GAAP for the disclosure of net selling prices, carrying amounts and the expected timing of receipt of the related cash flows in respect of the assets attributable to a discontinued operation for which the enterprise has entered into binding sale agreements.

Requirements for recognition and measurement of impairment of assets arising as a result of a decision to discontinue an operation are broadly similar in both IASs and UK GAAP. For further discussion of these requirements see **10.12**.

However, despite the fact that the requirements for recognition and measurement of restructuring provisions in FRS 12, *Provisions, Contingent Liabilities and Contingent Assets*, are similar to those in IAS 37, *Provisions, Contingent Liabilities and Contingent Assets*, provisions for discontinuance recognised in accordance with UK GAAP and IASs could differ. This is due to the fact that under UK GAAP the standard that deals more specifically with the subject of discontinued operations takes precedent over the standard which establishes general requirements for provisions. In this case, FRS 3, as the standard that specifically addresses accounting for discontinued operations, requires that a provision is made for:

(a) direct costs of the sale or termination;

and

(b) any operating losses of the operation up to the date of termination or sale;

less

(c) the aggregate profit, if any, to be recognised in the profit and loss account from the future profits of the operation.

As was mentioned above, IAS 37 does not allow future operating losses up to the date of termination or sale to be included in a provision for discontinuance.

5.14.6 Comparison with US GAAP

Similar to IAS 35, in accordance with APB 30, *Reporting the Results of Operations*, discontinued operations include business segments still in operation where the management commits itself to a formal plan of disposal. However, when this happens before entering into a binding sale agreement for substantially all of the assets of the discontinuing operation, IAS 35 requires initial disclosure of discontinuance when such commitment by the management is demonstrated by both approval and formal announcement of the plan. APB 30 does not explicitly require such announcement to be made although it could be argued that management is not committed until an announcement is made. Also, under US GAAP, discontinued operations include discontinued business segments related to a major class of customer. Depending on the particular circumstances, the definition in IAS 35 might or might not include such operations.

Under US GAAP, discontinued operations are presented on the face of the income statement below income from continuing operations after tax and are shown net of related income taxes. Separate line items are included for income or loss from operations and gain or loss on disposal. IAS 35 encourages but does not require the presentation of revenue, expenses, pre-tax results of ordinary activities and tax expense in relation to discontinuing operations on the face of the income statement.

Under US GAAP, if at the balance sheet date or at the date of the issuance of the financial statements, management intends to discontinue an operation and has committed itself to a formal plan of discontinuance, any expected loss on disposal including future losses from operations from the date of the decision to discontinue to the expected disposal date are accrued. Any expected income from operations may be accrued only to the extent of any expected loss on disposal. Any further income from operations or expected gain on disposal is not recognised until realised. IAS 37 explicitly prohibits generating provisions for future operating losses.

US GAAP requires a description to be given in the notes to financial statements, starting in the period of measurement date, of the remaining assets and liabilities of the segment at the balance sheet date. Many companies also segregate the assets and liabilities of discontinued operations from assets and liabilities of the continuing operations on the face of the balance sheet, and present them either as current and non-current or in a single line amount on a net basis. IAS 35 requires disclosure of the carrying amounts of the total assets and total liabilities to be disposed of in respect of the discontinuing operation but does not specify its placement.

5.14.7 *Examples from published financial statements*

Note that the excerpts given do not always comply in full with all aspects of IAS and as such are not necessarily examples of best practice but merely of current practice.

Example 5.10

Consolidated Income Statement (extract)

	Note	1.1.–31.12. 2000 € million	1999 € million
Net sales	1, 28	**2,486.0**	2,526.2
Share of associates' net income	2, 28	**–0.5**	2.8
Other income from operations	3	**30.9**	32.6
Cost of sales	4, 5	**–2,170.3**	–2,262.5
Depreciation	6, 28	**–171.3**	–188.1
Operating income	28	**174.8**	111.0
Financing income and expenses	7	**–30.5**	–52.4
Income before non-recurring items, taxes and minority interest		**144.3**	58.6
Non-recurring items from discontinuing operations	8, 22	**162.2**	–
Income before taxes and minority interests		**306.5**	58.6
Direct taxes	9	**–96.3**	–27.8
Income before minority interests		**210.2**	30.8
Minority interest		**–2.4**	–0.9
Net income		**207.8**	29.9
Earnings per share, €	10	**0.73**	0.23

The income statement has been split into continuing and discontinuing operations in Note 22

8. Discontinuing operations	*2000*	*1999*
Profit on sales	**244.7**	–
Shut down costs	**–82.5**	–
Total	**162.2**	–

22. Discontinuing Operations

The Kemira Pigments business and the CPS unit or the Tikkurila Group's colour processing business, were sold because they were not core businesses. Kemira Agro's production in Rozenburg was also closed. Kemira Pigments Inc. was sold on 31 March 2000 and Kemira Pigments BV on 30 April 2000. The remaining company, Kemira Pigments Oy, was transferred to the Kemira Chemicals business area as from 1 January 2001. The portion of the tinting machine business that belonged to the CPS group was sold on 31 August 2000, and the colour processing systems business was sold on 30 September 2000. The Board of Directors of Kemira Oyj decided to wind up Kemira Agro Rozenburg, and production was closed in December 2000. The closure of production resulted in a non-recurring charge to earnings of €82.5 million.

Income statement

The results of the above-mentioned companies are included in the income statements for discontinuing businesses up to the time they cease to be part of the Group. The net amount of the capital gains on divestments of the companies and the non-recurring expenses for Kemira Agro Rozenburg are stated within the income statements for discontinuing businesses.

Continuing operations	*2000*	*1999*
Net sales	**2,124.0**	1,920.2
Share of associates' net income	**–0.5**	2.7
Other operating income	**28.2**	29.7
Expenses	**–1,833.9**	–1,698.6
Depreciation	**–150.3**	–139.5
Operating income	**167.5**	114.5
Financing income and expenses	**–23.4**	–32.9
Income before Group contribution, taxes and minority interests	**144.1**	81.6
Group contribution	**–3.3**	6.7
Net income before taxes and minority interests	**140.8**	88.3
Income taxes	**–50.7**	–29.7
Minority interests	**–1.1**	–0.4
Net income after taxes	**89.0**	58.2

Discontinuing operations	*2000*	*1999*
Net sales	**362.0**	606.0
Share of associates' net income	–	0.1
Other operating income	**2.7**	3.0
Expenses	**–336.4**	–563.9
Depreciation	**–21.0**	–48.7
Operating income	**7.3**	–3.5
Financing income and expenses	**–7.1**	–19.5
Income before Group contribution, non-recurring items, taxes and minority interests	**0.2**	–23.0
Group contribution	**3.3**	–6.7
Income taxes	**1.1**	1.8
Minority interests	**–1.3**	–0.4
Net income before discontinuance	**3.3**	–28.3
Gain on discontinuance	**244.7**	–
Provision for employee termination	**–22.3**	–
Provision for cleaning and contracts	**–17.7**	–
Impairment loss	**–42.5**	–
Tax on discontinuance	**–46.7**	–
Net income after taxes	**118.8**	–28.3
Total Group net income from ordinary activities	92.3	29.9

Balance sheet, discontinuing operations		
Carrying amount of total assets (outside Group and intra-Group)	**43.7**	561.6
Carrying amount of total liabilities (outside Group companies)		
Interest-bearing liabilities	**0.4**	47.4
Interest-free liabilities	**52.2**	122.8
Total	**52.6**	170.2

Kemira Agro Rozenburg's total assets and liabilities are included in the balance sheet at 31 December 2000 and 31 December 1999 and the assets and liabilities of Kemira Pigments Inc., Kemira Pigments BV and Tikkurila CPS Group are given in the balance sheet at 31 December 1999.

Cash flow from discontinuing operations		
Cash flow from operations	**–**	34.9
Capital expenditure	**–16.7**	–36.3
Sales of assets	**493.9**	0.3
Cash flow before financing	**477.2**	–1.1
Financing	**–480.2**	3.6
Increase/decrease in liquid funds	**–3.0**	2.5

Kemira Group
Finland
31 December 2000
International Accounting Standards (with exception of IAS 19)

5.15 Changes in accounting estimates

Many items included in financial statements are based on estimates made by management of the enterprise. For example, stock obsolescence, bad debt, the useful lives of fixed assets and in many cases, the amount of a contingent liability, are all based on management estimates. Inevitably, in subsequent periods, management estimates may need to be revisited. When an estimate is revised the effect of the revision or change of the estimate is included in the determination of net profit or loss in the period of the change, if the change affects the period only; or the period of the change and future periods, if the change affects both. (IAS 8 (r1993).26) The standards and guidance in IAS 8 (r1993) refer only to current and future periods. IAS 8 (r1993) does not permit restatement of prior periods for changes in accounting estimates.

Although, a change in estimate is, by its nature, related to prior periods when the original estimate was made, financial statements of prior periods are still considered to be properly prepared since the estimate made could have only been based on information available at that time.

Example 5.11

At 31 December 20x1, an enterprise applies a particular formula to the amount of its sales for the year and as a result, estimates that its warranty provision should be £30,000. During 20x2, the enterprise receives warranty claims amounting to £5,000. Based on this experience, the enterprise decides that the formula was not an accurate predictor of actual results and decides to provide for £8,000 based on management judgement.

At 31 December 20x2, the warranty provision account has a balance of £25,000 (£30,000 – £5,000). In order to reduce the account balance to £8,000, £7,000 of the provision is released to the income statement of 20x2. No adjustment is made to the financial statements of 20x1. Under IAS 37 the enterprise will need to disclose the release of the provision in the notes to the financial statements.

'For consistency, the effect of a change in accounting estimate is required to be included in the same income statement classification as was used previously for the estimate.' (IAS 8 (r1993).28)

The guidance suggests that classification refers to the distinction between ordinary activities and extraordinary items. However, it is logical to apply the concept to the components of the income statement identified in IAS 1 (r1997), *Presentation of Financial Statements*, so that, for example, a change in estimate where the initial estimate was recognised as cost of sales would also be recognised as cost of sales.

> 'When the change in estimate has a material effect on the current income statement or is expected to have a material effect in the future, the nature and amount of the change of estimate should be disclosed. If it is impracticable to quantify the amount, this fact and the nature of the change should be disclosed.' (IAS 8 (r1993).30)

At times, it may be difficult to draw a distinction between a change in accounting policy and a change in estimate. When this is not clear, a more conservative approach is generally taken to treat such an item as a change in accounting estimate.

A change in the method of depreciation or amortisation due to the change in the expected pattern of economic benefits from the assets is required to be treated as a change in accounting estimate. (IAS 16 (r1998), *Property, Plant and Equipment*, para.52)

Example 5.12

In 20x2 an enterprise decided to change its depreciation policy for certain fixed assets which were previously depreciated using the diminishing balance method. Based on past experience management believes that the consumption of economic benefits associated with these assets is better reflected by using straight line method of depreciation. The resultant adjustment is treated as a change in accounting estimate, and therefore the depreciation charge for the current and future periods is adjusted. Comparative information is not restated. Thus, if at the start of 20x2 the net book value of the fixed assets was €10,000 and, at that date, the remaining useful economic lives of the assets was five years, depreciation of €2,000 would be charged in 20x2 and each of the years to 20x6. This applies even if the annual depreciation charge would have been, say, €2,500 had the straight-line method been used all along.

5.15.1 Comparison with UK GAAP and US GAAP

The treatment of changes in estimates under IAS 8 (r1993) is very similar to the treatment under both UK and US GAAP.

5.16 Fundamental errors

'Fundamental errors are errors discovered in the current period that are of such significance that the financial statements of one or more prior periods can no longer be considered to have been reliable at the date of their issue.' (IAS 8 (r1993).6) In other words, in light of the error, previous financial statements no longer can be considered to present fairly the financial position, performance or cash flows of the enterprise. Such errors are expected to occur only rarely and do not encompass immaterial items such as clerical errors, small defalcations, etc. Fundamental errors do not arise from a change in accounting estimate as described above since a change in estimate involves a revision of an approximation rather than an error. (IAS 8 (r1993).33)

It is suggested that a fundamental error should be recognised only in the very rare circumstances when it is acknowledged that the financial statements should not have been issued in the form in which they were. An error in an accounting estimate, however large, which is apparent with the benefit of hindsight is not a fundamental error if the estimate was reasonably made on the basis of the information available at the time.

IAS 8 (r1993) offers two treatments for fundamental errors, a benchmark, which is very similar to the treatment required by FRS 3, *Reporting Financial Performance*, in the UK and US GAAP, and an allowed alternative treatment, which is similar to the treatment required by law in many continental European countries.

5.16.1 Benchmark treatment

> 'The amount of the correction of a fundamental error that relates to prior periods should be reported by adjusting the opening balance of retained earnings. Comparative information should be restated, unless it is impracticable to do so.' (IAS 8 (r1993).34)

This treatment presents the financial statements as if the error had been corrected in the period in which it occurred. Thus, if an error occurred in a previous period which is not shown for comparative purposes, the opening balance of retained earnings of the earliest period presented is adjusted to correct the error.

Where prior period figures have been restated it is good practice to indicate this in the heading to the comparative figures on each page of the financial statements together with a reference to the note explaining the prior period adjustment (see *Example 5.9*).

The following disclosures should be made when the benchmark treatment is followed:

> '• the nature of the fundamental error;
> • the amount of the correction for the current period and for each prior period presented;
> • the amount of the correction relating to periods prior to those included in the comparative information; and
> • the fact that comparative information has been restated or that it is impracticable to do so.'
>
> (IAS 8 (r1993).37)

In addition, the cumulative effect of the correction of a fundamental error is required to be disclosed in the statement showing changes in equity (see Chapter **8**). (IAS 1 (r1997).86(c))

Example 5.13

When preparing its accounts for the year ended 31 December 20x2, management of an enterprise discovers that due to a systematic computer error reported revenues were overstated by £100,000 in 20x0 and £150,000 in 20x1. The tax rate is 30 per cent. The reported 20x1 income statement and statement of retained earnings are set out below:

Income statement (as reported previously)

	20x1
Revenue	£750,000
Cost of sales	(300,000)
Gross profit	450,000
Distribution costs	(50,000)
Administrative expenses	(55,000)
Profit from operating activities	345,000
Interest expense	(5,000)
Income tax	(102,000)
Net profit	£238,000

Reconciliation of retained earnings (as reported previously)

	20x1
Opening balance	£1,000,000
Net profit for year	238,000
Closing retained earnings	£1,238,000

Under the benchmark treatment:

- the correction relating to 20x0, net of tax, is made to the opening balance of retained earnings for 20x1 since the financial statements of 20x0 are not shown for comparative purposes;
- the error which occurred in 20x1 is corrected in the net profit figure for 20x1; and
- the cumulative effect of the errors is adjusted against the opening balance of retained earnings for 20x2.

Income statement – benchmark treatment

	20x2	*20x1 (as restated – see Note 5)*
Revenue	£700,000	£600,000
Cost of sales	(350,000)	(300,000)
Gross profit	350,000	300,000
Distribution costs	(60,000)	(50,000)
Administrative expenses	(60,000)	(55,000)
Profit from operating activities	230,000	195,000
Interest expense	(5,000)	(5,000)
Income taxes	(67,500)	(57,000)
Net profit	£157,500	£133,000

Reconciliation of retained earnings – benchmark treatment

	20x2	*20x1*
Opening balance as previously reported	£1,238,000	£1,000,000
Correction of fundamental error – see Note 5	(175,000)	(70,000)
Opening balance as restated	1,063,000	930,000
Net profit for year	157,500	133,000
Closing retained earnings	£1,220,500	£1,063,000

Note 5: During the year, management discovered that due to a systematic computer error, revenues were overstated in 20x1 by £150,000 and in 20x0 by £100,000. The after tax effect on net profit was £105,000 in 20x1 and £70,000 in 20x0. The error has been corrected by adjusting the opening balances of retained earnings for 20x2 and 20x1 and restating the comparative information for 20x1 as if revenue had not been overstated in that period.

5.16.2 *Allowed alternative treatment*

Under the allowed alternative treatment, 'the amount of the correction of a fundamental error should be included in the determination of net profit or loss for the current period. Comparative information should be presented as reported in the financial statements of the prior period. Additional pro forma information, prepared in accordance with the benchmark treatment should be presented unless it is impracticable to do so.' (IAS 8 (r1993).38)

The intent of the IASC Board in including this allowed alternative treatment was to allow preparers in countries where changes to comparative numbers may be prohibited by law to comply with IAS 8 (r1993) by including the cumulative amount of the correction of the error in the profit or loss of the current period. However, in order to provide information for users of financial statements which is comparable to that of other companies the additional pro forma information identical to the benchmark treatment is given.

When the allowed alternative treatment is followed, the following information should be disclosed:

- 'the nature of the fundamental error;
- the amount of the correction recognised in net profit or loss for the current period; and
- the amount of the correction included in each period for which pro forma information is presented and the amount of the correction relating to periods prior to those included in the pro forma information. If it is impracticable to present pro forma information, this fact should be disclosed.'

(IAS 8 (r1993).40)

Although no guidance is given on the presentation of this information, it would appear that if a fundamental error has occurred, it would fall into the category of items which by their nature are relevant to explain the performance of the enterprise and thus are required to be disclosed on the face of the current period income statement by IAS 1 (r1997) (see **5.4**). However, the correction of a fundamental error is not by its nature an extraordinary item unless the misstatement related to an item that was or should have been classified as an extraordinary item in the financial statements containing that error. Thus, the amount of the correction will generally be included in net profit or loss from ordinary activities.

Pro-forma information may be presented as separate columns in the financial statements alongside normal presentation (as suggested by IAS 8 (r1993).39) or in the notes thereto. In both cases, pro-forma information should be clearly identified as such.

Example 5.14

The same facts as in *Example 5.13* but using the allowed alternative treatment.

Income statement – allowed alternative treatment

	20x2	*20x1*
Revenue before correction of fundamental error	£700,000	£750,000
Correction of fundamental error – see note 5	250,000	–
Revenue	450,000	750,000
Cost of sales	(350,000)	(300,000)
Gross profit	100,000	450,000
Distribution costs	(60,000)	(50,000)
Administrative expenses	(60,000)	(55,000)
(Loss)/profit from operating activities	(20,000)	345,000
Interest expense	(5,000)	(5,000)
Income tax – see note 5	7,500	(102,000)
Net (loss)/profit	£(17,500)	£238,000

Reconciliation of retained earnings – allowed alternative treatment

	20x2	*20x1*
Opening balance	£1,238,000	£1,000,000
Net (loss)/profit for year	(17,500)	238,000
Closing retained earnings	£1,220,500	£1,238,000

Note 5: During the year, management discovered that due to a systematic computer error, revenues were overstated in 20x1 by £150,000 and in 20x0 by £100,000. The error has been corrected by reducing current year revenue by £250,000 and the tax charge by £75,000, resulting in an overall decrease of £175,000. Pro forma information is provided below which illustrates the effect of correcting the error by adjusting the opening balances of retained earnings for 20x2 and 20x1 and restating the comparative information for 20x1. (The statement of retained earnings and income statements under the benchmark treatment from Example 5.14 would be provided and clearly marked as 'pro forma.')

5.16.3 Comparison with UK GAAP and US GAAP

The requirements relating to fundamental errors are very similar under the benchmark treatment of IAS 8 (r1993), UK GAA5P and US GAAP.

5.17 Changes in accounting policies

Requirements for the selection of appropriate accounting policies, their consistent application for all similar items or items of the same category (where applicable), and the treatment of changes in accounting policies on the first-time application of IASs/IFRSs are discussed in Chapter **4.**

In order to achieve consistency in financial reporting, changes in accounting policies must be rare occurrences. As such,

> '• a change in accounting policy should be made only:
> - if required by statute or by an accounting standard setting body; or
> - if the change will result in a more appropriate presentation of events or transactions in the financial statements of the enterprise.'
>
> (IAS 8 (r1993).42)

In some cases, it could be necessary to change a particular accounting policy to comply with a statute or a national accounting standard. IASs allow such change when the new accounting policy is permitted by applicable International Accounting Standards. However, when this accounting policy is explicitly disallowed under IASs, the resultant financial statement presentation, while complying with the statute of national standard, can no longer be described as being in accordance with IASs. For further discussion see **4.7.1** and **4.7.9**.

A change in accounting policy does not occur when a policy is adopted to account for transactions which have not occurred previously or which differ in substance from previously occurring transactions.

When an enterprise initially adopts a new or revised IAS/IFRS, the transition provisions of the particular Standard are adopted. Generally these provisions provide an alternative to retrospective application since such application can be cumbersome. For example, when IAS 36, *Impairment of Assets*, was issued and became mandatory for the first time its transitional provisions required prospective application. If no transition provisions are given, the change is accounted for in accordance with either the benchmark or allowed alternative treatments described below. (IAS 8 (r1993).46)

If an IAS/IFRS is issued but is not yet effective and the enterprise does not elect to adopt the new IAS/IFRS early, it is considered best practice to disclose the nature of any resulting future change in accounting policy and an estimate of its effects if practicable. (IAS 8 (r1993).48)

The treatments offered in IAS 8 (r1993) for a change in accounting policy are similar to those for the correction of a fundamental error. The benchmark treatment is to account for the change by restating opening retained earnings as if the new accounting policy had always been in effect, and the allowed alternative treatment is to account for the change by adjusting the current period net profit or loss with the catch-up adjustment in respect of earlier years with a pro forma presentation of the benchmark treatment.

5.17.1 Benchmark treatment

> 'A change in accounting policy should be applied retrospectively unless the amount of any resulting adjustment that relates to prior periods is not reasonably determinable. Any resulting adjustment should be reported as an adjustment to the opening balance of retained earnings. Comparative information should be restated unless it is impracticable to do so.'
>
> (IAS 8 (r1993).49)

To apply an accounting policy retrospectively, a preparer must first determine what the effect on opening retained earnings would be if the entity had always adopted the new policy. The amount which relates to financial statement periods earlier than those shown is then adjusted against the opening balance of retained earnings of the earliest period presented. If it is not practicable to determine this amount, for example if accounting records do not exist to allow this amount to be calculated, then the change in accounting policy is accounted for prospectively, that is, the policy is applied to transactions occurring after the date of the change. Under prospective application, no previous periods are restated.

> 'When a change in accounting policy has a material effect on the current period or any prior period presented, or may have a material effect in subsequent periods, an enterprise should disclose the following:
>
> - the reasons for the change;
> - the amount of the adjustment for the current period and for each period presented;
> - the amount of the adjustment relating to periods prior to those included in the comparative information; and
> - the fact that comparative information has been restated or that it is impracticable to do so.'
>
> (IAS 8 (r1993).53)

In addition, the cumulative effect of the change in accounting policy is required to be disclosed in the statement showing changes in equity. (IAS 1(r1997).86(c))

Example 5.15

On 1 January 20x2, an enterprise decides to change its method of accounting for stock from the last-in, first-out method ('LIFO') to the first-in, first-out method ('FIFO') in order to be in line with the benchmark treatment in IAS 2 (r1993), *Inventories*, and to conform more closely to industry practice. Management has always kept FIFO cost records for information purposes and thus can determine that if FIFO had always been used:

- for all periods prior to 20x1, cost of sales would be £300,000 lower than previously reported and income taxes would have been £100,000 higher; and
- cost of sales for 20x1 would have been £30,000 lower than previously reported and income taxes would have been £10,000 higher.

Income statement (as previously reported)

	20x1
	£'000
Revenue	1,000
Cost of sales	(330)
Gross profit	670
Distribution costs	(100)
Administrative expenses	(80)
Profit from operating activities	490
Interest expense	(10)
Income taxes	(143)
Net profit	337

Reconciliation of retained earnings (as previously reported)

	20x1
	£'000
Opening balance	8,000
Net profit for year	337
Closing retained earnings	8,337

Income statement (benchmark treatment)

	20x2	*20x1*
	£'000	*£'000*
		(as restated – see Note 2)
Revenue	1,200	1,000
Cost of sales	(400)	(300)
Gross profit	800	700
Distribution costs	(120)	(100)
Administrative expenses	(100)	(80)
Profit from operating activities	580	520
Interest expense	(20)	(10)
Income taxes	(168)	(153)
Net profit	392	357

Reconciliation of retained earnings

	20x2 £'000	20x1 £'000
Opening balance as previously reported	8,337	8,000
Effect of change in accounting policy with respect to inventory, net of income taxes of £110,000 (20x1 – £100,000) – see Note 2	220	200
Opening balance as restated	8,557	8,200
Net profit for year	392	357
Closing retained earnings	8,949	8,557

Note 2: On 1 January 20x2, the company changed the method by which it accounts for the cost of inventory from the last-in, first-out method to the first-in, first-out method to be more closely in line with industry practice. Comparative information for 20x1 has been restated to conform to the changed policy. The effect of the change is to decrease cost of sales by £30,000 in 20x1 and in all periods prior to 20x1 by £300,000. The change was accounted for retrospectively by adjusting the opening balances of retained earnings for 20x2 by £220,000 (20x1 – £200,000) net of tax of £110,000 (20x1 – £100,000) as if the first-in, first-out method had always been used.

5.17.2 *Allowed alternative treatment*

Similar to the allowed alternative treatment for fundamental errors, the IASC Board provided this allowed alternative for preparers in countries where the alteration of comparative figures is prohibited by law. This does not, however, prohibit other IAS reporting entities from adopting this treatment.

Under the allowed alternative treatment, 'a change in accounting policy should be accounted for retrospectively unless the amount of any resulting adjustment that relates to prior periods is not reasonably determinable. Any resulting adjustment should be included in the determination of the net profit or loss for the current period.' (IAS 8 (r1993).54) To account for the change retrospectively, a preparer must first determine what the effect on opening retained earnings would be if the entity had always adopted the new policy. This amount is then included as an adjustment in the current year income statement. The effect of this adjustment is that at the end of the period, retained earnings will be stated as if the accounting policy had always been applied.

Separate presentation of the adjustment on the face of the income statement, although not required by IAS 8 (r1993), is required by IAS 1 (r1997) (see **5.4**).

> 'Comparative information should be presented as reported in the financial statements of the prior period. Additional pro forma comparative information, prepared in accordance with the benchmark treatment should be presented unless it is impracticable to do so.'
>
> (IAS 8 (r1993).54)

When it is impracticable to calculate the amount of the adjustment which would be required to account for the change in accounting policy, the change is accounted for prospectively by applying the new policy to all transactions occurring after the date of the change in policy and disclosing that fact.

When a material change in accounting policy takes place, an enterprise should disclose:

- ‘the reasons for the change;
- the amount of the adjustment recognised in net profit or loss in the current period; and
- the amount of the adjustment included in each period for which pro forma information is presented and the amount of the adjustment relating to periods prior to those included in the financial statements. If it is impracticable to present pro forma information, this fact should be disclosed.’

(IAS 8 (r1993).57)

Example 5.16

The same facts as in *Example 5.15* but using the allowed alternative treatment.

Income statement

	20x2 £'000	*20x1 £'000*	*20x2 £'000 Pro forma (see note 2)*	*20x1 £'000 Pro forma (see note 2)*
Revenue	£1,200	£1,000	£1,200	£1,000
Cost of sales	(400)	(330)	(400)	(300)
Cumulative effect of change in accounting policy – see note 2	330	–	–	–
Gross profit	1,130	670	800	700
Distribution costs	(120)	(100)	(120)	(100)
Administrative expenses	(100)	(80)	(100)	(80)
Profit from operating activities	910	490	580	520
Interest expense	(20)	(10)	(20)	(10)
Income taxes (20x2 includes tax effect of cumulative change in accounting policy of £110,000)	(278)	(143)	(168)	(153)
Net profit	612	337	392	357

Statement of retained earnings

	20x2 £'000	20x1 £'000	20x2 £'000 *Pro forma (see note 2)*	20x1 £'000 *Pro forma (see note 2)*
Opening balance as previously reported	8,337	8,000	8,337	8,000
Effect of change in accounting policy with respect to inventory net of income taxes of £110,000 (20x1 – £100,000) – see Note 2	–	–	220	200
Opening balance as restated	8,337	8,000	8,557	8,200
Net profit for year	612	337	392	357
Closing retained earnings	8,949	8,337	8,949	8,557

Note 2: On 1 January 20x2, the company changed the method by which it accounts for the cost of inventory from the last-in, first-out method to the first-in, first-out method to be more closely in line with industry practice. The change was accounted for retrospectively by including a cumulative adjustment in the net profit of the current year of £330,000 and additional income tax of £110,000. Pro forma information has been provided to illustrate the effect of adjusting the opening retained earnings of 20x2 and 20x1 as if the first-in, first-out method had always been used.

5.17.3 Comparison with UK GAAP

The treatment of a change in accounting policy is very similar to the benchmark treatment under IAS 8 (r1993).

5.17.4 Comparison with US GAAP

Under US GAAP, the treatment of most changes in accounting policy is to recognise the cumulative effect of the change in the income statement of the current period in line with the allowed alternative in IAS 8 (r1993). However, the following accounting changes require restatement of prior periods:

(a) a change from LIFO to any other pricing method;
(b) a change in the method of accounting for long-term construction contracts; and
(c) a change to or from the full-cost method of accounting in the extractive industries.

(APB 20, *Accounting Changes*, para.27)

5.17.5 Examples from published financial statements

Note that the excerpts given do not always comply in full with all aspects of IAS and as such are not necessarily examples of best practice but merely of current practice.

Example 5.17

32. CHANGES IN ACCOUNTING POLICY

The group adopted international accounting standards (IAS) for the first time during the current financial year. The financial statements have been prepared and presented as if they had always been prepared in accordance with the standards and interpretations effective for the first period of application.

32.1 Property, plant and equipment: IAS 16 (1998)

In terms of IAS 16 (revised 1998) the cost of an asset includes estimated costs of dismantling and removing the asset and restoring the site. Accordingly provisions have been raised for rehabilitation costs in respect of Pretoria Portland Cement Limited quarries. The related assets are amortised over the expected lives at the quarries.

32.2 Leases: IAS 17 (1997)

The accounting policy in respect of accounting for leases has been altered to comply with IAS 17 (revised 1997). A number of assets leased by Barloworld's leasing company to other group companies were previously not capitalised, although the assets were included in group receivables. As a result of adopting IAS 17 there has been a reallocation of these assets from receivables to property, plant and equipment. There is also a difference between the amounts previously expensed as lease charges and the amounts are now charged to depreciation and finance costs.

Another consequence of adopting IAS 17 from a lessor perspective has been an increase in the amount disclosed as an investment in finance leases and finance income.

32.3 Employee benefits: IAS 19 (1998)

IAS 19 (revised 1998) dealing with employee benefits has been adopted for the first time during the current financial year. This has resulted in an adjustment to the leave pay provision in some operations where it was not fully provided. A further consequence of adopting this standard has resulted in the surplus on defined benefit plans being brought on balance sheet. The income statement charge has also been adjusted to meet the requirements of IAS 19.

32.4 Foreign currencies: IAS 21 (1993)

During the year the group adopted IAS 21 (revised 1993), The Effect of Changes in Foreign Exchange Rates. Foreign currency denominated transactions are no longer accounted for at the forward rates as per forward exchange contracts.

32.5 Business combinations IAS 22 (1993) and intangible assets IAS 38 (1998)

The accounting for business combinations has been adjusted to comply with IAS 22 (revised 1993). In terms of this standard all goodwill arising in financial years beginning on or after 1 October 1995 is capitalised and amortised over its estimated useful life. Intangible assets have been restated at cost where appropriate and amortised on a straight-line basis over their estimated useful lives in accordance with IAS 38 (1998).

32.6 Elimination of intercompany profits: IAS 27 (1994)
During the year the company changed its policy in respect of intercompany transactions. In the past these were always included in turnover and operating profit because they were conducted on an arm's length basis. Revenue in respect of these transactions has been eliminated and disclosed separately in the segmental analysis. The margin in respect of these transactions has been eliminated and released to profit over the useful lives of the underlying assets.

32.7 Financial reporting in hyperinflationary economies: IAS 29 (1994)
This standard was applied for the first time in respect of Siberian and certain African countries for the first time in the current financial year. In terms of this standard, a measuring unit was identified for these operations as the US dollar.

32.8 Accounting for provisions: IAS 37 (1998)
In terms of IAS 37 (1998) provisions should only be recognised where the enterprise has a present obligation (legal or constructive) arising as a result of a past event. This has resulted in a number of provisions that were raised in the past being reversed. The bulk of these provisions related to provisions for maintenance expenditure. A further consequence of adopting this standard was the reversal of the dividend liability reflected in the 1999 accounts.

The aggregate effect of the changes in accounting policies on the financial statements for the year ended 30 September 1999 is as follows:

	Previously stated	*Adjustment*	*Restated 1999*
Income statement			
Adjustment to closing earnings – 1998	3,424	856	4,280
1999 earnings – gross	1,785	(108)	1,677
– taxation	209	(27)	182
– net	1,576	(81)	1,495
Balance sheet			
Interest of all shareholders	(6,990)	(808)	(7,798)
Goodwill and intangible assets		571	571
Property, plant and equipment	4,257	558	4,815
Other assets	9,828	(94)	9,734
Total liabilities	(7,095)	(227)	(7,322)

Barloworld Limited
South Africa
30 September 2000
International Accounting Standards

5.18 Dividends per share

'An enterprise should disclose, either on the face of the income statement or in the notes, the amount of dividends per share, declared or proposed, for the period covered by the financial statements.'

(IAS 1 (r1997).85)

IAS 1 (r1997) gives no guidance as to how this information should be presented. Where there is more than one dividend in a year and the number of shares changes between the two dividends, difficulties arise. The requirement would be satisfied if an enterprise disclosed separately for each class of shares, and for each dividend, the amount of dividends per share declared, proposed or paid and the actual number of shares entitled to receive these dividends. Alternatively, the enterprise could disclose just one dividend per share for each class of shares in issue, calculated by dividing the dividends in aggregate for that class of share by the weighted average number of shares in issue during the year. Where an enterprise chooses to present a single figure for dividends per share for each class of shares, the enterprise should disclose the method it used to calculate this number and, in particular, the number of shares included in the denominator of this calculation.

5.18.1 Comparison with UK and US GAAP

Dividends per share are permitted, but not required, to be disclosed under UK and US GAAP.

CHAPTER 6

Income statement – revenue recognition

6.1 Sources

IAS 11 (r1993)	*Construction Contracts.*
IAS 18 (r1993)	*Revenue.*
IAS 28 (r2000)	*Accounting for Investments in Associates.*
IAS 39 (r2000)	*Financial Instruments: Recognition and Measurement* (effective 1 January 2001).

6.2 Brief summary of the requirements

IAS 18 (r1993) sets out general revenue recognition criteria for revenue arising from:

- the sale of goods;
- the rendering of services; and
- the use by others of enterprise assets yielding interest, royalties and dividends.
- Specific revenue recognition criteria relating to government grants and construction contracts are discussed in Chapters **26** and **27**.

6.3 Development of the requirements

Originally approved in 1982, IAS 18 was amended in 1993 to remove the choice when accounting for the rendering of services between the completed contract method under which no contract revenue is recognised related to a contract until all work has been completed and the percentage of completion method under which contract revenue is recognised as work progresses. At the same time, IAS 11 was also revised to require the percentage of completion method when accounting for construction contracts.

6.4 Scope

The scope of IAS 18 (r1993) excludes certain kinds of revenue (some of which are specifically dealt with in other IASs). In particular, IAS 18 (r1993) does not deal with revenue arising from:

- lease agreements (see Chapter **24**);
- dividends arising from investments accounted for under the equity method (see Chapter **20**);
- insurance contracts of insurance enterprises (see **2.5.1**);
- changes in the fair value of financial assets and financial liabilities or their disposal (see Chapter **12**);
- changes in the value of other current assets (see Chapters **10** and **12**);
- initial recognition and from changes in the fair value of biological assets related to agricultural activity (see Appendix II);
- initial recognition of agricultural produce (see Appendix II); and
- the extraction of mineral ores (current IASB project – see **2.5**).

6.5 Definition of revenue

IAS 18 (r1993) defines revenue as 'the gross inflow of economic benefits during the period arising in the course of the ordinary activities of an enterprise when those inflows result in increases in equity, other than increases relating to contributions from equity participants.' (IAS 18(1993).7) Revenue includes such items as sales, fees, interest, dividends and royalties.

Revenue only includes gross inflows of economic benefits which are received and receivable on behalf of the enterprise itself. The word 'gross' in the definition is not intended to include amounts which are collected on behalf of others. For example, any sales tax which is collected on sales and remitted to a Customs and Excise Authority, would not be included as revenue. Likewise, collection agency revenue does not include the amounts actually collected on behalf of customers, but only the fee or commission relating to the collection.

6.5.1 Comparison with UK GAAP

In general, items which are considered to be revenue under IAS 18 (r1993) are considered revenue under UK GAAP.

6.5.2 Comparison with US GAAP

The definition of revenue in Concepts Statement No. 6 is similar to the definition in IAS 18 (r1993) and in practice most items which meet the definition under Concepts Statement No. 6 will also meet the definition under IAS 18 (r1993).

6.6 Measurement of revenue

'Revenue should be measured at the fair value of the consideration received or receivable.' (IAS 18(r1993).9) Fair value is defined as 'the amount for which an asset could be exchanged or a liability settled, between knowledgeable, willing parties in an arm's length transaction.' (IAS 18 (r1993).7)

6.6.1 Calculation of the fair value of the consideration received or receivable

In practice, revenue is normally measured at the nominal amount of consideration received or receivable. Thus, the amount of revenue recognised in relation to a transaction is net of any trade discounts, early payment discounts or volume rebates given since the amount of these discounts and rebates will not be received as consideration by the seller. In most cases, the nominal value of consideration received or receivable will not vary materially from its fair value because most trade receivables are due within a relatively short time frame.

In the unusual circumstances when consideration is to be received far in the future, the fair value of the consideration to be received will, due to the time value of money, be lower than the nominal amount of the consideration to be received. To calculate the fair value of the consideration to be received, future receipts are discounted using an imputed interest rate which is the more clearly determinable of:

- 'the prevailing rate for a similar instrument of an issuer with a similar credit rating; or
- a rate of interest that discounts the nominal amount of the instrument to the current cash sales price of the goods or services.'

(IAS 18 (r1993).11)

If material, the difference between the nominal amount of consideration to be received and the discounted amount is recognised as interest revenue as it becomes due and in accordance with IAS 39 (r2000).

Example 6.1

An enterprise sells a piece of heavy equipment for £10,000 under a financing agreement which has no stated interest rate.

Scenario A – Calculation of fair value using the prevailing rate for a similar instrument

Annual instalments of £2,000 are due each year for five years from the date of purchase. Another buyer paying cash would be charged £10,000 for the equipment, thus, it is a 'zero percent' financing arrangement. Based on the customer's credit rating, the seller believes the buyer would be able to obtain financing with an interest rate of 10 per cent from other sources.

Answer A

The enterprise must record the consideration to be received at its fair value. Since the consideration will not be received immediately but over a five year period, the fair value of the consideration is not the nominal amount received of £10,000 but a lesser amount which takes into account the time value of money by using an imputed rate of interest to calculate what the series of future payments is worth today. In essence, because the buyer is receiving financing at a below market rate, two transactions are taking place, a sale of goods and a financing transaction. The difference between the fair value of the consideration and its nominal amount is interest revenue from the financing transaction which is recognised as it becomes due each year.

Step 1 – Calculate the fair value of the stream of payments

Assuming no down payment, five annual instalments of £2,000, and an interest rate of 10 per cent, the fair value of the stream of payments which form the consideration is £7,581. Therefore, on the date of the sale, £7,581 is recorded as revenue from the sale of goods and a related debtor created.

Step 2 – Calculate the amount of interest earned each period

The difference between £10,000 and £7,581 of £2,419 will be recognised as interest revenue as it becomes due each year as calculated below. The table below shows each payment and the amount of the payment related to interest and to principal.

	Principal amount outstanding {A} £	*Interest element of payment {A*10%=B}* £	*Principal element of payment {C–B}* £	*Total payment {C}* £
Date of purchase	7,581	0	0	0
End of year 1	7,581	758	1,242	2,000
End of year 2	6,339	634	1,366	2,000
End of year 3	4,973	497	1,503	2,000
End of year 4	3,470	348	1,652	2,000
End of year 5	1,818	182	1,818	2,000
Total		**2,419**	**7,581**	**10,000**

Scenario B – Calculation of fair value using an interest rate that discounts the nominal amount of consideration to the cash price of goods

Annual instalments of £2,000 are due each year for five years from the date of purchase. If the buyer had paid cash for the equipment, the sales price would have been £8,000.

Answer B

Again, the selling enterprise must record the consideration to be received at its fair value. Since there is a £2,000 difference between the cash price of £8,000 and the amount due if the equipment is paid for in instalments of £10,000, the arrangement is effectively a financing transaction as well as a sale of goods. The amount of consideration attributable to the sale of goods is the cash price of £8,000. The remaining £2,000 is interest revenue and is recognised as it becomes due each year using the effective interest method as illustrated below.

Step 1 – Calculate the effective rate of interest

Since the cash price offered is £8,000, the fair value of the consideration is assumed to be £8,000 even though £10,000 of cash will eventually be received by the seller. Therefore, one must determine the interest rate which discounts £10,000 to £8,000 over a five year period assuming no down payment and five annual instalments of £2,000. This interest rate is 7.93 per cent.

Step 2 – Calculate the amount of interest earned each period

The difference of £2,000 between £10,000 and £8,000 will be recognised as interest revenue as it becomes due each year as calculated below. The table below shows each payment and the amount of the payment related to interest and to principal.

	Principal amount outstanding {A} £	*Interest element of payment {A*7.93%=B}* £	*Principal element of payment {C–B}* £	*Total payment {C}* £
Date of purchase	8,000	0	0	0
End of year 1	8,000	634	1,366	2,000
End of year 2	6,634	526	1,474	2,000
End of year 3	5,160	410	1,590	2,000
End of year 4	3,570	283	1,717	2,000
End of year 5	1,853	147	1,853	2,000
Total		**2,000**	**8,000**	**10,000**

6.6.2 Comparison with UK GAAP

No one accounting standard deals with revenue recognition under UK GAAP. However, the concept of recognising revenue at the fair value of the consideration received or receivable is consistent between IAS 18 (r1993) and UK GAAP. In practice, though, discounting as illustrated above is rare under UK GAAP.

6.6.3 Comparison with US GAAP

Under US GAAP, the general rule is that revenue is measured based on the exchange values of the assets, goods or services or liabilities involved. In practice, under US GAAP, discounting as illustrated above is more common than in the UK and guidance for its use has recently been formalised in Concepts Statement No. 7, *Using Cash Flow Information and Present Value in Accounting Measurements.*

6.6.4 Exchanges

When goods are exchanged or swapped for goods of a similar nature and value, no revenue is recognised since the earnings process is not considered to be complete. Such transactions occur in a limited number of commodity industries such as the oil or milk industries. These exchanges are generally made to help suppliers in the distribution of their products when they need a specific quantity of a commodity at a specific time in a particular location. (IAS 18 (1993).12) In practice, such similar exchanges of goods are expected to be very limited.

When goods are exchanged for dissimilar goods, the earnings process is considered complete; thus, a transaction which generates revenue has taken place and revenue is recognised. The revenue is measured as the fair value of the goods received adjusted for any cash payments made by either the buyer or the seller. If the fair value of the goods received cannot be measured reliably, revenue is recognised as the fair value of the goods given up adjusted for any cash payments made or received. (IAS 18 (r1993).12)

The SIC has an exposure draft out on barter transactions. SIC D-31, *Revenue – Barter Transactions Involving Advertising Services*, addresses how revenue from a barter transaction involving advertising should be measured, and the circumstances when the fair value of advertising services received or provided in a barter transaction should be reliably measured. The SIC agreed that:

- an enterprise providing advertising should measure revenue from a barter transaction based on the fair value of the advertising services it receives from its customer unless it is impracticable to measure the revenue reliably, in which case the enterprise should use the fair value of the advertising services it provides to the customer as the measurement of revenue. If the fair value of the advertising services of both enterprises is not reliably measurable, the seller should recognise revenue only to the extent of the carrying amount of assets given up;
- the fair value of advertising services received or provided in a barter transaction can be reliably measured only by reference to non-barter transactions that:
  - involve advertising similar to the advertising in the barter transaction; occur frequently;
  - are expected to continue occurring after the barter transaction;
  - represent a predominant source of revenue from advertising similar to the advertising in the barter transaction;
  - involve cash and/or another form of consideration (e.g., marketable securities, non-monetary assets and other services) that has a reliably measurable fair value; and
  - do not involve the same counterparty as in the barter transaction.

6.7 Identification of the transaction

The Framework identifies the need to represent the substance of transactions over their legal form. This concept is applied when considering whether a transaction is composed of several smaller transactions or conversely, if several transactions are linked and, in substance, form one transaction. For example, a contract to sell software may include an element related to after sale servicing over a period of time. In such a case, it would be appropriate to split the sale transaction into two parts, a sale element and a servicing element and to apply the revenue recognition criteria to each transaction individually. In other circumstances, several related transactions may, in substance, be part of one, larger transaction when the transactions are linked in such a way that the commercial effect cannot be understood without reference to the series of transactions as a whole. For example, a seller may enter into a contract to sell goods but agree in a separate contract to repurchase the goods at a later date. In such a case, the revenue recognition criteria are applied to both transactions together to determine if revenue is recognised. (IAS 18 (r1993).13)

6.8 Recognition criteria

IAS 18 sets out revenue recognition criteria for three types of transactions: the sale of goods, the rendering of services and the use by others of enterprise assets yielding interest, royalties and dividends. The criteria for each type of transaction are based on the recognition criteria in the Framework of probability of future economic benefit and reliable measurement.

6.8.1 Comparison with UK GAAP

Currently no general revenue recognition criteria exist in UK GAAP. However, in July 2001 the UK Accounting Standards Board published a Discussion Paper entitled '*Revenue Recognition*', as a first step towards the development of an accounting standard. The ASB expects the development process to be conducted in consultation with the International Accounting Standards Board and other standard setters, and this process may ultimately lead to a revision of IAS 18 (r1993).

The ASB's Statement of Principles issued in December 1999 states that the effect of a transaction or other event is recognised if:

> '(a) sufficient evidence exists that the new asset or liability has been created or that there has been an addition to an existing asset or liability; and
> (b) the new asset or liability or the addition to the existing asset or liability can be measured at a monetary amount with sufficient reliability.'
>
> (SOP Chapter 5, Principles)

Specifically, the SOP states that a gain (defined broadly to include revenue) is recognised when the effect of a transaction or other event is to increase the entity's recognised net assets (assuming that no contribution from owners and transfer to owners is involved). (SOP 5.26(a)) The SOP emphasises that the starting point for the recognition process is always the effect that a transaction or other event has had on the reporting entity's assets and liabilities. However, it explains that the notions of matching and the critical event in the operating cycle will often help in identifying these effects.

As discussed in Chapter **3**, these criteria are similar to those in the IASB Framework on which the recognition criteria in IAS 18 (r1993) are based. Thus, in general, items which qualify for recognition under IAS 18 (r1993) will qualify under UK GAAP.

6.8.2 Comparison with US GAAP

Under US GAAP, the general rule is that revenue must be both realised or realisable and earned in order to be recognised. Revenue is generally realised or realisable and earned when the following criteria are met:

- there is evidence of an arrangement;
- services have been provided or goods have been delivered;
- the price to the buyer is fixed or determinable; and
- the seller is reasonably assured of collecting the price from the buyer.

These criteria differ from those set out in IAS 18 (r1993) and while they may lead to revenue recognition at the same time in many cases, this will not always be the case. It is difficult to draw more specific, concise and meaningful comparisons between the recognition criteria in IAS 18 (r1993) and US GAAP since US GAAP contains over 90 documents providing guidance on revenue recognition. Most of these documents cover specific industries or problems that have arisen in practice.

6.9 Sale of goods

> 'Revenue from the sale of goods should be recognised when all the following conditions have been satisfied:
>
> (a) the enterprise has transferred to the buyer the significant risks and rewards of ownership of the goods;
> (b) the enterprise retains neither continuing managerial involvement to the degree usually associated with ownership nor effective control over the goods sold;
> (c) the amount of revenue can be measured reliably;
> (d) it is probable that the economic benefits associated with the transaction will flow to the enterprise; and
> (e) the costs incurred or to be incurred in respect of the transaction can be measured reliably.'
>
> (IAS 18.14)

6.9.1 Risks and rewards of ownership

Although each situation must be considered individually, in general, the risks and rewards of ownership pass when legal title or possession of the goods is transferred. However, if upon examination, the substance of the transaction does not entail a transfer of the risks and rewards when title or possession passes, revenue is not recognised.

The examples below illustrate some common situations when the risks have or have not been transferred.

Examples of the transfer of the risks and rewards of ownership

Example A

A manufacturing company gives a three month warranty which covers the cost of any amendments or repairs subsequent to delivery on its customised product. The product is likely to have some serious bugs which will need to be remedied after delivery due to the need to suit the particular customer's environment. It is impossible to estimate with reliability the cost to the seller of carrying out any such amendments or repairs, however, under the terms of the sales contract, title passes on delivery.

Answer A

The risks and rewards of ownership do not pass until the three month period has expired since it is impossible to estimate, and therefore accrue, any costs of repairs or amendments which could be material.

Example B

A magazine distributor sells and delivers magazines to a local shop. If the local shop does not sell the magazines, they are returned to the distributor for a refund or credit. It is impossible to estimate reliably at the time the magazines are delivered how many magazines the local shop will not sell.

Answer B

The risks and rewards of ownership do not pass from the distributor until the local shop has sold the magazines since the receipt of revenue by the distributor is contingent on the sale of the magazines by the local shop.

Example C

A manufacturing company sells a piece of machinery and agrees to install the machinery in the customer's factory. The cost of installation is material to the cost of the total sales price.

Answer C

Because the cost of installation is a material cost to the contract, the seller has not completed his obligation under the contract merely upon delivery. Thus, the risks and rewards of ownership will not pass until the installation is complete regardless of when the delivery of goods is made or when title passes.

Example D

A heavy equipment manufacturer sells a bulldozer to a customer who is anticipating being rewarded a particular road building contract from the government. In the sales contract, the seller gives the buyer the right to return the bulldozer if the customer does not win the contract. There is no way to estimate reliably whether the customer will return the bulldozer.

Answer D

The risks and rewards of ownership do not pass until the customer has been granted the road building contract from the government.

Example E

A retail shop offers a lifetime guarantee on its products. A customer may return any item for any reason at any time and have her money returned. Based on reliable, historical data, 2.05% of sales are returned under this policy.

Answer E

Based on historical data, the shop retains only insignificant risks and rewards of ownership by offering this guarantee. Providing the other revenue recognition criteria are met, revenue should be recognised at the time of sale and a corresponding return accrual of 2.05% of the amount of the sale should be made to cover the cost of expected sales returns.

Example F

As a matter of policy, a manufacturing company writes its sales contracts in such a way that legal title does not pass on delivery but when consideration for the goods is received. A sale is made and the related goods are delivered to a customer who is not a particular credit risk.

Answer F

The risks and rewards of ownership have passed even though title has not. Depending on the circumstances, the company may need to set up a general reserve for bad debts.

Note that additional examples which illustrate the appropriate time to recognise revenue from the sale of goods are included as an appendix to IAS 18 (r1993). The examples are relatively straight forward and provide guidance on:

- bill and hold sales;
- goods shipped subject to conditions;
- lay away sales;
- orders when payment (or partial payment) is received in advance;
- sale and repurchase agreements;
- sales to intermediate parties;
- subscription sales;
- instalment sales; and
- real estate sales.

6.9.2 Continuing managerial involvement and effective control

This criterion goes hand in hand with the risks and rewards of ownership. It would be highly unusual for an enterprise to retain managerial involvement to the degree usually associated with ownership or to retain effective control over the goods without retaining the risks and rewards of ownership. However, each situation must be considered individually. It may be the case that continuing managerial involvement does not constitute effective control. For example, a software consultancy firm may install a software system for a client and then oversee and manage the computer department which uses the software. This outsourcing of managerial control over the computer department which includes the newly installed software does not prohibit revenue recognition on the provision of the software as the risks and rewards stemming from this software are retained by the client who is now benefiting from the new software.

In some cases, although transfer of assets may qualify as a sale under IAS 18 (r1993) or another IAS, the role of the buyer has little economic substance other than to provide a vehicle for that transaction, with the seller retaining significant beneficial interest in the assets transferred. These situations raise difficult questions as to whether the buyer is, in economic substance, a subsidiary which should be consolidated. This issue is discussed further in Chapter **19** regarding the consolidation of special purpose entities.

6.9.3 Reliable measurement of revenue

Until the amount of revenue to be received can be measured reliably, revenue cannot be recognised. However, this does not imply that the consideration must actually be received in all cases for revenue to be recognised. Generally, consideration will be agreed in advance, and the revenue from a sale will be recognised when all of the other recognition criteria are met. However, if the amount of revenue to be received cannot be measured reliably, revenue cannot be recognised. For example, an electronic data provider may enter into a contract which allows a customer to access its database for an upfront, flat fee for one year. However, if the customer does not access the database a specified minimum number of times during the year, part of the fee will be returned. Similarly, if the customer accesses the database more than a specified maximum number of times during the year, additional fees will become payable. Under such a contract, if it is uncertain whether or not the customer will access the database the minimum number of required times, the refundable amount of the upfront fee cannot be recognised until the database has been accessed the minimum number of times since the amount of revenue related to the contract cannot be reliably estimated.

6.9.4 *Probability of receipt of economic benefits*

Revenue cannot be recognised unless it is probable that the economic benefits or consideration associated with the transaction will flow to the enterprise. For example, it may not be probable that consideration will be received from a particular customer due to exchange controls in the country in which the customer operates which limit the amount of currency which may leave that country. In such cases when it is not probable that the consideration will be received, revenue is not recognised until the consideration is received.

If revenue has been recognised and it later emerges that the related consideration will not be collectible, an expense for bad debts is recognised rather than reversing the related revenue.

6.9.5 *Measurement of costs incurred related to the transaction*

When the costs incurred or to be incurred in respect of a transaction cannot be measured reliably, revenue is not recognised. This criteria flows from the matching principle. Under this principle, when revenue is recognised, the related expenses, including an estimate of future expenses, are also recognised. A common example of this type of future expense which should be estimated and accrued relates to warranty costs. If future costs cannot be estimated reliably, revenue is deferred until the amount of such expenses can be more reliably estimated or have been incurred.

6.10 Rendering of services

IAS 18 (r1993) requires the use of the percentage of completion method when accounting for the rendering of services. Under the percentage of completion method, revenue is recognised as work progresses based on the percentage of work completed at the reporting date. IAS 18 (r1993) requires use of this method for revenue recognition but the recognition of related contract expenses is beyond its scope. The Standard refer users to IAS 11 (r1993), for further guidance on the percentage of completion method. A summary of the requirements and guidance in IAS 18 (r1993) is set out below with a more detailed discussion of the percentage of completion method in Chapter **27**.

When revenue is recognised by reference to the stage of completion of a transaction, it is often referred to as the percentage of completion method. The percentage of completion method may only be used when the outcome of a transaction involving the rendering of services can be estimated reliably. IAS 18 (r1993) lists the following conditions which must be met in order for the outcome of a transaction to be estimated reliably:

'(a) the amount of revenue can be measured reliably;
(b) it is probable that the economic benefits associated with the transaction will flow to the enterprise;
(c) the stage of completion of the transaction at the balance sheet date can be measured reliably; and
(d) the costs incurred for the transaction and the costs to complete the transaction can be measured reliably.'

(IAS 18 (r1993).20)

An enterprise is usually only able to make reliable estimates after it has agreed the following with the other parties in the transaction:

- each party's enforceable rights regarding the service to be provided and received by the parties;
- the consideration to be exchanged; and
- the manner and terms of settlement.

(IAS 18 (r1993).23)

In addition, it will usually be necessary for an enterprise to have an effective internal budgeting and reporting system in order for it to make reliable estimates and, in subsequent periods, to compare those estimates to the actual costs incurred to date.

The stage of completion of a transaction at the reporting date may be determined in a variety of ways. However, progress payments and advances received from customers are generally not reliable indicators of the stage of completion as these types of payments are often made for reasons other than compensating for work performed. Depending on the nature of the transaction, methods for determining the stage of completion may include:

- surveys of work performed;
- services performed to date as a percentage of total services to be performed; or
- the proportion of costs incurred to date bear to the estimated total costs of the transaction. However, only costs that reflect services performed to date are included in costs incurred to date.

IAS 18 (r1993) acknowledges that when services are performed by an indeterminate number of acts over a specified period of time, revenue may be recognised on a straight line basis. For example, if a service contract relates to daily cleaning services, for practical reasons, the revenue related to those services will be recognised on a straight line basis as the work is performed. However, if one specific act is more significant than any other act, the recognition of revenue is postponed until the significant act is completed. For example, a merchant bank may spend several months identifying a buyer for a subsidiary of one of its clients. However, until a buyer is located and the sale is complete, the bank does not recognise any revenue on the basis that if no buyer is found, no revenue will be earned.

When the outcome of a transaction involving the rendering of services cannot be estimated reliably, either:

- revenue is recognised only to the extent of expenses incurred which are likely to be recovered. Thus, no profit is recognised on the transaction; or
- revenue is not recognised and the costs incurred are recognised as an expense, if it is not probable that the costs incurred will be recovered.

When the uncertainties which led to no profit being recognised on the transaction no longer exist, revenue is recognised on the percentage of completion basis.

6.11 Interest revenue

'Interest should be recognised on a time proportion basis that takes into account the effective yield on the asset' (IAS 18 (r1993).30(a)) when:

> '(a) it is probable that the economic benefits associated with the transaction will flow to the enterprise; and
>
> (b) the amount of the revenue can be measured reliably.'
>
> (IAS 18 (r1993).29)

The guidance in IAS 18 (r1993) explains that, 'the effective yield on an asset is the rate of interest required to discount the stream of future cash receipts expected over the life of the asset to equate to the initial carrying amount of the asset.' (IAS 18(r1993).31)

On most short-term deposits and long-term deposits, this rate will not be materially different from the stated rate of interest paid on the deposit.

However, certain transactions may be structured so that the stated interest rate on an investment or loan is different from its effective rate. In such cases, the transaction is accounted for using its effective rate. Two common situations where this may arise are described below.

First, as discussed in **6.6.1**, if payment terms are offered to a customer under zero interest rate arrangements or below market rate arrangements, a financing transaction has often taken place which generates interest revenue. This type of interest revenue is recognised on the basis set out above. The calculation of such interest revenue using effective interest rates is discussed in **6.6.1**.

Second, if an enterprise purchases a debt security for more than or less than its maturity value, the difference between its initial carrying amount and its amount at maturity is referred to as a discount or premium. Due to the existence of this discount or premium, the yield earned by the enterprise on the debt security will differ from its stated interest rate. In order to recognise the interest revenue earned based on its effective yield in accordance with IAS 18 (r1993), the amount of the discount or premium is included in the calculation of interest revenue. (IAS 18 (r1993).31)

When unpaid interest has accrued before an interest-bearing investment is purchased by an enterprise, only the portion of interest which accrued subsequent to the purchase by the enterprise is recognised as interest revenue. (IAS 18 (r1993).32)

6.12 Royalty revenue

'Royalties should be recognised on an accrual basis in accordance with the substance of the relevant agreement' (IAS 18 (r1993).30(b)) when:

> '(a) it is probable that the economic benefits associated with the transaction will flow to the enterprise; and
>
> (b) the amount of the revenue can be measured reliably.'
>
> (IAS 18 (r1993).29)

Royalty agreements define the terms and conditions of royalty payments. Such payments may be based on sales, the passage of time, or some other basis. Royalty income is recognised as it accrues or becomes payable under the terms of the royalty agreement. Thus, if the agreement is based on the passage of time, the straight line method of revenue recognition would be appropriate. However, if royalty payments are based on particular sales levels by the other party to the agreement, it may be appropriate to accrue royalty revenue based on the budgeted sales of the other party with an adjustment to reflect actual sales at the year end.

In substance, some licensing agreements are sales rather than agreements under which royalties accrue. When an entity delivers a 'product' under a licensing agreement and has no further obligation under the agreement, a sale has taken place. For example, an entity which supplies software under the terms of a licensing agreement and which has no further obligation under the agreement has, in essence, made a sale and revenue is recognised.

6.13 Dividend revenue

Dividend revenue should be recognised when:

- it is probable that the economic benefits associated with a transaction will flow to the enterprise;
- the amount of the revenue can be measured reliably; and
- the shareholder's right to receive payment is established.

(IAS 18 (r1993).29&30(c))

The timing of the establishment of the shareholder's right to receive payment may vary based on the laws of particular countries. In some countries it may occur when the board of directors of an enterprise formally declares its intention to pay a dividend. In other countries it may occur only after such a declaration has been approved by shareholders. In any case, if subsequent to revenue recognition but before receipt of the dividend, it becomes apparent that the investee will not be able to pay the dividend, the amount of dividend revenue previously recognised is recognised as a bad debt expense rather than as a reversal of dividend revenue.

When the investee is an associate accounted for under the equity method in accordance with IAS 28 (r2000), the dividend received reduces the carrying amount of the investment. (See Chapter **20**.) However, the timing of recognition of the dividend would be the same as under the criteria set out above.

When dividends on an investment in equity securities are declared from income earned before the enterprise purchased the securities, only the portion of the dividends which are declared from income earned subsequent to the purchase by the enterprise is recognised as dividend revenue. (IAS 18 (r1993).32)

In practice, it is often difficult to make the distinction between dividends declared from income earned pre- and post-acquisition. When the distinction would be arbitrary, dividends are recognised as revenue unless they clearly represent a recovery of part of the cost of the equity securities.

6.14 Disclosure

The following disclosures are required relating to revenue:

'(a) the accounting policies adopted for the recognition of revenue including the methods adopted to determine the stage of completion of transactions involving the rendering of services;

(b) the amount of each significant category of revenue recognised during the period including revenue arising from:

(i) the sale of goods;

(ii) the rendering of services;
(iii) interest;
(iv) royalties;
(v) dividends; and

(c) the amount of revenue arising from exchanges of goods or services included in each significant category of revenue.'

(IAS 18 (r1993).35)

6.15 Examples from published financial statements

Note that the excerpts given do not always comply in full with all aspects of IAS (r1993) and as such are not necessarily examples of best practice but merely of current practice.

Example 6.2

Note 2.7 Revenue Recognition

Included in revenue are net invoiced sales to customers for goods and services, rentals from leasing fixed and moveable property, commission, hire purchase and finance lease income. Sales of goods are recognised when goods are delivered and title has passed. Revenue arising from services, commission, royalties and rebates is recognised on the accrual basis in accordance with the substance of the relevant agreements. Revenue excludes indirect taxes.

Interest income is accrued on a time basis, by reference to the principal outstanding and at the interest rate applicable.

Barloworld Limited
South Africa
30 September 2000
International Accounting Standards

Example 6.3

Note 1. Summary of significant accounting policies

Sales and cost of sales
Sales represent amounts received and receivable for goods supplied and services rendered to customers after deducting volume discounts and sales taxes. Cost of sales includes the corresponding direct production costs and related production overhead of goods manufactured and services rendered.

Roche Group
Switzerland
31 December 2000
International Accounting Standards

Example 6.4

Note 1. Revenue Recognition

The Group recognises sales when persuasive evidence of an arrangement exists, delivery has occurred, the fee is fixed and determinable, and collectability is probable. For Nokia Networks, substantially all sales are derived from contracts for products and services which involve solutions achieved through significant customisation and modification. The percentage of completion method is used for all such contracts, provided that the outcome of the contract can be assessed with reasonable certainty. Sales are recognised over the contract period based on the progress to completion as determined by relevant input measures or milestone activities. When it is probable that contract costs will exceed total contract revenue, the expected loss is expensed immediately.

Nokia
Finland
31 December 2000
International Accounting Standards

CHAPTER 7

Income statement: earnings per share

7.1 Sources

IAS 33	*Earnings per Share.*
SIC-24	*Earnings Per Share – Financial Instruments and Other Contracts that May be Settled in Shares.*

7.2 Brief summary of the requirements

IAS 33 requires the disclosure of basic and diluted earnings per share on the face of the income statement for each class of ordinary shares that has a different right to participate in the net profit for the period. Both figures are presented with equal prominence for all periods presented regardless of the fact that one or both of the figures may be negative (i.e., a loss per share).

As noted below IAS 33 was developed concurrently with national accounting standards of some countries, in particular, SFAS 128, *Earnings Per Share*, in the US and FRS 14, *Earnings Per Share*, in the UK. While being very similar to IAS 33 in principle, these standards include more guidance on certain specific matters within the scope of IAS 33. Throughout this Chapter we include such additional guidance of the UK and US standards for information purposes.

7.3 Development of the requirements

IAS 33 and the US standard, SFAS 128 *Earnings per Share*, are the fruit of the first joint project between the IASC and the FASB and as such represented an important step in co-operation between the two standard setters. In the UK, the ASB reproduced the full text of the IASC's exposure draft as a UK discussion paper. It subsequently issued FRS 14 *Earnings per Share* which replaces the earlier requirements of SSAP 3 and follows very closely not only the requirements of, but also the text of, IAS 33. While it is still too early in the international convergence process for the earnings portion of earnings per share figures to be standard across the world, with the issuance of IAS 33, SFAS 128, and FRS 14, a big step forward was made in the convergence of the calculation of the denominator in the earnings per share calculation. The earnings per share project is an excellent example of standard setters working together to issue substantially the same requirements.

7.4 Scope

IAS 33 applies to:

- enterprises whose ordinary shares or potential ordinary shares are publicly traded;
- enterprises which are in the process of issuing ordinary shares or potential ordinary shares in public securities markets; and
- enterprises which have neither ordinary shares nor potential ordinary shares which are publicly traded, but which disclose earnings per share.

(IAS 33.1 and .4)

When both parent and consolidated financial statements are presented, the disclosures in IAS 33 are only required for the consolidated information. (IAS 33.2)

7.5 Calculation of basic earnings per share

> 'Basic earnings per share should be calculated by dividing the net profit or loss for the period attributable to ordinary shareholders by the weighted average number of ordinary shares outstanding during the period.'
>
> (IAS 33.10)

7.5.1 Basic earnings

The net profit or loss for the period attributable to ordinary shareholders is calculated as:

(Net profit or loss for the period) – (preference dividends)

As discussed in Chapter 5, net profit or loss for the period is after tax, minority interest and extraordinary items.

Preference dividends include all dividends declared in respect of the period on non-cumulative preference shares as well as required preference dividends relating to the period on cumulative preference shares regardless of whether or not the dividend has been declared. However, dividends relating to cumulative preference shares which are paid or declared in the current period in respect of a previous period are not taken into account in the calculation since they do not relate to the current period. (IAS 33.13)

7.5.2 *Basic per share*

> 'For the purpose of calculating basic earnings per share, the number of ordinary shares should be the weighted average number of ordinary shares outstanding during the period.'
>
> (IAS 33.14)

IAS 33 defines an ordinary share as 'an equity instrument that is subordinate to all other classes of equity instruments.' (IAS 33.6) The guidance explains that ordinary shares participate in the net profit for the period only after other types of shares such as preference shares. Some enterprises may have different classes of ordinary shares. Ordinary shares within the same class have the same rights to receive dividends. See 7.7 for a discussion of calculation of earnings per share where an enterprise has two or more classes of ordinary shares.

The concept of using the weighted average number of shares outstanding during the period in an earnings per share calculation will be familiar to preparers and users of UK financial statements. The weighted average number of shares outstanding during a period is simply the number of shares outstanding at the beginning of the period plus the number of shares issued during the period less the number of shares bought back during the period with such additions and repurchases multiplied by a time weighting factor.

Example 7.1

At the beginning of its financial year on 1 January 20x2, an enterprise has 2,500,000 ordinary shares outstanding. On 25 April, it issues 3,000,000 new ordinary shares. On 7 June, it purchases 500,000 of its outstanding shares. On 6 October, it issues 20,000 new ordinary shares in connection with the exercise of share options at fair value under its executive share option scheme. Calculate the weighted average number of ordinary shares outstanding during the year.

Dates outstanding	*Number of shares outstanding*	*Days outstanding as a proportion of total days in year*	*Proportion of weighted average for year*
	{A}	*{B}*	*{A} * {B}*
1/1/x2–24/4/x2	2,500,000	114/365	780,822
25/4/x2–6/6/x2	5,500,000	43/365	647,945
7/6/x2–5/10/x2	5,000,000	121/365	1,657,534
6/10/x2–31/12/x2	5,020,000	87/365	1,196,548
Total		**365/365**	**4,282,849**

Thus the weighted average number of shares outstanding during the year which is the number to be used in the denominator of the basic earnings per share calculation is 4,282,849.

Alternatively, the calculation could have been done as:

$$2{,}500{,}000 + \frac{(3{,}000{,}000 \times 251)}{(365)} - \frac{(500{,}000 \times 208)}{(365)} + \frac{(20{,}000 \times 87)}{(365)} = 4{,}282{,}849.$$

Generally, shares are considered outstanding from the date that consideration for the shares becomes receivable which usually coincides with the date of issue. However, the terms of agreements to issue shares need to be examined to ensure that the substance of the agreement prevails over its legal form. The table below illustrates some common circumstances under which shares are issued and the date from which the shares are considered outstanding:

Consideration for issue of shares:	*Shares are considered outstanding:*
• cash	• when the cash is receivable
• voluntary reinvestment of dividends on ordinary or preference shares	• at the dividend payment date
• as a result of the conversion of a debt instrument to ordinary shares	• as of the date interest ceases accruing
• in place of interest or principal on other financial instruments	• as of the date interest ceases accruing on the other financial instruments
• in exchange for the settlement of a liability of the enterprise	• as of the settlement date of the liability
• in consideration for the acquisition of an asset other than cash	• as of the date on which the acquisition is recognised
• for the rendering of services to the enterprise	• as the services are rendered

(IAS 33.16)

Shares issued for cash

Even with the above guidance, it is not always clear from which date the shares should be included when they are issued for cash. Consider the following example.

Example 7.2

X plc is making a rights issue. Provisional allotment letters in respect of the new shares are posted, by first class post, on 19 October 20x2. Shareholders wishing to take up their entitlement must return the provisional allotment letter together with a remittance for the full amount payable so as to be received not later than 3.00pm on 17 November 20x2.

Consequently, X will receive cash on a number of days, up to and including 17 November. X's earnings will benefit from the date the cash is received; the cash being available for investment when received. However, IAS 33 requires the shares to be included in the weighted average calculation from the date the cash is receivable.

In this example 17 November 20x2 is the date the cash is receivable (since this is the date that X has asked to receive the cash by and if X received no cash until this date it would still validly issue the shares). Accordingly X should include the shares in its weighted average calculation from 17 November 20x2.

Ordinary shares issued as part of a business combination accounted for as an acquisition are included as of the date of the acquisition since that is the date on which the acquirer begins consolidating the results of the acquiree into its income statement. However, if a business combination is accounted for as a uniting of interests, the shares issued as part of the transaction are considered outstanding for all periods presented, since the combined financial statements are prepared as if the combined entity had always existed. Thus, 'the number of ordinary shares used for the calculation of basic earnings per share for an entity which has undergone a uniting of interests is the aggregate of the weighted average number of shares of the combined enterprises, adjusted to equivalent shares of the enterprise whose shares are outstanding after the combination.' (IAS 33.17)

Partly paid shares
Any partly paid shares outstanding are treated as a fraction of an ordinary share in proportion to the fraction of participation in dividends of an ordinary share to which they are entitled. (IAS 33.18)

Elsewhere in the text of the standard, the IASC position appears to have been to include shares in the calculation of earnings per share from the date the share proceeds start to generate earnings. The treatment of partly paid shares is slightly different. Rather than treat partly paid shares as a fraction of a share based on the proportion of the proceeds received, IAS 33 calls for them to be treated as a fraction of a share to the extent that they are entitled to participate in dividends relative to a fully paid up ordinary share during the period. Shares that are fully paid up are included in the earnings per share calculation from the date the consideration is receivable irrespective of whether they rank for dividends.

Thus, two £1 shares each ranking for dividend, one 100p paid and the other 1p paid, will be treated identically in the earnings per share computation.

Contingently issuable shares
Some enterprises may issue contingently issuable shares which are shares issuable upon the satisfaction of certain conditions. Contingently issuable shares are particularly common as part of executive remuneration contracts or in business combinations. Such contingently issuable shares are considered outstanding for the purpose of calculating basic earnings per share from the date when all necessary conditions for issue have been satisfied. Outstanding shares which are contingently returnable (that is subject to recall) are treated as contingently issuable shares. (IAS 33.19)

As indicated above, under IAS 33 contingently issuable shares are included in basic earnings per share from the date that all necessary conditions have been satisfied and thus, although issuing the shares is still a future transaction, it is no longer contingent; the reason is that there are no circumstances under which the shares will not be issued.

IAS 33 does not provide additional guidance in relation to the treatment of different types of contingencies that may be included in contingent share agreements. Such guidance can be found in the relevant US and UK standards. This guidance is illustrated in the two examples below.

Example 7.3

Contingency based on an event

Company A acquires company B on 1 January 20x2. Company A agrees to issue 100,000 shares to the vendor on 1 January 20x5 if at any point prior to that date a new product developed by B is granted a licence.

Company A's year end is 31 December. The 20x2 financial statements are approved on 22 March 20x3. The product is granted a licence on 4 March 20x3.

The 100,000 shares would be excluded from the basic earnings per share for 20x2 and would be included in the basic earnings per share for 20x3 as if the shares had been issued on 4 March 20x3 (the date the licence was granted).

Example 7.4

Contingency based on average profits

Company A acquires company B on 1 January 20x2. Company A agrees to issue 100,000 shares to the vendor on 1 January 20x5 if B's profits for the three years to 31 December 20x4 average £1m or more.

Company B's profits in each of 20x2 and 20x3 are £1.7m.

The shares are excluded from both the 20x2 and 20x3 basic earnings per share. Even if profits are expected for the year 20x4, so that the earnings condition will be met, the shares are excluded from basic earnings per share until the contingency period has ended; until thesn it is not known for certain whether all the necessary conditions will be satisfied since, however unlikely, a loss could be made in the year 20x4 and thus the earnings condition not be met.

Deferred shares

IAS 33 contains no guidance on how to deal with deferred shares. In this context, a distinction can be drawn between deferred shares and contingently issuable shares. Whereas contingently issuable shares are shares that will be issued at a future date only upon the satisfaction of certain conditions, deferred shares are shares that will be issued at a future date and are not subject to any conditions other than the passage of time. Deferred shares typically arise under acquisition agreements.

As discussed above under the general rules for when an ordinary share is considered to be outstanding for purposes of earnings per share, ordinary shares issued as consideration for the acquisition of an asset other than cash are included as of the date on which the acquisition is recognised. (IAS 33.16.(f)) Therefore, it appears appropriate to include such deferred shares in the calculation of basic earnings per share as if they had been issued on the acquisition date. It is correct to recognise the amount in both basic and diluted earnings per share since there are no conditions present other than the passage of time (see *Example 7.5*).

Example 7.5

X Enterprises purchased Y Limited paying 500,000 shares at the date of acquisition and a further 100,000 shares one year after the date of acquisition. All 600,000 shares should be included in the calculation of basic earnings per share from the date that Y Limited is brought into X plc's group financial statements.

An acquisition agreement may also provide for further shares to be issued but the exact number of shares has not been specified. For example, an agreement may provide that shares valued at £500,000 on a specified future date will be issued, the number of shares to be determined by dividing £500,000 by the share price on the specified future date. Under FRS 14 in the UK, such shares would be contingently issuable shares rather than deferred shares and it is therefore suggested that they would also be contingently issuable shares under IAS 33.

7.5.3 Changes in shares issued without a corresponding change in resources

In certain instances, an enterprise may issue ordinary shares or reduce the number of ordinary shares outstanding without a corresponding change in resources. When such changes, excluding those arising from the conversion of potential ordinary shares, occur, the weighted average number of ordinary shares outstanding is adjusted accordingly for all periods presented. (IAS 33.20)

Several examples of such changes in the number of outstanding shares without a corresponding change in resources are outlined below.

1. In different countries, various names including capitalisation, bonus issue, stock dividend or stock split are given to transactions in which an enterprise issues ordinary shares to current shareholders in equal proportions to the number of shares already held for no consideration. In order to reflect in the basic earnings per share calculation that no additional resources have been received and that holders of ordinary shares have not had their ownership interest diluted by the transaction,

the weighted average number of ordinary shares outstanding for each period for which an earnings per share figure is shown is adjusted in line with the terms of the transaction. For example, if a three-for-one share split occurs, the weighted average number of shares outstanding is multiplied by three to calculate the number of additional shares issued. The earnings per share figures for each period presented are adjusted accordingly.

Example 7.6

A three-for-one share split, in which three shares are awarded for every one share held, occurs on 1 January 20x2. Prior to the share split the enterprise had 300,000 ordinary shares outstanding. No other share movements have occurred in 20x2 or 20x1.

Net profit attributable to ordinary shareholders in 20x2 was £360,000 and in 20x1 £240,000. 20x1 basic earnings per share was reported as £0.80.

Basic earnings per share for 20x2 would be calculated as:

$$\frac{£360{,}000}{300{,}000 + (300{,}000 * 3)} = £0.30$$

Earnings per share for 20x1 would be recalculated and reported in 20x2 financial statements as:

$$\frac{£240{,}000}{1{,}200{,}200} = £0.20$$

2. In some countries, enterprises may issue instruments in the form of rights to existing ordinary shareholders which enable the shareholders to purchase ordinary shares at below market prices. These transactions are known as rights issues and because they give rise to an increase in the number of ordinary shares outstanding without a corresponding increase equal to the fair value of the ordinary shares issued, they are said to contain a 'bonus element.' Similar to the transactions in which ordinary shares are issued for no consideration as described in 1 above, this bonus element must be reflected in the earnings per share calculation for all periods for which earnings per share figures are presented. Note that rights issues differ from the exercise or conversion of potential ordinary shares, such as share options issued under an executive compensation scheme, because such potential ordinary shares generally have been issued for fair consideration (the executive's service) and thus do result in a corresponding change in the resources of the enterprise.

In order to reflect the bonus element, the number of weighted average ordinary shares outstanding for each period presented prior to the rights issue is multiplied by the following 'adjustment factor':

$$\frac{\text{Fair value per share immediately prior to the exercise of rights}}{\text{Theoretical ex-rights fair value per share}}$$

where the theoretical ex-rights fair value per share is calculates as:

$$\frac{\text{(aggregate fare value of shares outstanding immediately prior to the exercise of the rights + the proceeds from the exercise of the rights)}}{\text{the number of shares outstanding after the exercise of the rights}}$$

> 'Where the rights themselves are to be publicly traded separately from the shares prior to the exercise date, fair value for the purposes of this calculation is established at the close of the last day on which the shares are traded together with the rights.'
>
> (IAS 33.23)

Example 7.7

An enterprise launches a rights issue under which existing shareholders have the right to subscribe on 1 April 20x2 for one new share at £10 for every four shares currently held.

Before the rights issue, 100,000 ordinary shares are outstanding.

There have been no other movements in ordinary shares in 20x2 or 20x1.

The price per share on 31 March 20x2 is £15.

Net profit attributable to ordinary shareholders in 20x2 was £350,000 (20x1: £300,000)

Basic earnings per share for 20x1 was reported as £3.

Calculation of theoretical ex-rights fair value per share:

$$\frac{(£15 \times 100{,}000) + (25{,}000 \times £10)}{125{,}000} = £14$$

Calculation of the adjustment factor:

$$\frac{£15}{£14} = 1.07$$

Calculation of basic earnings per share for 20x2:

$$\frac{£350{,}000}{(100{,}000 \times 3/12 \times 1.07) + (125{,}000 \times 9/12)} = £2.90$$

Recalculation of basic earnings per share for 20x1:

$$\frac{£300{,}000}{100{,}000 \times 1.07} = £2.80$$

3. A reverse share split or a consolidation of shares occurs when the number of shares outstanding is consolidated. For example, shareholders may receive one new ordinary share for each three ordinary shares held previously. When this occurs, the number of ordinary shares outstanding is adjusted by dividing the weighted average number of ordinary shares outstanding by the ratio of the old shares to the new shares, in this case three, for each period for which earnings per share figures are presented.

When transactions which result in a change in the number of shares issued without a corresponding change in resources occur after the balance sheet date but before the financial statements are issued, the weighted average number of ordinary shares is adjusted for all periods presented and the fact that this adjustment has taken place is disclosed. (IAS 33.43)

Example 7.8

Post-balance sheet date issue of shares
A company has 1,000,000 ordinary shares in issue throughout 20x1 and 20x2. Earnings attributable to ordinary shareholders for 20x2 total £330,000 (20x1 – £220,000). On 1 February 20x3 the company issues 100,000 ordinary shares in a 1:10 bonus issue. The financial statements for 20x2 are not approved until 22 March 20x3.

In producing the 20x3 financial statements, IAS 33 requires the company to take account of the bonus issue as though it had taken place at the start of the earliest period for which an earnings per share is presented. Thus the 20x2 earnings per share that is presented as a comparative to the 20x3 earnings per share will be adjusted as if the bonus issue had been at the start of 20x2, making the 20x2 earnings per share 30 pence (£330,000 divided by 1,100,000 shares).

IAS 33 extends this principle and requires that if the bonus issue (or any other change in the number of shares in issue with no corresponding change in resources) takes place before the 20x2 financial statements are authorised for issue, the earnings per share disclosed in those 20x2 financial statements, together with any comparatives to the 20x2 earnings per share, are adjusted for the bonus issue (or other change in the number of shares with no corresponding change in resources) as if this took place at the start of the earliest period for which an earnings per share is presented. Consequently, in the 20x2 financial statements the earnings per share will be presented as:

20x2: 30 pence (£330,000 divided by 1,100,000 shares)
20x1: 20 pence (£220,000 divided by 1,100,000 shares)

This treatment means that in order to interpret a company's earnings per share for a year it is necessary to know the date that the financial statements were authorised for issue. The disclosure of the date of authorisation is now required by IAS 10 (r1999) (see Chapter **15**).

7.6 Calculation of diluted earnings per share

Diluted earnings per share is simply basic earnings per share adjusted for the effect on earnings (the net profit attributable to ordinary shareholders) and on the weighted average number of ordinary shares outstanding of the exercise of all dilutive potential ordinary shares.

> 'A potential ordinary share is a financial instrument or other contract that may entitle its holder to ordinary shares.'
>
> (IAS 33.6)

Common examples of potential ordinary shares include:

> '• debt or equity instruments, including preference shares, which are convertible into ordinary shares;
> • share warrants and options;
> • shares which may be issued to employees as part of their remuneration or as part of other share purchase plans; and
> • shares which would be issued upon the satisfaction of certain conditions resulting from contractual arrangements, such as the purchase of a business or other assets.'
>
> (IAS 33.8)

Not all potential ordinary shares are dilutive. Potential ordinary shares are considered dilutive when their conversion to ordinary shares would decrease net profit per share from continuing ordinary operations. (IAS 33.38) (Guidance on the determination of which potential ordinary shares are dilutive is in **7.6.3**).

7.6.1 Diluted earnings

When calculating diluted earnings per share, a preparer assumes the conversion of all dilutive potential ordinary shares. Therefore, if such instruments have given rise during the year to any income or expense, net profit must be adjusted to reverse its effect since the assumption is that the instruments were converted into ordinary shares at the beginning of the period and as such would not have given rise to that income or expense. Specifically, the net profit attributable to ordinary shareholders used in the basic earnings per share calculation is adjusted for the after-tax effects of:

- any preference dividends on dilutive convertible preference shares which have been deducted from net profit in the calculation of net profit attributable to ordinary shareholders, by adding such preference dividends back to net profit;
- interest expense recognised during the period related to any dilutive potential ordinary shares, such as convertible bonds, by adding the interest expense net of any related tax back to net profit; and

- any other consequential changes in income or expense that would result from the conversion of the dilutive potential ordinary shares. For example, if a company offers an employee profit sharing plan, the effect on net profit of adding back certain interest expense related to dilutive potential ordinary shares may trigger an increase or decrease in the remuneration expense related to the profit sharing plan. This change in remuneration expense is reflected by adjusting the net profit figure used in the calculation of diluted earnings per share.

(IAS 33.26&28)

No assumptions are made, and diluted earnings are not adjusted, for any potential effects of reinvesting the saved expense.

Example 7.9

In 20x2, an enterprise made a net profit of £500,000.

200,000 ordinary shares are outstanding for the entire year.

10% convertible debt of £3,000,000 is outstanding for the entire year.

The debt is convertible into one ordinary share for every £10 of debt outstanding.

The tax rate is 30%.

Calculate basic earnings per share and diluted earnings per share.

Calculation of basic earnings per share

$$\frac{£500{,}000}{200{,}000} = £2.50$$

Calculation of diluted earnings per share

The interest expense associated with the convertible bond must be added back net of tax to net profit attributable to ordinary shareholders and the additional shares issued must be included in the weighted average number of shares outstanding as follows:

$$\frac{£500{,}000 + (3{,}000{,}000 \times 10\%) - (3{,}000{,}000 \times 10\% \times 30\%)}{200{,}000 + 300{,}000} = £1.42$$

7.6.2 *Diluted per share*

The weighted average number of shares outstanding used in the computation of diluted earnings per share is the weighted average number of ordinary shares that would be issued on conversion of the dilutive potential ordinary shares added to the weighted average number of ordinary shares used for the basic earnings per share calculation.

When determining the number of ordinary shares which would be issued on the conversion of dilutive potential ordinary shares, the underlying terms of the potential ordinary shares are examined. When under the terms of the shares, assumptions relating to exercise price or conversion rate must be made, they are made to reflect the most favourable price or rate to the potential ordinary shareholder. (IAS 33.30)

When calculating the weighted average number of ordinary shares that would be issued on conversion of the dilutive potential ordinary shares:

- conversion of the potential ordinary shares is considered to have taken place at the beginning of the period or, if later, the date the potential ordinary shares were issued (IAS 33.29);
- potential ordinary shares which have lapsed or been cancelled during the period are included for the time they were outstanding (IAS 33.42); and
- potential ordinary shares which were converted during the period are included in the calculation as potential ordinary shares to the date of conversion and are then included in the weighted average number of ordinary shares outstanding for both basic earnings per share and diluted earnings per share. (IAS 33.42)

Similar to their treatment in the basic earnings per share computation, contingently issuable shares are considered to be converted in the computation of diluted earnings per share when all of the conditions for issuance have been met or would have been met had the end of the reporting period been the end of the contingency period. However, in the basic earnings per share calculation, they are included in the earnings per share calculation from the date the conditions are met whereas in the diluted computation they are assumed to have been converted from the beginning of the period or the date of the contingency agreement if later. If all of the conditions for issuance have not been met, the number of shares which would be issued if the period end date were the end of the contingency period is assumed to have been converted for the entire period or since the date of the contingency agreement if later. Restatement is prohibited in later periods even if the conditions for issuance are not met at the end of the contingency agreement. The same logic which governs contingently issuable shares is applied to contingently issuable potential ordinary shares such as share options which may be awarded to management if certain share price levels are reached. (IAS 33.31)

When potential ordinary shares issued by a subsidiary, associate or joint venture of the reporting entity have a dilutive effect on the earnings per share of the reporting entity, they are reflected in the calculation of diluted earnings per share. Such potential ordinary shares may be convertible into ordinary shares of the reporting entity, the subsidiary, joint venture or associate. (IAS 33.32)

Interestingly, IAS 33 refers to a dilutive effect on basic earnings per share rather than, as with potential ordinary shares issued by the reporting entity, a dilutive effect on continuing earnings per share. Refer to **7.6.3** for a description of the 'control number' used in determining if potential ordinary shares of the reporting entity are dilutive.

The Standard states that *to the extent* that partly paid shares are not entitled to participate in dividends during the financial period they are to be regarded as the equivalent of share warrants or options. (IAS 33.37)

The words 'to the extent', together with the guidance on how to include such shares in basic earnings per share (see **7.5.2**), imply that if a company has, say, 9,000 ordinary shares, two-thirds paid-up and entitled to two-thirds of the dividend declared on fully paid shares, then in calculating diluted earnings per share the company includes the partly-paid shares as if they were options over 3,000 shares (one-third of 9,000) where the exercise price of the options is equal to the amount remaining to be paid on the shares. The remaining 6,000 shares are treated as issued and should be included in the calculation of both basic and diluted earnings per share in the normal way.

For the purpose of calculating diluted earnings per share, the assumed proceeds from the exercise of share options and warrants (and the conversion of any other potential ordinary shares that result in the enterprise receiving cash in exchange for issuing ordinary shares) are considered to have been received from the issuance of ordinary shares at fair value. The difference between the number of shares actually issued and the number of shares that would have been issued at fair value is treated as an issue of ordinary shares for no consideration. (IAS 33.33) This approach produces the same results as the approach known in some countries, particularly the USA, as the 'treasury stock' method.[1] (IAS 33.36)

> 'Therefore, in order to calculate diluted earnings per share, each such arrangement is treated as consisting of:
>
> (a) a contract to issue a certain number of ordinary shares at their average fair value during the period. The shares so to be issued are fairly priced and are assumed to be neither dilutive nor anti-dilutive. They are ignored in the computation of diluted earnings per share; and

[1] The 'treasury stock' method is a theoretical computation for reflecting the dilutive effect on earnings per share of outstanding options and warrants (as if they have been exercised at the beginning of the period). It assumes that any 'proceeds' that could be obtained upon exercise of options and warrants would be used to purchase ('buy back') ordinary shares at the market price during the period. Those 'treasury shares' are then deducted from the total number of shares that would have been issued if options and warrants were in fact exercised to arrive at the number of incremental shares to be included in the denominator.

(b) a contract to issue the remaining ordinary shares for no consideration. Such ordinary shares generate no proceeds and have no effect on the net profit attributable to ordinary shares outstanding. Therefore such shares are dilutive and they are added to the number of ordinary shares outstanding in the computation of diluted earnings per share.'

(IAS 33.35)

Fair value for this purpose is calculated on the basis of the average price of the ordinary shares during the period. (IAS 33.34) IAS 33 does not provide any guidance as to how this average price is to be calculated. This is further discussed after the following example.

Example 7.10

An enterprise has 10,000 outstanding share options which were outstanding for the entire year each of which are convertible into one ordinary share for £5.

The average share price for the year was £10.

Net profit for the period was £100,000.

50,000 ordinary shares were in issue for the entire period.

There are no preference shares in issue.

Calculation of basic earnings per share:

$$\frac{£100{,}000}{50{,}000} = £2.00 \text{ per share}$$

Calculation of diluted earnings per share:

$$\frac{£100{,}000}{50{,}000 + 5{,}000^*} = £1.82 \text{ per share}$$

*To calculate diluted earnings per share, conversion of all dilutive potential ordinary shares is assumed therefore:

10,000 options × £5 conversion price = £50,000 assumed proceeds

£50,000	– assumed proceeds
/£10	– fair value of an ordinary share
5,000	– ordinary shares assumed issued at fair value. These shares are ignored in the diluted earnings per share calculation.
10,000	– assumed new ordinary shares
–5,000	– ordinary shares assumed issued at fair value
5,000	– dilutive ordinary shares included in the calculation of diluted earnings per share

Share options (and other share purchase arrangements) are treated as dilutive when their exercise price is less than the average fair value during the period.

Example 7.11

Identifying dilutive options

At 1 January and 31 December 20X2 an enterprise had the following options outstanding:

Number of shares under option	*Exercise price*	*Average share price during year*	*Dilutive or anti-dilutive*	*Number of shares deemed issued for no consideration*
10,000	£7	£10	D	3,000
5,000	£8	£10	D	1,000
15,000	£9	£10	D	1,500
10,000	£12	£10	A	–
20,000	£11	£10	A	–
				5,500

Alternatively, the enterprise could have calculated the 5,500 shares to be added to the numerator of the diluted earnings per share calculation as:

$$(10{,}000 + 5{,}000 + 15{,}000) - \frac{\{(10{,}000 \times £7) + (5{,}000 \times £8) + (15{,}000 \times £9)\}}{10}$$

Calculating average fair value during the period

In order to bring options into the adjustment for diluted earnings per share it is necessary for the enterprise to know the average fair value of its ordinary shares during the period. However, IAS 33 contains no guidance at all on how this should be calculated.

The US standard SFAS 128 does contain guidance. It starts by pointing out that the average shall represent a 'meaningful average' and that, theoretically, the average could be determined by using every market transaction in the enterprise's shares during the year. From a practical standpoint, however, it acknowledges that a simple average of weekly or monthly closing prices will usually be adequate. Where prices fluctuate widely over the period, week or month, being used, the US guidance suggests that an average of the high and low prices for the period would produce a more representative price than simply using the closing price for the period. The US guidance concludes with 'The method used to compute the average market price shall be used consistently unless it is no longer representative because of changed conditions. For example, an entity that uses closing market prices to compute the average market price for several years of relatively stable market prices might need to change to an average of high and low prices if prices start fluctuating greatly and the closing market prices no longer produce a representative average market price'.

Under IASs, it seems preferable in theory, where an average is not based on actual transactions, to calculate the average by using the price at the close of each day in the year. Where there has been very little change throughout the year then the closing price at the end of each week or month could instead be used. However, since the principles underlying the US standard are so similar to those underlying IAS 33, it would be acceptable for an entity to apply the US guidance, rather than calculate the average using daily information.

Options granted during the year

Options, as with any potential ordinary shares, are included in the calculation of diluted earnings per share as if conversion into ordinary shares had occurred on the first day of the accounting period or, if later, the date on which the option or other potential ordinary shares where granted. Where options are granted part way through a year, the question arises whether the average fair value is the average from the date the option is granted to the end of the year or the average for the entire accounting period.

The only references in IAS 33 are to the average price 'during the period' and are not to 'during the period they were outstanding'. It is suggested that the average for the whole reporting period should generally be used, but in cases where this gives a distorted answer, the average for the period the options are in issue may be used.

Options exercised during the year

Considerations similar to those applying when options are granted in the year apply when options are exercised during the year. Consequently, the fair value should be the average for the entire accounting period, and not the period during which the options were outstanding, unless this gives a distorted answer, in which case the average for the period the options were in issue may be used.

Employee share and incentive plans

Incentive plans forming part of employee remuneration may take different forms. A simple incentive plan might be comprised of a bonus payable in cash and/or share options with no conditions attaching. Alternatively, employee bonuses can have a performance period of, for example, three or four years. Also, while some bonuses are payable in cash, it is possible for long-term bonuses to be payable in the company's shares or with options only exercisable if certain performance conditions have been met.

IAS 33 does not produce any additional guidance for these circumstances. However, both the UK and the US standards do. FRS 14, *Earnings per Share*, and SFAS 128, *Earnings per Share*, draw a distinction between incentive schemes in which awards are based on performance criteria, and any other scheme generating potential ordinary shares:

- Performance-based awards are to be treated as contingently issuable shares, since their issue or exercise is contingent upon factors other than the passing of time, such as the level of future earnings;
- All other awards made under an employee share or other incentive scheme are regarded as options for the purpose of calculating diluted earnings per share. They are to be regarded as outstanding as of the grant date even though their exercise may be contingent upon vesting. They are to be included in the computation even if the employee may not receive (or be able to sell) the shares until some future date. Accordingly, all shares to be issued are included in calculating diluted earnings per share if the effect is dilutive. Where the awards are granted during the period, the shares to be issued are weighted to reflect that fact;
- Any bonuses to be settled in cash have no impact on earnings per share beyond the impact of payments on earnings.

Under the US standard, for entities that recognise a remuneration expense related to employee share options the assumed exercise price, for purposes of determining the number of incremental shares deemed issued for no consideration, would comprise the sum of:

- The amount the employee must pay upon exercise;
- The amount of remuneration expense attributable to future services and not yet recognised; and
- The amount of any tax benefits that may arise in some jurisdictions on the assumed exercise of the options.

Applying this method, initially, dilution is less because part of the consideration consists of future services not yet received. It becomes greater, over time, as the enterprise's earnings reflect the benefits of having received those services.

Contracts to be settled in cash or shares

An enterprise may have a financial instrument that may be settled in cash or shares. The question is then raised as to whether such instruments are potential ordinary shares under IAS 33. The IAS does not give guidance on such situations. However, in February 2000, the Standing Interpretations Committee issued SIC-24, effective on 1 December 2000.

SIC-24 clarifies that such instruments are potential ordinary shares, stating that 'All financial instruments or other contracts that may result in the issuance of ordinary shares of the reporting enterprise to the holder of the financial instrument or other contract, at the option of the issuer or the holder, are potential ordinary shares of the enterprise'. (SIC-24(4))

In explaining the conclusion, SIC-24 points out that IAS 33 defines a potential ordinary share as a financial instrument that *may entitle* its holder to ordinary shares. This implies that if it is possible that the holder will receive shares, the contract is considered to be a potential ordinary share. This is irrespective of whether it is the holder's or the issuer's choice.

SIC-24 also clarifies that the intended manner of settlement, or policy or past pattern of choosing a particular settlement manner, does not change the fact that the holder may be entitled to receive ordinary shares.

This differs from US and UK standards where FRS 14 and SFAS 128 state that, irrespective of whether the choice of cash or shares rests with the recipient or issuer, how this is reflected in diluted earnings per share depends upon the facts available in the particular accounting period. Past experience or a stated policy should be followed where that provides a reasonable basis for concluding how the contract will be satisfied. The contract is presumed to be settled by the more dilutive method where there is no stated policy or the entity has no past experience of settling such contracts.

Consequently if an entity reporting under IASs has issued convertible redeemable bonds that are dilutive, it should assume conversion when calculating diluted earnings per share even when the bondholder has stated an intention to redeem the bonds.

Written put options

IAS 33 does not provide any guidance for the treatment of share buy back transactions. SFAS 128 in the US provides specific guidance on how to reflect in the diluted earnings per share calculation contracts that require the reporting entity to repurchase its own stock, such as written put options or forward purchase contracts. If an enterprise grants options that require it to repurchase its own shares and those options are in the money (ie option holder has a present or future right to exercise the option at a price that is higher than the current market price of the share), SFAS 128 requires the incremental shares to be included in the denominator of diluted earnings per share calculation as of the beginning of the period, if dilutive, using the 'reverse treasury stock method'. This method assumes that the proceeds used to buy back ordinary shares (in accordance with the terms of a put option) will be raised from issuing shares at the average market price during the period. The difference between the number of shares that would be required to be issued based on average market price during the period to generate the proceeds necessary to settle the put option, and the number of ordinary shares to be repurchased, is treated as an issue of shares for no consideration.

7.6.3 Determining if potential ordinary shares are dilutive

Potential ordinary shares are dilutive if their conversion to ordinary shares would decrease the net profit per share from continuing ordinary activities. (IAS 33.38)

Potential ordinary shares are anti-dilutive when their conversion to ordinary shares would increase earnings per share from continuing ordinary operations or decrease loss per share from continuing ordinary operations. (IAS 33.40) If potential ordinary shares are considered to be anti-dilutive, they are ignored in the calculation of diluted earnings per share. Thus, if none of the potential ordinary shares of an enterprise are dilutive, diluted earnings per share will equal basic earnings per share.

Net profit from continuing ordinary activities is 'the control number' which is used to determine if potential ordinary shares are dilutive. In other words, if a type or issue of potential ordinary shares is dilutive in the calculation of diluted net profit from continuing ordinary activities per share, it will be used in the calculation of diluted earnings per share even if it is anti-dilutive in the diluted earnings per share calculation.

This peculiarity arises from harmonisation efforts with the US where diluted earnings per share is required to be shown for continuing operations activities as well as net income.

IAS 33 defines net profit from continuing ordinary activities as, 'the net profit from ordinary activities after deducting preference dividends and after excluding items relating to discontinued operations; therefore it excludes extraordinary items and the effects of changes in accounting policies and corrections of fundamental errors.' (IAS 33.39) This definition is somewhat confusing since the examples of the allowed alternative treatments included in IAS 8 (r1993), *Net Profit or Loss for the Period, Fundamental Errors and Changes in Accounting Policies*, relating to the correction of a fundamental error and a change in accounting policy include the effects of both in profit from ordinary activities. In any case, these items are not included in the calculation of net profit from continuing ordinary activities for purposes of this calculation.

Potential ordinary shares may be dilutive individually but anti-dilutive when included with other potential ordinary shares in calculating diluted earnings per share. In order to achieve maximum dilution, each type or issue of potential ordinary shares is considered in sequence from the most dilutive to the least dilutive. Thus, dilutive potential ordinary shares with the lowest incremental earnings per share are included in the calculation of diluted continuing earnings per share before those with a higher incremental earnings per share in order to determine which are dilutive for the purposes of calculating diluted earnings per share.

Example 7.12

An enterprise has:

- net profit after tax from continuing ordinary activities of £16,000,000
- net profit of £21,000,000
- 5,000,000 outstanding ordinary shares
- 1,000,000 outstanding convertible preference shares which pay a preference dividend of £1 per share and convert at a rate of 4 ordinary shares for each preference share outstanding
- 5,000,000 outstanding share options with an exercise price of £40
- £2,000,000 10 per cent convertible bonds which convert at a rate of 1 ordinary share for each £50 of debt outstanding
- a tax rate of 30 per cent

The average price of the ordinary shares during the period was £50.

Calculate diluted earnings per share

Step 1: Calculate basic earnings per share and net profit from continuing ordinary activities per share ('the control number')

$$\frac{£21{,}000{,}000 - £1{,}000{,}000}{5{,}000{,}000} = £4.00 \text{ basic earnings per share}$$

$$\frac{£16{,}000{,}000 - £1{,}000{,}000}{5{,}000{,}000} = £3.00 \text{ net profit from continuing ordinary activities per share (control number)}$$

Step 2: Determine dilution from conversion of each type of potential ordinary share

	Earnings effect of conversion	*Additional shares issued as a result of conversion*	*Earnings/ incremental share*
Preference shares	£1,000,000 *(1,000,000 × £1)*	4,000,000 *(1,000,000 × 4)*	£0.25
Options	£nil	1,000,000 *(£40 × 5,000,000 = £200,000,000)* *Proceeds from conversion* *(£200,000,000/£50 = 4,000,000)* *Ord. shares issued at fair value* *5,000,000 – 4,000,000 = 1,000,000* *Shares deemed issued for no consideration*	£nil
Convertible bonds	£140,000 *(£2,000,000 × 10% * (1–30%))*	£40,000 *(2,000,000/50)*	£3.50

When calculating diluted earnings per share, the potential ordinary shares are considered in the order of most dilutive to least based on the calculations above as follows:

Options	£nil
Preference shares	£0.25
Convertible bonds	£3.50

Step 3: Consider the effect on the control number of each potential ordinary share in order of dilution

	Earnings from continuing operations	*Number of shares*	*Continuing earnings per share*
Net profit from continuing ordinary activities per share (control number) (calculated in Step 1)	£15,000,000	5,000,000	£3.00
Options	£nil	1,000,000	
	£15,000,000	6,000,000	£2.50
Preference shares	£1,000,000	4,000,000	
	£16,000,000	10,000,000	£1.60
Convertible bonds	£140,000	40,000	
	£16,140,000	10,040,000	£1.61

Since the convertible bonds increase the amount of diluted net profit from continuing ordinary activities per share, they are not considered in the calculation of diluted earnings per share.

Step 4: Determine diluted earnings per share:

Basic earnings per share (calculated in Step 1)	£20,000,000	5,000,000	£4.00
Options	£nil	1,000,000	
Preference shares	£1,000,000	4,000,000	
Diluted earnings per share	£21,000,000	10,000,000	£2.10

Thus, diluted earnings per share is £2.10

A company might have granted options in each of the last, say, ten years and at its balance sheet date have some options outstanding from each of the ten issues. The question arises whether the company would have to consider each option issue separately or on an aggregated basis. The company should first decide, using the average price for the period, which options are dilutive – for a profitable company this will be those options with an exercise price below the average price for the period. Once the dilutive options have been identified these can then be dealt with on an aggregated basis (see *Example 7.11*).

7.7 Two or more classes of ordinary shares

As discussed below (see **7.8**), earnings per share has to be calculated and disclosed for each separate class of ordinary share, different classes having different rights to share in the net profit for the period. (IAS 33.47)

IAS 33 does not provide guidance on how to perform this computation. The following guidance is based on SFAS 128, *Earnings per Share*, in the US.

In addition to two or more classes of ordinary shares, an enterprise's capital structure may also include a security which entitles the holders to participate in dividends along with ordinary shareholders. Such participation may be defined in accordance with a predetermined formula (for example, two for one) with, at times, an upper limit on the extent of participation (for example, up to, but not beyond, a specified amount per share).

For the purpose of diluted earnings per share calculation, those participating securities that are convertible into ordinary shares are deemed converted if the effect is dilutive.

For those securities that are not convertible into a class of ordinary shares SFAS 128 requires the use of 'two class' method. Under this method the profits are divided between two (or more) classes of ordinary shares and other participating interests in undistributed earnings on the following basis:

- allocate the dividend(s) declared for the period to each class of share and the contractual amount of dividends (or interest on participating income bonds) and the amount that must be paid for the current period (for example, unpaid cumulative dividends) on participating securities; and
- allocate the retained profit between the classes of ordinary shares and participating securities as if it were distributed in full to the shareholders and holders of participating interests on the balance sheet date.

This principle is illustrated in the following example.

Example 7.13

Assume a company has two classes of ordinary shares, 'A' and 'B', and that the 'B' shares are entitled to half the dividend per share declared by the directors on the 'A' shares. Assuming that there were an equal number of 'A' and 'B' shares in issue throughout the period, the total amount of profit less non-equity appropriations would be divided into three with two-thirds used to calculate the earnings per share for the 'A' shares and the remaining third used to calculate the earnings per share for the 'B' shares.

What if there were 200,000 'A' shares and 100,000 'B' shares in issue throughout the period and the net profit after preference dividends totalled £300,000, but no ordinary dividends were paid for the period. If the total profit for the period were to be paid out to shareholders £240,000 would be paid to the 'A' shareholders and £60,000 to the 'B' shareholders. Accordingly, it appears appropriate to reflect the number of shares in the division of profits. Thus, in this example the profit of £300,000 would be split in the ratio of 4:1.

What if there were 200,000 'A' and 100,000 'B' shares in issue on the last day of the accounting period, but because of share transactions during the period the weighted average number of shares during the period was 120,000 'A' shares and 30,000 'B' shares? It is still appropriate to split the retained profit in the ratio of 4:1 and add to this the dividends actually declared in respect of the period for each class.

If the dividends declared for the period were £77,143 to the 'A' shareholders and £15,000 to the 'B' shareholders, the net profit of £300,000 would be divided as:

'A' shareholders	£243,429	(77,143 + $\frac{4}{5}$ (300,000 – 92,143))
'B' shareholders	£56,571	(15,000 + $\frac{1}{5}$ (300,000 – 92,143))
	£300,000	

7.8 Disclosure

> 'An enterprise should present basic and diluted earnings per share on the face of the income statement for each class of ordinary shares that has a different right to share in the net profit for the period. An enterprise should present basic and diluted earnings per share with equal prominence for all periods presented.'
>
> (IAS 33.47)

IAS 33 requires an enterprise to present basic and diluted earnings per share, even if the amounts disclosed are negative (a loss per share). (IAS 33.48)

IAS 33 also requires disclosure of the following:

'• the amounts used as the numerators in calculating basic and diluted earnings per share, and a reconciliation of those amounts to the net profit or loss for the period; and
• the weighted average number of ordinary shares used as the denominator in calculating basic and diluted earnings per share and a reconciliation of these denominators to each other.'

(IAS 33.49)

There is no example disclosure included in the Standard. The following example illustrates how this information can be presented.

Example 7.14

	Profit (numerator) £'000	*Shares (denominator) Number (000)*	*Per share amount Pence*
Profit for the financial year	57,500		
Less: preference dividends	(7,500)		
Basic EPS			
Profit attributable to ordinary shareholders	50,000	100,000	50p
Effect of dilutive potential			
Ordinary shares			
Options	–	10,000	
5 per cent convertible bonds	5,000	15,000	
Convertible preference shares	7,500	20,000	
Diluted EPS	62,500	145,000	43p

As illustrated above, in the requirement to reconcile the numerators used to calculate basic and diluted earnings per share to the net profit or loss for the period, the net profit or loss for the period is the profit or loss *before* deduction of any dividends or other appropriations.

An enterprise is permitted to disclose earnings per share figures other than the basic and diluted earnings per share figures required to be disclosed by IAS 33. Such figures may be calculated based on profit from ordinary activities or some other component of net profit or on another earnings figure such as a headline earnings figure. However, the weighted average number of shares outstanding used in these additional computations must be calculated in accordance with IAS 33 and if the numerator (earnings figure) used is not disclosed on the face of the income statement, a reconciliation is required between the numerator and a line item on the income statement. When such additional earnings per share figures are presented, both basic and diluted figures are required to be presented with equal prominence.

When material ordinary or potential ordinary share transactions occur after the balance sheet date but before the issuance of the financial statements, such events are encouraged to be disclosed if 'they are of such importance that non-disclosure would affect the ability of the users of the financial statements to make proper evaluations and decisions'. (IAS 33.45)

Such transactions, except for the issuance of shares without a corresponding change in resources as discussed in section **7.5.3**, do not affect the calculation of earnings per share because they have not affected the capital used to earn the net profit during the period and include:

- '• the issue of shares for cash;
- the issue of shares when the proceeds are used to repay debt or preference shares outstanding at the balance sheet date;
- the redemption of ordinary shares outstanding;
- the conversion or exercise of potential ordinary shares outstanding at the balance sheet date, into ordinary shares;
- the issue of warrants, options or convertible securities; and
- the achievement of conditions that would result in the issue of contingently issuable shares.'

(IAS 33.45)

IAS 33 disclosure of ordinary and potential ordinary share transactions occurring after the balance sheet date is consistent with the general approach in IAS 10 (r1999), *Events After the Balance Sheet Date* (see Chapter **15**). Specifically, in the context of IAS 33, it is best practise to disclose all transactions which would have changed materially the number of ordinary shares or potential ordinary shares outstanding at the end of the period if the transaction had occurred before the end of the period.

7.9 Comparison with UK GAAP

The provisions of IAS 33 are substantially the same as those found in UK GAAP in FRS 14, *Earnings per Share*. The differences between the two standards are mostly due to the fact that FRS 14 provides more guidance on certain specific issues including:

- computation of 'net profit from continuing operations', the control number with which to establish whether potential ordinary shares are dilutive or anti-dilutive; net profit from continuing operations is determined differently under IASs and UK GAAP;
- treatment, for earnings per shares purposes, of a special dividend combined with a share consolidation. IAS 33 does not address this issue;
- treatment of contingently issuable shares (compatible with US GAAP) (see guidance in **7.5.2**);
- treatment of shares held in an employee share scheme (compatible with US GAAP) (see also **7.6.2**);
- presentation of financial statistics in historical summaries.

Also, if additional amounts per share are presented for components of profit other than a line item in the profit and loss account, IAS 33 requires a reconciliation to a line item. FRS 14, on the other hand, requires that the additional amounts per share should be reconciled to the earnings per share figure required by FRS 14 and that the reconciliation should list the items for which adjustment is made, disclosing their individual effect on the calculation.

7.10 Comparison with US GAAP

The provisions of IAS 33 are substantially the same as those found in US GAAP in SFAS 128, *Earnings per share*. The computation of basic earnings per share is the same under both standards.

The differences between the two standards are mostly due to the fact that SFAS 128 provides more guidance on certain specific issues – mostly in the area of calculation of diluted earnings per share. SFAS 128 and FRS 14 in the UK are largely consistent with each other and calculation of diluted earnings per share is based on the same principles as in IAS 33. For this reason, this additional guidance of US and UK standards is included throughout this chapter where applicable. Therefore, in most cases, it is reasonable to expect that in the absence of specific guidance in IAS 33 preparers of financial statements in accordance with IASs will use guidance included in the US or UK standards. This will result in diluted earnings per share calculated under IAS 33 and SFAS 128 being consistent. However, different amounts may be computed under IAS 33 if the additional guidance of SFAS 128 is not followed. These potential differences are summarised below:

- IAS 33 does not address treatment of employee share options. Consistent with UK GAAP, SFAS 128 requires that unrecognised compensation expense related to such share options be included in the amount of 'proceeds' used in applying the treasury stock method. Thus, for entities that recognise compensation expense related to employee share options, the number of incremental shares reflected in the computation of diluted earnings per share may therefore differ (see **7.6.2**);
- SFAS 128 requires that the 'reverse treasury stock' method be applied for contracts that require the reporting entity to repurchase its own stock, such as written put options (see **7.6.2**);
- SFAS 128 provides additional guidance on determining the impact of different types of contingencies that may be included in contingent share issue agreements (see **7.5.2**);
- SFAS 128 provides specific guidance on whether and when to reflect contracts that may be settled in shares or cash in the computation of diluted earnings per share (see **7.6.2**);
- SFAS 128 provides more guidance than IAS 33 in determining how to reflect in the computation of basic and diluted earnings per share potential ordinary shares issued by a subsidiary and securities issued by a parent

company that are convertible into common stock of a subsidiary company or equity-method investee;

- SFAS 128 provides guidance on computing the average market price to be used in applying the treasury stock method. No similar guidance is provided in IAS 33 (see **7.6.2**);
- SFAS 128 describes the two-class method that should be used in computing earnings per share when an entity has participating securities or more than one class of ordinary shares (see **7.7**).

Additionally, some of the disclosure requirements of the two standards differ. In particular, per share figures are required for income from continuing operations, discontinued operations, extraordinary items and the cumulative effect of a change in accounting policy under SFAS 128.

7.11 Examples from published financial statements

Note that the excerpts given do not always comply in full with all aspects of IAS and as such are not necessarily examples of best practice but merely of current practice.

Example 7.15

Extract from Consolidated Profit and Loss Account

	Notes	*2000* €	*1999* €
Earnings per share	23		
Net profit			
Basic		0.84	0.56
Diluted		0.82	0.54
Average number of shares (1,000 shares)	23		
Basic		4,673,162	4,593,761
Diluted		4,792,980	4,743,184

1. Accounting principles – extract

Earnings per share
The Group calculates both basic and diluted earnings per share in accordance with the IAS 33, *Earnings per Share.* Under IAS 33 basic earnings per share is computed using the weighted average number of shares outstanding during the period. Diluted earnings per share is computed using the weighted average number of shares outstanding during the period plus the dilutive effect of warrants and stock options outstanding during the period. Share and per share data presented reflect the four-for-one stock split effective on 10 April 2000.

23. Earnings per share

	2000	*1999*
Numerator/€m		
Basic/Diluted:		
Income available to common shareholders	3,938	2,577
Denominator/1000 shares		
Basic:		
Weighted average shares	4,673,162	4,593,761
Effect of dilutive securities: warrants	119,818	149,423
Diluted:		
Adjusted weighted average shares and assumed conversions	4,792,980	4,743,184

Under IAS 33, basic earnings per share is computed using the weighted average number of shares outstanding during the period. Diluted earnings per share is computed using the weighted average number of shares outstanding during the period plus the dilutive effect of warrants and stock options outstanding during the period. Share and per share data presented reflect the four-for-one stock split effective on 10 April 2000.

Nokia
Finland
31 December 2000
International Accounting Standards

Example 7.16

Note 10 Earnings per share

	31.12.00	*31.12.99*
Basic earnings per share calculation		
Net profit for the period (CHF million)	7,792	6,153
Net profit for the period before goodwill amortisation (CHF million)[1]	8,459	6,493
Weighted average shares outstanding:		
Registered ordinary shares	433,486,003	430,497,026
Own shares to be delivered	2,058,212	–
Less: Treasury Shares	(32,514,906)	(25,754,544)[3]
Weighted average shares for basic earnings per share	**403,029,309**	**404,742,482**
Basic earnings per share (CHF)	**19.33**	**15.20**
Basic earnings per share before goodwill amortisation (CHF)[2]	**20.99**	**16.04**
Diluted earnings per share calculation		
Net profit for the year (CHF million)	7,778[5]	6,493
Net profit for the period before goodwill amortisation (CHF million)[2]	8,445[5]	6,493
Weighted average shares for basic earnings per share	403,029,309	404,742,482
Potential dilutive ordinary shares resulting from outstanding options, warrants and convertible debt securities[6]	5,496,591	3,632,670[4]
Weighted average shares for diluted earnings per share	**408,525,900**	**408,375,152**
Diluted earnings per share (CHF)	**19.04**	**15.07**
Diluted earnings per share before goodwill amortisation (CHF)[2]	**20.67**	**15.90**

1 The 1999 figure has been restated to reflect retroactive changes in accounting policy arising from newly applicable International Accounting Standards and changes in presentation (see Note 1: Summary of Significant Accounting Policies). 2 The amortisation of goodwill and other intangible assets is excluded from this calculation. 3 Treasury shares have increased by 11,371,720 for the period ended 31 December 1999, due to a change in accounting policy (see Note 1: Summary of Significant Accounting Policies). 4 Share amount has been adjusted by 1,414,114 representing other potentially dilutive instruments for the period ended 31 December 1999, due to a change in accounting policy (see Note 1: Summary of Significant Accounting Policies). 5 Net profit has been adjusted for the dilutive impact of own equity derivative activity in accordance with International Accounting Standards. 6 Total equivalent shares outstanding on options that were not dilutive for the respective periods but could potentially dilute earnings per share in future were 9,174,760 and 24,045,261 for the years ended 31 December 2000 and 31 December 1999 respectively.

1999 share figures are restated for the two-for-one share split, effective May 2000.

UBS Group
Switzerland
31 December 2000
International Accounting Standards

Example 7.17

21. Equity – extract

Share capital
At 31 December 2000 and 1999, the authorised and called-up share capital was 1,600,000 shares with a nominal value of CHF 100 each.

Non-voting equity securities (Genussscheine)
As of 31 December 2000 and 1999, 7,025,627 non-voting equity securities had been issued. Under Swiss company law these non-voting equity securities have no nominal value, are not part of the share capital and cannot be issued against a contribution which would be shown as an asset in the balance sheet of Roche Holding Ltd. Each non-voting equity security confers the same rights as any of the shares to participate in the net profit and any remaining proceeds from liquidation following repayment of the nominal value of the shares and, if any, participation certificates. In accordance with the law and the Articles of Incorporation of Roche Holding Ltd, the company is entitled at all times to exchange all or some of the non-voting equity securities into shares or participation certificates.

Own equity instruments
As at 31 December 2000 the Group held 284,566 (1999: 251,589) of its own non-voting equity securities and financial instruments to acquire these securities. These have been acquired primarily to meet the obligations that may arise in respect of certain of the Group's debt instruments. For 2000 the Group's holding in its own equity instruments is recorded as a deduction from equity.

22. Earnings per share and non-voting equity security

Basic and diluted earnings per share and non-voting equity security

	2000	*1999*
Net income (CHF million)	**8,647**	5,764
Number of shares (thousands) (see Note 21)	**1,600**	1,600
Number of non-voting equity securities (thousands) (see Note 21)	**7,026**	7,026
Weighted average number of own non-voting equity securities held (thousands)	**(277)**	–
Total (thousands)	**8,349**	8,626
Basic earnings per share and non-voting equity security (CHF)	**1,036**	668

Diluted earnings per share and non-voting equity

For the calculation of diluted earnings per share and non-voting equity security in 2000, the weighted average number of shares and non-voting equity securities outstanding is adjusted to assume conversion of all dilutive potential shares or non-equity voting securities.

	2000
Net income (CHF million)	8,647
Elimination of interest expense, net of tax, of convertible debt instruments, where dilutive (CHF million)	114
Net income used to calculate diluted earnings per share (CHF million)	8,761
Weighted average number of shares and non-voting equity securities in issue (thousands)	8,349
Adjustment for assumed conversion of convertible debt instruments, where dilutive (thousands)	203
Weighted average number of shares and non-voting equity securities in issue used to calculate dilutive earnings per share (thousands)	8,552
Diluted earnings per share and non-voting equity securities (CHF)	1,024

Roche Group
Switzerland
31 December 2000
International Accounting Standards

CHAPTER 8

Equity statement

8.1 Sources

IAS 1 (r1997)	*Presentation of Financial Statements.*
IAS 8 (r1993)	*Net Profit or Loss for the Period, Fundamental Errors and Changes in Accounting Policies.*
IAS 12 (r2000)	*Income Taxes.*
IAS 16 (r1998)	*Property, Plant and Equipment.*
IAS 21 (r1993)	*The Effects of Changes in Foreign Exchange Rates.*
IAS 39 (r2000)	*Financial Instruments: Recognition and Measurement* (effective 1 January 2001).

8.2 Brief summary of the requirements

IAS 1 (r1997) requires a separate, primary financial statement that discloses separately net profit or loss for the period; each item of income and expense, gain or loss which has been recognised directly in equity and thus bypassed the income statement; and the cumulative effect of changes in accounting policy and the correction of fundamental errors when these are recognised directly in equity. In addition, either within this statement or within the notes to the financial statements, an enterprise should present capital transactions with and distributions to owners; a reconciliation of accumulated profits; and a reconciliation between each class of equity capital, share premium and each reserve.

This separate financial statement may take the form of a traditional equity reconciliation. When this is the case, a subtotal of the items recognised directly in equity is required in the reconciliation. Alternatively, a separate financial statement may disclose the items recognised directly in equity and reconciliations of the other components of equity may be presented in the notes to the financial statements.

8.3 Development of the requirements

Prior to the issuance of IAS 1 (r1997) in August 1997, IAS 5 required various disclosures regarding each class of share capital and an equity reconciliation. However, a separate primary financial statement relating to equity was not required.

The revision of IAS 1 was a long project and during that time other standard setters, including the ASB in the UK and the FASB in the US, developed and issued requirements for new financial performance statements or indicators – the statement of total recognised gains and losses in the UK and comprehensive income in the US. These new statements and indicators provide financial statement users with a more broad performance indicator than net profit or loss for the period since they encompass gains and losses which bypass the income statement.

E53, the exposure draft which preceded IAS 1, proposed a new primary financial statement which aimed to capture this type of broad performance by including gains and losses not included in the income statement. However, based on the comments received on E53, the IASC Board decided it needed to consider further the implications of such a statement and as an interim step, approved IAS 1 (r1997) with a new requirement for a primary financial statement showing those gains and losses not currently presented in the income statement. Unlike what was proposed in the exposure draft, the new statement may be presented either as a 'traditional' equity reconciliation in a column form, or as a statement of performance in its own right. The IASC Board agreed in principle, in April 1997, to undertake a review of the way in which performance is measured and reported. In July 1999 this project was added to the Board's agenda. It will be based on a Position Paper developed by the G4+1 group of accounting standard setters (since disbanded) of which IASC was a member. The most significant proposal of the G4+1 Position Paper, *Reporting Financial Performance: Proposals for Change*, is that financial performance should be reported in a single statement – effectively combining the profit and loss account with the statement showing changes in equity. The statement would divide items into three main components:

- the results of operating (or trading) activities;
- the results of financing and other treasury activities; and
- other gains and losses.

The IASB staff are preparing a report on this subject in the form of a Draft Statement of Principles for consideration by the IASB and the requirements included in IAS 1 (r1997) relating to the new primary financial statement may change in due course.

IAS 1 (r1997) is effective for financial statements covering periods beginning on or after 1 July 1998. IAS 1 (r1997) supersedes IAS 1, IAS 5 and IAS 13.

8.4 Disclosure

> 'An enterprise should present, as a separate component of its financial statements, a statement showing:
>
> (a) the net profit or loss for the period;
> (b) each item of income and expense, gain or loss which, as required by other Standards, is recognised directly in equity, and the total of these items; and
> (c) the cumulative effect of changes in accounting policy and the correction of fundamental errors dealt with under the Benchmark treatments in IAS 8 (r1993).
>
> In addition, an enterprise should present, either within this statement or in the notes:
>
> (d) capital transactions with owners and distributions to owners;
> (e) the balance of accumulated profit or loss at the beginning of the period and at the balance sheet date, and the movements for the period; and
> (f) a reconciliation between the carrying amount of each class of equity capital, share premium and each reserve at the beginning and the end of the period, separately disclosing each movement.'
>
> (IAS 1 (r1997).86)

The above disclosure requirements may be met either by:

- including a primary financial statement of performance which includes items (a) to (c), showing separately in the notes to the financial statements items (d) to (f); or by
- including a 'traditional' equity reconciliation as a primary financial statement which includes a column disclosing items recognised directly in equity, i.e., items (a) to (f).

Presenting the total of (a) and (b), sometimes called 'comprehensive income', is optional; however, whichever approach is taken, a subtotal must be included of the items in (b) to enable users to derive the total gains and losses arising from the enterprise's activities during the period.

IAS 8 (r1993) requires that 'all items of income and expense recognised in a period should be included in the determination of the net profit or loss for the period unless an International Accounting Standard requires or permits otherwise.' (IAS 8 (r1993).7) When an IAS requires or permits an item of income or expense, which encompasses gains and losses, to be excluded from net profit or loss and recognised directly in equity, such items fall under (b) above and must be disclosed in a primary financial statement. Such items include:

(a) current and deferred tax which relates to items that are charged or credited directly to equity, including amounts arising on initial recognition of the equity component of a compound financial instrument (IAS 12 (r2000));

(b) certain revaluation surpluses and deficits arising on items of property, plant and equipment (IAS 16 (r1998));

(c) gains and losses arising on the translation of the financial statements of a foreign entity (IAS 21 (r1993)); and

(d) changes in fair values of certain financial instruments (IAS 39 (r2000)).

In addition, IAS 1 (r1997) requires disclosure of the cumulative effect of changes in accounting policy and the correction of fundamental errors dealt with under the benchmark treatments in IAS 8 (r1993). As discussed in **5.17**, these benchmark treatments require that the cumulative effect of such changes and corrections be recognised by adjusting the opening balance of retained earnings.

Additional disclosure requirements relating to the components of equity are discussed in Chapter **11**.

8.5 Examples

The equity statement examples given in the appendix to IAS 1 (r1997) are reproduced below:

Example 8.1

XYZ group – Statement of changes in equity for the year ended 31 December 20x2

(in thousands of currency units)

	Share capital	*Share premium*	*Revaluation reserve*	*Translation reserve*	*Accumulated profit*	*Total*
Balance at 31 December 20x0	X	X	X	(X)	X	X
Changes in accounting policy					(X)	(X)
Restated balance	X	X	X	(X)	X	X
Surplus on revaluation of properties			X			X
Deficit on revaluation of investments			(X)			(X)
Currency translation differences				(X)		
Net gains and losses not recognised in the income statement			X	(X)		X
Net profit for the period					X	X
Dividends					(X)	(X)
Issue of share capital	X	X				X
Balance at 31 December 20x1	X	X	X	(X)	X	X
Deficit on revaluation of properties			(X)			(X)
Surplus on revaluation of investments			X			X
Currency translation differences				(X)		(X)
Net gains and losses not recognised in the income statement			(X)	(X)		(X)
Net profit for the period					X	X
Dividends					(X)	(X)
Issue of share capital	X	X				X
Balance at 31 December 20x2	X	X	X	(X)	X	X

Example 8.1 illustrates a traditional equity reconcilation being adapted to meet the requirements in IAS 1 (r1997) for a primary financial statement. Note that a subtotal for net gains and losses not recognised in the income statement is given for each year presented.

An alternative method of presenting changes in equity is illustrated in the following example.

Example 8.2

XYZ group – Statement of recognised gains and losses for the year ended 31 December 20x2
(in thousands of currency units)

	20x2	*20x1*
Surplus/(deficit) on revaluation of properties	(X)	X
Surplus/(deficit) on revaluation of investments	X	(X)
Exchange differences on translation of the financial statements of foreign entities	(X)	(X)
Net gains not recognised in the income statement	X	X
Net profit for the period	X	X
Total recognised gains and losses	X	X
Effect of changes in accounting policy		(X)

The above example illustrates an approach which presents those gains and losses which have bypassed the income statement in a separate component of the financial statements. Under this approach, a reconciliation of opening and closing balances of share capital, reserves and accumulated profit, as illustrated above, is given in the notes to the financial statements.

8.6 Comparison with UK GAAP

Under UK GAAP, the statement of total recognised gains and losses ('STRGL') generally contains the same information as the separate financial statement required by IAS 1 (r1997) which presents gains and losses not recognised in the income statement. However, the UK statement is a performance statement, therefore once an item is reported as a gain or loss it cannot be reported a second time within either the profit and loss account or the statement of total recognised gains and losses. As under IAS 1 (r1997), an enterprise which presents a statement of total recognised gains and losses will present the additional equity reconciliations in the notes to the financial statements.

8.7 Comparison with US GAAP

In June 1997, the FASB issued SFAS 130, *Reporting Comprehensive Income*, which establishes standards for the reporting and display of comprehensive income and its components. Comprehensive income is defined as 'the change in equity (net assets) of a business enterprise during a period from transactions and other events and circumstances from nonowner sources. It

Example 8.3

Consolidated Statements of Stockholders' Equity
(€ million)

	Capital stock of Bayer AG	*Capital reserves of Bayer AG*	*Retained earnings*	*Net income interest*	*Bayer stockholders'*	*Translation differences interest*	*Minority stockholders'*	*Total*
Dec. 31 1998	1,867	2,945	7,121	1,614	13,547	(979)	211	12,779
Changes in stockholder's equity resulting from capital contributions and dividend payments								
Capital contributions	3	(3)			0			0
Dividend payments				(747)	(747)		(23)	(770)
	3	**(3)**		**(747)**	**(747)**		**(23)**	**(770)**
Other changes in stockholder's equity not recognised in income								
Exchange differences						1,206		1,206
Other differences			(23)		(23)		(28)	(51)
			(23)		**(23)**	**1,206**	**(28)**	**1,155**
Changes in stockholders' equity recognised in income								
Allocation to retained earnings			867	(867)	0			0
Income after taxes for 1999				2,002	2,002		16	2,018
			867	**1,135**	**2,002**		**16**	**2,018**
Dec. 31 1999	1,870	2,942	7,965	2,002	14,779	227	176	15,182
Changes in stockholder's equity resulting from capital contributions and dividend payments								
Capital contributions							2	2
Dividend payments				(949)	(949)		(4)	(953)
				(949)	**(949)**		**(2)**	**(951)**
Other changes in stockholder's equity not recognised in income								
Exchange differences						238		238
Other differences			29		29		37	66
			29		**29**	**238**	**37**	**304**
Changes in stockholders' equity recognised in income								
Allocation to retained earnings			1,053	(1,053)	0			0
Income after taxes for 2000				1,816	1,816		26	1,842
			1,053	**763**	**1,816**		**26**	**1,842**
Dec. 31 2000	**1,870**	**2,942**	**9,047**	**1,816**	**15,675**	**465**	**237**	**16,377**

Bayer Group
Germany
31 December 1998
International Accounting Standards

includes all changes in equity during a period except those resulting from investments by owners and distributions to owners.' (CON 6.70)

Thus, comprehensive income encompasses many of the items required to be included in a separate financial statement by IAS 1 (r1997). Specifically, it includes foreign currency translation gains and losses, certain minimum pension liability adjustments and unrealised gains and losses on certain investments in debt and equity securities.

Under SFAS 130, comprehensive income may be included either on the face of the income statement in a reconciliation below net profit or loss, or in a separate primary financial statement which discloses a reconciliation between net profit or loss for the period and comprehensive income, or in the statement of changes in shareholders' equity.

8.8 Examples from published financial statements

See **11.3.12** for examples of traditional equity reconciliations.

Note that the excerpts given do not always comply in full with all aspects of IAS and as such are not necessarily examples of best practice but merely of current practice.

CHAPTER 9

Balance sheet format

9.1 Sources

IAS 1 (r1997) *Presentation of Financial Statements.*
IAS 32 (r1998) *Financial Instruments: Disclosure and Presentation.*

9.2 Brief summary of the requirements

IAS 1 (r1997) allows a choice between a classified balance sheet presentation, one which presents assets and liabilities on the face of the balance sheet as current or non-current, and a presentation which does not make this distinction on the face of the balance sheet but discloses information about the maturities of assets and liabilities in the notes to the financial statements. It also requires specific line items to be disclosed on the face of the balance sheet and subclassifications of line items to be disclosed either on the face of the balance sheet or in the notes to the financial statements.

9.3 Development of the requirements

Prior to the issuance of IAS 1 (r1997) in July 1997, IASs did not prescribe a standard format for the balance sheet. Various IASs required the disclosure of certain items in the financial statements but no specific format was adopted. Accordingly, IAS 1 (r1997) greatly enhanced the ease with which a user can compare the balance sheets of different enterprises reporting under IASs. IAS 1 (r1997) became effective for financial statements covering periods beginning on or after 1 July 1998 and superseded IAS 1, IAS 5 and IAS 13.

9.4 Items presented on the face of the balance sheet

IAS 1 (r1997) requires that line items which present the items listed below be disclosed on the face of the balance sheet. However, the descriptions used and the ordering of items may be amended according to the nature of the enterprise and its transactions, to provide information that is necessary for an overall understanding of the enterprise's financial position. For example, some headings may not be applicable to certain enterprises, such as banks. Preparers of financial statements of banks should follow the more specific requirements of IAS 30, *Disclosures in the Financial Statements of Banks and Similar Financial Institutions* (see Appendix II). Similarly, if the amount of any item listed below is immaterial, it may be aggregated with another item and disclosed separately in the notes to the financial statements.

Required line items

- Property, plant and equipment.
- Intangible assets.
- Financial assets (excluding investments accounted for using the equity method, trade and other receivables and cash and cash equivalents).
- Investments accounted for using the equity method.
- Inventories.
- Trade and other receivables.
- Cash and cash equivalents.
- Trade and other payables.
- Tax liabilities and assets.
- Provisions.
- Non-current interest-bearing liabilities.
- Minority interest.
- Issued capital and reserves.

In general, additional line items are presented when they provide relevant information and add to the understandability of the financial statements. Specifically, additional line items are presented when:

(a) required by an International Accounting Standard (IAS 1 (r1997).68);
(b) the size, nature or function of an item is such that separate presentation is necessary to present fairly the enterprise's financial position (IAS 1 (r1997).68); or
(c) the nature, liquidity or function of a particular class of assets, or the nature or timing of a particular class of liabilities, is significantly different from other assets or liabilities included in a particular category. (IAS 1 (r1997).70)

In addition, when different measurement bases, such as historical cost or revaluation, are used to measure different classes of assets or liabilities, this usually indicates that the assets or liabilities differ in nature or function and thus should be shown separately if material. (IAS 1 (r1997).71)

Although IAS 1 (r1997) suggests that it is appropriate to segregate on the face of the balance sheet classes of property, plant and equipment which are accounted for using differing measurement bases, this presentation is not common in practice and not required.

9.5 Items required either on the face of the balance sheet or in the notes

> 'An enterprise should disclose, either on the face of the balance sheet or in the notes to the balance sheet, further sub-classifications of the line items presented, classified in a manner appropriate to the enterprise's operations. Each item should be sub-classified, when appropriate, by its nature and, amounts payable to and receivable from the parent enterprise, fellow subsidiaries and associates and other related parties should be disclosed separately.'
>
> (IAS 1 (r1997).72)

IAS 1 (r1997) does not provide an exhaustive list of all the balance sheet disclosures required in the notes to the financial statements since most such disclosures are addressed in other IASs. Instead, it states that the same criteria for inclusion of additional line items on the face of the balance sheet (see **9.4**) be considered when determining disclosure of sub-classifications of the balance sheet items in the notes. However, it does require separate disclosure of amounts payable to and receivable from the parent enterprise, fellow subsidiaries and associates, and other related parties.

9.6 Classified balance sheets

An enterprise has a choice of either presenting a classified balance sheet with assets and liabilities presented as current or non-current on the face of the balance sheet or disclosing the maturity dates of assets and liabilities in the notes to the financial statements. This choice is made based on the nature of the operations of an enterprise.

> 'Whichever method of presentation is adopted, an enterprise should disclose, for each asset and liability item that combines amounts expected to be recovered or settled both before and after twelve months from the balance sheet date, the amount expected to be recovered or settled after more than twelve months.'
>
> (IAS 1 (r1997).54)

When a classified balance sheet is not presented, assets and liabilities are required to be presented broadly in order of their liquidity. (IAS 1 (r1997).53) When a classified balance sheet is presented, assets and liabilities are classified according to the criteria and guidance described in the following two sections.

9.6.1 Assets

> 'An asset should be classified as a current asset when it:
>
> (a) is expected to be realised in, or is held for sale or consumption in, the normal course of the enterprise's operating cycle; or
> (b) is held primarily for trading purposes or for the short-term and expected to be realised within twelve months of the balance sheet date; or
> (c) is cash or a cash equivalent asset which is not restricted in its use.
>
> All other assets should be classified as non-current assets.'
>
> (IAS 1 (r1997).57)

However, IAS 1 (r1997), does not require the use of the term 'non-current' as long as the meaning of any alternative description is clear.

IAS 1 (r1997) defines an entity's operating cycle as, 'the time between the acquisition of materials entering into a process and its realisation in cash or an instrument that is readily convertible into cash.' (IAS 1 (r1997).59) For most enterprises the operating cycle will not exceed 12 months. However, some trade receivables and inventories may not be expected to be realised within 12 months of the reporting date, but they are still classified as current assets since they fall under the definition of an operating asset under (a) above. IAS 1 (r1997) requires disclosure of any amount included as a current asset which is not expected to be recovered within twelve months from the balance sheet date. (IAS 1 (r1997).54)

Current assets normally include: cash and cash equivalents, inventories, trade debtors, prepayments, accrued income and other financial assets expected to be realised within 12 months.

Assets which do not fall under (a), (b) or (c) above are classified as non-current and generally include tangible, intangible, operating and financial assets of a long-term nature. Line items typically included as non-current assets are property, plant and equipment, goodwill, development costs, other intangibles and long-term investments.

If an enterprise decides to dispose of assets which were originally classified as non-current it will result in a change in classification if those assets are now expected to be realised within the next 12 months.

9.6.2 Liabilities

> 'A liability should be classified as a current liability when it:
>
> (a) is expected to be settled in the normal course of the enterprise's operating cycle; or
> (b) is due to be settled within twelve months of the balance sheet date.
>
> All other liabilities should be classified as non-current liabilities.'
>
> (IAS 1 (r1997).60)

Some liabilities such as particular trade payables may not be expected to be settled within 12 months of the reporting date but are still classified as current since they fall under (a) above. However, IAS 1 (r1997) requires disclosure of any amount included as a current liability which is not expected to be settled within twelve months from the balance sheet date. (IAS 1 (r1997).54)

Current liabilities generally include: trade payables and accruals, accruals for wages and related payroll taxes, the current portion of interest-bearing liabilities, bank overdrafts, dividends payable, income taxes and other short-term non-trade payables.

Interest bearing liabilities which are due after 12 months from the reporting date are generally classified as non-current liabilities with the amount, if any, which is due to be repaid in the 12 months from the reporting date being classified as a current liability.

However, in certain circumstances, an enterprise may continue to classify long-term interest-bearing liabilities as non-current even when they are due to be settled within 12 months of the balance sheet date. See **11.6.6** for a discussion of these circumstances.

9.7 Equity capital and reserves

IAS 1 (r1997) requires that issued capital and reserves be presented on the face of the balance sheet and that numerous other disclosures be made either on the face of the balance sheet or in the notes to the financial statements. See Chapter **11** for a discussion of these disclosures.

IAS 32 (r1998) requires the substance of a financial instrument, rather than its legal form, to govern its classification on the balance sheet of the issuer. (IAS 32.19) Therefore, component parts of instruments such as convertible bonds may be required to be presented as part of equity rather than as a liability. The classification (and thus presentation) of items as either financial liabilities or equity is dealt with in **11.4**.

9.8 Example IAS, UK and US balance sheets

The following examples are provided to highlight differences in presentation between balance sheets prepared under IASs, UK GAAP and US GAAP. They are for illustration purposes only and should not be considered to be complete or appropriate for all circumstances. The IAS example is an expanded version of the example of the minimum requirements for a balance sheet included in the appendix to IAS 1 (r1997). A full set of IAS Model Financial Statements can be found in Appendix III.

Example 9.1
Company name
Balance Sheet
31 December 20x3
(IAS presentation)

	Note	*20x3* *£'000*	*20x2* *£'000*
ASSETS			
Non-current assets			
Property, plant and equipment		500	450
Goodwill		80	90
Manufacturing licences		20	30
Investments in associates		150	125
Pension fund asset due beyond one year		200	180
Other financial assets		150	125
		1,100	1,000
Current assets			
Inventories		100	80
Trade and other receivables		40	35
Prepayments		20	15
Other financial assets		10	5
Cash and cash equivalents		20	15
		190	150
Total assets		1,290	1,150
EQUITY AND LIABILITIES			
Capital and reserves			
Issued capital		75	75
Reserves		15	13
Accumulated profits/(losses)		140	12
		230	100
Minority interest		100	40
Non-current liabilities			
Interest bearing borrowings		350	400
Deferred tax		30	20
Retirement benefit obligation		350	(400)
		730	820
Current liabilities			
Trade and other payables		170	145
Short-term borrowings		10	5
Current portion of interest-bearing borrowings		20	20
Warranty provision		30	20
		230	190
Total equity and liabilities		1,290	1,150

Example 9.2

Company name
Balance Sheet
31 December 20x3
(UK GAAP presentation)

	Note	*20x3* *£'000*	*20x2* *£'000*
FIXED ASSETS			
Intangible fixed assets		100	120
Tangible fixed assets		500	450
Investments			
Investments in associate undertakings		150	125
Other investments		150	125
		300	250
		900	820
CURRENT ASSETS			
Stocks		100	80
Pension fund asset due beyond one year		200	180
Debtors		60	50
Investments		10	5
Cash at bank and in hand		20	15
		390	330
CREDITORS: amounts falling due within one year		(200)	(170)
NET CURRENT ASSETS		190	160
TOTAL ASSETS LESS CURRENT LIABILITIES		1,090	980
CREDITORS: amounts falling due after more than one year		(700)	(800)
PROVISIONS FOR LIABILITIES AND CHARGES		(60)	(40)
MINORITY INTERESTS			
Equity minority interests		(70)	(10)
Non-equity minority interests		(30)	(30)
		(100)	(100)
TOTAL NET ASSETS		230	100
CAPITAL AND RESERVES			
Called up share capital		30	30
Share premium account		45	45
Revaluation reserve		5	5
Other reserves		10	8
Profit and loss account		140	12
SHAREHOLDERS' FUNDS		230	100
Attributable to equity shareholders		200	70
Attributable to non-equity shareholders		30	30

Example 9.3

Company name
Balance Sheet
31 December 20x3
(US GAAP presentation)

	Note	*20x3* *$'000*	*20x2* *$'000*
ASSETS			
Current assets			
Cash and cash equivalents		900	800
Trade and other receivables, less allowance or doubtful accounts of $10 and $5, respectively		375	350
Inventory		400	150
Prepaid expenses		100	55
Deferred income taxes		250	150
Other		25	15
Total current assets		2,050	1,520
Non-current assets			
Property, plant and equipment – net of accumulated depreciation		750	550
Goodwill – net of amortisation		180	290
Manufacturing licences – net of amortisation		10	10
Investments in joint ventures		270	215
Pension fund assets		400	280
Total non-current assets		1,610	1,345
Total assets		3,660	2,865
LIABILITIES AND STOCKHOLDERS' EQUITY			
Current liabilities			
Trade and other payables		470	315
Short-term borrowings		110	55
Current portion of interest-bearing borrowings		20	20
Total current liabilities		600	390
Non-current liabilities			
Interest bearing borrowings		550	405
Deferred tax		130	20
Retirement benefit obligation		425	285
Total non-current liabilities		1,105	710
Stockholders' equity			
Common stock, par value $1 per share: Authorised 500,000,000 shares; issued and outstanding 75,000 and 70,000		75	70
Additional paid-in capital		1,450	1,312
Retained earnings		415	370
Accumulated other comprehensive income		15	13
Total stockholders' equity		1,955	1,765
Total liabilities and stockholders' equity		3,660	2,865

9.9 Comparison to UK GAAP

The above IAS example balance sheet differs from the balance sheet presentation which is most common in the UK, the Format 1 presentation of Schedule 4 of the Companies Act 1985, in that an asset total is presented which is equal to the presented total of liabilities plus equity and reserves rather than a presented net assets total which equals shareholders' funds. However, this does not imply that a Format 1 presentation is precluded under IAS 1 (r1997). As noted above, IAS 1 (r1997) does not prescribe the order of line items or the use of subtotals on the balance sheet. Thus, with care to ensure that all of the required disclosures of IAS 1 (r1997) and other IASs are made, it is possible for a balance sheet presented under the UK Format 1 presentation to comply with IAS 1 (r1997).

A slight difference arises between IAS 1 (r1997) and UK GAAP in the distinction between current and non-current assets. Generally, fixed assets under UK GAAP are equivalent to non-current assets under IAS 1 (r1997). However, under UK GAAP, a fixed asset is defined as one which is intended for use on a continuing basis in the activities of the enterprise whereas a current asset is one which is not intended for such use. Thus, an item which may be clearly of a long-term nature but not intended for use on a continuing basis in the activities of the enterprise, for example a deferred tax asset which is recoverable after more than one year, would be considered a current asset under UK GAAP but under the criteria set out in IAS 1 (r1997) discussed in **9.6.1**, such an asset would be considered non-current.

9.10 Comparison to US GAAP

A US style balance sheet is generally presented as two columns with assets on the left hand side which equal the total of liabilities and equity which are presented on the right hand side. The current/non-current distinction is similar to that defined in IAS 1 (r1997). Generally, the balance sheets of most US companies present separate classifications of current assets and liabilities in a classified balance sheet. There are several industries where the current/non-current distinction is not deemed relevant. In those cases, a non-classified balance sheet is prepared. Some common examples of enterprises with non-classified balance sheets are real estate companies, broker-dealers and finance institutions, and stock life insurance enterprises.

CHAPTER 10

Balance sheet assets

10.1 Sources

IAS 1 (r1997)	*Presentation of Financial Statements.*
IAS 2 (r1993)	*Inventories.*
IAS 7 (r1992)	*Cash Flow Statements.*
IAS 16 (r1998)	*Property, Plant and Equipment.*
IAS 17 (r1997)	*Leases.*
IAS 18 (r1993)	*Revenue.*
IAS 22 (r1998)	*Business Combinations.*
IAS 23 (r1993)	*Borrowing Costs.*
IAS 32 (r1998)	*Financial Instruments: Disclosure and Presentation.*
IAS 36	*Impairment of Assets.*
IAS 37	*Provisions, Contingent Liabilities and Contingent Assets.*
IAS 38	*Intangible Assets.*
IAS 39 (r2000)	*Financial Instruments: Recognition and Measurement* (effective 1 January 2001).
IAS 40	*Investment Property* (effective 1 January 2001).
SIC-1	*Consistency – Different Cost Formulas for Inventories.*
SIC-2	*Consistency – Capitalisation of Borrowing Costs.*
SIC-6	*Costs of Modifying Existing Software.*
SIC-14	*Property, Plant and Equipment – Compensation for the Impairment or Loss of Items.*
SIC-23	*Property, Plant and Equipment – Major Inspection or Overhaul Costs.*

10.2 Brief summary of the requirements

Assets are discussed in the following sections and chapters:

Non-current assets	**Section**
Property, plant and equipment	**10.3**
Borrowing costs	**10.4**
Investment property	**10.8**
Intangible assets	**10.7**

Goodwill	**10.5**
Negative goodwill	**10.6**
Impairment of assets	**10.12**
Investments in associates	Chapter **20**
Pension fund asset due beyond one year	Chapter **25**
Current assets	
Inventories	**10.9**
Trade and other receivables	**10.10**
Prepayments	**10.10**
Cash and cash equivalents	**10.11**

The requirements of IAS 39 (r2000) relating to financial assets are discussed in Chapter 12.

10.3 Property, plant and equipment

10.3.1 Sources

IAS 16 (r1998)	*Property, Plant and Equipment.*
IAS 36	*Impairment of Assets.*
IAS 37	*Provisions, Contingent Liabilities and Contingent Assets.*
IAS 38	*Intangible Assets.*
IAS 40	*Investment Property* (effective 1 January 2001).
SIC-6	*Costs of Modifying Existing Software.*
SIC-14	*Property, Plant and Equipment – Compensation for the Impairment or Loss of Items.*

10.3.2 Brief summary of the requirements

> 'Property, plant and equipment are tangible assets that:
>
> (a) are held by an enterprise for use in the production or supply of goods or services, for rental to others, or for administrative purposes; and
>
> (b) are expected to be used during more than one period.'
>
> (IAS 16 (r1998) 1998).6)

Property, plant and equipment may be carried at either historical cost (benchmark treatment) or a revalued amount (allowed alternative treatment).

Investment properties may be held either at fair value, with changes in fair value recognised in the income statement (see **10.8**), or at depreciated cost less any accumulated impairment losses.

10.3.3 Development of the requirements

Originally approved in 1981, IAS 16 was revised as part of the Comparability/Improvements project. The three main changes to IAS 16 related to a new requirement to ensure that revaluations are kept current; the initial measurement of property, plant and equipment acquired in exchange for another asset; and the recognition of a revaluation increase subsequent to a previous decrease. In addition, the text of IAS 4, *Depreciation Accounting*, dealing with the depreciation of property, plant and equipment was included in IAS 16. In November 1999, the IASC Board decided to withdraw IAS 4 since the subject is now addressed in IAS 16 (r1998), IAS 22 (r1998) and IAS 38.

During 1998, consequential amendments to IAS 16 were made as a result of the revision of IAS 22 and the issuance of IAS 36 and IAS 37. Two main revisions were made. First, the revised IAS 16 no longer covers the impairment of property, plant and equipment but contains references to IAS 36 (see **10.12**). Second, the revised IAS specifically states that the initial cost of an asset includes estimated dismantling and restoration costs to the extent that they are provided for under IAS 37. The revised IAS 16 is effective for annual financial statements covering periods beginning on or after 1 July 1999, which coincides with the effective dates for IAS 36 and IAS 37.

In October 1997, the IASC Board agreed that the choice of accounting treatment relating to investment properties should be eliminated. Under IAS 25, *Accounting for Investments*, since withdrawn, investment properties were required either to be carried at fair value and not depreciated, or to be accounted for as any other item of property, plant and equipment and carried at cost or a revalued amount and depreciated. The newly issued IAS 40, *Investment Property*, states that an investment property should either be measured at fair value with all changes in fair value recognised in the income statement, or measured at depreciated cost less any accumulated impairment losses in accordance with IAS 16 (r1998). IAS 25 was withdrawn following the introduction of IAS 40.

10.3.4 Recognition

The recognition criteria for property, plant and equipment are derived from the Framework and thus are the same as those for other assets. Specifically,

> 'an item of property, plant and equipment should be recognised as an asset when:
> (a) it is probable that future economic benefits associated with the asset will flow to the enterprise; and
> (b) the cost of the asset to the enterprise can be measured reliably.'
>
> (IAS 16 (r1998).7)

In practice, it can be difficult to establish when it is probable that future economic benefits will flow to the enterprise. IAS 16 (r1998) suggests that this probability is generally established when the risks and rewards of ownership have passed to the enterprise.

Example 10.1

An enterprise owns a building and contracts the day to day management of the building to a property management company. The property management company finds tenants, collects rental income and passes a fixed percentage of the income to the enterprise which owns the building. In this case, while the day to day operations are handled by the property management company, the risks and rewards associated with the building are retained by the owner of the building since the owner receives, for example, any benefit from an appreciation of the property or any risk of a fall in market value.

Segregation of assets

In some instances, it may be appropriate to segregate component parts of large assets into individual assets when the useful lives of the component parts are different or if the pattern of economic benefits provided differs. (IAS 16 (r1998).12) Each individual asset is then depreciated over its estimated useful life. Conversely, in other instances, it may be appropriate to aggregate many small component parts and recognise them as one asset when together they comprise a single asset with one useful life. (IAS 16 (r1998).11)

Example 10.2

1. An enterprise builds a cable telecommunications network in which the cable has a useful life of 40 years but the electronic equipment only has a useful life of seven years. Although part of the same asset, the cable telecommunication network, the cable in the network is recognised as a separate asset from the electronic equipment since the cable has a longer useful life than the electronic equipment.
2. An airline leases an aircraft under a finance lease. The aircraft, except for the cabin interior, is depreciated over the life of the lease of 20 years. The cabin interior is depreciated over its estimated useful life of five years. Although part of the same asset which was acquired as part of one transaction, the aircraft is recognised as a separate asset from the cabin interior since it has a different useful life.
3. An enterprise purchases numerous, individually inexpensive moulds and dies which are used in its production process. Generally, due to their size and similarity in nature, the cost of such items is carried in the balance sheet at an aggregate amount and depreciated over an average useful life.

In general, spare parts are carried in inventory and upon use are expensed. However, major spare parts and servicing equipment may be carried as items of property, plant and equipment when the enterprise expects to use them and thus derive future benefit from them for more than one period. Similarly, if particular spare parts and servicing equipment may only be used in connection with a certain item of property, plant and equipment, the parts and equipment may be included as property, plant and equipment and depreciated over the remaining useful life of the item to which they relate. (IAS 16 (r1998).11)

Comparison with UK GAAP and US GAAP

FRS 5 *Reporting the substance of transactions* includes general recognition criteria for both assets and liabilities. These criteria are very similar to those in IAS 16 (r1998). Similarly, the recognition criteria in IAS 16 (r1998) are similar to the definitions and criteria in the US Concepts Statements and, as a result, differences in practice are unlikely to occur between the two.

10.3.5 Initial measurement

As a general rule, when an item of property, plant and equipment qualifies for recognition as an asset, it is initially measured at its cost. However, this general initial measurement rule does not apply to or needs specific interpretation in respect of assets which are acquired:

(a) in connection with a business combination – see Chapter **18**;
(b) under finance leases – see Chapter **24**; or
(c) using funds obtained from government grants – see Chapter **26**.

Determination of cost of acquired assets

> 'Cost is the amount of cash or cash equivalents paid or the fair value of the other consideration given to acquire an asset at the time of its acquisition or construction.'
>
> (IAS 16 (r1998).6)

As a rule of thumb, any costs which either add to the value of the finished product or are unavoidably incurred in purchasing, installing and preparing an asset for use are *potentially* suitable for capitalising. If a doubt exists about whether these criteria apply to a certain expense, prudence requires expensing it instead. The following sections discuss the interpretation of this general rule related to assets which are acquired, exchanged or self-constructed.

The following items are generally included in the initial cost of an acquired asset:

(a) purchase price;
(b) duties and other non-refundable taxes paid;
(c) costs directly attributable to bringing the asset to working condition for its intended use including:
    (i) site preparation;
    (ii) freight and handling;
    (iii) installation costs; and
    (iv) professional fees such as for estate agents, surveyors, architects and engineers; and
(d) the estimated cost of dismantling and removing the asset and restoring the site, to the extent that it is recognised as a provision under IAS 37 (see **11.9.7**).

(IAS 16 (r1998).15)

As discussed further in **11.9.7**, when an enterprise has a present obligation upon constructing an asset to dismantle and remove an asset and perhaps to restore the site, the obligation is recognised as a provision and the cost of the dismantling, removal and restoration is included in the initial cost of the asset and depreciated over the asset's useful life.

In addition, an enterprise may choose to capitalise borrowing costs related to the acquisition of a qualifying asset (see **10.4**).

If the payment of purchase consideration is deferred, the current cash price of the item is capitalised and the remainder of the consideration paid is treated as interest and either expensed or capitalised depending on the accounting policy of the enterprise. (IAS 16 (r1998).16) If the cash price of the item is unknown, the future payments are discounted using an interest rate at which the enterprise could borrow funds. The amount of imputed interest is either expensed or capitalised depending on the accounting policy of the enterprise. See **6.6** for an example imputed interest computation.

Consistent with several other standard setters, IASC has introduced discounting into several of its IASs on a piecemeal basis with the result that there is currently no comprehensive guidance or framework to rely on for discounting.

The IASC adopted a project on discounting in April 1998 and its successor, the IASB, is expected to continue the work started by the IASC.

The initial cost of an acquired asset is net of any trade discounts or rebates received and generally does *not* include:

(a) general and administrative costs unless they are directly attributable to bringing the asset to its working condition;
(b) start-up and pre-production costs unless they are necessary to bring the asset to its working condition; and
(c) initial operating losses incurred prior to the asset achieving planned performance.

(IAS 16 (r1998).17)

Start-up and pre-production costs which *may* be capitalised include those incurred during the commissioning period for plant, when it is impossible for it to operate at normal levels because of the need to run in machinery, to test equipment and generally to ensure the proper functioning of the plant. These types of expenses are distinct from initial operating losses stemming from a lack of demand for the product which may *not* be capitalised. In addition, IAS 38 specifically prohibits capitalisation of start-up costs, unless such costs are included in the cost of an item of property, plant and equipment. As discussed above, the types of start-up costs permitted to be capitalised as part of property, plant and equipment are very narrow. See **10.7.8** for further discussion of start-up costs.

Example 10.3

An enterprise constructs a new hotel and it opens for business on 1 June. Operating losses are incurred in the first few months of operation due to a lack of demand. Experience teaches us that demand will build slowly (as the hotel is advertised, etc.) and full utilisation will be achieved only over the first year. However, such initial losses are not considered to be part of the cost of the hotel asset since they were not incurred as part of its construction. Therefore they are not capitalisable under IAS 16 (r1998) as part of property, plant and equipment nor under IAS 38 where they are specifically prohibited.

The application of these rules to specific items of property, plant and equipment is discussed below:

Land
Cost of land includes the purchase price, estate agents' commission, legal fees, surveying, draining, clearing and landscaping, and also demolition costs where the buildings on site were acquired with no intention of using them at that time.

Buildings
If a building is purchased, cost is the purchase price (excluding the cost of the land) plus all repair charges incurred in making good pre-acquisition dilapidations, as well as all costs of alterations and improvements.

Plant and machinery
The cost of plant and machinery includes the purchase price, freight, duty and installation costs. If there is a need to operate machinery for a time in order to run it in and test it, the costs of such work may be capitalised.

The costs of relocating machinery within a factory or to another location should not be capitalised, as it cannot add value in itself.

The costs of rectifying construction and installation errors should not be capitalised. These will duplicate (and on occasion will even be greater than) the original construction or installation costs, which will already have been capitalised. To add rectification costs would be double-counting, risking a significant overstatement of the real capital cost. Other examples of abnormal costs that should not be capitalised include those relating to design errors, industrial disputes, idle capacity, wasted materials or labour, production delays and operating losses occasioned by suspension of a revenue activity during construction.

Determination of cost of exchanged assets
When an item of property, plant and equipment is acquired in exchange for a *dissimilar* item of property, plant or equipment or other asset, the asset received is measured at its fair value which is the equivalent of the fair value

of the asset given up adjusted for any cash or cash equivalents transferred. (IAS 16 (r1998).21)

However, in the very rare situation when an item of property, plant and equipment is exchanged for a *similar* item of property, plant or equipment, the earnings process is not considered complete; and therefore, no gain or loss is recognised on the sale. The asset acquired is measured at the carrying value of the asset given up. A similar item of property, plant and equipment is one which:

(a) has a similar use in the same line of business; and
(b) has a similar fair value.

(IAS 16 (r1998).22)

An exchange of an item of property, plant and equipment for an equity interest in a similar item of property, plant and equipment may be considered an exchange of similar assets if the other criteria for similar assets are met, and thus no gain or loss is recognised on the exchange. (IAS 16 (r1998).22)

If the fair value of a similar asset received is less than the carrying value of the asset given up, it may indicate that the carrying value of the asset given up is impaired. In such cases, the carrying value of the asset given up is written down prior to the exchange. The asset acquired is then carried at the new, written-down carrying amount of the asset given up.

When cash consideration is exchanged along with items of property, plant and equipment, it generally indicates that the assets exchanged are not of similar fair value and, as such, the exchange is treated as an exchange of dissimilar assets.

Determination of cost of self constructed assets

If an asset is constructed for use by the enterprise, the determination of the initial cost of the asset is made using the same general principle of initial measurement at cost as outlined above in relation to acquired assets. Therefore, costs which are directly attributable to the construction of the asset may be capitalised including:

(a) work subcontracted;
(b) materials;
(c) labour;
(d) overheads which are directly attributable to the construction of the asset;
(e) building permits and licences; and
(f) professional fees.

In addition, an enterprise may choose to capitalise borrowing costs related to the construction of a qualifying asset (see **10.4**).

Any internal profit arising on construction of the asset is eliminated from the initial cost of the asset, if the enterprise is in the business of constructing similar assets for sale.

Similarly, any profit arising within a group between group enterprises is eliminated on consolidation. However, the intra-group profit may be considered part of the cost of the asset in the individual financial statements of one enterprise and profit in the individual financial statements of the other. For example, enterprise A, which is a fellow subsidiary in the same group as enterprise B, constructs a head office building for enterprise B. The contract is negotiated at arm's length with the result that enterprise A earns a profit on construction. In the individual entity financial statements, enterprise A recognises its profit on construction and enterprise B recognises the asset at its cost, which includes the profit of A. However, on consolidation, this intercompany profit must be eliminated and the asset of B written-down to its cost to enterprise A. In future years, this will necessitate an adjustment to depreciation on consolidation since the cost of the asset to enterprise B and to the group will differ.

Comparison with UK GAAP and US GAAP

Under UK GAAP, the determination of the initial cost of an item of property, plant or equipment follows the same general rules as those outlined above for assets purchased or constructed. However, differences arise in relation to items of property, plant and equipment which are acquired through an exchange of other items of property, plant and equipment.

While IAS 16 (r1998) contains specific requirements which deal with exchanges of similar items of property, plant and equipment where no gain or loss is recognised and dissimilar items where a gain or loss is recognised, UK GAAP does not have any specific requirements. As a result, current practice varies as to whether or not a gain or loss on disposal has been realised when an exchange takes place with the prudence concept dictating that gains are rarely recognised on the exchange of items of property, plant and equipment unless they are clearly dissimilar.

Under US GAAP, the determination of the initial cost of an item under current guidance would not vary significantly from IAS. However, differences will likely arise under the AICPA proposed SOP: *Accounting for Certain Costs and Activities Related to Property, Plant, and Equipment*. The proposed SOP will require all general and administrative expenses and costs incurred during the preliminary stage of development or acquisition to be expensed as incurred. The preliminary stage is the period prior to the time when the acquisition of the specific property, plant and equipment becomes probable. Under US GAAP as set out in APB 29, *Accounting for Nonmonetary Transactions*, EITF Abstract 86–29, *Nonmonetary Transactions: Magnitude of Boot and the Exceptions to the Use of Fair Value*, and EITF 00-5 *Determining Whether a Nonmonetary Transaction Is An Exchange of Similar Productive Assets*, the technical requirements relating to exchanges of similar assets vary somewhat from those of IAS 16 (r1998), and these variations could lead to material differences.

10.3.6 Subsequent expenditure on items of property, plant and equipment

Judgement is required in determining whether costs incurred subsequent to the initial purchase of an item of property, plant and equipment qualify for capitalisation. Such costs may only be capitalised and added to the cost of the original asset when 'it is probable that future economic benefits, in excess of the originally assessed standard of performance of the existing asset, will flow to the enterprise.' (IAS 16 (r1998).23)

Therefore, as a general rule, only expenditure which extends the useful life of an asset (i.e., restores an element already expensed as depreciation) or increases its productivity should be capitalised. Where this involves the retirement of a related asset or major component, its cost and accumulated depreciation should be removed from the financial statements, in order to avoid any element of cost being included in the balance sheet twice.

All other subsequent expenditure, with the exception of safety and environmental assets as discussed below, is expensed when incurred.

Examples of items which generally increase the standard of performance of an existing asset and therefore qualify for capitalisation include:

> '(a) modification of an item of plant to extend its useful life, including an increase in its capacity;
> (b) upgrading machine parts to achieve a substantial improvement in the quality of output; and
> (c) adoption of new production processes enabling a substantial reduction in previously assessed operating costs.'
>
> (IAS 16 (r1998).24)

Expenditure which merely restores or maintains the originally assessed standard of performance of the existing asset is expensed when incurred. This is often the case for routine repair and maintenance costs and other costs which management may have been aware of when the purchase of the original asset was made. Regular machine overhauls fall into this category when they merely restore the original standard of performance rather than increase output potential. However, the fact that an expenditure was not planned does not necessarily qualify the expenditure for capitalisation.

SIC-23 states that subsequent expenditure on an item of property, plant and equipment relating to a major inspection or overhaul of the asset occurring at regular intervals over the useful life of the asset and made to allow the continued use of the asset should be recogised as an expense in the income statement in the period in which it is incurred except when:

(a) the enterprise has separately identified a component of the asset representing the major inspection or overhaul and, whether the asset is carried at historical cost or revalued, has already depreciated that component to reflect the consumption of benefits which are replaced or restored by the major inspection or overhaul;
(b) it is probable that future economic benefits associated with the asset will flow to the enterprise; and
(c) the cost of the major inspection or overhaul to the enterprise can be measured reliably.

If these criteria are met by an enterprise which applies a component approach to the depreciation of an asset, the expenditure would be capitalised as a component of the asset.

Under IAS 37, in order to recognise a provision for repairs and maintenance an enterprise must have a present obligation to undertake the work as a result of a past event. Because future repairs and maintenance are not present obligations of the entity resulting from past events, no provision should be made for them, even if they are required by legislation if the asset is to continue to be used. There are no grounds for recognising a provision for future repairs and maintenance because the costs relate to the future operation of the business, and therefore must be either capitalised as assets or written off as incurred. The fact that the business could not continue as a going concern without the modification does not create either a legal or a constructive obligation. Where part of an asset can be identified as declining in service potential because of the need for repairs or maintenance, it should be depreciated to show the declining service potential. Subsequent expenditure on repairs and maintenance should then be capitalised to show the restoration of service potential (see *Example 10.4*).

Example 10.4

Ships and aircraft are required to undergo major work at regular intervals, for example, a ship may be required to undergo a dry dock overhaul every 5 years. However, no present obligation exists in respect of the cost of future overhauls, and thus no provision for overhauls should be recognised. However, the ship may be divided into two component assets in line with the SIC-23 approach when it is purchased, a ship and a clean hull (which will become dirty with use and require dry docking). The ship is depreciated over its estimated useful life, say 50 years, and the clean hull is depreciated over its estimated useful life of 5 years. When a dry docking is carried out in 5 years time, it will give rise to a new asset which is then depreciated over the next 5 years. See Chapter **11** for further examples and discussion.

For a discussion of subsequent expenditure on software in order for it to be Euro compliant, see **10.7.10**.

Safety and environmental assets

Certain items of property, plant and equipment may be purchased in order to enhance the safety or environmental friendliness of an asset already held by an enterprise. When considered on its own, such an item may not appear to encompass future economic benefits which will flow to the enterprise. If however, the item enables the enterprise to derive greater future economic benefits related to the original asset than would have been the case if the new asset had not been acquired, it is appropriate to capitalise the item in its own right. However, if such an item is capitalised, the net book amount of the new asset and the related asset already owned cannot exceed the total recoverable amount of the combined assets. (IAS 16 (r1998).13)

As discussed in **10.3.6** above the general rule in order to qualify for capitalisation of subsequent expenditure is that it must be probable that future economic *benefits in excess of the originally assessed standard of performance* of the existing asset will flow to the enterprise as a result of the expenditure. This is a more stringent test than that set out above for safety and environmental assets. It is unclear why this exception has been made for these types of assets.

Example 10.5

Due to new environmental regulations, a power plant is required to purchase electro-static precipitators to remove pollutants from steam which is released from its existing power plant.

When considered on their own, it would not appear that there are future economic benefits which will flow to the enterprise which directly relate to the precipitators. However, since the precipitators allow the enterprise to continue deriving economic benefit from its existing asset, the power plant, and the precipitators may be considered health and safety expenditure, the precipitators are recognised as assets.

Comparison with UK GAAP

The general principle described above that subsequent expenditure must increase the standard of performance of the related existing asset in order to be capitalised is consistent with FRS 15 *Tangible Fixed Assets.*

However, unlike IAS 16 (r1998), FRS 15 does *not* make an exception for subsequent expenditure on safety and environmental assets. Expenditure for such assets is subject to the same capitalisation criterion as other subsequent expenditure, namely it must provide an enhancement of the economic benefits in excess of the previously assessed standard of performance. Therefore, if the equipment in *Example 10.5* above did not enhance the previously assessed production capacity or life of the power plant, it would not qualify for capitalisation. The fact that the government requires such equipment does not mean that the equipment has extended the previously assessed standard of performance; it merely means that the power plant can continue to operate.

Comparison with US GAAP

US GAAP does not currently directly address subsequent expenditure. However, the proposed SOP: *Accounting for Certain Costs and Activities Related to Property, Plant, and Equipment,* will address accounting and disclosure requirements regarding routine repair and maintenance type expenditures. The proposed SOP will require that the costs of normal, recurring, or periodic repairs and planned major maintenance activities should be expensed unless the costs represent:

(a) the acquisition of additional components; or
(b) the replacement of existing components.

As a result of the proposed SOP, US GAAP will not differ significantly from IAS 16 (r1998) in this regard.

Compensation for the impairment or loss of items

SIC-14 addresses the accounting for compensation payments received related to an impairment of an asset. For example, compensation payments may arise as a result of reimbursement of a loss by an insurance company or indemnities from a government for items of property, plant and equipment that are expropriated. SIC-14 acknowledges that there are normally three transactions involved when compensation payments are received. Each transaction should be accounted for separately as follows:

1. Impairment of the asset should be recognised in accordance with IAS 36 (see **10.12**). Note that the compensation to be received is not included in the assessment of whether or not an impairment has

occurred since the impairment and the compensation are treated as separate transactions. The retirement and disposal of the asset should be accounted for in accordance with IAS 16 (r1998) (see **10.3.10**).
2. Compensation payments, whether monetary or non-monetary, should be included in the income statement in the period in which it becomes probable that the income will be received. If the compensation is contingent upon one or more future events which are out of the control of the enterprise, the compensation is a contingent asset and should not be recognised until it is virtually certain that the compensation will be received. See **11.9.12** for a further discussion of contingent assets.
3. The cost of the asset restored, purchased, constructed as a replacement, or received as compensation should be accounted for in accordance with IAS 16 (r1998) (see **10.3.5**). Effectively, items of property, plant and equipment purchased or constructed to replace impaired or lost assets are recorded at cost. Expenditure related to the restoration of impaired assets is capitalised to the extent that it is probable that future economic benefits in excess of the assessed standard of performance of the existing asset *after recognition of the impairment loss in 1.,* will flow to the enterprise.

Example 10.6

On 1 December 2001, a fire breaks out at a telephone call centre. The building is damaged but left largely intact but the communications equipment and other fixtures and fittings are completely destroyed. The day before the centre was destroyed, the building had a carrying value of £1.2 million and the communications equipment and other fixtures had a carrying value of £2.0 million. The fair value of a similar type of building in the area is around £1.5 million.

The enterprise which owned the centre was fully insured. However, the insurance company had become insolvent and at 31 December 2001, the balance sheet date, it was uncertain whether or not its claims would be covered by the relevant insurance regulator.

In January 2002, reconstruction of the building and its contents began and was completed by 31 March 2002. Costs of reconstruction totalled £1 million for the building and £3 million for the communications equipment and fixtures.

In June 2002, the claim for £4.0 million was paid by the insurance regulator.

In which periods and how should the above transactions be accounted for?

1. Recognition of impairment losses

During December 2001, an impairment loss related to the building should be recorded in the income statement calculated in accordance with IAS 36. (Assume that the appropriate carrying amount after the fire is £500,000. Therefore a loss of £700,000 is recognised). Since the communications equipment and the fixtures and fittings were destroyed, it is considered that they have been disposed of. Therefore, their carrying value at the date of the fire, £2.0 million, is recognised as a loss on disposal in the income statement.

2. Recognition of compensation payments

At 31 December, it is unclear whether or not compensation for the loss will be received. Therefore, the compensation is a contingent asset which may be disclosed in the notes to the financial statements but may not be recognised in the financial statements until it is virtually certain that the money will be received.

When the money is received in June 2002, it is recognised in the income statement.

3. Recognition of the restored asset

Before the restoration, the building has a carrying value of £500,000. £1 million is spent on its restoration. Since the fair value of a similar building in the area is approximately £1.5 million, it is appropriate to capitalise the £1 million restoration costs.

The communication equipment and fittings should be capitalised at their cost of £3 million.

10.3.7 Measurement subsequent to initial recognition – historical cost

IAS 16 (r1998) allows a free choice between valuing items of property, plant and equipment at historical cost (benchmark treatment) or at a revalued amount (allowed alternative treatment) in the balance sheet.

When an enterprise adopts the benchmark treatment for an item of property, plant and equipment, the item is carried in the balance sheet at its historical cost less any accumulated depreciation and any accumulated impairment losses.

Comparison with UK GAAP and US GAAP

Similar to IAS 16 (r1998), UK GAAP allows property, plant and equipment to be carried at either historical cost or a revalued amount. FRS 15, *Tangible Fixed Assets*, sets out the requirements relating to the revaluation of property, plant and equipment.

Revaluations of property, plant and equipment are generally not permitted under US GAAP outside of purchase accounting. Therefore, assets are normally carried at historic cost less accumulated amortisation and accumulated impairment losses.

10.3.8 Measurement subsequent to initial recognition – revaluation

When an enterprise adopts the allowed alternative treatment for an item of property, plant and equipment, the item is carried in the balance sheet 'at a revalued amount, being its fair value at the date of the revaluation less any subsequent accumulated depreciation and subsequent accumulated impairment losses.' (IAS 16 (r1998).29)

Basis for revaluation

Revaluations of items of property, plant and equipment are generally made on the basis of their fair value, which is usually their market value determined by appraisal. Fair value is defined as the amount for which an asset could be exchanged between knowledgeable, willing parties in an arm's length transaction. The guidance in IAS 16 (r1998) suggests that revaluations are normally undertaken by independent, professionally qualified valuers. If the market value cannot be reliably determined, as is often the case with plant and equipment due to the fact that these items are infrequently sold, the valuation is made on the basis of depreciated replacement cost.

Frequency of valuations

IAS 16 (r1998) does not set a specific requirement for the frequency of revaluations but states that they should be made with sufficient regularity such that the carrying amount does not differ materially from that which would be determined using fair value at the balance sheet date. (IAS 16 (r1998).29)

In order to meet this requirement, an enterprise must estimate the fair value of its revalued assets at each balance sheet date. However, this does not mean that a full valuation must be carried out every year, unless the estimate differs significantly from the carrying value.

This requirement could lead to some assets with volatile fair values being revalued each year. The guidance in IAS 16 (r1998) suggests that revaluations of assets with insignificant swings in fair value be carried out every three to five years.

Scope of revaluations

'When an item of property, plant and equipment is revalued, the entire class of property, plant and equipment to which that asset belongs should be revalued.' (IAS 16 (r1998).34) IAS 16 (r1998) defines a class of property, plant and equipment as, 'a grouping of assets of a similar nature and use in an enterprise's operations.' The following are examples of separate classes of property, plant and equipment:

'(a) land;
(b) land and buildings;
(c) machinery;
(d) ships;
(e) aircraft;
(f) motor vehicles;
(g) furniture and fixtures; and
(h) office equipment.'

(IAS 16 (r1998).35)

The intent of the requirement that all items in a class be revalued simultaneously is that all items in a class are carried on the same basis, either historical cost or fair value, and that the revaluations are as of the same date. It also acts to prohibit cherry-picking when revaluing assets, i.e., revaluing assets which have increased in value but not those which have decreased. However, some relief is provided in the guidance in IAS 16 (r1998) which states that revaluing assets on a rolling basis is acceptable as long as the revaluations are kept up to date. (IAS 16 (r1998).36)

Treatment of revaluation surplus

When a valuation indicates that the fair value of an asset is greater than its carrying amount, the amount of the surplus is credited to shareholders' equity under the heading of revaluation surplus. Under IAS 1 (r1997), items recognised directly in equity such as increases and decreases in the revaluation surplus due to revaluations are disclosed either in a reconciliation of movements of shareholders' funds or in a statement showing changes in equity.

At the date an asset is revalued, existing accumulated depreciation is either:

(a) restated proportionately with the change in the gross carrying amount of the assets so that the carrying amount of the asset after revaluation equals its revalued amount. This method is often used when an asset is revalued by means of an index to its depreciated replacement cost; or
(b) eliminated against the gross carrying amount of the asset and the net amount restated to the revalued amount of the asset. This is the appropriate method for buildings which are revalued to their market value. (IAS 16 (r1998).33)

Example 10.7 Initial revaluation surplus

An asset originally cost £500,000 and has a carrying value of £400,000 due to £100,000 of accumulated depreciation.

Based on the most recent valuation, the asset is to be revalued to £800,000. This can be achieved in two ways:

1. Increase historical cost and accumulated depreciation proportionally

The carrying value is increased to the revalued amount by increasing the cost and depreciation proportionally (i.e., following the above ratio of 5:1, cost:depreciation):

	Pre-Revaluation	*Post-Revaluation*
Cost	500,000	1,000,000
Accumulated depreciation	(100,000)	(200,000)
Net book value	400,000	800,000
The journal entries required are:		
Dr. Property, plant and equipment	500,000	
Cr. Revaluation surplus		500,000
Dr. Revaluation surplus	100,000	
Cr. Accumulated depreciation		100,000

2. Eliminate accumulated depreciation and increase cost with any remaining surplus

Cost	500,000	800,000
Accumulated depreciation	(100,000)	0
Net book value	400,000	800,000
The journal entries required are:		
Dr. Property, plant and equipment	300,000	
Cr. Revaluation surplus		300,000
Dr. Accumulated depreciation	100,000	
Cr. Revaluation surplus		100,000

In both of the above the cases, the balance on the revaluation surplus is £400,000 which equals the increase in the carrying value of the asset. The annual depreciation charge in the future will be the same no matter which method is chosen.

In addition, when a revaluation occurs, the useful life of the asset, its residual value and the appropriateness of the depreciation method are reconsidered. A change in any of the three is considered to be a change in estimate, and should be accounted for under IAS 8 (r1993), *Net Profit or Loss for the Period, Fundamental Errors and Changes in Accounting Policies* (See **5.15**).

However, if the increase in the fair value of the asset reverses a previously recognised decrease in the fair value of the same asset, the increase is recognised as income to the extent that the previous decrease was recognised as an expense. Any remaining increase is then credited to the revaluation surplus. (IAS 16 (r1998).37)

Example 10.8 Revaluation surplus reversing previously recognised decrease

A company purchased a parcel of land in 1990 for £125 million.

During 1992, the directors determined that the land had suffered a diminution in value to £100 million. Thus a £25 million charge to the income statement was made.

In 1995, the fair value of the land had increased to £160 million.

The excess of this revalued amount (£160 million) over the carrying value (£100 million) is £60 million.

The £60 million excess should be recognised by a £25 million credit to income to match the previous decrease in fair value recognised as an expense and crediting the remaining increase of £35 million to the revaluation surplus.

Treatment of revaluation deficit

When a revaluation indicates that the fair value of an asset is less than its carrying amount, the amount of the deficit is recognised in the income statement as an expense. (IAS 16 (r1998).38)

Example 10.9 Initial revaluation deficit

A company purchased a parcel of land in 1990 for £125 million. During 1992, the directors determined that the land had suffered a diminution in value to £100 million. Since no revaluation surplus existed with respect to this property, a charge to the income statement of £25 million is required.

However, if the decrease in the fair value of the asset reverses a previously recognised increase in the fair value of the same asset, the decrease is debited against the related revaluation surplus to the extent that the decrease does not exceed the amount held in the revaluation surplus in respect of that same asset. Any remaining decrease is then debited to the income statement. (IAS 16 (r1998).38)

Example 10.10 Revaluation deficit reversing previously recognised increase

A company purchased a parcel of land in 1990 for £125 million. During 1992, the directors determined that the land had a fair value of £200 million, resulting in a revaluation surplus of £75 million.

In 1995, the fair value decreased to £100 million.

The decrease in fair value of £100 million is recognised first by debiting the revaluation surplus of £75 million and then by debiting the income statement by the remaining £25 million.

Realisation of the revaluation surplus

The revaluation surplus may be transferred to retained earnings as or when the surplus is realised. The transfer from revaluation surplus to retained earnings is not made through the income statement but via an intra-reserve transfer. Such transfers are disclosed in the reconciliation of equity and reserves (see Chapter **8**). Realisation of the entire surplus occurs on disposal or retirement, when the asset is permanently withdrawn from use and no future economic benefits are expected from its disposal (see **10.3.10**). However, some realisation of the revaluation surplus may occur through the use of the asset. (IAS 16 (r1998).39)

The amount of the surplus which is realised through use of the asset is calculated as the difference between depreciation calculated on the historical cost of the asset and the depreciation calculated on the revalued amount. This difference may be transferred from the revaluation surplus to retained earnings in each period. As a result of such periodic transfers, when an item of revalued property, plant and equipment is fully depreciated in the balance sheet, the related revaluation surplus will have been reduced to zero.

Example 10.11

The stadium of a football club has a historical cost of £30 million, a useful life of 30 years and a residual value of £nil. After two years, the football club revalues its stadium to £56 million. On the date of revaluation, the carrying value of the stadium is as follows:

Cost	£30 million
Accumulated depreciation	2 million
Carrying value	£28 million

Thus, the revaluation generates a revaluation surplus of £28 million.

Annual depreciation charged on the asset prior to and post revaluation is as follows:

Depreciation on historical cost	£1 million per annum
Depreciation on revalued amount	£2 million per annum

The difference of £1 million per annum between depreciation on historical cost and the revalued amount is considered to be a realisation of the revaluation surplus and as such may be transferred from the revaluation surplus to retained earnings each year over the remaining useful economic life of the stadium. On this basis, when the asset is fully depreciated, the revaluation surplus will have been reduced to zero.

Comparison with UK GAAP

Both IAS 16 (r1998) and FRS 15, *Tangible Fixed Assets*, require revaluations to a current value. However, IAS 16 (r1998) refers to fair value whereas

FRS 15 defines current value as the *lower* of replacement cost and recoverable amount. Recoverable amount, in turn, is the *higher* of net realisable value and value in use. The following valuation bases are specified:

- non-specialised properties – valued at existing use value, with the addition of notional directly attributable acquisition costs, where material;
- specialised properties, being those which, due to their specialised nature, are rarely, if ever, sold on the open market outside of a business combination – depreciated replacement cost; and
- tangible fixed assets other than properties – market value, or depreciated replacement cost where market value is not available.

IAS 16 (r1998) does not address whether valuations should be on an existing use basis or whether material direct acquisition or selling costs should be added/deducted.

There are three further differences relating to the recognition of revaluation gains and losses. First, FRS 15 requires revaluation losses that are clearly caused by the consumption of economic benefit to be recognised in the income statement since they are operating costs similar to depreciation. Second, revaluation losses should be recognised in the statement of total recognised gains and losses, and thus bypass the income statement, to the extent that an asset's recoverable amount is greater than its revalued amount. Such losses are not impairments under FRS 11, *Impairment of Fixed Assets and Goodwill*. As discussed above, IAS 16 (r1998) generally requires revaluation losses to be recognised in the income statement unless they represent a reversal of a previously recognised gain, and revaluation gains are recognised in equity unless they reverse a previously recognised loss. Finally, differences can arise between IAS 16 (r1998) and FRS 15 in the precise allocation of gains and losses between the income statement and equity. Unlike IAS 16 (r1998), FRS 15 takes account of subsequent depreciation when allocating revaluation gains that reverse earlier losses. In addition, the allocation of revaluation losses between the income statement and equity will apparently be affected, under IAS 16 (r1998), by whether an enterprise has previously chosen to transfer realised surpluses out of the revaluation surplus; under FRS 15, the allocation is not affected by this choice.

Comparison with US GAAP

As noted previously, outside of purchase accounting, revaluations are not generally permitted under US GAAP.

10.3.9 Depreciation

'The depreciable amount of an item of property, plant and equipment should be allocated on a systematic basis over its useful life.' (IAS 16 (r1998).41)

Depreciation charges are made in order to recognise that the economic benefits related to an asset are being consumed by the enterprise as the asset is being used. Depreciation charges are not made in an attempt to reflect the fair value of the asset to the enterprise. Therefore, depreciation is charged even when the fair value of an asset exceeds its carrying amount.

Only two types of property, plant and equipment are exempt from the requirement to depreciate, land and investment property. Under IAS 40, an enterprise has a choice when accounting for investment property between measuring the investment property at depreciated cost less any accumulated depreciation and any accumulated impairment losses, in accordance with the benchmark treatment in IAS 16 (r1998), and measuring the asset at fair value and thereby avoiding depreciation (see **10.8**).

In order to calculate depreciation, a preparer must identify:

(a) the depreciable amount of the asset which is its cost or revalued amount less its residual value. Similarly, if impairment provisions have been made against the asset, these are deducted in arriving at the remaining depreciable amount;
(b) the residual value of the asset which is, 'the net amount which the enterprise expects to obtain for an asset at the end of its useful life after deducting the expected costs of disposal.' (IAS 16 (r1998).6) When assets are valued at historical cost, this residual amount is not revised in later periods to take account of subsequent increases. However, when assets are carried at revalued amounts, a new estimate of residual value is made at each revaluation date; and
(c) the useful life of the asset which is either:

> '(a) the period of time over which an asset is expected to be used by the enterprise; or
> (b) the number of production or similar units expected to be obtained from the asset by the enterprise.' (IAS 16 (r1998).6)

The determination of the useful life of an asset requires management judgement and IAS 16 (r1998) suggests that the following factors be considered in making this estimation:

> '(a) the expected usage of the asset by the enterprise. Usage is assessed by reference to the asset's expected capacity or physical output;
> (b) the expected physical wear and tear, which depends on operational factors such as the number of shifts for which the asset is to be used and the repair and maintenance programme of the enterprise, and the care and maintenance of the asset while idle;
> (c) technical obsolescence arising from changes or improvements in production, or from a change in the market demand for the product or service output of the asset; and

(d) legal or similar limits on the use of the asset, such as the expiry dates of related leases.'

(IAS 16 (r1998).43)

The estimated useful life is required to be reviewed periodically and if current estimates vary significantly from previous estimates, a new useful life is used to calculate depreciation on a prospective basis. In other words, the new useful life is applied to the carrying amount of the item from the date the new estimated useful life is adopted. Since the useful life of an asset is estimated on acquisition, a change in useful life is a change in estimate, not a change in accounting policy.

Depreciation method

'The depreciation method used should reflect the pattern in which the asset's economic benefits are consumed by the enterprise.' (IAS 16 (r1998).41) As such, management should consider this pattern and choose the depreciation method which best matches the consumption of benefits with the charges calculated under each method. Several depreciation methods are acceptable including:

(a) straight-line;
(b) diminishing balance; and
(c) sum-of-the-digits.

The most commonly employed depreciation methods are the straight-line method and the diminishing balance method. The straight-line method is the most frequently used because it is simpler than the diminishing balance method.

Another useful basis is the unit of production method which apportions the cost of the fixed asset over its productive life measured in terms of the units produced or machine hours utilised in relation to the total of such units or hours estimated to comprise the productive life of the asset. This method is theoretically superior to the straight-line and diminishing balance methods in that it more accurately matches costs with benefits where the life of the asset can be measured with some precision in terms of its ultimate total output. One regular application of this method is in oil, gas and other extractive industries, where the production assets have no further value once mineral reserves have been extracted. However, in that case, its actual precision depends entirely on the accuracy of the prediction of total extractable reserves.

Some considerations regarding the methods of depreciation are discussed below:

Freehold land
Freehold land which is not subject to depletion (by, for example, the extraction of minerals) does not have a limited useful life and therefore should not be depreciated. In consequence it is necessary where freehold property is purchased to allocate the purchase consideration between the value of the land and that of the buildings. Similarly, any revaluations of freehold property should distinguish between land and buildings (valuers should provide a figure for the depreciable element in the value).

While land is not depreciated, where the value of freehold land is adversely affected by long-term environmental factors, it should be written down to reflect any diminution in value in accordance with IAS 36 (see **10.12**).

Freehold buildings
Buildings have limited useful economic lives and are no different from other depreciable assets. Although their estimated useful lives are usually significantly longer than other tangible fixed assets, they should nevertheless be depreciated in a similar manner, generally on the straight-line basis. An exception to this requirement applies to buildings which qualify as investment properties (see **10.8**).

Leasehold properties (including improvements)
Depreciation should be charged over the unexpired period of the lease, or the useful life of the asset if shorter. Provision should be made for the estimated cost of any contractual requirement to make good any dilapidations over the period of the lease, using latest estimates of the cost of repairs at current prices.

It is normal to use the straight-line method for this depreciation. It is sometimes argued that there is evidence that leases commonly maintain value well until the latter third of their life, and that value then plunges steeply towards the end. However, this evidence has been strongest during a period of rising property prices and high inflation. Consequently it is unlikely to be appropriate to apply a depreciation method to leases which loads later periods with a higher amortisation charge. In any event, as noted earlier, depreciation is not charged in an attempt to reflect the fair value of an asset, but rather in order to recognise that economic benefits are being consumed.

Plant and machinery, tools and equipment, ships, vehicles, etc.
Provision for depreciation is in general computed using the straight-line method, but the diminishing balance and unit of production methods are also suitable in appropriate circumstances. Assets of very short effective lives, such as loose tools, jigs and patterns, may be dealt with more satisfactorily by other methods such as revaluation or valuation at a fixed amount (see *Example* **10.2**).

The depreciation method used must be reviewed periodically to determine if the method selected continues to reflect the pattern in which the asset's economic benefits are consumed by the enterprise. If management determines that a change in the pattern of benefits has occurred and that a different depreciation method is appropriate, the change is accounted for as a change in estimate. (IAS 16 (r1998).52) Therefore, the new depreciation method is applied prospectively to the carrying amount of the asset at the date of the change and in future periods over the remaining useful life of the asset. See **5.15** for a discussion of changes in estimate.

Accounting for the depreciation charge

Depreciation charges are normally recognised as an expense unless the related asset was used in the production of another asset in which case it is included in the carrying amount of the asset being produced.

Example 10.12

1. A widget making enterprise incurs depreciation charges related to items of equipment located on the shop floor. These items of machinery are only used in the production of widgets.

   The enterprise may absorb the depreciation expense related to the widget-making machinery directly into the cost of the inventory rather than expensing it in accordance with IAS 2 (r1993), *Inventories* (see **10.9.6**).

2. A pharmaceutical company uses specific laboratory equipment in development activities. This laboratory equipment is used only in relation to development activities.

   When the costs of the development activities qualify for capitalisation, the depreciation related to the laboratory equipment is capitalised as a component of development cost in accordance with IAS 38 (see **10.7.8**).

Comparison with UK and US GAAP

The concept that depreciation represents the consumption of the economic benefits of an item of property, plant and equipment rather than a measurement of the value of the asset is consistent throughout IAS 16 (r1998), UK GAAP and US GAAP. Under both IAS and UK GAAP, exemptions from recognising depreciation are made for investment properties, on the basis that the consumption of economic benefits (i.e., depreciation) is included within, and not analysed separately from, other changes in fair value.

Depreciation is calculated in substantially the same manner under IAS 16 (r1998), UK GAAP and US GAAP. However, a change in the depreciation method used is accounted for prospectively as a change in accounting estimate under IAS 16 (r1998) and UK GAAP but as a change in accounting policy under US GAAP.

Also, FRS 15, *Tangible Fixed Assets*, contains further requirements around depreciation which are not included in IAS 16 (r1998). Namely, an annual impairment review will be required if an enterprise does not charge depreciation on the grounds of immateriality or if the estimated useful life is greater than 50 years. These requirements were added to deal with specific abuses that had arisen in the UK prior to FRS 15.

10.3.10 Retirements and disposals

An item of property, plant and equipment, whether carried at historical cost or a revalued amount, is removed from the balance sheet on disposal or when the asset is permanently withdrawn from use and no future economic benefits associated with the asset are expected to flow to the enterprise. (IAS 16 (r1998).55)

The gain or loss on disposal is calculated as the difference between the estimated net disposal proceeds and the carrying amount of the asset and is recognised in the income statement. (IAS 16 (r1998).56)

As discussed previously, the revaluation surplus may be transferred to retained earnings when the surplus is realised. The transfer from revaluation surplus to retained earnings is not made through the income statement but via an intra-reserve transfer. Such transfers are disclosed in the reconciliation of equity and reserves (see Chapter **8**).

Example 10.13

An item of plant and machinery is purchased by an enterprise for £100,000 and has a useful life of ten years. The straight-line method of depreciation will be used giving annual depreciation of £10,000 per annum.

At the end of year two, the asset has a carrying value of £80,000 (£100,000 cost and £20,000 accumulated depreciation). The asset is revalued to £200,000 thus creating a revaluation surplus of £120,000.

The new depreciation charge per year is £25,000 being £200,000 depreciated over the remaining economic life of eight years. Each year, a transfer from the revaluation surplus to retained earnings will be made of £15,000, being the difference between the historical cost depreciation charge of £10,000 per annum and the depreciation charge after revaluation of £25,000.

Sale of asset

At the end of year six, the asset is sold, and proceeds of £120,000 are received. The carrying value of the asset at the date of sale is:

Revalued amount	200,000
Accumulated depreciation	(100,000)
Carrying value	100,000

The revaluation surplus at the date of sale is:

Revaluation surplus	120,000
Reserve transfer (£15k × 4yrs)	(60,000)
Revaluation surplus	60,000

The excess of sale proceeds of £120,000 over carrying value of £100,000 generates a profit on the sale of £20,000. This profit is recognised in the income statement since it is a realised gain.

The balance of £60,000 in the revaluation surplus account is transferred to retained earnings via an intra-reserve transfer.

If an asset is removed from use and is held for sale, the asset remains at its carrying amount at the date the asset is retired from active service. At least at each financial year end, the asset is tested for impairment according to IAS 36 and any impairment losses are recognised accordingly (see **10.12**). (IAS 16 (r1998).59)

Comparison with UK GAAP and US GAAP

Under IAS 16 (r1998), UK GAAP and US GAAP, the difference between the carrying amount of an asset and the proceeds received on its sale less any costs of disposal is recognised as the profit or loss on the sale of the asset.

Under IAS 16 (r1998), when an asset is no longer in use and is held for sale or disposal, the asset is held at its carrying amount at the date when the asset is retired from active use. At least at each financial year end, an impairment review is carried out. Under UK GAAP, items of property, plant and equipment which are surplus to an entity's requirements and which are taken out of use permanently are normally valued at the lower of carrying amount and net realisable value. Under US GAAP, assets which are part of a segment which is to be disposed of are also valued at the lower of carrying amount and net realisable value. (APB 30, *Reporting the Results of Operations*) However, other non-current assets to be disposed of are carried at the lower of cost and fair value less costs to sell. (SFAS 121, *Accounting for the Impairment of Long-Lived Assets and for Long-Lived Assets to be Disposed Of*)

The FASB has issued a new statement on asset retirement obligations: Statement No. 143, *Accounting for Asset Retirement Obligations.* The objective of the asset retirement obligations (ARO) statement is to provide accounting requirements for retirement obligations associated with tangible long-lived assets. The obligations included within the scope of the statement are those for which there is a legal obligation to settle as a result of existing or enacted law, statute, written or oral contract or by legal construction under the doctrine of promissory estoppel. The major issues in the project relate to:

(a) liability recognition;
(b) initial measurement of that liability;
(c) allocation of an asset retirement cost, that is, the debit side of the entry;
(d) subsequent measurement of an ARO liability;
(e) financial statement disclosures; and
(f) effective date and transition.

The Statement is effective for fiscal years beginning after 15 June 2002. Upon adoption of the Statement, an entity will use a cumulative-effect approach to recognise transition amounts for any existing ARO liabilities, asset retirement costs and accumulated depreciation. All transition amounts are to be measured using current (as of the date of adoption of the final Statement) information, current assumptions and current interest rates.

10.3.11 Disclosure

For each class of property, plant and equipment, the financial statements should disclose:

(a) the measurement bases used for determining the gross carrying amount. When more than one basis has been used, the gross carrying amount for that basis in each category should be disclosed;
(b) the depreciation methods used;
(c) the useful lives or the depreciation rates used;
(d) the gross carrying amount and the accumulated depreciation (including accumulated impairment losses) at the beginning and end of the period;
(e) a reconciliation of the carrying amount at the beginning and end of the period showing:
    (i) additions;
    (ii) disposals;
    (iii) acquisitions through business combinations;
    (iv) increases or decreases resulting from revaluations and from impairment losses recognised or reversed directly in equity during the period;
    (v) impairment losses recognised or reversed in the income statement during the period;
    (vi) depreciation;
    (vii) the net exchange differences arising on the translation of the financial statements of a foreign entity; and
    (viii) other movements.

(IAS 16 (r1998).60)

Note that comparative information is not required for the reconciliation described in (e) above.

'The financial statements should also disclose:

(a) the existence and amounts of restrictions on title, and property, plant and equipment pledged as security for liabilities;
(b) the accounting policy for the estimated costs of restoring the site of items of property, plant or equipment;
(c) the amount of expenditures on account of property, plant and equipment in the course of construction; and
(d) the amount of commitments for the acquisition of property, plant and equipment.'

(IAS 16 (r1998).61)

When items of property, plant and equipment are stated at revalued amounts the following disclosures are required:

(a) the basis used to revalue the assets;
(b) the effective date of the revaluation;
(c) whether an independent valuer was involved;
(d) the nature of any indices used to determine replacement cost;
(e) the carrying amount of each class of property, plant and equipment that would have been included in the financial statements had the assets been carried at historical cost less depreciation and impairment losses; and
(f) the revaluation surplus, indicating the movement for the period and any restrictions on the distribution of the balance to shareholders.

(IAS 16 (r1998).64)

IAS 16 (r1998) lists the following disclosures which are not required but that users of financial statements would find relevant and which, therefore, should be viewed as best practice:

(a) the carrying amount of temporarily idle property, plant and equipment;
(b) the gross carrying amount of any fully depreciated property, plant and equipment that is still in use;
(c) the carrying amount of property, plant and equipment retired from active use and held for disposal; and
(d) when the benchmark treatment is used, the fair value of property, plant and equipment when this is materially different from the carrying amount.

In addition to the disclosures in IAS 16 (r1998), if there has been a change in estimate, the disclosures set out in IAS 8 (r1993), *Net Profit or Loss for the Period, Fundamental Errors and Changes in Accounting Policies*, will be required (See **15.5**). Changes in estimate related to items of property, plant and equipment may include changes in:

(a) residual values;
(b) the estimated costs of dismantling and removing items of property, plant and equipment and restoring the site;
(c) useful lives; and
(d) depreciation method.

If an item of property, plant and equipment has suffered an impairment loss, the disclosures included in IAS 36 will be required (see **10.12**).

10.3.12 Examples from published financial statements

Note that the excerpts given do not always comply in full with all aspects of IAS and as such are not necessarily examples of best practice but merely of current practice.

Property, plant and equipment carried at historical cost

Example 10.14

Property, plant and equipment is carried at the cost of acquisition or construction. Assets subject to depletion are depreciated over their estimated useful lives. Write-downs are made for any declines in value that are expected to be permanent, aside from those reflected in depreciation. Assets are written back if the reasons for previous years' write-downs no longer apply.

The cost of construction of self-constructed property, plant and equipment comprises the direct cost of materials, direct manufacturing expenses, appropriate allocation of material and manufacturing overheads, and an appropriate share of the depreciation and write-downs of assets used in construction. It includes the shares of expenses for company pension plans and discretionary employee benefits that are attributable to construction.If the construction phase of property, plant or equipment extends over a long period, the interest incurred on borrowed capital up to the date of completion is capitalised as part of the cost of acquisition or construction.

Expenses for the repair of property, plant and equipment are normally charged against income, but they are capitalised if they result in an enlargement or substantial improvement of the respective assets.

Property, plant and equipment is depreciated by the straight-line method, except where the declining-balance method is more appropriate in light of the actual utilisation period.

The following depreciation periods, based on the estimated useful lives of the respective assets, are applied throughout the Group:

Buildings	20 to 50 years
Outdoor infrastructure	10 to 20 years
Plant installations	6 to 20 years
Machinery and apparatus	6 to 12 years
Laboratory and research facilities	3 to 5 years
Storage tanks and pipelines	10 to 20 years
Vehicles	4 to 8 years
Computer equipment	3 to 5 years
Furniture and fixtures	4 to 10 years

Changes in property, plant and equipment in 2000 were as follows:

(€ million)	*Land and buildings*	*Machinery and technical equipment*	*Furniture, fixtures and other equipment*	*Construction in progress and advance payments to vendors and contractors*	*Total*
Gross carry amounts, Dec. 31, 1999	7,529	17,860	2,360	1,458	29,207
Exchange differences	129	399	28	49	605
Changes in companies consolidated	(32)	98	1	–	67
Acquisitions	57	207	10	317	591
Capital expenditures	115	522	295	1,361	2,293
Retirements	(142)	(589)	(276)	(17)	(1,204)
Transfers	322	1,489	95	(1,906)	–
Gross carrying amounts, Dec. 31, 2000	**7,978**	**19,986**	**2,513**	**1,262**	**31,739**
Accumulated depreciation and write-downs, Dec. 31, 1999	3,867	11,742	1,605	7	17,221
Exchange differences	42	122	17	–	181
Changes in companies consolidated	(18)	77	1	–	60
Depreciation and write-downs in 2000	238	1,174	283	–	1,695
– of which write-downs	[5]	[11]	[–]	[–]	[16]
Write-backs	–	(2)	–	–	(2)
Retirements	(37)	(530)	(194)	–	(761)
Transfers	–	–	–	–	–
Accumulated depreciation and write-downs, Dec. 31, 2000	**4,092**	**12,583**	**1,712**	**7**	**18,394**
Net carrying amounts, Dec. 31, 2000	**3,886**	**7,403**	**801**	**1,255**	**13,345**
Net carrying amounts, Dec. 31, 1999	3,622	6,118	755	1,451	11,986

The exchange differences are the differences between the carrying amounts at the beginning and the end of the year that result from translating foreign companies' figures at the respective different exchange rates and changes in their assets during the year at the average rate for the year.

Capitalised property, plant and equipment includes assets with a total net value of €199 million held under finance leases. The gross carrying amounts of these assets total €277 million. These assets are mainly furniture and fixtures where the present value of the minimum lease payments covers substantially all of the cost of acquisition, or buildings where title passes to the lessee on expiration of the lease.

Also included are products leased to other parties, except where the lessee is to be regarded as the economic owner and the relevant agreements therefore constitute finance leases as defined in IAS 17, *Leases*; in this case a receivable is recognised in the balance sheet in the amount of the discounted future lease payments.

Bayer
Germany
31 December 2000
International Accounting Standards

Property, plant and equipment carried at revalued amounts

Example 10.15

1(e) Premises and equipment

Premises and equipment are stated at cost or as revalued to approximate market values in the case of freehold land and buildings based on valuations by independent firms of professional surveyors. The surplus, net of tax if any, on revaluation is directly credited to revaluation reserves in equity. Any decrease in revaluation is charged first against any previous surplus, in respect of that asset held in revaluation reserve, and where such surpluses are insufficient, the shortfall is charged to the statement of income.

Freehold land is not depreciated. Depreciation on other premises and equipment is provided on a straight-line basis over their estimated useful lives.

5 Premises and equipment

	Land and buildings (US$ million)	*Equipment and other assets (US$ million)*	*Total (US$ million)*
Cost or valuation:			
At 1 January 2000	401	242	643
Additions	19	34	53
Disposals	(14)	(17)	(31)
Foreign exchange translation and other adjustments	(12)	(11)	(23)
At 31 December 2000	**394**	**248**	**642**
Depreciation			
At 1 January 2000	48	148	196
Provided during the year	5	21	26
Disposals	(2)	(9)	(11)
Foreign exchange translation and other adjustments	(1)	(8)	(9)
At 31 December 2000	**50**	**152**	**202**
Net book value			
At 31 December 2000	**344**	**96**	**440**
At 31 December 1999	353	94	447

Arab Banking Corporation BSC
Bahrain
31 December 2000
International Accounting Standards

10.4 Borrowing costs

10.4.1 Sources

IAS 23 (r1993) *Borrowing Costs.*
SIC-2 *Consistency – Capitalisation of Borrowing Costs.*

10.4.2 Brief summary of the requirements

IAS 23 (r1993) allows a free choice between expensing borrowing costs in the period in which they are incurred (benchmark treatment) and capitalising borrowing costs incurred in connection with the borrowing of funds that are directly attributable to the acquisition, construction or production of a qualifying asset (allowed alternative treatment). However, in order to ensure consistency, once an enterprise has adopted the allowed alternative treatment, it must capitalise borrowing costs related to all qualifying assets. It is not appropriate to capitalise such costs associated with some assets but not others.

10.4.3 Development of the requirements

Initially approved in 1983, IAS 23 allowed a free choice between expensing and capitalising borrowing costs related to qualifying assets. As part of the Comparability/Improvements project, the IASC Board reviewed IAS 23 and issued an exposure draft, E39, which proposed a requirement to capitalise borrowing costs related to qualifying assets. However, in light of the comments received on the exposure draft and the failure of the IASC Board to reach a consensus in favour of either capitalisation or recognition as an expense, the revised IAS 23 includes a benchmark treatment of expensing all borrowing costs and an allowed alternative of capitalising borrowing costs related to qualifying assets.

10.4.4 Borrowing costs

Borrowing costs are defined as, 'interest and other costs incurred by an enterprise in connection with the borrowing of funds.' (IAS 23 (r1993).4) This definition is broad and encompasses more costs than merely interest expense, such as:

(a) interest on bank overdrafts and short-term and long term borrowings;
(b) amortisation of discounts or premiums relating to borrowings;
(c) amortisation of ancillary costs incurred in connection with the arrangement of borrowings;
(d) finance charges in respect of finance leases recognised in accordance with IAS 17 (r1997), *Leases* (see **24.7.1**);
(e) exchange differences arising from foreign currency borrowings to the extent that they are regarded as an adjustment to interest costs.

(IAS 23 (r1993).5)

10.4.5 Qualifying assets

In order for borrowing costs related to the acquisition, construction or production of an asset to be capitalised, the asset must be a qualifying asset which is, 'an asset that necessarily takes a substantial period of time to get ready for its intended use or sale.' (IAS 23 (r1993).4) Thus, a qualifying asset could be an item of inventory or an item of property, plant and equipment such as a manufacturing plant, power generation facility or an investment property. IAS 23 (r1993) specifically prohibits treating other investments, inventories which are routinely manufactured over a short period of time and assets which are ready for their intended use or sale when acquired as qualifying assets.

While IAS 23 (r1993) does not define 'a substantial period of time,' it is unlikely that such a period would be significantly less than one year.

10.4.6 Recognition

IAS 23 (r1993), allows a free choice regarding the treatment of borrowing costs incurred relating to the acquisition, construction or production of a qualifying asset.

The benchmark treatment requires such costs to be expensed in the period in which they are incurred. (IAS 23 (r1993).7)

The allowed alternative treatment requires such costs to be capitalised as part of the cost of the asset to which the borrowings relate. (IAS 23 (r1993).11)

In order to ensure consistency, once an enterprise has adopted the allowed alternative treatment, it must capitalise borrowing costs related to all qualifying assets. It is not appropriate to capitalise such costs associated with some assets but not others. (SIC-2)

10.4.7 Measurement of borrowing costs capitalised

In general, borrowing costs which are capitalised are those borrowing costs which would have been avoided if the related acquisition, construction or production of the qualifying asset had not taken place. (IAS 23 (r1993).13) When borrowings are made specifically to finance a qualifying asset, it is relatively easy to identify the borrowing costs which could have been avoided. The amount capitalised as a cost of the asset is simply the amount of borrowing costs which would have been avoided less any interest earned related to the principal borrowed. (IAS 23 (r1993).15)

Example 10.16

An enterprise borrows £1,000,000 to finance the construction of a new building. However, the first progress payment is only £250,000. If the remaining £750,000 is invested in short-term investments until the next payment is due, any interest earned on these investments is offset against the amount of borrowing costs capitalised as part of the cost of the building.

However, frequently an enterprise will not finance a qualifying asset with one, specific borrowing but from the working capital of the enterprise which may be financed by various borrowings. When this is the case, the amount of borrowing costs capitalised is calculated by applying a capitalisation rate to the related capital expenditure on the qualifying asset. This capitalisation rate is calculated as:

> 'the weighted average of the borrowing costs applicable to the borrowings of the enterprise that are outstanding during the period, other than borrowings made specifically for the purpose of obtaining a qualifying asset.' (IAS 23 (r1993).17)

The related capital expenditure is generally estimated as the average carrying value of the related asset, including borrowing costs capitalised in previous periods, during the period and is limited to those capital expenditures that have resulted in payments of cash, transfers of other assets or the assumption of interest-bearing liabilities less any progress payments received or grants received in connection with the asset. (IAS 23 (r1993).21)

When borrowings are not specifically related to the purchase, construction or acquisition of an asset, any interest income earned during the period is disregarded due to the difficulty of allocating interest income when multiple borrowings exist.

Example 10.17

An enterprise has incurred £850,000 in capital expenditure during the year constructing a mobile phone network. At year end, £100,000 related to the construction of the network is included in creditors. The network is considered to be a qualifying asset under IAS 23 (r1993), and the enterprise has elected to capitalise borrowing costs related to qualifying assets.

The enterprise has borrowings outstanding as follows:

- Bank overdraft (£100,000: 15%)
- Long term loan (£250,000: 7%)
- Debentures (£1,000,000: 8%)

To calculate the amount of borrowing costs to be capitalised, the enterprise applies a weighted average interest rate to the average carrying amount of the related asset during the year as follows:

$$\frac{(£100{,}000 \times 15\%) + (£250{,}000 \times 7\%) + (£1{,}000{,}000 \times 8\%)}{(£100{,}000 + £250{,}000 + £1{,}000{,}000)} = 8.3\% = \text{weighted average interest rate}$$

£750,000 / 2 = £375,000 = average carrying amount of related asset during the year (Note only cash payments qualify for capitalisation.)

£375,000 × 8.3% = £31,125 = amount of borrowing costs capitalised

The amount of borrowing costs capitalised may not exceed the amount of borrowing costs actually incurred during the period. When applying a capitalisation rate to the related capital expenditures, sometimes the result will be an amount which is greater than the amount of borrowing costs incurred during the period. In such cases, only the amount of the borrowing costs incurred is capitalised.

Example 10.18

If the enterprise in the previous example did not have the debentures outstanding, the weighted average interest rate would be:

$$\frac{(£100{,}000 \times 15\%) + (£250{,}000 \times 7\%)}{(£100{,}000 + £250{,}000)} = 9.3\% = \text{weighted average interest rate}$$

£375,000 × 9.3% = £34,875 = potential amount of borrowing costs capitalised

However, borrowing costs incurred on the two borrowings during the year were only £32,500 = ((£100,000 × 15%) + (£250,000 × 7%)).

Therefore, the amount of borrowing costs capitalised is the lower of the two amounts, £32,500.

Since the amount of borrowing costs capitalised may not exceed the amount of borrowing costs actually incurred, 'notional' interest charges may not be capitalised. This point has special relevance to group accounts. Some groups have centralised banking arrangements whereby the 'banking' company charges or credits interest to the group companies on the basis of its balances with these companies. Interest charged by one group company to another cannot be capitalised in the consolidated financial statements except to the extent that it represents interest actually borne by the group on capital borrowed to finance the production of the relevant asset. Intra-group interest will be eliminated on consolidation.

In some instances, if expenditures have been made unevenly throughout the year, it may be necessary to apply the capitalisation rate to the weighted average carrying amount of the related asset rather than to the simple average of the related expenditure in order to achieve a fair presentation (see *Example* **10.19**).

Example 10.19

Capital expenditure of £125,000 is made in January, and a further £300,000 is expended in July. In December, there is additional expenditure of £1.2 million. If a capitalisation rate of 9.5 per cent is applied to the total capital expenditure incurred during the year, then the borrowing costs to be capitalised are as follows:

(125,000 + 300,000 + 1,200,000)/2 = £812,500 × 9.5% = **£77,188**
= amount capitalised using a simple average carrying amount

However, given the uneven nature of the capital expenditure during the year, it is appropriate to apply the capitalisation rate to the weighted average capital expenditure incurred in the year. When the weighted average capital expenditure is used, the costs eligible for capitalisation are more prudently stated at **£35,625** (see below).

Expenditure	*Period outstanding*	*Weighted Average Expenditure*
£125,000	12/12	125,000
£300,000	6/12	150,000
£1,200,000	1/12	100,000
		375,000

£375,000 × 9.5% = **£35,625**

10.4.8 Capitalisation period

Commencement of capitalisation

> 'The capitalisation of borrowing costs as part of the cost of a qualifying asset should commence when:
>
> (a) expenditures for the asset are being incurred;
> (b) borrowing costs are being incurred; and
> (c) activities that are necessary to prepare the asset for its intended use or sale are in progress.'
>
> (IAS 23 (r1993).20)

It may be the case that for several accounting periods, expenditures related to a qualifying asset are being incurred and activities that are necessary to prepare the asset for its intended use or sale are in progress but borrowing costs are not being incurred. If in a later period, borrowing costs are incurred, they may only be capitalised from that point forward. In other words, the capitalisation rate is only applied to expenditures incurred after the borrowings have been made.

Example 10.20

An enterprise began construction of a property in January and consequently incurred capital expenditure of £100k per month from this point. The sources of financing for the specific borrowing for the project were finalised and the funds received on 1 June. The weighted average capitalisation rate for the enterprise is 10.2 per cent, but this rate may only be applied to the capital expenditure incurred from 1 June onwards.

Activities necessary to prepare the asset for its intended use or sale include any activities that change the condition of the asset. Such activities encompass more than physical changes such as construction of the asset. For example, technical and administrative work prior to the commencement of physical construction such as the procurement of permits would be considered an activity necessary to prepare the asset for its intended use or sale. However, if no activities are being carried out to change the condition of the asset subsequent to its purchase, borrowing costs may not be capitalised. (IAS 23 (r1993).22)

Suspension of capitalisation

> 'Capitalisation of borrowing costs should be suspended during extended periods in which active development is interrupted.'
>
> (IAS 23 (r1993).23)

If activities that are necessary to prepare an asset for its intended use or sale are delayed for an extended period and borrowing costs continue to be incurred, these borrowing costs are not eligible for capitalisation. Since borrowing costs incurred during the suspension of activity are associated with the holding of a partially complete asset, they are expensed as they are incurred. However, capitalisation does not cease during shorter, temporary delays when substantial technical or administrative work is being carried out. (IAS 23 (r1993).24)

Cessation of capitalisation

> 'Capitalisation of borrowing costs should cease when substantially all the activities necessary to prepare the qualifying asset for its intended use or sale are complete.'
>
> (IAS 23 (r1993).25)

When the qualifying asset has been constructed, this cessation is generally when building work is finished despite the fact that some decorating or landscaping may still be required.

If a qualifying asset is completed in stages and each stage is able to be used independently, capitalisation related to each stage ceases on the completion of each stage rather than at the end of the entire project. For example, a cable company may be building a cable network covering many franchise areas. As substantially all the activities necessary to prepare the cable network in each franchise area for use are completed, capitalisation of borrowing costs related to expenditures in that franchise area ceases, although the capitalisation of borrowing costs in other franchise areas which are still under construction may continue.

10.4.9 Impairment

IAS 36 requires that the recoverable amount of an asset should be estimated whenever there is an indication that the asset may be impaired. Assets under construction or in production are not exempt from this periodic assessment. When management determines that the recoverable amount of an asset on which related borrowing costs are being capitalised exceeds its carrying amount, borrowing costs continue to be capitalised, but the carrying amount of the related asset is written down to its recoverable amount to recognise the impairment. (SIC-2) This rule effectively requires an enterprise to capitalise borrowing costs as part of an asset and then recognise any impairment at the balance sheet date.

10.4.10 Disclosure

When borrowing costs are material and the benchmark treatment is adopted (i.e. borrowing costs are expensed as incurred), an enterprise is required to disclose its accounting policy adopted for borrowing costs. (IAS 23 (r1993).29)

When the allowed alternative treatment is adopted (i.e. borrowing costs are capitalised), an enterprise is required to disclose its accounting policy adopted for borrowing costs as well as:

(a) the amount of borrowing costs capitalised during the period; and
(b) the capitalisation rate used to determine the amount of borrowing costs eligible for capitalisation.

(IAS 23 (r1993).29)

10.4.11 Comparison with UK GAAP

Under UK GAAP, in practice both the benchmark and allowed alternative treatments can be found, although the benchmark treatment of expensing borrowing costs as they are incurred is the more common. This practice is not expected to change in light of FRS 15, *Tangible Fixed Assets*, which became effective for financial statements ending on or after 23 March 1999, and which allows either capitalisation or recognition as an expense.

10.4.12 Comparison with US GAAP

Unlike IAS 23 (r1993) which allows a free choice of whether or not to capitalise borrowing costs related to qualifying assets, under SFAS 34 *Capitalization of Interest Cost,* borrowing costs incurred related to the construction of a qualifying item of property, plant and equipment are *required* to be capitalised. However, items which qualify for capitalisation differ between US GAAP and IAS 23 (r1993). One notable difference is that under US GAAP, qualifying assets include investments (equity, loans, and advances) accounted for by the equity method while the investee has activities in progress necessary to commence its planned principal operations provided that the investee's activities include the use of funds to acquire qualifying assets for its operations. Under IAS 23 (r1993), such investments are not considered to be qualifying assets. Another difference is that under US GAAP, exchange differences arising from foreign currency borrowings would not be considered a borrowing cost eligible for capitalisation.

In addition, unlike IAS 23 (r1993), under US GAAP, interest earned on specifically borrowed funds before they are expended is not deducted from the amount of borrowing costs capitalised.

10.4.13 Examples from published financial statements

Note that the excerpts given do not always comply in full with all aspects of IAS and as such are not necessarily examples of best practice but merely of current practice.

Benchmark treatment

Example 10.21

Excerpt from property, plant and equipment note:

Borrowing costs are not capitalised.

Roche Holdings
Switzerland
31 December 2000
International Accounting Standards

Allowed alternative treatment

> **Example 10.22**
>
> MINING
>
> Capitalised mine development cost includes expenditure incurred to develop new mining operations, to define further mineralisation in existing ore bodies and to expand the capacity of the mine. Costs include interest capitalised during the construction period where financed by borrowings and the net present value of future decommissioning costs. Amortisation is first charged on new mining ventures from the date on which the mining ventures reach commercial productions quantities, at which time capital work-in-progress costs are transferred to mining property, plant and equipment. Development costs to maintain production are capitalised and amortised over the estimated useful life of the asset.
>
> *Anglo Platinum*
> *South Africa*
> *31 December 2000*
> *South African GAAP/International Accounting Standards*

> **Example 10.23**
>
> *Excerpt from Property, plant and equipment note*
>
> Financing costs directly associated with the construction or acquisition of qualifying assets are capitalised at interest rates relating to loans specifically raised for that purpose, or at the average borrowing rate where the general pool of group borrowings was utilised. Capitalisation of borrowing costs ceases when the asset is substantially complete.
>
> *ISCOR*
> *South Africa*
> *International Accounting Standards/South African GAAP*
> *30 June 2000*

10.5 Goodwill

10.5.1 Source

IAS 8 (r1993)	*Net Profit or Loss for the Period, Fundamental Errors and Changes in Accounting Policies.*
IAS 22 (r1998)	*Business Combinations.*
IAS 36	*Impairment of Assets.*
IAS 37	*Provisions, Contingent Liabilities and Contingent Assets.*
IAS 38	*Intangible Assets.*

10.5.2 Brief summary of the requirements

Goodwill arises as the result of a business combination accounted for as an acquisition and is the excess of the cost of the acquisition over the fair value of the identifiable assets and liabilities acquired. Goodwill is capitalised and amortised over its estimated useful life. There is a rebuttable presumption that the useful life of goodwill will not exceed 20 years from initial recognition. This presumption may be overcome, with the result that goodwill is amortised over a period exceeding 20 years. However, when the useful life of goodwill is estimated to be longer than 20 years, an annual impairment test must be carried out in accordance with IAS 36 (see **10.12**).

The capitalisation of internally generated goodwill is not permitted.

Note: The discussion of goodwill in this chapter will focus on how to account for goodwill once it has been recognised as an asset in the balance sheet at the date of the exchange transaction. See **18.6** for a discussion of how to calculate the cost of an acquisition and the fair value of the identifiable assets and liabilities acquired. See **10.6** for a discussion of the treatment of negative goodwill.

10.5.3 Development of the requirements

Originally approved in November 1983, IAS 22 was revised as part of the Comparability/Improvements project in 1993. The main changes in relation to positive goodwill were the removal of choice between capitalising goodwill as an asset and writing it off against equity and the inclusion of a 20 year limit on the amortisation period of goodwill. IAS 22 (r1993) required that goodwill arising on a business combination be capitalised and amortised. However, the change was not required to be made retrospectively. Thus, some financial statements which comply with IASs may have pre-1995 goodwill written-off in equity.

In 1998, the IASC Board again revisited IAS 22 and amended it to be consistent with IAS 36, IAS 37 and IAS 38. The treatment of negative goodwill was also amended. To be consistent with the amortisation of other intangible assets (IAS 38), the 20 year maximum useful life for goodwill was converted into a rebuttable presumption that the useful life of goodwill does not exceed 20 years. If the presumption is overcome and goodwill is amortised over more than 20 years, the goodwill must be tested for impairment annually and disclosure should be made of the reasons why the presumption has been rebutted.

When revising IAS 22 (r1993), the IASC Board intentionally set very similar rules for the amortisation of intangible assets (included in IAS 38) and goodwill to curb accounting arbitrage between goodwill and other intangible assets since it is often difficult to distinguish between the two. Only two differences exist between the requirements for goodwill and for other intangible assets:

1. IAS 38 permits the revaluation of intangible assets, while IAS 22 (r1998) does not permit goodwill to be revalued; and
2. in certain circumstances, IAS 38 requires a residual value to be estimated when determining the depreciable amount of an intangible asset. IAS 22 (r1998) does not entertain the notion of a residual value for goodwill.

The IASC Board does not believe that the above two differences will result in many differences in practice since the revaluation of intangible assets and intangible assets with residual values are expected to be rare.

10.5.4 Recognition and measurement

IAS 22 (r1998) defines goodwill as any excess of the cost of the acquisition over the acquirer's interest in the fair value of the identifiable assets and liabilities acquired as at the date of the exchange transaction. (IAS 22 (r1998).41)

Successful businesses are worth more than the sum of the net assets they control and so generate their own goodwill (through commercial connections, regular customers, good reputation, efficient management, etc.), but such internally-generated goodwill does not appear in the financial statements, and companies are precluded from including it in their balance sheets. Throughout the rest of the section, 'goodwill' refers to purchased goodwill.

Goodwill is recognised as an asset and subsequently carried at cost less any accumulated amortisation and any accumulated impairment losses. (IAS 22 (r1998).43)

It is necessary at the outset to be able to distinguish between transactions for the purchase of a business, in which goodwill may or may not arise, and the purchase of specific assets. In order to treat a transaction as the purchase of a business, it is considered that two criteria should be met – the benefit of customers' accounts should have passed to the purchaser and employees should continue in the same employment, albeit with the acquiring company. In other words, the business carries on substantially as before under the responsibility of the new owners.

Where specific assets are purchased, the total consideration represents the cost of those assets to the purchaser, irrespective of the values attributed to them in the books of the vendor, and therefore no goodwill arises. Where more than one asset or group of assets is acquired, it will be necessary to allocate the purchase price to the respective assets on the basis of fair values, in order to record their cost to the purchaser as required by IAS 16 (r1998). Where there is a vending agreement which attributes values to the various assets, this may give some guidance but it is unlikely to be authoritative.

There is the possibility that the process of attribution may be driven by tax or other considerations, rather than by the need to attribute fair values. Such values should always be considered carefully, in the light of all the circumstances, to check that they represent fair and arm's length prices, before they may safely be adopted as costs to the purchaser.

Unlike other intangible assets, goodwill is not permitted to be revalued subsequent to initial recognition. In the view of the IASC Board, the requirement that there be an active market which can be used to determine the fair value of an intangible asset in IAS 38 will never be met for goodwill; and therefore, the option of revaluation is not permitted.

10.5.5 *Subsequent adjustments to goodwill*

As discussed more fully in **18.6.5**, subsequent to initial recognition, goodwill may be adjusted as a result of subsequent changes to the amount of purchase consideration or the subsequent identification of changes in the fair value of assets and liabilities acquired. However, adjustments to goodwill arising from adjustments to the fair values of the assets and liabilities acquired may only be made before the end of the first annual accounting period commencing after the acquisition and cannot result in the carrying amount of goodwill exceeding its recoverable amount. (IAS 22 (r1998).71) After this date, with the exception of deferred tax, any adjustments related to fair value are recognised in the income statement of the current period. See **18.6.5** for a discussion of subsequent recognition of deferred tax assets.

Subsequent changes to the fair value of the purchase consideration will always result in an adjustment to goodwill, regardless of the period in which the adjustment is made.

10.5.6 *Amortisation*

Similar to other intangible assets, goodwill is required to be amortised over its useful life with the amortisation charges recognised as an expense. (IAS 22 (r1998).44 and 46)

By not specifying where on the income statement goodwill is to be charged, IAS 22 (r1998) provides many options. For example, it does not specify whether or not goodwill amortisation charges should be included within operating profit. However, since paragraph 88 (d) requires disclosure of the line item(s) in which goodwill amortisation is included on the face of the income statement, it appears that it may be included either before or after operating profit as long as it is clearly disclosed in the notes where the amount has been charged in the income statement. The fact that the disclosure requirement refers to 'line item(s)' would indicate that it is not required to include the amortisation charge in only one line item. Therefore, it would appear appropriate to look to the nature of the goodwill to determine where on the income statement the related amortisation charges should be shown.

Amortisation period

The useful life of goodwill should reflect the best estimate of the period during which future economic benefits are expected to flow to the enterprise. Factors to consider in estimating the useful life of goodwill include:

> '(a) the nature and foreseeable life of the acquired business;
> (b) the stability and foreseeable life of the industry to which the goodwill relates;
> (c) public information on the characteristics of goodwill in similar businesses or industries and typical lifecycles of similar businesses;
> (d) the effects of product obsolescence, changes in demand and other economic factors on the acquired business;
> (e) the service life expectancies of key individuals or groups of employees and whether the acquired business could be efficiently managed by another management team;
> (f) the level of maintenance expenditure or of funding required to obtain the expected future economic benefits from the acquired business and the company's ability and intent to reach such a level;
> (g) expected actions by competitors or potential competitors; and
> (h) the period of control over the acquired business and legal, regulatory or contractual provisions affecting its useful life.'
>
> (IAS 22 (r1998).48)

IAS 22 (r1998) concedes that choosing an appropriate useful life for goodwill is difficult and notes that estimates of useful life become less reliable as the length of the useful life increases. Therefore, a rebuttable presumption is included that the useful life of goodwill will not exceed 20 years. In rare cases, this presumption can be overcome if there is persuasive evidence that the goodwill will last for a specific period of more than 20 years. (IAS 22 (r1998).44) This may be the case when the goodwill is so closely related to another identifiable asset or group of assets that its life is likely to coincide with that of the related identifiable assets. For example, if the principal asset of an acquired business is a 25 year cable broadcasting licence, a useful life of 25 years for the related goodwill may be appropriate.

However, the sting in the tail is that the carrying amount of goodwill which is being amortised over more than 20 years is subject to an *annual* impairment review in accordance with IAS 36. (IAS 22 (r1998).56) (see **10.12**). In addition, the enterprise must disclose in the notes to the financial statements the reasons why the presumption is rebutted and the factor(s) that played a significant role in determining the useful life of the goodwill.

At first sight, the opportunity to lessen goodwill amortisation charges in the income statement by lengthening the useful life of goodwill seems an attractive one. However, in practice, many acquirers will not try to justify lives exceeding 20 years for acquired goodwill, even where it would be possible to do so. Instead, they will simply amortise the goodwill over a period of 20 years or less.

The reasons why they might choose to do so are:

(a) *to avoid annual impairment reviews.* The calculations that have to be undertaken to perform impairment reviews can be relatively detailed. Some enterprises may find that the cost of the exercise exceeds the benefit of lower amortisation charges.

(b) *to report more stable earnings patterns.* If goodwill is amortised over a period exceeding 20 years, its carrying value is more exposed to future impairment write-downs. The recognition of large one-off charges for impairment makes earnings patterns more volatile and may necessitate explanations that management might prefer to avoid. In contrast, a regular amortisation charge contributes to a smooth earnings pattern.

(c) *because amortisation charges may be ignored by analysts and other users of accounts.* There is a view that analysts, who are increasingly concentrating on cash flows to measure business performance, may ignore goodwill amortisation charges when assessing earnings, on the grounds that the charge has no economic meaning or cash consequences. Some company directors believe that if this is the case, they will present their results in a better light by regular amortisation charges than they would do by exposing themselves to the risk of irregular impairment charges.

Although goodwill may have a useful life of more than 20 years, goodwill is always considered to have a finite life, and therefore amortisation will always be required. (IAS 22 (r1998).51)

Amortisation method

The amortisation method chosen should reflect the pattern in which the future economic benefits arising from goodwill are expected to be consumed. (IAS 22 (r1998).45) In almost all cases, this will be the straight-line method.

At least at each financial year end, the estimated useful life of goodwill and the related amortisation methods should be reviewed. If a change in either is deemed appropriate, it is accounted for as a change in estimate in accordance with IAS 8 (r1993), *Net Profit or Loss for the Period, Fundamental Errors and Changes in Accounting Policies*, (IAS 22 (r1998).54) by adjusting current and future periods (see **5.15**). If a change in the estimated useful life of goodwill results in the goodwill having an estimated useful life of greater than 20 years from the date of the original exchange transaction, annual impairment tests will be required as discussed above.

10.5.7 Impairment and reversals of impairment

An enterprise follows the guidance in IAS 36 to determine whether goodwill is impaired and to measure such an impairment. As explained in IAS 36 since goodwill does not generate cash flows independently from other assets or groups of assets, its recoverable amount cannot be separately estimated. Therefore, when there is an impairment indicator related to goodwill, the recoverable amount of the entire cash-generating unit which includes the goodwill is determined. When this recoverable amount is less than the cash-generating unit's carrying amount, an impairment loss is recognised. IAS 36 includes specific guidance on the allocation of the impairment loss to goodwill (see **10.12.14**).

IAS 36 also contains specific requirements around the reversal of impairment losses related to goodwill. The situations in which reversals of goodwill impairment losses are permitted are fewer than for other types of assets (see **10.12.15**).

10.5.8 Disclosure

The financial statements should disclose:

(a) the amortisation periods used for goodwill;
(b) when the useful life of goodwill exceeds 20 years, the reasons why the rebuttable presumption that goodwill has a useful life not exceeding 20 years has been overcome, including the factors that played a significant role in determining the useful life of the goodwill;
(c) when the amortisation method used for goodwill is not the straight-line method, the reasons why the method chosen is superior;
(d) the line item(s) of the income statement in which the amortisation of goodwill is included; and
(e) a reconciliation of the carrying amount of goodwill at the beginning and end of the period showing:
    (i) the gross amount and the accumulated amortisation (aggregated with accumulated impairment losses) at the beginning of the period;
    (ii) any additional goodwill recognised during the period;
    (iii) any adjustments resulting from subsequent identification or changes in value of identifiable assets and liabilities acquired;
    (iv) any goodwill disposed of during the period;
    (v) amortisation recognised during the period;
    (vi) any impairment losses recognised or reversed during the period;
    (vii) any other changes in carrying amount during the period; and

(viii) the gross amount and the accumulated amortisation (aggregated with accumulated impairment losses) at the end of the period.

Comparative information is not required for the items included in the reconciliation.

(IAS 22 (r1998).88)

When goodwill is impaired or a reversal of an impairment occurs, the disclosures required by IAS 36 are also applicable (see **10.12.16**).

10.5.9 Transitional provisions

Due to the fact that IAS 22 has been amended several times, the transitional provisions are many and confusing. IAS 22 (r1998) includes a table to clarify how the transitional provisions work in various scenarios.

Broadly:

(1) Goodwill written off to reserves during accounting periods beginning before 1 January 1995 may either be:
   (a) left in reserves; or
   (b) brought onto the balance sheet as an asset. If it is restated as an asset:
      (i) a prior period adjustment is made in accordance with IAS 8 (r1993) (see **5.17**);
      (ii) the amount included as an asset on the balance sheet is net of any amortisation or impairment losses which would have accumulated from the date of acquisition to the date of the restatement; and
      (iii) the amount of goodwill will need to be calculated using the rules on assigning fair values to identifiable assets and liabilities included in IAS 22 (r1998).

(2) Goodwill capitalised as an asset during accounting periods beginning before 1 January 1995 which is not calculated in accordance with IAS 22 (r1998) may be either:
   (a) unadjusted and deemed to be recorded correctly; or
   (b) adjusted to the amount which would have been calculated had the rules on assigning fair values to identifiable assets and liabilities included in IAS 22 (r1998) been in effect at the date of acquisition. The adjustment and any consequential adjustment to accumulated amortisation would be shown as a prior period adjustment;

(3) Goodwill arising during accounting periods beginning on or after 1 January 1995 should be treated as follows:
   (a) if the goodwill has been calculated in accordance with the rules on assigning fair values to identifiable assets and liabilities included in

IAS 22 (r1998), no adjustment to initial carrying amount required. However, amortisation charges may need to be revised. See 4 or 5 below;

(b) if the goodwill has not been calculated in accordance with the rules on assigning fair values to identifiable assets and liabilities included in IAS 22 (r1998), determine the amount which would have been capitalised and adjust it for the related accumulated amortisation of the goodwill that would have been recognised under IAS 22 (r1993) (i.e. the 20 year maximum limit on the useful life of goodwill applies); and

(c) amortise any remaining goodwill in accordance with IAS 22 (r1998) from the period of adoption of IAS 22 (r1998) forward.

(4) If goodwill was capitalised in periods prior to the adoption of IAS 22 (r1998) but not amortised, the carrying amount of the goodwill and related accumulated amortisation should be restated as if the amortisation of goodwill had always been determined under IAS 22 (r1998) and reflected as a prior period adjustment.

(5) If goodwill was previously capitalised and amortised, do not restate the carrying amount of goodwill for any difference between accumulated amortisation calculated in prior years and that which would be calculated under IAS 22 (r1998). Instead, treat the change as a change in estimate and amortise any carrying amount of the goodwill over its remaining useful life determined under IAS 22 (r1998).

Although not specifically stated in the transitional provisions, if goodwill had been capitalised and amortised over 20 years under IAS 22 (r1993) and the management believes that a useful life of greater than 20 years is appropriate and supportable, the change should be reflected as a change in estimate and thus effected prospectively rather than a change in accounting policy which would be reflected retrospectively (Scenario 5 above).

One issue not addressed by IAS 22 (r1998) is the treatment of pre-1995 goodwill which has been written off to reserves on disposal or partial disposal of the related investment. Such an amount could either be added to the carrying amount of the assets disposed of and thus decrease the gain or increase the loss on disposal or simply transferred from the goodwill reserve to retained earnings. Since the goodwill has never been recognised in either the income statement or the other performance statement which shows gains and losses not included in the income statement, it would seem to be most appropriate for it to be taken into account in calculating the gain or loss on disposal.

10.5.10 Comparison with UK GAAP

Under UK GAAP goodwill arising on a business combination accounted for as an acquisition is calculated on the same basis as under IAS 22 (r1998), namely, it is the excess of the purchase price over the fair value of the assets acquired. However, this similarity does not necessarily mean that goodwill calculated under IAS 22 (r1998) will be equal to goodwill calculated under UK GAAP as differences may arise between IAS 22 (r1998) and UK GAAP on the calculation of the fair value of the consideration given and of the assets acquired (see Chapter **18**).

FRS 10, *Goodwill and Intangible Assets,* which became effective for financial statements relating to accounting periods ending on or after 23 December 1998, requires that goodwill be capitalised as an asset. The previous standard, SSAP 22, *Accounting for Goodwill*, allowed a choice in accounting for goodwill between immediate elimination against shareholders' reserves and capitalisation of the asset in the balance sheet. Goodwill arising prior to the adoption of FRS 10 may either be restated as an asset or remain in equity.

Similar to IAS 22 (r1998), under FRS 10, goodwill is amortised over its estimated useful life. FRS 10 also contains a rebuttable presumption that the useful life of goodwill does not exceed 20 years. However, as under IAS 22 (r1998), this presumption may be overcome and a longer life used, but the goodwill will become subject to an annual impairment test. Unlike IAS 22 (r1998) under FRS 10, a life of more than 20 years can include an indefinite life, when no amortisation will be charged.

Early indications in the UK are that the additional obligations imposed on entities that are successful in rebutting the '20 years or less' assumption are discouraging a high proportion of managements from attempting the rebuttal. Non-amortisation will, it seems, be very much the exception to the rule.

As under IAS 22 (r1998), under UK GAAP, subsequent changes made to the fair value of the assets and liabilities purchased may be adjusted to goodwill only before the end of the first annual accounting period commencing after the acquisition. (FRS 7, *Fair Values in Acquisition Accounting*)

Lastly, FRS 10 requires an impairment review to be carried out related to goodwill at the end of the first full financial year following acquisition. Such a review would only be required under IAS if there were impairment indicators present or if the useful life of goodwill was estimated as greater than 20 years.

10.5.11 Comparison with US GAAP

Under US GAAP, goodwill arising on a business acquisition accounted for as a purchase is calculated on the same basis as under IAS 22 (r1998), namely, it is the excess of the purchase price over the fair value of the net identifiable assets acquired. However, this similarity does not necessarily mean that goodwill calculated under IAS 22 (r1998) will be equal to goodwill calculated under US GAAP as differences may arise between IAS 22 (r1998) and US GAAP on the calculation of the fair value of the consideration given and of the assets acquired (see Chapter **18**).

On 29 June 2001, the FASB approved the following Statements as a result of its project to reconsider the accounting for business combinations:

- FASB Statement No. 141, *Business Combinations* ('Statement 141');
- FASB Statement 142, *Goodwill and Other Intangible Assets* ('Statement 142').

These Statements change the accounting for business combinations and goodwill in two significant ways. First, Statement 141 requires that the purchase method of accounting be used for all business combinations initiated after 30 June 2001. Use of the pooling-of-interests method for those business combinations is prohibited. Second, Statement 142 changes the accounting for goodwill from an amortization method to an impairment-only approach. Thus, amortisation of goodwill, including goodwill recorded in past transactions, will cease upon adoption of Statement 142.

On 20 July 2001, the FASB issued Statement 141 and Statement 142. Statement 141 was effective on 1 July 2001. Statement 142 will be applied in fiscal years beginning after 15 December 2001, with early adoption permitted for entities with fiscal years beginning after 15 March 2001 provided that the first interim financial statements have not been previously issued.

Given the transition provisions, the Statements will have an immediate impact on many entities. Applying the provisions of the Statements will require the use of significant judgement. Significant judgements include, but are not limited to:

- identification of intangible assets;
- determining the useful lives of identifiable intangible assets;
- identification of reporting units;
- allocation of assets, liabilities and goodwill to reporting units;
- identification of events or circumstances that will trigger an interim impairment test for either goodwill or other intangible assets;
- fair value measurements.

Statement 141 provides for the following transition provisions to business combinations for which the acquisition date was before 1 July 2001, that were accounted for using the purchase method:

(a) The carrying amount of acquired intangible assets that do not meet the criteria in paragraph 39 for recognition apart from goodwill (and any related deferred tax liabilities if the intangible asset is non-deductible for tax purposes) shall be reclassified as goodwill as of the date Statement 142 is initially applied in its entirety.

(b) The carrying amount of:
   (i) any recognised intangible assets that meet the recognition criteria in paragraph 39, or
   (ii) any unidentifiable intangible assets recognised in accordance with paragraph 5 of FASB Statement No. 72, *Accounting for Certain Acquisitions of Banking or Thrift Institutions,* that have been included in the amount reported as goodwill (or as goodwill and intangible assets)

   shall be reclassified and accounted for as an asset apart from goodwill as of the date Statement 142 is initially applied in its entirety.

(c) Other than as set forth in (a) and (b), an entity shall not change the amount of the purchase price assigned to the assets acquired and liabilities assumed in a business combination for which the acquisition date was before 1 July 2001.

In applying Opinion 16, entities sometimes did not separately allocate amounts to identifiable intangible assets for financial reporting purposes. Justification for this presentation may have been that:

(a) The identifiable intangible assets remaining within goodwill had a useful life identical to or consistent with goodwill. (For example, if an acquired patent has a useful life of four years and goodwill had a useful life of five years, a separate allocation to the patent for financial reporting purposes may not have been made.)

(b) The useful life determined for goodwill was a composite life that reflected the inclusion of the identifiable intangible assets. (For example, in the banking industry, sometimes entities did not separately assign a value to the acquired core deposit intangible asset and instead used a shorter amortisation period for goodwill that reflected the inclusion of the asset within goodwill).

Consistent with recent reminders to registrants that 'APB Opinion No. 16 requires that **all** identifiable intangibles be assigned a fair value in the purchase price allocation of a purchase business combination', on 13 August 2001, the SEC staff indicated the expectation that identifiable intangible assets recognisable under Opinion 16 that were previously subsumed into goodwill be separated upon adoption of Statement 142. Sufficient accounting records are expected to exist in support of the original accounting to now support separate recognition. Restatement of prior financial statements are not, however, required in connection with the adoption of Statement 142.

As indicated in the Basis for Conclusions section of Statement 141, at the inception of the project the Board observed that intangible assets make up an increasing proportion of the assets of many (if not all) entities. The Board also observed that intangible assets acquired in a business combination often were included in the amount recognised as goodwill, despite the provisions of APB Opinion No. 16 that required they be recognised apart from goodwill. The Board concluded that Statement 141 should provide explicit criteria for determining whether an acquired intangible asset should be recognised apart from goodwill to enhance the decision usefulness of financial statements and to prevent finite-lived intangible assets from being included in the amount recognised as goodwill which will not be amortised under Statement 142.

This revised definition of an identifiable intangible asset has implications to both entities performing purchase price allocations for business combinations after the effective date of Statement 141 as well as in performing the second step of the goodwill impairment test under Statement 142.

Statement 142 provides that an intangible asset whose life extends beyond the foreseeable horizon be classified as having an indefinite life. An intangible asset that is determined to have an indefinite useful life shall not be amortised until its useful life is determined to be no longer indefinite. If no legal, regulatory, contractual, economic, or other factors limit the useful life of an intangible asset to the reporting entity, the useful life of the asset shall be considered to be indefinite.

Appendix A of Statement 142 provides examples describing an acquired intangible asset and the facts and circumstances surrounding the determination of its useful life. The following examples of an acquired intangible asset with a determined indefinite life are provided: an acquired broadcast licence, an acquired airline route authority and an acquired trade mark. The examples in Appendix A of Statement 142 are for illustration purposes only. The determination of useful life can only be made based on a consideration of the facts and circumstances unique to each acquired intangible asset.

Close SEC staff scrutiny is expected with regard to the determination of the useful life of an acquired intangible asset, especially those decisions that the useful life is deemed to be indefinite.

The following fair value measurements are required under the Statements for goodwill and intangibles:

(1) Purchase Price Allocations – At the time of each business combination, fair value measurements are required in order to assign amounts to the assets acquired and liabilities assumed.
(2) Goodwill Impairment Test (Step 1) – Upon adoption of Statement 142, annually thereafter, and on an interim basis when events or

circumstances warrant, it is necessary to determine the fair value of each reporting unit to determine if the fair value of the reporting unit exceeds its carrying amount.

(3) Goodwill Impairment Test (Step 2) – At any point in time when Step 1 of the goodwill impairment test indicates that the fair value of a reporting unit is less than its carrying amount, fair value measurements are required to allocate the fair value of a reporting unit determined in Step 1 to all of the assets and liabilities of that unit (including any unrecognised intangible assets) as if the reporting unit had been acquired in a business combination and the fair value of the reporting unit determined in Step 1 was the price paid to acquire the reporting unit.

(4) Identifiable Intangible Assets Not Subject to Amortisation – Upon adoption of Statement 142, annually thereafter, and on an interim basis when events or circumstances warrant, it is necessary to determine the fair value of each identifiable intangible asset not subject to amortisation to test the assets for impairment

(5) Disposal of a Portion of a Reporting Unit – When a portion of a reporting unit that constitutes a business is to be disposed of, goodwill associated with that business shall be included in the carrying amount of the business in determining the gain or loss on disposal. The amount of goodwill to be included in that carrying amount shall be based on the relative fair values of the business to be disposed of and the portion of the reporting unit that will be retained.

(6) Reorganisation of Reporting Structure – When an entity reorganises its reporting structure in a manner that changes the composition of one or more of its reporting units, goodwill shall be reassigned to the reporting units affected using a relative fair value allocation approach similar to that used when a portion of a reporting unit is to be disposed of.

The new Statements are detailed and complex. However, despite the existence of numerous implementation issues related to the Statements, to date the FASB has announced no intention to provide further implementation guidance.

SFAS 38, *Accounting for Preacquisition Contingencies of Purchased Enterprises*, sets a time limit of one year from the date of acquisition to make adjustments to goodwill resulting from subsequent amendments to the fair value of assets and liabilities acquired. This is a shorter time period than under IAS 22 (r1998).

10.5.12 Examples from published financial statements

Note that the excerpts given do not always comply in full with all aspects of IAS and as such are not necessarily examples of best practice but merely of current practice.

Example 10.24

Intangible assets and business combinations

Goodwill is recorded as an intangible asset and is the surplus of the cost of acquisition over the fair value of identifiable assets acquired. Any goodwill and fair value adjustments are treated as assets and liabilities of the acquired company and are recorded in the local currency of that company.

Patents, licences, trade marks and other intangible assets are initially recorded at fair value. Where these assets have been acquired through a business combination, this will be the fair value allocated in the acquisition accounting. Where these have been acquired other than through a business combination, the initial fair value will be cost.

All intangible assets are amortised over their useful lives on a straight-line basis.

Roche
Switzerland
International Accounting Standards
31 December 2000

Example 10.25

Intangible assets

In the case of business combinations, the excess of the purchase price over the fair value of net identifiable assets acquired is recorded as goodwill in the balance sheet. Goodwill, which is denominated in the local currency of the related acquisition, is amortised to income through administration and general overheads on a straight-line basis over its useful life. The amortisation period is determined at the time of the acquisition, based upon the particular circumstances, and ranges from 5 to 20 years. Goodwill relating to acquisitions arising prior to 1 January 1995 has been fully written off against reserves.

Novartis Group
Switzerland
International Accounting Standards
31 December 2000

For examples of the reconciliation of opening and closing goodwill, see **10.7.17**.

10.6 Negative goodwill

10.6.1 Sources

IAS 22 (r1998) *Business Combinations.*

10.6.2 Brief summary of the requirements

Negative goodwill arises when the cost of an acquired business is less than the aggregate fair values of the identifiable assets and liabilities within that business. When an enterprise suspects that it may have made an acquisition resulting in negative goodwill, it must take the following three steps:

(1) review the fair values assigned to identified assets and liabilities acquired to ensure that the negative goodwill does not arise from errors in the fair value exercise;
(2) identify negative goodwill which relates to future losses and expenses which are not liabilities at the acquisition date. This portion of negative goodwill will be recognised as income when the future losses and expenses are recognised. If the losses and expenses do not occur when expected, this portion of negative goodwill is treated as in step 3.
(3) for any negative goodwill not assigned in step 2, one of two treatments is required:
    (a) for the amount of negative goodwill not exceeding the fair values of acquired identifiable non-monetary assets, recognise it as income on a systematic basis over the remaining weighted average useful life of the identifiable acquired depreciable/amortisable assets;
    (b) for any amount of negative goodwill exceeding the fair values of acquired identifiable non-monetary assets, recognise it as income immediately.

Negative goodwill is presented as a deduction from assets in the same balance sheet classification as goodwill.

Note: The discussion of negative goodwill in this chapter focuses on how to account for negative goodwill once its amount has been determined in accordance with IAS 22 (r1998). See **18.6.3** and **18.6.4** for a discussion of how to calculate the cost of an acquisition and the fair value of the identifiable assets and liabilities acquired. See **10.5** for a discussion of the treatment of positive goodwill (simply referred to as goodwill).

10.6.3 Development of the requirements

The treatment of negative goodwill has been the subject of much debate at the IASC, resulting in several changes over the years in its treatment.

Originally issued in 1983, IAS 22 allowed a choice between crediting negative goodwill immediately to reserves or capitalising it and amortising it over its useful life. As part of the Comparability/Improvements project in 1993, the option of crediting negative goodwill immediately to reserves was removed.

The resulting revised Standard, IAS 22 (r1993) contained a benchmark and allowed alternative treatment. Under the benchmark treatment, when the cost of the acquisition was less than the acquirer's interest in the fair values of the identifiable assets and liabilities acquired, the fair values of the non-monetary assets acquired were reduced proportionally until the excess was eliminated. Any residual excess was classified as negative goodwill and treated as deferred income and recognised as income over a period not normally exceeding five years unless a longer period, not exceeding 20 years from the date of acquisition could be justified. Under the allowed alternative treatment, the total amount of negative goodwill was treated as deferred income as described under the benchmark treatment.

In 1998, IAS 22 was again revised and the IASC Board decided that neither the benchmark nor the allowed alternative treatment in IAS 22 (r1993) were appropriate. Instead the three step plan outlined above was adopted.

10.6.4 Negative goodwill arising on acquisition

Negative goodwill arises when the cost of an acquired business is less than the aggregate fair values of the identifiable assets and liabilities within that business. Typically negative goodwill is attributed to either:

- *a bargain purchase:* the acquirer has managed to purchase the assets at less than their fair values, perhaps because the vendor needed to achieve a quick sale; or
- *future costs or losses:* the purchase price has been reduced to take account of future costs, such as reorganisation costs, or losses that do not represent identifiable liabilities at the balance sheet date.

Step 1: Review fair values assigned to identified assets and liabilities
Bargain purchases are not necessarily as common as optimistic acquirers might believe them to be. Therefore, IAS 38, *Intangible Assets*, suggests that the existence of negative goodwill may indicate that identifiable assets have been overstated and identifiable liabilities have been omitted or understated. When negative goodwill arises, a review of the fair value exercise is generally in order. (IAS 22(r1998).60)

The most subjective asset values are likely to be those of certain types of intangible assets, i.e. those for which an active market does not exist. So

IAS 38 restricts the values assigned to such intangible assets to amounts that do not increase or create negative goodwill. See *Example 10.28* in **10.7.7.**

IAS 22 (r1998) appears to encourage an approach whereby assets with subjective values (i.e. the non-monetary assets) are assigned conservative fair values and a lower amount is attributed to negative goodwill. It might be possible to eliminate the negative goodwill altogether, which would make the balance sheet presentation and subsequent accounting simpler and, as explained below, would not normally impact on future profits: although there would be no income on releasing negative goodwill, there would be increased margins on the sale or use of the assets. This does not however, mean that assets should ever be stated at less than reasonably objective fair values: to do so would breach the measurement requirements of IAS 22 (r1998) (see **18.6.4**) and overstate the profits on sale or use of these assets.

Step 2: Identify negative goodwill relating to future losses and expenses

As discussed above, negative goodwill generally arises due to future losses or expenses which do not meet the recognition criteria for a liability at the date of exchange. When these losses and expenses are identified in the acquirer's plan for the acquisition and can be measured reliably, an equivalent amount of negative goodwill is recognised as income in the income statement in the period when the future losses and expenses are recognised. If the future losses and expenses do not materialise as planned, the associated negative goodwill is treated as any other residual negative goodwill as described in step 3. (IAS 22(r1998).61)

Step 3: Deal with the remainder

After steps 1 and 2 have been completed, any remaining negative goodwill is treated in one of two ways:

- the amount which does not exceed the fair values of acquired non-monetary assets should be recognised as income on a systematic basis over the remaining weighted average useful life of the identifiable acquired depreciable/amortisable assets. Such negative goodwill is a gain which is recognised as income when the future economic benefits embodied in the identifiable depreciable/amortisable assets acquired are consumed; and
- the amount in excess of the fair values of acquired identifiable non-monetary assets is recognised as income immediately. The gain on this type of negative goodwill relates to monetary assets and therefore is recognised immediately. However, this type of negative goodwill is expected to be extremely rare in practice.

(IAS 22(r1998).62)

10.6.5 *Presentation*

Negative goodwill is presented as a deduction from assets in the same balance sheet classification as goodwill. (IAS 22(r1998).64)

IAS 1 (r1997), *Presentation of Financial Statements*, requires that, at a minimum, a line item representing intangible assets is included on the face of the balance sheet. Therefore, several possibilities exist for the presentation of negative goodwill. It may be:

- included in intangible assets on the face of the balance sheet and shown in the notes as a deduction from the other intangible assets;
- included within goodwill on the face of the balance sheet, if goodwill is shown on the face of the balance sheet; or
- it may be presented as a deduction from the line item including goodwill on the face of the balance sheet.

The magnitude of the negative goodwill will be the largest factor in determining the most appropriate presentation.

Example 10.26

Sample excerpt from balance sheet

		1998
		£
ASSETS		
Non-current assets		
Property, plant and equipment		133
Intangible assets		
Development costs		19
Goodwill	80	
Negative goodwill	(25)	
		55
Investment in associates		60
		267

IAS 22 (r1998) does not prescribe where on the income statement the gain on the release of negative goodwill is to be presented. However, as discussed in the next section, disclosure is required of the income statement line item in which the release of negative goodwill is included.

Given that negative goodwill is treated as a 'negative asset' on the balance sheet, it could be argued that consistency would best be achieved by offsetting the amortisation of negative goodwill against the heading in which any positive goodwill amortisation is charged. However, if the amount of negative goodwill offset against the positive amortisation charge were material, it would be necessary to disclose it separately within the total to avoid breaching the requirements of IAS 1 (r1997) not to offset positive and negative items.

10.6.6 Disclosure

The financial statements should disclose:

(a) a description, the amount and the timing of the expected future losses and expenses where negative goodwill is being recognised in the income statement when such losses and expenses occur;
(b) the period(s) over which negative goodwill is recognised as income;
(c) the line item(s) of the income statement in which negative goodwill is recognised as income; and
(d) a reconciliation of the carrying amount of negative goodwill at the beginning and end of the period showing:
    (i) the gross amount of negative goodwill and the accumulated amount of negative goodwill already recognised as income, at the beginning of the period;
    (ii) any additional negative goodwill recognised during the period;
    (iii) any adjustments resulting from subsequent identification or changes in value of identifiable assets and liabilities;
    (iv) any negative goodwill derecognised on the disposal of all or part of the business to which it relates during the period;
    (v) negative goodwill recognised as income during the period, showing separately the portion of negative goodwill recognised as income when the identified related losses and expenses were recognised;
    (vi) other changes in the carrying amount during the period (if any); and
    (vii) the gross amount of negative goodwill and the accumulated amount of negative goodwill already recognised as income, at the end of the period.

Comparative information is not required for this reconciliation.

(IAS 22 (r1998).91)

10.6.7 Transitional provisions

Due to the fact that IAS 22 has been amended several times, the transitional provisions are many and confusing. IAS 22 (r1998) includes a table to clarify how the transitional provisions work in various scenarios.

Broadly:

(1) Negative goodwill written off to reserves during accounting periods beginning before 1 January 1995 may either be:
   (a) left in reserves; or
   (b) brought onto the balance sheet as a negative asset. If it is restated:
      (i) a prior period adjustment is made in accordance with IAS 8 (r1993), Net Profit or Loss for the Period, Fundamental Errors and Changes in Accounting Policies (see **5.17**);
      (ii) the amount included as a negative asset on the balance sheet is net of any amounts recognised as income which would have accumulated from the date of acquisition to the date of the restatement; and
      (iii) the amount of negative goodwill will need to be calculated using the rules on assigning fair values to identifiable assets and liabilities included in IAS 22 (r1998).
(2) Negative goodwill recognised on the balance sheet as deferred income during accounting periods beginning before 1 January 1995 which is not calculated in accordance with IAS 22 (r1998) may be either:
   (c) unadjusted and deemed to be recorded correctly; or
   (d) adjusted to the amount which would have been calculated had the rules on assigning fair values to identifiable assets and liabilities included in IAS 22 (r1998) been in effect at the date of acquisition. The adjustment and any consequential adjustment to the related accumulated amount of negative goodwill that would have been recognised as income would be shown as a prior period adjustment;
(3) For negative goodwill arising during accounting periods beginning on or after 1 January 1995 and for which:
   (e) the benchmark treatment in IAS 22 (r1993) was adopted, (i.e., the fair values of the identifiable non-monetary assets acquired were reduced to eliminate the excess):
      (i) restatement of negative goodwill is encouraged, but not required. If the restatement route is chosen, negative goodwill arising on all acquisitions after 1 January 1995 is required. If restatement is chosen:
         (1) determine the amount which would have been assigned to negative goodwill at the date of acquisition and adjust it for the related accumulated amount of negative goodwill that would have been recognised in income under IAS 22 (r1993) (i.e., the 20 year maximum limit on negative goodwill applies); and
         (2) recognise any remaining negative goodwill as income over the remaining weighted average useful life of the identifiable depreciable/amortisable non-monetary assets acquired). See (5) below.
   (f) the allowed alternative treatment in IAS 22 (r1993) was adopted,

(i.e., the fair values of the identifiable non-monetary assets acquired were not reduced to eliminate the excess):

(i) if the negative goodwill has been calculated in accordance with the rules on assigning fair values to identifiable assets and liabilities included in IAS 22 (r1998), no adjustment to initial carrying amount required. However, the related accumulated amounts recognised as income may need to be revised. See 4 or 5 below;

(ii) if the negative goodwill has *not* been calculated in accordance with the rules on assigning fair values to identifiable assets and liabilities included in IAS 22 (r1998), determine the amount which would have been assigned and adjust it for the related accumulated amount of negative goodwill that would have been recognised in income under IAS 22 (r1993) (i.e., the 20 year maximum limit on negative goodwill applies). Recognise any remaining negative goodwill as income, (i.e. recognise as income over the remaining weighted average useful life of the identifiable depreciable/amortisable non-monetary assets acquired). See (5) below.

(4) If negative goodwill was recognised in the balance sheet in periods prior to the adoption of IAS 22 (r1998) but not subsequently recognised as income, the carrying amount of the negative goodwill should be restated as if the amount of negative goodwill recognised as income had always been determined under IAS 22 (r1998) and reflected as a prior period adjustment.

(5) If negative goodwill was previously recognised in the balance sheet and recognised as income, do not restate the carrying amount of negative goodwill for any difference between accumulated amounts recognised as income as calculated in prior years and that which would be calculated under IAS 22 (r1998). Instead, treat the change as a change in estimate and recognise any remaining carrying amount of the negative goodwill as income over the remaining weighted average useful life of the identifiable depreciable/amortisable non-monetary assets acquired.

10.6.8 Comparison with UK GAAP

Under FRS 10, *Goodwill and Intangible Assets,* when negative goodwill arises on an acquisition, an impairment review is required of the assets acquired. While IAS 22 (r1998) recommends such a review, it is not mandatory.

FRS 10 is similar to IAS 22 (r1998) in that both Standards treat negative goodwill as a negative asset. However, FRS 10 is more specific in its presentation requirements than IAS 22 (r1998). FRS 10 requires negative goodwill to be shown separately on the face of the balance sheet, immediately below the goodwill heading and followed by a subtotal showing the net amount of positive and negative goodwill.

Unlike under IAS 22 (r1998), negative goodwill which can be identified as relating to future costs or losses is not released as income when those costs/losses occur. Instead, negative goodwill up to the values of the non-monetary assets acquired is recognised as income over the period in which the non-monetary assets are recovered. Where the non-monetary assets are being depreciated, the negative goodwill will be released over the same period as that used for depreciation purposes. Where the non-monetary assets are intended for sale, the negative goodwill will be released as they are sold. FRS 10 does not prescribe how negative goodwill in excess of the fair values of the non-monetary asset is treated. Rather, it simply states that the negative goodwill should be released over the periods expected to be benefited and requires the source of the negative goodwill and the reasons for the period of its release to be explained. While these requirements are somewhat similar to those of IAS 22 (r1998), differences will arise in practice.

10.6.9 Comparison with US GAAP

US GAAP takes a completely different approach from IAS 22 (r1998) to the recognition of negative goodwill. Statement 141, *Business Combinations*, provides that negative goodwill must be:

> 'allocated as a pro rata reduction of the amounts that otherwise would have been assigned to all of the acquired assets except (a) financial assets other than investments accounted for by the equity method, (b) assets to be disposed of by sale, (c) deferred tax assets, (d) prepaid assets relating to pension or other post-retirement benefit plans, and (e) any other current assets.'

Further:

> 'if any negative goodwill remains after reducing to zero the amounts that otherwise would have been assigned to those assets, that remaining excess shall be recognised as an extraordinary gain as described in paragraph 11 of APB Opinion No. 30, *Reporting the Results of Operations—Reporting the Effects of Disposal of a Segment of a Business, and Extraordinary, Unusual and Infrequently Occurring Events and Transactions*. The extraordinary gain shall be recognised in the period in which the business combination is completed unless the combination involves contingent consideration that, if paid or issued, would be recognised as an additional element of cost of the acquired entity. If an extraordinary gain is recognised before the end of the period, any subsequent adjustments to that extraordinary gain that result from changes to the purchase price allocation shall be recognised as an extraordinary item.'

Statement 141 also addresses the issue of contingent consideration when negative goodwill remains after the business combination.

> 'If a business combination involves a contingent consideration agreement that might result in recognition of an additional element of cost of the acquired entity when the contingency is resolved (a contingency based on earnings), an amount equal to the lesser of the maximum amount of contingent consideration or the excess shall be recognised as if it was a liability. When the contingency is resolved and the consideration is issued or becomes issuable, any excess of the fair value of the contingent consideration issued or issuable over the amount that was recognised as if it was a liability shall be recognised as an additional cost of the acquired entity. If the amount initially recognised as if it was a liability exceeds the fair value of the consideration issued or issuable, that excess shall be allocated as a pro rata reduction of the amounts assigned to assets acquired. Any amount that remains after reducing those assets to zero shall be recognised as an extraordinary gain.'

10.6.10 Example from published financial statements

Note that the excerpts given do not always comply in full with all aspects of IAS and as such are not necessarily examples of best practice but merely of current practice.

Example 10.27

1.9 Negative goodwill

Any negative goodwill that arises where the fair value of the group's interest in the identifiable assets and liabilities of the subsidiary exceed the cost of acquisition is taken to profit. It is taken to profit immediately in the case of an expectation of future losses or in respect of monetary assets. To the extent that negative goodwill relates to depreciable assets, it is recognised as profit over the useful life of those assets.

Barlow Limited
South Africa
30 September 2000
International Accounting Standards

10.7 Intangible assets

10.7.1 Source

IAS 36	*Impairment of Assets.*
IAS 38	*Intangible Assets.*
SIC-6	*Costs of Modifying Existing Software.*

10.7.2 Brief summary of requirements

IAS 38 requires an enterprise to recognise an intangible asset at cost if, and only if, it is probable that the future economic benefits that are attributable to the asset will flow to the enterprise and the cost of the asset can be measured reliably. These criteria apply to both internally generated assets and those purchased, although additional criteria apply to internally generated intangible assets. However, internally generated goodwill cannot be capitalised.

In very limited circumstances, IAS 38 allows intangible assets to be revalued in a similar manner to items of property, plant and equipment.

IAS 38 requires an intangible asset to be amortised over its estimated useful life. There is a rebuttable presumption that the useful life of an intangible asset will not exceed 20 years from initial recognition. This presumption may be overcome with the result that the intangible is amortised over a period exceeding 20 years. However, when the useful life of an intangible is estimated to be longer than 20 years, an annual impairment test must be carried out in accordance with IAS 36 (see **10.12**).

The following table summarises the situation:

Capitalise as goodwill	*Capitalise as intangible assets*	*Do not capitalise*
(1) Purchased goodwill.	(1) Intangible assets purchased separately from a business.	(1) Internally generated goodwill.
(2) Intangible assets purchased with a business if they are not identifiable as distinct from the goodwill or their values cannot be measured reliably.	(2) Intangible assets purchased with a business providing they are identifiable as distinct from the goodwill and their values can be measured reliably.	
	(3) Internally developed intangible assets which meet definition of an intangible asset and the recognition criteria in paragraphs 19 and 45 of IAS 38.	(2) Internally developed intangible assets which do not meet the definition of an intangible asset or the recognition criteria in paragraphs 19 and 45 of IAS 38.

10.7.3 Development of the requirements

Issued in 1998, IAS 38 required two exposure drafts due to the varying practices related to intangible assets around the world. The IASC Board structured IAS 38 in a manner very similar to IAS 16 (r1998), *Property, Plant and Equipment*, and aligned the requirements for intangible assets closely with those for goodwill.

When revising IAS 22, *Business Combinations*, in 1998, the IASC Board intentionally set very similar rules for the amortisation of intangible assets (included in IAS 38) and goodwill to curb accounting arbitrage between goodwill and other intangible assets since it is often difficult to distinguish between the two. Only two differences exist between the requirements for goodwill and for other intangible assets:

(1) IAS 38 permits the revaluation of intangible assets, while IAS 22 (r1998) does not permit goodwill to be revalued; and
(2) in certain circumstances, IAS 38 requires a residual value to be estimated when determining the depreciable amount of an intangible asset. IAS 22 (r1998) does not entertain the notion of a residual value for goodwill. The IASC Board does not believe that the above two differences will result in significant differences in practice since the revaluation of intangible assets and intangible assets with residual values are expected to be rare.

IAS 38 supersedes IAS 9, although the changes introduced by IAS 38 to research and development costs are peripheral in nature and should not lead to changes in practice. IAS 38 also supersedes IAS 4 with respect to the amortisation of intangible assets.

10.7.4 Scope

IAS 38 does not apply to:

(1) intangible assets that are covered by another IAS, for example:
   (a) intangible assets held by an enterprise for sale in the ordinary course of business (IAS 2 (r1993), *Inventories*, see **10.9** or IAS 11 (r1993), *Construction Contracts*, see Chapter **27**);
   (b) deferred tax assets (IAS 12 (r2000), *Income Taxes*, see Chapter **23**);
   (c) leases that fall within the scope of IAS 17 (r1997), *Leases* (see Chapter **24**);
   (d) assets arising from employee benefits (IAS 19 (r2000), *Employee Benefits* (see Chapter **25**); and
   (e) goodwill arising on a business combination (IAS 22 (r1998), *Business Combinations*, see Chapter **18**);
(2) financial assets (which are dealt with in IAS 27, *Consolidated Financial Statements and Accounting for Investments in Subsidiaries*, IAS 28 (r2000), *Accounting for Investments in Associates*, IAS 31 (r2000), *Financial Reporting of Interests in Joint Ventures*, IAS 32 (r1998), *Financial Instruments: Disclosure and Presentation* and IAS 39 (r2000), *Financial Instruments: Recognition and Measurement*, see Chapters **19**, **20**, **21** and **12**);
(3) mineral rights and expenditure on the exploration for, or development and extraction of, minerals, oil, natural gas and similar non-regenerative resources (separate IASB project underway); and
(4) intangible assets arising in insurance enterprises from contracts with policyholders (separate IASB project underway).

(IAS 38.1 and 2)

When an intangible asset is contained in or on a physical substance such as computer software on a compact disk or a motion picture on film, management must assess which element is more significant. For example software which controls machinery would normally be considered an integral part of the machinery and therefore would be treated as property, plant and equipment rather than an intangible asset. The same would normally be true for the operating system of a computer. Where the software does not form an integral part of the machinery or computer hardware to which it relates, it is separately accounted for under IAS 38. (IAS 38.3)

10.7.5 Definition of an intangible asset

> 'An intangible asset is an identifiable non-monetary asset without physical substance held for use in the production or supply of goods or services, for rental to others, or for administrative purposes.'
>
> (IAS 38.7)

There are several components of this definition which should be considered:

(1) identifiability;
(2) non-monetary; and
(3) asset (the definition of which encompasses control).

Identifiability

In a business acquisition, it is often difficult to determine whether an intangible item qualifies for recognition as an intangible asset or whether it is merely part of goodwill. The word 'identifiable' in the definition is intended to help in such situations. In some countries such as the UK, in order to qualify for separate recognition as an asset, the intangible item must be separable, or capable of being rented, sold, exchanged or distributed, without also disposing of a business of the enterprise. While an asset which is separable meets the identifiability criteria in the definition of an intangible asset in IAS 38, there are other ways to meet the identifiability criteria. For example, a legal right, such as a broadcasting license, may give rise to future benefits which are 'identifiable' under IAS 38 even if they are not separable from the underlying broadcasting business, since it is unlikely that the broadcasting license could be sold without disposing of the underlying broadcasting business. In other words, the separability criterion prescribed in the UK is more restrictive than that of identifiability.

In summary, an individual intangible asset should be recognised, even if the asset is *not* separable from the business in which it is used, as long as:

(1) the asset is identifiable;
(2) it is probable that the asset, albeit in combination with other assets, will generate future economic benefits; and
(3) the cost of the asset can be measured reliably.[1]

[1] Basis for Conclusions: *IAS 38, Intangible Assets*; IAS 22 (Revised 1998) *Business Combinations*; and Summary of Changes to E60 and IAS 22. A document prepared by the IASC Stff; Paragraph 28(b).

Non-Monetary

> 'Monetary assets are money held and assets to be received in fixed or determinable amounts of money.'
>
> (IAS 38.7)

Assets which do not meet this definition are considered non-monetary. Non-monetary assets include *inter alia*:

- items of property, plant and equipment;
- research and development costs;
- patents;
- licences; and
- brands.

Asset (control)

The Framework and IAS 38 define an asset as 'a resource controlled by the enterprise as a result of past events and from which future economic benefits are expected to flow to the enterprise.' (Framework.49) In the context of intangible assets, it is sometimes difficult to determine whether or not an enterprise can exert *control* over the expected future benefits. Control in this context means that the entity has a right to the economic benefits that the asset will generate and can restrict the access of other to those benefits.

Normally, control of an intangible asset is achieved through legal rights: a brand name is protected by a trademark, a publishing title by copyright, a licence by contract etc. Less frequently, an intangible asset may be controlled merely through custody: a product formulation or intellectual property may be controlled simply by keeping it a secret from outsiders.

Certain intangible items of value to an entity may not be controlled by it. For example, it is unusual for an entity to have control over its employees: usually employee contracts can be terminated with a short period of notice and without penalty. Therefore, when a business combination is accounted for as an acquisition, the benefit of an assembled workforce is more likely to fall to be treated as goodwill than as an intangible asset since the workforce cannot normally be controlled.

Exceptions do however occur. For example, the transfer fees paid for footballers secure rights to their services for a number of years. Such fees could be potentially treated as giving rise to intangible assets.

Similarly, an established customer base is not usually controlled by the entity: there may be an expectation that customers will continue to buy from the entity, but usually, they are under no obligation to do so. The value of a customer base will therefore normally be treated as goodwill rather than as a separate intangible asset.

For example, in some industries, such as those providing mobile telephone services, one service provider may purchase subscriber bases from another. The price paid for the subscriber bases usually exceeds the value of the existing contracts, the difference representing the expectation that existing subscribers will renew their contracts. This difference may not represent a separable intangible asset in its own right if the existing customers are under no obligation to renew their contracts.

Comparison with UK GAAP
At first, the definitions of an intangible asset included in FRS 10, *Goodwill and Intangible Assets,* and IAS 37 appear very similar. However, there is an important distinction in the interpretation of one key word, 'identifiability.' FRS 10 defines an intangible asset as one that does not have physical substance but is identifiable and is controlled by the entity through custody or legal rights. An identifiable asset is defined by UK companies legislation as one that can be disposed of separately without disposing of a business of the entity. In IAS terminology, this characteristic is referred to as separability. As discussed above, the IAS definition includes a requirement that an asset be identifiable; however, identifiable is defined more broadly than it is in FRS 10. See discussion under **'Identifiability'** above. Therefore, assets which may meet the definition of an intangible asset under IAS 37 may not meet the definition included in FRS 10.

Comparison with US GAAP
US GAAP, as set out principally in FASB Statement No. 141, *Business Combinations* ('Statement 141'), and FASB Statement 142, *Goodwill and Other Intangible Assets* ('Statement 142'). Under these statements, an identifiable intangible asset shall be recognised as an asset apart from goodwill if it arises from contractual or other legal rights (regardless of whether those rights are transferable or separable from the acquired entity or from other rights and obligations). If an intangible asset does not arise from contractual or other legal rights, it shall be recognised as an asset apart from goodwill only if it is separable, that is, it is capable of being separated or divided from the acquired entity and sold, transferred, licensed, rented, or exchanged (regardless of whether there is an intent to do so). An intangible asset that cannot be sold, transferred, licensed, rented or exchanged individually is considered separable if it can be sold, transferred, licensed, rented, or exchanged in combination with a related contract, asset, or liability. Statement 142 carries forward the guidance under APB 17, *Intangible Assets,* which does state that internally generated intangible assets are not specifically identifiable and are expensed as incurred.

Certain items under the new statements would be unlikely to meet the definition of an intangible asset under IAS 38 since they would not be considered to be 'controlled' by the enterprise. Therefore, in practice differences may arise between which intangible assets are recognised when a business combination is accounted for as an acquisition under IAS and US GAAP.

10.7.6 Recognition

An intangible asset may only be recognised if it:

(1) meets the definition of an intangible asset (see **10.7.5**);
(2) is probable that the future economic benefits that are attributable to the asset will flow to the enterprise; and
(3) is capable of being reliably measured (see **10.7.7**).

(IAS 38.18 and 19)

Otherwise, costs related to intangible items are expensed when incurred. (IAS 38.56)

Additional criteria must be met in order to recognise internally generated intangible assets (see **10.7.8**).

Comparison with UK GAAP and US GAAP
The differences arising around when recognition of an intangible asset is appropriate stem from the definition of an intangible asset and are discussed in **10.7.5.**

10.7.7 Measurement

Intangible assets are initially recorded at cost. (IAS 38.22) Specific guidance is included on the measurement of cost in the following specific situations:

(1) separate acquisition;
(2) acquisition as part of a business combination;
(3) acquisition by way of a government grant;
(4) exchange of assets; and
(5) internally generated intangible assets (see **10.7.8**).

Separate acquisition
When an intangible asset is purchased and the consideration given is in the form of cash or other monetary assets, the determination of cost is relatively straight forward. The cost of the intangible asset includes:

(1) purchase price;
(2) import duties;
(3) non-refundable purchase taxes; and
(4) any directly attributable expenditure on preparing the asset for its intended use, for example professional fees for legal services.

Any trade discounts taken or rebates received are deducted in the calculation of the cost of the asset. (IAS 38.24)

If the payment of consideration is deferred, the asset is recorded at the equivalent cash price and the difference between this amount and the amount actually paid is treated as interest expense and either expensed or capitalised in accordance with circumstances and the accounting policy of the enterprise (see **10.4**). (IAS 38.25)

If the purchase consideration for the intangible asset is satisfied by the issuance of equity instruments of the reporting enterprise, the cost of the intangible asset is recorded at the fair value of the equity instruments. (IAS 38.26)

Acquisition as part of a business combination

When a business combination is accounted for as an acquisition, even if an intangible asset has not been previously recorded by the acquiree, the acquirer recognises an intangible asset when the definition and recognition criteria for an intangible asset are met. If the recognition criteria are not met, the asset is not recognised separately but is included as part of goodwill. (IAS 38.31)

An identifiable asset acquired in a business combination is recorded at its fair value determined as follows:

(1) By reference to an active market (see **10.7.11** for a definition of an active market). While quoted market prices (current bid price) in an active market provide the most reliable measurement of fair value, for many intangible assets, no such market exists. If there has been a similar recent transaction, it may provide a basis on which to determine fair value as long as there has not been a significant change in economic circumstances since the date of the original transaction; (IAS 38.28) or

(2) If no active market exists, the fair value reflects the amount the enterprise would have paid in an arm's length transaction between knowledgeable and willing parties, based on the best information available. (IAS 38.29) In certain industries where unique intangible assets are regularly traded techniques have been developed for estimating their fair values indirectly. Such techniques may be used if their objective is to estimate fair value and if they reflect current transactions and practices in the industry. Such techniques include applying multiples reflecting current market transactions to certain indicators driving the profitability of the asset or discounting estimated future net cash flows from the asset. (IAS 38.30) However, if there is no active market for an intangible asset, its cost is limited to an amount that does not create or increase any negative goodwill arising at the date of acquisition. (IAS 38.32)

Example 10.28

Enterprise A acquires Enterprise B. Enterprise B publishes newspapers and has several established titles or 'mastheads' to which Enterprise A is assigning a fair value as part of its acquisition accounting. Since each masthead is individual, no active market exists for mastheads. However, in the publishing industry, mastheads are often bought and sold with the sales price based on a multiple of the current year's operating profit. The multiple is based on the industry or geographic segment in which the masthead operates.

Enterprise A assigns a multiple of 11 to the masthead obtained through the acquisition of Enterprise B. The newspaper involved had operating profits of £1million in the year before purchase. Therefore, the fair value tentatively assigned to the masthead intangible asset is £11 million.

The fair value of the other net assets acquired is £50 million and the purchase consideration is £55 million. Therefore, before taking the masthead intangible asset into account, the goodwill arising on the acquisition is £5 million.

When the intangible asset is added to the £50 million of other net assets, negative goodwill of £6 million (£50m + £11 m – £55 m) arises on the acquisition. Since the masthead is not an intangible which is traded on an active market, its fair value cannot create or increase negative goodwill. Therefore, the fair value assigned to the masthead is limited to £5m (– £6m + £11m).

Acquisition by way of a government grant

Sometimes an intangible asset may be granted to an enterprise free of charge or for nominal consideration by a government. This may be the case for assets such as airport landing rights, broadcasting licences, import licences or quotas, or rights to access other restricted resources. Under IAS 20, *Accounting for Government Grants and Disclosure of Government Assistance*, paragraph 23 (see Chapter **26**), an enterprise may either record both the grant and the intangible asset at its fair value or record both the intangible asset and the grant at a nominal amount which includes any expenditure that is directly attributable to preparing the asset for its intended use. (IAS 38.33)

Exchanges of assets

When an intangible asset is acquired in exchange or part exchange for a *dissimilar* intangible asset or other asset, the asset received is measured at its fair value which is the equivalent of the fair value of the asset given up adjusted for any cash or cash equivalents transferred. (IAS 38.34)

However, in the very rare situation when an intangible asset is exchanged for a *similar* intangible asset or other asset, the earnings process is not considered complete; and therefore, no gain or loss is recognised on the sale. The asset acquired is measured at the carrying value of the asset given up. A similar intangible asset is one which is:

(a) used in the same line of business; and
(b) of a similar fair value.

An exchange of an intangible asset for an equity interest in a similar intangible asset may be considered an exchange of similar assets if the other criteria for similar assets are met, and thus no gain or loss is recognised on the exchange.

If the fair value of a similar asset received is less than the carrying value of the asset given up, it may indicate that the carrying value of the asset given up is impaired. In such cases, the carrying value of the asset given up is written down prior to the exchange. The asset acquired is then carried at the new, written-down carrying amount of the asset given up.

Comparison with UK GAAP

The initial measurement rules under FRS 10, *Goodwill and Intangible Assets*, are quite similar to those in IAS 38 for intangible assets purchased either singly or as part of a business combination and differences in practice should be uncommon. However, if an intangible asset, such as an airport landing right, is received by way of government grant, IAS encourages use of a fair value measurement (but would accept recording a nominal amount), whereas UK GAAP has no specific requirement and practice tends towards recording such a right at its nominal value rather than assigning a fair value.

As opposed to the specific requirements of IAS 38 which deal with exchanges of similar intangible assets (where no gain or loss is recognised) and dissimilar intangible assets (where a gain or loss is recognised), under UK GAAP, specific requirements related to such exchanges do not exist. As a result, current practice varies as to whether or not a gain or loss on disposal has been realised when an exchange takes place with the prudence concept dictating that gains are rarely recognised on the exchange of intangible assets unless they are clearly dissimilar.

Comparison with US GAAP

The initial measurement rules under US GAAP are quite similar to those in IAS 38 for intangible assets purchased either singly or when received as a government grant. However, if an intangible asset is acquired as part of a business combination, and the intangible asset is not traded in an active market, IAS 38 limits the amount which can be assigned to the intangible asset to an amount which does not create or increase negative goodwill. Statements 141 and 142 do not contain such a restriction. The asset would be valued at its fair value.

Under US GAAP as set out in APB 29, *Accounting for Non-Monetary Transactions*, EITF Abstract 86–29, *Non-Monetary Transactions: Magnitude of Boot and the Exceptions to the Use of Fair Value*, and EITF 00-5, *Determining Whether a Non-Monetary Transaction Is an Exchange of Similar Productive Assets*, the technical requirements relating to exchanges of similar assets vary somewhat from those of IAS 16 (r1998) and these variations could lead to material differences.

10.7.8 Internally generated intangible assets

As noted above, IAS 38 includes additional recognition criteria for internally generated intangible assets which expand on the general recognition criteria. It is assumed that these additional criteria are met implicitly whenever an enterprise acquires an intangible asset.

Which internally generated intangible assets can be capitalised?
Certain internally generated intangible assets are specifically identified in IAS 38 as not being capable of being distinguished from the cost of developing the business as a whole and therefore are banned from being capitalised as *internally* generated intangible assets. Such assets include:

- brands;
- mastheads;
- publishing titles;
- customer lists; and
- items similar in substance to any of the above.

(IAS 38.51)

Although IAS 38 bans these items from recognition as internally generated assets, when such an asset is purchased either individually or as part of a business combination, it may meet the general recognition criteria for intangible assets and therefore potentially may be recognised. This difference will allow certain acquired items, such as a brand, to be capitalised but require it to be expensed if it is internally generated. Therefore, similar items may be treated differently among various enterprises.

Given the types of assets specifically excluded, the recognition of internally generated intangible assets should be uncommon. Most items which meet the additional criteria will be the types of development assets which were previously recognised under IAS 9 (r1993), *Research and Development Costs (withdrawn).*

The Standard distinguishes between two phases within the generation of an internal intangible asset: the research phase and the development phase. Capitalisation is only permitted during the development phase. The additional recognition criteria are discussed under **'Development phase'** below.

Distinction between research and development

In colloquial speech, the terms research and development are often used interchangeably. However, in the context of IAS 38, an important distinction lies between research and development.

> 'Research is original and planned investigation undertaken with the prospect of gaining new scientific or technical knowledge and understanding.'
>
> (IAS 38.7)

Whereas, 'development is the ***application*** (emphasis added) of research findings or other knowledge to a plan or design for the production of new or substantially improved materials, devices, products, processes, systems or services prior to the commencement of commercial production or use.' (IAS 38.7)

The following examples given in the IAS of research activities illustrate the fact that the main objective of research activities is the discovery of something new:

> '(a) activities aimed at obtaining new knowledge;
> (b) the search for, evaluation and final selection of, applications of research findings or other knowledge;
> (c) the search for alternatives for materials, devices, products, processes, systems or services; and
> (d) the formulation, design, evaluation and final selection of possible alternatives for new or improved materials, devices, products, processes, systems or services.'
>
> (IAS 38.44)

The following examples of development activities illustrate the fact that the main objective of development activities is to apply research findings for a business purpose:

> '(a) the design, construction and testing of pre-production or pre-use prototypes and models;
> (b) the design of tools, jigs, moulds and dies involving new technology;
> (c) the design, construction and operation of a pilot plant that is not of a scale economically feasible for commercial production; and
> (d) the design, construction and testing of a chosen alternative for new or improved materials, devices, products, processes, systems or services.'
>
> (IAS 38.47)

Research phase

Research costs are, by their nature, incurred with the intent of gaining new knowledge rather than creating a practical application from which future economic benefits will flow. Therefore, research costs will not meet the criteria for recognition of an internally generated asset. Therefore, costs incurred during the research phase are required to be expensed. (IAS 38.42)

Development phase (additional recognition criteria)

In some cases, during the development phase of a project, an enterprise will be able to identify an intangible asset and demonstrate that the asset will generate probable future economic benefits. This is due to the fact that the development stage is further advanced than the research phase. (IAS 38.46) However, as noted above, criteria in addition to those for externally acquired intangible assets must be met to recognise an internally generated intangible asset. Specifically, an intangible asset arising from development (or from the development phase of an internal project) should be recognised if, and only if, an enterprise can demonstrate all of the following:

> '(a) the technical feasibility of completing the intangible asset so that it will be available for use or sale;
> (b) its intention to complete the intangible asset and use or sell it;
> (c) its ability to use or sell the intangible asset;
> (d) how the intangible asset will generate probable future economic benefits. Among other things, the enterprise should demonstrate the existence of a market for the output of the intangible asset or the intangible asset itself or, if it is to be used internally, the usefulness of the intangible asset;
> (e) the availability of adequate technical, financial and other resources to complete the development and to use or sell the intangible asset; and
> (f) its ability to measure the expenditure attributable to the intangible asset during its development reliably.'
>
> (IAS 38.45)

IAS 38 does not provide any guidance in respect of criterion (a) on when technical feasibility is established. While it is difficult to set one guideline due to the differing types of internally generated intangible assets, when the asset is the fruit of 'traditional' research and development activities or software development activities, an appropriate point may be when the enterprise has completed all the planning, designing and testing activities that are necessary to establish that an asset can be produced to meet its design specifications including functions, features and technical performance requirements.

In respect of criterion (d), IAS 38 recommends that an enterprise can demonstrate that the asset will generate future economic benefits by using the principles in IAS 36 relating to the estimation of future cash flows. As discussed in more detail in **10.12.11**, cash flow projections should be based on reasonable and supportable assumptions that represent management's best estimate of the set of economic conditions that will exist over the useful life of the asset, with greater weight given to external evidence. Such projections should not normally cover a period of more than five years. The cash flows should be discounted using a pre-tax rate that reflects current market assessments of the time value of money and the risks specific to the asset. If the internally generated intangible asset will only produce economic benefits together with other assets, for example new computer software which will significantly reduce overhead costs, its cash flows cannot be independently assessed.

Therefore, it is included in its cash generating unit and the unit as a whole is evaluated. See **10.12.10** for further discussion of cash generating units.

Criterion (e) will normally be met by a business plan which details the planned expenditure on the project and the resources which will be available to fund it. If the project is being financed externally, a lender's indication that it will finance the business plan may be sufficient. (IAS 38.49)

In order to meet criterion (f), an enterprise will need a cost system to track costs incurred related to the specific development project. In many cases, this will be a simple system based on the time sheets of the employees involved in the development of the intangible asset, but on more complex projects the system will also need to track direct expenses incurred as well.

Cost

The requirement that an intangible asset be initially recorded at its cost applies to internally generated intangible assets as well as purchased intangible assets. Cost includes all costs incurred from the date on which all of the recognition criteria (those for purchased as well as internally generated intangible assets) are met. If costs have been expensed in periods prior to the recognition criteria being met, they may *not* be reinstated upon satisfaction of the criteria. (IAS 38.53 and 59)

Similar to self-constructed items of property, plant and equipment, the cost of an internally generated intangible asset includes all directly attributable costs, as well as those allocated on a reasonable and consistent basis, of creating, producing and preparing the asset for its intended use. This cost may include:

(a) expenditure on materials and services used or consumed in generating the intangible asset;
(b) the salaries, wages and other employment related costs of personnel directly engaged in generating the asset;
(c) any expenditure that is directly attributable to generating the asset, such as fees to register a legal right and the amortisation of patents and licences that are used to generate the asset; and
(d) overheads that are necessary to generate the asset and that can be allocated on a reasonable and consistent basis to the asset (for example, an allocation of the depreciation of property, plant and equipment, insurance premiums and rent). Allocations of overheads are made on bases similar to those used in allocating overheads to inventories (see **10.9.6**). IAS 23 (r1993) establishes criteria for the recognition of interest as a component of the cost of an internally generated intangible asset (see **10.4**).

(IAS 38.54)

IAS 38 specifically prohibits the inclusion in the cost of an internally generated intangible asset of the following items:

(1) selling, administrative and other general overhead expenditure unless this expenditure can be directly attributed to preparing the asset for use;
(2) clearly identified inefficiencies and initial operating losses incurred before an asset achieves planned performance; and
(3) expenditure on training staff to operate the asset.

(IAS 38.55)

Research and development activities under contract for others

IAS 9 (r1993), *Research and Development Costs (withdrawn)*, which was superseded by IAS 38, included guidance on how to account for enterprises carrying out research and development activities under contract for others. While this guidance is not included in IAS 38, it may still be useful to enterprises which are in this situation and has been summarised below.

When enterprises carry out research and development activities for other enterprises, the substance of the arrangement dictates the accounting treatment of the research and development costs for both enterprises. If the enterprise carrying out the research and development activities is retaining the risks and rewards of the activities, it accounts for the costs of the research and development activities in accordance with IAS 38. However, if the enterprise carrying out the research and development activities is not retaining the risks and rewards of the activities and they lie with the other party, the enterprise carrying out the activities accounts for its costs in accordance with IAS 2, (r1993), *Inventories* (see Chapter **27**). The following factors may indicate that the risks and rewards of the research and development activities are retained by the enterprise carrying out the activities:

(a) the enterprise conducting the research and development activities is contractually obliged to repay any of the funds provided by the other enterprise, regardless of the outcome of the research and development activities; and
(b) even though the contract does not require the enterprise conducting the research and development activities to repay any of the funds provided by the other enterprise, repayment could be required at the option of the other enterprise or the surrounding conditions indicate that repayment is probable.

Websites

The SIC is currently addressing the issue of website development costs. SIC-D32, *Intangible Assets – Web Site Costs*, addresses the accounting for an internal expenditure to develop, enhance and maintain a web site by an enterprise for its own use. Specifically, it addresses the application of IAS 38, *Intangible Assets*, to website development costs.

SIC-D32 identifies the following stages of website development:

- planning;
- application and infrastructure development;
- graphical design and content development;
- operating.

SIC-D32 proposes that:

- A website developed by an enterprise for its own use is an internally generated intangible asset that is subject to the requirements of IAS 38.
- The planning stage of website development is similar in nature to the research phase described in IAS 38.42–44 and, therefore, an expenditure incurred in this stage should be recognised as an expense when it is incurred.
- The application and infrastructure development stage and the graphical design and content development stage of website development are similar in nature to the development phase in IAS 38.45–52. Therefore, expenditures incurred in these stages are eligible for recognition as an intangible asset if, first, they meet the general requirements of IAS 38 for recognition and initial measurement of an intangible asset and, second, the enterprise can demonstrate that the conditions in IAS 38.45 are met. In addition:
  - an enterprise may be able to demonstrate how its website will generate probable future economic benefits under IAS 38.45(d) by using the principles in IAS 36, Impairment of Assets. This includes situations where the website is developed solely or primarily for promoting and advertising an enterprise's own products and services; and
  - an enterprise may incur an expenditure to enable use of content, which had been purchased or created for another purpose, on its website (e.g., acquiring a license to reproduce information) or may purchase or create content specifically for use on its website prior to the website becoming available for use. In such circumstances, an enterprise should determine whether a separate asset is identifiable with respect to such content (e.g., copyrights and licences), and if a separate asset is not identifiable, then the expenditure should be included in the cost of developing the website when the expenditure meets the conditions in IAS 38.54.
- The operating stage commences once the website is available for use, and therefore an expenditure to maintain or enhance the website after development has been completed should be recognised as an expense when it is incurred unless it meets the criteria in IAS 38.60.

The Draft Interpretation was issued for public comment on 9 July 2001. The comment deadline was 10 September 2001.

Comparison with UK GAAP

Unlike IAS 38, under FRS 10, *Goodwill and Intangible Assets*, an internally generated intangible asset may only be recognised if it has a readily ascertainable market value. Under IAS 38, several additional criteria must be met to recognise an internally generated asset but having a readily ascertainable market value is not one of them. However, given the list in IAS 38 of intangible assets which may not be recognised when they are internally generated, in practice this should not lead to many differences.

FRS 10 does not include research and development costs in its scope. Research and development costs are covered in SSAP 13, *Accounting for Research and Development*. Similar to IAS 38, SSAP 13 requires that costs associated with research activities or projects be expensed as incurred. However, SSAP 13 allows a choice between capitalisation and recognition as an expense for development costs which meet certain criteria whereas IAS 38 *requires* capitalisation of development costs which meet certain criteria. Both standards require amortisation of capitalised development costs, although SSAP 13 does not include a rebuttable presumption that the useful life does not exceed 20 years as IAS 38 does.

Unlike IAS 38, SSAP 13 does not prohibit the reinstatement in the balance sheet of development costs expensed in periods before the asset recognition criteria were met. However, in practice, this reinstatement is rare.

In February 2001, the UITF issued UITF Abstract 29, *Website Development Costs*. The UITF concluded that, subject to the provisions below, website costs should be capitalised as tangible fixed assets under the provisions of FRS 15. This asset should then be subject to annual depreciation and reviews for impairment. The UITF states that the useful life of a website is inherently short, and the depreciation rate should reflect this.

The costs incurred in developing a website are divided into planning, application and infrastructure, design and contents costs. The UITF states that planning costs do not give rise to any future economic benefits for the company and should therefore be expensed as incurred.

Application and infrastructure, design and content costs of the website should be capitalised as tangible fixed assets in accordance with FRS 15. However, this treatment is only possible for design and content costs where the costs lead to the creation of an enduring asset (i.e., an asset to be used on a continuing basis), and it can be demonstrated that the entity will receive economic benefits at least as great as the amounts capitalised. The Abstract states that this will only be the case where:

(a) the expenditure is separately identifiable;
(b) the technical feasibility and commercial viability of the website have been assessed with reasonable certainty in the light of factors such as likely market conditions (including competing products), public opinion and possible legislation;
(c) the website will generate sales or other revenues directly and the expenditure makes an enduring contribution to the development of the revenue-generating capabilities of the website;
(d) there is a reasonable expectation that the present value of the future cash flows (i.e., future revenues less attributable costs) to be generated by the website will be no less than the amounts capitalised in respect of that revenue-generating activity; and
(e) adequate resources exist, or are reasonably expected to be available, to enable the website project to be completed and to meet any consequential need for increased working capital.

Comparison with US GAAP

Under SFAS 2 *Accounting for Research and Development Costs* both research and development costs are required to be expensed as incurred. However, certain costs related to the development of software and websites are required to be capitalised in accordance with SFAS 86 *Accounting for the Costs of Computer Software to Be Sold, Leased or Otherwise Marketed*, SOP 98-1, *Accounting for the Costs of Computer Software Developed or Obtained for Internal Use*, or EITF 00-2 *Accounting for Web Site Development Costs.*

The general requirement to write off expenditure on research and development as incurred extends to the situation where part of the price paid for an acquired business can be attributed to the value of research or development previously undertaken by the business. That part of the purchase price is charged through the consolidated income statement in the year of acquisition.

This has become a significant feature of acquisition accounting amongst the technology companies in the US. It has been said that acquirers have increasingly been attributing large proportions of the price of an acquisition to research and development, possibly in the belief that analysts might ignore the 'one-off' charge. The SEC has recently criticised some companies for attributing too much of the purchase price to research and development and the FASB is considering this aspect of acquisition accounting as part of its more general review of accounting for business combinations.

The requirements of IAS 22 (r1998), *Business Combinations*, would prohibit the costs of research and development purchased with a business from being written off as an expense at the date of acquisition. Rather, the costs should be capitalised as development expenditure if the recognition criteria are met, or otherwise form part of the residual goodwill. Thus, where a material portion of the value of an acquired business is attributed to the value of research or development, the value of goodwill under US GAAP may be different than the value measured under IAS 22 (r1998) and IAS 38.

10.7.9 Items to be recognised as an expense

As a general rule, expenditure related to intangible items should be expensed as incurred unless:

(1) it forms part of the capitalisable cost of an intangible asset which meets the appropriate definition and recognition criteria; or
(2) the item is acquired in a business acquisition and does not meet the criteria for separate recognition. In such cases, any cost which may be attributable to the item forms part of the goodwill or negative goodwill arising on the acquisition.

(IAS 38.56)

IAS 38 states that some types of expenditure will never fall into category (1) above and therefore should always be expensed. Such items include expenditure on:

(1) research;
(2) start-up activities, unless the expenditure is included in the cost of an item of property, plant and equipment. Start-up costs include:
    (a) establishment costs such as legal and secretarial costs incurred in establishing the legal entity;
    (b) pre-opening costs or expenditure to open a new facility or business;
(3) training activities;
(4) advertising and promotional activities; and
(5) relocating or re-organising part or all of an enterprise.

(IAS 38.57)

However, IAS 38.56 does not preclude the capitalisation of *bona fide* prepaid costs when payment for the delivery of goods or services has been made in advance of the delivery of goods or the rendering of services.

Some argue that start-up costs, training costs, advertising costs and relocation/ reorganisation costs are prepaid assets since the benefit of the expenditure will be recognised in future periods when the business is up and running, the benefits of the training are recognised, sales increase due to advertising, etc. They argue that the matching principle requires recognition of this expenditure when the related revenue is generated. However, in the view of the IASC Board, such expenditure does not meet the recognition criteria for an intangible asset included in IAS 38. In addition, such expenditure is likely to be difficult to distinguish from internally generated goodwill (which must always be expensed). For the avoidance of doubt, the Board makes its interpretation of the recognition criteria explicit in the Standard.

Comparison with UK GAAP
Although FRS 10, *Goodwill and Intangible Assets*, is not as explicit as IAS 38 about items which should be expensed, in practice, the items discussed above would normally be expensed as incurred. Certain 'preliminary' expenses of a company may be written off against a company's share premium account. These expenses normally include any legal fees and other expenses associated with the process of company registration. However, operating losses in the first years of operation may not be treated in this manner.

Comparison with US GAAP
Although US GAAP does not have one comprehensive standard on the above types of expenses, in most cases, they would be expensed as incurred. In particular, SOP 98-5, *Reporting on the Costs of Start-Up Activities*, specifically requires start-up costs to be expensed as incurred. However, in very limited circumstances, SOP 93-7 requires capitalisation of certain advertising and promotional costs.

10.7.10 Subsequent expenditure

In almost all cases, subsequent expenditure on an intangible asset will be expensed as incurred unless the following criteria are met:

> '(a) it is probable that this expenditure will enable the asset to generate future economic benefits in excess of its originally assessed standard of performance; and
> (b) this expenditure can be measured and attributed to the asset reliably.'
> (IAS 38.60)

If these two criteria are met, the expenditure is added to the cost of the intangible asset. However, given the nature of most intangible assets, it will be difficult to establish that it is probable that additional economic benefits will be reaped by the enterprise. Therefore, the capitalisation of such subsequent expenditure is expected to be rare.

Consistent with the prohibition on capitalising internally generated brands, mastheads, publishing titles, customer lists and similar items, subsequent expenditure on such items, whether they were originally purchased or internally generated, must also be expensed. (IAS 38.62)

Euro and Other Software Modification Costs

SIC-6 clarifies that capitalisation is not appropriate for expenditure incurred in order to restore or maintain the future economic benefits that an enterprise can expect from the originally assessed standard of performance of existing software systems (for example, to enable them to operate as intended after the introduction of the Euro). The Interpretation extends to software the guidance in IAS 16 (r1998), *Property, Plant and Equipment*, related to maintenance work undertaken on items of property, plant and equipment.

Determining whether expenditure restores or maintains the originally assessed standard or performance or results in a new, capitalisable asset can be difficult. Many companies have opted for purchasing new software systems rather than modifying their old systems to cope with the introduction of the Euro. In such cases, the old system would generally be disposed of and the new system capitalised. Therefore, the accounting is straightforward. However, other companies may upgrade existing systems mainly to cope with the Euro but also take advantage of the opportunity to add new systems capabilities. Each situation will need to be assessed carefully to determine if any costs qualify for capitalisation or if the additional benefits of the upgrade over and above Euro compliance are peripheral in nature. The following criteria which are based on the Framework guidance on the recognition of assets contained in paragraphs 89 and 90 should be met in order to qualify for capitalisation:

(a) it is probable that the costs will enable the software to generate specifically attributable future economic benefits in excess of its originally assessed standard of performance; and
(b) the costs can be measured and attributed to the asset reliably.

In the case of a modification merely to enable a system to operate as originally intended after the introduction of the Euro, the criteria are not met.

This policy was applied during the Year 2000 compliance upgrades. Companies were required to expense amounts incurred in making systems Y2K compliant as this modification did not enhance the originally assessed standard of performance of the systems.

In addition, SIC-6 states that such expenditure may be recognised as an expense when, and only when, the restoration or maintenance work is carried out. (SIC-6.4) Therefore it is not appropriate to create a provision for costs related to work which has not been carried out since no present obligation exists. The fact that the business could not continue as a going concern without the modification does not create either a legal or a constructive obligation. Liabilities such as creditors or accruals may only be recognised as third parties undertake the work. The Interpretation clearly states that it is inappropriate to recognise provisions before any work is carried out based on commitments made or contracts entered into with third parties. (SIC-6.7) This guidance on provisioning is consistent with the Standard on provisions, IAS 37, *Provisions, Contingent Liabilities and Contingent Assets* (see **11.9**).

Comparison with UK GAAP
The same general rules for subsequent expenditure are found in practice in the UK and therefore, it would normally be expensed.

UITF Abstract 21 deals with software modification costs in preparation for the Euro. Consistent with SIC-6, the UITF establishes the principle that Euro software modification costs should be expensed as incurred unless the expenditure clearly represents an enhancement of an asset beyond that originally assessed rather than merely maintaining its service potential. In addition, the requirement that such expenditure may only be recognised as an expense when the work is carried out and may not be provided for in advance is consistent with IAS 37.

Comparison with US GAAP
EITF D-71, *Accounting Issues Relating to the Introduction of the European Economic and Monetary Union (EMU)*, states that the accounting for costs related to the software modification necessary for Euro conversion should be consistent with the accounting principles established in EITF 96-14, *Accounting for the Costs Associated with Modifying Computer Software for the Year 2000*. EITF 96-14 generally required software modification costs to be expensed as incurred.

10.7.11 Measurement subsequent to initial recognition

IAS 38 allows a choice between accounting for intangible assets at historical cost (benchmark treatment) or revalued amounts (allowed alternative treatment).

If an intangible asset is accounted for at historical cost, it is carried in the balance sheet at its cost less any accumulated amortisation and any accumulated impairment losses. (IAS 38.63)

If the allowed alternative treatment is adopted, the intangible asset is carried at a revalued amount, which is its fair value at the date of the revaluation less any subsequent accumulated amortisation and any subsequent accumulated impairment losses.

Which intangibles can be revalued?
In order for an intangible asset to be revalued, first it must have been recognised at its cost. The option for revaluation does not permit initial

recognition at a revalued amount (fair value). Initial recognition must always be at cost.

However, IAS 38 does not prohibit recognition of an intangible asset at its cost (if it meets the definition and appropriate recognition criteria) with an immediate revaluation to fair value (if an active market exists – see below).

As discussed below, a revaluation is made by reference to an active market. IAS 38 specifically states that active markets cannot exist, due to their unique nature, for the following items:

(1) brands;
(2) newspaper mastheads;
(3) music and film publishing rights; and
(4) patents or trade marks.

Therefore, the above items cannot be revalued once recognised.

(IAS 38.67)

Basis for revaluation

When an intangible asset is revalued, it is revalued to its fair value, which is defined as the amount for which the asset could be exchanged between knowledgeable, willing parties in an arm's length transaction. (IAS 38.7) IAS 38 requires fair value to be determined by reference to an active market. An active market is defined as a market where all the following conditions exist:

> '(a) the items traded within the market are homogeneous;
> (b) willing buyers and sellers can normally be found at any time; and
> (c) prices are available to the public.'

(IAS 38.7)

No other technique for estimating fair value is permitted. It will be relatively unusual for an active market to exist for many intangible assets. Therefore, the revaluation of intangible assets is not expected to be common. As discussed in the previous section, due to their unique nature, certain intangible assets will never be able to be revalued due to the lack of an active market. While such assets may be traded in private transactions, each intangible will be unique and therefore there cannot be a market where the traded items are homogeneous.

Example 10.29

Taxi licences

The taxi licences granted within a certain city give identical rights to each licence holder. The licences are traded actively and, at any point in time, there will be a clearly defined market price. Such licences therefore are traded in an active market.

Example 10.30

Cable television operating licences

Cable television operating licences cover different regions with different populations and geographies and hence may not be homogeneous. Although such licences change hands, it is unlikely that the value of one licence would equal the prices at which others have been traded. Such licences are not considered to be traded in an active market.

Example 10.31

Databases of names and addresses

A market research company builds up databases of names and addresses of individuals with certain socio-economic characteristics. It sells the names and addresses on the list to consumer goods companies wishing to market their products. The fact that the company sells the rights to use the names and addresses does not mean that the database itself is traded. Only if there is a market in which the databases are sold outright to other market research companies and there is an established market price for such databases (say, £x per 1,000 names) could the database be considered to be traded in an active market.

Frequency of revaluations

IAS 38 does not set a specific time requirement for the frequency of revaluations but states that they should be carried out with sufficient regularity so that at each balance sheet date, the carrying amount of a revalued intangible asset does not differ materially from its fair value. (IAS 38.64)

In order to meet this requirement, an enterprise must estimate the fair value of its revalued intangible assets at each balance sheet date. However, this does not mean that a full valuation must be carried out every year, unless the estimate differs significantly from the carrying value.

Scope of revaluations

Consistent with items of property, plant and equipment, when an intangible asset is revalued, all the other assets in its class should also be revalued, unless there is no active market for those assets. (IAS 38.70) If there is no active market for a particular intangible asset which is included in a revalued class of intangible assets, it is carried at its historical cost less accumulated amortisation and accumulated impairment losses.

The intent of the requirement that all items in a class which qualify for revaluation be revalued simultaneously is that all items in a class are carried on the same basis, either historical cost or fair value, and that the revaluations are as of the same date. It also acts as to prohibit cherry-picking when revaluing assets, i.e., revaluing assets which have increased in value but not those which have decreased.

If the fair value of a revalued intangible asset can no longer be assessed by reference to an active market, the intangible asset is carried at its fair value at the date of the last valuation less accumulated amortisation and impairment losses. The disappearance of the active market may be an indicator of impairment which triggers an impairment review (see **10.12**). If the active market resurfaces, the intangible asset should once again be revalued by reference to the active market. (IAS 38.75)

Treatment of revaluation surplus

When a valuation indicates that the fair value of an intangible asset is greater than its carrying amount, the amount of the surplus is credited to shareholders' equity under the heading revaluation surplus. (IAS 38.76) Under IAS 1 (r1997), *Presentation of Financial Statements*, items recognised directly in equity such as increases and decreases in the revaluation surplus due to revaluations are disclosed either in a reconciliation of movements of shareholders' funds or in a statement showing changes in equity.

At the date an intangible asset is revalued, existing accumulated amortisation is either:

(a) restated proportionately with the change in the gross carrying amount of the asset so that the carrying amount of the asset after revaluation equals its revalued amount; or
(b) eliminated against the gross carrying amount of the asset and the net amount restated to the revalued amount of the asset. (IAS 38.69)

These treatments are similar to those permitted for depreciation when an item of property, plant and equipment is revalued. See *Example* **10.7** for a comparison of the two methods described above.

However, if the increase in the fair value of the asset reverses a previously recognised decrease in the fair value of the same asset, the increase is recognised as income to the extent that the previous decrease was recognised as an expense. (IAS 38.76)

Treatment of revaluation deficit

When a revaluation indicates that the fair value of an intangible asset is less than its carrying amount, the amount of the deficit is recognised in the income statement as an expense. (IAS 38.77)

However, if the decrease in the fair value of the intangible asset reverses a previously recognised increase in the fair value of the same asset, the decrease is debited against the related revaluation surplus to the extent that the decrease does not exceed the amount held in the revaluation surplus in respect of that asset. Any remaining decrease is then debited to the income statement. (IAS 38.77)

The treatments of revaluation surpluses and deficits arising on intangible assets are the same as those for items of property, plant and equipment (see *Examples* **10.7–10.10**).

Realisation of the revaluation surplus

The revaluation surplus may be transferred to retained earnings as or when the surplus is realised. The transfer from revaluation surplus to retained earnings is not made through the income statement but via an intra-reserve transfer. Such transfers are disclosed in the reconciliation of equity and reserves (see Chapter **8**). Realisation of the entire surplus occurs on disposal or retirement, when the asset is permanently withdrawn from use and no future economic benefits are expected from its disposal (see **10.7.14**). However, some realisation of the revaluation surplus may occur through the use of the intangible asset. (IAS 38.78)

The amount of the surplus which is realised through use of the asset is calculated as the difference between amortisation calculated on the historical cost of the asset and the amortisation calculated on the revalued amount. This difference may be transferred from the revaluation surplus to retained earnings in each period. As a result of these periodic transfers, when a revalued intangible asset is fully amortised in the balance sheet, the related revaluation surplus will have been reduced to zero.

Comparison to UK GAAP

The requirements around the recognition and measurement of revalued intangible assets are similar under FRS 10, *Goodwill and Intangible Assets*, and IAS 38. However, FRS 10 restricts recognition of the reversal of an impairment loss related to an intangible assets which was previously caused by an external event such that the loss may only be reversed when subsequent *external* events clearly and demonstrably reverse the effects of that event in a way that was unforeseen in the original impairment calculations. In effect, FRS 10 is prohibiting the capitalisation of an internally generated asset by reinstatement of an impairment loss. IAS 38 does not contain a similar restriction although such a reinstatement could be seen as against the spirit of the Standard.

Comparison to US GAAP

Outside of purchase accounting, revaluations are not generally permitted.

10.7.12 Amortisation

All intangible assets are required to be amortised over their estimated useful lives. In the majority of cases, the amortisation charges are recognised as an expense. However, if the economic benefits of the intangible asset are used by the enterprise in the production of other assets, the amortisation charge is added to the cost of the other assets and included in their carrying amount. For example, if a patented production process has been capitalised as an intangible asset, as the relevant inventory items are produced using the patented process, the amortisation of the intangible asset is added to the cost of the inventory.

By not specifying where on the income statement amortisation is to be charged, IAS 38 provides many options. For example, it does not specify whether or not amortisation charges should be included within operating profit. However, since paragraph 107 (d) requires disclosure of the line item(s) in which amortisation is included on the face of the income statement, it appears that it may be included either before or after operating profit as long as it is clearly disclosed in the notes where the amount has been charged in the income statement. The fact that the disclosure requirement refers to 'line item(s)' would indicate that it is not required to include the amortisation charge in only one line item. It would appear appropriate to look to the nature of the intangible asset to determine where on the income statement the related amortisation charges should be shown.

Amortisation period

An intangible asset is required to be amortised over its estimated useful life. Amortisation commences from the date the asset is available for use. (IAS 38.79)

The useful life of an intangible asset should reflect the best estimate of the period during which future economic benefits are expected to flow to the enterprise. Factors to consider in estimating the useful life of an intangible asset include:

> '(a) the expected usage of the asset by the enterprise and whether the asset could be efficiently managed by another management team;
> (b) typical product life cycles for the asset and public information on estimates of useful lives of similar types of assets that are used in a similar way;
> (c) technical, technological or other types of obsolescence;
> (d) the stability of the industry in which the asset operates and changes in the market demand for the products or services output from the asset;
> (e) expected actions by competitors or potential competitors;
> (f) the level of maintenance expenditure required to obtain the expected future economic benefits from the asset and the company's ability and intent to reach such a level;
> (g) the period of control over the asset and legal or similar limits on the use of the asset, such as the expiry dates of related leases; and
> (h) whether the useful life of the asset is dependent on the useful life of other assets of the enterprise.'

(IAS 38.80)

Choosing an appropriate useful life for an intangible asset is difficult and IAS 38 notes that estimates of useful life become less reliable as the length of the useful life increases. Therefore, a rebuttable presumption is included that the useful life of an intangible asset will not exceed 20 years. In rare cases, this presumption can be overcome if there is pervasive evidence that the intangible asset will last for a specific period of more than 20 years. (IAS 38.83) This may be the case, for example, when the intangible asset is a legal right which extends for a period greater than 20 years.

However, the carrying amount of an intangible asset which is being amortised over more than 20 years is subject to an *annual* impairment review in accordance with IAS 36 (see **10.12**). (IAS 38.83) In addition, the enterprise must disclose in the notes to the financial statements the reasons why the presumption is rebutted and the factor(s) that played a significant role in determining the useful life of the intangible asset.

Often control over the future economic benefits from an intangible asset is achieved through legal rights that have been granted for a finite period. Under most circumstances, the estimated useful life of the intangible asset is the shorter of the period of the legal rights and the period over which economic benefits are expected to be generated. However, in some cases, the legal rights may be renewable. The question then arises whether or not it is appropriate to assume that the legal rights will be extended. IAS 38 clearly states that such a renewal can only be included when estimating an asset's useful life if the renewal is virtually certain. (IAS 38.85) The following factors are listed which indicate that renewal of a legal right is virtually certain:

> '(a) the fair value of the intangible asset does not reduce as the initial expiry date approaches, or does not reduce by more than the cost of renewing the underlying right;
> (b) there is evidence (possibly based on past experience) that the legal rights will be renewed; and
> (c) there is evidence that the conditions necessary to obtain the renewal of the legal right (if any) will be satisfied.'
>
> (IAS 38.87)

Virtually certain is a very high threshold. The probability would certainly have to be near 100 per cent to obtain it.

Amortisation method

The amortisation method chosen should reflect the pattern in which the future economic benefits arising from an intangible asset are expected to be consumed. If this pattern cannot be determined reliably, the straight-line method is required. (IAS 38.88)

At least at each financial year end, the estimated useful life of intangible assets and their related amortisation methods should be reviewed. If a change in either is deemed appropriate, it is accounted for as a change in estimate in accordance with IAS 8 (r1993), *Net Profit or Loss for the Period, Fundamental Errors and Changes in Accounting Policies*, by adjusting current and future periods (see **5.15**). If a change in the estimated useful life of an intangible asset results in the asset having an estimated useful life of greater than 20 years from the date the asset became available for use, annual impairment tests will be required as discussed above.

Residual value

Under most circumstances, the residual value of an intangible asset will be zero. However, a residual value is required if:

> '(a) there is a commitment by a third party to purchase the asset at the end of its useful life; or
> (b) there is an active market for the asset and:
> (i) residual value can be determined by reference to that market; and
> (ii) it is probable that such a market will exist at the end of the asset's useful life.'
>
> (IAS 38.91)

When an intangible asset is carried at historical cost, the residual value is estimated using prices prevailing at the date of acquisition of the asset for the sale of a similar asset which has operated under similar conditions and has reached the end of its estimated useful life. The residual value is not subsequently updated for changes in prices or value. If the asset is carried at a revalued amount, a new estimate of residual amount is made whenever the asset is revalued, based on prices prevailing at that date. (IAS 38.93)

Comparison with UK GAAP

Similar to IAS 38, under FRS 10, *Goodwill and Intangible Assets*, an intangible asset is amortised over its estimated useful life. FRS 10 also contains a rebuttable presumption that the useful life of an intangible asset does not exceed 20 years. However, as under IAS 38, this presumption may be overcome and a longer life used, but the intangible asset will become subject to an annual impairment test. Unlike IAS 38, under FRS 10 a life of more than 20 years can include an indefinite life, when no amortisation will be charged.

Comparison with US GAAP

Statement 142 provides that an intangible asset whose life extends beyond the foreseeable horizon be classified as having an indefinite life. An intangible asset that is determined to have an indefinite useful life shall not be amortised until its useful life is determined to be no longer indefinite. If no legal, regulatory, contractual, economic, or other factors limit the useful life of an intangible asset to the reporting entity, the useful life of the asset shall be considered to be indefinite. Intangible assets that have finite useful lives will continue to be amortised over their useful lives, but without the constraint of an arbitrary ceiling.

Appendix A of Statement 142 provides examples describing an acquired intangible asset and the facts and circumstances surrounding the determination of its useful life. The following examples of an acquired intangible asset with a determined indefinite life are provided: an acquired broadcast licence, an acquired airline route authority and an acquired trade mark. The examples in Appendix A of Statement 142 are for illustration purposes only. The determination of useful life can only be determined based on a consideration of the facts and circumstances unique to each acquired intangible asset.

10.7.13 Impairment

An enterprise follows the guidance in IAS 36 to determine whether an intangible asset is impaired and to measure any such an impairment (see **10.12**). In addition to the impairment reviews required by IAS 36, an enterprise is required to estimate the recoverable amount in accordance with IAS 36 of the following two categories of intangible assets at least at each financial year end, regardless of whether or not any impairment indicators are present:

(1) any intangible asset which is not yet ready for use; and
(2) any intangible asset that is amortised over a period greater than 20 years from the date when the asset is available for use.

Any impairment loss is then recognised following the provisions of IAS 36.

10.7.14 Retirements and disposals

An intangible asset, whether carried at historical cost or a revalued amount, is removed from the balance sheet on disposal or when no future economic benefits associated with the asset are expected to flow to the enterprise from its use or disposal. (IAS 38.103)

The gain or loss on disposal is calculated as the difference between the estimated net disposal proceeds and the carrying amount of the asset and is recognised in the income statement. (IAS 38.104)

As discussed previously, the revaluation surplus may be transferred to retained earnings as or when the surplus is realised. The transfer from revaluation surplus to retained earnings is not made through the income statement but via an intra-reserve transfer. Such transfers are disclosed in the reconciliation of equity and reserves (see Chapter **8**).

If an intangible asset is removed from use and is held for sale, the asset remains at its carrying amount at the date the asset is retired from active service. At least at each financial year end, the asset is tested for impairment according to IAS 36 and any impairment losses are recognised accordingly (see **10.12**). (IAS 38.106)

10.7.15 Disclosure

The extensive disclosure requirements of IAS 38 can be broken down into:

(1) those which apply to all intangible assets;
(2) additional requirements for intangible assets carried at a revalued amount;
(3) additional requirements for research and development expenditure; and
(4) encouraged disclosures.

All intangible assets
The following disclosures should be made for each class of intangible assets, distinguishing between internally generated intangible assets and other intangible assets:

(a) the useful lives or the amortisation rates used;
(b) the amortisation methods used;
(c) the gross carrying amount and the accumulated amortisation (aggregated with accumulated impairment losses) at the beginning and end of the period;
(d) the line item(s) of the income statement in which the amortisation of intangible assets is included;
(e) a reconciliation of the carrying amount at the beginning and end of the period showing:
    (i) additions, indicating separately those from internal development and business combinations;
    (ii) retirements and disposals;
    (iii) increases or decreases during the period resulting from revaluations and from impairment losses recognised or reversed directly in equity;
    (iv) impairment losses recognised or reversed in the income statement during the period;
    (v) amortisation recognised during the period;
    (vi) net exchange differences arising on the translation of the financial statements of a foreign entity; and
    (vii) other changes in the carrying amount during the period.

Comparative figures are not required for the items included in the reconciliation. (IAS 38.107)

A class is defined as a grouping of assets of a similar nature and use in the operations of an enterprise. Examples of separate classes include:

(1) brand names;
(2) mastheads and publishing titles;
(3) computer software;
(4) licences and franchises;
(5) copyrights, patents and other industrial property rights, service and operating rights;
(6) recipes, formulae, models, designs and prototypes; and
(7) intangible assets under development.

These classes may be disaggregated or aggregated if this results in more relevant information. (IAS 38.108)

The financial statements should also disclose:

(a) if an intangible asset is amortised over more than 20 years, the reasons why the presumption that the useful life of an intangible asset will not exceed 20 years from the date when the asset is available for use is rebutted. In giving these reasons, the enterprise should describe the factor(s) that played a significant role in determining the useful life of the asset;
(b) a description, the carrying amount and remaining amortisation period of any individual intangible asset that is material to the financial statements of the enterprise as a whole;
(c) for intangible assets acquired by way of a government grant and initially recognised at fair value:
   - the fair value initially recognised for these assets;
   - their carrying amount; and
   - whether they are carried under the benchmark or the allowed alternative treatment for subsequent measurement;
(d) the existence and carrying amounts of intangible assets whose title is restricted and the carrying amounts of intangible assets pledged as security for liabilities; and
(e) the amount of commitments for the acquisition of intangible assets.

(IAS 38.111)

In addition to the disclosures included in IAS 38, if there has been a change in estimate during the period, the disclosures set out in IAS 8 (r1993), *Net Profit or Loss for the Period, Fundamental Errors and Changes in Accounting Policies*, will be required (see **5.15**). Changes in estimates related to intangible assets include changes in:

(a) residual values;
(b) amortisation period; and
(c) amortisation method.

If an intangible asset has suffered an impairment loss, the disclosures included in IAS 36 will be required (see **10.12.16**).

Additional requirements for intangible assets carried at a revalued amount

In addition to the disclosures listed above, if an enterprise carries its intangible assets at revalued amounts, it is required to disclose:

(a) by class of intangible assets:
    (i) the effective date of the revaluation;
    (ii) the carrying amount of revalued intangible assets; and
    (iii) the carrying amount that would have been included in the financial statements had the revalued intangible assets been carried at historical cost less any accumulated amortisation and any accumulated impairment losses; and
(b) the amount of the revaluation surplus that relates to intangible assets at the beginning and end of the period, indicating the changes during the period and any restrictions on the distribution of the balance to shareholders.

(IAS 38.113)

Additional requirements for research and development expenditure

The amount of research and development expenditure recognised as an expense during the period should be disclosed. (IAS 38.115) Such expenditure includes all expenditure that is directly attributable to research or development activities or that can be allocated on a reasonable and consistent basis to such activities.

Encouraged disclosures

The following disclosures are encouraged but not required:

(a) a description of any fully amortised intangible asset that is still in use; and
(b) a brief description of significant intangible assets controlled by the enterprise but not recognised as assets because they did not meet the recognition criteria in IAS 38 or because they were acquired or generated before IAS 38 became effective.

10.7.16 Examples from published financial statements

Note that the excerpts given do not always comply in full with all aspects of IAS and as such are not necessarily examples of best practice but merely of current practice.

Intangible asset example

Example 10.32

[17] Intangible assets Acquired intangible assets other than goodwill are recognised at cost and amortised over a period of four to five years, depending on their estimated useful lives. Write-downs are made for any declines in value that are expected to be permanent. Assets are written back if the reasons for previous years' write-downs no longer apply.

Goodwill, including that resulting from capital consolidation, is capitalised in accordance with IAS 22 and amortised on a straight-line basis over a maximum estimated useful life of 20 years. The value of goodwill is reassessed regularly and written down if necessary.

Self-created intangible assets are not capitalised.

Changes in intangible assets in 2000 are as follows:

(€ million)	*Acquired concessions, industrial property rights, similar rights and assets, and licenses thereunder*	*Acquired goodwill*	*Advance payments*	*Total*
Gross carrying amounts, Dec. 31 1999	1,903	944	84	2,931
Exchange differences	126	22	6	154
Changes in companies consolidated	5	36	–	41
Acquisitions	2,268	301	–	2,569
Capital expenditures	293	5	56	354
Retirements	(95)	(28)	–	(123)
Transfers	66	9	(75)	–
Gross carrying amounts, Dec. 31, 2000	**4,566**	**1,289**	**71**	**5,926**
Accumulated amortisation and write-downs, Dec. 31 1999	479	239	–	718
Exchange differences	39	5	–	44
Changes in companies consolidated	1	(3)	–	(2)
Amortisation and write-downs in 2000	345	99	–	444
– *of which write-downs*	[–]	[1]	[–]	[1]
Write-backs	(1)	(1)	–	(2)
Retirements	(91)	(28)	–	(119)
Transfers	–	–	–	–
Accumulated amortisation and write-downs, Dec. 31, 200	**722**	**311**	**–**	**1,083**
Net carrying amounts, Dec. 31, 2000	**3,794**	**978**	**71**	**4,843**
Net carrying amounts, Dec. 31, 1999	1,424	705	84	2,213

The exchange differences are the differences between the carrying amounts at the beginning and the end of the year that result from translating foreign companies' figures at the respective different exchange rates and changes in their assets during the year at the average rate for the year.

Bayer Group
Germany
International Accounting Standards
31 December 2000

Research and development examples

Example 10.33

Research development

Research and development expenses are fully charged to the income statement. The Group considers that the regulatory and other uncertainties inherent in the development of its key products preclude it from capitalizing development costs. Laboratory buildings and equipment in tangible fixed assets are depreciated over their estimated useful lives.

Novartis Group
Switzerland
International Accounting Standards
31 December 2000

Example 10.34

Research and development

Research and development costs are expensed in the financial period during which they are incurred, except for certain development costs which are capitalized when it is probable that a development project will be a success, and certain criteria, including commercial and technological feasibility, have been met. Capitalized development costs are amortized on a systematic basis over their expected useful lives. The amortization period is between two and five years.

10. Intangible assets	*2000* *€m*	*1999* *€m*
Capitalized development costs		
Acquisition cost Jan. 1	811	650
Additions	394	271
Disposals	–108	–110
Accumulated depreciation Dec. 31	–457	–398
Net carrying amount Dec. 31	640	413
Intangible rights		
Acquisition cost Jan. 1	187	137
Additions	77	50
Disposals	–19	–
Accumulated depreciation Dec. 31	–134	–103
Net carrying amount Dec. 31	111	84
Goodwill		
Acquisition cost Jan. 1	554	347
Additions	1,016	210
Disposals	–	–3
Accumulated depreciation Dec. 31	–458	–318
Net carrying amount Dec. 31	1,112	236
Other intangible assets		
Acquisition cost Jan. 1	164	66
Additions	55	116
Disposals	–12	–20
Translation differences	7	2
Accumulated depreciation Dec. 31	–83	–59
Net carrying amount Dec. 31	131	105

Nokia Corporation
International Accounting Standards
Finland
31 December 2000

10.8 Investments and investment property

This section on investments does not deal with investments in subsidiaries (see Chapter **19**), associates (see Chapter **20**) or joint ventures (see Chapter **21**); intangible assets (see **10.5–10.7**); investments of retirement benefit plans (see Appendix II) and life insurance enterprises; finance leases (see Chapter **24**); or financial assets to which IAS 32 (r1998), and IAS 39 (r2000) apply (see Chapter **12**). Consequently this chapter deals only with the provisions of IAS 40 on Investment Properties.

10.8.1 Sources

IAS 1 (r1997)	*Presentation of Financial Statements.*
IAS 16 (r1998)	*Property, Plant and Equipment.*
IAS 32 (r1998)	*Financial Instruments: Disclosure and Presentation.*
IAS 39 (r2000)	*Financial Instruments: Recognition and Measurement* (effective 1 January 2001).
IAS 40	*Investment Property* (effective 1 January 2001).

10.8.2 Brief summary of the requirements

Investments which meet the definition of financial assets included in IAS 32 (r1998) will be subject to its presentation and disclosure requirements as well as the requirements of IAS 39 (r2000) (See Chapter **12**).

Investment properties may be held either at fair value, with changes in fair value recognised in the income statement, or at depreciated cost, less any accumulated impairment losses, as described in **10.8.9**.

10.8.3 Development of the requirements

Originally approved in 1985, IAS 25, *Accounting for Investments*, was reformatted in 1994 but no substantive changes were made to the original approved text. IAS 25 was originally included in the scope of the Comparability/Improvements project but the IASC Board decided that the accounting issues would be covered in the financial instruments project and therefore, IAS 25 was not amended as part of the project except to be reformatted.

IAS 25 originally covered recognition and measurement of debt and equity investments, as well as investments in land and buildings and other tangible and intangible assets held as investments. However, several new IASs subsequently superseded IAS 25. Specifically:

- IAS 38 superseded IAS 25 with respect to investments in intangible assets (see **10.7**).

- IAS 39 (r2000) superseded IAS 25 with respect to investments in debt and equity investments (see Chapter **12**).
- IAS 40, *Investment Property* (see below), superseded IAS 25 with respect to investment properties.

On adoption of IAS 38, IAS 39 (r2000) and IAS 40, IAS 25 would only have covered investments in commodities and in tangible assets such as vintage cars and other collectors' items as well as a few other specialised areas. The IASC Board did not believe that there was a need for an IAS covering such items and therefore IAS 25 was withdrawn as of 1 January 2001.

In October 1997, the IASC Board agreed that the choice of accounting treatment relating to investment properties should be eliminated. Under IAS 25 investment properties could be carried at fair value and not depreciated or accounted for as any other item of property, plant and equipment and carried at cost or a revalued amount and depreciated. IAS 40 *Investment Property* states that an investment property should either be measured at fair value, with all changes in fair value recognised in the income statement, or at depreciated cost, less any accumulated impairment losses.

Despite the IASC Board's initial views, a (reduced) choice of treatment of investment property still exists as comments received on E64, the exposure draft of IAS 40, made it clear that it could be impracticable to require a fair value model at present.

IAS 40 becomes operative for annual financial statements covering periods beginning on or after 1 January 2001. Earlier adoption is encouraged; if management apply IAS 40 for periods beginning before 1 January 2001, the financial statements should disclose that fact. (IAS 40.74)

10.8.4 Scope

IAS 40 applies in the recognition, measurement and disclosure of investment property. In addition, IAS 40 deals with the measurement in a lessee's financial statements of investment property held under a finance lease and with the measurement in a lessor's financial statements of investment property leased out under an operating lease. IAS 40 does not deal with matters covered in IAS 17 (r1997), *Leases*, including:

'(a) classification of leases as finance leases or operating leases;
(b) recognition of lease income earned on investment property;
(c) measurement in a lessee's financial statements of property held under an operating lease;
(d) measurement in a lessor's financial statements of property leased out under a finance lease;

(e) accounting for sale and leaseback transactions; and
(f) disclosure about finance leases and operating leases.'

(IAS 40.2)

Leases are discussed in Chapter **24**.

The following are also beyond the scope of IAS 40:

(a) biological assets attached to land related to agricultural activity (see IAS 41, *Agriculture*, see Appendix II); and
(b) mineral rights, the exploration for and extraction of minerals, oil, natural gas and similar non-regenerative resources (separate IASB project underway. See Chapter **2**).

(IAS 40.3)

10.8.5 Definition

IAS 40 defines investment property as:

> 'property (land or a building – or part of a building – or both) held (by the owner or by the lessee under a finance lease) to earn rentals or for capital appreciation or both, rather than for:
>
> (a) use in the production or supply of goods or services or for administrative purposes; or
> (b) sale in the ordinary course of business.'

(IAS 40.4)

Investment properties are held to earn rentals or for capital appreciation or both. Therefore, an investment property generates cash flows largely independently of the other assets held by an enterprise. (IAS 40.5)

IAS 40 cites the following as examples of investment property:

(a) land held for long-term capital appreciation rather than for short-term sale in the ordinary course of business;
(b) land held for a currently undetermined future use;
(c) a building owned by the reporting enterprise and leased out under one or more operating leases; and
(d) a building that is vacant but is held to be leased out under one or more operating leases.

(IAS 40.6)

Investment property that is being redeveloped for continued future use as investment property is also defined as investment property and is therefore within the scope of IAS 40.

The following are examples given in IAS 40 which are not investment property and therefore fall outside the scope of IAS 40:

(a) property held for sale in the ordinary course of business or in the process of construction or development for such sale, e.g., property acquired exclusively with a view to subsequent disposal in the near future or for development and resale;
(b) property being constructed or developed on behalf of third parties (see Chapter **27**);
(c) owner-occupied property, including property held for future use as owner-occupied property, property held for future development and subsequent use as owner-occupied property, property occupied by employees and owner-occupied property awaiting disposal; and
(d) property that is being constructed or developed for future use as investment property – IAS 16 (r1998) applies until the construction or development is complete at which time the property is deemed to be investment property and IAS 40 applies.

(IAS 40.7)

Where properties include a portion that is held for investment purposes, i.e., to earn rentals or for capital appreciation, and another portion is held for use in the ordinary course of business, then the portions should be accounted for separately if the portions could be sold or leased out separately. If this is not the case, then the property is only treated as investment property if an insignificant portion is held for use in the ordinary course of business. (IAS 40.8)

Where ancillary services are provided by the owners of a property to the occupants of a property, e.g., the owner of an office building provides security and maintenance services to the lessees who occupy the building, then the property is investment property if the services are a relatively insignificant component of the arrangement as a whole. (IAS 40.9) Where the services provided are a more significant component, e.g., services provided by the owner of a hotel to guests, the property is owner-occupied rather than investment property. (IAS 40.10)

However, it can be difficult to determine the significance of the services provided. For example, the owner of a hotel sometimes transfers certain responsibilities to third parties under a management contract, and the terms of such contracts can be very different. The owner may be a passive investor or may have simply outsourced certain day-to-day functions while retaining significant exposure to variation in the cash flows generated by the operations of the hotel. (IAS 40.11)

Therefore, judgement is required to determine whether a property is investment property or not. Management should develop their own criteria and apply these criteria on a consistent basis. IAS 40.66(a) requires these criteria to be disclosed when classification is difficult.

In some cases, an enterprise owns property that is leased to, and occupied by, its parent or another subsidiary. The property does not therefore qualify as investment property in the consolidated financial statements that include both enterprises, as the perspective of the group as a whole needs to be considered and the property would be classified as owner-occupied. However, provided the property meets the definition for investment property, detailed above, for the enterprise which owns the property, the property is classified as investment property in the individual financial statements of the owning enterprise. (IAS 40.14)

10.8.6 Recognition

Investment property should be recognised as an asset when, and only when:

(a) it is probable that the future economic benefits that are associated with the investment property will flow to the enterprise; and
(b) the cost of the investment property can be measured reliably.

(IAS 40.15)

Management needs to assess the degree of certainty attaching to the flow of future economic benefits on the basis of the evidence available at the time of initial recognition. (IAS 40.16)

10.8.7 Initial measurement

Investment properties are initially measured at cost. In addition to the purchase price of the investment property, cost includes any directly attributable expenditure, e.g., legal fees and property transfer taxes. The cost is not increased by start-up costs unless they are necessary to bring the property to its working condition. Initial operating losses incurred before the investment property achieves the planned level of occupancy or abnormal amounts of wasted resources (such as labour and materials) incurred in constructing or developing the property should not be capitalised as part of the cost. (IAS 40.18 and 20)

The cost of a self-constructed investment property is its cost at the date when the construction or development is complete. As discussed in **10.8.5**, until that date IAS 16 (r1998), *Property, Plant and Equipment*, applies. At that date, the property becomes investment property and IAS 40 applies. (IAS 40.19)

If payment for an investment property is deferred, its cost is the cash price equivalent. The difference between this amount and the total payments is recognised as interest expense over the period of credit. (IAS 40.21)

10.8.8 Subsequent expenditure

Subsequent expenditure relating to an investment property that has already been recognised should be added to the carrying amount of the investment property when it is probable that future economic benefits, in excess of the originally assessed standard of performance of the existing investment property, will flow to the enterprise. All other subsequent expenditure should be recognised as an expense in the period in which it is incurred. (IAS 40.22)

When determining the appropriate accounting treatment for subsequent expenditure, management should consider the circumstances which were taken into account on the initial measurement and recognition of the related investment.

For example, if the carrying amount of an investment property already takes into account a loss in future economic benefits, subsequent expenditure to restore the future economic benefits expected from the asset should be capitalised. Similarly, where the purchase price reflects the need for subsequent expenditure to bring the asset to working condition, that subsequent expenditure will be capitalised when incurred.

10.8.9 Measurement subsequent to initial recognition

A choice is allowed on the subsequent measurement of investment property. Investment property may be valued either using the fair value model or the cost model. (IAS 40.24)

Management should apply the model chosen to all the enterprise's investment properties. A change from one model to the other model should be made only if the change will result in a more appropriate presentation. This is highly unlikely to be the case for a change from the fair value model to the cost model. (IAS 40.25)

Whichever model is chosen, management is required to determine the fair value of investment property. This is for the purpose of measurement if the fair value model is adopted, or disclosure if the cost model is adopted. Management is encouraged, but not required, to determine the fair value of investment property on the basis of a valuation by an independent valuer who holds a recognised and relevant professional qualification and who has recent experience in the location and category of the investment property being valued. (IAS 40.26)

Fair value model

Fair value is defined as 'the amount for which an asset could be exchanged between knowledgeable, willing parties in an arm's length transaction'. (IAS 40.4)

'Knowledgeable' means that both parties are reasonably informed about the nature and characteristics of the investment property, its actual and potential uses, and the state of the market as of the balance sheet date. (IAS 40.34)

A 'willing' buyer is motivated, but not compelled, to buy, and is neither over-eager nor determined to buy at any price, i.e., the willing buyer will take the realities of the current market into account. (IAS 40.35) A 'willing' seller is neither an over-eager nor a forced seller, prepared to sell at any price, nor one prepared to hold out for a price not considered reasonable in the current market. The willing seller is motivated to sell the investment property at market terms for the best price obtainable in the open market, whatever that price may be, after the investment property has been exposed to the market in the most appropriate manner to effect its disposal at the best price reasonably obtainable. This means that the investment property would have been brought to the attention of an adequate number of potential purchasers. (IAS 40.36 and 37)

An arm's length transaction is one between parties who do not have a particular or special relationship that makes prices of transactions uncharacteristic of the market. The transaction is presumed to be between unrelated parties, each acting independently. (IAS 40.38)

After initial recognition, if management chooses the fair value model then it should measure all investment property at its fair value, except in the exceptional circumstances detailed below. (IAS 40.27) A gain or loss arising from a change in the fair value of investment property should be included in net profit or loss for the period in which it arises. (IAS 40.28)

However, there is a rebuttable presumption that management will be able to determine the fair value of an investment property reliably on a continuing basis. In exceptional cases there is clear evidence when an investment property is first acquired (or when an existing property first becomes investment property following the completion of construction or development, or after a change in use) that management will not be able to determine the fair value of the investment property reliably on a continuing basis.

This only arises when comparable market transactions are infrequent and alternative estimates of fair value, e.g., based on discounted cash flow projections, are not available. In such cases, management should measure that investment property using the benchmark treatment in IAS 16 (r1998), i.e., depreciated cost less any accumulated impairment losses, and assume the residual value of the investment property to be zero. IAS 16 (r1998) should continue to be applied until the investment property has been disposed of. (IAS 40.47)

If management is compelled to apply IAS 16 (r1998) to measure a particular investment property, then all other investment property should still be measured at fair value. (IAS 40.48) If management has previously measured an investment property at fair value then management should continue to do so until the property has been disposed of or reclassified, even if comparable market transactions become less frequent or market prices become less readily available. (IAS 40.49)

The fair value of investment property is usually its market value and should reflect the actual market state and circumstances as of the balance sheet date, not as of either a past or future date. (IAS 40.31) Consideration therefore needs to be given to factors such as rental income from current leases, but the estimate of fair value should specifically exclude an estimated price inflated or deflated by special terms or circumstances. (IAS 40.29) The fair value of an investment property does not reflect future capital expenditure that will improve or enhance the property and does not reflect the related future benefits from this future expenditure. (IAS 40.45)

Management should avoid double counting of assets or liabilities that are recognised in the balance sheet as separate assets or liabilities. For example:

(a) equipment such as elevators or air-conditioning is often an integral part of a building and is generally included in the investment property, rather than being recognised separately as property, plant and equipment;
(b) if an office is leased on a furnished basis, the fair value of the office generally includes the fair value of the furniture, because the rental income relates to the furnished office. When furniture is included in the fair value of the investment property, an enterprise does not recognise that furniture as a separate asset; and
(c) the fair value of investment property excludes prepaid or accrued operating lease income, as the enterprise recognises it as a separate liability or asset.

(IAS 40.44)

Fair value should not be confused with value in use, as defined in IAS 36, *Impairment of Assets.* Fair value is based on general factors, whereas value in use is estimated using factors which are quite specific to the enterprise. For example, fair value does not reflect any:

(a) additional value derived from the creation of a portfolio of properties in different locations;
(b) synergies between investment property and other assets;
(c) legal rights or legal restrictions that are specific only to the current owner; and
(d) tax benefits or burdens that are specific to the current owner.

(IAS 40.43)

The best evidence of fair value is normally given by current prices on an active market for similar property in the same location and condition and subject to similar lease and other contracts. In the absence of such information, management should consider information from a variety of sources, including:

(a) current prices on an active market for properties of different nature, condition or location, adjusted to reflect those differences;
(b) recent prices on less active markets, with adjustments to reflect any changes in economic conditions since the date of the transactions that occurred at those prices; and
(c) discounted cash flow projections based on reliable estimates of future cash flows, supported by the terms of any existing lease and other contracts and, where possible, by external evidence such as current market rents for similar properties in the same location and condition, and using discount rates that reflect current market assessments of the uncertainty in the amount and timing of the cash flows.

(IAS 40.40)

If the above sources of information suggest different conclusions as to the fair value of an investment property, then management should consider the reasons for those differences in order to arrive at the 'most reliable estimate of fair value within a relatively narrow range of reasonable fair value estimates'. (IAS 40.41)

Cost model
If management chooses to adopt the cost model, then it should measure all investment property using the benchmark treatment in IAS 16 (r1998), i.e., at cost less any accumulated depreciation and any accumulated impairment losses. (IAS 40.50)

10.8.10 Transfers

IAS 40.51 stipulates that transfers to, or from, investment property should be made when, and only when, there is a change in use, evidenced by:

(a) commencement of owner-occupation, for a transfer from investment property to owner-occupied property;
(b) commencement of development with a view to sale, for a transfer from investment property to inventories;
(c) end of owner-occupation, for a transfer from owner-occupied property to investment property;
(d) commencement of an operating lease to another party, for a transfer from inventories to investment property; or
(e) end of construction or development, for a transfer from property in the

course of construction or development (covered by IAS 16 (r1998)) to investment property.

When an enterprise decides to dispose of an investment property without development, the enterprise continues to treat the property as an investment property until it is derecognised, i.e., eliminated from the balance sheet, and does not treat it as inventory. Similarly, if an enterprise begins to redevelop an existing investment property for continued future use as investment property, it remains an investment property and is not reclassified as owner-occupied property during the redevelopment. (IAS 40.52)

For a transfer from investment property carried at fair value to owner-occupied property or inventories, the property's cost for subsequent accounting under IAS 16 (r1998) or IAS 2 (r1993), *Inventories*, should be its fair value at the date of change in use. (IAS 40.54)

If an owner-occupied property becomes an investment property that will be carried at fair value, an enterprise should apply IAS 16 (r1998) up to the date of change in use. The enterprise should treat any difference at that date between the carrying amount of the property under IAS 16 (r1998) and its fair value in the same way as a revaluation under IAS 16 (r1998). (IAS 40.55)

Up to the date when an owner-occupied property becomes an investment property carried at fair value, an enterprise continues to depreciate the property and to recognise any impairment losses that have occurred. The enterprise treats any difference at that date between the carrying amount of the property under IAS 16 (r1998) and its fair value in the same way as a revaluation under IAS 16 (r1998). In other words:

(a) any resulting decrease in the carrying amount of the property is recognised in net profit or loss for the period. However, to the extent that an amount is included in revaluation surplus for that property, the decrease is charged against that revaluation surplus; and
(b) any resulting increase in the carrying amount is treated as follows:
  (i) to the extent that the increase reverses a previous impairment loss for that property, the increase is recognised in net profit or loss for the period. The amount recognised in net profit or loss for the period does not exceed the amount needed to restore the carrying amount to the carrying amount that would have been determined (net of depreciation) had no impairment loss been recognised; and
  (ii) any remaining part of the increase is credited directly to equity under the heading of revaluation surplus. On subsequent disposal of the investment property, the revaluation surplus included in equity may be transferred to retained earnings. The transfer from

revaluation surplus to retained earnings is not made through the income statement.

(IAS 40.56)

For a transfer from inventories to investment property that will be carried at fair value, any difference between the fair value of the property at that date and its previous carrying amount should be recognised in net profit or loss for the period. (IAS 40.57) This treatment is consistent with the treatment of sales of inventories. (IAS 40.58)

When the construction or development of a self-constructed investment property that will be carried at fair value is completed, any difference between the fair value of the property at that date and its previous carrying amount should be recognised in net profit or loss for the period. (IAS 40.59)

The above is summarised as follows:

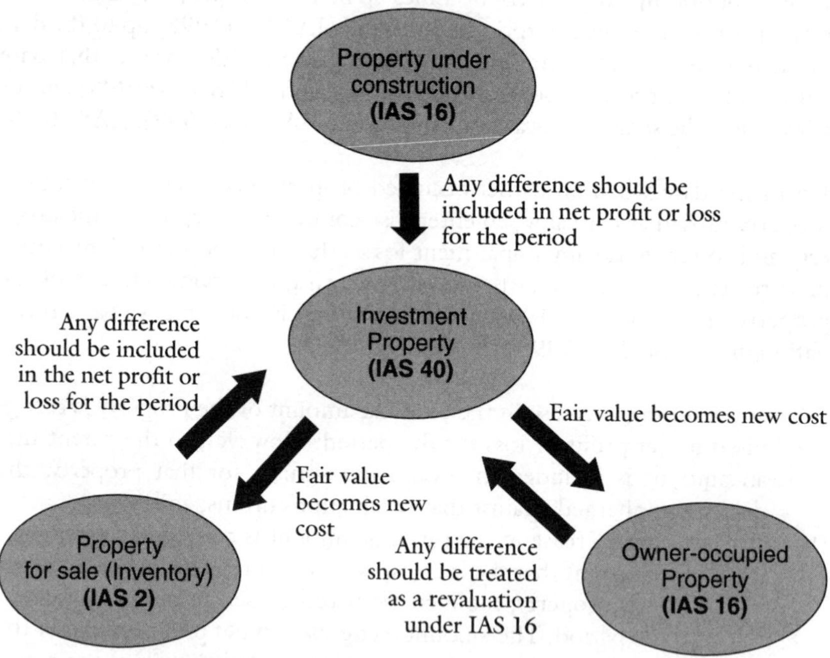

10.8.11 Disposals

IAS 40.60 requires an investment to be derecognised, i.e., eliminated from the balance sheet, on disposal or when the investment property is permanently withdrawn from use and no future economic benefits are expected from its disposal.

An investment property is disposed of via sale or by entering into a finance lease. When determining the date of disposal, the relevant Standard should be applied: IAS 18 (r1993), *Revenue*, for disposals via sale and IAS 17 (r1997), *Leases*, for disposals via entering into a finance lease or a sale and leaseback. (IAS 40.61)

Gains or losses arising from the retirement or disposal of investment property should be calculated as the difference between the net disposal proceeds and the carrying amount of the asset, and should be recognised as income or expense in the income statement, unless IAS 17 (r1997) requires different treatment on a sale or leaseback. (IAS 40.62)

IAS 40.63 stipulates that the consideration receivable on disposal of an investment property is recognised initially at fair value. If payment for an investment property is deferred, the consideration received is recognised initially at the cash price equivalent. The difference between the nominal amount of the consideration and the cash price equivalent is recognised as interest revenue under IAS 18 (r1993) on a time proportion basis that takes into account the effective yield on the receivable.

10.8.12 Disclosure

Fair value model and cost model

The disclosures detailed below are in addition to any disclosures required by IAS 17 (r1997), *Leases*. The requirements of IAS 40 (paragraphs 66 to 69) are to disclose:

(a) when classification is difficult (see **10.8.5**), the criteria developed by the enterprise to distinguish investment property from owner-occupied property and from property held for sale in the ordinary course of business;

(b) the methods and significant assumptions applied in determining the fair value of investment property, including a statement whether the determination of fair value was supported by market evidence or was more heavily based on other factors (which should be disclosed) because of the nature of the property and lack of comparable market data;

(c) the extent to which the fair value of investment property, as measured or disclosed in the financial statements, is based on a valuation by an independent valuer who holds a recognised and relevant professional qualification and who has recent experience in the location and category of the investment property being valued. If there has been no such valuation, that fact should be disclosed;

(d) the amounts included in the income statement for:
   (i) rental income from investment property;

(ii) direct operating expenses, including repairs and maintenance, arising from investment property that generated rental income during the period; and
(iii) direct operating expenses, including repairs and maintenance, arising from investment property that did not generate rental income during the period;

(e) the existence and amounts of restrictions on the realisability of investment property or the remittance of income and proceeds of disposal; and
(f) material contractual obligations to purchase, construct or develop investment property or for repairs, maintenance or enhancements.

Fair value model only

Where management has decided to adopt the fair value model, the financial statements should also disclose a reconciliation of the carrying amount of investment property at the beginning and end of the period showing the following (comparative information is not required):

(a) additions, disclosing separately those additions resulting from acquisitions and those resulting from capitalised subsequent expenditure;
(b) additions resulting from acquisitions through business combinations;
(c) disposals;
(d) net gains or losses from fair value adjustments;
(e) the net exchange differences arising on the translation of the financial statements of a foreign entity;
(f) transfers to and from inventories and owner-occupied property; and
(g) other movements.

In the exceptional cases when an enterprise measures a particular investment property using the benchmark treatment in IAS 16 (r1998), *Property, Plant and Equipment*, because of the lack of a reliable fair value (see **10.8.9**), the reconciliation detailed above should disclose the amounts relating to that investment property separately from amounts relating to other investment property. The following should also be disclosed:

(a) a description of the investment property;
(b) an explanation of why fair value cannot be reliably measured;
(c) if possible, the range of estimates within which fair value is highly likely to lie; and
(d) on disposal of investment property not carried at fair value:
    (i) the fact that the enterprise has disposed of investment property not carried at fair value;
    (ii) the carrying amount of that investment property at the time of sale; and
    (iii) the amount of gain or loss recognised.

Cost model only
Where management has decided to adopt the cost model, the financial statements should also disclose:

(a) the depreciation methods used;
(b) the useful lives or the depreciation rates used;
(c) the gross carrying amount and the accumulated depreciation (aggregated with accumulated impairment losses) at the beginning and end of the period;
(d) a reconciliation of the carrying amount of investment property at the beginning and end of the period showing the following (comparative information is not required):
    (i) additions, disclosing separately those additions resulting from acquisitions and those resulting from capitalised subsequent expenditure;
    (ii) additions resulting from acquisitions through business combinations;
    (iii) disposals;
    (iv) depreciation;
    (v) the amount of impairment losses recognised, and the amount of impairment losses reversed, during the period under IAS 36, *Impairment of Assets*;
    (vi) the net exchange differences arising on the translation of the financial statements of a foreign entity;
    (vii) transfers to and from inventories and owner-occupied property; and
    (viii) other movements; and
(e) the fair value of investment property. In the exceptional cases detailed in **10.8.9**, when management cannot determine the fair value of the investment property reliably, the enterprise should disclose:
    (i) a description of the investment property;
    (ii) an explanation of why fair value cannot be determined reliably; and
    (iii) if possible, the range of estimates within which fair value is highly likely to lie.

10.8.13 Transitional provisions

IAS 40 (paragraphs 70 to 73) stipulates the transitional provisions for each of the models adopted.

Fair value model
Under the fair value model, the financial statements should report the effect of adopting IAS 40 on its effective date (or earlier) as an adjustment to the opening balance of retained earnings for the period in which IAS 40 is first adopted. In addition:

(a) if the enterprise has previously disclosed publicly (in financial statements or otherwise) the fair value of its investment property in earlier periods

(determined on a basis that satisfies the definition of fair value and the guidance detailed in **10.8.9**), the enterprise is encouraged, but not required, to:
   (i) adjust the opening balance of retained earnings for the earliest period presented for which such fair value was disclosed publicly; and
   (ii) restate comparative information for those periods; and

(b) if the enterprise has not previously disclosed publicly the information described in (a), the enterprise should not restate comparative information and should disclose that fact.

IAS 40 requires a different treatment from the benchmark and allowed alternative treatments for changes in accounting policies under IAS 8 (r1993), *Net Profit or Loss for the Period, Fundamental Errors and Changes in Accounting Policies.* IAS 8 (r1993) requires comparative information to be restated (benchmark treatment) or additional pro forma comparative information on a restated basis to be disclosed (allowed alternative treatment) unless it is impracticable to do so (see Chapter **5**).

When IAS 40 is first adopted, the adjustment to the opening balance of retained earnings includes the reclassification of any amount held in revaluation surplus for investment property.

Cost model

IAS 8 (r1993) applies to any change in accounting policies that occurs when an enterprise first adopts IAS 40 and chooses to use the cost model. The effect of the change in accounting policies includes the reclassification of any amount held in revaluation surplus for investment property.

10.8.14 Comparison with UK GAAP

Under SSAP 19, *Accounting for Investment Properties*, investment properties are carried at fair value and are not subject to depreciation whereas under IAS 40, investment properties may be accounted for either at fair value, exempt from depreciation, or at depreciated cost less any accumulated impairment losses.

10.8.15 Comparison with US GAAP

Under US GAAP, investment properties are not exempt from depreciation whereas under IAS 40, investment properties may be accounted for either at fair value, exempt from depreciation, or at depreciated cost less any accumulated impairment losses.

10.9 Inventories

10.9.1 Sources

IAS 2 (r1993) *Inventories.*
SIC-1 *Consistency – Different Cost Formulas for Inventories.*

10.9.2 Brief summary of the requirements

Inventories are carried at the lower of cost and net realisable value. Cost may be assigned to individual items of inventory either by specific identification or by use of a cost formula. IAS 2 (r1993) gives a free choice among three cost formulas: the weighted average formula and first-in, first out ('FIFO') formula which are both denoted as benchmark treatments or the last-in, first-out ('LIFO') formula which is the allowed alternative treatment.

10.9.3 Development of the requirements

Originally approved in 1975, IAS 2 was revised as part of the Comparability/Improvements project. E32 *The Comparability of Financial Statements*, proposed that the FIFO and weighted average cost formulas be designated as benchmark treatments with LIFO as the allowed alternative and the base stock method no longer permitted. However, upon further deliberation, the IASC Board decided that LIFO should not be allowed and when the revised IAS 2 was exposed as E38, the proposals did not allow the use of LIFO. Comments on E38 were unfavourable from many parts of the world including the US, Germany, Italy and Japan, and in light of the comments received, the IASC Board decided to permit the use of LIFO as an allowed alternative but to require disclosure of the difference between the amount of inventory stated in the balance sheet and either: the lower of the amount arrived at in accordance with the FIFO or weighted average cost formula and net realisable value; or the lower of current cost at the balance sheet date and net realisable value. (Insight, December 1992, p.1)

In October 1997, the SIC approved SIC-1. This SIC requires that the same cost formula be used for inventories having the same characteristics. However, where the nature or use of items differs, the application of different formulas is allowed.

10.9.4 Definition

'Inventories are assets:

(a) held for sale in the ordinary course of business;
(b) in the process of production for such sale; or
(c) in the form of materials or supplies to be consumed in the production process or in the rendering of services.'

(IAS 2 (r1993).4)

Inventories held for sale include inventories held by retailers or unallocated finished goods of a manufacturer. Inventories in the process of production for such sale may include both work-in-progress of a manufacturing enterprise and labour costs of a service provider related to a particular project which has not yet been completed and revenue recognised. Inventories in the form of materials or supplies to be consumed in the production process or in the rendering of services are often referred to as raw materials.

This section does not deal with:

- work in progress arising under long-term construction or service contracts (see Chapter **27**);
- financial instruments (see Chapter **12**);
- producers' inventories of agricultural and forest products, mineral ores and agricultural produce to the extent that they are measured at net realisable value in accordance with well-established practices in certain industries (IASB has a separate project underway for Extractive Industries); and
- biological assets related to agricultural activity (see Appendix II).

10.9.5 Measurement

> 'Inventories should be measured at the lower of cost and net realisable value.'
>
> (IAS 2 (r1993).6)

10.9.6 Components of cost

> 'The cost of inventories should comprise all costs of purchase, costs of conversion and other costs incurred in bringing the inventories to their present location and condition.'
>
> (IAS 2 (r1993).7)

Each of these types of costs is considered below.

Costs of purchase

The costs of purchase which are capitalised as part of inventory include:

(a) purchase price;
(b) import duties and other non-recoverable taxes;
(c) transport and handling costs; and
(d) other costs directly attributable to the acquisition of finished goods, materials and services.

Any trade discounts or rebates received are deducted in determining the cost of purchase of an item.

Normally, foreign exchange gains and losses arising on the purchase of inventory are considered to be transaction gains and losses and are recognised in the income statement in the period they occur. However, in the rare circumstances that an enterprise is following the allowed alternative treatment of IAS 21 (r1993), *The Effects of Changes in Foreign Exchange Rates*, in relation to exchange differences resulting from a severe devaluation or depreciation of a currency against which there is no practical means of hedging and that affects liabilities which cannot be settled and which arise on the recent acquisition of the inventories, such exchange differences may be included in the cost of purchase of the inventory. (IAS 2 (r1993).9) See Chapter **22** for further discussion of such circumstances.

Costs of conversion

The costs of conversion which are capitalised as part of inventory include costs directly related to the units of production such as:

(a) direct materials;
(b) direct labour including all related employment taxes and benefits; and
(c) a systematic allocation of the fixed and variable production overheads incurred in converting materials into finished goods.

The practice of omitting some or all overheads from valuation on the grounds of prudence is not acceptable. Equally, the valuation of inventory on a 'marginal costing' basis, whereby only costs which vary directly with volume of output are included and costs which accrue on a time basis are excluded, is not acceptable.

'Fixed production overheads are those indirect costs of production that remain relatively constant regardless of the volume of production'. (IAS 2 (r1993).10) Fixed production overheads may include:

(a) depreciation;
(b) rent and rates of the factory building;
(c) maintenance of the factory building and equipment; and
(d) factory management and administration.

'Variable production overheads are those indirect costs of production that vary directly, or nearly directly, with the volume of production'. (IAS 2 (r1993).10) Variable overheads may include indirect materials and indirect labour.

Fixed and variable production overheads may be allocated to each unit of production based on the standard cost method which is described below under **'Techniques for the measurement of cost.'**

Sometimes two products may result from the production process, e.g., when joint products are produced or when a product and a by-product are produced. In such cases, when it is difficult to allocate costs between the two, a rational and consistent allocation method is chosen. For example, the cost of joint products may be allocated on the basis of relative sales values either at the stage in production when each product becomes identifiable or when production is complete. If an immaterial by-product results from production of the main product, the net realisable value of the by-product is often deducted from the cost of the main product. Since the value of the by-product is immaterial, this deduction does not result in the cost of the main product being understated. (IAS 2 (r1993).12)

Other costs

Other costs are capitalised as part of the cost of inventories only to the extent that they are incurred in bringing the inventories to their present location and condition. IAS 2 (r1993) states that it may be appropriate to capitalise non-production overheads. Such overheads might include an allocation of the costs of general and administrative expenses such as the payroll function or design costs related to a specific item of inventory.

Overheads other than production overheads should only be included in inventory valuation where this is justified by exceptional circumstances: those which are properly classified as selling or administrative overheads should not be included. An exception is made in circumstances where firm sales contracts have been entered into for the provision of goods or services to customer specification; in these circumstances, overheads relating to design, and marketing and selling costs incurred before manufacture, may be included in arriving at cost.

In addition, some enterprises may choose to capitalise borrowing costs related to inventory which is considered a qualifying asset. 'A qualifying asset is an asset that necessarily takes a substantial period of time to get ready for its intended use or sale.' (IAS 23.4 (r1993), *Borrowing Costs*) When inventories meet this requirement and are not routinely manufactured or otherwise produced in large quantities on a repetitive basis over a short period of time, they may be considered qualifying assets and related borrowing costs may be capitalised (see **10.4**).

Generally interest should not be included in inventory valuations, since capital is borrowed to finance the activities of the business as a whole and not specifically to finance inventory during the period of production. Normally, interest may only be included in the cost of inventory under the same conditions as are appropriate for capitalising interest in other situations, namely the underlying asset is one which necessarily takes a substantial period of time to get ready for its intended sale or use.

An exception to the general rule that interest is not included in inventory valuation arises when a company holds significant quantities of maturing stocks such as whisky. The maturing period is clearly part of the period of production and attributable to bringing the product to its existing condition and the addition of interest is therefore permissible.

> 'Examples of costs excluded from the cost of inventories and recognised as expenses in the period in which they are incurred are:
>
> (a) abnormal amounts of wasted materials, labour, or other production costs;
> (b) storage costs, unless those costs are necessary in the production process prior to a further production stage;
> (c) administrative overheads that do not contribute to bringing inventories to their present location and condition; and
> (d) selling costs.'
>
> (IAS 2 (r1993).14)

In addition, where the manufacturing process involves the transfer of work from one department to another, the transfer may be made at a price different from the cost incurred by the transferring department, either for reasons of convenience in accounting or as part of the system of management control. Where this takes place, it is necessary for the purpose of valuing closing inventory to adjust the valuations to actual cost by eliminating any profits or losses arising at the separate department levels.

Example 10.39

The following table illustrates the types of costs which may, or may not be, included in the cost of inventory.

PURCHASE COST	YES	NO
Purchase price		
discounts/rebates on purchase price	✓	
penalty or interest charge for overdue payments		×
travel expenses of the purchasing department		×
Taxes		
Recoverable VAT		×
Irrecoverable VAT	✓	
Import duties	✓	
Transport		
forwarding charges for external transport	✓	
transport insurance	✓	
internal storage costs after receiving materials		×
internal transport between stock locations		×
Other costs		
costs for a letter of reference (e.g., quality certificate for drugs)	✓	
costs for commission, brokerage	✓	

CONVERSION COSTS	YES	NO
Social security costs for staff in production	✓	
Voluntary security contributions	✓	
Salaries of construction department	✓	
Christmas bonus, vacation bonus	✓	
Factory supplies, auxiliary material	✓	
External consulting (e.g., process reengineering)		×
Depreciation of plant and machines	✓	
Costs of legal assistance (e.g., patent infringement)		×
Costs of leasing a machine	✓	
Costs of scrap production (exceeds normal level)		×
Rework of finished products (because of quality defects)		×
Salaries of the sales department		×
Costs of maintaining a canteen in the factory	✓	
Warranty cost		×
Costs for using a patent	✓	
Research for new products		×
Wages of purchase department	✓	
Audit fees		×
Ordinary maintenance of the factory	✓	
Restructuring of the whole plant		×

Costs of service providers

The costs of inventories of service providers consist mainly of labour and overhead costs related to service projects which have not been completed and on which revenue has not been recognised. For example, in an accountancy firm, amounts in inventory would represent costs incurred related to audits or other assignments which are not yet complete and on which revenue has not been recognised or only partially recognised. The bulk of such costs would relate to labour costs incurred by the personnel performing the work with other overheads such as costs associated with photocopying and faxing allocated to each assignment as appropriate. General and administrative expenses such as rent and rates are expensed as incurred.

Techniques for the measurement of cost

Techniques for the measurement of cost such as the standard cost method or the retail method, may be used as long as the results approximate actual cost. (IAS 2 (r1993).17)

The standard cost method is a method often used by manufacturing enterprises to allocate fixed and variable production overheads to each item of inventory produced. The standard cost of a unit of production is based on the budgeted amount of fixed production overheads and the normal capacity of the production facilities. Normal production is determined by reference to production over several years or periods so that unusual fluctuations in a particular period do not unduly affect the allocation. As such, normal losses in production due to planned maintenance and repair are taken into account when making this allocation. The use of actual capacity is permitted if it is similar to normal capacity.

Standard costs are revised to take account of variances which arise when actual performance varies from the budgeted figures on which the standard cost was based. For example, during periods of abnormally high production, the amount of fixed production overheads allocated to each unit of production is decreased to prevent inventory being stated above cost. However in keeping with the prudence principle, during periods of abnormally low production, the amount of fixed overheads allocated to each unit of production is not increased.

Variable production overheads are allocated to each unit of production on the basis of the actual use of the production facilities. Unallocated overheads are recognised as an expense in the period incurred.

Example 10.40

A small enterprise owns one building which houses both its head office and its production facilities. The head office occupies 40 per cent of the building and the production facilities the remaining 60 per cent. When allocating the fixed overhead of depreciation on the building:

- First the budgeted depreciation figure for the entire building is obtained, £100,000.
- Second, since the production facilities occupy 60 per cent of the building, 60 per cent of the depreciation charge, £60,000, is allocated to production facilities.
- Third, the budgeted amount of the overhead, £60,000 is allocated to each unit of production using the normal capacity of the enterprise, 20,000 units.
- Therefore, the cost of each unit produced will include £3 (£60,000/20,000 units) for depreciation of the production facility.

The retail method is often used by retailers who sell a large number of relatively homogeneous items which have a similar gross profit margin. The cost of inventory is determined by deducting the average margin from the selling price of the inventory. Such average margins take into account any reductions from the original selling price of items due to sales or other promotions. When the retail method is used, average margins are often determined on a departmental basis. (IAS 2 (r1993).18)

Example 10.41

	Cost	*Retail*
Beginning inventory	£200,000	£400,000
Purchases	1,000,000	1,600,000
Total	£1,200,000	£2,000,000
	Sales	(1,500,000)
	Ending inventory at retail	500,000

To convert ending inventory at retail to ending inventory at cost, multiply by the ratio of cost:retail for the year as follows:

£1,200,000/£2,000,000 = 60%
60% × £500,000 = **£300,000** = ending value of inventory

The retail method only works satisfactorily for an entire department or shop if all the lines held are expected to generate a similar profit margin. For example, the inventory of a newsagent and confectioner normally includes lines of widely differing profit margins and, to arrive at an acceptable inventory figure by the retail method, it is necessary to divide the stocks into categories according to the profit margin achieved. A further problem with the retail method arises if the selling price on slow moving items has been marked down. If the normal gross profit percentage is then deducted from such items, this will result in their being valued below cost, giving a result that may well be excessively prudent. It is therefore necessary to ensure that the volume of marked down items is insignificant or, alternatively, they should be segregated and valued separately. Sometimes, the margin that is deducted from selling price is the net rather than the gross margin. This would only be acceptable where the difference between the two is too small to make a material difference.

10.9.7 Cost formulas

Cost may be assigned to individual items of inventory either by the specific identification method or by use of a cost formula. When the use of the specific identification method is inappropriate, as discussed below, IAS 2 (r1993) gives a free choice among three cost formulas: the weighted average formula and first-in, first out ('FIFO') formula which are both denoted as benchmark treatments or the last-in, first-out ('LIFO') formula which is the allowed alternative. However, the same cost formula must be used for inventories having the same characteristics. Where the nature or use of items differs, the application of different formulas is allowed. (SIC-1)

Example 10.42

A car manufacturer makes the same model car in its factories in Asia, Mexico and Europe. If it applies the FIFO cost formula to its inventory in Europe, it must use FIFO at its other two factories.

However, if the same enterprise also produces watches, it may use a different cost formula for the watches since the nature of the two products differs.

Regardless of the formula used to assign cost to an item of inventory, the cost of an item of inventory may never exceed its net realisable value (See **10.9.8**).

Specific identification

> 'The cost of inventories of items that are not ordinarily interchangeable and goods or services produced and segregated for specific projects should be assigned by using specific identification of their individual costs.'
>
> (IAS 2 (r1993).19)

The specific identification method entails assigning the specific cost of an item of inventory to that particular item of inventory and is only feasible when each item of inventory can be separately identified. Thus, this method is only appropriate when items of inventory are allocated to specific projects and when other items of inventory held could not be substituted for that item, for example antique cars or works of art. This method is generally not appropriate in the routine production of inventory where raw materials are constantly being purchased and used, since specific identification in these circumstances could allow for a manipulation of profits through the selection of particular items of inventory to be used.

The specific identification method is rarely used in practice due to the complexity of many manufacturing or retail environments.

Weighted average cost

The weighted average cost formula assigns a value to each item of inventory based on the weighted average of items in inventory at the beginning of the period and the weighed average of items of inventory purchased or produced during the period. Depending on the inventory systems of the enterprise, the weighted average cost is calculated either on a periodic basis or on a perpetual basis as the inventory is received.

Example 10.43

An enterprise has opening inventory of 15,000 units at £4 and made the following purchases during the year:

Date	*Number of Units*	*Cost per Unit*	*Total Cost*
1 January	15,000	£4.20	£63,000
1 April	20,000	4.50	90,000
1 May	25,000	4.10	102,500
1 July	10,000	4.40	44,000
1 October	5,000	4.50	22,500
Total	75,000		£322,000

Ending inventory comprised 20,000 units.

Under the weighted average formula, multiply the number of units in ending inventory by the weighted average cost per unit for the year:

	Number of Units	*Cost per Unit*	*Total Cost*
Beginning inventory	15,000	£4.00	£60,000
Purchases:			
1 January	15,000	£4.20	£63,000
1 April	20,000	4.50	90,000
1 May	25,000	4.10	102,500
1 July	10,000	4.40	44,000
1 October	5,000	4.50	22,500
Total	90,000		£382,000

Thus, the weighted average cost per unit for the year is:

£382,000/90,000 = £ 4.24

The value of ending inventory is:

£4.24 × 20,000 = **£84,800.**

FIFO

The FIFO cost formula assumes that the items of inventory which were purchased or produced first were used first. Therefore, at the end of the period, the items in inventory are valued at the most recent purchase prices. The classic example of inventory accounted for under the FIFO formula is perishable goods such as fruit. When an enterprise holds perishable fruit, it is in its best interest to sell the oldest fruit first and thus the stock of fruit at any given time is the most recently purchased. However, IAS 2 (r1993) does not require cost formulas to be assigned in order to match the physical flow of goods, because this would be equivalent to specific identification and could be used to manipulate reported results. Thus a fruit retailer may sell its oldest fruit first but account for its inventory under the LIFO or weighted average cost formula.

Example 10.44

Same facts as in *Example 10.43.*

Under the FIFO formula, the first units in stock are the first units out, therefore, ending inventory is valued at the cost per unit of the last purchases.

Therefore, if ending inventory is 20,000 units, the value of ending inventory is calculated as follows:

Date	*Number of Units*	*Cost per Unit*	*Total Cost*
October purchases	5,000	4.50	£22,500
July purchases	10,000	4.40	44,000
May purchases	5,000	4.10	20,500
	20,000		£87,000

Thus, ending inventory is valued at **£87,000**.

LIFO

The LIFO cost formula assumes that the items of inventory which were purchased or produced last were used first. Therefore, at the end of the period, the items in inventory are those purchased first. The classic example of inventory accounted for under the LIFO formula is coal located in a large coal pile. When an enterprise uses coal from the pile, it takes the coal from the top of the pile which is where the coal which was purchased last was deposited. Thus, at any given time the coal in the pile is the oldest coal since the most recently purchased coal has been taken from the top of the pile and used. However, as noted earlier, IAS 2 (r1993) does not require cost formulas to be assigned in order to match the physical flow of goods, because this would be equivalent to specific identification and could be used to manipulate reported results. Thus the enterprise holding the coal may sell its newest coal first but account for its inventory of coal under the FIFO or weighted average cost.

Example 10.45

Same facts as in *Example 10.43.*

Under the LIFO formula, the last units in stock are the first units out, therefore, ending inventory is valued at the cost per unit of the first purchases.

Therefore, if ending inventory is 20,000 units, the value of ending inventory is calculated as follows:

Date	*Number of Units*	*Cost per Unit*	*Total Cost*
Beginning inventory	15,000	£4.00	60,000
January purchases	5,000	4.20	21,000
	20,000		£81,000

Thus, ending inventory is valued at **£81,000**.

Example 10.46

In summary, in the above examples, ending inventory was valued at:

Weighted average	£84,800
FIFO	£87,000
LIFO	£81,000

In times of rising prices, FIFO will generally give a higher ending inventory cost than LIFO with weighted average in between the two. In times of falling prices, the reverse will be true.

10.9.8 Subsequent measurement

Inventories are carried at the lower of cost and net realisable value. 'Net realisable value is the estimated selling price in the ordinary course of business less the estimated costs of completion and the estimated costs necessary to make the sale.' (IAS 2 (r1993).4)

The net realisable value of an item of inventory may fall below its cost for many reasons including damage, obsolescence, a decline in selling prices or an increase in the estimate of costs to complete and market the inventory.

Determination of net realisable value
Generally estimates of net realisable value are made, and thus items of inventory are written down, on an item by item basis. However, it may be appropriate to group items of similar or related inventory. This may be the case when items of inventory:

(a) relate to the same product line and have similar purposes or end uses;
(b) are produced and marketed in the same geographical area; and
(c) cannot be practicably evaluated separately from other items in that product line.

(IAS 2 (r1993).26)

However, IAS 2 (r1993).26 indicates that it is generally inappropriate to write-down entire classifications of inventory such as finished goods.

Service providers generally accumulate cost in respect of each service for which a separate selling price is charged. Thus, when determining net realisable value, it is appropriate to group by category of service. (IAS 2 (r1993).26)

When estimating the net realisable value of inventory, management must consider all the facts pertaining to the inventory and the operating environment at the time the estimates are made. If events or price fluctuations occur after the balance sheet date which confirm the net realisable value at the balance sheet date, such events or fluctuations are taken into account when making the estimation. (IAS 2 (r1993).28)

When estimating the net realisable value of inventory, the purpose for which the inventory is held is taken into consideration. For example, if the inventory is held to satisfy firm sales contracts, the sales prices agreed in those contracts form the basis of the estimation. (IAS 2 (r1993).28)

Recognition of impairment

When the net realisable value of an item of inventory is less than its cost, the excess is written off immediately in the income statement. (IAS 2 (r1993).31)

Net realisable value estimates are made at each balance sheet date and when the circumstances prevailing at the time of the write-down reverse or no longer exist, the amount of the write-down should be reinstated through the income statement. (IAS 2 (r1993).31) However, since inventory is carried at the lower of cost or net realisable value, upon reinstatement, the inventory may not be valued at above its historical cost.

The cost of materials and other supplies used in the production of inventory is not written down unless the finished goods into which the items will be incorporated will be sold at less than cost. Thus, a fall in the current purchase price of raw materials does not cause inventories of those materials to be written down unless the related finished goods will be sold at less than their cost. Where this is the case, the replacement value of the raw materials may be the best estimate of net realisable value. (IAS 2 (r1993).29)

10.9.9 Recognition as a cost of sales

'When inventories are sold, the carrying amount of those inventories should be recognised as an expense in the period in which the related revenue is recognised.' (IAS 2 (r1993).31) In accordance with the Framework, this process results in the matching of revenues and expenses.

If inventories are used by the enterprise, their cost may be capitalised as part of the cost of another asset, for example property, plant and equipment. Their cost is then recognised as an expense through depreciation.

10.9.10 Disclosure

The financial statements should disclose:

(a) the accounting policies adopted in measuring inventories, including the cost formula used;

(b) the total carrying amount of inventories and the carrying amount in classifications appropriate to the enterprise;
(c) the carrying amount of inventories carried at net realisable value;
(d) the amount of any reversal of any write-down that is recognised as income in the period;
(e) the circumstances or events that led to the reversal of a write-down of inventories; and
(f) the carrying amount of inventories pledged as security for liabilities.

(IAS 2 (r1993).34)

Common classifications of inventories are:

(a) merchandise;
(b) production supplies;
(c) materials;
(d) work in progress; and
(e) finished goods.

(IAS 2 (r1993).35)

When the cost of inventories is determined using the LIFO formula, the financial statements should disclose the difference between the amount of inventories as shown in the balance sheet and either:

(a) the lower of the amount arrived at in accordance with either the FIFO or weighted average formulas and net realisable value; or
(b) the lower of current cost at the balance sheet date and net realisable value.

(IAS 2 (r1993).36)

IAS 1 (r1997), *Presentation of Financial Statements*, requires that a line item which represents inventories be included on the face of the balance sheet. (IAS 1 (r1997).66(c)) When an enterprise chooses to present a classified balance sheet, inventory is normally classified as a current asset. However, in the unlikely circumstances that particular inventory is expected neither to be realised in, nor held for sale in, the enterprise's normal operating cycle, that inventory would be classified as non-current. IAS 1 (r1997) requires that an enterprise disclose for each asset that combines amounts expected to be recovered both before and after twelve months from the balance sheet date, the amount expected to be recovered after more than twelve months. (IAS 1 (r1997).54) Therefore, it is appropriate for an enterprise to disclose the amount of inventories which is expected to be recovered after more than one year from the balance sheet date. (IAS 1 (r1997).56)

10.9.11 Comparison with UK GAAP

Despite the fact that IAS 2 (r1993) refers to inventories while UK GAAP, principally SSAP 9, *Stocks and long-term contracts*, refers to stocks, the two Standards are similar in many respects. The definition of inventory/stock, cost in relation to inventory/stock, cost of purchase and cost of conversion are nearly identical. Thus, the guidelines governing the amounts which may be included related to the purchase and conversion of inventory are also very similar. However, in rare circumstances, under IAS 2 (r1993) certain foreign exchange gains and losses may be included in the cost of inventory which generally would not be permitted under UK GAAP.

Under both IAS 2 (r1993) and UK GAAP the retail cost method or the standard cost method may be used for assigning cost to inventory. However, while both IAS 2 (r1993) and UK GAAP allow the specific identification method, FIFO and the weighted average formula, LIFO is generally not appropriate under UK GAAP whereas IAS 2 (r1993) offers LIFO as an allowed alternative treatment. In addition, whereas IAS 2 (r1993) restricts use of the specific identification method to certain types of inventory, its use is not restricted under SSAP 9, though FRS 18, *Accounting Policies,* discourages the determination of cost on an asset-by-asset basis (i.e., specific identification) for fungible assets.

10.9.12 Comparison with US GAAP

IAS 2 (r1993) and US GAAP, principally Accounting Research Bulletin No. 43, Chapter 4, *Inventory Pricing*, with respect to the accounting for inventories are broadly similar. Although US GAAP does not specifically address accounting for the inventory of service providers, the provisions of IAS 2 (r1993) relating to service providers are generally consistent with US GAAP and practice in the US. Both IAS 2 (r1993) and US GAAP permit a choice of cost formulas among the specific identification method, FIFO, weighted average cost and LIFO and allow the use of the retail cost method or the standard cost method in estimating the cost of inventory.

IAS 2 (r1993) requires subsequent measurement of inventory at the lower of cost and net realisable value with net realisable value being based on estimated selling prices less costs to complete. US GAAP requires inventory to be carried at the lower of cost and market with market generally meaning replacement cost. Therefore, while both IAS 2 (r1993) and US GAAP require impairment write-downs to be recognised in the income statement, the calculation of impairment and indeed whether or not impairment has occurred may differ between the two.

In addition, IAS 2 (r1993) allows subsequent reinstatement of an amount written-down when circumstances have changed while US GAAP prohibits reinstatement.

10.9.13 Examples from published financial statements

Note that the excerpts given do not always comply in full with all aspects of IAS and as such are not necessarily examples of best practice but merely of current practice.

Example 10.47

[20] Inventories Raw materials, supplies, and goods purchased for resale are valued at the cost of acquisition; work in process and finished goods are valued at the cost of production. If the inventory values are lower at the closing date because of a drop in market prices, for example, the lower amounts are shown. Of the €6,095 million of inventories carried as of 31 December 2000, €431 million represents those included at their net realisable value.

Inventories are normally valued by the weighted-average method.

The cost of production comprises the direct cost of materials, direct manufacturing expenses, appropriate allocations of material and manufacturing overheads, and an appropriate share of the depreciation and write-downs of assets used for production. It also includes the shares of expenses for company pension plans and discretionary employee benefits that are attributable to production. Administrative costs are included where they are attributable to production.

Work in process and finished goods are grouped together in light of the production sequences characteristic of the chemical industry

Inventories are comprised as follows:

(€ million)	*31 Dec, 2000*	*31 Dec, 1999*
Raw materials and supplies	1,041	978
Work in process, finished goods and goods purchased for resale	5,046	4,006
Advance payments	8	8
	6,095	**4,992**

Bayer
Germany
International Accounting Standards
31 December 2000

Example 10.48

Inventories

Inventories are stated at the lower of cost and net realisable value. Cost is determined on a first in first out (FIFO) basis. Net realisable value is the amount that can be realised from the sale of the inventory in the normal course of business after allowing for the costs of realisation.

In addition to the cost of materials and direct labor, an appropriate proportion of production overheads is included in the inventory values.

14. Inventories	*2000* *€m*	*1999* *€m*
Raw materials, supplies and other	1,057	1,020
Work in progress	685	446
Finished goods	521	306
Total	**2,263**	1,772

Nokia
Finland
International Accounting Standards
31 December 2000

10.10 Trade and other receivables

10.10.1 Sources

IAS 1 (r1997) *Presentation of Financial Statements.*
IAS 18 (r1993) *Revenue.*
IAS 32 (r1998) *Financial Instruments: Presentation and Disclosure.*
IAS 39 (r2000) *Financial Instruments: Recognition and Measurement* (effective 1 January 2001).

10.10.2 Recognition

Trade and other receivables will normally meet the definition of a financial asset. Therefore, they are accounted for in accordance with IAS 39 (r2000). Under IAS 39 (r2000), an enterprise recognises a financial asset such as a trade receivable when, and only when, it becomes a party to the contractual provisions of the instrument. (IAS 39 (r2000).27) This is normally when the enterprise has a legal right to receive cash. (IAS 39 (r2000).29(a))

Normally this will be when the enterprise has performed (i.e., shipped goods or performed services, etc) under the contract. The issuance of IAS 39 (r2000) will not affect the timing of recognition of trade receivables for most enterprises. For example, for most manufacturing enterprises, a debtor will continue to be recognised when the goods are shipped, for a service provider, on completion of a job, etc.

However, trade receivables are *not* recognised as a result of a firm commitment to sell goods or services until the enterprise has performed under the agreement and therefore is entitled to receive an asset in return. (IAS 39 (r2000).29(b)) One exception to this rule relates to a forward contract which is defined as a commitment to purchase or sell a specified financial instrument or commodity on a future date at a specified price. This is dealt with in Chapter **12**.

10.10.3 Measurement

A trade or other receivable should be initially recognised at its cost, which is the fair value of the consideration given for it. (IAS 39 (r2000).66) Normally cost is determined by reference to the invoice price. However, when receivables are due in more than one year, the terms of the agreement need to be examined to determine if interest revenue is being recognised appropriately in accordance with IAS 18 (r1993) (see **6.6**).

Unlike some other financial assets, trade receivables fall into a category of assets which is not required to be remeasured to fair value at each balance sheet date. However, an allowance may be needed in order to reflect properly the amount of cash which is expected to be collected related to the trade receivable balance. In practice, the trade receivable balance is generally shown net of such an allowance (sometimes called bad debt allowance or bad debt provision), although in some countries the amount of the allowance is disclosed on the face of the balance sheet. Disclosure of such an allowance is not required by IAS.

10.10.4 Disclosure

IAS 1 (r1997) requires that a line item which represents trade and other receivables be included on the face of the balance sheet. (IAS 1 (r1997).66(f)) While IAS 1 (r1997) recognises that the appropriate subclassifications of receivables which will need to be disclosed will vary depending on individual circumstances, it suggests that the following subclassifications are generally appropriate:

(a) amounts receivable from trade customers;
(b) prepayments;
(c) other receivables; and
(d) amounts due from:
    (i) parent;
    (ii) fellow subsidiaries or associates; or
    (iii) other related parties.

Note that separate disclosure is *required* of (d) (i), (ii) and (iii). (IAS 1 (r1997).72)

Most trade and other receivables will meet the definition of a financial asset included in IAS 32 (r1998) and thus are subject to its disclosure requirements (see Chapter **12**). In particular, IAS 32 (r1998) requires disclosure of the fair value of all financial assets.

Since trade and other receivables generally have a maturity of within one year, under normal circumstances, their fair value will not vary materially from their carrying value.

If an enterprise chooses to present a classified balance sheet, trade and other receivables which are expected to be realised in the normal course of an enterprise's operating cycle are classified as current assets. Thus, if trade and other receivables are due in over one year but are expected to be realised in the normal course of the operating cycle of the enterprise, they are classified as current. However, IAS 1 (r1997).54 requires that an enterprise disclose for each asset that combines amounts expected to be received both before and after 12 months from the balance sheet date, the amount expected to be recovered after 12 months.

10.10.5 Comparison with UK GAAP

Under UK GAAP, receivables are generally referred to as debtors. The accounting treatment and disclosures relating to trade and other debtors are similar under IASs and UK GAAP.

10.10.6 Comparison with US GAAP

The accounting treatment and disclosures relating to trade and other debtors are very similar under IASs and US GAAP. However, listed companies (that is those falling within the jurisdiction of the Securities and Exchange Commission), are required to disclose any component of trade receivables which exceeds five per cent of the total line item. In practice, the five per cent guideline is used by most companies, not only those which are listed.

10.10.7 Examples from published financial statements

Note that the excerpts given do not always comply in full with all aspects of IAS and as such are not necessarily examples of best practice but merely of current practice.

Example 10.49

[21] Trade accounts receivable

Trade accounts receivable are stated at nominal value, less write-downs of €204 million (1999: €173 million) for amounts unlikely to be recovered.

Trade accounts receivable as of 31 December 2000 include €6,235 million (1999: €5,325 million) maturing within one year and €8 million (1999: €8 million) maturing after one year. Of the total, €11 million (1999: €25 million) is receivable from subsidiaries, €87 million (1999: €77 million) from other affiliated companies and €6,146 million (1999: €5,231) from other customers.

Bayer
Germany
International Accounting Standards
31 December 2000

10.11 Cash and cash equivalents

10.11.1 Sources

IAS 7 (r1992) *Cash Flow Statements.*
IAS 39 (r2000) *Financial Instruments: Recognition and Measurement* (effective 1 January 2001).

10.11.2 Definition

As discussed further in Chapter **13**, IAS 7 (r1992) defines cash as comprising 'cash on hand and demand deposits,' whereas cash equivalents are 'short-term, highly liquid investments that are readily convertible to known amounts of cash and which are subject to an insignificant risk of changes in value.' (IAS 7 (r1992).6)

As a rule of thumb, cash equivalents generally have a maturity of three months or less from the date of acquisition.

IAS 7 (r1992) distinguishes bank borrowings from bank overdrafts, and notes that when bank overdrafts which are repayable on demand are an integral part of an enterprise's cash management, such overdrafts are considered a component of cash and cash equivalents rather than a separate liability.

10.11.3 Measurement

Cash is carried at its face value which is equivalent to fair value. (For a discussion of cash denominated in a foreign currency, see Chapter **22**.) Cash equivalents are accounted for under IAS 39 (r2000) (see Chapter **12**).

10.11.4 Disclosure

IAS 1 (r1997) requires that a line item which represents cash and cash equivalents be presented on the face of the balance sheet. (IAS 1 (r1997).66(g))

IAS 7 (r1992) also requires disclosure of *inter alia*:

(a) the components of cash and cash equivalents (IAS 7 (r1992).45);
(b) the accounting policy adopted in determining the composition of cash and cash equivalents (IAS 7 (r1992).46);
(c) a reconciliation of the amount of cash and cash equivalents at the end of the period as shown in the cash flow statement to the amount of cash and cash equivalents disclosed on the face of the balance sheet (IAS 7 (r1992).45); and
(d) the amount of significant cash and cash equivalent balances held by the enterprise that are not available for use by the enterprise. (IAS 7 (r1992).48)

10.11.5 Comparison with UK GAAP

Under UK GAAP, 'cash at bank and in hand' is required to be disclosed on the face of the balance sheet and normally includes legal tender, amounts due by banks, items such as cheques, postal orders, bank credit card vouchers held in the ordinary course of collection, and demand deposits and deposits on seven day call with banks and similar institutions including building societies. It should be noted that the definition of cash used in the UK cash flow statement does not include demand deposits unless they can be withdrawn without notice and penalty within 24 hours. The definition used for cash and cash equivalents in IAS 7 (r1992) is used for both the cash flow statement and in the balance sheet and includes cash equivalents which would not be included in either definition under UK GAAP. For more detail on the cash flow statement, and a comparison with UK GAAP (see Chapter **13**).

10.11.6 Comparison with US GAAP

Under US GAAP, the definition of cash equivalents is similar to that found in IAS 7 (r1992). However, bank overdrafts which may be included in cash equivalents under IAS 7 (r1992) would generally be considered liabilities under US GAAP. For more detail on the cash flow statement, and a comparison with US GAAP (see Chapter **13**).

10.11.7 Examples from published financial statements

Note that the excerpts given do not always comply in full with all aspects of IAS and as such are not necessarily examples of best practice but merely of current practice.

Example 10.50

Cash and cash equivalents

Cash equivalents consist of time deposits with financial institutions with an initial term of less than three months.

China Petroleum & Chemical Corporation
China
International Accounting Standards
31 December 2000

Example 10.51

Cash and marketable securities

Cash comprises cash on hand and time, call and current balances with banks and similar institutions. This definition is also used for the cash flow statement. Marketable securities are shown at the lower of cost or market value.

Cash and marketable securities in millions of CHF (Swiss francs)

	2000	*1999*
Equity securities	**11,347**	12,593
Bonds and debentures	**4,669**	2,700
Money market instruments	**2,070**	1,521
Total marketable securities	**18,086**	16,814
Total cash	**2,562**	2,052
Total cash and marketable securities	**20,648**	18,866

Equity securities: These consist primarily of readily saleable securities.

Bond and debentures:

	Amount	*Range of interest rates*
2000		
Contracted maturity		
Within one year	1,054	3.0%–9.8%
Between one and five years	1,163	1.0%–11.8%
Over five years	2,452	2.0%–7.6%

Roche
Switzerland
International Accounting Standards
31 December 2000

10.12 Impairment of assets

10.12.1 Sources

IAS 22 (r1998)	*Business Combinations.*
IAS 36	*Impairment of Assets.*
IAS 38	*Intangible Assets.*

10.12.2 Brief summary of the requirements

IAS 36 requires that a review for impairment be carried out if events or changes in circumstances indicate that the carrying amount of an asset may not be recoverable. However, in the case of goodwill or intangible assets which are amortised over a period greater than 20 years, such an impairment review must be carried out every year. In each case, the review will compare the carrying amount of the asset with its recoverable amount which is the higher of its net selling price (if known) and value in use.

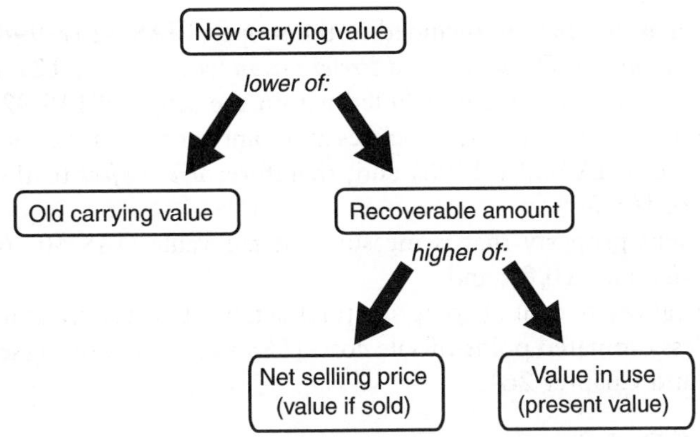

Any shortfall is deemed an impairment loss and recognised in the income statement for assets carried at cost and treated as a revaluation decrease (which may or may not lead to a charge in the income statement) for assets carried at a revalued amount.

10.12.3 Development of the requirements

Approved by the IASC Board in April 1998, IAS 36 became effective for financial statements covering periods beginning on or after 1 July 1999. It replaced the requirements for assessing the recoverability of an asset and recognising impairment losses that were included in:

- IAS 16 (r1993), *Property, Plant and Equipment*, related to property, plant and equipment;

- IAS 22 (r1993), *Business Combinations*, related to goodwill;
- IAS 28 (r1994), *Accounting for Investments in Associates*, related to investments in associates; and
- IAS 31 (r1994), *Financial Reporting of Interests in Joint Ventures*, related to interests in joint ventures.

All of the above Standards were revised during 1998, and the previous guidance relating to impairment removed and references to IAS 36 added.

10.12.4 Scope

IAS 36 applies to all assets *except*:

- inventories (IAS 2 (r1993), *Inventories*) (see **10.9**);
- assets arising from construction contracts (IAS 11 (r1993), *Construction Contracts*) (see Chapter **27**);
- deferred tax assets (IAS 12 (r2000), *Income Taxes*) (see Chapter **23**);
- assets arising from employee benefits (IAS 19 (r2000), *Employee Benefits*) (see Chapter **25**);
- financial assets that are included in the scope of IAS 32 (r1998), *Financial Instruments: Disclosure and Presentation* (see Chapter **12**). Note that *not all* financial assets are included within the scope of IAS 32 (r1998). For example, subsidiaries, associates and joint ventures are excluded from the scope of IAS 32 (r1998) and, therefore, *are subject* to the requirements of IAS 36;
- investment property that is measured at fair value (IAS 40, *Investment Properties*) (see **10.8**); and
- biological assets related to agricultural activity that are measured at fair value less estimated point-of-sale costs (IAS 41, *Agriculture*) (see Appendix II and Chapter **26**).

10.12.5 Definitions

The terms used in IAS 36 have specific meanings within the context of the Standard. Therefore, the more important definitions have been reproduced below for reference. (IAS 36.5)

Recoverable amount is the higher of an asset's net selling price and its value in use.

Value in use is the present value of estimated future cash flows expected to arise from the continuing use of an asset and from its disposal at the end of its useful life.

Net selling price is the amount obtainable from the sale of an asset in an arm's length transaction between knowledgeable, willing parties, less the costs of disposal.

Costs of disposal are incremental costs directly attributable to the disposal of an asset, excluding finance costs and income tax expense.

An ***impairment loss*** is the amount by which the carrying amount of an asset exceeds its recoverable amount.

Carrying amount is the amount at which an asset is recognised in the balance sheet after deducting any accumulated depreciation (amortisation) and accumulated impairment losses thereon.

Depreciable amount is the cost of an asset, or other amount substituted for cost in the financial statements, less its residual value.

A ***cash-generating unit*** ('CGU') is the smallest identifiable group of assets that generates cash inflows from continuing use that are largely independent of the cash inflows from other assets or groups of assets.

Corporate assets are assets other than goodwill that contribute to the future cash flows of both the cash-generating unit under review and other cash-generating units.

An ***active market*** is a market where all the following conditions exist:

(a) the items traded within the market are homogeneous;
(b) willing buyers and sellers can normally be found at any time; and
(c) prices are available to the public.

10.12.6 When is an impairment review required?

An impairment review is required:

(1) when at the balance sheet date, there is an indication that an asset or cash-generating unit ('CGU') may be impaired (IAS 36.8);
(2) at each financial year end for goodwill or intangible assets which are being amortised over a period greater than 20 years (IAS 22 (r1998).56 and IAS 38.99);
(3) at each financial year end for an intangible asset which is not yet available for use (IAS 38.99); and
(4) at least at each financial year end for items of property, plant and equipment held for sale. (IAS 16(r1998).59)

Indications of impairment
The Standard requires that at each balance sheet date an enterprise assesses whether any indications exist that an asset is impaired. When such indications are present, the enterprise must carryout an impairment review. At a

minimum, IAS 36 requires that the following indications should be considered. However, the list is not exhaustive and not all items will apply to all types of enterprises. If an impairment indicator which is not on this list exists at the balance sheet date, an impairment review is required nonetheless.

Impairment indicators

External sources of information

1. During the period, an asset's market value has declined significantly more than would be expected as a result of the passage of time or normal use;

   Such a decline could be caused by either a decrease in the external market value for an asset such as a head office building or a decrease in the sales price of items produced by an asset, such as a factory.

2. Significant changes with an adverse effect on the enterprise have taken place during the period, or will take place in the near future, in the technological, market, economic or legal environment in which the enterprise operates or in the market to which an asset is dedicated;

   For example, if a factory produces coal burning furnaces, and the government bans the use of such equipment after a phase-out period in favour of a more environmentally friendly alternative, the value of the factory would need to be assessed.

3. Market interest rates or other market rates of return on investments have increased during the period, and those increases are likely to affect the discount rate used in calculating an asset's value in use and decrease the asset's recoverable amount materially;

   If, in prior years, an asset has been the subject of an impairment test, and in the current period, there is a change in the market interest rates which will affect the discount rate used in the previous calculation, it is appropriate to revisit the calculation. However, this does not necessarily mean that once an impairment review has been carried out, it must be revisited each year or whenever market rates move. The review is required only when the change in rates is likely to affect *materially* the recoverable amount of the asset.

   IAS 36 specifically states that no formal review is required when the discount rate used in performing the impairment review is:

   (a) unlikely to be affected by the increase in these market rates. For example, increases in short-term interest rates may not have a material effect on the discount rate used for an asset that has a long remaining useful life; or
   (b) likely to be affected by the increase in these market rates but previous sensitivity analysis of recoverable amount shows that:

(i) it is unlikely that there will be a material decrease in the recoverable amount because future cash flows are also likely to increase. For example, in some cases, an enterprise may be able to demonstrate that it adjusts its revenues to compensate for any increase in market rates; or

(ii) the decrease in recoverable amount is unlikely to result in a material impairment loss.

(IAS 36.13)

4. The carrying amount of the net assets of the reporting enterprise is more than its market capitalisation;

In such cases, a write-down of the net assets of the reporting enterprise is not necessarily required. However, an impairment review should be undertaken to evaluate whether or not the value in use of the business is greater than its market price. If this is not the case, a write-down would be required. In some cases, the business prospects of the reporting enterprise may not have changed, but the sector in which the enterprise operates may be 'out of favour' with the market analysts and therefore, its share price has dropped. For example, in London in the late 1990s, small companies were 'out of favour' with the analysts causing market capitalisations across the sector to drop, in some cases without reference to the underlying business prospects of the enterprises in the sector. In such situations, a write-down may not ultimately be required, but a formal review would be.

Internal sources of information

5. Evidence is available of obsolescence or physical damage of an asset;

These may be the easiest impairment indicators to identify since they physically can be observed. Items such as unused factory equipment or equipment which has been damaged by fire are two examples which may indicate impairment.

6. Significant changes with an adverse effect on the enterprise have taken place during the period, or are expected to take place in the near future, in the extent to which, or manner in which, an asset is used or is expected to be used. These changes include plans to discontinue or restructure the operation to which an asset belongs or to dispose of an asset before the previously expected date;

Prior to IAS 36, assets held for sale were carried at the lower of their carrying amount and their net realisable value. Under the revised IAS 16 (r1998), *Property, Plant and Equipment*, assets held for sale remain at their carrying amount but at least at each financial year end, a formal impairment review is required.

7. Evidence is available from internal reporting that indicates that the economic performance of an asset is, or will be, worse than expected.

   Such evidence may include:

   (a) 'cash flows for acquiring the asset, or subsequent cash needs for operating or maintaining it, that are significantly higher than those originally budgeted;
   (b) actual net cash flows or operating profit or loss flowing from the asset that are significantly worse than those budgeted;
   (c) a significant decline in budgeted net cash flows or operating profit, or a significant increase in budgeted loss, flowing from the asset; or
   (d) operating losses or net cash outflows for the asset, when current period figures are aggregated with budgeted figures for the future.' (IAS 36.11)

When an impairment indicator exists, the facts surrounding the indicator should be considered when making the annual review of the remaining useful life of the asset, the depreciation or amortisation method and its estimated residual value. These items may need to be adjusted even if no impairment loss is recorded. (IAS 36.14)

10.12.7 How are impairment reviews performed?

Impairment is measured by comparing the carrying amount of an asset, or a cash-generating unit, with its recoverable amount.

Recoverable amount = *higher* of net selling price and value in use.

See **10.12.5** for definitions of these terms.

In order to measure an impairment it may therefore be necessary to calculate both net realisable value and value in use. However, simplifications will often be possible:

- if either net selling price or value in use is found to be higher than the carrying amount, the asset is not impaired and there is no need to calculate the other amount;
- if no reliable estimate of net selling price is available, recoverable amount is measured by reference to value in use alone;
- the detailed calculations involved in measuring value in use may be avoided if a simple estimate is sufficient to show that either value in use is higher than the carrying amount (in which there is no impairment) or that it is lower than net selling price (in which case the recoverable amount is the net selling price).

If however, an estimate of net selling price is required (see **10.12.8**). If an estimate of value in use is required, the estimation process can be broken down into four stages as discussed in **10.12.9**.

10.12.8 Net selling price

In descending order, the following represent the best evidence of the net selling price of an asset:

(1) a price in a binding sale agreement in an arm's length transaction, adjusted for incremental, directly attributable disposal costs (IAS 36.21);
(2) bid price in an active market less costs of disposal. If current bid prices are unavailable, the price of the most recent transaction may provide a basis from which to estimate net selling price, if there has not been a significant change in economic circumstances between the transaction date and the estimation date (IAS 36.22);
(3) the best information available to reflect the amount that an enterprise could obtain, at the balance sheet date, for the disposal of the asset in an arm's length transaction after deducting the costs of disposal. The outcome of recent transactions for similar assets within the same industry may provide a basis for the estimate. Unless management is compelled to sell immediately, the estimate does not reflect a forced sale (IAS 36.23).

Costs of disposal are deducted in arriving at net selling price and include:

(1) legal costs;
(2) stamp duty and similar transaction taxes;
(3) costs of removing the asset;
(4) other direct, incremental costs to bring an asset into condition for its sale.

Costs such as termination benefits and reorganisation expenses following a disposal are not considered direct, incremental costs of sale and as such, are not deducted in arriving at net selling price. (IAS 36.24)

Revalued assets
When considering revalued assets such as a revalued item of property, plant and equipment, it is important to remember that the carrying amount of such an asset under the revaluation rules of IAS 16 (r1998) may not always be equivalent to net selling price under IAS 36. For example, if such an asset is revalued to its fair value based on market prices whether or not this is equal to net selling price will depend on the size of the related disposal costs. If disposal costs are material, then net selling cost will be less than the market value

of the asset. Unless value in use is greater than this net selling price, the asset will be impaired. (IAS 36.4) However, some assets will be revalued based on something other than market value. Where this is the case, if an indication of impairment exists, an impairment test will need to be performed and recoverable amount assessed as for any other asset.

10.12.9 Value in use

The calculation of value in use can be broken down into four stages:

(1) Identify cash-generating units (see **10.12.10**);
(2) Estimate expected future cash flows (see **10.12.11**);
(3) Determine the appropriate discount rate (see **10.12.12**);
(4) Discount expected cash flows and total to arrive at value in use (see **10.12.13**).

10.12.10 Stage 1: Identify cash-generating units ('CGUs')

In large enterprises, it is often impossible to estimate the recoverable amount of an individual asset since assets usually generate cash when working together rather than singly. When this is the case, an enterprise should determine the recoverable amount of the cash-generating unit ('CGU') to which the asset belongs. (IAS 36.65) However, if the recoverable amount of an asset can be individually determined, Stage 1 may be omitted.

> 'A ***cash-generating unit*** is the smallest identifiable group of assets that generates cash inflows from continuing use that are largely independent of the cash inflows from other assets or groups of assets.'
>
> (IAS 36.5)

IAS 36 states that the recoverable amount of an individual asset cannot be determined when the following two conditions exist:

(1) the value in use of the asset cannot be estimated to be close to its net selling price (for example, when the future cash flows from continuing use of the asset are not negligible); and
(2) the asset does not generate cash inflows from continuing use that are largely independent of those from other assets.

(IAS 36.66)

When the recoverable amount of an individual asset cannot be estimated, its CGU should be identified as the lowest aggregation of assets that generates largely independent cash inflows from continuing use. (IAS 36.67)

In general terms, cash inflows are likely to follow the way in which management monitors and makes decisions about continuing or closing the different lines of business of the enterprise. Unique intangible assets, such as brands and mastheads, are generally seen to generate cash independently of each other and are usually monitored separately. Hence they can often be used to identify CGUs. Further cash inflows may be identified by reference to major products or services.

Cash flows from continuing use – internal vs. external cash flows
Cash inflows from continuing use are inflows of cash and cash equivalents received from parties *outside* the reporting enterprise. However, if an active market exists for the output produced by an asset or a group of assets, it should be identified as a CGU, even if some or all of the output is used internally. When this is the case, management estimates the *market* value for the output of the unit not only when determining the value in use of the unit itself but also when determining the value in use of the other CGU which is using its output internally. (IAS 36.69) In other words, market prices rather than internal transfer prices are used when estimating recoverable amount of a CGU.

Consistency
CGUs should be identified consistently from period to period for the same asset or types of assets, unless a change is justified. When a change is made during a year in which an impairment loss is recognised or reversed, disclosure is required of the current and former way of aggregating assets and the reasons for changing the way the CGU is identified. (IAS 36.71)

Example 10.52

Examples of identifying CGUs

(1) Interchangeable products
A publisher owns a particular publishing title. The title is sold in both paper and electronic form. In general customers will purchase either the paper or the electronic version, not both, depending upon their own circumstances. Therefore, demand for one affects demand for the other.

The assets used for production of both paper and electronic versions of the title comprise one CGU.

(2) Spare capacity
A company owns a warehouse to store its products. When the company has spare warehouse capacity it sells the capacity externally. The income from selling warehouse space externally only arises when there happens to be spare capacity and is not a largely independent income stream.

The warehouse represents one CGU.

(3) Service companies
Service companies such as telecom companies will have substantial assets to support their services. The arrangement and use of the assets will generally indicate appropriate CGUs.

Other service companies, especially if office buildings are leased, may have very few net assets. In such companies the importance of identifying CGUs is not in determining how to allocate assets to the CGUs, but in being able to make accurate estimates of levels of demand for the various services provided.

If a company provides regional services, it may be appropriate to identify each region as a separate CGU if economic decisions are taken by region. In contrast, if unprofitable regional offices are supported because overall coverage is necessary to the business as a whole then 'countrywide' CGUs may be appropriate.

In addition, Appendix A of IAS 36 includes several examples of CGU allocation.

Allocation of assets and liabilities to CGUs

As a general rule, the carrying amount of a CGU:

> '(a) includes the carrying amount of only those assets that can be attributed directly, or allocated on a reasonable and consistent basis, to the cash-generating unit and that will generate the future cash inflows estimated in determining the cash-generating unit's value in use; and
>
> (b) does not include the carrying amount of any recognised liability, unless the recoverable amount of the cash-generating unit cannot be determined without consideration of this liability.'
>
> (IAS 36.75)

This allocation is consistent with the calculation of the net selling price and value in use of a CGU which both exclude cash flows that relate to assets outside the CGU and liabilities that have already been recognised in the financial statements (see Stage 2 at **10.12.11**).

However, IAS 36.78 states that for practical purposes sometimes it is necessary to include assets that are not part of the CGU or will not generate future cash inflows from continuing use (for example, receivables/debtors or other financial assets) or liabilities that have already been recognised in the financial statements (for example, payables/creditors, pensions and other provisions). When this is the case, these items are also included in the carrying amount of the CGU.

Therefore, it appears as though best practice is to exclude these items, but if they are included, they should be included consistently, that is both in the carrying amount of the CGU and in the estimation of recoverable amount. To do otherwise would be to compare apples and pears, or unlike items.

In other situations due to the nature of a particular recognised and recorded liability, it may be appropriate to include it in the carrying amount and recoverable amount of a CGU. This would be the case when a CGU could not be sold without the assumption of the related liability by the buyer. In such a situation, the net selling price of the CGU is the estimated sales price for the assets and the liability together, less disposal costs. In order to be consistent and compare like with like, the carrying amount of the liability would also be deducted in determining both the value in use and carrying amount of the CGU. (IAS 36.77) IAS 36 gives an example of a mine where legislation requires site restoration on completion of mining activities. Since the mine could not be disposed of without the buyer assuming the restoration liability, when performing an impairment review, the liability would be included in the carrying amount of the CGU as well as in estimating both net selling price and value in use.

The following sections discuss the allocation of goodwill and corporate assets to CGUs.

Allocation of goodwill to CGUs

The recoverable amount of goodwill as an individual asset cannot be determined since goodwill does not generate cash flows independently from other assets. Therefore, if an indication exists that goodwill is impaired, it must be reviewed in the context of a CGU.

IAS 36 takes a 'two test' approach to the allocation of goodwill to a CGU. If a CGU is being tested for impairment, and there is any goodwill in the financial statements relating to that CGU:

(1) a 'bottom-up' test is performed. This requires the enterprise to determine whether the carrying amount of goodwill can be allocated on a reasonable and consistent basis to the CGU under review.

    If such an allocation *is* possible (for example if the goodwill relates entirely to an acquisition which is 100 per cent included in the CGU), the portion of goodwill related to the CGU is simply included in the carrying amount of the CGU for impairment testing purposes. No further 'top down' test is required.

    If goodwill *cannot* be allocated to the CGU, the carrying amount of the CGU (excluding any allocation of goodwill) is compared to its recoverable amount to ensure that any impairment of the assets other than goodwill included in the CGU is identified. Since goodwill is not included in this assessment, a 'top-down' test is then undertaken;

(2) if goodwill cannot be reasonably allocated to the CGU in the 'bottom up' test, a further 'top down' test is performed. This requires the enterprise to identify the smallest CGU under review and to which the amount of goodwill can be allocated on a reasonable and consistent basis (the 'larger' CGU). The carrying amount of this 'larger' CGU (including the allocated goodwill) is then compared to its recoverable amount.

Example 7 of Appendix A to IAS 36 includes an example of the bottom-up and top-down tests.

Allocation of corporate assets to CGUs
Corporate assets are assets other than goodwill that contribute to the future cash flows of both the CGU under review and other CGUs. Such assets may include group or divisional assets such as the building of a headquarters or a division of the enterprise, EDP equipment or a research centre. Key characteristics of corporate assets are that:

(1) they do not generate cash inflows independently from other assets or groups of assets; and
(2) their carrying amount cannot be fully attributed to the cash-generating unit under review.

(IAS 36.84)

When attempting to perform an impairment test for CGUs with associated corporate assets, the approach adopted for the allocation of goodwill is again appropriate. As detailed above, this would involve a 'bottom-up' test where such assets are split between the CGUs involved, followed, if necessary, by a 'top-down' test where a 'larger CGU' is formed (and used in the impairment test).

Example 8 in Appendix A to IAS 36 includes an example of the bottom-up and top-down approach to allocation of corporate assets.

10.12.11 Stage 2: Estimate expected future cash flows

Use of forecasts/budgets/cash flow projections
When estimating expected future cash flows, the following rules apply. Cash flow projections:

(1) should be based on reasonable and supportable assumptions that represent management's best estimate of the set of economic conditions that will exist over the remaining useful life of the asset. Greater weight should be given to external evidence;
(2) should be based on the most recent financial budgets/forecasts that have been approved by management. Projections based on these budgets/forecasts should cover a *maximum period of five years*, unless a longer period can be justified. The IASC Board takes the view that detailed budgets/forecasts are not generally available for a period of greater than five years and that as the time covered by a budget/forecast increases, it is less likely to be accurate. However, if management has produced budgets/forecasts for a period greater than five years and can demonstrate based on past experience that its forecasting methods are reliable for such extended periods, it can use forecasts for periods exceeding five years. It is expected that this will very much be the exception, not the rule; and

(3) beyond the period covered by the most recent budgets/forecasts should be estimated by extrapolating the projections based on the budgets/forecasts using a steady or declining growth rate for subsequent years, unless an increasing rate can be justified based on objective information about patterns over a product or industry lifecycle. This growth rate should not exceed the long-term average growth rate for the products, industries, or country or countries in which the enterprise operates, or for the market in which the asset is used, unless a higher rate can be justified. In some cases, it may be appropriate for the growth rate to be zero or negative.

Care should be taken to ensure that the growth rate used is not overly optimistic. For example, it would be likely where conditions are very favourable and growth rates high for competitors to enter the market and restrict growth. Therefore, the IAS states that it will be difficult to exceed the average historical growth rate over the long term (say, 20 years) for the products, industries, or country or countries in which the enterprise operates, or for the market in which the asset is used. (IAS 36.27–30)

(4) should be consistent with the discount rate assumptions related to price increases due to general inflation. Thus, if the discount rate includes the effect of price increases due to general inflation, future cash flows are estimated in nominal terms. However, if the discount rate excludes the effect of price increases due to general inflation, cash flows are estimated in real terms but include future specific price increases or decreases. (IAS 36.33)

Which cash flows are included?
Estimates of future cash flows *include*:

(a) projections of cash inflows from the continuing use of the asset;
(b) projections of cash outflows that are necessarily incurred to generate the cash inflows from continuing use of the asset. This includes cash outflows to prepare the asset for use if it is not yet completed, for example a building under construction, and future overheads that can be directly attributed, or allocated on a reasonable and consistent basis, to the asset; and
(c) net cash flows, if any, to be received (or paid) for the disposal of the asset at the end of its useful life. This is the amount that an enterprise expects to obtain from the disposal of the asset in an arm's length transaction between knowledgeable, willing parties, after deduction of the estimated costs of disposal. In estimating these net cash flows:
    (i) prices prevailing at the date of the estimate for similar assets that have reached the end of their useful life and that have operated under similar conditions are used; and

(ii) those prices are adjusted for the effect of both future price increases due to general inflation and specific future price increases/decreases. However, if estimates of future cash flows from the asset's continuing use and the discount rate exclude the effect of general inflation, this effect is also excluded from the estimate of net cash flows on disposal.

(IAS 36.32–35 and 46)

Which cash flows are excluded?

Estimates of future cash flows *exclude*:

(1) cash inflows from assets that generate cash inflows from continuing use that are largely independent of the cash inflows from the asset under review (for example, financial assets such as receivables/debtors) (IAS 36.36);

(2) cash outflows that relate to obligations that have already been recognised as liabilities (for example, payables/creditors, pensions or provisions) (IAS 36.36);

(3) cash outflows or related costs savings (for example reductions in staff costs) or benefits that are expected to arise from a future restructuring to which an enterprise is not yet committed. The guidance in IAS 37, *Provisions, Contingent Liabilities and Contingent Assets*, should be used to determine when an enterprise is committed (see **11.9**). Once an enterprise is committed, estimates of future cash inflows and cash outflows reflect the cost savings and other benefits from the restructuring based on the most recent financial budgets/forecasts that have been approved by management (IAS 36.37–40);

(4) estimated future cash inflows/outflows related to future capital expenditure that will improve or enhance the asset in excess of its originally assessed standard of performance. However, estimates of future cash flows do include future capital expenditure necessary to maintain or sustain an asset at its originally assessed standard of performance (IAS 36.37 and 42);

Example 10.53

Capital expenditure included in cash flow forecasts

The assets of the CGU comprise a factory and plant and machinery. The factory is expected to last 50 years, but will need a new roof in 30 years, and the machinery needs to be replaced every 10 years. The company expects to be able to reduce costs per unit of production by extending the factory to double production in a few years time.

The replacement expenditure for the 50 years including the new roof should be included in the cash flows, but neither the expenditure to double the size of the factory nor the additional income and revenue expenditure consequent on that expansion should be included.

(5) cash inflows or outflows from financing activities (IAS 36.43); and
(6) income tax receipts or payments (IAS 36.43). The assumptions underlying the discount rate must be consistent with the estimated future cash flows. Therefore, since the time value of money is considered by discounting the estimated future cash flows, these cash flows exclude cash inflows/outflows from financing activities. Similarly, as discussed in *Stage 4* below, a pre-tax discount rate is used; and therefore, future cash flows are also estimated on a pre-tax basis.

Foreign currency cash flows

Future cash flows are estimated in the currency in which they will be generated and then discounted using a discount rate appropriate for that currency. The cash flows are then translated to the net present value obtained using the spot or closing exchange rate at the balance sheet date. (IAS 36.47)

10.12.12 Stage 3: Determine the appropriate discount rate

> 'The discount rate (or rates) should be a pre-tax rate (or rates) that reflect(s) current market assessments of the time value of money and the risks specific to the asset. The discount rate(s) should not reflect risks for which future cash flow estimates have been adjusted.'
>
> (IAS 36.48)

Effectively, the discount rate used is an estimate of the rate that the market would expect on an equally risky investment. This rate is *ideally* estimated from either:

(a) the rate implicit in current market transactions for similar assets; or
(b) from the weighted average cost of capital ('WACC') of a listed enterprise that has a single asset (or a portfolio of assets) similar in terms of service potential and risks to the asset under review. (IAS 36.49)

In practice, a rate under (a) above will seldom be available due to the unique nature of different transactions. For (b), there may be few listed companies that offer a readily usable comparison since listed companies are likely to have a wider product/service base, wider markets and potentially lower risk profile.

When neither (a) nor (b) is available, a discount rate must be estimated. The rate being estimated should reflect a market estimate of the time value of money for the periods until the end of the useful life of the asset and the risks that the future cash flows will differ in amount or timing from estimates.

Estimation of a market rate

The enterprise may consider one of the following rates as a 'starting point' for its estimation. The rates would then be adjusted as discussed below. The 'starting point' rates include:

(1) the WACC of the enterprise. IAS 36 suggests using a technique such as the Capital Asset Pricing Model to determine the WACC of the enterprise. This technique and several others are discussed under **Calculating weighted average cost of capital ('WACC')** below;
(2) the incremental borrowing rate of the enterprise; and
(3) other market borrowing rates.

(IAS 36.51)

This 'starting point' rate is then adjusted:

(a) to reflect the way that the market would assess the specific risks such as country risk, currency risk, price risk and cash flow risk associated with the future cash flows; and
(b) to exclude risks that are not relevant to the projected cash flows.

(IAS 36.52)

If the 'starting point' rate is post-tax, remember to adjust it to a pre-tax rate. See '**Converting from a post-tax rate to a pre-tax rate**' below.

As discussed under *Stage 2*, the choice of discount rate and estimate of cash flows must be consistent. Therefore, the discount rate should not reflect risks for which future cash flow estimates have been adjusted. (IAS 36.53)

The discount rate is independent of the capital structure of the enterprise and the way the enterprise financed the purchase of the asset because the future cash flows expected to arise from an asset do not depend on the way in which the enterprise financed the purchase of the asset. (IAS 36.54)

Calculating weighted average cost of capital ('WACC')
The WACC can be defined as the weighted average of the returns required by each of a company's classes of securities. The WACC (post-tax) can be illustrated in its simplest form as follows:

WACC = (proportion of equity × cost of equity) + (proportion of debt × cost of debt)

$$\text{or WACC} = \frac{V_e}{V_e + V_d} \times K_e + \frac{V_d}{V_e + V_d} \times K_d \times (1-T)$$

where:

V_e = Market value of equity
K_e = cost of equity
T = effective corporate rate of tax
V_d = Market value of debt
K_d = cost of debt

There are a number of theoretical approaches to deriving the various constituents of a WACC. Some of the most practical and commonly used approaches are discussed below. The end of the section lists sources of information to assist in estimating some of the components of the models.

Cost of Equity ('Ke')

The cost of equity is commonly estimated by use of either the Capital Asset Pricing Model, the Arbitrage Pricing Theory or some other method. Each is discussed below.

1. Capital Asset Pricing Model ('CAPM')

One of the most common approaches to estimating a cost of equity is the CAPM. This model is based on the premise that, on average, investors in equity shares expect to receive an extra return over risk-free assets, to compensate for the additional risk inherent in such shares. It can be set out below:

$$K_e = R_f + \beta \times (R_m - R_f)$$

$\mathbf{R_f}$	Risk free rate
$\boldsymbol{\beta}$	Beta
$\mathbf{(R_m - R_f)}$	Market Risk Premium.

Common sources for these factors are detailed later in the chapter.

2. Arbitrage Pricing Theory ('APT')

CAPM is based on a single 'risk factor', the beta, which measures the level of market risk of a minority investment in a particular listed company (i.e., it is a measure of the volatility of a particular share price or investment return) in relation to the returns of a broad market portfolio of leading listed companies. Market risk includes inflation, interest rates, fiscal policy, state of economy, etc. Arbitrage Pricing Theory (APT) can be considered an extension of CAPM to incorporate certain additional risk factors which may affect a cost of equity. One of the main practical problems in using APT is that there is no consensus as to what these risk factors are. Most models attempt to link risk to macroeconomic factors such as interest rates, inflation or yield spreads.

The resulting equity return only reflects market risk. Adjustment for additional non-market risks particular to the company in question (such as size, lack of diversity, access to capital markets, etc.) must then be made to the extent these are not already reflected in the cash flows. These are a matter of informed investment judgement.

3. Other

Other methods may include more intuitive approaches, based on, for example, observations of rates of return evidenced in market transactions. This can be highly subjective but can be important as a safety cross-check.

Cost of debt ('K_d')

The cost of debt can be derived by looking at the cost to the company of its interest bearing debt. In general all interest bearing debt (ignoring non-interest bearing debt) used to finance the business should be included, although short-term 'working capital' (for example overdrafts) which are not part of the ongoing financing requirements of the company should not be included. Where the company holds quoted debt instruments, K_d can be estimated with reference to the market yields on those securities.

Debt/Equity ratio ('V_d/V_e')

The debt/ equity ratio of a company is the ratio of the *market value* of debt, V_d, to the *market value* of equity, V_e. In developing this ratio it is necessary to determine an economically appropriate capital structure for the company. This will provide a *target ratio*. Strictly, because the beta risk factor already reflects the actual gearing of the listed stock in question, it should be 'degeared' before application of the target gearing for the business unit.

This target ratio is the appropriate combination of the various sources of financing that optimises the value of the company and, specifically, the value of the equity.

A *target ratio* needs to be developed for two reasons:

(1) the current capital structure may not reflect the structure expected to prevail over the company's medium to long-term future. This may be the case if, for example, a recent transaction has distorted the current capital structure, or management would logically plan to change the mix of debt and equity; and

(2) it may be difficult to obtain the current market value of V_e. It is more appropriate to estimate the target ratio rather than attempt to estimate V_e and the current ratio.

Taxation ('T')

The effective corporate tax rate should be used in the calculation of WACC. This reduces the cost of debt based on the fact that interest on debt is an allowable deduction against corporation tax.

WACC estimated as above is a post-tax rate. Converting from a post-tax to a pre-tax rate is discussed below.

Quoted companies

Calculating WACC for a quoted company is a relatively simple exercise. As noted above the most difficult element to determine is normally the cost of equity, K_e, for which most entities will use the CAPM as detailed above. Most independent studies indicate that the market equity return over the risk-free rate for the smallest 20-30% of listed shares is somewhat higher than the average due to a lack of size. A premium may be added to reflect this.

Unquoted companies

It can be a more difficult and judgmental exercise to determine WACC for an unlisted company because of the lack of readily available comparable market data. Risk premiums can vary substantially – up to 40–50 per cent – which therefore makes the adjustment for non-market risk from the comparable cost of equity in a listed company to that appropriate to the business in question highly subjective. Companies may therefore wish to consider taking specialist advice when they need to determine such a discount factor. Although there are no clear universally accepted methods for determining WACC for an unquoted company, one possible route that may be considered is:

- To take an industry average beta factor for quoted companies, or the beta factor of the quoted company with the most similar risk profile. However, with the exception of larger successful businesses (or businesses with strong profit potential) which are likely to be suitable for listing, this can be a very crude starting point.
- Make the major judgmental adjustment to reflect any additional non-market risk due to the nature of products or market the unquoted company is considered to have, including the lack of marketability.

Example 10.54

Estimate of WACC for an unquoted company

Assume the company is in the retail food sector.

Cost of long term debt 12 per cent

Using the CAPM the cost of equity is expressed as:

$K_e = R_f + \beta \times (R_m - R_f)$

The following values have been assigned to these factors:

R_f	= 5.1%	Average yield to redemption of UK Gilts over 15 years – per Financial Times UK Gilts prices 14 September 1998.
β	= 0.8	Based on betas for listed companies in food retailing business – London Business School risk measurement service July–September 1998 (average taken from three measures given 0.82, 0.8 and 0.78).
$(R_m - R_f)$	= 5.5%	Average return over last 20 years – 1998 BZW Equity – Gilt Study Exhibit 2.1.

For a listed company in the food retailing industry the cost of equity could therefore be estimated as:

$K_e = 5.1\% + 0.8 \times 5.5\% = 9.5\%$

A further premium (possibly substantial) is then required to reflect non-market risks that are peculiar to the particular business compared to the listed comparable company. These involve: size, product and market diversity, market share, access to capital markets, maturity, etc. Accordingly, the range in which such an additional risk premium may fall is necessarily wide and it is not possible to give anything other than the broadest guidance. With a listed cost of equity at 10 per cent, and venture capital start-ups around 50 per cent, an appropriate rate of return will clearly depend on a careful risk analysis of the differences between the comparable company and the business in question.

Sources of information

Detailed below are some of the more common sources for the parameters used in the estimation of a WACC.

R_f The risk-free rate of return

The redemption yields on long–term UK Gilts are often used as a guide to the risk-free rate of return, with terms matching the investment period.

Recognised sources:
Financial Times
Datastream (on-line service)
Bloomberg Financial Markets

β Beta

Recognised sources:
London Business School, Risk Measurement Service, published quarterly
Datastream (on-line service)
Bloomberg Financial Markets
Barra

$R_m - R_f$ The market risk premium or ERP

Recognised sources:
Barclays Capital Equity – Gilt Study, published annually
Investment Banks

Converting from a post-tax rate to a pre-tax rate

Often, WACC will be calculated on a post-tax basis. When this is the case, the rate will need to be converted to a pre-tax rate. However, as the examples below illustrate, a simple grossing-up of the post-tax rate is only likely to be reliable where the pattern of tax cash flows is similar to the pattern of pre-tax operating cash flows.

Two factors which will impact on the relationship between pre and post tax return are whether assets are deductible for tax, i.e., are capital/writing down allowances available, and the timing of any such allowances.

Example 10.55

Tax deductible asset

Assume:

A CGU with a single asset. The asset generates cash flows for 5 years and is then worth nil. Cash flows are taxed at a standard rate of 30 per cent. Tax allowances are given at 25 per cent writing down allowance per year with a final year balancing credit.

	Year 0	*Year 1*	*Year 2*	*Year 3*	*Year 4*	*Year 5*
Pre-tax cash flow (asset cost)	–620	160	170	180	200	210
W/down allowance given on balance of:		155.00	116.25	87.19	65.39	196.17
W/down allowance		46.50	34.88	26.16	19.62	58.85
Tax on cash flow		–48.00	–51.00	–54.00	–60.00	–63.00
Post tax cash flow		158.50	153.88	152.16	159.62	205.85

Post tax return 10 per cent (IRR of post-tax cash flows incl. original cost).

Actual pre-tax return 14.01 per cent (IRR of pre-tax cash flows incl. original cost).

The relationship between pre-tax and post tax return in the example above can be compared with that achieved through simply grossing up for the rate of tax.

A post-tax rate of 10 per cent grossed up for a standard tax rate of 30 per cent equates to a pre-tax rate of 14.28 per cent. [10%/(1–0.3)]. The reason for the difference between this and the rate of 14.01 per cent seen in the example is that the tax deductions for the asset are not even over its life.

In a CGU comprised of a group of assets acquired at different times it is likely that the overall pattern of tax deduction for assets will even out and the actual pre-tax rate of return will then be closer to a simple grossed up post-tax rate.

Example 10.56 and *Example 10.57* below give an indication of the impact that the non-deductibility of an asset for tax has on the relationship of post-tax to pre-tax rates based on differing asset lives.

Example 10.56

Asset not deductible for tax.

Assume:

A CGU has only one asset not allowable for tax. Tax on cash flows is at 30 per cent. The asset generates cash for five years and is then worth nil.

	Year 0	*Year 1*	*Year 2*	*Year 3*	*Year 4*	*Year 5*
Pre-tax cash flow (asset)	–1000	356	370	380	390	400
Tax on cash flow		–107	–111	–114	–117	–120
Post-tax cash flow		249	259	266	273	280
Discounted at 10%		226	214	200	186	174

Post tax return 10 per cent (IRR of post-tax cash flows incl. original expenditure).

Actual pre-tax return 25.33 per cent (IRR of pre-tax cash flows incl. original expenditure).

Example 10.57

Asset not deductible for tax – effect of differing life.

The same assumptions as in *Example 10.56* above, i.e., the CGU has only one asset not deductible for tax. Tax on cash flows is at 30 per cent but this time the asset is assumed to have 10, 15 and 20 years' life (and be worth nil at the end of that life). A post-tax return of 10 per cent equates to the following pre-tax return rates:

Assumed life	Pre-tax return
10 years	18.80%
15 years	16.83%
20 years	15.37%

Normally a non-deductible asset such as goodwill or another intangible will be used within a group of other assets. The impact of such a non-deductible asset on the pre-tax return for the CGU will depend on its size relative to the carrying value of the CGU and, as demonstrated, its expected life.

10.12.13 Stage 4 Discount expected cash flows and total to arrive at value in use

The formulae for calculating value in use are derived from three formulae:

Single cash flow

Present value of a single cash flow occurring in *n* years = $\frac{Cash\ flow}{(1 + d)^n}$

Series of cash flows

Present value of *n* annual cash flows = *Cash flow* × $\frac{1 - (1 + d)^{-n}}{d}$

Perpetuity

Present value of annual cash flow to perpetuity = $\frac{Cash\ flow}{d}$

Where d = discount rate

Notes:

(1) In the first (single cash flow) formula, the cash flow is an actual cash flow. The discount rate will therefore be a nominal rate, matching the cash flow by including a compatible estimate of the effect of inflation.

(2) In the second (series) and third (perpetuity) formulae, it is assumed that all cash flows are the same, with the first cash flow occurring at the end of year 1. Where these cash flows will increase due to growth and inflation, this effect can be achieved by using a cash flow for year 1, and reducing the nominal discount rate by both growth and inflation rates. Where actual cash flow for the previous period is used, it will first be necessary to increase it by the first year's growth and inflation in order to find cash flow at the end of year 1. (This adjustment of the discount rate for growth is a substitute for building growth into the cash flows. It should not be confused with a real rate of return which would adjust for inflation only).

(3) At a discount rate of 20 per cent, a perpetuity can be assumed to approximate to 20 years or more, and at 10 per cent to 35 years or more, since any amounts beyond those horizons will be immaterial.

Situation 1 – Assumed steady growth in cash flows to perpetuity

The calculation is based on the perpetuity formula. Cash flow is for year 1, thus where the previous year's actual cash flow is used it is first necessary to increase it to reflect growth and inflation in year 1.

Value in use = $\frac{CF_0}{d_a}(1 + g)(1 + i)$

Where:

CF_0 = actual cash flow for previous period

i = annual inflation rate

g = annual growth rate in cash flows

d_a = pre-tax discount rate adjusted to reflect inflation and growth in cash flows.

Situation 2 – Cash flows forecast for 5 years, and assumed steady growth thereafter

The calculation is the sum of individual present values for the first 5 years, plus a perpetuity from year 6 onwards re-expressed from year 5 back to present value at time 0.

Value in use = Present value of each cash flow for years 1–5
+ Present value of cash flows for year 6 onwards

$$\frac{CF_1}{1+d_n} + \frac{CF_2}{(1+d_n)^2} + \frac{CF_3}{(1+d_n)^3} + \frac{CF_4}{(1+d_n)^4} + \frac{CF_5}{(1+d_n)^5} + \frac{CF_5(1+g)(1+i)}{d_a \times (1+d_n)^5}$$

Where:

CF_n = Cash flow in n^{th} year
i = annual inflation rate after year 5
g = annual growth rate in cash flows after year 5
d_n = pre-tax nominal discount rate
d_a = pre-tax discount rate adjusted to reflect growth and inflation in cash flows

Note

The sixth term in the formula, $\frac{CF_5(1+g)(1+i)}{d_a \times (1+d_n)^5}$, is a compound of two functions: $\frac{CF_5(1+g)(1+i)}{d_a}$ is the present value of cash flows from year 6 onwards expressed as a present value at the beginning of year 6; the further adjustment to multiply by $\frac{1}{(1+d_n)^5}$ re-expresses this as a present value at the beginning of year 1.

Example 10.58

Cash flows are forecast for 2 years

Assume:

Cash flow for year 1	£20m
Cash flow for year 2	£24m
Assumed steady growth thereafter	2.5%
Inflation	2.5%
Nominal pre-tax discount rate	15%
Adjusted pre-tax discount rate	10%

$$\text{Value in use} = \frac{£20m}{1.15} + \frac{£24m}{1.15^2} + \frac{£24m \times 1.025 \times 1.025}{0.1 \times 1.15^2} = £226\text{m}$$

10.12.14 Recognition and measurement of an impairment loss

The following sections discuss the recognition and measurement of an impairment loss for an individual asset and for a CGU, respectively.

Individual asset

> 'If, and only if, the recoverable amount of an asset is less than its carrying amount, the carrying amount of the asset should be reduced to its recoverable amount. That reduction is an impairment loss.'
>
> (IAS 36.58)

An impairment loss should be recognised in the income statement immediately unless it relates to an asset carried at a revalued amount. If an asset has been revalued, for example an item of property, plant and equipment, the impairment loss is dealt with in accordance with that particular IAS, in this case IAS 16 (r1998), *Property, Plant and Equipment* (see **10.3**). Generally, an impairment loss will first result in a decrease in any revaluation surplus related to the asset. This decrease is shown in the statement showing changes in equity rather than the income statement. Second, where no related revaluation surplus exists or to the extent that the impairment loss is greater than the related revaluation surplus, the excess impairment loss is expensed in the income statement.

If the impairment loss is greater than the carrying amount of the asset, a provision may only be made if it is required by another IAS. (IAS 36.61) In general, provisions are only recognised when they represent obligations arising as a result of past events. IAS 37, *Provisions, Contingent Liabilities and Contingent Assets*, includes the recognition criteria for provisions (see Chapter **11**).

IAS 16 (r1998) and IAS 37 both require that the estimated useful life, the depreciation/amortisation method and residual value of an item of property, plant and equipment or an intangible asset, respectively, be reviewed at each balance sheet date. After an impairment loss is recognised, these three items are reviewed, and the new carrying amount is depreciated/amortised over the remaining useful life. (IAS 36.62)

Since an impairment loss affects the carrying amount of an asset, it affects the relationship between an asset's carrying amount and tax base. Therefore, any deferred tax asset or liability related to the asset will need to be revisited (see Chapter **23**).

Example 10.59

This example is taken from Example 3 (Appendix A) of IAS 36.

An enterprise has an asset with a carrying amount of 1,000. Its recoverable amount is 650. The tax rate is 30 per cent and the tax base of the asset is 800. Impairment losses are not deductible for tax purposes. The effect of the impairment loss is as follows:

	Before impairment	*Effect of impairment*	*After impairment*
Carrying amount	1,000	(350)	650
Tax base	800	–	800
Taxable (deductible) temporary difference	200	(350)	(150)
Deferred tax liability (asset) at 30%	60	(105)	(45)

In accordance with IAS 12 (r2000), Income Taxes, the enterprise recognises the deferred tax asset to the extent that it is probable that taxable profit will be available against which the deductible temporary difference can be utilised.

Cash generating unit

> 'An impairment loss should be recognised for a cash-generating unit if, and only if, its recoverable amount is less than its carrying amount. The impairment loss should be allocated to reduce the carrying amount of the assets of the unit in the following order:
>
> (a) first, to goodwill allocated to the cash-generating unit (if any); and
> (b) then, to the other assets of the unit on a pro-rata basis based on the carrying amount of each asset in the unit.'
>
> (IAS 36.88)

These reductions in carrying amounts should be treated as impairment losses on individual assets as discussed in the previous section.

When allocating an impairment loss to individual assets within a CGU, the carrying amount of an individual asset should not be reduced below the highest of:

(a) its net selling price (if determinable);
(b) its value in use (if determinable); and
(c) nil.

If this results in an amount being allocated to an asset which is less than its pro-rata share of the impairment loss, the excess is allocated to the remaining assets on a pro-rata basis.

(IAS 36.89)

If the recoverable amount of an individual asset cannot be determined:

(a) an impairment loss is recognised for the asset if its carrying amount is greater than the higher of its net selling price and the results of the allocation procedures described above; and
(b) no impairment loss is recognised for the asset if the related CGU is not impaired. This applies even if the asset's net selling price is less than its carrying amount. (IAS 36.92)

10.12.15 Reversals of impairment losses

An enterprise is required to assess at each balance sheet date whether there is any indication that an impairment loss recognised for an asset in prior years may no longer exist or may have decreased. If such an indication exists, the enterprise should estimate the recoverable amount of that asset.

The 'reversal of impairment indicators' listed in IAS 36 are broadly the mirror image of the impairment indicators discussed in **10.12.6**. They are reproduced below:

> '*External sources of information*
>
> (a) the asset's market value has increased significantly during the period;
> (b) significant changes with a favourable effect on the enterprise have taken place during the period, or will take place in the near future, in the technological, market, economic or legal environment in which the enterprise operates or in the market to which the asset is dedicated;
> (c) market interest rates or other market rates of return on investments have decreased during the period, and those decreases are likely to affect the discount rate used in calculating the asset's value in use and increase the asset's recoverable amount materially;
>
> *Internal sources of information*
>
> (d) significant changes with a favourable effect on the enterprise have taken place during the period, or are expected to take place in the near future, in the extent to which, or manner in which, the asset is used or is expected to be used. These changes include capital expenditure that has been incurred during the period to improve or enhance an asset in excess of its originally assessed standard of performance or a commitment to discontinue or restructure the operation to which the asset belongs; and
> (e) evidence is available from internal reporting that indicates that the economic performance of the asset is, or will be, better than expected.'
>
> (IAS 36.96)

An impairment loss may be reversed if, and only if, there has been a change in the estimates used to determine the recoverable amount of the asset since the last impairment loss was recognised. When this is the case, the carrying amount of the asset is increased to its recoverable amount. (IAS 36.99)

A reversal of an impairment loss must reflect an increase in the estimated service potential of an asset, either from use or sale. Examples of such changes in estimate include:

(1) a change in the basis for recoverable amount (i.e., whether recoverable amount is based on net selling price or value in use);
(2) if recoverable amount was based on value in use, a change in the amount or timing of estimated future cash flows or in the discount rate; or
(3) if recoverable amount was based on net selling price, a change in estimate of the components of net selling price.

(IAS 36.100)

However, an increase in the recoverable amount of the asset due to the passage of time, does *not* represent an increase in the estimated service potential of an asset and therefore it is not acceptable to recognise a reversal of an impairment loss on this basis. In other words, the value in use of an asset may increase simply because the present value of future cash inflows increases as they become closer. However, this does not represent an economic change in the value of the asset. Therefore, a reversal of an impairment loss may not be recognised on this basis. (IAS 36.101)

Reversal for an individual asset

'The increased carrying amount of an asset due to a reversal of an impairment loss should not exceed the carrying amount that would have been determined (net of amortisation or depreciation) had no impairment loss been recognised for the asset in prior years.' (IAS 36.102) Any increase in excess of this amount would be a revaluation and would be accounted for under the appropriate IAS (i.e., IAS 16 (r1998) for an item of property, plant and equipment or IAS 37 for an intangible asset).

Reversals of impairment losses are recognised in the income statement unless the asset is carried at a revalued amount. When an asset is carried at a revalued amount, the reversal is considered a revaluation increase and treated accordingly. Normally, a revaluation increase is credited directly to equity and recognised in the statement showing changes in equity. However, to the extent that an impairment loss on the same revalued asset was previously recognised as an expense in the income statement, a reversal of that impairment loss is recognised as income in the income statement. (IAS 36.105)

After the reversal of an impairment loss, the estimated useful life, residual value and the depreciation/amortisation method should be reviewed. The new carrying amount is then depreciated/amortised over the remaining useful life.

Reversal for a CGU

A reversal of an impairment loss for a CGU should be allocated to increase the carrying amount of the assets of the unit in the following order:

(a) first, assets other than goodwill on a pro-rata basis based on the carrying amount of each asset in the unit; and
(b) then, to goodwill allocated to the CGU *if* the requirements discussed under **'Reversal for goodwill'** are met.

These increases in carrying amounts should be treated as reversals of impairment losses for individual assets and recognised as discussed above under **'Reversal for an individual asset'.** (IAS 36.107)

In allocating a reversal of an impairment loss for a CGU, the carrying amount of an asset should not be increased above the *lower* of:

(a) its recoverable amount (if determinable); and
(b) the carrying amount that would have been determined (net of amortisation/depreciation) had no impairment loss been recognised for the asset in prior years. (Any further increase would constitute a revaluation.)

The amount of the reversal of the impairment loss that would otherwise have been allocated to the asset should be allocated to the other assets of the unit on a pro-rata basis. (IAS 36.108)

Example 10.60

An intangible asset costing £10 million is amortised over 20 years. Two years after it is purchased, it becomes impaired and is written down from its carrying value of £9 million to its estimated recoverable amount of £5 million. Two years after that the impairment reverses in a manner that can be recognised in the financial statements. The recoverable amount of the intangible asset is now estimated to be £10 million. However, the amount that can be recognised as the reversal of an impairment loss is only the £3 million that increases the carrying amount of the intangible asset up to the £8 million at which it would have been recorded had the original impairment loss not occurred.

Reversal for goodwill

Due to the fact that the IASC Board did not support the recognition of internally generated goodwill (IAS 38 specifically prohibits it), it set two criteria which must be met in order to recognise a reversal of an impairment loss related to goodwill. The Board's reasoning is that unless the two criteria are met, the reversal must represent newly created internally generated goodwill and therefore recognition would be inappropriate. The two criteria are:

(1) the impairment loss was caused by a specific external event of an exceptional nature that is not expected to recur; and
(2) subsequent external events have occurred that reverse the effect of that event.

(IAS 36.109)

A specific external event must be one that is outside the enterprise's control. IAS 36 gives as an example new regulations that significantly curtail the operating activities, or decrease the profitability, of the business to which the goodwill relates. (IAS 36.112) The Standard also specifically prohibits a reversal of an impairment loss related to goodwill due to a change in estimate such as a change in the discount rate or in the amount and timing of future cash flows. (IAS 36.111)

In practice, the situations where it will be possible to recognise the reversal of an impairment loss on goodwill and intangible assets will be very limited. Typically, an impairment loss reflects a downturn in the profitability of the business, perhaps because the market has become more competitive or the products have become outdated. If the value of the goodwill or intangible asset subsequently recovers, it is probably because action has been taken by the company, perhaps to update the products, reorganise the business, improve efficiency or refocus a brand. In such circumstances, the recovery in the value of the goodwill or intangible asset is not attributable to the reversal of an external event. Rather, it is attributable to the creation of internally generated goodwill or intangible asset value. So it would not be possible to write back the loss.

A fairly extreme example is necessary to illustrate the circumstances in which it would be possible to recognise the reversal of an impairment loss as a gain:

Example 10.61

An acquired business produces bottled mineral water. Just before the year end, a consumer group tests the water and publicises the fact that it contains dangerous levels of a harmful chemical. Sales of the mineral water plummet.

Situation 1

Suppose that there is great uncertainty about the validity of the consumer group's claim, but it is assumed to be valid and that sales of the product will recover only after the problem is sorted out and the product is re-tested and re-marketed. The future cash flows indicate that the goodwill is worth much less than before: it is written down.

But in the next period, further tests demonstrate that the consumer group had been wrong in its claims and it retracts them publicly. Sales of the mineral water recover very quickly and soon are back to previous levels. *The assumptions made in forecasting future cash flows at the time of the impairment review had been wrong.*

In this specific case, it is clear that an external event caused the impairment and that a subsequent external event has reversed it in a way that was not foreseen when measuring the original impairment loss. The goodwill can be written back up to the lower of its present value and its amortised historical cost.

Situation 2

As in situation 1, it is assumed that the claims of the consumer group may be valid and that sales will recover only once the problem has been sorted out and the product re-marketed. The goodwill is written off.

Suppose this time, that in the next period, it transpires that the consumer group was correct. The product is withdrawn until the problem is resolved and then relaunched with substantial marketing support. Sales recover and the value of the goodwill gradually rises back towards its original level. The recovery cannot be recognised because it has not been caused by unforeseen external events. Rather, it has been caused by the creation of internally generated goodwill.

Situation 3

Suppose this time that, by the year end, the mineral water company has conducted its own tests and satisfied both itself and independent experts that the consumer group was wrong in its claims. So the company forecasts that, although there has been a temporary reduction in the sales, these will soon recover as the consumer group retracts the claims.

The temporary reduction in sales has caused a small temporary impairment in the value of the goodwill as measured at the balance sheet date. The goodwill is written down by this small amount.

In the next period, the sales increase back to their previous levels in line with expectations and the value of the goodwill recovers to its original level. But the (small) impairment loss cannot be reversed in the accounts: its reversal was foreseen in the original impairment calculations and has occurred simply because of the passing of time.

10.12.16 Disclosure

For each class of assets (defined as a grouping of assets of similar nature and use in the operations of the enterprise), the financial statements should disclose the amount of:

(1) impairment losses recognised in the income statement during the period and the line item(s) of the income statement in which those impairment losses are included;
(2) reversals of impairment losses recognised in the income statement during the period and the line item(s) of the income statement in which those impairment losses are reversed;
(3) impairment losses recognised directly in equity during the period; and
(4) reversals of impairment losses recognised directly in equity during the period.

(IAS 36.113)

This information may be presented in the reconciliation of the carrying amounts of property, plant and equipment, intangible assets, investments or elsewhere as appropriate.

When an enterprise applies IAS 14 (r1997), *Segment Reporting*, (see Chapter **16**), it is required to disclose the following for each reportable segment based on the primary reporting format:

(1) the amount of impairment losses recognised in the income statement and directly in equity during the period; and
(2) the amount of reversals of impairment losses recognised in the income statement and directly in equity during the period.

(IAS 36.116)

When an impairment loss for an individual asset or a CGU is recognised or reversed *which is material to the financial statements taken as a whole*, the following disclosures are required:

(a) the events and circumstances that led to the recognition (reversal) of the loss;
(b) the amount of the loss recognised (reversed);
(c) for an individual asset:
    (i) the nature of the asset; and
    (ii) the reportable segment to which the asset belongs based on the primary reporting format of the enterprise (see Chapter **16**);
(d) for a CGU:
    (i) a description of the CGU (such as whether it is a product line, a

plant, a business operation, a geographical area, a reportable segment as in IAS 14 (r1997) or other);

(ii) the amount of the loss recognised or reversed by class of assets and by reportable segment based on the primary reporting format of the enterprise; and

(iii) if the aggregation of assets for identifying the CGU has changed since the previous estimate of the CGU's recoverable amount (if any), a description of the current and former way of aggregating assets and the reasons for changing the way the CGU is identified;

(e) whether the recoverable amount of the asset or CGU is its net selling price or its value in use;

(f) if recoverable amount is net selling price, the basis used to determine net selling price (such as whether selling price was determined by reference to an active market or in some other way); and

(g) if recoverable amount is value in use, the discount rate(s) used in the current estimate and previous estimate (if any) of value in use.

(IAS 36.117)

If impairment losses recognised (reversed) during the period are material in aggregate to the financial statements taken as a whole, an enterprise discloses a brief description of the following:

(1) the main classes of assets affected by impairment losses (reversals) for which no information is disclosed under the above paragraph (i.e., that are not material to the financial statements taken as a whole in their own right); and

(2) the main events and circumstances that led to the recognition (or reversal) of these impairment losses for which no information is disclosed under the above paragraph.

(IAS 36.118)

Finally, an enterprise is encouraged, but not required, to disclose key assumptions used to determine the recoverable amount of assets (CGUs) during the period.

10.12.17 Comparison with UK GAAP

UK GAAP requires an impairment test as follows:

- for tangible fixed assets where a useful life of greater than 50 years is used (FRS 15, *Tangible Fixed Assets*);
- for goodwill and intangible assets where a useful life of greater than 20 years is used (FRS 10, *Goodwill and Intangible Assets*); and
- for all tangible and intangible fixed assets where there is an indication of impairment (FRS 10 and 18).

FRS 11, *Impairment of Fixed Assets and Goodwill*, deals with the methodology of impairment tests.

Broadly, IAS 36 and FRS 11 are similar with both measuring impairment by comparing the carrying value of assets with the higher of net selling price (equivalent to net realisable value in FRS 11) and value in use. However, the following differences in detail exist:

- the FRS requires impairments of revalued assets that are clearly caused by the consumption of economic benefits to be recognised in the income statement. In contrast, the IAS requires such impairments to be recognised in the income statement only to the extent that the loss exceeds the balance on the revaluation surplus relating to the assets in question.
- to be consistent with FRS 10, FRS 11 aligns the treatment of intangible assets with that of goodwill, whereas IAS 36 treats intangibles as being more similar to items of property, plant and equipment. This has two consequences:
  (1) FRS 11 allocates impairment losses in an income-generating unit (similar to a cash-generating unit under IAS 36) first to goodwill, secondly to intangible assets and then to tangible fixed assets, while the IAS allocates impairment losses first to goodwill and then pro rata to intangible and tangible assets; and
  (2) FRS 11 restricts the recognition of reversals of impairment losses on intangible assets (except those with a readily ascertainable market value) to the same limited circumstances in which reversals of impairments of goodwill are recognised. IAS 36 recognises reversals of impairments of intangible assets under the same conditions that apply to reversals of impairments of tangible fixed assets.
- FRS 11 has a general rule that in all but exceptional circumstances, longer-term cash flow projections should assume that within five years a steady or declining growth rate of no more than the relevant country average growth rate is achieved. It requires disclosure if these assumptions are not made. IAS 36 includes a similar general rule but does not require disclosure if the assumptions are not made. Also, FRS 11 restricts growth rates to those of the relevant country, while IAS 36 restricts them to those of the relevant products, industry or country.
- if an acquired business has been merged with existing operations, the FRS requires any subsequent impairment to be allocated between the acquired goodwill and the goodwill in the existing operations at the time of merging the two businesses. IAS 36 does not include this requirement.
- FRS 11 requires the accuracy of previous estimates of value in use to be monitored for five years following an impairment review. Any impairment that should have been recognised at the time must be recognised in the current period unless it has since reversed, in which case its

non-recognition in past years should be disclosed. The IAS does not include these requirements.
- IAS 36 requires the amounts recognised as impairment losses and reversals of impairment losses to be disclosed in more detail than does FRS 11.

10.12.18 Comparison with US GAAP

SFAS 121, *Accounting for the Impairment of Long-Lived Assets and for Long-Lived Assets to Be Disposed Of,* is similar in scope to IAS 36 and takes a similar approach to initially identifying impaired assets. However, the two Standards take significantly different approaches to recognising, measuring and reversing impairment losses and to assets held for disposal.

Both Standards require that an impairment loss be recognised when the carrying amount of an asset (or cash-generating unit) exceeds an impairment recognition 'trigger'. However, the recognition trigger differs between the two Standards. IAS 36 uses the recoverable amount of the asset (the higher of the value in use of an asset and its net selling price). As discussed previously, value in use is based on estimated future *discounted* cash flows. The trigger in SFAS 121 is the sum of an asset's *undiscounted* future cash flows. In most cases, this will lead to recognition of an impairment loss sooner under IAS 36 than SFAS 121.

When measuring an impairment loss, under IAS 36, the loss is measured as the excess of the carrying amount of the asset over its recoverable amount. Under SFAS 121, the loss is measured as the amount by which the carrying amount of an asset exceeds its fair value. When there is insufficient market information available to estimate fair value, under SFAS 121, a surrogate of fair value is estimated based on estimated, *discounted* future cash flows. Thus, depending on the circumstances, the two Standards may or may not lead to calculation of the same amount of impairment loss.

SFAS 121 prohibits the reversal of an impairment loss while, in certain situations, IAS 36 requires it.

And finally, IAS 36 applies to all assets which are held for disposal whilst SFAS 121 applies only to most assets to be disposed of. Segments of a business which are to be disposed of are covered under APB 30, *Reporting the Results of Operations* (see Chapter **5**). Also, under SFAS 121, an asset is not depreciated while it is held for disposal, whereas under IAS 36, an asset continues to be depreciated until it is disposed of.

After Statement 121 was issued, significant implementation issues were raised by members of the EITF and others. As a result, the FASB has issued an Exposure Draft to address significant implementation questions and to develop a single accounting model based on the framework established in Statement 121 for the disposal of long-lived assets, whether previously held and used or newly acquired.

The Board has issued an Exposure Draft of a proposed Statement, *Accounting for the Impairment or Disposal of Long-Lived Assets and for Obligations Associated with Disposal Activities*, in July 2000. The proposed Statement would supersede Statement 121. The proposed Statement also would supersede the provisions of APB Opinion No. 30, *Reporting the Results of Operations – Reporting the Effects of Disposal of a Segment of a Business, and Extraordinary, Unusual and Infrequently Occurring Events and Transactions*, for the disposal of segments of a business and nullify most of the guidance provided by EITF Issue No 94-3, *Liability Recognition for Certain Employee Termination Benefits and Other Costs to Exit an Activity (including Certain Costs Incurred in a Restructuring)*.

CHAPTER 11

Balance sheet – equity and liabilities

11.1 Sources

Framework for the Preparation and Presentation of Financial Statements.

IAS 1 (r1997)	*Presentation of Financial Statements.*
IAS 10 (r1999)	*Events After the Balance Sheet Date.*
IAS 12 (r2000)	*Accounting for Taxes on Income.*
IAS 16 (r1998)	*Property, Plant and Equipment.*
IAS 21 (r1993)	*The Effects of Changes in Foreign Exchange Rates.*
IAS 22 (r1998)	*Business Combinations.*
IAS 32 (r1998)	*Financial Instruments: Disclosure and Presentation.*
IAS 37	*Provisions, Contingent Liabilities and Contingent Assets.*
IAS 39 (r2000)	*Financial Instruments: Recognition and Measurement* (effective 1 January 2001).
IAS 40	*Investment Property* (effective 1 January 2001).
SIC-5	*Classification of Financial Instruments – Contingent Settlement Provisions.*
SIC-16	*Share Capital – Reacquired Own Equity Instruments (Treasury Shares).*
SIC-17	*Equity – Costs of an Equity Transaction.*

11.2 Brief summary of the requirements

Equity and liabilities are not covered by one, specific IAS but by several. For a number of items, a specific IAS has not been developed which covers recognition and measurement issues. In such cases, it is appropriate to look to the Framework for guidance. Many components of liabilities will meet the IAS 32 (r1998) definition of a financial instrument included in IAS 32 (r1998) and IAS 39 (r2000) and thus be subject to the recognition and measurement rules of IAS 39 (r2000) and the extensive disclosure requirements of IAS 32 (r1998). Rather than reproduce these requirements in this chapter, they are included in Chapter **12**.

An excerpt from the example IAS balance sheet in Chapter **9** and the section in which the related discussion can be found is set out below:

EQUITY AND LIABILITIES	*Section*
Capital and reserves	
Issued capital	**11.3.4**
Reserves	**11.3.6**
Retained earnings/accumulated profits	**11.3.8**
Minority interest	**11.10**
Non-current liabilities	
Interest-bearing liabilities	**11.6**
Deferred tax	Chapter **23**
Retirement benefit obligation	Chapter **25**
Current liabilities	
Trade and other payables	**11.8**
Short-term borrowings	**11.6**
Current portion of interest-bearing liabilities	**11.6**
Total equity and liabilities	

11.3 Equity

11.3.1 Brief summary of the requirements

IAS 1 (r1997) requires that at a minimum, line items which present issued capital and reserves be included on the face of the balance sheet. Numerous other disclosures are required in the notes to the financial statements.

11.3.2 Development of the requirements

Due to the fact that the presentation, use and accounting treatment of equity is inextricably linked to company law in many countries, it has been difficult for the IASC Board to prescribe detailed rules in this area. For example, IASs do not address which reserves may be distributable or used for other purposes. Rather, the approach taken in IAS 1 (r1997) is to require minimum disclosure on the face of the balance sheet to allow most countries to meet its requirements, but to require extensive disclosure in the notes to the financial statements to aid transparency.

11.3.3 Definition and presentation

'Equity is the residual interest in the assets of the enterprise after deducting all its liabilities.' (Framework.49(c)) Equity may contain many subcomponents including:

(a) funds contributed by shareholders (Framework.65);
(b) share premium (IAS 1 (r1997).86(f));
(c) retained earnings (Framework.65), also referred to as accumulated profits (IAS 1 (r1997).86(e); and
(d) other reserves (IAS 1 (r1997).86(f)).

In respect of the presentation of equity, IAS 1 (r1997) requires that, at a minimum, line items which present issued capital and reserves be disclosed on the face of the balance sheet. (IAS 1 (r1997).66(m)) Various disclosures are required in the notes to the financial statements as set out in this chapter.

11.3.4 Issued capital

As noted above, issued capital is required to be disclosed on the face of the balance sheet. IAS 1 (r1997) does not require that the term 'issued capital' necessarily be included on the face of the balance sheet but only that a line item or line items which present this information be included on the face of the balance sheet.

In addition to disclosing issued capital on the face of the balance sheet, IAS 1 (r1997) further requires that the following be disclosed either on the face of the balance sheet or in the notes, for each class of share capital:

> '(a) the number of shares authorised;
> (b) the number of shares issued and fully paid, and issued but not fully paid;
> (c) par value per share, or that the shares have no par value;
> (d) a reconciliation of the number of shares outstanding at the beginning and at the end of the year;
> (e) the rights, preferences and restrictions attaching to that class including restrictions on the distribution of dividends and the repayment of capital;
> (f) shares in the enterprise held by the enterprise itself or by subsidiaries or associates of the enterprise; and
> (g) shares reserved for issuance under options and sales contracts, including the terms and amounts.'
>
> (IAS 1 (r1997).74)

In addition, a reconciliation between the opening and closing balance of the share premium account is required. This reconciliation is required to be included either in a statement showing changes in equity or to be disclosed separately in the notes to the financial statements. (IAS 1 (r1997).86(f))

11.3.5 Treasury shares

When an enterprise holds its own equity shares, they are referred to as 'treasury shares'. SIC-16 applies when the shares (or other own equity instrument) are:

- classified as equity under IAS 32 (r1998) (see **11.4**);
- acquired and held by the enterprise or by a consolidated subsidiary; *and*
- legally available for re-issue or re-sale, even if the enterprise *intends* to cancel them.

Accounting for treasury shares
The re-acquisition and cancellation of an enterprise's own shares represents a transfer between those holders of equity instruments who have given up their equity interest and those who continue to hold an equity interest. Similarly, a re-sale or issuance of such shares is another transfer of equity interest. Therefore, none of the transactions give rise to a gain or loss to the enterprise which would be reflected in the income statement. Instead, all transactions are accounted for as changes in equity and shown in the statement showing changes in equity or equity reconciliation.

Presentation
Treasury shares are presented either on the face of the balance sheet, or in the notes, as a deduction from equity. (SIC 16.4) Treasury shares are not presented as a financial asset.

As discussed above, IAS 1 (r1997) requires that for each class of share capital, treasury shares be disclosed separately. SIC-16 notes that this may be accomplished in one of three ways:

(1) the total costs may be shown as a one line adjustment to equity;
(2) the par value, if any, may be shown as a deduction from share capital, with adjustment of premiums or discounts against other categories of equity; or
(3) each category of equity may be adjusted.

11.3.6 Reserves

IAS 1 (r1997) requires disclosure of a description of the nature and purpose of each reserve within equity (IAS 1 (r1997).74.(b)) and a reconciliation between the opening and closing balance of each such reserve. (IAS 1 (r1997).86(f))

Although the creation of other reserves is not prohibited, IASs require or refer to the following reserves:

(a) reserves representing appropriations of retained earnings (Framework. 65);
(b) reserves representing capital maintenance adjustments (Framework. 65);
(c) other reserves required by statute such as creditor protection reserves (Framework.66);
(d) revaluation reserves on items of property, plant and equipment (IAS 16 (r1998)); certain financial assets or financial liabilities (IAS 39 (r2000)); certain investment properties that cannot be measured reliably under the fair value model (IAS 40); and
(e) foreign currency translation reserves (IAS 21 (r1993)).

Some reserves may be required by a specific IAS. For example, revaluation surpluses arising on the revaluation of property, plant and equipment in accordance with IAS 16 (r1998), certain financial assets or financial liabilities in accordance with IAS 39 (r2000), investment properties that cannot be measured reliably using the fair value model in accordance with IAS 40; or translation reserves arising on the translation of the financial statements of a foreign entity in accordance with IAS 21 (r1993). Otherwise, IASs do not prescribe when a reserve may or may not be created but only that the nature and purpose of each reserve be disclosed. This flexibility allows the creation of statutory reserves where required. Similarly, IASs do not provide guidance on which reserves are distributable (i.e., may be paid as dividends to shareholders), because this is generally governed by company law which varies in different countries.

The reconciliation of the opening and closing balance of each reserve may be included in the statement showing changes in equity or be separately disclosed in the notes to the financial statements.

11.3.7 Costs of an equity transaction

SIC-17 addresses the costs of issuing or acquiring an enterprise's own instruments classified as equity under IAS 32 (r1998) when the transaction results in a net increase or decrease to equity. It does not apply to the cost of issuing an equity instrument that is directly attributable to an acquisition of a business. (IAS 22 (r1998))

Transaction costs are only those incremental external costs directly attributable to the equity transaction that would otherwise have been avoided. The transaction costs of an equity transaction should be accounted for as a deduction from equity, net of any related income tax benefit. The costs of a transaction which fails to be completed should be expensed. Transaction costs that relate to the issuance of a compound instrument that contains both a liability and an equity element should be allocated to the component parts in proportion to the allocation of proceeds. Transaction costs that relate jointly to more than one transaction, for example, costs of a concurrent offering of some shares and stock exchange listing of other shares, should be allocated to those transactions using a basis of allocation which is rational and consistent with similar transactions. (SIC-17.5 – 8)

11.3.8 Retained earnings / accumulated profits

IAS 1 (r1997) is unclear whether or not retained earnings or accumulated profits are considered to be a reserve. (The terms retained earnings and accumulated profits are used interchangeably in various IASs.) In any case, as with other reserves, a reconciliation of the opening and closing balance of retained earnings or accumulated profits is required and may be presented either in the statement of changes in equity or be separately disclosed in the notes to the financial statements.

11.3.9 Dividends paid

Dividends or other distributions to holders of a financial instrument classified as an equity instrument are required to be debited directly to equity. (IAS 32 (r1998).30) However, as discussed in **11.4**, under IAS 32 (r1998), some financial instruments such as redeemable preference shares may be classified as financial liabilities. Dividends paid relating to such financial liabilities are recognised in the income statement as an expense. See Chapter **5** for further discussion of the income statement treatment.

In addition, the following disclosures are required:

> '(a) the amount of dividends that were proposed or declared after the balance sheet date but before the financial statements were authorised for issue; and
>
> (b) the amount of any cumulative preference dividends not recognised.'
>
> (IAS 1 (r1997).74)

Note that IAS 1 (r1997) does not prohibit the recognition of dividends before they have been formally approved for payment, but IAS 10 (r1999) does (see Chapter **15**). IAS 1 (r1997) requires the disclosure detailed above to be made either on the face of the balance sheet as a separate component of equity, or in the notes to the financial statements.

11.3.10 Comparison with UK GAAP

Under UK GAAP, similar disclosures to those contained in IAS 1 (r1997) exist regarding the amount of authorised share capital, the number of shares issued and fully paid and issued but not fully paid, and movements during the period, although there are minor differences between the two. Under UK GAAP and the Companies Act, there are many rules relating to which reserves are distributable, which amounts may be set off against share premium, etc. As noted in **11.3.2**, since these requirements often result from company law, IASs do not currently address such issues.

In the UK, dividends paid on equity instruments are deducted from the net profit or loss for the period to arrive at the retained profit or loss for the period. This deduction is shown on the face of the income statement. This presentation is not forbidden by IASs but net profit or loss for the period must be clearly noted on the face of the income statement and the presentation must make clear that dividends paid are not part of net profit or loss for the period but are being debited directly to equity.

Under UK GAAP, dividends paid relating to non-equity shares, such as redeemable preference shares are recognised in the same manner as dividends paid on equity shares as described above. Under IAS 32 (r1998), dividends paid relating to redeemable preference shares not classified as equity are recognised in the income statement.

In the UK when own shares are legally acquired they would be shown as an asset on the balance sheet in accordance with the Companies Act 1985 formats for accounts. Under SIC-16, treasury shares are presented either on the face of the balance sheet, or in the notes, as a deduction from equity. (SIC-16.4) Treasury shares, under IAS, are not presented as a financial asset.

Under UK GAAP, when dividends are proposed but have not been formally approved for payment by the balance sheet date, they are recorded as a liability. Such dividends are not considered a liability under IAS 10 (r1999).

11.3.11 Comparison with US GAAP

Under US GAAP, similar disclosures to those contained in IAS 1 (r1997) regarding the amount of authorised share capital, the number of shares issued and fully paid and issued but not fully paid, and movements during the period, exist, although there may be minor differences between the two.

Consistent with IAS 32 (r1998), under US GAAP, dividends paid are normally debited directly to equity and presented in the statement of stockholders' equity. However, this includes dividends paid related to redeemable preference shares which are not classified as equity. Under IAS 32 (r1998), dividends paid related to redeemable preference shares not classified as equity are included in the income statement.

Under US GAAP, when dividends are proposed but not formally approved for payment (declared), they are not recorded as a liability. This is consistent with IAS 10 (r1999).

11.3.12 Examples from published financial statements

Throughout this chapter there are examples from published financial statements. Note that the excerpts given do not always comply in full with all aspects of IAS and as such are not necessarily examples of best practice but merely of current practice.

Example 11.1

24 Share capital

			2000 US$ m	1999 US$ m
Authorised:				
1,000,000,000 shares of US¢ 25 each			250.0	250.0

	Ordinary shares in millions 2000	1999	2000 US$ m	1999 US$ m
Issued and fully paid:				
At 1st January	**807.9**	784.7	**202.0**	196.2
Scrip issued in lieu of dividends	**21.4**	20.5	**5.4**	5.1
Issued under share incentive schemes	**2.8**	2.7	**0.7**	0.7
Repurchased and cancelled	**(196.2)**	–	**(49.1)**	–
At 31st December	**635.9**	807.9	**159.0**	202.0
Outstanding under share incentive schemes	**(13.1)**	(10.7)	**(3.3)**	(2.7)
	622.8	797.2	**155.7**	199.3

During the year the Company repurchased 181.1 million ordinary shares through a tender offer and from the stock market at a total cost of US$992.0 million. In addition, the Company also repurchased 15.1 million ordinary shares from a subsidiary undertaking at a cost of US$88.9 million. After elimination of intercompany profit of US$15.7 million, the net cost of US$1,065.2 million had been dealt with by charging US$49.1 million to share capital, US$342.4 million to share premium and contributed surplus, and US$673.7 million to revenue and other reserves.

25 Senior Executive Share Incentive Schemes

The Senior Executive Share Incentive Schemes were set up in order to provide selected executives with options to purchase ordinary shares in the Company. Under the Schemes ordinary shares are issued to the Trustee of the Schemes, Clare Investment and Trustee Company Limited, a wholly-owned subsidiary undertaking, which holds the ordinary shares until the options are exercised. Ordinary shares are issued at prices based on the average market price for the five trading days immediately preceding the date of grant of the options, which are exercisable for up to ten years following the date of grant.

As the shares issued under the Schemes are held on trust by a wholly-owned subsidiary undertaking, for presentation purposes they are netted off the Company's share capital in the consolidated balance sheet (*refer note 24*) and the premium attached to them is netted off the share premium account (*refer note 26*).

	Ordinary shares in millions			
	2000	*1999*	*2000 US$ m*	*1999 US$ m*
At 1st January	10.7	8.4	61.0	53.4
Granted	2.8	2.7	10.5	8.7
Exercised	(0.4)	(0.4)	(1.3)	(1.1)
At 31st December	**13.1**	**10.7**	**70.2**	**61.0**

The exercise price of share options exercised during the year were in the range of US$3.2 to US$4.3 (1999: US$2.3 to US$3.2) per share.

Outstanding at 31st December:

Expiry date	*Exercise Price US$*	*Ordinary shares in millions*	
		2000	*1999*
2000	3.2–10.1	–	0.9
2001	3.2–8.0	**0.3**	0.7
2002	6.9–7.9	**0.2**	0.2
2003	7.7	**0.3**	0.3
2004	6.6–10.1	**1.0**	1.1
2005	7.5–8.0	**0.4**	0.5
2006	7.2	**0.3**	0.3
2007	6.1–7.7	**1.0**	1.1
2008	2.0–4.5	**0.6**	0.7
2009	3.2–3.3	**1.9**	2.3
2010	3.7–5.0	**2.7**	–
Unallocated	1.2–10.1	**4.4**	2.6
		13.1	10.7

26 Share Premium and Contributed Surplus

	2000 US$ m	*1999 US$ m*
At 1st January	403.4	400.5
Capitalisation arising on scrip issued in lieu of dividends	(3.9)	(5.1)
Arising from shares issued under share incentive schemes	9.8	8.0
Repurchase of shares (refer note 24)	(342.4)	–
At 31st December	66.9	403.4
Outstanding under share incentive schemes	(66.9)	(58.3)
	–	345.1

The contributed surplus was set up on the formation of the Company in 1984 and, under the Bye-Laws of the Company is not distributable.

27 Revenue and Other Reserves

	Revenue Reserves US$ m	*Capital Reserves US$ m*	*Property Revaluation Reserves US$ m*	*Exchange Reserves US$ m*	*Total US$ m*
2000					
At 1st January	2,533.3	60.1	653.6	(195.8)	3,051.2
Property revaluation	–	–	556.3	–	556.3
Deferred tax on property revaluation	–	–	(1.0)	–	(1.0)
Net exchange translation differences					
– amount arising in year	–	–	–	(85.9)	(85.9)
– disposal of subsidiary undertakings, associates and joint ventures	–	–	–	55.6	55.6
Net profit	930.8	–	–	–	930.8
Dividends (refer note 28)	(137.3)	–	–	–	(137.3)
Scrip issued in lieu of dividends (refer note 28)	104.2	–	–	–	104.2
Capitalisation arising on scrip issued in lieu of dividends	(1.5)	–	–	–	(1.5)
Repurchase of shares (refer note 24)	(613.6)	(60.1)	–	–	(673.7)
Change in attributable interests	2.2	–	–	–	2.2
Other	1.3	–	–	–	1.3
Transfer	11.6	–	(11.3)	(0.3)	–
At 31st December	2,831.0	–	1,197.6	(226.4)	3,802.2
of which:					
Company	722.9	–	–	–	722.9
Associates and joint ventures	295.5	–	853.6	(77.5)	1,071.6
1999					
At 1st January	2,362.5	60.1	586.0	(187.9)	2,820.7
Property revaluation	–	–	78.0	–	78.0
Deferred tax on property revaluation	–	–	(2.8)	–	(2.8)
Net exchange translation differences					
– amount arising in year	–	–	–	(13.5)	(13.5)
– disposal of subsidiary undertakings, associates and joint ventures	–	–	–	0.6	0.6
Net profit	207.4	–	–	–	207.4
Dividends (refer note 28)	(130.6)	–	–	–	(130.6)
Scrip issued in lieu of dividends (refer note 28)	88.8	–	–	–	88.8
Change in attributable interests	2.2	–	–	–	2.2
Other	0.4	–	–	–	0.4
Transfer	2.6	–	(7.6)	5.0	–
At 31st December	2,533.3	60.1	653.6	(195.8)	3,015.2
of which:					
Company	1,455.7	60.1	–	–	1,515.8
Associates and joint ventures	601.1	–	326.9	(84.8)	848.2

The capital reserves represent the balance of the share premium account of Jardine Matheson & Co Limited, the holding company of the Group prior to the reorganisation in 1984, when Jardine Matheson Holdings Limited became the new holding company, and are non-distributable.

The capital reserves represent the balance of the share premium account of Jardine Matheson & Co., Limited, the holding company of the Group prior to the reorganisation in 1984 when Jardine Matheson Holdings Limited became the new holding company, and are non-distributable.

The property revaluation arising during the year includes surpluses of US$517.8 million and US$46.2 million (1999: US$27.1 million and US$43.2 million) relating to Hongkong Land and Mandarin Oriental respectively.

28 Dividends

	2000 *US$ m*	*1999* *US$ m*
Final dividend in respect of 1999 of US¢17.20 (1998: US¢13.80) per share	137.1	107.1
Interim dividend in respect of 2000 of US¢7.80 (1999: US¢7.80) per share	49.3	61.6
	186.4	168.7
Less Company's share of dividends paid on the shares held by subsidiary undertakings	(49.1)	(38.1)
	137.3	130.6
Shareholders elected to receive scrip in respect of the following:		
Final dividend in respect of previous year	71.1	55.4
Interim dividend in respect of current year	33.1	33.4
	104.2	88.8

A final dividend in respect of 2000 of US¢18.70 (1999: US¢17.20) per share amounting to a total of US$116.5 million (1999: US$137.1 million) is proposed by the Board. The dividend proposed will not be accounted for until it has been approved at the Annual General Meeting. The net amount after deducting the Company's share of the dividends payable on the shares held by subsidiary undertakings of US$43.2 million (1999: US$32.1 million) will be accounted for as an appropriation of revenue reserves in the year ending 31st December 2001.

29 Own shares held

Own shares held represent the Company's share of the cost of 312.7 million (1997: 312.4 million) ordinary shares in the Company held by subsidiary undertakings and are deducted in arriving at shareholders' funds.

Jardine Matheson Holdings Limited
Hong Kong
31 December 2000
International Accounting Standards

Example 11.2

Statement of Changes in Equity

GROUP

	Share capital and debentures R'000	*Non distributable reserves R'000*	*Distributable Reserves R'000*	*Total unitholders' funds R'000*
– Balance at 30 June 1998	353,882	34,585	12,346	400,813
– Changes in accounting policies	(58)	322,368	(23,208)	299,102
– Deferred taxation		322,707	(18,896)	303,811
– Consolidation of the Primedia Trust	(58)	(467)	(1,626)	(2,151)
– Depreciation of building		128	(2,686)	(2,558)
– Restated balance at 30 June 1998	353,824	356,953	(10,862)	699,915
– Units issued	189,708			189,708
	(162,775)	19,650	(23,223)	(166,348)
– Write off of intangibles	(162,775)		(38,594)	(201,369)
– Taxation relief on intangible		19,650	15,371	35,021
– Net profit for the year			65,054	65,054
– Translation reserve movement		(20,087)		(20,087)
– Transfer from non-distributable reserves		(2,401)	2,401	–
– Other		445		445
– Restated balance at 30 June 1999	380,757	354,560	33,370	768,687
– Units held in The Primeval Trust	(5,372)	(15,147)		(20,519)
– Units issued (net of repurchase)	2,285			2,285
		18,117	(60,118)	(42,001)
– Write off of intangibles			(60,118)	(60,118)
– Taxation relief on intangible assets		18,117		18,117
– Net loss for the year			(13,256)	(13,256)
– Translation reserve movement		10,678		10,678
– Transfer to non-distributable reserves		1,421	(1,421)	–
– Other		308		308
Balance at 30 June 2000	377,670	369,937	(41,425)	706,182

COMPANY

	Share capital and debentures R'000	*Non distributable reserves R'000*	*Distributable Reserves R'000*	*Total unitholders' funds R'000*
– Balance at 30 June 1998	353,882	–	114,253	468,135
– Units issued	189,708			189,708
– Write off of intangibles	(162,775)			(162,775)
– Net profit for the year			78,954	78,954
– Balance at 30 June 1999	380,815	–	193,207	574,022
– Units issued (net of repurchase)	2,285			2,285
– Net loss for the year			(125,545)	(125,545)
– Other		323		323
– Balance at 30 June 2000	383,100	323	67,662	451,085

Primedia Limited
South Africa
30 June 2000
South African GAAP

Example 11.3

28. Dividends

Dividends payable are not accounted for until they have been ratified at the Annual General Meeting. At the meeting on 5 April 2001, the following dividend in respect of 2000 will be proposed:

Dividend per share	CHF 55.-
Resulting in a total dividend of[a]	CHF 2,171,990,095.-

The accounts for the year ended 31 December 2000 do not reflect this proposed distribution, which will be treated as an appropriation of profit in the year ending 31 December 2001.

(a) Number of shares with right to dividend: see annual report of Nestlé SA.

Nestlé Group
Switzerland
31 December 2000
International Accounting Standards

11.4 Distinction between equity and liabilities

Substance over form

The Framework indicates the need to reflect the substance of transactions over their legal form. IAS 32 (r1998) recognises that while substance and legal form are commonly consistent, in some cases they are not. For example, some financial instruments legally referred to as equity, such as preference shares, may, in substance, have characteristics of both liabilities and equity, only equity or only liabilities. The objective of IAS 32 (r1998) is to require such instruments to be classified according to their substance; and therefore, financial instruments which are legally referred to as equity instruments may be classified or partly classified as liabilities.

Consistency

The classification of a financial instrument is made based upon its substance when it is issued and is not revised in later periods even though circumstances regarding the likelihood of conversion or other factors may have changed. (IAS 32 (r1998).19)

Definitions

IAS 32 (r1998) defines an equity instrument as, 'any contract that evidences a residual interest in the assets of an enterprise after deducting all of its liabilities'. (IAS 32 (r1998).5)

A financial liability is defined as,

> 'any liability that is a contractual obligation:
> (a) to deliver cash or another financial asset to another enterprise; or
> (b) to exchange financial instruments with another enterprise under conditions that are potentially unfavourable.'
>
> (IAS 32 (r1998).5)

Thus the critical feature in differentiating a financial liability from an equity instrument is that a financial liability contains a contractual obligation which *requires the transfer* of cash or another financial asset or an exchange of financial instruments under conditions that are potentially unfavourable, whereas an equity instrument does not contractually obligate the issuer to transfer cash or other financial instruments but merely evidences a residual interest in the assets of the enterprise.

When contractual obligations exist which require the transfer of cash or another financial asset or an exchange of financial instruments under conditions that are potentially unfavourable, a financial liability exists regardless of the manner in which the obligation will be settled. Therefore, a restriction on the ability of the issuer of a financial liability to satisfy an obligation, such as lack of access to foreign currency or the need to obtain approval for payment from a regulatory authority, does not negate the issuer's obligation or the holder's right under the instrument. (IAS 32 (r1998).20)

When *no* contractual obligation exists which requires the transfer of cash or another financial asset, or an exchange of financial instruments under conditions that are potentially unfavourable, the financial instrument is classified as equity. Subsequent to issue, an enterprise may declare dividends on an equity instrument, for example common ordinary shares, which will legally entitle their holders to cash or other financial instruments, but as long as the declaration of such dividends is at the discretion of the issuer, the payment of such dividends does not indicate that a financial instrument is a liability. (IAS 32 (r1998).21)

Normally, making the distinction between equity instruments and financial liabilities is straightforward since substance is often consistent with legal form. For example, bonds which pay a contractually fixed amount of interest and which will be redeemed on a contractually agreed date are clearly financial liabilities of the issuer. Another example where the distinction between a liability and equity is relatively easy is for common ordinary shares, which are normally classed as equity instruments since they contain no contractual obligation to deliver cash or another financial instrument.

Preferred shares

In some cases, the terms of particular preferred shares will cause them to be classified as financial liabilities rather than equity. A preferred share meets the definition of a liability and is classified as such when it:

(a) provides for mandatory redemption by the issuer for a fixed or determinable amount at a fixed or determinable future date;
(b) gives the holder the right to require the issuer to redeem the share at or after a particular date for a fixed or determinable amount;
(c) gives the holder an option to require redemption upon the occurrence of a future event that is highly likely to occur; or
(d) indirectly gives the holder the contractual right to receive either cash or another financial instrument or to exchange another financial instrument with the issuer under conditions that are potentially unfavourable. (IAS 32 (r1998).22)

As regards (d) above, a preferred share which may not explicitly give the holder the contractual right to receive either cash or another financial instrument or to exchange another financial instrument with the issuer under conditions that are potentially unfavourable may give it indirectly. For example, a preferred share which has a contractually provided accelerating dividend structure so that within the foreseeable future, the dividend yield is scheduled to be so high that the issuer will be economically compelled to redeem the instrument. (IAS 32 (r1998).22) In such cases, although the issuer may not have a contractual obligation to redeem the instrument, when it is economically unfeasible for an issuer not to redeem, the instrument is accounted for as though such an obligation does exist and classified as a liability.

When preference shares are non-redeemable, their classification is determined based on their other contractual rights. 'When distributions to holders of the preferred shares whether cumulative or non-cumulative, are at the discretion of the issuer, the shares are equity instruments.' (IAS 32 (r1998).A21)

Obligations settled by cash or equity instruments

Generally, an enterprise's obligation to issue its own equity instruments in exchange for financial assets of another party is *not* potentially unfavourable since it results in an increase in equity and cannot result in a loss to the enterprise. The possibility that existing holders of an equity interest in the enterprise may find the fair value of their interest reduced as a result of the obligation does not make the obligation unfavourable to the enterprise itself. (IAS 32 (r1998).A7) Therefore, generally such obligations are not financial liabilities.

Example 11.4

Scenario 1

Enterprise A acquires the trade debtors (with recourse) of Enterprise C. Under the terms of the sale agreement, the consideration for the sale will be 10,000 equity shares of Enterprise A. On the balance sheet date, the sale agreement is signed and the trade debtors transferred, but the issuance of shares is not made until three days after year end.

Result: Unpaid consideration would be considered equity since Enterprise A's obligation to issue its own shares in exchange for a financial asset (the trade debtors) is *not* potentially unfavourable since it results in an increase in equity and cannot result in a loss to the enterprise.

However, if the enterprise can settle the obligation either by payment of financial assets (such as cash) *or* by issuance of its own equity securities *and* the number of equity securities required to settle the obligation varies with changes in their fair value with the result that the total fair value of the securities to be issued always equals the amount of the contractual obligation, the obligation is accounted for as a financial liability. The obligation is a financial liability since the holder of the obligation is not exposed to gain or loss from fluctuations in the price of its equity securities. (IAS 39 (r2000).11)

Example 11.5

Scenario 2

Enterprise A acquires the trade debtors of Enterprise C. Under the terms of the sale agreement, the consideration for the sale will be either £500,000 cash or £500,000 worth of equity shares of Enterprise A based on the share price of Enterprise A in three months time. On the balance sheet date, the sale agreement is signed and the trade debtors transferred, but the issuance of shares is not made until after year end.

Result: The obligation is a financial liability since the holder of the obligation is not exposed to gain or loss from fluctuation in the price of its equity securities.

Contingent settlement provisions

As a general rule, where the rights and obligations regarding the manner of settlement of a financial instrument depend on the occurrence or non-occurrence of uncertain future events or on the outcome of uncertain circumstances that are beyond the control of both the issuer and the holder, the financial instrument should be classified as a liability. (SIC-5.5) The exception to the rule occurs when the possibility of the issuer being required to settle in cash or another financial asset is remote at the time of issuance. In such a case, the contingent settlement provision is ignored and the obligation is classified as equity. (SIC-5.6)

Example 11.6

Scenario 3

Enterprise A acquires the printing operations of Enterprise C. Under the terms of the sale agreement, the consideration for the sale is in the form of shares of Enterprise A. The consideration is deferred for one year and will be the greater of £1 million or 500,000 equity shares of Enterprise A based on its fair value in one year's time.

Result: The consideration should be recorded as a liability since the share price of Enterprise A is beyond the control of both the issuer and holder.

Disclosure

When the balance sheet presentation of a financial instrument differs from the instrument's legal form, IAS 32 (r1998) encourages enterprises to explain in the notes to the financial statements the nature of the instrument. (IAS 32 (r1998).50)

11.4.1 Compound financial instruments

Some financial instruments may contain both a liability and an equity component. In order to represent substance over form, the components are classified separately on initial recognition of the financial instrument.

The example of such an instrument given in IAS 32 (r1998) is of a bond which contains an option to the holder of the bond to convert it into shares. In the balance sheet of the issuer, the bond would be recognised as a financial liability and the option would be recognised as an equity instrument. (IAS 32 (r1998).25)

Since the economic effect of issuing such an instrument is substantially the same as issuing simultaneously a debt instrument with an early settlement provision and warrants to purchase common shares, or issuing a debt instrument with detachable share purchase warrants, the issuer presents the liability and equity elements separately on its balance sheet.

Similar to the classification of a non-compound financial instrument, the determination of the classification between equity and liabilities of a compound financial instrument is made at the date of issue and is not revised subsequently.

Since IAS 32 (r1998) does not deal with the measurement of financial instruments, it does not prescribe one manner to apportion the value of a financial instrument between liabilities and equity. It does suggest that either of the following methods may be used:

> '(a) assigning to the less easily measurable component (often an equity instrument), the residual amount after deducting from the instrument as a whole the amount separately determined for the component that is more easily measurable; or
>
> (b) measuring the liability and equity components separately and, to the extent necessary, adjusting these amounts on a pro rata basis so that the sum of the components equals the amount of the instrument as a whole.
>
> The sum of the carrying amounts assigned to the liability and equity components on initial recognition is always equal to the carrying amount that would be ascribed to the instrument as a whole. No gain or loss arises from recognising and presenting the components of the instrument separately.'
>
> (IAS 32(r1998).28)

A24 of the appendix to IAS 32 (r1998) illustrates each of the two methods described above.

11.4.2 Comparison with UK GAAP

Under UK GAAP, shares of an enterprise are required to be shown within equity, with one exception as discussed in the next paragraph. However, in accordance with FRS 4, *Capital Instruments,* shares which have certain characteristics of a liability are classified as non-equity shares. For example, if shares are redeemable either according to their terms or because the holder, or any party other than the issuer, can require their redemption, they are classified as non-equity shares. Thus, some non-equity shares may be similar to the redeemable preference shares that are classified as liabilities under IAS 32 (r1998). However, under UK GAAP, other characteristics besides redeemability, for example the rights of the shares to participate in payments such as dividends or in a surplus on winding up, may cause shares to be classified as non-equity. Under IAS 32 (r1998), such features may or may not require shares to be classified as equity. Therefore, one cannot assume that non-equity shares under UK GAAP are necessarily equivalent to shares classified as a liability under IAS 32 (r1998).

An exception to the general rule in UK GAAP of classifying shares within equity exists in consolidated financial statements where the group, taken as a whole, has an obligation to transfer economic benefits in connection with particular shares issued by a subsidiary (unless the shares are held by companies within the group). For example, when a parent has given a guarantee of payments, such as dividends, to be made in respect of shares of a subsidiary, the shares are accounted for in the consolidated financial statements as a liability, irrespective of the financial condition of the subsidiary, since the group as a whole will be unable to avoid the transfer of economic benefits if the subsidiary does not perform. In all other cases, such shares are recognised as minority interests.

Under UK GAAP, any instrument which is capable of being separately transferred or redeemed is separately accounted for. For example, if a debt instrument is issued with warrants and the warrants are capable of being separately transferred, a value is allocated to the warrants and reported within equity. This concept is consistent with IAS 32 (r1998). However, under UK GAAP, the instrument must be capable of being separately transferred in order to be separately accounted for. This is more restrictive than the requirements for separate accounting of a single instrument under IAS 32 (r1998). For example, under IAS 32 (r1998), convertible debt is accounted for as two instruments, a debt instrument and share options. Under UK GAAP, if the option to convert cannot be transferred separately from the debt, the debt is accounted for as a single instrument.

11.4.3 Comparison with US GAAP

In the US, listed companies (that is those falling within the jurisdiction of the SEC) are required to classify redeemable preference shares separately from debt, common stock, and other stockholders' equity. Under IAS 32, such shares are classified as liabilities.

Under US GAAP, in accordance with APB Opinion No. 14 *Accounting for Convertible Debt and Debt Issued with Stock Purchase Warrants*, convertible debt and debt with *nondetachable* stock purchase warrants are accounted for as liabilities rather than split into their component parts as required by IAS 32. However, when debt with *detachable* warrants is issued, the convertible debt is classified as a liability while the warrants are classified as equity based on the relative fair values of the two securities at time of issuance. While the splitting into component parts in this circumstance is consistent with IAS 32 (r1998), as discussed previously, IAS 32 (r1998) does not deal with measurement issues.

11.5 Non-current liabilities

The distinction between current and non-current assets and liabilities is discussed in Chapter **9**.

11.6 Interest-bearing liabilities including short-term borrowings

11.6.1 Sources

IAS 1 (r1997)	*Presentation of Financial Statements.*
IAS 32 (r1998)	*Financial Instruments: Disclosure and Presentation.*
IAS 39(r 2000)	*Financial Instruments: Recognition and Measurement* (effective 1 January 2001).

11.6.2 Brief summary of the requirements

An interest-bearing liability (including short-term borrowings) will normally meet the definition of financial liability. As such, numerous disclosures are required regarding their terms, repayment schedules, covenants, related risks, etc. An interest-bearing liability is initially measured at cost and subsequently measured at amortised cost.

11.6.3 Development of the requirements

Issued in 1995 and revised in 1998 for consequential amendments due to the issuance of IAS 39, IAS 32 (r1998) covers the disclosure requirements for financial liabilities including interest-bearing liabilities and short-term borrowings. Issued in 1998 and revised in 2000, IAS 39 (r2000) covers the recognition and measurement of financial liabilities including interest-bearing liabilities and short-term borrowings.

11.6.4 Recognition

Interest-bearing liabilities (including short-term borrowings) will normally meet the definition of a financial liability. Therefore, they are accounted for in accordance with IAS 39 (r2000). Under IAS 39 (r2000), an enterprise recognises a financial liability such as an interest-bearing liability when, and only when, it becomes a party to the contractual provisions of the instrument. (IAS 39(r2000).27) This is normally when the enterprise has a legal obligation to pay cash at some point in the future.

In practice, IAS 39 (r2000) will probably not have an impact on the timing of the recognition of interest-bearing liabilities. Such liabilities are usually recognised from the date that the principal amount is received, since at that date, the enterprise has a present obligation to repay in the future the principal borrowed.

11.6.5 Measurement

An interest-bearing liability should be initially recognised at its cost, which is the fair value of the consideration received for it. (IAS 39 (r2000).66) Transaction costs are included in initial cost and include incremental costs that are directly attributable to the acquisition or disposal of the interest-bearing liability. (IAS 39 (r2000).10) Such costs may include fees and commissions paid to agents, advisers, brokers, and dealers; levies by regulatory agencies and securities exchanges; and transfer taxes and duties. However, transaction costs do *not* include debt premium or discount, financing costs, or allocations of internal administrative costs. (IAS 39 (r2000).17)

After initial recognition, an enterprise should measure an interest-bearing liability, other than those held-for-trading, at amortised cost. (IAS 39 (r2000).93) Amortised cost is the amount at which the interest-bearing liability was measured at initial recognition minus principal repayments, plus or minus the cumulative amortisation of any premium or discount.

11.6.6 Presentation and disclosure

Classification

In general, the classification of liabilities as current or non-current depends on when they fall due for repayment. However, in certain circumstances liabilities due within one year may be classed as non-current. Specifically,

> 'An enterprise should continue to classify its long-term interest-bearing liabilities as non-current, even when they are due to be settled within twelve months of the balance sheet date if:
>
> (a) the original term was for a period of more than twelve months;
> (b) the enterprise intends to refinance the obligation on a long-term basis; and
> (c) that intention is supported by an agreement to refinance, or to reschedule payments, which is completed before the financial statements are approved.
>
> The amount of any liability that has been excluded from current liabilities in accordance with this paragraph, together with information in support of this presentation, should be disclosed in the notes to the balance sheet.'
>
> (IAS 1 (r1997).63)

Most non-current, interest-bearing liability agreements contain covenants which may be financial such as minimum net asset levels or ratios, or operational such as a requirement to have the financial statements audited within a certain number of days after year end. When such covenants are breached, the terms of the agreement often cause the debt to become repayable on demand. In such a case, the debt is reclassified as current unless:

> '(a) the lender has agreed, prior to the approval of the financial statements, not to demand payment as a consequence of the breach; and
> (b) it is not probable that further breaches will occur within twelve months of the balance sheet date.'
>
> (IAS 1 (r1997).65)

Disclosures about financial instruments

Interest-bearing liabilities will normally be considered to be financial liabilities and thus be subject to the disclosure requirements of IAS 32 (r1998). In many cases, short-term borrowings will form a separate category of financial liability for disclosure purposes. See Chapter **12** for a summary of the requirements.

11.6.7 Comparison with UK GAAP

Under UK GAAP, interest-bearing liabilities are carried at proceeds net of issue costs, adjusted for cumulative finance costs less payments made. FRS 4, *Capital Instruments,* requires issue costs related to interest-bearing liabilities to be recognised as prepaid expenditure and amortised over the life of the liability as interest expense. As under FRS 4, under IAS 39 (r2000), issue costs are treated as transaction costs and deducted from the original cost of the liability.

Under FRS 4, an enterprise may continue to classify its long-term, interest-bearing liabilities as non-current, even when they are due to be settled within twelve months of the balance sheet date if all of the following conditions are met:

(a) the debt and the committed facility which permits the refinancing of debt for a period beyond its maturity are under a single agreement or course of dealing with the same lender or group of lenders;
(b) the finance costs of the new debt are on a basis that is not significantly higher than that of the existing debt;
(c) the obligations of the lender (or group of lenders) are firm; the lender is not able legally to refrain from providing funds except in circumstances the possibility of which can be demonstrated to be remote;
(d) the lender (or group of lenders) is expected to be able to fulfil its obligations under the facility.

(FRS 4.35)

These criteria differ from those set out in IAS 32 (r1998), and in some circumstances, may lead to a different result. In addition, the criteria in FRS 4 specifically cover multi-option facilities, where a group of parties agree that one of them will always provide a facility, although the particular lender may change without notice. IAS 1 (r1997) does not specifically cover these types of facilities.

UK GAAP contains similar, but fewer, disclosures regarding interest-bearing liabilities as those required by IAS 32 (r1998). See Chapter **12** for a discussion of those requirements.

11.6.8 Comparison with US GAAP

Under US GAAP, interest-bearing liabilities are carried at historical cost and are shown net of issue costs. Issue costs are amortised to interest expense over the life of the interest-bearing liability. This is consistent with IAS 39 (r2000).

Under US GAAP, if, before the balance sheet is issued, the enterprise has entered into a financing agreement that clearly permits the enterprise to refinance the short-term obligation on a long-term basis on terms that are readily determinable, and all of the following conditions are met, an enterprise may continue to classify its long-term, interest-bearing liabilities as non-current:

(a) the agreement does not expire within one year (or operating cycle) from the date of the enterprise's balance sheet and during that period the agreement is not cancellable by the lender or the prospective lender or investor (and obligations incurred under the agreement are not callable during that period) except for violation of a provision with which compliance is objectively determinable or measurable;
(b) no violation of any provision in the financing agreement exists at the balance-sheet date and no available information indicates that a violation has occurred thereafter but prior to the issuance of the balance sheet, or, if one exists at the balance-sheet date or has occurred thereafter, a waiver has been obtained; and
(c) the lender or the prospective lender or investor with which the enterprise has entered into the financing agreement is expected to be financially capable of honouring the agreement.

(SFAS 6.11)

Except for (c), these conditions are similar to those set out in IAS 32 (r1998).

US GAAP contains similar, but fewer, disclosures regarding interest-bearing liabilities to those required by IAS 32 (r1998) (see Chapter **12**).

11.6.9 Examples from published financial statements

Note that the excerpts given do not always comply in full with all aspects of IAS and as such are not necessarily examples of best practice but merely of current practice.

Example 11.7

[29] Financial Obligations

Financial obligations are carried at nominal or redemption value, whichever is higher. They comprise the following:

Million	*Dec. 31, 2000*	*Total*	*Dec. 31, 1999*	*Total*
		Maturing in 2001		*Maturing in 2000*
Debentures	2,168	283	1,809	10
Liabilities to banks	1,458	932	1,959	1,658
Liabilities under lease agreements	199	34	181	23
Liabilities from the issuance of promissory notes	2	2	1	1
Commercial paper	1,812	1,812	314	314
Other financial obligations	1,026	799	202	101
	6,665	3,862	4,466	2,107

The financial obligations are predominantly in US, dollars, which account for 4.0 billion (1999: 2.5 billion). US dollar borrowings represent 61 per cent (1999: 55 per cent) of total financial obligations.

Debentures include the following:

		Volume Million
Bayer Capital Corporation BV		
2.50% Bonds with Warrants Attached 1987/2002	CHF 250 million	164
Bayer Corporation		
6.50% Notes 1995/2002	USD 400 million	430
7.125% Notes 1995/2015	USD 200 million	215
6.75% Notes 1996/2001	USD 250 million	269
6.56% Bonds 1997/2002	CHF 200 million	131
6.20% Bonds 1998/2028	USD 250 million	269
Bayer Ltd, Japan		
3.75% Bonds 2000/2005	CHF 400 million	239
Other debentures		26
		2,168

The other debentures are due between 2000 and 2011; their average interest rate is 10.9 per cent.

Liabilities under finance leases are recognised as financial obligations if the leased assets are capitalised under property, plant and equipment. They are stated at present values. Lease payments totalling 285 million (1999: 277 million), including 86 million (1999: 96 million) in interest, are to be made to the respective lessors in future years. The liabilities mature as follows:

	Million *Lease payments*	*Of which interest*	*Liability*
2001	44	10	34
2002 to 2005	100	38	62
After 2005	141	38	103
	285	86	199

The other financial obligations include 42 million (1999: 43 million) to non-consolidated subsidiaries.

Bayer Group
Germany
31 December 2000
International Accounting Standards

Example 11.8

20 Borrowings

	2000 *US$ m*	*1999* *US$ m*
Current		
– bank overdrafts	**58.2**	53.1
– other bank advances	**104.6**	117.7
– other borrowings	**69.0**	49.9
	231.8	220.7
Current portion of long-term borrowings		
– bank	**151.7**	328.0
– other	**0.2**	6.9
	151.9	334.9
	383.7	555.6
Long-term borrowings		
– bank	**2,249.8**	1,538.6
– guaranteed bonds	**470.8**	–
– convertible bonds	**20.4**	–
– other	**1.4**	15.1
	2,742.4	1,553.7
	3,126.1	2,109.3
Secured	**856.3**	350.5
Unsecured	**2,269.8**	1,758.8
	3,126.1	2,109.3
Due dates of repayment		
Within one year	**383.7**	555.6
Between one and two years	**1,043.2**	514.9
Between two and five years	**1,122.9**	950.1
Beyond five years	**576.3**	88.7
	3,126.1	2,109.3

Fixed rate borrowings

Currency:	*Weighted average interest rates %*	*Weighted average period outstanding years*	*US$m*	*Floating rate borrowings US$m*	*Total US$m*
2000					
Australian Dollar	6.9	1.3	77.6	199.5	277.1
Hong Kong Dollar	7.1	2.3	378.2	468.0	846.2
Malaysian Ringgit	6.6	–	–	32.2	32.2
New Taiwan Dollar	5.8	0.2	9.1	63.1	72.2
New Zealand Dollar	7.0	1.0	26.4	30.8	57.2
Singapore Dollar	3.6	–	–	28.1	28.1
United Kingdom Sterling	6.4	0.1	56.1	272.3	328.4
United States Dollar	7.5	8.4	519.0	917.5	1,436.5
Other	6.3	5.6	34.1	14.1	48.2
			1,100.5	**2,025.6**	**3,126.1**

1999					
Australian Dollar	6.1	0.9	101.1	150.6	251.7
Hong Kong Dollar	7.4	1.4	258.8	542.0	800.8
Malaysian Ringgit	7.6	–	–	26.3	26.3
New Taiwan Dollar	5.8	1.1	11.1	78.8	89.9
New Zealand Dollar	6.3	1.6	46.8	36.4	83.2
Singapore Dollar	3.3	–	–	36.6	36.6
United Kingdom Sterling	6.3	0.1	47.5	367.2	414.7
United States Dollar	6.8	1.6	20.2	343.1	363.3
Other	9.8	2.0	26.4	16.4	42.8
			511.9	1,597.4	2,109.3

All borrowings were within subsidiary undertakings.

In September 2000, JMH Finance Limited, a wholly-owned subsidiary undertaking, issued US$550 million 4.75% guaranteed bonds due 2007. The bonds are guaranteed by the Company. Proceeds of the bonds were used to finance the repurchase of the Company's shares. The bonds are exchangeable, at the option of the holders, into shares of common stock of J P Morgan Chase & Co. on the basis of 15.83 shares for each US$1,000 principal amount of the bonds from 6 September 2001 until 30 August 2007. The bonds will mature on 6 September 2007. The fair values of the liability component and option component are determined on issue of the bond. The fair value of the liability component, included in long-term borrowings, is calculated using a market interest rate for an equivalent non-convertible bond. The residual amount, representing the value of the conversion option component, is included in other non-current liabilities (refer note 22).

In March 2000, Mandarin Oriental issued US$75.8 million 6.75% convertible bonds due 2005. Proceeds of the bonds were used to finance the acquisition of the Rafael Group. The bonds are convertible up to and including 23 February 2005 into fully paid ordinary shares of Mandarin Oriental at a conversion price of US$0.671 per ordinary share. At 31 December 2000, US$60.7 million of the bonds were held by Jardine Strategic and were netted off the carrying amount of the bonds.

Secured borrowings at 31 December 2000 included US$354.0 million (1999: US$309.4 million) which were secured against Mandarin Oriental's tangible fixed assets. The net book value of these assets at 31 December 2000 was US$951.2 million (1999: US$837.5 million).

The weighted average interest rates and period of fixed rate borrowings are stated after taking account of hedging transactions.

Jardine Matheson Holdings Limited
Hong Kong
31 December 2000
International Accounting Standards

11.7 Current liabilities

The distinction between current and non-current assets and liabilities is discussed in Chapter **9**.

11.8 Trade and other payables

11.8.1 Sources

IAS 1 (r1997)	*Presentation of Financial Instruments.*
IAS 32 (r1998)	*Financial Instruments: Disclosure and Presentation.*
IAS 39 (r2000)	*Financial Instruments: Recognition and Measurement* (effective 1 January 2001).

11.8.2 Recognition

Trade and other payables will normally meet the definition of a financial liability. Therefore, they are accounted for in accordance with IAS 39 (r2000). Under IAS 39 (r2000), an enterprise recognises a financial liability such as a trade payable when, and only when, it becomes a party to the contractual provisions of the instrument. (IAS 39 (r2000).27) This is normally when the enterprise has a legal obligation to pay cash. (IAS 39 (r2000).29(a))

Normally this will be when the enterprise has received goods or services under the contract. The issuance of IAS 39 (r2000) will not affect the timing of recognition of trade payables for most enterprises. For example, for most manufacturing enterprises, a payable will continue to be raised when the goods are received; for a service provider, on rendering of services, etc.

However, trade payables are *not* recognised as a result of a firm commitment to purchase goods or services, until the enterprise is obligated to disburse an asset which is usually when the ordered goods or services have been shipped, delivered, or rendered. (IAS 39 (r2000).29(b)) One exception to this rule relates to a forward contract which is defined as a commitment to purchase or sell a specified financial instrument or commodity on a future date at a specified price. These are dealt with in Chapter **12**.

Since IAS 1 (r1997) requires financial statements (except the cash flow statement) to be prepared on the accrual basis of accounting, at each period end, it may be necessary to estimate the amount of expenses incurred for which invoices have not been received and set up an accrual for such amounts. For example, if an enterprise has not received its electricity bill at year end but it has used electricity during the period, an estimate of the amount of the electricity bill relating to the period is made and an expense and an accrual are recognised.

11.8.3 Measurement

A trade or other payable should be initially recognised at its cost, which is the fair value of the consideration given for it. (IAS 39 (r2000).66) Normally cost is determined by reference to the invoice price.

Unlike some other financial liabilities, trade payables fall into a category of liabilities which is not required to be remeasured to fair value at each balance sheet date. (IAS 39 (r2000).93)

11.8.4 Disclosure

Enterprises commonly include the following items as trade and other payables and disclose them separately in the notes to the financial statements:

(a) trade payables;
(b) accruals;
(c) income taxes payable;
(d) the current portion of non-current interest-bearing borrowings;
(e) dividends payable;
(f) other non-trade payables;
(g) amounts due to:
  (i) the parent enterprise;
  (ii) fellow subsidiaries or associates; and
  (iii) other related parties.

The above list is not exhaustive and all items are not required for all enterprises. The only required disclosures in the list relate to amounts due to the parent enterprise, fellow subsidiaries and associates and other related parties which must each be disclosed separately. (IAS 1 (r1997).72)

If the size, nature or function of a component of trade and other payables is such that separate presentation would assist in presenting fairly the enterprise's financial position, separate disclosure of the component on the face of the balance sheet is required. (IAS 1 (r1997).67)

IAS 32 (r1998) does require the disclosure of the fair value of all financial liabilities including trade and other payables. (IAS 32 (r1998).77) However, as the payment terms are generally within one year or one operating cycle, for most trade and other payables fair value would normally equal cost.

11.8.5 Comparison with UK GAAP

Under UK GAAP, in practice, recognition of trade payables will generally be in line with that under IASs. Measurement under UK GAAP is also likely to be similar, at historic cost, due to the short-term nature of such payables.

Under UK GAAP, all current liabilities are often presented in one line item, 'creditors due within one year' on the face of the balance sheet with the components disclosed in the notes. The requirements concerning the disclosure of the components are more prescriptive under UK GAAP than under IAS 1 (r1997) and are set out in the Companies Act 1985. If an enterprise follows the Companies Act format for disclosure of the components of creditors due within one year, they will most likely be in compliance with IASs. However, in the rare circumstance that a component of creditors due within one year is so material that it is necessary to disclose it on the face of the balance sheet in order to present fairly the enterprise's financial position, IAS 1 (r1997) would require presentation which might go beyond the Companies Act requirements.

11.8.6 Comparison with US GAAP

Under US GAAP, in practice, the recognition of trade payables will generally be in line with that under IASs. Measurement under US GAAP is also likely to be similar, at historic cost, due to the short-term nature of such payables. The requirements regarding the disclosure of the components of trade and other payables are similar under both IAS 1 (r1997) and US GAAP in that significant components are required to be disclosed in the notes to the financial statements. However, US GAAP is more prescriptive in that listed companies (that is those falling within the jurisdiction of the Securities and Exchange Commission (the 'SEC')), are required to disclose any component of trade payables which exceeds five percent of the total line item. In practice, the five percent guideline is used by most companies, not only those which are listed.

11.8.7 Examples from published financial statements

Example 11.9

19 Creditors and Accruals 2000

	2000 *US$ m*	*1999* *US$ m*
Trade creditors	**1,095.9**	1,245.5
Accruals	**657.4**	654.8
Agency creditors	**280.0**	348.9
Amounts due to associates and joint ventures	**18.0**	3.2
Deposits accepted	**16.7**	17.2
Deferred warranty income	**31.0**	27.8
Other	**30.2**	22.2
	2,192.2	2,320.6

Jardine Matheson Holdings Limited
Hong Kong
31 December 2000
International Accounting Standards

Example 11.10

	GROUP		*COMPANY*	
	2000	*1999 restated*	*2000*	*1999*
	R'000	*R'000*	*R'000*	*R'000*
21. ACCOUNT PAYABLE				
– Trade creditors and accruals	321,841	310,910	3,732	3,961
– Provisions	105,796	74,088	710	600
	427,637	384,998	4,442	4,561

Primedia Limited
South Africa
30 June 2000
South African GAAP

Example 11.11

(29) Trade accounts payable

Trade accounts are payable mainly to third parties; they are carried at nominal or redemption value, whichever is higher.

Trade accounts payable as of December 31, 2000 include 2,013 million (1999: 1,556 million) maturing within one year and 3 million (1999: 0 million) maturing after one year. Of the total, 8 million (1999: 6 million) is payable to subsidiaries, 16 million (1999: 12 million) to other affiliated companies and 1,992 million (1999: 1,538 million) to other suppliers.

(30) Miscellaneous liabilities

Miscellaneous liabilities are carried at nominal or redemption value, whichever is higher. The individual items are as follows:

(DM million)	*Dec. 31 2000*		*Dec. 31 1999*	
	Total	*Maturing in 2001*	*Total*	*Maturing in 2000*
Payroll liabilities	537	422	526	419
Tax liabilities	291	289	209	206
Liabilities for social expenses	114	114	126	125
Accrued interest on liabilities	73	46	79	54
Advance payments received	24	24	28	28
Liabilities from the acceptance of drafts	14	14	10	10
License liabilities	32	32	26	26
Other miscellaneous liabilities	1,385	1,333	1,029	933
	2,470	**2,274**	**2,033**	**1,801**

Tax liabilities include not only Group companies' own tax liabilities, but also taxes withheld by them for paying over to the authorities on behalf of third parties.

Liabilities for social expenses include, in particular, social insurance contributions that had not been paid over by the closing date.

The other miscellaneous liabilities comprise numerous individual items such as guarantees, commissions to customers, and expense reimbursements.

The total of miscellaneous liabilities includes DM 76 million (1999: DM 67 million) to non-consolidated subsidiaries and DM 12 million (1999: DM 16 million) to other affiliated companies.

Bayer Group
Germany
31 December 1998
International Accounting Standards

11.9 Provisions and contingencies

11.9.1 Source

IAS 37 *Provisions, Contingent Liabilities and Contingent Assets.*

11.9.2 Brief summary of the requirements

IAS 37 gives guidance on recognition, measurement and disclosure of certain provisions, contingent liabilities and contingent assets.

The Standard defines provisions as liabilities of uncertain timing or amount. A provision can only be recognised when an enterprise has a present obligation (legal or constructive) arising as a result of a past event; it is probable that an outflow from the enterprise of resources embodying economic benefits will be required to settle the obligation; and a reliable estimate can be made of the amount of the obligation.

In summary then, the recognition conditions for a provision cover two elements: the existence of a liability and measurement of that liability.

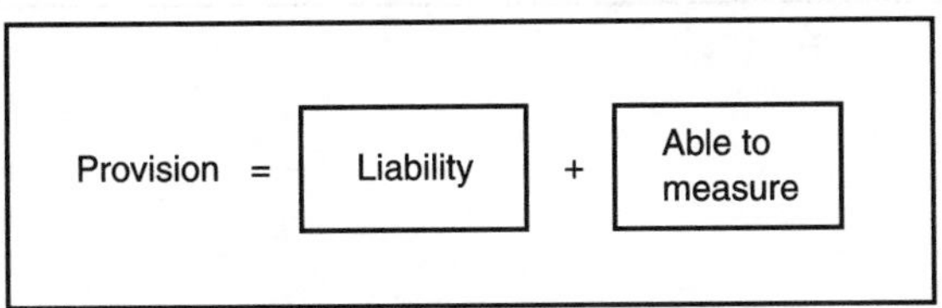

The existence element is further subdivided by IAS 37 into two conditions.

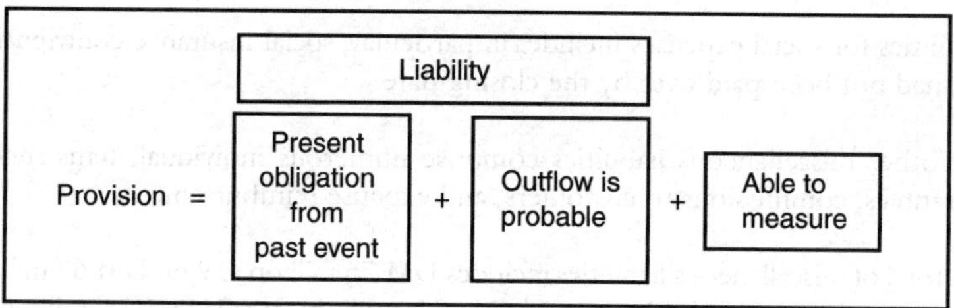

With respect to contingencies, a contingent liability, which is not recognised but disclosed by way of note, results when one or more of the three recognition conditions for a provision is not met.

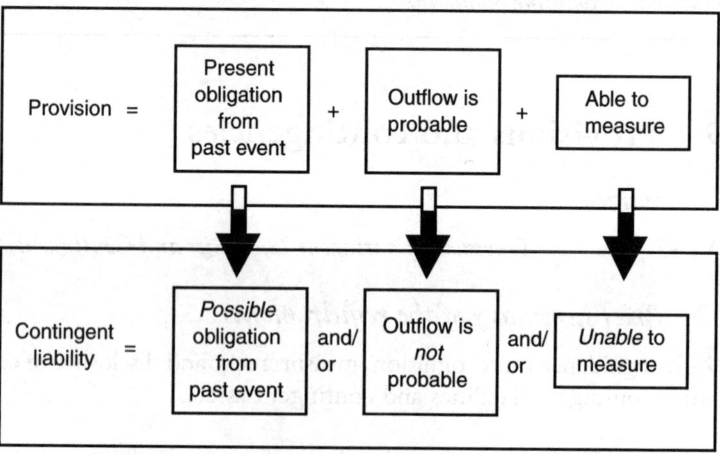

A contingent asset is not recognised but disclosed by way of note:

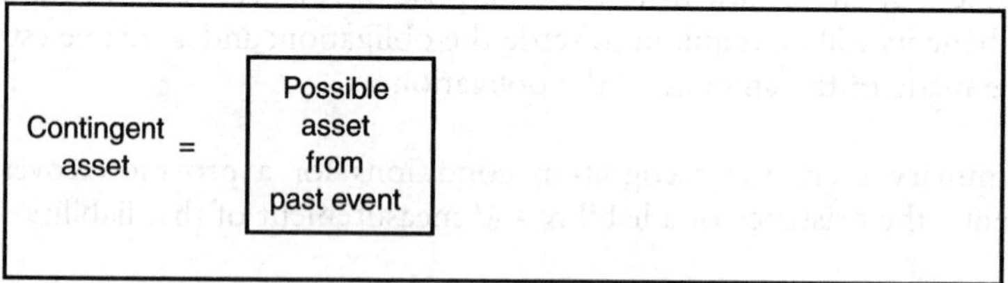

11.9.3 Development of the requirements

There has been no International Accounting Standard on provisions in the past, and therefore the situation has been one in which there was a lack of guidance and a need for clarification. In part because of a lack of guidance, the practice had developed under the general banner of 'prudence' of aggregating liabilities with expected liabilities of future years, and sometimes with expected expenditures related to ongoing operations, in one large provision, often reported as an exceptional item. This practice resulted in very large provisions, colloquially known as 'big bath' provisions, which presented a distorted liability position on the balance sheet and subsequently, when released, boosted profits in an unrealistic manner. Future liabilities, which had already been taken into account in such a big bath provision, were therefore not matched to the periods in which they were occurring.

In summary, three practices are banned by IAS 37:

- creation of provisions where there is no liability;
- undisclosed use of old provisions created for one purpose to meet new expenditure of a different purpose; and
- undisclosed release of provisions into the profit and loss account.

Common practices adopted before IAS 37 which are either no longer permitted, or which will require a different approach include: provision for restructuring based only on a board decision, provision for future losses or other items which smooth profits, and provision for repairs.

11.9.4 Scope

The requirements of the IAS apply to all provisions, contingent liabilities and contingent assets other than:

> '• those resulting from financial instruments that are carried at fair value;
> • those resulting from executory contracts, except where the contract is onerous;
> • those arising in insurance enterprises from contracts with policy holders; or
> • those covered by another International Accounting Standard'.
>
> (IAS 37.1)

Those resulting from financial instruments that are not carried at fair value (including guarantees) do come within the scope of the Standard.

An executory contract is not strictly defined in the Standard, but an explanation is given:

> 'Executory contracts are contracts under which neither party has performed any of its obligations or both parties have partially performed their obligations to an equal extent.'
>
> (IAS 37.3)

This exemption covers contracts such as:

- employee contracts in respect of continuing employment;
- contracts for future delivery of services such as gas and electricity;
- obligations to pay council tax and similar levies; and
- most purchase orders.

IAS 37 does not apply to executory contracts unless they are onerous. An onerous contract is defined as follows: 'a contract in which the unavoidable costs of meeting the obligations under the contract exceed the economic benefits expected to be received under it.' See **11.9.9** for further discussion of onerous contracts.

The rules of the Standard do apply to provisions, contingent liabilities and contingent assets of insurance enterprises, other than those arising from contracts with policy holders. The IASB currently has a project on Insurance on its agenda (see Chapter **2**).

There will be occasions where another International Accounting Standard deals with a specific type of provision, contingent liability or contingent asset. Examples might be construction contracts falling under IAS 11 (r1993), *Construction Contracts* (see Chapter **27**), tax falling under IAS 12 (r2000), *Income Taxes* (see Chapter **23**), leases falling under IAS 17 (r1997), *Leases* (see Chapter **24**) (unless the lease is an onerous operating lease in which case IAS 37 applies) or employee benefits falling under IAS 19 (r2000), *Employee Benefits* (see Chapter **25**). Where these circumstances arise, then the enterprise applies that Standard instead of IAS 37.

Use of the term 'provision' is restricted in the Standard to items that are disclosed in a balance sheet under headings for liabilities. It does not cover adjustments to assets, such as depreciation, impairment and doubtful debts, which may be popularly referred to as provisions.

Other International Accounting Standards specify whether expenditures are treated as assets or expenses, so IAS 37 does not address these issues. It neither prohibits nor requires capitalisation of costs recognised when a provision is made.

IAS 37 applies to provisions for restructuring (including discontinuing operations). Where a restructuring meets the definition of a discontinuing operation, additional disclosures may be required by IAS 35, *Discontinuing Operations* (see Chapter **5**).

11.9.5 Definitions

IAS 37 defines a provision as a liability of uncertain timing or amount. A liability is defined as 'a present obligation of the enterprise arising from past events, the settlement of which is expected to result in an outflow from the enterprise of resources embodying economic benefits'. (IAS 37.10) This is consistent with the explanation of a liability given in the Framework.

Provisions can be distinguished from other types of liability by considering the events which give rise to the obligation, and the degree of certainty over the amount. In each case, the definition of a liability will be met through the existence of a present obligation arising from a past event. For example, trade payables are liabilities to pay for goods/services already received/supplied and which have been invoiced or formally agreed with the supplier. Accruals, on the other hand, are liabilities to pay for goods/services received/supplied but which have not been paid, invoiced or formally agreed with the supplier. Although it is sometimes necessary to estimate the amount or timing of accruals, the uncertainty is generally much less than for provisions. Accruals are often reported as part of trade and other payables, whereas provisions are reported separately.

Example	**Classification**	**Degree of uncertainty**
Goods or services received and invoiced	Trade payable	None
Goods or services received, but not invoiced	Accrual	Some
Legal claim from supplier for breach of exclusive supply agreement	Provision (if conditions met)	Significant

A contingent liability is:

'(a) a possible obligation that arises from past events and whose existence will be confirmed only by the occurrence or non-occurrence of one or more uncertain future events not wholly within the control of the enterprise; or

(b) a present obligation that arises from past events but is not recognised because:

(i) it is not probable that an outflow of resources embodying economic benefits will be required to settle the obligation; or

(ii) the amount of the obligation cannot be measured with sufficient reliability.'

(IAS 37.10)

A contingent asset is 'a possible asset that arises from past events and whose existence will be confirmed only by the occurrence or non-occurrence of one or more uncertain future events not wholly within the control of the enterprise.' (IAS 37.10)

The important point of distinction between provisions and contingent liabilities and assets, is that provisions are recognised on the balance sheet, whilst contingent liabilities are not recognised, merely disclosed under certain circumstances (see **11.9.12**).

11.9.6 Recognition of provisions

The Standard sets out three conditions which must all be satisfied in order to recognise a provision:

> '(a) an enterprise has a present obligation (legal or constructive) as a result of a past event;
> (b) it is probable that an outflow of resources embodying economic benefits will be required to settle the obligation; and
> (c) a reliable estimate can be made of the amount of the obligation.'
>
> (IAS 37.14)

The first two of these criteria derive from the definition of a liability. The third derives from the conditions for recognising a liability.

Each criterion is discussed in turn below.

11.9.7 Recognition – present obligations and past events

A present obligation and a past event are key considerations when trying to determine whether a provision or a contingent liability is the more appropriate. The terms 'present obligation' and 'past obligating event' are not actually defined in the Standard, but there is a considerable amount of narrative devoted to explaining the concepts.

In order for there to be a present obligation, the IAS requires that an obligating event has taken place. An obligating event means that the enterprise has no realistic alternative but to settle the obligation created by the event. Such obligations will be either:

- a legal obligation – that is, enforceable by law; or
- a constructive obligation – that is, the event creates a valid expectation in another party such that the enterprise has no realistic alternative to settling that obligation.

It may be that an event which happens does not immediately give rise to an obligation. However, where a subsequent obligation arises, which can be traced back to the event, then the event becomes an obligating event. For example, an unexpected legal claim is received after the balance sheet date in respect of damage alleged to have occurred before the balance sheet date.

The following paragraphs discuss the implications of recognising provisions only when they are present obligations arising as a result of past events.

Events before the balance sheet date

Financial statements deal with the financial position of an enterprise at the end of its reporting period and not its possible position in the future. The only liabilities recognised in an enterprise's balance sheet are those that exist at the balance sheet date. Therefore no provision is recognised for costs that need to be incurred to operate in the future, notwithstanding that such costs may be necessary to continue as a going concern.

Future actions

It is only obligations which exist independently of the enterprise's future actions which fall to be recognised as provisions. One example where a provision is recognised might be clean-up costs for environmental damage. Even if the enterprise changed its future business, it would still incur the expenses relating to cleaning up because of its past activities. In contrast, if an airline was legally required to service its planes every 2000 flying hours, in theory it could stop flying planes, or stop flying that particular plane, and therefore no present obligation exists.

Role of third parties

An obligation always involves a commitment to another party. Sometimes the identity of the party will not be known, or sometimes it may be the public at large.

Management decision

It is because of the requirement for a clear commitment to another party, that a decision made by management before the balance sheet date does not of itself give rise to a present obligation, unless it is communicated to those affected by it in a sufficiently specific manner to raise a valid expectation in them that the enterprise will discharge its responsibilities.

New legislation

Where details of new legislation have yet to be finalised, an obligation arises only when the legislation is virtually certain to be enacted as drafted. Under IAS 37, such expectation is treated as a legal obligation.

Smoothing of results

The Standard seeks to stop artificial 'smoothing' of results. Through basing the recognition of a provision on the existence of a present obligation, the IAS rules out the recognition of any provision made simply to allocate results over more than one period, or otherwise to smooth the results reported. For example, companies will no longer be able to provide in advance for items such as future repairs. The cost will instead be charged to the income statement when it is actually incurred, i.e., when the work is done. However, the

IAS could have the opposite effect by encouraging the smoothing of results: 'big bath' provisions for restructuring resulted in large hits to the income statement, so a move towards recognising smaller but more frequent hits will actually stabilise earnings.

Prudence

An enterprise may be aware of some future commitment to spend money but future expenditure, however necessary, does not justify the recognition of a provision unless a liability exists at the period end.

Repairs and maintenance

Example 11A in IAS 37 Appendix C illustrates the application of the IAS to repairs and maintenance for property, plant and equipment. Because future repairs and maintenance are not present obligations of the enterprise resulting from past events, no provision should be made for them, even if they are required by legislation if the asset is to continue to be used. There are no grounds for recognising a provision for future repairs and maintenance expenditures because these relate to the future operation of the business and the restoration of service potential, and therefore they are either to be capitalised as assets or written off as operating expenses when incurred. Where a part of the asset can be identified as declining in service potential because of the need for repairs or maintenance, it should be depreciated to show the declining service potential. Subsequent expenditure on repairs and maintenance should then be capitalised to show the restoration of service potential.

This treatment is recommended in SIC-23, *Property, Plant and Equipment – Major Inspection or Overhaul Costs.* SIC-23 confirms that the cost of a major inspection or overhaul generally should be expensed as incurred. The exception is where the enterprise treats the cost of a major inspection or overhaul as a separate 'component' asset for accounting purposes and depreciates that component to reflect the consumption of benefits resulting from the major inspection or overhaul.

Complex situations

IAS 37 states that there will, on rare occasions, be circumstances where it is unclear whether a present obligation has arisen. In order to determine whether a present obligation exists under such rare circumstances, the Standard advises that account be taken of all available evidence. Such evidence may include, by way of example, the opinion of experts. When examining evidence, events occurring after the balance sheet date should also be taken into consideration. The advice contained in the Standard is basically to look at all the available evidence and come to a reasoned judgement on whether or not there is a present obligation. If it is more likely than not that a present obligation exists at the balance sheet date, then it is appropriate to conclude that there is a present obligation. If there is, then a provision is recognised; if not, a contingent liability is disclosed, unless the possibility of any outflow of resources embodying economic benefits in settlement is remote.

Recognition – outflow of resources embodying economic benefits

An essential part of the definition of a liability is the existence of an obligation to transfer resources embodying economic benefits. Recognition of a provision is conditional on such an outflow being 'probable'. The interpretation which IAS 37 adopts for the meaning of probable is more likely than not to occur, i.e., the probability that the event will occur is greater than the probability that it will not. Where a number of similar obligations exist (for example product warranties) the overall probability that an outflow of resources embodying economic benefits will be made is determined by looking at the class of obligations as a whole. A typical situation will be that despite the likelihood of an outflow of resources for any one item being small, it may well be probable that some outflow of resources will be needed to settle the class of obligations as a whole. Where this is the case, assuming that the other recognition criteria apply, then a provision is recognised.

Note that the 'more likely that not' concept is peculiar to IAS 37 and may have a different interpretation in other IASs.

Recognition – reliable estimate

The use of estimates is an inherent part of preparing financial statements. Provisions are clearly uncertain by nature, but IAS 37 emphasises that it should not be impossible to determine a range of possible outcomes and from this range to reach an appropriate conclusion which is sufficiently reliable for the provision to be recognised.

Despite this optimistic view, it is likely that this area will be open to vigorous debate between auditors and their clients. The Standard does allow for the possibility that a reliable estimate may not be able to be made. In this instance, because the three general criteria are not met, it falls to be disclosed as a contingent liability.

Recognition criteria for provisions: summary

The table below aims to illustrate the application of the three criteria described in the paragraphs above.

Situation	Provision?	Action
Past event has occurred resulting in a ***possible*** obligation for which a transfer of benefits is possible but not probable.	×	Unless the possibility of a transfer of benefits is remote, disclose a contingent liability.
Past event has occurred resulting in a present obligation for which there may ***possibly*** be a transfer of benefits, but there probably will not.	×	Unless the possibility of a transfer of benefits is remote, disclose a contingent liability.
Past event has occurred resulting in a present obligation for which it is likely there will be a transfer of benefits, but a ***reliable estimate cannot be made*** of the amount of the obligation.	×	Disclose a contingent liability (NB this situation is likely to be very rare).
Past event has occurred resulting in a present obligation for which it is likely there will be a transfer of benefits, and a reliable estimate can be made of the amount of the obligation.	✓	Disclosures are required in respect of the provision.
An obligating ***event has not taken place by the balance sheet date***, but it takes place after the balance sheet date resulting in an obligation for which it is likely there will be a transfer of benefits, and a reliable estimate can be made of the amount of the obligation.	×	Consider whether IAS 10 (r1999), *Events After the Balance Sheet Date*, requires the disclosure of the non-adjusting event which has arisen.

11.9.8 Application of recognition criteria – future operating losses

IAS 37 contains two prohibitions on the recognition of provisions for future operating losses:

- a general prohibition, on grounds that there is no present obligation and thus no liability (however, it may indicate a need to test whether assets have been impaired under IAS 36 (see **10.12**)); and
- a specific prohibition in respect of future operating losses up to the date of a restructuring, again on grounds that there is no present obligation, unless the losses relate to an onerous contract.

In both cases, future operating losses relate to an activity which will continue, albeit in a restructured form, and are presumed to be avoidable (for example, by an immediate closure of the loss-making activities). They are therefore appropriately recognised as the activity occurs.

11.9.9 Application of recognition criteria – onerous contracts

Provision is required for the present obligation under an onerous contract. However, where assets dedicated to a contract are involved, a separate provision is recognised only after any impairment loss has been recognised on those assets under IAS 36, *Impairment of Assets* (see **10.12**).

An onerous contract is defined as 'a contract in which the unavoidable costs of meeting the obligations under the contract exceed the economic benefits expected to be received under it'. The unavoidable costs under a contract reflect the least net cost of exiting from the contract, i.e., the lower of:

- the cost of fulfilling the contract; and
- any compensation or penalties arising from failure to fulfil the contract.

Example 11.12

Long-term supply contract

Long-term contracts for the supply of goods or services where costs have risen or current market prices have fallen are onerous, and provision recognised, to the extent that future supplies must be made at a loss. No provision is recognised under a contract for the supply of goods which is profitable, but at a reduced margin compared to other contracts, since there is no probable net outflow of resources embodying economic benefits by the enterprise.

Vacated property

A lease for property which has been vacated is onerous, and a provision recognised, to the extent that rentals continue which are not recoverable from subleasing the property. The provision should represent the best estimate of the expenditure required to settle the obligation at the balance sheet date, which in this case might be the amount the landlord would accept to terminate the lease.

Examples of contracts which do not meet the criteria for recognition of a provision are:

- routine purchase orders, and similar contracts, which realistically could be cancelled by agreement with the vendor without paying compensation; and
- purchase orders where the future benefits from use of the asset exceed its cost, notwithstanding that compensation must be paid if the order is cancelled.

11.9.10 Application of recognition criteria – restructuring

IAS 37 provides specific guidance on how the general recognition criteria for provisions apply to restructuring.

IAS 37 defines restructuring as a programme that is planned and controlled by management, and materially changes either (a) the scope of a business undertaken by an enterprise; or (b) the manner in which that business is conducted. However, restructuring in the Standard is used in a wider set of circumstances than the definition would suggest, and includes events such as:

(a) sale or termination of a line of business;
(b) the closure of business locations in a country or region or the relocation of business activities from one country or region to another;
(c) changes in management structure, for example, eliminating a layer of management; and
(d) fundamental reorganisations that have a material effect on the nature and focus of the enterprise's operations.

(IAS 37.76)

Although a restructuring may encompass both closure of an operation and the opening of a new operation, the effect of IAS 37.80(b) will be to allow provision only for the closure element. (This is discussed in **11.9.11**).

Application of general recognition criteria
The two principal requirements for recognition of a provision in respect of a restructuring are:

- a detailed plan; and
- a valid expectation that the plan will be implemented.

Requirement for detailed plan
The detailed plan must specify:

(i) the business or part of a business concerned;
(ii) the principal locations affected;
(iii) the location, function, and approximate number of employees who will be compensated for terminating their services;
(iv) the expenditures that will be undertaken; and
(v) when the plan will be implemented.

(IAS 37.72a (i)–(v))

In order to give rise to a constructive obligation when it is communicated to those affected by it, implementation of the plan should commence as soon as possible, and be completed within a timeframe that makes significant change to the plan unlikely. Where either there is a long delay before commencement, or execution of the plan will take a long time, the timeframe allows opportunities for the plan to be changed, and thus it is unlikely that the enterprise has raised a valid expectation that it is presently committed to the restructuring.

Requirement for valid expectation

IAS 37 requires that the enterprise has raised a valid expectation in those affected that it will carry out the restructuring by:

(a) actually starting to implement that plan; or
(b) announcing its main features to those affected by it.

(IAS 37.72(b))

The existence of a valid expectation in those affected relates to the situation at the balance sheet date. The fact that implementation has commenced by the date financial statements are approved does not give rise to a present obligation at the balance sheet date unless some other event gave rise to a valid expectation at that date. Actually starting to implement the plan at the balance sheet date would be evidenced by, for example, dismantling plant, the sale of assets or a public announcement. To constitute a constructive obligation, a public announcement must be made in such a way and in sufficient detail that it gives rise to valid expectations in other parties such as customers, suppliers and employees (or their representatives) that the enterprise will carry out the restructuring.

A management or board decision to go ahead with its plan will not, by itself, constitute a constructive obligation unless it is accompanied by a valid expectation in those affected by either (a) or (b) above, that is commencement of the plan or a suitable announcement. Similarly, events involving third parties which occur before a board decision is taken or approval given to a detailed plan, for example negotiations with employee representatives for termination payments or with purchasers for the sale of an operation, do not amount to a constructive obligation without a valid expectation in those affected. However, a constructive obligation could arise where, as happens in some countries, a board includes non-management representatives such as employees with the effect that notification to those affected and approval by the board of a detailed plan satisfies the requirement for a valid expectation being raised with those employees affected.

A valid expectation is unlikely to exist in the following cases:

- management has developed a detailed plan, but has not notified those affected by it, even though it can point to previous instances where it has proceeded with a plan; and

- management has developed a plan which involves closure of one of two possible sites, and has made general indications to employees that one site will close, but has not communicated which of the two sites will close in order to avoid alienation of employees at that site before implementation commences.

Restructuring – sale of an operation
The IAS specifies that an obligation does not exist for the sale of an operation until the enterprise is committed to the sale, i.e., there is a binding sale agreement. Until there is such an agreement, the enterprise will be able to change its mind and indeed will have to take another course of action if a purchaser cannot be found on acceptable terms.

When a sale is only part of a restructuring, a constructive obligation can arise for the other parts of the restructuring before a binding sale agreement exists. In this case, the assets of the operation are reviewed for impairment, under IAS 36 (see **10.12**).

Where, at the year end, an enterprise had signed heads of agreement to dispose of a loss-making part of its business, but a binding sale agreement was not signed until a month later, no provision may be made under IAS 37 at the balance sheet date. However, an impairment review should be carried out and this may cover much of the provision which would otherwise have been made. Also, consideration should be given to whether the business has onerous contracts for which provision should be made.

Restructuring provision flowchart
The following flowchart shows when it is appropriate to make a provision in a restructuring situation.

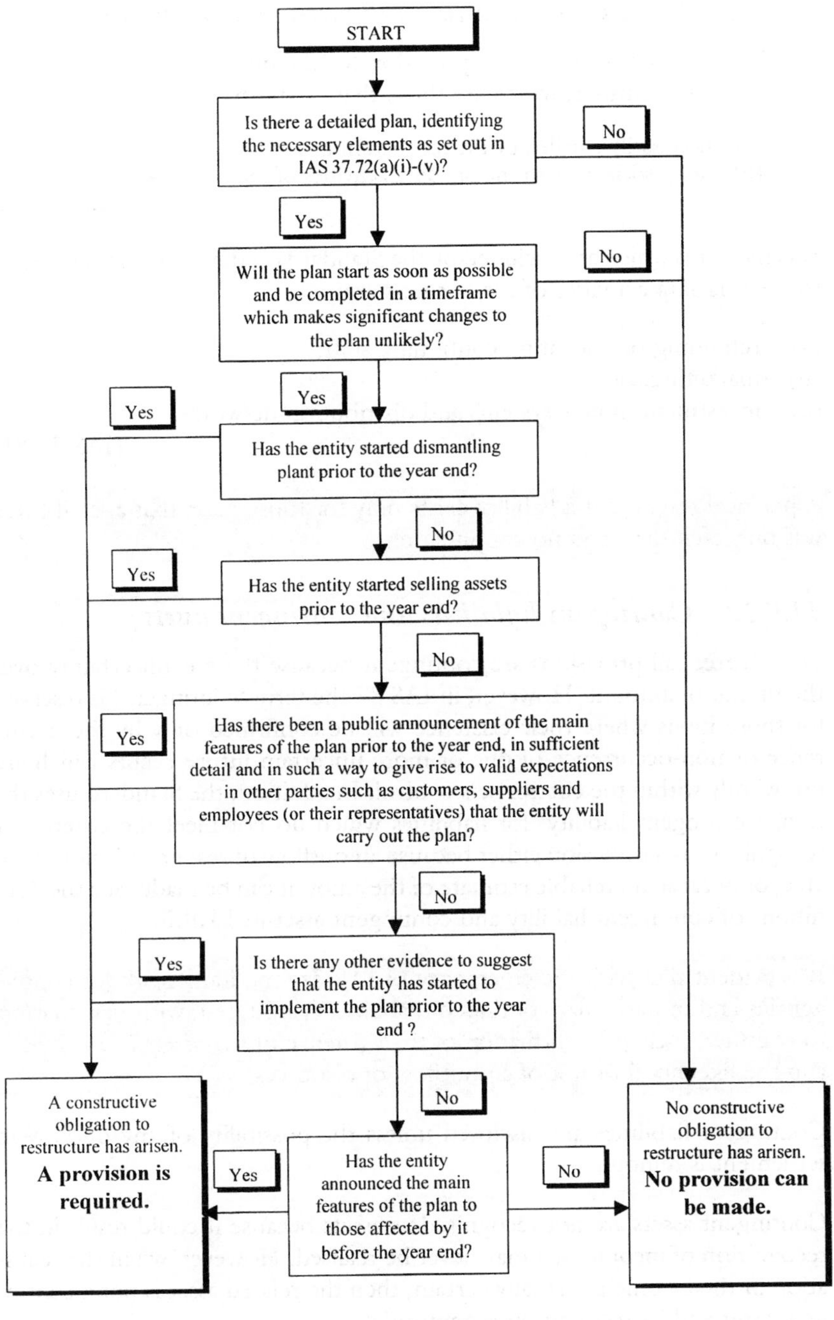
START
Is there a detailed plan, identifying the necessary elements as set out in IAS 37.72(a)(i)-(v)?
No
Yes
Will the plan start as soon as possible and be completed in a timeframe which makes significant changes to the plan unlikely?
No
Yes
Yes
Has the entity started dismantling plant prior to the year end?
No
Yes
Has the entity started selling assets prior to the year end?
No
Yes
Has there been a public announcement of the main features of the plan prior to the year end, in sufficient detail and in such a way to give rise to valid expectations in other parties such as customers, suppliers and employees (or their representatives) that the entity will carry out the plan?
No
Yes
Is there any other evidence to suggest that the entity has started to implement the plan prior to the year end ?
No
A constructive obligation to restructure has arisen.
A provision is required.
Yes
Has the entity announced the main features of the plan to those affected by it before the year end?
No
No constructive obligation to restructure has arisen.
No provision can be made.

11.9.11 What is included in a restructuring provision?

IAS 37 restricts a restructuring provision to 'the direct expenditures arising from the restructuring, which are those that are both:

> '(a) necessarily entailed by the restructuring; and
> (b) not associated with the ongoing activities of the enterprise.'
>
> (IAS 37.80)

Specific items which are excluded by the Standard on the basis that they relate to the ongoing activities of the business are:

(a) retraining or relocating continuing staff;
(b) marketing; or
(c) investment in new systems and distribution networks.

(IAS 37.81)

A practical test is that a liability exists only for those costs that arise if there was only a closure, and no continuation.

11.9.12 Contingent liabilities and contingent assets

To a degree, all provisions are contingent because there is uncertainty over the timing or amount. However, in IAS 37 the term 'contingent' is reserved for those items where their existence will be confirmed only by the occurrence or non-occurrence of one or more uncertain future events which are not wholly within the enterprise's control. In addition, the Standard uses the term 'contingent liability' for liabilities which do not meet the criteria for recognition as a provision either because an outflow of resources is not probable, or because no reliable estimate of the amount can be made. See the definitions of contingent liability and contingent asset in **11.9.5**.

It is evident that with the emergence of IAS 37, the framework for contingencies and in particular contingent liabilities has altered, with new matters to consider, such as confirmation of the existence of the assets and liabilities and the likelihood or not of an outflow of resources.

Contingent liabilities are disclosed unless the possibility of any outflow in settlement is remote.

Contingent assets are not recognised as assets because it could result in the recognition of income that may never be realised. However, when the realisation of the income is virtually certain, then the related asset is not a contingent asset and its recognition is appropriate.

Contingent assets are disclosed where an inflow of economic benefits is probable.

Both contingent liabilities and contingent assets should be assessed continually to measure changes in the probability of outflows/inflows as appropriate and hence consequential changes in the disclosure. For details of the disclosure requirements see **11.9.17**.

11.9.13 Measurement

Best estimate
The measurement principle of IAS 37 is the familiar 'best estimate' of expenditure required to settle the present obligation at the balance sheet date. The reference to balance sheet date does not preclude use of later additional evidence or better information, but indicates that the best estimate will be the amount that an enterprise would rationally pay to have the obligation go away – by settlement, or by transfer to a third party. The addition of 'rationally' in paragraph 37 of the Standard suggests that although it may be difficult to arrange settlement or transfer, there is nevertheless a point of balance, and thus a price at which management would be willing to settle.

Ultimately, judgement will be that of management and will reflect experience of similar transactions. In reaching their judgement, reports of independent experts may be required. Examples of relevant independent experts are:

- solicitors and barristers;
- surveyors and valuers;
- loss adjusters;
- actuaries; and
- technical experts (e.g., regarding a decommissioning process).

Use of expected value
Where the provision relates to a large population of items, it is valid to use an 'expected value'. This is the amount that takes account of all possible outcomes using probabilities to weight the outcomes. Expected value as a method of estimation has a number of desirable features. The method provides an estimate that reflects the entire probability distribution, i.e., all the possible outcomes weighted by their probabilities. For a given assessed distribution, the method has the advantage of objectivity in that different measurers would calculate the same estimate. Furthermore, expected value is additive (i.e., the expected value of a number of items is the sum of the expected values of the individual items).

Example 11.13

An enterprise faces 100 legal claims, each with a 40 per cent likelihood of success in defending the claim with no cost, and a 60 per cent likelihood of failure with a cost of each claim of £1m.

Using expected value, the statistical likelihood is that 60 per cent of claims will result in a cost of £1m, thus the provision should be 60% × 100 × £1m = £60m.

Where the provision relates to a single event, or a small number of events, expected value is not a valid technique.

Example 11.14

An enterprise faces a single legal claim, with a 40 per cent likelihood of success in defending the claim with no cost, and a 60 per cent likelihood of failure with a cost of £1m.

Expected value is not valid in this case since the outcome will never be a cost of £600,000 (60% × £1m). It will either be nil or £1m. Paragraph 40 of the Standard states that the provision should represent whichever is the most likely of these two outcomes. In this example, it is more likely that a cost of £1m will result, and therefore full provision would be made.

As a general rule of thumb, where the most likely outcome is close to expected value, it will be appropriate to provide the most likely outcome since expected value provides evidence of the probable outflow of benefits.

Example 11.15

An enterprise is required to replace a major component in an asset under a warranty. Each replacement costs £1m. From experience, there is a 30 per cent chance of a single failure, 50 per cent chance of two failures, and a 20 per cent chance of three failures.

The most likely outcome is two failures, costing £2m. The expected value is £1.9m (30% × £1m + 50% × £2m + 20% × £3m). The expected value supports the provision for the most likely outcome of £2m.

A second rule of thumb, implied by IAS 37.40, is that where most likely outcome and expected value are not close together, it will often be appropriate to provide for whichever possible outcome is nearest to the expected value.

Example 11.16

An enterprise is required to replace a major component in an asset under a warranty. Each replacement costs £1m. From experience, there is a 40 per cent chance of a single failure, 30 per cent chance of two failures, and a 30 per cent chance of three failures.

The most likely outcome is a single failure, costing £1m. The expected value is £1.9m (40% × £1m + 30% × £2m + 30% × £3m). In this case, the most likely outcome of £1m has only a 40 per cent probability. There is a 60 per cent probability that the cost will be higher. The outcome closest to expected value is £2m, that is two failures.

Tax

Under IAS 37, provisions are measured before tax. The tax consequences of the provision, and of changes in the provision, are dealt with under IAS 12, *Income Taxes* (r2000) (see Chapter **23**).

Risks and uncertainties

IAS 37 contains a rather vague requirement that 'risks and uncertainties that inevitably surround many events and circumstances should be taken into account in reaching the best estimate of a provision'. (IAS 37.42) The explanatory guidance suggests that a balance needs to be struck between, on the one hand, being imprudent (resulting in overstated assets or profits or understated liabilities or expenses) and on the other hand being over prudent (resulting in excessive provisions or overstated liabilities). Also, adjustment for risk and uncertainty should not be double-counted. The most obvious situation when this may happen is when risk is reflected both in estimated future cash flows and in the discount. Disclosures concerning uncertainty required by IAS 37.85(b) would act as a safeguard against obvious error.

Future events

In many cases, future events do not represent present obligations, and therefore provision is not generally made. However, future events may affect the measurement of a present obligation. A common example cited in IAS 37 is the impact of future technology changes on site clean-up costs at the end of the site's life. A similar example would be decommissioning. IAS 37 requires the current provision to reflect reduced costs of technology expected to be available at the time of a future clean-up.

This allows cost reductions to be recognised for:

- increased experience in applying existing technology; and
- applying existing technology to a larger or more complex clean-up operation than has been carried out to date.

However, a completely new technology should only be assumed where there is sufficient objective evidence that it will be available and will be effective for the claimed cost.

New legislation should be reflected in the measurement of a provision for an existing obligation when there is sufficient objective evidence that the legislation is virtually certain to be exercised. Paragraph 50 specifies that this will include:

- evidence of what the legislation will demand; and
- evidence that the legislation will be enacted and implemented.

In practice, there is no single event in the passage of new legislation prior to enactment which provides a general trigger point.

Present value
IAS 37 requires provisions to be discounted to present value when the time value of money is material.

Quantifying materiality will depend on a range of factors, for example, the size of the provision relative to other items in the balance sheet, the impact of any adjustment on profit for the year, etc. The following table summarises the impact of discounting a single future cash flow for a range of future dates, and for a range of possible discount rates. The table indicates that discounting reduces an amount by around 10 per cent over a 1–2 year period. However, over a 40 year period, discounting reduces an amount to less than 10 per cent of its nominal amount (with the effect that most of the charge would be recognised through the unwinding of the discount).

	Discount rate		
	5%	7.5%	10%
Cash flow of 100 after: 1 year	95	93	91
2 years	91	87	83
3 years	86	80	75
4 years	82	75	68
5 years	78	70	62
10 years	61	49	39
15 years	48	34	24
20 years	38	24	15
40 years	14	6	2

Choice of discount rate
Discount rate (or rates) should:

- be pre-tax;
- reflect current market assessments of the time value of money; and
- reflect risks specific to the liability.

Under IAS 37, it is acceptable to reflect risk either in estimation of cash flows, or by adjusting the discount rate. Use of an adjusted discount rate will normally be the easiest method. However, practical experience of estimating discount rates for use in impairment tests suggests that it is a most imprecise science. There is therefore a good case, on grounds of simplicity and avoiding spurious accuracy, for dealing with risk through a detailed estimation of cash flows to include the impact of risk, coupled with use of a risk-free discount rate. Whichever method is used, care should be taken to avoid double-counting the effect of risk.

It follows that where risk is reflected in estimates of cash flows, the appropriate discount rate will be a pre-tax risk-free rate such as a current government bond rate.

The following is a general guide:

- a risk free rate, based on government bond rates, reflects the discount that a creditor will accept to receive a risk-free cash flow now rather than at the due date;
- a risk-adjusted rate based on a general corporate bond rate will reflect general corporate credit risk and will be appropriate for 'blue-chip' entities;
- a risk adjusted rate based on an enterprise specific corporate bond rate or weighted average cost of capital (adjusted to a gross tax basis) will reflect risk factors specific to an enterprise and will be appropriate for most enterprises where risk is not specifically considered in the estimation of cash flows.

Example 11.17

Risk-free rate

An enterprise sells goods subject to a warranty. A provision is calculated for warranty claims based on detailed records of past faults in products. Since the estimation of cash flows takes account of enterprise specific risks, the appropriate discount rate will be a risk free rate, for example, a government bond rate.

Risk-adjusted rate

An enterprise vacates a leased property, and identifies a liability in respect of continuing rentals due. Estimated cash flows are lease rentals stipulated in the lease, and as such do not reflect risk. The appropriate discount rate is a rate which reflects the credit-risk of the enterprise such as a rate derived from weighted average cost of capital (grossed-up for tax).

Care should be taken in determining a pre-tax discount rate by adjusting a post-tax rate. Because the tax consequences of different cash flows may be different, the pre-tax rate of return is not always the post-tax rate of return grossed up by the standard rate of tax.

Where estimated cash flows are expressed in current prices, a real discount rate (that is, reduced for the impact of future inflation) will be used. Where, alternatively, cash flows are expressed in expected future prices (normally higher than current prices) a nominal discount rate will be used. The effects of inflation on the present value will be the same provided one of these methods is used:

- current (lower) prices discounted at a real (lower) rate; or
- future (higher) prices discounted at a nominal (higher) rate.

Expected disposal of assets

Gains from the expected disposal of assets should not be taken into account in measuring a provision.

Example 11.18

At the end of year 1, an enterprise is demonstrably committed to closures of some facilities, having drawn up a detailed plan and made announcements. The plan shows the effects to be:

	Year 1	*Year 2*	*Year 3*
	£m	*£m*	*£m*
Direct costs	10	100	
Gain from sale of property			–20

Prior to IAS 37, a provision at the end of year 1 would be made for £80m (being 100 – 20). In practice, this treatment would result in the balance sheet at the end of year 2 recognising as an asset the £20m expected gain on sale irrespective of whether this qualified for recognition.

Under IAS 37, the provision at the end of year 1 is £100m. The gain on sale of the property is dealt with separately under the principles of asset recognition.

The treatment of estimated future operating losses in a closure provision is considered in **11.9.8**.

11.9.14 Reimbursements

An enterprise with a present obligation requiring a provision to be recognised may be able to seek reimbursement of part or all of the expenditure from another party. For example:

- an insurance contract arranged to cover a risk;
- an indemnity clause in a contract; and
- a warranty provided by a supplier.

Recognition of a reimbursement is on the basis that any asset arising is separate from the related obligation. Consequently, such a reimbursement should be recognised only when it is virtually certain that it will be received consequent upon the settlement of the obligation. This treatment is consistent with guidance on contingent assets.

Reporting of a reimbursement is as follows:

- in the balance sheet, a separate asset is recognised (which must not exceed the amount of the provision); and
- in the income statement, a net amount may be presented being a provision for the obligation less the reimbursement.

Offset of a provision and related reimbursement is only appropriate where an enterprise can avoid making payment in respect of its obligation such that it has no liability.

Where an enterprise is jointly and severally liable for an obligation, it should provide for that part of the obligation for which payment by it is probable. The remainder, which is expected to be paid by other parties, is a contingent liability.

If an enterprise has a provision and a matching reimbursement, and the time value of money is material to both, the question arises whether both should be discounted. In principle, both the asset and the liability should be discounted. If there will be a significant interval between the cash outflows and receiving the reimbursement, the reimbursement will be more heavily discounted – so on initial recognition there will be a net cost. If (presumably rarely) the reimbursement will be received first, IAS 37.53 will restrict the discounted amount of the reimbursement so that it does not exceed the discounted amount of the provision. In the income statement, the expense relating to a provision may be presented net of the amount recognised for a reimbursement.

11.9.15 Changes in provisions

Provisions should be reviewed at each balance sheet date and adjusted to reflect the current best estimate.

Adjustments arise from three sources:

- revision to estimated cash flows (both amount and likelihood);
- change to present value due to the passage of time; and
- revision of discount rate to prevailing current market conditions.

Where a provision is no longer required, for example, if it is no longer probable that an outflow of resources embodying economic benefits will be required to settle the obligation, the provision should be reversed.

When discounting to present value is used, the carrying amount of a provision increases in each period to reflect the passage of time. This increase is recognised as an interest expense.

Disclosure of changes in provisions is dealt with in **11.9.17**.

11.9.16 Use of provisions

One of the objectives of IAS 37 is to increase the transparency of accounting for provisions, and in particular, prevent the use of an existing provision to meet a different, undisclosed obligation. Accordingly, the Standard requires provisions to be used only for expenditures for which the provision was originally recognised.

Increased disclosure requirements (see paragraph **11.9.17**), especially the requirement to identify movements on each class of provision, are intended to reinforce this requirement.

11.9.17 Disclosure requirements

Objective
The objective of IAS 37 with respect to disclosure is to ensure that sufficient information is disclosed in the notes to the financial statements to enable users to understand the nature, timing and amount of provisions, contingent liabilities and contingent assets. IAS 37 sets out the disclosure requirements for contingent liabilities and contingent assets alongside those for provisions, making clear the consistent basis for the requirements.

Provisions
With respect to provisions, the thinking behind the requirements is to supply information about their significance, any changes during the year, and explanation of how a provision has been used as expenditure is incurred during the year. The general requirements are set out in the following paragraphs.

For each class of provision there should be disclosed:

- brought and carried forward balances;
- changes during the period (showing separately additional provisions made; amounts incurred and charged against the provision; and unused amounts reversed);
- increase during the period in the discounted amount arising from the passage of time and the effect of any change in the discount rate;

- the nature of the obligation and expected timing of outflows;
- uncertainties surrounding the amount or timing of outflows;
- major assumptions concerning future events (if considered necessary to provide adequate information); and
- expected reimbursement, including amount of any asset recognised for that reimbursement.

Comparative information is not required for the numerical disclosures in the first three bullet points above.

Contingent liabilities

With respect to each class of contingent liability the following table of disclosures applies:

- estimate of the financial effect;
- uncertainties relating to the amount or timing of any outflow; and
- the possibility of any reimbursement.

Aggregation

There may be confusion about whether a group of provisions or contingent liabilities may be aggregated to form a class. Under these circumstances it is necessary to consider whether the nature of the items is sufficiently similar for a single statement about them to fulfil the requirements outlined above with respect to nature and uncertainties.

Linkage

One important point to note is that where a provision and contingent liability arise from the same set of circumstances, an enterprise should make the disclosure so that it clearly shows the link between the provision and the contingent liability.

Contingent assets

For contingent assets, where an inflow of economic benefits is probable, a brief description of the nature of the contingent assets and, where practicable, their estimated financial effect should be given, taking care to avoid giving misleading indications of the likelihood of income arising.

Non-disclosure of information

Where any of the information on contingencies is not disclosed because it is not practicable to do so, that fact should be stated.

In extremely rare cases, it is conceivable that some or all of the disclosures required for provisions and contingencies can be expected to prejudice seriously the position of the enterprise in a dispute with other parties on the subject matter of the provision. In such cases an enterprise need not disclose the information, but it should disclose the general nature of the dispute, together with the fact that, and reason why, the information has not been disclosed.

11.9.18 Transitional provisions

The effect of adopting IAS 37 'should be reported as an adjustment to the opening balance of retained earnings for the period in which the Standard is first adopted. Enterprises are encouraged, but not required, to adjust the opening balance of retained earnings for the earliest period presented and to restate comparative information. If comparative information is not restated, this fact should be disclosed.' (IAS 37.93)

11.9.19 Examples from IAS 37

IAS 37 Appendix C gives examples designed to illustrate application of the standard. The examples are reproduced below, but in a tabular format in order to identify reasons why particular items meet, or do not meet, the definition of a provision. In all cases it is assumed that a reliable estimate can be made.

Example 11.20

Type of risk or cost	*Present obligation as a result of a past event?*	*Probable transfer?*	*Conclusion*
1. Warranty given by a manufacturer under the terms of a contract for sale. Past experience shows claims will be received.	✓	✓	*Provide at date of sale sale for legal obligation.*
2A. Contaminated land (1) – enterprise cleans up only to meet legal requirements which are virtually certain to be enacted soon after the year end.	✓	✓	*Provide for expected legal obligation*
2B. Contaminated land (2) – enterprise has no legal obligation, but meets widely published clean-up policy.	✓	✓	*Provide for constructive obligation.*
3. Decommissioning – terms of a licence impose a legal obligation to remove an oil rig at the end of its life.	✓	✓	*Provide on commissioning of asset, and include in cost.*
4. Refunds – retail store follows a published policy of providing refunds even though there is no legal obligation.	✓	✓	*Provide for constructive obligation.*
5A. Closure of a division (1) – board decision taken before the balance sheet date, but not communicated to those affected, and plan not commenced.	✗		*No obligating event before the balance sheet date.*
5B. Closure of a division (2) – board decision, detailed plan completed, staff and customers notified before the balance sheet date.	✓	✓	*Provide for expected costs of closure.*

Type of risk or cost	*Present obligation as a result of a past event?*	*Probable transfer?*	*Conclusion*
6. Installation of new equipment – legal requirement to fit smoke filters within 6 months of balance sheet date.	✘		*No obligating event until filters fitted. Capitalise cost when incurred.*
7. Staff retraining – need to retrain staff to meet new system requirements imposed by change in the law.	✘		*No obligating event until training occurs.*
8. Onerous contract – operating lease rental payments on vacated property.	✓	✓	*Provide for unavoidable lease payments.*
9A. Guarantee (1) – guarantee provided for another enterprise's borrowings, and that entity is in a sound financial condition.	✓	✘	*No outflow of benefits is probable.*
9B. Guarantee (2) – guarantee provided for another enterprise's borrowings, and that entity has filed for protection from creditors.	✓	✓	*Provide for estimated call on guarantee.*
10A. Court case (1) – unsettled case where lawyers advise that no liability will be proved.	✘		*No obligation exists based on evidence.*
10B. Court case (2) – unsettled case where lawyers advise that liability will be proved.	✓	✓	*Provide for estimated settlement.*
11A. Repairs and maintenance – a furnace has a lining that needs to be replaced every five years for technical reasons. At the balance sheet date, the lining had been in use for three years.	✘		*No obligation exists independently of future actions. Expenditure capitalised and depreciated.*
11B. Refurbishment costs – legislative requirement – an airline is required by law to overhaul its aircraft once every three years.	✘		*No obligation exists Expenditure capitalised. and depreciated.*

11.9.20 Specific problem area: repairs and maintenance obligations under leases

In some operating leases the lessee is required to incur periodic charges for maintenance of the leased asset or to make good dilapidations or other damage occurring during the rental period. Since the lease is a legal contract it may give rise to legal obligations. Accordingly, the principles of IAS 37 which preclude the recognition of provisions for repairs and maintenance generally do not preclude the recognition of such liabilities in a lease, once the event giving rise to the obligation under the lease has occurred. This would include provision for rental payments for a lease where the property has been vacated by the lessee. In assessing the best estimate of the provision, a judgement would be made of the period for which rentals will be paid which will not be covered by rentals received from a sub-lease.

Aircraft leases provide a useful source of examples to examine circumstances when an obligation under the lease has arisen. For example, an enterprise leases an aircraft under an operating lease. The aircraft has to undergo an expensive 'C check' after every 2,400 flying hours. Should provision be made for the cost of these checks?

The requirement to perform a 'C check' does not give rise to a present obligation at the time the lease is signed because, until 2,400 hours have been flown, there is no obligation which exists independently of the enterprise's future actions. Even the intention to incur the cost of a 'C check' depends on the enterprise deciding to continue flying the aircraft. The cost of each successive 'C check' will therefore be capitalised as it is incurred, and amortised over the period to the next 'C check'.

This leaves the question of the condition in which the aircraft must be returned to the lessor at the end of the lease, and whether this creates a present obligation, thus a provision, at the time the lease is signed. The answer depends on what the lease terms say happens when the aircraft is returned at the end of the lease. If no final 'C check' is required (i.e., in the final period the enterprise can use the aircraft for up to 2,399 flying hours and then return it without bearing any cost), no provision should be made, since there is no legal obligation. Since the income statement will first be charged with amortisation of costs after the first 'C check', this will mean the first 2,400 flying hours are effectively a 'free period'.

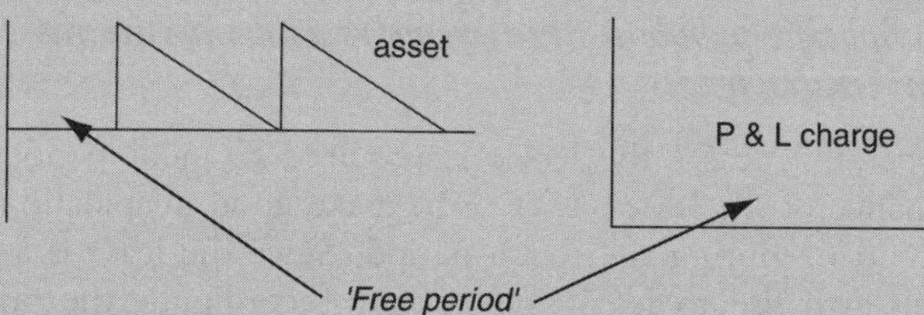

If a 'C check' is required at the end of the lease irrespective of how many hours have been flown, full provision for the cost should be made at the start of the lease. The costs should be carried forward and written off over the shorter of the next 2,400 flying hours and the number of flying hours to the end of the lease – and similarly each time a 'C check' is carried out. (This will fill the 'free period' above).

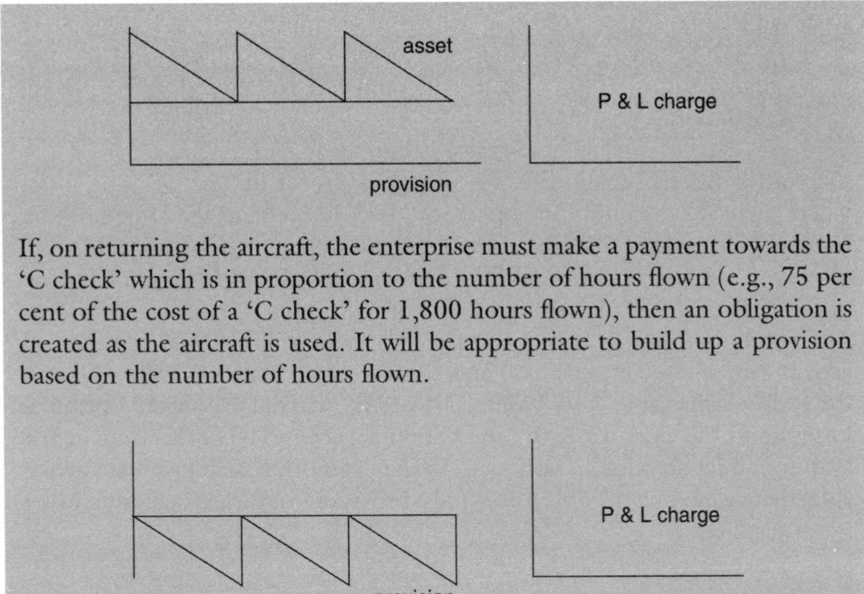

If, on returning the aircraft, the enterprise must make a payment towards the 'C check' which is in proportion to the number of hours flown (e.g., 75 per cent of the cost of a 'C check' for 1,800 hours flown), then an obligation is created as the aircraft is used. It will be appropriate to build up a provision based on the number of hours flown.

11.9.21 Specific problem area: directors' bonuses

Many enterprises pay directors' bonuses where the amount to be paid is not finalised until after the year end. For owner managed enterprises (where the directors are the shareholders) both directors' bonuses and dividends may be paid, determining the balance between the two on the basis of (amongst other things) the draft audited financial statements.

IAS 37 may not prohibit a provision for such bonuses. The fact that the amount is not finalised until after the year end is not inherently a problem – provision would still be made if there is a constructive obligation to pay the bonuses. A constructive obligation might be supported by the pattern of past practice, but it might also be a good idea for the enterprise to distinguish this from mere board intention by writing to individual directors prior to the year end to indicate that a bonus will be paid, of an amount yet to be determined.

Each case should be determined based on the set of facts presented and the circumstances specific to an entity.

11.9.22 Comparison with UK GAAP

In September 1998, the UK ASB issued FRS 12, *Provisions, Contingent Liabilities and Contingent Assets,* which was developed in parallel with IAS 37. FRS 12 contains all the requirements of IAS 37 and there are no differences of substance between the common requirements. However, FRS 12 contains some additional material dealing with the circumstances under which an asset should be recognised when a provision is recognised and it gives more guidance than IAS 37 on the discount rate to be used in the present value calculation.

One other difference is in the area of provisions for future operating losses where there is a discontinuing operation. FRS 12 contains the same prohibitions on recognition of provisions for future operating losses as IAS 37. However, under UK GAAP FRS 3, *Reporting Financial Performance*, paragraph 18 permits the inclusion of such losses in a provision for restructuring. The conditions which must exist are that there will be total cessation of activity (by sale or termination) and the sale or termination will happen at the earliest achievable date. Under UK GAAP unavoidable future operating losses up to the date of sale or termination are seen to be of the same nature as losses under an onerous contract. To the extent that such losses are avoidable, there is no present obligation and a provision for future operating losses is not justified.

11.9.23 Comparison with US GAAP

Individual sections of IAS 37 have counterparts in many US pronouncements, but there is no single FASB statement which covers the area of provisions. Whilst many of the definitions and concepts in IAS 37 are similar to those found in US GAAP, some are not directly comparable. One large area of difference is that the recognition criteria for provisions under IAS 37 rely on an event being 'more likely than not' to occur. Under US GAAP, liabilities are generally recognised when it is 'probable' that they will occur. This could lead to provisions being recognised under IAS 37 when they might not under US GAAP since 'more likely than not' can be interpreted to be less restrictive than 'probable.'

Whilst IAS 37 covers provisions recorded as a consequence of a restructuring, including a provision resulting from discontinued operations, US GAAP treats separately the recognition and measurement of discontinued operations and the disposal of a segment of a business (APB 30) and other restructurings (EITF 94-3).

APB 30 permits a provision arising on the discontinuance of an operation to include anticipated losses between the measurement date and the date of expected disposal. Under IAS 37, a provision for such losses would be prohibited.

Related to other restructurings, IAS 37 includes a requirement that management must either begin implementation of its restructuring plan or announce the plan to affected parties before it can provide for the costs of reorganisation. Other than for costs related to employee termination, EITF 94-3 does not include this requirement.

After Statement 121 was issued, significant implementation issues were raised by members of the EITF and others. As a result, the FASB has issued an Exposure Draft to address significant implementation questions and to develop a single accounting model based on the framework established in Statement 121 for the disposal of long-lived assets, whether previously held and used or newly acquired.

The Board issued an Exposure Draft of a proposed Statement, *Accounting for the Impairment or Disposal of Long-Lived Assets and for Obligations Associated with Disposal Activities*, in July 2000. The proposed Statement would supersede Statement 121. The proposed Statement would also supersede the provisions of APB Opinion No 30, *Reporting the Results of Operations – Reporting the Effects of Disposal of a Segment of a Business, and Extraordinary, Unusual and Infrequently Occurring Events and Transactions*, for the disposal of segments of a business and nullify most of the guidance provided by EITF Issue No 94–3, *Liability Recognition for Certain Employee Termination Benefits and Other Costs to Exit an Activity (including Certain Costs Incurred in a Restructuring)*.

The FASB is to issue this Statement in the third quarter of 2001. The Statement will be effective for financial statements issued for fiscal years beginning after 15 December 2001, and interim periods within those fiscal years, with early application encouraged.

11.9.24 Examples from published financial statements

Note that the excerpts from published financial statements given below do not always comply in full with all aspects of IAS and as such are not necessarily examples of best practice but merely of current practice.

Example 11.20

26. Provisions in millions of CHF (Swiss Francs)

	Restructuring provisions	*Other provisions*	**2000** *Total*	*1999 Total*
At beginning of year	748	3,606	**4,354**	3,352
Changes in Group organisation and Givaudan spin-off	16	(10)	**6**	(54)
Additional provisions created	75	368	**443**	2,673
Unused amounts reversed	(69)	(96)	**(165)**	(62)
Utilised during the year	(338)	(632)	**(970)**	(1,903)
Increase in discounted amount due to passage of time or change in discounting rate	–	77	**77**	–
Currency translation effects and other	(4)	254	**250**	348
At end of year	428	3,567	**3,995**	4,354
Current portion of provisions	216	1,743	**1,959**	2,660
Non-current portions of provisions	212	1,824	**2,036**	1,694
Total provisions	428	3,567	**3,995**	4,354

Restructuring provisions arise from planned programmes that materially change the scope of business undertaken by the Group or the manner in which business is conducted. Such provisions include only the costs necessarily entailed by the restructuring which are not associated with the ongoing activities of the Group. The creation of such provisions is recorded as a charge against other operating income, except where they arise from the restructuring or newly acquired companies, in which case they are included in the acquisition and hence form part of the goodwill.

Other provisions consist mainly of legal, environmental and similar matters. Other provisions include provisions in respect of the vitamin case (see Note 5).

27. Contingent liabilities

The operations and earnings of the Group continue, from time to time and in varying degrees, to be affected by political, legislative, fiscal and regulatory developments, including those relating to environmental protection, in the countries in which it operates. The industries in which the Group is engaged are also subject to physical risks of various kinds. The nature and frequency of these developments and events, not all of which are covered by insurance, as well as their effect on future operations and earnings are not predictable.

Provisions have been recorded in respect of the vitamin case, as disclosed in Note 5. These provisions are the Groups best current estimate of the total liability that may arise. As the various investigations outside the United States of America and private civil suits are still in progress it is possible that the ultimate liability may be different form this.

Roche Group
Switzerland
31 December 2000
International Accounting Standards

Example 11.21

7. Net interest	***2000***	*1999*	*1998*
Interest payable:	***£m***	*£m*	*£m*
On loans wholly repayable within five years	215	280	303
On loans any part repayable after five years	187	92	60
Interest payable re transportation prepayment	11	24	26
Termination of a bond obligation	–	–	8
Finance lease (income)/charges	(1)	1	(2)
Interest receivable	(52)	(39)	(58)
Other net interest	12	12	–
Less: interest capitalised (a)	(13)	(21)	(5)
	359	349	332
Unwinding of discount on provisions (see note 22, page 88(b))	**54**	56	56
Unwinding of discount on deferred income	**11**	11	2
Net interest payable – Group	**424**	416	390
– joint ventures	**15**	4	–
– associated undertakings	**20**	25	26
	459	445	416

(a) Interest is capitalised at a rate 7% per annum.
(b) Relates to the interest charge arising on discounted provisions; they are certain long-term gas sales contracts £26m (1999 £22m; 1998 £22m), environmental costs £14m (1999 £15m; 1998 £14m)

22 PROVISIONS FOR LIABILITIES AND CHARGES

	As at 1 Jan 2000 £m	*Profit and loss (credit)/ charge £m*	*Unwinding of discount £m*	*Paid £m*	*Transfers and other adjustments £m*	*Demerged £m*	*As at 31 Dec 2000 £m*
The Group							
Decommissioning costs	224	–	14	(9)	26(a)	–	255
Pension costs	423	(52)	–	(13)	–	(300)	58
Long-term gas contract	217	–	26	(28)	–	–	215
Deferred petroleum revenue tax	83	2	–	–	–	–	85
Deferred corporation tax	128	–	–	–	–	–	128
Environmental costs	310	–	14	(12)	–	(312)	–
Property restructuring costs	69	–	–	(8)	–	(61)	–
Other	87	29	–	–	19	(57)	78
	1,541	(21)	54	(70)	45	(730)	819
The Company							
Pension costs	423	(60)	–	(13)	–	(300)	50
	423	(60)	–	(13)	–	(300)	50

	As at 1 Jan 1999 £m	*Profit and loss (credit)/ charge £m*	*Unwinding of discount £m*	*Paid £m*	*Transfers and other adjustments £m*	*As at 31 Dec 1999 £m*
The Group						
Decommissioning costs	205	–	15	(4)	8	224
Pension costs	519	(77)	–	(19)	–	423
Long-term gas contract	222	–	22	(27)	–	217
Deferred petroleum revenue tax	76	7	–	–	–	83
Deferred corporation tax	143	(16)	–	–	1	128
Environmental costs	313	–	19	(21)	(1)	310
Property restructuring costs	83	–	–	(14)	–	69
Other	58	24	–	(25)	30	87
	1,619	(62)	56	(110)	38	1,541
The Company						
Pension costs	–	(7)	–	(2)	432	423
	–	(7)	–	(2)	432	423

(a) Includes £(2)m relating to the disposal of British Gas Qatar Limited.

A brief description of each provision together with estimates of the timing of expenditure is given below.

Decommissioning costs

The estimated cost of decommissioning at the end of the producing lives of fields is based on engineering estimates and reports from independent experts. Provision is made for the estimated cost of decommissioning at the balance sheet date. The payment dates of total expected future decommissioning costs is uncertain, but are currently anticipated to be between 2000 and 2030.

Pension costs

These represent the difference between the charge or credit to the profit and loss account in respect of pension costs and the contributions to the pension schemes (see *Principal accounting policies*, page 57 and note 27, page 93). The pension provision as at 31 December 2000 is the amount attributable to the existing employees of the Group following the demerger.

Long-term gas sales contract loss provisions

These represent forecast future losses under certain gas purchase and supply sales contracts assigned to BG on the demerger of Centrica plc in 1997. Some of the contracts terminated this year, with others due to terminate in 2009. The estimated net losses have been discounted at around 10% and are dependent upon factors such as prices, which vary with a basket of indices, and supply and demand volumes. BG also uses its own gas to supply these contracts. To account for BG's own gas sales and transportation of all gas at the contract prices, the difference between the market and contract prices is included within Other activities.

Deferred petroleum revenue tax

The provision for tax on gas and oil activities is calculated on a unit of production basis and represents liabilities expected to crystallise on certain North Sea fields. The first payment is expected to be made in 2005.

Deferred tax

This represents the provision for the tax attributable to timing differences between profits and losses compiled for tax purposes and results as stated in the financial statements. The following potential deferred tax liabilities have not been provided for on the basis that the differences will not reverse in the foreseeable future:

	2000	*1999*
	£m	*£m*
UK corporation tax at 30% (1999 30%):		
Accelerated capital allowances	**592**	1,949
Other timing differences	**(75)**	(71)
	517	1,878
Overseas tax	**3**	3
	520	1,881
Less: UK deferred corporation tax provided	**(128)**	(128)
Unprovided potential deferred tax liabilities	**392**	1,753

In December 2000 the Accounting Standards Board issued Financial Reporting Standard (FRS 19) *Deferred Tax*. This FRS requires deferred tax to be provided for on a "full provision" basis. BG plc will adopt this standard for the year ended 31 December 2001.

In the event of the distribution of the unappropriated profits or reserves of certain overseas subsidiary undertakings, joint ventures and associated undertakings; additional liabilities to UK and overseas tax of approximately £270m (1999 £210m) might arise. Such potential deferred taxation liabilities have not been provided because it is currently not intended to remit the profits.

Environmental costs

The provision for statutory decontamination costs of old gas manufacturing sites was transferred to Lattice on demerger. It was determined by periodic assessments undertaken by environmental specialists. The provision was discounted at 6%.

Property restructuring costs

These were transferred to Lattice on demerger. They consisted primarily of provisions for disposal of surplus leasehold interests and rent and rates payable on surplus properties.

Other

The balance as at 31 December 2000 represents the provision acquired in respect of employee benefits on the acquisition of Integral Holdings SA and its subsidiary undertaking Companhia de Gas de São Paulo SA (Comgas) in 1999 and restructuring costs arising from the renegotiation of power purchase agreements at Premier Power Limited (see note 6, page 75).

The provision as at 31 December 1999 included estimates of liabilities in respect of past events incurred by BG's insurance subsidiary undertaking, which was transferred to Lattice on demerger.

BG Plc
United Kingdom
31 December 2000
UK GAAP

Example 11.22

21 Provisions

	2000	*1999*
	SA Rands	
Post-retirement medical funding	**756**	746

The provision for post-retirement medical funding represents the provision for healthcare benefits for employees and retired employees and their registered dependants.

The post-retirement benefit costs are assessed in accordance with the advice of independent professionally qualified actuaries. The actuarial method used is the projected unit credit funding method.

The main assumptions used in calculating the costs were an annual discount rate of 13.5 per cent, healthcare inflation of 10.5 per cent, normal retirement age of 63 years, and fully eligible age of 55 years. The last valuation was performed as at 31 December 2000.

Environmental rehabilitation obligations		
Provision for decommissioning		
Balance at beginning of year	**312**	297
Unwinding of decommissioning obligation (note 3)	–	15
Balance at end of year	**312**	312
Provision for restoration		
Balance at beginning of year	**392**	337
Charge to income statement	**(54)**	55
Balance at end of year	**338**	392
Total provision	**1,396**	1,450

22 Deferred taxation

Deferred taxation relating to temporary differences is made up as follows:		
Deferred taxation liabilities		
Mining assets	**4,294**	4,460
Inventories	**142**	121
Other	**4**	10
	4,440	4,591
Deferred taxation assets		
Provisions	**573**	676
Net deferred taxation	**3,867**	3,915
The movement on the deferred tax balance is as follows:		
The balance at the beginning of year	**3,915**	4,311
Income statement charge (note 8)	**148**	27
Taxation on impairment (note 8)	**(196)**	–
Taxation rate change (note 8)	–	(423)
Balance at end of year	**3,867**	3,915

Anglo Gold
South Africa
31 December 2000
International Accounting Standards/South African GAAP

11.10 Minority interest

In the balance sheet, minority interest is that part of the net assets of a subsidiary attributable to interests which are not owned, directly or indirectly through subsidiaries, by the parent. (IAS 27.6) It is required to be disclosed on the face of the balance sheet (IAS 1 (r1997), *Presentation of Financial Statements*, para.66(l)). The illustrative examples in IAS 1 (r1997) place minority interest in between capital and reserves and liabilities to illustrate that minority interest is neither part of capital and reserves, since it does not relate to the equity of the shareholders of the enterprise, nor is it a liability of the enterprise. See Chapters **18** and **19** for a discussion of the measurement of minority interest.

11.10.1 Comparison with UK GAAP

Under UK GAAP, minority interest is included either in total net assets or underneath capital and reserves on the face of the balance sheet. Since IAS 1 (r1997) is silent on the issue of placement, it can be assumed that this is consistent with IAS 1 (r1997). In addition, FRS 4, *Capital Instruments*, requires minority interests to be analysed between the aggregate amount attributable to equity interests and amounts attributable to non-equity interests. Where the underlying shares are equity shares, the relevant amount of minority interests will be the proportionate share of net identifiable assets. If the underlying shares are non-equity shares, the amount of capital and reserves attributable to the shares will correspond to the amount determined by the requirements of FRS 4, namely, the net proceeds plus recognised finance costs less payments made.

11.10.2 Comparison with US GAAP

Under US GAAP, minority interest is generally disclosed between liabilities and shareholders' equity which is consistent with the illustrative example in IAS 1 (r1997).

CHAPTER 12

Balance sheet: financial instruments

12.1 Sources

IAS 1 (r1997)	*Presentation of Financial Statements.*
IAS 32 (r1998)	*Financial Instruments: Disclosure and Presentation.*
IAS 39 (r2000)	*Financial Instruments: Recognition and Measurement* (effective 1 January 2001).

12.2 Brief summary of the requirements

IAS 39 (r2000) requires that all financial assets and financial liabilities, including derivatives, should be recognised on the balance sheet. They are initially measured at cost, which is the fair value of the consideration exchanged. Subsequent to initial recognition, all financial assets should be remeasured to fair value, except for the following, which should be carried at amortised cost subject to a test for impairment:

- loans and receivables originated by the enterprise and not held for trading;
- other fixed maturity investments, such as debt securities and mandatorily redeemable preferred shares, that the enterprise intends and is able to hold to maturity; and
- financial assets whose fair value cannot be reliably measured (limited to some equity instruments with no quoted market price and some derivatives that are linked to and must be settled by delivery of such unquoted equity instruments).

Except for derivatives and liabilities held for trading, after acquisition, most financial liabilities should be measured at original recorded amount (cost) less principle repayments and amortisation.

For those financial assets and liabilities that are remeasured to fair value, an enterprise will have a single enterprise-wide option either to recognise the entire adjustment in net profit or loss for the period or recognise in net profit or loss for the period only those changes in fair value relating to financial assets and liabilities held for trading, with the value changes for non-trading instruments reported in equity until the financial asset is sold, at which time the realised gain or loss is reported in net profit or loss. For this purpose, derivatives are always deemed held for trading unless they are part of a hedging relationship that qualifies for hedge accounting.

IAS 39 (r2000) also establishes conditions for determining when control over a financial asset or liability has been transferred to another party and for hedge accounting.

IAS 32 (r1998) contains certain requirements for presentation of financial instruments and identifies the information that should be disclosed about them. The specific disclosures required include:

- their extent and nature, including significant terms and conditions that may affect the amount, timing and certainty of future cash flows;
- the accounting policies and methods applied;
- the enterprise's exposure to interest rate risk from financial assets and liabilities, including information about contractual repricing or maturity dates and effective interest rates;
- the enterprise's exposure to credit risk, including the amount that best represents the maximum exposure at the balance sheet date, without taking account of any collateral, and information about significant concentrations of credit risk; and
- the fair value of financial assets and liabilities.

12.3 Development of the requirements

In 1989, the IASC undertook a joint project with the Accounting Standards Board of The Canadian Institute of Chartered Accountants (CICA). This project resulted in two exposure drafts which both dealt with recognition and measurement as well as presentation and disclosure issues. In November 1994, based on the comments received, the IASC decided to complete the Financial Instrument project in two stages – a disclosure based standard and a separate recognition and measurement based standard. To that end, the IASC Board approved IAS 32 in March 1995, which deals with presentation and disclosure. To begin the second stage, in March 1997, the IASC issued a Discussion Paper which set out a framework for recognition and measurement standards for financial assets and liabilities. This Discussion Paper was intended to form the basis of an exposure draft to be issued later in 1997.

However, in November 1997, the IASC Board decided to join with national standard setters to develop an integrated and harmonised international accounting standard on financial instruments. At the same time, recognising the urgency of the matter, the Board also agreed to work to complete an interim international solution on recognition and measurement of financial instruments in 1998. IAS 39 (r2000) represents the interim solution related to recognition and measurement of financial instruments and partially incorporates the Discussion Paper's proposal to require fair value accounting for all financial instruments. At that time, the IASC committed to continue working with national standard setters throughout the world to achieve a solution to the issue of fair value accounting for all financial instruments within a reasonable time.

It is to this end that the IASC, together with other members of the Financial Instruments Joint Working Group of Standard Setters (JWG), published for public comment, in December 2000, the JWG's 'Draft Standard and Basis for Conclusions – Accounting for Financial Instruments and Similar Items'. This document builds on certain of the principles contained in the IASC's 1997 Discussion Paper and proposes some far-reaching changes to current accounting standards for financial instruments. The JWG Draft Standard, however, reflects the views of JWG members representing accounting standard setters and professional organisations in 10 jurisdictions, and does not necessarily reflect the views of the IASB. The JWG document does not therefore have the status of an IASB draft standard or exposure draft and is being treated by the IASB as a discussion paper for comment by 30 June 2001 (comments will be accepted until 30 September 2001).

Because of the complex nature of IAS 39 (r2000), in a bid to assist companies implementing the standard, the IASC approved the formation of the IAS 39 Implementation Guidance Committee ('IGC') in March 2000. The IGC, which first met in April 2000, has published a series of Questions and Answers on IAS 39. The implementation guidance, which does not have the status of either a standard or official interpretation, has not been considered by the Board and therefore does not necessarily represent the IASB's views. The detailed IGC guidance may be found and downloaded from the IASC's website at www.iasb.org.uk.

The guidance issued by the IGC has been included in this Chapter under the appropriate sections and is separately referenced based on the relevant paragraph of IAS 39 (r2000) and question number relating to that paragraph. Hence, for example, IGC 10-19 refers to question 19 relating to IAS 39 (r2000).10 and provides guidance relating to that particular paragraph. The guidance referred to in this Chapter includes both the consolidated batch (containing batches one through five), as of 1 July 2001, as well as batch six, containing further proposed questions and answers. Batch six was published on the IASB's website on 22 June 2001 for comment by 24 August 2001. As such, these interpretations in batch six could be amended.

A further function of the IGC was to identify any issues that it believed should be referred to the SIC for a formal interpretation, or to recommend to the IASC possible amendments to IAS 39 where these could provide further clarity and assistance. As a result, in October 2000, the IASC approved five limited revisions to IAS 39 and other related International Accounting Standards (IAS 27, IAS 28(r2000), IAS 31(r2000) and IAS 32 (r1998)) to improve specific paragraphs and to help ensure that the standards are applied consistently. These changes become effective when an enterprise applies IAS 39 (r2000) for the first time. The nature and purpose of these amendments are detailed under the relevant sections below.

12.4 Scope

IAS 32 (r1998) and IAS 39 (r2000) apply to all financial instruments, as defined in **12.5**, subject to a limited number of exceptions. These IAS standards should be applied by *all* enterprises to *all* financial instruments *except*:

Equity Instruments of the Issuer	Including options, warrants and other financial instruments that are classified as shareholders' equity of the reporting enterprise (however, the *holder* of such instruments is required to apply IAS 39 (r2000) to those instruments); (IAS 39 (r2000).1(e) and IAS 32 (r1998).16)
Employee Benefit Plans	Employers' assets and liabilities under employee benefit plans, which are subject to IAS 19 (r2000), *Employee Benefits* (see Chapter **25**); (IAS 39 (r2000).1(c) and IAS 32 (r1998).1(d))
Certain Aspects of Leases	Rights and obligations under leases, to which IAS 17 (r1997), *Leases* (see Chapter **24**) applies are excluded. However: • lease receivables recognised on a lessor's balance sheet are subject to the derecognition provisions of IAS 39 (r2000) (see **12.12**); and • IAS 39 (r2000) does apply to derivatives that are embedded in leases. (IAS 39 (r2000).1(b))
Certain Financial Guarantee Contracts	This category includes letters of credit and other financial guarantee contracts that provide for payments to be made if the debtor fails to make

	payment when due, provided that the holder of the financial guarantee contract is exposed to a loss on the debt asset that is referenced in the financial guarantee contract (IGC 1–5). Such contracts are covered by IAS 37, *Provisions, Contingent Liabilities and Contingent Assets* (see **11.9.12**). However, financial guarantee contracts are subject to IAS 39 (r2000) if they provide for payments to be made in response to changes in a specified interest rate, security price, commodity price, credit rating, foreign exchange rate, index of prices or rates, or other variable (sometimes called the 'underlying'). Also, IAS 39 (r2000) *does* require recognition of financial guarantees incurred or retained as a result of its derecognition provisions (see **12.12.2**). (IAS 39 (r2000).1(f)) For further discussion of this exemption, see **12.16.3**.
Business Combinations	Contracts for contingent consideration in a business combination are excluded (see **18.6.3**); (IAS 39 (r2000).1(g))
Interests in Subsidiaries, Associates and Joint Ventures	Those interests in subsidiaries, associates, and joint ventures that are accounted for under IAS 27, *Consolidated Financial Statements and Accounting for Investments in Subsidiaries* (see Chapter **19**); IAS 28 (r2000), *Accounting for Investments in Associates* (see Chapter **20**); and IAS 31 (r2000), *Financial Reporting of Interests in Joint Ventures* (see Chapter **21**); are excluded (IAS 39 (r2000).1(a) and IAS 32 (r1998).1(d) Following an amendment to IAS 28 in October 2000, investments in associates that are held exclusively with a view to their disposal in the near future, and those which operate under severe long term restrictions that significantly impair its ability to transfer funds to the investor, are not accounted for under IAS 28 (r2000), and instead are accounted for under IAS 39. (IAS 39 (r2000).1(a) and IGC 1-4) A similar amendment was made to IAS 31. Previously, IAS 28

	and IAS 31 required that such investments be accounted for using the cost method. This amendment achieved consistency between IAS 28 (r2000), IAS 31 (r2000) and IAS 27 in the treatment of enterprises, whether they be subsidiaries, associates or joint ventures, that are held temporarily or operate under severe long term restrictions. IAS 32 (r1998) and IAS 39 (r2000) do *not* change the requirements relating to: (a) accounting by a parent for investments in subsidiaries in the parent's separate financial statements; (b) accounting by an investor for investments in associates in the investor's separate financial statements; or (c) accounting by a joint venturer for investments in joint ventures in the venturer's or investor's separate financial statements. An enterprise, in its separate financial statements, may elect under IAS 27 and IAS 28 (r2000) to treat its investments in associates and subsidiaries according to the provisions in IAS 39 (r2000) relating to available-for-sale and held-for-trading financial assets. (IAS 27. 29 and IAS 28 (r2000). 12 and 14). Both IAS 32 (r1998) and IAS 39 (r2000) apply to financial instruments held by a subsidiary, and thus included in the parent's consolidated financial statements, and to financial instruments held by a joint venture and included in a venturer's financial statements either directly or through proportionate consolidation. (IAS 32 (r1998).2)
Certain Aspects of Insurance Contracts	Rights and obligations under insurance contracts as defined in IAS 32 (r1998) are excluded. (IAS 39 (r2000).1(d) and IAS 32 (r1998).1(f)) IAS 32 (r1998).3 defines an insurance contract as 'a contract that exposes the insurer to identified risks of loss from events or circumstances occurring or discovered within a specified

	period, including death (in the case of an annuity, the survival of the annuitant), sickness, disability, property damage, injury to others and business interruption.' Contracts which take the form of insurance contracts but which principally involve the transfer of financial risk (such as currency, interest rate, market, liquidity, certain forms of credit or cash flow risk) are within the scope. (IAS 32 (r1998).3, IAS 39 (r2000).5 and IGC1-3) Examples of such contracts include some types of financial reinsurance and guaranteed investment contracts issued by insurance and other enterprises. (IAS 39 (r2000)) IAS 39 (r2000) *does apply* to the financial assets and liabilities of insurance companies other than rights and obligations arising under insurance contracts and to derivatives that are embedded in insurance contracts. (IAS 39 (r2000).1(d)) A separate IASB project on accounting for insurance contracts is currently under way, which will address rights and obligations arising under insurance contracts (see Chapter **2**).
Contracts Based on Physical Variables	Contracts that require a payment based on climatic, geological, or other physical variables which are commonly used as insurance policies are excluded. (Those based on climatic variables are sometimes referred to as weather derivatives.) In such cases, the payment made is based on an amount of loss to the enterprise. However, IAS 39 (r2000) *does apply* to other types of derivatives that are embedded in such contracts. (IAS 39 (r2000).1(h)) Where a contract contains more than one underlying variable, one of which is excluded from the scope of IAS 39 (r2000), such as a climatic variable or weather index, while one of the other variables falls within the scope of IAS 39 (r2000), and the embedded derivative based on the latter cannot be separated, the whole contract is accounted for under IAS 39 (r2000) (IGC 1-6).

Although not specifically excluded from the scope of IAS 39 (r2000), paragraph 3 confirms that IAS 39 (r2000) does not change the requirements relating to employee benefit plans that comply with IAS 26, *Accounting and Reporting by Retirement Benefit Plans* (see Appendix II).

12.4.1 Non-financial assets and liabilities

Non-financial assets and liabilities are not financial instruments and are outside the scope of IAS 39 (r2000). Non-financial assets and liabilities include:

- physical assets such as inventories, property, plant and equipment, leased assets and intangible assets such as patents and trademarks (IAS 32 (r1998).11);
- assets, such as prepaid expenses, for which the future economic benefit is the receipt of goods or services rather than the right to receive cash or another financial asset and similarly, items such as deferred revenue and most warranty obligations since the probable outflow of economic benefits associated with them is the delivery of goods and services rather than cash or another financial asset. (IAS 32 (r1998).12);
- liabilities or assets that are not contractual in nature, such as income taxes that are created as a result of statutory requirements imposed by governments (IAS 32 (r1998).13);
- the minority interest that may arise on an enterprise's balance sheet from consolidating a subsidiary (IAS 32 (r1998).17); and
- servicing assets (which are intangible assets) or obligations (IAS 39 (r2000).50).

12.4.2 Commodities

Commodities themselves, such as gold bullion, do not meet the definition of a financial instrument and therefore are excluded from the provisions of IAS 39 (r2000) since there is no contractual right to receive cash or another financial asset from another enterprise. These are non-financial assets (IGC 8-1).

However, IAS 39 (r2000) *does* apply to commodity-based contracts that give either party the right to settle in cash or some other financial instrument, with the exception of commodity contracts that:

(1) were entered into and continue to meet the enterprise's expected purchase, sale or usage requirements;
(2) were designated for that purpose at their inception; and
(3) are expected to be settled by delivery.

(IAS 39 (r2000).6 and IAS 32 (r1998).5)

See **12.16.2** for further discussion of this exemption.

12.4.3 *Comparison with UK GAAP*

UK GAAP does not include one comprehensive standard dealing with the recognition and measurement of financial instruments. However, FRS 13, *Derivatives and Other Financial Instruments: Disclosures* covers disclosure; FRS 5, *Reporting the Substance of Transactions,* covers recognition and derecognition of certain financial assets and liabilities; FRS 4, *Capital instruments,* covers certain financial liabilities; and companies legislation covers certain types of investments which may often meet the definition of a financial instrument. Currently, derivative instruments are not comprehensively dealt with in UK GAAP. However, the ASB has expressed its concern that accounting practice is finding it difficult to cope with the rapid growth in the use of financial instruments and the increasingly complex types of financial instruments that are being used. To address these needs, the ASB is a participant in the international Joint Working Group on Financial Instruments.

12.4.4 *Comparison with US GAAP*

The structure of US GAAP as it applies to financial instruments is spread over several pronouncements (principally, SFAS 107, *Disclosures about Fair Value of Financial Instruments*; SFAS 115, *Accounting for Certain Investments in Debt and Equity Securities*; SFAS 125, *Accounting for Transfers and Servicing of Financial Assets and Extinguishment of Liabilities*; SFAS 133, *Accounting for Derivative Instruments and Hedging Activities*; SFAS 138, *Accounting for Certain Derivative Instruments and Certain Hedging Activities*; SFAS 140, *Accounting for Transfers and Servicing of Financial Assets and Extinguishment of Liabilities*, and related EITF issues) whereas the primary provisions in IAS are contained within IAS 39 (r2000) (and to a limited extent IAS 32 (r1998)). The scope of these provisions as they relate to financial instruments, and the definitions, are generally similar to those under IAS, however, there are some specific differences with the provisions in US GAAP being largely *form* driven whereas those in IAS 32 (r1998) and IAS 39 (r2000) focus to a greater extent on the *substance* of transactions.

All of the IAS provisions relating to financial instruments are premised on the primary definitions of financial assets and financial liabilities. Other related definitions set out the treatment in respect of specific financial instruments (such as derivatives and equity instruments). The scope of IAS 32 (r1998) and IAS 39 (r2000) therefore covers all financial assets and liabilities (unless specifically exempted).

IAS 39 (r2000) does not provide a similar exception since it is not relevant whether the contract can be settled net in cash. The test is whether the enterprise intends to take or make delivery and whether there has been a past practice of settling net in cash.

SFAS 133 contains a similar exemption to IAS 39 (r2000) for contracts where the settlement is based on a climatic or geological variable or on some other physical variable. However, this exemption is limited to contracts that are not exchange traded. As a result of the increased use of these contracts, further guidance has been issued in EITF Issues 98-10, *Accounting for Contracts Involved in Energy Trading and Risk Management Activities*, and 99-2, *Accounting for Weather Derivatives*, to address specifically the accounting for weather derivatives. EITF 99-2 requires that entities that enter into weather derivatives for trading purposes or for the purpose of speculation should account for such contracts at fair value (i.e., following the provisions of SFAS 133 in the absence of the specific exemption).

12.5 Key definitions

12.5.1 Financial instrument

'A *financial instrument* is any contract that gives rise to both a financial asset of one enterprise and a financial liability or equity instrument of another enterprise.' (IAS 32 (r1998).5 and IAS 39 (r2000).8)

As used in IAS 32 (r1998) and IAS 39 (r2000), 'the terms 'contract' and 'contractual' refer to an agreement between two or more parties that has clear economic consequences that the parties have little, if any, discretion to avoid, usually because the agreement is enforceable at law. Contracts, and thus financial instruments, may take a variety of forms and need not be in writing.' (IAS 32 (r1998).6) For the purposes of the definitions in IAS 32 (r1998) and IAS 39 (r2000), the term 'enterprise' includes individuals, partnerships, incorporated bodies and government agencies. (IAS 32 (r1998).7 and IAS 39 (r2000).9) This differs from the normal use of the term 'enterprise' within IAS literature. See **12.5.2** for discussion of the normal definition.

Even where an arrangement may not be enforceable at law, the existence of clear economic consequences or disincentives for non-performance of either party could imply that a contractual arrangement nevertheless does exist.

Financial instruments include both primary instruments such as debtors (receivables), creditors (payables) and equity securities as well as derivative instruments such as financial options, currency swaps, etc. (IAS 32 (r1998).9) The following section, **12.5.2**, gives more examples of financial assets and liabilities. Several examples of common non-financial assets and liabilities and commodity based contracts are discussed in **12.4.1** and **12.4.2** respectively.

12.5.2 *Financial asset and financial liability*

'A financial asset is any asset that is:

(a) cash;
(b) a contractual right to receive cash or another financial asset from another enterprise;
(c) a contractual right to exchange financial instruments with another enterprise under conditions that are potentially favourable; or
(d) an equity instrument of another enterprise.'

(IAS 32 (r1998).5 and IAS 39 (r2000).8)

'A financial liability is any liability that is a contractual obligation:

(a) to deliver cash or another financial asset to another enterprise; or
(b) to exchange financial instruments with another enterprise under conditions that are potentially unfavourable.'

(IAS 32 (r1998).5 and IAS 39 (r2000).8)

The definitions of a financial instrument, financial asset and financial liability included in IAS 32 (r1998) are very broad and encompass many items commonly found on the balance sheet of most enterprises including:

(a) cash and amounts included in deposit accounts;
(b) trade accounts receivable and payable;
(c) notes receivable and payable, including notes payable in government bonds;
(d) loans receivable and payable; and
(e) bonds receivable and payable.

(IAS 32 (r1998), Appendix A3, A4 and A5)

Obligations to be settled by the issue of securities

In general, an enterprise's obligation to issue its own equity instruments in exchange for financial assets of another party *is not* potentially unfavourable (and therefore *not* a financial liability) since it results in an increase in equity and cannot result in a loss to the enterprise. Any resulting dilution suffered by existing shareholders does not make the obligation unfavourable to the enterprise itself. (IAS 32 (r1998), Appendix.A7)

However, when a contractual obligation may be settled *either* by payment of financial assets *or* by payment in the form of its own equity securities, *and* the number of equity securities required to settle the obligation varies with changes in their fair value with the effect that the total fair value of the equity securities paid always equals the amount of the contractual obligation, the holder of the obligation is not exposed to gain or loss from fluctuations in the price of its equity securities; and therefore, the obligation is accounted for as a financial liability. (IAS 32 (r1998).5 and IAS 39 (r2000).11)

No guidance is given for the phrase 'always equals'. However, it is reasonable to interpret this to mean 'substantially the same'; and, therefore, 'always equals' need not imply that the amounts must equal exactly.

The following table summarises the appropriate classification of an obligation based on its method of settlement:

Method of Settlement (IAS reference)	*Classification by the Issuer*
Cash or other financial assets (gross and net settlements)	Financial liability (follows from IAS 39 (r2000).8)
Shares (physical settlement): Fixed number of shares (e.g., share options, warrants)	Equity instrument (IAS 32 (r1998).16)
Number of shares to be issued is indexed to share price (i.e., total fair value of obligation is substantially fixed)	Financial liability (IAS 39 (r2000).11)
Net Share Settlement – the net gain/loss on the change in the value of the shares is settled in shares (e.g., put options on own shares)	Equity instrument 32 (r1998) (IGC 11-1)
Derivative is settled in shares but the value of the derivative is not indexed to changes in the price of the enterprise's equity	Financial asset or liability (i.e., is treated as a derivative instrument) instruments (IAS 39 (r2000).12)
Optional settlement method (cash or shares): Counterparty alone can select method of settlement	Financial liability because counterparty can force cash settlement (IAS 32 (r1998)) and IAS 39 (r2000).11)
Issuer can elect to settle in shares or other financial assets where number of shares to be issued is indexed to share price	Assumed to be a financial liability unless number of shares to be issued is fixed in which case it is an equity instrument
Contingent settlement method: Event triggering the method of settlement is beyond both the issuer and the holder's control	Financial liability (SIC – 5.8)
The possibility of issuer having to settle in a financial asset as a result of the contingency is remote	Equity instrument (contingent settlement provision is ignored). (SIC – 5.5 and 6)

Options to reacquire own shares and treasury shares

An option or other similar instrument that gives an enterprise the right to reacquire its own equity instruments is not a financial asset but an equity instrument since the enterprise will not receive cash or any other financial asset through exercise of the option. The change in equity resulting from reacquiring and cancelling an enterprise's own equity instruments represents a transfer between those holders of equity instruments who have given up their equity interest and those who continue to hold an equity interest, rather than a gain or loss by the enterprise. (IAS 32 (r1998), Appendix.A8) Similarly, the cost incurred by an enterprise to reacquire its own shares, known as treasury shares, is shown as a deduction from equity rather than an asset. See **11.3.5** for further discussion of treasury shares.

Preferred shares

Whether or not a preferred share meets the definition of a financial liability or an equity instrument depends on the terms of the individual share. See **11.4** for further discussion of the distinction between equity instruments and financial liabilities.

12.5.3 Equity instruments and compound instruments

IAS 32 (r1998) contains requirements and guidance relating to the distinction between equity instruments and financial liabilities and covers compound instruments which contain characteristics of both. See **11.4** for the related discussion.

12.6 Classification of financial instruments

IAS 39 (r2000) identifies and defines four primary categories of financial instruments. These categories are used to determine how a particular financial instrument is measured and recognised in the financial statements. The four primary categories are:

(1) Held for trading ('HFT') (financial assets or liabilities)
(2) Held-to-maturity investments ('HTM') (financial assets)
(3) Loans and receivables originated by the enterprise ('OLR') (financial assets)
(4) Available-for-sale financial assets ('AFS')

Three additional categories, for which the Standard prescribes special rules, are:

- Derivative instruments (see **12.16**)
- Equity instruments of the issuer (see **11.3**)
- Compound instruments of the issuer (see **11.4.1**)

Each of the four primary categories are discussed in turn in the following sections. Recognition and measurement is discussed in **12.8–12.10**.

12.6.1 Held for trading

> 'A financial asset or liability held for trading is one that was acquired or incurred principally for the purpose of generating a profit from short-term fluctuations in price or dealer's margin. A financial asset should be classified as held for trading if, regardless of why it was acquired, it is part of a portfolio for which there is evidence of a recent actual pattern of short-term profit-taking . . . Derivative financial assets and derivative financial liabilities are always deemed held for trading unless they are designated and effective (as) hedging instruments.'
>
> (IAS 39 (r2000).10)

See **12.18** to **12.26** for a discussion of hedge accounting.

The term portfolio, although not explicitly defined, refers to a group of financial assets that are managed as part of that group (for example, could be managed by a separate trading desk in an enterprise). Hence, even if an individual instrument in a portfolio may be held for a longer period of time, if there is evidence of a recent actual pattern of profit taking on other financial instruments included in that portfolio, the whole portfolio would be classified as held for trading (IGC 10-21).

The phrase 'profit from short term fluctuations' in the description of financial assets or liabilities held for trading would seem to contemplate a holding period generally measured in hours, days or weeks rather than months or years. However, IAS 39 (r2000) does not define 'short-term' and does not limit the time period in which an instrument designated on acquisition as held for trading can be held. Provided that on acquisition of an instrument there is an intent to profit from short-term price fluctuations, that instrument will be designated as HFT (IGC 10-15).

Derivative transactions are always deemed held-for-trading. Embedded derivatives that require separation from the host contract are therefore required to be included in the held-for-trading category unless they qualify for certain hedge accounting treatment. Similarly, hybrid instruments for which the embedded derivative cannot be reliably separated should be classified as HFT (IGC 10-15) (see **12.17**).

Whilst it is financial assets that are often categorised as held for trading, financial liabilities may be considered held for trading too. Examples include:

(1) derivative liabilities that are not hedging instruments (IAS 39 (r2000).18);
(2) the obligation to deliver securities borrowed by a short seller (an

enterprise that sells securities that it does not yet own) (IAS 39 (r2000).18); and

(3) the obligation to deliver a financial asset that is not a security borrowed by a short seller (IGC 18-2).

If an enterprise sells an asset short, i.e., sells an asset it has borrowed, it accounts for the proceeds received as an asset with a corresponding obligation to return the asset to the lender as a held for trading liability measured at fair value (IGC 18-1).

However, the fact that a liability is used to fund trading activities does not make that liability one held for trading. (IAS 39 (r2000).18)

Characteristics of trading activities

The term 'trading' generally reflects active and frequent buying and selling. Determining whether or when an enterprise is involved in trading activities is a matter of judgement that depends on the relevant facts and circumstances. The facts and circumstances can be assessed based on an evaluation of various activities of the enterprise rather than solely on the terms of the individual transactions. Inherent in that assessment is an evaluation of the enterprise's intent in entering into financial instrument contracts and using particular types of financial instruments.

Indications that financial instruments are entered into for trading purposes, are set out below. These indications are based on guidance contained in EITF 98-10, *Accounting for Contracts Involved in Energy Trading and Risk Management Activities*, under US GAAP but should be helpful in interpreting IAS 39 (r2000). The absence of any or all of the indicators in any category, by itself, would not necessarily avoid the classification of financial assets or liabilities as held-for-trading. All available evidence should be considered to determine whether, based on the weight of that evidence, an operation is involved in trading activities.

Organisational characteristics (nature of operations)

- The primary assets/liabilities of the operation are financial instrument contracts.
- The operation does not use its own capital as the primary source of funding its activities and instead makes extensive use of other techniques such as leveraging and credit enhancement as sources of risk capital.
- The operation offers financial instruments as a dealer, not as a 'user'.

Customers, counterparties, and competitors

- The majority of the counterparties to the financial instrument contracts and competitors are banks, brokers/traders or fund managers.

Volume and prevalent direction (buying/selling) of transactions

- The volume of transactions differs significantly from the operation's historical requirements for such contracts.
- There has been a change in the volume of transactions that is significant relative to the change in demand arising from the entity's primary operating environment and financial structure.
- Contracted quantities far exceed normal needs and exposure levels or result in opposite exposures.
- The operation does not consume the financial instruments to meet its normal needs (or make use of physical delivery to settle the contracts).
- There is a high turnover rate in the portfolio of financial instrument contracts (IGC 10-22).

IGC 10-9 deals with whether activities involving periodically rebalancing portfolios should be classified as available for sale or as held for trading. Mere authorisation to buy and sell alone is not sufficient to qualify for held for trading. The trading category should be used where the pattern of transactions involves buying and selling for short-term profit. Classification as available for sale is appropriate if there is intent to sell but not to trade for short-term profit (for example where certain portfolio managers rebalance their portfolios to stay within prescribed investment guidelines but where there is no past pattern or intention to actively trade).

Example 12.1

Consideration of investment strategy

Assume enterprise L, a non-public entity, has an investment portfolio of debt and equity securities with a market value of €400 million. The documented portfolio guidelines specify that the equity exposure of the portfolio should be limited to between 60 and 90 per cent of total portfolio value. The investment manager of the portfolio is authorised to balance the portfolio within the designated guidelines by buying and selling equity and debt securities, to change the effective asset allocation of the underlying portfolio. The portfolio manager actively buys and sells securities to generate short-term profits, and the portfolio turnover is typically a few days.

The financial instruments in the investment portfolio in this example should be classified as held for trading. In actively balancing the portfolio, the investment manager's objective is to generate short-term profits based on his view of the market. The approach to accomplishing this objective is to implement a dynamic investment strategy, transacting a significant volume of purchase and sales transactions over a short period (IGC 10-9).

Management and controls

- Compensation and/or performance measures are tied to the short-term results generated from financial instrument transactions (that is, the operation is measured based on trading profits or changes in the market values of its positions).
- The operation communicates internally in terms of 'trading strategy' (that is, management reports identify contractual positions, fair values, hedging activities, risk exposure etc.).
- The operation sets limits on market positions and related strategies, sets policies governing what types of contracts it will transact in, and sets the controls it will follow; in addition, management is involved in reviewing compliance with those limits, strategies, policies, and controls on a daily or frequent basis.
- The word 'trading' appears in the name of or documentation of the operation for internal or external purposes.
- Employees of the operation are referred to as 'traders' or 'dealers' or have prior experience in banking, broking, derivative trading or risk management activities.
- Assessment of net market positions of the operation is done on a regular and frequent basis (for example hourly or overnight).
- Infrastructure of the operation is similar to that of a trading operation of a bank or investment bank's front office, middle office, and back office (that is, there is a segregation of back office processing and front office trading functions).
- An infrastructure exists that enables the operation to capture price and other risks on a real-time basis.
- The activities are managed on a portfolio or 'book' basis.
- Management searches for opportunities to take advantage of favourable price spreads, arbitrage opportunities, or outright positions in the market-place.

The transactions/contracts

- The operation has a history of pairing off (entering into offsetting contracts) or otherwise settling the transactions without physically receiving or delivering the underlying item. In other words, past practices of the operation have resulted in net cash settlement, offsetting, as well as netting out, and the type of settlement has changed quickly from one type to another to maximise profits/mitigate losses.
- The contracts do not permit physical delivery and must be settled net in the market or in cash.
- The financial instrument contracts are not customarily used for general commercial (operational) business purposes or by the industry in general.

Comparison with UK GAAP
UK GAAP does not specifically refer to a separate HFT category except for specialised industries such as banks. However, the generally accepted practice is to mark to market trading transactions. IAS 39 (r2000)

Comparison with US GAAP
The classification of HFT financial assets is the same under US GAAP and IAS. However, under US GAAP, this classification only applies to securities held, whereas under IAS 39 (r2000) it applies to all HFT financial assets and liabilities. Certain differences also exist between US GAAP and IAS 39 (r2000) in the classification of securitised mortgage loans. US GAAP currently contains specific provisions applicable to securitised mortgage loans which are not specified by IAS provisions. SFAS 115, *Accounting for Certain Investments in Debt and Equity Securities*, considers two types of mortgage-backed securities (resulting from the securitisation of mortgage loans):

- securitisations of mortgage loans held for sale; and
- securitisations of mortgage loans reported at amortised cost.

US GAAP specifically requires that securities that result from the securitisation of a mortgage loan held for sale must be classified as a trading security at fair value since these loans were originated or acquired specifically with the intent to resell. This intent is more akin to the trading concept in SFAS 115 than the available-for-sale (AFS) category (SFAS 115, 125 and 140). Loans reported at amortised cost, once securitised, may be designated as held for trading, AFS or held-to-maturity (HTM) upon satisfaction of the relevant HTM or AFS criteria. (SFAS 115.12)

Under IAS 39 (r2000), only loans and receivables originated with the intent to be sold immediately or in the short term should be classified as held for trading. Where loans are securitised, the derecognition provisions in IAS 39 (r2000) are applied and, in the event that a new financial asset or liability has been created, the classification of that asset or liability is required to be made based on the classification criteria for purchased loans in IAS 39 (r2000).

12.6.2 Held-to-Maturity (HTM)

The decision to classify a financial investment as held-to-maturity (HTM) is indicative that the investor is indifferent to future profit opportunities, and therefore to the purchase prices offered by others, over the investment's term since the investor has the positive intent to hold the security to maturity irrespective of market value fluctuations. *Held-to-maturity investments* are defined as 'financial assets with fixed or determinable payments and fixed maturity that an enterprise has the positive intent and ability to hold to maturity other than loans and receivables originated by the enterprise.' (IAS 39 (r2000).10)

The key criteria in the definition are:

- fixed or determinable payments and a fixed maturity;
- positive intent; and
- ability.

'Fixed or determinable payments' and 'fixed maturity' mean a contractual arrangement that defines the amounts and dates of payments to the holder, such as interest and principal payments on debt. (IAS 39 (r2000).80)

Positive intent and ability are discussed in the following sections.

As discussed in **12.10**, the HTM category is attractive to many enterprises since it is measured at amortised cost rather than fair value. However, the stringent tests of positive intent and ability to hold to maturity are supplemented by harsh ramifications if an asset is sold from the HTM category before its maturity. With certain exceptions, such a sale will call into question the intention of management to hold any asset to maturity and 'taint' the entire HTM category with the result that all assets in the category will be required to be reclassified immediately as available-for-sale or as held for trading (carried at fair value) and no further assets may be classified as HTM for two financial years. Sales out of HTM and their consequences are discussed in a separate section below.

An enterprise is required to assess its intent and ability to hold its HTM investments to maturity not only when those financial assets are initially acquired but also at each balance sheet date. (IAS 39 (r2000).89)

Stand-alone derivatives may not be classified as held to maturity investments. However, embedded derivatives that are not required to be separated from the host, are classified together with the host instrument, and thus could fall into the HTM category.

Positive intent

> 'An enterprise does not have the positive intent to hold to maturity an investment in a financial asset with a fixed maturity if any one of the following conditions is met:
>
> (a) the enterprise has the intent to hold the financial asset for only an undefined period;
>
> (b) the enterprise stands ready to sell the financial asset (other than if a situation arises that is non-recurring and could not have been reasonably anticipated by the enterprise) in response to changes in market interest rates or risks, liquidity needs, changes in the availability of and the yield on

alternative investments, changes in financing sources and terms, or changes in foreign currency risk; or

(c) the issuer has a right to settle the financial asset at an amount significantly below its amortised cost.'

(IAS 39 (r2000).79)

The intent criterion above involves an expectation that is beyond the mere absence of an intention to sell.

If a sale or transfer of a security classified as held-to-maturity occurs subsequent to the issue of financial statements for reasons other than those permitted under paragraph 86 of IAS 39 (r2000) (i.e., those specific changes in circumstances that do not call into question an enterprise's intent to hold other debt securities to maturity in the future), a question arises whether the previous financial statements were issued in error.

Generally, because the accounting for financial instruments is based primarily on a representation of intent by management, the sale or transfer of a security classified as held-to-maturity does not represent an error of previously issued financial statements, provided there was no evidence that existed at the time the financial statements were issued demonstrating that the entity did not have the positive intent and ability to hold the security to maturity. Such sale or transfer may call into question the enterprise's intent to hold other debt securities to maturity in the future.

An example of evidence that would contradict management's stated intention might be the existence of an investment policy that indicates investment objectives to manage the investment portfolio to meet liquidity needs for asset-liability management purposes, for specific tax positions, or for other objectives that would be inconsistent with the notion of holding securities to maturity. Another example of evidence that might be viewed as contradictory to management's positive intent to hold certain securities to maturity is a history of selling held-to-maturity securities for reasons not specifically permitted in IAS 39 (r2000).86.

Financial assets classified as held-to-maturity (HTM) may be pledged as collateral for a borrowing without calling into question the enterprise's intent and ability to hold these assets to maturity provided that the enterprise intends and expects to be able to repay the borrowing and recover access to its collateral. Additionally, HTM securities may be subject to a repurchase agreement or a securities lending agreement if the transaction is accounted for as a secured borrowing. Under IAS 39 (r2000), paragraphs 35-65, repurchase and securities lending agreements are accounted for as either secured borrowings or as sales, depending on the terms of the repurchase agreement. The underlying securities may be classified as HTM if the repurchase or securities lending agreement is reported as a secured borrowing, provided that the enterprise intends and expects to be able to repay the borrowing and recover access to its collateral (IGC 87-1).

Ability

> 'An enterprise does *not* have a demonstrated ability to hold to maturity an investment in a financial asset with a fixed maturity if either one of the following conditions is met:
>
> (a) it does not have the financial resources available to continue to finance the investment until maturity; or
>
> (b) it is subject to an existing legal or other constraint that could frustrate its intention to hold the financial asset to maturity (however, an issuer's call option does not necessarily frustrate an enterprise's intent to hold a financial asset to maturity).'
>
> (IAS 39 (r2000).87)

For financial assets classified as held-to-maturity (HTM), management of financial institutions should consider whether the enterprise has both the financial ability as well as the regulatory ability to obviate the need to dispose of HTM securities prior to maturity. An enterprise's financial ability takes into account factors such as its funding position and its ability to maintain any over-collateralisation requirements. An enterprise's regulatory ability takes into account factors such as its regulatory capital requirements, its liquidity position (including specified holdings of liquid assets), its loans-to-one-borrower ratio, growth prospects and financing related requirements and its investment authority (and permitted asset-mix).

Application to certain instruments

Instrument	Qualifies as HTM?
Variable rate debt instruments	If the other terms of the debt do not disqualify it, the variable interest rate will not prohibit HTM classification. (IAS 39 (r2000).80)
Equity instruments	Generally cannot be HTM since most have an indefinite life (such as ordinary shares) or because the amounts the holder may receive can vary in a manner that is not predetermined (such as share options, warrants, and rights). (IAS 39 (r2000).80)
An instrument that is callable by the issuer (issuer call option)	Yes, if the holder intends and is able to hold the instrument until it is called or until maturity and if the holder would recover substantially all of its carrying amount. The call

	option, if exercised, simply accelerates the asset's maturity. However, if the holder would not recover substantially all of its carrying amount if the option were called, the financial asset is not classified as HTM. Any premium paid and capitalised transaction costs should be considered in determining whether the carrying amount would be substantially recovered. (IAS 39 (r2000).81)
An instrument that is puttable (the holder has the right to require that the issuer repay or redeem the financial asset before maturity)	Yes, but only if the holder has the positive intent and ability to hold the instrument until maturity and not to exercise the put feature. (IAS 39 (r2000).82) However, classification as HTM requires great care since this is generally inconsistent with the intention of purchasing a puttable debt instrument, which involves paying for the put (IGC 83-3).
Convertible and redeemable securities	Generally no. Convertible debt securities usually bear a lower interest rate, because the investor hopes to benefit from appreciation in value of the option embedded in the debt security. Given the opportunity for profit when the market value of the underlying share increases, it would generally be contradictory to assert the positive intent and ability to hold a convertible debt investment to maturity and forego the opportunity to exercise the conversion feature (IGC 23-2). Classification as HTM may, however, be appropriate where conversion may only occur on redemption date of the security.
Instruments with high risk of default	The likelihood of default is not a consideration for HTM qualification provided there is an intent and ability, in view of the credit condition existing at the acquisition

	date, to hold the instrument to maturity (IGC 10-16).
Certain high risk instruments subject to regulatory rules	Certain financial institution regulators have designated specific financial instruments (such as certain collateralised mortgage obligations (CMOs) or other, similar stripped securities (e.g., interest-only and principal-only securities)) as high-risk securities, and may require a regulated entity to sell such securities as a result of changes in interest rates. If a financial instrument is subject to such regulatory provisions, classification as held-to-maturity may not be appropriate since management would not be able to demonstrate the ability to hold to maturity. Note that, absent regulatory requirements, an interest- or principal-only strip could be classified as HTM provided the enterprise can demonstrate the intent and ability to hold the security until it is either redeemed or prepaid. The risk of prepayment itself does not preclude classification as HTM.

Example 12.2

Assume Enterprise X has a portfolio of debt securities classified as HTM. Also assume that the terms of one security in the portfolio contains a put feature allowing Enterprise X to require the issuer to redeem the security under certain conditions. Initial classification of that security as HTM is appropriate, provided that X has demonstrated a positive intent and ability to hold the security to maturity. Exercise of the put option, however, would call into question its intent to hold other debt securities to maturity in the future.

Sales out of HTM

'An enterprise should not classify any financial assets as held-to-maturity if the enterprise has, during the current financial year or during the two preceding financial years, sold, transferred, or exercised a put option on more than an insignificant amount of held-to-maturity investments before maturity (more than insignificant in relation to the total held-to-maturity portfolio) other than by:

(a) sales close enough to maturity or exercised call date so that changes in the market rate of interest did not have a significant effect on the financial asset's fair value;

(b) sales after the enterprise has already collected substantially all of the financial asset's original principal through scheduled payments or prepayments; or

(c) sales due to an isolated event that is beyond the enterprise's control and that is non-recurring and could not have been reasonably anticipated by the enterprise.'

(IAS 39 (r2000).83)

Whenever a sale (including sales in response to unsolicited offers (IGC 83-4), or transfer including reclassifications out of the held to maturity category prior to maturity (IGC 83-2), or an exercise of a put option (IGC 83-3)) of more than an insignificant amount of financial assets classified as HTM occurs for a reason other than those specified above, no instruments should continue to be classified in that category.

Accordingly, any remaining HTM instruments should immediately be reclassified as either available-for-sale or held for trading. The reclassification would be recorded in the reporting period in which the sale or transfer occurred and would be accounted for as a change in classification (See **12.10.2**). The sale would not impact the treatment of similar instruments held outside the HTM portfolio. IAS 39 (r2000).83 makes it clear that at least two full financial years must pass after a 'taint' to its HTM classification before an enterprise can again classify securities as HTM (IGC 83-4).

An enterprise may not separately apply the HTM tainting provisions to different categories of HTM assets, such as those contained in other HTM portfolios, since the tainting rule affects all HTM assets held by the enterprise (IGC 83-5).

If a subsidiary is not permitted to use the HTM category as a result of a sale out of it, the HTM category also cannot be used in the consolidated financial statements of the enterprise (IGC 83-6).

Although in paragraph 83(a) 'close enough to maturity' is not defined, it is designed to address situations where interest rate risk is substantially eliminated as a pricing factor (for example, near a call date when the issuer is expected to exercise the call option). In other words, this relates to where an enterprise would be indifferent whether to hold or sell a financial asset because of movements in interest rates after substantially all of the original principal has been collected. In such situations, a sale would not affect reported net profit or loss, and no price volatility would be expected in the remaining time to maturity. To illustrate this principle, an enterprise which sells an instrument less than three months prior to its maturity would generally qualify for the use of this exception because the impact on the fair value of the instrument for the difference between the stated interest rate and the market rate would generally be small for an instrument that matures in three months relative to an instrument that matures in several years (IGC 83-1). Depending on the level of interest rates, however, it could be argued that interest rate risk is still substantially eliminated for some period of time beyond this three-month period.

The condition of having collected 'substantially all' of the original principal provides guidance as to when a sale is for not more than an insignificant amount. If an enterprise sells a financial asset after having collected 90 per cent or more of the original principal amount through scheduled payments or prepayments, that would generally qualify for this exemption. However, if the enterprise has collected only 10 per cent of the original payment, this condition would clearly not be met (IGC 83-1). IAS 39 (r2000) does concede that a 'disaster scenario' that is extremely remote, such as a run on a bank or a similar situation affecting an insurance company, should not be anticipated when deciding whether an enterprise has the positive intent and ability to hold an investment to maturity. (IAS 39 (r2000).85) A sale or transfer of a held to maturity security in response to such an event would therefore not be considered to taint an enterprise's intent to hold other investments to maturity. Although the phrase 'extremely remote' is not defined further, the wording in IAS 39 (r2000).83(c) is stringent, implying that the event is rare, beyond the control of the enterprise and will often threaten the viability of the enterprise.

Permitted sales

Sales before maturity could satisfy the condition in paragraph 83(c) (and therefore not taint the HTM category) if they are due to:

'(a) a significant deterioration in the issuer's creditworthiness;

(b) a change in tax law that eliminates or significantly reduces the tax-exempt status of interest on the held-to-maturity investment (but not a change in tax law that revises the marginal tax rates applicable to interest income);

(c) a major business combination or major disposition (such as sale of a segment) that necessitates the sale or transfer of held-to-maturity investments to maintain the enterprise's existing interest rate risk position or credit risk policy (although the business combination itself is an event within the enterprise's control, the changes to its investment portfolio to maintain interest rate risk position or credit risk policy may be consequential rather than anticipated);

(d) a change in statutory or regulatory requirements significantly modifying either what constitutes a permissible investment or the maximum level of certain kinds of investments, thereby causing an enterprise to dispose of a held-to-maturity investment;

(e) a significant increase by the regulator in the industry's capital requirements that causes the enterprise to downsize by selling held-to-maturity investments; or

(f) a significant increase in the risk weights of held-to-maturity investments used for regulatory risk-based capital purposes.'

(IAS 39 (r2000).86)

If an enterprise plans to sell a security from the HTM category in response to one of the conditions listed in paragraph 86 above, there is no requirement in IAS 39 (r2000) for the security to be reclassified to the available-for-sale or held for trading category prior to the sale.

Permitted sales – deterioration in issuer creditworthiness – paragraph 86(a)

Paragraph 86(a) above considers 'evidence of a significant deterioration in the issuer's creditworthiness' as acceptable justification for a sale of that issuer's debt security without compromising the holder's classification of the investment as HTM. For example, if an enterprise holds a debt instrument that is classified as HTM, and that security is downgraded by a rating agency, then a sale or transfer of that security would not call into question the entity's intent to hold other debt securities to maturity in the future.

To meet this exemption, a sale should be in response to an actual deterioration rather than in advance of a deterioration in creditworthiness and should not be based on mere speculation or in response to industry statistics. The deterioration should be supported by evidence about the issuer's creditworthiness though the enterprise need not await the formal notification of an actual downgrading in the issuer's published credit rating or inclusion on a 'credit watch' list.

A security that is downgraded one level would not generally meet the significant deterioration criteria. However, a decline in credit rating of two grades or more (whether based on internal or external ratings) may, depending on the security and market involved, constitute a 'significant deterioration' (IGC 83-7 and 83-8).

Although judgement is required, the following factors should be considered in determining whether a significant deterioration in the issuer's creditworthiness has occurred as envisaged in paragraph 86:

- the deterioration in the issuer's creditworthiness should have occurred after the security was acquired. Low credit ratings or creditworthiness concerns existing at acquisition would generally not provide a basis for a subsequent sale from the held-to-maturity category (IGC 83-7); and
- there should be evidence of actual deterioration of the issuer's creditworthiness. An expectation of deterioration should be supported by objective evidence. Some of the concrete financial measures that may provide objective evidence are:
  - cash flows from operations (i.e., declines in cash flows, available cash flows, liquidity);
  - broker/analyst reports on the issuer;
  - adverse performance compared to projections;

- sustained decline in net profit or loss or other key measures; and
- violation of covenants or other evidence that the issuer is in peril of violating covenants.

A downgrade of the internal rating of an issuer by an enterprise does not in itself provide evidence of a significant deterioration unless the enterprise can demonstrate that its approach to assigning internal ratings and changes in those ratings provides a consistent, reliable and objective measure of the credit quality of issuers and that deterioration is significant (IGC 83-8).

In many situations, an effective measure of a significant deterioration is a significant increase in the yield on the debt of an entity when compared to the change in the yield of a risk-free security of a similar maturity. An increase in yield relative to a risk-free rate may be indicative of the market's evaluation of the total mix of information including the risk associated with holding the issuer's debt.

Guidance related to impairment may also be useful in assessing a significant decline in the issuer's creditworthiness. (IAS 39 (r2000).110) Information, such as the current and near-term projected financial condition and performance of the issuer, the issuer's dividend payment and net profit performance, the general market conditions and prospects of the region and industry in which the issuer operates, and specific adverse news or events affecting the issuer may also be used as general guidelines.

General market or industry prospects or events should have a direct or demonstrable effect on a specific issuer to provide evidence of a decline in creditworthiness for that issuer. For instance, widespread difficulties experienced by others in the industry (e.g., due to over-leveraging or weak assets), but which are not expected to affect the issuer more adversely than its peers, would not be relevant. In contrast, the development of severe competition, adverse tax or regulatory developments, or declining markets may have a direct bearing on the creditworthiness of specific issuers.

As a remedy to protect the investor from the issuer's violation of a debt covenant, a contractual right of foreclosure that was negotiated at arm's-length at the issuance date would not preclude an investor classifying an investment as held-to-maturity (HTM). Similarly, the exercise of such a right or foreclosure on the violation of a substantial covenant would not taint an investor's remaining HTM portfolio. However, this conclusion does not apply to a refinancing evidenced by any continuing debtor/creditor relationship.

If an exchange of debt securities classified as held-to-maturity is being contemplated pursuant to a bankruptcy where the investor does not control the outcome, such exchange would not call into question the investor's intent to hold other financial assets to maturity.

Example 12.3 Significant deterioration in creditworthiness of the issuer

Violation of debt covenants

Assume enterprise M, an insurance company, has a portfolio of private placement debt securities classified as HTM. The securities contain normal debt covenants that, in the event of default or non compliance, permit M to exercise an embedded put option to sell the securities back to the issuer (initiate foreclosure). Trigger events for such covenants may include a change in control of the issuer and financial and operating covenants that may or may not have resulted in an actual credit deterioration.

If, in a subsequent period, the issuer violates a substantial debt covenant, Enterprise M may exercise its right to sell the security back to the issuer without tainting its remaining HTM portfolio.

Sale of securities in response to insurance claim

Assume an insurance enterprise sells financial assets that have been classified as HTM due to cash needs arising from the failure of one of its principal reinsurers. This situation is not analogous to significant deterioration in an issuer's creditworthiness, because the deterioration does not relate specifically to the issuer of the security sold but to the enterprise's reinsurer. A sale from the HTM portfolio for this reason would be inconsistent with the positive intent and ability to hold the security to maturity. The failure of an insurance enterprise's principal reinsurer would also not be considered an event that is 'extremely remote' or isolated, non-recurring, and unusual, given the environment in which an insurance enterprise operates.

Financial restructuring

Assume N, a life insurance enterprise, purchased debt in a private placement offering. At acquisition, N classified the debt as HTM. The issuer, a private company, is currently in bankruptcy proceedings and is restructuring its debt. The issuer is contemplating swapping its debt to N in exchange for new debt and stock. N has no control over the outcome of the issuer's restructuring arrangements.

Prior to the issuer's determination of the final restructuring arrangements, N can continue to classify the debt security as HTM. The HTM classification is acceptable because the issuer's termination of the original debt is not under N's control. N should determine whether impairment has occurred (see **12.11**) and if so, write down the financial instrument to its net recoverable amount.

Prior to the issuer's determination of the final restructuring arrangements, N may also transfer the debt security from the held-to-maturity (HTM) to the available-for-sale category without tainting its HTM portfolio. This conclusion is based on the guidance contained in paragraph 86(a), which concludes that a transfer resulting from evidence of a significant deterioration in the issuer's creditworthiness will not call into question an enterprise's intent to hold other financial assets to maturity in the future.

Permitted sales – changes in tax law affecting tax-exempt status – paragraph 86(b)

Paragraph 86(b) above identifies a change in tax law, which eliminates or reduces the tax-exempt status of interest on a held-to-maturity investment, as a circumstance that permits an investor to reclassify these securities from the HTM category without calling into question the enterprise's ability and intent to hold other investments to maturity.

A reclassification in anticipation of future tax law changes that have not become law, however, does not qualify under this exception. Also precluded are reclassifications resulting from tax law changes that impact the marginal tax rate applicable to interest income on HTM debt securities.

Example 12.4 Changes in tax law affecting tax-exempt status

Assume Enterprise X, a company operating in Canada, has a portfolio of financial assets classified as HTM which contains a Malaysian bond issue. Also assume that at the date that Enterprise X purchased the security, a tax treaty existed between the Canadian tax jurisdiction and Malaysia. This treaty allowed the use of Canadian foreign tax credits to reduce the onerous tax consequences that would otherwise result from inclusion of interest on the Malaysian security in taxable income in both tax jurisdictions (assuming Enterprise X is also taxed on the income in Malaysia). Enterprise X cannot reclassify the security from its HTM category in anticipation of the treaty's expiration without calling into question the intent to hold other financial assets to maturity. However, if the treaty does expire, reclassification is permitted and no tainting will occur in respect of any remaining HTM securities.

Permitted sales – major business combinations or disposals – paragraph 86 (c)

Although IAS 39 (r2000) does not specify a quantitative threshold to be applied in respect of the paragraph 86(c) exception for a major business combination or disposal, paragraph 86(c) refers to a sale of a segment as an example of a major disposal. Guidance on the definition of a segment is contained in IAS 14 (r1997), *Segment Reporting*, which refers to a distinguishable component of an enterprise that is engaged in providing products or services and that is subject to risks and returns different from those of other business segments or of other components operating in different economic environments. It is unlikely that a purchase or sale of a large pool of financial assets (e.g., conforming mortgages) or liabilities (e.g., deposit liabilities) would be considered a major business combination or disposal that would justify the sale of HTM securities.

It is important to emphasise that paragraph 86(c) permits sales of HTM securities only when the combination or disposal necessitates the sale or transfer of HTM securities to maintain the enterprise's existing interest rate risk position or credit risk policy, changes to which are consequential rather than anticipated. Sales of HTM securities to fund an acquisition (or a disposal if, for example, deposit liabilities are being assumed by the other party) are inconsistent with paragraph 86. Spin-offs and other corporate reorganisations that may change the tax attributes of the enterprise are *not* considered to be isolated or non-recurring events.

By referring to consequential rather than anticipated changes arising from a business combination or disposal, an enterprise may reassess the classification of HTM securities concurrently with or shortly after a major business combination and not call into question its intent to hold other securities to maturity in the future. Following a major acquisition, some of the acquiring enterprise's HTM investments may need to be transferred or sold because of the nature of the liabilities assumed - even though all of the acquired financial instruments are classified anew following such a business combination. As time passes, it becomes increasingly difficult to demonstrate that the business combination, and not other events or circumstances, necessitated the transfer or sale of HTM securities.

Permitted sales – regulatory capital requirements – paragraph 86 (d)–(f)

One objective of financial reporting is that the assumptions used in preparing financial statements are consistent. It would be inconsistent under IAS 39 (r2000) for an insurance company or other regulated enterprise to classify financial assets as held-to-maturity and also indicate to regulators that those investments could be sold to meet liquidity needs in a defined interest rate scenario whose likelihood of occurrence is reasonably possible but not probable.

A sale out of HTM to meet entity-specific capital requirements generally would cause the held-to-maturity portfolio to be tainted since it may be difficult to demonstrate that an entity-specific requirement could not have been anticipated (IGC 86-2).

Permitted sales – intercompany sales of held-to-maturity investments

In consolidated financial statements, intercompany sales would generally not taint the HTM portfolio from a group perspective, as long as the business purpose of the transfer and the investment policies of the 'buyer' are consistent with a positive intent and ability to hold to maturity. The impact on each entity's stand-alone financial statements should be assessed separately.

Permitted sales – catastrophic losses

Catastrophic losses or high levels of policy surrenders are not generally considered to be isolated, non-recurring, and unusual events for an insurance company. As a result, the sale of investments classified as held-to-maturity in order to meet excessive levels of claim obligations or because of policyholder withdrawals would taint the HTM classification.

Permitted sales – change in management
A change in management is not specifically identified under paragraph 86 as an instance where sales or transfers of financial assets from HTM do not compromise the HTM classification. Sales in response to such a change would therefore call into question the enterprise's intent to hold investments to maturity (IGC 86-1).

Example 12.5 Change in management

Enterprise X has a portfolio of financial assets that is classified as HTM. In the current period, a significant restructuring has been implemented by the board of directors. As part of the restructuring, the senior management team has been replaced. The new management wishes to sell a portion of the HTM securities in order to carry out an expansion strategy designated and approved by the board. Although the previous management team had been in place since the company's inception and enterprise X had never before undergone a major restructuring, the sale of HTM securities nevertheless calls into question X's intent to hold remaining HTM securities to maturity.

Permitted sales – asset-liability risk management considerations
An enterprise shall not classify a financial instrument as held to maturity (HTM) if the enterprise has the intent to hold the security for only an indefinite period as part of its interest rate or liquidity risk management policy. For example, it is inconsistent with IAS 39 (r2000) to have a documented policy to initially classify all debt securities as HTM and then automatically transfer every security to available-for-sale when it reaches a predetermined point before maturity as part of managing duration.

A debt security should not, for example, be classified as held-to-maturity if the enterprise anticipates that the security would be available-for-sale in response to:

- changes in market interest rates and related changes in the security's prepayment risk;
- needs for liquidity (e.g., due to the withdrawal of deposits, increased demand for loans, surrender of insurance policies, or payment of insurance claims);
- changes in the availability of and the yield on alternative investments;
- changes in funding sources and terms; and
- changes in foreign currency risk exposures.

Although its asset-liability management framework and methodology may include consideration of the maturity and repricing characteristics of all financial assets, an enterprise may decide that it can accomplish the necessary adjustments under its asset-liability management strategy without having all of its financial assets available for disposal. In that case, the enterprise may choose to maintain a separate portfolio of certain financial assets which are classified as available-for-sale to accomplish those ongoing adjustments deemed necessary under its asset-liability management. The remaining financial assets could then be accounted for at amortised cost on the basis of a positive intent and ability to hold them to maturity.

Example 12.6

Impact on other held-to-maturity investments

Assume Enterprise X has a portfolio of HTM financial assets comprising both municipal and corporate bonds. A sale or transfer of a single corporate bond that does not meet the specific exceptions in paragraph 86 of IAS 39 (r2000) causes a taint of all remaining municipal and corporate bonds. These securities would be transferred into the available-for-sale or held-for-trading categories as appropriate.

Tainting of the held-to-maturity portfolio after the balance sheet date

Enterprise X, with a 31 December year-end, has a portfolio of financial assets classified as HTM. Early in January 20x2, prior to the issuance of the 20x1 financial statements, Enterprise X sells a portion of the financial assets held, and the factors motivating the sale do not qualify under the exceptions provided in IAS 39 (r2000).83. Accordingly, the entire HTM securities portfolio is required to be reclassified as either available-for-sale or held for trading in the balance sheet as at 31 December 20x1 since the actions in January call into question the enterprise's assertion of intent at year-end.

Comparison with UK GAAP

UK GAAP does not include similar classifications to IAS 39 (r2000). However, most financial assets categorised as HTM under IAS 39 (r2000) will be treated as investments under UK GAAP. The rules for investments under UK GAAP are outlined in **10.8.16.**

Comparison with US GAAP

Under IAS 39 (r2000), the HTM category can include purchased loans that would not be classified as securities under US GAAP and therefore which are not subject to the classification provisions contained in SFAS 115, *Accounting for Certain Investments in Debt and Equity Securities*, (for example, whole commercial mortgage loans and revolving loans that were purchased in the secondary market). Under IAS 39 (r2000), these loans would be subject to the classification scheme regardless of their form and since these loans were purchased in the secondary market, they would not qualify for classification in the 'loans originated by the enterprise category'. US GAAP does not permit such loans to be classified in the HTM category and although both Standards would achieve the same accounting on an amortised cost basis, the IAS enterprise that holds HTM assets cannot sell them without 'tainting' this category.

Securities acquired by an investor in connection with their initial offering (origination) are considered to be originated loans and may not be classified as HTM, held for trading or available-for-sale under IAS 39 (r2000). All securities must be classified in one of these three categories under US GAAP since there is no originated loans category under US GAAP.

12.6.3 Originated loans and receivables

IAS 39 (r2000) defines loans and receivables originated by the enterprise as 'financial assets that are created by the enterprise by providing money, goods or services directly to a debtor, other than those that are originated with the intent to be sold immediately or in the short term, which should be classified as held for trading. Loans and receivables originated by the enterprise are not included in held-to-maturity investments, but, rather, are classified separately.' (IAS 39 (r2000).10)

As discussed further in **12.10.2**, originated loans and receivables which are not held for trading are not required to be carried at fair value but are carried at cost or amortised cost, as appropriate.

Originated loans and receivables include normal trade debtors. However, loans or receivables *purchased* by an enterprise, as opposed to being originated, are classified as HTM, available for sale or held for trading, as appropriate. IAS 39 (r2000).19 contains the following guidance related to determining when a loan or receivable has been purchased or acquired or when it has been originated:

Description of loan/receivable	IAS 39 (r2000) classification
A loan acquired by an enterprise as a participation in a loan from another lender.	Originated by the enterprise provided it is funded by the enterprise on the date that the loan is originated by the other lender.
An interest in a pool of loans or receivables acquired, for example, in connection with a securitisation.	HTM, available-for-sale or held-for-trading, as appropriate. This is a purchase, not an origination, because the enterprise did not provide money, goods, or services directly to the underlying debtors nor acquire

	its interest through a participation with another lender on the date the underlying loans or receivables were originated.
A transaction that is, in substance, a purchase of a loan that was previously originated – for example, a loan to an unconsolidated special purpose entity that is made to provide funding for its purchases of loans originated by others.	HTM, available-for-sale or held-for-trading, as appropriate. This is not a loan originated by the enterprise for the reasons in the above example.
A loan acquired by an enterprise in a business combination.	Originated by the acquiring enterprise provided that it was similarly classified by the acquired enterprise. The loan is measured at acquisition at fair value under the rules of IAS 22 (r1998), *Business Combinations* (see Chapter **18.6.4**).
A loan acquired through a syndication.	An originated loan because each lender shares in the origination of the loan and provides money directly to the debtor.
A term deposit made by a bank with a central bank.	An originated loan regardless of whether the deposit is negotiable (IGC 10-7).
A bond or debt security purchased at original issuance (including issues of sovereign debt).	An originated loan (IGC 10-11a and 10-20).
Funds transferred directly to the issuer to acquire its equity securities which are, in substance, debt because they have fixed or determinable payments and a fixed maturity.	An originated loan (IGC 10-11b).

Comparison with UK GAAP

UK GAAP does not under IAS 39 (r2000) refer to originated loans as a separate category. However, originated loans and receivables would generally be carried at cost or amortised cost in line with IAS 39 (r2000).

Comparison with US GAAP
Although this specific classification does not exist in US GAAP, the effect of other classification provisions could produce the same accounting result. For example, loans that are not included in the definition of securities (such as ordinary mortgage loans) are excluded from the scope of SFAS 115, *Accounting for Certain Investments in Debt and Equity Securities,* and hence are recorded at amortised cost.

12.6.4 Available-for-Sale (AFS)

'*Available-for-sale financial assets* are those financial assets that are not (a) loans and receivables originated by the enterprise, (b) held-to-maturity investments, or (c) financial assets held for trading.' (IAS 39 (r2000).10) Thus, this category is for all financial assets which do not meet the criteria for another category. However, as discussed in **12.6.1**, if a financial asset is part of a portfolio of similar assets for which there is a pattern of trading for the purpose of generating a profit from short-term fluctuations in price or dealer's margin, it is appropriately classed as held for trading rather than AFS (IGC 10-9). (IAS 39 (r2000).21)

As discussed further in **12.10.2**, financial assets classified as AFS are carried at fair value but changes in fair value may be recognised in the statement of changes in equity rather than the income statement based on an upfront election by the enterprise.

If an enterprise holds equity securities that are classified as AFS and, in connection with a merger, those shares are exchanged for the shares of the merged entity, and the fair value amount is recorded in equity under the enterprise's policy for accounting for available-for-sale assets, a gain or loss is recognised on the exchange in the income statement (IGC 103-2).

Comparison with UK GAAP
UK GAAP does not under IAS 39 (r2000) refer to AFS assets as a separate category. However, most AFS financial assets under IAS 39 (r2000) will be treated as investments under UK GAAP. The rules for investments under UK GAAP are outlined in **10.8.16.**

Comparison with US GAAP
Both IAS 39 (r2000) and US GAAP permit classification of securities as AFS. This classification, while an option under US GAAP, only results by default under IAS 39 (r2000) (although the representation of intent provides some latitude in determining this classification). Hence whereas an entity may, to a certain extent, make an election between held-for-trading and AFS based on management's intent under US GAAP, the use of AFS under IAS 39 (r2000) is solely the result of the transaction not meeting the criteria for

classification in the other three categories. IAS 39 (r2000) does not permit an entity to make a prima facie election to use the AFS classification based on management's intent.

Whereas the IAS 39 (r2000) classification of AFS applies to all financial assets, application of the SFAS 115, *Accounting for Certain Investments in Debt and Equity Securities*, definition of the AFS category is restricted to securities (as defined). By virtue of the fact that both Standards require the recording at fair value of financial instruments meeting the AFS definition, a mortgage loan could be recorded at fair value under IAS 39 (r2000) since this is a financial asset (assuming it is not further classified as a loan originated by the entity), yet be recorded at amortised cost under US GAAP because the loan is not a security as defined. Differences also exist in the subsequent recognition of AFS financial assets between US GAAP and IAS 39 (r2000) (see **12.10.5**).

12.7 Offsetting

Offsetting financial assets and financial liabilities in the balance sheet is a matter of presentation. IAS 1 (r1997) permits offsetting of assets and liabilities only when offsetting is required or permitted by a specific IAS (IAS 1 (r1997).33). IAS 32 (r1998) *requires* financial assets and financial liabilities to be offset and the net amount to be reported in the balance sheet when an enterprise both:

> '(a) has a legally enforceable right to set off the recognised amounts; and
> (b) intends either to settle on a net basis, or to realise the asset and settle the liability simultaneously.'
>
> (IAS 32 (r1998).33)

> 'Offsetting a recognised financial asset and a recognised financial liability and presenting the net amount differs from ceasing to recognise a financial asset or a financial liability (extinguishment). While offsetting does not give rise to the recognition of a gain or a loss, ceasing to recognise a financial instrument not only results in the removal of the previously recognised item from the balance sheet but may also result in recognition of a gain or a loss.'
>
> (IAS 32 (r1998).35)

Each criterion is discussed below.

Legal right of set-off

Criterion (a) refers to the legal right of set-off. 'A right of set-off is a debtor's legal right, by contract or otherwise, to settle or otherwise eliminate all or a portion of an amount due to a creditor by applying against that amount an amount due from the creditor. In unusual circumstances, a debtor may have a legal right to apply an amount due from a third party against the amount due to a creditor provided that there is an agreement among the three parties that clearly establishes the debtor's right of set-off. Since the right of set-off is a legal right, the condition supporting the right may vary from one legal jurisdiction to another and care must be taken to establish which laws apply to the relationships between the parties.' (IAS 32 (r1998).36)

IAS 32 (r1998) does not provide any guidance either as to what constitutes unusual circumstances or regarding the nature of the agreement amongst the parties. IAS 32 (r1998) It is not clear whether the legal rights need to be established in a document amongst the three parties. For example, a debtor might obtain set-off rights separately from the third party and from the creditor. In establishing the validity of the legal right to set-off, it is necessary to understand the terms of the particular contracts as well as the context within which set-off is to be applied. The legal right to set-off could, inter alia, be evidenced with reference to a legal opinion, or to established statutory or regulatory provisions which have been clearly established and demonstrated as governing the particular transaction.

Intention to settle net or simultaneously

In addition to the legal right of set-off, in order to offset financial assets and liabilities, an enterprise must intend to either settle on a net basis or to realise the asset and settle the liability simultaneously.

However, an intention by one or both of the parties to settle on a net basis without the legal right is not sufficient grounds to offset.

Intention may be demonstrated through management representations that are not contradicted by past experience or other relevant circumstances and may also take into account reference to the enterprise's risk management policies, if appropriate. There is no requirement for an assessment of the counterparty's intent and as long as the reporting entity has the legal right, intent need only be considered from the reporting enterprise's perspective.

> 'Simultaneous settlement of two financial instruments may occur through, for example, the operation of a clearing house in an organised financial market or a face-to-face exchange. In these circumstances the cash flows are, in effect, equivalent to a single net amount and there is no exposure to credit or liquidity risk. In other circumstances, an enterprise may settle two instruments by receiving and paying separate amounts, becoming exposed to credit risk for the full amount of the asset or liquidity risk for the full amount of the liability. Such risk exposures may be significant even though relatively brief. Accordingly, realisation of a financial asset and settlement of a financial liability are considered simultaneous only when the transactions occur at the same moment.' (IAS 32 (r1998).39)

Enterprises which enter into a number of financial instrument transactions with a single counterparty often enter into master netting arrangements. Such arrangements (for example, the widely used ISDA and ISMA Master agreements) usually provide the legal right of set off in the event of bankruptcy or other events which result in the counterparty being unable to meet its obligations. However, such arrangements are generally entered into as a precaution catering for default events, and unless an enterprise actually intends to settle on an ongoing net basis under the master netting arrangement, offsetting is not permitted. Therefore, the mere existence of such an arrangement is not sufficient grounds for offsetting. (IAS 32 (r1998).41)

Although master netting agreements often provide the ability for enterprises to settle net across multiple product types, it is unlikely that enterprises will be able to demonstrate the intention (or often even have the systems capability) to settle net across different products. In such cases, the application of set-off should be assessed on a contract by contract, instrument by instrument basis.

Example 12.7 Offsetting multiple cash flows

Assume that the legal right of set-off exists in the following scenario. Company X owes company Y four payments of €10 million each at the end of each calendar quarter (31 March, 30 June, 31 August, 31 December), totalling €40 million. As part of another contract, company Y owes company X two payments of €15 million at 30 June and 31 December, totalling €30 million.

The intention to settle simultaneously can only be demonstrated in respect of the 30 June and 31 December cash flows. At the beginning of the year, company X will therefore reflect a financial liability of €20 million (being the 31 March and 30 September payments) and a separate financial asset of €10 million (representing the difference between the €10 million payable and €15 million receivable from company Y on 30 June and 31 December). Although company X's net position over the whole year is a financial liability of €10 million, since it cannot demonstrate the intention to settle net or simultaneously for all payments, the criteria for offset are not satisfied in respect of those unmatched payments and separate presentation is required. Company Y correspondingly has an asset of €20 million and a liability of €10 million.

Example 12.8 Intention to offset

Option premiums

Company X, a gold producer in South Africa, manages its exposure to changes in the gold price and locks in the cost of funding future capital expenditure by entering into option strategies with several investment banks. These strategies require company X to both purchase call options and to write put options at various strike prices and with various maturity dates. The transactions are expected to be settled in cash and meet the definition of a derivative in IAS 39 (r2000). The investment banks require company X to enter into ISDA Master Netting agreements (drafted by the International Swaps and Derivatives Association) which give either party the legal right of set-off on termination of the contract, or on default of the other party. These agreements do not provide for the set-off of settlements in the ordinary course of business.

Company X may not offset the premiums paid and received with each investment bank, or the financial assets and financial liabilities arising from the subsequent measurement of these options to fair value. Since the master netting agreement establishes a legally enforceable right of set-off only if there is a contingent event (i.e., default or on termination by one of the parties) and not in respect of ongoing settlements, the requirement in IAS 32 (r1998).33(a) is not satisfied. Additionally, by virtue of the different maturity dates, the company does not demonstrate the intention to settle on a net basis or to realise the asset and liability simultaneously and therefore the requirement in IAS 32 (r1998).33(b) is not satisfied.

Interest rate swap agreements

Bank A, an investment bank enters into several swap transactions having different reset dates to manage the interest rate risk arising from its corporate loans portfolio. Although these transactions are with a range of other banks as counterparties, Bank A's systems aggregate all exposures on a daily basis to enable them to recognise the net profit or loss due to the change in fair value of all open (i.e., unexpired) contracts. Certain contracts have a positive fair value while others are in a loss position. ISDA Master Netting Agreements are in place with some, but not all of these counterparties. Bank A does not net the settlements across swap positions with counterparties on reset dates.

Bank A does not meet the criteria for offsetting financial assets and liabilities related to its swap positions. It does not settle on a net basis and, due to the mismatch in reset dates across its swaps book, cannot demonstrate the simultaneous settlement of swap cash flows. The ISDA Master Netting Agreements are not, in themselves sufficient to provide the Bank with the legal right to set off its settlement cash flows across contracts except in the conditional event of default or termination by one of the parties.

If, in order to maximise the use of available credit lines, Bank A entered into credit enhancement agreements (annexes to its ISDA Master Netting Agreements) with its counterparties by placing or receiving daily margin to the extent of the change in fair value on all open contracts with a particular counterparty, this would typically satisfy the requirements for netting in respect of individual counterparties. This is because the margin payments and receipts represent settlement on an ongoing net basis. Bank A could not, however, net financial assets and liabilities across counterparties in terms of these agreements.

Situations when offsetting is inappropriate

The offsetting criteria are generally not met and thus offsetting is generally not appropriate when:

'(a) several different financial instruments are used to emulate the features of a single financial instrument (i.e., a 'synthetic instrument');

(b) financial assets and financial liabilities arise from financial instruments having the same primary risk exposure (for example, assets and liabilities within a portfolio of forward contracts or other derivative instruments) but involve different counterparties;

(c) financial or other assets are pledged as collateral for non-recourse financial liabilities;

(d) financial assets are set aside in trust by a debtor for the purpose of discharging an obligation without those assets having been accepted by the creditor in settlement of the obligation (for example, a sinking fund arrangement); or

(e) obligations incurred as a result of events giving rise to losses are expected to be recovered from a third party by virtue of a claim made under an insurance policy.'

(IAS 32 (r1998).40)

Comparison with UK GAAP

FRS 5, *Reporting the Substance of Transactions*, contains three conditions which must be met in order to offset. These conditions differ from those in IAS 39 (r2000), in particular they do not require intent to settle either simultaneously or on a net basis, and thus may or may not lead to the same conclusion regarding the appropriateness of offsetting:

'(1) The reporting entity and another party owe each other determinable monetary amounts, denominated either in the same currency, or in different but freely convertible currencies. For this purpose a freely convertible currency is one for which quoted exchange rates are available in an active market that can rapidly absorb the amount to be offset without significantly affecting the exchange rate.

(2) The reporting entity has the ability to insist on a net settlement. In determining this, any right to insist on a net settlement that is contingent should be taken into account only if the reporting entity is able to enforce net settlement in all situations of default by the other party.

(3) The reporting entity's ability to insist on a net settlement is assured beyond reasonable doubt. It is essential that there is no possibility that the entity could be required to transfer economic benefits to another party whilst being unable to enforce its own access to economic benefits. For this to be the case it is necessary that the debit balance matures no later than the credit balance. It is also necessary that the reporting entity's ability to insist on a net settlement would survive the insolvency of the other party'.

(FRS 5.29)

FRS 5 does not deal with hedging. However, in many cases, the ability to account realistically for a hedge transaction will depend on two or more items being presented together within financial statements. For example, a company may have a sterling loan, together with a sterling/dollar swap contract that has been acquired as an effective hedge to switch exposure from sterling into dollar currency movements; arguably, the most appropriate presentation of these items will be as a single balance sheet liability denominated in dollars and a single interest charge also denominated in dollars, with note disclosure providing the analysis into two separate legal instruments. Until a UK standard on recognition of derivatives is in place, disclosure on a net basis is acceptable only where it portrays the commercial substance of the hedged position and is therefore necessary to give a true and fair view.

Comparison with US GAAP

US GAAP differs from IAS 32 (r1998) with respect to offsetting in two principal areas, namely the ability to offset where a third party is involved and the exception in respect of master netting agreements.

FASB Interpretation, FIN 39, *Offsetting of Amounts Related to Certain Contracts*, sets out the criteria for offsetting amounts related to certain financial instrument contracts. These criteria are broadly similar to those under IAS 32 (r1998) in requiring that a right of set-off must exist. This is demonstrated when all of the following conditions are met:

(a) each of the two parties owes the other determinable amounts;
(b) the reporting party has the right to set off the amount owed with the amount owed by the other party;
(c) the reporting party intends to set off; and
(d) the right of set-off is enforceable at law. (FIN 39.5)

By restricting the ability to offset to where the right of set-off exists between two parties (i.e., where a debtor-creditor relationship exists), US GAAP does not permit set-off under third-party netting agreements.

The second area of difference relates to master netting agreements. FIN 39.10 provides an exception to the above requirements where a master netting arrangement exists and the reporting entity has multiple contracts (whether in respect of multiple types of financial instruments or only single contract types). Even though the master netting agreement may only provide for the net settlement of all contracts through a single payment in a single currency in the event of default or on termination of any one contract, fair value amounts may be offset. This is also the case even where the reporting enterprise's intention is only to offset in the case of default or termination. This exception recognises that the net presentation is consistent with the credit exposures under such an arrangement and which constitutes useful information for users of the financial statements. Presentation of the aggregate fair values of the individual contracts executed under that arrangement does not provide any extra information about the uncertainty of future cash flows from those contracts other than that which is already contained in disclosure of the net amounts.

12.8 Initial recognition

> The general recognition rule in IAS 39 (r2000) provides that 'an enterprise should recognise a financial asset or financial liability on its balance sheet when, and only when, it becomes a party to the contractual provisions of the instrument.' (IAS 39 (r2000).27)

The previous paragraph results in all derivatives, unless specifically excluded from the scope of IAS 39 (r2000), being recognised in the balance sheet and hence not being treated as 'off balance sheet' items.

The following are some examples of applying the principle in paragraph 27:

'(a) unconditional receivables and payables are recognised as assets or liabilities when the enterprise becomes a party to the contract and, as a consequence, has a legal right to receive, or a legal obligation to pay, cash;

(b) assets to be acquired and liabilities to be incurred as a result of a firm commitment to purchase or sell goods or services are not recognised under present accounting practice until at least one of the parties has performed under the agreement such that it either is entitled to receive an asset or is obligated to disburse an asset. For example, an enterprise that receives a firm order does not recognise an asset (and the enterprise that places the order does not recognise a liability) at the time of the commitment but, rather, delays recognition until the ordered goods or services have been shipped, delivered, or rendered;

(c) in contrast to (b) above, however, a forward contract – a commitment to purchase or sell a specified financial instrument or commodity subject to this Standard on a future date at a specified price – is recognised as an asset or a liability on the commitment date, rather than waiting until the closing date on which the exchange actually takes place. When an enterprise becomes a party to a forward contract, the fair values of the right and obligation are often equal, so that the net fair value of the forward is zero, and only any net fair value of the right and obligation is recognised as an asset or liability. However, each party is exposed to the price risk that is the subject of the contract from that date. Such a forward contract satisfies the recognition principle of paragraph 27, from the perspectives of both the buyer and the seller, at the time the enterprises become parties to the contract, even though it may have a zero net value at that date. The fair value of the contract may become a net asset or liability in the future depending on, among other things, the time value of money and the value of the underlying instrument or commodity that is the subject of the forward;

(d) financial options are recognised as assets or liabilities when the holder or writer becomes a party to the contract;

(e) planned future transactions, no matter how likely, are not assets and liabilities of an enterprise since the enterprise, as of the financial reporting date, has not become a party to a contract requiring future receipt or delivery of assets arising out of the future transactions' (IAS (39 (r2000).29); and

(f) cash received as collateral for another transaction, e.g. a securities borrowing transaction, is recognised as an asset; a payable, i.e. an obligation to return that asset, is also recognised. (IGC 27-2)

In the case of many derivatives, when an enterprise becomes a party to the contract, the consideration (and hence net fair value) is zero since the fair values of the related rights and obligations are often equal (see IAS 39 (r2000).29(c)). This is, however, not an impediment to initial recognition or measurement.

IAS 39 (r2000) does not address the situation when an enterprise should recognise an obligation to issue its own equity instruments in settlement of a financial liability. US Guidance exists in EITF 96-18, *Accounting for Equity Instruments that are Issues to Other Than Employees for Acquiring, or in Conjunction with Selling, Goods or Services.* Ordinarily, the date on which the exchange of the equity instruments occurs should be used as the date to measure the equity instrument (or when the service is rendered or performance is complete). The existence of an agreement is not usually sufficient in and of itself to permit recognition of the equity instrument on the date the contract/ agreement is signed.

12.9 Initial measurement

> 'When a financial asset or financial liability is recognised initially, an enterprise should measure it at its cost, which is the fair value of the consideration given (in the case of an asset) or received (in the case of a liability) for it. Transaction costs directly attributable to the acquisition of a financial asset on a financial liability are *included* in the initial measurement of all financial assets and liabilities.' (IAS 39 (r2000).66)

Note that where a loan is granted which either bears interest at an off-market interest rate, or carries no interest in return for some implicit right to obtain expected future economic benefits other than the right to receive payment on the loan asset, the fair value of the loan is generally not equal to the consideration exchanged. Under IAS 39 (r2000), in such cases the imputed interest charge should be taken into account by adjusting the value at which the loan is recognised to the present value of the future cash flows on the loan. Although IAS 39 (r2000).74 and 111 state that cash flows relating to short-term receivables are not generally discounted, where the discounting effect is considered significant, an adjustment to the consideration exchanged should be recognised to arrive at the initial recorded amount which is the fair value of the consideration exchanged. The imputed interest charge is then expensed over the life of the loan (IGC 66-3).

As an exception to the general measurement rule above, IAS 39 (r2000).160 requires that certain hedging gains and losses are included as part of the initial measurement of the cost of the related hedged asset (see **12.24.2 Basis Adjustment**).

As discussed in **12.9.2**, the value initially recorded related to a financial instrument depends on whether an enterprise adopts trade date or settlement date accounting.

12.9.1 Transactions costs

'*Transaction costs* are incremental costs that are directly attributable to the acquisition or disposal of a financial asset or liability.' (IAS 39 (r2000).10) Such costs include:

(1) fees and commissions paid to agents, advisers, brokers, and dealers;
(2) levies by regulatory agencies and securities exchanges; and
(3) transfer taxes and duties.

Transaction costs do not include debt premium or discount, financing costs, or allocations of internal administrative or holding costs. (IAS 39 (r2000).17)

IAS 39 (r2000).69 includes a clarification that transaction costs *expected* to be incurred on transfer or disposal of a financial instrument are not included in any subsequent measurement of the financial instrument. This was confirmed by the IGC which further stated that transaction costs to be incurred upon sale of a financial instrument are not included in the measurement of the financial instrument (IGC 66-1).

Example 12.9 Transaction costs

IAS 39 (r2000).77 includes this example which illustrates how transaction costs relate to the initial and subsequent measurement of a financial asset held for trading.

An asset is acquired for 100 plus a purchase commission of 2. Initially it is recorded at 102. At the next financial reporting date, the quoted market price of the asset remains at 100. If the asset were sold a commission of 3 would be paid. At the financial reporting date, the asset is measured at 100 (without regard to the possible commission on sale) and a loss of 2 is recognised in net profit or loss for the period.

The effect of including transaction costs in the initial measurement of the financial instrument is that, for subsequent measurement, the method of recognising transaction costs in net profit or loss is driven by the classification of the underlying financial instrument (IGC 66-1).

For instruments which are held-to-maturity, financial liabilities which are neither derivatives nor held for trading and for loans and receivables originated by the enterprise and not held for trading, these costs will be amortised over the life of the instrument.

For available-for-sale instruments where the enterprise has opted to recognise all changes in fair value directly in equity, these costs are amortised from equity into the income statement using the effective interest method over the life of the instrument. If, however, the instrument does not have a fixed maturity, the costs are only recognised in net profit or loss at the time of sale (IGC 66-1).

For the remaining categories (held for trading and available-for-sale instruments where the enterprise has opted to recognise all changes in fair value in the income statement), the full amount of the transactions costs will be recognised in net profit or loss in the reporting period in which the financial instrument is acquired. See *Example 12.9* above.

Comparison with UK GAAP

Under UK GAAP, transaction costs would generally be included in initial recognition of a financial instrument. For capital instruments FRS 4, *Capital Instruments*, specifies that subsequent to initial recognition transaction costs are included in the calculation of the effective interest rate and, in effect, are amortised through profit and loss account. Costs to be incurred on transfer or disposal of the financial instrument are not included in the measurement of the financial instrument unless the enterprise is contractually committed to sell or transfer that instrument.

Comparison with US GAAP

US GAAP is silent about transaction costs subsequent to initial recognition.It does not prohibit deduction of costs to be incurred on transfer or disposal of a financial instrument in the fair value of that financial instrument. Therefore, enterprises following IAS 39 (r2000) may reflect higher fair values than US GAAP entities because those following US GAAP may choose to deduct anticipated transaction costs relating to sales in arriving at a fair value.

12.9.2 Trade date v *settlement date accounting*

Regular-way contracts

As an exception to the general recognition rule in IAS 39 (r2000), an enterprise may elect to use either trade date or settlement date accounting when initially recognising either purchases or sales of 'regular way' financial assets. The method chosen should be applied consistently for all purchases and sales of financial assets that belong to the same category of financial assets. (IAS 39 (r2000).30) Note that prior to the amendment to IAS 39 in October 2000, enterprises were only able to elect the use of trade or settlement date accounting in respect of regular way purchases of financial assets. The amendment extended this election to regular way sales of financial assets to prevent inconsistencies in the reporting of those assets and to cater for differences in legal systems across countries where ownership may be transferred and change in control occur at different points in time between trade and settlement date.

Although IAS 39 (r2000) does not make specific reference to financial liabilities, since the general recognition and derecognition rules apply, settlement date accounting should generally be used to recognise and derecognise financial liabilities. Settlement date is typically the date when each of the parties become a contractual party to the agreement on initial recognition, and when the liability is extinguished on derecognition (IGC 27-1).

'Regular-way contracts' are agreements to buy financial assets on terms that require delivery of the asset within the time frame established generally by regulation or convention in the market place. The term 'market place' is not limited to a formalised exchange or organised over the counter market but rather means the environment in which the financial asset is customarily exchanged. An acceptable timeframe would be the period reasonably and customarily required for the parties to complete the transaction and prepare and execute closing documents (IGC 16-1). Where an enterprise's securities trade in more than one market, the exemption for regular way is determined by following the convention of the market in which the contract will be settled (IGC 16-3).

Whilst regular-way contracts may meet the definition of a derivative instrument under IAS 39 (r2000) (they are effectively forward contracts), such contracts are not recognised as derivatives due to the short duration of the commitment. (IAS 39 (r2000).31) Where, however, the settlement term exceeds the normal settlement term in the market, the contract is accounted for as a derivative (IGC 16-2). Similarly, a contract that requires or permits net settlement cannot be accounted for as a regular way transaction (IGC 30-2). Furthermore, if an option is exercised, but delivery of the underlying is beyond the term of regular market place convention, the forward resulting from the exercise of the option is accounted for as a derivative until settlement (IGC 16-4).

The exemption for regular way transactions is intended to apply to purchase and sales commitments relating to financial assets that, because of constraints in the market place, cannot be settled immediately at the trade date or commitment date. The exemption is not available to forward and option contracts that have a term that extends beyond the necessary time to settle the underlying financial asset to take advantage of, or protect against market movements (IGC 30-1).

Although loan commitments meet the definition of derivative instruments, these are not accounted for as such if they are required to be settled in the customary or regulatory time frame established in the market and therefore meet the definition of regular-way contracts (IGC 30-1).

Trade date accounting
Trade date accounting refers to the recognition of the asset to be received and the liability to pay for it on the date that an enterprise commits to purchase the asset. Generally, interest does not start to accrue on the asset and corresponding liability until the settlement date when title passes. (IAS 39 (r2000).32)

Settlement date accounting
Settlement date accounting refers to the recognition of the asset on the day it is transferred or delivered to the enterprise. When settlement date accounting is applied, an enterprise will account for any change in the fair value of the asset to be received during the period between the trade date and the settlement date in the same way as it will account for the acquired asset (which depends on which category the assets falls into). For example, the value change is not recognised for assets carried at cost or amortised cost; it is recognised in net profit or loss for assets classified as trading; and it is recognised in net profit or loss or in equity (depending on the accounting policy of the enterprise) for assets classified as available-for-sale. (IAS 39 (r2000).33)

Under settlement date accounting for assets which are remeasured to fair value (i.e., the available-for-sale and held-for-trading categories), since the asset is only recognised in the balance sheet on settlement date, changes in the fair value between trade and settlement date are recorded as a receivable or payable and not as a fair value adjustment to the investment account. It would be inappropriate to recognise the change as an offset to the investment accounts where the asset has not yet been recognised.

If an enterprise uses settlement date accounting, a change between the trade date and the settlement date in the fair value of a financial asset that is sold on a regular way basis under a fixed price contract is not recognised until settlement date. If there is a risk that settlement will not occur, the enterprise will assess whether there has been an impairment (IGC 106-1).

Derivative instruments (whether they be financial assets or liabilities) do not qualify for settlement date accounting. This is because both the buyer and seller (or writer in the case of an option) become parties to the contract on the trade date and changes in fair value between trade and settlement date are automatically recognised in the balance sheet under IAS 39 (r2000). This applies regardless of whether the transaction may provide for an initial consideration (such as an option's premium) which may be settled in accordance with a regular way convention.

If an enterprise enters into an agreement to exchange non-cash financial assets and it recognises sales using settlement date accounting, it accounts for the purchase of the asset being acquired in the exchange based on its policy of trade date or settlement date for the category of asset being acquired (IGC 106-2).

IGC 34-1 sets out an illustration of trade and settlement date accounting for the sale of a financial asset. When trade date accounting is used for a sale, the asset is removed from the balance sheet and replaced with a receivable (an originated loan) from the purchaser.

The following additional examples also illustrate the application of the initial measurement rules and some subsequent measurement rules that specify measurement and recognition of changes in fair values for various types of financial assets.

Example 12.10 Settlement *v* trade date accounting

On 29 December 20x1, an enterprise commits to purchase a financial asset for 1,000 (including transaction costs), which is its fair value on commitment (trade) date. On 31 December 20x1 (financial year end) and on 4 January 20x2 (settlement date) the fair value of the asset is 1,002 and 1,003, respectively. The amounts to be recorded for the asset will depend on how it is classified and whether trade date or settlement date accounting is used, as shown in the two tables below: (IAS 39 (r2000).34)

Settlement date accounting

Balances	**Held-to-maturity investments – carried at amortised cost**	**Available-for-sale assets – remeasured to fair value with changes in equity**	**Assets held for trading and available-for-sale assets – remeasured to fair value with changes in profit or loss**
29 December 20x1			
Financial asset	–	–	–
Liability	–	–	–
31 December 20x1			
Receivable	–	2	2
Financial asset	–	–	–
Liability	–	–	–
Equity (fair value adjustment)	–	(2)	–
Retained earnings (through net profit or loss)	–	–	(2)
4 January 20x2			
Receivable	–	–	–
Financial asset	1,000	1,003	1,003
Liability	–	–	–
Equity (fair value adjustment)	–	(3)	–
Retained earnings (through net profit or loss)	–	–	(3)

Trade date accounting			
Balances	**Held-to-maturity investments – carried at amortised cost**	**Available-for-sale assets – remeasured to fair value with changes in equity**	**Assets held for trading and available-for-sale assets – remeasured to fair value with changes in profit or loss**
29 December 20x1			
Financial asset	1,000	1,000	1,000
Liability	(1,000)	(1,000)	(1,000)
31 December 20x1			
Receivable	–	–	–
Financial asset	1,000	1,002	1,002
Liability	(1,000)	(1,000)	(1,000)
Equity (fair value adjustment)	–	(2)	–
Retained earnings (through net profit or loss)	–	–	(2)
4 January 20x2			
Receivable	–	–	–
Financial asset	1,000	1,003	1,003
Liability	–	–	–
Equity (fair value adjustment)	–	(3)	–
Retained earnings (through net profit or loss)	–	–	(3)

Example 12.11 Sale of a security carried at fair value

Enterprise X has a portfolio of debt securities which are classified as held-for-trading. This portfolio contains a Danish government bond with a carrying value (corresponding to its fair value) of €80 million that the enterprise sells on 30 March for settlement on 2 April. Assuming that the bonds were sold for €80 million and that the market value of the bonds was €76 million on both 31 March and 1 April and €82 million when the transaction was settled on 2 April.

The following journal entries would be recorded if settlement date accounting is adopted:

30 March	*Debit*	*Credit*
No entries are passed (since the asset is carried at its fair value).		
31 March		
Unrealised loss – Held-for-trading securities (Income statement)	4,000,000	
Held-for-trading securities (Balance sheet)		4,000,000
To record the change in fair value between 30 and 31 March.		
2 April		
Cash	80,000,000	
Held-for-trading securities (Balance sheet)		76,000,000
Realised gain – Held-for-trading securities		4,000,000

Following trade debt accounting, the enterprise would record the receivable from the buyer of €80 million and no further entries would be passed until 2 April, when the cash is received (Dr cash €80 million, Cr receivable €80 million).

Comparison with UK GAAP

In the UK, trade date accounting is the norm based on industry practice.

Comparison with US GAAP

For US GAAP, the use of trade or settlement date accounting is generally based on industry practice. Trade date accounting is used for purchases and sales of securities as well as commitments to buy and sell securities in a trading account. Settlement date accounting is used for loan origination commitments and sales of loans and securities out of the available-for-sale category. Under US GAAP, derecognition (and therefore the use of trade or settlement date accounting) only occurs once the transfer criteria in SFAS 140, *Accounting for Transfers and Servicing of Financial Assets and Extinguishment of Liabilities*, have been met (based on the need to give up control).

IAS 39 (r2000) requires, for those instruments reflected at fair value, recognition of changes in fair value between trade and settlement date for situations where settlement date accounting is used. This is not required under US GAAP. (SFAS 133.274)

12.10 Subsequent recognition and measurement

12.10.1 General subsequent measurement rule

The general rule is that 'after initial recognition, an enterprise should measure financial assets, including derivatives that are assets, at their fair values, without any deduction for transaction costs that it may incur on sale or other disposal.' (IAS 39 (r2000).69)

The exceptions to the general rule which are measured either at cost or amortised cost include:

(a) loans and receivables originated by the enterprise and not held for trading;
(b) held-to-maturity investments; and
(c) any financial asset that does not have a quoted market price in an active market and whose fair value cannot be reliably measured.

(IAS 39 (r2000).69)

12.10.2 Recognition and measurement table

A summary of the measurement and recognition principles of IAS 39 (r2000) for each category of financial asset or liability subsequent to initial recognition is provided below. Discussions of the meaning of 'fair value', 'amortised cost' and 'cost' follow in the sections after the table.

Held-to-maturity investments (financial assets)	
Basis of subsequent measurement	Amortised cost. (IAS 39 (r2000).69, 73 and 84)
Remeasurement gains/ losses	Remeasurement gains/losses consists of the amortisation amount (determined using the effective interest rate method) which is reflected in net profit or loss for the period. (IAS 39 (r2000).108, 73 and 10)
Impairment	If it is probable that an enterprise will not be able to collect all amounts due (principal and interest) according to the contractual terms of loans, receivables or held-to-maturity investments carried at amortised cost, an impairment or bad debt loss has occurred. The amount of the loss is the difference between the asset's carrying amount and the present value of expected future cash flows discounted at *the*

original effective interest rate (the estimated recoverable amount). The carrying amount is reduced to its estimated recoverable amount either directly by writing the asset down or through an allowance account which is netted off the investment for presentation purposes. The amount of the loss is included in net profit or loss for the period. (IAS 39 (r2000).111)

Specific guidance is not provided for assessing the probability that the amounts due will be uncollectable and considerable judgement is required. The wording implies, however, that this envisages situations where the likelihood of impairment is beyond a mere possibility. If the impairment is expected to be temporary and therefore is not expected to impact negatively on the ability to collect *all* amounts due, an impairment loss would not normally be recognised. However, since IAS 39 (r2000) refers to collecting all amounts due according to the contractual terms of the financial asset, it implies that a history of failure to meet scheduled payments on time could indicate that an impairment loss has occurred even if it is probable that all amounts will eventually be recovered. This scenario may be aggravated in a high interest rate environment due to the present value effect on the scheduled cash flows.

Impairment of a financial asset carried at amortised cost is measured using the financial instrument's original effective interest rate because discounting at the current market rate of interest would, in effect, impose fair-value measurement on financial assets that IAS 39 (r2000) would otherwise measure at amortised cost. Nevertheless, market price may provide evidence of credit deterioration (IGC 113.3). If a loan, receivable, or held-to-maturity investment has a variable interest rate, the discount rate for measuring recoverable amount is the current effective interest rate(s) determined under the contract. As a surrogate for such a fair value calculation, a creditor may measure

	impairment based on an instrument's fair value using an observable market price. If an asset is collateralised and foreclosure is probable, then the holder measures impairment based on the fair value of the collateral. (IAS 39 (r2000).113) Subsequent write-backs of impairment losses are permitted if the recovery can be objectively related to an event occurring after the write-down (such as an improvement in the debtor's credit rating). Such write-backs are adjusted against net profit or loss either directly against the carrying amount of the asset or the allowance account as appropriate. These may not exceed the equivalent amortised cost carrying amount had impairment not occurred. (IAS 39 (r2000).114) See **12.11** for further discussion of impairment.
Changes in classification	Except in limited circumstances (due to either a change in intent or ability to hold the asset to maturity), IAS 39 (r2000) does not permit reclassification out of the held-to-maturity category. When this designation is no longer appropriate, the asset is remeasured to fair value. Gains or losses are then recognised based on whether it is subsequently classified as held-for-trading or available-for-sale. (IAS 39 (r2000).83, 84 and 90) Remember, sales or transfers out of the held-to-maturity category, that are considered to taint an enterprise's intent, result in the reclassification of all instruments in this category as either available-for-sale or held for trading. (IAS 39 (r2000).83) (See **12.6.2**).
Available-for-sale financial assets (AFS)	
Basis of subsequent measurement	Fair value. (IAS 39 (r2000).69)
Remeasurement gains/ losses	An enterprise is permitted to make an upfront election in respect of all AFS assets either to include such gains/losses:

(1) in net profit or loss in the period it occurs; or
(2) directly in equity (via the statement of changes in equity) until the asset is disposed of at which time the cumulative gain/loss previously recognised in equity is included in net profit or loss for the period. (IAS 39 (r2000).103(b))

Note that the election relates to *all* assets in the AFS category. For example it would be inappropriate to elect option 1 for all bonds held but option 2 for all equity securities held.

Under IAS 8 (r1993), *Net Profit or Loss for the Period, Fundamental Errors and Changes in Accounting Policies*, a voluntary change in accounting policy may be made only if the change results in a more appropriate presentation of events or transactions. The IASC Board believe that this is highly unlikely to be the case for a change from option 1 to option 2. (IAS 39 (r2000).105)

Where, the change in fair value of an AFS security includes a time related component, this benefit is effectively realised over the life of the instrument and should therefore be reported in net profit or loss on that basis. For example, where a debt security is remeasured to fair value, the gains or losses recognised as a result of changes in fair value contain two components. These components are the change in fair value arising from the movement in market interest rates as well as the change relating to the passage of time which would reflect the accrual of any coupon as well as the amortisation of any premium or discount. Although IAS 39 (r2000) does not specifically provide for the separate recognition of the components of fair value which are not related to market movements, but which instead are a function of time, IGC 103-1 permits this. Accordingly, the change in fair value attributable to the

	accrual of coupons and the amortisation of any premium or discount on available-for-sale assets should be taken out of equity and recognised in net profit or loss in the period in which it occurs on an effective yield basis. IAS 12 (r2000), *Income Taxes*, provides guidance on reporting the tax effects of items charged directly to equity and therefore also covers the tax effects of unrealised holding gains and losses reported directly in equity for certain hedging activities and available for sale securities. It concludes that current tax and deferred tax should be charged directly to equity if the tax relates to items that are credited or charged, in the same or a different period, directly to equity. (IAS 12 (r2000).61) Similarly, the effect on minority interests of those items reflected directly in equity occurring during the year should be adjusted against minority interest in the consolidated balance sheet. (IAS 27.15 (c) and 26) See *Example 12.13* for an example of a sale of an available-for-sale security.
Impairment	If a loss on remeasurement to fair value is recognised directly in equity (option 2 above), and it can be objectively determined that the asset is impaired (see **12.11**), the cumulative net loss, including any portion attributable to foreign currency changes, previously recognised in equity for that asset is recognised in net profit or loss for the period even though the asset is not derecognised. (IAS 39 (r2000).117 and IGC 117-2) The amount of the loss to be removed from equity is the excess of the acquisition cost (net of any principal repayment and amortisation) over the current fair value (for equity instruments) or recoverable amount (for debt instruments), less any impairment loss on that asset previously recognised in net profit or loss. (IAS 39 (r2000).118)

	The recoverable amount is calculated as the present value of expected future cash flows discounted using the current market rate of interest for a similar financial asset. (IAS 39 (r2000).118) The current market rate of interest for a similar financial asset is its effective yield. The effective yield is already adjusted by the market for the impairment loss it expects, and therefore if this rate is used, cash flows should not be adjusted for expected impairment loss (IGC 118-1). Subsequent write-backs of the impairment loss are permitted if the recovery can be objectively related to an event occurring after the write-down and are adjusted against net profit or loss. (IAS 39 (r2000).119) Note that a fall in fair value of an AFS asset is not necessarily evidence of impairment, and cumulative negative amounts can be reported in equity until there is objective evidence of impairment (IGC 117-1). See **12.11** for further discussion of impairment.
Changes in classification	Instruments may only be reclassified into the AFS category from the held-to-maturity category since transfers out of the held-for-trading category are prohibited by IAS 39 (r2000).107 and originated loans may not be classified as AFS (IAS 39 (r2000).75). It may become appropriate to carry a financial asset as held-to-maturity rather than at fair value (available for sale or held for trading) under the following circumstances: • there has been a change of intent or ability; • a reliable measure of fair value is no longer available (expected to be rare); or • two financial years have passed since the HTM category was tainted. In such cases, the fair value carrying amount of the financial asset on the date of change

	becomes its new amortised cost. Any previous gain or loss that has been recognised in equity should be accounted for as follows: (a) in the case of an asset with a fixed maturity, such gains/losses are amortised over the remaining life of the investment. Any difference between the new amortised cost and maturity amount should be amortised over the remaining life of the financial asset as an adjustment of yield, similar to amortisation of premium and discount; and (b) in the case of an asset without a fixed maturity, such gains/losses are left in equity until the asset has been sold or otherwise disposed of, at which time it should enter into the determination of net profit or loss. (IAS 39 (r2000).92) In the case of transfers from the available-for-sale category to the held-for-trading category, where the changes in fair value have been recognised in equity for the available-for-sale security, it would be inappropriate to recognise a gain or loss on the transfer since this would provide scope to manage the timing of revenue recognition in net profit or loss. Instead, the gain or loss on transfer should remain in equity until the instrument is disposed of, at which stage the full amount is recognised in net profit or loss in accordance with the principle set out in paragraph 92(b) above (IGC 107-1).
Loans and receivables originated by the enterprise and not held-for-trading (financial assets)	
Basis of subsequent measurement	Amortised cost unless the asset does not have a fixed maturity in which case it is measured at cost. (IAS 39 (r2000).69 and 73)
Remeasurement gains/ losses	Not applicable if assets are carried at cost. For assets carried at amortised cost, the amortisation amount (determined using the effective interest rate method) is reflected in

	net profit or loss for the period. (IAS 39 (r2000).108, 73 and 10)
Impairment	The treatment is the same as that for held-to-maturity investments. See above table.
Changes in classification	This is not specifically addressed but since these may only be reclassified into the held-for-trading category (IAS 39 (r2000).10 and .75), this would result in these being carried at fair value with changes in fair value recognised in net profit or loss in the period in which they occur. The guidance related to reclassifications out of held-to-maturity investments would appear to be applicable. See above table.
Financial assets and liabilities held-for-trading (including derivatives)	
Basis of subsequent	Fair value. (IAS 39 (r2000).69)
Remeasurement gains/ losses	Recognised in net profit or loss in the period in which it arises. (IAS 39 (r2000).103(a))
Impairment	Not applicable since the full loss is already recognised in net profit or loss.
Changes in classification	Since the designation as held for trading is based on the objective for initially acquiring it, reclassifications out of this category are not permitted. (IAS 39 (r2000).107) Reclassification of a financial asset into the trading category are made only if there is evidence of a recent actual pattern of short-term profit taking that justifies such reclassification. (IAS 39 (r2000).107)
Financial assets/liabilities carried at fair value where fair value cannot be reliably determined	
Basis of subsequent measurement	Cost or amortised cost depending on whether the instrument has a specified maturity. (IAS 39 (r2000).69 and 73)
Remeasurement gains/ losses	In respect of assets carried at amortised cost, the amortisation amount (determined using the effective interest rate method) is reflected in net profit or loss for the period. (IAS 39 (r2000).108, 73 and 10)

Impairment	Use the same procedure as for held-to-maturity investments, with the exception that the impairment loss is determined based on the difference between the asset's carrying amount and the present value of expected future cash flows discounted at the current market interest rate for a similar financial asset (rather than using the original effective interest rate). (IAS 39 (r2000).115) If subsequently the enterprise has objective evidence that the asset is no longer impaired, the impairment loss may be reversed (DIGC 115-1).
Changes in classification	Changes in classification in respect of this category are based solely on whether fair value is reliably determinable. Once this becomes reliably determinable, these instruments are treated as either AFS or as held for trading, as appropriate. Gains or losses are then recognised based on whether it is subsequently classified as held-for-trading or available-for-sale and, in the case of available-for-sale, on the company's policy for recognising changes in either equity or net profit or loss. (IAS 39 (r2000).91) In the rare circumstances that this is permitted under IAS 39 (r2000).92 (see available-for-sale table) if it is subsequently classified as held-to-maturity, the fair value carrying amount becomes its new amortised cost. Amortisation is based on the difference between the maturity amount and the new carrying value. Previous gains/losses recognised directly in equity are amortised over the remaining life of the held to maturity investment or, if the instrument does not have a fixed maturity, are kept in equity until the instrument is disposed of when the full amount is recognised in net profit/ loss. (IAS 39 (r2000).92)
Financial liabilities (except held-for-trading and derivative liabilities)	
Basis of subsequent measurement	Amortised cost. (IAS 39 (r2000).93)

Remeasurement gains/ losses	The amortisation amount (determined using the effective interest rate method) is reflected in net profit or loss for the period. (IAS 39 (r2000).108, and 10; IGC 93-1)
Changes in classification	Not specifically addressed under IAS 39 (r2000), however, if these are subsequently classified as held-for-trading, the treatment should follow that discussed under changes in classification for held-to-maturity investments (see above).
Hedges	
Basis of subsequent measurement	Fair value (see **12.18–12.26** on Hedging).
Remeasurement gains/ losses	Fair value hedges: the gain/loss in respect of both the hedging instrument and hedged item are recognised in net profit or loss in the period in which these arise (regardless of the classification of the underlying item) and the carrying amount of the hedged item is adjusted accordingly). (IAS 39 (r2000).153–157) Cash flow hedges: the gain/loss on the hedging instrument is recognised directly in equity to the extent the hedge is effective. The ineffective portion (as defined) is recognised immediately in net profit or loss if the hedging instrument is a derivative, or directly in equity if it is the enterprise's policy and the hedging instrument is not a derivative. (IAS 39 (r2000).158–163) Refer to **12.18–12.26** on Hedging for the subsequent treatment of the portion recognised directly in equity and for the treatment of hedges of a net investment in a foreign entity.
Impairment	Not specifically addressed, however, this would be taken into account in determining the fair value of the hedging instrument and would therefore affect hedge effectiveness.
Changes in classification	Changes in treatment are based on the failure of a hedge's effectiveness in offsetting changes in fair value or cash flows of the hedged item. Refer to **12.18–12.26** on Hedge accounting for more details.

12.10.3 Examples of sales of securities held for trading and available for sale

Since all changes in the fair value of financial instruments classified as 'held for trading' are reported in net profit or loss as they occur, the sale of a trading security does not necessarily give rise to a gain or loss. Generally, a debit to cash (or settlement date receivable) is recorded for the sales proceeds and a credit is recorded to remove the security at its fair value (or sales price) (see **12.9.2** and *Example 12.11*). If the enterprise is not taxed on a mark-to-market basis (i.e., is not taxed on unrealised gains or losses), the deferred tax accounts would be adjusted.

Example 12.12 Sale of securities held for trading

Enterprise X has an investment in an equity security, Y, that was acquired late in 20x1 with a cost of £1,000 and which was classified as 'held for trading'. Assume that X's effective tax rate is 40 per cent and the enterprise is not taxed on a market-to-market (fair value) basis. At the close of 20x1, X's investment in Y shares had a fair value of £1,100; thus, X increased the carrying amount of the trading security by £100, recording a gain in income of £100. Enterprise X also recognised deferred tax expense (and a deferred tax liability) of £40 (£100 × 40%) in 20x1. If X sells its shares in Y for £1,100 early in 20x2, no gain or loss would be recognised and the following journal entry would be made:

		Debit	*Credit*
Cash		£1,100	
Deferred tax liability		40	
Current tax expense		40	
	Investment in trading security		£1,100
	Deferred tax expense		40
	Current tax liability		40

(To record the sale of trading securities carried at fair value in 20x2)

Enterprises have different bookkeeping methods for available-for-sale securities. Generally, a debit to cash (or trade date receivable) is recorded for the sales proceeds and a credit is recorded to remove the security at its fair value (or sales price). The amount recorded in equity, representing the unrealised gain or loss at the date of sale, is released into net profit or loss and the deferred tax accounts are adjusted. Some adjustment to this procedure will be necessary for enterprises that have not yet recorded the security's change in value up to the point of sale (perhaps because fair value changes are recorded at the end of each interim period) or when write-downs for impairment have been recognised.

Example 12.13 Sale of available for-sale-security

Enterprise X has an investment in Y, an equity security, that was acquired in 20x1 with a cost of €1,000 that is classified as AFS. X's effective tax rate is 40 per cent, and the enterprise is not taxed on a marked-to-market basis. At the close of 20x1, X's investment in Y shares had a fair value of €1,100; thus, X increased the carrying amount of the AFS securities by €100 and recorded a gain, net of related deferred income tax expense, of €60 (€100 – [€100 × 40%]) in the separate component of shareholders' equity; additionally, a deferred tax liability of €40 was recorded at the end of 20x1. If X sells its shares in Y for €1,100 in 20x2, the gain previously reported in stockholders' equity is reversed and the deferred tax accounts are adjusted as shown in the following journal entry:

	Debit	*Credit*
Cash	€1,100	
Deferred tax liability	40	
Current tax expense (Income Statement)	40	
Shareholders' equity	60	
Investment in AFS security		€1,100
Realised gain (Income Statement)		100
Current tax liability		40

(To record the sale of AFS securities in 20x2)

In the case of interest based financial instruments where changes in fair value are recognised directly in net profit or loss (whether AFS or HFT), certain enterprises determine the fair value taking interest accrued to date into account (sometimes referred to as marking-to-fair value based on the 'all-in' or 'dirty' price). When coupon cash flows are received in respect of these instruments prior to maturity, since the accrual of these cash flows is already included in the fair value adjustments recognised in net profit or loss, the receipt of cash represents the realisation of a portion of the asset's value and there is no additional entry to net profit or loss. If, however, the enterprise determines the mark-to-market on a 'clean' price basis which does not include the interest accrued to date, an additional journal entry would be required to recognise this interest in the income statement. Each of these methods should provide an identical net result in the income statement and balance sheet, although the specific journal entries would differ.

12.10.4 Comparison with UK GAAP

UK GAAP does not include similar classifications to IAS 39 (r2000). Some financial assets are treated as investments under UK GAAP; some financial instruments are treated as current assets and current liabilities, e.g., receivables and payables, some financial liabilities are capital instruments and are treated following the rules in FRS 4, *Capital Instruments*. As a result, most assets and liabilities are carried at cost or amortised. Exceptions, are assets and liabilities held for trading and some investments which are carried at valuation.

12.10.5 Comparison with US GAAP

IAS 39 (r2000) provides a one-time election to record the change in fair value of available-for-sale (AFS) financial assets in either net profit or loss or equity. US GAAP requires that until realised the changes in value of AFS securities and certain deferred taxes be recorded in equity, which under US GAAP is referred to as Other Comprehensive Income (OCI). An entity following US GAAP could achieve the same result as IAS 39 (r2000) by initially classifying securities in the trading category, since the related unrealised gains and losses are recorded in earnings.

IAS 39 (r2000) also provides that 'financial liabilities held for trading' (including short sales) are recorded at fair value with the changes in value recorded in earnings. (IAS 39 (r2000).18) US GAAP does not have a held-for-trading category for financial liabilities, although certain entities, such as broker dealers, are subject to fair value accounting for liabilities. Under US GAAP, all liabilities are accounted for at amortised cost with the only exception being for derivative financial liabilities, which are recorded at fair value.

12.10.6 Fair value accounting in certain financial services industries

In some countries, either based on national law or accepted industry practice, enterprises in certain financial services industries measure substantially all financial assets at fair value. Examples of such industries include, in certain countries, mutual funds, unit trusts, securities brokers and dealers, and insurance companies. Under IAS 39 (r2000), such an enterprise will be able to continue to measure its financial assets at fair value if its financial assets are classified under this Standard as either available-for-sale or held-for-trading. (IAS 39 (r2000).120)

12.10.7 Fair value measurement

Under IAS 39 (r2000), fair value is a more appropriate measure for most financial assets than amortised cost. The exceptions to fair value accounting are listed above. In addition to most financial assets, financial liabilities held for trading and derivatives that are liabilities are also measured at fair value, except for a derivative that is linked to and that must be settled by delivery of an unquoted equity instrument whose fair value cannot be reliably measured, which should be measured at cost. (IAS 39 (r2000).93)

'*Fair value* is the amount for which an asset could be exchanged, or a liability settled, between knowledgeable, willing parties in an arm's length transaction.' (IAS 39 (r2000).10)

'The existence of published price quotations in an active market is normally the best evidence of fair value. The appropriate quoted market price for an asset held or liability to be issued is usually the current bid price and, for an asset to be acquired or liability held, the current offer or asking price. When current bid and offer prices are unavailable, the price of the most recent transaction may provide evidence of the current fair value provided that there has not been a significant change in economic circumstances between the transaction date and the reporting date. When an enterprise has matching asset and liability positions, it may appropriately use mid-market prices as a basis for establishing fair values.' (IAS 39 (r2000). 99)

IAS 39 (r2000) does not define mid-market prices further but this is interpreted to mean the mid (or average) of both the bid and ask prices rather than the average of the bid prices or the average of the ask prices.

Assets that do not form part of matching asset-liability positions must be valued at the bid price. The use of mid-market prices is not permitted even if, for example, required by the regulations governing an investment fund. The existence of regulations requiring a different basis of measurement for specific purposes does not justify a departure from the general requirement in IAS 39 (r2000) (IGC 99-1).

An enterprise is free to choose which prices are used to measure fair value within the constraints of IAS 39 (r2000).99, however, the enterprise's fair value measurement policy should be applied consistently across instruments and within instrument classes (this is particularly important in the construction of yield curves). Where there is a considerable difference (or spread) between the bid and offer prices, there should be some objective basis for selecting a particular estimate.

Market quotations can ordinarily be obtained from several different sources such as quoted prices on a financial exchange, prices from market makers who are willing to quote and trade at their own prices (sometimes referred to as a dealer market), or from independent brokers (sometimes referred to as brokered markets). Valuations may also be obtained from appraisers, from specialists firms that offer pricing services or from database services (such as Bloombergs™). Where market quotations can be obtained from several different markets or different sources, the price in the most active market or from the most active source will generally be the best indicator of fair value.

However, market quotations that are obtained from any source other than the exchange market (typically described as the over the counter or OTC market), are generally not as precise or as reliable as the exchange market quotations. In addition, different price quotes might be obtained from different participants in the same non-exchange market. Since these can vary widely between participants, enterprises that place reliance on independent quotations should obtain more than one quotation to ensure that the fair value estimate is appropriate. The market price of an exchange-traded financial instrument is determined only when an actual transaction occurs. The price of the most recent transaction, however, does not necessarily mean that the next transaction will settle for the same amount. This is because the factors that determine a financial instrument's fair value may change and would typically be affected by other considerations such as available depth (liquidity in respect of the individual instrument) and breadth (liquidity across instruments and number of willing participants) of the particular market. However, an active exchange market will generally provide a good indicator of market value at a given point in time.

Fair value is not adjusted for any costs required to close out positions since the definition of fair value is premised on the assumption of an exchange as a going concern. Fair value is not, therefore, the amount that an enterprise would receive or pay in a forced transaction, involuntary liquidation, or distress sale. (IAS 39 (r2000).98)

Reliability of measurement of fair value

There is a presumption that fair value can be reliably determined for most financial assets classified as available-for-sale or held-for-trading. There is a further presumption that fair values can be determined reliably even for complex derivatives, with the exception of those linked to an unquoted equity instrument as described below (IGC 70-1).

The presumption is based on the premise that an enterprise is unlikely to purchase a financial instrument for which it does not expect to be able to obtain a reliable measure of fair value after acquisition. However, that presumption can be overcome for an investment in an equity instrument (including an investment that is in substance an equity instrument) that does not have a quoted market price in an active market and for which other methods of reasonably estimating fair value are clearly inappropriate or unworkable. The presumption can also be overcome for a derivative that is linked to and that must be settled by delivery of such an unquoted equity instrument. (IAS 39 (r2000).70) When the presumption is overcome, the instrument is carried at cost if it has no specific maturity date or at amortised cost if it does have a specified maturity. (IAS 39 (r2000).69 and 73) If, however, an enterprise is able to estimate reliably the fair value of an unquoted equity instrument, it should measure such instrument at fair value. It should further document its methodology for estimating fair value as well as its basis for concluding that the fair value can be determined reliably, and apply that methodology consistently (IGC 70-2).

If an equity instrument is represented solely by underlying investments in assets for which fair values can be determined reliably, the fair value of that equity instrument can be measured reliably.

> 'The fair value of a financial instrument is reliably measurable if:
>
> (a) the variability in the range of reasonable fair value estimates is not significant for that instrument; or
>
> (b) if the probabilities of the various estimates within the range can be reasonably assessed and used in estimating fair value.'
>
> (IAS 39 (r2000).95)

> 'Situations in which fair value *is* reliably measurable include:
>
> (a) a financial instrument for which there is a published price quotation in an active public securities market for that instrument;
>
> (b) a debt instrument that has been rated by an independent rating agency and whose cash flows can be reasonably estimated; and
>
> (c) a financial instrument for which there is an appropriate valuation model and for which the data inputs to that model can be measured reliably because the data come from active markets.'
>
> (IAS 39 (r2000).96)

Before the presumption is overcome, whether in respect of equity instruments or other financial assets or liabilities, there is an initial requirement that all available and appropriate valuation and estimation techniques have been assessed. It should be capable of demonstration that other methods of reasonably estimating fair value are clearly inappropriate or unworkable.

It is possible that in situations where valuation techniques require sophisticated assumptions or comprehensive data sets to arrive at reliable estimates of fair value, enterprises, particularly smaller ones, will be forced to incur significant additional costs. In this case, provided that the criteria in IAS 39 (r2000).95 are satisfied, it may be more appropriate to use simplified assumptions (subject to adequate disclosure) to provide a reliable estimate of fair value at a reasonable cost. Sensitivity analysis should be performed to determine the sensitivity of the outcome to changes in key variables. This sensitivity information should be disclosed if it is material to the enterprise.

Techniques for estimating fair value

> 'If there is infrequent activity in a market, the market is not well established (for example, some 'over the counter' markets) or small volumes are traded relative to the number of trading units of a financial instrument to be valued, quoted market prices may not be indicative of the fair value of the instrument. In some cases where the volume traded is relatively small, a price quotation for a larger block may be available from the market maker in that instrument. In other circumstances, as well as when a quoted market price is not available, estimation techniques may be used to determine fair value with sufficient reliability to satisfy the requirements of this Standard. Techniques that are well established in financial markets include reference to the current market value of another instrument

that is substantially the same, discounted cash flow analysis, and option pricing models. In applying discounted cash flow analysis, an enterprise uses the discount rate(s) equal to the prevailing rate of return for financial instruments having substantially the same terms and characteristics, including the creditworthiness of the debtor, the remaining term over which the contractual interest rate is fixed, the remaining term to repayment of the principal, and the currency in which payments are to be made.' (IAS 39 (r2000).100)

IGC 100-1 requires the use of current market quotations to determine fair value unless there is objective, reliable evidence that validates the existence of an adjustment to fair value in respect of a control premium or blockage factor in pricing a particular asset. An example of such evidence would be a contract with a third party to sell at a specified price. An independent quote, of itself, is not considered to be objective or reliable to justify such an adjustment.

'If a market does not exist for a financial instrument but a market exists for a similar financial instrument, fair value is constructed on the basis of the market price of the similar financial instrument.' (IAS 39 (r2000).101)

Similarly, 'if a market price does not exist for a financial instrument in its entirety but markets exist for its component parts, fair value is constructed on the basis of the relevant market prices.' (IAS 39 (r2000).101)

Valuation techniques should incorporate the assumptions that market participants would use in their estimates of fair values, including assumptions about prepayment rates, rates of estimated credit losses, and interest or discount rates. (IAS 39 (r2000).97)

In the event that fair value has to be estimated based on certain assumptions in the absence of objective and verifiable external supporting information, that estimation should be based on the best available information. This should not take into account any additional adjustment for uncertainty in either the valuation variables or for modelling error. In addition, the determination of fair value should be applied consistently by the enterprise in accordance with predefined, appropriate and documented valuation methodologies.

Where the capability exists to price transactions independently, the basis used to value financial instruments that have been acquired from external parties in arms-length transactions, should be consistent with that used by the entity in pricing the initial transactions (and adjusted for any subsequent changes to the terms of the contracts).

A number of decisions must be made when using models to estimate fair value. These decisions involve the selection of methods, formulas, and assumptions (including the probability distributions of key variables and the required data sets). Each of these decisions requires judgement, and these decisions will vary depending on the characteristics of the particular instrument. Although the models used to estimate the value of financial instruments will differ depending on the type of instrument being valued, many market valuation techniques are founded on arbitrage arguments, which are based on the premise that a risk-free profit cannot occur in the market-place. If risk-free arbitrage profits cannot occur, the theoretical value of a financial instrument must be equal to the value of an equivalent alternative investment. This assumption may not be appropriate for nascent and emerging markets where various sources of inefficiency could exist which could distort the results of models developed under assumptions of efficient markets.

Where fair value is calculated based on the price of a similar instrument, certain adjustments to fair value may be required to take into account the effect of unearned credit spreads, differences in credit risk, basis risk or liquidity risk (which is a particularly difficult and extremely subjective exercise). These adjustments should only be made where a sufficiently reliable basis exists for doing so (for example, taking into account liquidity differentials on similar instruments where a high degree of correlation can be demonstrated). IAS 39 (r2000).96(c) states that where an appropriate valuation model exists, for fair value to be reliably measurable, the data inputs to that model should come from active markets. No guidance is provided regarding what constitutes active markets and judgement is required in determining the integrity and appropriateness of the various inputs.

When valuation techniques are used, the determination of fair value should incorporate those assumptions that market participants would use in their estimates of value. Conceptually, if the timing and amounts of future cash flows could be determined absolutely, the discount rate would be the risk-free rate. However, an adjustment to the risk-free rate or risk premium is necessary to recognise that defaults, prepayments and other adjustments cannot be estimated precisely.

There are a number of methods that can be used to determine the appropriate discount rate for each cash flow. For example, rates may be constructed by building each component, starting with the risk-free rate. The components would include factors for accepting risk (e.g., risk of credit losses and prepayments), unavoidable expenses (e.g., servicing), volatility (e.g., volatility relating to credit and prepayments) and liquidity considerations. Rates also can be obtained directly or developed from market interest rates of comparable instruments. Discount rates are developed by isolating the risk premium of the comparable instrument and adding it to the applicable risk-free rate. The risk premium can be isolated by computing the embedded spread to a risk-free rate or the implied option-adjusted spread.

Techniques for estimating fair value include matrix pricing (which estimates fair value based on adjusted prices of similar instruments), option-adjusted spread models, and fundamental analysis.

Models can produce results that range from extremely precise to less precise depending on the sophistication of the model and the use of simplifying assumptions to facilitate computation. It must be recognised that no model is a perfect substitute for values evidenced by active market transactions and all models must be adjusted to comprehend the unique characteristics of the instrument being modelled. There is an unavoidable trade-off between simple, inexpensive models that are easy to use and complex, system intensive and sophisticated models that are difficult to use. Regardless of the level of sophistication, a model produces only a theoretical representation of market value and its effectiveness should be judged based on the necessity of obtaining the desired level of provision (through techniques such as backtesting). These limitations must be understood in the determination of fair value and should be assessed in determining the variability in the range of reasonable fair value estimates.

Example 12.14 Adjustments to fair value

Assume that enterprise X has an equity investment comprising 15 per cent (1.5 million shares) of company Y, whose equity shares are traded on the Sydney Stock Exchange (a public market). The current market capitalisation of Y is A$1 billion based on 10 million total shares outstanding (i.e., company Y's shares are currently trading at A$100 per share). Due to the significant size of the investment, several independent bids are obtained which provide a reliable measure of fair value, if X sold its entire 1.5 million company Y shares over a short space of time. These techniques indicate that X would be forced to accept a 15 per cent discount to the prevailing market price (A$85). X cannot depart from the quoted market price solely because independent bids indicate that a different price could be obtained. Unless a bid represented a firm contract to purchase the shares for A$85 in the immediate future, it would be very difficult to justify an adjustment to the quoted price.

Comparison with UK GAAP

This is an area that is not addressed to any significant extent by UK requirements, though mid-market prices are often used to fair value financial instruments.

Comparison with US GAAP

Under US GAAP, SFAS 107, *Disclosures About Fair Value of Financial Instruments*, sets out detailed provisions for the disclosure of, and examples relating to the estimation of, fair values for disclosure purposes. Fair value measurement provisions relating to specific instruments are contained in the relevant SFAS statements (principally SFAS 115, *Accounting for Certain Investments in Debt and Equity Securities*, and SFAS 133, *Accounting for Derivative Instruments and Hedging Activities*).

Unquoted equity instruments
US GAAP provides an exemption from fair value requirements for equity securities that are not traded, including forwards and options on unquoted equity instruments that are required to be settled by delivery. The exemption is not permitted for derivative instruments that have net settlement provisions. Accordingly, under US GAAP, restricted stock is not carried at fair value. Restricted stock for the purpose of applying US GAAP (SFAS 115) includes equity securities for which sale is restricted by governmental or contractual requirement (other than in connection with being pledged as collateral). However, it excludes instances where the requirement terminates within one year or if the holder has the power by contract or otherwise to cause the requirement to be met within one year. Any portion of the security that can reasonably be expected to qualify for sale within one year is not considered restricted.

Also, under US GAAP, an enterprise does not look beyond the form of an equity investment to determine whether fair value can be readily determined. Accordingly, if the net assets that underlie the unquoted equity instrument have readily determinable fair values, they are not used and the unquoted equity instrument is carried at cost.

Equity instruments traded only in a foreign market
Under US GAAP, the fair value of an equity security which is traded only in a foreign market is not considered to be readily determinable and, therefore, it is carried at cost unless the breadth and scope of that foreign market are comparable to one of the US markets. (SFAS 115.3(b)) There is no equivalent requirement under IAS 39 (r2000). Instead, IAS 39 (r2000).100 requires the adjustment of published price quotations to arrive at a reliable measure of fair value where this is not represented in the published price quotation as a result of insufficient depth or scope in the foreign market.

Use of estimates
IAS 39 (r2000) provides an exemption from fair value requirements for any financial asset for which there is no price quotation in an active market and whose fair value cannot be measured reliably. In contrast, US GAAP requires fair value accounting for all derivative instruments and does not permit a fair value exclusion based on the inability to measure fair value reliably. US GAAP requires that an entity provide its best estimate of fair value based on the information available even where considerable judgement is required about the methods and assumptions to be used in various circumstances. (SFAS 107.22 and 59)

Blockage adjustment
US GAAP does not permit an adjustment for blockage when a company has a significant investment in a particular security and believes that an attempt to sell the entire investment at one time would significantly affect the security's market price. If a quoted market price is available, for an

instrument, the fair value to be used is the product of the number of trading units of the instrument times its market price. (SFAS 115.37)

Although an adjustment for blockage is permitted under IAS 39 (r2000).100, IGC 100-1 makes it clear that this would be difficult to do reliably in the absence of quotations from market makers and hence the circumstances in which this would be applied are expected to be extremely rare.

12.10.8 Amortised cost measurement

In **12.10.1** the following financial assets are excluded from the requirement to be carried at fair value:

(a) loans and receivables originated by the enterprise and not held for trading;
(b) held-to-maturity investments; and
(c) any financial asset that does not have a quoted market price in an active market and whose fair value cannot be reliably measured.

Subsequent to initial recognition, the financial assets that are excluded from fair value *and* that have a fixed maturity should be measured at amortised cost using the effective interest method. (IAS 39 (r2000).73) Additionally, all financial liabilities, other than liabilities held-for-trading and derivative that are liabilities should be measured at amortised cost using the effective interest rate method. (IAS 39 (r2000).93 and IGC 93-1)

> 'The *effective interest method* is a method of calculating amortisation using the effective interest rate of a financial asset or financial liability.' (IAS 39 (r2000).10)
>
> 'The *effective interest rate* (effective yield) is the rate that exactly discounts the expected stream of future cash payments through maturity or the next market-based repricing date to the current net carrying amount of the financial asset or financial liability. That computation should include all fees and points paid or received between parties to the contract. The effective interest rate is sometimes termed the level yield to maturity or to the next repricing date, and is the internal rate of return of the financial asset or financial liability for that period.' (IAS 39 (r2000).10) 'The rate is a historical rate for a fixed rate instrument carried at amortised cost and a current market rate for a floating rate instrument or an instrument carried at fair value.' (IAS 32 (r1998).61) IGC 76-1 confirms that the amortisation of a variable rate debt instrument issued at a premium or discount, is calculated to the next repricing date if fair value will become par value at that date; otherwise it is calculated over the remaining life of the instrument. In the latter case, the premium or discount most likely relates to credit factors and not market interest rate factors and hence should be amortised over the life of the instrument.

For a portfolio of loans that is subject to prepayment, the effective interest rate is based on the expected cash payments rather than the contractual cash payments (IGC 10-19).

> '*Amortised cost of a financial asset or financial liability* is the amount at which the financial asset or liability was measured at initial recognition minus principal repayments, plus or minus the cumulative amortisation of any difference between that initial amount and the maturity amount, and minus any write-down (directly or through the use of an allowance account) for impairment or uncollectability.' (IAS 39 (r2000).10)

When an instrument has stepped interest payments, amortisation is still calculated based on the effective yield to achieve a level yield to maturity (i.e., a constant interest rate on the carrying amount) (IGC 10-12).

If an instrument is not required to be repaid and has a contractual fixed rate or market rates to perpetuity, it is carried at cost and not at amortised cost since there are no repayments of principal (IGC 10-13). If, however, the instrument is not required to be repaid and the contractual fixed rate becomes zero after a specified period of time, the instrument must be amortised over the period in which it pays interest. The interest payment is considered to have a principal payment embedded in it (IGC 10-14). Such an instrument can be classified as held-to-maturity provided the principal is required to be amortised over a specified period of time (IGC 10-17).

See **6.6.1** for a numerical example of the effective interest method. A further example is set out in IGC 73-1.

All financial assets are subject to review for impairment as discussed in **12.11**.

12.10.9 Cost measurement

In **12.10.1** the following financial instruments were stated to be excluded from the requirement to be carried at fair value:

(a) loans and receivables originated by the enterprise and not held for trading;
(b) held-to-maturity investments; and
(c) any financial asset that does not have a quoted market price in an active market and whose fair value cannot be reliably measured.

Subsequent to initial recognition, the financial instruments that are excluded from fair value *and* that *do not* have a fixed maturity should be measured at cost. (IAS 39 (r2000).73)

Cost is the fair value of the consideration given (in the case of an asset) or received (in the case of a liability) for it. Transaction costs are included in cost. (IAS 39 (r2000).66)

> 'The fair value of the consideration given or received normally is determinable by reference to the transaction price or other market prices. If such market prices

are not reliably determinable, the fair value of the consideration is estimated as the sum of all future cash payments or receipts, discounted, if the effect of doing so would be material, using the prevailing market rate(s) of interest for a similar instrument (similar as to currency, term, type of interest rate, and other factors) of an issuer with a similar credit rating'. (IAS 39 (r2000).67)

All financial assets are subject to review for impairment as discussed in **12.11**.

12.11 Impairment

'A financial asset is impaired if its carrying amount is greater than its estimated recoverable amount.' (IAS 39 (r2000).109)

An enterprise is required to assess at each balance sheet date whether there is any objective evidence that a financial asset or group of assets may be impaired. IAS 39 (r2000) lists several indicators of such evidence, which are discussed below. If any such evidence exists, the enterprise estimates the recoverable amount of that asset or group of assets and recognises an impairment loss. The recognition and measurement of an impairment loss depends on the category in which the asset is held (HTM, AFS, etc.) The table in **12.10.2** sets out the impairment recognition and measurement principles for each category of asset.

IGC 111-3 makes it clear that fixed provisioning loss ratios (often based on regulatory requirements) cannot be used as the basis for recognising an impairment, unless they are determined in accordance with the provisions of IAS 39 (r2000), that is, based on the present value of estimated future cash flows. Similarly, impairment amounts do not include unsupported amounts, sometimes referred to as 'general contingency reserves' (IGC 111-4).

Estimates of recoverable cash flows should take into account cash flows that may result from foreclosure (such as collateral), whether or not foreclosure is probable (IGC 113-1). If foreclosure is probable, the collateral is not recognised as an asset separate from the impaired asset until it qualifies for recognition, which is usually when the transfer of the collateral is completed (IGC 113-2).

12.11.1 Objective evidence of impairment

'Objective evidence that a financial asset or group of assets is impaired or uncollectable includes information that comes to the attention of the holder of the asset about:

(a) significant financial difficulty of the issuer;
(b) an actual breach of contract, such as a default or delinquency in interest or principal payments;
(c) granting by the lender to the borrower, for economic or legal reasons

relating to the borrower's financial difficulty, of a concession that the lender would not otherwise consider;

(d) a high probability of bankruptcy or other financial reorganisation of the issuer;

(e) recognition of an impairment loss on that asset in a prior financial reporting period;

(f) the disappearance of an active market for that financial asset due to financial difficulties; or

(g) a historical pattern of collections of accounts receivable that indicates that the entire face amount of a portfolio of accounts receivable will not be collected.'

(IAS 39 (r2000).110)

However, the disappearance of an active market because an enterprise's securities are no longer publicly traded is not evidence of impairment. Similarly, a downgrade of an enterprise's credit rating is not, of itself, evidence of impairment, though it may be evidence of impairment when considered with other available information. (IAS 39 (r2000).110)

It is not necessary to identify a single, distinct, past causative event to conclude that it is probable that the entity will not be able to collect all amounts due on a financial asset. Although a credit downgrade of itself may not be sufficient to conclude that an asset is impaired, other factors should also be considered, such as: liquidity, solvency, business and financial risk exposures, levels of and trends in delinquencies in similar assets, national and local economic trends and conditions, and the fair value of collateral and guarantees (IGC 109-1).

Following the amendment to IAS 39 (r2000), impairment and uncollectability are measured and recognised individually for financial assets that are individually significant and may be measured and recognised on a portfolio basis for a group of similar financial assets, provided none of those financial assets are individually significant. (IAS 39 (r2000).112) Prior to the amendment, it was unclear whether enterprises had a choice between assessing impairment and uncollectibility on an individual or portfolio basis and hence the amendment was designed to provide clarity in line with the IASC's original intention. IGC 112-1 further states that impairment must be considered on an individual asset basis for known losses, while the portfolio approach may be used to recognise impairment for a group of similar assets and impairment cannot be identified with an individual asset in that group. A financial asset that has been individually assessed or identified as impaired cannot be included in a group of similar assets for which impairment is recognised and measured on a portfolio basis (IGC 112-2).

An immediate impairment loss is not recognised in connection with making a loan unless the loan contains off-market conditions in connection with other rights or privileges. For example, where an enterprise granting loans expects (based on past experience) that a certain percentage of the principal will not be collected, an immediate impairment loss is not recognised (IGC 110-1).

Objective evidence of the impairment of debt instruments is typically triggered by the enterprise not being able to collect an amount when due. For example, when a borrower fails to make a coupon payment on a bond, impairment should be assessed.

However, with equity instruments, there is no trigger event since there are usually no contractually specified payments to be made. In this case, an enterprise should conduct its impairment assessment at each reporting date or more frequently if required using other evidence.

Example 12.15 Objective evidence of impairment

Company B has receivables arising from sales to Company X. Company B's normal credit terms specify that payment must be made within 30 days of invoice date. Company X receivables are currently aged at 90 days, however, Company X is the largest producer in the industry and wields significant buying power over its suppliers. As part of its financing strategy, Company X usually only settles amounts due to suppliers within 60 to 90 days, however, it has no history of defaulting on payments.

Company B would not perform an impairment test since it is probable that it will be able to collect all amounts due. Although these sales fall outside Company B's normal credit terms, the short term nature of the receivable is not considered to result in a carrying amount that exceeds the net recoverable amount and there is no past history of default.

If, however, after 120 days, Company B had still not received payment from Company X, this would be considered objective evidence of impairment and Company B would conduct an impairment assessment of these receivables.

IGC 111-1 provides an example of assessing impairment in a loan restructuring situation.

Where fair value hedge accounting is applied and the carrying amount of the hedged asset is adjusted, impairment is assessed on the adjusted basis (see **12.23** for a discussion of fair value hedge accounting). The original effective yield is adjusted to take into account the adjusted basis of the loan (IGC 111-2).

12.11.2 Income recognition after impairment

Once a financial asset has been written down to its estimated recoverable amount, interest income is thereafter recognised based on the rate of interest that was used to discount the future cash flows for the purpose of measuring the recoverable amount. (IAS 39 (r2000).116)

12.11.3 Comparison with UK GAAP

This is an area that is not addressed to any significant extent by UK requirements. FRS 11, *Impairment of Fixed Assets and Goodwill*, excludes financial instruments from its scope.

12.11.4 Comparison with US GAAP

Impairment testing based on other than temporary conditions
Impairment testing under US GAAP for available-for-sale and held-to-maturity securities is based on circumstances where the impairment is considered to be 'other than temporary' and therefore involves an assessment of the probability of the impairment being reversed. Although impairment under IAS 39 (r2000) is also based on the probability of loss, it does not include the requirement that the impairment is other than temporary.

Impairment losses adjust the basis of the asset
Under US GAAP, if an impairment loss is recognised, it is reflected as a basis adjustment of the asset. Any subsequent recovery is not permitted to be recognised until the asset is sold or when it matures. IAS 39 (r2000) impairment guidelines permit reversing previous impairment-related write-downs through earnings.

12.12 Derecognition of financial assets

Historically, the accounting for sales of financial assets, in which following the sale the seller does not have any continuing involvement, has not been controversial. The accounting for the sale of securities to a third party is often without continuing involvement and is relatively straightforward. However, if the enterprise continues to have some involvement with the assets after the transfer, the appropriate accounting is not always clear and the derecognition criteria have been developed to address these instances. Examples of continuing involvement are recourse, other financial guarantees, servicing, agreements to reacquire assets, written or held options on the transferred assets, and pledges of collateral.

> '*Derecognise* means remove a financial asset or liability, or a portion of a financial asset or liability, from an enterprise's balance sheet.' (IAS 39 (r2000).10)
>
> 'An enterprise should derecognise a financial asset or a portion of a financial asset when, and only when, the enterprise loses control of the contractual rights that comprise the financial asset (or a portion of the financial asset). An enterprise loses such control if it realises the rights to benefits specified in the contract, the rights expire, or the enterprise surrenders those rights.' (IAS 39 (r2000).35)
>
> '*Control* of an asset is the power to obtain the future economic benefits that flow from the asset.'

The contractual rights comprising a financial asset are described in the definition of a financial asset as a contractual right to receive cash or another financial asset from another enterprise or a contractual right to exchange financial instruments with another enterprise under conditions that are potentially favourable.

If a financial asset is transferred to another enterprise but the transferor does *not* lose control of the contractual rights that comprise the asset, the transaction is accounted for as a collateralised (secured) borrowing (see **12.13**). (IAS 39 (r2000).36) The transferee then records the asset as an originated loan and not as a purchase of a financial asset (IGC 35-4).

In respect of 'wash-sale' transactions, whereby an asset is repurchased immediately before or soon after the sale of the same asset, the repurchase does not invalidate the original sale since the original sale had to meet the derecognition requirements to qualify as a sale (IGC 35-5).

As discussed in **12.4**, the derecognition principles in IAS 39 (r2000) do not change the requirements for sales by a parent company of an interest in a subsidiary or in respect of investments for which proportionate consolidation or the equity method of accounting was appropriate. However, derecognition principles should be applied to sales of financial assets, financial liabilities (see **12.15**), securitisations, repurchase agreements and securities lending agreements (see **12.13**).

12.12.1 Assessing control

> 'Determining whether an enterprise has lost control of a financial asset depends both on the enterprise's position and that of the transferee. Consequently, if the position of either enterprise indicates that the transferor has retained control, the transferor should not remove the asset from its balance sheet.' (IAS 39 (r2000).37)

It is important to note that the accounting between the transferor and transferee is intended to be symmetrical. If the transferor surrenders control over the transferred assets, the transferee must also have obtained control and therefore the transaction should be accounted for as a sale by the transferor and a purchase by the transferee. Otherwise, when control has not been surrendered, the transferor should account for the transaction as a borrowing, and the transferee should account for it as secured lending.

The derecognition approach in IAS 39 (r2000) is a combination of a control approach and a risks and returns approach. The Standard does not clearly indicate, however, which approach takes precedence and instead alternates between attributes of each approach in the various provisions. Therefore, both the substance of control and the extent to which the risks and returns are transferred (i.e., whether the transferee is free to pledge or exchange substantially the full fair value of the asset) should be assessed in determining whether derecognition is appropriate. Because of the complexities in assessing the transfer of control several important IGC issues provide further clarity in understanding the practical application of the provisions in IAS 39 (r2000). These are discussed in more detail in the sections below.

The control approach involves an analysis of the contractual rights comprising the transferred financial asset by examining the component assets and liabilities that exist subsequent to the transfer. The determination of control is therefore broader than just a physical ownership or custody notion. Certain elements of a risk and rewards approach have been included in the derecognition model prescribed in IAS 39 (r2000).

Derivatives are often included in transfers of financial assets, either explicitly or implicitly. The identification and evaluation of derivatives that are included in a transfer of financial assets requires a thorough understanding of the transfer structure, terms and conditions, and is crucial in applying the derecognition criteria because certain derivatives have control elements that may preclude sale treatment.

Derivatives commonly found in transfers of financial assets include put options, call options, forward or repurchase contracts, forward sales contracts and swap agreements. Put options provide the transferee with the right to require the transferor to repurchase some or all of the financial assets that were sold, for example, to repurchase delinquent receivables. Call options provide the transferor with the right to repurchase some or all of the financial assets sold to the transferee. Forward or repurchase agreements require the transferee to sell and the transferor to buy some or all of the financial assets that were sold before their scheduled maturity. Forward sales contracts require the transferor to sell and the transferee to buy additional financial assets in the future. Swap agreements effectively change one or more cash flows of the underlying transferred assets (or debt issued by a special purpose entity). For example, an interest rate swap may convert a variable rate asset to a fixed rate.

Any derivative instrument that constrains a transferee from using a transferred asset in a manner that best realises the economic benefits encompassed in the asset should be carefully evaluated in the context of control. In most situations, it will be appropriate to evaluate derivatives based on their type or form. However, different types of derivatives can result in identical economic outcomes. There are a number of factors to consider when evaluating derivatives.

Derivatives (whether stand alone or embedded), which serve as impediments to a transfer of control, are not accounted for as derivatives if they have no impact on the transferor. For example, a transferor cannot have a call option on its own assets. Such derivatives may, however, have an impact on the resultant financing liability. For example, a call on the asset may have the effect of putting the liability back to the investor/lender, in which case, it is evaluated to determine whether it is closely related to the liability (IGC 36-1).

Derivatives can operate automatically or require exercise by one of the parties; they can be exercised freely or only after the occurrence of a future event. Such a future event may be certain of occurring, such as the passage of time, or may be conditional upon an event, such as a loan becoming delinquent. Some conditional events may be probable of occurring, possible of occurring, or their occurrence may be considered remote. In some instances, it may not be possible to assess the likelihood of occurrence. The exercise price of a derivative can be fixed above, below, or equal to the market value of the financial assets at inception or it can be variable, equal to the market value at exercise date, or the result of a formula that is a function of market conditions or other future events. Derivatives can be combined to form different types of derivatives. Each of these factors impacts the degree of control retained by the transferor over the financial assets that have been transferred and the degree of control obtained by the transferee. Judgement is required in making these assessments.

There are many different terms that can be incorporated in a transaction which result in the transferor retaining control and/or economically constraining a transferee from actually selling the transferred assets, even if there is no legal constraint. A call option does not have to be in-the-money, and a put option does not have to be deep in-the-money to constrain the transferee. A very short time period to the exercise date of a call option or put option, for example, may be sufficient to constrain a transferee when the assets transferred are not readily obtainable, even though a transferee has the legal right to sell the assets subject to the call or repurchase agreement.

IAS 39 (r2000) contains specific derecognition rules to help determine when the derecognition criteria are met related to following derivatives:

- repurchase or call options;
- repurchase agreements or forward contracts;
- total return swaps/put options (retention of risks and returns).

In addition, the position of the transferee must be considered and specific guidance is provided related to the transferee.

The guidance related to each of the above four items is discussed in the following sections.

Comparison with UK GAAP

Under FRS 5, *Reporting the Substance of Transactions*, in order to derecognise an asset, the following must be transferred to others:

(a) all significant rights or other access to benefits relating to that asset, and
(b) all significant exposure to the risks inherent in those benefits.

Total derecognition thus depends on the effective removal of both control and exposure to risk of change in benefits. Removal of control alone with continued exposure to some risks prevents total derecognition, but partial derecognition may still be appropriate.

In addition, it is necessary for derecognition to demonstrate that any funds received in respect of the asset do not constitute either a liability (requiring continued gross presentation) or a form of non-recourse finance that meets the conditions for linked presentation (see below) but which does not qualify for removal from the balance sheet.

Linked presentation is relevant where non-recourse finance has been received, which is repayable only out of the proceeds of the asset(s) financed. The commercial effect for the reporting entity must be that it is committed to the disposal of the asset, but that the sale process is not yet complete. Receipt of non-recourse finance is thus the first stage of a two-stage disposal of the asset. The seller may receive further profit from the second stage of disposal, but is not required to return proceeds received. Linked presentation is not appropriate for any asset which remains in use by the seller or which the seller can reacquire. Where detailed conditions are met, the finance is shown deducted from the gross amount of the asset on the face of the balance sheet. Legally, the seller's asset is the net amount. Linked presentation therefore provides a presentation that shows the net asset on the balance sheet, supported by disclosure of the asset on a gross basis, less non-recourse finance received. IAS 39 (r2000) does not contain a similar concept of linked presentation.

Comparison with US GAAP

US GAAP relating to derecognition of financial assets is set out in SFAS 140, *Accounting for Transfers and Servicing of Financial Assets and Extinguishments of Liabilities*, which supersedes SFAS 125, *Accounting for Transfers and Servicing of Financial Assets and Extinguishments of Liabilities*, and in a FASB Staff document that provides additional guidance on over 100 related issues. Although, like IAS 39 (r2000), these provisions are defined in terms of whether a transfer of control has occurred, they differ significantly from the IAS 39 (r2000) guidelines in determining when a transferor loses control and transferred assets should be derecognised.

One of the major differences with IAS 39 (r2000) currently is that US GAAP focuses on physical considerations and legal ownership (requiring legal isolation), giving lesser weight to economic constraints on either party. Whereas IAS 39 (r2000) is based on control but also considers risks and returns, US GAAP defines transfers as the conveyance of a non-cash financial asset by and to someone other than the issuer of that financial asset. Transferring connotes the act of delivering the financial asset to another party and does not necessarily mean that the transferor has given up (economic) control or that the transferee has acquired economic control of the asset.

IAS 39 (r2000) does not require that assets be transferred to a legally isolated entity in order to meet the requirements of a sale and is instead based on the (economic) substance of control. This difference is magnified by the provisions of SIC 12, *Consolidation – Special Purpose Entities*, which effectively looks through the legal structure of these entities in determining whether control has, in reality, been transferred. There are no such comparable provisions under US GAAP (see **19.6.3** and **19.6.5**).

Transfers of investments accounted for under the equity method are generally included within the scope of the derecognition principles under US GAAP but not under IAS 39 (r2000). However, under US GAAP, there are exceptions for exchanges of similar equity method investments and for transfers of investments that are in substance real estate.

IAS 39 (r2000) guidance in respect of the control implications of derivative instruments is founded on risks and rewards as well as control and in this regard, may be more restrictive than that under US GAAP. US GAAP does not consider risks and returns and is silent regarding transfers subject to put options and total return swaps whereas IAS 39 (r2000) makes specific mention of these as instances where the transferor has not surrendered control.

Repurchase or call options

> 'A transferor has not lost control of a transferred financial asset and, therefore, the asset is *not* derecognised if, for example, the transferor has the right to reacquire the transferred asset *unless* either:
>
> (i) the asset is readily obtainable in the market; or
> (ii) the reacquisition price is fair value at the time of reacquisition.'
>
> (IAS 39 (r2000).38(a))

Where the transferor is entitled (but not obligated) to repurchase or redeem transferred assets and those assets are not readily obtainable, the transferor retains control over the contractual rights comprising the assets and sale accounting is not permitted. Instead, the transfer is accounted for as a secured borrowing (see **12.13**). Agreements that entitle the transferor to repurchase transferred financial assets are regarded as call options and are distinguished from contracts where the transferor is both entitled and obligated to reacquire the financial asset (such as forward contracts) which are dealt with in the next section.

Generally, whenever a call option on transferred assets is held by a transferor and the transferred assets are not readily obtainable elsewhere, the transferee's right to enjoy all the benefits of ownership has been diminished. If the transferee is compelled to hold the transferred assets to enable it to transfer them back to the original transferor pursuant to a call option, the transferee is constrained from exchanging those assets with a third party and the transferor has not therefore surrendered control over the right to the benefits comprising the asset.

However, if the assets are readily obtainable, the transfer will generally be accounted for as a sale since the transferee is usually not constrained legally or economically by a call option. This is because the existence of a liquid market enables the transferee to freely exchange or pledge the transferred assets within a short period of time to realise their full value (and also to obtain other assets necessary to satisfy the call option if exercised). When assets that are callable by the transferor are readily obtainable, the transferor clearly has surrendered control because of the potential to get back assets that are not identical to the assets sold. The transferee may deliver assets that are substantially the same but not necessarily exactly same assets that were sold, for example shares in a particular publicly traded company.

Readily obtainable in the market

The term, 'readily obtainable in the market' is not defined or otherwise explained in IAS 39 (r2000) and, as a result, application of this provision involves some judgement. Ordinarily, it is expected that in order to qualify under this test, a market must exist where the assets are either traded on a formal exchange or are considered liquid and trade in a market where price quotations either are published or are obtainable through another verifiable source. In other words, the determination of whether an asset is readily obtainable in the market reflects whether the transferee has access to a market where it can easily obtain a replacement asset (DIGC 38-6).

In addition, the following factors provide useful guidance in determining whether the assets are readily obtainable from the perspective of the transferee:

- whether the financial assets that would satisfy the call option or forward contract may have to be purchased from a third party at a price significantly above its estimated fair value, thus indicating that the assets are not liquid;
- whether the normal settlement period for obtaining financial assets that would satisfy the call option or forward contract is approximately equal

to or greater than the period within the delivery terms of the option or forward contract (e.g., the normal settlement period requires 30 days to obtain an asset, and the forward contract requires delivery of the asset within 15 days of the original transfer);

- whether the quantity of financial assets available for satisfying the call option or forward contract is insufficient in comparison to the quantity required in the call option or forward contract;
- whether the majority of the financial assets available to satisfy the call option or forward contract are held by one or a few entities, thus indicating that the assets are not liquid.

Intuitively, the wider the range of assets that may be used to satisfy the call option, the more likely the requirement of being readily obtainable will be satisfied. For instance, assets identical to those originally transferred may not be readily obtainable, but, if the call option permits delivery of assets that are similar to the transferred assets, they may be readily obtainable, and the condition would be satisfied.

Some call options may permit settlement in cash as an alternative to delivering the financial asset. Since cash is a readily obtainable asset, call options and forward contracts that permit settlement in cash will not preclude sale treatment, provided that the cash settlement alternative does not contain an economic penalty rendering this alternative unfeasible.

Right to reacquire at fair value

Where there is an agreement entitling the transferor to reacquire the transferred asset at a price other than its fair value, the transferor has not lost control and derecognition is not permitted.

Example 12.16 In substance call options and first right of refusal

Sale accounting is not permitted where a transferor retains a call option on transferred assets that are not readily obtainable. However, a transferor may obtain an in-substance call option through a combination of contracts and sale accounting may be appropriate depending on the particular terms and conditions of the various contracts. For example, the transferor may have a right of first refusal that permits the transferor to purchase the transferred assets at their market value should the transferee decide to sell them. The transferor may also have an arrangement that effectively allows it to force the transferee to sell the assets. The combination of the right of first refusal and an arrangement in which the transferor can effectively require the transferee to sell the transferred assets is equivalent to a call option with a strike price equal to market value at the date it is exercised. Sale accounting is appropriate in these instances because the reacquisition price is at fair value. However, in and of itself, a transferor's first right of refusal to purchase at fair value, should the transferee decide to sell the assets, does not preclude derecognition (IGC 38-1).

If a call option on transferred assets causes the transaction to be accounted for as a secured borrowing rather than a sale and the transferor allows the call option to expire unexercised, thereby releasing the transferor's control over the transferred assets, the assets which were subject to the call option should be treated as sold by the transferor. For the transferor, this requires the derecognition of these assets and the related borrowing. The transferee should recognise the financial assets and eliminate the receivable due from the transferor.

Example 12.17 Call option on readily obtainable assets

Transferor X transfers Euro bonds maturing in 2015 to a third party, Transferee Y. Transferor X also has an agreement with Transferee Y that permits it to repurchase the bonds at any time prior to maturity. Because identical securities can be readily obtained from a third party in the market-place, the call option does not prevent accounting for the transfer as a sale.

Example 12.18 Call option on not-readily obtainable assets

Assume the same facts as in the above *Example 12.17*, except that the transferred assets subject to Transferor X's call option are a pool of mortgage loans and the mortgage loans are not readily obtainable elsewhere. Under this circumstance, the call option would prevent accounting for the transfer as a sale and both parties would be required to report the transaction as a secured borrowing. The agreement contains no explicit conditions restraining Transferee Y from selling, exchanging or pledging the assets to a third party; however, it cannot prudently do so since it must have access to the original mortgage loans that were transferred in the event Transferor X exercises its purchased call option. In other words, at the exercise date of the call option, the buyer must have the assets on hand; since they are not readily obtainable from another source, the buyer can only perform under the contract if the assets are held. In this situation, the transferor has not surrendered control of the assets and the transaction should be accounted, by the transferor as a secured borrowing (see **12.13**).

Example 12.19 Call option with economic penalty

Transferor X transfers not readily obtainable financial assets to Transferee Y. The sales price and fair value of the financial assets is ¥1 billion. The transfer agreement contains a call option that allows Transferor X to repurchase the assets for ¥1.02 billion. If the call option is exercised, Transferee Y has the alternative of delivering the assets or delivering cash equal to the fair value of the assets plus an additional 25 per cent. Since the cash settlement alternative contains an economic penalty making it a highly improbable scenario, the original transfer should be considered to be a secured borrowing (see **12.13**).

Call option on beneficial interests

Where assets are transferred to a special purpose entity (SPE) created for the purpose of securitising these assets and selling securities to investors, the beneficial interests issued by a securitisation entity (an SPE) may contain a call option held by the original transferor. Similar to other call options, the call option on the beneficial interests may constrain the beneficial interest holders from exchanging their interests. In this case, the securitisation should be accounted for as a secured borrowing by the original transferor (IGC 41-1).

Comparison with UK GAAP

Under UK GAAP, whilst there is no specific exemption which permits derecognition where an option exists for reacquisition when the price is fair, if in substance such a provision means that the significant rights or access to benefits and significant exposure to risks inherent in the benefits have been transferred, derecognition would be appropriate.

Comparison with US GAAP

US GAAP does not include the exception which permits sale accounting where the reacquisition price of the call option is fair value at the time of reacquisition.

In addition, US GAAP provides a specific exception by permitting sale accounting in the case of 'clean-up calls' and 'clean-ups' structured as forwards. No such exception is provided under IAS 39 (r2000). These features would generally preclude sale accounting under IAS 39 (r2000) to the extent of the call (IGC 38-5). (Clean-up calls are options *held by a servicer*, who may also be the transferor, to purchase transferred financial assets when the amount of outstanding assets falls to a level at which the cost of servicing those assets becomes burdensome).

Repurchase agreements (forward contracts)

'A transferor has not lost control of a transferred financial asset and, therefore, the asset is not derecognised if, for example, the transferor is both entitled and obligated to repurchase or redeem the transferred asset on terms that effectively provide the transferee with a lender's return on the assets received in exchange for the transferred asset. A lender's return is one that is not materially different from that which could be obtained on a loan to the transferor that is fully secured by the transferred asset.' (IAS 39 (r2000).38(b)) Note that if this is the case, derecognition is not permitted regardless of whether the asset is readily obtainable since the transferor generally retains substantially all of the risks and returns of ownership of the transferred asset irrespective of whether the transferee has the ability to transfer it to a third party (DIGC 38-6).

IAS 39 (r2000) does not provide any guidance with respect to what would be considered as materially different from a lender's return and it is difficult to specify this in either absolute or relative terms given the different levels of interest rates in different countries (particularly between emerging and developed markets) and how they apply to different instruments. Professional judgement is therefore required in making this assessment.

> 'A transferor may be both entitled and obligated to repurchase or redeem an asset by:
>
> (a) a forward purchase contract;
> (b) a call option held and a put option written with approximately the same strike price; or
> (c) in other ways.
>
> However, neither the forward purchase contract in (a) nor the combination of options in (b) is sufficient, by itself, to maintain control over a transferred asset if the repurchase price is fair value at the time of repurchase.'
>
> (IAS 39 (r2000).40)

(a) Forward purchase contracts

An agreement that both entitles and obligates the transferor to repurchase or redeem transferred financial assets before their maturity, on terms that effectively provide a lender's return on the assets, maintains the transferor's control over those assets. These transactions should be accounted for as secured borrowings. Repurchase agreements and securities lending transactions are common agreements that fall under this provision. (IGC 38-3).

Financial institutions and other enterprises often transfer financial assets with a concurrent forward contract to reacquire the transferred assets, commonly referred to as repurchase agreements. In a typical repurchase agreement, the enterprise might, for example, own government securities that it sells to a third party with an agreement to repurchase the securities at a specified price, generally within a short period of time. At inception, the transferor (lender of the security) transfers the securities to the borrower of the security and receives cash or other consideration as collateral; if the consideration is cash, it is then invested in other assets that earn a return. At a defined date, the transferor repurchases the securities. Dollar repurchase agreements (dollar rolls) are similar transactions in which the transferor repurchases similar but not identical assets to those originally sold. Economically, the lender is motivated in these transactions by the liquidity afforded by the agreement and/or the excess returns it expects to earn on the collateral. These transactions historically have been viewed as secured financing by some entities (e.g., depository institutions) while being treated as sales and purchases by others (e.g., broker-dealers).

Repurchase agreements are commonly referred to as repos. In many countries, these are actively traded on listed exchanges or in the over the counter market and are often used as a source of funding or yield enhancement mechanism. The terminology, however, varies from country to country and the form taken can also be different. In some countries, a distinction is made between a repurchase agreement where legal title passes (also known as 'sell/buy-backs') and a carry (typically a short term repo that is sometimes also known as a classic repo) where title does not pass. Terminology also differs depending on which party is 'buying' or 'selling' the security (hence the use of terms such as reverse repos, inward and outward carries). For the purpose of applying the derecognition criteria, rather than specifying the treatment of specific types of repo which are likely to differ from country to country, the particular terms (and market conventions where appropriate) should be analysed to determine whether or not the substance of control is transferred.

Some enterprises also enter into securities lending transactions on a regular basis. In these transactions, the transferor (lender of the security) transfers a security to the transferee (borrower of the security) for a period of time. The transferee is generally required to provide collateral, which may be cash, other securities, or a standby letter of credit with a value that can be slightly higher than the value of the security borrowed (sometimes referred to as a 'haircut'). These transactions are typical when an entity needs a specific security to cover a short sale or a customer's failure to deliver securities sold. The transferor is compensated for lending the security by earning a fee or a return on the collateral invested if the collateral is cash. Note that, unlike the case of an interest rate-based return in the case of repurchase agreements, the fee is often only a nominal charge based on the market value of the scrip lent. This is still considered to represent a lender's return for the purpose of IAS 39 (r2000) and hence would preclude derecognition in such cases, even where the charge is significantly lower than current market rates.

IAS 39 (r2000) provides that the above-mentioned arrangements are not automatically accounted for as secured borrowings by the transferor and that of itself, a forward purchase contract (whether synthetic or otherwise) is not sufficient to demonstrate that control has been retained where the repurchase price is defined in terms of fair value at the time of repurchase. A transaction should be accounted for as a secured borrowing if the transferor retains control over the assets. If the transferor does not retain control over the financial assets, the transferor and transferee would account for this arrangement as a sale and purchase of financial assets and a separate forward commitment to purchase (for the transferor) or sell (for the transferee) the financial assets. Thus, in a repurchase agreement accounted for as a sale, an enterprise would record the original transfer of its securities as a sale with any gain or loss recognised in income; in addition, it would account for its obligation to repurchase the securities as a forward commitment. The transferee's accounting would be symmetrical. It would record the purchase of the securities with a forward commitment to sell them. As most enterprises entering into these arrangements seek to avoid sale accounting treatment, these arrangements generally will be structured so that the transferor retains control over the transferred financial assets.

(b) A call option held and a put option written with approximately the same strike price

A put option and a call option can be combined to be equivalent to a forward (also known as a synthetic forward); a forward and a put option can be combined to create the equivalent of a call option. Different combinations of derivatives may impact the degree of control that the transferee has over the financial assets that have been transferred. Combinations of derivatives that may be created in connection with a transfer of financial assets should be carefully evaluated to ensure that control rests with the transferee and that the transferee is not physically, legally or economically constrained. Factors to consider in evaluating combinations of derivatives include whether the transferred assets are readily obtainable and how the derivatives affect the transferee's ability to use the transferred assets.

The assessment of whether the strike prices of combined put and call options are approximately equal should be evaluated relative to a forward which would result in the same exposure to changes in fair value of the underlying. Combination put and call options transacted with a single counterparty which result in both of the parties being exposed to changes in value of the underlying (even if this exposure is limited for one of the parties) would typically not meet the requirement of having approximately equal strikes. However, depending on the circumstances, such options may preclude sale accounting if they result in the transferor retaining substantially all the risks and returns or in the transferee being constrained.

Comparison with UK GAAP – repurchase agreements (forwards)
Similarly to IAS 39 (r2000), under FRS 5, *Reporting the Substance of Transactions*, derecognition is inappropriate if the transferor is both entitled and obligated to repurchase or redeem the transferred asset on terms that effectively provide the transferee with a lender's return. In such a case, linked presentation would also be inappropriate.

Comparison with US GAAP – repurchase agreements (forwards)
US GAAP follows a slightly different approach where the transferor is both entitled and obligated to repurchase or redeem an asset. Its starting point is based on specific, narrowly defined criteria that need to be satisfied for the agreement to be accounted for as a secured borrowing. IAS evaluates these transactions from the perspective of whether or not the transferee receives a lender's return and whether or not the repurchase is to be effected at fair value. US GAAP does not specify the requirement that the terms of the transfer effectively provide the transferee with a lender's return on the assets received in exchange for the transferred asset.

Additionally, US GAAP specifies that where a forward purchase contract can be satisfied with readily obtainable assets, further criteria must be met to treat it as a secured borrowing. These criteria require that the assets to be repurchased or redeemed must be substantially the same, the transferor must be able to repurchase or redeem the assets on substantially the agreed terms, even in the event of default by the transferee, the agreement to repurchase or redeem must be at a fixed or determinable price and the agreement must be entered into concurrently with the transfer. (SFAS 140, *Accounting for Transfers and Servicing of Financial Assets and Extinguishments of Liabilities*) Further guidance is provided in SOP 90-3 as interpretation of the term 'substantially the same'.

Under US GAAP, in order for the transferor to be able to redeem financial assets subject to a repurchase agreement on substantially the agreed terms, even in the event of default by the transferee, the transferor must at all times have obtained sufficient collateral to fund substantially all (90 per cent or greater) of the purchase price of replacement securities from other parties in case the transferee defaults. The determination of whether this requirement has been met requires judgement and should be made based on the contract provisions, and facts and circumstances at the transfer date.

IAS 39 (r2000) neither specifically mentions any requirement in respect of whether or not the asset is readily obtainable where the transferor is entitled and obligated to repurchase or redeem the asset, nor sets out additional criteria to be satisfied over and above the agreement providing a lender's return. Although IAS 39 (r2000) does not include these requirements, by virtue of its focus on the substance of control, the treatment in most cases would likely provide similar results to those achieved under US GAAP.

Total return swaps/put options (retention of risks and returns)

> 'A transferor has not lost control of a transferred financial asset and, therefore, the asset is not derecognised if, for example, the asset transferred:
>
> (a) is not readily obtainable in the market; and
> (b) the transferor has retained substantially all of the risks and returns of ownership through a total return swap with the transferee; or
> (c) has retained substantially all of the risks of ownership through an unconditional put option on the transferred asset held by the transferee
>
> (a total return swap provides the market returns and credit risks to one of the parties in return for an interest index to the other party, such as a LIBOR payment).'
>
> (IAS 39 (r2000).38(c))

Put options

Put options provide the transferee with the ability to require the transferor to repurchase some or all of the transferred assets. They generally do not preclude sale accounting because the transferee controls whether the option is exercised and, therefore, has control over the assets. In-the-money and even deep in-the-money put options on assets that are readily obtainable generally do not preclude the transferee from using the transferred asset. Assets can be readily obtained to satisfy exercise of the put option, and the transferred assets can be exchanged or pledged by the transferee without economic constraints or penalties. In these instances, the transferor has not retained control over those assets.

However, in-the-money put options on assets that are not readily obtainable may constrain a transferee from selling or exchanging the transferred assets if the transferee's only rational course of action is to exercise the put option. For example, if a transferor transfers bonds that are not readily obtainable to a transferee and provides the transferee with a deep in-the-money put option that expires in a short period of time, it is likely that the transferee is constrained economically (IGC 38-4). Although the transferee may have the freedom to exercise or not to exercise its put option, the deep in-the-money feature coupled with the short exercise period limits the alternatives and virtually compels the transferee to put the assets back to the transferor.

The primary factor to consider is whether the transferor has retained control because the assets transferred are not readily obtainable and the option features, such as the exercise period and strike price, limit the transferee from taking any action other than to exercise the put option. These conditions are indicative that the transferor has retained substantially all of the risks and rewards of ownership. In making this assessment, the probability that an in-the-money option will not be exercised is ordinarily not a consideration, because the transferee generally will be constrained until such time in the future when the option actually is no longer in-the-money or expires worthless.

It should be noted that debt instruments that are not traded and are not readily obtainable typically are not rated and tend to have values that fluctuate more with movements in credit than with movements in interest rates. In this situation, it would be difficult enough to resell assets that are not readily obtainable because there is usually a wide bid-ask difference (spread). It would be much more difficult to sell such assets at a price in excess of the estimated value, which would be required for the transferee to recoup the value of its put option. A potential investor would be reluctant to purchase such assets and pay an additional amount for an in-the-money put option without obtaining assurance that the investment would be realised. It would also be difficult, if not impossible, to sell the put separately in the marketplace and realise any value for it. Even if the put option is in-the-money, it has no value without access to the referenced assets because they are necessary to satisfy the put. If a transaction involves an in-the-money put option, the only rational action a transferee may be able to take to realise its investment is to exercise the option. Although it is necessary to assess the extent to which the value attributed to the put option constrains the transferee, in the absence of any evidence to the contrary, the transferee will always be constrained economically to some extent if the assets are not readily obtainable.

A transferee's ability to exercise a put option to return the transferred assets back to the transferor as a result of credit deterioration, actual credit default or interest rate changes is considered to be an unconditional put option because the transferor retains substantially all the risks and rewards of ownership. This transaction would therefore be accounted for as a secured borrowing (IGC 38-2).

Transfers subject to recourse

If the risk retained by the transferor, through a put option, is limited to credit recourse (in respect of actual credit defaults), a transfer is recognised as a sale since the transferor does not retain substantially all of the risks and rewards of ownership through an unconditional put option or a total return swap. In such a case, the guarantee is treated as a separate financial instrument to be recognised as a financial liability by the transferor (IGC 37-1).

Swaps

Swaps may be used to provide a transferor with the economic risks and returns of ownership of the transferred assets even where physical control over the contractual rights to the benefits of the underlying assets is passed to the transferee. An example of this is a total return swap referenced to the transferred assets between the transferor and the transferee. This situation is specifically described under paragraph 38(c) where, in the event that the asset is not readily obtainable in the market, the transferor is considered to have retained control and hence derecognition is not considered appropriate. However, IAS 39 (r2000) does not provide any guidance in respect of the phrase 'substantially all of the risks and returns of ownership'.

Swap agreements should be carefully evaluated to determine that the terms of such agreements do not limit the transferee's control over the underlying assets transferred. Total return swaps in respect of assets that are readily obtainable in the market do not compromise the transferee's effective control of the asset and sale accounting is appropriate since the transferee may sell the asset, thereby obtaining the associated benefits. On the other hand, if the asset is not readily obtainable, the transferee may not have the practical ability to transfer the asset to a third party (DIGC 38-6).

Example 12.20 In-the-money put option

Transferor X sells South African government bonds that are readily obtainable in the market-place with a book value of R100 to Transferee Y for R103. The transfer includes an option for Transferee Y to put the assets back to Transferor X up to one year after the transfer date at R103.50. Transferee Y exercises its option 30 days after the initial sale. The option had a fair value of R2 at the exchange date consisting of time value of R1.50 and intrinsic value of R0.50. Should the transfer be accounted for as a sale?

In this example, the transferor has not retained control because the assets are readily obtainable. This put option does not therefore preclude sale treatment.

Example 12.21 Deep in-the-money put option, asset not readily obtainable

Transferor X transfers receivables with a carrying value of US$90 and a put option which expires in ten days to Transferee Y. Transferee Y pays US$150 for the receivables which have a fair value of US$100. Under the terms of the put option, Transferee Y may put the receivables to Transferor X for US$151. The possibility of the fair value of the receivables increasing to US$151 in ten days is considered remote and, therefore, exercise of the option appears virtually assured at inception so that the arrangement is more like a forward repurchase agreement than an option (IGC 38-4).

If Transferor X were permitted to record this transaction as a sale, it would derecognise the receivables, recognise US$150 in cash, recognise a put option liability of US$51 (exclusive of the time value inherent in the option for simplicity), and recognise a gain of US$9.

However, because at inception it appears virtually assured that the put option will be exercised, Transferor X has retained substantially all of the risks of ownership over the receivables, and this transaction should be accounted for as a secured borrowing of US$150.

Comparison with UK GAAP

Generally, a sale with a total return swap would not meet the derecognition criteria.

Comparison with US GAAP

The transfer of the risks and returns associated with ownership is not a determining criterion under US GAAP in evaluating whether a transfer should be accounted for as a sale.

The transfer of control in respect of total return swaps is not specifically addressed under US GAAP. However, the retention of risk under a total return swap may cause the transfer to fail the isolation test under US GAAP and result in the transfer being accounted for as financing.

Transferee's position

> 'A transferor generally has lost control of a transferred financial asset only if the transferee has the ability to obtain the benefits of the transferred asset. That ability is demonstrated, for example, if the transferee:
>
> (a) is free either to sell or to pledge approximately the full fair value of the transferred asset; or
>
> (b) is a special-purpose entity whose permissible activities are limited, and either the special purpose entity itself or the holders of beneficial interests in that entity have the ability to obtain substantially all of the benefits of the transferred asset.
>
> That ability may be demonstrated in other ways.'

(IAS 39 (r2000).41)

'Beneficial interests' refer to the rights issued by the special-purpose entity (usually in the form of a debt instrument, an equity instrument, a participation right, a residual interest or a lease) and not the transferred assets held by the special-purpose entity.

The condition in paragraph 41(a) encompasses the notion that an entity that has recorded an asset can use it in various ways to recover the future economic benefits in the financial asset. Thus, recovery by the transferee not only involves holding and collecting cash inflows according to the underlying original contractual terms inherent in those assets, but the transferee must also have the right to obtain the benefits through other alternatives, such as exchanging them either for other assets, including future goods and services, or in satisfaction of an obligation; or through an assignment to a third party. A transferee may be able to use a transferred asset in some of these ways but not others. A transferee that does not have all these alternatives available to it may control the transferred asset if the alternatives that are available allow the transferee to realise the full fair value of the economic benefits that comprise the asset. For example, if the transferee is prohibited from pledging the financial asset but may exchange it, sale treatment would not be precluded because the transferee could obtain the full fair value of the transferred asset through an exchange. Similarly, if the transferee is prohibited from exchanging the transferred asset, the asset may still be considered controlled by the transferee if it could realise the full economic value inherent in the cash flows of the asset by pledging it.

The assessment of control is more complex where the financial assets being transferred are not readily obtainable and are subject to put options, call options, or repurchase agreements. These features may constrain the transferee economically even though the transferee is not contractually precluded from selling or pledging the transferred assets and thus may permit the transferor to retain control over the transferred asset. In such a case, IAS 39 (r2000).41(a) would be satisfied, indicating that the transferee has the ability to obtain the benefits of the asset and therefore that the transferor has lost control of the asset. However, since the transferor has a right to reacquire the transferred asset, in terms of IAS 39 (r2000).38(a), the transferor is considered to have retained control and the asset would therefore not be derecognised. Where the position of either enterprise indicates that the transferor has retained control, IAS 39 (r2000) requires that the transferor should not remove the asset from its balance sheet.

Many transferor-imposed conditions on a transferee's contractual right to pledge or exchange a transferred asset constrain the transferee from taking advantage of that right. Some transferor-imposed conditions may not be indicative of a failure to transfer control to a transferee. The following exceptions are examples of minor constraints that generally do not preclude sale treatment since they presumptively do not constrain a transferee from exercising its right to pledge or exchange approximately the full fair value of the transferred asset:

- a right of first refusal granted to transferors that allows reacquisition of transferred financial assets whenever a transferee solicits a bona fide offer of purchase from a third party (IGC 38-1);
- a stipulation contained in an agreement of sale that requires permission of the transferor to sell or pledge financial assets transferred, which, in the case of the transferor, is not to be unreasonably withheld; or
- qualifications prohibiting the transferee from subsequently selling or assigning transferred financial assets to competitors of the transferor and the transferee is able to sell or assign its beneficial interests to a number of third parties who do not compete with the transferor.

Elimination of constraints subsequent to transfer

Some constraints on the transferee's ability to exchange or pledge a financial asset may expire automatically upon the passage of time or upon the occurrence of a certain event. One example is a restriction against exchanging or pledging a financial asset for a period of time when the asset has a maturity date that extends past the time restriction. In these circumstances, sale treatment is precluded while the transferee is constrained from exchanging or pledging the asset. A sale should be recorded, however, once the constraint no longer exists and the transferee is able to sell or pledge the financial asset.

Example 12.22 External constraint that does not preclude sale treatment

Entity X owns shares in entity B. Entity B wants to restrict the number of shareholders; thus, a condition contained in the shareholder agreement requires that holders of B's shares cannot transfer such shares without B's approval or the shares must be sold to B. X transfers the shares to Y, a buyer approved by B, for cash and has no other involvement with such shares. The shareholder agreement precludes Y from selling the shares without the approval of B. The transfer should be accounted for as a sale (provided the transfer meets all other derecognition criteria) because X surrendered all control it had in the financial asset to Y and the external constraint does not involve X, provide X with a means for repurchasing the shares from Y, or permit X to obtain any other advantage with respect to the shares.

Example 12.23 Time constraint on financial assets

Transferee Y is prohibited by Transferor X from pledging or exchanging, for the first year after the transfer, a financial asset that matures in five years. X otherwise controls the risks and returns of the asset. Upon expiration of this time period, the transferee is free to pledge or exchange approximately the full fair value of the asset. In this example, the transferor and transferee should account for this transfer as a secured borrowing along with a forward sale/purchase contract until the restriction expires. Upon the expiration of the constraint, both parties should account for the transfer as a sale.

Transfers with disproportionate risk sharing

In a transfer of financial assets, a forward or call option may pertain to only a portion of the transferred assets. For example, a transferor may retain a call option on 20 per cent of the transferred assets. Similarly, where a portion of a financial asset is sold and the remainder is retained, the transferor often retains custody of the asset and the transferee is unable to sell or pledge it. In such a case, to protect the interests of all parties having ownership rights in the assets, restrictions are generally placed on the sale and use of those assets and hence although the transferor retains custody of the asset, neither party has the ability to sell or pledge the asset. IAS 39 (r2000).35 does not prohibit derecognition in such cases and specifically provides for the sale of a portion of an asset when an enterprise loses control of the contractual rights that comprise it.

This scenario is dealt with in IGC 35-1. Under IAS 39 (r2000).35, an enterprise loses control if it realises the rights to benefits specified in the contract, the rights expire, or the enterprise surrenders those rights while IAS 39 (r2000).41 states that a transferor 'generally' loses control only if the transferee has the ability to obtain the benefits of the transferred asset. The examples given of this are if the transferee is free to sell or pledge the financial asset or, if the transferee is a special purpose entity (SPE), the holders of the beneficial interests in the SPE have the ability to obtain substantially all of the benefits of the transferred assets. However, IAS 39 (r2000).41 does not limit sale accounting to these two conditions and it recognises that control is not just a physical or custody notion. There are other factors to consider, particularly the ability to realise the beneficial interests.

To illustrate the principle, IGC 35-1 contains a detailed example. Company A purchases loans in the market-place at par with an effective yield at the time of purchase equal to its coupon of 11 per cent and a maturity of 10 years. It later sells a portion of those loans to investors. Under the terms of the sales agreement, the investors purchase at par 80 per cent of the total principal amount of the loan with interest at 6 per cent. Company A retains the remaining 20 per cent of the principal with coupon interest at 11 per cent, and the excess interest of 5 per cent due on the underlying loans that were sold to the investors. Company A's retained interests in the loans are pledged as collateral on a first-loss basis to the investors and, therefore, are subordinated to the 80 per cent portion of the loans sold to the investors. Company A also agrees to continue to collect interest and principal payments from the borrowers and remit the payments to the investors for their share of the cash flows (a servicing arrangement). Since the loans cannot be physically separated, the portion sold cannot be delivered to the investors. Company A also retains physical custody of the loans; however, to protect the interests of each of the parties, Company A is prohibited under the agreement from selling or pledging the loans that were the subject of the partial sale.

Company A has relinquished control of the 80 per cent interest in the loans that it sold. Even though Company A retains custody of the loans, it gave up its right to sell or pledge the loans. Company A also realised the benefits of the portion of the loans that were sold, and the investors obtain the risks and rewards of ownership of the portion of the asset that they purchased. Neither Company A nor the investors have the right to sell or pledge the underlying loans, but both Company A and the investors are free to sell or pledge their respective interests. Accordingly, they have control over their respective economic benefits in the interests that they own in the loans.

Although Company A has pledged its 20 per cent portion of the loans on a first-loss basis to the investors and therefore has retained credit risk on 100 per cent of the loans, significant interest rate risk has been transferred to the investors on the 80 per cent portion of the loans that were sold to the investors. Therefore, assuming that there are no other rights or obligations relating to this transaction that would preclude sale accounting, Company A accounts for this transaction as a sale even though it retains custody of the loans and the investors do not have the ability to sell or pledge the loans.

Related to IGC 35-1, IGC 35-2 provides further factors to consider in assessing whether the transferor has surrendered control. Factors supporting the transfer of control include:

- the transferor has no legal right to reacquire the portion of the transferred assets sold. This condition is often evidenced by legally documenting the transfer as a sale;
- the transferor is prohibited from selling or pledging the underlying financial assets that are the subject of the transfer;
- if the transferor retains custody of the assets that are the subject of the transfer, it is not entitled to benefit from collecting cash flows due to the transferee by reinvesting those cash flows for its own account.

The following factors limit the extent to which the transferred portion of financial assets qualifies for derecognition:

- there is no derecognition to the extent of put or call options or forwards on the transferred assets;
- there is no derecognition to the extent that the transferor retains substantially all the risks and rewards of ownership.

For the purpose of applying tests related to call options and forwards involving a sale of a portion of an asset, beneficial interests are considered to be 'not readily obtainable' if the underlying financial assets cannot be sold by either the transferor or the transferee (IGC 35-2).

If the transfer of financial assets is made to a special purpose entity, and the transfer meets the tests for derecognition under IAS 39 (r2000), the SPE may be required to be consolidated under SIC-12, *Consolidation – Special Purpose Entities*, in which case, the accounting effect of the sale is eliminated on consolidation. However, if the transaction between the SPE and the investors is consistent with the guidance in IGC 35-1 and 35-2, there is a transfer at the SPE level and even on consolidation, the portion of the financial assets sold or transferred to the third-party investors in the SPE is derecognised (IGC 35-3).

12.12.2 Accounting for derecognition

IAS 39 (r2000) sets out the accounting treatment for transactions that meet the derecognition criteria in respect of three scenarios, namely:

(1) complete derecognition of a financial asset;
(2) partial derecognition of a financial asset; and
(3) derecognition of a financial asset coupled with a new financial asset or liability.

In the last two scenarios, special consideration (and professional judgement) is required in identifying the various financial assets and liabilities subsequent to the transfer and in determining and allocating the appropriate fair values to the identified financial assets and liabilities. This must be done prior to determining any gain or loss to be reported in net profit or loss in respect of the transferred asset.

(1) Complete derecognition of a financial asset

> 'On derecognition, the difference between (a) the carrying amount of an asset (or portion of an asset) transferred to another party and (b) the sum of (i) the proceeds received or receivable and (ii) any prior adjustment to reflect the fair value of that asset that had been reported in equity should be included in net profit or loss for the period.'
>
> (IAS 39 (r2000).43)

Thus, any fair value adjustments reported in equity relating to the asset being derecognised are recycled through the income statement on derecognition.

For a discussion of determining fair value, see **Determining fair value on derecognition** below.

As discussed in **12.12.1**, the important question in accounting for derecognition of financial assets involves the determination of whether the transaction should be accounted for as a sale or a secured borrowing. This determination is critical, since the accounting treatment for a sale is significantly different from the accounting treatment for a secured borrowing for both the transferor and transferee. If the transfer is considered a sale, the transferor removes the transferred assets from the balance sheet and records a gain or loss in net profit or loss for the period in which the exchange occurs. For this same transaction, the transferee records the transferred assets at the fair value of the consideration paid. If the transfer is a secured borrowing, the assets remain on the balance sheet of the transferor, and a liability is recognised for the proceeds with no effect on income on the transfer date. In a secured borrowing, the transferee recognises a receivable due from the transferor and does not recognise the transferred assets.

(2) Partial derecognition of a financial asset

> 'If an enterprise transfers a part of a financial asset to others while retaining a part, the carrying amount of the financial asset should be allocated between the part retained and the part sold based on their relative fair values on the date of sale. A gain or loss should be recognised based on the proceeds for the portion sold.
>
> In the rare circumstance that the fair value of the part of the asset that is retained cannot be measured reliably, then that asset should be recorded at zero. The entire carrying amount of the financial asset should be attributed to the portion sold, and a gain or loss should be recognised equal to the difference between (a) the proceeds and (b) the previous carrying amount of the financial asset plus or minus any prior adjustment that had been reported in equity to reflect the fair value of that asset (a 'cost recovery' approach).'
>
> (IAS 39 (r2000).47)

Thus, any fair value adjustments reported in equity relating to the portion of the asset being derecognised are recycled through the income statement.

For a discussion of determining fair value, see **Determining fair value on derecognition** below.

IAS 39 (r2000) gives the following examples of transfers involving the partial derecognition of a financial asset:

(a) separating the principal and interest cash flows of a bond and selling some of them to another party while retaining the rest; and
(b) selling a portfolio of receivables while retaining the right to service the receivables profitably for a fee, resulting in an asset for the servicing right.

(IAS 39 (r2000).48)

Although no further guidance is provided regarding what constitutes a part of a financial asset, paragraph 35 makes reference to the contractual rights that comprise the asset or a portion of the asset. Where these contractual rights (to receive cash or another financial asset or to exchange financial instruments with another enterprise under conditions that are potentially favourable) can be separately identified and separated out from a financial asset, this would represent a part of a financial asset.

To illustrate, assume receivables with a carrying amount of 100 are sold for 90. The selling enterprise retains the right to service those receivables for a fee that is expected to exceed the cost of servicing, but the fair value of the servicing right cannot be measured reliably. In that case, a loss of 10 would be recognised and the servicing right would be recorded at zero. (IAS 39 (r2000).49)

The following example from IAS 39 (r2000) illustrates how a transferor accounts for a sale or securitisation in which servicing is retained.

Example 12.24 Sale in which servicing is retained

An enterprise originates 1,000 of loans that yield 10 per cent interest for their estimated lives of 9 years. The enterprise sells the 1,000 principal plus the right to receive interest income of 8 per cent to another enterprise for 1,000. The transferor will continue to service the loans, and the contract stipulates that its compensation for performing the servicing is the right to receive half of the interest income not sold (that is, 100 of the 200 basis points). The remaining half of the interest income not sold is considered an interest only strip receivable. At the date of the transfer, the fair value of the loans, including servicing, is 1,100, of which the fair value of the servicing asset is 40 and the fair value of the interest only strip receivable is 60. Allocation of the 1,000 carrying amount of the loan is computed as follows:

	Fair Value	*Percentage of Total Fair Vale*	*Allocated Carrying Amount*
Loans sold	1,000	91.0	910
Servicing asset	40	3.6	36
Interest-only strip receivable	60	5.4	54
Total	1,100	100.0	1,000

The transferor will recognise a gain of 90 on the sale of the loan – the difference between the net proceeds of 1,000 and the allocated carrying amount of 910. Its balance sheet will also report a servicing asset of 36 and an interest-only strip receivable of 54. The servicing asset is an intangible asset subject to the provisions of IAS 38, *Intangible Assets.* (IAS 39 (r2000).50)

Carrying amount

While IAS 39 (r2000) does not define the term 'carrying amount,' this term is defined in various other pronouncements, including IAS 36, *Impairment of Assets*, para.5 and IAS 38, *Intangible Assets*, para.7. In these Standards, the carrying amount is defined to encompass unamortised premiums or discounts, acquisition costs, and impairment amounts, such as an allowance for uncollectable amounts.

When only a portion of the financial assets is transferred, the allocation of any valuation allowances and impairment amounts to those assets transferred and retained should generally be done based on the relative fair values of the portion of the asset sold and the portion retained. For example, the percentage of the fair value of credit card loans transferred determined by dividing the fair value of the amount transferred by the total fair value of all credit card loans held at the time of the transfer, is used to allocate a portion of the allowance for uncollectable amounts to the amount transferred.

Accrued interest is a separate financial asset that may or may not be transferred in the same transaction. Accrued interest that is retained is not included in the carrying amount of the transferred asset because it is a separate financial asset and a present benefit that has already been recognised.

Retained interests

When the allocation of the carrying amount of the transferred assets to its components is required, identifying retained interests and sold interests becomes a necessity. Retained interests relate to identifiable, contractual rights to receive the economic benefits (or cash flows) that comprise financial assets over which the transferor does not relinquish control. Examples of retained interests in a transfer of financial assets include servicing assets, retained undivided interests in the transferred assets (e.g., a retained interest-only strip or a percentage interest in the subject receivables), securities backed by the transferred assets and retained interests in securitisation trusts. Distinguishing characteristics of retained interests are that they are always assets held by the transferor and represent the portion of those expected cash flows from the assets being transferred that is retained by the transferor.

Forms of continuing involvement with transferred assets which do *not* represent retained interests include liabilities incurred and derivatives resulting from the transfer. For example, recourse provisions, put options and guarantees of a specific return are considered to be new liabilities and not retained interests. Liabilities and derivatives that are not part of the original financial asset are not considered retained interests.

Servicing assets and liabilities

Servicing assets are a common form of retained interest. Servicing refers to activities associated with the collection of cash flows from receivables or other financial assets after origination and the distribution of that cash to investors if the receivables are owned by other entities. Servicing may include the temporary investment and distribution to the financial asset owners of all or a portion of the cash collected. Servicing activities also may include monitoring delinquencies, advancing delinquent payments, restructuring receivables, and foreclosing on the collateral underlying the receivables when necessary. If the receivables are mortgage loans, servicing activities often include collecting and disbursing payments for taxes and insurance. Servicing activities are inherent in all receivables; however, they do not need to be performed by the owner of the receivables. If the receivables are being serviced for another entity, the servicer generally receives a fee for performing these activities. This fee is usually a contractual amount received based on a fixed percentage of the outstanding receivables for the period. Servicers may also receive additional compensation by retaining late charges, other ancillary fees, and the float, which is the net interest earned on funds held by the servicer before disbursement. The compensation received by the servicer is referred to as the benefits of servicing.

Servicing becomes a distinct asset or liability when it is contractually separated from the related receivables, and thus, becomes a servicing contract. The following are examples of servicing that are separated from the related receivables under a servicing contract:

- the owner of the receivables sells the servicing rights to another entity and retains the receivables.
- the owner of the receivables sells the receivables but retains the right to service those receivables.
- receivables are exchanged for securities (backed by the receivables) that may be sold at a later date, and the securities do not include the right to service the underlying receivables.

If an enterprise transfers receivables and retains the right to a portion of the interest payments, the amount allocated to the servicing asset or liability is the portion of the interest payments that the servicer would lose on termination or transfer of the servicing contract. The portion of the interest payments that the servicer would not lose is an interest-only strip receivable (IGC 50-1). The fair values of the servicing asset and interest-only strip receivable are then used in allocating the carrying amount of the receivables between the part of the asset transferred and the part retained.

The servicing asset is an intangible asset subject to the provisions of IAS 38, ***Intangible Assets.*** (IAS 39 (r2000).50) Under IAS 38, an intangible asset should only be recognised if, and only if, it is probable that the future economic benefits that are attributable to the asset will flow to the enterprise, and the cost of the asset can be measured reliably. (IAS 38.19) Intangible assets should initially be measured at cost (IAS 38.22) and are subject to impairment testing. See **10.7** for further discussion of intangible assets.

Once the servicing has been separated from the related financial assets, it may represent an economic benefit (asset) to, or obligation (liability) of, the servicer. A servicing asset is a contract to service financial assets under which the estimated future revenues from contractually specified servicing fees, late charges, and other ancillary revenues are expected to have a positive fair value. A servicing liability is a contract to service financial assets under which the estimated future cash flows are expected to have a negative fair value. The servicing in this instance represents an obligation, an onerous contract, because the servicer would have to pay another entity to assume the servicing contract or use its assets in the future to perform under the servicing contract.

Servicing liabilities initially have a negative fair value to the servicer. When the estimated future revenues will enable the servicer to perform the servicing but provide no additional benefits, the servicer has neither an asset nor a liability and the fair value of this servicing contract is zero. A servicing contract with a positive fair value is considered to be one that would not be unfavourable for a substitute servicer should one be required, and includes the profit that would be demanded in the market-place. One approach in determining whether a servicing contract has a positive fair value is to use the servicing costs of an average servicer plus a reasonable profit margin if this information is available.

An entity should recognise a servicing asset or servicing liability to service financial assets (provided its value is not zero) whenever it undertakes an obligation to service financial assets pursuant to a servicing contract, provided the recognition criteria in IAS 38 are satisfied. Where the servicing asset has arisen as a result of contractually separating it as part of the transfer, it is likely that the first criteria in IAS 38.19 (i.e., it is probable that economic benefits in the asset will flow to the enterprise) will be satisfied. Provided then that the cost of the servicing asset can be measured reliably in terms of the second criterion in IAS 38.19, the recognition criteria would be satisfied and the servicing asset would be recognised at cost.

A servicing asset retained in a sale or securitisation of financial assets should initially be recognised at its cost based on the allocated carrying amount determined using relative fair values at the date of the sale or securitisation. However, if the servicer obtains a servicing asset by purchase or a servicing liability by assumption (including servicing liabilities resulting from sales or securitisation of financial assets), the servicing contract is initially recognised in the balance sheet at its fair value. The fair value of servicing assets and liabilities can be estimated using a present value model when quoted market prices are unavailable. One of the difficulties in using this model is estimating the expected future cash inflows and outflows because many different factors affect these amounts. The expected cash inflows normally comprise the contractual servicing fee, ancillary income (e.g., late fees, returned cheque fees), and earned float (e.g., float on escrow accounts, monthly payments, pay-offs).

These cash inflows should be adjusted for the expected effects of prepayments, changes in interest rates, and defaults. The expected cash outflows are normally composed of servicing costs, foreclosure costs and interest paid (e.g., on escrows, advances, pay-offs). These cash outflows should also be adjusted for the effects of prepayments, changes in interest rates and defaults.

Because this calculation attempts to measure what a third-party investor would pay for these rights, any inefficiencies or efficiencies particular to the servicer should be ignored, and the calculation should include a profit component equal to the amount that would be demanded in the market-place by an investor.

While the above methodology may be used for allocating basis, this would not meet the criteria for subsequent remeasurement to fair value as set out in IAS 38 which only permits the use of fair values where price information can be derived from an active market.

Example 12.25 Partial derecognition of a financial asset – allocation between sold and retained interests

Company A owns US$1,000,000 face amount of loans that contractually yield 10 per cent interest over their life. The carrying amount of these loans after considering the US$20,000 allowance for loan losses is US$980,000. Company A sells without recourse 90 per cent of the principal and the right to receive interest income of 8 per cent, to an investor for US$900,000 in cash. The transfer meets all the criteria for a sale. Company A retains the right to service these loans, and the servicing contract stipulates a 1 per cent fee as compensation for performing the servicing. Company A therefore also retains an interest-only strip for the portion of the interest coupon not sold (1 per cent). At the date of transfer, the fair value of the retained 10 per cent of the loan is US$100,000; the fair value of the servicing asset is US$15,000; and the fair value of the interest-only strip is US$35,000.

The following table demonstrates the allocation of this loan between the sold and retained interests.

Interest	*Fair value (US$)*	*Percentage of total fair value (%)*	*Allocated carrying amount (US$) (1)*	*Sold interests (US$)*	*Retained interests (US$)*
Loans sold	900,000	85.71	840,000	840,000	
Loans retained	100,000	9.53	93,333		93,333
IO strip	35,000	3.33	32,667		32,667
Servicing asset	15,000	1.43	14,000		14,000
Total	**1,050,000**	**100.00**	**980,000**	**840,000**	**140,000**

(1) The allocated carrying amount is calculated as the interest's percentage of total fair value times the aggregate carrying amount prior to the transfer (US$980,000).

Comparison with UK GAAP
Unlike IAS 39 (r2000), on complete derecognition of an asset or partial derecognition of an asset, any revaluation gain or loss recognised directly in equity would *not* be recycled through the income statement. Such an amount would be reclassified from equity to retained earnings via a reserve transfer.

Comparison with US GAAP
Under US GAAP, servicing rights are specifically treated as non-financial assets or liabilities. US GAAP records servicing rights initially at fair value, but then amortises the basis over the related loan terms. Under IAS 38, although the benchmark treatment subsequent to initial recognition is to carry the asset at amortised cost, the allowed alternative treatment permits the recognition of servicing rights at fair value where, and only where this value can be determined by reference to an active market for the asset. (IAS 38.64)

Transfers where the owner of receivables sells the servicing rights to another entity and retains the receivables are not subject to the derecognition criteria for financial instruments under US GAAP since servicing is regarded as a non-financial asset to which the derecognition provisions of SFAS 140, *Accounting for Transfers and Servicing of Financial Assets and Extinguishments of Liabilities* do not apply.

Under US GAAP, a reasonable estimate of fair value is considered sufficient where it is not practicable to determine fair value when allocating basis. IAS 39 (r2000)'s requirement of a reliable estimate represents a higher threshold in the determination of fair value though IAS 39 (r2000) presumes that a reliable estimate of fair value can be obtained.

(3) Derecognition of a financial asset coupled with a new financial asset or liability

> 'If an enterprise transfers control of an entire financial asset but, in doing so, creates a new financial asset or assumes a new financial liability, the enterprise should recognise the new financial asset or financial liability at fair value and should recognise a gain or loss on the transaction based on the difference between:
>
> (a) the proceeds; and
> (b) the carrying amount of the financial asset sold plus the fair value of any new financial liability assumed, minus the fair value of any new financial asset acquired, and plus or minus any adjustment that had previously been reported in equity to reflect the fair value of that asset.'
>
> (IAS 39 (r2000).51)

> 'In the rare circumstance that the fair value of the new financial asset or new financial liability cannot be measured reliably, then:
>
> (a) if a new financial asset is created but cannot be measured reliably, its initial carrying amount should be zero, and a gain or loss should be recognised

equal to the difference between (i) the proceeds and (ii) the previous carrying amount of the derecognised financial asset plus or minus any prior adjustment that had been reported in equity to reflect the fair value of that asset; and

(b) if a new financial liability is assumed but cannot be measured reliably, its initial carrying amount should be such that no gain is recognised on the transaction and, if IAS 37, *Provisions, Contingent Liabilities and Contingent Assets*, requires recognition of a provision, a loss should be recognised.'

(IAS 39 (r2000).54)

In the rare circumstances described above, the excess of the proceeds over the carrying amount is not recognised in net profit or loss. Instead it is recorded as a liability in the balance sheet. (IAS 39 (r2000).55)

Note that, any fair value adjustments reported in equity relating to the asset being derecognised are recycled through the income statement on derecognition.

For a discussion of determining fair value, see **Determining fair value on derecognition** below.

See **12.10.7** for guidance as to when fair value is reliably measurable.

If a guarantee is recognised as a liability under IAS 39 (r2000), for example as a result of its derecognition rules, it continues to be recognised as a liability of the guarantor, measured at its fair value (or at the greater of its original recorded amount and any provision required by IAS 37, if fair value cannot be reliably measured), until it expires. If the guarantee involves a large population of items, the guarantee should be measured by weighting all possible outcomes by their associated probabilities. (IAS 39 (r2000).56)

Examples of transfers involving the derecognition of a financial asset or a portion of a financial asset and the simultaneous recognition of a new financial asset or liability given in IAS 39 (r2000) are:

(a) selling a portfolio of receivables while assuming an obligation to compensate the purchaser of the receivables if collections are below a specified level; and

(b) selling a portfolio of receivables while retaining the right to service the receivables for a fee, and the fee to be received is less than the costs of servicing, thereby resulting in a liability for the servicing obligation. (IAS 39 (r2000).52)

No further guidance is provided in IAS 39 (r2000) as to what constitutes a new financial asset or liability and judgement will be necessary to determine the extent to which the terms of the asset subsequent to the transfer differ from those prior to the transfer. Both form and substance must be assessed and the component parts of resultant assets and liabilities may need to be analysed carefully.

The term 'proceeds' refers to those assets obtained, less any liabilities incurred as consideration for the transfer.

Cash and other non-derivative assets received are easily identified as part of the sales proceeds. Common items that are obtained or incurred in sales of financial assets that should be included as part of the proceeds include:

- holdbacks of cash sales proceeds that belong to the transferor but are held in escrow or held by the transferee. Holdbacks are generally used to enhance credit and ensure performance on guarantees of the transferor. This does not include initial cash deposits put up by the transferor, out of its own cash or debtor deposits, as a performance guarantee.
- call options held on the transferred financial assets (e.g., a call option on financial assets that are readily obtainable).
- put options written on the transferred assets (e.g., guarantees or recourse obligations).
- forward commitments (e.g., commitments to deliver additional receivables in a revolving-period securitisation), but only to the extent that they are off-market.
- swaps (e.g., provisions that convert interest rates from fixed to variable or vice versa, or exchange currencies).

If a derivative financial instrument is entered into concurrently with and as part of a transfer of financial assets, it is either an asset obtained or a liability incurred in a transfer and should be considered part of the sales proceeds.

It should further be noted that incurred liabilities which are recognised as part of the proceeds (e.g., recourse obligations) may not be offset against assets, retained or newly obtained, unless the requirements of IAS 32 (r1998) for the right of set-off are satisfied (see **12.7**).

On completion of a transfer which meets the criteria for sale accounting, the transferee enterprise recognises all assets obtained and liabilities incurred in its balance sheet.

IAS 39 (r2000) includes the following example of derecognition coupled with a new financial liability.

Example 12.26 Derecognition coupled with a guarantee

A transfers certain receivables to B for a single, fixed cash payment. A is not obligated to make future payments of interest on the cash it has received from B. However, A guarantees B against default loss on the receivables up to a specified amount. Actual losses in excess of the amount guaranteed will be borne by B. As a result of the transaction, A has lost control over the receivables and B has obtained control. B now has the contractual right to receive cash inherent in the receivables as well as a guarantee from A. Under paragraph 51:

(a) B recognises the receivables on its balance sheet, and A removes the receivables from its balance sheet because they were sold to B; and
(b) the guarantee is treated as a separate financial instrument, created as a result of the transfer, to be recognised as a financial liability by A and a financial asset by B. For practical purposes, B might include the guarantee asset with the receivables. (IAS 39 (r2000).53)

Securitisations

'*Securitisation* is the process by which financial assets are transformed into securities.' (IAS 39 (r2000).10)

In most revolving-period securitisations, a trust purchases short-term receivables (e.g., credit card or 90-day receivables) from the transferor, but issues long-term beneficial interests (e.g., five-year certificates). The funds collected on the short-term receivables are used first to provide a return to the holders of the beneficial interests and then to purchase new receivables from the transferor. This procedure of purchasing new receivables with funds collected from previously transferred receivables continues until the liquidation period begins (funds collected from the receivables held by the trust will be used to redeem the securities). Often the transferor is the servicer; therefore, the transferor will in effect use the funds it collected to purchase its own receivables on behalf of the trust.

If the securitisation meets the sales criteria, each transfer of receivables to the trust (i.e., the initial sale and each subsequent transfer using collected funds) is a separate sale of financial assets and should be accounted for as such. The gain or loss on each sale is limited to the gain or loss on only those receivables that exist and have been sold. Similarly, any servicing asset or liability and interest-only strip is limited to the servicing and excess interest on the receivables that exist and have been sold. Therefore, servicing on new receivables may not be included in the balance sheet until those receivables have been originated and sold to the trust.

The recording of a servicing asset or liability and/or interest-only strip for each new sale makes the accounting complex, because each servicing asset or liability and interest-only strip resulting from the separate sales should be tracked separately. Intuitively, the greater the number of sales that make up a pool of assets, the more complex the accounting will become. In order to decrease the complexity, the transferor may group sales that occur in a week or a month provided the method is consistently applied, and the results will not be materially different than if the sales are accounted for separately.

The accounting for the initial sale in a revolving-period securitisation is very similar to the accounting for a standard securitisation. One primary difference is that the transferor would also recognise an asset or liability for the implicit forward contract if its fair value is other than zero. The forward contract represents the transferor's commitment to sell, and the trust's commitment to purchase, new receivables using funds collected during the revolving period. If the forward is entered into on terms other than market terms, it has a value, which is included as a component in the sales proceeds, and should be recognised initially at that value in the transferor's statement of the financial position.

An issue arises when a transferor commits to sell non interest-bearing trade receivables into the revolving-period securitisation whether the value of the forward should encompass any loss to be recognised from the sale of future receivables.

Future receivables do not exist at the measurement date and, therefore, the loss is not recognised until the receivables are generated – at that point the transferor's commitment to sell them on the pre-agreed terms is crystallised.

A transferor in a revolving-period securitisation may use a master trust for many securitisations. The transferor can achieve additional securitisations by transferring receivables to the existing trust in consideration for new securities and then selling those securities to investors. This transfer of new receivables to the trust is neither a sale nor a borrowing because the transfer only increases the transferor's beneficial interests in the transferred assets. It is not until the transferor sells the beneficial interests to investors that the transferor can record a sale.

Desecuritisations

In a desecuritisation, a holder of a security rescinds the securitisation in order to obtain the assets underlying the security. For example, an entity may desecuritise mortgage-backed securities to obtain the underlying mortgage loans or desecuritise related interest-only and principal-only strips in order to obtain the underlying security. Similar to a securitisation in which the transferor retains all the beneficial interests not being treated as a sale, a desecuritisation in which the entity retains all the underlying assets is also not accounted for as a sale. Thus, if an entity were to transfer the securities or beneficial interest in a pool of financial assets in exchange for the financial assets underlying those securities or beneficial interests, the financial assets received would be accounted for as retained interests, and no gain or loss on the transfer would be recognised.

Determining fair value on derecognition

When a transfer of financial assets is accounted for as a sale, the use of fair value is required in measuring the financial components sold, retained, or incurred and in determining any gain or loss on disposal. Fair value of an asset or liability is determined using the principles set out in IAS 39 (r2000) paragraphs 95–102 (see **12.10.7**). IGC 47-1 and IGC 47-2 provide further guidance and illustrative examples relating to the estimation of fair values when a portion of a bond or loan is sold. When there is no active market for the retained interests the best estimate of the fair value of the retained interests is the market value for bonds or loans as a whole, either based on prices of similar bonds or loans or arrived at by using a valuation model, less the proceeds in respect of the portion sold. While there is considerable subjectivity in estimating fair values of components, without objective evidence of values, it would be inappropriate to recognise a gain from allocating the basis between the various elements such that the carrying value of the sum of the parts, plus the recognised gain, is greater than the fair value of the total asset without substantiating market transactions. In instances where the value of the parts exceeds the value of the whole, it is likely that some aspect of the valuation is not being fully comprehended by the model, or a financial asset or a liability is not recognised, or there is a measurement error.

Financial guarantees and recourse

When financial guarantees and recourse obligations arise on a transfer of assets, they are initially recognised at fair value. With respect to determining the fair value of financial guarantees on the basis of probabilities of possible outcomes, IAS 39 (r2000) provides no guidance as to what constitutes a large population of items and judgement will be required in assessing this. This assessment should take into account both the number of observations as well as the monetary amount. Statistically, it is difficult to attribute reliably characteristics to a population where the population consists of a small number of observations (typically less than between 20 or 30 individual items), and it is typically only for populations larger than these that the full benefits of diversification and correlation are derived.

Alternatively, the present value model can be used. For financial guarantees and recourse, the determination of the appropriate discount rate may, however, be difficult because these items are not generally traded. Using the risk-free rate to estimate the fair value of these liabilities may be considered conservative, because it will produce a higher fair value. Judgement should be exercised to ensure that the rate used will produce a reliable estimate of fair value, not just a conservative one.

Allocation when fair value cannot be determined reliably

If the fair value of the new financial asset or financial liability cannot be measured reliably, the fair value of these interests shall be assumed to be zero for purposes of this allocation and the initial carrying amount of this asset in the balance sheet is zero.

Example 12.27 Determining fair value on derecognition

Company A owns US$1,000,000 face amount of loans that contractually yield 10 per cent interest over their life. The carrying amount of these loans after considering the US$20,000 allowance for loan losses is US$980,000. Company A sells 90 per cent of the principal, plus the right to receive interest income of 8 per cent without recourse to an investor for US$900,000 in cash. The transfer meets all the criteria for a sale. Company A retains the right to service these loans, and the servicing contract stipulates a 1 per cent fee as compensation for performing the servicing. Company A also retains an interest-only strip for the portion of the interest coupon not sold (1 per cent). At the date of transfer, the fair value of the retained 10 per cent of the loan is US$100,000; the fair value of the servicing asset is US$15,000; and the fair value of the interest-only strip could not be measured reliably.

The following table demonstrates the allocation of this loan between the sold and retained interests:

Interest	*Fair value (US$)*	*Percentage of total fair value (%)*	*Allocated carrying amount (US$)*	*Sold interests (US$)*	*Retained interests (US$)*
Loans sold	900,000	88.67	868,965	868,965	
Loans retained	100,000	9.85	96,552		96,552
Interest Only (IO) strip	0	0	0	0	0
Servicing asset	15,000	1.48	14,883		14,883
Total	**1,015,000**	**100.00**	**980,000**	**868,965**	**111,035**

12.13 Accounting for secured borrowings

If a financial asset is transferred to another enterprise but the transfer does not satisfy the conditions for derecognition, the transferor accounts for the transaction as a collateralised (secured) borrowing. In such a case, the transferor's right to reacquire the asset is not a derivative. (IAS 39 (r2000).36 and IGC 36-1)

12.13.1 Accounting for repurchase agreements

Under a repurchase agreement accounted for as a secured borrowing, the transferor should recognise the cash received and a payable due to the transferee. The difference between the amount of cash initially exchanged and the amount of cash exchanged upon maturity of the agreement (the repurchase transaction) should be recognised as interest expense. The transferor should continue to recognise the transferred financial asset in its balance sheet. The accounting for the financial asset and the interest expense in the transferor's books is determined based on its classification as held-to-maturity, available-for-sale, held-for-trading or as a loan or receivable originated by the enterprise.

The accounting by the transferee for a repurchase agreement that is a secured borrowing is symmetrical to the transferor's accounting. The transferee should record a receivable for the cash initially paid for the financial asset. The difference between the amount of cash initially exchanged and the amount of cash exchanged upon maturity of the agreement (the repurchase transaction) should be recognised as interest income by the transferee. The transferred asset is considered collateral held by the transferee and, therefore, should not be recorded by the transferee in its balance sheet.

12.13.2 Accounting for securities lending transactions

In a securities-lending transaction accounted for as a financing (secured borrowing), any cash received from the transferee is considered to be the amount borrowed by the transferor. The treatment of securities lending transactions accounted for as secured borrowings is similar to the accounting for repurchase agreements if the asset received from the transferee is cash.

However, in securities lending transactions, the transferee may give the transferor other assets, such as letters of credit or other securities, instead of cash as collateral for the security borrowed. Subsequent to the amendment to IAS 39 (r2000), the transferor does not record either these securities in its balance sheet or an obligation for their return (see **12.14**).

If the transferee exchanges cash for the financial assets, the accounting for the sale of the financial assets is exactly the same as for repurchase agreements accounted for as sales. If the transferee surrenders control over other financial assets in return for the transferor's financial assets, both parties should derecognise the financial assets surrendered and recognise, initially at fair value, the financial assets received.

12.13.3 Other transfers accounted for as secured borrowings

If an exchange of financial assets for cash or other consideration (excluding beneficial interests) does not meet the criteria for a sale, the transferor and transferee shall account for the transfer as a secured borrowing. The accounting for these transfers is very similar to the accounting for repurchase and securities lending agreements accounted for as secured borrowings.

For the transferor/debtor, this requires the establishment of a liability initially equal to the fair value of the proceeds received. Conversely, the transferee/lender should recognise a receivable equal to the cash and other consideration paid. Subsequently, both the transferor and transferee should recognise remittances by the transferor to the transferee as debt service payments consisting of principal and interest.

12.14 Accounting for collateral

IAS 39.44–46 initially required the separate recognition and disclosure of collateral in both the debtor's and creditor's accounting records where the creditor was permitted to sell or repledge the collateral without constraint.

These paragraphs were deleted from the standard in the amendment to IAS 39 in October 2000. The disclosure requirements for collateral have, however, been expanded, requiring increased disclosure by both debtors and creditors that was not formerly required under IAS 32 (r1998) or IAS 39. These additional disclosure requirements include the disclosure by the creditor of the fair value of any collateral received which it is permitted to sell or repledge as well as any portion that has, in fact, been sold or repledged.

Cash held as collateral is always recorded as an asset by the secured party, with a corresponding obligation for its return, because it is impossible to determine whether it has been used by the secured party, and it cannot be distinguished from borrowed cash.

Offsetting collateral
IAS 32 (r1998).40(c) specifically precludes netting in the disclosure of assets pledged as collateral for non-recourse financial liabilities.

12.14.1 Comparison with UK GAAP

Rules in FRS 5, *Reporting the Substance of Transactions*, result in accounting for sale and repurchase agreements and securities lending transactions as secured borrowings. Treatment of collateral is the same as it is under the revised provisions of IAS 39 (r2000).

12.14.2 Comparison with US GAAP

Following the replacement of SFAS 125 by SFAS 140, *Accounting for Transfers and Servicing of Financial Assets and Extinguishments of Liabilities,* US GAAP no longer requires accounting for collateral by debtors and creditors, mirroring the amended collateral accounting provisions under IAS 39 (r2000).

12.15 Derecognition (extinguishment) of financial liabilities

12.15.1 Derecognition criteria

The derecognition criteria in respect of financial liabilities differ from those relating to financial assets in that they are not based on control.

> 'An enterprise should remove a financial liability (or a part of a financial liability) from its balance sheet when, and only when, it is extinguished – that is, when the obligation specified in the contract is discharged, cancelled, or expires.'
>
> (IAS 39 (r2000).57)

> 'This condition is met when either:
>
> (a) the debtor discharges the liability by paying the creditor, normally with cash, other financial assets, goods, or services; or
>
> (b) the debtor is legally released from primary responsibility for the liability (or part thereof) either by process of law or by the creditor (the fact that the debtor may have given a guarantee does not necessarily mean that this condition is not met).'
>
> (IAS 39 (r2000).58)

If a debtor reacquires its own outstanding debt securities, regardless of whether the securities are cancelled or held either as an investment or available for re-issue, the debt is discharged since the creditor has been paid in cash and the enterprise cannot have a liability to itself. Any difference between the carrying amount and the amount paid to the creditor is included in net profit or loss. The intention to resell the bonds does not create a contractual obligation to deliver cash or another financial asset (IGC 57-2).

The issuance of equity instruments of the debtor that are *not* mandatorily redeemable or redeemable at the option of the holder in full satisfaction of the obligation would also be considered extinguishments. However, under IAS 32 (r1998).22 equity instruments of the debtor that are mandatorily redeemable or redeemable at the option of the holder are debt instruments (see **11.4**), and as such, the issuance of these instruments in satisfaction of a debt obligation should be accounted for as an exchange of debt instruments. As discussed in **12.15.2** an exchange of one debt instrument in satisfaction of another debt instrument is not always accounted for as an extinguishment.

When a debtor is released by the creditor from being the primary obligor on the condition that a third party assumes the original debt obligation (often for a fee), the release constitutes an extinguishment of the original debtor's liability provided the debtor is legally released from the liability by the creditor (IGC 57-3). If, however, the debtor agrees to continue to make payments to the original creditor on behalf of the third party, a new debt with the third party is recognised (IGC 57-1).

In-substance defeasance

IAS 39 (r2000).59 clarifies that payment to a third party including a trust (referred to in the USA as 'in-substance defeasance') does not by itself relieve the debtor of its primary obligation to the creditor, in the absence of legal release. Such an arrangement fails because in the event of default by a debtor, the mere fact that the debtor has placed assets with a third party or trust does not affect the other creditors' right(s) to claim payment from the debtor.

Recognition of a new liability

In some cases, a liability may meet the criteria and be derecognised, but the non-cash financial asset used to settle the liability may not meet the financial asset derecognition criteria. In such a case, the transferred assets remain on the transferor's balance sheet, and the transferor recognises a new liability relating to the transferred assets which may be equal to the derecognised liability. (IAS 39 (r2000).60)

12.15.2 Debt exchange/modification

> 'An exchange between an existing borrower and lender of debt instruments with substantially different terms is an extinguishment of the old debt that should result in derecognition of that debt and recognition of a new debt instrument. Similarly, a substantial modification of the terms of an existing debt instrument (whether or not due to the financial difficulty of the debtor) should be accounted for as an extinguishment of the old debt.'
>
> (IAS 39 (r2000).61)

The terms of the instruments are considered 'substantially different' if the discounted present value of the cash flows under the new terms, including any fees paid net of any fees received, is at least 10 per cent different from the discounted present value of the remaining cash flows of the original debt instrument. (IAS 39 (r2000).62)

A modification of debt terms may include, inter alia, any one or a combination of the following:

- reduction (absolute or contingent) of the stated interest rate for the remaining original life of the debt;
- extension of the maturity date or dates at a stated interest rate lower than the current market rate for new debt with similar risk;
- reduction (absolute or contingent) of the face amount or maturity amount of the debt as stated in the instrument or other agreement; and
- reduction (absolute or contingent) of accrued interest.

Cash flows, therefore, can be affected by changes in principal amounts, interest rates or maturity. They can also be affected by fees exchanged between the debtor and creditor to effect changes in:

- recourse or non-recourse features;
- priority of the obligation;
- collateralised (including changes in collateral) or non-collateralised features;
- debt covenants and/or waivers;
- the guarantor (or elimination of the guarantor);
- option features.

If the terms of a debt instrument are changed or modified in any of the ways described above and the cash flow effect on a present value basis is less than 10 per cent, the debt instruments are not considered to be substantially different and the difference between the present values under the new and old terms is amortised over the remaining term of the debt instrument. IAS 39 (r2000) does not address whether the present values should be determined based on the effective interest rate of the old debt that is being modified or exchanged, or on the effective interest rates of the new debt. Accordingly, either method may be used provided the method is applied consistently to all modifications or exchanges of debt instruments (IGC 62-1).

The new debt instrument should be initially recorded at fair value and that amount should be used to determine the debt extinguishment gain or loss to be recognised. Any costs or fees incurred are recognised as part of the gain or loss on the extinguishment.

If it is determined that the original and new debt instruments are not substantially different, then a new effective interest rate is to be determined based on the carrying amount of the original debt instrument and the revised cash flows. Any costs or fees incurred are an adjustment to the carrying amount of the liability and are amortised over the remaining term of the modified loan. (IAS 39 (r2000).62)

12.15.3 Derecognition of part of a financial liability

If an enterprise transfers a part of a financial liability to others while retaining a part, or if an enterprise transfers an entire financial liability and in so doing creates a new financial asset or assumes a new financial liability, the enterprise should account for the transaction as it would for a derecognition of part of a financial asset (see **(2) Partial derecognition of a financial asset** within **12.12.2**) or a derecognition coupled with a new financial asset or liability (see **(3) Derecognition of a financial asset coupled with a new financial asset or liability** also within **12.12.2**. (IAS 39 (r2000).65)

> 'The difference between the carrying amount of a liability (or part of a liability) extinguished or transferred to another party, including related unamortised costs, and the amount paid for it should be included in net profit or loss for the period.'
>
> (IAS 39 (r2000).63)

When a creditor releases a debtor from its obligation to make payments, but the debtor assumes an obligation to pay if the party assuming primary responsibility defaults, the debtor:

(a) recognises a new financial liability based on the fair value of its obligation for the guarantee; and recognises a gain or loss based on the difference between (i) any proceeds and (ii) the carrying amount of the original financial liability (including any related unamortised costs) minus the fair value of the new financial liability. (IAS 39 (r2000).64)

IAS 39 (r2000) is not explicit in the treatment of instances where extinguishment of part of a financial liability occurs simultaneously with a modification of the terms of the remaining debt. Paragraph 65 requires the allocation of basis based on relative fair values between the extinguished and the modified portions in determining the gain or loss on extinguishment and the new carrying amounts. However, there is no guidance as to whether the 10 per cent rule should be applied first in determining whether the aggregate transaction (the reduction in principal together with the modification of terms) represents a substantial modification in terms of paragraph 61. If the 10 per cent test is met, full extinguishment of the financial liability is required and the new financial liability is recognised at its fair value. The determination of whether extinguishment has occurred should be made prior to allocating fair value between the relevant portions.

12.15.4 Comparison with UK GAAP

Derecognition of liabilities in the UK follows similar rules.

Although there are no specific rules in the UK on fees paid to extinguish a liability, the general requirement in FRS 4, *Capital Instruments*, that a profit or loss arising on the repayment of a loan is recognised in the income statement immediately would imply that any such fees are treated in the same way. Modification of the terms of debt, and treatment of any fees incurred on such modification, is also similar, though UK GAAP does not contain a 10 per cent rule or any similar definitive guidance in this area.

12.15.5 Comparison with US GAAP

The treatment of costs or fees under US GAAP is identical to that under IAS 39 (r2000) in the case of fees exchanged between the debtor and creditor. However, differences arise in the treatment of fees paid to third parties which IAS 39 (r2000) treats identically to fees exchanged between the debtor and creditor.

Under US GAAP, where fees are paid to a third party associated with an extinguishment these fees are considered to be related to the new debt instrument and are amortised over the term of the new instrument using the effective interest rate method. Where the exchange or modification is not accounted for as an extinguishment, these fees are expensed as incurred. (EITF 96-19, *Debtor's Accounting for a Modification or Exchange of Debt Instruments*)

IAS 39 (r2000) does not contain guidance in calculating the 10 per cent limitation. US GAAP provides the following guidance on calculating the present value of the cash flows to determine whether or not a substantial modification has occurred:

- The cash flows of the new debt instrument include all cash flows specified by the terms of the new debt instrument, plus any amounts paid by the debtor to the creditor less any amounts received by the debtor from the creditor as part of the exchange or modification.
- If the original debt instrument and/or the new debt instrument has a floating interest rate, the variable rate in effect at the date of the exchange or modification is to be used to calculate the cash flows of the variable-rate instrument.
- If either the new debt instrument or the original debt instrument is callable or puttable, separate cash flow analyses are to be performed assuming exercise and non-exercise of the call or put. The cash flow assumptions that generate the smaller change would be the basis for determining whether the 10 per cent threshold is met.
- If the debt instruments contain contingent payment terms or unusual interest rate terms, judgement should be used to determine the appropriate cash flows.
- The discount rate to be used to calculate the present value of the cash flows is the effective interest rate, for accounting purposes, of the original debt instrument. It would not be considered appropriate to use the current market rate applied to the new debt as the discount rate.
- If within a year of the current transaction the debt has been exchanged or modified without being deemed to be substantially different, the debt terms that existed a year earlier should be used to determine whether the current exchange or modification is substantially different. (EITF 96-19)

12.16 Derivative instruments

The key aspects of IAS 39 (r2000) related to derivatives are:

- all derivatives and certain embedded derivatives are reported on the balance sheet at fair value;
- changes in fair value of derivatives are recorded in net profit or loss;
- special accounting rules are provided for:

- fair value hedges;
- cash flow hedges; and
- hedges of a net investment of a foreign entity.

12.16.1 Definition

Rather than defining derivatives in terms of the various types and forms currently found in the financial markets, IAS 39 (r2000) sets out a broad definition based on the distinguishing characteristics of derivative contracts. This definition is designed to cater for the various different forms that derivatives can take and to keep pace with ongoing innovation in financial markets and product structuring. As a result, certain contracts which have typically not historically been regarded as derivatives are now included in the scope of the definition of a derivative under IAS 39 (r2000).

> 'A derivative is a financial instrument:
>
> (a) whose value changes in response to the change in a specified interest rate, security price, commodity price, foreign exchange rate, index of prices or rates, a credit rating or credit index, or similar variable (sometimes called the 'underlying');
>
> (b) that requires no initial net investment or little initial net investment relative to other types of contracts that have a similar response to changes in market conditions; and
>
> (c) that is settled at a future date.'
>
> (IAS 39 (r2000).10)

> 'A derivative usually has a notional amount, which is an amount of currency, a number of shares, a number of units of weight or volume, or other units specified in the contract. Alternatively, a derivative could require a fixed payment as a result of some future event that is unrelated to a notional amount.'
>
> (IAS 39 (r2000).13)

Thus, there are four components of a derivative instrument:

(1) an underlying index or variable;
(2) the notional amount or payment provision;
(3) no or little initial net investment; and
(4) future settlement.

> 'Derivative financial instruments create rights and obligations that have the effect of transferring between the parties to the instrument one or more of the financial risks inherent in an underlying primary financial instrument. Derivative instruments do not result in a transfer of the underlying primary financial instrument on inception of the contract and such a transfer does not necessarily take place on maturity of the contract.'
>
> (IAS 32 (r1998).10)

Unlike many other financial instruments, derivatives, which often have a fair value of zero on inception, may be either financial assets or financial liabilities at a given stage during their life, depending on their fair value. On inception, derivative financial instruments give one party a contractual right to exchange financial assets with another party under conditions that are potentially favourable, or a contractual obligation to exchange financial assets with another party under conditions that are potentially unfavourable. Some instruments embody both a right and an obligation to make an exchange. Since the terms of the exchange are determined on inception of the derivative instrument, as prices in financial markets change, those terms may become either favourable or unfavourable. (IAS 32 (r1998), Appendix.A9)

Common types of derivative financial instruments include:

(a) financial options;
(b) futures contracts and forward foreign exchange contracts;
(c) interest rate swaps;
(d) currency swaps;
(e) put and call options;
(f) interest rate caps, collars and floors;
(g) loan commitments ;
(h) forward contracts to purchase fixed rate debt (for example, a mortgage);
(i) note issuance facilities; and
(j) letters of credit.

(IAS 32 (r1998).9, and A12, IGC 10-5 and IGC 30.1)

The following sections discuss the four characteristics of derivative instruments.

(1) Underlying index or variable

An underlying is a variable that, along with either a notional amount or a payment provision, determines the settlement of a derivative, though in many instances, the underlying is not delivered at settlement. Examples of an underlying include:

- a security price or security price index;
- a commodity price or commodity price index;
- an interest rate or interest rate index;
- a credit rating or credit index;
- an exchange rate or exchange rate index; or
- an insurance index or catastrophe loss index.

An underlying may be any variable whose changes are observable or otherwise objectively verifiable.

The following are examples of common derivative contracts and the respective underlying (IGC 10-1):

Type of Contract	Pricing/settlement variable (Underlying)
Interest rate swap	Interest rates
Currency swap	Currency (exchange) rates
Commodity swap	Commodity prices
Equity swap	Equity prices
Credit (or default) swap	Credit rating or credit value
Total return swap	Total fair value of the reference asset and interest rates
Bond option (call or put, purchased or written)	Interest rates
Currency option (call or put, purchased or written)	Currency (exchange) rates
Commodity option (call or put, purchased or written)	Commodity prices
Stock option or warrant (call or put, purchased or written)	Equity prices
Bond futures (e.g., Treasury or Eurodollar futures)	Interest rates
Forward rate agreements	Interest rates
Currency futures	Currency (exchange) rates
Commodity futures	Commodity prices
Bond forwards	Interest rates
Currency forwards	Currency (exchange) rates
Commodity forwards	Commodity prices
Equity futures and forwards	Equity prices

Example 12.28 Underlying index or variable

Company ABC enters into a contract with a counterparty that requires ABC to purchase one share of XYZ common stock in one year for €110, the market forward price. The current price of XYZ common stock is €105 per share. In this example, common stock is the underlying variable.

(2) Notional amount or payment provision

'A derivative usually has a notional amount, which is an amount of currency, a number of shares, a number of units of weight or volume, or other units specified in the contract. However, a derivative instrument does not require the holder or writer to invest or receive the notional amount at the inception of the contract. Alternatively, a derivative could require a fixed payment as a result of some future event that is unrelated to a notional amount. For example, a contract may require a fixed payment of US$1,000 if six-month LIBOR increases by 100 basis points. In this example, a notional amount is not specified.'

(IAS 39 (r2000).13)

The settlement of a derivative instrument with a notional amount is determined by the interaction of that notional amount with the underlying. The interaction may be simple multiplication, or it may involve a formula with leverage factors or other constants. A payment provision specifies a fixed or determinable settlement to be made if the underlying behaves in a specified manner (see also IGC 10-6).

The easiest way to understand the concepts of notional amounts, underlyings and payment provisions is to work through a few examples.

Example 12.29 Notional amount and underlying

XYZ enters into an interest rate swap that requires XYZ to pay a fixed rate of interest and receive a variable rate of interest. The fixed interest rate amount is 7.50 per cent, while the variable interest rate amount is three month LIBOR, reset on a quarterly basis. The notional amount of the swap is US$100 million. In this example, the underlying is an interest rate index, the difference between 7.50 per cent and three month LIBOR. Payments are based on the multiplication of this underlying by the US$100 million notional amount.

Example 12.30 Payment provision

XYZ enters into a contract that requires XYZ to pay £10 million if ABC stock increases by £5 per share during a six month period; XYZ will receive £10 million if ABC stock decreases by £5 per share during the same six month period. In this example, the underlying is the price of ABC stock. However, there is no notional amount to determine the settlement amount. Instead, there is a payment provision of £10 million that is based on changes in the underlying.

(3) No or little initial net investment

> 'One of the defining conditions of a derivative is that it requires little initial net investment relative to other contracts that have a similar response to market conditions. An option contract meets that definition because the premium is significantly less than the investment that would be required to obtain the underlying financial instrument to which the option is linked.' (IAS 39 (r2000).15)

Providing the opportunity to participate in the price changes of an underlying such as shares without actually having to own an associated asset or owe an associated liability (leverage) is a basic feature that distinguishes most traditional derivative instruments from non-derivative instruments. Therefore, a contract that requires the holder or writer to invest or receive an amount approximating the notional amount of the contract at inception is not a derivative instrument. For example, entering into a commodity futures contract generally requires no net investment, while purchasing the same commodity requires an initial net investment equal to its market price.

However, both contracts reflect changes in the price of the commodity in the same way (i.e., similar gains or losses will be incurred).

The phrase initial net investment is stated from the perspective of only one party to the contract, but it determines the application of the Standard for both parties. This term should be interpreted on a relative and not absolute basis and therefore refers to circumstances where the investment is less than that needed to acquire a traditional financial instrument with a similar exposure to market conditions. This reflects the inherent leverage feature typical of derivative agreements compared to the underlying instruments (IGC 10-10).

A swap or forward contract does not generally require an initial net investment unless the terms favour one party over the other. An option generally requires that one party make an initial net investment (a premium), because that party has the rights under the contract and the other party has the obligations.

Some contracts require gross exchanges of currencies (e.g., currency swaps that require an exchange of different currencies at both inception and maturity). The definition of a derivative instrument includes such currency swaps. The initial exchange of currencies of equal fair values in those arrangements does not constitute an initial net investment in the contract. Instead, it is the exchange of one kind of cash for another kind of cash of equal value. The balance of the agreement, a forward contract that obligates and entitles both parties to exchange specified currencies, on specified dates, at specified prices, is a derivative instrument indexed to the currencies (IGC 10-3).

Many derivative instruments require margin accounts, such as futures contracts and exchange traded written options. The margin account is not part of the initial net investment in a derivative instrument. Margin accounts are a form of collateral for the counterparty or clearinghouse and may take the form of cash, securities, or other specified assets, typically liquid assets. Margin accounts are distinct financial assets that are accounted for separately (IGC 15-2).

Derivatives with initial net investment (prepayment provisions)
However, many contracts do require an initial investment that may be significant and therefore may not meet the initial net investment criterion. For example, a deep-in-the-money purchased option, a prepaid forward, and a prepaid interest rate swap all may require a significant initial investment. The prepayment of an equity forward at the spot price is not a derivative since it fails the 'little or no initial net investment' criterion. The initial net investment in this case approximates the investment that would be required for other types of contracts having a similar exposure to market risk. (IGC 15-1) Determining whether a contract meets the initial net investment criterion

requires judgement when the investment is significant, but is less than the notional amount or the notional amount applied to the underlying.

Prepaid interest rate swap

Instead of entering into a pay-fixed, receive-variable swap that is settled each quarter, an enterprise can enter into a prepaid swap and pay the entire present value of the fixed leg of the swap at inception of the contract in return for the quarterly variable payments. Such a swap has both an underlying (the variable rate) and a notional amount, is settled at a future date (at each quarterly reset) and since the prepaid leg is settled based on the present value of the future cash flows, the initial investment is smaller than both the notional amount and what would be required relative to other contracts to provide a similar exposure to changes in value of the underlying (IGC 10-4a).

Since the whole contract represents a derivative instrument, it would not be appropriate under IAS 39 (r2000) to separate out ('bifurcate') the prepaid amount which is equivalent to a loan and therefore the whole contract should be accounted for as a derivative. The principles relating to bifurcating the derivative component of a financial instrument are discussed more fully in **12.17**.

If, however, a pay-variable, receive-fixed swap is prepaid (i.e., the variable leg is prepaid in return for the contracted fixed rate payments), this transaction is not a derivative. It is no different from investing in fixed rate debt. It does not meet the definition of a derivative since the initial investment required is identical to that which would be incurred to invest in a non-derivative contract that has a similar response to changes in market conditions (IGC 10-4b).

Initial net investment – offsetting loans

Where transactions have been entered into to circumvent the definition of a derivative, the separate legs should be viewed as an aggregate unit. For example, Entity A makes a five-year fixed rate loan to entity B, while entity B makes a five-year variable rate loan to entity A. Each party has a receivable and payable for the same amount and has entered into a netting agreement which satisfies the criteria for netting as set out in IAS 32 (r1998), paragraph 33. The net effect of offsetting the contracts for entities A and B is the economic equivalent of an interest rate swap arrangement (entity A pays fixed, receives variable) where there is no exchange of notional amount (i.e., no initial net investment). The criteria to be considered in determining whether the transaction is entered into to circumvent the provisions of IAS 39 (r2000) may include (IGC 10-8):

- Are the transactions entered into at the same time and in contemplation of one another?

- Are the transactions executed with the same counterparty (or structured through an intermediary)?
- Do the transactions relate to the same risk?
- Is there no apparent economic need or substantive business purpose for structuring the transactions separately that could not also have been accomplished in a single transaction?

Example 12.31 Initial net investment – interest rate swap

Company A enters into a contract with a counterparty that requires it to pay a LIBOR based variable rate of interest on a notional amount of ¥10 billion while the counterparty pays A an 8 per cent fixed rate of interest. The contract is a typical interest rate swap with a notional amount of ¥10 billion. The contract does not require an initial net investment by either party. In some instances, the terms of the interest rate swap may be favourable or unfavourable and would require one of the parties to make an upfront initial investment in the contract. If the initial investment represents a premium or discount for market conditions, the initial net investment would normally not approximate the notional amount of the contract and, thus, the contract meets the initial net investment criteria of a derivative instrument.

Example 12.32 Initial net investment – equity

ABC wishes to participate in the changes in the fair value of 10,000 shares of Company XYZ. ABC can either purchase 10,000 shares of XYZ common stock or enter into a forward purchase contract with a notional amount of 10,000 shares of XYZ common stock and an underlying that is the forward price of XYZ. Purchasing the shares would require an initial investment equal to the current price for 10,000 shares and would result in benefits such as the receipt of dividends, if any, and the ability to vote the shares. This would not represent a derivative instrument. A simple forward contract entered into at the current forward price for 10,000 shares of the equity instrument would not require an initial investment equal to the notional amount, but would offer the same opportunity to benefit or lose from changes in the price of that security and would qualify as a derivative instrument.

(4) Future settlement

Another defining characteristic of a derivative financial instrument is that it is settled at a future date. This criterion in the definition of a derivative is all encompassing. It means that any forward commitment in which neither party has yet performed is a derivative. IAS 39 (r2000) provides two very significant exceptions, however, that limit the extent to which settlement at a future date results in a contract being a derivative. Normal commitments to purchase and sell non-financial assets and regular-way purchase contracts that require delivery of a financial asset (see **12.16.2**) are exempted from the derivatives requirements under IAS 39 (r2000).

Under IAS 39 (r2000), unless one of the exceptions is met, executory contracts that are founded in an index, underlying, or variable are treated as derivatives. Since neither party has yet performed, there is little or no initial net investment and settlement will be at a future date. For example, a forward contract to purchase a fixed rate debt instrument is an executory contract because neither party has performed. It is a derivative because there is no initial net investment, there is an underlying (interest rates), and it will be settled in the future. The contract would usually be exempt, however, because regular-way delivery, as discussed below, generally is required.

Executory contracts based on agreements to perform services where there is an underlying would not fall under the definition of a derivative since these are settled by physical delivery in the normal course of business. Assets to be acquired and liabilities to be incurred as a result of a firm commitment to purchase or sell goods or services are not recognised under present accounting practice until at least one of the parties has performed under the agreement such that it either is entitled to receive an asset or is obligated to disburse an asset. (IAS 39 (r2000).29(b))

Under IAS 39 (r2000), it is not important whether an option is expected to be exercised or not (for example, if the contract is deeply out of the money) for the contract to meet this criterion of future settlement since expiration at maturity is a form of settlement even though there is no further exchange of consideration between the parties (IGC 10-18).

In the case of a swap, whether the regular resets are settled on a net or gross basis does not affect the application of the future settlement criterion since under IAS 39 (r2000) there is no requirement for settlement on a net basis to meet the definition of a derivative (IGC 10-2).

Example 12.33 Settlement at a future date – interest rate swap

Company ABC enters into an interest rate swap with a counterparty that requires ABC to pay a fixed rate of 8 per cent and receive a variable rate of three month LIBOR, reset on a quarterly basis. The fixed and variable amounts are determined based on a A$100 million notional amount. ABC and the counterparty do not exchange the notional amount. XYZ pays or receives a net cash amount each quarter based on the difference between 8 per cent and three month LIBOR, reset quarterly. The contract meets the definition of a derivative because there is no initial net investment, under the terms of the swap, settlements are made in cash, not by delivery of a financial instrument on a regular-way basis, and they occur at future quarterly dates.

Comparison with UK GAAP
There are no specific UK GAAP rules that relate to this area.

Comparison with US GAAP
Net settlement provisions
Under US GAAP, the definition of a derivative is similar to the definition in IAS 39 (r2000) with the exception that under US GAAP, contracts that have an explicit or implicit net settlement provision are also regarded as derivatives.

Under US GAAP, a contract is considered to have a net settlement provision if delivery of the underlying is not required (even if it can be settled in cash as a result of a default of one of the parties), if there is an established market mechanism that facilitates net settlement outside the contract (for example, if the security is publicly traded), or if the asset is readily convertible to cash or is itself a derivative. A contract that permits net settlement is a derivative unless there exists a significant penalty as a disincentive for non-performance (non delivery).

Under IAS 39 (r2000), the ability to settle net is not a consideration in determining whether a contract is a derivative. Instead, it focuses on an enterprise's intent to make or take delivery and the practice of the enterprise. It excludes contracts that require delivery of a non-financial asset (providing among other things that there is no practice of not taking or making delivery) and it excludes contracts that require delivery of a financial asset (providing the contract specifies a regular-way delivery) (see **12.16.2**).

The general definition of a derivative, however, is narrower under IAS 39 (r2000) than under US GAAP. IAS 39 (r2000) requires settlement at a future date and therefore appears to exclude contracts for goods and services that are prepaid.

12.16.2 Financial instruments excluded from the scope of IAS 39 (r2000) or not treated as derivatives

Certain financial instruments and other contracts described below that may otherwise meet the definition of a derivative instrument are not treated as derivatives because they are either excluded from the scope of IAS 39 (r2000) or are not accounted for under IAS 39 (r2000) as a derivative. These instruments are discussed in the following sections and include:

- normal purchases and sales;
- regular-way contracts;
- certain financial guarantees;
- insurance contracts;
- contracts based on physical variables;

- unquoted equity instruments;
- certain equity instruments of an issuer;
- equity-based compensation contracts; and
- royalty contracts.

Normal purchase and sales commitments

> 'Commitments to buy or sell non-financial assets and liabilities that are intended to be settled by the reporting enterprise by making or taking delivery in the normal course of business, and for which there is no practice of settling net (either with the counterparty or by entering into offsetting contracts), are not accounted for as derivatives but rather as executory contracts. Settling net means making a cash payment based on the change in fair value.'
>
> (IAS 39 (r2000).14)

Pure commodities themselves (e.g., gold bullion) fall outside the scope of IAS 39 (r2000) and are accounted for under IAS 2 (r1993), *Inventories*, if they are held as inventory (IGC 8-1). Certain commodity contracts do, however, fall within the scope of IAS 39 (r2000) and must be accounted for as derivative instruments.

IAS 39 (r2000) does apply to commodity-based contracts that give either party the right to settle in cash or some other financial instrument, with the exception of commodity contracts that:

(a) were entered into and continue to meet the enterprise's expected purchase, sale, or usage requirements,
(b) were designated for that purpose at their inception, and
(c) are expected to be settled by delivery. (IAS 39 (r2000).6)

However, if an enterprise follows a pattern of entering into offsetting contracts that effectively accomplish settlement on a net basis, those contracts are not entered into to meet the enterprise's expected purchase, sale, or usage requirements and thus would be subject to the rules of IAS 39 (r2000). (IAS 39 (r2000).7)

Where a contract to purchase or sell a commodity has a cash settlement alternative, and there is a past practice of either offsetting or settling in cash, such contract meets the definition of a derivative and does not qualify for the 'normal' exemption (IGC 14-1). Even if the contract is required to be settled by delivery, where there is a past pattern of entering into offsetting contracts and settling the net difference between the contract price and market value in cash, the contract does not meet the 'normal' exemption and must be accounted for as a derivative (IGC 14-2).

In the case of an option to exercise a put in respect of a non-financial asset where the issuer has the right to settle either in cash or by physical delivery, the holder (issuer) of the option that gives it the right to settle net in cash can meet the 'normal' exemption. The counterparty to the option contract who cannot control settlement must treat the option as a derivative. However, if the option contract requires a physical settlement, then neither party would treat the option as a derivative instrument unless there is a past practice of settling such contracts on a net basis (IGC 14-3).

Example 12.34 Commodity-based forward contract

Company X enters into a fixed-price forward contract to purchase one million pounds of copper. Copper is traded on the London Metals Exchange (LME) and is readily convertible to cash. The contract permits X to take physical delivery of the copper at the end of twelve months or to pay or receive a net settlement in cash, based on the change in fair value of copper. The contract is a derivative instrument because there is no initial net investment, the contract is based on an index, the price of copper, and it is to be settled at a future date. However, if Company X intends to settle the contract by delivery and has no history of settling in cash or entering into offsetting contracts, the contract qualifies for the exemption and is not considered a derivative under IAS 39 (r2000). If this contract was not convertible to cash but there was a pattern of entering into offsetting contracts, it would be a derivative.

Example 12.35 Pattern of net settlement

Company A enters into a forward contract to purchase an asset. The contract requires physical settlement. Company A has an established pattern of settling such contracts on a net basis prior to delivery by entering into an offsetting position with the counterparty. The pattern of settling on a net basis prohibits Company A from qualifying for the exemption based on normal delivery.

Example 12.36 Inability to settle by delivery

Company XYZ owns an office building in Milan. XYZ enters into a European put option with an investor that permits XYZ to exercise the option to sell the building to the investor for €150 million. The current value of the building is €175 million. The option expires in five years. The option, if exercised, may be settled through physical delivery or net cash, at XYZ's option. Although the contract meets the definition of a derivative, it is not accounted for as a derivative if XYZ intends to settle the contract by delivering the building if it exercised its option.

The investor, however, must account for the contract as a derivative because it does not control whether settlement is by delivery or in cash.

Regular-way contracts

Regular-way contracts (discussed in detail in **12.9.2**) are agreements to buy financial assets on terms that require delivery of the asset within the time frame established generally by regulation or convention in the market place. During the period between trade and settlement date of a security, the buyer and seller essentially have entered into a forward contract that might meet the definition of a derivative. However, these contracts are not recognised under IAS 39 (r2000) as derivatives due to the short duration of commitment. (IAS 39 (r2000).31)

The notion of a regular-way security trade is based on market-place regulations or conventions rather than on the normal practices of an individual enterprise. For example, if it is either required or customary for certain securities on a specified exchange to settle within three days, a contract that requires settlement in more than three days is not a regular-way security trade even if the enterprise customarily enters into contracts to purchase such securities more than three days forward. Regulations or conventions may be more difficult to determine for less developed markets or less active exchanges.

IAS 39 (r2000) provides no guidance for situations in which the instrument is not traded. The application of the regular-way exemption in those situations is considered appropriate providing the transaction ultimately will result in the delivery of a financial asset and the time period of the forward commitment is not longer than reasonably required for the parties to complete normal underwriting and prepare and execute closing documents.

Example 12.37 Regular-way contracts

Equity securities

A contract to purchase or sell a publicly traded equity security in the United States customarily requires settlement within three business days ('t+3'). If a contract for purchase of that type of security requires settlement in three business days, the regular-way exception applies, but if the contract requires settlement in a period greater than three business days, the regular-way exception does not apply. Trades of financial instruments with settlement terms outside those prescribed by normal market convention do not typically qualify for the regular-way exception and are considered derivative instruments if the other criteria are satisfied.

Equity purchases in different markets

Company X purchases one million shares of Company B, a NYSE listed entity, through a US broker on 1 October 2001. The settlement date of the contract is 9 October 2001. Trades for equity securities on US exchanges customarily settle in three business days. Because the trade settles in six business days, it does not meet the exemption as a regular-way contract.

Assume X purchases the same one million shares of Company B on a foreign exchange with a customary settlement period of six business days. The contract to purchase B on the foreign exchange would meet the exemption for a regular-way trade.

Certain financial guarantees

Financial guarantee contracts, including letters of credit, that provide for payments to be made if the debtor fails to make payment when due generally are excluded from IAS 39 (r2000) but fall under IAS 37 *Provisions, Contingent Liabilities and Contingent Assets* (see **11.9**). In contrast, financial guarantee contracts are subject to IAS 39 (r2000) if they provide for payments to be made in response to changes in a specified interest rate, security price, commodity price, credit rating, foreign exchange rate, index of prices or rates, or other variable (sometimes called the 'underlying'). Also, IAS 39 (r2000) does require recognition of financial guarantees incurred or retained as a result of its derecognition standards (see **12.12.2**).

To qualify for this exemption, there is a prerequisite that a debtor-creditor relationship must exist and that the creditor (holder of the contract) must be exposed to loss in the event of default by the debtor (IGC 1-5a). This analysis applies equally to the perspective of the issuer of the credit contract in that the holder must be exposed to the loss for the contract to be exempt from IAS 39 (r2000) (IGC 1-5b). In such a case, neither the issuer nor the holder account for it as a derivative. Credit (default) swaps traded between counterparties will typically not qualify under this exemption unless there is an underlying debtor-creditor relationship. These instruments are therefore accounted for as derivatives. Similarly, in the case of other credit derivative instruments such as credit rating guarantees, total return swaps and credit spread products, since the trigger events for payments under these instruments are not based on an underlying debtor-creditor relationship or on the creditor being exposed to loss in the event of default by the debtor, they typically will not qualify for the exemption and instead are accounted for as derivative instruments (IGC 1-1 and 1-2).

Example 12.38 Financial guarantees

Credit rating contract

Company B owns £100 million of Company X bonds that mature in twenty years. Company X is rated BBB by the rating agencies. Company B is concerned that X may be downgraded and the value of bonds would decline in value. To protect against such a decline, Company B enters into a contract with a banker that will pay Company B for any decline in the fair value of the Company X bonds related to a credit downgrade to B or below. The contract is for a five-year period. Company B pays £2 million for the credit contract. Because the contract pays Company B in the event of a downgrade, and not in the event of a failure by Company X to pay, it is a derivative instrument.

Actual credit loss contract

Company X owns £100 million of single family residential mortgage loans. Company X is concerned that defaults may increase as a result of a recession and purchases a guarantee contract from Company B, a mortgage insurance entity. The contract requires Company B to pay any loan deficiency to Company X upon a default and foreclosure by Company X. The contract has a £5 million cap. Company X pays Company B a £2 million fee for the contract. Because the contract provides for payments to Company X in the event of a failure of a debtor to pay when due, it is exempt from the scope of IAS 39 (r2000).

Insurance contracts

Rights and obligations under insurance contracts as defined in IAS 32 (r1998) are excluded from the scope of IAS 39 (r2000). The IASB currently has a separate project on its agenda dealing with Insurance Contracts (see Chapter **2**). However, derivatives embedded in such contracts are not excluded from IAS 39 (r2000). (IAS 39 (r2000). 1(d))

> 'An insurance contract is a contract that exposes the insurer to identified risks of loss from events or circumstances occurring or discovered within a specified period, including death (in the case of an annuity, the survival of the annuitant), sickness, disability, property damage, injury to others and business interruption.' (IAS 32 (r1998).3)

Similarly, when a financial instrument takes the form of an insurance contract but principally involves the transfer of financial risks (for example, some types of financial reinsurance and guaranteed investment contracts issued by insurance and other enterprises), they do fall within the scope of IAS 32 (r1998) and IAS 39 (r2000). (IAS 32 (r1998).3) (See also **12.4**.)

Examples of insurance contracts that contain embedded derivatives include contracts whose payout is linked to an underlying variable (such as an equity index). Where insurance contracts contain embedded derivatives that are not considered to be closely related to the host contract, the embedded derivative is required to be separated out from the host instrument and separately accounted for in accordance with the provisions of IAS 39 (r2000) (see **12.17**).

Contracts based on physical variables

Contracts that require a payment based on climatic, geological, or other physical variables are commonly used as insurance policies and are excluded from the scope of IAS 39 (r2000). (Those based on climatic variables are sometimes referred to as weather derivatives.) In such cases, the payment made is based on an amount of loss to the enterprise. As discussed above, rights and obligations under insurance contracts are excluded from the scope of IAS 39 (r2000).

Examples of climatic, geological, and other physical variables include the number of inches of rainfall or snow in a particular area, temperature in a particular area or for a specified period of time, and the severity of earthquakes.

If the underlying is a physical variable, the contract is not subject to the scope and requirements of IAS 39 (r2000).

If a contract's underlying is the combination of two or more variables, and one or more would not qualify for the exception for physical variables discussed above, the application of the definition of a derivative instrument depends on the predominant characteristics of the combined variable. The contract is considered a derivative instrument if the changes in its combined underlying are highly correlated with changes in one of the component variables that would not qualify for an exception (IGC 1-6).

Example 12.39 Contracts based on physical variables

Heating degree days

A utility company in the United States enters into a contract with an intermediary or counterparty that is based on heating degree days. A heating degree day in the United States is defined as the deviation of a day's average temperature from 65 degrees Fahrenheit. The utility company knows that if its heating degree days exceed a certain level, profit margins increase due to higher consumption. However, if heating degree days are below a certain level, the company will suffer a loss due to lower consumption. The contract requires no initial investment and requires a payment by the counterparty if heating degree days are less than a specified amount during January, February, and March. If heating degree days exceed a specified amount during January, February, and March, the utility company will make a fixed payment to the intermediary or counterparty. Because the underlying on which settlement is based is a physical variable, heating degree days, the utility company is not subject to the provisions of IAS 39 (r2000) in respect of the contract which would otherwise meet the definition of a derivative. The counterparty is also not subject to the provisions of IAS 39 (r2000).

Unquoted equity instruments

IAS 39 (r2000) includes a presumption that fair value can be reliably determined for most financial assets classified as available for sale or held for trading and by default derivatives related to such assets. However, the presumption can be overcome for a derivative that is linked to and that must be settled by delivery of an unquoted market investment (see **12.10.7**). Unquoted market investments refer to those equity instruments that are not traded on either active markets or established exchanges and therefore in respect of which no quoted market price exists.

If the presumption is overcome, the instrument is not accounted for as a derivative.

Example 12.40 Unquoted equity instruments

Call option on an unquoted equity security

Company B purchases a call option from a counterparty on Company X's ordinary shares. Company X is a private company whose shares are not traded and for which no market quotation exists. The call option requires physical settlement, if exercised. The contract is a derivative instrument. However, since the underlying is represented by, and requires settlement by delivery of Company X's unquoted equity, it is not accounted for as a derivative if the fair value of the equity instrument cannot be reliably determined.

Certain equity instruments of an issuer

Certain equity instruments, some of which would otherwise meet the definition of a derivative, are specifically excluded from the scope of the Standard. The exclusion includes equity instruments of the issuer as well as derivative instruments that are indexed to the enterprise's own equity that can be settled by the enterprise in its own equity securities including options, warrants and other financial instruments that are classified as shareholders' equity of the reporting enterprise. However, the holder of the instruments does apply IAS 39 (r2000).

However, an enterprise may have a forward, option or other derivative instrument whose value changes in response to something other than the market price of the enterprise's own equity securities but that the enterprise can choose to settle or is required to settle in its own equity securities. In such case, the enterprise accounts for the instrument as a derivative instrument, not as an equity instrument, because the value of such an instrument is unrelated to the changes in the equity of the enterprise. (IAS 39 (r2000).12)

Example 12.41 Instruments settled in equity shares

Option settled in but not indexed to equity

Company X enters into a contract with counterparty B. The contract is a call option indexed to gold prices with a strike of US$400 per ounce. B pays a premium to X to purchase the call option. If settlement is required X will settle the call option by issuing its own shares at a value equal to the intrinsic value of the option upon exercise. The call option does not meet the exception because it is indexed to gold. The settlement provision that requires X to issue its own shares does not exempt the contract from the scope of IAS 39 (r2000) because the contract is not indexed to X's equity.

Equity swap settled in shares

Company X enters into an equity swap with a counterparty. The notional amount of the equity swap is one million of X's ordinary shares. The equity swap requires

X to pay the counterparty a LIBOR rate based on a notional amount while receiving the total return on its ordinary shares. The payments may be cash or net share settled at X's option. Accordingly, the derivative instrument is exempt from the scope of IAS 39 (r2000) for Company X since the contract is indexed to both the enterprise's own securities and to LIBOR. The counterparty, however must account for the instrument as a derivative because the instrument is not indexed to the counterparty's equity and is not settled by its own equity instruments.

Equity based compensation contracts

Derivative instruments issued in connection with equity-based compensation arrangements are not specifically addressed in IAS 39 (r2000). However, equity instruments of an issuer are not treated as derivatives under IAS 39 (r2000). Therefore, many such instruments are exempt because they are classified in shareholders' equity. IAS literature does not specify the issuer's accounting for those contracts. The holder of the contract would, however, be required to account for the contract as a derivative instrument that is subject to IAS 39 (r2000) if the holder prepares financial statements in accordance with IAS.

Royalty contracts

No guidance is provided in IAS 39 (r2000). The treatment of these should follow IAS 18 (r1993), *Revenue*, even if these contracts would otherwise meet the definition of a derivative instrument under IAS 39 (r2000) (IGC 13-1). IAS 18 (r1993).33 states that 'royalties accrue in accordance with the terms of the relevant agreement and are usually recognised on that basis unless, having regard to the substance of the agreement, it is more appropriate to recognise revenue on some other systematic and rational basis.'

A foreign currency contract with a pay-off based on sales volumes has two underlyings, being foreign currency and sales, and therefore is a derivative instrument. Sales volume is not exempt from being considered an underlying (IGC 13-2).

Example 12.42 Royalty contracts

Company X enters into a royalty arrangement with Company B that allows X the exclusive rights to manufacture and market B's software product. Company X is required to pay B an annual royalty equal to 4 per cent of sales for the first €10 million in sales and 2 per cent for all sales above €10 million. The royalty arrangement is for a ten-year period. At the end of ten years, the rights to the software revert to B.

Because the royalty arrangement has an underlying (sales volume), a payment provision, no initial net investment and will be settled in the future, it meets the definition of a derivative instrument. However, the guidance in IAS 18 (r1993), *Revenue*, which prescribed the accounting treatment in respect of royalty contracts has not been amended by IAS 39 (r2000) and therefore should prevail over the provisions of IAS 39 (r2000) such that royalty arrangements should not be accounted for as derivative instruments. IAS 18 (r1993).33 states that 'royalties accrue in accordance with the terms of the relevant agreement and are usually recognised on that basis unless, having regard to the substance of the agreement, it is more appropriate to recognise revenue on some other systematic and rational basis.' This treatment is consistent with the rationale of IAS 39 (r2000).

Comparison with UK GAAP

There are no specific rules in the UK relating to this area.

Comparison with US GAAP

Normal purchases and sales

Like IAS 39 (r2000), US GAAP also provides an exception for normal purchases and normal sales of non-financial instruments and non-derivative instruments. Following the FAS 138, *Accounting for Certain Derivative Instruments and Certain Hedging Activities* amendment to SFAS 133, *Accounting for Derivative Instruments and Hedging Activities*, the exemption is available in respect of contracts where it is probable (both at inception and during the contract's term), that the contract will not settle net and will result in physical delivery. The exception is further limited to contracts that provide for delivery of quantities that are expected to be used or sold by the reporting entity over a reasonable period in the normal course of business. Contracts must also not have a price based on an underlying index that is not clearly and closely related to the asset. Contracts that require cash settlement of the gains or losses or are otherwise settled net on a periodic basis do not qualify for this exception. Net settlement of contracts in a group of contracts classified as 'normal' would call into question the classification of all such contracts. Entities are required to document the basis for concluding that it is probable that the contract will result in physical delivery. IAS 39 (r2000) does not specify these limitations.

Non-financial assets and liabilities

Under US GAAP, if the underlying of a contract that is not exchange traded is the price or value of a non-financial asset or liability as described below, the contract is exempted from scope of SFAS 133:

- a non-financial asset of one of the parties to the contract provided that the asset is not readily convertible to cash; or
- a non-financial liability of one of the parties to the contract provided that the liability does not require delivery of an asset that is readily convertible to cash.

IAS 39 (r2000) does not provide a similar exception because it is not relevant whether the contract can be settled in net cash. The test is whether the enterprise intends to take or make delivery and whether there has been a past practice of settling in cash.

Regular-way contracts
Under US GAAP, an exception is also made for regular-way contracts, but it is limited to contracts for the purchase of securities that are readily convertible to cash. However, the exception is only available if the contract has no net settlement provision (as defined) and there is no market mechanism (as defined) that facilitates net settlement. IAS 39 (r2000) provides the exception for contracts to buy financial assets, not just securities, and in situations in which there are net settlement provisions and market mechanisms that facilitate net settlement.

Contracts based on physical variables – climactic, geological or other
Under US GAAP, an exemption is provided for physical variables similar to IAS 39 (r2000). However, the exemption is limited to contracts that are not traded on an exchange. To cater for the growing popularity of such contracts and to prevent abuse of the exemption in SFAS 133, EITF 99-2, *Accounting for Weather Derivatives* was issued to specifically address the accounting for weather derivatives. EITF 99-2 requires that entities that enter into weather derivatives for trading purposes or for the purpose of speculation should account for such contracts at fair value (which mirrors the provisions of SFAS 133 in the absence of the specific exemption). Contracts entered into under non-trading activities (such as for risk management purposes by end-users) are not required to be marked to fair-value.

12.17 Embedded derivatives

12.17.1 Definition

> 'Sometimes, a derivative may be a component of a hybrid (combined) financial instrument that includes both the derivative and a host contract – with the effect that some of the cash flows of the combined instrument vary in a similar way to a stand-alone derivative. Such derivatives are sometimes known as 'embedded derivatives'. An embedded derivative causes some or all of the cash flows that otherwise would be required by the contract to be modified based on a specified interest rate, security price, commodity price, foreign exchange rate, index of prices or rates, or other variable.'
>
> (IAS 39 (r2000).22)

12.17.2 Interaction of IAS 32 (r1998) and IAS 39 (r2000)

IAS 32 (r1998) and IAS 39 (r2000) contain two significant provisions relating to embedded derivatives and compound instruments. These provisions, although related, operate independently of each other, are designed to achieve different objectives and do not result in the same treatment of compound instruments between the issuer and the holder of the financial instrument.

IAS 32 (r1998) requires the separation of the equity and liability elements of a compound instrument for presentation purposes by the issuer of the financial instrument. Certain instruments that are comprised of both an equity and a liability component, may contain embedded derivatives. However, the embedded derivative provisions in IAS 39 (r2000) only relate to hybrid instruments in which one of the components meets the definition of a derivative. The hybrid instrument provisions in IAS 32 (r1998), operate regardless of whether or not the embedded derivative provisions in IAS 39 (r2000) apply and vice versa. Since IAS 32 (r1998) does not deal with recognition and measurement, the embedded derivative provisions of IAS 39 (r2000) provide a useful basis for determining the classification of the amounts required for presentation purposes. The treatment of compound instruments under IAS 32 (r1998) is discussed in **11.4.1** (see also IGC 11-1).

12.17.3 Separation ('bifurcation') conditions

> 'An embedded derivative should be separated from the host contract and accounted for as a derivative under this Standard if all of the following conditions are met:
>
> (a) the economic characteristics and risks of the embedded derivative are *not* closely related to the economic characteristics and risks of the host contract;
> (b) a separate instrument with the same terms as the embedded derivative would meet the definition of a derivative; and
> (c) the hybrid (combined) instrument is not measured at fair value with changes in fair value reported in net profit or loss.'
>
> (IAS 39 (r2000).23)

If an enterprise is required to separate an embedded derivative from its host contract but is unable to measure the embedded derivative separately either at acquisition or at a subsequent financial reporting date, it treats the entire combined contract as a financial instrument held for trading (see **12.6.1.**). (IAS 39 (r2000).26) IGC 25-1 emphasises that combinations of a cash instrument and a derivative cannot be treated as a unit, for example, to avoid the use of fair value accounting for the derivative.

Under IAS 39 (r2000), many but not all embedded derivative features are required to be accounted for separately from the host contract. The requirement to separate the derivative from the host contract is based on a determination of whether the embedded derivative is closely related to the host. Considerable judgement is required to make this determination because most of the guidance provided is in the form of examples. These examples are included below and many of them are further illustrated. In the absence of conditions and terms that are specifically addressed by IAS 39 (r2000), the determination is based on analogy to such examples. More than one embedded derivative may be identified and separated from a hybrid instrument providing they have different risk exposures and are readily separable and independent of each other (IGC 23-8). IAS 39 (r2000) does not permit an enterprise to separate embedded derivatives where IAS 39 (r2000) does not require such separation (IGC 23-4).

If a derivative can be contractually transferred separately from the hybrid instrument, it is not an embedded derivative. Instead, it is considered to be a stand-alone derivative instrument and is accounted for as such (IGC 23-6). Similarly, a derivative that is attached to a host instrument by a third party does not represent an embedded derivative. Such a derivative is treated as a freestanding derivative, even if it cannot be sold or transferred separately from the host contract (IGC 23-7).

Where separation is required, although IAS 39 (r2000) does not require separate disclosure of each component in the balance sheet, separate disclosure is required of assets carried at cost and those carried at fair value (IGC 23-1).

Host is a derivative
In terms of the embedded derivative provisions in IAS 39 (r2000), embedded derivatives are only separated from instruments if the other component (the host) is not a derivative.

Determining the host instrument
IAS 39 (r2000) does not provide guidance for making the determination whether a host instrument is debt or equity in nature where both features are present. However, there is guidance in US GAAP that provides a reasonable basis for making the distinction on whether or not the equity-indexed component provides a holder with residual equity rights. Under US GAAP, if the host contract encompasses a residual interest in an entity, its economic characteristics and risks should be considered that of an equity instrument, and an embedded derivative would need to possess equity characteristics (related to the same entity) to be closely related to the host contract.

However, most commonly, a financial instrument host contract will not embody a claim to the residual interest in an entity and, thus, the economic characteristics and risks of the host contract should be considered that of a debt instrument. For example, even though the overall hybrid instrument that provides for repayment of principal may include a return based on the market price of shares, the host contract does not involve any existing or potential residual interest rights (i.e., rights of ownership) and, thus, would not be an equity instrument. The host contract would instead be considered a debt instrument, and the embedded derivative that incorporates the equity-based return would not be closely related to the host contract. If the embedded derivative is considered not to be closely related to the host contract, the embedded derivative must be separated from the host contract and accounted for as a derivative instrument by both parties to the hybrid instrument, except in the case where it is an equity instrument of the issuer. (SFAS 133, paragraph 60)

Treatment of host

If an embedded derivative is separated, the host contract itself should be accounted for (a) under this IAS 39 (r2000) if it is, itself, a financial instrument and (b) in accordance with other appropriate IASs if it is not a financial instrument (IAS 39 (r2000).23).

Upon separation from the host contract, the embedded derivative may be designated as a hedging instrument, if desired, provided it meets the hedge accounting criteria.

Allocation ('bifurcation') methods

IAS 39 (r2000) does not provide any guidance in respect of allocating a hybrid instrument between its host and embedded derivative components in the event that separation is required.

The IGC concluded that the allocation method which records the embedded derivative at fair value and determines the initial carrying value assigned to the host contract as the difference between the basis of the hybrid instrument and the fair value of the embedded derivative should be used to determine the carrying values of the host contract component and the embedded derivative component of a hybrid instrument when separate accounting for the embedded derivative is required (see IGC 23-3).

This conclusion is supported by the fact that there is a presumption (in IAS 39 (r2000).70) that fair value can be determined reliably in respect of derivative instruments. It is only in unusual circumstances that an entity would conclude that it cannot reliably separate an embedded derivative from its host contract.

Separation of the embedded derivative from its host contract should not result in recognition of an immediate gain or loss in earnings.

If an enterprise is unable to measure an embedded derivative independently of the host contract, for example because the derivative is based on an unquoted equity instrument whose fair value cannot be reliably determined, the enterprise may measure the derivative at fair value by reference to the fair value of the hybrid instrument and deducting the fair value of the host contract. In such cases, the difference between the two values provides reliable evidence of the fair value of the embedded component (DIGC 23-10). If the enterprise concludes that the embedded derivative is sufficiently significant to preclude it from obtaining a reliable estimate of the fair value of the entire instrument, the combined instrument is measured at cost less impairment (IGC 70-3).

Enterprises are encouraged to use the same method adopted for the bifurcation of embedded derivatives and, whatever method is used, to apply it consistently.

Assumptions regarding valuation of the embedded derivative
When an embedded derivative is at-the-market (which would typically result in a fair value of zero at inception for forwards and futures) and the host is a debt instrument, the use of different discount rates in pricing the forward and the debt host will result in the sum of the components being different to the value of the combined instrument. When a forward contract is entered into in-the-money (i.e., other than at-the-market), the contract contains a financing component. One party to the contract must pay the other party for the favourable term. A financing component also exists if a forward contract is entered into at-the-money and the market price of the underlying subsequently changes.

When a financing component is present, some or all of it can be separated from the forward contract. However, the amount of interest to be recognised on the financing component will vary not only as a function of the portion being separated, but also as a function of the discount rates used to value each component. A forward is typically valued using a risk free rate, while financing transactions are typically valued at the risk adjusted discount rate. Although the total return and weighted average yield on the instrument will not change, irrespective of how the components are allocated, different assumptions as to whether the forward is at- ,in- or out-of-the-money can significantly affect the allocation of basis between the components.

As a result of the potentially significant effect of these assumptions and in the absence of explicit guidance in IAS 39 (r2000), IGC 22-1 and DIGC 22-2 provide detailed guidance for identifying the terms of a host debt instrument and the requirement to separate out both an option-based and a non-option based embedded derivative. Based on this guidance, the terms of the debt instrument should reflect the stated or implied substantive terms of the hybrid instrument. In the absence of implied or stated terms, the enterprise must make its own judgement of the terms, for example whether the host instrument is a fixed, variable or zero coupon instrument. An enterprise may not identify a component that is not specified or separate an embedded derivative that is not already clearly present in the hybrid instrument, that is it cannot create a cash flow that does not exist.

In separating a non-option based embedded derivative from the host contract, the terms of the non-option embedded derivative should be determined in a manner that results in its fair value being equal to zero at the inception of the hybrid instrument. Often, simply adjusting the referenced forward price (pursuant to documented legal terms) to be at-the-market for the purpose of separately accounting for the embedded derivative will result in that non-option embedded derivative having a fair value of zero at inception of the hybrid instrument.

If it was permitted to separate non-option embedded derivatives on other terms, a single hybrid instrument could be decomposed into an infinite variety of combinations of host debt instruments and embedded derivatives, for instance, by separating embedded derivatives with terms that create leverage, asymmetry or some other risk exposure not already present in the hybrid instrument. The determination of the terms of the embedded derivative is based on the conditions existing when the financial instrument was issued (IGC 22-1). If a non-option embedded derivative has stated terms that are off-market at inception, that amount should be quantified and allocated to the host contract since it effectively represents a borrowing.

The economic nature of an option-based embedded derivative is fundamentally different from a forward-based derivative (including forwards and swaps), because the terms of a forward are such that a payment based on the difference between the price of the underlying and the forward price will occur at a specified date, while the terms of an option are such that a payment based on the difference between the price of the underlying and the strike price may or may not occur. Adjusting the strike price of an option-based derivative therefore alters the nature of the hybrid instrument (DIGC 22-2).

Therefore, in separating an embedded option-based derivative, there is no requirement to assume terms which would result in the derivative having a fair value of zero or an intrinsic value of zero at inception of the hybrid instrument. The separation should be based on the stated terms of the option feature documented in the hybrid instrument (IGC 22-2).

12.17.4 Economic characteristics and risks which are closely related

IAS 39 (r2000).25 lists the examples below where the economic characteristics and risks of an embedded derivative are considered to be closely related to the economic characteristics and risks of the host contract. In these circumstances, an enterprise does *not* account for the embedded derivative separately from the host contract (IAS 39 (r2000).25). Additional guidance related to the examples is given in the sections following the table.

Debt Instruments Interest Rates	(a) the embedded derivative is linked to an interest rate or interest rate index that can change the amount of interest that would otherwise be paid or received on the host debt contract (in other words, IAS 39 (r2000) does not permit floating rate debt to be treated as fixed rate debt with an embedded derivative);
Debt Instruments Interest Rate Options (Caps and Floors)	(b) an embedded floor or cap on interest rates is considered to be closely related to the interest rate on a debt instrument if the cap is at or above the market rate of interest or if the floor is at or below the market rate of interest when the instrument is issued, and the cap or floor is not leveraged in relation to the host instrument (see **12.17.5**);
Debt Instruments Foreign Currency Interest and Principal Payments	(c) the embedded derivative is a stream of principal or interest payments that are denominated in a foreign currency. Such a derivative is not separated from the host contract because IAS 21 (r1993), *The Effects of Changes in Foreign Exchange Rates*, requires that foreign currency translation gains and losses on the entire host monetary item be recognised in net profit or loss. Similarly, dual currency bonds, where interest and principal are denominated in different currencies, do not contain an embedded derivative that is separated from the host contract (IGC 25-3);
Non Financial Instruments Foreign Currency	(d) the host contract is not a financial instrument and it requires payments denominated in (i) the currency of the primary economic environment in which any substantial party to that contract operates or (ii) the currency in which the price of the related good or service that is acquired or delivered is routinely denominated in international commerce (for example, the US dollar for crude oil transactions). That is, such contract is not regarded as a host contract with an

	embedded foreign currency derivative (see **12.17.6**);
Debt Instruments Prepayment Options	(e) the embedded derivative is a prepayment option with an exercise price that would not result in a significant gain or loss;
Debt Instruments Interest-only and Principal-only Strips	(f) the embedded derivative is a prepayment option that is embedded in an interest-only or principal-only strip that (i) initially resulted from separating the right to receive contractual cash flows of a financial instrument that, in and of itself, did not contain an embedded derivative and that (ii) does not contain any terms not present in the original host debt contract (see **12.17.7**);
Lease Payments Indexed Rentals	(g) with regard to a host contract that is a lease, the embedded derivative is (i) an inflation-related index such as an index of lease payments to a consumer price index (provided that the lease is not leveraged and the index relates to inflation in the enterprise's own economic environment), (ii) contingent rentals based on related sales, and (iii) contingent rentals based on variable interest rates (see **12.17.8**); or
Debt Instruments Recoverability of Principal and Return to Investors	(h) the embedded derivative is an interest rate or interest rate index that does not alter the net interest payments that otherwise would be paid on the host contract in such a way that the holder would not recover substantially all of its recorded investment or (in the case of a derivative that is a liability) the issuer would pay a rate more than twice the market rate at inception (see **12.17.9**). (IAS 39 (r2000).25)

12.17.5 (b) Caps and floors – debt and other hosts

Floors or caps on interest rates and the interest rate on a debt instrument are considered to be closely related, provided the cap is at or above the current market price (or rate) and the floor is at or below the market price (or rate) at issuance of the instrument and is not leveraged in relation to the host instrument. Thus, the derivative embedded in a variable-rate debt instrument that has a floor on the interest rate (i.e., the floor option) would not be separated from the host contract and accounted for separately even though, in a falling interest rate environment, the debt instrument may have a return to the investor that is a significant amount above the market return of a debt instrument without the floor provision.

If, instead of a debt host, the host contract is a sales or purchase contract (including for non-financial assets) and the embedded derivative is a cap or floor (i.e., establishes a higher or lower limit) on the price of the asset that is subject to the sales or purchase contract, the cap or floor is considered closely related and therefore is not separated from the host provided the cap or floor is out of the money at inception (IGC 25-8).

Example 12.43 Interest rate options – caps and floors

Company X issues US$1 million variable rate debt with a five-year maturity. The variable rate is indexed to LIBOR, which is 4.5 per cent at the date of issue. Embedded in the debt is a clause that caps the variable rate at 10 per cent. The cap would not be accounted for separately because the cap is both related to interest rates and above the market rate when the debt is issued. Thus, the cap is considered to be closely related to the host instrument.

12.17.6 (d) Embedded foreign currency derivatives

An embedded foreign currency derivative instrument is *not* separated from the host contract if the host contract is a non-financial instrument and it requires payment(s) denominated in:

(1) the currency of the primary economic environment in which any substantial party to that contract operates (i.e., its functional currency); or
(2) the currency in which the price of the related good or service that is acquired or delivered is routinely denominated in international commerce (e.g., the US dollar for crude oil transactions).

This is designed to ensure that the foreign currency is integral to the arrangement and thus considered to be closely related to the terms of the host contract. A contract with payments denominated in a currency that is not the primary currency of any substantial party to that contract includes an embedded derivative that is not considered to be closely related to the host contract and would be accounted for separately (IGC 25-2).

The currency of the primary economic environment refers to the currencies used in measuring items in the financial statements of any substantial party to the contract (measurement currency as determined in SIC-19, *Reporting Currency*), or the currencies of the countries in which any substantial party to the contract is domiciled (IGC 25-6). In countries that are subject to significant inflation, it is common for contracts to be denominated in a hard currency such as the US dollar (USD). In these circumstances, assuming the USD is not the measurement currency of any substantial party to the transaction and not the currency in which such contract is routinely denominated, the embedded USD/local currency derivative must be separated from the host supply contract (DIGC 25-9).

A currency of international commerce exists if it is the only currency in which the underlying asset is exchanged in similar transactions worldwide, not just in a local area. This does not therefore represent a currency that is routinely used for a certain commodity or service in commerce within the local area of one of the substantial parties to the contract. Oil is clearly an example of an asset that is exchanged based on a single currency of international commerce (the US dollar). If a commodity or service trades in different markets in different currencies, there is no single currency which can be said to represent a currency in which the item is routinely denominated in international commerce (IGC 25-5).

This exemption only applies in respect of non-financial instruments (including executory contracts) and implies that all other aspects of the contract must be closely related. For example, a leveraged embedded foreign currency forward (for example where the foreign currency feature exceeds the notional amount of the contract), would be required to be separated from a foreign currency based goods or services contract (IGC 25-4).

Example 12.44 Equity instruments – embedded foreign currency derivatives

Embedded foreign currency provision

Company X, a Dutch company, leases property from Company Y, a UK company. The lease payments are denominated in Sterling (£). The primary currency of X is the Euro and the primary currency of Y is Sterling. The provision to pay in Sterling would not require separate accounting because Sterling is the currency of the primary economic environment of Y, who is a substantial party to the lease. As discussed in **12.4**, an operating lease is not a financial instrument. (IAS 32 (r1998).14)

Embedded foreign currency provision

Company X, a New Zealand company, leases property under an operating lease from Company Y, an Australian company. The lease payments are denominated in US dollars. The primary currency of X is the New Zealand dollar (NZ$) and the primary currency of Y is the Australian dollar (A$). The provision to pay in US dollars would require separate accounting because it is not the currency of the primary economic environment of any substantial party to the contract and the price of this asset is not routinely denominated in that currency in international commerce. If the property was leased under a finance lease (which is a financial instrument), the lease payments would represent monetary items in terms of IAS 21 (r1993), *The Effects of Changes in Foreign Exchange Rates.*

Because gains or losses measured using spot rates on such items are recognised in net profit or loss under IAS 21(r1993), the embedded derivative would not be separated from the host contract since the condition in IAS 39 (r2000).23(c) is not met. Under this condition if the combined instrument is measured at fair value with changes in fair value reported in net profit, the embedded derivative is not separated.

Embedded foreign currency provision – Involvement of a third party

Company X would like to lease property from Company Y under an operating lease and have the payments denominated in US dollars. The primary currency of both companies is the Brazilian real. To accomplish a US dollar-denominated lease, Company Y leases the property to an investment banker whose functional currency is US dollars. The investment banker then subleases the property to Company X. The sublease agreement requires Company X to pay US dollars. The investment banker cannot offset the lease transactions. The provision to pay in US dollars would not require separate accounting because the US dollar is the functional currency of investment banker who is acting as a principal, that is, the party that is subject to the risk of loss.

If, however, the investment banker were to be acting as an agent (i.e., the investment banker would be indemnified for any losses incurred due to a default by Company X), the parties would look through the investment banker to determine if the foreign currency provision would be a derivative. In this example, the foreign currency provision would require separate accounting because the US dollar is not the primary currency of any substantial party to the contract.

Comparison with UK GAAP – embedded foreign currency derivatives

There are no specific UK requirements relating to this area. It is extremely rare to find a hybrid instrument separated into its parts for accounting purposes.

Comparison with US GAAP – embedded foreign currency derivatives

Under US GAAP, unsettled foreign currency transactions, including financial instruments, that are monetary items and have their principal payments, interest payments, or both of these denominated in a foreign currency are subject to the requirement in SFAS 52, *Foreign Currency Translation*, to recognise any foreign currency transaction gain or loss in earnings and are not be considered to contain embedded foreign currency derivative instruments. The same rule applies to available-for-sale or trading securities that have cash flows denominated in a foreign currency. (SFAS 133.15)

IAS 39 (r2000) does not specify guidance in this area. However, applying IAS 21 (r1993).15 results in the same treatment as under US GAAP. IAS 21 (r1993) states that any foreign currency gains or losses on unsettled foreign currency transactions that are monetary items are recognised in net profit or loss. As a result, the condition in IAS 39 (r2000).23(c) is not satisfied. As a result, there is no requirement to separate the embedded derivative from the host contract.

12.17.7 (f) Interest-only and principal only (I/O and P/O) strips)

An interest-only or principal-only strip does not contain an embedded derivative under IAS 39 (r2000) that should be separated, if it:

(1) initially resulted from separating the rights to receive contractual cash flows of a financial instrument that, in and of itself, did not contain an embedded derivative; and
(2) does not contain any terms not present in the original host debt contract.

Example 12.45 Debt instruments I/O and P/O strips

Qualifying interest-only strip

Transferor X securitises £100 million of financial assets with an 8 per cent coupon in a securitisation structure that meets the requirements for sale accounting. The beneficial interests issued consist of Class A and B and an interest-only certificate. The Class A and B certificates have a principal amount of £100 million and a 6 per cent coupon. The interest-only strip is entitled to any residual interest cash flows after the Class A and B certificate holders are paid. As an embedded derivative, the interest-only strip is not considered to be closely related in terms of IAS 39 (r2000).25(e) since it could potentially cause the holder to recover less than substantially all of its initial investment. However, the interest-only certificate contains no unusual features. The interest-only strip results from separating the rights to receive contractual cash flows from a financial instrument that did not contain an embedded derivative that otherwise would be required to be accounted for separately and did not incorporate any new terms. Thus, the interest-only strip would not be accounted for as a derivative since paragraph 25(f) considers the prepayment option to be closely related to the debt host.

Non-qualifying interest-only strip

Transferor X securitises £100 million of mortgage loans with an 8 per cent coupon in a securitisation structure that meets the requirements for sale accounting. The issued beneficial interests consist of a principal-only strip of £100 million and an interest-only strip that pays 8 per cent based on the principal amount. Transferor X received proceeds of £60 million for the principal-only strip. If market 30-year mortgage rates exceed 10 per cent, the coupon on the interest-only strip increases to 10 per cent. The additional 2 per cent will be paid from the principal-only cash receipts. The conditional 2 per cent payment is an option, sometimes referred to as a caplet. In this example, the embedded caplet is required to be separated because it was not present in the original financial instrument. If the fair value of the components cannot be measured reliably, the entire instrument would be accounted for separately under the held-for-trading classification.

12.17.8 (g) Lease payments – indexed rentals

With regard to a host contract that is a lease, the most common form of embedded derivative is an inflation-related index such as the indexing of lease payments to a consumer price index. Provided the lease is not leveraged and the index relates to inflation in the enterprise's own economic environment, such embedded derivatives are considered closely related and not separated from the host contract. Under IAS 39 (r2000), rentals for the use of leased assets and adjustments in the enterprise's own environment for inflation on similar property are considered to be closely related.

IAS 39 (r2000).25(g) specifies that lease contracts that include contingent rentals based on certain sales of the lessee are not considered to have an embedded derivative in the form of the contingent rental.

An obligation to make future payments for the use of leased assets and the adjustment of those payments to reflect changes in a variable interest-rate index is an embedded derivative that is considered to be closely related to the lease. An example of this is a rental adjusted for changes in LIBOR.

Example 12.46 Leased payments – indexed rentals

Inflation-indexed payments – domestic environment

Company X leases property with a lease term of ten years. The primary currency of Company X is the Euro. Lease payments are also to be made in Euros. Embedded in the lease is a provision that requires the lease payment to be adjusted every two years for the change in a specified local consumer price index. The provision has no additional unusual features. The embedded inflation indexed payment would not be accounted for separately because the rate of inflation is not leveraged and is in the same economic environment of the enterprise.

Leveraged inflation-indexed payments

Company X leases property with a lease term of ten years. The functional currency of Company X is the Hong Kong dollar. Lease payments are also to be made in Hong Kong dollars. Embedded in the lease is a provision that requires the lease payment to be adjusted every two years for two times the change in the consumer price index. The embedded inflation indexed payment would be accounted for separately because the rate of inflation is leveraged. In this instance, the leveraged portion of the embedded inflation provision would be accounted for as a derivative. This would be valued based on the extent to which it is leveraged over and above the change in the consumer price index since the non-leveraged portion is not a derivative which is separated. (IAS 39 (r2000))

12.17.9 (h) Recoverability of principal and return to investors

IAS 39 (r2000) specifies that an embedded derivative is considered closely related to its host debt instrument if it is an interest rate or interest rate index that does not alter the net interest payments that otherwise would be paid on the host contract in such a way that the holder would not recover substantially all of its recorded investment or, (in the case of a derivative that is a liability) the issuer would pay a rate more than twice the market rate at inception.

IAS 39 (r2000) does not specify what is meant by the term 'substantially all'. Under US GAAP, the term 'substantially all' generally has been interpreted to mean greater than or equal to 90 per cent and the use of 90 per cent, although not required under IAS 39 (r2000), provides an appropriate indicator of how this term should be interpreted.

Even though the above conditions focus on the investor's rate of return and the investor's recovery of its investment, the existence of either of those conditions would result in the embedded derivative instrument not being considered closely related to the host contract by *both* parties to the hybrid instrument. Because the existence of those conditions is assessed at the date that the hybrid instrument is acquired (or incurred) by the reporting enterprise, the acquirer of a hybrid instrument in the secondary market could potentially reach a different conclusion than the issuer of the hybrid instrument due to applying the conditions in this paragraph at different points in time.

A holder's ability (but not obligation) to settle at a substantial loss (for instance with a puttable debt instrument) is not an embedded derivative that requires separation from the host contract if the holder is not required to make such an election. The condition that 'the holder would not recover substantially all of its recorded investment' therefore applies to situations where the holder can be forced to accept settlement (IGC 25-7).

In evaluating whether the holder would recover substantially all of its recorded investment, IAS 39 (r2000) does not specify how this test should be applied. However, if the likelihood of the investor losing substantially all of its investment or of obtaining a rate more than twice the market rate at inception, is judged to be remote, it seems reasonable to conclude that the embedded derivative does not alter the cash flows in such a way as to meet the loss or recoverability tests, thereby requiring the bifurcation of the embedded derivative.

Note also that with a variable rate instrument, although the issuer could potentially pay a rate more than twice the market rate at inception, this is not an embedded derivative that requires bifurcation since the interest rate is always equal to the current market rate.

Example 12.47 Recovery of principal and return to investors

Issuer's rate doubles

Company A issues 30-year zero coupon debt with principal of €10,000,000 due at maturity. The bonds are issued to yield five percent, excluding the impact of a written option, embedded in the debt. The option is a five-year written cap with a notional amount of €460,000,000 and a strike of 10 per cent indexed to 6-month LIBOR. The debt holder receives payments, if any, from the cap component during the first five years and €10,000,000 at maturity. For example, if rates go to 12 per cent the holder receives two percent of €460,000,000. The embedded cap would be accounted for separately because it could result in a rate of return on the host contract that is at least double the issuer's initial rate on the host contract.

12.17.10 Characteristics and risks not closely related

IAS 39 (r2000).24 lists the examples below where the economic characteristics and risks of an embedded derivative are *not* considered to be closely related to those of the host contract. In these circumstances, assuming the conditions in paragraphs 23(b) (a separate instrument with same terms would be a derivative) and 23(c) (the hybrid instrument is not measured at fair value with changes reported in net profit) are also met, an enterprise accounts for the embedded derivative separately from the host contract. (IAS 39 (r2000).24) Additional guidance related to the examples is given in the sections following the table.

Equity Instruments Put Options	(a) a put option on an equity instrument held by an enterprise is not closely related to the host equity instrument (see **12.17.11**);
Equity Instruments Call Options	(b) a call option embedded in an equity instrument held by an enterprise is not closely related to the host equity instrument from the perspective of the holder (from the issuer's perspective, the call option is an equity instrument of the issuer if the issuer is required to or has the right to require settlement in shares, in which case it is excluded from the scope of IAS 39 (r2000)) (see **12.17.11**);
Debt Instruments Term Extending Options	(c) an option or automatic provision to extend the term (maturity date) of debt is not closely related to the host debt contract held

	by an enterprise unless there is a concurrent adjustment to the market rate of interest at the time of the extension (see **12.17.12** and **12.17.13**);
Debt Instruments Equity Indexed Interest and Principal Payments	(d) equity-indexed interest or principal payments – by which the amount of interest or principal is indexed to the value of equity shares – are not closely related to the host debt instrument or insurance contract because the risks inherent in the host and the embedded derivative are dissimilar (see **12.17.14**);
Debt Instruments Commodity Indexed Interest and Principal Payments	(e) commodity-indexed interest or principal payments – by which the amount of interest or principal is indexed to the price of a commmodity – are not closely related to the host debt instrument or insurance contract because the risks inherent in the host and the embedded derivative are dissimilar (see **12.17.15**);
Equity Instruments Conversion Features	(f) an equity conversion feature embedded in a debt instrument is not closely related to the host debt instrument;
Debt instruments Put and Call Options	(g) a call or put option on debt that is issued at a significant discount or premium is not closely related to the debt except for debt (such as a zero coupon bond) that is callable or puttable at its accreted amount (see **12.17.16**); and
Debt Instruments Credit Indexed Payments	(h) arrangements known as credit derivatives that are embedded in a host debt instrument and that allow one party (the 'beneficiary') to transfer the credit risk of an asset, which it may or may not actually own, to another party (the 'guarantor') are not closely related to the host debt instrument. Such credit derivatives allow the guarantor to assume the credit risk associated with a reference asset without directly purchasing it. (IAS 39 (r2000).24)

	In such a case, the hybrid instrument cannot be classified as a held-for-trading liability in its entirety since the host contract is a debt instrument (IGC 18-3).

12.17.11 (a) and (b) Call and put options on equity instruments

A put option that enables the holder to require the issuer of an equity instrument to reacquire that equity instrument for cash or other assets is *not* closely related to that equity instrument. Thus, such a put option embedded in the equity instrument to which it relates should be separated from the host contract by the holder of the equity instrument. That put option should also be separated from the host contract by the issuer of the equity instrument except in those cases in which the put option is not considered to be a derivative instrument because it is classified in shareholders' equity.

A purchased call option that enables the **issuer** of an equity instrument to reacquire that equity instrument would not be considered to be a derivative instrument by the issuer of the equity instrument. Thus, if the call option were embedded in the related equity instrument, it would not be separated from the host contract by the issuer. However, for the **holder** of the related equity instrument, the embedded written call option *would not be* considered to be closely related to the equity instrument and would be separated from the host contract.

Example 12.48 Equity instruments – put and call options and conversion features

Put option embedded in an equity security

Company A issues ordinary shares to investors that are puttable to the Company at the end of three years. The put option can be settled in net cash or shares at the option of the investors. Assume that the investors classify such securities as available-for-sale and recognise changes in the fair value directly in equity. The embedded put option would be separated from the host contract and accounted for as a derivative by both the issuer and the holder because the ability to settle the option on a net cash basis is inconsistent with the notion of residual equity.

Since the net cash or net share settlement option is held by the investor, it would not be considered to be an equity instrument of the issuer.

However, if the terms of the put option specified settlement in net shares of the company, the issuer would not separate the put option from the host contract because a separate instrument with the same terms would be classified in shareholders' equity and would not be a derivative. A financial instrument indexed to a company's own shares that is to be settled in shares is recorded as an equity instrument. A financial instrument that can be settled in net cash or shares at the option of the investors would be recorded as an asset or liability.

Puttable redeemable preferred shares

Company A issues US$100 million mandatorily redeemable preferred shares to investors with a dividend rate of 10 per cent. The preferred shares are puttable to the Company for cash if interest rates move 200 basis points. The embedded put option would not be separated from the host contract under the embedded derivative provisions because mandatorily redeemable preferred shares would be classified as a debt instrument rather than an equity instrument under IAS 32 (r1998). The option is a prepayment option that would be considered to be closely related to the debt host if, upon redemption, it does not result in a significant gain or loss.

Convertible preferred shares

Company X issues non-redeemable preferred shares convertible into ordinary shares at the option of the holder. The conversion feature represents an embedded call option on Company X's shares. Company X would not account for the embedded option separately because on a free-standing basis, the option would be an equity instrument of Company X. However, the investor would have to account for the embedded option separately.

Comparison with UK GAAP

There are no specific rules relating to embedded derivatives in the UK.

Comparison with US GAAP

Under US GAAP, because the changes in fair value of an equity interest and interest rates on a debt instrument are not clearly and closely related, the terms of the preferred stock (other than the conversion option) must be analysed to determine whether the preferred stock (and, thus, the potential host contract) is more akin to an equity instrument or a debt instrument. A typical cumulative fixed-rate preferred stock that has a mandatory redemption feature is more akin to debt, whereas cumulative participating perpetual preferred stock is more akin to an equity instrument.

Although IAS 39 (r2000) does not specifically address mandatorily redeemable preferred stock, IAS 32 (r1998) requires the identification of the debt and equity components from the perspective of the issuer. Guidance contained in IAS 32 (r1998) would result in a similar conclusion to that obtained under US GAAP. However, IAS 32 (r1998) takes it a step further by requiring the separation of these two components for the purpose of presentation on the issuer's balance sheet.

12.17.12 (c) Term extending options

An embedded derivative provision that either:

- enables one party to extend the remaining term to maturity; or
- automatically extends the remaining term,

is ***not*** closely related to the interest rate on a debt instrument unless the interest rate is concurrently reset to the approximate current market rate for the extended term.

> **Example 12.49 Term extending options**
>
> *Term extending option*
>
> Company X issues US$10 million in debt at par with an 8 per cent coupon and maturity of five years. However, if LIBOR increases by 250 basis points or more during the term of the debt, the issuer of the bonds has the option to extend the maturity for an additional three years. If the issuer exercises its option to extend the maturity, the coupon will reset to the current market rate for a company with a similar credit rating. The embedded derivative is closely related and would not be accounted for separately from the host contract because, although it significantly extends the maturity of the debt instrument, the coupon will reset to the current market rate for a company with a similar credit rating.
>
> *Contingent embedded derivative*
>
> Company X issues US$10 million in debt with an 8 per cent coupon and a maturity of five years. However, if LIBOR increases by 250 basis points within any one year, the maturity of the bonds will be extended for another three years at the stated coupon rate. The embedded derivative would be accounted for separately from the host contract because the term is extended but the coupon does not reset to the current market rate at each renewal date.

Comparison with UK GAAP

There are no specific rules in the UK on embedded derivatives.

Comparison with US GAAP

Under US GAAP, a term extending option is not closely related if it significantly extends the remaining term to maturity. IAS 39 (r2000) does not qualify its guidance by the extent to which the term is extended.

12.17.13 (f) Conversion features

The changes in fair value of an equity interest and the interest rates on a debt instrument are not closely related. Thus, for a debt security that is convertible into a specified number of shares of the debtor's equity or another enterprise's equity instruments, the embedded derivative (i.e., the conversion option) must be separated from the debt host contract and accounted for as a derivative instrument provided that the conversion option would, as a free-standing instrument, meet the definition of a derivative instrument (IGC 23-2). This would not be the case from the issuer's perspective if the conversion is into the issuer's own equity.

In some instances, venture capital companies providing subordinated loans agree that if and when the borrower lists its shares on a Stock Exchange, the venture capital company is entitled to receive shares of the borrowing enterprise for free or at a very low price (an equity kicker) in addition to interest and repayment of principal. As a result of the equity kicker feature, the interest on the subordinated loan is lower than it otherwise would be. Assuming the subordinated loan is not carried at fair value, the embedded equity derivative must be separated even though it is contingent upon the future listing of the borrower since the risks of an equity return are not closely related to the economic characteristics and risks of a host debt instrument (DIGC 23-9).

If an enterprise issues puttable, convertible bonds at par where the investor may put the convertible bonds back to the issuer at their par value, the issuer does not separate the written put option as an embedded derivative liability and instead allocates the par value of the convertible bonds between its equity and liability components in accordance with IAS 32 (r1998). The equity conversion feature is an equity instrument of the issuer and therefore falls outside the scope of IAS 39 (r2000) (DIGC 23-11).

Example 12.50 Conversion features

Convertible debt

Company X issues debt that is convertible into its ordinary shares in five years. The conversion feature represents an embedded call option on Company X's shares, settled in shares. Company X would not account for the embedded option separately because, on a free-standing basis, the option would be an equity instrument of Company X which is exempted from the scope of IAS 39 (r2000). However, the investor would have to account for the embedded option separately.

12.17.14 (d) Equity indexed principal and interest payments

Equity-indexed interest or principal payments – by which the amount of interest or principal is indexed to the value of equity shares – are not closely related to the host debt instrument or insurance contract because the risks inherent in the host and the embedded derivative are dissimilar and therefore they must be separated.

In certain cases, judgement may be required in identifying whether the host contract is an equity instrument or a debt instrument. In such cases, if the hybrid debt instrument has a stated maturity, this would not meet the definition of an equity instrument (see **11.3**) and would instead be treated as a debt instrument (DIGC 23-12).

Example 12.51 Equity indexed principal and interest payments

Equity indexed interest payments

Company X issues ten-year notes to a bank. The notes have no stated coupon rate. However, embedded in the notes is a provision that requires interest to be paid or received based on changes in Company Y's share price. Payments will be net cash settled. The embedded equity related derivative would be accounted for separately by both parties because the interest payments are based on changes in another company's share price and are therefore not closely related to the host debt instrument.

Equity indexed interest payments

Company X issues ten-year notes with a coupon of 5 per cent to a bank. At maturity, the investor receives cash equal to the higher of the initial proceeds or an amount based on the S&P 500. The embedded cash settled call option would be accounted for separately by both the issuer and the holder because payments made based on changes in the S&P are not closely related.

12.17.15 (e) Commodity indexed interest or principal payments

The changes in fair value of a commodity (or other asset) and the interest yield on a debt instrument are not closely related. Thus, a commodity-related derivative embedded in a commodity-indexed debt instrument must be separated from the non-commodity host contract and accounted for as a derivative instrument (IGC 23-5).

Example 12.52 Embedded commodity

Commodity-indexed interest payments

Company X issues ten-year notes with no stated coupon. Embedded in the notes is a provision that requires interest to be paid or received based on the changes in the price of corn. The embedded commodity related derivative would be accounted for separately because interest payments made based on changes in a commodity price are not closely related to the host debt instrument.

12.17.16 (g) Put and call options on debt instruments

Call options or put options that can accelerate the repayment of principal on a debt instrument are considered to be closely related to a debt instrument that requires principal repayments unless the debt involves a significant premium or discount (which is common with zero-coupon bonds). Thus, if a premium or discount is not involved, embedded calls and puts would not be separated from the host contract.

Significant premium or discount

IAS 39 (r2000) does not specify what is meant by a 'significant premium or discount.' Although judgement is necessary, 10 per cent of the par value generally would be considered substantial. Until further guidance is provided regarding the relationship between the interest rate on the debt, the fair value and rights attaching to the embedded option and the impact of these factors on the determination of the level of the discount or premium, considerable judgement will be required.

Example 12.53 Put and call options on debt instruments

Embedded put option

Company X issues ten-year bonds with a par value of R100 million and a coupon of 16 per cent. Embedded in the bonds is a provision that allows the investors to put the bonds in the event that Company X defaults on its financial debt ratio covenants. Assuming that the bonds were not issued at a substantial discount or premium, the embedded put option would not be accounted for separately because the option relates to credit risk which is closely related to the debt. The embedded put option also would be considered closely related if the settlement price would not result in a significant gain or loss on repayment as per IAS 39 (r2000).25(e).

Puttable debt

Company X issues ten-year bonds with a par value of €1 million for proceeds of €800,000. The bonds have a coupon of 8 per cent. Embedded in the bonds is a provision that allows the investors to put the bonds back to Company X in the event interest rates move 150 basis points. The embedded put option would be accounted for separately because the bonds were issued at a substantial discount. However, if the bonds were not issued at a substantial discount, for example, for proceeds of €950,000, the put option would not be accounted for separately.

Callable debt

Company X issues ten-year bonds with a par value of ¥1 billion for proceeds of ¥1.2 billion. The bonds have a coupon of 2 per cent. Embedded in the bonds is a provision that allows the issuer to call the bonds in the event interest rates move 150 basis points. The embedded call option would be accounted for separately because the bonds were issued at a significant premium (greater than 10 per cent).

Puttable debt indexed to the FTSE

Company X issues ten-year bonds with a par value of £1 million for proceeds of £950,000. The bonds have a coupon of 10 per cent. Embedded in the bonds is a provision that allows the investors to put the bonds in the event the FTSE declines 20 per cent.

The embedded put option would not be accounted for separately even though the put is indexed to a trigger that is not considered closely related to the host instrument (i.e., a trigger other than interest rates or credit). The tests in IAS 39 (r2000) are whether the bonds were issued at a significant premium or discount and whether the prepayment resulted in a significant gain or loss.

Comparison with UK GAAP

There are no specific requirements relating to this area.

Comparison with US GAAP

Under US GAAP, a put or call option is not considered to be closely related to a debt instrument if, in addition to the substantial premium or discount, the put or call option is only contingently exercisable. US GAAP also specifies that for contingently exercisable calls and puts to be considered clearly and closely related, they can be indexed only to interest rates or credit risk, not some extraneous event or factor. There are no similar requirements under IAS 39 (r2000).

US GAAP specifies that call options or put options that do not accelerate the repayment of principal on a debt instrument, but instead require a cash settlement that is equal to the price of the option at the date of exercise, would not be considered to be clearly and closely related to the debt instrument in which it is embedded and would be separated from the host contract. (SFAS 133, *Accounting for Derivative Instruments and Hedging Activities*, para.61d) In this case, the cash settlement provision effectively achieves an adjustment to the interest rate on the debt. There is no similar requirement under IAS 39 (r2000).

12.18 Hedge accounting

IAS 39 (r2000) recognises three types of hedge accounting:

(1) fair value hedge (see **12.23**);
(2) cash flow hedge (see **12.24**); and
(3) hedge of a net investment in a foreign entity (see **22.6.6**).

When approaching a potential hedging relationship, to determine if the transaction will qualify for special hedge accounting, the following steps should be taken:

(1) Identify the nature of the exposure to determine the type of hedge accounting (see above);
(2) Ensure that the qualifying criteria for hedge accounting are met (see **12.20**);

(3) Ensure that the hedged item is allowable under IAS 39 (r2000) (see **12.21**); and
(4) Ensure that the hedging instrument is allowable under IAS 39 (r2000) (see **12.22**).

12.19 Definition

> '*Hedging*, for accounting purposes, means designating one or more hedging instruments so that their change in fair value is an offset, in whole or in part, to the change in fair value or cash flows of a hedged item.'
>
> (IAS 39 (r2000).10)

A hedged item can be an asset, liability, firm commitment or forecasted future transaction that is exposed to risk of change in value or changes in future cash flows. Hedge accounting recognises the offsetting effects on net profit or loss symmetrically.

IAS 39 (r2000) identifies three types of hedges: fair value hedges, cash flow hedges and hedges of a net investment in a foreign entity. Hedge accounting differs depending on the type of hedge. For fair value hedges, the hedged item is adjusted for changes in its fair value to offset the changes in the fair value of the hedging instrument. For cash flow hedges and hedges of a net investment in a foreign entity, changes in the fair value of the hedging instrument are recognised in equity.

If a hedge does not qualify for special hedge accounting because it fails to meet the criteria discussed in **12.20**, gains and losses arising from changes in the fair value of a hedged item that is measured at fair value subsequent to initial recognition are reported either in net profit or loss or equity depending on the accounting policy of the enterprise and the classification of the instrument. Fair value adjustments of a hedging instrument that is a derivative, but does not qualify for special hedge accounting, would be reported in net profit or loss. (IAS 39 (r2000).165)

IAS 39 (r2000) does not require risk reduction on an enterprise-wide basis. Transactions that increase enterprise-wide risk can qualify for hedge accounting provided all the relevant criteria are satisfied (IGC 137-6).

12.19.1 Summary table of hedge accounting for asset, liability, and future transaction-related exposures

The following table provides examples of assets, liabilities and future transactions, the earnings exposures including exposures of their components, and the type of hedge accounting that can be used when a hedging relationship is established. (See **12.23** and **12.24** for a discussion of the types of hedge accounting.)

Fixed Rate Assets and Liabilities

Examples

- Fixed rate loans and receivables.
- Investments in debt securities.
- Fixed rate debt of the enterprise.
- Fixed rate deposit liabilities.

Exposure	Hedge Accounting
Overall fair value	FV (Fair Value)
Interest rates	FV[4]
Credit of the issuer	FV or CF
Foreign currency	FV or CF[2]
Termination options	FV

Variable Rate Assets and Liabilities

Examples

- Variable rate loans and receivables.
- Variable rate debt securities.
- Variable rate debt of the enterprise.
- Variable rate deposit liabilities.

Exposure	Hedge Accounting
Overall fair value	FV (Fair Value)
Interest rates	CF (Cash Flow)[3]
Credit of the issuer	FV or CF[3]
Foreign currency	CF
Termination options	FV

Firm Commitments to Purchase or Sell Financial Instruments[1]

Examples

- Commitment to purchase fixed rate debt.
- Fixed rate loan commitments.

Exposure[1]	Hedge Accounting
Overall fair value	CF (Cash Flow)
Interest rates	CF
Credit	CF
Foreign currency	CF

Forecasted Purchases and Sales of Financial Instruments

Examples

- Forecasted purchase of fixed rate debt.
- Forecasted loan originations.

Exposure	Hedge Accounting
Overall fair value	CF (Cash Flow)
Interest rates	CF
Credit	CF
Foreign currency	CF

Firm Commitment to Purchase or Sell Non-Financial Assets[1]

Examples

- Forecasted Sale of Inventory.
- Forecasted Purchase of Inventory.

Exposure[1]	Hedge Accounting
Overall fair value	CF (Cash Flow)
Credit	CF
Foreign currency	CF

Forecasted Purchase and Sales of Non-Financial Instruments

Examples

- Forecasted Sale of Inventory.
- Forecasted Purchase of Inventory.

Exposure	Hedge Accounting
Overall fair value	CF (Cash Flow)
Credit	CF
Foreign currency	CF

Other Assets

Examples

- Inventories.
- Equity Instruments (held by the enterprise).

Exposure[1]	Hedge Accounting
Overall fair value	FV (Fair Value)

(1) IAS 39 (r2000) recognises that firm commitments create a fair value exposure. However, it requires that hedges of firm commitments be accounted for as cash flow hedges. (IAS 39 (r2000).137 (b))

(2) Note that a forward foreign exchange contract hedging a foreign currency loan payable can be designated as a fair value hedge of the revaluation to the spot rate or a cash flow hedge of the amount to be settled in future in the foreign currency. The income statement impact is similar because the gain or loss on the remeasurement of the forward contract, which is recognised in equity under a cash flow hedge, is included in net profit or loss when the payable is remeasured (IGC 137-9). Changes in the fair value of the derivative related to the forward points (the time value) are recognised directly in net profit or loss (IGC 137-10).

(3) A portion of a variable rate debt instrument can qualify as a hedged item in a fair value hedge, such as its credit risk exposure and interest payments which have a fair value exposure to interest rate changes after they are reset and before they are paid (IGC 137-11).

(4) A fixed rate cash flow cannot qualify as a hedged item in a cash flow hedging relationship because it does not create a cash flow exposure that affects net profit or loss. However, the forecasted reinvestment of the cash flow can qualify for cash flow hedge accounting because the reinvestment of the cash flow at the then current market interest rate creates a cash flow exposure (IGC 137-7). For a similar reason, a receive-variable, pay-fixed forward rate agreement does not qualify as a cash flow hedge of the forecasted receipt of interest payments on a fixed rate debt instrument because the fixed-rate cash flow does not create a cash flow exposure. It could, however, qualify as a fair value hedge of the interest payments (IGC 137-8).

12.19.2 Comparison with UK GAAP – firm commitments

There are no detailed rules on hedge accounting in the UK. Gains and losses on hedges of firm commitments are often ignored.

12.19.3 Comparison with US GAAP – firm commitments

Under US GAAP, hedges of firm commitments are accounted for as fair value hedges. However, hedges of foreign currency risk in foreign currency denominated firm commitments can be accounted for as fair value hedges or cash flow hedges.

IAS 39 (r2000) requires hedges of firm commitments to be accounted for as cash flow hedges.

12.20 Qualifying criteria

Under IAS 39 (r2000), a hedging relationship qualifies for special hedge accounting if, and only if, all of the following conditions are met:

Formal documentation of hedging relationship	(a) at the inception of the hedge there is formal documentation of the hedging relationship and the enterprise's risk management objective and strategy for undertaking the hedge. That documentation should include identification of the hedging instrument, the related hedged item or transaction, the nature of the risk being hedged, and how the enterprise will assess the hedging instrument's effectiveness in offsetting the exposure to changes in the hedged item's fair value or the hedged transaction's cash flows that is attributable to the hedged risk (see **12.20.1**, **12.21.7** and IGC 121-2c);
Expectation of high effectiveness	(b) the hedge is expected to be highly effective (see **12.25**) in achieving offsetting changes in fair value or cash flows attributable to the hedged risk, consistent with the originally documented risk management strategy for that particular hedging relationship (see **12.10.2**);
High probability of occurrence	(c) for cash flow hedges, a forecasted transaction that is the subject of the hedge must be highly probable and must present an exposure to variations in cash flows that could ultimately affect reported net profit or loss (see **12.20.3**);
Reliably measurable	(d) the effectiveness of the hedge can be reliably measured, that is, the fair value or cash flows of the hedged item and the fair value of the hedging instrument can be reliably measured (see **12.20.4**); and
Ongoing assessment and actual offset	(e) the hedge was assessed on an ongoing basis and determined actually to have been highly effective throughout the financial reporting period (see **12.20.2**). (IAS 39 (r2000).142)

These criteria are discussed in the following sections.

12.20.1 (a) Formal documentation of the hedging relationship

The concurrent designation and documentation of a hedge is critical; without it, an enterprise could retroactively identify a hedged item, a hedged transaction, or a method of measuring effectiveness to achieve a desired accounting result. Retrospective designation is not permitted under IAS 39 (r2000) and hence an enterprise may only apply hedge accounting once it has completed the necessary documentation of the hedging relationship, including identification of the hedging instrument, the related hedged item or transaction, the nature of the risk being hedged and how hedge effectiveness will be assessed (IGC 142-4). An enterprise may, however, designate and formally document a derivative contract as a hedging instrument subsequent to entering into the derivative contract (IGC 142-7). Since hedge accounting is applied prospectively, designation is only required at inception of the hedge relationship (being the date from which hedge accounting will be applied). As a result, it need not coincide with the inception of the economic hedging relationship, or when the enterprise acquires the hedging instrument.

Identifying the nature of the risk being hedged and using a hedging derivative consistent with an enterprise's established policy for risk management are essential components of risk management and are necessary to add verifiability to the hedge accounting model. To document the hedging relationship as required by IAS 39 (r2000), enterprises must first formulate risk management policies. Those policies will be not only an integral part of managing risk but also the basis for the use of hedge accounting for those activities. All hedging activities must be consistent with an enterprise's *written* risk management policies and must be documented in writing at the date the hedge activities are initiated. An enterprise's failure to establish written risk management policies and designation at the inception of a hedge will invalidate hedge accounting.

Under IAS 39 (r2000)'s transition provisions, in the financial year in which the standard is initially applied, hedge accounting is no longer permitted for previously designated hedges that do not meet the hedge criteria under IAS 39 (r2000). The hedge accounting provisions are not applied retrospectively. In the event that ongoing hedging transactions were entered into prior to the implementation of IAS 39 (r2000) but were not previously designated and documented as such, they would not qualify for hedge accounting. Subsequent documentation of the hedging relationship is necessary to qualify in the future but it does not change the past.

Where a forecasted transaction is the subject of the hedge, the documentation must be sufficient to specifically identify the hedging relationship and comply with the other qualifying criteria to ensure that the timing and amounts recognised in net profit or loss are appropriate. For example, it is not sufficient to document a hedge of the purchase or sale of the last 15,000 units of a product in a specified period or as a percentage of purchases or sales during a specified period. The hedged item must be documented so that when the transaction occurs, it is clear whether the transaction is or is not the hedged transaction. Therefore, a forecasted transaction could be identified as the first 15,000 units in the above example, but not the last 15,000 units since the last units cannot be identified when they occur (IGC 142-5).

An enterprise may hedge an exposure on an after-tax basis provided this fact is adequately documented in the designation of the hedge and hedge effectiveness is assessed on an after tax basis (IGC 142-2).

Example 12.54 Formal documentation of the hedging relationship

Designation and documentation of hedging activities

Company XYZ has €500 million in short-term (30 day) commercial paper ('CP') borrowings. XYZ wants to hedge the interest rate risk on the forecasted rollover of the CP for a five-year period. On 1/1/x0, XYZ enters into a five-year pay seven per cent fixed, receive 30-day CP interest rate swap.

The hedging strategy is consistent with XYZ's written risk management policy that specifically permits the use of swaps to hedge interest rate risk on forecasted rollovers of CP borrowings. The policy permits such hedging strategies for periods of up to seven years.

XYZ prepares the following written documentation, formally designating the hedging relationship at the date the hedge is initiated:

XYZ Company Hedging Files

Date: 1/1/x0

On 1/1/x0, XYZ Company entered into a pay seven per cent fixed, receive 30 day CP interest rate swap. The swap is designated as a cash flow hedge of the interest rate risk on the forecasted rollover of the bottom €100 million layer of 30 day CP borrowings. There is an assumption of no ineffectiveness because all of the critical terms of the hedged item (bottom layer of CP) and the hedging instrument match. The assumption of no ineffectiveness is discussed in **12.25.4**.

XYZ specified that the swap was designated against the bottom layer of the CP borrowings. XYZ could have designated the swap on a proportionate basis. However, XYZ must specify which layer is being hedged when the entire asset, liability, firm commitment, or forecasted transaction is not being hedged. Because the critical terms of the hedged item and hedging instrument are the same, XYZ can assume 100 per cent effectiveness (see **12.25**). If the terms of the hedge were not the same, XYZ would be required to specify how effectiveness would be measured.

12.20.2 (b) and (e) High effectiveness

See **12.25**.

12.20.3 (c) High probability of occurrence

For cash flow hedges, a forecasted transaction that is the subject of the hedge must be highly probable and must present an exposure to variations in cash flows that could ultimately affect reported net profit or loss.

The phrase 'highly probable' implies a significantly greater likelihood of occurrence than the phrase 'more likely than not'. The highly probable criterion suggests that the future event or events are likely to occur (IGC 142-1).

An assessment of the likelihood that a forecasted transaction will take place should not be based solely on management's intent because intent is not verifiable. A transaction's probability should be supported by observable facts and the attendant circumstances.

In assessing the likelihood that a transaction will occur, consideration should be given to the following circumstances (IGC 142-1):

(a) the frequency of similar past transactions;
(b) the financial and operational ability of the enterprise to carry out the transaction;
(c) substantial commitments of resources to a particular activity (for example, a manufacturing facility that can be used in the short run only to process a particular type of commodity);
(d) the extent of loss or disruption of operations that could result if the transaction does not occur;
(e) the likelihood that transactions with substantially different characteristics might be used to achieve the same business purpose (for example, an enterprise that intends to raise cash may have several ways of doing so, ranging from a short-term bank loan to a common stock offering); and
(f) the enterprise's business plan.

In addition, both the length of time until a forecasted transaction is projected to occur and the quantity of the forecasted transaction should be considered in determining probability. Other factors being equal, the more distant a forecasted transaction is, the less likely it is that the transaction would be considered probable and the stronger the evidence that would be needed to support an assertion that it is probable. For example, a transaction forecasted to occur in five years may be less likely than a transaction forecasted to occur in one year. However, forecasted interest payments for the next 20 years on variable-rate debt typically would be probable if supported by an existing contract (IGC 142.1).

For an asset or liability that does not exist, in other words that is not on the balance sheet, it may be difficult to demonstrate the likelihood of the transaction occurring beyond a forecasted period of five to seven years.

Additionally, other factors being equal, the greater the physical quantity or future value of a forecasted transaction in proportion to the enterprise's transactions of the same nature, the less likely it is that the transaction would be considered highly probable and the stronger the evidence that would be required to support an assertion that it is highly probable. For example, less evidence generally would be needed to support forecasted sales of 100,000 units in a particular month than would be needed to support forecasted sales of 950,000 units of the same product in that month by an enterprise, even if its recent sales have averaged 950,000 units per month for the past three months.

A history of having designated hedges of forecasted transactions and the determining that the hedged forecasted transactions are no longer expected to occur would call into question both an enterprise's ability to predict accurately forecasted transactions and the propriety of using hedge accounting in the future for similar transactions (IGC 142-1).

For a hedge of forecasted transaction, the documentation of the hedging relationship that is established at inception of the hedge should identify the date on or time period in which the transaction is expected to occur. Without this, the hedge would not qualify for hedge accounting since it would not be possible to measure effectiveness reliably. Although the forecasted date need not be an exact date, the expected timing should be documented within a reasonably specific and generally narrow range of time from a most probable date as a basis for assessing hedge effectiveness (IGC 142-8).

Example 12.55 High probability of occurrence

Long-term forecasted purchase of oil

Company Z uses oil to run electrical generators that supply its manufacturing facilities. Z's production estimates and long-term business plan call for the use of at least 2 million barrels of oil annually for the next 20 years. Z wants to hedge its purchase of oil for the next 15 years and, accordingly, must consider whether the forecasted purchase of oil is a probable transaction.

Z has used its own generators for the past 10 years and on average purchases 2 million barrels of oil a year; without the generators Z's manufacturing facilities would close. However, Z has a contract to buy electricity from the local utility if it were unable to run its generators. In this instance, Z's ability to demonstrate that the acquisition of oil for a 15 year period is highly probable would be difficult because of the time period of the forecasted transaction and the availability of alternative transactions with substantially different characteristics, i.e., the ability to purchase electricity from the local utility. If Z's contract were for a period of 3 to 5 years, Z could reasonably conclude that the forecasted purchase of oil is highly probable.

12.20.4 (d) Reliable measurement

A hedge of the risk of obsolescence of a physical asset or the risk of expropriation of property by a government would not be eligible for hedge accounting since effectiveness cannot be measured because those risks are not capable of being measured reliably. (IAS 39 (r2000).149)

12.21 Hedged items

> 'A *hedged item* is an asset, liability, firm commitment or forecasted future transaction that;
>
> (a) exposes the enterprise to risk of changes in fair value or changes in future cash flows and that;
>
> (b) for hedge accounting purposes, is designated as being hedged.'
>
> (IAS 39 (r2000).10)

As discussed below, a hedged item can be a recognised asset or liability, an unrecognised firm commitment, or an uncommitted but highly probable anticipated future transaction ('forecasted transaction'). The hedged item can be:

(a) a single asset, liability, firm commitment, or forecasted transaction; or
(b) a group of assets, liabilities, firm commitments, or forecasted transactions with similar risk characteristics.

(IAS 39 (r2000).127)

12.21.1 Instruments that qualify as hedged items

The following instruments and activities *may* qualify as hedged items:

(a) firm commitments (see **12.21.2**);
(b) forecasted transactions (see **12.21.2**);
(c) financial assets and liabilities (including portfolios) (see **12.21.3**);
(d) non-financial assets (**12.21.4**);
(e) components or ingredients of non-financial assets and liabilities (foreign currency risk only) (see **12.21.4**);
(f) held-to-maturity instruments (see **12.21.5**);
(g) multiple risks hedged with a single instrument (see **12.21.6**); and
(h) portfolio hedges (see **12.21.7**); and
(i) certain macro hedging alternatives (see **12.21.8**).

The following instruments and activities do *not* qualify as hedged items:

(a) derivative instruments since these are always deemed held for trading (IGC 127-5);

(b) items with no earnings exposure such as equity instruments or inter-company transactions in consolidated financial statements (see **12.21.9**);
(c) equity method investments (see **12.21.10**);
(d) investments in subsidiaries (see **12.21.11**);
(e) business acquisition commitments (except for foreign exchange risk) (see **12.21.12**);
(f) macro hedging (see **12.21.13**);
(g) the risk of transactions not occurring (such as future sales) (IGC 149-1); and
(h) unrecognised assets (such as certain intangible assets, for example core deposit intangibles (IGC 137-3).

The following sections discuss the above items in more detail.

12.21.2 (a) and (b) Firm commitments and forecasted transactions

> 'A *firm commitment* is a binding agreement for the exchange of a specified quantity of resources at a specified price on a specified future date or dates.'
>
> (IAS 39 (r2000).10)

> 'A *forecasted transaction* is an uncommitted, but highly probable, anticipated future transaction.'
>
> (IAS 39 (r2000).127)

Both a firm commitment and a forecasted transaction that are designated as a hedged item are accounted for as cash flow hedges (see **12.24**). However, it is important to distinguish between the two because an additional assessment of probability is required for a forecasted transaction which is not required for a firm commitment.

Firm commitments

IAS 39 (r2000) states that a commitment is firm if it is binding, specifies the terms of the commitment (quantity, price, timing and the delivery or settlement date). A commitment is binding if it is legally enforceable. Commitments among related parties are not generally legally enforceable. To be legally enforceable, the agreement should generally provide for legal remedies that are available to the parties to the contract in the event of non-performance. For example, a penalty could be specified at a fixed amount or equal to the change in market price of the item under the contract. Alternatively, the penalty may not be specifically stipulated in the agreement but may otherwise be applicable (for example remedies under law).

The definition of a firm commitment requires that the price be specified. The price may be expressed as a specified amount of an enterprise's functional currency or of a foreign currency. It may also be expressed as a specified interest rate or specified effective yield.

A price that varies with the market price of the item which is the subject of a commitment, results in a transaction that has a cash flow exposure rather than a fair value exposure. Therefore, such a contract is considered to be a forecasted transaction rather than a firm commitment and can be hedged using a cash flow hedge.

For example, an agreement to purchase 500 automobiles on 1 September 2002, for a price specified in British pounds and a sufficient penalty for non-performance would meet the definition of a firm commitment because, among the other requirements that are met, the price is specified in a currency. However, if the price for the automobiles were variable, the contract would not be a firm commitment because IAS 39 (r2000) requires that a firm commitment must have a fixed price based on currency or interest rates. A variable price (i.e., an amount that could change outside of changes in currency), is not considered to be a fixed price commitment.

Forecasted transaction
A forecasted transaction is a transaction that is expected to occur for which there is no firm commitment. Because no transaction or event has yet occurred and the transaction or event will be at the prevailing market price when it occurs, a forecasted transaction does not give an enterprise any present rights to future benefits or a present obligation to surrender future benefits.

A forecasted transaction can qualify for cash flow hedge accounting, if the enterprise specifically identifies the forecasted transaction that gives rise to the cash flow exposure. That information is necessary to:

(a) assess the likelihood that the transaction will occur;
(b) determine if the cash flows of the designated derivative are expected to be highly effective at offsetting the change in expected cash flow of the forecasted transaction attributable to the risk being hedged; and
(c) assess the hedge's effectiveness on an ongoing basis.

The forecasted transaction must be specifically identified as a single transaction or a group of individual transactions that share the same risk exposure for which they are designated as being hedged. An enterprise is required to identify the hedged forecasted transaction with sufficient specificity to make it clear whether a particular transaction is a hedged transaction when it occurs (IGC 142-5).

An example of a forecasted transaction which could qualify for (cash flow) hedge accounting is the anticipated issuance of fixed rate debt. An illustrative example is provided in IGC 137-2.

Hedge accounting of future foreign currency revenue streams is permitted under IAS 39 (r2000) provided the revenues are highly probable. While it is unlikely that an enterprise can reliably predict 100 per cent of revenues for a future year, it is possible that a portion of predicted revenues, normally those expected in the short term, will meet the 'highly probable' criterion (IGC 137-4).

Example 12.56 Firm commitments and forecasted transactions

Firm commitment to buy inventory (forward contract)

Company E is a discount grocery chain with over 400 stores in the USA and which enters into forward contracts to purchase various inventory items for its stores. On 1 June 2002, Company E enters into a forward contract to purchase 300,000 bushels of wheat for a fixed price of US$1.40 per bushel on 1 August 2002. Company E will use the wheat in its bakery operations. If Company E was to fail to take delivery of the wheat, it would both be required to pay for any increase in the value of the wheat and would be subject to legal remedies. Accordingly, this transaction meets the requirements of a firm commitment because it specifies all significant terms of the transaction, including quantity, fixed price and timing. However, the forward contract is not accounted for as a derivative because Company E intends to take delivery and the purchase is considered to be normal given the operations of E. Under IAS 39 (r2000), E could hedge the fair value exposure of the firm commitment relating to the change in the price of wheat between 1 June 2002 and 1 August 2002 by entering into a forward contract that qualifies as a derivative to sell wheat for a fixed price on 1 August.

Mortgage loan commitments

In possession of the necessary approvals, Bank M issues interest rate lock commitment letters for mortgage loans to prospective borrowers. Each commitment letter details the principal to be borrowed, related fees and the fixed interest rate. The commitment letter has a stated maturity date, typically 60 to 90 days. The borrower is not required to accept and finalise the mortgage loan and there is no penalty if the borrower does not make use of the offered facility. Bank M can estimate the number of commitments that it projects will be finalised. Bank M would like to hedge the projected fair value exposure related to its fixed rate loan commitments. Loan commitments are contracts that are binding on one party but not on the other and, thus, a loan commitment is not considered to be a firm commitment since a sufficiently large disincentive for non-performance does not exist which would make the commitment legally enforceable. However, these commitment letters may be hedged as a cash flow exposure by purchasing options provided that the company can demonstrate hedge effectiveness.

Hedge of anticipated purchase of copper

Company C uses copper as part of its manufacturing process. On 1 January 2002, Company C entered into a forward contract to purchase 100 tonnes of copper to hedge the forecasted purchase of copper in the fourth quarter of 2002. The forward contract meets the definition of a derivative. Company C designates the forward as a hedge of the first 100 tonnes of copper purchased in the fourth quarter. Company C could not designate the forward contract as a hedge of the last 100 tonnes purchased because Company C cannot identify which 100 tonnes will be purchased last.

Comparison with UK GAAP – firm commitments and forecasted transactions

There are no specific requirements in the UK in this area.

Comparison with US GAAP – firm commitments and forecasted transactions

Under US GAAP, firm commitments are accounted for as fair value hedges. US GAAP requires that for a firm commitment to exist, and therefore for performance to be probable, there needs to be a sufficiently large disincentive for non-performance. This criterion is necessary under US GAAP because the absence of such a penalty could result in a net settlement, which would cause the instrument to meet the definition of a derivative instrument. This would also preclude fair value hedge accounting if it is a non-derivative, although it could qualify as a cash flow hedge.

Under IAS 39 (r2000), a net settlement provision does not necessarily mean the instrument is a derivative. IAS 39 (r2000) focuses on the history and practice of delivery and on the use of the underlying in the normal operations of the enterprise. Accordingly, under IAS 39 (r2000), it is not necessary to require a significant, fixed penalty for the commitment to be firm, however, the existence of a penalty for default is an indication that the commitment is legally enforceable. Also, under IAS 39 (r2000), it does not matter whether the commitment is firm because in either case, it can only qualify for cash flow hedge accounting. If a commitment is firm, however, there is no requirement to assess whether the transaction is probable of occurring.

12.21.3 (c) Financial assets and liabilities

Provided that effectiveness can be measured (see **12.25**), financial assets or liabilities may be designated as hedged items with respect to the risk associated with either the total amount of, or only a portion of, their cash flows or fair value. (IAS 39 (r2000).128) Examples of the designated risk that may be hedged include:

(1) the risk of changes in the overall fair value or cash flows of the entire hedged item;

(2) the risk of changes in its fair value or cash flows attributable to changes in market interest rates;

(3) the risk of changes in its fair value or cash flows attributable to changes in the related foreign currency exchange rates;
(4) the risk of changes in its fair value or cash flows attributable to changes in the obligor's creditworthiness; or
(5) the option component of a pre-payable instrument.

Hedge accounting is permitted for components of risk, for example, the risk free component of interest rate risk, credit spread risk or the exposure to changes in fair value due to changes in three-month interbank offered rates associated with a debt instrument, provided hedge effectiveness can be measured and the other hedge accounting conditions are met (IGC 128-3).

IAS 39 (r2000) does not specifically address whether a portion of a firmly committed unrecognised transaction can be a hedged item. However, using the criteria for financial assets and liabilities, a portion of such unrecognised firmly committed transactions would qualify as a hedged item, provided that effectiveness can be measured.

Normally, a hedging relationship is designated between an entire hedging instrument and a hedged item so that there is a single measure of fair value for the hedging instrument. If the risk designated as being hedged is not the risk of changes in the overall fair value of the entire hedged item, two or more of the other risks (market interest rate risk, foreign currency exchange risk, and credit risk) may simultaneously be designated as being hedged. For example, companies commonly use a cross-currency interest rate swap (also known as a combined interest rate and currency swap, or 'CIRCUS') to convert a variable rate position in a foreign currency to a fixed rate position in the reporting currency. This swap may be designated separately as a fair value hedge of the currency risk and a cash flow hedge of the interest rate risk (IGC 131-1).

Although IAS 39 (r2000).145 prohibits the designation of a hedging relationship for only a portion of the time period in which a hedging instrument is outstanding, a portion of the time period to maturity of a hedged item may be designated as part of a hedging relationship, if effectiveness can be measured. For example, a three-year interest rate swap could qualify as a hedge of the effect of interest rate changes for three years of a debt instrument which has five years remaining to maturity (IGC 128-2).

If an entire instrument is designated as being hedged, the effect of an embedded derivative must be considered in designating a hedge of an individual risk. For example, the effect of an embedded prepayment option in a debt host must be considered in designating a hedge of market interest rate risk of the debt to be able to demonstrate high correlation. If the entire asset or liability is designated as being hedged, for the hedging instrument to be effective, it would have to contain an option that coincides with the prepayment option on the debt allowing the entity to terminate the hedge. However, the hedging relationship could be designated for just the fixed portion of the term of the instrument, that is for the period, if any, before the prepayment option can be exercised (assuming effectiveness can be measured). Embedded derivatives which are separated from the host contract may be designated as hedging instruments provided all the hedging criteria are satisfied.

With a financial asset subject to prepayment risk, cash flows resulting from a prepayment of the asset cannot be designated in a cash flow hedging relationship because the prepayment cannot be determined to be probable. However, hedge accounting may be appropriate if the cash flows being hedged are part of a portfolio of financial assets that are subject to prepayment risk and prepayments can be estimated reliably, or a 'bottom level' of cash flows is being hedged, for example, the cash flows of the instruments that are expected to remain outstanding after prepayments occur over a specified period of time (IGC 128-1).

Example 12.57 Financial assets and liabilities

Hedge of the entire fair value

Company XYZ owns 1,000 shares of Company ABC's publicly traded common stock and has classified the securities as available-for-sale. At 1 January 2000, these shares are trading at A$50 per share and Company XYZ has an unrealised gain of A$25,000 recognised directly in equity. XYZ would like to lock in the unrealised gain and purchases a put option on Company ABC's common stock from Counterparty A for A$9,000. The purchased put option allows XYZ to put its 1,000 shares to Counterparty A at A$50 per share on 31 December 2002. The purchased put option may be appropriately designated as a hedge of the entire exposure to the decline in the fair value of the investment in ABC.

Hedge of credit risk

Company F purchased €2,500,000 in BBB rated corporate bonds on 1 March. The securities will be classified as available-for-sale. Company F realises that if the issuer's credit standing is downgraded, the fair value of the fixed rate bonds will decrease. On 1 March, Company F also enters into a credit swap to hedge the fair value exposure associated with changes in the issuer's credit rating. The terms of the swap call for Company F to pay a fixed amount and receive or pay a variable amount based on changes in the credit fair value of the bonds. The portion of the risk of the bonds related to credit exposure qualifies as a hedged item and the credit swap may appropriately be designated as a fair value hedge.

Hedge of selected cash flows

Company R is replacing maturing debt with a new NZ$100 million ten-year fixed rate borrowing. Company R believes that interest rates will be volatile for the next three years and will decline in years 4–10. Company R issued the new debt on 4 January 2000, with a fixed rate of 8.25 per cent. Interest on the debt is payable annually beginning 31 December 2000. At the same time that Company R issued the debt, it entered into a forward starting interest rate swap to convert the last seven years of the debt from fixed to variable. The forward starting interest rate swap may appropriately be designated as a hedge of the fair value in years 4–10 of the ten-year debt. The change in fair value is based on the changes in the yield curve in years 4–10.

Hedge of interest rate risk with an embedded prepayment option

Bank G has a fixed-rate commercial loan maturing in five years. The borrower can prepay the loan without penalty after year two. If Bank G wants to hedge the fair value of the loan due to changes in interest rate risk, it must consider the effect on fair value of the embedded option (a prepayment option is a sub-component of overall interest rate risk). A five-year receive variable, pay fixed swap might or might not be sufficiently effective to qualify as a hedge. A swap, cancellable at Bank G's option after year two, would be a more effective hedging instrument because it hedges all of the interest rate risk, including the embedded prepayment option.

Hedge of multiple risks

Company M's functional currency is the Israeli Shekel. On 1 April , company M entered into a firm commitment to invest in fixed rate debt to be issued by Company D with delivery of the bond on 1 May. The price of the corporate bond is set at €270,000. Company M would like to hedge its fair value exposure related to interest rate risk and foreign exchange risk. M enters into a forward contract on 1 April to purchase €270,000 on May 1 and designates this contract as the hedge of the foreign exchange risk. M also enters into a forward starting interest rate swap that calls for M to pay a fixed amount and receive a variable amount. The swap is designated as a hedge of the interest rate risk. Subject to the other criteria being satisfied, both the foreign exchange contract and the forward starting interest rate swap would qualify for hedge accounting.

Comparison with UK GAAP – financial assets
There are no specific rules in this are in the UK.

Comparison with US GAAP – financial assets
Hedging credit and interest rate risk.
SFAS 138, *Accounting for Certain Derivative Instruments and Certain Hedging Activities*, redefined the SFAS 133, *Accounting for Derivative Instruments and Hedging Activities*, definition of interest rate risk under US GAAP. SFAS 133 defined interest rate risk as the changes attributable to changes in interest rates and changes in prevailing spreads over market interest rates. This resulted in credit spread risk being a source of ineffectiveness that was either included in current income or could result in the hedge failing to qualify for hedge accounting. Under SFAS 138, changes in

prevailing spreads over market interest rates and specific events affecting the creditworthiness of a particular debt issuer are now classified as credit risk. Interest rate risk has been redefined as arising from changes in a benchmark interest rate (which is limited in the USA to the interest rate on direct treasury obligations of the US Government or the LIBOR swap rate). This amendment has significantly expanded the extent to which both interest rate risk and credit risk now qualify for hedge accounting.

Partial term hedges

Under US GAAP, partial-term hedge transactions of fair value exposures do not qualify for hedge accounting because only specified portions of risk (credit, interest rate, prepayment) are permitted to be hedged. Partial term fair value hedges are permitted under IAS 39 (r2000) provided that effectiveness can be demonstrated and the other qualifying requirements are met.

12.21.4 (d) and (e) Hedged non-financial assets, components or ingredients

If a hedged item is a non-financial asset or liability, due to the difficulty of isolating and measuring the appropriate portion of the cash flows or fair value changes attributable to specific risks other than foreign currency risks, it should be designated as a hedged item either:

(a) for foreign currency risks; or
(b) in its entirety for all risks

(IAS 39 (r2000).129)

Because changes in the price of an ingredient or component of a non-financial asset or liability generally do not have a predictable, separately measurable effect on the price of the item as a whole that is comparable to the effect of, say, a change in market interest rates or the price of a bond, a non-financial asset or liability is a hedged item only in its entirety except for foreign currency risks which may be separately identified and hedged. (IAS 39 (r2000).130)

If the future sale of a non-financial asset (carried at cost) is hedged for its foreign currency exposure, the asset is not remeasured to fair value. It is a cash flow hedge with the derivative gain or loss in equity. The non-financial asset itself does not have a foreign currency exposure unless it is transacted internationally in only one currency and that currency is not the measurement currency of the entity that is selling the asset (IGC Other-4).

Example 12.58 Non-financial assets, components or ingredients

Hedge of forecasted purchase of inventory

Company B purchases bronze for its inventory of raw materials used in manufacturing its products. Company B enters into a forward contract indexed to copper and designates it as a hedge of the copper component in forecasted purchases of bronze.

The hedge does not qualify for hedge accounting because the exposure to changes in the price of copper is only a portion of the exposure to changes in the price of bronze. For non-financial assets or liabilities to qualify for hedge accounting, only the foreign currency risk or the overall fair value risk may qualify for hedge accounting.

Comparison with UK GAAP – non-financial assets, components or ingredients
There are no specific rules in the UK in this area.

Comparison with US GAAP – non-financial assets, components or ingredients
US GAAP provides an exception to its requirement for hedging non-financial assets in their entirety and permits a portion of the risk to be hedged for recognised loan servicing rights and non-financial firm commitments with financial components. For hedges of non-financial assets or liabilities, the designated risk being hedged must be the risk of changes in the fair value or cash flows of the entire hedged asset or liability or foreign currency risk.

These exceptions are not provided for IAS 39 (r2000).

12.21.5 (f) Held-to-maturity investments

For hedges of a debt instrument or a portfolio of similar debt instruments that are classified as held-to-maturity, the designated risk being hedged, provided all qualifying criteria are met, may be the risk of either:

- changes in the issuer's creditworthiness; or
- the risk of changes in foreign currency exchange rates.

Unlike originated loans and receivables, a held-to-maturity investment cannot be a hedged item with respect to interest-rate risk because designation of an investment as held-to-maturity involves not accounting for associated changes in interest rates since the investment is carried at cost or amortised cost. (IAS 39 (r2000).127) This prohibition includes the hedging of variable rate interest payment on a held-to-maturity investment (IGC 127-2). Cash flow hedge accounting is, however, permitted for the reinvestment of the interest and principal cash flows because they expose an entity to interest rate upon reinvestment. The source of the funds forecasted to be reinvested is not relevant in determining whether the reinvestment risk can be hedged. The same principle applies to hedging the cash flow risk associated with forecasted future interest receipts on debt instruments resulting from the reinvestment of interest receipts on fixed rate assets classified as held to maturity (IGC 127-4).

A hedging relationship involving a forecasted purchase of a financial asset that will be classified as held to maturity can qualify for cash flow hedge accounting. This is because, whilst IAS 39 (r2000) prohibits hedge accounting for HTM assets with respect to interest rate risk, classification only occurs when the asset is acquired (IGC 127-3).

Prepayment risk hedged by a purchased call option does not qualify for hedge accounting in a hedging relationship involving a financial asset that is callable and classified as held to maturity. Prepayment risk is primarily a function of interest rate changes and is more akin to interest rate risk than foreign currency or credit risk (IGC 127-6).

Note, however, that the above prohibition of hedging interest rate risk in a held-to-maturity asset does not apply to originated loans and receivables. Changes in interest rates can affect earnings on an originated loan because the lender does not commit to hold it to maturity. Therefore, interest rate risk on an originated loan can qualify as a hedged item (IGC 137-1).

Comparison with UK GAAP – held-to-maturity investments
There are no specific rules in the UK in this area.

Comparison with US GAAP – held-to-maturity investments
Under US GAAP, the risk of changes in foreign currency exchange rates may not be hedged if the hedged item is classified as held-to-maturity. However, US GAAP permits hedge accounting for the change in the fair value of a prepayment option component embedded in the held-to-maturity instrument. IAS 39 (r2000) permits the foreign currency exposures to be hedged for an instrument classified as held-to-maturity but it does not provide an exception to permit hedge accounting for prepayment risk in a held-to-maturity instrument. Both IAS 39 (r2000) and US GAAP permit the credit risk in a held-to-maturity instrument to be designated as a hedged item.

12.21.6 (g) Hedging multiple risks with a single instrument

A single hedging instrument may be designated as a hedge of more than one type of risk provided that:

(a) the risks hedged can be clearly identified;
(b) the effectiveness of the hedge can be demonstrated (see **12.25**); and
(c) it is possible to ensure that there is a specific designation of the hedging instrument and the different risk positions.

(IAS 39 (r2000).131)

A single derivative, appropriately constructed, could be designated as hedging multiple foreign currency exposures, multiple interest rate risks, and aggregated forecasted purchases and sales transactions, with different instruments and various components of different instruments. For example, a currency and interest rate swap (known as a 'CIRCUS') is commonly used as a hedge of foreign currency denominated debt instruments issued in cross-border financing transactions where the debt obligation, including interest and principal, is swapped back into the local functional currency and changes the debt from fixed to variable and vice versa. These instruments can qualify as a hedge of the fair value of the currency risk and a cash flow hedge of the interest rate risk (IGC 131-1).

Example 12.59 Hedging multiple risks with a single instrument

Hedge of a portfolio of variable rate loans

Bank B has a US$1 billion portfolio of 10-year variable rate loans. The loans are indexed to various indices including LIBOR. B also has prime based debt. B enters into an interest rate swap to hedge the cash flow exposure related to the future interest payments. The swap is a US$1 billion, 10 year pay LIBOR, receive 7 per cent fixed interest rate swap. The pay and receive legs of the swap match the interest receipt dates on the loans. The swap can qualify as a hedge of the LIBOR based indexed loans and the prime based debt.

12.21.7 *(h) Portfolio hedges*

IAS 39 (r2000) permits portfolio hedging but requires that the individual assets or liabilities in the portfolio share the risk exposure for which they are designated as being hedged and that the hedged risk for each individual item is expected to respond approximately proportionately to changes in the hedged risk for the portfolio as a whole. (IAS 39 (r2000).132)

Although IAS 39 (r2000) does not provide specific guidance as to what is approximately proportional, US GAAP provides useful guidance in this regard. US GAAP interprets proportionately strictly, but the term does not mean identically. A group of assets would not be considered to respond proportionately to a change in interest rates if a 100 basis point increase in interest rates is expected to result in percentage decreases in the fair values of the individual items ranging from 7 per cent to 13 per cent. However, percentage decreases within a range of 9 per cent to 11 per cent could be considered proportionate if that change in interest rates reduced the fair value of the portfolio by 10 per cent. (SFAS 133.144)

Additionally, this provision should be considered in view of the overall limitation on effectiveness. IAS 39 (r2000) specifies that a hedge is effective if it is in the range of 80 per cent to 125 per cent. If all items in the portfolio were individually within the range of 80 per cent to 125 per cent of the change in the value of the hedging instrument, each would qualify for hedge accounting regardless of how closely they moved in proportion to each other. The approximately proportional test becomes significant when, on average, effectiveness is at the limits (i.e., close to 80 per cent or 125 per cent). In these circumstances, some of the items in the portfolio may be outside of the range of 80 per cent to 125 per cent, yet on average the portfolio is within the limits. For example, if the average effectiveness is 80 per cent (representing the hedge gain or loss divided by the average portfolio gain or loss), an individual item that is 110 per cent of the portfolio average would by itself have an effectiveness of 72.7 per cent (80%/110%). Although IAS 39 (r2000) does not provide specific guidance, a movement more than 10 per cent from the average portfolio when the average is close to the minimum acceptable limits suggests that the hedged item should not be part of the portfolio.

At inception, an entity should perform a sensitivity analysis of all individual items to be included in a portfolio that will be designated as a hedged item. The sensitivity analysis should use a broad range of expected changes and should be applied to all items individually. The entity should continue this analysis process over the term of the hedge to determine that no changes have occurred that would cause the individual items to respond differently compared to the initial expectations or to fall outside the acceptable range.

Individual items that respond to changes outside the 90 to 110 per cent range when the average effectiveness of the portfolio is at the minimum acceptable limit, but that are not material to the portfolio, should not result in the entire portfolio becoming ineffective. In the event that ineffectiveness is determined for individual items that are, in aggregate, not material, that amount should be marked to market through earnings.

If some items within a pool respond within the range of 90 to 110 per cent while others do not, we believe that judgement will be required to determine if the portfolio qualifies as a hedged item. For example, if in a pool of 2,000 loans, 20 (1 per cent) of the loans do not respond within 90 to 110 per cent, the portfolio as a whole may continue to qualify as a hedged item. In the same pool, if 200 (10 per cent) of the loans do not respond within 90 to 110 per cent, the portfolio would not qualify as a hedged item because the individual items within the portfolio did not respond proportionately to the total change in fair value of the hedged portfolio. An entity could then achieve the required range of change for individual items and in aggregate through further subdivision of the items in the portfolio.

IAS 39 (r2000) does not provide guidance for aggregating loans in a portfolio to be hedged. This can be done by classifying according to any predominant risk characteristic, including date or origination or geographic location. An enterprise may choose to consider some of the following characteristics, as appropriate, in the case of loans:

- loan type;
- loan size;
- nature and location of collateral;
- interest rate type (fixed or variable) and the coupon interest rate (if fixed);
- scheduled maturity, prepayment history of the loans; and
- expected prepayment performance in varying interest rate scenarios.

Hedging a specified portion of a portfolio of assets or liabilities
If an entity hedges a specified portion of a portfolio of similar assets or similar liabilities, that portion should relate to every item in the portfolio. If an entity wishes to hedge only certain similar items in a portfolio, it should first identify a smaller portfolio of only the items it wishes to hedge.

When identifying the risk exposure that is shared by individual items in a group, risk should be assessed at the lowest individual level. If a forecasted transaction does not share the risk exposure for which the group of items is being hedged, it should not be part of the group. This is considered necessary to ensure that a single derivative will be effective as a hedge of the aggregated transactions.

A portfolio of equity securities cannot be hedged with an equity-indexed derivative (for example where a stock index is used to replicate a portfolio of shares), even if high correlation can be demonstrated. Hedge accounting is prohibited because a portfolio of different equity securities do not share the same risk and, therefore, the fair value of each item in the portfolio would not change in proportion to the portfolio as a whole (IGC 132-1).

Management of interest rate risk in financial institutions
An enterprise that manages its interest rate risk on a net (or portfolio) basis can potentially qualify for hedge accounting, provided the derivative instruments that hedge the net exposure are designated in a hedging relationship as a hedge gross exposure relating to assets, liabilities, forecasted cash inflows or outflows giving rise to the net exposure. Banks and other financial institutions often manage liquidity risk and interest rate risk on an aggregate basis for all or parts of their activities. They have developed systems to

accumulate critical information throughout the enterprise about their financial assets, financial liabilities and forward commitments, including loan commitments. This information is used to develop estimates of aggregate cash flows and to schedule such estimated cash flows into applicable future periods in which they are expected to be paid or received. The systems generate an estimate of cash flows based on the contractual terms of the instruments and other factors, including estimates of prepayments and defaults. For risk management purposes, derivative contracts are often used to offset some, or all, of the exposure to interest rate risk on a net basis.

IAS 39 (r2000) prohibits net hedging (see **12.21.8**). However, a net exposure can often be defined and documented to meet the qualifying criteria for hedge accounting.

IGC 121-2 sets out the key factors that an enterprise must consider for hedge accounting purposes if it manages interest rate risk on a net basis. These are summarised as follows:

- A derivative that is used to manage interest rate risk on a net basis can be designated as either a fair value hedge or a cash flow hedge. However, it is typically easier to document and track cash flow hedges because under fair value hedge accounting the carrying values ('basis') of individual assets and liabilities in the balance sheet and the effective yield of the hedged items will need to be adjusted each time there is a change in fair value (IGC 121-2a).
- The effects of prepayments may make it more difficult to demonstrate effectiveness in a fair value hedge, and it may be more difficult to implement a system to track the fair value changes and associate them with individual assets and liabilities that require adjustment and changes to their amortisation rates (IGC 121-2b).
- The documentation required for all hedging relationships to qualify for hedge accounting must include (IGC 121-2c):
  1. the hedging relationship;
  2. the enterprise's risk management objective and strategy;
  3. the type of hedge;
  4. the hedged item;
  5. the hedged risk;
  6. the hedging instrument; and
  7. the method used to assess effectiveness (including the basis and frequency of assessment).
- An enterprise may demonstrate an expectation of high effectiveness by preparing an analysis demonstrating high historical and expected future correlation between the interest rate risk designated as being hedged and the interest rate index of the hedging instrument (IGC 121-2d).
- A high probability of the forecasted transaction occurring can be

demonstrated by preparing a cash flow maturity schedule showing that sufficient levels of cash flows exist, including the effects of the resetting of interest rates for assets and liabilities (IGC 121-2e).

- Effectiveness is required to be measured when financial statements are prepared, but management may wish to monitor results more frequently, perhaps daily or monthly. The schedule used to determine effectiveness is maintained and used as the basis for determining the period in which the hedging gains and losses are reclassified out of equity into net profit or loss (IGC 121-2f).
- The portions of the hedging gains and losses that are effective are recognised in equity; ineffective portions of gains and losses are recognised in net profit and loss (IGC 121-2g).
- Hedging gains or losses remain in equity until the transaction occurs or it appears probable that the transaction will not occur, in which case it is reported in net profit or loss (IGC 121-2h).
- A derivative can be redesignated in a new hedging relationship after a hedge failure, provided it is designated for the entire term of its remaining life (IGC 121-2i).
- There is no basis adjustment in a cash flow hedge of forecasted cash flows if the derivative is hedging net exposure to interest rate risk and is designated as a cash flow hedge of forecasted interest cash flows on a gross basis. The reason for this is that the hedged forecasted transactions do not result in the recognition of assets or liabilities and the effect of interest rate changes are recognised in net profit or loss in the period in which the forecasted transaction occurs (IGC 121-2j).
- A financial asset or liability may be a hedged item with respect to the risks associated with a portion of its cash flows or fair value if effectiveness can be measured (IGC 121-2k).
- Although the overall risk exposures may be different for the individual items in the group, a specific risk inherent in each of the items in the group can be designated as being hedged. A common risk typically shared by a portfolio of debt instruments is exposure to changes in the risk-free interest rate or to changes in a specified rate that has a credit exposure equal to the highest credit-rated instrument in the portfolio (IGC 121-2l).

Due to the complexities involved in designating cash flow hedges under these circumstances, a detailed annex to IGC 121-2 provides comprehensive illustrative examples of applying the above approach, including indicating how the cash flow exposures are identified, assessed and reduced, as well as providing additional hedge accounting considerations relating to designation of the hedging relationship. Also included in the annex is an example of hedge designation and documentation, designation objectives, systems, effectiveness and accounting considerations.

Example 12.60 Portfolio hedges

Portfolio hedges – assessing proportional changes

Bank D has a portfolio of motor vehicle loans that it wishes to designate as a hedged item. All of the loans in the portfolio have an 8 per cent fixed rate and a maturity of 48–60 months. Bank D wants to hedge the fair value interest rate risk on the motor vehicle loans. Bank D performs a sensitivity analysis on the portfolio and concludes that the individual items in the portfolio respond proportionately to overall changes in the portfolio (i.e., within a range of 90–110 per cent). The portfolio may therefore qualify as a hedged item because each item is expected to respond to changes in interest rates within a narrow range.

Portfolio hedges – separating the ineffective portion

On 1 April 2002, Bank S has a €100 million portfolio of corporate bonds that have a range of coupons from 7.5 per cent–9 per cent and a maturity range of 10–11 years. Bank S would like to hedge the interest rate exposure on the €100 million bond portfolio. Bank S performs a sensitivity analysis and determines that the price of all of the items individually respond within a range of 90 to 110 per cent of the overall change in price of the portfolio as a whole. Bank S enters into an interest rate swap with a €100 million notional that requires S to pay 9 per cent fixed and receive Euribor (Euro inter-bank offer rate) variable for ten years. Bank S designates this interest rate swap as a hedge of the interest rate risk exposure. On 30 June 2003, Bank S performs its regular, quarterly sensitivity analysis of the individual items in the €100 million portfolio. Interest rates have unexpectedly decreased significantly and the sensitivity analysis indicated that 65 per cent of the individual loans responded to change within the range of 90 to 110 per cent. The remaining 35 per cent are considered to be ineffective. Bank S can de-designate the hedge and redesignate 65 per cent of the notional as a hedge of the portion of the portfolio that responds to changes in a range of 90 to 110 per cent. The remaining fair value of the derivative should be marked to market through net profit along with any other ineffectiveness. Alternatively, Bank S could de-designate the hedge and re-designate specific portions (such as the AA-interest rate and specified portions of the remaining term to maturity common to all loans) of 100 per cent of the loans, as being hedged.

12.21.8 (i) Macro hedging alternatives

For a definition and discussion of macro hedging see **12.21.13**.

> 'Macro hedging is not permitted under IAS 39 (r2000). However, approximately the same effect on net profit or loss of hedge accounting for this kind of hedging relationship can be achieved by designating part of the underlying items as the hedged position. For example, if a bank has 100 of assets and 90 of liabilities with risks and terms of a similar nature and wishes to hedge the net 10 exposure, it can designate 10 of those assets as the hedged item. This designation could be used if such assets and liabilities are fixed rate instruments, in which case it is a fair value hedge, or if they are both variable rate instruments, in which

case it is a cash flow hedge. Similarly, if an enterprise has a firm commitment to make a purchase in a foreign currency of 100 and a firm commitment to make a sale in the foreign currency of 90, it can hedge the net amount of 10 by acquiring a derivative and designating it as a hedging instrument associated with 10 of the firm purchase commitment of 100.'

(IAS 39 (r2000).133)

12.21.9 (k) *Items with no earnings exposure*

'To qualify for hedge, the hedge must relate to a specific identified and designated risk, and not merely to overall enterprise business risks, and must ultimately affect the enterprise's net profit or loss.' (IAS 39 (r2000).149) Excluded items include equity instruments of the enterprise as well as most intercompany transactions in consolidated financial statements.

Equity instruments of the enterprise
An enterprise cannot hedge transactions in its own equity because an entity's own equity does not expose it to a risk (whether relating to changes in fair value or cash flow risk) that will ultimately affect net profit or loss (IGC 137-16). These transactions do not therefore qualify as hedged items. For example, forecasted dividends from a subsidiary do not affect an enterprise's consolidated net profit or loss.

Additionally, certain of these items, such as the issuance of and subsequent repurchase of an enterprise's own equity instruments, would not qualify for hedge accounting because they do not present a cash flow risk that could affect net profit or loss.

In the case of mandatorily redeemable preferred shares, since IAS 32 (r1998) regards these as debt instruments, the dividend on these shares is, by nature, interest. The distinction between debt and equity is based on whether the enterprise is obligated to make the payment, thus dictating whether it is recorded through net profit or loss. Hedging dividends on mandatorily redeemable preferred shares and on equity instruments which are classified as debt instruments, is therefore permitted under IAS 39 (r2000).

An equity security can be hedged for its foreign currency risk exposure provided that the equity instrument is not traded on an exchange on which trades are denominated in the same currency as the measurement currency of the holder and dividends are not denominated in the currency of the holder (IGC 128-4).

Example 12.61 Items with no earnings exposure

Hedge of equity instruments

Company S has issued debt with detachable share warrants. The warrants were assigned a fair value and are recorded in shareholders' equity. The price of Company S's common shares has improved significantly in the market in the current year, and S believes that the warrants will be in the money within the next 3 months. The exercise of the warrants will have a dilution effect for Company S's shareholders; and therefore, Company S would like to hedge the fair value exposure associated with the warrants. S purchases call options on its own shares as a hedge of the written call options (warrants) that it issued. Since the warrants are considered equity instruments, the warrants do not qualify as hedged items under IAS 39 (r2000) because the exchange or settlement of the warrants will not affect net profit or loss.

Intercompany transactions

Such transactions do not expose the consolidated enterprise to fair value or cash flow risks since they are eliminated on consolidation and, therefore, do not qualify as hedged items in the consolidated financial statements. However, foreign currency intercompany balances and transactions are translated at the subsidiary level into its currency and such translated amounts are not eliminated on consolidation. Accordingly, foreign currency intercompany transactions may qualify for hedge accounting as hedged items in the consolidated financial statements. IGC 134-2 clarifies that hedge accounting is permitted if a parent company hedges a foreign currency exposure of a subsidiary, since IAS 39 (r2000) does not require that the operating unit that is exposed to the risk being hedged be a party to the hedging instrument.

IGC 134-1 deals with offsetting internal derivative hedging instruments. Internal hedges cannot qualify for hedge accounting in the consolidated financial statements unless they are offset with an external party (see **12.22.9**).

An intragroup monetary item can be designated at the group level as the hedged item in either a foreign currency fair value hedge or a cash flow hedge, even though the intragroup monetary item is eliminated on consolidation, provided it results in an exposure to exchange differences that cannot be eliminated on consolidation, for example where a transaction involves two group companies that have different measurement currencies (IGC 137-13).

A forecasted intragroup foreign currency transaction may be designated as the hedged item in a foreign currency cash flow hedge provided the transaction is highly probable and will result in the recognition of an intragroup monetary item for which exchange differences cannot be eliminated in consolidated net profit or loss (IGC 137-14).

Example 12.62 Intercompany transactions

Intercompany forecasted transaction

Company ABC sells steel to its wholly owned subsidiary S. The sales to S are priced at market levels at the date of sale. ABC expects to sell S 100,000 tonnes of steel in each of the next 4 quarters. ABC has a long history of steel sales to S and wants to hedge its exposure to sales price variability. ABC enters into a forward contract that effectively locks in the anticipated sales price at the current forward prices for each of the next 4 quarters. The anticipated sales do not qualify as a hedgeable item in the consolidated financial statements of ABC because the forecasted transaction is with a wholly owned subsidiary and therefore does not expose the group as a whole to fair value or cash flow risks. As an alternative, Company ABC could hedge its steel inventory as a fair value hedge.

12.21.10 (l) Equity method investments

> 'An equity method investment cannot be a hedged item in a fair value hedge because the equity method recognises the investor's share of the associate's accrued net profit or loss, rather than fair value changes, in net profit or loss. If it were a hedged item, it would be adjusted for both fair value changes and profit and loss accruals – which would result in double counting because the fair value changes include the profit and loss accruals.'
>
> (IAS 39 (r2000).150)

Example 12.63 Equity method investments

Hedge of an equity method investment

Company P has a 20 per cent investment in the publicly traded common stock of Company Q and since it exercises significant influence over Company Q's activities, Company P accounts for its investment using the equity method. Company Q's share price has appreciated significantly in recent years and Company P wants to hedge the current price. Company P enters into cash settled forward contracts to sell Company Q's shares. Because P uses the equity method of accounting for its investment in Q, the investment may not be a hedged item in a fair value hedge.

12.21.11 (m) Investments in subsidiaries

Similarly to an equity method investment, an investment in a consolidated subsidiary cannot be a hedged item in a fair value hedge because consolidation recognises the parent's share of the subsidiary's accrued net profit or loss, rather than fair value changes, in net profit or loss. However, a hedge of a net investment in a foreign subsidiary is different. There is no double counting because it is a hedge of the foreign currency exposure, not a fair value hedge of the change in the value of the investment. (IAS 39 (r2000).150) (See **22.6.6**.)

Comparison with UK GAAP – investments in consolidated subsidiaries
The UK standard on foreign currency translation, SSAP 20, *Foreign Currency Translation*, allows a hedge of an equity instrument to be offset by the movement on translation on the investment itself, both in the consolidated accounts and in the company's own accounts. These rules are written in very general terms and there are no further detailed requirements.

Comparison with US GAAP – investments in consolidated subsidiaries
In permitting hedging of forecasted transactions, US GAAP contains a proviso that the forecasted transaction must not relate to a forecasted purchase or sale involving a parent company's interests in consolidated subsidiaries or of a minority interest in a consolidated subsidiary. These items do not qualify as hedged items. IAS 39 (r2000) does not specifically exclude these items from qualifying as hedged items and hence the foreign currency exposure, though only foreign currency exposure, relating to these forecasted transactions may qualify for hedge accounting.

12.21.12 (n) Business acquisition commitments

Only a foreign exchange risk resulting from a firm commitment to acquire a business in a business combination is eligible to be a hedged item. The commitment itself cannot be a hedged item since the other risks potentially being hedged cannot be specifically identified and measured. Therefore, it would represent a hedge of a general business risk which is not permitted. (IAS 39 (r2000).135)

12.21.13 (o) Macro hedging

> 'Because hedge effectiveness must be assessed by comparing the change in value or cash flow of a hedging instrument (or group of similar hedging instruments) and a hedged item (or group of similar hedged items), comparing a hedging instrument to an overall net position rather than to a specific hedged item (for example, the net of all fixed rate assets and fixed rate liabilities with similar maturities), does not qualify for hedge accounting.' (IAS 39 (r2000).133)

For example, a forecasted purchase and a forecasted sale cannot both be included in the same group of individual transactions and still qualify as a hedged item. Although they may be based on the same underlying, they have opposite exposures and are considered a macro exposure, the hedging of which is not permitted. Similarly, an enterprise may not group financial assets and financial liabilities together for the purpose of determining the net cash flow exposure to be hedged for hedge accounting purposes. Although the enterprise's hedging strategy and risk management practices may assess cash flow risk on a net basis, designation for hedge accounting purposes must be done on a gross basis, even where a portfolio is being hedged (IGC 127-1).

See also **12.21.7** and **12.21.8**.

12.22 Hedging instruments

> 'A *hedging instrument,* for hedge accounting purposes, is a designated derivative or (in limited circumstances) another financial asset or liability whose fair value or cash flows are expected to offset changes in the fair value or cash flows of a designated hedged item. Under this Standard, a non-derivative financial asset or liability may be designated as a hedging instrument for hedge accounting purposes only if it hedges the risk of changes in foreign currency exchange rates.'
>
> (IAS 39 (r2000).10)

The following types of instruments are discussed below:

(1) derivatives (see **12.22.1**);
(2) non-derivatives (see **12.22.2**);
(3) instruments where time and intrinsic values have been split (see **12.22.3**);
(4) proportions of hedging instruments (see **12.22.4**);
(5) an enterprise's own equity instruments (see **12.22.5**);
(6) written and combination options (see **12.22.6**);
(7) held-to-maturity investments (see **12.22.7**);
(8) instruments with fair value not reliably determinable (see **12.22.8**); and
(9) intercompany derivatives (see **12.22.9**).

12.22.1 Hedging with derivatives

As long as the hedge criteria are met (see **12.20**), IAS 39 (r2000) does not restrict the circumstances in which a derivative may be designated as a hedging instrument, except for certain written options see **12.22.6** below. (IAS 39 (r2000).122)

Two or more derivative instruments, or proportions thereof, may be viewed in combination and designated as the hedging instrument provided, however, that the derivatives do not result in a net written option. If they are with different counterparties, they should not be offset in the balance sheet (IGC 122-1).

A cross-currency interest swap in which neither leg of the swap is indexed to the measurement currency of the entity can be designated in a hedging relationship if each leg of the swap offsets a designated foreign currency exposure, provided that effectiveness can be measured (IGC 131-2). Similarly, a cross-currency interest swap can be designated as a hedge of a foreign currency receivable and foreign currency payable, each of which has a different currency. However, since the foreign currency receivable and payable are remeasured to their respective foreign currency spot rates, hedge accounting is unnecessary. A derivative can hedge more than one type of risk if the risk can be clearly identified, effectiveness can be demonstrated and there is a specific designation of the hedging instrument with the different risk exposures (IGC 131-1 and 131-3).

A concurrent, offsetting swap can be designated as a hedging instrument provided that either the second offsetting swap was not entered into in contemplation of the first swap or there is a substantive business purpose for structuring the transactions separately. In such a case, the swaps would not be viewed as a single unit (IGC 137-15).

A derivative that will be settled by physical delivery of an underlying asset can be designated as the hedging instrument in a cash flow hedge of the variability of the consideration to be paid or received in the future transaction that is the subject of delivery under the derivative contract (also known as all-in-one hedges) (IGC 137-5).

12.22.2 Hedging with non-derivatives

A non-derivative financial asset or liability may be designated as a hedging instrument, for hedge accounting purposes, only for a hedge of a foreign currency risk. The reason for this limitation is the different bases for measuring derivatives and non-derivatives. Under IAS 39 (r2000) derivatives are always classified as held for trading or hedging and, therefore, are (unless they are linked to and must be settled by delivery of an unquoted equity instrument whose fair value is not reliably measurable) remeasured to fair value, with changes in fair value included in net profit or loss or in equity if the instrument is a cash flow hedge. On the other hand, non-derivatives are measured either at fair value with changes in fair value included in net profit or loss; at fair value with changes in fair value reported in equity; or at amortised cost. To allow non-derivatives to be designated as hedging instruments in more than limited circumstances would create measurement inconsistencies. (IAS 39 (r2000).122)

A foreign currency debt instrument, for example an asset, can be designated as a hedge of a foreign currency exposure of another foreign currency debt instrument, for example a liability. However, it cannot hedge the entire fair value of the other instrument. For a non-derivative, only the foreign currency component qualifies as a hedging instrument (IGC 122-2).

A non-derivative asset or liability can be designated as a hedging instrument in a cash flow hedge of the foreign currency exposure of a firm commitment.

In a hedge of a net investment in a foreign entity, the hedging instrument must qualify under IAS 39 (r2000) regardless of whether it qualified under IAS 21 (1993), *The Effects of Changes in Foreign Exchange Rates*, before the adoption of IAS 39 (r2000) (IGC Other-2).

Example 12.64 Hedging a foreign currency purchase with cash deposits

Company A, with a Euro functional currency, has a firm commitment to invest 300 million Yuan in a joint venture in China. Company A currently has 300 million Yuan on deposit with a Hong Kong bank on which it currently recognises transaction gains and losses at each balance-sheet date. Company A is permitted to designate its Chinese Yuan-denominated deposit balances as a hedge of foreign currency exposure on its firm commitment to invest in the joint venture.

Comparison with UK GAAP – hedging with non-derivatives
There are no specific rules in this area in the UK.

Comparison with US GAAP – hedging with non-derivatives
US GAAP limits the use of non-derivatives as hedging instruments to hedges of a net investment in a foreign entity and hedges of a firm commitment. In contrast, IAS 39 (r2000) permits non-derivatives to be used to hedge all foreign currency exposures.

12.22.3 Splitting time and intrinsic values

> 'There is normally a single fair value measure for a hedging instrument in its entirety, and the factors that cause changes in fair value are co-dependent. Thus a hedging relationship is designated by an enterprise for a hedging instrument in its entirety. The only exceptions permitted are:
>
> (a) splitting the intrinsic value and the time value of an option and designating only the change in the intrinsic value of an option as the hedging instrument, while the remaining component of the option (its time value) is excluded; and
>
> (b) splitting the interest element and the spot price on a forward.'
>
> (IAS 39 (r2000).144)

Those exceptions recognise that the intrinsic value of the option and the premium on the forward generally can be measured separately. A dynamic hedging strategy under which quantity of the hedging instrument is constantly adjusted (such as delta-neutral hedging) that assesses both the intrinsic and the time value of an option can qualify for hedge accounting provided sufficient documentation is maintained to evidence the effectiveness of the relationship (IGC 144-2).

An enterprise may not separate a derivative into components representing different risks and designate specific components as the hedging instruments. IAS 39 (r2000) does not permit the bifurcation of derivative instruments.

Similarly, the premium or discount (forward points) on a forward foreign exchange contract that is designated as a hedge may not be amortised to profit or loss over the life of the instrument. The change in the forward points is reported in net profit or loss on a mark-to-market basis over the life of the contract. (IGC 164-1).

IGC 158-5 provides a detailed example demonstrating the accounting journal entries in respect of a hedge of a forecasted foreign currency sale and resulting receivable using a foreign exchange contract. This example illustrates both the situation where the critical terms match (see **12.25.4**) as well as where the hedging relationship is designated for changes in the spot component of the forward exchange contract and the interest element is excluded from the designated hedging relationship.

Comparison with UK GAAP – splitting time value
There are no specific rules in this area in the UK.

Comparison with US GAAP – splitting time value
Although US GAAP prohibits separating a compound derivative into component parts and designating any such component as the hedging instrument, it provides an exception to this rule and permits the foreign currency component of a compound derivative to be separated at the date of initial application of SFAS 133 by the transition provisions. (SFAS 133.18) There is no equivalent transition provision in IAS 39 (r2000).

12.22.4 Hedging with a proportion of a hedging instrument

> 'A proportion of the entire hedging instrument, such as 50 per cent of the notional amount, may be designated in a hedging relationship. However, a hedging relationship may not be designated for only a portion of the time period in which a hedging instrument is outstanding.'
>
> (IAS 39 (r2000).145)

When designating a part of a derivative as a hedging instrument, there is a distinction between the terms 'portion' and 'proportion'. A proportion refers to a percentage of the entire derivative financial instrument whereby any gains and losses on the entire derivative financial instrument relate to the separate pieces as a percentage of their notional amounts. A portion refers to any part of a derivative financial instrument, for example, the first three years of the life of a five-year life of an interest rate swap, or the risk free interest rate component in an A-rated bond. Gains and losses on the entire derivative instrument relate to the separate components based on their specific terms and characteristics and, accordingly, are not proportional to the notional amounts of the pieces.

In the case of foreign exchange risk, a non-derivative financial asset or financial liability can potentially qualify as a hedging instrument. An enterprise may not, however, treat the cash flows for specified periods during which a financial asset or financial liability remains outstanding as a proportion of a hedging instrument and exclude other cash flows from the designated hedging relationship. For example, the first three years for a 10-year foreign currency-denominated borrowing cannot qualify as a hedging instrument in a cash flow hedge of the first three years of revenue in the same foreign currency since a hedging instrument may not be designated for only a portion of the time period in which the hedging instrument is outstanding. A non-derivative financial asset or financial liability denominated in a foreign currency may potentially qualify as a hedging instrument in a hedge of foreign currency risk associated with a hedged item that has a remaining time period until maturity that is equal to or longer than the remaining maturity of the hedging instrument (DIGC 145-1).

Example 12.65 Hedging with a proportion of a hedging instrument

Designating a proportion of a derivative

Company X enters into a R200 million five-year pay variable, receive fixed interest rate swap to hedge R100 million in five-year fixed rate debt. Company X designates the 50 per cent of the swap as a fair value hedge of the debt. 50 per cent of the swap may be designated as a hedge because it is a proportion of the entire derivative.

12.22.5 Hedging with an enterprise's own equity instruments

An enterprise's own equity securities are not financial assets or liabilities and therefore are not hedging instruments. (IAS 39 (r2000).123)

Enterprises may engage in share buy back programs for various reasons and repurchase their outstanding shares traded in the market place. They may also wish to lock in their current share price and attempt to accomplish this by purchasing call options or entering into forward contracts indexed to their own stock. Such forwards and options, to the extent that they are considered equity instruments of the enterprise, are not eligible to be used as hedging instruments because they do not create a fair value or cash flow exposure to net profit or loss.

12.22.6 Hedging with written options and combination options

Written options do not qualify as hedging instruments under IAS 39 (r2000) unless they are designated as an offset to a purchased option(s), including one that is embedded in another financial instrument, for example a written option used to hedge callable debt. However, a purchased option can qualify as a hedging instrument. (IAS 39 (r2000).124)

A written option exposes its writer to the possibility of unlimited loss but limits the gain to the amount of premium received. A written option serves only to reduce the potential for gain in the hedged item or hedged transaction. It leaves the potential for loss on the hedged item or hedged transaction unchanged except for the amount of premium received on the written option. Consequently, on a net basis, an enterprise may be worse off as a result of trying to hedge with a written option and will not be able to achieve hedge effectiveness. Therefore, written options generally do not qualify for hedge accounting.

Where a compound derivative contains an embedded written option, unless this option is designated as an offset to a purchased option (i.e., a combination option), the compound derivative is regarded as a written option and cannot be classified as a hedging instrument. The embedded option may not be separated from the derivative to enable the residual component to be designated as a hedging instrument. Judgement may be required to determine whether the terms and conditions of a compound derivative result in an equivalent exposure to that of a net written option (i.e., greater exposure to losses than to gains) and therefore whether the compound derivative qualifies as a hedging instrument.

Combination options

Two or more derivatives, or proportions thereof, may also be viewed in combination and jointly designated as the hedging instrument. Although IAS 39 (r2000) does not specifically address hedging with combination options, the use of combination option strategies is acceptable, providing the combination is not the equivalent of a net *written* option and effectiveness can be demonstrated. Ordinarily, the individual components of a combination option would need to be entered into contemporaneously to qualify as a hedging instrument. A combination of a written option and a purchased option documented in a single derivative that is economically a net written option cannot be split into their respective components with the purchased option component qualifying for hedge accounting. A derivative instrument can be designated as a hedging instrument only in its entirety and a net written option does not qualify for hedge accounting except in the limited circumstance where it is offsetting a purchased option (IGC 144-1).

Under certain circumstances, a written option component may be considered to offset a purchased option component in a combination option thereby permitting the combination option to be designated as a hedging instrument. This interpretation specifically deals with the requirements for a combination to be classified as a net *purchased* option or a zero cost collar. A combination of options, in which the strike price and the notional amount in both the written option component and the purchased option component remain constant over the life of the respective component, would be considered a net purchased option or a zero cost collar provided all of the following three conditions are met:

(1) no net premium is received;
(2) except for the strike prices, the critical terms and conditions of the

written option component and the purchased option component are the same (including the underlying variable(s), the currency denomination and maturity date);

(3) the notional amount of the written option component is not greater than the notional amount of the purchase option component.

(IGC 124-1)

Under these conditions, for example, a combination of options having different underlying indices, such as a collar containing a written floor based on three-month Treasury rates and a purchased cap based on three-month LIBOR would *not* be considered a net purchased option or a zero cost collar even though the indices may be highly correlated.

Example 12.66 Splitting time and intrinsic value and written options

Separation of a derivative – embedded termination option

Company A enters into a pay variable, receive fixed interest rate swap that has an early termination feature that permits the counterparty to terminate the swap prior to its maturity at a specified price. The termination feature is an embedded written option that would require the entire derivative instrument to be viewed as a written option because the potential loss on the swap is greater than the potential gain. Company A may not separate the embedded written option from the swap and designate the swap component as a hedge.

Note that in the above example, if the termination feature merely specified that the counterparty could terminate the transaction at the market price (i.e., an 'early termination' or 'break' clause), this would not represent a written option because there is no value attached to it. If the option merely enables the parties to terminate the derivative contract at market price, there is no exposure to gain or loss.

12.22.7 Hedging with held-to-maturity investments

Held-to-maturity investments carried at amortised cost may be effective hedging instruments with respect to risks from changes in foreign currency exchange rates (IAS 39 (r2000).125) but are not permitted to be designated as hedges of other risks. (IAS 39 (r2000).122)

The fair value adjustment resulting from remeasuring the hedging instrument (i.e., the held-to-maturity instrument) under hedge accounting does not include the effect on fair value of changes in other sources of exposure. Since the remeasurement is only based on the change in the designated risk being hedged (i.e., the foreign currency exposure), changes in the entire instrument's fair value, changes in interest rates (to the extent not reflected in exchange rates) and changes as a result of the instrument's credit exposure are therefore not taken into account.

12.22.8 Hedging with instruments with fair value not reliably determinable

'A financial asset or financial liability whose fair value cannot be reliably measured cannot be a hedging instrument except in the case of a non-derivative instrument:

(a) that is denominated in a foreign currency,
(b) that is designated as a hedge of foreign currency risk, and
(c) whose foreign currency component is reliably measurable.'

(IAS 39 (r2000).126)

12.22.9 Hedging with intercompany derivatives

'For hedge accounting purposes, only derivatives that involve a party external to the enterprise can be designated as hedging instruments. Although individual companies within a consolidated group or divisions within a company may enter into hedging transactions with other companies within the group or divisions within the company, any gains and losses on such transactions are eliminated on consolidation. Therefore, such intra-group or intra-company hedging transactions do not qualify for hedge accounting treatment in consolidation.'

(IAS 39 (r2000).134)

Intercompany and related party derivatives do not qualify for hedge accounting under IAS 39 (r2000) because they do not affect the enterprise's net profit or loss on consolidation. However, intercompany derivatives could qualify to be used as hedging instruments for the stand-alone financial statements of an enterprise (IGC 134-1) (See also **12.21.9**).

Similarly, an intra-company derivative (that is, a derivative instrument contract between operating units within a single legal entity) cannot be designated as the hedging instrument. Derivatives entered into with enterprises which the entity accounts for under the equity method or using proportionate consolidation are not considered to be third-party derivatives under IAS 39 (r2000).

Although intra-group derivatives are defined within the specific context of members or divisions within a consolidated group, the same principles would apply to derivatives transacted on behalf of affiliates other than subsidiaries. If a transaction between entities is required to be eliminated on consolidation, it is not considered to be a third-party derivative.

The IGC addressed the treatment of intra-group hedges where the related party derivative used as a hedge by one member of a consolidated group is offset by a derivative entered into by the other member of the consolidated group with a third party (IGC 134-1). This situation is fairly common with centralised treasury operations where affiliates are required to hedge exposures with the central treasury, which itself then takes responsibility for hedging these transactions externally in the market. In these instances, the central treasury operation may be viewed as an agent of the related party, hedging on their behalf. The net effect where a central treasury enters into internal contracts with subsidiaries or divisions is that the division or subsidiary holds an equal and opposite position to treasury which net off on consolidation. What remains is the underlying exposures in the subsidiary or division and the external contracts transacted by treasury in the market.

Where a single external derivative is used as a hedging instrument to offset the net cash flow exposure of an enterprise, it qualifies for hedge accounting only to the extent that it is designated as an offset of cash inflows or cash outflows on a gross basis (IGC 134-3). Where the enterprise enters into several third-party external derivatives with a single third party to offset internal derivatives used in hedging relationships and uses a master netting agreement, it may settle the cash flows under those contracts on a net basis. The enterprise may also hedge the exposure created by entering into the external contracts with a single third party by entering into a single offsetting derivative with the same external party (IGC 134-4).

When assessing whether internal derivative contracts can qualify for hedge accounting, it is important to distinguish between situations where a central treasury is hedging exposures of group companies relating to foreign currency risk, and those where other risks are being hedged by the central treasury since netting of exposures is only permitted under limited circumstances in the hedging of foreign currency risk. For other risks, such as interest rate risk, where a central treasury enters into internal derivative contracts with subsidiaries or divisions within the consolidated group to manage risk on a centralised basis, the treasury may not first net off internal contracts before hedging the net exposure in the market through external derivative contracts. In those cases an intra-group derivative can be designated as the hedging instrument provided that the counterparty (that is, the other member of the consolidated group) has entered into a contract with an unrelated third party that offsets the intercompany derivative completely. The reason for different treatment of foreign currency risk as compared to other risks is based on the fact that the internal derivative represents the transfer of foreign currency risk on underlying non-derivative financial assets and liabilities, and IAS 39 (r2000) permits a non-derivative instrument to be designated as a hedging instrument for hedge accounting only for a hedge of foreign currency risk (IGC 134-1a and b).

12.23 Fair value hedges

A *fair value hedge* is defined as 'a hedge of the exposure to changes in the fair value of a recognised asset or liability, or an identified portion of such an asset or liability, that is attributable to a particular risk and that will affect reported net income.' (IAS 39 (r2000).137(a))

Fair value exposures arise from existing assets, liabilities and firm commitments. For example, fixed-rate financial assets and liabilities have a fair value exposure to changes in market rates of interest and changes in credit quality. See **12.19.1** for examples of items which may be hedged as part of a fair value hedge.

12.23.1 Accounting for fair value hedges

If a fair value hedge meets the conditions for hedge accounting (see **12.20**), the hedged item is permitted (see **12.21**), and the hedging instrument is acceptable (see **12.22**), it should be accounted for as follows:

(a) the gain or loss from remeasuring the hedging instrument at fair value should be recognised immediately in net profit or loss; and
(b) the gain or loss on the hedged item attributable to the hedged risk should adjust the carrying amount of the hedged item and be recognised immediately in net profit or loss. This applies even if a hedged item is otherwise measured at fair value, with changes in fair value recognised directly in equity. It also applies if the hedged item is otherwise measured at cost or amortised cost.

(IAS 39 (r2000).153)

Changes in the fair values of inventories can qualify as a hedged item in a hedge of changes in fair value due to changes in the price of inventory. The adjusted carrying amount of the inventory becomes the cost basis for the purpose of applying the lower of cost or net realised value test under IAS 2 (r1993), *Inventories* (IGC 137-12).

If a non-derivative financial instrument, which is classified as a held to maturity asset, originated loan or non-trading liability, is designated as a hedging instrument (only permitted in the case of hedges of foreign currency risk), the non-derivative is remeasured for changes in its fair value attributable to changes in foreign exchange rates under IAS 21 (r1993), *The Effects of Changes in Foreign Exchange Rates*, but not for other changes in its fair value that do not affect its cost (IGC 153-1).

If a foreign currency denominated asset or liability is designated as a hedged item under a fair value hedge of the exposure to changes in foreign currency rates, it is reported at the closing (spot) rate even if it otherwise would have been reported using a historical rate under IAS 21 (r1993), *The Effects of Changes in Foreign Exchange Rates*. It may also be reported at fair value if the entire fair value of the asset or liability is designated as being hedged (IGC Other-5).

IAS 39 (r2000) provides the following example of the application of the above paragraph.

Example 12.67 Accounting for fair value hedges

The following illustrates the accounting for a hedge of exposure to changes in the fair value of an investment in fixed rate debt as a result of changes in interest rates. This example is presented from the perspective of the holder.

In Year 1 an investor purchases for 100 a debt security that is classified as available-for-sale. At the end of Year 1, current fair value is 110.

Therefore, the 10 increase is reported in equity (assuming the investor has elected this method), and the carrying amount is increased to 110 in the balance sheet.

To protect the 110 value, the holder enters into a hedge by acquiring a derivative.

By the end of Year 2, the derivative has a gain of 5, and the debt security has a corresponding decline in fair value.

Investor's Books Year 1:	*Debit*	*Credit*
Investment in debt security	100	
Cash		100
To reflect the purchase of the security.		
Investment in debt security	10	
Increase in fair value (included in equity)		10
To reflect the increase in fair value of the security.		

Investor's Books Year 2:	*Debit*	*Credit*
Derivative asset	5	
Gain (included in net profit or loss)		5
To reflect the increase in fair value of the derivative.		
Loss (included in net profit or loss)	5	
Investment in debt security		5
To reflect the decline in fair value of the debt security.		

The carrying amount of the debt security is 105 at the end of Year 2, and the carrying amount of the derivative is 5.

Hedge accounting adjustments to the carrying amount of hedged assets and liabilities are subsequently reported in net profit or loss in the same manner as other adjustments of the carrying amount of the hedged item. For example, gains and losses on an interest-bearing debt instrument that are attributable to interest rate risk would generally be amortised over the life of the instrument as a yield adjustment. For some unrecognised firm commitments, such as a firm commitment to purchase inventory, the nature of the hedged item will specify a basis for recognising hedge accounting adjustments in net income. For others, such as an operating lease with substantial cancellation penalties, there will be no obvious pattern of income recognition for hedge accounting adjustments. An enterprise should specify as part of its initial hedge designation how hedge accounting adjustments will be subsequently recognised in net income.

Hedge of only certain risks

If only certain risks attributable to a hedged item have been hedged, recognised changes in the fair value of the hedged item unrelated to the hedge are reported depending on the classification of the item (e.g., held-for-trading, available-for-sale, etc). (IAS 39 (r2000).155)

Hedge of an interest-bearing instrument

> 'An adjustment to the carrying amount of a hedged interest-bearing financial instrument should be amortised to net profit or loss. Amortisation should begin no later than when the hedged item ceases to be adjusted for changes in its fair value attributable to the risk being hedged. The adjustment should be fully amortised by maturity.'
>
> (IAS 39 (r2000).157)

Theoretically, amortisation should start immediately since the adjustment of the carrying amount affects the calculation of the effective interest of the hedged item, but it is not required under IAS 39 (r2000) because it may be administratively burdensome (IGC 157-1).

In the example above, the gain of 10 would be amortised to net profit or loss over the remaining life of the debt security.

Hedge ineffectiveness

If a fair value hedge is fully effective, the gain or loss on the hedging instrument, adjusted for the component, if any, of that gain or loss that is excluded from the assessment of effectiveness, will exactly offset the loss or gain on the hedged item attributable to the hedged risk. Any difference that does arise would be the effect of hedge ineffectiveness, which is recognised immediately in net profit or loss (see **12.25**). Although a hedging relationship must comply with an enterprise's established policy range of what is considered 'highly effective' and fall within the 80 per cent–125 per cent range in order for that relationship to qualify for hedge accounting, that compliance does not assure zero ineffectiveness. Any hedge ineffectiveness directly affects net profit or loss because there will be no offsetting adjustment of a hedged item's carrying amount for the ineffective aspect of the gain or loss on the related hedging instrument.

Discontinuing fair value hedge accounting

An enterprise should discontinue prospectively fair value hedge accounting if any one of the following occurs:

(a) the hedging instrument expires or is sold, terminated, or exercised (for this purpose, the replacement or a rollover of a hedging instrument into another hedging instrument is not considered an expiration or termination if such replacement or rollover is part of the enterprise's documented hedging strategy); or

(b) the hedge no longer meets the criteria for qualification for hedge accounting.

(IAS 39 (r2000).156)

The enterprise may elect to designate prospectively a new hedging relationship with a different hedging instrument, a different hedged item or a hedged transaction if the new hedging relationship meets the requirements for a fair value hedge.

Example 12.68

Hedge of mortgage loans held for sale

Bank J has a ¥100 million fixed rate mortgage portfolio that is classified as available-for-sale. Bank J hedged the fair value exposure of the portfolio using forward contracts. As a result of the hedge, the mortgage portfolio has been adjusted for changes in the fair value of the risk being hedged. The adjustment represents the change in fair value of the hedged portfolio and is recognised in net profit or loss. This adjustment will remain as part of the mortgage loans held for sale, until the loans are sold or until the loans are no longer hedged. If hedge accounting ceases prior to the loans being sold, the fair value adjustment of the mortgage loans will be amortised as a yield adjustment over the expected remaining life of the mortgage loans.

12.24 Cash flow hedges

'*Cash flow hedge*: a hedge of the exposure to variability in cash flows that:

(i) is attributable to a particular risk associated with a recognised asset or liability (such as all or some future interest payments on variable rate debt) or a forecasted transaction (such as an anticipated purchase or sale); and

(ii) will affect reported net profit or loss.

A hedge of an unrecognised firm commitment to buy or sell an asset at a fixed price in the enterprise's reporting currency is accounted for as a cash flow hedge even though it has a fair value exposure.'

(IAS 39 (r2000).137(b))

Examples of cash flow hedges are:

(a) a hedge of the future foreign currency risk in an unrecognised contractual commitment by an airline to purchase an aircraft for a fixed amount of a foreign currency;

(b) a hedge of the change in fuel price relating to an unrecognised contractual commitment by an electric utility to purchase fuel at a fixed price, with payment in its domestic currency; and

(c) use of a swap to, in effect, change floating rate debt to fixed rate debt (this is a hedge of a future transaction; the future cash flows being hedged are the future interest payments).

(IAS 39 (r2000).139)

A hedge of a firm commitment in an enterprise's own reporting currency is not a hedge of a cash flow exposure but rather of an exposure to a change in fair value. Nonetheless, such a hedge is accounted for as a cash flow hedge under IAS 39 (r2000), rather than as a fair value hedge, to avoid recognising as an asset or a liability a commitment that otherwise would not be recognised as an asset or liability under current accounting practice. (IAS 39 (r2000).140)

Example 12.69 Definition of a cash flow hedge

Hedge of an anticipated fixed rate debt issuance

Company R periodically issues new bonds to refinance maturing bonds, provide working capital and for various other purposes. When company R knows it will be issuing bonds in the future, it may hedge the risk of changes in the long-term interest rate from the date company R decides to issue the bond to the date the bonds are issued. As a result of the hedge, the effective interest rate of the forecasted bond is locked-in. If long-term interest rates go up, the bond will be issued either at a higher rate or with a higher discount or smaller premium than was originally expected. The higher rate being paid or decrease in proceeds is normally offset by the gain on the hedge. If long-term interest rates go down, the bond will be issued either at a lower rate or with a higher premium or a smaller discount than was originally expected. The lower rate being paid or increase in proceeds is normally offset by the loss on the hedge.

12.24.1 Accounting for cash flow hedges

If a cash flow hedge meets the conditions for hedging set out in **12.20** during the financial reporting period, it should be accounted for as follows:

(a) the portion of the gain or loss on the hedging instrument that is determined to be an effective hedge (see **12.25**) should be recognised directly in equity through the statement of changes in equity; and
(b) the ineffective portion (even if the hedge is considered highly effective) should be reported:
   (i) immediately in net profit or loss if the hedging instrument is a derivative; or
   (ii) in the limited circumstances in which the hedging instrument is not a derivative, in accordance with the policy on reporting changes in fair value of that type of financial asset or liability.

(IAS 39 (r2000).158 and IGC 146-2)

More specifically, a cash flow hedge is accounted for as follows:

(a) the separate component of equity associated with the hedged item is adjusted to the lesser of the following (in absolute amounts):
    (i) the cumulative gain or loss on the hedging instrument necessary to offset the cumulative change in expected future cash flows on the hedged item from inception of the hedge excluding the ineffective component related to a hedging instrument which is not a derivative; and
    (ii) the fair value of the cumulative change in expected future cash flows on the hedged item from inception of the hedge;
(b) any remaining gain or loss on the hedging instrument (which is not an effective hedge) is included in net profit or loss or directly in equity as appropriate; and
(c) if an enterprise's documented risk management strategy for a particular hedging relationship excludes a specific component of the gain or loss or related cash flows on the hedging instrument from the assessment of hedge effectiveness, that excluded component of gain or loss is recognised in accordance with the policy on reporting changes in fair value of that type of financial asset or liability.

If the change in the fair value of a derivative instrument used in a cash flow hedge of interest rate risk (IAS 39 (r2000).159) arises due to a change in market interest rates and also a change in the creditworthiness of the counterparty, ineffectiveness is recognised based on the cumulative change in fair value of the derivative. A derivative cannot be separated into component parts or into portions in order to qualify for hedge accounting (IGC 158-1).

If, however, the change in the value of the hedged item exceeds the change in the fair value of a derivative instrument, no ineffectiveness is recognised. For a cash flow hedge, only the excess of the change in value of the derivative over the change in value of the hedged item is recognised in net profit or loss (IGC 158-2). This is known as 'underperformance' of the derivative as a hedge of the underlying exposure.

If an enterprise enters into a derivative as a cash flow hedge of a forecasted transaction (for example, a sale of a commodity) and subsequently the transaction is expected to occur prior to the original period specified, the enterprise may conclude that this transaction is the same as the one designated as being hedged. The change in timing of the forecasted transaction does not affect the validity of the designation. It may, however, affect the assessment of the effectiveness of the hedging relationship (see **12.25**) and the hedging instrument would need to be designated as a hedging instrument for the whole remaining period of its existence (DIGC 158-3).

Basis adjustment

When the hedged firm commitment or forecasted transaction results in the recognition of an asset or a liability, the associated cash flow hedge gains or losses that were previously recognised directly in equity should be removed from equity and included in the initial measurement of the acquisition cost or other carrying amount of the new asset or liability. (IAS 39 (r2000).160)

The gain or loss on the hedging instrument that was included in the initial measurement of the acquisition cost or other carrying amount of the asset or liability is subsequently included in net profit or loss when the asset or liability affects net profit or loss (such as in the periods that depreciation , interest income or expense, or cost of sales is recognised). The provisions of other IASs with respect to impairment of assets (IAS 36, *Impairment of Assets* – see **10.12**) and net realisable values of inventories (IAS 2 (r1993), *Inventories* – see **10.9.8**) apply to these assets. (IAS 39 (r2000).161)

Hedge accounting is permitted for a hedge of the foreign currency exposure on a forecasted issuance of a foreign currency debt. The gain or loss on the derivative results in a basis adjustment of the debt when the transaction occurs (IGC 160-1).

For all cash flow hedges relating to firm commitments or forecasted transactions where no asset or liability is recognised, amounts that had been recognised directly in equity should be included in net profit or loss in the same period or periods during which the hedged firm commitment or forecasted transaction affects net profit or loss (for example, when a forecasted sale actually occurs). (IAS 39 (r2000).162)

Example 12.70 Amounts recorded in equity

Company S is hedging the forecasted issuance of fixed rate debt using a Eurodollar future (a derivative). The debt was expected to be issued in three months.

At the end of three months the derivative has accumulated losses of US$2 million because of a decline in Eurodollar deposit rates. The discounted or fair value of the cumulative positive change in expected future cash flows on the anticipatory debt issuance was US$1.8 million.

As a result, Company S should recognise US$200,000 of the hedging loss immediately in net profit or loss because that portion of the hedge was ineffective and the derivative is considered to have 'overperformed'. Eurodollar deposit rates declined faster than rates on Company S's anticipated debt issuance. The remaining US$1.8 million is recognised directly in equity in accordance with company S's policy. At the end of three months S issued fixed rate debt and closed-out the Eurodollar futures position by paying the clearing agent on the exchange US$2 million. The US$1.8 million is reclassified out of equity and recorded as a reduction of the proceeds on the debt, thereby recording the debt at a discount.

Example 12.71 Forecasted sale of wheat

Forecasted Sale of Wheat

On 4 January 2000 Company B has forecasted to sell 500 tonnes of wheat on or about 31 December 2000. On 4 January 2000 company B designates the cash flows of the forecasted sale as a hedged item and entered into a wheat futures contract to sell 500 tonnes at US$1.1 million on 31 December 2000. At hedge inception, the derivative is at–the-money (fair value is zero). The terms of the commodity and the derivative match. On 31 December 2000, the wheat futures contract has a fair value of US$25,000 and is closed out. Company B sells the inventory for US$1,075,000.

The journal entries are as follows:

31 December 2000

		Debit	*Credit*
Wheat futures contract		25,000	
	Equity		25,000

To record the wheat futures contract at fair value (note the changes in fair value of the derivative are recorded in Equity until the hedged forecasted sale occurs)

Cash		25,000	
	Wheat futures contract		25,000

To record the settlement of the wheat futures contract

Cash		1,075,000	
Cost of goods sold		1,000,000	
	Revenue		1,075,000
	Inventory		1,000,000

To record the inventory sale

Equity		25,000	
	Revenue		25,000

To record the amount reclassified from Equity to earnings upon the inventory sale

The forecasted cash flows were US$1,100,000 and the actual cash flows are US$25,000 from the derivative and US$1,075,000 from the sale of inventory, which totals US$1,100,000. The variability of the cash flows related to the forecasted inventory sale is offset by the change in the value of the derivative.

Example 12.72 Hedge of variable rate debt with an interest rate cap

Hedge of Variable Rate debt with an Interest Rate Cap

On 4 January 2000, Company X issued a five-year US$100 million variable rate bond. The bond pays interest based on LIBOR plus a spread of 200 basis points on an annual basis, reset on December 31. Company X wants to hedge against increases in the interest expense on the bonds by capping the maximum interest expense at 9.00 per cent (LIBOR of 7.00% + 2.00% spread). Company X purchased an interest rate cap that is indexed to LIBOR with a US$100 million notional amount. The cap pays company X the difference between 7.00 per cent and LIBOR if LIBOR rises above 7.00 per cent. The interest rate cap is designated as a cash flow hedge of the variable rate debt. The terms of the cap are as follows:

Notional amount	$100 million
Trade date	04/01/00
Start date	04/01/00
Expiration date	31/12/04
Strike rate	7.00%
Index	12 month LIBOR
Initial LIBOR	5.56%
Premium	$1.44 million
Caplet expirations	31 December 2000, 2001, 2002, and 2003

The payments on each caplet are made 12 months after the expiration. For example, the caplet that expires on 31 December 2000 will be paid, if applicable, on 31 December 2001.

The fair value of the cap throughout the term of the cap is summarised below:

	LIBOR	*Cap rate*	*Fair value of cap*	*Intrinsic value of cap*(1)	*Time value of cap*	*Cap cash payments*
4 January 2000	5.56%	7.00%	1,440,000	-	1,440,000	-
31 December 2000	5.00%	7.00%	1,000,000	-	1,000,000	-
31 December 2001	5.50%	7.00%	850,000	-	850,000	-
31 December 2002	7.50%	7.00%	1,500,000	895,000	605,000	500,000
31 December 2003	8.00%	7.00%	925,000	925,000	-	1,000,000

(1) Intrinsic fair value is computed on a discounted basis.

The following journal entries are made:

4 January 2001

		Debit	*Credit*
Cash		100,000,000	
	Debt		100,000,000

To record the issuance of debt

Option asset		1,440,000	
	Cash		1,440,000

To record the purchase of the interest rate cap

31 December 2000

		Debit	*Credit*
Interest expense		7,560,000	
	Cash		7,560,000

To record the interest expense (LIBOR at reset plus 200 basis points (5.56% + 2.00%)) on the 100 million principal amount.

Hedge loss		440,000	
	Option asset		440,000

To record the cap option asset at fair value with changes in time value recognised in income (there was no intrinsic value to record).

31 December 2001

		Debit	*Credit*
Interest expense		7,000,000	
	Cash		7,000,000

To record the interest expense (LIBOR at reset plus 200 basis points (5.00% + 2.00%)) on the 100 million principal amount.

Hedge loss		150,000	
	Option asset		150,000

To record the cap option asset at fair value with changes in time value recognised in income (there was no intrinsic value to record).

31 December 2002

		Debit	*Credit*
Interest expense		7,500,000	
	Cash		7,500,000

To record the interest expense (LIBOR at reset plus 200 basis points (5.50% + 2.00%)) on the 100 million principal amount.

Option asset		650,000	
Hedge loss		245,000	
	Equity		895,000

To record the cap option asset at fair value with changes in time value recognised in income and changes in intrinsic value recognised in equity.

31 December 2003

		Debit	*Credit*
Interest expense		9,500,000	
	Cash		9,500,000

To record the interest expense (LIBOR at reset plus 200 basis points (7.50% + 2.00%)) on the 100 million principal amount.

Cash		500,000	
Hedge loss		605,000	
	Equity		30,000
	Option asset		575,000
	Interest expense		500,000

To record the cap option asset at fair value with changes in time value recognised in income and changes in intrinsic value recognised in equity and to record the receipt on the interest rate cap ((7.50% LIBOR – 7.00% cap rate) × 100 million) – the effect of the cap is a 9.00% ceiling on the interest expense.

31 December 2004

		Debit	Credit
Interest expense		10,000,000	
	Cash		10,000,000

To record interest expense (LIBOR at reset plus 200 basis points (8.00% + 2.00%)) on the 100 million principal amount.

		Debit	Credit
Cash		1,000,000	
Equity		925,000	
	Cap asset		925,000
	Interest expense		1,000,000

To recognise the cap asset at fair value and equity at intrinsic (zero) and to record the receipt on the interest rate cap ((8.00% LIBOR – 7.00% cap rate) × 100 million) – the effect of the cap is a 9.00 per cent ceiling on the interest expense

Discontinuing cash flow hedge accounting

An enterprise should discontinue prospectively cash flow hedge accounting if any one of the following occurs:

(a) the hedging instrument expires or is sold, terminated, or exercised (for this purpose, the replacement or a rollover of a hedging instrument into another hedging instrument is *not* considered an expiration or termination if such replacement or rollover is part of the enterprise's documented hedging strategy). In this case, the cumulative gain or loss on the hedging instrument that initially had been reported directly in equity when the hedge was effective should remain separately in equity until the forecasted transaction occurs. When the transaction occurs, either the amount is included in the initial carrying amount of the new asset/liability or the amount is included in net profit or loss. See **Basis adjustment** above;

(b) the hedge no longer meets the criteria for qualification for hedge accounting. In this case, the cumulative gain or loss on the hedging instrument that initially had been reported directly in equity when the hedge was effective should remain separately in equity until the committed or forecasted transaction occurs; or

(c) the committed or forecasted transaction is no longer expected to occur, in which case any related net cumulative gain or loss that has been reported directly in equity should be reported in net profit or loss for the period. (IAS 39 (r2000).163)

If a forecasted transaction designated as being hedged is no longer highly probable of occurring but is still expected to occur, the hedge accounting is required to be terminated prospectively but any net cumulative gain or loss that had been reported directly in equity remains in equity either until the transaction occurs or it becomes probable that the transaction will not occur (IGC 163-1).

If, on transition, an enterprise had deferred gains or losses on cash flow hedges in respect of a forecasted transaction that is no longer highly probable of occurring, the cumulative gain or loss is reported in equity, but no further hedge accounting is permitted. If the forecasted transaction is no longer expected to occur, any cumulative hedging gains or losses should be reclassified out of equity into net profit or loss on initial application (IGC 172-2).

Example 12.73 Discontinuing cash flow hedge accounting

Forecasted transaction no longer probable

Company D is hedging the anticipated issuance of £100 million of 10 year, fixed rate debt using a rate lock agreement (a derivative). Company D expects to issue the debt in the second quarter of 2002. Company D's credit rating is BB. In the first quarter of 2002 the spreads between government and corporate bond rates widen significantly. As a result Company D does not expect to issue its bonds in the second quarter. Company D's advisors believe that the markets will stabilise in the third or fourth quarter of 2002 or the first quarter of 2003. Once the markets stabilise and spreads return to 'normal' levels, Company D will issue its bonds.

Company D closed its rate lock agreement in the first quarter because of the widening of spreads and significant losses incurred on the derivative. The loss at 31 March 2002 was £8 million of which £4 million was ineffective because of the widening of spreads.

Company D should recognise the entire £8 million loss in net profit or loss because the original forecasted transaction is not expected to occur. While it is possible that D will issue debt later in 2002 or early 2003, the original transaction will not occur.

Hedge no longer meets hedge accounting criteria

MNO Incorporated enters into an interest rate swap (Swap 1) and designates it as a hedge of the variable interest payments on a series of US$5 million notes with 90-day terms. MNO plans to continue issuing new 90-day notes over the next five years as each outstanding note matures. The interest on each note will be determined based on LIBOR at the time each note is issued. Swap 1 requires a settlement every 90 days, and the variable interest rate is reset immediately following each payment. MNO pays a fixed rate of interest (6.5 per cent) and receives interest at LIBOR. MNO neither pays nor receives a premium at the inception of Swap 1. The notional amount of the contract is US$5 million, and it expires in 5 years.

At the end of the second year of the 5-year hedging relationship, MNO discontinues its practice of issuing 90-day notes. Instead, MNO issues a 3-year, US$5 million note with a fixed rate of interest (7.25 per cent). Because the interest rate on the three-year note is fixed, the variability of the future interest payments has been eliminated. The hedging relationship qualified for hedge accounting until the end of the second year when MNO issued 3-year debt, at which time a cash flow exposure to interest rates no longer exists. Thus, Swap 1 no longer qualifies for cash flow hedge accounting. However, the net gain or loss on Swap 1 is recognised in equity and is not reclassified to net profit or loss immediately. Immediate reclassification is required if the forecasted hedged transactions (future interest payments) are no longer expected to occur. The variability of the payments has been eliminated, but it still is probable that cash flows at the rates established at the end of year two will occur. Thus, the gain or loss on the swap that has been incurred up to the date in which the 3-year note is issued are not recognised in net profit or loss. Instead the gain or loss is an adjustment to the basis of the fixed rate note that was issued. Unless the swap is redesignated as a cash flow hedge of another exposure, subsequent changes in the fair value of the swap will be recognised in net profit or loss because it no longer qualifies as a hedge.

Hedge no longer meets hedge accounting criteria

Assume the same background facts described in the example above. At the end of the second year of the 5-year hedging relationship, MNO discontinues its practice of issuing 90-day notes and instead issues a 3-year, US$5 million note with a rate of interest that adjusts every 90 days to the prime rate quoted on that day. Swap 1 is no longer effective as a cash flow hedge because the receive-variable rate on the swap is LIBOR, and the prime rate and LIBOR are expected to change differently. MNO wants to continue the hedging relationship and fully offset changes in cash flows caused by changes in the prime rate. Rather than liquidate Swap 1 and obtain a separate derivative to hedge the variability of the prime-rate-based interest payments, MNO enters into a pay-LIBOR, receive-prime basis swap. The basis swap has a US$5 million notional amount and a 3-year term and requires a settlement every 90 days. MNO designates Swap 1 and the basis swap in combination as the hedging instrument in a cash flow hedge of the variable interest payments on the three-year note. Although IAS 39 does not specifically deal with whether combinations of derivatives qualify for designation as hedging instruments, it similarly does not restrict the use of derivatives for hedging purposes except in limited circumstances. On the three-year note, MNO pays interest at prime. On the basis swap, MNO receives interest at prime and pays interest at LIBOR. On Swap 1, MNO receives interest at LIBOR and pays interest at 6.5 per cent. Together, the cash flows from the two derivatives are effective at offsetting changes in the interest payments on the three-year note. Changes in fair values of the two swaps are recognised directly in equity and are reclassified to net profit or loss when the hedged forecasted transactions (the variable interest payments) affect earnings.

12.25 Assessing hedge effectiveness

As discussed in **12.20**, one of the principal criteria for a hedge transaction to qualify for special hedge accounting is that the hedge must be assessed, both at inception and on an ongoing basis, to determine that the hedge is highly effective throughout the financial reporting period. (IAS 39 (r2000).142(b) and (e))

> '*Hedge effectiveness* is the degree to which offsetting changes in fair value or cash flows attributable to a hedged risk are achieved by the hedging instrument.'
>
> (IAS 39 (r2000).10)

A hedge is normally regarded as *highly effective* if, at inception and throughout the life of the hedge, the enterprise expects changes in the fair value or cash flows of the hedged item to be almost fully offset by the changes in the fair value or cash flows of the hedging instrument, and actual results are within a range of 80 per cent to 125 per cent. For example, if the loss on the hedging instrument is 120 and the gain on the cash instrument being hedged is 100, offset can be measured by 120/100, which is 120 per cent, or by 100/120, which is 83 per cent. In such a case, the enterprise will conclude that the hedge is highly effective. (IAS 39 (r2000).146)

In assessing whether a hedging relationship will be highly effective, the creditworthiness of the counterparty to the hedging instrument must be considered. (IGC 142-6)

Hedging relationships frequently will not be fully effective. Assessing hedge effectiveness and measuring the ineffective part of the hedge can be complex. For example, hedge ineffectiveness would result from the following circumstances, among others:

(a) a difference between the basis of the hedging instrument and the hedged item or hedged transaction (e.g., a dollar-based hedging instrument and euro-based hedged item) to the extent that those bases do not move in tandem;
(b) differences in critical terms of the hedging instrument and hedged item or hedged transaction.

If the principal terms of the hedging instrument and of the entire hedged asset or liability or forecasted transaction are the same, the changes in fair value and cash flows will offset fully (the hedge will be highly effective). For instance, an interest rate swap is likely to be an effective hedge if the notional and principal amounts, term, repricing dates, date of interest and principal receipts and payments and index for measuring interest rates are the same for the hedging instrument and the hedged item. In other cases, the hedging instrument will offset the hedged risk only partially. For example, a hedge would not be fully effective if the hedging instrument and hedged item are denominated in different currencies and the two do not move in tandem. (IAS 39 (r2000).148)

At a minimum, an enterprise is required to assess hedge effectiveness when it prepares it interim and annual financial reports. (IAS 39 (r2000).151)

12.25.1 Measurement methods

Measuring effectiveness can be quite complicated. However, for some hedges, a 'short-cut method' is available which is straight forward and less time consuming than normal measurement methods. The short-cut method and the criteria to qualify are discussed in **12.25.4**.

Otherwise, IAS 39 (r2000) does not prescribe a single method for assessing hedge effectiveness. The method an enterprise adopts to measure effectiveness for the purpose of initially qualifying and continuing to qualify for hedge accounting will depend on its risk management strategy and policy (IGC 146-1). It may be appropriate and is permissible for different methods of assessment to be adopted for different types of hedges. When documenting its hedging strategy, an enterprise is required to set out its procedures for assessing effectiveness including, for example, whether the assessment will include all of the gain or loss on a hedging instrument or whether the time value of the instrument will be excluded. (IAS 39 (r2000).151) The policy and hedge documentation should be consistent with and reflect the enterprise's policy. Effectiveness can be measured on a cumulative or period-to-period basis and, therefore, even if a hedge is not expected to be highly effective in a particular period, hedge accounting may be continued if effectiveness is expected to remain sufficiently high over the life of the hedging relationship. Any ineffectiveness will be recognised as it occurs (IGC 142-3).

If any component, such as the time value of money, is excluded from assessing hedge effectiveness, this portion of the movement in fair value is recognised in each period in net profit or loss regardless of the effectiveness of the remaining portion of the hedge.

In assessing the effectiveness of a hedge, the time value of money generally needs to be taken into consideration. The fixed rate on a hedged item need not exactly match the fixed rate on a swap designated as a fair value hedge. Nor does the variable rate on an interest-bearing asset or liability need to be the same as the variable rate on a swap designated as a cash flow hedge. A swap's fair value comes from its net settlements. The fixed and variable rates on a swap can be changed without affecting the net settlement if both are changed by the same amount. (IAS 39 (r2000).152)

> 'In the case of interest rate risk, hedge effectiveness may be assessed by preparing a maturity schedule that shows a reduction of all or part of the rate exposure, for each strip of maturity schedule, resulting from the aggregation of elements, the net position of which is hedged, providing such net exposure can be associated with an asset or liability giving rise to such net exposure and correlation can be assessed against that asset or liability.'
>
> (IAS 39 (r2000).143)

IGC 121-1 and 121-2 provide guidance on hedge accounting when the enterprise manages interest rate risk on an enterprise-wide basis (see **12.21.7**).

If an enterprise identifies an improved effectiveness measurement method and wants to apply that method prospectively, it must discontinue the existing hedging relationship and designate the relationship anew using the improved method.

Example 12.74 Assessment of hedge effectiveness

Hedge of forecasted foreign currency purchase of equipment

Company X's functional currency is the Singapore Dollar. Company X's forecasted purchase of equipment is expected to cost €100,000. Company X wishes to hedge its foreign currency risk. Since the company believes that the British pound (sterling) will broadly move in tandem with the Euro and since the Sterling/Singapore Dollar currency market is more liquid than the Euro/Singapore dollar currency market, Company X enters into a forward contract to receive £60,000 and pay 165,000 Singapore Dollars. The Sterling will then be converted into Euro in the liquid, spot market. The currency exchange rate between Sterling and the Euro is 0.6:1 and the currency exchange rate between the Euro and the Singapore Dollar is 1:1.8.

Because the basis of the equipment and the forward are different (Euro v Sterling), Company X may not assume that the hedge will be highly effective in achieving offsetting changes in fair value (i.e., it may not use the short-cut method – see **12.25.4**). In its documentation of the hedge strategy, Company X measures effectiveness based on the correlation between Sterling and the Euro. To qualify for hedge accounting therefore, Company X will be required to demonstrate effectiveness at inception and on an ongoing basis using a correlation method (such as regression or ratio analysis – see next section). However, even if the effectiveness test is met and hedge accounting is permitted, Company X may experience ineffectiveness in its hedge due to the difference in the basis, and such ineffectiveness is recognised in net profit or loss in the period in which it arises.

Assessing effectiveness of a hedge of fair value with a put option

Company X owns 1,000 shares of Company A worth £50 each. Company X classifies these securities as available-for-sale and has elected to record changes in the fair value of these securities directly in equity. Company X would like to hedge its downside price risk. Company X purchases an at-the-money put option (i.e., the put option has a strike price of £50) on 1,000 Company A shares expiring in three years.

The premium paid for the option is £9,000. Company X appropriately designates the intrinsic value of the put option as a hedge of its investment in Company A, and the hedge strategy is consistent with X's established risk management strategies. Company X measures effectiveness by comparing decreases in fair value of the investment below the £50 strike price with changes in the intrinsic value (the difference between the spot rate and the strike price) of the option on a quarterly basis. The time value of the option is not included in the assessment of effectiveness.

Because the hedging instrument and the hedged item have the same basis and are on the same number of shares, increases in the intrinsic value of the option are expected to be fully effective in offsetting decreases in the fair value of the investment. In this example, the entire £9,000 is time value because the option was purchased at-the-money. Changes in time value are recognised directly in net profit or loss. Note that in this example, effectiveness of the hedge is assessed based on the intrinsic value rather than the fair value of the option. To the extent that the fair value of the option changes due to other variables such as volatility and the risk free rate, Company X calculates the fair value of the option and then deducts the intrinsic value to arrive at the 'time' value component that is recognised in net profit or loss. In other words, the time value component reflects the effect of all variables on the option's price other than the intrinsic value. Based on Company X's designation of effectiveness, all of these other components represent ineffectiveness of the hedge and are therefore recognised directly in net profit or loss.

In some circumstances, it may be possible to demonstrate effectiveness within the designated range even where there is a difference between the basis of the hedging instrument and the hedged item. For example, it may be demonstrated that there is a significant (and increasing) degree of correlation between the Euro and the currencies of certain Scandinavian countries due to regional proximity and similar economic policies and fundamentals. A further example might be a variable rate debt instrument with an embedded pre-payment option that is hedged by a vanilla (standard) swap. In this instance, it might be possible that the fair value of the prepayment option is so insignificant relative to the fair value of the host contract that even though this feature is not replicated in the swap, that it does not negatively impact on hedge effectiveness. Provided that effectiveness can be clearly and rigorously demonstrated in these instances, the use of hedge accounting may be permitted. Generally, however, this would not be a good hedge.

Ratio and regression analysis

Effectiveness is assessed both retrospectively, based on historical relationships that are expected to continue in the future, and prospectively, based on actual results validating that expectation. The appropriateness of a given method of assessing hedge effectiveness can depend on the nature of the risk being hedged and the type of hedging instrument used. An entity should ordinarily assess effectiveness for similar hedges in a similar manner; use of different methods for similar hedges should be justified. It is essential that an entity document at the inception of the hedge how effectiveness will be assessed for each hedge and then apply that effectiveness test on a consistent basis for the duration of the designated hedge.

Several mathematical techniques can be used to make comparisons of hedging gains and losses with the hedged item for the purpose of determining whether the highly effective test has been met including both ratio and regression analysis as well as combinations of these approaches (IGC 146-1). The common definition of highly effective seems to imply some form of ratio analysis, which is a comparison of hedging gains and losses to the corresponding losses and gains on the hedged item. Ratio analysis is a point-in-time measure. It is relatively simple to compute and seems to be well suited for measuring the effectiveness of short-term hedges and for measuring the level of actual offset. Statistical measurement techniques, such as regression analysis, are more complex. They require appropriate interpretation and understanding of the statistical inferences. Regression analysis seems to be best suited for measuring the strength of empirical relationships, assessing probability of offset, and establishing hedge ratios based on such historical relationships.

The use of regression analysis to measure effectiveness is more complex than the use of ratio analysis, because valid conclusions cannot be made solely on the basis of a single regression statistic, such as r^2 (also known as goodness-of-fit). Regression typically works best where there is basis risk in the hedging relationship. The statistical level of effectiveness means little without an understanding of the regression formula and other statistical results. The constant and slope of the regression formula and standard errors of the regression should be interpreted and understood to arrive at appropriate conclusions. Assuming a constant of zero, the slope of the regression equation is equivalent to the ratio of effectiveness and should therefore also lie within the range of 0.8 to 1.25 (corresponding to a ratio of 80 per cent to 125 per cent). In the absence of anything to the contrary, a correlation coefficient (r^2) lying between the values of 0.8 to 1 is typically representative of a highly effective offsetting relationship between the hedged item and the hedging instrument.

A regression analysis can generally be performed to determine whether there is a probability of achieving offset. Such analysis is essential for indirect hedges, whereby the commodity or index underlying the futures or options contract is not the same commodity or index as the item being hedged (e.g., oil as a hedge of petrol). After the hedge has commenced, a ratio analysis can be performed on a cumulative basis to ensure that substantial offset has occurred and should be used to measure ineffectiveness.

12.25.2 Comparison with UK GAAP

There are no specific rules in this area in the UK.

12.25.3 Comparison with US GAAP

US GAAP permits the measurement of the effectiveness of a hedge with an option contract based on the option's minimum value. An option's minimum value is defined as its intrinsic value plus the effect of discounting. If effectiveness is measured in this manner, the change in the volatility value of the contract is excluded in the determination of effectiveness. (SFAS 133.63(b)) It appears that the use of an option's minimum value is not permitted under IAS 39 (r2000).

12.25.4 *Assuming no ineffectiveness*

If the critical terms of the hedging instrument and the entire hedged asset or liability (as opposed to selected cash flows) or hedged forecasted transaction are the same, an enterprise could conclude that changes in fair value or cash flows attributable to the risk being hedged are expected to completely offset at inception and on an ongoing basis and use the 'short-cut method'. For example, an enterprise may assume that a hedge of a forecasted purchase of a commodity with a forward contract will be highly effective and that there will be no ineffectiveness to be recognised in net profit or loss if:

(a) the forward contract is for purchase of the same quantity of the same commodity at the same time and location as the hedged forecasted purchase;
(b) the fair value of the forward contract at inception is zero; and
(c) either the change in the discount or premium on the forward contract is excluded from the assessment of effectiveness and included directly in net profit or loss or the change in expected cash flows on the forecasted transaction is based on the forward price for the commodity.

(IAS 39 (r2000).151)

IAS 39 (r2000) specifies that an enterprise can conclude that there is an expectation of complete offset if the critical terms are the same. This does not, however, equate to the short-cut method permitted under US GAAP which may be used to assess hedge effectiveness on an ongoing basis. IAS 39 (r2000) does not contain a similar provision for a short-cut method, instead requiring hedge effectiveness to be assessed on an ongoing basis (IAS 39 (r2000).142(e)) even if the principal terms of the hedging instrument and the hedged item are the same, since in a hedging relationship ineffectiveness could arise because of other attributes such as credit risk and liquidity factors affecting a particular hedging instrument. In such cases, IAS 39 (r2000) permits an enterprise to designate only certain risks in an overall exposure as being hedged, thereby improving the effectiveness of the hedging relationship (IGC 147-1).

IAS 39 (r2000) does not provide guidance as to what constitutes critical terms or what conditions are necessary to be able to conclude that there is an expectation of complete offset of the changes in the fair value or cash flows of the hedging instrument and hedged item. The following conditions are set out in US GAAP and are not required in IAS 39 (r2000) but may be helpful when considering whether there is an expectation of complete offset under IAS 39 (r2000). Under US GAAP, an entity may assume no ineffectiveness in a hedging relationship of interest rate risk involving an interest-bearing asset or liability and an interest rate swap if all of the applicable conditions in the following list are met (SFAS 133.68):

Conditions applicable to both fair value hedges and cash flow hedges

(1) The notional amount of the swap matches the principal amount of the interest-bearing asset or liability.
(2) The fair value of the swap at its inception is zero.
(3) The formula for computing net settlements under the interest rate swap is the same for each net settlement. (That is, the fixed rate is the same throughout the term, and the variable rate is based on the same index and includes either the same constant adjustment or no adjustment.)
(4) The interest-bearing asset or liability is not pre-payable.
(5) Any other terms in the interest-bearing financial instruments or interest rate swaps are typical of those instruments and do not invalidate the assumption of no ineffectiveness.

Conditions applicable to fair value hedges only

(1) The expiration date of the swap matches the maturity date of the interest-bearing asset or liability.
(2) There is no floor or ceiling on the variable interest rate of the swap.
(3) The intervals between the repricing of the variable interest rate in the swap are frequent enough to justify an assumption that the variable payment or receipt is at a market rate (generally, three to six months or less).

Conditions applicable to cash flow hedges only

(1) All interest receipts or payments on the variable-rate asset or liability during the term of the swap are designated as hedged, and no interest payments beyond the term of the swap are designated as hedged.
(2) There is no floor or cap on the variable interest rate of the swap unless the variable-rate asset or liability has a floor or cap. In that case, the swap must have a floor or cap on the variable interest rate that is comparable to the floor or cap on the variable-rate asset or liability. (For this purpose, comparable does not necessarily mean equal. For example, if a swap's variable rate is LIBOR and an asset's variable rate is LIBOR plus two per cent, a ten per cent cap on the swap would be comparable to a 12 per cent cap on the asset.)
(3) The repricing dates match those of the variable-rate asset or liability.
(4) The index on which the variable rate is based matches the index on which the asset or liability's variable rate is based.

Example 12.75 Conclusion of no ineffectiveness

Fair value hedge of a firm commitment

Company X enters into a firm commitment to buy 10,000 ounces of gold at the current six-month forward rate of US$310. On the same day, Company X enters into a forward contract (which is a derivative) to sell 10,000 ounces of gold at the current six-month forward rate of US$310. Company X appropriately documents the hedging strategy and states that effectiveness will be measured based on changes in the six month forward price of gold. Because the critical terms of the firm commitment and the forward contract match, Company X may assume that the changes in the fair value of the firm commitment are expected to completely offset the change in the fair value of the derivative.

Evaluation of interest rate swap

On 1 January 2000, Company X issued R100 million of five-year 15 per cent fixed rate debt. Interest on the debt is payable annually. X enters into a fair value hedge of its debt with an interest rate swap.

The terms of both instruments follow:

	Debt	*Swap*
Notional/principal amount	R100 million	R100 million
Trade date		01/01/00
Start date	01/01/00	01/01/00
Maturity date	31/12/04	31/12/04
Company X pays	15.00% Fixed	JIBAR
Company X receives		15.00%
Pay and receive dates	Annually	Annually
Variable reset		Annually
Initial JIBAR		16.69%
First pay/receive date	31/12/00	31/12/00
Last pay/receive date	31/12/04	31/12/04

All of the critical terms match; therefore, Company X may assume no ineffectiveness, provided there are no significant differences in credit that are part of the designated hedging relationship.

Comparison with UK GAAP

There are no equivalent rules in the UK.

Comparison with US GAAP

IAS 39 (r2000) does not provide guidance as to what constitutes critical terms for the use of the short-cut method. US GAAP specifies critical terms.

IAS 39 (r2000) permits an entity to conclude that a hedge will be fully effective if the critical terms of the hedging instrument match the terms of the hedged item. US GAAP has a similar rule but it is only specified for interest rate swaps.

Under US GAAP, if the critical terms match and certain other conditions are met, no ineffectiveness is required to be recognised. This approach is referred to as the 'short-cut method' under US GAAP. It permits an entity that qualifies for its use to ignore certain differences such as credit that would otherwise cause ineffectiveness in the hedging relationship. Since credit is not identified as a critical term under US GAAP, changes in the fair value of the hedged instrument as a result of credit changes that create ineffectiveness are not recognised. An assumption of no ineffectiveness is especially important because it significantly simplifies the computations necessary to make the accounting entries. The purpose of the exception is to provide relief from the burden of computing the change in fair value for both the derivative instrument and the hedged item.

Although under IAS 39 (r2000), it can be concluded that there will be no ineffectiveness when critical terms match, if there is ineffectiveness in a hedging relationship it cannot be ignored. To the extent that there would be significant ineffectiveness as a result of credit differences, critical terms do not match and it cannot be concluded that there will be no ineffectiveness.

However, IAS 39 (r2000) provides another method of limiting ineffectiveness. It permits an entity to designate portions of assets, liabilities and transactions as the hedged items, which can have the effect of eliminating risks, such as credit risk that could not be hedged effectively, from the hedging relationship. US GAAP does not permit hedge accounting for portions of risks except as specifically provided.

By permitting the designation of specific portions of risks as the hedged item, the portion of the risk being hedged can often be limited and equal to the risk of the hedging instrument. This approach reduces the ineffectiveness that would otherwise result from being required to hedge the whole instrument.

12.26 Hedges of net investment in a foreign entity

See **22.6.6**.

12.27 Disclosure

Both IAS 32 (r1998) and to a lesser extent IAS 39 (r2000) prescribe certain requirements for the presentation of financial instruments and identify the information that should be disclosed about financial instruments and exposures. Neither IAS 32 (r1998) nor IAS 39 (r2000) prescribe either the format or the location in the financial statements of the disclosures they require.

Some information may be appropriately given in tables while other information may be better suited to narrative disclosure. Management considers the clarity to a user of the financial statements when choosing the manner of presentation of the disclosures. Accordingly, methods of presentation vary among enterprises since the objective for holding financial instruments and therefore, the types and their significance will vary.

Similarly, the level of detail given about particular financial instruments is a matter of judgement. Management must strike a balance between overburdening financial statements with excessive detail which is unhelpful to users in assessing the performance, financial position or future cash flows of the enterprise and obscuring significant information as a result of too much aggregation. 'For example, when an enterprise is a party to large numbers of financial instruments with similar characteristics and no one contract is individually significant, summarised information by reference to particular classes of instruments is appropriate. On the other hand, specific information about an individual instrument may be important when that instrument represents, for example, a significant element in an enterprise's capital structure.' (IAS 32 (r1998).45) Management may classify financial instruments having similar characteristics together such as whether they are carried at cost or fair value.

Relatively few of the disclosures discussed in IAS 32 (r1998) are mandatory and instead have been designed more in line with providing recommended best practice. Judgement is required in determining the appropriate classes of financial instruments, assessing the extent to which a reporting enterprise's disclosures meet the requirements and in evaluating the exact nature and format of information to be provided.

When supplementary schedules given in the notes relate to items recognised in the balance sheet, sufficient information is given to allow a user to reconcile the schedule given to the notes to a line item in the balance sheet. (IAS 32 (r1998).46)

In addition to the requirements in IAS 32 (r1998) and IAS 39 (r2000), IGC 170-1 provides guidance relating to the required disclosure of the amounts and changes in fair values during a reporting period. As part of the amendments to IAS 39 (r2000), the disclosure requirements in IAS 32 relating to hedges of anticipated transactions (IAS 32.91-93) were deleted, having been superseded by the disclosure requirements of IAS 39 (r2000).

12.27.1 Mandatory disclosure requirements

Financial risk management objectives and policies	An enterprise should describe its financial risk management objectives and policies, including its policy for hedging each major type of forecasted transaction for which hedge accounting is used. (IAS 32 (r1998).43A) The disclosure of management's policies and activities in respect of hedging risk exposures does not relate solely to those transactions that qualify under the rules of IAS 39 (r2000) for special hedge accounting. Disclosure should also include the economic aspects of hedging and hedging relationships which might not qualify for special hedge accounting but which are integral to obtaining an understanding of the enterprise's activities in financial instruments. See **12.27.2** for a discussion of the types of risk.
Terms, conditions and accounting policies	For each class of financial asset, financial liability and equity instrument, both recognised and (unrecognised, an enterprise should disclose: (a) information about the extent and nature of the financial instruments, including significant terms and conditions that may affect the amount, timing and certainty of future cash flows; and (b) the accounting policies and methods adopted, including the criteria for recognition and the basis of measurement applied. (IAS 32 (r1998).47) The following should be included in the disclosures of the enterprise's accounting policies as part of the disclosure required by IAS 32 (r1998).47(b) and IAS 39 (r2000).170: (a) the methods and significant assumptions (including prepayment rates, rates of estimated credit losses and interest or discount rates) applied in estimating fair values of financial assets and financial liabilities that

	are carried at fair value, separately for significant classes of financial assets (IAS 32 (r1998).46 provides guidance for determining classes of financial assets for disclosure purposes); (b) whether gains and losses arising from changes in the fair value of those available-for-sale financial assets that are measured at fair value subsequent to initial recognition are included in net profit or loss for the period or are recognised directly in equity until the financial asset is disposed of; and (c) for each of the four categories of financial assets, whether 'regular way' purchases and sales of financial assets are accounted for at trade date or settlement date. (IAS 39 (r2000).167) If the enterprise has entered into a securitisation or repurchase agreement, disclose, separately for such transactions occurring in the current financial reporting period and for remaining retained interests from transactions occurring in prior financial reporting periods: (i) the nature and extent of such transactions, including a description of any collateral and quantitative information about the key assumptions used in calculating the fair values of new and retained interests; (ii) whether the financial assets have been derecognised; (IAS 39 (r2000).170(d)) See **12.27.3** for further discussion of disclosing terms, conditions and accounting policies.
Interest rate risk	For each class of financial asset and financial liability, both recognised and unrecognised, an enterprise should disclose information about its exposure to interest rate risk, including: (a) contractual repricing or maturity dates, whichever dates are earlier; and

	(b) effective interest rates, when applicable. (IAS 32 (r1998).56) See **12.27.4** for further discussion.
Credit risk	For each class of financial asset, both recognised and unrecognised, an enterprise should disclose information about its exposure to credit risk, including: (a) the amount that best represents its maximum credit risk exposure at the balance sheet date, without taking account of the fair value of any collateral, in the event other parties fail to perform their obligations under financial instruments; and (b) significant concentrations of credit risk. (IAS 32 (r1998).66) See **12.27.5** for further discussion.
Fair values and impairments	For each class of financial asset and financial liability, an enterprise should disclose information about fair value. When it is not practicable within constraints of timeliness or cost to determine the fair value of a financial asset or financial liability with sufficient reliability, that fact should be disclosed together with information about the principal characteristics of the underlying financial instrument that are pertinent to its fair value. (IAS 32 (r1998).77) However, if an instrument is measured at fair value under IAS 39 (r2000), this disclosure is not required. (IAS 39 (r2000).166) If a gain or loss from remeasuring available-for-sale financial assets to fair value (other than assets relating to hedges) has been recognised directly in equity, through the statement of changes in equity, disclose: (i) the amount that was so recognised in equity during the current period; and (ii) the amount that was removed from equity and reported in net profit or loss for the period; (IAS 39 (r2000).170(a))

	If the presumption that fair value can be reliably measured for all financial assets that are available for sale or held for trading has been overcome and the enterprise is, therefore, measuring any such financial assets at amortised cost, disclose that fact together with a description of the financial assets, their carrying amount, an explanation of why fair value cannot be reliably measured, and, if possible, the range of estimates within which fair value is highly likely to lie. Further, if financial assets whose fair value previously could not be measured reliably are sold, that fact, the carrying amount of such financial assets at the time of sale, and the amount of gain or loss recognised should be disclosed. (IAS 39 (r2000).170(b)) When an enterprise carries one or more financial assets at an amount in excess of their fair value, the enterprise should disclose: (a) the carrying amount and the fair value of either the individual assets or appropriate groupings of those individual assets; and (b) the reasons for not reducing the carrying amount, including the nature of the evidence that provides the basis for management's belief that the carrying amount will be recovered. (IAS 32 (r1998).88) Disclosure in respect of the above paragraph is not required for those instruments measured at fair value in terms of the provisions of IAS 39 (r2000) (see IAS 39 (r2000).166). Financial statements should disclose the nature and amount of any impairment loss or reversal of an impairment loss recognised for a financial asset, separately for each significant class of financial asset (IAS 32 (r1998).46 provides guidance for determining classes of financial assets). (IAS 39 (r2000).170(f))
Hedging	Financial statements should include all of the following additional disclosures relating to hedging:

(a) a description of the enterprise's policy for hedging each major type of forecasted transaction;

For example, in the case of hedges of risks relating to future sales, that description indicates the nature of the risks being hedged, approximately how many months or years of expected future sales have been hedged, and the approximate percentage of sales in those future months or years;

(b) disclosure of the following separately for designated fair value hedges, cash flow hedges, and hedges of a net investment in a foreign entity:
   (i) a description of the hedge;
   (ii) a description of the financial instruments designated as hedging instruments for the hedge and their fair values at the balance sheet date;
   (iii) the nature of the risks being hedged; and
   (iv) for hedges of forecasted transactions, the periods in which the forecasted transactions are expected to occur, when they are expected to enter into the determination of net profit or loss, and a description of any forecasted transaction for which hedge accounting had previously been used but that is no longer expected to occur; and

(c) if a gain or loss on derivative and non-derivative financial assets and liabilities designated as hedging instruments in cash flow hedges has been recognised directly in equity, through the statement of changes in equity, disclosure of:
   (i) the amount that was so recognised in equity during the current period;
   (ii) the amount that was removed from equity and reported in net profit or loss for the period; and
   (iii) the amount that was removed from equity and added to the initial measurement of the acquisition cost

	or other carrying amount of the asset or liability in a hedged forecasted transaction during the current period. (IAS 39 (r2000).169)
Other disclosures	
Reacquired own equity instruments	Shares (including the effects of treasury shares) held by the enterprise itself or by subsidiaries or associates of the enterprise. The amounts of reductions to equity for treasury shares held should be disclosed separately either on the face of the balance sheet or in the notes. (SIC-16.6)
Interest, dividends, gains and losses	Significant items of income, expense, and gains and losses resulting from financial assets and financial liabilities, whether included in net profit or loss or as a separate component of equity. For this purpose: (i) total interest income and total interest expense (both on a historical cost basis) should be disclosed separately. Even if an asset or liability is adjusted for changes in fair value as a result of hedge accounting, interest income on a historical basis must be disclosed (IGC 170-2); (ii) with respect to available-for-sale financial assets that are adjusted to fair value after initial acquisition, total gains and losses from derecognition of such financial assets included in net profit or loss for the period should be reported separately from total gains and losses from fair value adjustments of recognised assets and liabilities included in net profit or loss for the period (a similar split of 'realised' versus 'unrealised' gains and losses with respect to financial assets and liabilities held for trading is not required); (iii) the enterprise should disclose the amount of interest income that has been accrued on impaired loans pursuant to paragraph 116 and that has not yet been received in cash. (IAS 39 (r2000).170(c))

Collateral	A borrower should disclose the carrying amount of financial assets pledged as collateral for liabilities and any conditions relating to pledged assets. (IAS 39 (r2000).170(g)) A lender should disclose the fair value of collateral that it has accepted and that is permitted to sell or repledge, and the fair value of collateral that it has sold or repledged, and any significant terms and conditions associated with its use of collateral. (IAS 39 (r2000).170(h))
Changes in categories	If the enterprise has reclassified a financial asset as one required to be reported at amortised cost rather than at fair value, disclose the reason for that reclassification. (IAS 39 (r2000).170 (e))

12.27.2 Types of risk

The disclosures required by IAS 32 (r1998) focus on the financial risks related to the financial instruments held by an enterprise and the strategies used to mitigate these risks. The following definitions are given of each type of risk.

> 'Price risk – There are three types of price risk: currency risk, interest rate risk and market risk.
>
> Currency risk is the risk that the value of a financial instrument will fluctuate due to changes in foreign exchange rates.
>
> Interest rate risk is the risk that the value of a financial instrument will fluctuate due to change in market interest rates.
>
> Market risk is the risk that the value of a financial instrument will fluctuate as a result of changes in market prices whether those changes are caused by factors specific to the individual security or its issuer or factors affecting all securities traded in the market.
>
> The term "price risk" embodies not only the potential for loss but also the potential for gain.
>
> Credit risk – Credit risk is the risk that one party to a financial instrument will fail to discharge an obligation and cause the other party to incur a financial loss.
>
> Liquidity risk – Liquidity risk, also referred to a funding risk, is the risk that an enterprise will encounter difficulty in raising funds to meet commitments associated with financial instruments. Liquidity risk may result from an inability to sell a financial asset quickly at close to its fair value.
>
> Cash flow risk – Cash flow risk is the risk that future cash flows associated with a monetary financial instrument will fluctuate in amount. In the case of a floating rate debt instrument, for example, such fluctuations result in a change in the effective interest rate of the financial instrument, usually without a corresponding change in its fair value.'
>
> (IAS 32 (r1998).43)

12.27.3 Disclosure of terms, conditions and accounting policies

Terms and conditions

As noted earlier, the disclosure requirements of IAS 32 (r1998) apply not only to derivative financial instruments, but to all financial instruments. Therefore, the disclosures discussed below are made for financial assets such as trade or notes receivable, financial liabilities such as trade or notes payable or bank loans, and derivative financial instruments.

When financial instruments are 'important, either individually or as a class, in relation to the current financial position of an enterprise or in future operating results, their terms and conditions are disclosed. If no single instrument is individually significant to the future cash flows of a particular enterprise, essential characteristics of the instruments are described by reference to appropriate groupings of like instruments.' (IAS 32 (r1998).48)

> 'When financial instruments held or issued by an enterprise, either individually or as a class, create a potentially significant exposure to price, credit, liquidity or cash flow risk (which they generally always will), terms and conditions that may warrant disclosure include:
>
> (a) the principal, stated, face or other similar amount which, for some derivative instruments, such as interest rate swaps, may be the amount (referred to as the notional amount) on which future payments are based;
> (b) the date of maturity, expiry or execution;
> (c) early settlement options held by either party to the instrument, including the period in which, or date at which, the options may be exercised and the exercise price or range of prices;
> (d) options held by either party to the instrument to convert the instrument into, or exchange it for, another financial instrument or some other asset or liability, including the period in which, or date at which, the options may be exercised and the conversion or exchange ratio(s);
> (e) the amount and timing of scheduled future cash receipts or payments of the principal amount of the instrument, including instalment repayments and any sinking fund or similar requirements;
> (f) stated rate or amount of interest, dividend or other periodic return on principal and the timing of payments;
> (g) collateral held, in the case of a financial asset, or pledged, in the case of a financial liability;
> (h) in the case of an instrument for which cash flows are denominated in a currency other than the enterprise's reporting currency, the currency in which receipts or payments are required;
> (i) in the case of an instrument that provides for an exchange, information described in items (a) to (h) for the instrument to be acquired in the exchange; and
> (j) any condition of the instrument or an associated covenant that, if contravened, would significantly alter any of the other terms (for example, a minimum debt-to-equity ratio in a bond covenant that, if contravened, would make the full principal amount of the bond due and repayable immediately).'
>
> (IAS 32 (r1998).49)

When the balance sheet presentation of a financial instrument differs from its legal form, for example when redeemable preferred shares are classified as financial liabilities rather than as equity instruments as described in Chapter **11**, an enterprise is encouraged to explain in the notes to the financial statements the nature of the instrument. (IAS 32 (r1998).50)

The relationships between financial instruments often need to be explained to provide users with a complete picture of the transactions of the enterprise and to assist in assessing the future cash flows of the enterprise. 'For example, it is important to disclose hedging relationships such as might exist when an enterprise holds an investment in shares for which it has purchased a put option. Similarly, it is important to disclose relationships between components of 'synthetic instruments' such as fixed rate debt created by borrowing at a floating rate and entering into a floating to fixed interest rate swap. In each case, an enterprise presents the individual financial assets and financial liabilities in its balance sheet according to their nature, either separately or in the class of financial asset or financial liability to which they belong.' (IAS 32 (r1998).51)

Accounting policies

IAS 1 (r1997), *Presentation of Financial Statements*, requires disclosure of the measurement basis (or bases) used in preparing the financial statements and each specific accounting policy that is necessary for a proper understanding of the financial statements. (IAS 1 (r1997).97)

In the case of financial instruments, such disclosures include:

'(a) the criteria applied in determining when to recognise a financial asset or financial liability on the balance sheet and when to cease to recognise it;
(b) the basis of measurement applied to financial assets and financial liabilities both on initial recognition and subsequently; and
(c) the basis on which income and expense arising from financial assets and financial liabilities is recognised and measured.'

(IAS 32 (r1998).52)

Essentially, the disclosures given need to cover the recognition, derecognition, measurement and income statement treatment of financial instruments.

IAS 32 (r1998) specifically notes that it may be necessary to disclose the accounting policies for the related types of transactions:

'(a) transfers of financial assets when there is a continuing interest in, or involvement with, the assets by the transferor, such as securitisations of financial assets, repurchase agreements and reverse repurchase agreements;
(b) transfers of financial assets to a trust for the purpose of satisfying liabilities when they mature without the obligation of the transferor being discharged at the time of the transfer, such as an in-substance defeasance trust;

(c) acquisition or issuance of separate financial instruments as part of a series of transactions designed to synthesise the effect of acquiring or issuing a single instrument;
(d) acquisition or issuance of financial instruments as hedges of risk exposures; and
(e) acquisition or issuance of monetary financial instruments bearing a stated interest rate that differs from the prevailing market rate at the date of issue.'

(IAS 32 (r1998).53)

The Appendix to IAS 32 (r1998) lists additional circumstances in which an enterprise discloses its accounting policies in relation to financial instruments.

Measurement

In addition to stating the basis on which an enterprise accounts for a financial instrument, information is disclosed about the application of that basis.

> 'For example, for financial instruments carried on the cost basis, an enterprise may be required to disclose how it accounts for:
>
> (a) costs of acquisition or issuance;
> (b) premiums and discounts on monetary financial assets and financial liabilities;
> (c) changes in the estimated amount of determinable future cash flows associated with a monetary financial instrument such as a bond indexed to a commodity price;
> (d) changes in circumstances that result in significant uncertainty about the timely collection of all contractual amounts due from monetary financial assets;
> (e) declines in the fair value of financial assets below their carrying amount; and
> (f) restructured financial liabilities.
>
> For financial assets and liabilities carried at fair value, an enterprise indicates whether carrying amounts are determined from quoted market prices, independent appraisals, discounted cash flow analysis or another appropriate method, and discloses any significant assumptions made in applying those methods.'
>
> (IAS 32 (r1998).54)

> 'In the case of uncertainty about the collectability of amounts realisable from a monetary financial asset or a decline in the fair value of a financial asset below its carrying amount due to other causes, an enterprise indicates its policies for:
>
> (a) when to reduce the carrying amount of the asset;
> (b) the amount to which it reduces the carrying amount;
> (c) how to recognise any income from the asset; and
> (d) whether the reduction in carrying amount may be reversed in the future if circumstances change.'
>
> (IAS 32 (r1998).A27)

Income statement treatment

> 'An enterprise discloses the basis for reporting in the income statement realised and unrealised gains and losses, interest and other items of income and expense associated with financial assets and financial liabilities.'
>
> (IAS 32 (r1998).55)

For example, as part of its accounting policy related to financial assets in the available-for-sale category, an enterprise discloses whether changes in fair value are recognised in net profit or loss or equity. Another disclosure which is given relates to the basis on which income and expense arising from financial instruments held for hedging purposes is recognised. In addition, 'when an enterprise presents income and expense items on a net basis even though the corresponding financial assets and financial liabilities on the balance sheet have not been offset, the reason for that presentation is disclosed if the effect is significant.' (IAS 32 (r1998).55)

12.27.4 Interest rate risk disclosures

Summary
An enterprise indicates which of its financial assets and financial liabilities are exposed to interest rate price risk, interest rate cash flow risk and which are not exposed to interest rate risk. (IAS 32 (r1998).60) Some financial assets which have been removed from the balance sheet are still subject to interest rate risk and this risk is disclosed.

Sensitivity analysis may provide useful additional information in some cases.

Maturity dates
As noted above, an enterprise is required to disclose, for each class of financial asset and financial liability, contractual repricing or maturity dates, whichever dates are earlier. When an enterprise expects repricing and maturity dates which are earlier than those which are contractually agreed, it may elect to disclose these expected dates in addition to the required contractual dates. For example, a mortgage lender may be able to predict, with reasonable reliability, the amount of fixed rate mortgage loans that will be repaid prior to maturity. Since management uses this information to control its exposure to interest rate risk, such information will assist a user in understanding the enterprise's strategy towards mitigating this risk, and thus it is relevant (although optional) information to disclose. When expected repricing and maturity dates are given, an enterprise discloses that the dates are based on management's expectations and explains the assumptions made and how those assumptions differ from the contractual dates. (IAS 32 (r1998).59)

Effective interest rates
As noted above, an enterprise is required to disclose, for each class of financial asset and financial liability, the related effective interest rates, when applicable.

> 'The effective interest rate (effective yield) of a monetary financial instrument is the rate that, when used in a present value calculation, results in the carrying amount of the instrument. The present value calculation applies the interest rate

to the stream of future cash receipts or payments from the reporting date to the next repricing (maturity) date and to the expected carrying amount (principle amount) at that date. The rate is a historical rate for a fixed rate instrument carried at amortised cost and a current market rate for a floating rate instrument or an instrument carried at fair value. The effective interest rate is sometimes termed the level yield to maturity or to the next repricing date, and is the internal rate of return of the instrument for that period.'

(IAS 32 (r1998).61)

Effective interest rates will normally be disclosed by both holders and issuers of bonds, notes and similar monetary financial instruments which involve future payments that create a return to the holder, and a cost to the issuer, reflecting the time value of money. However, some non-monetary and derivative instruments, for example interest rate derivatives such as forward rate agreements and options, while mitigating against interest rate risk, do not bear a determinable effective interest rate and thus no such rate is disclosed. However, the effect of such derivative instruments on the effective interest rates of other financial instruments is disclosed, for example the effect on the effective interest rates of financial liabilities which are hedged. (IAS 32 (r1998).62)

Financial assets and liabilities exposed to interest rate risk

'An enterprise indicates which of its financial assets and financial liabilities are:

(a) exposed to interest rate price risk, such as monetary financial assets and financial liabilities with a fixed interest rate;
(b) exposed to interest rate cash flow risk, such as monetary financial assets and financial liabilities with a floating interest rate that is reset as market rate change; and
(c) not exposed to interest rate risk, such as some investments in equity securities.'

(IAS 32 (r1998).60)

The identification of fixed assets and fixed liabilities which are exposed to interest rate price risk and interest rate cash flow risk is relatively straight forward for financial assets and financial liabilities which are recognised in the balance sheet. However, IAS 32 (r1998) applies to unrecognised financial assets and financial liabilities as well. IAS 32 (r1998) specifically addresses two situations of unrecognised items which expose an enterprise to interest rate risk, certain securitisations and commitments to lend funds.

'An enterprise may retain an exposure to the interest rate risks associated with financial assets removed from its balance sheet as a result of a transaction such as a securitisation.' (IAS 32 (r1998).63) In such cases or when a similar transfer of financial assets occurs, an enterprise discloses:

(a) the nature of the assets transferred;
(b) their stated principal, interest rate and term to maturity; and

(c) the terms of the transaction giving rise to the retained exposure to interest rate risk.

(IAS 32 (r1998).63)

'Similarly an enterprise may become exposed to interest rate risk as a result of a transaction in which no financial asset or financial liability is recognised on its balance sheet, such as a commitment to lend funds at a fixed interest rate which qualifies for the regular way exemption.' (IAS 32 (r1998).63) In such cases, an enterprise discloses:

(a) the stated principal, interest rate and term to maturity of the amount to be lent; and
(b) the significant terms of the transaction.

(IAS 32 (r1998).63)

Presentation

> 'The nature of an enterprise's business and the extent of its activity in financial instruments will determine whether information about interest rate risk is presented in narrative form, in tables, or by using a combination of the two. When an enterprise has a significant number of financial instruments exposed to interest rate price or cash flow risks, it may adopt one or more of the following approaches to presenting information.
>
> The carrying amount of financial instruments exposed to interest rate price risk may be presented in tabular form, grouped by those that are contracted to mature or be repriced:
>
> (a) within one year of the balance sheet date;
> (b) more than one year and less than five years from the balance sheet date; and
> (c) five years or more from the balance sheet date.'
>
> (IAS 32 (r1998).64)

However, when the performance of an enterprise, such as a bank, is significantly affected by the level of its exposure to interest rate price risk or changes in that exposure, more detailed information is desirable. Such an enterprise may disclose, for example, separate groupings of the carrying amounts of financial instruments contracted to mature or be repriced:

(a) within one month of the balance sheet date;
(b) more than one and less than three months from the balance sheet date; and
(c) more than three and less than twelve months from the balance sheet date.

(IAS 32 (r1998).64)

> 'Similarly, an enterprise may indicate its exposure to interest rate cash flow risk through a table indicating the aggregate carrying amount of groups of floating rate financial assets and financial liabilities maturing within various future time periods.'
>
> (IAS 32 (r1998).64)

> 'Interest rate information may be disclosed for individual financial instruments or weighted average rates or a range of rates may be presented for each class of financial instrument. An enterprise groups instruments denominated in different currencies or having substantially different credit risks into separate classes when these factors result in instruments having substantially different effective interest rates.'
>
> (IAS 32 (r1998).64)

Sensitivity analysis

Sensitivity analysis indicates the effect of a hypothetical change in the prevailing level of market interest rates of the fair value of the financial instruments, future earnings and cash flows of an enterprise. Such analysis is generally based on an assumed one per cent change in market interest rates occurring at the balance sheet date. 'The effects of a change in interest rates includes changes in interest income and expense relating to floating rate financial instruments and gains or losses resulting from changes in the fair value of fixed rate instruments. The reported sensitivity analysis may be restricted to the direct effects of an interest rate change on interest-bearing financial instruments on hand at the balance sheet date since the indirect effects of a rate change on financial markets and individual enterprises cannot normally be predicted reliably. When disclosing interest rate sensitivity information, an enterprise indicates that basis on which it has prepared the information, including any significant assumptions.'(IAS 32 (r1998).65)

12.27.5 Credit risk disclosures

Credit risk exposure

For most recognised financial assets, the carrying amount of the assets in the balance sheet, net of any applicable provisions for loss, usually represents the amount exposed to credit risk. For example, under normal circumstances, the maximum amount of trade debtors exposed to loss due to credit risk is the amount of trade debtors included in the balance sheet, net of any allowances for doubtful accounts. In the case of an interest rate swap carried at fair value, the maximum exposure to loss at the balance sheet date is normally the carrying amount since it represents the cost, at current market rates, of replacing the swap in the event of default. In such circumstances, no additional disclosure beyond that provided on the balance sheet is necessary.

However, in some circumstances, the maximum exposure to loss related to a recognised financial asset at the balance sheet date varies significantly from the carrying amount of the asset. Such variances may arise when a legal right of set-off exists related to the financial asset and a financial liability of an enterprise or when master netting arrangements are in place. In such cases, IAS 32 (r1998) describes additional disclosures which are needed.

Similar to recognised financial assets, when there is no credit risk associated with unrecognised financial assets or when the maximum exposure is equal to the principal, stated, face or other similar contractual amount of the instrument, no additional disclose is required related to credit risk. However, for some unrecognised financial assets, the maximum loss that would be recognised upon default by the other party to the underlying instrument may differ substantially from the principal, stated, face or fair value of the instrument. For example, an enterprise may have a legal right of set-off which substantially mitigates its risk. In such cases, the details of the set-off arrangements are disclosed.

When an enterprise guarantees an obligation of another party, it exposes itself to credit risk and the disclosures required relating to credit risk, as described above, are required. In the case of an enterprise guaranteeing an amount for a subsidiary, the enterprise simply discloses the maximum amount it would have to pay if the other party failed to perform its obligation (i.e., repay the amount borrowed). In more complex transactions, such as a securitisation, an enterprise may remain exposed to the credit risk associated with the financial assets that have been removed from its balance sheet. 'If the enterprise is obligated under recourse provisions of the transaction to indemnify the purchaser of the assets for credit losses, it discloses the nature of the assets removed from its balance sheet, the amount and timing of the future cash flows contractually due from the assets, the terms of the recourse obligation and the maximum loss that could arise under that obligation.' (IAS 32 (r1998).73)

Significant concentrations of credit risk

> 'Concentrations of credit risk are disclosed when they are not apparent from other disclosures about the nature and financial position of the business and they result in a significant exposure to loss in the event of default by other parties. Identification of significant concentrations is a matter for the exercise of judgement by management taking into account the circumstances of the enterprise and its debtors.'
>
> (IAS 32 (r1998).74)

When management identifies a concentration of credit risk, it discloses a description of the shared characteristic that identifies each concentration (i.e., geographic area or industry) and the amount of the maximum credit risk exposure associated with all recognised and unrecognised financial assets sharing that characteristic.

Concentrations of credit risk may arise from:

(a) exposure to a single, significant debtor;
(b) groups of debtors in the same geographic region;
(c) groups of debtors in the same industry; or
(d) the level of creditworthiness of a group of debtors.

(IAS 32 (r1998).75)

12.28 Other disclosures

'Additional disclosures are encouraged when they are likely to enhance financial statements users' understanding of financial instruments. It may be desirable to disclose such information as:

(a) the total amount of the change in the fair value of financial assets and financial liabilities that has been recognised as income or expense for the period; and

(b) the average aggregate carrying amount during the year of recognised financial assets and financial liabilities, the average aggregate principal, stated notional or other similar amount during the year of unrecognised financial assets and financial liabilities and the average aggregate fair value during the year of all financial assets and financial liabilities, particularly when the amounts on hand at the balance sheet date are unrepresentative of amounts on hand during the year.'

(IAS 32 (r1998).94)

12.29 Transitional provisions

When comparative information for prior periods is not available when IAS 32 (r1998) is first adopted, such information need not be presented. (IAS 32 (r1998).95)

The transition to IAS 39 (r2000) is as follows:

(a) recognition, derecognition, measurement, and hedge accounting policies followed in financial statements for periods prior to the effective date of IAS 39 (r2000) should not be reversed and, therefore, those financial statements should not be restated.

The 'tainting' provisions relating to sales of held to maturity assets do not apply to transactions which occurred prior to the adoption of IAS 39 (r2000) (IGC 172-7).

Where an enterprise measured impairment of financial assets carried at cost on an undiscounted basis, IAS 39 (r2000) requires that impairment be measured on a discounted basis. On transition, therefore, an adjustment is made to the carrying amount of impaired assets to reflect the discounting of expected future cash flows. The adjustment is recognised as part of the adjustment to opening retained earnings on initial adoption. The transition amount only relates to the extent it results from adopting IAS 39 (r2000) and does not take into account changes in expected future cash flows as part of a revised impairment measurement (IGC 172-10);

(b) for those transactions entered into before the beginning of the financial year in which IAS 39 (r2000) is initially applied that the enterprise did previously designate as hedges, the recognition, derecognition, and measurement provisions of IAS 39 (r2000) should be applied prospectively. Therefore, if the previously designated hedge does not meet the conditions for an effective hedge and the hedging instrument is still held, hedge accounting will no longer be appropriate starting with the beginning of the financial year in which IAS 39 (r2000) is initially applied. Accounting in prior financial years should not be retrospectively changed to conform to the requirements of IAS 39 (r2000). Paragraphs 156 and 163 of IAS 39 (r2000) explain how to discontinue hedge accounting.

Retrospective application of hedge accounting is not permitted. Continued designation is permitted if the previous designation met the conditions under IAS 39 (r2000) (IGC 172-5).

In the case of fair value hedges, if the previous adjustment was to an asset or liability that was accounted for at amortised cost, the adjustment is amortised to net profit or loss. If the instrument is an equity instrument that was not carried at fair value, the fair value adjustment is recorded in equity (IGC 172-6).

To qualify for hedge accounting when IAS 39 (r2000) becomes effective, the designation and documentation of the hedging relationship must be completed at the effective date. Hedge accounting may only be applied prospectively from the designation date (IGC 172-8).

Internal derivative instruments used in a hedging relationship prior to the adoption of IAS 39 (r2000) are not grandfathered (phased in) and do not qualify as hedges for any ongoing hedging activities initiated prior to the adoption of IAS 39 (r2000). They may qualify for hedge accounting prospectively if they are validated by a third-party derivative (IGC 172-9);

(c) At the beginning of the financial year in which IAS 39 (r2000) is initially applied, an enterprise should recognise all derivatives in its balance sheet as either assets or liabilities and should measure them at fair value (except for a derivative that is linked to and that must be settled by delivery of an unquoted equity instrument whose fair value cannot be measured reliably). Because all derivatives, other than those that are designated hedging instruments, are considered held-for-trading, the difference between previous carrying amount (which may have been zero) and fair value of derivatives should be recognised as an adjustment of the balance of retained earnings at the beginning of the financial year in which IAS 39 (r2000) is initially applied (other than for a derivative that is a designated hedging instrument);

(d) at the beginning of the financial year in which IAS 39 (r2000) is initially applied, an enterprise should apply the criteria in IAS 39 (r2000) to identify those financial assets and liabilities that should be measured at fair value and those that should be measured at amortised cost, and it should remeasure those assets as appropriate. Any adjustment of the previous carrying amount should be recognised as an adjustment of the balance of retained earnings at the beginning of the financial year in which IAS 39 (r2000) is initially applied.

Amounts reported in equity for available for sale financial assets, including the adjustment to retained earnings on initial application of IAS 39 (r2000) are reclassified to net profit or loss when the asset is sold (IGC 172-1).

In respect of revaluations under IAS 25, retained earnings is adjusted if the asset is classified as trading, or as available for sale with changes in fair value reported in net profit or loss. If the asset is classified as available for sale with changes in fair value reported in equity, the gain or loss remains in equity (IGC 172-3);

(e) at the beginning of the financial year in which IAS 39 (r2000) is initially applied, any balance sheet positions in fair value hedges of existing assets and liabilities should be accounted for by adjusting their carrying amounts to reflect the fair value of the hedging instrument;

(f) if an enterprise's hedge accounting policies prior to initial application of IAS 39 (r2000) had included deferral, as assets and liabilities, of gains or losses on cash flow hedges, at the beginning of the financial year in which IAS 39 (r2000) is initially applied, those deferred gains and losses should be reclassified as a separate component of equity to the extent that the transactions meet the criteria in paragraph 142 and, thereafter, accounted for as set out in paragraphs 160–162;

(g) transactions entered into before the beginning of the financial year in which IAS 39 (r2000) is initially applied should not be retrospectively designated as hedges.

Retrospective designation is not permitted. Retrospective de-designation is also not permitted (IGC 172-10);

(h) if a securitisation, transfer, or other derecognition transaction was entered into prior to the beginning of the financial year in which IAS 39 (r2000) is initially applied, the accounting for that transaction should not be retrospectively changed to conform to the requirements of IAS 39 (r2000) (IGC 172-4); and

(i) at the beginning of the financial year in which IAS 39 (r2000) is initially applied, an enterprise should classify a financial instrument as equity or as a liability in accordance with IAS 39 (r2000).11. (IAS 39 (r2000).172)

12.30 Comparison with UK GAAP

Features of IAS 32 (r1998) are covered by FRS 4, *Capital Instruments*, FRS 5, *Reporting the Substance of Transactions*, FRS 13, *Derivatives and other financial instruments: disclosures* and UK companies legislation. Compliance with those FRSs and companies legislation will ensure compliance in all material respects with IAS 32 (r1998) except in respect of the matters set out below.

Scope
IAS 32 (r1998) applies to the financial statements of all entities. FRS 13 on the other hand:

(a) applies only to entities that have a capital instrument listed or publicly traded and to banks, banking groups and similar institutions and groups; and
(b) does not apply to insurance companies or groups, certain small reporting entities or to a parent's own financial statements where they are presented together with its consolidated financial statements.

IAS 32 (r1998) applies to all financial instruments held or issued by entities, other than those instruments specifically excluded from its scope. The same approach is adopted in FRS 13 although there are certain differences in the financial instruments excluded.

(a) whilst IAS 32 (r1998) exempts all interests in subsidiaries, associates and joint ventures, FRS 13 exempts only those not held exclusively with a view to subsequent resale;
(b) FRS 13 exempts certain equity shares issued by the reporting entity and certain warrants and options on such shares that are issued by the reporting entity. IAS 32 (r1998) has no similar exemption;
(c) FRS 13 permits short-term debtors and creditors to be excluded from the disclosures. IAS 32 (r1998) has no similar exemption; and
(d) FRS 13 requires all the financial assets and financial liabilities of an insurance company or group to be excluded from the disclosures. IAS 32 (r1998) exempts obligations arising under insurance contracts only.

In addition, FRS 13 requires certain contracts and instruments that are not financial assets and financial liabilities – in particular non-equity shares issued by the reporting entity that are equity instruments and certain types of commodity contracts – to be dealt with in the disclosures. IAS 32 (r1998) has no similar requirement.

Disclosure

Generally speaking, the disclosure requirements of FRS 13 are more specific than the requirements in IAS 32 (r1998). They are also more extensive in certain respects. For example, IAS 32 (r1998) does not require the narrative disclosures required by FRS 13. Therefore, compliance with IAS 32 (r1998) will not ensure compliance with FRS 13. On the other hand, compliance with FRS 13 will ensure compliance with the disclosure requirements of IAS 32 (r1998) except as discussed below.

IAS 32 (r1998) requires, for each class of financial asset, financial liability and equity instrument, information to be provided on the extent and nature of the instruments, including specific terms and conditions that may affect the amount, timing and certainty of future cash flows. FRS 13 does not require the disclosure of significant terms and conditions, although it does require disclosures that show the effect of the instruments on the entity's interest rate and currency profiles, liquidity position and other market price risk exposures.

IAS 32 (r1998) requires numerical disclosures to be provided about credit risk exposures. FRS 13 does not require numerical disclosures on these matters although, where an entity has significant exposure to credit risk, a discussion of the entity's policy for controlling and managing the risk is required.

IAS 32 (r1998) requires that, when an entity carries one or more financial assets at an amount in excess of fair value, the entity should disclose the carrying amount and the fair value involved and the reasons for not reducing the carrying amount. FRS 13 does not require a similar disclosure.

Presentation

There are differences in the way in which offsetting is dealt with.

(a) Whilst IAS 32 (r1998) treats offsetting as a matter of presentation, FRS 5 treats it as a recognition issue. Therefore, whilst IAS 32 (r1998) permits financial assets and financial liabilities to be offset in certain limited cases, under FRS 5 assets and liabilities should not be offset, although a debit and credit balance are required to be added together when they constitute a single asset or liability.

(b) IAS 32 (r1998) requires a financial asset and a financial liability to be offset and the net amount reported in the balance sheet only when an entity has a legally enforceable right to set off the recognised amounts and it intends either to settle on a net basis, or to realise the asset and settle the liability simultaneously. This reference to an intention to settle either net or simultaneously is not included in FRS 5.

12.31 Comparison with US GAAP

In general, more disclosure is required by IAS 32 (r1998) and IAS 39 (r2000) than by the various US GAAP pronouncements. For example, IAS require specific items of disclosure about terms, conditions, accounting policies, assumptions in arriving at fair value and whether trade date or settlement date has been adopted by class of instrument. The US GAAP requirement is more broad and requires all significant accounting policies to be disclosed.

Disclosure about hedging are similar under IAS 39 (r2000) and US GAAP. However, additional disclosures are required by enterprises listed in the US with the SEC. Overall, IAS require a greater level of disclosure about financial instruments that are not derivatives but IAS and US GAAP have similar (although not exactly the same) levels of disclosure related to derivatives.

IAS 32(r1998) requires disclosure about and enterprise's exposure to interest rate risk for each class of financial instrument, including contractual repricing or maturity dates and effective interest rates. US GAAP does not require similar disclosures. In cases in which an enterprise retains exposure to interest rate risk when a financial asset is removed from the balance sheet (for example, in a securitisation) or when exposure exists without a recognised financial asset or liability, IAS 32 (r1998) requires disclosure of information designed to permit users to understand the nature and extent of its exposure. US GAAP has no similar requirement.

IAS 32 (r1998) requires disclosure of information about maximum credit risk exposure (the full value of the enterprise's exposure without regard to collateral) which US GAAP does not.

When a financial asset is carried at an amount in excess of its fair value, IAS 32 (r1998) requires that the reporting enterprise disclose the fair value and carrying amount and the reasons for not writing down the carrying amount, whereas US GAAP does not.

12.32 Examples from published financial statements

The first example is taken from the financial statements of an enterprise which is not in the financial industry. The second example reflects an interim report referring to the impact of the adoption of IAS 39 (r2000) while the third, extensive example, is from the financial statements of a financial institution.

Note that the excerpts given do not always comply in full with all aspects of IAS and, as such, are not necessarily examples of best practice but merely of current practice.

Example 12.76 (excerpt)

28. Financial instruments

In its ordinary operations, the Renault Group is exposed to various financial risks, such as foreign currency risks, interest rate risks and credit risks. The Group has devised on a central basis a set of specific policies for managing these exposures. When managing financial risk, the Group uses derivative financial instruments, but never acts as market maker in such instruments. Since most transactions are intended to hedge positions taken in the course of normal business, the market risk of the instruments used is largely offset on the hedged positions by equal and opposite movements.

A. Management of currency and interest rate risk

The corresponding commitments, expressed in national amounts where appropriate, are broken down as follows:

(€ million)	*2000*	*1999*	*1998*
Foreign exchange risk:			
Currency swap			
Purchases	1,192	840	461
Sales	1,224	846	460
Forward exchange contracts and options:			
Purchases	13,936	12,087	12,551
Sales	13,969	11,967	12,411
Interest rate risk:			
Interest rate swap	29,532	25,941	27,609
FRAs			
Purchases	369	4,264	1,398
Sales	197	4,237	1,198
Other interest rate hedging instruments:			
Purchases	557	1,197	3,250
Sales	633	1,389	3,311

In addition, in the course of its ordinary business, Renault has entered into a number of financial contracts, including guarantees accompanying sales of receivables, financial guarantees and letters of credit, that may represent a potential risk. On 31 December 2000, neither the amounts involved nor the risks inherent in such contracts are considered to pose any significant risk.

B. Counterparty risk

The Group controls the counterparty risk inherent in using of financial instrument contracts by dealing solely with leading financial institutions and by establishing limits for each institution.

Renault has commercial relations with customers, dealers and partners throughout the world. Accordingly, its receivables and customer guarantees are highly diversified and, in many cases, collateralised by sureties and other pledges. As a result, the Group considers that it is not exposed to any notable concentration of credit risk.

C. Market value of financial instruments

The carrying amounts on the balance sheet and the estimated market values of the Group's financial instruments are broken down as follows:

(€ million)	*2000*		*1999*		*1998*	
	Book value	*Market value*	*Book value*	*Market value*	*Book value*	*Market value*
Assets						
Other listed securities (a)	514	543	69	161	69	124
Other unlisted equity securities (b)	208	NA	107	NA	98	NA
Other equity securities (I)	722	NA	176	NA	167	NA
Securities included in other financial assets (II)	10	10	1			
Trading securities	21	21	59	59	78	78
Other securities	445	470	415	441	225	272
Marketable securities (III)	466	491	474	500	303	350
Total investment portfolio (I+II+III)	1,198	NA	651	NA	470	NA
Investment loans	2,019	1,989	2,204	2,167	6,160	6,173
Sales financing receivables	15,513	15,309	15,110	15,144	10,898	10,869
Cash and cash equivalents	1,812		1,046		1,087	
Liabilities						
Redeemable shares						
Bonds	(336)	(633)	(346)	(696)	(353)	
Other interest bearing debts	(17,417)	(17,588)	(15,080)	(15,130)	(12,041)	(12,099)
	(2,755)	NA	(1,334)	NA	2,985	NA

(a) The differences between market and book value consists of unrealised:
- capital losses: €67 million for 2000;
- capital gains: €97 million for 1999 and E55 million for 1998.

(b) It has not been possible to determine the market value of equity stakes in some unlisted companies with which the Group does business and for which comparisons with listed companies are unavailable.

Estimated market value of off-balance sheet instruments:

(€ million)	*2000*		*1999*		*1998*	
	Assets	*Liabilities*	*Assets*	*Liabilities*	*Assets*	*Liabilities*
Forward exchange contracts	13,692	13,727	11,087	11,109	12,629	12,594
Currency swaps	1,193	1,228	847	841	470	479
Interest rate swaps	27	(47)	350	365	412	302
Interest rate futures	0	0	2	2	1	

Assumptions and methods adopted:

Estimated market values are based on information available on the markets and arrived at using valuation methods appropriate to the types of instrument in question. However, the methods and assumptions used are theoretical by nature, and judgement plays a major role in interpreting market data. Adopting different assumptions or pricing methods could therefore have a significant impact on the values estimated.

Market values have been determined on the basis of information available at the end of the fiscal year and do not therefore take account of subsequent movements.

The main assumptions and valuation methods are as follows:

- Securities (marketable securities, redeemable securities and other securities).

The market value of securities is determined mainly by reference to market prices. Redeemable securities and other securities for which there is no traded price have been estimated by reference to the market price of similar securities, if such exist.

- Investment loans.

For loans with an original maturity of less than three months and for floating-rate loans, the value recorded on the balance sheet is considered to be the market value. Other fixed-rate loans have been estimated by discounting future cash flows using the rates offered to Renault on December 31, 1998, December 31, 1997 and December 31, 1996 for loans having similar conditions and maturities.

- Sales-finance receivables.

Sales-finance receivables at fixed rates have been estimated by discounting future cash flows at rates that would be applicable to similar loans (conditions, maturity and debtor quality) as at December 31, 2000, December 31, 1999 and December 31, 1998.

- Cash and cash equivalents.

The value recorded on the balance sheet is considered the market value.

- Bonds and other financial debt.

The market value of listed bonds has been estimated at year end market prices. As regards the Finance Division's debts evidenced by securities issued with a life of less than 90 days, the value recorded on the balance sheet is considered the market value. The market value of other financial debt was determined by discounting future cash flows at the rates offered to Renault on December 31, 2000, December 31, 1999 and December 31, 1998 for loans having similar conditions and maturities.

- Off-balance sheet foreign exchange instruments.

The market value of forward contracts is estimated on the basis of prevailing market conditions. The market value of currency swaps is determined by discounting cash flows using exchange rates and interest rates prevailing on December 31, 2000, December 31, 1999 and December 31, 1998 for the contracts' residual lives.

- Off-balance sheet interest rate instruments.

The market value of interest rate swaps represents the amount Renault would receive (or pay) if it settled outstanding contracts at the end of the fiscal year. Unrealised capital gains or losses, determined on the basis of prevailing interest rates and the quality of the counterparty to each contract, is taken into account on December 31, 2000, December 31, 1999 and December 31, 1998.

20. Loans and marketable securities

(€ million)	*2000*	*1999*	*1998*
Investment loans	2,019	2,204	6,160
Marketable securities	214	310	272
Renault treasury shares	252	164	31
Total	2,485	2,678	6,463

Investment loans essentially consist of interbank loans between the financial companies and correspond principally to the investment of cash surpluses from industrial and commercial activities.

Maturity over one year	209	197	227
Maturity within one year	1,810	2,007	5,933
Total	2,019	2,204	6,160

Certain marketable securities are reclassified as cash equivalents. The amounts concerned are €176 million for 2000, €75 million for 1999, and €67 million for 1998.

Renault Group
France
31 December 2000
International Accounting Standards (with exception of IAS 38 and SIC 16)

Example 12.77

Change in accounting and valuation methods due to IAS 39

IAS 39, which became effective January 1, 2001, requires that all financial instruments, including derivatives, be reported on the balance sheet either at their accrued value or their fair value according to certain tests under this new accounting standard. The application of hedge accounting is restricted, subject to these tests.

One impact on Deutsche Bank is that certain derivatives used as economic hedges are reported on the balance sheet at their fair value, with the change from the prior period recognised in net profit. However, in certain circumstances the corresponding non-trading assets or liabilities continue to be carried at their accrued value.

Another impact is that the changes in the fair value of securities classified as 'available for sale' (including our industrial holdings) are reported on the balance sheet in a separate section within a separate section of equity and not recognised in net profit until the gain or loss is realised. By contrast, the changes in the value of any related economic hedges are recognised in net profit in each period.

Deutsche Bank
Germany
Interim Results as at 31 March 2001
International Accounting Standards

Example 12.78

Note 53 Fair value of financial instruments

In € bn	*31.12.2000* *Fair value*	*Book value*	*31.12.1999* *Fair value*	*Book value*
Assets				
Cash reserve	18.0	18.0	21.9	21.9
Placements with, and loans and advances to, other banks	117.2	117.2	114.8	114.9
Related derivatives	0	–	0	–
Loans and advances to customers	369.0	367.1	347.7	345.7
Related derivatives	0	–	0	–
Assets held for dealing purposes	290.4	290.4	233.0	233.0
Investments	73.1	71.6	63.4	62.2
Related derivatives	(0.7)	–	(0.6)	–
Liabilities				
Deposits from other banks	178.0	177.8	174.8	174.7
Related derivatives	(0.1)	–	(0.1)	–
Amounts owed to other depositors	335.1	334.6	291.5	291.0
Related derivatives	(0.2)	–	(0.3)	–
Liabilities evidenced by paper	200.8	200.7	162.9	164.1
Related derivatives	0.2	–	0.6	–
Liabilities from dealing activities	127.1	127.1	123.3	123.3
Subordinated capital	15.6	15.4	15.7	15.5
Related derivatives	(0.2)	–	–	–
Other positions				
Contingent liabilities	34.7	34.7	36.9	36.9
Credit commitments and placement obligations	113.5	113.4	107.5	107.5
Non-attributable derivatives	0.2	–	0.4	–

The fair value of amounts receivable and amounts payable of non-fixed term and at short term with maturities and/or fixed interest periods of up to 180 days was either recognised at book value or calculated using the present value method depending on the product or the market situation.

The stated values correspond in our opinion to the amounts at which the financial instruments could have been traded on a fair basis on balance sheet date between knowledgeable, willing parties in arm's length transactions.

Market prices were taken where available. This was largely the case for securities and derivatives traded on Stock Exchanges and on active markets. For other financial instruments we used internal valuation models, in particular the present value method. Shareholdings in the non-bank sector as well as insurance companies' assets and liabilities were not taken into account.

As at December 31, 2000, the aggregate difference between the fair value and the book value of financial instruments amounted to €2.1bn (1999: €3.1bn). The development of this figure over time depends on movements in the market parameters which are included in the valuation, as well as additions to and disposals of financial instruments.

Note 55 Relevant maturity groupings based on the remaining period

The table shows selected loans and advances and liabilities in maturity groupings based on the remaining period:

In € m	*Up to 3 months*		*>3 months–1 year*		*>1 year–5 years*		*More than 5 years*	
	31.12.2000	*31.12.1999*	*31.12.2000*	*31.12.1999*	*31.12.2000*	*31.12.1999*	*31.12.2000*	*31.12.1999*
Loans and advances								
Loans and advances to customers	183,280	180,922	43,425	34,446	68,557	62,219	78,343	74,784
Dated placements with, and loans and advances to, other banks								
Loans and advances	4,003	2,645	2,175	2,218	2,893	3,465	5,530	6,464
Money market	36,269	43,879	4,376	7,995	6,880	601	–	–
Bonds and other fixed income securities in investments	17,005	9,294	4,312	9,540	19,834	17,648	20,175	13,953
Total	**240,607**	**236,740**	**54,288**	**54,199**	**98,164**	**83,933**	**104,048**	**95,201**
Liabilities								
Time deposits from other banks	86,789	96,433	15,842	16,541	12,337	7,131	10,624	9,664
Savings deposits and building savings deposits	16,622	16,855	6,692	5,081	4,536	4,478	488	467
Other dated amounts owed to depositors	115,056	107,789	26,041	16,680	13,528	9,331	16,949	13,625
Liabilities evidenced by paper	49,057	53,848	57,881	25,792	60,557	53,844	33,246	30,576
Subordinated capital	220	128	159	512	5,234	5,132	9,797	9,732
Total	**267,744**	**275,053**	**106,615**	**64,606**	**96,192**	**79,916**	**71,104**	**64,064**

Note 57 Assets pledged as security

Assets were pledged as security in the amounts stated for the following liabilities and contingent liabilities.

In € m	*31.12.2000*	*31.12.1999*
Deposits from other banks	21,054	21,657
Amounts owed to other depositors	12,235	10,700
Liabilities evidenced by paper	1,304	278
Contingent liabilities	28	22
Total	34,621	32,657

The assets pledged as security were made up as follows.

In € m	*31.12.2000*	*31.12.1999*
Debt instrument of public sector entities and bills of exchange eligible for refinancing at central banks	666	1,460
Placements with, and loans and advances to, other banks	1,970	346
Loans and advances to customers	8,696	7,881
Assets held for dealing purposes	22,238	19,968
Investments	668	3,002
Property and equipment	383	–
Total	34,621	32,657

Risk report (excerpt)

Types of risk

The most important risks Deutsche Bank is exposed to are specific banking risks and risks that arise from general entrepreneurial activity or business risks. In addition, there are insurance risks in the Group's insurance companies. Risk is an inherent part of the bank's business and activities. The bank distinguishes between credit risk, market risk, liquidity risk and operational risk.

Credit risk reflects the potential that customers might not fulfil their contractual payment obligations to the bank. For Deutsche Bank, this is the largest single risk and is comprised of the following types:

- default risk: the failure of customers to meet contractual payment obligations;
- country risk: the inability of customers to fulfil their payment obligations owing to government measures (e.g., transfer restrictions) or country-specific economic factors (e.g., currency devaluation);
- settlement risk: the risk that arises if financial obligations are not settled on time or at all, either for the bank or when the banks acts as intermediary for its clients or other third parties.

Market risk arises from the uncertainty about changes in market prices and rates (interest rates, equity prices, exchange rates, commodity prices) and the correlations between them and their levels of volatility.

Liquidity risk refers to the possibility that the bank's payment obligations are not met fully and punctually when due. It also covers potential losses from being forced to borrow at excessive interest rates or to invest surplus funds at rates below market.

Operational risk is the potential for incurring losses through unmanageable events, business disruption, inadequately defined controls or control-system failure in relation to staff, customer relationships, technology, assets, other third parties/regulators as well as project and other risks.

Risk management tools

Deutsche Bank uses a comprehensive range of tools for monitoring and managing risk. Some of these tools are common to a number of risk factors, while others are tailored to the particular features of specific risk categories. These quantitative tools generate information to:

- quantify the susceptibility of the market value of single positions or portfolios to changes in market parameters (commonly referred to as sensitivity analysis);
- measure aggregate risk (taking into account interdependencies and correlations, using statistical techniques);
- capture exposure to risks from extreme movements in market prices through scenario analysis.

Deutsche Bank's policies and risk limits are aligned with such quantitative tools across the Group divisions to effectively manage risks. As a matter of policy, Deutsche Bank continuously assesses the appropriateness and reliability of tools in light of the evolving risk environment.

The following are the most important quantitative tools used to measure, manage and report risk:

- The equity capital that appears in the balance sheet serves to absorb any losses that result from the risks assumed in the group divisions. Deutsche Bank uses economic capital as the primary tool to allocate the book capital to its five Group Divisions and to assess their profitability and their relative abilities to employ capital efficiently. Economic capital is a measure designed to state, with a high degree of certainty, the amount of equity capital needed at any given date to absorb unexpected losses arising from exposure at that date. It is used to show an aggregated view of the bank's risk position at each level from individual business divisions up to the Group level. Deutsche Bank calculates economic capital for credit risk, market risk, operational risk and general business risk.
- Deutsche Bank uses expected loss as a measure of the default and country risk components of credit risk. Expected loss represents the potential losses from credit defaults within a one-year period based on the bank's historical loss experience.
- Value at risk and stress testing is explained in the market risk section.

Credit risk

Credit risk is the largest component of the bank's overall risk position. Credit risk arises when Deutsche Bank places reliance on another counterparty to perform contractual obligations that are of economic value to the bank.

Deutsche Bank has established a set of principles to define its appetite for default risk and to measure and actively manage this risk. Approval of transactions and management of exposures that result in credit risk takes place within the framework of portfolio guidelines and the bank's credit strategies arising from these principles. The bank has implemented a number of core principles in this respect.

The bank bases its lending decisions for each counterparty on the aggregate credit exposure to that counterparty and – in the case of companies – to all related group entities.

A primary element of the credit approval process is a detailed risk assessment. For a corporate counterparty, the risk assessment consists of an analysis of the obligor's financial condition and market position, the business environment in which the obligor operates and the quality of the obligor's management. For cross-border transactions, the bank also conducts an analysis of country risk.

The risk assessment process generates a risk rating for each exposure. Deutsche Bank has different risk rating scales for different groups of customers, such as corporates, banks, non-bank financial institutions, insurance companies, commercial real estate finance companies, private customers, and self-employed individuals.

The risk rating not only affects the outcome of the credit decision, but also influences the level of decision making authority required to extend the credit and terms and conditions of the transaction.

Credit limits set the upper boundary of exposures to a customer and are further broken down by product and tenor.

The credit portfolio is well diversified by industry sector. Banks and other financial institutions, together with G10 sovereigns, account for more than half of the counterparty risk in the trading business, underpinning a strong credit profile and minimal loss experience in these products. Within wholesale and middle market corporate credit business, industry exposure is well spread.

Each year a formal review of total group exposure to each major industry is undertaken, covering trends and outlook and their likely impact on the portfolio. Industry exposure strategy and risk appetites for the largest counterparty groups are affirmed or adjusted at this time (or more frequently if conditions require). Certain industry exposures are managed within explicit industry caps.

Credit risk profile by credit rating category

Products by Standard & Poors rating equivalent

	Total credit extended(1)		*Contingent liabilities*		*OTC derivatives*(2)		*Tradable assets*(3)	
In € bn	*31.12.2000*	*31.12.1999*	*31.12.2000*	*31.12.1999*	*31.12.2000*	*31.12.1999*	*31.12.2000*	*31.12.1999*
AAA–AA	31.20	26.07	3.02	3.92	18.42	12.51	127.50	113.65
A	42.82	32.66	3.91	4.27	20.54	32.72	36.58	13.06
BBB	66.87	65.52	14.18	15.88	8.72	8.08	7.65	20.37
BB	115.16	107.10	10.98	11.01	2.68	4.42	4.69	11.13
B	23.07	28.52	2.52	1.76	0.66	2.72	2.81	3.86
CCC and below	2.28	1.58	0.13	0.08	0.16	0.90	0.06	0.71
Total	281.40	261.45	34.74	36.92	51.18	61.35(2)	179.29	162.78

(1) In the Risk Report, total risk extended excludes receivables from brokers and clearing houses, other amounts receivable and accrued interest totalling approximately €25 billion.

(2) For OTC derivatives, the positive market values are shown after netting. Recalculating 1999 figures in accordance with current netting would reduce the total to €42 billion.

(3) Bonds and other fixed income products, except for securities with special purpose entities in the amount of €24 billion which are not considered a bank risk.

Western Europe and North America accounted for more than 85% of the overall credit portfolio. Likewise, exposures in the Asia/ Pacific region were predominantly in Japan, Australia and other investment grade countries. Borrowers in emerging market regions included a significant share of business with subsidiaries of multinational corporations and international financial institutions.

Credit risk profile by region (borrower's domicile)

	Total credit extended		*Contingent liabilities*		*OTC derivatives*	
In € bn	*31.12.2000*	*31.12.1999*	*31.12.2000*	*31.12.1999*	*31.12.2000*	*31.12.1999*
Eastern Europe	3.46	4.19	0.69	0.70	0.28	0.26
Western Europe	221.11	198.70	25.00	23.47	26.33	28.61
Africa	0.30	0.58	0.38	0.60	0.46	0.36
Asia Pacific	13.48	17.49	3.21	5.65	7.48	7.23
North America	38.92	35.15	4.56	5.46	13.15	16.73
Central and South America	4.10	5.27	0.90	0.99	3.09	4.56
Other	0.03	0.07	0	0.05	0.39	3.60
Total	281.40	261.45	34.74	36.92	51.18	61.35*

* For OTC derivatives, the positive market values are shown after netting. Recalculating 1999 figures in accordance with current netting would reduce the total to €42 billion.

The allowance for credit losses is available to absorb losses arising from credit risks. The allowance for credit losses is created and maintained at a level considered appropriate in relation to the risk of credit loss inherent in the portfolio. Management determines the adequacy of the allowance on the basis of:

- credit risk in the portfolio;
- prevailing economic conditions;
- the quality of the portfolio according to Asset Quality Review (independent internal credit quality review team at work in parts of Global Corporate and Institutions);
- the actual loss experience and the overall level of the allowance.

Allowance for credit losses by Group division

	Global Corporate and Institutions	*Coporates and real estate*	*Retain and private banking*	*Other*	*Total*	
In € bn	*31.12.2000*	*31.12.2000*	*31.12.2000*	*31.12.2000*	*31.12.2000*	*31.12.1999*
Credit risks	229.62	183.08	62.07	5.29	480.06	466.40
Allowance/provisioning						
For specific risks*	1.459	3.340	1.370	0.046	6.214	6.264
For country risks	0.274	0.016	0.004	0.000	0.294	0.756
For general value adjustments	0.199	0.348	0.110	0.032	0.690	0.830
Total allowances/ provisioning	**1.932**	**3.704**	**1.484**	**0.078**	**7.198**	**7.850**
Credit risks net of allowances	227.69	179.38	60.58	5.21	472.86	458.55

* Includes allowances for contingent liabilities

Trading activities in OTC derivatives by counterparty group

	Positive market values after netting	
In € bn	*31.12.2000*	*31.12.1999*
OECD central governments	1.70	1.89
OECD credit institutions	21.60	39.05
OECD financial institutions	11.09	6.70
Other (e.g., enterprises, private individuals)	9.65	9.93
Non-OECD central governments	0.01	0.04
Non-OECD credit institutions	3.01	1.82
Non-OECD financial institutions	1.11	1.92
Total	**51.18**	**61.35**

Recalculating 1999 figures in accordance with current netting would reduce the total to €42 billion.

Trading activities in derivatives

December 31, 2000

In € m	Nominal amount with remaining life of				Positive market values*	Negative market values*	Net market market value*	Average values for 2000		
	Up to 1 year	>1–5 years	Over 5 years	Total				Notional Volume	Positive market values	Negative market value
Interest rate related transactions										
FRAs	646,730	61,292	0	708,022	394	283	111	754,416	485	471
Interest rate swaps (same currency)	2,013,576	1,899,169	1,373,344	5,286,089	60,455	65,341	(4,886)	5,241,699	57,062	62,454
OTC products										
Interest rate option purchases	179,798	346,321	90,244	616,363	7,610		7,610	590,020	6,842	73
Interest rate option sales	222,331	342,201	116,571	681,103		(6,751)	(6,751)	660,834	88	6,965
Other interest rate trades				0			0	163	20	40
Subtotal	**3,062,435**	**2,648,983**	**1,580,159**	**7,291,577**	**68,459**	**72,375**	**(3,916)**	**7,247,132**	**64,497**	**70,003**
Exchange-traded products										
Interest rate futures	1,283,688	436,851	55,894	1,776,433				2,290,138		
Interest rate option purchases	127,586	15,897	–	143,483				193,416		
Interest rate option sales	86,570	22,235	–	108,805				201,438		
Subtotal	**4,560,279**	**3,123,966**	**1,636,053**	**9,320,298**	**68,459**	**72,375**	**(3,916)**	**9,932,124**	**64,497**	**70,003**
Currency rate related transactions										
OTC products										
Forward exchange trades	1,142,305	35,356	1,187	1,178,848	30,764	27,969	2,795	1,477,095	31,948	29,146
Cross-currency swaps	308,206	146,114	101,652	555,972	19,892	18,849	1,043	328,163	16,067	15,037
Forex option purchases	152,807	17,499	392	170,698	4,625		4,625	175,561	4,649	9
Forex option sales	120,493	10,628	527	131,648		3,256	(3,256)	136,836	13	2,652
Other forex trades				0			0		0	0
Subtotal	**1,723,811**	**209,597**	**103,758**	**2,037,166**	**55,281**	**50,074**	**5,207**	**2,117,655**	**52,677**	**46,844**
Exchange-traded products										
Forex futures	2,386	636	2	3,024				4,328		
Forex option purchases	460	–	–	460				719		
Forex option sales	741	–	–	741				5,659		
Subtotal	**1,727,398**	**210,233**	**103,760**	**2,041,391**	**55,281**	**50,074**	**5,207**	**2,128,361**	**52,677**	**46,844**

Trading activities in derivatives (continued)

December 31, 2000

In € m	*Up to 1 year*	*>1–5 years*	*Over 5 years*	*Total*	*Positive market values**	*Negative market values**	*Net market value**	*Notional Volume*	*Positive market values*	*Negative market value*
	Nominal amount with remaining life of							*Average values for 2000*		
Equity/index related transactions										
OTC products										
Equity/index swaps	42,726	12,539	2,268	57,533	3,262	4,010	(748)	55,289	3,616	4,073
Equity/index option purchases	28,627	49,705	6,538	84,870	9,644		9,644	65,121	11,855	–
Equity/index option sales	30,955	57,425	14,268	102,648	10,682		(10,682)	70,308	4	13,379
Other equity/index trades	22	–	–	22	20	21	(1)	675	292	304
Subtotal	**102,330**	**119,669**	**23,074**	**245,073**	**12,926**	**14,713**	**(1,787)**	**191,393**	**15,767**	**17,756**
Exchange-traded products										
Equity/index futures	72,839	131	–	72,970				60,712		
Equity/index option purchases	18,825	1,618	12	20,455				32,144		
Equity/index option sales	15,850	2,995	44	18,889				24,961		
Subtotal	**209,844**	**124,413**	**23,130**	**357,387**	**12,926**	**14,713**	**(1,787)**	**309,210**	**15,767**	**17,756**
Other transactions										
OTC products										
Precious metal trades (including gold)	17,405	17,481	4,688	39,574	1,591	1,426	165	49,961	851	822
Commodities	6,069	5,288	216	11,573	3,727	3,252	475	12,108	2,265	2,221
Subtotal	**23,474**	**22,769**	**4,904**	**51,147**	**5,318**	**4,678**	**640**	**62,069**	**3,116**	**3,043**
Exchange-traded products										
Futures	9,889	1,733	–	11,622				11,705		
Equity/ index option	2,405	348	–	2,753				1,407		
Equity/ index option	2,706	332	–	3,038				1,771		
Subtotal	**38,474**	**25,182**	**4,904**	**68,560**	**5,318**	**4,678**	**640**	**76,952**	**3,116**	**3,043**
Total excluding exchange traded products	**4,912,050**	**3,001,018**	**1,711,895**	**9,624,963**	**141,984**	**141,840**	**144**	**9,618,249**	**136,057**	**137,646**

* Market values given for OTC derivatives only

Market risks

At Deutsche Bank, the trading units in the Global Division Global Corporates and Institutions, as well as a designated unit, also in Global Corporates and Institutions responsible for the management of interest rate risk arising from the non-trading businesses, are authorised to assume market risks within the scope of their authority to manage assets, liabilities and liquidity. In certain subsidiaries, interest rate risk arising from the non-trading businesses is managed by the responsible business division under the overall responsibility of Group Market Risk Management.

Value at risk

The value-at-risk approach is used to derive a quantitative measure specifically for market risk under normal conditions. For a given portfolio, value-at-risk measures the potential future loss (in terms of market value) which, under normal market conditions, will not be exceeded in a certain period and with a certain probability. The value-at-risk measure enables a consistent and uniform measure to be applied across all the trading businesses and products. This facilitates comparisons of the risk estimate both across time and with actual daily trading results.

Deutsche Bank's value-at-risk model uses a Monte Carlo process. The volatilities and correlations of market parameters are observed over the most recent twelve month period and used on an unweighted basis. The value-at-risk estimates are made at a 99% confidence level and for a one-day time horizon. Deutsche Bank has obtained approval from the German Banking Supervisory Authority to use its proprietary value-at-risk models for the regulatory reporting and calculation of required capital for market risk.

The meaningfulness of the value-at-risk procedure, based on historical market movements, is verified by back-testing, whereby the daily profits and losses are compared with the estimates forecast using the value-at-risk procedure.

A back-testing committee that meets on a quarterly basis discusses back-testing results at Group, divisional and business area levels.

The committee consists of risk managers, risk controllers and business area controllers. They analyse performance fluctuations and assess the predictive power of the bank's value-at-risk models. Using the outcome of statistical analyses of the back-testing results, the committee contributes to improving the risk estimation process.

The Group's value-at-risk comprises the market risks of the trading units in Global Corporates and Institutions as well as the interest rate risks and foreign exchange risks of the non-trading units.

In € m	*Total value-at-risk*(1)		*Interest rate risk*		*Equity price risk*		*Commodity price risk*		*Foreign exchange risk*	
	2000	*1999*	*2000*	*1999*	*2000*	*1999*	*2000*	*1999*	*2000*	*1999*
Year-end value-at-risk	37.7	61.3	35.2	58.0	12.3	17.8	2.9	1.4	5.0	8.0
Minimum value-at-risk	30.9	33.8	25.8	31.0	10.8	9.0	1.3	0.6	3.5	2.7
Maximum value-at-risk	65.5	61.3	62.6	58.0	42.2	27.4	6.8	3.8	11.8	19.9
Average value-at-risk	43.6	47.8	38.3	44.5	18.7	14.5	3.5	1.9	7.5	8.6

(1) One day holding period, confidence interval 99%

Back-testing shows that there were no down-side value-at-risk band breaks in the year 2000.

While value-at-risk, calculated on a daily basis, supplies forecasts for maximum losses under normal market movements, extreme market movements are simulated by weekly stress tests on trading portfolios. Such stress tests, including event risk scenarios, form the basis of the assessment of Economic Capital required to support the market risks of the different businesses and Group divisions.

The analysis of country-specific event risks, for example, has great importance for the risk management of portfolios in emerging markets. Large movements in the equity, interest rate, and foreign exchange markets of various countries are simulated and their probability estimated by the assignment of an event risk rating. The (internal) event risk ratings, with their greater frequency and shorter term observation horizon (one to three months) must be distinguished from the longer term country ratings for the assessment of credit. A downgrading of the country event risk rating leads, via limit management, to a reduction in the trading positions that may be taken.

Deutsche Bank calculated country specific event risk scenarios for all of the major emerging Markets where it takes material risk. Event risk ratings are assessed weekly and a committee reviews the ratings and the limits bi-weekly. Group Market Risk Management can alter these limits, just as they can alter any other market risk limits at any time.

Liquidity risks

In view of the significant increase in the Group's balance sheet over the recent years, liquidity management has taken centre stage. Liquidity risk management ensures the protection of the bank's solvency and the ability to support asset portfolios with funding of appropriate term and at reasonable cost.

Deutsche Bank monitors net cash flows by currency and location as well as globally. An internal system used for cash flow monitoring captures future expected cash flows, both by day and by currency. The monitoring process also includes the ongoing assessment of the ability to sell liquid assets, mostly trading inventories.

The bank finances a substantial portion of its balance sheet on a collateralised basis by taking advantage of available security inventories. As a result, reliance on unsecured funding in the money and capital markets is limited.

The liquidity of assets held in the balance sheet is an important element in protecting the bank against short-term liquidity squeezes. It is monitored on an ongoing basis. The securities inventory consists of a large variety of liquid securities, which can, even in times of market stress, be converted into cash. These liquid assets also protect the bank against unexpected liquidity squeezes resulting from customer drawings under committed credit facilities. In addition, the bank maintains an average portfolio of about €30 billion of highly liquid securities at several major locations to supply collateral in support of substantial cash clearing activities in euro, US dollar, and other major currencies.

Based on its global presence, the bank has access to many different funding sources which are well diversified in terms of geographic region, currency, instrument and maturity. They include retail and fiduciary deposits as well as other customer deposits and funds raised through long term capital market issues. The strong diversification of funding sources has enabled Deutsche Bank to replace funding from more volatile money markets.

Overall risk position

To calculate the overall risk position, the Economic Capital figures for all types of risk are added up without taking into account diversification between types of risk, i.e., the basis taken is a conservative assumption that extreme losses occur simultaneously in all types of risk.

As at December 31, 2000, the Group's Economic Capital usage came to €15.8 billion (1999: €15.2 billion) taking into account cross-divisional diversification effects of credit risks. This figure does not yet include liquidity risk, settlement risk, insurance risk and the industrial holdings of DB Investor.

Capital and reserves

Capital and reserves according to BIS are shown in the following table:

With a capital ratio of 12.6%, Deutsche Bank is well above the minimum ratio of 8% required by BIS.

In € m	*31.12.2000*	*30.09.2000*	*30.06.2000*	*31.03.2000*	*31.12.1999*
Core capital (Tier I)	21,575	22,143	21,302	18,421	17,338
Supplementary capital (Tier II)	15,382	17,207	17,185	18,212	17,338
Available Tier III funds	0	0	0	0	496
Total eligible capital and reserves	36,957	39,350	38,487	36,633	35,172
Core capital ratio (including market risks)	7.4%	7.2%	7.3%	6.0%	5.9%
BIS capital ratio	12.6%	12.8%	13.2%	11.8%	12.0%

Deutsche Bank
Germany
31 December 2000
International Accounting Standards

CHAPTER 13

Cash flow statements

13.1 Source

IAS 7 (r1992) *Cash Flow Statements.*

13.2 Brief summary of the requirements

IAS 1 (r1997), *Presentation of Financial Statements*, para .07 defines a complete set of financial statements as including a cash flow statement. The standard does not detail how this statement is to be prepared or presented. IAS 7 (r1992) requires a cash flow statement to be presented as a primary financial statement classifying the cash flows (defined as inflows and outflows of cash *and cash equivalents*) during the period as those arising from operating activities, those arising from investing activities and those arising from financing activities. IAS 7 (r1992) gives preparers guidance on the preparation and presentation of the cash flow statement.

13.3 Development of the requirements

The original IAS 7, published in 1977, was entitled 'Statement of Changes in Financial Position' and required the presentation of a funds flow statement. The current version of the IAS was issued in 1992 and requires a cash flow statement to be presented as a primary statement.

To make it easier for foreign registrants to participate in American markets, the US SEC now accepts from them, without supplement, modification or reconciliation, a cash flow statement prepared in accordance with IAS 7 (r1992).

13.4 Scope

There are no exemptions on the grounds of size or business activity. All entities preparing financial statements in accordance with International

Accounting Standards are required to prepare a cash flow statement in accordance with IAS 7 (r1992) and to present it as an integral part of the financial statements.

13.5 Requirements of the Standard

13.5.1 General requirement

The basic requirement of IAS 7 (r1992) is that enterprises should prepare and present a cash flow statement which reports the cash flows (defined as inflows and outflows of cash ***and cash equivalents***) of the enterprise during the period, and each comparative period included in the financial statements, classified into operating, investing and financing activities.

The classification of cash flows between the three categories should be done in the way which is most appropriate to the enterprise's business. Thus, for example, the purchase of an investment might be an investing activity for a manufacturing enterprise but might be part of the operating activities of a financial institution.

Where a single payment or receipt of cash represents two smaller payments or receipts, each should be classified according to its nature.

Example 13.1

A company makes a payment of £100,000 under a finance lease. In its financial statements the company allocates £20,000 to interest and £80,000 as a repayment of loan capital.

Accordingly, in its cash flow statement £80,000 is categorised as a financing cash flow and £20,000 is included wherever the company includes interest (see **13.5.6**).

Example 13.2

A company receives £100,000 on 1 January 20x3, when it issues a zero coupon bond. On 31 December 20x7 it redeems the bond by paying cash of £140,255 to the bondholder. In its income statements for each of the five years ended 31 December 20x7, the company has classified the £40,255 as interest expense.

Accordingly, in its cash flow statement for the year ended 31 December 20x7 £100,000 is categorised as a financing cash flow and £40,255 is included wherever the company includes interest (see **13.5.6**).

The cash flows from operating activities should be reported using either:

- the direct method – under this method each major class of cash flow is reported separately and, subject to specified exceptions, inflows are reported separately from outflows (see **13.5.3** and *Example 13.4*); or
- the indirect method – this method starts with the net profit or loss and adjusts it for: any non-cash items included in its calculation (such as depreciation or movements in provisions); any cash flows in the year that were reported in net profit or loss of an earlier year or will be reported in net profit or loss of a future year; and any items of income and expense that are related to investing or financing cash flows. There is an alternative method of presenting this (see *Examples 13.5* and *13.6*).

IAS 7 (r1992) ***encourages*** enterprises to use the ***direct*** method.

Cash flows reported under the investing and financing cash flows sections should be reported separately for each major class of cash flow and, subject to specified exceptions, inflows should be reported separately from outflows.

13.5.2 Cash and cash equivalents

Cash flows are defined as 'inflows and outflows of cash and cash equivalents'. (IAS 7 (r1992).6).

Cash comprises 'cash on hand and demand deposits'. (IAS 7 (r1992).6).

'Demand deposits' are not explained in the IAS. It seems appropriate to interpret the term to mean deposits where the reporting enterprise can withdraw cash without giving any notice and without suffering any penalty. Because it is undefined, the term is not restricted to deposits with banks.

Cash equivalents are defined in IAS 7 (r1992) as 'short-term, highly liquid investments that are readily convertible to known amounts of cash and which are subject to an insignificant risk of changes in value'. (IAS 7 (r1992).6).

The Standard explains that cash equivalents are held for the purpose of meeting short-term cash commitments rather than for investment or other purposes. Thus an enterprise might hold an investment meeting the definition of a cash equivalent but not classify it as a cash equivalent because its purpose in holding the instrument is for investment purposes.

The definition of cash equivalents includes the requirement that it is a short-term, highly liquid, investment. The IAS goes on to explain that, to qualify as a cash equivalent, the investment will ***normally*** have a maturity of three months or less from the date of acquisition.

Example 13.3

A company has an account with its bank under which the company has to give 90 days' notice to the bank before it can withdraw any money. Does this meet the definition of either cash or cash equivalents?

The account does not meet the definition of cash since it is not a demand deposit account. However, only 90 days' notice needs to be given and thus it meets the definition of cash equivalents.

The IASC's thinking here is presumably that the risk of changes in value as a result of interest rate changes are not likely to be significant over the final three months of an investment's life. A company purchasing a two year bond in the market when the bond only has three months remaining before its redemption date would therefore be able to classify the bond as a cash equivalent (assuming there were no other factors that would cause it to be subject to a significant risk of change in value). However, the reference to three months or less 'from the date of acquisition' means that if the company instead purchased the same two year bond when it had four months remaining before maturity, the company would not be able to classify the bond as a cash equivalent either at the date of purchase or at any time thereafter, including once it has less than three months remaining to maturity (unless it could justify a departure from the three month guide, in which case the instrument would be classified as a cash equivalent throughout the entire four months).

Providing the definition of cash equivalent is met, there is no reason why a foreign currency investment could not be classified as a cash equivalent. Indeed, IAS 7 (r1992) specifically refers to 'cash and cash equivalents held or due in a foreign currency'. (IAS 7 (r1992).28)

Equity investments will not normally meet the definition of a cash equivalent, although there are exceptions. The example given in the Standard is preferred shares with a specific redemption date, which, when acquired are close to maturity. The majority of equity instruments will not meet the definition, however, and therefore cannot be classified as cash equivalents.

Although certain investments within three months of maturity when acquired are classified as cash equivalents, there is no provision in the definition for the inclusion of bank borrowings of three months or less. Paragraph 8 of IAS 7 (r1992), however, acknowledges that bank overdrafts repayable on demand and forming an integral part of an enterprise's cash management are included as a component of cash and cash equivalents. The IASC points out that a characteristic of such banking arrangements is that the bank balance often fluctuates from being positive to being overdrawn.

Where an enterprise uses cash to purchase a short term investment meeting the cash equivalents definition, that purchase is not shown in the cash flow statement as a purchase since the total of cash and cash equivalents combined has not altered as a result of the purchase.

Where an enterprise changes its policy on the components of cash and cash equivalents, the effect of the change in policy is to be reported in accordance with IAS 8 (r1993). However, this disclosure will not be triggered simply because one year an enterprise has an instrument included in its balance of cash and cash equivalents that was not there in any previous year. For example, an enterprise might include a 90 day notice account with its bank within its balance of cash and cash equivalents at 31 December 1997, but such balances have never been included in the past. If the balances are included on 31 December 1997 for the first time because it is only during 1997 that such an account was opened, then the change is not a change in accounting policy. However, if the enterprise had such balances in the past, but classified as investing, and during 1997 decided that they were, after all, cash equivalents, then this is a change in accounting policy (provided there has been no change of substance in the accounts and the level of funds kept in them) and the disclosure requirements of IAS 8 (r1993) are triggered (see **5.17**).

13.5.3 Operating activities

Operating activities are defined in IAS 7 (r1992) as the 'principal revenue-producing activities of the enterprise and other activities that are not investing or financing activities'. (IAS 7 (r1992).6)

Examples of cash flows from operating activities are:

- cash received in the year from customers (in respect of sales of goods or services rendered either in the year or in an earlier year or received in advance in respect of the sale of goods or services to be rendered in a later year);
- cash payments in the year to suppliers (for raw materials or goods for resale whether supplied in the current or an earlier year or to be supplied in a later year);
- the payment of wages and salaries to employees;
- tax and other payments on behalf of employees;
- the payment of rent on property used in the business's operations;
- the payment of hire charges for plant and equipment;
- royalties received in the year;
- the payment of insurance premiums;
- cash payments or refunds of income taxes that cannot be specifically identified with financing or investing activities (see **13.5.7**);

- cash flows arising from futures contracts, forward contracts, option contracts or swap contracts hedging a transaction that is itself classified as operating; and
- cash flows arising from the purchase and sale of securities and loans held for dealing or trading purposes.

Although an enterprise classifies its cash flows consistently from one period to another, there may be differences in classification between different enterprises. In addition, transactions which are financed in different ways by different enterprises can result in a different classification in the cash flow statement. This can be a problem when trying to compare cash flow statements, and, in particular, operating cash flows, for different enterprises. IAS 7 (r1992).14 states that the operating cash flows generally derive from transactions that are reported in the income statement in arriving at net profit or loss. It goes on to state, however, that interest paid and interest and dividends received can either be reported as operating cash flows or interest paid can be reported as financing with interest and dividends received being reported as investing cash flows. (IAS 7 (r1992).33) This illustrates the argument for including them in operating cash flows is that they are recognised in the income statement in arriving at the net profit or loss. Contrary to this, however, it argues that although a profit or loss on the disposal of property, plant or equipment is recognised in the income statement in arriving at the net profit or loss, the disposal proceeds are to be included in the cash flow statement within investing activities, not operating activities. Thus an enterprise that directly purchases its property, plant and equipment for cash will include the cash flows in respect of the asset in the investing activities section whereas an enterprise that purchases its property, plant and equipment by means of finance lease will include the cash flows (in subsequent years in respect of the repayment of principal to the lessor) in the financing activities section. On the other hand, an enterprise that obtains the use of such assets by means of operating leases will include the cash flows in respect of these assets in the operating activities section of the cash flow statement.

As discussed above, the cash flows from operating activities can be included in the cash flow statement using either the direct method or the indirect method. IAS 7 (r1992) *encourages* enterprises to use the *direct* method.

Direct method

An example of the operating cash flows section of a cash flow statement using the direct method is:

Example 13.4

	20x2	*20x2*
	£000	*£000*
Cash flows from operating activities		
Cash receipts from customers	252,376	
Cash paid to suppliers	(127,045)	
Cash paid to and on behalf of employees	(78,014)	
Other cash payments	(12,038)	
Cash generated from operations	35,279	
Interest paid	(5,933)	
Income taxes paid	(13,447)	
Net cash from operating activities		15,899

The data for inclusion in the direct method of presentation can be obtained from either:

- the enterprise's accounting records; or
- by adjusting sales, cost of sales and other items recognised in the income statement for: changes in operating receivables, inventories and operating payables during the period; other non-cash items; and other items which are to be reported as investing or financing cash flows.

Indirect method

There are two methods of presenting operating cash flows using the indirect method. The first starts with net profit or loss and then adjusts it for: any non-cash items included in its calculation (such as depreciation or movements in provisions); any cash flows in the year that were reported in net profit or loss of an earlier year or will be reported in net profit or loss of a future year; and any items of income and expense that are related to investing or financing cash flows. An example of this presentation is:

Example 13.5

	20x2 £000	20x2 £000
Cash flows from operating activities		
Net profit before taxation	19,696	
Adjustments for:		
Depreciation	6,174	
Foreign exchange loss	829	
Interest expense*	7,305	
Operating profit before working capital changes	34,004	
Increase in trade and other receivables	(7,601)	
Increase in trade payables	5,224	
Decrease in inventories	3,652	
Cash generated from operations	35,279	
Interest paid*	(5,933)	
Income taxes paid	(13,447)	
Net cash from operating activities		15,899

* 'Interest expense' is included above as an 'adjustment' to net profit before tax. If interest is considered an operating activity, the adjustment from profit to cash flow is the difference between the interest expense in the income statement and the interest actually paid during the period, i.e., £1,372,000. However, in order that the amount of interest paid can be disclosed separately as required by IAS 7 (r1992).31, the example in the appendix to IAS 7 (r1992) uses the approach illustrated above, i.e., to add back the interest expense in full and then deduct the full amount of interest paid.

The alternative method of presentation shows the revenues and expenses that are disclosed in the income statement and adjusts these for the changes during the period in operating receivables and payables and in inventories. An example is:

Example 13.6

	20x2 £000	20x2 £000
Cash flows from operating activities		
Revenues	259,376	
Operating expenses excluding depreciation	(225,372)	
Operating profit before working capital changes	34,004	
Increase in trade and other receivables	(7,601)	
Increase in trade payables	5,224	
Decrease in inventories	3,652	
Cash generated from operations	35,279	
Interest paid	(5,933)	
Income taxes paid	(13,447)	
Net cash from operating activities		15,899

13.5.4 Investing activities

Investing activities are defined in IAS 7 (r1992) as 'the acquisition and disposal of long-term assets and other investments not included in cash equivalents'. (IAS 7 (r1992).6). Examples of cash flows arising from investing activities include:

- payments in respect of the purchase of property, plant and equipment, intangible assets and other long-term assets;
- payments in respect of development costs that have been capitalised;
- payments in respect of the construction of property, plant and equipment;
- cash received from the sale of property, plant and equipment, intangible fixed assets and other long-term assets;
- payments to acquire equity or debt instruments of other enterprises or interests in joint ventures (although in some circumstances, these may need to be classified either as cash equivalents or as operating cash flows (if they were held for dealing purposes));
- cash received from the sale of equity or debt instruments of other enterprises or interests in joint ventures (although again, the cash received from the sale of the instruments may instead need to be classified either as cash equivalents or as operating cash flows (if they were held for dealing purposes));
- cash advances and loans made to another enterprise;
- cash received following the repayment of advances and loans made to another enterprise;

- payments for futures contracts, forward contracts, option contracts and swap contracts provided the contracts are not held for dealing or trading purposes, financing in nature, or hedging a transaction that itself is classified as operating or financing; and
- receipts from futures contracts, forward contracts, option contracts and swap contracts provided the contracts are not held for dealing or trading purposes, financing in nature, or hedging a transaction that itself is classified as operating or financing.

13.5.5 Financing activities

Financing activities are defined as 'activities that result in changes in the size and composition of the equity capital and borrowings of the enterprise'. (IAS 7 (r1992).6) Examples of cash flows arising from financing activities are:

- cash receipts from issuing shares or other equity instruments in the enterprise;
- payments to owners to purchase or redeem shares in the enterprise;
- cash flows arising from futures contracts, forward contracts, option contracts or swap contracts hedging a transaction that is itself classified as financing;
- cash receipts from issuing debentures, loans, notes, bonds, mortgages and other borrowings, whether short or long-term;
- repayment of borrowings; and
- where the reporting enterprise is a lessee, the payments under a finance lease that will be classified in the balance sheet as a repayment of the loan from the lessor (i.e., the principal portion).

13.5.6 Interest and dividends

The requirements of IAS 7 (r1992).31 are as follows:

- cash flows from interest and dividends paid and received should each be disclosed separately;
- the cash flows should be classified in a consistent manner from period to period as either operating, investing or financing activities.

In which of the three categories should the dividends and interest be reported? IAS 7 (r1992) permits each enterprise to choose how it wishes to classify its interest and dividends. IAS 7 (r1992) suggests that dividends paid could be reported in either financing or operating activities. The argument in favour of financing activities is that the dividends are a cost of obtaining financial resources and the argument in favour of operating activities is that it will 'assist users to determine the ability of an enterprise to pay dividends out of operating cash flows'. (IAS 7 (r1992).34) The example of a full cash flow statement reproduced in **13.10** (*Example 13.14*) includes dividends paid in the financing section of the cash flow statement. *Example 13.15* also reproduces just the operating activities section of another cash flow statement; here dividends paid have been included within operating activities.

Interest paid and interest and dividends received would generally be classified as operating by a financial institution. For other enterprises the IAS 7 (r1992) suggests that the cash flows might similarly be classified as operating because the items are included in arriving at net profit or loss in the income statement. IAS 7 (r1992) does, however, point out that interest paid could be classified as a financing activity and interest and dividends received could be classified as investing activities because the former is a cost of obtaining financial resources and the latter two are returns on investments.

Interest paid in cash must be included in the cash flow statement whether the expense is charged in the income statement or whether the cost is capitalised as part of the acquisition, construction or production of a qualifying asset. Where the interest is capitalised, it is suggested that it is included in the cash flow statement in operating activities if the qualifying asset is inventory, and is included in investing activities where the qualifying asset is property, plant or equipment or an intangible asset.

13.5.7 Taxes

Unless they can be specifically identified with financing or investing activities, cash flows in respect of taxes should be classified as operating cash flows. Cash flows in respect of tax are required to be separately disclosed. (IAS 7 (r1992).35)

Clearly, transactions of all natures, operating, investing or financing, might have tax consequences. Identifying whether each amount of income or expense included in the tax computation derives from operating, investing or financing activities might be a reasonably easy task. However, identifying the *cash flows* is not always so easy.

IAS 7 (r1992) points out that because it is often impracticable to identify cash flows in respect of investing and financing activities and the fact that such cash flows often arise in a different period from the cash flows of the underlying transaction, 'taxes paid are usually classified as cash flows from operating activities'. (IAS 7 (r1992).36)

When it is practicable to identify a tax cash flow with an individual transaction that is classified as investing or financing, the tax cash flow will be classified as investing or financing in accordance with the underlying transaction. In these cases, the total amount of taxes paid is also disclosed.

Example 13.7

A company paid tax in the year of £90,000, being taxable profits of £300,000 at 30 per cent. Within the calculation of the taxable profit there was a deduction of £40,000 in respect of a loss on disposal of a property.

The disposal proceeds of the property were included in the cash flow statement (last year's cash flow statement) in the investing activities section.

The tax expense of £90,000 appearing in the financial statements could be allocated between the amount in respect of the property disposal, a tax credit of £12,000 (being £40,000 at 30 per cent) and the balance (assume it is all in respect of operating activities), a tax charge of £102,000 (being £340,000 at 30 per cent). However, in cash flow terms there has not been a payment of £102,000 and a receipt of £12,000; there was only one cash flow, being a payment of £90,000. Accordingly, in this instance it is not possible to recognise the tax consequences of the property disposal in the investing activities section of the cash flow statement. Had the £300,000 taxable profit been made up of taxable profit of £50,000 arising on the profitable disposal of a property and £250,000 in respect of operating activities, then the tax cash flow could have been divided into two components, £15,000 in respect of property disposal and £75,000 in respect of operating activities.

13.5.8 Can any cash flows be reported on a net basis?

IAS 7 (r1992) permits the following cash flows to be reported on a net basis:

(a) receipts and payments on behalf of customers when the cash flows reflect the activities of the customer rather than those of the enterprise; and

(b) receipts and payments for items in which the turnover is quick, the amounts are large and the maturities are short.

(IAS 7 (r1992).22)

Examples where cash flows may be reported net are:

In respect of (a) above:

- rents collected on behalf of, and paid over to, the owners of properties;
- funds held for customers by an investment enterprise; and
- the acceptance and repayment of demand deposits of a bank;

In respect of (b) above:

- commercial paper with a maturity of three months or less and a quick turnover;

- other short-term borrowings with a maturity period of three months or less;
- principal amounts relating to credit card customers;
- the purchase and sale of investments.

Where the reporting enterprise is a financial institution, it is permitted to report additional cash flows on a net basis. The circumstances are set out in IAS 7 (r1992).24.

13.5.9 Investments in subsidiaries, associates and joint ventures

Where an enterprise has an interest in a subsidiary, associate or joint venture, the impact on its cash flow statement depends on how that interest has been accounted for, as set out below:

Type of investment	*Accounting treatment in financial statements*	*Treatment in cash flow statement*
Associate or subsidiary	Cost or equity method	Report the cash flows between the reporting enterprise and its investee, e.g., dividends and advances
Jointly controlled entity	Proportionate consolidation	Include the reporting enterprise's proportionate share of its jointly controlled entity's cash flows
Jointly controlled entity	Equity method	Report the cash flows between the reporting enterprise and its jointly controlled entity, e.g., distributions and advances
Subsidiary	Consolidated	Include the subsidiary's cash flows but exclude any that are intra-group. Where a subsidiary is only partly owned by the group, the dividends paid to the minority shareholders (but not the dividends to the group companies) are included in cash outflows and classified as financing

13.5.10 Acquisitions and disposals of subsidiaries and other business units

Where an enterprise acquires or disposes of a subsidiary or other business unit, the aggregate cash flows arising should be presented separately and classified as investing activities. The single line entry in the cash flow statement comprises the amount of cash paid or received as purchase or sale consideration net of the cash and cash equivalents in the subsidiary or business unit at the date of acquisition or disposal. The cash flow effects of disposals are not to be deducted from those of acquisitions; instead each is to be shown separately.

Example 13.8

On 30 June 20x2 company X sells its 100 per cent holding in company Y for £900,000. At that date, the net assets of Y included in the consolidated balance sheet were:

	£
Property, plant equipment	500,000
Inventories	150,000
Accounts receivable	230,000
Cash	80,000
Cash equivalents	100,000
Trade payables	(110,000)
Long-term debt	(300,000)
	650,000

The consideration received was all received during the year ended 31 December 20x2 and comprised cash of £300,000 and equity shares of £600,000.

In the investing activities section of the cash flow statement for the year ended 31 December 20x2, the entry in respect of the disposal of the subsidiary will be an inflow of £120,000 (being £300,000 cash received less cash and cash equivalents of £180,000 in the subsidiary at the date of sale). The cash and cash equivalents of £180,000 in the subsidiary at the date of sale is deducted from the cash received because the cash and cash equivalents of the reporting group is reduced by this amount as a result of the sale of the subsidiary.

Had the cash consideration of £300,000 been received over two years with £150,000 being received in 20x2 and £150,000 being received in 20x3, the investing section of the cash flow statement would record an outflow in 20x2 of £30,000 (being £150,000 less the cash and cash equivalents of £180,000) and an inflow in 20x3 of £150,000.

The group's property, plant and equipment is reduced by £500,000 as a result of the sale. However, this does not appear in the cash flow statement as a sale of property, plant and equipment for cash.

Where the indirect method is used to present the operating activities section, the increase or decrease in inventories and accounts receivable and payable will need to be adjusted for the disposal of the subsidiary. Let us consider inventories as an example. On 31 December 20x2, the inventories in X's consolidated balance sheet totalled £950,000 and at 31 December 20x1 totalled £1,000,000. In the adjustments from net profit to the operating cash flow in the indirect method, the movement in inventories will be an increase of £100,000 (being closing inventories of £950,000 less opening inventories of £1,000,000 plus the inventories in the consolidated balance sheet at the date of disposal in respect of the subsidiary of £150,000).

Each of the following should be disclosed, in aggregate, in respect of both acquisitions and disposals of subsidiaries or other business units during the period:

- the total of each of purchase and disposal consideration;
- the portion of each of the purchase and disposal consideration discharged by means of cash and cash equivalents;
- the amount of cash and cash equivalents in the subsidiary or business units acquired and, separately, in those disposed of; and
- the amount of the assets and liabilities other than cash or cash equivalents in the subsidiary or business unit acquired and, separately, in those disposed of, summarised by each major category.

(IAS 7 (r1992).40)

13.5.11 Foreign currency cash flows

Foreign currency cash flows arise in two instances: where the reporting enterprise directly enters into a transaction involving inflows or outflows in a foreign currency; and where the reporting group includes an overseas subsidiary.

Where the reporting enterprise directly enters into a transaction involving inflows or outflows in a foreign currency, the cash flows should be recorded

Example 13.9

A company, whose reporting currency is sterling, buys an item of plant for $600,000. It records the purchase in its accounting records on the date of delivery of the plant. The rate of exchange on that date resulted in the plant being recorded at £390,000. The invoice for the plant was settled by bank transfer 30 days later, at which date £410,000 was needed to settle the liability. The exchange difference of £20,000 was charged in the income statement.

The acquisition of plant will be recorded in the cash flow statement as an *investing* cash outflow of £410,000. Thus, if the *operating* cash flows are shown using the *indirect* method, one of the adjustments to net profit will be to adjust out the exchange difference of £20,000.

Had the item purchased been goods for resale, then the cash flow for the purchase should be reported in *operating* (not investing) cash flows. Under the rules in IAS 7 (r1992), a cash outflow of £410,000 should be included in the operating cash flows section of the cash flow statement in respect of the purchase. In the income statement, the cost of the goods, recorded at £390,000, will have been included in purchases and the exchange difference of £20,000 will have been charged in arriving at net profit. Thus the full £410,000 will have already been recognised in the income statement in arriving at the net profit for the year. Consequently if the operating cash flows are shown using the indirect method, there will be no need to adjust out the exchange difference of £20,000.

in the cash flow statement by translating the foreign currency cash flow at the rate of exchange applying on the date of the cash flow. (IAS 7 (r1992).25)

The cash flows of a foreign subsidiary should be included in the group cash flow statement translated at the exchange rates ruling on the dates of the cash flows. (IAS 7 (r1992).26)

IAS 7 (r1992) points out that cash flows denominated in a foreign currency are to be reported in a manner consistent with IAS 21 (r1993), *The Effects of Changes in Foreign Exchange Rates.* IAS 21 (r1993) permits the use of an average exchange rate that approximates to the actual rate. For example, a weighted average exchange rate for a period may be used for recording foreign currency transactions or the translation of the cash flows of a foreign subsidiary. IAS 21 (r1993) does not permit the cash flows of a foreign subsidiary to be translated using the rate of exchange ruling on the balance sheet date.

Unrealised exchange gains and losses are not cash flows.

Example 13.10

Consider in *Example 13.9* above, the purchase of goods for resale costing $600,000, which translated to £390,000 when the goods were first recorded in the accounting records. Now assume that the invoice for the goods is still unpaid at the balance sheet date and at that date the exchange rate is such that the liability to the creditor translates to £410,000. As above, both the £390,000 and the £20,000 will have been charged in the income statement in arriving at net profit. However, since there has been no cash flow, there should be no cash flow recorded in the cash flow statement. If the indirect method is used to arrive at operating cash flows, both the £390,000 and the £20,000 need to be reversed out; this will be done with one entry, the increase or decrease in trade payables. The trade payable for the liability will be included in the balance sheet translated at £410,000, thus when it is reversed out in the adjustments to net profit it will automatically adjust out both the original entry of £390,000 and the unrealised exchange loss of £20,000.

Unrealised gains and losses from movements in exchange rates do not represent 'cash flows'. However, the effect of exchange rate changes on cash and cash equivalents held or due in a foreign currency is reported in the cash flow statement in order to reconcile the balance of cash and cash equivalents at the start and end of the period. This amount is to be presented separately from cash flows from operating, investing and financing activities. The amount includes the differences, if any, had those cash flows been reported using the rate of exchange ruling at the end of period. (IAS 7 (r1992).28)

13.5.12 Extraordinary items

The cash flows associated with an extraordinary item should be classified as operating, investing or financing as appropriate. They should be separately disclosed. Even though this disclosure will enable users to understand the nature and effect of the extraordinary item on the present and future cash flows of the enterprise, it is additional to that required by IAS 8 (r 1993), *Net Profit or Loss for the Period, Fundamental Errors and Changes in Accounting Policies* (see **5.11**).

13.6 Pro forma cash flow statement

The following proforma cash flow statement is taken from the direct method example in appendix 1 to IAS 7 (r1992); the accompanying notes have not been reproduced. Immediately following it is the operating activities section reproduced from the indirect method example in Appendix 1 to IAS 7 (r1992).

Direct method cash flow statement

Example 13.11

	20x2	*20x2*	*20x1*	*20x1*
Cash flows from operating activities				
Cash receipts from customers	x		x	
Cash paid to suppliers and employees	(x)		(x)	
Cash generated from operations	x		x	
Interest paid	(x)		(x)	
Income taxes paid	(x)		(x)	
Cash flow before extraordinary item	x		x	
Proceeds from earthquake disaster settlement	x		x	
Net cash from operating activities		x		x
Cash flows from investing activities				
Acquisition of subsidiary X, net of cash acquired (Note A)	(x)		(x)	
Purchase of property, plant and equipment (Note B)	(x)		(x)	
Proceeds from sale of equipment	x		x	
Interest received	x		x	
Dividends received	x		x	
Net cash used in investing activities		(x)		(x)
Cash flows from financing activities				
Proceeds from issuance of share capital	x		x	
Proceeds from long-term borrowings	x		x	
Payment of finance lease liabilities	(x)		(x)	
Dividends paid*	(x)		(x)	
Net cash used in financing activities		(x)		(x)
Net increase in cash and cash equivalents		x		x
Cash and cash equivalents at beginning of period (Note C)		x		x
Cash and cash equivalents at end of period (Note C)		x		x

* This could also be shown as an operating cash flow.
Refer to IAS 7 (r1992) Appendix 1 for the notes to the cash flow.

Indirect method cash flow statement (extract)

Example 13.12

	20x2	*20x2*	*20x1*	*20x1*
Cash flows from operating activities				
Net profit before taxation, and extraordinary item	x		x	
Adjustments for:				
Depreciation	x		x	
Foreign exchange loss	x		x	
Investment income	(x)		(x)	
Interest expense	x		x	
Operating profit before working capital changes	x		x	
Increase in trade and other receivables	(x)		(x)	
Decrease in inventories	x		x	
Decrease in trade payables	(x)		(x)	
Cash generated from operations	x		x	
Interest paid	(x)		(x)	
Income taxes paid	(x)		(x)	
Cash flow before extraordinary item	x		x	
Proceeds from earthquake disaster settlement	x		x	
Net cash from operating activities		x		x

13.7 Disclosure

In addition to the disclosures outlined in **13.5.10** above that are required when there is an acquisition or disposal of a subsidiary or other business unit, the disclosures set out in this section are to be given.

Where an enterprise enters into an investing or financing transaction that does not involve the use of cash or cash equivalents, the transaction is omitted from the cash flow statement and the enterprise should disclose sufficient information in the financial statements to give a user all the relevant information about the transaction. (IAS 7 (r1992).43) Examples of non-cash transactions are:

- the acquisition of an asset using a finance lease;
- the purchase of the equity in another enterprise by the issue of equity in the reporting enterprise;
- the conversion of debt to equity; and
- the acquisition of an asset where the consideration is satisfied by the reporting enterprise assuming directly related liabilities.

The components of cash and cash equivalents should be disclosed and a reconciliation between the amounts in the cash flow statement and the equivalent items reported in the balance sheet should be presented. (IAS 7 (r1992).45)

In order to comply with IAS 1 (r1997), *Presentation of Financial Statements*, the policy adopted by an enterprise in determining the composition of cash and cash equivalents must be disclosed. (IAS 7 (r1992).46 and IAS 1 (r1997).99)

The amount of significant cash and cash equivalent balances that are not available for use by the group should be disclosed, together with a commentary by management. (IAS 7 (r1992).48) Such disclosure might be triggered when a subsidiary operates in a country where exchange controls or other legal restrictions apply and thus the cash and cash equivalents in that subsidiary are not available for general use by other members of the group. Another example might be where substantial amounts of cash are held in escrow accounts and are only available for use on a particular project.

IAS 7 (r1992) suggests that:

> 'additional information may be relevant to users in understanding the financial position and liquidity of an enterprise. Disclosure of this information, together with a commentary by management, is encouraged and may include:
>
> (a) the amount of undrawn borrowing facilities that may be available for future operating activities and to settle capital commitments, indicating any restrictions on the use of these facilities;
>
> (b) the aggregate amounts of the cash flows from each of operating, investing and financing activities related to interests in joint ventures reported using proportionate consolidation;
>
> (c) the aggregate amount of cash flows that represent increases in operating capacity separately from those cash flows that are required to maintain operating capacity; and
>
> (d) the amount of the cash flows arising from the operating, investing and financing activities of each reported industry and geographical segment' (see IAS 14 (r1997), *Segment Reporting*).
>
> (IAS 7 (r1992).50)

13.8 Comparison with UK GAAP

A cash flow statement is required to be presented as a primary statement under UK GAAP. The extant Standard on the topic is FRS 1 (revised 1996), *Cash Flow Statements*. As can be seen by its title, the original standard was revised in 1996. The revised version of the Standard was further revised (in 1997) by FRS 9, *Associates and Joint Ventures*.

An important difference between FRS 1 (revised) and IAS 7 (r1992) is their definitions of cash flows. Under FRS 1 (revised), cash flows are defined as increases or decreases in cash. Cash is defined as 'cash in hand and deposits repayable on demand with any qualifying financial institution, less overdrafts from any qualifying financial institution repayable on demand'. FRS 1 (revised) goes on to state that deposits are repayable on demand if they can be withdrawn at any time without notice and without penalty or if a maturity or period of notice of not more than 24 hours or one working day has been agreed. This is a more restrictive definition than the definition of cash flows in IAS 7 (r1992), which includes cash equivalents as well as cash. In addition, under IAS 7 (r1992) there is some flexibility as to whether overdrafts are part of cash and cash equivalents.

As opposed to the three headings of IAS 7 (r1992), FRS 1 (revised) requires the cash flows to be reported under the following nine headings:

- operating activities;
- dividends from joint ventures and associates;
- returns on investment and servicing of finance;
- taxation;
- capital expenditure and financial investment;
- acquisitions and disposals;
- equity dividends paid;
- management of liquid resources; and
- financing.

The first seven of these headings are required to be shown in the order set out above, while the three headings specified by IAS 7 (r1992) are not required to be presented in any particular order. The cash flows reported under each of the headings can generally be compared to their position within a cash flow statement prepared in accordance with IAS 7 (r1992) as follows:

FRS 1 (r1996)	**IAS 7 (r1992)**
Operating activities	Operating activities
Dividends from joint ventures and associates	*Either* operating activities; *or* investing activities
Returns on investment and servicing of finance	*Either* operating activities; *or* interest paid = financing interest and dividends received = investing
Taxation	Operating activities unless the cash flows can be specifically identified with financing or investing activities (in which case classify as such)

Capital expenditure and financial investment	Investing activities
Acquisitions and disposals	Investing activities
Equity dividends paid	*Either* financing activities *or* operating activities
Management of liquid resources	*Either* investing activities *or* will be part of cash equivalents
Financing	Financing activities

Similar to IAS 7 (r1992), the cash flows from operating activities can be presented by either the direct or the indirect method. However, FRS 1 (revised) requires a reconciliation from operating profit to operating cash flows regardless of whether the direct or indirect method is used (FRS 1 (revised).58), while IAS 7 (r1992) only requires it when the indirect method is applied. Also, unlike IAS 7 (r1992), FRS 1 (revised) does not permit the reconciliation to be presented *as part of* the cash flow statement; it must be presented as a note, although the note may be presented *adjoining* the cash flow statement, so long as it is clearly labelled and kept separate.

Unlike IAS 7 (r1992), the FRS does contain some exemptions to the requirement to present a cash flow statement. The entities exempted include:

- subsidiary undertakings where 90 percent or more of the voting rights are controlled within the group, provided that consolidated financial statements in which the subsidiary undertakings are included are publicly available;
- certain small entities, namely those companies incorporated under companies legislation and entitled to file abbreviated financial statements with the Registrar of Companies, and other entities that would be so entitled had they been incorporated under companies legislation;
- mutual life assurance companies;
- pension funds; and
- certain open-ended investment funds.

Although FRS 1 (revised) permits some cash flows to be reported on a net basis (see FRS 1.9), it would not allow netting off of cash receipts and payments on behalf of customers when the cash flows reflect the activities of the customer rather than those of the enterprise. Nor would it always allow netting of 'receipts and payments for items in which the turnover is quick, the amounts are large and the maturities are short'. As set out in **13.5.8**, such cash flows are reported net under IAS 7 (r1992). Note, however, that the netting of cash inflows and outflows within financing *is* specifically permitted by FRS 1 (revised), if they either relate to a single financing transaction or are due to short maturities and high turnover, occurring from a rollover or reissue.

FRS 1 (revised) requires a reconciliation of the movement in cash flows to the movement in net debt to be presented. Such reconciliation is not required by IAS 7 (r1992).

Another difference between the two standards is in the treatment of the cash flows of a foreign subsidiary. FRS 1 (revised) requires the cash flows to be translated using the same rate of exchange that is used to translate the profit and loss account (which will be the average or closing rate) but allows the use of actual rates or an approximation thereto for intra-group transactions. IAS 7 (r1992) requires cash flows of a foreign subsidiary to be translated using the rates of exchange prevailing on the date of the cash flows and permits this to be approximated by the use of a weighted average exchange rate.

The following example illustrates the presentation of a cash flow statement prepared in accordance with FRS 1 (revised).

Example 13.13

	Note	*20x2* *£'000*	*20x1* *£'000*
Net cash inflow from operating activities	27	x	x
Dividends received from associates		x	x
Returns on investments and servicing of finance	28	(x)	(x)
Taxation	28	(x)	(x)
Capital expenditure and financial investment	28	(x)	(x)
Acquisitions and disposals	28	x	(x)
Equity dividends paid		(x)	(x)
Cash outflow before use of liquid resources and financing		x	(x)
Management of liquid resources		x	x
Financing		x	(x)
Increase in cash		x	(x)

13.9 Comparison with US GAAP

A cash flow statement is also required to be presented as part of US GAAP. The relevant standard is SFAS 95 *Statement of Cash Flows*. SFAS 95 has been subsequently amended by:

- SFAS 102 *Statement of Cash Flows – Exemptions of Certain Enterprises and Classification of Cash Flows from Certain Securities Acquired for Resale*;
- SFAS 104 *Statement of Cash Flows – Net Reporting of Certain Cash*

Receipts and Cash Payments and Classification of Cash Flows from Hedging Transactions;
- SFAS 117 *Financial Statements of Not-for-Profit Organisations*; and
- SFAS 133 Accounting for Derivative Instruments and Hedging Activities.

Under US GAAP, the cash flows (being inflows and outflows of cash and cash equivalents) are reported under the same three headings as under IAS 7 (r1992), namely: operating activities; investing activities; and financing activities. Cash flows from investing and financing activities are defined under US GAAP. All other cash flows not specifically identified as either investing or financing are treated as operating, including extraordinary items. In general, the items included in each category will be the same. However, there are some exceptions which mainly arise due to the alternatives permitted by IAS 7 (r1992) as discussed below.

- Although under IAS 7 (r1992) interest paid and interest and dividends received could be reported as operating cash flows, they are not required to be so reported, whereas under US GAAP they are required to be reported as operating cash flows. Similarly, dividends paid are required to be reported as a financing cash flow under US GAAP and, although they could be so reported under IAS 7 (r1992), they are not required to be classified as financing.
- All cash flows in respect of taxes are classified as operating under SFAS 95 whereas under IAS 7 (r1992) cash flows that can be specifically identified with financing or investing activities are classified as financing or investing respectively. EITF 00-15 states that the SFAS 95 classification also applies to the reduction of income taxes paid as a result of the deduction triggered by employee exercise of stock options.
- Where a single payment or receipt of cash represents two smaller payments or receipts, each should be classified according to its nature under IAS 7 (r1992), whereas under SFAS 95 both the cash flows should be classified in accordance with the activity that is likely to be the predominant source of cash flows for the item.
- Under IAS 7 (r1992), bank overdrafts that are payable on demand and are an integral part of the enterprise's cash management are explicitly permitted to be included as an element of cash equivalents. SFAS 95 does not address bank overdrafts, but generally they would not be treated as part of cash equivalents; movements in overdrafts would instead be recorded in the financing section of the cash flow statement. The only time overdrafts would form part of cash and cash equivalents under US GAAP is when the overdraft is in an account that can be netted with another, positive, account balance with the same financial institution; here the net of the two accounts would be included in cash and cash equivalents.

As discussed in **13.3**, to make it easier for foreign registrants to participate in American markets, the US SEC now accepts from them, without supplement, modification or reconciliation, a cash flow statement prepared in accordance with IAS 7 (r1992).

13.10 Examples from published financial statements

Note that the excerpts given do not always comply in full with all aspects of IAS and, as such, are not necessarily examples of best practice but merely of current practice.

Example 13.14

Consolidated cash flow statement, IAS

Financial year ended December 31	*Note*	*2000 €m*	*1999 €m*
Cash flow from operating activities			
Operating profit		**5,776**	3,908
Adjustments, total	28	**967**	597
Operating profit before change in net working capital		**6,743**	4,505
Change in net working capital	28	**−1,377**	−21
Cash generated from operations		**5,366**	4,484
Interest received		**255**	189
Interest paid		**−115**	−212
Other financial income and expenses		**−454**	−113
Income taxes paid		**−1,543**	−1,246
Net cash from operating activities		**3,509**	3,102
Cash flow from investing activities			
Acquisition of Group companies, net of acquired cash		**−400**	−178
Treasury shares acquired		**−160**	−25
Investments in other shares		**−111**	−37
Additions in capitalised development costs		**−393**	−271
Capital expenditures		**−1,580**	−1,302
Proceeds from disposal of shares in Group companies, net of disposed cash		**4**	27
Proceeds from sale of other shares		**75**	121
Proceeds from sale of fixed assets		**221**	318
Dividends received		**51**	6
Net cash used in investing activities		**−2,293**	−1,341
Cash flow from financing activities			
Share issue		**72**	152
Capital investment by minority shareholders		**7**	28
Proceeds from (+), payments of (−) long-term liabilities		**−82**	−6
Proceeds from (+), payments of (−) short-term borrowings		**133**	−126
Proceeds from (+), payments of (−) long-term receivables		**−776**	−171
Proceeds from (+), payments of (−) short-term receivables		**378**	128
Dividends paid		**−1,004**	−597
Net cash used in financing activities		**−1,272**	−592
Net increase in cash and cash equivalents		**−56**	1,169
Cash and cash equivalents at beginning of period		**4,239**	2,990
Cash and cash equivalents at end of period		**4,183**	4,159

The above figures cannot be directly traced from the balance sheet without additional information as a result of acquisitions and disposals of subsidiaries and net foreign exchange differences arising on consolidation.

The schedule shown below reconciles cash and cash equivalents at the end of the previously reported period to cash and cash equivalents reported for the beginning of the current period.

Reconciliation

As previously reported for 1999 and 1998, respectively	**4,159**	2,891
Foreign exchange adjustment	**80**	99
	4,239	2,990
Net decrease/increase in cash and cash equivalents	**−56**	1,169
As reported for 2000 and 1999	**4,183**	4,159

28. Notes to cash flow statement

	2000 *€m*	*1999* *€m*
Adjustments for:		
Depreciation	**1,009**	665
Other operating income and expenses	**−42**	−68
Adjustments, total	**967**	597
Change in net working capital		
Short-term trade receivables, increase (−), decrease (+)	**−2,304**	−982
Inventories, increase (−), decrease (+)	**−422**	−362
Interest-free short-term liabilities, increase (+), decrease (−)	**1,349**	1,323
Change in net working capital	**−1,377**	−21
Non-cash investing activities		
Acquisition of:		
Network Alchemy	**336**	–
DiscoveryCom	**223**	–
Rooftop	–	42
	559	42

Nokia Corporation
Finland
31 December 2000
International Accounting Standards

Example 13.15

Cash flow statements (excerpt)

	Notes	GROUP *2000* *Rm*	*1999* *Rm*
CASH FLOWS FROM OPERATING ACTIVITIES			
Cash generated from/(utilised by) operations	31.1	**1,703**	1,610
Finance costs		**(244)**	(293)
Dividends received		**60**	38
Interest received		**195**	258
Taxation paid	31.2	**(291)**	(168)
Cash available from operations		**1,423**	1,445
Dividends paid (including outside shareholders)		**(381)**	(324)
Net cash from/(used in) operating activities		**1,042**	1,121

Barloworld Limited
South Africa
30 September 2000
International Accounting Standards

Example 13.16

UBS Group statement of cash flows (excerpt)

CHF million

For the year ended	*31.12.00*	*31.12.99*	*31.12.98*
Net increase/(decrease) in cash equivalents	**(8,907)**	18,599	(8,675)
Cash and cash equivalents, beginning of the year	**102,277**	83,678	92,353
Cash and cash equivalents, end of the year	**93,370**	102,277	83,678
Cash and cash equivalents comprise:			
Cash and balances with central banks	**2,979**	5,073	3,267
Money market paper	**66,454**	69,717	18,390
Due from banks maturing in less than three months	**23,937**	27,487	62,021
Total	**93,370**	102,277	83,678

UBS
Switzerland
31 December 2000
International Accounting Standards

CHAPTER 14

Disclosure: notes to the financial statements

14.1 Source

IAS 1 (r1997) *Presentation of Financial Statements.*

14.2 Brief summary of the requirements

The notes to the financial statements should present information in a systematic manner. The notes should show the basis of preparation of the financial statements, the accounting policies used and any additional information that is not presented elsewhere in the financial statements, whether required by International Accounting Standards or otherwise necessary for fair presentation. Other specific disclosures about the enterprise, its legal form, its domicile, etc. are required to be made either in the financial statements or in information which is published with the financial statements.

14.3 Development of the requirements

Prior to the issuance of IAS 1 (r1997), the disclosure of accounting policies was dealt with in IAS 1 *Disclosure of Accounting Policies*, and general disclosure requirements were set out in IAS 5. IAS 1 (r1997) replaced IAS 1 and IAS 5 as well as IAS 13.

14.4 Structure of financial statements

To assist users in understanding the financial statements, the notes to the financial statements are required to be presented in a systematic manner. Each item on the face of the balance sheet, income statement and cash flow statement is cross-referenced to any related information in the notes. (IAS 1 (r1997).92)

Notes are normally presented in the following order:

(1) statement of compliance with International Accounting Standards (see **4.7.1** for a discussion of this statement);
(2) statement of the measurement basis (bases) adopted and accounting policies applied;
(3) supporting information and detail for items presented on the face of each financial statement in the order in which each line item and each financial statement is presented; and
(4) other disclosures, including:
   (a) contingencies, commitments and other financial disclosures; and
   (b) non-financial disclosures.

(IAS 1 (r1997).94)

In some cases, an enterprise may vary the order of the specific items or combine required disclosures within the notes. For example, an enterprise may disclose interest rate and fair value information related to certain interest-bearing financial liabilities along with maturity information relating to the same liabilities even though the former relates to the income statement while the latter relates to the balance sheet.

IAS 1 (r1997) does not prohibit information about the basis of preparation of the financial statements and the accounting policies adopted being presented as a separate component of the financial statements. (IAS 1 (r1997).96)

14.5 Presentation of accounting policies

The accounting policies section of the notes to the financial statements includes the following two items:

(a) the measurement basis (or bases), such as historical cost, current cost, realisable (settlement) value, fair value or present value, used in preparing the financial statements. When an enterprise adopts more than one measurement basis, for example if it revalues items of property, plant and equipment but carries all other assets and liabilities at historical cost, it provides an indication of the categories of assets and liabilities to which each measurement basis is applied; and
(b) each specific accounting policy that is necessary for a proper understanding of the financial statements.

(IAS 1 (r1997).97 and 98)

> 'In deciding whether a specific accounting policy should be disclosed, management considers whether disclosure would assist users in understanding the way in which transactions and events are reflected in the reported performance and financial position. The accounting policies that an enterprise might consider presenting include, but are not restricted to, the following:

(a) revenue recognition;
(b) consolidation principles, including subsidiaries and associates;
(c) business combinations;
(d) joint ventures;
(e) recognition and depreciation/amortisation of tangible and intangible assets;
(f) capitalisation of borrowing costs and other expenditure;
(g) construction contracts;
(h) investment properties;
(i) financial instruments and investments;
(j) leases;
(k) research and development costs;
(l) inventories;
(m) taxes, including deferred taxes;
(n) provisions;
(o) employee benefit costs;
(p) foreign currency translation and hedging;
(q) definition of business and geographical segments and the basis for allocation of costs between segments;
(r) definition of cash and cash equivalents;
(s) inflation accounting ; and
(t) government grants.

Other International Accounting Standards specifically require disclosure of accounting policies in many of these areas.'

(IAS 1 (r1997).99)

In addition, in consolidated financial statements, the policy used for determining goodwill and minority interest is disclosed. (IAS 1 (r1997).100)

It is important to note that an accounting policy may need to be disclosed even if the related amounts shown for current and prior periods are not material. This may be the case when the amounts are expected to be material in the future or when the accounting policy explains why the amounts are immaterial, such as the disclosure of a deferred tax policy which explains the enterprise's policy for recognition of deferred tax assets. It is also important to disclose accounting policies adopted when no specific IASs address a particular issue or when there is a choice of accounting policies when applying a certain IAS. For example, an enterprise will need to disclose whether it expenses borrowing costs as incurred in accordance with the benchmark treatment in IAS 23 or whether it capitalises them when the criteria in IAS 23 are met under the allowed alternative treatment.

14.6 Other disclosures

'An enterprise should disclose the following if not disclosed elsewhere in information published with the financial statements:

(a) the domicile and legal form of the enterprise, its country of incorporation and the address of the registered office (or principal place of business, if different from the registered office);

(b) a description of the nature of the enterprise's operations and its principal activities;

(c) the name of the parent enterprise and the ultimate parent enterprise of the group; and

(d) either the number of employees at the end of the period or the average for the period.'

(IAS 1 (r1997).102)

14.7 Comparison with UK GAAP

In the UK, FRS 18, *Accounting Policies*, states that an entity's financial statements should describe each of the accounting policies that is material in the context of those financial statements. (FRS 18.55(a)) This Standard was issued in December 2000 and is effective for accounting periods ending on or after 22 June 2001. Prior to FRS 18, SSAP 2, *Disclosure of Accounting Policies*, set out similar requirements in this area.

The Companies Act also requires the accounting policies adopted by a company to be stated, and, moreover, requires the notes to the accounts to state whether the accounts have been prepared in accordance with applicable accounting standards, although small and medium-sized companies are exempt from the latter requirement.

There is no requirement in the UK for the notes to the accounts to be presented in any particular order, although it is usual for companies to adopt the same logical order as set out in IAS 1 (r1997). It is considered good practice for the accounting policies adopted to be identified in the first note to the accounts, although, again, there is no requirement for this. It is also customary to disclose, either in the accounting policy note or separately, the accounting convention (i.e., measurement basis or bases) used in preparing the financial statements and any modifications thereto. Disclosure of the measurement bases adopted would, in any event, generally be appropriate as part of the description of accounting policies under FRS 18.

As regards the other disclosures listed in **14.6** above:

- the Companies Act likewise requires disclosure of the principal activities of the company and its subsidiaries and additionally requires disclosure of any significant change in those activities, an indication of future developments in the business, a review of the development of the group's business during the year, and other matters;
- FRS 8, *Related Party Disclosures*, requires disclosure of the name of the controlling party and ultimate controlling party of an entity;

- the Companies Act requires disclosure of the monthly average number of persons employed in the year and the number employed in each category selected by the directors, as well as the aggregate amounts of wages and salaries, social security costs and other pension costs.

14.8 Comparison with US GAAP

The notes to the financial statements requirements are generally not formalised in the US. However, formats have developed through practice and specifically by the SEC. US Concepts Statement 5 does emphasise the importance and usefulness of the notes to the financial statements. Some information can only be provided by the notes to the financial statements, such as significant accounting policies, alternative measures for assets and liabilities, or explanations of elements of the financial statements.

In US GAAP there is flexibility as to where the accounting policies are listed. The Accounting Principles Board, however, expresses a preference for locating the description of the accounting policies in a 'Summary of Significant Accounting Policies' preceding the notes to financial statements or as the initial note.

14.9 Examples from published financial statements

Examples of many accounting policies will be given in the relevant chapters. However, the *overall* measurement basis chosen is not discussed in other chapters, so examples of this disclosure are provided below. Note that the excerpts given do not always comply in full with all aspects of IAS and, as such, are not necessarily examples of best practice but merely of current practice.

Example 14.1

1. Accounting policies and basis of preparation (excerpt)

The financial statements are prepared under the historical cost convention.

The financial statements are prepared in accordance with International Accounting Standards (IAS) and South African Statements of Generally Accepted Accounting Practice.

The principal accounting policies adopted are set out below.

Barloworld Limited
South Africa
30 September 2000
International Accounting Standards

Example 14.2

2. Basis of preparation and Reporting Currency (excerpt)

The consolidated financial statements are prepared in accordance with International Accounting Standards ('IAS') and Interpretations of the International Accounting Standards Committee. The consolidated financial statements are prepared under the historical cost convention.

For the reporting period 1999, implementation of several revised or new standards became mandatory, some of which require restatement of prior year data. This includes in particular IAS 1 (revised 1997) – *Presentation of Financial Statements*, IAS 19 (revised 1998) – *Employee Benefits* and IAS 35 – *Discontinuing Operations.*

Effective January 1, 1999, the Group adopted the following IAS in advance of their effective date:

- IAS 22 (revised 1998) – *Business Combinations*
- IAS 36 – *Impairment of Assets*
- IAS 37 – *Provisions, Contingent Liabilities and Contingent Assets*
- IAS 38 – *Intangible Assets*
- IAS 16 (revised 1998) – *Property, Plant and Equipment**
- IAS 28 (revised 1998) – *Accounting for Investments in Associates**
- IAS 31 (revised 1998) – *Financial Reporting of Interests in Joint Ventures**

*as amended by IAS 22, IAS 36, IAS 37 and IAS 38

The implementation of the new standards resulted in a number of changes to the financial statements . . .

As required by IAS, unless impracticable, comparative information has been restated and/or reclassified to conform the financial information reported in 1998 to the changes in measurement and presentation.

Hoechst Group
Germany
31 December 1999
International Accounting Standards

CHAPTER 15

Events after the balance sheet date

15.1 Source

IAS 1 (r1997)	*Presentation of Financial Statements.*
IAS 10 (r1999)	*Events After the Balance Sheet Date.*
IAS 37	*Provisions, Contingent Liabilities and Contingent Assets.*

15.2 Brief summary of the requirements

IAS 10 (r1999) sets out the accounting and disclosure requirements for events after the balance sheet date.

Events after the balance sheet date fall into two categories:

(a) those that provide evidence of conditions that existed at the balance sheet date (adjusting events after the balance sheet date); and
(b) those that are indicative of conditions that arose after the balance sheet date (non-adjusting events after the balance sheet date).

15.3 Development of the requirements

IAS 10, *Contingencies and Events Occurring After the Balance Sheet Date*, was originally approved in November 1974. The Standard was reformatted in 1994 in order to bring it into line with the presentation adopted for International Accounting Standards. No substantive changes were made to the original approved text.

In September 1998 the IASC published IAS 37. This superseded the guidance on contingencies contained in IAS 10 (r1999). IAS 10 (r1999) was published in May 1999 and it replaces those parts of IAS 10 not already superseded by IAS 37. It also makes a number of limited changes as follows:

- new disclosures about the date of authorisation of the financial statements for issue;
- banning the recognition of a liability for dividends that are stated to be in respect of the period covered by the financial statements and are proposed or declared after the balance sheet date, but before the financial statements are authorised for issue;
- confirmation that an enterprise should update disclosures that relate to conditions that existed at the balance sheet date in the light of any new information that it receives after the balance sheet date about those conditions;
- deletion of the requirement to adjust the financial statements where an event after the balance sheet date indicates that the going concern assumption is not appropriate for part of the enterprise (see **15.7**);
- refinements to the examples of adjusting and non-adjusting events; and
- various drafting improvements.

See **11.9.12** for a discussion of the accounting treatment of contingencies.

15.4 Definition of events after the balance sheet date

IAS 10 (r1999) defines events after the balance sheet date as 'those events, both favourable and unfavourable, that occur between the balance sheet date and the date when the financial statements are authorised for issue'. (IAS 10 (r1999).2)

In some circumstances, an enterprise must submit its financial statements to its shareholders for approval after the financial statements have already been issued. In such cases, the financial statements are authorised for issue on the date of original issuance, not on the date when shareholders approve the financial statements. (IAS 10 (r1999).4)

In other cases, the management of an enterprise may be required to issue its financial statements to a supervisory board (made up solely of non-executives) for approval. In such cases, the financial statements are authorised for issue when the management authorises them for issue to the supervisory board. (IAS 10 (r1999).5)

Events after the balance sheet date include all events up to the date when the financial statements are authorised for issue, even if those events occur after the publication of a profit announcement or of other selected financial information. (IAS 10 (r1999).6)

15.5 Recognition of events after the balance sheet date

Events after the balance sheet date fall into two categories:

(a) those that provide evidence of conditions that existed at the balance sheet date (adjusting events after the balance sheet date); and
(b) those that are indicative of conditions that arose after the balance sheet date (non-adjusting events after the balance sheet date).

Adjusting events
The following are examples of adjusting events after the balance sheet date that require an enterprise to adjust the amounts recognised in its financial statements, or to recognise items that were not previously recognised:

(a) the resolution after the balance sheet date of a court case which, because it confirms that an enterprise already had a present obligation at the balance sheet date, requires the enterprise to adjust a provision already recognised, or to recognise a provision instead of merely disclosing a contingent liability;
(b) the receipt of information after the balance sheet date indicating that an asset was impaired at the balance sheet date, or that the amount of a previously recognised impairment loss for that asset needs to be adjusted. For example, the insolvency of a customer which occurs after the balance sheet date may confirm a loss that already existed at the balance sheet date on a trade receivable account and the enterprise needs to adjust the carrying amount of that account accordingly. Another example might be sale of inventories after the balance sheet date which may give evidence about their net realisable value at the balance sheet date;
(c) the determination after the balance sheet date of the cost of assets purchased, or the proceeds from assets sold, before the balance sheet date;
(d) the determination after the balance sheet date of the amount of profit sharing or bonus payments, if the enterprise had a present legal or constructive obligation at the balance sheet date to make such payments as a result of events before that date (see **11.9.21**); and
(e) the discovery of fraud or errors that show that the financial statements were incorrect.

IAS 10 (r1999).8

There is no specific requirement in IAS 10 (r1999) to disclose adjusting events after the balance sheet date, presumably on the basis that once the requisite adjustment has been made to the assets or liabilities concerned no further disclosure is necessary. It may, nevertheless, be appropriate to include a note of explanation within the financial statements where there has been a very significant adjustment arising from an event after the balance sheet date.

Non adjusting events

> 'An enterprise should not adjust the amounts recognised in its financial statements to reflect non-adjusting events after the balance sheet date.'
>
> (IAS 10 (r1999).9).

The underlying principle here is that adjustment ought not to be made to assets and liabilities in the light of events after the balance sheet date, if these events do not relate to conditions existing at the balance sheet date. A good example of this is the decline in market value of listed investments between the balance sheet date and the date when the financial statements are authorised for issue. The fall in market value does not normally reflect conditions at the balance sheet date, but circumstances which have arisen since then. No adjustment is therefore made to the carrying value of the investments. Similarly, the enterprise does not update the amounts disclosed, although it may need to give additional disclosure as set out in **15.8.3**. (IAS 10 (r1999).10)

However, all facts should be considered in each case to determine if an event is adjusting or non-adjusting. For example, if the investments in the paragraph above had not been listed or traded heavily, a sale of the shares after the balance sheet date, but before the financial statements have been authorised for issue, may indicate their value at the balance sheet date and therefore be an adjusting event.

15.6 Dividends

If dividends to holders of equity instruments (as defined in IAS 32 (r1998), *Financial Instruments: Disclosure and Presentation*, see Chapter **12**) are proposed or declared after the balance sheet date, an enterprise should not recognise those dividends as a liability at the balance sheet date. (IAS 10 (r1999).11)

IAS 1 (r1997) requires an enterprise to disclose the amount of dividends that were proposed or declared after the balance sheet date but before the financial statements were authorised for issue. IAS 1 (r1997) permits an enterprise to make this disclosure either:

(a) on the face of the balance sheet as a separate component of equity; or
(b) in the notes to the financial statements.

See **11.3.9** for further discussion of dividends.

15.7 Going concern

Events after the balance sheet date may also indicate whether the whole or part of the enterprise is no longer a going concern. IAS 1 (r1997) requires management, when preparing financial statements, to make an assessment of an enterprise's ability to continue as a going concern. Events after the balance sheet date form an important part of the evidence which management considers when making this assessment.

> 'An enterprise should not prepare its financial statements on a going concern basis if management determines after the balance sheet date either that it intends to liquidate the enterprise or to cease trading, or that it has no realistic alternative but to do so.'
>
> (IAS 10 (r1999).13)

IAS 10 (r1999) advises that deterioration in operating results and financial position after the balance sheet date may indicate a need to consider whether the going concern assumption is still appropriate. If that assumption is no longer appropriate, the Standard requires a fundamental change in the basis of accounting, rather than an adjustment to the amounts recognised within the original basis of accounting.

IAS 1 (r1997) requires certain disclosures if the financial statements are not prepared on a going concern basis, or if there are significant doubts about the enterprise's ability to continue as a going concern. The events or conditions requiring disclosure may arise after the balance sheet date. See **4.7.3** for a discussion of the going concern basis.

15.8 Disclosure

15.8.1 Date of authorisation for issue

> 'An enterprise should disclose the date when the financial statements were authorised for issue and who gave that authorisation. If the enterprise's owners or others have the power to amend the financial statements after issuance, the enterprise should disclose that fact.'
>
> (IAS 10 (r1999).16)

It is important for users to know when the financial statements were authorised for issue, as the financial statements do not reflect events after this date.

This information may be included as a disclosure, or, in some countries, a member of the board actually signs and dates the balance sheet or a separate report.

15.8.2 Updating disclosure about conditions at the balance sheet date

> 'If an enterprise receives information after the balance sheet date about conditions that existed at the balance sheet date, the enterprise should update disclosures that relate to these conditions, in the light of the new information.'
>
> (IAS 10 (r1999).18)

Sometimes an enterprise needs to update the disclosures in its financial statements to reflect information received after the balance sheet date. This can occur even when the information does not affect the carrying amounts of the assets and liabilities in the accounts. One example of the need to update disclosures is when evidence becomes available after the balance sheet date about a contingent liability that existed at the balance sheet date. In addition to considering whether a provision should be recognised under IAS 37, an enterprise may need to update its disclosures about the contingent liability in the light of that evidence. (IAS 10 (r1999).19)

15.8.3 Non-adjusting events after the balance sheet date

> 'Where non-adjusting events after the balance sheet date are of such importance that non-disclosure would affect the ability of the users of the financial statements to make proper evaluations and decisions, an enterprise should disclose the following information for each significant category of non-adjusting event after the balance sheet date:
>
> (a) the nature of the event; and
> (b) an estimate of its financial effect, or a statement that such an estimate cannot be made.'
>
> (IAS 10 (r1999).20)

The Standard gives examples of non-adjusting events after the balance sheet date that may be of such importance that non-disclosure would affect the ability of the users of the financial statements to make proper evaluations and decisions. The list is as follows:

(a) a major business combination after the balance sheet date (IAS 22 (r1998), *Business Combinations*, requires specific disclosures in such cases, **18.8.1**) or disposing of a major subsidiary;
(b) announcing a plan to discontinue an operation, disposing of assets or settling liabilities attributable to a discontinuing operation or entering into binding agreements to sell such assets or settle such liabilities (IAS 35, *Discontinuing Operations*, **5.14.3**);
(c) major purchases and disposals of assets, or expropriation of major assets by government;
(d) the destruction of a major production plant by a fire after the balance sheet date;
(e) announcing, or commencing the implementation of, a major restructuring (IAS 37, see **11.9.10**);

(f) major ordinary share transactions and potential ordinary share transactions after the balance sheet date (IAS 33, *Earnings Per Share*, encourages an enterprise to disclose a description of such transactions other than capitalisation issues and share splits, see **7.8**);
(g) abnormally large changes after the balance sheet date in asset prices or foreign exchange rates;
(h) changes in tax rates or tax laws enacted or announced after the balance sheet date that have a significant effect on current and deferred tax assets and liabilities (IAS 12 (r2000), *Income Taxes*, see **23.6**);
(i) entering into significant commitments or contingent liabilities, for example by issuing significant guarantees; and
(j) commencing major litigation arising solely out of events that occurred after the balance sheet date.

(IAS 10 (r1999).21)

15.9 Comparison with UK GAAP

The rules set out in IAS 10 (r1999) regarding events after the balance sheet date are very similar to those in the corresponding UK standard, SSAP 17, *Accounting for Post Balance Sheet Events*. There is, for instance, almost no difference in substance and very little difference in wording between the definitions used in the IAS and its UK counterpart.

However, the following differences between the respective standards should be noted:

- IAS 10 (r1999) prohibits the recognition of dividends proposed or declared after the balance sheet date as liabilities, but IAS 1 (r1997) requires their disclosure. (IAS 10 (r1999).11) The UK Companies Act Sch 4:3(7) requires the aggregate amount of any dividends paid and proposed to be shown in the profit and loss account. Consequently, SSAP 17 includes in its definition of adjusting events, 'events which because of statutory or conventional requirements are reflected in financial statements'. These include not just proposed dividends but also dividends receivable from subsidiary and associated companies and amounts appropriated to reserves.
- The UK standard requires disclosure as a non-adjusting event of the reversal or maturity after the period end of transactions entered into before the period end, the substance of which is primarily to alter the appearance of the balance sheet. (SSAP 17.23) This rule is designed principally to catch so-called 'window dressing' transactions. IAS 10 (r1999) requires that an enterprise should update disclosures that relate to conditions that existed at the balance sheet date in the light of any new information that it receives after the balance sheet date about those conditions. This could be seen as weaker than SSAP 17 in terms of preventing window dressing.

- SSAP 17 requires disclosure of each non-adjusting event separately (SSAP 17.24), while under IAS 10 (r1999) the disclosure is only required for each significant category of non-adjusting event. SSAP 17 also requires the tax effect of non-adjusting events to be disclosed.
- The new UK standard, FRS 18, *Accounting Policies*, states in FRS 18.21 that an entity should prepare its financial statements on the going concern basis, unless:
  (a) the entity is being liquidated or has ceased trading, or
  (b) the directors have no realistic alternative but to liquidate the entity or to cease trading.
- In these circumstances the entity *may*, if appropriate, prepare its financial statements on a basis other than that of a going concern. The decision as to whether or not another basis should be adopted then depends on the directors' view of whether another basis is more appropriate in providing information that is relevant, reliable and understandable, when balanced against the aim of comparability with earlier accounting periods. IAS 10 (r1999), differs in two respects. Firstly, as explained in paragraph **15.7** above, it extends category (a) above by introducing an element of management *intent* and secondly it states that if the entity is determined by management to be in either category (a) or (b) above, then it *should not* use the going concern basis.
- As regards authorisation for issue of the financial statements, s233 of the UK Companies Act requires that the annual financial statements must be approved by the board of directors and signed on their behalf by a director on the face of the balance sheet. The name of the signatory must also be stated. This is a more specific requirement than that set out in IAS 10 (r1999) (see **15.8.1**).

15.10 Comparison with US GAAP

US coverage of post balance sheet events is to be found mainly in AU (audit) section 560 *Subsequent Events* (*Codification of Statements on Auditing Standards)* with additional discussion of the going concern concept in AU section 341. There do not appear to be any significant differences between IAS 10 (r1999) and US auditing and reporting requirements. Under US GAAP, dividends are recorded as liabilities in the period in which they are formally declared by the Board of Directors or equivalent body. Thus, if dividends are declared after the balance sheet date, disclosure of this fact is the appropriate treatment. This is consistent with IAS 10 (r1999) and IAS 1 (r1997).

Note, however, that following Staff Accounting Bulletin 40 (Topic 4C), where an entity is SEC registered and there is a change in capital structure after the balance sheet date but before the financial statements are issued, as a result of a stock dividend, stock split or reverse split, this must be reflected in the balance sheet.

15.11 Examples from published financial statements

Note that the excerpts given do not always comply in full with all aspects of IAS and as such are not necessarily examples of best practice but merely of current practice.

Example 15.1

45. Events after the balance sheet date

On January 25, 2000, Biochimica Opos SpA ('Opos'), an indirect subsidiary of Hoechst AG, announced that it had finalized an agreement with Eli Lilly and Company ('Lilly') that resolved all outstanding litigation between Lilly and Opos and certain of Opos' affiliated companies that related to the production and sale of bulk cefaclor. In fulfilment of the settlement agreement Hoechst paid US$110 million (see Note 43). This payment has already been reflected in the consolidated financial statements 1999 in form of a provision.

On February 16, 2000 Aventis Pharmaceuticals, Inc. (formerly Hoechst Marion Roussel, Inc), the US subsidiary of Hoechst Pharma, reached a settlement with 3M on certain disputes arising under an agreement on the supply, distribution, co-promotion and licensing of asthma inhalators, which was concluded in 1998. The financial burden associated with the settlement has been reflected in the consolidated financial statements 1999 by impairment of intangible assets and in form of a provision.

On February 28, 2000 the Nobel Tower, the former administrative building of Hoechst Pharma in France, was sold by way of a purchase promise (*'promesse de vente'*) to a consortium led by Caisse des Dépôts et Consignations. The final purchase agreement will be concluded upon fulfilment of certain suspensive conditions, e.g., the waiver by the relevant community of its pre-emption right. The purchase price amounts to €107 million (FF 700 million) in the aggregate.

On March 8, 2000 Aventis Pharma AG (formerly Hoechst Marion Roussel AG) announced plans to form an alliance with DuPont Pharmaceuticals Company, a wholly owned independent subsidiary of DuPont, to discover, develop and market pharmaceuticals in certain therapeutic areas, in Europe. Final negotiations on an exclusive basis have already started and the transaction is expected to be completed in mid-2000, subject to consultations of work councils and approvals of the boards and relevant authorities. As part of the agreement, DuPont Pharmaceuticals would acquire the Aventis Pharma research and development facility in Romainville, France, and would assume responsibility for Aventis Pharma employees associated with this facility. DuPont Pharmaceuticals also would acquire current research and development projects as well as exclusive marketing rights in several European countries to eight products with combined annual sales in excess of US$250 million.

Hoechst Group
Germany
31 December 1999
International Accounting Standards

Example 15.2

Note 37 Post Balance Sheet Events

There have been no material post balance sheet events which would require disclosure or adjustment to the December 2000 financial statements.

Long-term debt, excluding medium-term notes, has decreased by CHF 582 million since the balance sheet date to 5 March 2001.

On 14 February 2001, the Board of Directors reviewed the financial statements and authorised them for issue. These financial statements will be submitted to the Annual General Meeting of Shareholders to be held on 26 April 2001 for approval.

UBS
Switzerland
31 December 2000
International Accounting Standards

CHAPTER 16

Disclosure: segment reporting

16.1 Source

IAS 14 (r1997) *Segment Reporting*

16.2 Brief summary of the requirements

IAS 14 (r1997) requires companies with publicly traded equity or debt securities to report data for business segments (groups of related products or services) and geographical segments. Based on the structure of its internal reporting system, management identifies one of those bases of segmentation as primary and the other as secondary, with fewer disclosures required for the secondary basis. An enterprise looks to its internal organisational structure and internal reporting system for the purpose of identifying its segments (the 'management approach'). In those rare circumstances where internally reported segments are not along either product/service or geographical lines, management looks to the next lower level of internal segmentation that reports information along product/service lines or geographical lines, as appropriate.

Segments are generally separately reportable if the majority of their sales are to external customers *and* they constitute 10 per cent or more of: revenue from sales (both external and internal), 'result' as defined in IAS 14 (r1997); or total assets. Total external revenue reported by segments must constitute at least 75 per cent of total revenue.

16.3 Development of the requirements

Originally adopted in 1981, IAS 14 has been subsequently revised, and the revised Standard is effective for periods beginning on or after 1 July 1998. Changes to the original IAS 14 include: (1) exclusion of all non-public companies from the scope of the Standard; (2) clearer definitions of business and geographical segments, including use of the 'management approach' to identify reportable segments; (3) a new requirement that segments should comprise at least 75 per cent of the enterprise total; (4) standardised definition of segment result; (5) specification that segment data should follow the accounting policies used in the consolidated financial statements; and (6) 'two-tier' disclosure, with expanded information only for primary segments.

IAS 14 was included in the list of core standards identified by IOSCO as necessary for IASs to be acceptable for financial statements used in cross-border financing transactions (see **2.2.5**). Concurrent with the revision of IAS 14, the US FASB and the Canadian Accounting Standards Board, jointly revised their standards on segment reporting. As discussed in **16.14**, several differences arise between IAS 14 (r1997) and the new US standard, SFAS 131, *Disclosures about Segments of an Enterprise and Related Information.* The SEC has indicated that both approaches have substantial merit and that the FASB, the CICA and IASC should undertake a joint study of the resulting quality of segmentation and related disclosures after the standards have been in use for five years. (*Insight*, March 1997, p21)

16.4 Scope

Enterprises whose equity or debt securities are publicly traded and enterprises that are in the process of issuing equity or debt securities in public securities markets are required to apply IAS 14 (r1997). (IAS 14 (r1997).3)

Enterprises whose securities are not publicly traded are encouraged, but not required, to include the segment information required by IAS 14 (r1997). However, if such an enterprise chooses to disclose segment information, it must comply fully with IAS 14 (r1997). Thus, it is inappropriate for such an enterprise to disclose some, but not all, of the segment information required by IAS 14 (r1997) or to disclose segment information calculated using different methods from those set out in IAS 14 (r1997) without also making the disclosures required by and calculated in accordance with IAS 14 (r1997).

When one financial report contains both the consolidated financial statements of an enterprise whose securities are publicly traded and separate financial statements of the parent or one or more subsidiaries, segment information is required only on the basis of the consolidated information. Likewise, if one financial report contains the financial statements of an enterprise whose securities are publicly traded and the financial statements of an equity method associate or joint venture, segment information is required only for the enterprise itself. (IAS 14 (r1997).6 and 7) Of course, if a subsidiary, associate or joint venture itself is publicly traded, it will present the appropriate segment disclosures in its own financial statements.

16.5 Management approach

IAS 14 (r1997) is based on the premise that the predominant sources of risks and returns affect how most enterprises are organised and managed. Therefore, to give financial statement users insight into these risks and returns, the organisational structure and internal financial reporting system of an enterprise form the basis on which segments are identified for external reporting purposes. This method is often referred to as the management approach.

At the same time, IAS 14 (r1997) anticipates that, for most enterprises, the predominant sources of risk and returns are related either to differences in the products and services that it produces or differences in the geographical areas in which it operates, or both. Therefore, by looking to an enterprise's internal organisational structure and internal financial reporting system to identify segments, in most cases that will lead directly to segmentation along product and service lines and/or along geographical lines.

16.6 Definitions of business segment, geographical segment and reportable segment

16.6.1 Business segment

> 'A business segment is a distinguishable component of an enterprise that is engaged in providing an individual product or service or a group of related products or services and that is subject to risks and returns that are different from those of other business segments. Factors that should be considered in determining whether products and services are related include:
>
> (a) the nature of the products or services;
> (b) the nature of the production processes;
> (c) the type or class of customer for the products or services;
> (d) the methods used to distribute the products or provide the services; and
> (e) if applicable, the nature of the regulatory environment, for example, banking, insurance, or public utilities.'
>
> (IAS 14 (r1997).9)

Examples of business segments for a publishing enterprise might include consumer books, consumer magazines, business magazines, etc. Examples of business segments for a conglomerate might include coal mining, chemicals, material handling, tobacco products, propane, forest products, building materials and any other business in which it is engaged which meet the definition above.

Example 16.1

Lufthansa, the German airline company, has divided itself into seven major business segments, two of which are each further split: Passenger Travel (divided into two segments); Cargo; Maintenance, Repairs, and Overhaul; Catering; Leisure Travel Services; IT Services (divided into two segments); and Ground Services.

16.6.2 Geographical segment

> 'A geographical segment is a distinguishable component of an enterprise that is engaged in providing products or services within a particular economic environment and that is subject to risks and returns that are different from those of components operating in other economic environments. Factors that should be considered in identifying geographical segments include:
>
> (a) similarity of economic and political conditions;
> (b) relationships between operations in different geographical areas;
> (c) proximity of operations;
> (d) special risks associated with operations in a particular area;
> (e) exchange control regulations; and
> (f) the underlying currency risks.'
>
> (IAS 14 (r1997).9)

Depending on the circumstances, a geographical segment may be a country, a group of countries or a region within a country.

Example 16.2

Gucci Group uses a mix of individual countries and regions as its geographical segments: United States, Italy, France, Rest of Europe, Japan, Rest of Asia and Rest of World.

With reference to *Example 16.1*, Lufthansa's seven geographical segments are Germany, Europe, North America, Central and South America, Asia Pacific, Middle East, and Africa.

When identifying geographical segments, management must consider whether the risks and returns of the enterprise are more greatly influenced by the geographic location of its assets/operations (where its products are produced or where its service delivery activities are based) or by the location of its customers/markets (where its products are sold or services are rendered). In practice, risks and returns arise from each. However, an enterprise's organisation and internal reporting structure will normally provide evidence of whether its dominant source of geographic risks results from the location of its assets (the origin of its sales) or the location of its customers (the destination of its sales).

If geographical segments are defined on the basis of location of customers, how is location of customer defined? Possibilities include:

(a) location from which the order was placed and to which the invoice is sent;
(b) location to which the goods are shipped;
(c) location of the ultimate consumer if known.

IAS 14 (r1997) does not address this specifically. The broad principle in IAS 14.14 is that geographical segments should be determined by the 'dominant source of geographical risks'. That principle would seem to suggest that location of the ultimate consumer if known is the best indicator of risks. But because this information is often not known to the seller, IAS 14 (r1997) does not suggest that geographical segments be defined in this matter. The fallback would be (b) above, location to which goods are shipped.

As a general rule, a single segment, either business or geographical, does not contain operations with significantly differing risks and returns. Therefore, a business segment does not include products and services with significantly differing risks and returns and a geographical segment does not include operations in economic environments with significantly differing risks and returns.

When identifying business or geographical segments, it is unlikely that all of the factors listed above will be met for any particular potential segment. Normally, when the majority of the factors listed are present, it indicates that a separate segment exists. However, management will need to keep the objective of identifying segments with differing risks and returns in mind during the identification process.

16.6.3 Reportable segment

> 'A reportable segment is a business segment or a geographical segment identified based on the foregoing definitions for which segment information is required to be disclosed by this Standard'.
>
> (IAS 14 (r1997).9)

As discussed in **16.7.3**, not all business segments or geographical segments are required to be separately disclosed primarily because either they are considered insignificant or they earn a majority of their revenues from intra-enterprise transfers rather than from outside sales. In some cases, it is appropriate to combine identified segments for reporting purposes.

16.7 Identification of segments for external reporting

IAS 14 (r1997) takes a three step approach to the identification of segments for external reporting purposes:

(1) Identification of primary and secondary reporting formats.
(2) Identification of business segments and geographical segments.
(3) Identification of reportable segments.

16.7.1 Step 1: identification of primary and secondary reporting formats

To identify its primary and secondary reporting formats, an enterprise determines whether the dominant source and nature of the risks and returns of an enterprise lie in the products and services its sells (business segments) or in the fact that it operates in different countries or geographic areas (geographic segments). (IAS 14 (r1997).26) The dominant source, either business segments or geographical segments, is identified as the segment type which will be used in the primary reporting format with the remaining source identified as the secondary reporting format. (As discussed in **16.10** and **16.11**, more information is required to be disclosed for the primary reporting format than the secondary reporting format.)

Therefore, if the risks and rates of return of an enterprise are affected predominantly by differences in the products and services it produces, its primary format for reporting segment information is business segments, with secondary information reported geographically.

However, if the risks and rates of return of an enterprise are affected predominantly by the fact that it operates in different countries or other geographical areas, its primary format for reporting segment information is geographical segments, with secondary information reported for business segments.

Normally, the determination of the primary reporting format of an enterprise is based on:

(a) the internal organisation and management structure; and
(b) its system of internal financial reporting to the board of directors and the chief executive officer.

(IAS 14 (r1997).27)

As discussed in **16.5**, IAS 14 (r1997) is based on the premise that the predominant sources of risks and returns affect how most enterprises are organised and managed. Therefore, an enterprise's organisational structure and its internal financial reporting system should form the basis on which segments are identified for external reporting purposes, including the identification of the primary and secondary reporting formats.

Example 16.3

Mandarin Oriental International Limited considers its primary reporting segment to be geographic. 'The Group is operated on a worldwide basis in four regions: Hong Kong and Macau, Southeast Asia, Europe and North America. In addition, the Group has two distinct business segments: hotel ownership and hotel management.' Business segments are this enterprise's secondary basis of segment reporting.

There are two exceptions to the general rule, and they are expected to occur only infrequently.

First, if an enterprise reports internally to the board of directors and the chief executive officer using both business segment information and geographical segment information, the 'matrix approach,' because its risks and rates of return are strongly affected by both differences in the products and services it produces and by differences in the geographical areas in which it operates, then the enterprise is required to use business segments as its primary segment reporting format and geographical segments as its secondary reporting format. (IAS 14 (r1997).27(a)) However, an enterprise may wish to present both business segments and geographical segments as primary segment reporting formats with full segment disclosures on each basis ('the matrix presentation'). Such a presentation is neither required nor prohibited by IAS 14 (r1997).

Second, if an enterprise reports internally to the board of directors and the chief executive officer based neither on business segments nor geographical segments, then the directors and management of the enterprise should determine the primary and secondary reporting formats based on whether the enterprise's risks and returns are related more to the products and services it produces (in which case business segments are the primary segment reporting format) or more to the geographical areas in which it operates (in which case geographical segments are the primary segment reporting format). This situation is expected to be rare but may arise, for example, when internal reporting is based solely on legal entity. Such reporting often results in internal segments composed of groups of unrelated products and services. Therefore, these internal segments will not meet the definitions of business or geographical segments set out in IAS 14 (r1997). As such, the directors and management are required to determine whether the enterprise's risks and returns are more product/service driven or geographically driven and to choose either business segments or geographical segments as the enterprise's primary basis of segment reporting. The guidance in IAS 14 (r1997) suggests that management's objective when making the determination is to achieve a reasonable degree of comparability with other enterprises, enhance understandability of the resulting information and meet the expressed needs of investors, creditors, and others for information about product/service-related and geographically-related risks and returns. (IAS 14 (r1997).30)

16.7.2 Step 2: identification of business and geographical segments

As a general rule, an enterprise's business and geographical segments for external reporting purposes are those organisational units for which information is reported to the board of directors (particularly the non-executive directors) and to the chief executive officer (or other senior operating decision maker, which in some cases may be a group of several people) for the purpose of evaluating the unit's past performance and for making decisions about future allocations of resources.

In practice, such information may take the form of monthly or quarterly management accounts or board packages. When this is the case, segments are identified based on the units for which financial information is included in such packages.

Example 16.4

To illustrate, Deutsche Bank identifies in a note to its financial statements the specific management report that forms the basis for its business segmentation: 'The Group's reporting of segment information according to IAS relates in its primary format to the results of the Group Divisions. The basis is the internal management information system "Divisional Profitability Calculation", which has central importance as a planning, steering and control instrument within the scope of the bank's divisional management organization.'

However, if the internal organisational and management structure of an enterprise and its system of internal financial reporting to the board of directors and chief executive officer are based neither on products or services nor on geography, as discussed in the previous section, the directors and management first determine the primary reporting format. Then they determine the business and geographical segments of the enterprise based on the factors discussed in **16.6**, rather than on the basis of its system of internal financial reporting to the board of directors and chief executive officer. In such situations, when determining business and geographical segments, the following rules apply:

(a) for those segments reported internally to the directors and management that satisfy the definitions of a business segment or a geographical segment, management does not need to look to a lower level of internal information as described in (b). In other words, IAS 14 (r1997) does not require the further segmentation of an internally identified segment which meets the IAS 14 (r1997) definition of a segment;

(b) for those segments reported internally to the directors and management that do not satisfy the definitions of a business segment or a geographical segment, management looks to the next lower level of internal segmentation that reports information along product and service lines or geographical lines.

(IAS 14 (r1997).32)

The presumption of (b) above is that at some internal level, an enterprise will track and report financial information about individual products and services or groups of related products and services, and information about operations in individual countries, such that products/services and countries of diverse risks and prospects are not commingled. A consequence of 'digging deeper' into an enterprise's internal reporting system is that the internally reported segments get smaller and smaller. As the next section explains, it may be appropriate or even necessary to combine those smaller segments into groups of products and services and geographical areas of similar risks and prospects for IAS 14 (r1997) reporting purposes.

Example 16.5

An enterprise has acquired ten insurance companies operating in 10 different countries. Each insurance company sells life insurance and property and casualty insurance. Management is decentralised, and the enterprise's board of directors receives reports with financial information by subsidiary. The managers of each insurance subsidiary receive financial reports broken down by life and property/casualty insurance. For purposes of identifying its business segments, the enterprise will look to the product/service line information reported to the managers of the subsidiaries. Because many of these segments may be individually insignificant, it may be appropriate to combine all of the life insurance segments and all of the property/casualty insurance segments – but only if the risks in those lines of business are not dissimilar from subsidiary to subsidiary.

16.7.3 Step 3: identification of reportable segments

Once a primary reporting format has been determined and the business segments and geographical segments have been identified, an enterprise must determine which segments are reportable, that is, are required by IAS 14 (r1997) to be disclosed in the financial statements.

'A business or geographical segment should be identified as a reportable segment if a majority of its revenue is earned from sales to external customers *and*:

(a) its revenue from sales to external customers and from transactions with other segments is 10 per cent or more of the total revenue, external and internal, of all segments; or
(b) its segment result, whether profit or loss, is 10 per cent or more of the combined result of all segments in profit or the combined result of all segments in a loss, whichever is the greater in absolute amount; or
(c) its assets are 10 per cent or more of the total assets of all segments.'

(IAS 14 (r1997).35)

The definitions of segment revenue, segment result and segment assets are discussed in **16.9**.

Segments below the 10 per cent threshold
When an internally reported segment is below all of the thresholds of significance set out above, the segment may be:

(a) designated as a reportable segment despite its size;
(b) combined into a separately reportable segment with one or more other similar internally reported segments(s) that are also below all of the 10 per cent thresholds (but only if the internally reported segments are substantially similar as defined below); or
(c) included as an unallocated reconciling item.

(IAS 14 (r1997).36)

In respect of (a):

> 'a segment identified as a reportable segment in the immediately preceding period because it satisfied the relevant 10 per cent thresholds should continue to be a reportable segment for the current period notwithstanding that its revenue, result, and assets all no longer exceed the 10 per cent thresholds, if the management of the enterprise judges the segment to be of continuing significance.'
>
> (IAS 14 (r1997).42)

IAS 14 (r1997) provides no guidance on the meaning of continuing significance. Presumably, one would look to profit and cash flow forecasts or the strategic plans of the enterprise to determine the continuing significance of a previously reported segment.

Aggregation
As noted in (b) above, in some cases, it may be appropriate to combine two or more business segments or geographical segments if they are substantially similar. IAS 14 (r1997) states that such segments are substantially similar only if:

(a) they exhibit similar long-term financial performance; and
(b) they are similar in all of the factors in the relevant definition of that type of segment (i.e. business segment or geographical segment).

(IAS 14 (r1997).34)

75 per cent threshold

After an enterprise has identified its reportable segments, if total external revenue attributable to reportable segments constitutes less than 75 per cent of the total consolidated or enterprise revenue, additional segments must be identified as reportable segments, even if they do not meet the 10 per cent thresholds, until at least 75 per cent of total consolidated or enterprise revenue is included in reportable segments.

(IAS 14 (r1997).37)

Comparative information

> 'If a segment is identified as a reportable segment in the current period because it satisfies the relevant 10 per cent thresholds, prior period segment data that is presented for comparative purposes should be restated to reflect the newly reportable segment as a separate segment, even if that segment did not satisfy the 10 per cent thresholds in the prior period, unless it is impracticable to do so.'
>
> (IAS 14 (r1997).43)

Vertically integrated operations

Because IAS 14 (r1997) bases the identification of a reportable segment on external revenue, vertically integrated operations will not necessarily be required to be reported. IAS 14 (r1997) acknowledges this fact and encourages, but does not require, reporting of vertically integrated activities as separate segments with appropriate description.

> 'If an enterprise's internal reporting system treats vertically integrated activities as separate segments and the enterprise does not choose to report them externally as business segments, the selling segment should be combined into the buying segment(s) in identifying externally reportable business segments unless there is no reasonable basis for doing so, in which case the selling segment would be included as an unallocated reconciling item.'
>
> (IAS 14 (r1997).41)

Example 16.6

An oil company has subsidiaries which concentrate on each of the following:

- exploration and production; and
- refining and marketing.

In the normal course of business, the only operating revenue of the exploration and production subsidiary is from intercompany sales of crude oil to the refining and marketing subsidiary. Therefore, the exploration and production subsidiary would not meet the definition of a reportable segment and its revenue and expenses would be combined with that of the refining and marketing subsidiary for purposes of segment disclosure. However, IAS 14 (r1997) would encourage disclosure as if the exploration and production subsidiary were a reportable segment with appropriate description of the basis of pricing inter-segment transfers.

16.8 Segment accounting policies

Segment accounting policies are defined in IAS 14 (r1997).16 as, 'the accounting policies adopted for preparing and presenting the financial statements of the consolidated group or enterprise as well as those accounting policies that relate specifically to segment reporting'. Thus, segment accounting policies in the context of IAS 14 (r1997) is a broad term which includes all the accounting policies of an enterprise including those which related to segment reporting.

'Segment information should be prepared in conformity with the accounting policies adopted for preparing and presenting the financial statements of the consolidated group or enterprise.' (IAS 14 (r1997).44) However, this rule does not imply that the accounting policies are applied to each segment as if it were a stand-alone entity. Some accounting policies may be applied on an enterprise basis and allocated to the appropriate segments on a consistent and rational basis. For example, pension costs may be determined for an enterprise as a whole and allocated to each segment based on salary and demographic data.

IAS 14 (r1997) does not prohibit the presentation of ***additional*** segment information prepared using differing accounting policies from that of the enterprise as long as:

(a) the information is reported internally to the board of directors and the chief executive officer for the purposes of making decisions about allocating resources to the segment and assessing its performance; and
(b) the basis of measurement for the additional information is clearly described.

(IAS 14 (r1997).46)

In other words, information which is not reported internally will probably not be useful to external users of financial statements and thus would be extraneous and potentially misleading. However, if information is reported internally to help the chief executive officer and the board of directors manage the business and the risks of the enterprise, it probably would be useful and relevant information for external financial statement users as well; and therefore, IAS 14 (r1997) allows such information to be presented in addition to the normal segment reporting disclosures.

When IAS 14 (r1997) was being developed (1995 to 1997), the US Financial Accounting Standards Board and the Canadian Accounting Standards Board were jointly developing their own segment reporting standard. IASC worked closely with FASB and CICA to try to harmonise their standards to the extent possible. However, a fundamental disagreement was reached with respect to the accounting principles used in preparing segment information. As noted earlier, IAS 14 (r1997).44 requires that segment information be prepared using the same accounting policies as are used in the consolidated financial statements.

SFAS 131, *Disclosures about Segments of an Enterprise and Related Information*, has no such requirement. In fact, it requires that segment information reported to investors and creditors be prepared using the same accounting practices as were used in preparing segment information reported to top management, even if those practices were different from consolidated accounting policies or at variance with national GAAP.

Once the IASC and FASB acknowledged that their final standards would differ in this regard, IASC agreed to add paragraph 46 to its standard so that SFAS 131 disclosures would not be in violation of IAS 14 (r1997). Thus an enterprise would be able to comply with both IAS 14 (r1997) and SFAS 131 by including in its segment information the data required by IAS 14 and the data required by SFAS 131. Paragraph 46 clarifies this point.

16.9 Definitions of segment revenue, expense, result, assets and liabilities

These definitions encompass amounts that are directly attributable to a segment and amounts that can be allocated to a segment on a reasonable basis. The starting point for identifying such items is the internal financial reporting system. It is presumed that amounts that have been identified with segments for internal financial reporting purposes are directly attributable or can be allocated on a reasonable basis to those segments. However, an enterprise may use a system of allocation that management understands but that results in an improper allocation of assets, liabilities, revenue and expenses to segments for purposes of IAS 14 (r1997). As such, the definitions and guidance provided in IAS 14 (r1997) must be considered when an enterprise makes segment disclosures to ensure that any required adjustments to internal financial reporting segments are identified and properly reflected in its external segment reporting.

16.9.1 Inter-company balances

Segment revenue, segment expense, segment assets, and segment liabilities are determined before intra-group balances and intra-group transactions are eliminated as part of the consolidation process, except to the extent that such intra-group balances and transactions are between group enterprises within a single segment. (IAS 14 (r1997).24)

16.9.2 Segment revenue

> 'Segment revenue is revenue reported in the enterprise's income statement that is directly attributable to a segment and the relevant portion of enterprise revenue that can be allocated on a reasonable basis to a segment whether from sales to external customers or from transactions with other segments of the same enterprise.'
>
> (IAS 14 (r1997).16)

Therefore, segment revenue includes:

(a) an enterprise's share of profits or losses of associates, joint ventures, or other investments accounted for under the equity method only if those items are included in consolidated or total enterprise revenue; and
(b) a joint venturer's share of the revenue of a jointly controlled entity that is accounted for by proportionate consolidation.

By definition, revenue is a 'gross' figure – total inflow from sales of goods and services. On the other hand, by definition, under the equity method the enterprise's share of investee profits is a 'net' figure – revenue minus all expenses. It would not seem appropriate to add the net figure of equity method income to the enterprise's gross revenues and report the total as revenues, whether in consolidation or for purposes of segment reporting. However, when the IASC was debating the segment reporting standard, it realised that:

(a) some companies were, in fact, including equity method income at the top of their consolidated income statements as revenue;
(b) this is not clearly prohibited under the Framework or IAS 18 (r1993), *Revenue*; and
(c) this is an issue that goes beyond segment reporting and should not be addressed in the segment reporting standard.

Consequently, IAS 14 (r1997).16 does not close the door to reporting equity method income as revenue, but this can be done for segment reporting purposes only if it is also done in the consolidated income statement.

Segment revenue does not include:

(a) extraordinary items;
(b) interest or dividend income, including interest earned on advances or loans to other segments, unless the operations of the segment are primarily of a financial nature; or
(c) gains on sales of investments or gains on extinguishment of debt unless the operations of the segment are primarily of a financial nature.

(IAS 14 (r1997).16)

16.9.3 Segment expense

> 'Segment expense is expense resulting from the operating activities of a segment that is directly attributable to the segment and the relevant portion of an expense that can be allocated on a reasonable basis to the segment, including expenses relating to sales to external customers and expenses relating to transactions with other segments of the same enterprise.'
>
> (IAS 14 (r1997).16)

Therefore, segment expense includes a joint venturer's share of the expenses of a jointly controlled entity that is accounted for by proportionate consolidation.

Segment expense does not include:

(a) extraordinary items;
(b) interest, including interest incurred on advances or loans from other segments, unless the operations of the segment are primarily of a financial nature;
(c) losses on sales of investments or losses on extinguishment of debt unless the operations of the segment are primarily of a financial nature;
(d) an enterprise's share of losses of associates, joint ventures, or other investments accounted for under the equity method;
(e) income tax expense; or
(f) general administrative expenses, head-office expenses, and other expenses that arise at the enterprise level and relate to the enterprise as a whole. However, costs are sometimes incurred at the enterprise level on behalf of a segment. Such costs are segment expenses if they relate to the operating activities of the segment and they can be directly attributed or allocated to the segment on a reasonable basis.

When the operations of a segment are primarily of a financial nature, interest income and interest expense may be reported as a single net amount for segment reporting purposes only if those items are netted in the consolidated or enterprise financial statements. See Chapter **12** for a discussion of when this presentation is appropriate.

(IAS 14 (r1997).16)

16.9.4 Segment result

> 'Segment result is segment revenue less segment expense and is determined before any adjustments for minority interest.'
>
> (IAS 14 (r1997).16)

In summary, segment result is normally a measure of operating profit before corporate head office expenses, interest income or expense (except for financial segments), income taxes, extraordinary items, investment gains and losses (again, except for financial segments), and minority interest. As mentioned in 16.9.2(a), income and losses of equity method associates and joint ventures are not normally included in revenue and therefore will not normally be included in the segment result.

IAS 1 (r1997), *Presentation of Financial Statements*, para 75(b) requires that the pre-tax results of operating activities be reported on the face of an enterprise's income statement. Even though the concept of segment result adopted in IAS 14 (r1997) is pre-tax operating profit or loss, the sum of those amounts for each of the segments will not aggregate to enterprise-wide pre-tax operating profit or loss because segment expenses do not include general administrative expenses, head office expenses, and other expenses that arise at enterprise level and relate to the enterprise as a whole. These latter expenses are operating expenses, but only at the corporate level.

16.9.5 Segment assets

Segment assets are those operating assets that are employed by a segment in its operating activities and that:

(a) either are directly attributable to the segment; or
(b) can be allocated to the segment on a reasonable basis.

(IAS 14 (r1997).16)

Therefore, segment assets include, but are not limited to:

(a) investments accounted for under the equity method only if the profit or loss from such investments is included in segment revenue;
(b) a joint venturer's share of the operating assets of a jointly controlled entity that is accounted for by proportionate consolidation;
(c) goodwill that is directly attributable to a segment or that can be allocated on a reasonable basis;
(d) current assets that are used in the operating activities of the segment;
(e) property, plant and equipment;
(f) assets that are the subject of finance leases; and
(g) other intangible assets.

IAS 14 (r1997) requires 'symmetry' in the inclusion of items in segment result and in segment assets. For example, if the results of a segment include:

(a) interest or dividend income, its segment assets include the related receivables, loans, investments or other income-producing assets;
(b) depreciation expense for a particular item of property, plant and equipment, that item of property, plant and equipment is included in its segment assets; or
(c) amortisation expense for a particular amount of goodwill, that amount of goodwill is included in its segment assets.

Segment assets do not include income tax assets or assets used for general enterprise or head-office purposes. Income tax assets are excluded from segment assets (and, as **16.9.6** notes income tax liabilities are excluded from segment liabilities) because segment result is measured on a pre-tax basis. That 'symmetry' enables financial statement users to make more meaningful assessments of return on assets or return on net investment by segment.

Segment assets are determined after deducting related allowances that are reported as direct offsets in the enterprise's balance sheet, such as an allowance for bad debt or inventory obsolescence.

Measurements of segment assets include adjustments to the prior carrying amounts of the identifiable segment assets and segment liabilities of a company acquired in a business combination accounted for as a purchase (fair value adjustments), even if those adjustments are made only for the purpose of preparing consolidated financial statements and are not recorded in either the parent's or the subsidiary's separate financial statements. Similarly, if property, plant and equipment has been revalued subsequent to acquisition, then segment assets reflect those revaluations.

16.9.6 Segment liabilities

> 'Segment liabilities are those operating liabilities that result from the operating activities of a segment and that either are directly attributable to the segment or can be allocated to the segment on a reasonable basis.'
>
> (IAS 14 (r1997).16)

Therefore segment liabilities include, but are not limited to:

(a) a joint venturer's share of the liabilities of a jointly controlled entity that is accounted for by proportionate consolidation;
(b) trade and other payables;
(c) accrued liabilities;
(d) customer advances; and
(e) product warranty provisions and other claims relating to the provision of goods and services.

Segment liabilities do not include:

(a) borrowings;
(b) liabilities related to assets that are the subject of finance leases;
(c) other liabilities that are incurred for financing rather than operating purposes; and
(d) income tax liabilities.

Application of the symmetry principle set out above means that if the result of a segment includes interest expense, its segment liabilities include the related interest-bearing liabilities. However, application of the symmetry principle does not lead to the conclusion that if segment assets include items which are the subject of finance leases, then segment liabilities must include the related finance lease obligations. This anomaly arises from the fact that segment liabilities are operating liabilities and thus do not include financing liabilities such as finance lease obligations.

Measurement of segment liabilities include fair value adjustments, even if those adjustments are made only for the purpose of preparing consolidated financial statements and are not recorded in either the parent's or the subsidiary's separate financial statements.

16.10 Disclosure in the primary reporting format

The following disclosures are required for each reportable segment based on an enterprise's primary reporting format:

(a) segment revenue (IAS 14 (r1997).51), showing separately:
  (i) segment revenue from sales to external customers (IAS 14 (r1997).51);
  (ii) segment revenue from transactions with other segments (IAS 14 (r1997).51);
(b) segment result (IAS 14 (r1997).52);
(c) the total carrying amount of segment assets (IAS 14 (r1997).55);
(d) segment liabilities (IAS 14 (r1997).56);
(e) the total cost incurred during the period to acquire segment assets that are expected to be used during more than one period (property, plant and equipment and intangible assets) for each reportable segment. This is measured on an accrual basis rather than a cash basis (IAS 14 (r1997).57);
(f) the total amount of expense included in segment result for depreciation and amortisation of segment assets for the period (IAS 14 (r1997).58);
(g) the total amount of significant non-cash expenses, other than depreciation and amortisation, that were included in segment expense (IAS 14 (r1997).61);
(h) the aggregate of the enterprise's share of the net profit or loss of associates, joint ventures, or other investments accounted for under the equity method if substantially all of the operations of the associate, joint venture or other investment are within that single segment. While this disclosure is a single amount, the determination of whether or not the operations of an associate, joint venture or other investment are within a single segment is made on an individual basis (IAS 14 (r1997).64 and 65);

(i) when (h) is disclosed, the aggregate investments in those associates and joint ventures should also be disclosed by reportable segment (IAS 14 (r1997).66);

(j) a reconciliation between the information disclosed for reportable segments and the aggregated information in the consolidated or enterprise financial statements. In presenting the reconciliation:
   (i) segment revenue is reconciled to enterprise revenue from external customers (including disclosure of the amount of enterprise revenue from external customers not included in any segment's revenue);
   (ii) segment result is reconciled to a comparable measure of enterprise operating profit or loss as well as to enterprise net profit or loss;
   (iii) segment assets are reconciled to enterprise assets; and
   (iv) segment liabilities are reconciled to enterprise liabilities; (IAS 14 (r1997).67)

(k) the amount of impairment losses recognised in the income statement and directly in equity during the period (IAS 36.116); and

(l) the amount of reversals of impairment losses recognised in the income statement and directly in equity during the period. (IAS 36.116)

IAS 14 (r1997) encourages, but does not require, the following disclosures:

(a) in addition to segment result, segment net profit or loss or some other measure of segment profitability, such as gross profit or profit or loss from ordinary activities, if it can be computed without arbitrary allocations and is appropriately described (IAS 14 (r1997).53);

(b) the nature and amount of any items of segment revenue or segment expense that are of such size, nature, or incidence that their disclosure is relevant to explain the performance of each reportable segment for the period. (IAS 14 (r1997).59) As discussed in **5.10**, these types of items are required to be disclosed on a consolidated or enterprise basis by IAS 8 (r1993), *Net Profit or Loss for the Period, Fundamental Errors and Changes in Accounting Policies.* This encouraged disclosure does not change the status of such items to extraordinary, but in the context of a segment rather than the consolidated or enterprise financial statements, items which were not required to be disclosed under IAS 8 (r1993) may become relevant and thus be disclosed. Examples of such items include: write-downs of inventories and property, plant, and equipment, provisions for restructuring, disposals of property, plant, and equipment and long-term investments, discontinued operations, litigation settlements, and reversals of provisions;

(c) the amount of the cash flows arising from the operating, investing and financing activities of each reported business segment and geographical segment. Enterprises which disclose this information do not need to disclose segment depreciation and amortisation expense or segment non-cash expenses (IAS 14 (r1997).63); and

(d) significant non-cash revenues that were included in segment revenue and, therefore, added in measuring segment result (IAS 14 (r1997).62).

16.11 Disclosure in the secondary reporting format

The disclosure requirements for the secondary reporting format depend on which type of segment, business segment or geographical segment, is identified as the primary format.

If the primary format is business segments, then the secondary format will be geographical segments, and an enterprise is required to disclose:

(a) segment revenue from external customers by geographical area based on the geographical location of its customers, for each geographical segment whose revenue from sales to external customers is 10 per cent or more of total enterprise revenue from sales to all external customers;
(b) the total carrying amount of segment assets by geographical location of assets, for each geographical segment whose segment assets are 10 per cent or more of the total assets of all geographical segments; and
(c) the total cost incurred during the period to acquire segment assets that are expected to be used during more than one period (property, plant, equipment and intangible assets) by geographical location of assets, for each geographical segment whose segment assets are 10 per cent or more of the total assets of all geographical segments.

(IAS 14 (r1997).69)

Example 16.7

Danisco, the large Danish food products and packaging company, uses 'location of assets' as the basis for its secondary geographical segments. Those segments are Denmark, other EU countries, rest of western Europe, eastern Europe, North America, central and South America, and rest of the world. It reports the carrying amounts of, and new investments in, assets located in those geographical areas as required by (b) and (c) above. In addition, Danisco reports sales revenue by geographical market (location of customers) as required by (a) above, using those same geographical areas as the market segments.

If the primary format is geographical segments, the secondary format will be business segments, and an enterprise is required to disclose the following for each business segment whose revenue from sales to external customers is 10 per cent or more of total enterprise revenue from sales to all external customers or whose segment assets are 10 per cent or more of the total assets of all business segments:

(a) segment revenue from external customers;
(b) the total carrying amount of segment assets; and
(c) the total cost incurred during the period to acquire segment assets that are expected to be used during more than one period (property, plant, equipment, and intangible assets).

(IAS 14 (r1997).70)

In addition, when the primary reporting format of an enterprise is geographical segments based on the location of its assets, and the location of its customers is different from the location of its assets, then the enterprise is required to disclose revenue from sales to external customers for each customer-based geographical segment whose revenue from sales to external customers is 10 per cent or more of total enterprise revenue from sales to all external customers. (IAS 14 (r1997).71) When the primary reporting format of an enterprise is geographical segments based on the location of its customers, and if the assets of the enterprise are located in different geographical areas from its customers, then the enterprise is required to disclose the following for each asset-based geographical segment whose revenue from sales to external customers or segment assets are 10 per cent or more of related consolidated or total enterprise amounts:

(a) the total carrying amount of segment assets by geographical location of the assets; and
(b) the total cost incurred during the period to acquire segment assets that are expected to be used during more than one period (property, plant, equipment, and intangible assets) by location of the assets.

(IAS 14 (r1997).72)

16.12 Other disclosures

Other required disclosures are discussed below.

16.12.1 Segments which are not reportable but for which revenue from sales to external customers is 10 per cent or more of total enterprise revenue

If a business segment or geographical segment for which information is reported to the board of directors and chief executive officer is not a reportable segment because it earns a majority of its revenue from sales to other segments, but nonetheless its revenue from sales to external customers is 10 per cent or more of total enterprise revenue from sales to all external customers, the enterprise is required to disclose:

(a) that fact;
(b) the amount of revenue from sales to external customers; and
(c) internal sales to other segments.

(IAS 14 (r1997).74)

16.12.2 *Types of products and services included in each segment*

An enterprise is required to disclose the types of products and services included in each reported business segment and indicate the composition of each reported geographical segment, both primary and secondary, if not otherwise disclosed in the financial statements or elsewhere in the financial report. (IAS 14 (r1997).81)

16.12.3 *Previously reported segments*

Segments reported in the immediately preceding period that no longer satisfy the quantitative thresholds established in IAS 14 (r1997) are not reported separately. However, IAS 14 (r1997) notes that it may be helpful to financial statement users for an enterprise to explain the reasons why a previously reported segment is no longer reported. To be useful, such an explanation would not be simply that the quantitative thresholds are no longer being met, but an explanation of the factors that contributed to the situation such as a decline in demand or a change in management strategy or because a part of the operations of the segment has been sold or combined with other segments.

16.12.4 *Inter-segment transfer pricing*

When measuring and reporting segment revenue from transactions with other segments, inter-segment transfers must be measured on the basis that the enterprise actually used to price those transfers. The basis of pricing inter-segment transfers and any change therein is required to be disclosed. (IAS 14 (r1997).75)

16.12.5 *Changes in accounting policies*

When an enterprise changes the method that it uses to price inter-segment transfers, it is not a change in accounting policy for which comparative segment data is required to be restated (as discussed below) but the nature of the change is required to be disclosed. (IAS 14 (r1997).76)

Two types of changes in accounting policy may effect segment reporting:

(a) a change in an accounting policy adopted for segment reporting; and
(b) a change in accounting policy at the enterprise level.

Changes in accounting policies adopted for segment reporting
Some changes in accounting policies relate specifically to segment reporting, for example, changes in identification of segments and changes in the basis for allocating revenues and expenses to segments. However, such changes will not affect the information reported at the aggregate consolidated or enterprise level. When an enterprise changes an accounting policy adopted for segment reporting and the change has a material effect on segment information, the comparative segment information is required to be restated in line with the new policy, unless it is impracticable to do so, and the following is required to be disclosed:

(a) the nature of the change;
(b) the reasons for the change;
(c) the fact that comparative information has been restated or that is impracticable to do so; and
(d) the financial effect of the change, if it is reasonably determinable.

(IAS 14 (r1997).76)

If an enterprise changes the identification of its segments and it does not restate comparative segment information on the new basis on the grounds of impracticality, then the enterprise is required to report segment data for both the old and the new bases of segmentation in the year in which it changes the identification of its segments. (IAS 14 (r1997).76)

Financial analysts have said repeatedly that the ability to analyse trends in segment operations is critical to their work. When an enterprise changes its segments, trend analysis is adversely affected. That is why IAS 14 (r1997) requires restatement, if practicable. If restatement is deemed impracticable, the dual basis reporting requirement of IAS 14 (r1997).76 is intended as a 'second best' way to facilitate trend analysis.

Changes in accounting policy at the enterprise level
As discussed in **5.17**, changes in accounting policy at the enterprise level are accounted for in accordance with IAS 8 (r1993), *Net Profit or Loss for the Period, Fundamental Errors and Changes in Accounting Policies.* If the benchmark treatment in IAS 8 (r1993) is followed, prior period comparative information is required to be restated, unless it is impracticable to do so. If the allowed alternative treatment is followed, the cumulative adjustment that is included in determining the enterprise's net profit or loss is included in segment result if it is an operating item that can be attributed or reasonably allocated to segments.

16.13 Comparison with UK GAAP

IAS 14 (r1997) and the relevant UK GAAP, contained primarily in SSAP 25, *Segmental Reporting*, have similar objectives; however, SSAP 25 does not take a management approach to segment reporting as IAS 14 (r1997) does. That said, use of the management approach is not precluded as long as it satisfies the objectives and definitions included in SSAP 25. Thus, with careful choices, and use of paragraph 46 of IAS 14 (r1997) which allows disclosure of additional segment information in certain cases and with appropriate disclosure, it may be possible to comply with both IAS 14 (r1997) and SSAP 25. The primary differences between the two standards are set out below.

- IAS 14 (r1997) is required for public enterprises or enterprises in the process of going public whereas SSAP 25 applies to enterprises which are public limited companies or enterprises which have a subsidiary which is a public limited company, banking or insurance companies or groups or enterprises which exceed certain size criteria.
- IAS 14 (r1997) defines business and reportable segments in a similar, but expanded, fashion in comparison with SSAP 25 and the factors to be considered when identifying each type of segment are broadly similar between the two.
- SSAP 25 does not require the management approach to the identification of segments to be taken; however, its use is not precluded as long as it satisfies the objectives and definitions included in SSAP 25. Instead, segments are determined by reference to their differing returns, risks, rates of growth and potential for development.
- SSAP 25 requires disclosure of segment information for segments which are significant, that is account for 10 per cent or more of the total third party revenue, results or net assets of the enterprise. IAS 14 (r1997).35 requires disclosure of segment information for segments which earn the majority of their revenue from external customers *and* comprise 10 per cent or more of total revenue, result or assets.
- SSAP 25 does not identify a primary and secondary reporting format as IAS 14 (r1997) does. Instead, it requires the same disclosures for both business and geographical segments if both types of segments exist, though these disclosures are less extensive than those in the IAS.
- SSAP 25 requires different disclosures for segments from either the primary or secondary reporting format of IAS 14 (r1997). SSAP 25 requires disclosure of segment turnover (distinguished between external and internal); results; and net assets. Not all of these disclosures are required for secondary segments under IAS 14 (r1997), while far more disclosure is required for primary segments. In particular, SSAP 25 does not require disclosure of capital expenditure, depreciation, amortisation and other non-cash expenses. Nor does it require separate disclosure of segment assets and segment liabilities. IAS 14 (r1997) also requires

disclosure of the aggregate share of net profit or loss of associates, joint ventures and other equity method investments when substantially all the operations are within a segment. SSAP 25 only requires this if associated undertakings account for at least 20 per cent of the reporting entity's total result or 20 per cent of its total net assets.

- IAS 14 (r1997) requires disclosure of the basis of pricing intersegment transfers and changes therein. SSAP 25 does not require this.
- SSAP 25 does not have such detailed definitions as IAS 14 (r1997) of those elements required to be disclosed.
- In general, segment assets and segment liabilities determined in accordance with IAS 14 (r1997) would be appropriate in determining segment net assets under UK GAAP. However, given the very detailed definitions of segment assets and segment liabilities in IAS 14 (r1997), the reverse will not always be true.
- Under UK GAAP, FRS 3, *Reporting Financial Performance*, para 53 requires additional segment disclosures relating to material acquisitions, sales or terminations. IAS 14 (r1997) contains no equivalent requirements.
- SSAP 25 allows an exemption from making disclosures when the directors believe disclosure would be seriously prejudicial to the interests of the reporting entity. There is no such exemption in IAS 14 (r1997).

16.14 Comparison with US GAAP

IAS 14 (r1997) and SFAS 131, *Disclosures about Segments of an Enterprise and Related Information*, start with different objectives for segment information. The objective of IAS 14 (r1997) is to provide insight into how the diversity of a company's products and services and its operations in different geographical areas affect its overall risks and returns. The US objective is more general – to provide information about an enterprise's different types of business activities and different economic environments. The different objectives lead to differences between the two standards, the most significant of which are detailed below:

- IASC and FASB start with different objectives for segment information. The IASC's objective is quite specific: information about different types of products and services and information about different geographical areas – to provide insight into how the diversity of products and services and geographical operations affects an enterprise's overall risks and returns. This objective led IAS 14 (r1997) to define segments in terms of products and services and geographical areas. The stated objective in SFAS 131, on the other hand, is to provide information about business activities and economic environments. Neither of those is defined in SFAS 131. Rather, it is left to each enterprise to decide, based entirely on its internal financial reporting system.

- Similar to IAS 14 (r1997), SFAS 131 identifies externally reportable segments by looking to the internally reported segments of an enterprise, but only for the primary basis of segment reporting. SFAS 131 does not identify a secondary reporting format based on management segment reporting but requires enterprises to provide up to three types of additional segment data:
  (i) segmentation of the enterprise into groups of similar products and services;
  (ii) segmentation of the enterprise by geographical areas; and
  (iii) information about major customers (IAS 14 (r1997) does not require disclosure of information about major customers or any other economic dependencies).
- Along similar lines, IAS 14 (r1997) acknowledges that sometimes internally reported segments do not meet the definition of business or geographical segments included in the Standard. Under IAS 14 (r1997), an enterprise is required to look to the next lower level of management information to identify appropriate reportable segments. Under SFAS 131, the disclosures described above compensate for the disclosure of such segment information;
- IAS 14 (r1997) requires separate business segment and geographical segment information. SFAS 131 permits a mixed segmentation (some of each) if that is how it is reported internally;
- IAS 14 (r1997) includes definitions of segment revenue, segment expense and segment result. SFAS 131 does not include a standardised measure of performance for segments. Instead, it looks to segment performance measures used internally.
- IAS 14 (r1997) requires segment data to be prepared using the same accounting policies as the consolidated or enterprise financial statements. SFAS 131 requires use of the accounting policies used for internal reporting purposes, which may involve imputed costs, cash basis measurements, or even policies that are otherwise prohibited under authoritative accounting standards.
- IAS 14 (r1997) requires a reasonable basis for all revenue and expense allocations to segments. SFAS 131 accepts whatever is reported internally.
- IAS 14 (r1997) requires symmetry between segment assets and segment result. SFAS 131 does not explicitly require such symmetry.
- SFAS 131 requires the same information required by IAS 14 (r1997) for the primary reporting format plus interest revenue, interest expense, unusual items and extraordinary items.
- SFAS 131 requires separate disclosure of vertically integrated segments that meet the appropriate definitions and criteria. IAS 14 (r1997) only encourages such disclosure.
- SFAS 131 allows different accounting policies to be used in interim and annual segment data, if done internally. IAS 14 (r1997) does not.
- SFAS 131 suggests that as the number of reportable segments increases

above 10, the enterprise should consider whether a practical limit has been reached. While IAS 14 (r1997) does not mention or impose a limit on the number of segments, its 10 per cent materiality thresholds are likely to lead to a result similar to that under SFAS 131.

16.15 Examples from published financial statements

Note that the excerpts given do not always comply in full with all aspects of IAS and, as such, are not necessarily examples of best practice but merely of current practice.

Example 16.8

Note 3a Segment reporting by business group (excerpt)

The Business Group results have been presented on a management reporting basis. Consequently, internal charges and transfer pricing adjustments have been reflected in the performance of each business. The basis of the reporting reflects the management of the business within the Group. Revenue sharing agreements are used to allocate external customer revenues to a Business Group on a reasonable basis. Transactions between Business Groups are conducted at arms length.

For the year ended 31 December 2000

CHF million	*UBS Switzerland*	*UBS Asset Manage't*	*UBS Warburg*	*Corporate Centre*	*UBS Group*
Income	14,182	1,953	19,779	358	36,272
Credit loss recovery/(expense)[1]	(784)	0	(247)	1,161	130
Total operating income	13,398	1,953	19,532	1,519	36,402
Personnel expenses	4,759	880	11,002	522	17,163
General and administrative expenses	2,394	439	3,501	431	6,765
Depreciation	508	49	731	320	1,608
Amortisation of goodwill and other intangible assets	62	263	298	44	667
Total operating expenses	7,723	1,631	15,532	1,317	26,203
Business Group performance before tax	**5,675**	**322**	**4,000**	**202**	**10,199**
Tax expense					2,320
Net profit before minority interests					**7,879**
Minority interests					(87)
Net profit					**7,792**
Other information as of 31 December 2000[2]					
Total assets	281,780	6,727	870,608	(71,563)	1,087,552
Total liabilities	272,134	5,513	846,451	(81,379)	1,042,719

[1] In order to show the relevant Business Group performance over time, adjusted expected loss figures rather than the net credit expense/recovery are reported for all Business Groups. The statistically derived adjusted expected losses reflect the inherent counterparty and country risks in the respective portfolios. The difference between the statistically derived adjusted expected loss figures and the net IAS credit loss expenses recorded at Group level for financial reporting purposes is reported in the Corporate Centre. The divisional breakdown of the net credit recovery/(expense) for financial reporting purposes of CHF 130 million for the year ended 31 December 2000 is as follows: UBS Switzerland CHF 695 million, UBS Warburg CHF (565) million.
[2] The funding surplus or requirement is reflected in each Business Group and adjusted in Corporate Centre.

Note 3b Segment reporting by geographic location

The geographic analysis of total assets is based on customer domicile whereas operating income and capital investment is based on the location of the office in which the transactions and assets are recorded. Because of the global nature of financial markets the Group's business is managed on an integrated basis worldwide, with a view to profitability by product line. The geographical analysis of operating income, total assets, and capital investment is provided in order to comply with International Accounting Standards, and does not reflect the way the Group is managed. Management believes that analysis by Business Group, as shown in Note 3a to these financial statements, is a more meaningful representation of the way in which the Group is managed.

For the year ended 31 December 2000

	Total operating income		*Total assets*		*Capital investment*	
	CHF million	*Share %*	*CHF million*	*Share %*	*CHF million*	*Share %*
Switzerland	15,836	44	211,851	19	1,135	43
Rest of Europe	10,907	30	305,342	28	311	12
Americas	6,976	19	474,617	44	1,169	44
Asia Pacific	2,626	7	87,831	8	36	1
Africa/Middle East	57	0	7,911	1	8	0
Total	**36,402**	**100**	**1,087,552**	**100**	**2,659**	**100**

Comparatives for the above information in Notes 3a and 3b were also given. These figures have not been reproduced here on grounds of length.

UBS
Switzerland
31 December 2000
International Accounting Standards

Example 16.9

2. Segment information

Nokia is organized on a worldwide basis into three primary business segments: Nokia Networks, Nokia Mobile Phones and Nokia Ventures Organization. As of January 1, 2000, the Nokia Ventures Organization has been segregated into a separate segment as a result of the increased activity in this segment. Nokia's reportable segments are strategic business units that offer different products and services for which monthly financial information is provided to the Board.

Nokia Networks develops, manufactures and supplies cellular network mobile internet and broadband solutions for mobile operators, corporate customers, ASPs and ISPs.

Nokia Mobile Phones develops, manufactures and supplies mobile phones and wireless data products, including a complete range of cellular phones for all major digital and analog standards worldwide.

Nokia Ventures Organization comprises new business areas, the largest of which is Nokia Internet Communications, which offers enterprises and managed ISPs strategic IP-oriented products and solutions.

Common Group Functions consists of common research and general Group functions.

The accounting policies of the segments are the same as those described in Note 1. Nokia accounts for intersegment revenues and transfers as if the revenues or transfers were to third parties, that is, at current market prices. Nokia evaluates the performance of its segments and allocates resources to them based on operating profit.

2000, €m	*Nokia Networks*	*Nokia Mobile Phones*	*Nokia Ventures Organizations*	*Common Group Functions*	*Total reportable segment*	*Eliminations*	*Group*
Income Statement Information							
Net sales to external customers	7,708	21,844	824	–	30,376		30,376
Net sales to other segments	6	43	30	–	79	−79	–
Depreciation and amortisation	354	467	102	86	1,009		1,009
Operating profit	1,358	4,879	−387	−74	5,776		5776
Share of result of associated companies	–	–	–	−16	−16		−16
Balance Sheet Information							
Capital expenditure	304	902	38	336	1,580		1,580
Segment assets (1)	5,076	7,108	709	1,577	14,470	−688	13,782
of which:							
Investments in associated companies	–	–	–	61	61		61
Unallocated assets							5,543
Total assets (2)							19,325
Segment liabilities (3)	1,936	4,602	256	686	7,480	−685	6,795
Unallocated liabilities							1,771
Total liabilities (4)							8,566

(1) Comprises intangible assets, property, plant and equipment, investments, inventories and accounts receivable as well as prepaid expenses and accrued income except those related to interest and taxes.
(2) Total assets excluding prepaid expenses and accrued income related to taxes and deferred tax assets.
(3) Comprises accounts payable, prepaid income, accrued expenses and provisions except those related to interest and taxes.
(4) Total liabilities excluding prepaid income and accrued expenses related to taxes and deferred tax liabilities.

Comparatives for the above information were also given. These have not been reproduced here on grounds of length.

	2000	*1999*
Net sales to external customers by market area	***€m***	*€m*
Finland	**494**	479
USA	**5,312**	3,360
China	**3,065**	2,332
Great Britain	**2,828**	1,855
Germany	**2,579**	1,679
Other	**16,098**	10,067
Total	**30,376**	19,772

	2000	*1999*
Segment assets by location of assets	***€m***	*€m*
Finland	**4,688**	3,144
USA	**2,774**	1,894
China	**2,030**	1,312
Great Britain	**654**	476
Germany	**909**	748
Other	**8,270**	6,276
Total	19,325	13,850

	2000	*1999*
Capital expenditure by market area	***€m***	*€m*
Finland	**587**	487
USA	**279**	313
China	**157**	121
Great Britain	**75**	54
Germany	**133**	124
Other	**349**	259
Total	**1,580**	1,358

Nokia
31 December 2000
International Accounting Standards

CHAPTER 17

Related party disclosures

17.1 Sources

IAS 1 (r1997)	*Presentation of Financial Statements.*
IAS 14 (r1997)	*Segmental Reporting.*
IAS 24	*Related Party Disclosures.*

17.2 Brief summary of the Standard

IAS 24 requires disclosure of related party relationships irrespective of whether there have been transactions between the related parties. If there have been transactions between related parties, the reporting enterprise is required to disclose the nature of the related party relationships as well as the types of transactions and the elements of the transactions necessary for an understanding of the financial statements.

17.3 Development of the Standard

IAS 24 was originally approved in July 1984. The Standard was reformatted in 1994 in order to bring it into line with the presentation adopted for International Accounting Standards from 1991 onwards. No substantive changes were made to the original approved text.

17.4 Scope

IAS 24 deals only with the following related party relationships:

(a) enterprises that directly or indirectly control, or are controlled by, or are under common control with, the reporting enterprise.

This definition not only covers group relationships, but also appears to cover the situation where one individual controls two enterprises. That is to say, two enterprises which are subject to common control from the same source will be deemed to be related parties, even if the controlling party is an individual, rather than an enterprise;

(b) associates (see Chapter **20**);
(c) individuals owning, directly or indirectly, an interest in the voting power of the reporting enterprise which gives them significant influence over the enterprise, and close members of the family of any such individual. Close members of the family of an individual are those that may be expected to influence, or be influenced by, that person in their dealings with the enterprise;
(d) key management personnel (i.e., persons having authority and responsibility for planning, directing and controlling the activities of the reporting enterprise), including directors and officers of companies and close members of their families.

Although not addressed specifically by IAS 24, it appears that transactions under management remuneration contracts and other transactions with key management would come within the scope of IAS 24 and the disclosures required therein. IAS 19 (r2000) paragraph 23 implies that this is the case; and

(e) enterprises in which a substantial interest in the voting power is owned, directly or indirectly, by any individual having significant influence over or occupying a key management position in the reporting enterprise, as described above. This includes enterprises owned by directors or major shareholders of the reporting enterprise, and enterprises that have a member of key management in common with the reporting enterprise. (IAS 24.3)

IAS 24 states that no disclosure of transactions is required:

> (a) 'in consolidated financial statements in respect of intra-group transactions;
> (b) in parent financial statements when they are made available or published with the consolidated financial statements;
> (c) in financial statements of a wholly-owned subsidiary if its parent is incorporated in the same country and provides consolidated financial statements in that country; and
> (d) in financial statements of state-controlled enterprises of transactions with other state-controlled enterprises.'
>
> (IAS 24.4)

17.5 Definitions

IAS 24.5 contains the following definitions of key terms used in the Standard.

Related party:

> 'parties are considered to be related if one party has the ability to control the other party or exercise significant influence over the other party in making financial and operating decisions.'

This definition does not specify whether the relationship should exist at the year end in order for the two parties to be considered related. Consequently, it is unclear whether transactions between parties should be disclosed if they were related parties during the year but have ceased to be related at the year end. Equally, it is unclear how to treat the situation where parties were not related at the point in time when a transaction took place between them, but they are related parties by the year end. It seems likely, however, that parties should be considered related, for the purposes of giving the disclosures required by IAS 24, if they are related at any time during the reporting period.

Related party transaction:

> 'a transfer of resources or obligations between related parties, regardless of whether a price is charged.'

Control:

> 'ownership, directly, or indirectly through subsidiaries, of more than one half of the voting power of the enterprise, or a substantial interest in voting power and the power to direct, by statute or agreement, the financial and operating policies of the management of the enterprise.'

Significant influence:

> 'participation in the financial and operating policy decisions of an enterprise, but not control of those policies. Significant influence may be exercised in several ways, usually by representation on the board of directors but also by, for example, participation in the policy making process, material inter-company transactions, interchange of managerial personnel or dependence on technical information. Significant influence may be gained by share ownership, statute or agreement. With share ownership, significant influence is presumed in accordance with the definition contained in IAS 28 (r2000), *Accounting for Investments in Associates*.'

The definition in IAS 28 presumes significant influence if an investor holds, directly or indirectly through subsidiaries, 20 per cent or more of the voting power of the investee, unless it can be clearly demonstrated that the investor does not have such influence (See Chapter **20**).

In the context of IAS 24, the following are deemed not to be related parties:

- two companies simply because they have a director in common. This exclusion from the definition of related party is in apparent contradiction with the scope of related party relationships set out in paragraphs 3(d) and 3(e) of IAS 24 (see **17.4**). Paragraph 3(e), in particular, includes as a related party 'enterprises that have a member of key management in common with the reporting enterprise', with directors having been defined as part of key management for this purpose. IAS 24 does not fully resolve this apparent contradiction, but points out that it is necessary in this situation to consider the possibility, and to assess the likelihood, that the director would be able to affect the policies of both companies in their dealings with each other;
- providers of finance, trade unions, public utilities, and government departments and agencies, in the course of their dealings with an enterprise by virtue only of those dealings (although they may circumscribe the freedom of action of an enterprise or participate in its decision-making process);
- a single customer, supplier, franchisor, distributor, or general agent with whom an enterprise transacts a significant volume of business, merely by virtue of the resulting economic dependence.

(IAS 24.6)

17.6 The related party issue

IAS 24 includes discussion of the rationale for disclosure of related party relationships and transactions. The Standard notes that related party relationships are a normal feature of business and commerce. It is common, for example, for enterprises to operate separate parts of their activities through subsidiaries or associates. Again, many enterprises acquire interests in other enterprises as investments or for commercial reasons, which means that the investing enterprise can control or exercise significant influence over the investee.

Such relationships can have an effect on the operating results and financial position of the reporting enterprise. They may lead to transactions being undertaken between the related parties which would not be undertaken between unrelated parties; or to transactions being effected at different amounts from those which would prevail between unrelated parties.

Even if there are no transactions between the related parties, it is still possible for the operating results and financial position of an enterprise to be affected by the relationship. For example, a newly acquired subsidiary company may be required by its parent to terminate or change an existing trading relationship to benefit another group company.

While IAS 24 considers at some length the issue of pricing of transactions between related parties, it does not require that one particular basis or method be adopted. It does, however, require disclosure of the pricing policy irrespective of the method used, i.e., even when normal trading terms are applied. IAS 14 (r1997).75 also requires the disclosure of the basis of pricing inter-segment transfers and any change in that basis.

17.7 Disclosure

IAS 24 requires disclosure of controlling party relationships, irrespective of whether there have been transactions between the related parties. (IAS 24.20) As discussed in **17.6**, even if there are no transactions between the related parties, it is still possible for the operating results and financial position of an enterprise to be affected by a controlling party relationship. For example, the management of an enterprise may be able to influence its trading relationships with other group enterprises or with third parties. For this reason, in order for the reader of the financial statements to form a view about the effects of such a relationship on a reporting enterprise, it is appropriate to disclose the relationship where control exists. In addition, IAS 27, *Consolidated Financial Statements and Accounting for Investments in Subsidiaries,* and IAS 28 (r2000), *Accounting for Investments in Associates,* require disclosure of a list of significant subsidiaries and associates, respectively.

When there have been transactions between related parties, the reporting enterprise is required to disclose:

- the nature of the related party relationships;
- the types of transactions; and
- the elements of the transactions necessary for an understanding of the financial statements.

(IAS 24.22)

The guidance in IAS 24 suggests that elements of transactions necessary for an understanding of the financial statements normally include the following items:

'• an indication of the volume of transactions, either as an amount or as an appropriate proportion;
• amounts or appropriate proportions of outstanding items; and
• pricing policies.'

(IAS 24.23)

It may be noted that this list of elements is not exhaustive. Disclosure of transactions may therefore be tailored to fit individual circumstances. As noted above, IAS 14 (r1997) requires the disclosure of the basis of pricing of inter-segment transfers as well as any change in that basis.

In addition, IAS 1 (r1997), *Presentation of Financial Statements*, requires separate disclosure of amounts payable to and receivable from the parent enterprise, fellow subsidiaries and associates and other related parties.

IAS 24 provides a list of examples of situations where related party transactions may lead to disclosures by a reporting enterprise in the period which they affect, as follows:

'• purchases or sales of goods (finished or unfinished);
- purchases or sales of property and other assets;
- rendering or receiving of services;
- agency arrangements;
- leasing arrangements;
- transfer of research and development;
- licence agreements;
- finance (including loans and equity contributions in cash or in kind);
- guarantees and collateral; and
- management contracts.'

(IAS 24.19)

Again, the above list is not exhaustive. It is worth noting that it includes situations where no transactions involving the transfer of resources occur, such as the giving of a guarantee by one enterprise on behalf of another enterprise in the same group.

IAS 24 permits aggregation of similar types of related party transactions, stating 'Items of a similar nature may be disclosed in aggregate except when separate disclosure is necessary for an understanding of the effects of related party transactions on the financial statements of the reporting enterprise.'(IAS 24.24)

The Standard is not specific on the circumstances which might lead to separate disclosure of items of a similar nature, but if a transaction is individually significant it may well be worthy of separate disclosure. The principal objective of the Standard on this matter is to avoid excessive disclosure where the related party transactions comprise many items of a routine nature, such as in normal trading relationships between group enterprises.

Finally, IAS 24 states that disclosure of transactions between members of a group is unnecessary in consolidated financial statements, because these present information about the group as a single reporting enterprise. However, transactions with associated enterprises accounted for under the equity method are not fully eliminated and therefore require separate disclosure as related party transactions. (IAS 24.25)

Example 17.1

Enterprise A is a 75 per cent owned subsidiary of Enterprise B, which is itself a wholly-owned subsidiary of Enterprise C. During the financial year Enterprise A made sales in the ordinary course of business totalling £1,200,000 to Enterprise B, from which an amount receivable of £80,000 was outstanding at the year end. Enterprise A also sold a property at its market value of £500,000 to Enterprise C. Director X of Enterprise A purchased a car from the enterprise at its book value of £10,000, while Director Y received a temporary loan of £50,000 at a commercial rate of interest towards the purchase of a house which was fully repaid during the year. The minority shareholder M of Enterprise A has made a loan of £150,000 to the enterprise on which interest is payable at the rate of 10 per cent per annum. The relevant disclosure notes in the accounts of Enterprise A might read as follows:

Controlling parties

The immediate parent and controlling party is Enterprise B, and the ultimate parent and controlling party is Enterprise C. (It is optional under IAS 24 to provide further information about the immediate and ultimate controlling parties, such as their countries of operation and incorporation. Additional information is, however, required by UK companies legislation and accounting standards.)

Related party transactions

During the financial year, the enterprise made sales totalling £1,200,000 to Enterprise B. These sales were made on an arm's-length basis in the ordinary course of trading operations. At the year end there was a balance outstanding of £80,000 receivable from Enterprise B in respect of sales.

The enterprise sold a property to Enterprise C at its market value of £500,000.

Director X purchased a motor vehicle from the enterprise at its book value of £10,000.

During the year the enterprise made a temporary loan of £50,000 to Director Y for the purpose of house purchase. Interest was charged on the loan at a commercial rate, and amounted to £3,000. The loan was fully repaid at the year end. The minority shareholder M has made a loan of £150,000 to the enterprise. Interest of £15,000 for the year, representing a rate of 10 per cent per annum, was charged on this loan.

17.8 Comparison with UK GAAP

The UK standard FRS 8 *Related Party Disclosures* was issued in October 1995. Except for the exemptions allowed in respect of subsidiary enterprises and certain other matters detailed below, the disclosure requirements of FRS 8 are very similar to those of IAS 24.

The main differences between FRS 8 and IAS 24 may be summarised as follows:

- If the parties are related *at any time* during the financial period, then they are treated by FRS 8 as related parties for the whole of that period. (FRS 8.2.5(a)) For example, if a parent company acquires a subsidiary part way through a financial period, transactions with that subsidiary during that period but prior to acquisition are treated as related party transactions in the same way as transactions which take place after acquisition. IAS 24 is silent on this matter.
- Under FRS 8, related parties are presumed to include persons acting in concert in such a way as to be able to exercise control or influence over the reporting entity, unless it can be shown that neither party has influenced the financial and operating policies of the other in such a way as to inhibit the pursuit of separate interests. IAS 24 does not mention persons acting in concert.
- FRS 8 does not require disclosure in the financial statements of a subsidiary, 90 per cent or more of whose voting rights are controlled within the group, of transactions with entities that are part of the group or investees of the group qualifying as related parties, provided that the consolidated financial statements in which that subsidiary is included are publicly available. (FRS 8.3(c)) There is no restriction as to the country in which the parent undertaking is incorporated or in which the consolidated financial statements are made available. Reporting entities taking advantage of this exemption are required to state that fact. IAS 24, on the other hand, grants the same exemption only to a wholly owned subsidiary whose parent is incorporated in the same country and provides consolidated financial statements in the same country as the subsidiary. (IAS 24.4(c))
- FRS 8 grants an exemption from the requirement to disclose related party transactions in respect of pension contributions paid to a pension fund (though other transactions with a pension fund are not exempt). (FRS 8.3(d)) The scope exclusions included in IAS 24 might exclude some pension contributions, depending on the nature of the pension plan to which the reporting enterprise is contributing and whether or not the reporting enterprise controls the plan. However, IAS 19 (r2000), *Employee Benefits*, requires disclosure of pension expense or income during a period.
- FRS 8 does not require disclosure of emoluments for services as an employee of the reporting entity. However, entities still need to comply with the specific disclosure requirements of the UK Companies Act 1985 in respect of UK company directors. The exemption in FRS 8 does, however, extend to the emoluments of directors of entities in other jurisdictions where FRS 8 may be applied, and which do not have the same statutory disclosure requirements in respect of directors' emoluments. As

discussed in the Scope section, it would appear that transactions with key management *are* within the scope of IAS 24 and consequently that the remuneration of directors and key management is required to be disclosed. Although the IAS does not state this *specifically*, it points out that local laws or stock exchange regulations will often require these disclosures to be made.

- Under IAS 24 a state-controlled enterprise is exempt from the requirement to disclose related party transactions with other state-controlled enterprises. FRS 8 has no equivalent exemption.
- FRS 8.16 gives an exemption from disclosure where compliance with the FRS would breach a reporting entity's duty of confidentiality arising by operation of law. Banks are given as an example, since they have a duty of confidentiality in respect of their customers' affairs. There is no such exemption in IAS 24.
- FRS 8 stipulates that when the reporting entity is controlled by another party, there should be disclosure of the related party relationship and the name of that party and, if different, that of the ultimate controlling party. If the controlling party or ultimate controlling party is not known, that fact should be disclosed. (FRS 8.5) IAS 24 requires instead the disclosure of 'related party relationships where control exists' (IAS 24.20), which appears to cover not only the controlling party of the reporting entity, but also subsidiaries and other enterprises over which the reporting entity has control. IAS 24 contains no requirement to disclose the fact that a controlling party is not known in those instances where this applies.
- FRS 8 sets out specific disclosures in respect of material transactions with a related party, including:

  (a) the names of the transacting related parties;
  (b) a description of the relationship between the parties;
  (c) a description of the transactions;
  (d) the amounts involved;
  (e) any other elements of the transaction necessary for an understanding of the financial statements;
  (f) the amounts due to or from related parties at the balance sheet date and provisions for doubtful debts due from such parties at that date; and
  (g) amounts written off in the period in respect of debts due to or from related parties.

  (FRS 8.6)

IAS 24 is significantly less prescriptive in its disclosure requirements for transactions, stating that 'the reporting enterprise should disclose the nature of the related party relationships as well as the types of transactions and the elements of the transactions necessary for an understanding of the financial statements'. (IAS 24.22) IAS 24 does list the elements of transactions that would normally be included (see **17.7**), but the elements are indicative rather than prescriptive, and the list is not as extensive as that in FRS 8. It can be seen from this list that the IAS permits disclosure of the volume of transactions and outstanding items to be in terms of proportions, rather than amounts, as required by FRS 8, and, unlike FRS 8, it does not require disclosure of write-offs. However, as mentioned in **17.7** above, IAS 24 is tougher in one area: it does require the disclosure of pricing policies for related party transactions, while FRS 8 only requires this where a major asset has been transferred between related parties at an amount materially different from that obtainable on normal commercial terms.

- In determining whether an item is sufficiently material to be disclosed, FRS 8.20 requires preparers of accounts to consider not only whether the transaction is material to the reporting entity, but also its significance to the *other* related party, when that party falls into certain categories (broadly, a director or other individual accountable for the stewardship of the reporting entity). There is no guidance in IAS 24 in this area.

17.9 Comparison with US GAAP

There are few significant differences between IAS 24 and its US counterpart, SFAS 57, *Related Party Disclosures.* The more important points of difference between IAS 24 and SFAS 57 are:

- SFAS 57 does not include the exemption granted by IAS 24 to a wholly-owned subsidiary from disclosure of transactions if its parent provides consolidated financial statements. Such an exemption is only permitted under SFAS 57 if the financial statements of the subsidiary are presented in the same financial report as the financial statements of the parent which gives the appropriate disclosures.
- IAS 24 sets out a definitive list of related party relationships, and types of relationships not contained within that list are outside the scope of the Standard. SFAS 57 does not contain a definitive list. Instead, SFAS 57 sets out examples of transactions involving related parties. Although there is much overlap of the related party relationships set out in IAS 24 with the examples in SFAS 57, there are some differences. For instance, SFAS 57 makes specific mention of trusts for the benefit of employees, such as pension and profit-sharing trusts, as examples of related party relationships, whereas these come within the scope of IAS 24 only if one or more of the related party relationships set out in paragraph 3 of the Standard apply.
- Like IAS 24, the US standard includes a list of types of transaction for which disclosure is required. While the types of transaction listed by both standards are similar, SFAS 57 specifically excludes from disclosure compensation payments, expense allowances, and other similar items in the ordinary course of business. (SFAS 57.2)

17.10 Examples from published financial statements

Note that the excerpts given do not always comply in full with all aspects of IAS and, as such, are not necessarily examples of best practice but merely of current practice.

Example 17.2

36 Related parties

Related parties include the Board of Directors, the Group Executive Board, the Group Managing Board, close family members and enterprises which are controlled by these individuals as well as certain persons performing similar functions.

Total remuneration of related parties recognized in the income statement amounted to CHF 272.3 million in 2000 and CHF 193.1 million in 1999, including accrued pension benefits of approximately CHF 30.0 million in 2000 and CHF 21.2 million in 1999.

The number of long-term sock options outstanding from equity plans was 1,564,486 at 31 December 2000 and 274,616 at 31 December 1999. This scheme is further explained in Note 35 Equity Participation Plans.

The external members of the Board of Directors do not have employment or service contracts with UBS, and thus are not entitled to benefits upon termination of their service on the Board of Directors. The full-time Chairman and Vice-Chairman have top-management employment contracts and receive pension benefits upon retirement.

The total amounts of shares and warrants held by members of the Board of Directors, Group Executive Board and Group Managing Board were 2,527,728 and 69,504,577 as of 31 December 2000 and 2,456,092 and 11,424,514 as of 31 December 1999.

Total loans and advances receivable (mortgages only) from related parties were as follows:

CHF million	*2000*	*1999*
Mortgages at the beginning of the year	**28**	27
Additions	**9**	6
Reductions	**(1)**	(5)
Mortgages at the end of the year	**36**	28

Members of the Board of Directors, Group Executive Board and Group Managing Board are granted mortgages at the same terms and conditions as other employees. Terms and conditions are based on third party conditions excluding credit margin.

Loans and advances to significant associated companies were as follows:

CHF million	*2000*	*1999*
Loans and advances at the beginning of the year	**62**	165
Additions	**0**	42
Reductions	**(62)**	(145)
Loans and advances at the end of the year	**0**	62

Note 38 provides a list of significant associates.

UBS Group

Switzerland

International Accounting Standards

31 December 2000

Example 17.3

27 Related party transactions

The Group has entered into a variety of transactions with the subsidiary undertakings of Jardine Matheson Holdings Limited ('Jardine Matheson group members'). The most significant of these transactions are as follows:

Management fee

The management fee payable by the Group under an agreement entered into in 1995 with Jardine Matheson Limited was US$1.8 million (1999: US$1.3 million), being 0.5% per annum of the Group's net profit in consideration for management consultancy services provided by Jardine Matheson Limited, a wholly-owned subsidiary of Jardine Matheson Holdings Limited.

Banking services

Jardine Matheson group members provided banking services to the Group. The Group's net deposits with Matheson Bank Limited at 31st December 2000 amounted to US$47.2 million (1999: US$48.1 million).

Property and other services

The Group rented properties to Jardine Matheson group members. Gross rents on such properties in 2000 amounted to US$5.5 million (1999: US$6.5 million).

Jardine Matheson group members provided property maintenance and other services to the Group in 2000 in aggregate amounting to US$21.4 million (1999: US$21.5 million).

Disposal of interest in an associate

In December 2000, Hongkong Land International Holdings Limited, a wholly-owned subsidiary of the Company, disposed of its 45% interest in Connaught Investors Limited to Jardine Strategic Holdings Limited, the parent undertaking of the Company, for a consideration of US$207.9 million. The consideration was based on the value of the assets held by Connaught Investors Limited and was confirmed as fair and reasonable by PricewaterhouseCoopers acting as an independent adviser.

Hongkong Land Holdings Limited
Hong Kong
International Accounting Standards
31 December 2000

CHAPTER 18

Consolidated financial statements: business combinations

18.1 Sources

IAS 12 (r2000)	*Accounting for Income Taxes.*
IAS 22 (r1998)	*Business Combinations.*
IAS 27	*Consolidated Financial Statements and Accounting for Investments in Subsidiaries.*
IAS 36	*Impairment of Assets.*
IAS 37	*Provisions, Contingent Liabilities and Contingent Assets.*
IAS 38	*Intangible Assets.*
SIC-9	*Business Combinations – Classification either as Acquisitions or Unitings of Interests.*
SIC-18	*Consistency – Alternative Methods.*
SIC-22	*Business Combinations – Subsequent Adjustment of Fair Values and Goodwill Initially Reported.*

18.2 Brief summary of the requirements

IAS 22 (r1998) differentiates between a business combination which is an acquisition and one which is a uniting of interests. An acquisition occurs when one enterprise obtains control over the net assets and operations of another enterprise. A uniting of interests occurs when shareholders of the combining enterprises combine control over their net assets and operations to achieve a continuing mutual sharing in the risks and benefits attaching to the combined entity. Given the narrow definition and description of a uniting of interests, they are expected to be extremely rare. The standard does not deal with transactions among enterprises under common control and thus does not encompass group reorganisations. (IAS 22 (r1998).7a)

Acquisitions are accounted for by the purchase method. Under the purchase method, identifiable assets and liabilities acquired are measured at their fair values. The difference between the cost of the acquisition and the fair values of the identifiable assets and liabilities acquired is either goodwill or negative goodwill. Both amounts are shown in the asset section of the balance sheet.

Uniting of interests are accounted for by the pooling of interests method. Under the pooling method, the financial statements of the combining enterprises are aggregated with very few adjustments. The net assets united are aggregated at their carrying amounts rather than fair value. Thus, no goodwill or negative goodwill results from a uniting of interests. Prior period financial statements are restated as if the combination had always been in place.

18.3 Development of the requirements

Originally issued in November 1983, IAS 22 has been amended several times, the most recent of these being in October 1998.

IAS 22 was originally revised in 1993 as part of the Improvements project when the following changes were made:

(a) the use of the purchase method in accounting for acquisitions and the pooling of interests method in accounting for uniting of interests were required;
(b) the option to eliminate goodwill or negative goodwill arising on an acquisition against equity was removed;
(c) the previously required treatment for minority interests arising on a business combination of measurement at its proportion of the fair value of the net assets at the date of acquisition was designated as an allowed alternative and a new benchmark treatment requiring measurement at the minority's proportion of the pre-acquisition carrying amounts was added; and
(d) a five year limit (extended to 20 years where justified) on the amortisation period for goodwill was introduced.

Issued in October 1996, IAS 12 (r1996) made two small changes to IAS 22. The first prohibits the use of discounting of deferred tax assets and liabilities resulting from a business combination and the second conforms with the guidance and terms used in IAS 22 with that of IAS 12 (r1996).

IAS 22 was then revised again in October 1998 in order to become more consistent with IAS 36, 37 and 38. IAS 22 (r1998) became operative for accounting periods beginning on or after 1 July 1999. The limited changes made to the Standard were as follows:

(a) the 20 year ceiling on the amortisation period of goodwill became a rebuttable presumption, rather than an absolute limit. As a consequence, if an enterprise amortises goodwill over more than 20 years from initial recognition, the enterprise discloses the evidence that rebuts the presumption and tests goodwill for impairment at least annually in accordance with IAS 36 (see **10.5** for a discussion of goodwill);

(b) goodwill has to be tested for impairment, in accordance with IAS 36;

(c) the 'benchmark' treatment of negative goodwill was removed. This means that any excess of the acquirer's interest in the fair values of the identifiable assets and liabilities acquired over the cost of acquisition must be disclosed, as negative goodwill, on the balance sheet as a deduction from assets, and can no longer be used to reduce the fair values of identifiable assets acquired. Guidance was added on how and when to recognise the balance in the income statement;

(d) in order to be consistent with IAS 37, the identifiable liabilities which are recognised as part of acquisition accounting were, apart from one exception, limited to those of the acquiree that existed at the date of acquisition. This is to prohibit recognition, as part of the fair value exercise, of provisions for future operating losses and for reorganisation and integration costs expected to be incurred as a result of the acquisition; and

(e) the recognition, in accordance with IAS 38, of intangible assets existing at the acquisition date at their fair values which are to be determined by an active market, or an arm's length price (if no active market exists). These requirements greatly restrict the recognition of intangible assets on acquisition over those previously allowed.

In July 1998, the SIC issued SIC-9 which stated that in almost all cases, an acquirer could be identified, and so acquisition accounting should be used. It did not give any additional guidance on the size criteria which must be met in order to qualify as a unitings of interests.

In January 2000 SIC published SIC-18 which states that, if one or more accounting policies are available an enterprise should choose and apply consistently one of those policies, unless the IAS or SIC specifically requires or permits categorisation of items for which different policies may be appropriate.

SIC-22, effective for periods ending on or after 15 July 2000, states that any fair value adjustments made subsequent to the date of acquisition, as a result of the requirements of IAS 22 (r1998), should be calculated as if the newly assigned values had been used from the date of acquisition.

In late December 1998, the IASC published a Discussion Paper on the convergence of methods of accounting for business combinations. The paper contained the text of a Position Paper prepared by the G4+1 Group of standard setters and addressed the issue of whether a single method of accounting for business combinations was preferable to the current two methods used. The preferred method in the Discussion Paper is acquisition accounting, therefore, removing the option to use the uniting of interests method when no acquirer can be identified. The IASB is currently considering the responses to the paper and a project on business combinations is part of the new IASB agenda (see Chapter **2**).

18.4 Definition of a business combination

> 'A business combination is the bringing together of separate enterprises into one economic entity as a result of one enterprise uniting with or obtaining control over the net assets and operations of another enterprise.'
>
> (IAS 22 (r1998).8)

A business combination may result in a parent-subsidiary relationship in which the acquirer is the parent and the acquiree is the subsidiary. In such cases, the acquirer applies IAS 22 (r1998) in its consolidated financial statements. If the enterprise prepares separate financial statements, it includes its interest in the acquiree as an investment in a subsidiary in accordance with IAS 27 (See Chapter **19**). (IAS 22 (r1998).3)

In some cases, a business combination may be achieved by the purchase of the net assets, including any goodwill, of another enterprise rather than the purchase of shares in the other enterprise. Such a business combination does not result in a parent-subsidiary relationship. In such cases, the acquirer applies IAS 22 (r1998) in its separate financial statements and consequently, if applicable, in its consolidated financial statements. (IAS 22 (r1998).4) See **10.5.4** for a discussion of the distinction between a purchase of a business and a purchase of assets.

IAS 22 (r1998) does not deal with business combinations arising between enterprises under common control. Neither does it deal with interests in joint ventures (See Chapter **21**). (IAS 22 (r1998).7) The SIC had been considering establishing guidance to deal with such transactions. This project has been removed from the SIC agenda, and will probably be addressed in the IASB projects on Business Combinations.

18.5 Distinction between an acquisition and a uniting of interests

All business combinations under IAS 22 (r1998) are either an 'acquisition' or a 'uniting of interests' (SIC 9.6).

IAS 22 (r1998).8 defines each as follows:

> 'An acquisition is a business combination in which one of the enterprises, the acquirer, obtains control over the net assets and operations of another enterprise, the acquiree, in exchange for the transfer of assets, incurrence of a liability or issue of equity.'
>
> 'A uniting of interests is a business combination in which the shareholders of the combining enterprises combine control over the whole, or effectively the whole, of their net assets and operations to achieve a continuing mutual sharing in the risks and benefits attaching to the combined entity such that neither party can be identified as the acquirer.'

The Framework identifies the need to account for the substance of a transaction and not merely its legal form. In line with the Framework, IAS 22 (r1998) requires the substance of a business combination to be reflected in its accounting treatment rather than its legal form. Therefore, despite the fact that a transaction may be legally classified as a merger, under IAS 22 (r1998), such a transaction may be accounted for as an acquisition rather than a uniting of interests. Therefore, when an enterprise enters into a business combination, it must consider the substance of the exchange agreement and the rights of each of the combining enterprises *after* the transaction to determine the appropriate accounting treatment.

It is important to consider that the characteristics of acquisitions and uniting of interests discussed in IAS 22 (r1998) (and set out in **18.5.1** and **18.5.2**) are presented as indicators which may lead to a particular classification. SIC-9.5 states 'the classification of a business combination should be based on an overall evaluation of all relevant facts and circumstances of the particular transaction. The guidance given in IAS 22 (r1998) provides examples of important factors to be considered, not a comprehensive set of conditions to be met. Single characteristics of a combined enterprise such as voting power or relative fair values of the combining enterprises should not be evaluated in isolation in order to determine how a business combination should be accounted for.' Additionally, IAS 22 (r1998) does not set arbitrary numerical criteria. Rather, it presents the characteristics as items which will generally be indicative of one treatment to guide preparers in accounting for the substance of transactions over their legal form. A discussion of the characteristics of an acquisition and a uniting of interests is set out below.

18.5.1 Acquisitions

The critical feature in differentiating between an acquisition and a uniting of interests is the existence of control by one of the combining enterprises, the acquirer, over the other combining enterprise, the acquiree. IAS 22 (r1998) refers to this characteristic as the ability to identify an acquirer. When such control exists, which in almost all circumstances it will, an acquirer can be identified, and the business combination is accounted for as an acquisition. Control is defined as 'the power to govern the financial and operating policies of an enterprise so as to obtain benefits from its activities'. (IAS 22 (r1998).8)

As a general rule, when one of the combining enterprises obtains more than 50 per cent of the voting rights of the other enterprise, it is presumed that this enterprise is the controlling enterprise, the acquirer, and the business combination is accounted for as an acquisition.

However, in exceptional circumstances, an enterprise may be able to demonstrate clearly that control has not passed when more than 50 per cent of the voting rights are acquired and the transaction may qualify as a uniting of interests. Conversely, when less than 50 per cent of one of the combining enterprises is acquired, in substance, control may still be obtained. Control exists even when less than 50 per cent of the voting rights are acquired when there is:

> '(a) power over more than one half of the voting rights of the other enterprise by virtue of an agreement with other investors;
> (b) power to govern the financial and operating policies of the other enterprise under a statute or an agreement;
> (c) power to appoint or remove the majority of the members of the board of directors or equivalent governing body of the other enterprise; or
> (d) power to cast the majority of votes at meetings of the board of directors or equivalent governing body of the other enterprise.'
>
> (IAS 22 (r1998).11 and IAS 27.12)

Additional factors which generally indicate that control has been acquired by one of the combining enterprises and thus the business combination is an acquisition include:

> '(a) the fair value of one enterprise is significantly greater than that of the other combining enterprise. In such cases, the larger enterprise is the acquirer;
> (b) the business combination is effected through an exchange of voting common shares for cash. In such cases, the enterprise giving up cash is the acquirer; or
> (c) the business combination results in the management of one enterprise being able to dominate the selection of the management team of the resulting combined enterprise. In such cases, the dominant enterprise is the acquirer.'
>
> (IAS 22 (r1998).11)

There has been much debate over the meaning of criterion (a). In response to the continuing debate over the interpretation of this criteria, the SIC issued SIC-9. However, the SIC refrained from adding numerical guidelines, and instead, clarified that in almost all cases an acquirer can be identified, and therefore acquisition accounting will be required. It stresses that all relevant facts and circumstances must be considered and that one criterion, such as relative fair values, should not be considered in isolation.

18.5.2 Uniting of interests

In exceptional circumstances, one of the combining enterprises may not obtain control over the other. Instead of one of the enterprises emerging as the acquirer, the enterprises may 'join in a substantially equal arrangement to share control over the whole, or effectively the whole, of their net assets and operations. In addition, the managements of the combining enterprises participate in the management of the combined entity. As a result, the shareholders of the combining enterprises share mutually in the risks and benefits of the combined entity.' (IAS 22 (r1998).13) In such circumstances, the combination is accounted for as a uniting of interests.

An enterprise should classify a business combination as an acquisition, unless *all* of the following three characteristics are present:

> '(a) the substantial majority, if not all, of the voting common shares of the combining enterprises are exchanged or pooled;
> (b) the fair value of one enterprise is not significantly different from that of the other enterprise; and
> (c) the shareholders of each enterprise maintain substantially the same voting rights and interests in the combined entity, relative to each other, after the combination as before.'
>
> (IAS 22 (r1998).15)

Even if all of the three characteristics are present, an enterprise should classify a business combination as a uniting of interests only if the enterprise can demonstrate that an acquirer cannot be identified. (SIC-9.6)

As mentioned above, it is very rare for two combining enterprises to meet these criteria. Specifically,

> 'The mutual sharing of the risks and benefits of the combined entity diminishes and the likelihood that an acquirer can be identified increases when:
> (a) the relative equality in fair values of the combining enterprises is reduced and the percentage of voting common shares exchanged decreases;
> (b) financial arrangements provide a relative advantage to one group of shareholders over the other shareholders. Such arrangements may take effect either prior to or after the business combination; and
> (c) one party's share of the equity in the combined entity depends on how the business which it previously controlled performs subsequent to the business combination.'
>
> (IAS 22 (r1998).16)

Some enterprises may try to avoid accounting for a business combination as an acquisition by structuring a transaction in such a way that it appears, in form, to be a uniting of interests. However, it is important that all the terms surrounding each business combination be considered individually. For example, with respect to (b), arrangements made by either combining enterprise immediately prior to the transaction with the purpose of making a transaction appear to be a uniting of interests will need to be considered when looking at the substance of the transaction. In addition, the existence of contingency clauses as described in (c) usually indicates that the risks and benefits will not be shared equally after the combination and thus the transaction is not a uniting of interests. Furthermore, a combination which may appear to meet the criteria for a uniting of interests will not, if the terms of the exchange agreement contain a significant reduction in the rights attaching to the shares of one of the combining enterprises which would weaken the influence of that party. (IAS 22 (r1998).14)

18.5.3 Comparison with UK GAAP

Under UK GAAP, the terms merger and merger accounting are similar to the terms uniting of interests and the pooling of interests method.

The Companies Act criteria to qualify for merger accounting in the UK are much more prescriptive than the broad criteria found in IAS 22 (r1998). Under UK GAAP, the Companies Act (Schedule 4A:10) requires that merger accounting may be used only if all the following conditions are met:

- (i) at least 90 per cent of the nominal value of the relevant shares in the undertaking acquired is held by or on behalf of the parent and its subsidiaries;
- (ii) the proportion referred to in (i) above was attained pursuant to an arrangement providing for the issue of equity shares by the parent or its subsidiaries;
- (iii) the fair value of any consideration other than the issue of equity shares given pursuant to the arrangement by the parent and its subsidiaries did not exceed 10 per cent of the nominal value of the equity shares issued; and
- (iv) the merger method adopted accords with generally accepted accounting principles or practice.

Criterion (iv) encompasses the five criteria included in FRS 6 *Acquisitions and Mergers*, which must also be met in order to merger account. The five criteria relate to:

- the role of the parties and whether or not an acquirer can be identified. Consistent with IAS 22 (r1998), if an acquirer can be identified, the transaction as an acquisition;
- the dominance of management selection. Consistent with IAS 22 (r1998), if one party dominates the selection of management of the combined entity, the transaction is accounted for as an acquisition;
- the relative size of the parties. Consistent with IAS 22 (r1998), if one

party dominates by virtue of relative size, the transaction is accounted for as an acquisition. Under UK GAAP, this is interpreted as one party being more than 50 per cent larger than each of the other parties to the combination, judged by reference to the ownership interests. IAS 22 (r1998) does not mention specific percentages;

- the size of non-equity consideration. Under FRS 6, the amount of cash or other non-equity consideration exchanged should be immaterial to the total transaction. While IAS 22 (r1998) does not specifically address the size of non-equity consideration, it does note that in order to achieve a mutual sharing of the risks and benefits, the substantial majority, if not all, of the voting common shares of the combining enterprises are exchanged or pooled and that when one enterprise purchases common shares for cash, it is usually an indication that the enterprise giving up cash is the acquirer; and
- how the profits of the combined entity are shared. The criterion requires that merger accounting may be used for a combination only when no equity shareholders of any of the combining entities retain any material interest in the future performance of only part of the combined entity. (FRS 6.11) IAS 22 (r1998).16 contains similar guidance (see **18.5.2**). The FRS 6 criterion would not be met if a material minority in one of the parties did not accept the terms of the combination offer. This aspect is not specifically mentioned in IAS 22 (r1998).

Thus, the objectives of FRS 6 and of IAS 22 (r1998) are similar in that mergers or uniting of interests will only occur when there is a true merger and acquisition accounting would be inappropriate. However, due to the complexity of individual transactions, each case will need to be examined separately to determine whether or not it meets the criteria under UK GAAP and/or under IAS 22 (r1998).

The ASB issued the G4+1 discussion paper in December 1998 which supported adopting only one method (the acquisition method) of accounting for business combinations. The majority of the respondents to the discussion paper opposed the proposal to ban merger accounting. However, the ASB shares the concerns of the G4+1 about the application of merger accounting in cases where it is not appropriate. It is therefore examining FRS 6 to see whether changes are required and monitoring international developments. Any movements on this issue by the ASB will most likely mirror the developments at the IASB.

18.5.4 Comparison with US GAAP

Under US GAAP, accounting for business combinations is principally set out in APB 16 *Business Combinations.* However, numerous additional interpretative pronouncements and EITFs have been issued to clarify specific issues within APB 16. Under US GAAP, the term pooling of interests is similar to the term uniting of interests.

The FASB recently finalised two Statements (Statement 141, *Business Combinations,* and Statement 142, *Goodwill and Other Intangible Assets*). The new statement on business combinations, which is effective for any business combinations completed after 30 June 2001, eliminates the pooling method of accounting for business combinations. Transactions initiated after 30 June 2001 must use the purchase method of accounting for business combinations. The following definition of 'initiated' from Paragraph 46 of APB 16 *Business Combinations* should be used in determining the effective date of this statement:

> 'A plan of combination is initiated on the earlier of (1) the date that the major terms of a plan, including the ratio of exchange of stock, are announced publicly or otherwise formally made known to the stockholders of any one of the combining companies or (2) the date that stockholders of a combining company are notified in writing of an exchange offer.'

The other provisions of the business combinations statement (including the recognition of identifiable intangible assets separately from goodwill) are to be effective for any business combination accounted for by the purchase method completed after 30 June 2001 (that is, if the acquisition date was on or after 1 July 2001).

18.6 Accounting for acquisitions

A business combination which is an acquisition is accounted for by the purchase method. Under the purchase method, the identifiable assets and liabilities acquired are measured at their fair values. The difference between the cost of the acquisition and the fair values of the identifiable assets and liabilities acquired is either goodwill or negative goodwill.

18.6.1 Recognition

> 'As from the date of the acquisition, an acquirer should:
>
> (a) incorporate into the income statement the results of operations of the acquiree; and
>
> (b) recognise in the balance sheet the assets and liabilities of the acquiree and any goodwill or negative goodwill arising on the acquisition.'
>
> (IAS 22 (r1998).19)

Date of acquisition

'The date of acquisition is the date on which control of the net assets and operations of the acquiree is *effectively* transferred to the acquirer and the date when application of the purchase method commences.' (IAS 22 (r1998).20) Therefore, the substance of each agreement needs to be considered in determining when control of the net assets and operations has passed, since this date does not necessarily coincide with the date that a transaction closes or is finalised at law. In some countries, it may take several months after the exchange of purchase consideration for a transaction to be finalised at law. However, in many cases, the acquirer will assume control when purchase consideration is paid. In such cases, the date of acquisition is the date the acquirer assumes control.

Results of operations of the acquiree

As discussed in **18.6.4**, under the purchase method, the net assets acquired are measured at fair value. Thus, the profits and losses earned prior to the acquisition date are reflected in the fair value of the net assets acquired. As such, the results of the operations of the acquiree are only included in the income statement of the acquirer from the date of acquisition to avoid double counting.

Identifiable assets and liabilities of the acquiree

IAS 22 (r1998).26 requires that the acquired identifiable assets and liabilities recognised should only be those of the acquiree that *existed* at the date of the acquisition. However, the Standard also allows some additional provisions, which have resulted from the acquirer's intentions, to be recognised as liabilities of the acquiree at the date of acquisition. The conditions for these provisions are discussed below.

The identifiable assets and liabilities should only be recognised separately as at the date of acquisition if:

(a) it is probable that any associated future economic benefits will flow to, or resources embodying economic benefits will flow from, the acquirer; and
(b) a reliable measure is available of their cost or fair value.

IAS 22 (r1998).26

Such assets and liabilities are referred to as *identifiable* assets and liabilities. Most identifiable assets and liabilities will have been recognised previously by the acquiree in its financial statements. However, when the above recognition criteria are met, assets and liabilities which were not recognised previously by the acquiree are recognised on acquisition. (IAS 22 (r1998).28) Such assets and liabilities may not previously have met the recognition criteria or may have arisen as a result of the acquisition.

For example, a deferred tax benefit related to tax losses which did not qualify for recognition in the books of the acquiree may qualify for recognition as an identifiable asset under the criteria set out above if the acquiring enterprise earns sufficient taxable income, and thus it is recognised as an asset on acquisition. Another example of items which are frequently not recognised in the books of an acquiree which may qualify for recognition on acquisition is certain intangible assets, for example, broadcasting licences, software development costs, patents, etc. (IAS 38.31) However, IAS 38 has introduced new recognition criteria for intangible assets (See **10.7**).

As noted above, one of the main changes in the 1998 revision of IAS 22, was to ensure that liabilities should not be recognised at the date of acquisition if they result from the acquirer's intentions or actions. This change makes IAS 22 (r1998) consistent with both IAS 37 and the Framework's definition of a liability (i.e., in order to recognise the liability at the acquisition date, there has to be a present obligation arising from a past event).

The old Standard stated that 'assets and liabilities requiring recognition at the date of acquisition may also include those arising as a result of the acquisition.' This guidance, taken along side the fact that the fair values of identifiable assets and liabilities were, under the old Standard, determined by reference to their *intended* use by the acquirer, had been interpreted by some enterprises as permitting the recognition, as part of the fair value exercise, of provisions for future operating expenses and reorganisation and integration costs expected to be incurred as a result of the acquisition. To prevent this continuing, the revised Standard makes it very clear that, with one exception, liabilities should not be recognised at the acquisition date if they result from:

- the acquirer's intentions;
- the acquirer's actions;
- expected future losses;
- other costs expected to be incurred as a result of the acquisition.

(IAS 22 (r1998).29)

The exception, given in IAS 22 (r1998).31, relates to restructuring and allows a provision to be included in the identifiable assets and liabilities of the acquiree at the date of acquisition even if the liability did not exist in the acquiree at that time. There are strict conditions attaching to this exception. Such a liability can only be included in the fair values of the acquiree where the acquirer has:

> '(a) at or before, the acquisition date, developed the main features of a plan that involves terminating or reducing the activities of the acquiree and that relates to:
> (i) compensating employees of the acquiree for termination of their employment;
> (ii) closing facilities of the acquiree;
> (iii) eliminating product lines of the acquiree;
> (iv) terminating contracts of the acquiree that have become onerous because the acquirer has communicated to the other party at, or before, the date of acquisition that the contract will be terminated;
>
> (b) by announcing the main features of the plan at, or before, the date of acquisition, raised a valid expectation in those affected by the plan that it will implement the plan; and

(c) by the earlier of three months after the date of acquisition and the date when the annual financial statements are authorised for issue, developed the main features into a detailed formal plan identifying at least;
  (i) the business or part of a business concerned;
  (ii) the principal locations affected;
  (iii) the location, function and approximate number of employees who will be compensated for terminating their services;
  (iv) the expenditures which will be undertaken; and
  (v) when the plan will be implemented.

Any provision recognised under this paragraph should cover only the costs of the items in (a)(i) to (iv) above.'

(IAS 22 (r1998).31)

Goodwill or negative goodwill is also recognised at the date of acquisition. See **18.6.6** for a discussion of its calculation.

Reverse acquisitions

In a reverse acquisition, one combining enterprise may issue shares to 'acquire' another enterprise. However, in the process, the enterprise issues enough shares so that control of the resulting combined enterprise lies with the enterprise whose shares were acquired. In such cases, although legally the enterprise which issued the shares may be the parent entity, in substance, the other enterprise, whose shares were purchased, now has control of the combined enterprise and, for accounting purposes, is identified as the acquirer and applies the purchase method of accounting to the assets and liabilities of the enterprise which issued the shares. (IAS 22 (r1998).13) These transactions are often undertaken by enterprises to obtain a stock exchange listing without going through the full registration process. Such enterprises are 'acquired' by shell public companies with the result that the combined enterprise is listed.

Under a reverse acquisition:

(a) the acquiree's net assets continue to be recorded at book value;
(b) an adjustment within shareholders' funds is required to eliminate the cost of acquisition in the issuing company's books, and introduce a notional cost of acquiring the smaller issuing company based on the fair value of its shares;
(c) the acquirer's net assets are restated to fair value;
(d) goodwill is the difference between the adjusted cost of acquisition in (b) less the combining share of (c);
(e) performance statements (including comparatives) disclose the pre- and post-combination results of the acquirer; and
(f) the comparatives to the consolidated balance sheet show the acquiree's net assets.

Example 18.1

Enterprise Y has 50,000 ordinary shares outstanding.

In order to 'acquire' Enterprise Z, it issues 70,000 new ordinary shares to the shareholders of Enterprise Z in exchange for all the shares of Enterprise Z.

Although in some countries, Enterprise Y has legally acquired Enterprise Z, in substance, Enterprise Z now controls Enterprise Y since it owns 70,000 of the 120,000 Enterprise Y shares outstanding.

Therefore, under IAS 22 (r1998), Enterprise Z would apply the purchase method of accounting to the assets and liabilities of Enterprise Y.

Comparison with UK GAAP

Consistent with IAS 22 (r1998), under UK GAAP the fair values of the identifiable assets and liabilities acquired are recognised and the results of operations of an acquisition are incorporated by the acquirer from the date of acquisition which is the date on which control of the acquiree passes to the acquirer.

Consistent with IAS 22 (r1998), under UK GAAP assets and liabilities which were not recorded on the books of the acquiree may be recognised on acquisition by the acquirer. Under UK GAAP, provisions for future operating expenses, including all reorganisation and redundancy expenses arising from the acquirer's intentions are also prohibited. There is no exception in UK GAAP for restructuring provisions which result from the acquirer's intentions as there is in IAS 22 (r1998).

Appendix II to FRS 6 *Acquisitions and Mergers* notes that reverse acquisition accounting is incompatible with companies legislation in the UK. However, a subsequent UITF Information Sheet announced that there could be instances where it would be right and proper to invoke the true and fair override and apply reverse acquisition accounting and, therefore, each case should be considered on its merits. So both accounting in terms of the legal form and the substance of a transaction could be seen in the UK, the latter following the use of the true and fair override.

Comparison with US GAAP

Under US GAAP, the fair values of the assets and liabilities acquired are recognised and the results of operations of an acquisition are incorporated by the acquirer from the date when assets are received and other assets are given or securities are issued as consideration. In most cases, this will coincide with the date of acquisition as defined in IAS 22 (r1998). However, in some cases, effective control may pass before or after the exchange of consideration. In such cases, the date of acquisition may differ between IAS 22 (r1998) and US GAAP.

Consistent with IAS 22 (r1998), under US GAAP, assets and liabilities which were not recorded on the books of the acquiree may be recognised on acquisition by the acquirer. However, provisions for future operating expenses, including many expenses arising from reorganisation and redundancy costs of the acquirer, are prohibited. However, certain costs to exit an activity of an acquired company are permitted to be recognised as liabilities at the acquisition date when certain criteria are met. EITF 95-3 *Recognition of Liabilities in Connection with a Purchase Business Combination* sets out the criteria which may or may not lead to the same conclusion about recognition as IAS 22 (r1998) does, depending on the individual circumstances.

18.6.2 Measurement

When an acquisition takes place, management must determine:

(a) the cost of acquisition;
(b) the fair values of the identifiable assets and liabilities acquired; and
(c) the value of any goodwill or negative goodwill arising on the transaction.

18.6.3 Measurement of the cost of acquisition

> 'An acquisition should be accounted for at its cost, being the amount of cash or cash equivalents paid or the fair value, at the date of exchange, of the other purchase consideration given by the acquirer in exchange for control over the net assets of the other enterprise, plus any costs directly attributable to the acquisition.'
>
> (IAS 22 (r1998).21)

In practice, the date of the exchange transaction referred to in the benchmark treatment often coincides with the date of acquisition referred to in the allowed alternative treatment. However, a difference arises between the two when acquisitions are achieved through successive share purchases (see **18.6.7**).

When calculating the cost of an acquisition, IAS 22 (r1998) provides the following guidelines:

Consideration given:	*Measured at:*
Monetary assets	Fair value at the date of exchange (IAS 22 (r1998).23). Fair value is, 'the amount for which an asset could be exchanged or a liability settled between knowledgeable, willing parties in an arm's length transaction.' (IAS 22 (r1998).8)
Deferred consideration	Present value of the consideration. (IAS 22 (r1998).23)
Marketable securities issued by acquirer	Fair value measured as their market price at the date of exchange, provided that undue fluctuations or the narrowness of the market do not make the market price an unreliable indicator. If market price is unreliable, use price movements for a reasonable period before and after the announcement of the terms of the acquisition. If market is unreliable or no quotes exist, estimate by reference to their proportional interest in the fair value of the acquirer's enterprise or by reference to the proportional interest in the fair value of the enterprise acquired, whichever is the more clearly evident. All aspects of the acquisition, including significant factors influencing the negotiations, need to be considered. In practice, it is unlikely that an acquisition will be agreed without both parties understanding the value of the purchase consideration being exchanged. For this reason, it may be helpful to consider factors influencing the negotiations in determining the fair value of the securities issued. For example, purchase consideration which is paid in cash as an alternative to securities may also provide evidence of the value of the securities. In addition, independent valuations may be used in the determination of the fair value of the securities. (IAS 22 (r1998).24)

The cost of an acquisition includes direct costs relating to the acquisition such as:

(a) costs of registering and issuing equity shares; and
(b) professional fees paid to accountants, legal advisers, valuers and other consultants to effect the acquisition.

(IAS 22 (r1998).25)

Indirect general administrative costs such as the cost of maintaining an acquisitions department or other costs which cannot be directly attributable to the acquisition are expensed as incurred. (IAS 22 (r1998).25)

Contingent purchase consideration

Often acquisition agreements contain clauses which will vary the amount of purchase consideration dependent on specified future events. Such clauses commonly relate to the future earnings level of the enterprise acquired; the outcome of a contingent liability of the acquired enterprise, such as a lawsuit; the market price of the securities issued as purchase consideration; or other future events.

'When the acquisition agreement provides for an adjustment to the purchase consideration contingent on one or more future events, the amount of the adjustment should be included in the cost of the acquisition as at the date of acquisition if the adjustment is probable and the amount can be measured reliably.' (IAS 22 (r1998).65) In practice, it is normally possible to estimate the amount of any adjustment to the purchase consideration which may arise from contingency clauses and thus calculate the cost of acquisition accordingly.

When such a contingency is resolved at a date subsequent to the acquisition with the result that it becomes probable that an adjustment to the purchase consideration will be made and its amount can be reliably estimated, the cost of the acquisition is adjusted accordingly. (IAS 22 (r1998).68) Normally, this results in an adjustment to the goodwill or negative goodwill arising on the transaction. IAS 22 (r1998) does not prescribe a time limit on these types of adjustments. Also no guidance is included in IAS as to whether adjustments should also be made to accumulated goodwill amortisation, however, we would recommend that an adjustment is made effective from the date of acquisition, as this is consistent with SIC-22 (see **18.6.5**).

However, when the acquirer guarantees the market value of debt or equity securities issued as purchase consideration, their value subsequently falls and the acquirer issues additional debt or equity securities as compensation, the cost of the acquisition to the acquirer has not changed. The market value of the securities issued as consideration has merely fallen. Therefore, no adjustment to goodwill or negative goodwill is made. Instead, the value of the new issue of securities is adjusted against the premium or discount arising on the initial issue of securities. Thus, the value of a further issue of equity securities is adjusted against the share premium arising on the original issue while the value of a further issue of debt is adjusted against any premium or discount arising on the original issue of the debt.

(IAS 22 (r1998).70)

Shares issued as purchase consideration

The SIC has a draft interpretation out on IAS 22 (r1998) at present. SIC-D28 *Business Combinations – Measurement of Shares Issued as Purchase Consideration* addresses when the date of exchange occurs in a purchase business combination in which shares are issued as the purchase consideration. If an acquisition is achieved in a single exchange transaction, the date of exchange is the date on which the acquirer obtains control over the net assets and operations of the acquiree. If an acquisition is achieved in stages by successive share purchases, the fair value of the shares issued as purchase consideration should be determined at the date that each exchange is recognised.

SIC-D28 also addresses when it is appropriate to use a price other than a published price at the date of exchange when determining the fair value of an acquirer's shares that are quoted in an active market. SIC-D28 proposes that the published price of a share in an active market at the date of exchange should be considered the best evidence of the share's fair value. Another price should be used only if it can be demonstrated that a price fluctuation is undue and that the other price provides a more reliable measure of the share's fair value.

Comparison with UK GAAP

The measurement of the cost of an acquisition under UK GAAP is generally consistent with that under IAS 22 (r1998). UK GAAP provides more guidance relating to discounting than IAS 22 (r1998) and also requires that when contingent consideration is to be paid in the form of shares, rather than raising a liability for the estimated amount, since there is no obligation to transfer economic benefits, amounts recognised be reported as part of shareholders' funds under a caption such as shares to be issued. IAS 22 (r1998) contains no equivalent requirements or guidance. In practice in the UK, contingent consideration is not normally based on the future market values of securities issued as purchase consideration and as such the treatment of such transactions has not been established.

As under IAS 22 (r1998), under UK GAAP, acquisition costs are treated as part of the cost of acquisition. However, some items which may be included as acquisition costs under IAS 22 (r1998) will not qualify as acquisition costs under UK GAAP. For example, the issue costs of shares or other securities issued as part of the payment of consideration are accounted for as a reduction in the proceeds of a capital instrument rather than as acquisition costs under UK GAAP.

FRS 7 *Fair Values in Acquisition Accounting*, para.84 provides guidance on determining whether the substance of additional payments under the acquisition, such as non-competition payments or bonuses to the vendors who continue to work for the acquired company, is payment for the business acquired, or an expense such as compensation for services or profit sharing.

Comparison with US GAAP

The measurement of the cost of an acquisition under US GAAP is generally consistent with that under IAS 22 (r1998), including the treatment of contingent consideration based on the market value of securities issued. However, EITF 95-8 *Accounting for Contingent Consideration Paid to Shareholders of an Acquired Enterprise in a Purchase Business Combination* provides guidance on determining when additional consideration paid to former shareholders who are now employees constitutes an adjustment to the purchase price and when it is compensation expense.

18.6.4 Initial measurement of identifiable assets and liabilities acquired

Minority interests

IAS 22 (r1998) allows a free choice when measuring the identifiable assets and liabilities acquired with respect to the measurement of any minority interest arising on the transaction.

The benchmark treatment requires the proportion of the identifiable assets and liabilities acquired to be measured at their fair values as at the date of the exchange transaction, and minority interest to be stated at its pre-acquisition carrying amount. Therefore, under the benchmark treatment, the carrying amount of each identifiable asset or liability is comprised of a proportion of its fair value at the date of exchange and a proportion of its pre-acquisition carrying amount. (IAS 22 (r1998).32, 33)

Under the allowed alternative treatment, identifiable assets and liabilities are measured at their fair values as at the date of acquisition. Minority interest is also stated at its fair value at the date of acquisition. In practice, the allowed alternative treatment is the more straightforward since the entire carrying amount of each identifiable asset or liability is its fair value at the date of acquisition. (IAS 22 (r1998).34, 35)

Example 18.2

Acquirer purchases 90 per cent of the outstanding ordinary shares of acquiree.
At the date of acquisition and date of exchange,
Acquiree has net assets with a carrying amount of £40,000.
Acquiree has net assets with a fair value of £100,000.

Under the benchmark treatment:

Acquirer's 90 per cent interest is valued at:	£90,000	(£100,000 × 90%)
Minority interest of 10 per cent is valued at:	£4,000	(£ 40,000 × 10%)
Therefore, the net assets of acquiree are recorded in the books of the acquirer at the date of the exchange transaction at:	£94,000	

Under the allowed alternative treatment:

Acquirer's 90 per cent interest is valued at:	£90,000	(£100,000 × 90%)
Minority interest of 10 per cent is valued at:	£10,000	(£100,000 × 10%)
Therefore, the net assets of acquiree are recorded in the books of the acquirer at the date of acquisition at:	£100,000	

In practice, the date of the exchange transaction referred to in the benchmark treatment often coincides with the date of acquisition referred to in the allowed alternative treatment. However, a difference arises between the two when acquisitions are achieved through successive share purchases (see **18.6.7**).

SIC-18 requires that, where a choice of accounting policies exists, an enterprise should choose and apply one of those policies consistently. This would mean from an IAS 22 (r1998) perspective, that an enterprise should choose whether it wants to adopt the benchmark or the alternative treatment and apply this to all subsidiaries consistently. It is no longer possible to adopt the benchmark treatment for one subsidiary and the alternative treatment for another.

Comparison with UK GAAP

Under UK GAAP, the allowed alternative treatment is the required treatment of minority interests on acquisition.

Comparison with US GAAP

In practice, under US GAAP, both the benchmark and the allowed alternative treatments are used. According to informal consultation with the SEC staff, it would appear that the SEC generally would prefer use of the benchmark treatment.[1]

[1] The IASC-U.S. Comparison Project: A Report on the Similarities and Differences between IASC Standards and U.S. GAAP. page 341 footnote 16.

Determination of the fair values of identifiable assets and liabilities acquired

In order to calculate goodwill, the fair values of the identifiable assets and liabilities acquired need to be determined. IAS 22 (r1998) defines fair value as, 'the amount for which an asset could be exchanged or a liability settled between knowledgeable, willing parties in an arm's length transaction'. (IAS 22 (r1998).8) Prior to the 1998 revision of the Standard, the fair values were determined by reference to their *intended use by the acquirer*. This meant that fair values could be based, not on the asset's existing use in the business, but on whatever probable plans the acquirer had for the asset. In the main, this basis for determining the fair value has been removed by the 1998 revision. Fair values are now based on the *existing use* of the asset. The one exception is where a specific restructuring provision, which results from the acquirer's intentions, meets the strict conditions in IAS 22 (r1998).31. In this situation, the fair value of the liability is still based on the acquirer's intentions. This exception is discussed in more detail in **18.6.1**.

General guidelines for assigning fair value to the assets and liabilities acquired in a business combination, once it has established that they qualify for recognition (see **18.6.1**), as set out in IAS 22 (r1998) are as follows:

Asset/liability	*Fair value*
Marketable securities	Current market values. Market value is defined in IAS 32 (r1998) *Financial Instruments: Disclosure and Presentation* as, 'the amount obtainable from the sale, or payable on the acquisition, of a financial instrument in an active market'. (IAS 32.5)
Non-marketable securities	Estimated values taking into consideration features such as price earnings ratios, dividend yields and expected growth rates of comparable securities of enterprises with similar characteristics.
Receivables	Present values of the amounts to be received, determined at appropriate current interest rates, less allowances for uncollectability and collection costs, if necessary. Discounting is not required for short-term receivables when the difference between the nominal amount of the receivable and the discounted amount is immaterial.
Inventories – finished goods and merchandise	Selling prices less the sum of the costs of disposal and a reasonable profit allowance for the selling effort of the acquirer based on the profit for similar finished goods and merchandise.

Inventories – work in progress	Selling prices of finished goods less the sum of costs to complete, costs of disposal, and a reasonable profit allowance for the completing and selling effort based on profit for similar finished goods.
Inventories – raw materials	Current replacement cost.
Land and buildings	Market value.
Plant and equipment	Market value normally determined by appraisal. When there is no evidence of market value because of the specialised nature of the plant and equipment or because the items are rarely sold, except as part of a continuing business, they are valued at their depreciated replacement cost.
Intangible assets (as defined in IAS 38)	At fair values determined by reference to an active market (as defined in IAS 38) or, if no active market exists, on a basis that reflects the amount the enterprise would have paid for the asset in an arm's length transaction between knowledgeable willing parties, based on the best information available. However, if the fair value of an intangible asset cannot be measured by reference to an active market, the amount recognised for that intangible asset at the date of the acquisition should be limited to an amount that does not create or increase negative goodwill that arises on the acquisition. (IAS 22 (r1998).40) See Chapter **10** for a further discussion of intangibles acquired as part of a business combination.
Net pension assets or obligations for defined benefit plans	Present value of defined benefit obligation less the fair value of any plan assets. However, an asset is only recognised to the extent that it is probable that it will be available to the enterprise in the form of refunds from the plan or a reduction in future contributions.[a]
Tax assets and liabilities (current and deferred)	The amount of the tax benefit arising from tax losses or the taxes payable in respect of the net profit or loss, assessed from the perspective of the combined entity or group resulting from the acquisition.[b] The tax asset or liability is determined after allowing for the tax effect of restating identifiable assets and liabilities to their fair values and is not discounted.[c] The tax assets include any deferred tax asset of the acquirer that was not recognised prior to the business combination, but which, as a consequence of

	the business combination, now satisfies the recognition criteria in IAS 12 (r2000) *Income Taxes.*
Accounts payable and notes payable Long term debt Liabilities Accruals and other claims payable	Present value of amounts to be disbursed in meeting the liability determined at appropriate current interest rates. However, discounting is not required for short-term liabilities when the difference between the nominal amount of the liability and the discounted amount is not material.
Onerous contracts and other identifiable liabilities of the acquiree	Present values of amounts to be disbursed in meeting the obligation determined at appropriate current interest rates.
Provisions for terminating or reducing activities where an acquirer has plans at, or before, the acquisition date which, by a specified time, turn into detailed plans. (IAS 22 (r1998).31) Discussed in **18.6.1**.	The amount which can be included as a liability at the date of acquisition is determined under IAS 37 *Provisions, Contingent Liabilities and Contingent Assets.*

[a] The valuation on acquisition of net pension assets or obligations for defined benefit plans differs from the valuation which would normally be carried out under IAS 19 (r1998) *Employee Benefits* which in some cases, does not allow the immediate recognition of assets and liabilities in respect of surpluses of deficiencies, but requires them to be recognised systematically over the expected remaining working lives of the employees. This difference arises because IAS 19 (r1998) is primarily concerned with the allocation of retirement benefit costs to the income statement of an enterprise on a continuing basis over several financial years whereas acquisition accounting requires the assignment of fair values to all identifiable assets and liabilities as of a specific date (See Chapter **25**).

[b] At the end of the accounting period in which the acquisition occurred, the deferred tax assets and liabilities of the combined group will be calculated using assumptions applicable to the combined group. The deferred tax relating to the acquired enterprise at the date of acquisition is calculated using the same assumptions, with the result that the post-acquisition income statement will reflect only 'real' changes in the circumstances of the combined group and not any effects of changing from one set of assumptions to another (See Chapter **23**).

[c] When applying the purchase method of accounting, the fair value adjustments made to the identifiable assets and liabilities acquired give rise to temporary differences and IAS 12 (r2000) requires an enterprise to recognise the resulting deferred tax liability or (subject to the probability criterion for recognition) deferred tax asset with a corresponding effect on the determination of the amount of goodwill or negative goodwill. 'For example, when the carrying amount of an asset is increased to fair value but the tax base of the asset remains at cost to the previous owner, a taxable temporary difference arises which results in a deferred tax liability.' (IAS 12 (r2000).19) Deferred tax assets arise when an identifiable liability is recognised on acquisition but the related costs are not deducted in determining taxable profits until a later period or when the fair value of an identifiable asset acquired is less than its tax base. (IAS 12 (r2000).26 (c)) In each of the above three cases, the amount of goodwill or negative goodwill arising on the acquisition is affected by the recognition of the deferred tax asset or liability. However, an enterprise does not recognise deferred tax liabilities arising from goodwill itself (if amortisation of the goodwill is not deductible for tax purposes) or deferred tax assets arising from non-taxable negative goodwill which is treated as deferred income (See Chapter **23**). (IAS 12 (r2000).66)

Comparison with UK GAAP

Consistent with IAS 22 (r1998), under UK GAAP, identifiable assets and liabilities are measured at their fair value at the date of acquisition. Since the latest revision of IAS 22, the calculation of the fair values of identifiable assets and liabilities should be substantially the same under UK GAAP and IAS 22 (r1998). One area of difference relates to the fair value of inventory where, previously, differences arose from the fact that under the old Standard, assets were valued based on their *intended* use by the combined enterprise. As IAS 22 (r1998) does not reflect any changes (with one exception), resulting from the acquirer's intentions, the requirements are now more similar to UK GAAP. The exception in IAS 22 (r1998) relates to restructuring provisions. This is discussed in more detail in **18.6.1**.

Differences may arise relating to deferred tax assets and liabilities due to differences between IAS 12 (r2000) and UK GAAP (See chapter **23**).

Comparison with US GAAP

Consistent with IAS 22 (r1998), under US GAAP, identifiable assets and liabilities are measured at their fair values at the date of acquisition. The methods of determining fair values of individual assets and liabilities are generally consistent between the two. However, some differences may arise on the calculation of the fair value of a pension asset or liability, intangible assets or items of property, plant and equipment. In particular, IAS 22 (r1998) requires intangible assets to be valued at fair values in an active market or reasonable independent estimate if no active market exists, as opposed to US GAAP which requires intangible assets acquired to be valued at appraised values. Thus, in practice in the US, outside valuers report on the fair value of any identifiable intangible assets acquired such as brands, the value of the workforce, patents, etc. and those fair values are incorporated into the accounting for the acquisition. The result of assigning individual values to each of these assets rather than aggregating them as goodwill is that each will have a different useful life and thus amortisation period. If no such exercise were undertaken, all of these assets would be aggregated as goodwill, with the risk that some of the intangible assets acquired but not separately identified would not be appropriately amortised over a period estimating their useful lives. This exercise is particularly important in light of the new FASB statement on Goodwill and Intangibles. The new statements provide specific guidance on the recognition of intangible assets. An identifiable intangible asset must be recognised separately from goodwill if *either* of the following criteria are met:

(a) control over the future economic benefits of the asset results from contractual or other legal rights (regardless of whether those rights are transferable or separable from other rights and obligations); and
(b) the asset is capable of being separated or divided and sold, transferred,

licensed, rented, or exchanged (regardless of whether there is an intent to do so).

An intangible asset that cannot be sold, transferred, licensed, rented, or exchanged individually meets the criteria for recognition apart from goodwill if it can be sold, transferred, licensed, rented, or exchanged along with a related contract, asset or liability. For example, a financial institution customer relationship cannot be separated from the deposits, however, this intangible asset must be separated from goodwill and recognised appropriately.

Additionally, the new statement requires that goodwill is no longer amortised. Goodwill must be assessed for impairment at least annually. Any impairment must be recorded in the income statement as an impairment loss. The useful economic life of previously recognised intangible assets should be reassessed upon adoption of the Statement, and remaining amortisation periods should be adjusted accordingly. Intangible assets deemed to have an indefinite life would no longer be amortised.

The new goodwill and intangible assets statement are effective for fiscal years beginning after 15 December 2001. Early adoption would be permitted for companies with a fiscal year beginning after 15 March 2001 provided that the first quarter financial statements have not been previously issued. In all cases, the statement must be adopted as of the beginning of a fiscal year.

A company whose annual reporting period ends on 31 December (a calendar-year company) would be required to adopt the goodwill and intangible assets Statement on 1 January 2002 (the beginning of its annual reporting period). Early adoption would not be permitted for calendar-year companies.

A company whose annual reporting period ends on 30 June would be required to adopt the Statement on 1 July 2002 (the beginning of its annual reporting period). However, that company would be permitted to adopt the Statement on 1 July 2001.

A company whose annual reporting period ends on 31 March would be required to adopt the Statement on 1 April 2002 (the beginning of its annual reporting period). However, that company would be permitted to adopt the Statement on 1 April 2001 provided it had not previously issued its financial statements for the quarter ended 30 June 2001.

Goodwill and intangible assets acquired in a transaction completed after 31 June 2001 but before the Statement is initially applied would be accounted for in accordance with the amortisation and non-amortisation provisions of the Statement.

> **Example 18.3**
>
> A company with a 31 December 2001 year-end that completes an acquisition on 15 October 2001 will not amortise goodwill acquired in that acquisition. However, previously acquired goodwill would continue to be amortised until 1 January 2002. The impairment provisions of the Statement would not be applicable to the recently acquired goodwill until 1 January 2002.

See **10.7** for further discussion of intangibles acquired in a business combination.

18.6.5 Subsequent identification or changes in value of assets and liabilities

Often, information which either confirms the existence of identifiable assets and liabilities acquired but not previously recognised or clarifies the fair values of the identifiable assets and liabilities when the transaction was initially accounted for, becomes available subsequent to the assignment of fair values to those assets and liabilities. In general:

- identifiable assets and liabilities acquired which do not satisfy the criteria for separate recognition on acquisition are recognised subsequently as and when they satisfy the criteria;
- the carrying amounts of identifiable assets and liabilities acquired are adjusted when additional evidence becomes available to assist with the estimation of the amounts assigned to those identifiable assets and liabilities when the acquisition was initially accounted for; and
- the goodwill or negative goodwill amount is adjusted, when necessary, to the extent that the amount of the adjustment does not increase the carrying amount of goodwill above its recoverable amount (as defined in IAS 36) and such adjustment is made by the end of the first annual accounting period commencing after acquisition; otherwise the adjustment should be recognised as income or expense. (IAS 22 (r1998).71)

Thus, goodwill or negative goodwill (including associated amortisation) may only be adjusted as a result of the adjustment of the fair values of the identifiable assets and liabilities before the end of the first annual accounting period (excluding interim periods) commencing after acquisition. Any adjustments made to the fair values of the identifiable assets and liabilities acquired after this date are recognised in the income statement. An example of an adjustment which would affect the carrying value of goodwill is an impairment loss which did not relate to specific events or changes in circumstances occurring after the acquisition date. (IAS 22 (r1998).73)

SIC-22, effective for periods ending on or after 15 July 2000, states that any fair value adjustments made subsequent to the date of acquisition as a result of the above requirements of IAS 22 (r1998) should be calculated as if the newly assigned values had been used from the date of acquisition. Consequently, the adjustment not only includes the effect of the change in fair value but also the effect of depreciation and other changes that would have been recognised had the revised fair value been included all along. It further clarifies that adjustments to amounts included in the income statement, such as depreciation of the asset whose value has been adjusted or amortisation of goodwill, are included in the corresponding category of income or expense presented on the face of the income statement. SIC-22 requires, *inter alia*, disclosure of the amount of an adjustment recognised in the income statement of the current period which relates to comparative and prior periods. For example, if the adjustment increases depreciation expense in the current period by $150 and $75 of the increase results from the recalculation of the effects of the adjustment to identifiable assets over the comparative year, that fact would be disclosed.

When an adjustment to the fair values of the identifiable assets and liabilities is made, before goodwill can be increased, an assessment is made whether the adjustment increases the carrying amount of goodwill above its recoverable amount. (IAS 22 (r1998).71) If the increased amount would result in the goodwill balance exceeding its recoverable amount, then the excess above recoverable amount is recognised in the income statement rather than as an addition to goodwill.

There are two exceptions to the rule about adjusting goodwill or negative goodwill before the end of the first annual accounting period:

(1) restructuring provisions; and
(2) deferred tax.

Each is discussed below.

Restructuring provision

Where a provision for restructuring has been set up on acquisition, IAS 22 (r1998).75 states it 'should be reversed if, and only if:

(a) the outflow of economic benefits is no longer probable; or
(b) the detailed formal plan is not implemented:
    (i) in the manner set out in the detailed formal plan; or
    (ii) within the time established in the detailed formal plan.

Such a reversal should be reflected as an adjustment to goodwill or negative goodwill (and minority interests, if appropriate), so that no income or expense is recognised in respect of it.'

IAS 22(r1998) notes that such reversals should be rare since a detailed formal plan is required to identify the expenditures that will be undertaken in order to raise the provision in the first place. If subsequently, there is any obligation that is required to be recognised as a provision, the enterprise recognises a corresponding expense. (IAS 22 (r1998).76)

Deferred tax

IAS 12 (r2000) amends the guidance in IAS 22 (r1998) to the effect that when the potential benefit of income tax loss carryforwards, or other deferred tax assets, of an acquired enterprise which were not recognised as an identifiable asset by the acquirer at the date of acquisition are subsequently realised, the acquirer recognises the benefit as income. In addition, the acquirer:

> '(a) adjusts the gross carrying amount of the goodwill and the related accumulated amortisation to the amounts that would have been recorded if the deferred tax asset had been recognised as an identifiable asset at the date of the business combination; and
>
> (b) recognises the reduction in the net carrying amount of the goodwill as an expense.

However, this procedure does not create negative goodwill, nor does it increase the carrying amount of negative goodwill.' (IAS 22 (r1998).85)

The effect of these adjustments is that no gain is recognised in the income statement. Instead, goodwill is adjusted as if the deferred tax asset had been recognised at the date of acquisition.

Comparison with UK GAAP

The time limit to adjust the fair value of identifiable assets and liabilities acquired against goodwill is consistent between UK GAAP and IAS 22 (r1998) other than that there is no exception in UK GAAP for deferred tax. The exception for restructuring would not arise under UK GAAP because such a provision could not be set up in the first place.

SIC-22 contains more detailed guidance than is in UK GAAP on recognising the adjustments; the approach adopted in SIC-22 would not be precluded by UK GAAP.

Comparison with US GAAP

Under US GAAP, the time limit to adjust the fair value of the identifiable assets and liabilities acquired against goodwill is one year from the date of acquisition as opposed to a period ending on the first annual accounting period commencing after the acquisition under IAS 22 (r1998). The exception to this guidance relates to the accounting for income taxes associated with a purchase business combination.

As indicated in Question 17 of the FASB Special Report *A Guide to Implementation of Statement No. 109 on Accounting for Income Taxes* deferred tax assets and liabilities at the date of a purchase business combination should be based on management's best estimate of the ultimate tax basis that will be accepted by the tax authority, and liabilities for prior tax returns of the acquired entity should be based on management's best estimate of the ultimate settlement. At the date of a change in management's best estimate of the ultimate tax basis of acquired assets, liabilities, and carry-forwards, and at the date that the tax basis is settled with the tax authority, deferred tax assets and liabilities should be adjusted to reflect the revised tax basis and the amount of any settlement with the tax authority for prior-year income taxes. Similarly, at the date of a change in management's best estimate of items relating to the acquired entity's prior tax returns, and at the date that the items are settled with the tax authority, any liability previously recognised should be adjusted. The effect of those adjustments should be applied to increase or decrease the remaining balance of goodwill attributable to that acquisition. If goodwill is reduced to zero, the remaining amount of those adjustments should be applied initially to reduce to zero other non-current intangible assets related to that acquisition, and any remaining amount should be recognised in income.

18.6.6 Measurement of goodwill and negative goodwill

'Any excess of the cost of the acquisition over the acquirer's interest in the fair value of the identifiable assets and liabilities acquired as at the date of the exchange transaction should be described as goodwill and recognised as an asset.' (IAS 22 (r1998).41) As discussed in greater detail in **10.7** goodwill is required to be capitalised and amortised over a period not exceeding twenty years unless a longer period can be justified.

'Any excess, as at the date of the exchange transaction, of the acquirer's interest in the fair values of the identifiable assets and liabilities acquired over the cost of the acquisition, should be recognised as negative goodwill.' (IAS 22 (r1998).59) As discussed in greater detail in Chapter **10**, once it has been established that negative goodwill exists, it needs to be determined whether the negative goodwill relates to any identifiable expected future losses and expenses of the acquiree which have been predicted at the date of acquisition.

If any such losses/expenses have been identified, the negative goodwill should be matched in the same period as the losses/expenses are recognised.

If no such losses/expenses have been identified, the negative goodwill is credited to the income statement, first in relation to the acquired non-monetary assets weighted average useful life, and second, if any negative goodwill is in excess of the fair values of the identifiable acquired non-monetary assets, recognised as income immediately. (IAS 22(r1998).62)

Comparison with UK GAAP

Consistent with IAS 22 (r1998), under UK GAAP, goodwill or negative goodwill is the difference between the cost of acquisition and the fair value of identifiable assets and liabilities acquired at the date of acquisition. However, as discussed in previous sections, the calculation of the cost of acquisition and the fair value of identifiable assets and liabilities may differ between UK GAAP and IAS 22 (r1998) which could give rise to a different goodwill figure (the difference is mainly due to the treatment of restructuring provisions as discussed in **18.6.1**). See Chapter **10** for a discussion of the UK GAAP treatment of goodwill and negative goodwill.

Comparison with US GAAP

Consistent with IAS 22 (r1998), under US GAAP, goodwill or negative goodwill is the difference between the cost of acquisition and the fair value of identifiable assets and liabilities acquired at the date of acquisition. However, as discussed in previous sections, the calculation of the cost of acquisition and the fair value of identifiable assets and liabilities may differ between US GAAP and IAS 22 (r1998) which would give rise to a different goodwill figure. See **10.7** for a discussion of the US GAAP treatments of goodwill and negative goodwill.

18.6.7 Successive share purchases

Sometimes an acquisition is achieved through several, successive share purchases rather than one transaction. When this is the case, the cost of the acquisition is the aggregate cost of the individual transactions. (IAS 22 (r1998).22) Similarly, in order to calculate any goodwill or negative goodwill arising on each share purchase, the cost of the individual transaction is compared to the fair value at the date of the exchange transaction of the assets and liabilities acquired in that individual transaction. (IAS 22 (r1998).41, 59) The total goodwill related to an acquisition is the aggregate of the goodwill amounts calculated at each successive share purchase date. However, the value assigned as part of the purchase accounting exercise to the assets and liabilities acquired depends on whether the enterprise has adopted the benchmark or allowed alternative treatment as described in **18.6.4**. Under the benchmark treatment, identifiable assets and liabilities acquired are recorded at the aggregate of their fair values as at the date of each exchange transaction. In other words, the proportion of the net assets owned prior to each successive purchase of shares is not marked to fair value at each successive purchase date as part of purchase accounting. If an enterprise wishes to revalue previous share purchases in order that its entire investment is valued as of the same date, it may revalue the previously owned interest as a separate exercise from that of purchase accounting.

Example 18.4

In 19x0, enterprise A purchases 80 per cent of the ordinary shares of enterprise B for £130,000. The fair value of the identifiable net assets of enterprise B at the date of acquisition is £100,000 (and these are recorded in B's books at £75,000).

Therefore, goodwill arising on this transaction is £50,000.
(£130,000 – (£100,000 × 80%))

In 19x2, enterprise A purchases the remaining 20 per cent of the ordinary shares of enterprise B for £60,000.

The fair value of the identifiable net assets of enterprise B at the date of this acquisition is £200,000 (and these are recorded in B's books at £150,000).

Therefore, goodwill arising on this transaction is £20,000.
(£60,000 – (£200,000 × 20%)

After the second transaction, enterprise A owns 100 per cent of enterprise B.

The cost of acquisition is £190,000 (£60,000 + £130,000).

The goodwill arising on the acquisition is £70,000 (£20,000 + £50,000)

It is important to note that, after the second acquisition, the assets and liabilities of enterprise B existing at the date of the initial acquisition and those acquired between the first and second acquisitions will be valued in the books of enterprise A at 80 per cent of their historic cost to enterprise A (which would be either their fair value at the date of the first acquisition or their historic cost if obtained by B after the first acquisition) and 20 per cent of their fair value at the date of the second acquisition, i.e., £180,000 assuming that all the fair value adjustments from the 19x0 acquisition relate to land which is not being depreciated, and was not disposed of between the two acquisition dates.

Thus, there is no step-up in basis of the first 80 per cent acquired merely because the second purchase took place.

Under the allowed alternative treatment, identifiable assets and liabilities acquired are recorded at their fair values as at the date of acquisition, which is the date that the acquirer gains control. (IAS 22 (r1998).34) Thus, at first glance, it would appear that all assets and liabilities, regardless of when they were acquired, should be fair valued as part of the purchase accounting when the acquirer initially gains control over the investee. However, the guidance in IAS 22 (r1998).36 explains that in the case of successive share purchases, each significant transaction is treated separately for the purpose of determining the fair values of the identifiable assets and liabilities acquired. Therefore, all of the previously acquired identifiable assets and liabilities are not fair valued as part of the purchase accounting. In order to meet the requirement that identifiable assets and liabilities acquired be measured at their fair values as at the date of acquisition, an enterprise revalues all of the identifiable assets and liabilities purchased prior to the date of acquisition as a separate exercise from purchase accounting. Any surplus of the fair value of the previously acquired net assets over their carrying amount is taken to a revaluation surplus in reserves and any deficit is recognised in the income statement. Goodwill or negative goodwill arising on the previous share purchases is not adjusted unless the revaluation exercise indicates that such goodwill is impaired.

Prior to qualifying as an acquisition (or an associate), an investment may qualify for fair value accounting in accordance with IAS 39 (r2000) *Financial Instruments: Recognition and Measurement.* When this is the case, the cost of the investment for IAS 22 (r1998) purposes is the fair value under IAS 39 (r2000) at the date of change in classification plus the cost of the investment which triggers the application of IAS 22 (r1998). As a successive share purchase, the two separate transactions should not be treated separately for the purposes of determining the fair value of the identifiable assets and liabilities acquired, and for determining the amount of goodwill or negative goodwill in accordance with IAS 22 (r1998). As the fair value of the initial investment has already been adjusted for in the 'deemed cost', the fair value and goodwill calculation should be performed as at the date of the latest exchange.

Alternatively, prior to qualifying as an acquisition, an acquiree may qualify as an investment in an associate and be accounted for by use of the equity method in accordance with IAS 28 (r2000) *Accounting for Investments in Associates* (See Chapter **20**). When this is the case, the fair values of the identifiable assets and liabilities acquired and the goodwill or negative goodwill arising on the investment will initially have been determined at the date the equity method was first applied. However, use of the equity method over time leads to the recognition by the acquirer of an increase or decrease in the value of the investment due to its participation in the profits and losses made by the investee. If, on a subsequent share purchase resulting in an associate becoming a subsidiary, the allowed alternative treatment of accounting for business combinations is used (see **18.6.4**) the revaluation of the identifiable assets and liabilities of the subsidiary will be partly recognised in the consolidated accounts of the parent. That part of the revaluation relating to the original share of the identifiable assets and liabilities, which has not been previously recognised through equity accounting, should be recognised as a revaluation surplus in equity, in a similar manner to revaluations of property, plant and equipment, in the consolidated financial statements (See *Example 18.5*). The same principles will also apply when an enterprise increases a stake in an existing subsidiary.

Example 18.5

Same facts as in *Example 18.4*, but concurrently with the second purchase, enterprise A revalues its original 80% interest in the assets and liabilities of enterprise B to fair value.

Historic cost (fair value at date of acquisition) of original 80 per cent of net assets of enterprise B:	£80,000	
Fair value of original 80 per cent at the date of the second purchase based on fair values assigned for second purchase:	£160,000	(£200,000 × 80%)
Apparent increase	£80,000	
However, some of the increase in fair value is due to profits earned and retained during the two years between each share purchase.		
Profits earned by Enterprise B during this period were £70,000.		
Since enterprise A was accounting for enterprise B as a subsidiary during these two years, it has already recognised 80 per cent of these profits:	(£56,000)	
Therefore, the increase in fair value of the identifiable assets and liabilities relating to enterprise A's original 80% is:	£ 24,000	

This amount is recognised in a revaluation surplus in equity in a similar manner to revaluations of property, plant and equipment.

Comparison with UK GAAP

Under UK GAAP, the general rule for the calculation of goodwill is that successive share purchases are accounted for under the piecemeal approach as described above. When an investor increases its share in an associate with the result that it becomes a subsidiary, a slightly different treatment is required. Goodwill is still calculated as the sum of the goodwill arising on each previous investment based on the cost and fair values at each acquisition date, but in order to comply with the Companies Act, the difference between this amount of goodwill and the amount of goodwill calculated as if the entire acquisition had taken place at the final acquisition date has to be disclosed.

Under UK GAAP, when further shares are purchased in an investment which is already classified as a subsidiary, FRS 2 *Accounting for Subsidiary Undertakings* requires that, prior to the further investment, the identifiable assets and liabilities of the subsidiary are revalued to current fair values when this differs materially from their carrying amounts. Under IAS 22 (r1998), such a revaluation is optional.

Comparison with US GAAP
Under US GAAP, the general rule is that successive share purchases, known as step acquisitions, are accounted for under the piecemeal approach as described above. However, revaluations of previous share purchases would generally not be permitted. In addition when a subsequent purchase results in an investment being accounted for under the equity method for the first time, an adjustment is made to increase the amount of the investment (assuming the investee has been profitable) with a corresponding increase to retained earnings as if the investment had always been accounted for under the equity method. No corresponding requirement or guidance exists in IAS 22 (r1998).

18.7 Accounting for a uniting of interests

In order to achieve a uniting of interests, normally either one combining enterprise issues shares in exchange for the shares of the other combining enterprise or a new enterprise is created which issues shares to each of the combining enterprises in exchange for their shares. In either case, the conditions described in **18.5.2** will need to be met in order to account for the transaction as a uniting of interests.

A uniting of interests is accounted for by the pooling of interests method.

> 'The substance of a uniting of interests is that no acquisition has occurred and there has been a continuation of the mutual sharing of the risks and benefits that existed prior to the business combination. Use of the pooling of interests method recognises this by accounting for the combined enterprises as though the separate businesses were continuing as before, though now jointly owned and managed. Accordingly, only minimal changes are made in aggregating the individual financial statements.'
>
> (IAS 22 (r1998).80)

18.7.1 Presentation

Under the pooling of interests method, the financial statement items of the combining enterprises for the period in which the combination occurs and for any prior periods presented are included in the financial statements of the combined enterprise as if the two enterprises had been combined from the beginning of the earliest period presented. (IAS 22 (r1998).78)

18.7.2 Recognition and measurement of the combined assets and liabilities

Under the pooling of interests method, the existing carrying amounts of the assets, liabilities and equity of the two combining enterprises are aggregated, with three adjustments as described below, to arrive at the assets, liabilities and equity of the combined enterprise. No fair value adjustments are made and thus, no goodwill arises, under the pooling of interests method. The three adjustments are:

(1) Since the retained earnings of the combined enterprises are aggregated to arrive at the retained earnings of the combined enterprise, any previous transactions between the combining enterprises are eliminated.
(2) 'Any difference between the amount recorded as share capital issued plus any additional consideration in the form of cash or other assets and the amount recorded for the share capital acquired should be adjusted against equity.' (IAS 22 (r1998).79) Under the pooling of interests method, shares issued are recorded at their par value rather than their fair value. Any difference between the par value of the shares issued plus any additional consideration and the par value of the shares acquired is adjusted against equity. IAS 22 (r1998) is not specific about which accounts in equity are adjusted. Presumably, this is due to the legal restrictions surrounding the use of various components of equity in different countries.
(3) Since the combined enterprises will present one set of consolidated financial statements, a uniform set of accounting policies is adopted which may result in adjustments to the assets, liability and equity of the combining enterprises.

18.7.3 Costs of a uniting of interests

Expenditures incurred in relation to a uniting of interests are required to be expensed in the period in which they are incurred. (IAS 22 (r1998).82) Such expenses may include:

(a) registration fees;
(b) costs of furnishing information to shareholders;
(c) finders and consultants fees; and
(d) salaries and other expenses related to services of employees involved in achieving the business combination.

Similarly, any costs or losses incurred in combining the operations of the enterprises are expensed as incurred.

18.7.4 Comparison with UK GAAP

Merger accounting in the UK is similar to that of a uniting of interests under IAS 22 (r1998).

18.7.5 Comparison with US GAAP

Pooling of interests accounting in the US was similar to that of a uniting of interests under IAS 22 (r1998). The FASB has finalised two Statements (Statement 141, *Business Combinations,* and Statement 142, *Goodwill and Other Intangible Assets*). The new statement on business combinations, which was effective for any business combinations completed after 30 June 2001, eliminates the pooling method of accounting for business combinations.

18.8 Disclosure

18.8.1 All business combinations

'For all business combinations, the following disclosures should be made in the financial statements for the period during which the combination has taken place:

(a) the names and descriptions of the combining enterprises;
(b) the method of accounting for the combination;
(c) the effective date of the combination for accounting purposes; and
(d) any operations resulting from the business combination which the enterprise has decided to dispose of.'

(IAS 22 (r1998).86)

For material business combinations effected after the balance sheet date but before the issuance of the financial statements of either enterprise, the disclosures required if the business combination had taken place before the balance sheet date (found in paragraphs 86–94 and reproduced above and below) are required to be made in the enterprise's financial statements. If this is impracticable, this fact is required to be disclosed. (IAS 22 (r1998).96, 97)

When a business combination allows one of the enterprises to continue as a going concern, disclosure of this fact is made in the financial statements of the enterprise which would not have been able to continue as a going concern without the business combination. (IAS 22(r1998).98) For example, a small technology enterprise, which has many plans for future products but little cash to fund them, is having cash flow difficulties and will not be able to continue as a going concern. If this small enterprise is acquired by a larger enterprise with access to cash to fund these future products, the small technology enterprise discloses that the ability to continue as a going concern was in doubt before the business combination.

18.8.2 Acquisitions

> 'For a business combination which is an acquisition, the following additional disclosures should be made in the financial statements for the period during which the acquisition has taken place:
>
> (a) the percentage of voting shares acquired; and
> (b) the cost of acquisition and a description of the purchase consideration paid or contingently payable.'
>
> (IAS 22 (r1998).87)

If a provision for restructuring, terminating or reducing the activities of an acquiree has been made, then the disclosure requirements of IAS 37 apply (see Chapter **11**). These provisions should be treated as a separate class of provisions for the purpose of disclosure under IAS 37. In addition, the aggregate carrying amount of these provisions should be disclosed for each individual business combination. (IAS 22 (r1998).92)

> 'If the fair values of the identifiable assets and liabilities or the purchase consideration can only be determined on a provisional basis at the end of the period in which the acquisition took place, this should be stated and reasons given. When there are subsequent adjustments to such provisional fair values, those adjustments should be disclosed and explained in the financial statements of the period concerned.'
>
> (IAS 22 (r1998).93)

For required disclosures related to goodwill and negative goodwill, see **10.7**.

SIC-22.8 requires that adjustments to the carrying amounts of identifiable assets or liabilities or goodwill or negative goodwill should be disclosed and explained in the financial statements of the period in which the adjustment is made. The amount of an adjustment which relates to prior and comparative periods should also be disclosed.

18.8.3 Uniting of interests

> 'The following additional disclosures should be made in the financial statements for the period during which the uniting of interests has taken place:
>
> (a) description and number of shares issued, together with the percentage of each enterprise's voting shares exchanged to effect the uniting of interests;
> (b) amounts of assets and liabilities contributed by each enterprise; and
> (c) sales revenue, other operating revenues, extraordinary items and the net profit or loss of each enterprise prior to the date of the combination that are included in the net profit or loss shown by the combined enterprise's financial statements.'
>
> (IAS 22 (r1998).94)

18.9 Examples from published financial statements

Note that the excerpts given do not always comply in full with all aspects of IAS and as such are not necessarily examples of best practice but merely of current practice.

Example 18.6

Basis of accounting

The consolidated financial statements are stated in Swiss francs, the currency of the country in which UBS is incorporated. The consolidated financial statements have been prepared in accordance with and comply with International Accounting Standards.

UBS AG was formed on 29 June 1998 when Swiss Bank Corporation and Union Bank of Switzerland merged. The UBS consolidated financial statements were prepared using the pooling of interests method of accounting. Due to the merger, the Group harmonised its accounting policies which have then been retrospectively applied for the restatement of comparative information and opening retained earnings as 1 January 1997.

Note 2 Harmonisation of Accounting Policies

The business combination of Union Bank of Switzerland and Swiss Bank Corporation was accounted for under the pooling of interests method of accounting. Under the pooling of interests method of accounting, a single uniform set of accounting policies was adopted and applied to all periods presented. As a result of harmonising these policies, adjustments were required for the accounting for treasury shares, netting of balance sheet items, repurchase agreements, depreciation and employee share schemes.

The impact on the financial statements is shown in the table below. Details of the shares issued to effect the pooling of interests are shown in Note 27.

CHF million	*1997*
Shareholders' equity as at 1 January 1997	
Former Union Bank of Switzerland	22,707
Former Swiss Bank Corporation	11,742
Total Shareholders' equity as previously reported	34,449
Impact of accounting policy harmonisation	(293)
Shareholders' equity restated as at 1 January 1997	**34,156**
Net loss for the 12 month period ended 31 December 1997	
Former Union Bank of Switzerland	(129)
Former Swiss Bank Corporation	(248)
Total as previously reported	(377)
Impact of accounting policy harmonisation	(290)
Net loss restated for the 12 month period ended 31 December 1997	(667)

Total assets restated as at 31 December 1997	
Former Union Bank of Switzerland	577,576
Former Swiss Bank Corporation	438,948
Total assets as previously reported	1,016,524
Impact of accounting policy harmonisation	69,890
Total assets restated as at 31 December 1997	1,086,414

UBS
Switzerland
31 December 1998
International Accounting Standards

Example 18.7

Basis of consolidation

The consolidated financial statements incorporate the financial statements of the Company, its subsidiaries, associates and joint ventures on the basis set out below.

Subsidiaries. Subsidiaries are companies over which the Group has control. Control is the power to govern the financial and operating policies of a company so as to obtain benefits from its activities. The results of subsidiaries are included or excluded from their effective dates of acquisition or disposal respectively.

All intercompany transactions, balances and unrealised surpluses and deficits on transactions between group companies have been eliminated. Minority interests represent the proportion of the results and net assets of subsidiaries not attributable to the Group.

Associates and joint ventures. Associates are companies, not being subsidiaries over which the Group exercises significant influence.

Joint ventures are companies where the Group has a contractual arrangement with third parties to undertake an economic activity which is subject to joint control.

Associates and joint ventures are included on the equity basis of accounting. The results of associates and joint ventures are included or excluded from their effective dates of acquisition or disposal respectively, and are based on their latest financial statements.

Goodwill. Goodwill represents the difference between the cost of an acquisition and the fair value of the Group's share of the net assets of the acquired subsidiary, associate or joint venture at the effective date of acquisition. Goodwill on acquisitions occurring on or after 1st January 1995 is reported in the balance sheet as an intangible asset or included within associates or joint ventures, as appropriate, and is generally amortised using the straight line method over a period not exceeding twenty years. Goodwill on acquisitions which occurred prior to 1st January

1995 was taken directly to reserves. The carrying amount of goodwill is reviewed annually and written down for permanent impairment where it is considered necessary.

Own shares. The cost of shares held in the Company by a wholly-owned subsidiary and dividends thereon are eliminated from shareholders' funds.

Hongkong Land Holdings Limited
Hong Kong
31 December 2000
International Accounting Standard

CHAPTER 19

Consolidated financial statements: subsidiaries

19.1 Sources

IAS 12 (r2000)	*Accounting for Income Taxes.*
IAS 21 (r1993)	*The Effects of Changes in Foreign Exchange Rates.*
IAS 27	*Consolidated Financial Statements and Accounting for Investments in Subsidiaries.*
IAS 36	*Impairment of Assets.*
IAS 39 (r2000)	*Financial Instruments: Recognition and Measurement (effective 1 January 2001).*
SIC-12	*Consolidation – Special Purpose Entities.*
SIC-16	*Share Capital – Reacquired Own Equity Instruments (Treasury Shares).*

19.2 Introduction

Under International Accounting Standards, the accounting treatment of investments is determined by the substance of the relationship between the investor and the investee. Certain criteria must be met in order to account for investments in a particular manner. Often, these criteria will be met when certain ownership percentages or voting right percentages are met. However, under IASs, the substance of the arrangements will ultimately determine the appropriate accounting treatment. The following table summarises the classification of investments, the substantive criterion applicable to each particular class, the ownership percentages which are likely to lead to the particular classification, the accounting treatment required for each class, and the IASs and chapters in this book which discuss each classification.

Classification	Substantive criterion	Voting rights %	Accounting treatment	Covered by IAS/chapter
Investment	No significant influence	<20	Cost or fair amount	IAS 39/Chapter **12** value
Associate	Significant influence	20–50	Equity method	IAS 28 (r2000)/ Chapter **20**
Subsidiary	Control	>50	Consolidation	IAS 27/Chapter **19**
Joint venture	Joint control	n/a	Proportional consolidation or equity method	IAS 31 (r2000)/ Chapter **21**

19.3 Brief summary of the requirements

A subsidiary is an enterprise that is controlled by another enterprise (the parent). Control is generally presumed to exist when an investor owns more than 50 per cent of the voting rights of the investee. However, the substance of the relationship between the investor and the investee may be such that this is not always the case.

Consolidated financial statements are required to be prepared by all parent enterprises unless the parent enterprise is itself a wholly owned or virtually wholly owned (90 per cent or more) subsidiary of another enterprise.

All investments in subsidiaries are required to be consolidated unless control over an investment is intended to be temporary or it operates under severe long-term restrictions which significantly impair its ability to transfer funds to the parent.

A special purpose entity is consolidated when the substance of the relationship between this entity and the enterprise indicates that the enterprise effectively controls the special purpose entity even where it owns little or none of the special purpose entity's equity.

If an enterprise presents its own separate financial statements, its subsidiaries should be either accounted for using the equity method, carried at cost or accounted for as available-for-sale financial assets in accordance with IAS 39 (r2000).

19.4 Development of the requirements

Issued in 1989, IAS 27 *Consolidated Financial Statements and Accounting for Investments in Subsidiaries* and IAS 28 *Accounting for Investments in Associates* replaced IAS 3 *Consolidated Financial Statements and the Equity*

Method of Accounting. Both IAS 27 and IAS 28 were reformatted in 1994, but no substantive changes were made.

In April 1998 the IASC approved IAS 36 *Impairment of Assets* which sets out guidelines for measuring impairment, including the impairment of investments in subsidiaries. In November 1998 the Standing Interpretations Committee issued SIC-12 dealing with consolidation of special purpose entities.

In December 1998 the IASC approved IAS 39 which establishes principles for recognising, measuring and disclosing information about financial assets and financial liabilities. With the approval of IAS 39, IAS 25 *Accounting for Investments* was withdrawn.

In January 1999 the Standing Interpretations Committee issued SIC-16 dealing with the presentation of an enterprise's holding of its own equity instruments ('treasury shares').

19.5 Scope

IAS 27 deals with accounting for subsidiaries in consolidated financial statements and accounting for subsidiaries in a parent's own separate financial statements.

SIC-12 applies to all special purpose entities with the exception of post-employment benefit plans and equity compensation plans.

19.5.1 Comparison with UK GAAP

Similar concepts of consolidated financial statements and separate parent-only financial statements exist under UK GAAP.

19.5.2 Comparison with US GAAP

Under US GAAP, consolidated financial statements are the only generally accepted financial statements. As such, in practice, separate financial statements of a parent enterprise are virtually non-existent.

19.6 Definitions, control, special purpose entities and limited partnerships

19.6.1 Definitions

> 'A subsidiary is an enterprise that is controlled by another enterprise (known as the parent).'
>
> (IAS 27.6)

'Control (for the purpose of this Standard) is the power to govern the financial and operating policies of an enterprise so as to obtain benefits from its activities.'
(IAS 27.6)

Operating and financial policies are not defined in IASs. They are not the decisions taken by management on a day to day basis, but are the strategic decisions such as: should the group expand into a particular area; should the group pull out of an area; how does the group finance a particular project or expansion plan; at what level should the debt-equity ratio be set; what level of earnings are to be retained and what level are to be paid out as dividends.

'A parent is an enterprise that has one or more subsidiaries.'
(IAS 27.6)

'A group is a parent and all its subsidiaries.'
(IAS 27.6)

19.6.2 Control

As a general rule, control is presumed to exist when an investor owns, either directly or indirectly through subsidiaries, more than 50 per cent of the voting power of an enterprise. However, in exceptional cases, it may be possible to demonstrate that such ownership does not constitute control. The substance of the arrangements in each case will need to be considered.

Control may also exist if a parent owns 50 per cent or less of the voting power of an enterprise when there is:

(a) 'power over more than one half of the voting rights by virtue of an agreement with other investors;
(b) power to govern the financial and operating policies of the enterprise under a statute or an agreement;
(c) power to appoint or remove the majority of the members of the board of directors or equivalent governing body; or
(d) power to cast the majority of votes at meetings of the board of directors or equivalent governing body.'

(IAS 27.12)

Additionally, control exists, and therefore consolidation is required, for certain special purpose entities when few or no voting rights are held (see below). Note, though, that economic dependence, such as that created through a supplier-customer relationship, by itself will not give rise to a parent/subsidiary relationship.

In May 2001 the SIC discussed whether the existence of potential voting rights (e.g., share options) should be considered when determining whether control or significant influence exists, and preliminarily concluded that such rights, if presently exercisable, should be considered. The SIC discussed various circumstances when potential voting rights indicate control or significant influence, and plans to consider these circumstances further at future meetings.

19.6.3 Special purpose entities

A special purpose entity ('SPE') is a corporation, trust or unincorporated entity that has been created to accomplish a narrow and well-defined objective such as to effect a lease, research and development or a securitisation of financial assets. SPEs are often created with legal arrangements that impose strict legal limits on the decision-making powers of their governing body over the operations of the SPE. Frequently, these provisions specify that the policy guiding the ongoing activities of the SPE cannot be modified, other than perhaps by its creator or sponsor (i.e., they operate on so-called 'autopilot'). (SIC-12.1) The sponsor (or enterprise on whose behalf the SPE was created) may transfer assets to the SPE, obtain the right to use assets held by the SPE or perform services for the SPE, while other parties may provide the funding for the SPE. (SIC-12.2)

A beneficial interest in an SPE may, for example, take the form of a debt instrument, an equity instrument, a participation right, a residual interest or a lease. Some beneficial interests may simply provide the holder with a fixed or stated rate of return, while others give the holder rights or access to other future economic benefits of the SPE's activities. In most cases, the creator or sponsor retains a significant beneficial interest in the SPE's activities, even though it may own little or none of the SPE's equity. (SIC-12.3)

SIC-12 requires that 'an SPE should be consolidated when the substance of the relationship between an enterprise and the SPE indicates that the SPE is controlled by that enterprise.' (SIC-12.8) In this context, control may arise through the predetermination of the activities of the SPE (operating on 'autopilot') or otherwise. This is possible even in cases where an enterprise owns little or none of the SPE's equity. (SIC-12.9)

In addition to situations (a)-(d) (described in **19.6.2**) where control may be seen to exist where an enterprise owns 50 per cent or less of the voting power of another enterprise, the SIC concluded that the following circumstances may indicate a relationship in which an enterprise controls an SPE and consequently should consolidate the SPE:

(a) 'in substance, the activities of the SPE are being conducted on behalf of the enterprise according to its specific business needs so that the enterprise obtains benefits from the SPE's operation;
(b) in substance, the enterprise has the decision-making powers to obtain

the majority of the benefits of the activities of the SPE or, by setting up an 'autopilot' mechanism, the enterprise has delegated these decision making powers;

(c) in substance, the enterprise has rights to obtain the majority of the benefits of the SPE and therefore may be exposed to risks incident to the activities of the SPE; or

(d) in substance, the enterprise retains the majority of the residual or ownership risks related to the SPE or its assets in order to obtain benefits from its activities'.

(SIC-12.10)

The effect of SIC-12 is that many SPE arrangements will be consolidated. A potential inconsistency arises where assets which may meet the derecognition criteria of IAS 39 (r2000), would continue to be consolidated if they were structured within an SPE.

Further examples and guidance are included in the appendix to the SIC-12. However, the list above and the further guidance in the appendix to the SIC-12 are not intended to be a comprehensive checklist of conditions that must be met cumulatively in order to require consolidation of an SPE. These conditions are only the indicators of the underlying substance of the relationship between the enterprise and the SPE. Each such arrangement should be analysed individually to determine the substance of the relationship.

19.6.4 Limited partnerships

In the case of limited partnerships in the UK, situations may arise where the limited partners are the majority equity interest holders. By definition, limited partners do not have any involvement in the management of the partnership and are therefore not the parent of the partnerships. The general partners, despite holding minority equity interests, will often exercise control over the partnerships and, if so, this would make them the parent under IAS 27.

19.6.5 Comparison with UK GAAP

In accordance with FRS 2 *Accounting for Subsidiary Undertakings*, an enterprise is considered a parent of another enterprise if it holds a majority of the voting rights in the undertaking. This differs from IAS 27 which merely presumes control when greater than 50 per cent of the voting rights of an enterprise are owned. Although it may be rare in practice, this presumption in IAS 27 may be rebutted. Similar to IAS 27, under UK GAAP, when an enterprise does not own a majority of the voting rights of another enterprise, it may still be considered a parent when the substance of the arrangement indicates that it has dominant influence (dominant influence is a concept very similar to that of control in IAS 27). Provisions of FRS 5

Reporting the Substance of Transactions, regarding identification and accounting for quasi-subsidiaries would generally result in consolidation of SPEs in accordance with SIC-12.

However, while FRS 5 permits a net presentation ('linked presentation') for certain non-recourse arrangements held through an SPE, SIC-12 would require full consolidation.

19.6.6 Comparison with US GAAP

ARB 51 *Consolidated Financial Statements*, as amended by SFAS 94 *Consolidation of All Majority-Owned Subsidiaries*, is the main source of US GAAP relating to consolidations. As under IAS 27, under US GAAP, control is the basis for defining subsidiaries. However, this statement may be slightly misleading since the definitions of control differ between US GAAP and IAS 27. US GAAP refers to control as, 'the usual condition for a controlling financial interest (which) is ownership of a majority voting interest.' (SFAS 94.13) In practice, under US GAAP, when ownership of a majority voting interest is held, an investment is considered a subsidiary. However, under IAS 27, the definition of control does not hinge on a particular level of voting interest. It is based on the substance of the relationship between the investor and investee. Thus, while IAS 27 refers to the presumption that control exists when greater than 50 per cent of the voting power of an enterprise is held, it is merely a presumption. That presumption may be rebutted when it can be clearly demonstrated that control does not exist when greater than 50 per cent of the voting power of an investee is held or conversely when it can be clearly demonstrated that control does exist when less than 50 per cent of the voting power of an investee is held.

Existing US GAAP rules on consolidation of special purpose entities are complex and not very clear. Generally, under US GAAP a sponsor or transferee must consolidate an SPE except where the majority owner of the SPE is an independent third party who has made a substantive capital investment in the SPE, has control of the SPE, and has substantive risks and rewards of ownership of the assets of the SPE (including residuals).

Specific rules apply to 'qualified SPEs' as defined by SFAS 140 *Accounting for Transfers and Servicing of Financial Assets and Extinguishments of Liabilities – a replacement of FAS 125*. EITF 90-15 *Impact of Nonsubstantive Lessors, Residual Value Guarantees, and Other Provisions in Leasing Transactions* specifically addresses the use of SPEs in leasing transactions and requires a lessee to consolidate a special-purpose entity lessor when certain conditions exist. For other SPEs control is determined within the meaning of SFAS 94 as mentioned above. The variety of specific arrangements under which SPEs are created and certain vagueness of the rules in both US GAAP and IASs could result in some cases in different treatments adopted under these accounting regimes.

19.7 Presentation of consolidated financial statements

'Consolidated financial statements are the financial statements of a group presented as those of a single enterprise.' (IAS 27.6) In some countries consolidated financial statements may not be required while in other countries, only consolidated financial statements are required.

As a general rule, IAS 27 requires that a parent enterprise present consolidated financial statements. (IAS 27.7) An exception to the rule is made and consolidated financial statements are not required when a parent is:

(a) a wholly owned subsidiary; or
(b) a virtually wholly owned subsidiary (its parent owns 90 per cent or more of its voting power), and the parent obtains the approval of the owners of the minority interest.

When a parent takes advantage of this exception, it must disclose:

(a) the reasons why consolidated financial statements are not presented;
(b) the bases on which subsidiaries are accounted for in its separate financial statements (cost, fair value or the equity method); and
(c) the name and registered office of its parent that publishes consolidated financial statements.

(IAS 27.8)

If the parent of the intermediate parent company does not publish consolidated financial statements, we recommend that a note to this effect is given in the financial statements of the intermediate parent, together with the name and registered office of the parent.

19.7.1 Comparison with UK GAAP

The Companies Act 1985 requires that an enterprise which is a parent company at the balance sheet date prepares consolidated financial statements. However, exceptions are made for:

(a) certain enterprises which head what are defined as eligible small and medium-sized groups;
(b) certain enterprises which are subsidiaries of other groups within the European Union; and

(c) certain enterprises whose subsidiaries are all exempt from consolidation as discussed in the next section.

19.7.2 Comparison with US GAAP

As noted earlier, under US GAAP, consolidated financial statements are required for all parent enterprises. Separate financial statements are not generally permitted.

19.8 Scope of consolidated financial statements

As a general rule, when preparing consolidated financial statements, all subsidiaries, foreign and domestic, are required to be consolidated. (IAS 27.11) However, exceptions to the general rule are made in two circumstances. Subsidiaries are not required to be consolidated when:

(a) control is intended to be temporary because the subsidiary is acquired and held exclusively with a view to its subsequent disposal in the near future. Thus, deciding to hold an existing investment in a subsidiary for sale is not enough to qualify for this exemption from consolidation; or
(b) it operates under severe long-term restrictions which significantly impair its ability to transfer funds to the parent.

Such subsidiaries should be accounted for in accordance with IAS 39 (r2000) *Financial Instruments: Recognition and Measurement*. (IAS 27.13) See Chapters **10** and **12**, respectively.

The temporary control exemption would apply, for example, to transactions that are in substance an acquisition of interest by the enforcement of a security. For instance, an enterprise may have initially lent money on the security of a property. The borrower subsequently defaults on the loan and enters into a financial restructuring whereby the lender receives a majority of shares in the borrower. The lender should exclude the subsidiary from consolidation on the ground that effectively it was acquired as a result of the enforcement of a security, unless, of course, the interest has, or is to, become part of the investor's continuing activities.

Determining temporary control is a matter of professional judgement and careful analysis of the facts and circumstances in each case is required. Normally, the expectation should be that the disposal would normally take place within one year of the date of acquisition. Where the disposal has not been achieved within that period, consideration should be given to whether the parent entity has identified or is continuing to actively seek a purchaser and the extended period can be justified on the basis of the particular circumstances of the subsidiary and the prevailing economic environment.

It is inappropriate to exclude subsidiaries from consolidation on the grounds that their activities are substantially different from those of the parent and/or the rest of the group. As long as the parent retains control over such subsidiaries, they are required to be consolidated. Information regarding the different nature of the activities of a subsidiary may be appropriately disclosed in accordance with IAS 14 (r1997), *Segment Reporting*. (IAS 27.14)

Note that SPEs operating on 'autopilot' are not excluded from consolidation on the basis of (b) above.

19.8.1 Comparison with UK GAAP

Under UK GAAP, subsidiaries may be excluded from consolidation on the basis of:

(a) materiality. However, two or more subsidiaries may be excluded only if they are not material taken together. This is consistent with IASs which do not apply to immaterial items;
(b) 'severe long-term restrictions (which) substantially hinder the exercise of the rights of the parent company over the assets or management of that undertaking.' (s229(3(a))) This exclusion is required by FRS 2, *Accounting for Subsidiary Undertakings*, and is consistent with IAS 27. However, the exclusion in IAS 27 is more broad in that it refers to restrictions which significantly impair the subsidiary's ability to transfer funds to the parent and thus would encompass subsidiaries operating in countries with restrictions on the amount of currency able to leave the country;
(c) temporary control. This exclusion is required and is more prescriptive than the exclusion included in IAS 27 in that, other than on the enforcement of a security, it may only be invoked if the investment is reasonably expected to be disposed of within one year from its date of acquisition. It also only applies if the subsidiary has not previously been consolidated in group accounts prepared by the parent; or
(d) differing activities. This exclusion is defined very narrowly in FRS 2 with the effect that no examples can be identified. There is no corresponding exclusion in IAS 27.

Although the Companies Act 1985 permits the exclusion of subsidiaries on the grounds of disproportionate expense or undue delay, FRS 2 effectively repeals the exclusion.

19.8.2 Comparison with US GAAP

Both IAS 27 and US GAAP require exclusion from consolidation when control is temporary, involves severe foreign exchange restrictions or governmentally imposed uncertainties. SEC Staff Accounting Bulletin 93 clarified the meaning of temporary control by indicating that this exception to consolidation is not applicable to situations involving the planned dispositions of subsidiaries that have previously been consolidated. Rather, the temporary control exception to consolidation is only applicable if control is likely to be lost in the near term as a result of the probable occurrence of events that lie outside the company's control, or the subsidiary will be sold within a year after it is acquired. For non-public entities, the issue of whether control is temporary is largely a matter of judgement, based on the specific facts and circumstances. However, at a minimum, the following criteria must be met:

(a) the investor must have the intent and ability to relinquish its control over a majority voting interest in the investee (e.g., by sale of all or a portion of its interest in the investee, such that it controls 50 per cent or less of the investee);
(b) it must be probable that the investor will relinquish control over the investee within one year from the balance-sheet date; and
(c) the necessary approvals (e.g., board approval) to cause such actions to occur must have been obtained prior to issuing the financial statements.

It is unclear whether or not the exclusion in US GAAP for subsidiaries over which control is temporary encompasses as many scenarios as those included in IAS 27 relating to restrictions on the ability of a subsidiary to transfer funds to the parent.

19.9 Preparation of consolidated financial statements

IAS 27 briefly outlines consolidation procedures and states other general requirements about the preparation of consolidated financial statements. The guidance is summarised below.

19.9.1 Consolidation procedures

When preparing consolidated financial statements, the individual items in the financial statements of the parent and its subsidiaries are aggregated on a line-by-line basis and then certain consolidation adjustments are made. (IAS 27.15) For example, the cash, trade receivables and prepayments of the parent and each subsidiary are added together to arrive at the cash, trade receivables and prepayments of the group before consolidation adjustments are made.

The consolidation adjustments required will vary depending on the circumstances. Normally adjustments (the list is not exhaustive) are required to:

(a) eliminate the carrying amount of the parent's investment in each subsidiary and the parent's portion of equity of each subsidiary. Any resultant goodwill is recognised in accordance with IAS 22 (r1998) (see Chapter **18**) (IAS 27.15(a));
(b) amortise any goodwill or negative goodwill arising from step (a);
(c) eliminate the minority interest in the net income of consolidated subsidiaries for the reporting period. (IAS 27.15(b)) If the losses applicable to the minority interests in a consolidated subsidiary exceed the minority interest in the equity of the subsidiary, the excess, and any further losses applicable to the minority interests, are charged against the majority except to the extent that the minority has a binding obligation to, and is able to, make good the losses. When the subsidiary subsequently reports profits, the minority interests do not participate until the majority has recovered all of the losses of the minority it previously absorbed (IAS 27.27);
(d) eliminate all intragroup balances and intragroup transactions and resulting unrealised profits in full including sales, expenses, dividends, etc. Unrealised losses resulting from intragroup transactions are also eliminated in full unless their cost cannot be recovered. (IAS 27.17) Unrealised profits which are included in the assets of the group such as items of property, plant and equipment or inventory, are also eliminated in full; and
(e) eliminate from consolidated profits dividends related to outstanding cumulative preference shares of a subsidiary when such shares are held outside of the group regardless of whether the dividends have been declared. (IAS 27.28)

Deferred tax

Deferred tax assets or liabilities may arise on consolidation. A temporary difference arises when the carrying amount of an investment in a subsidiary becomes different from the tax base, often the cost, of the investment. Such differences may arise due to undistributed profits of subsidiaries, changes in foreign exchange rates when the parent and subsidiary are based in different countries or other reasons. IAS 12 (r2000) sets out the criteria for recognition of deferred tax assets and liabilities arising on consolidation (see Chapter **23**).

Minority interest

> 'Minority interest is that part of the net results of operations and of net assets of a subsidiary attributable to interests which are not owned, directly or indirectly through subsidiaries, by the parent.'
>
> (IAS 27.6)

As indicated above the basic consolidation process involves the aggregation of the assets, liabilities, income and expenditure of the individual group undertakings. Therefore where the group does not hold the whole of the share capital of a subsidiary, an adjustment is necessary to take account of the interests of the outside shareholders. Their interests in the capital and reserves of the subsidiary need to be recognised in the group balance sheet and their share of the subsidiary's profit or loss for the year needs to be taken into account in arriving at the group profit or loss.

The amount of minority interest included in the balance sheet is calculated as:

(a) the amount of minority interest arising at the date of acquisition (see Chapter **18**); plus
(b) the share of the minority interest in movements in equity since the date of acquisition.

(IAS 27.15(c) and IAS 27.26)

As it is possible that a parent has control over a subsidiary without majority ownership of shares, there is no upper limit to the proportion of net assets and profits or losses that may be attributable to 'minority' shareholders. Thus, in certain situations, the term 'outside shareholders interests' appears to be more appropriate than the term 'minority interests'.

Subsidiary holding shares in parent

When a subsidiary holds shares in its parent, SIC-16 requires the use of the treasury stock method whereby consolidated shareholders' equity is reduced by the cost of shareholdings by the subsidiary in its parent. The acquisition of treasury shares is presented in the consolidated financial statements as a change in equity. (SIC-16) For further discussion of the treatment of treasury shares and relevant disclosures see Chapter **11**.

19.9.2 Comparison with UK GAAP

As under IAS 27, under UK GAAP, full elimination of intercompany transactions is required. The other consolidation procedures outlined above are generally followed in the UK. However, in the UK, companies legislation does not generally allow a subsidiary to hold shares in its parent. However, shares of the parent held in a trust controlled by the group (for example, to provide employee benefits) are generally shown as an asset rather than deducted from equity.

19.9.3 Comparison with US GAAP

US GAAP does not specifically prescribe the consolidation procedures outlined above. However, in practice, they are generally followed. The only exception relates to intercompany transactions. IAS 27 requires full (100 per cent) elimination of intercompany transactions. US GAAP does not address this point and varying practices have developed. Some enterprises eliminate

100 per cent in line with IAS 27 but some enterprises eliminate only their proportionate share. Similarly to SIC-16, ARB 51 *Consolidated Financial Statements* in the US requires that shares of a parent company held by a subsidiary are not treated as outstanding shares in the consolidated balance sheet of the parent.

19.10 General requirements and guidance

19.10.1 Reporting dates

Usually the reporting dates of a parent and its subsidiaries coincide. However, 'When the financial statements used in the consolidation are drawn up to different reporting dates, adjustments should be made for the effects of significant transactions or other events that occur between those dates and the date of the parent's financial statements. In any case the difference between reporting dates should be no more than three months.' (IAS 27.19)

When a subsidiary and its parent have differing reporting dates, the subsidiary normally prepares financial statements as of the reporting date for the parent for consolidation purposes unless it is impracticable to do so. As indicated above, when financial statements with different reporting dates are used for consolidation purposes, the difference between reporting dates can be no greater than three months. The time lag must be consistent from year to year.

There are circumstances, however, which make it necessary or appropriate to have different dates. Some reasons which may be justifiable are:

- companies in remote territories may be unable to comply with the parent company's timetable for preparing annual financial statements which will usually be framed with a view to avoiding undue delay in publication. This may result in some foreign subsidiaries closing their accounts one or two months earlier than the parent in order to allow time to complete and transmit information for consolidation;
- legislation in certain countries requires financial statements to be prepared to a specified date;
- the normal trading cycle in certain trades (e.g., agriculture) may make it desirable for subsidiaries to have financial years which end at a particular time of the year (e.g., when crops have been harvested). In addition, subsidiaries with cyclical trade such as retail businesses may wish to avoid a year end routine during busy pre-Christmas trading when stock levels are high; and
- a change in accounting date may have serious adverse tax consequences, or significant tax advantages may arise from having a different accounting date.

In any of the cases above, the time lag between reporting dates of longer than three months is not permitted.

IAS 21 (r1993) states that when a subsidiary is a foreign entity and it draws up its accounts at a different date from that of its parent, the exchange rate used is the rate in effect at the subsidiary's reporting date. However, if there are significant movements in exchange rates up to the balance sheet date of the parent, adjustments are made to reflect these movements. (IAS 21 (r1993).35) See Chapter **22** for further discussion of exchange gains and losses related to subsidiaries operating in foreign countries.

19.10.2 Uniform accounting policies

> 'Consolidated financial statements should be prepared using uniform accounting policies for like transactions and other events in similar circumstances. If it is not practicable to use uniform accounting policies in preparing the consolidated financial statements, that fact should be disclosed together with the proportions of the items in the consolidated financial statements to which the different accounting policies have been applied.'
>
> (IAS 27.21)

The following are examples of circumstances where it is impracticable or inappropriate to adopt uniform accounting policies in the individual financial statements of each undertaking in the group:

- the policy is prohibited by legislation in another country;
- the policy is contrary to generally accepted accounting principles in the relevant country; and
- the policy would result in serious adverse tax consequences.

In practice, when subsidiaries adopt different accounting policies from the parent, an adjustment is made on consolidation to bring the accounting policies into line. When such adjustments are made, the above disclosures are not required.

However, most group companies usually adopt uniform policies in order to provide consistent bases for reporting management information, and also to minimise the level of consolidation adjustments necessary.

19.10.3 Acquisitions and disposals

As discussed in Chapter **18**, the results of operations of a subsidiary are included in the consolidated financial statements from the date of acquisition, which is the date on which control effectively passes to the acquirer/parent. Such results are included in the consolidated financial statements until the date of disposal which is the date on which the parent ceases to have control of the subsidiary.

The difference between the carrying amount of the net assets of a subsidiary including goodwill capitalised as an asset, at its date of disposal and the fair value of the consideration received for its sale is recognised as a gain or loss in the income statement of the parent at the date of disposal. (IAS 27.23)

It is not clear whether pre-1995 goodwill written off to reserves is included in calculation of the gain or loss on disposal of a subsidiary. Such an amount could either be added to the carrying amount of the assets disposed of and thus decrease the gain or increase the loss on disposal or simply transferred from the goodwill reserve to retained earnings. Since the goodwill has never been recognised in either the income statement or the other performance statement which shows gains and losses not included in the income statement, the preferable view would seem to be that it should be taken into account in calculating the gain or loss on disposal.

The date of disposal is the date on which the parent ceases to have control of the subsidiary. (IAS 27.23)

The date of disposal cannot be artificially altered, for example, by indicating in the purchase agreement some other date. Although the date on which the consideration is paid is often an important indication of the date on which a subsidiary undertaking is acquired or disposed of, it does not give conclusive evidence of the date of the transfer of control because this date can be set to fall on a date other than that on which control is transferred, with compensation for any lead or lag included in the consideration. It is important to consider all the circumstances in order to determine when control passes. In some countries, it may take several months after the exchange of purchase consideration for a transaction to be finalised at law. However, in many cases, the acquirer will assume control when purchase consideration is paid. In such cases, the date of acquisition is the date the acquirer assumes control.

On disposal of a subsidiary additional disclosures are required (as discussed in **19.12**).

If an investment ceases to meet the definition of a subsidiary and does not meet the definition of an associate (see Chapter **20**), the investment is accounted for as an investment in accordance with IAS 39 (r2000) (see Chapters **10** and **12**, respectively). (IAS 27.24) The carrying amount of the investment at the date it ceases to be a subsidiary is regarded as cost thereafter. (IAS 27.25)

IASs are silent on the issue of how to account for gains or losses, generally referred to as dilution gains and losses, arising from the issuance by a subsidiary of equity shares. In October 1997, the SIC considered whether such gains or losses should be recognised in equity or net profit or loss and determined that to require one over the other would require a choice between the fundamental accounting concepts of the parent company approach and the economic unit approach. Since such a choice was at that time beyond the mandate of the SIC, the SIC decided not to add the project to its agenda. The IASB has added a two-phase project on Business Combinations to its agenda, and will probably address this issue in one of these projects.

19.10.4 Comparison with UK GAAP

UK GAAP is consistent with IAS 27 regarding reporting dates of a parent and its subsidiaries. However, under UK GAAP, when the financial statements of a subsidiary used in consolidation are not prepared as of the reporting date of the parent, additional disclosures are required which are not required under IAS 27.

Under UK GAAP, uniform accounting policies between a parent and its subsidiaries are required in the consolidated financial statements in all but exceptional circumstances. Under IAS 27, consistent accounting policies are required unless it is not practicable. However, when policies are not consistent, both UK GAAP and IAS 27 require certain disclosures to be made; these required disclosures differ.

19.10.5 Comparison with US GAAP

US GAAP is consistent with IAS 27 regarding reporting dates of a parent and its subsidiaries.

Under IAS 27, parent and subsidiary enterprises are required, unless it is not practicable, to adopt the same accounting policies in the preparation of the consolidated financial statements. This issue is not addressed in US GAAP. An exception to this general rule arises when a subsidiary adopts, for its separate financial statements, a standard in a period different from the period in which the parent adopts the standard or uses a different transition method. In these circumstances, the separate financial statements of the subsidiary should conform to those of the parent in consolidation.

19.11 Accounting for investments in subsidiaries in a parent's separate financial statements

As noted earlier, some enterprises may present separate parent financial statements. IASs do not require or preclude the preparation of such financial statements. When separate financial statements of a parent enterprise are prepared, investments in subsidiaries that are included in the consolidated financial statements should be either:

(a) carried at cost;
(b) accounted for using the equity method (see Chapter **20**); or
(c) accounted for as available-for-sale financial assets in accordance with IAS 39 (r2000) (see Chapter **12**).

(IAS 27.29)

Similarly, investments in subsidiaries that are excluded from consolidation are accounted as either (a), (b) or (c) above in the separate parent financial statements. (IAS 27.30) As discussed in **19.8**, a subsidiary may be excluded from consolidation if control is intended to be temporary or if it operates under severe long-term restrictions which significantly impair its ability to transfer funds to the parent.

IAS 36 requires an impairment review to be carried out if there is indication that the carrying amount of an asset may not be recoverable (see **10.12**).

19.11.1 Comparison with UK GAAP

Under UK GAAP, investments in subsidiaries are normally carried in the separate financial statements of the parent at cost but may be revalued on any basis permitted by law.

19.11.2 Comparison with US GAAP

As discussed previously, separate financial statements are not generally permitted or required under US GAAP.

19.12 Disclosure

As discussed in **19.7**, when a parent enterprise does not present consolidated accounts, the reason and bases on which subsidiaries have been accounted for in its separate financial statements is required to be disclosed.

As discussed in **19.10**, when subsidiaries are consolidated which have not adopted consistent accounting policies with the parent, this fact is required to be disclosed together with the proportions of the items in the consolidated financial statements to which the different accounting policies have been applied.

In addition, the following disclosures are required:

(a) 'in consolidated financial statements a listing of significant subsidiaries including the name, country of incorporation or residence, proportion of ownership interest, and if different, proportion of voting power held;
(b) in consolidated financial statements, where applicable:
    (i) the reasons for not consolidating a subsidiary;

(ii) the nature of the relationship between the parent and a subsidiary of which the parent does not own, directly or indirectly through subsidiaries, more than one half of the voting power;

(iii) the name of an enterprise in which more than one half of the voting power is owned, directly or indirectly through subsidiaries, but which, because of the absence of control, is not a subsidiary; and

(iv) the effect of the acquisition and disposal of subsidiaries on the financial position at the reporting date, the results for the reporting period and on the corresponding amounts for the preceding period.

(c) in the parent's separate financial statements, a description of the method used to account for subsidiaries.'

(IAS 27.32)

In respect of (b) (iv) above, when a subsidiary which has been disposed of meets the definition of a discontinuing operation included in IAS 35 (r1998) *Discontinuing Operations*, the disclosure requirements of that Standard are also applicable (see Chapter **5**).

The minority interests in the net assets of the enterprise is required to be disclosed on the face of the balance sheet separately from liabilities and issued capital and reserves. (IAS 1 (r1997) *Presentation of Financial Statements*, para.66 and IAS 27.26) See Chapter **9**. Minority interest in the net profit or loss of consolidated subsidiaries for the reporting period is disclosed on the face of the income statement. (IAS 1(r1997).75 and IAS 27.26) See Chapter **5**.

19.13 Examples from published financial statements

Note that the excerpts given do not always comply in full with all aspects of IAS and as such are not necessarily examples of best practice but merely of current practice.

Example 19.1

Principles of consolidation

The assets, liabilities and equity of consolidated companies are added together on a line-by-line basis, eliminating the book value of the related investment against the Group's share of equity.

In the case of subsidiaries not 100% owned, the Group recognises a minority interest consisting of the portion of net income and net assets attributable to the interest owned by third parties.

All significant intercompany balances, transactions and unrealised profits and losses are eliminated.

The balance sheets of subsidiaries denominated in foreign currencies are translated into US Dollars using year-end exchange rates, while average exchange rates for the year are used for the translation of the statements of the income and cash flows. Significant individual transactions are translated at the rate of exchange prevailing on the date of the transaction. Translation gains and losses, including the differences arising as a result of translating opening shareholders' equity using exchange rates at the close of the period rather than exchange rates at the beginning of the period, are reported as a separate component of shareholders' equity.

Any goodwill arising on the acquisition of a foreign entity and any fair value adjustments to the carrying amount of the assets and liabilities arising on the acquisition of that foreign entity are translated using the closing exchange rate.

Acquisitions

In November 1999, the Group acquired 70% of Sergio Rossi S.p.A., a company which manufactures and distributes shoes and accessories principally under the Sergio Rossi trademark, for approximately US$96 million. In December 1999, the Group acquired 100% of the shares of Artemis IV S.A., a company which controls the Yves Saint Lauren fashion and accessory business (hereafter 'Yves Saint Laurent Couture') as well as the Sanofi Beaute perfume, cosmetics and skin care business (hereafter 'YSL Beaute'), which includes the wholly owned trademarks Yves Saint Laurent and Roger & Gallet as well as licenses for the trademarks Van Cleef & Arpels, Oscar de la Renta and Fendi. The price for this company was approximately US$1,100 million.

In January 2000, the Group acquired 66.7% of the shares of Mendes S.A., a company involved in production, distribution, retail sales and licensing of products with the trademark Yves Saint Laurent Rive Gauche. The remaining 33.3% of the shares were already held by Yves Saint Laurent Couture. The price paid for these shares was not material.

The acquisitions have been accounted for utilising the purchase method and, accordingly, the operating results of the new businesses have been included in the consolidated statements of income since acquisition. The purchase prices have been preliminarily allocated to identified assets (including trademarks) and liabilities of the acquired companies based on their estimated fair values on the date of acquisition. The residual value has been recorded as goodwill.

The value and expected useful life of each brand acquired have been determined by the specialist brand valuation expert Interbrand Newell and Sorrell Ltd. Based on their appraisals, the Group has determined that the trademarks Yves Saint Laurent, Yves Saint Laurent Rive Gauche and Sergio Rossi will be amortised over a period of 20 years, the maximum permitted by IAS.

After allocation of the purchase price to the identified assets and liabilities, the residual amount of US$ 268.9 million was attributed to goodwill, which will be amortised over 20 years.

Gucci
Netherlands
31 December 1999
International Accounting Standards

Example 19.2

Acquisitions/Sales of companies

The year 2000 was one of considerable activity in the acquisition and sale of companies. Overall, acquisitions made total DKK 14.3 billion and companies have been divested for a total of DKK 13.6 million. There has been a significant impact on the financial statements, and the principal transactions are described below.

Effective August 10, GN Great Nordic sold its 53.5% shareholding in SONOFON to Norwegian telecommunications operator Telenor. The value of the transaction was DKK 14.7 billion on an enterprise value basis, giving GN Great Nordic an accounting gain of approx. DKK 12.8 billion in the 2000 fiscal year.

On June 7, 2000, GN Great Nordic acquired the US company Beltone Electronics Corporation at a price of DKK 3.1 billion. Beltone has now been integrated into GN ReSound, enhancing that company's market position in the United States and Japan by a substantial margin. The estimated goodwill amounts to DKK 3,442 million and other intangibles amount to DKK 277 million. The annual impact on income will be DKK 172 million in amortisation of goodwill and DKK 22 million in amortisation of other intangibles.

On November 10, 2000, NetTest acquired French company Photonetics S.A., and that company is now a part of NetTest. The acquisition price was DKK 9.1 billion. The parties also agreed a potential additional payment of up to USD 100 million to be paid with NetTest shares depending on NetTest's market capitalisation on an IPO. The additional payment is not included in debt at December 31, 2000, as it is not considered likely that the amount will fall due for payment given the current stock market price levels. Photonetics S.A. is a provider of equipment and systems for testing and monitoring optical communications networks. Goodwill amounts to DKK 8,254 million and other intangibles amount to DKK 1,234 million, equal to an annual impact on income of DKK 413 million in the amortisation of goodwill and of DKK 136 million in the amortisation of other intangibles.

GN Netcom acquired JABRA Corporation on August 25 at a price of USD 40 million plus earn-out payments totalling a maximum of USD 35 million depending on JABRA's future earnings. The amount of USD 62 million is recognised in the financial statement in respect of this acquisition.

JABRA is the largest and the leading supplier of advanced hands-free headsets for cell phones in the United States. Goodwill amounts to DKK 369 million and other intangibles amount to DKK 173 million. The annual impact on income will be DKK 18 million in amortisation of goodwill and DKK 12 million in amortisation of other intangibles.

In November, GN Netcom acquired Hello Direct, a US company listed on NASDAQ (ticker: HELO) at a price of 95 million in cash. Hello Direct develops, manufactures and markets desktop telephony solutions, including headsets. Goodwill amounts to DKK 473 million and other intangibles amount to DKK 164 million. The annual impact on income will be DKK 24 million in amortisation of goodwill and DKK 23 million in amortisation of other intangibles.

NetTest acquired two French companies, GM Iris and Optran S.A. on September and October respectively. The company paid FRF 80 million for GM Iris, while Optran S.A. was acquired at a price of FRF 94 million plus earn-out payments of up to FRF 46 million over the next three years. This amount includes DKK 46 million in additional costs at December 31, 2000. GM Iris most important product is COMPASS, a software system for troubleshooting in mobile GSN networks. Optran S.A. specialises in testing high-speed data transmission.

The overall gain on the sale of companies in 2000 amounted to DKK 12,836 million.

The overall investment in companies acquired in 2000 amounted to DKK 14,258. Goodwill on the year's acquisitions amounts to DKK 13,099 million and other intangibles amount to DKK 1,850 million. The impact on income in 2000 will be DKK 205 million in amortisation of goodwill and DKK 43 million in amortisation of other intangibles.

The useful life of goodwill is determined by assessing each acquisition, including the company's strategic nature, customers, and technologies. Goodwill from major acquisitions is usually amortised over 20 years, while minor acquisitions are typically amortised over a fewer number of years.

Other intangibles acquired through acquisitions are amortised over their estimated useful lives.

GN Great Nordic
Denmark
31 December 2000
International Accounting Standards

CHAPTER 20

Consolidated financial statements: associates

20.1 Source

IAS 1 (r1997)	*Presentation of Financial Statements.*
IAS 27	*Consolidated Financial Statements and Accounting for Investments in Subsidiaries.*
IAS 28 (r2000)	*Accounting for Investments in Associates.*
IAS 36	*Impairment of Assets.*
IAS 39 (r2000)	*Financial Instruments: Recognition and Measurement* (effective 1 January 2001).
SIC-3	*Elimination of Unrealised Profits and Losses on Transactions with Associates.*
SIC-20	*Equity Accounting Method – Recognition of Losses.*

20.2 Brief summary of the requirements

An associate is an enterprise in which an investor has significant influence and is neither a subsidiary nor a joint venture of the investor. The definition of an associate is dependent on an investor being able to exercise significant influence over the investee. Significant influence is generally presumed to exist when an investor owns between 20 per cent and 50 per cent of the voting rights of the investee. However, the substance of the relationship between the investor and the investee may be such that this is not always the case.

An investment in an associate is accounted for using the equity method in consolidated financial statements, unless control over the investment is intended to be temporary or it operates under severe long-term restrictions which significantly impair its ability to transfer funds to the parent.

If an enterprise presents separate financial statements, its investments in associates are either accounted for using the equity method, carried at cost or accounted for as an available-for-sale financial asset, as described in IAS 39 (r2000) (see Chapter **12**).

20.3 Development of the requirements

Issued in 1989, IAS 27 and IAS 28, replaced IAS 3 *Consolidated Financial Statements and the Equity Method of Accounting*. Both IAS 27 and IAS 28 were reformatted in 1994, but no substantive changes were made.

In December 1997 the Standing Interpretations Committee issued SIC-3 dealing with the elimination of unrealised profits and losses resulting from the transaction between an investor and associates accounted for using the equity method.

In April 1998 IASC approved IAS 36 which sets out guidelines for measuring impairment, including the impairment of investments in associates. In July 1998 IAS 28 was revised to be consistent with IAS 36.

In December 1998 the IASC approved IAS 39, which establishes principles for recognising, measuring and disclosing information about financial assets and financial liabilities, and superseded IAS 25 *Accounting for Investments.*

In June 2000 the Standing Interpretations Committee issued SIC-20 dealing with the recognition of the investor's share of losses of an associate.

20.4 Associates and significant influence

> 'An associate is an enterprise in which the investor has significant influence and which is neither a subsidiary nor a joint venture of the investor.'
>
> (IAS 28 (r2000).3)
>
> 'Significant influence is the power to participate in the financial and operating policy decisions of the investee but is not control over those policies.'
>
> (IAS 28 (r2000).3)

As a general rule, significant influence is presumed to exist when an investor holds, directly or indirectly through subsidiaries, 20 per cent or more of the voting power of the investee. However, as with the classification of any investment, the substance of the arrangements in each case will need to be considered. If it can be clearly demonstrated that an investor which holds less than 20 per cent of the voting power of the investee exercises significant influence, its investment will be accounted for as an associate. Conversely, if it can be clearly demonstrated that an investor which holds more than 20 per cent of the voting power of the investee does not have the power to exercise significant influence, its investment will not be accounted for as an associate but as an investment in accordance with IAS 39 (r2000) (see Chapters **10** and **12,** respectively).

For example, an investor may hold more than 20 per cent of the voting rights of an enterprise but not be able to exert significant influence due to the existence of another shareholder who holds all or substantially all of the remaining shares in the enterprise, and therefore the investment is not accounted for as an associate. Another common example arises when an investor purchases more than 20 per cent of an enterprise in a hostile take-over bid which subsequently fails. Although the investor may hold more than 20 per cent of the voting rights, it may well not be able to exert significant influence over the investee.

When an investor exercises significant influence over the investee one or more of the following indicators are usually present:

(a) 'representation on the board of directors or equivalent governing body of the investee;
(b) participation in policy making process;
(c) material transactions between the investor and the investee;
(d) interchange of managerial personnel; or
(e) provision of essential technical information.'

(IAS 28 (r2000).5)

In some circumstances, it may be difficult to distinguish between significant influence and control. As discussed in Chapter **19**, 'Control is the power to govern the financial and operating policies of an enterprise so as to obtain benefits from its activities.' (IAS 28 (r2000).3) When an investor exercises control over an investee, the investment is accounted for as a subsidiary as discussed in Chapter **19**. In each case, the substance of the arrangements between the investor and the investee is examined to determine whether significant influence or control exists.

An investor may hold, say, a 30 per cent shareholding in an investee which is a subsidiary of another entity (which is unrelated to the investor). The question arises whether the investee can be both a subsidiary of one entity and an associate of another at the same time. The obvious assumption is that since a subsidiary is controlled by its parent, there is no scope for another investor to be in a position to exercise a significant influence. However, this assumption may be rebutted if it can be demonstrated that the parent has allowed the investor some degree of influence.

20.4.1 Comparison with UK GAAP

Consistent with IAS 28 (r2000), under FRS 9 *Associates and Joint Ventures* an associate is an investment over which the investor exercises significant influence, and significant influence is presumed when an investor owns between 20 per cent and 50 per cent of the voting rights of the investee. Under both IAS 28 (r2000) and FRS 9, this is a rebuttable presumption. In addition, FRS 9 includes a requirement that an investor must hold a participating interest in order for the investment to qualify as an associate. However in practice, this requirement should not lead to investments being accounted for as associates under IAS 28 (r2000) but not under FRS 9. However, a slight difference in emphases does exist between IAS 28 (r2000) and FRS 9 in that IAS 28 (r2000) merely requires an investor to have the power to participate in the financial and operating policy decisions of the investee whereas under FRS 9 an investor must actually be participating and exercising significant influence.

20.4.2 Comparison with US GAAP

As in IAS 28 (r2000), under US GAAP, as principally set out in APB 18 *The Equity Method of Accounting for Investments in Common Stock*, an associate is an investment over which the investor exercises significant influence, and significant influence is presumed when an investor owns between 20 per cent and 50 per cent of the voting rights of the investee. Under both IAS 28 (r2000) and US GAAP, when the substance of the arrangements indicates that significant influence is present and an enterprise owns less than 20 per cent, the investee is still considered an associate. However, as discussed in the previous chapter, under IAS 28 (r2000), in certain circumstances when an investor holds less than 50 per cent of the voting rights of an enterprise, but retains control of the enterprise, it accounts for its investment as a subsidiary. Under US GAAP when less than 50 per cent of the voting rights of the enterprise is owned, the investment is accounted for as an associate.

20.5 Equity method

As described in **20.10** and **20.11**, associates are generally required to be accounted for under the equity method. Under the equity method, an investment is initially recorded at cost and is adjusted thereafter for the post acquisition change in the investor's share of net assets of the investee. Most of these adjustments will result from the operations of the investee and will be reflected by recognising the investor's share of the results of operations of the investee in its income statement. However, as described in the steps below, some changes in the net assets of the investee are not due to items recognised in its income statement.

20.5.1 Procedures

Many of the procedures appropriate for the application of the equity method are similar to the consolidation procedures discussed in Chapter **19**. The investment is initially recognised at its cost at the date the investment becomes an associate and goodwill or negative goodwill is recorded as appropriate. Both the value of the consideration paid and the goodwill or negative goodwill arising on acquisition is calculated in the manner described in Chapter **18** for business combinations.

At the end of each accounting period, the investor makes adjustments to the carrying amount of its investment (this list is not exhaustive) to:

(a) recognise the investor's proportionate share of the post-acquisition profits or losses of the associate. If the associate has outstanding cumulative preferred shares held by outside interests, the investor computes its share of the net profit or loss after adjusting for the preferred dividends whether declared or not. (IAS 28 (r2000).21) IAS 28 (r2000) does not specify which element of profit or loss of an associate an investor recognises in its income statement. For example, an investor's share of the profits or losses of an associate could be included as part of operating profit or after operating profit but before financing costs or before profit before tax. The example income statements included in IAS 1 (r1997) disclose income from associates after finance costs and before profit before tax. However, no requirement or guidance exists in IAS 28 (r2000) to suggest that this placement is preferable to another;

(b) record an adjustment to its proportion of the depreciation expense of the associate, if appropriate. Such an adjustment is necessary when the associate carries its non-monetary assets at different carrying amounts from the investor. This is often the case since the investor carries its proportionate share of the non-monetary assets at fair value at the date of acquisition (IAS 28 (r2000).17);

(c) amortise any goodwill or negative goodwill (as appropriate) arising on acquisition. (IAS 28 (r2000).17)

IAS 28 (r2000).17 suggests that items (a) to (c) would be netted into one figure to be recognised in the income statement;

(d) recognise the investor's proportionate share of changes in the net assets of the associate not recognised in the income statement of the associate, for example, changes in the net assets of the associate which are recognised directly in equity, such as a revaluation surplus arising on the revaluation of items of property, plant and equipment or investments or foreign exchange translation differences. (IAS 28 (r2000).6)

IAS 28 (r2000) does not prescribe the method of accounting for such changes, but the logical treatment is to recognise them separately in a statement of changes in equity;

(e) recognise a decrease in value equal to any distributions, such as dividends, received by the investor from the associate (IAS 28 (r2000).6); and

(f) eliminate, to the extent of the investor's interest in the associate, unrealised profits and losses resulting from transactions between the investor or its consolidated subsidiaries and the associate. However, unrealised losses are not eliminated to the extent that the transaction provides evidence of an impairment (SIC-3).

Example 20.1

If an investor purchases inventory from an associate and the inventory has not been sold by the investor to a third party at period end, the journal entry to eliminate the unrealised profit on the inventory would be:

DR Income from associate accounted for under the equity method;

CR Inventory, with the investor's share of the unrealised profit on the inventory.

If an investor sells inventory to an associate and the inventory has not been sold by the associate to a third party at period end, the journal entry to eliminate the unrealised profit on the inventory would be:

DR Revenue;

CR Cost of sales;

CR Investments accounted for using the equity method, with the investor's share of the unrealised profits.

Deferred tax

Deferred tax assets or liabilities may arise from the use of the equity method. A temporary difference arises when the carrying amount of an investment in an associate becomes different from the tax base, often the cost, of the investment. Such differences may arise due to undistributed profits of associates, a reduction in the carrying amount of an associate to its recoverable amount or other reasons. IAS 12 (r2000), *Income Taxes*, sets out the criteria for recognition of deferred tax assets and liabilities and contains some specific guidance regarding differences arising on investments in associates (see Chapter **23**).

Discontinuance of the equity method

When the carrying value of an associate being accounted for under the equity method is reduced to zero due to the investor's participation in the losses of the associate, the investor normally discontinues use of the equity method. If the investor has incurred obligations or made payments on behalf of the associate to satisfy obligations of the associate that the investor had guaranteed or otherwise committed, additional losses are provided for in the accounts of the investor. If the associate subsequently reports profits, the investor does not include its proportionate share of these profits until it equals the amount of losses it did not previously recognise. (IAS 28 (r2000).22 and SIC-3.6)

SIC-20 requires that for the purpose of applying the above rule, the carrying amount of the investment in an associate comprises only those instruments which provide unlimited rights of participation in earnings or losses and a residual equity interest in the associate. This is likely to include all common shares, and some (but not all) preference shares.

Financial interests in an associate which are not included in the carrying amount of the investment in an associate would be accounted for in accordance with other applicable IASs. (SIC-3.7)

> 'An investor should discontinue the use of the equity method from the date that:
>
> (a) it ceases to have significant influence in an associate but retains, either in whole or in part, its investment; or
>
> (b) the use of the equity method is no longer appropriate because the associate operates under severe long-term restrictions that significantly impair its ability to transfer funds to the investor.
>
> The carrying amount of the investment at that date should be regarded as cost thereafter.'
>
> (IAS 28 (r2000).11)

20.6 General rules and guidance under the equity method

20.6.1 Reporting dates

When applying the equity method, the investor uses the most recent financial statements of the associate. Ideally, when the associate has a different reporting date from the investor, the associate will prepare financial statements as of the reporting date of the investor for the use of the investor, unless it is impracticable to do so. (IAS 28 (r2000.18) 'When financial statements (of an associate) with a different reporting date are used, adjustments are made for the effects of any significant events or transactions between the investor and the associate that occur between the date of the associate's financial statements and the date of the investor's financial statements.' (IAS 28 (r2000).19)

IAS 28 (r2000) does not specify a maximum time period that reporting dates may differ by, but the three month rule for subsidiaries specified by IAS 27 is probably a good rule of thumb. In any case, to ensure consistency, the time lag must be consistent from year to year.

When financial statements (of an associate) with a different reporting date are used, in addition to the adjustments mentioned above, we recommend adjusting for any material transactions entered into by the associate between its reporting date and the date of the investor's financial statements.

IAS 21 (r1993) *The Effects of Changes in Foreign Exchange Rates* states that when an associate is a foreign entity and it draws up its accounts at a different date from that of the investor, the exchange rate used by the investor in applying the equity method is the rate in effect at the associate's reporting date. However, if there are significant movements in exchange rates up to the balance sheet date of the parent, adjustments are made to reflect these movements. (IAS 21 (r1993).35) See Chapter **22** for a discussion of foreign exchange gains and losses arising relating to associates.

20.6.2 Uniform accounting policies

An associate may adopt similar accounting policies to that of its investor(s). It is considered best practice, when different accounting policies are adopted, for the investor to make appropriate adjustments to the financial statements of the associate before applying the equity method, when practicable. When an investor does not make such adjustments, this fact is disclosed in the notes to the financial statements.

20.6.3 Comparison with UK GAAP

The application of the equity method of accounting is very similar between UK GAAP and IAS 28 (r2000). However, FRS 9 *Associates and Joint Ventures* specifies that the investor's share of an associates' operating results are brought into its consolidated income statement immediately after the line showing group operating profit or loss but after its share of the operating results of its joint venture, if any. The investor's share of any exceptional items (which are disclosed after this point on the face of the income statement) is disclosed separately from those of the investor. As discussed above, IAS 28 (r2000) is silent on this point. In addition, as described in Chapter **18**, the treatment of goodwill may differ between UK GAAP and IASs. Therefore, accounting for the goodwill arising on an associate may differ accordingly.

The treatment of an associate being accounted for under the equity method which has net assets of nil or negative net assets is more stringent under FRS 9 than IAS 28 (r2000). Under FRS 9, an investor continues to account for an investment in an associate when the associate has net assets of nil or negative net assets unless there is sufficient evidence that an event has irrevocably changed the relationship between the investor and the associate, marking the investor's irreversible withdrawal from the associate. Under IAS 28 (r2000), when the carrying value of an associate being accounted for under the equity method is reduced to zero due to the investor's participation in the losses of the associate, the investor normally discontinues use of the equity method. However, if the associate subsequently reports profits, the investor does not recognise its proportionate share of these profits until it equals the amount of losses it did not previously recognise.

Under UK GAAP, financial statements of an associate which are used in applying the equity method should not be prepared as of a date more than three months before the reporting date of the investor, unless the associate is listed in which case the associate's financial statements can be used providing they are not drawn up to a date more than six months before the reporting date of the investor. IAS 28 (r2000) does not set such a maximum period.

Under UK GAAP, FRS 9 requires consistent accounting policies to be applied. IAS 28 (r2000) requires adjustment only where it is practical to do so.

20.6.4 Comparison with US GAAP

The application of the equity method of accounting is very similar between US GAAP, as principally set out in APB 18 *The Equity Method of Accounting for Investments in Common Stock*, and IAS 28 (r2000). However, the guidance in IAS 28 (r2000) suggests that when an investor applies the equity method to financial statements of an associate with a different reporting date from its own, it adjusts for the effects of any significant events or transactions between the investor and the associate that occur between the date of the associate's financial statements and the date of the investor's financial statements. No equivalent guidance exists in US GAAP. However, the time lag must be consistent from period to period and should not exceed three months. In addition, the guidance in IAS 28 (r2000) discusses the need for uniform accounting policies. US GAAP does not address this issue.

Under both US GAAP and IAS 28 (r2000), use of the equity method ceases when the carrying amount of the investment is reduced to zero due to the investor participating in the losses of the associate. If the investee subsequently reports net income, the investor should resume applying the equity method only after its share of that net income equals the share of net losses not recognised during the period the equity method was suspended. However, equity in losses would still be recognised if the investor is committed to provide further financial support to the investee, such as through legal obligations or assumption of liabilities or other indications, such as having funded losses in the past. Additionally, an investor should provide for additional losses when the imminent return to profitable investee operations seems assured. A footnote to paragraph 19(i) of APB Opinion 18 states:

> 'An investor should, however, provide for additional losses when the imminent return to profitable operations by an investee appears to be assured. For example, the material, non-recurring loss of an isolated nature may reduce an investment below zero even though the underlying profitable operating pattern of an investee is unimpaired.'

The rationale of this provision of APB Opinion 18 is that investors should record the effect of an investee's losses to the extent of their risk; that is, to the extent that the consequences of continued losses will ultimately be borne by them. This would also include other amounts the investee owes the investor. For example, where investor's equity investment in a joint venture was $2 million, but the investor also held $8 million in subordinated debentures, the $8 million in subordinated debentures should be considered as 'capital at risk'. Accordingly, the investor should not discontinue recording losses once $2 million of losses have been recorded. The SEC staff interprets SAB Topic 5.E in a manner consistent with this position.

20.7 Presentation under the equity method

Investments in associates accounted for using the equity method are disclosed as a separate item in the balance sheet. Enterprises which present classified balance sheets, which differentiate between current and non-current assets and liabilities, classify investments accounted for under the equity method as long term. (IAS 28 (r2000).28)

An investor's share of profits and losses of associates accounted for using the equity method is required to be disclosed separately on the face of the income statement. Depending on the materiality of the items, this amount may be aggregated with the investor's share of profits and losses of joint ventures accounted for using the equity method with separate disclosure in the notes to the financial statements. (IAS 1 (r1997).75)

In addition, the investor's share of any extraordinary items, fundamental errors or changes in accounting policies is required to be separately disclosed. (IAS 28 (r2000).28)

20.7.1 Comparison with UK GAAP

Under UK GAAP, as under IAS 28 (r2000), investments in associates are disclosed as a separate line item on the face of the balance sheet and income from associates is a separate line item on the face of the income statement. However, extraordinary items, exceptional items shown below operating result and the investor's share of any associate interest expense are included with similar group items on the face of the income statement and are disclosed separately if material. Under IAS 28 (r2000), such items are required to be disclosed, although IASs do not apply to immaterial items, and their placement is not prescribed.

20.7.2 Comparison with US GAAP

Under US GAAP, as under IAS 28 (r2000), investments in associates are disclosed as a separate line item on the face of the balance sheet and income from associates is a separate line item on the face of the income statement. However, under US GAAP, if the investor's share of any corrections of fundamental errors, changes in accounting policies or extraordinary items would be material in the financial statements of the investor, these amounts are to be separately presented in the investor's financial statements and disclosed on the face of the income statement. Under IAS 28 (r2000), such items are required to be disclosed, but their placement is not prescribed.

20.8 Cost method

As described in section **20.11**, in certain situations associates may be accounted for under the cost method. Under the cost method of accounting, an investment is recorded at its cost. The income statement of the investor reflects income from the investment only to the extent that the investor receives distributions (normally dividends) from accumulated net profits of the investee arising subsequent to the date of acquisition. If dividends are received which are paid in excess of such profits, for example, from pre-acquisition profits of the investee, in substance, they are not income but a reduction of the cost of investment and are accounted for as such. (IAS 28 (r2000).7)

20.8.1 Comparison with UK GAAP

The application of the cost basis is not permitted in consolidated financial statements under UK GAAP. The cost basis is, however, used in the investor's own single entity financial statements. Under UK GAAP, dividends made from pre-acquisition profits are not treated as a reduction in the cost of an investment in an associate. However, after such a dividend is received, an enterprise reviews the carrying amount of its investment to determine if an impairment has occurred and when an impairment loss is recorded, this will have the same net effect as the IAS 28 (r2000) treatment.

20.8.2 Comparison with US GAAP

The application of the cost basis is broadly consistent with US GAAP. However, as described in sections **20.10** and **20.11**, there appears to be very limited circumstances under US GAAP where the use of the cost basis for accounting for investments in associates is appropriate.

20.9 Impairment

IAS 36 requires an impairment review to be carried out if there is indication that the carrying amount of an asset may not be recoverable.

Impairment indicators
IAS 28 (r2000) gives no additional guidance to assist in determining when a decline in value of an associate has occurred. The general guidance in IAS 36 should be used (see **10.12**).

Value in use

As discussed further in **10.12**, if an impairment indicator is present, an impairment review is required. This review compares the carrying value of the asset to its recoverable amount which is defined as the higher of the net selling price of the asset and its value in use. The calculation of an asset's value in use can be complicated. In relation to the value in use of an associate, an enterprise has two options:

- to estimate its share of the present value of the estimated future cash flows expected to be generated by the investee as a whole, including the cash flows from the operations of the investee and the proceeds on the ultimate disposal of the investment; or
- to estimate the present value of the estimated future cash flows expected to arise from dividends to be received from the investment and from its ultimate disposal.

In theory, under appropriate assumptions, both methods give the same result. Any resulting impairment loss for the investment is allocated in accordance with IAS 36. Therefore, it is allocated first to any remaining goodwill. (IAS 28 (r2000).23) See also **10.12**.

The first option is unlikely to be appropriate if the associate is being accounted for using the cost method described in **20.8**.

Cash generating units ('CGUs')

Under IAS 36, recoverable amount is estimated for an individual asset, in this case an individual associate. When this is not possible an enterprise determines the recoverable amount of the smallest identifiable group of assets that generates cash inflows from continuing use that are largely independent from the cash inflows from other assets or groups of assets.

IAS 28 (r2000) confirms that normally, the recoverable amount of an investment in an associate is assessed for each individual associate. However, when an individual associate does not generate cash inflows from continuing use that are largely independent of those from other assets of the reporting enterprise, it is grouped with other assets into a CGU. The recoverability of the CGU, including the associate, is then assessed. (IAS 28 (r2000).24)

In most circumstances, an investment in an associate will generate independent cash flows and therefore, be individually assessed for impairment. However, this may not always be the case. For example, if a manufacturer has a plant which produces a product which is purchased solely by an associate, it may be necessary to review the net book value of the plant and the investment in the associate together.

20.9.1 Comparison with UK GAAP

UK GAAP contains no special guidance or requirements related to the impairment of associates. However, the guidance above is not inconsistent with FRS 11 *Impairment of Fixed Assets and Goodwill.* For a full discussion of the differences between FRS 11 and IAS 36, see **10.12.**

20.9.2 Comparison with US GAAP

SFAS 115 *Accounting for Certain Investments in Debt and Equity Securities* requires that each equity security, not marked-to-market through income, is evaluated to determine whether a decline in fair value below the original cost basis is other than temporary. If the decline in fair value is judged to be other than temporary, SFAS 115 requires that the cost basis of the individual security is written down to fair value as a new cost basis, and the amount of the write-down is included in earnings in the period in which the determination of other-than-temporary impairment is made. The SEC staff, in various public forums, has noted that a six to nine month period of time where market value is below cost indicates that a decline in value is other-than-temporary. Evidence of a loss in value might include, but would not necessarily be limited to, absence of an ability to recover the carrying amount of the investment or inability of the investee to sustain an earnings capacity which would justify the carrying amount of the investment. These requirements are not inconsistent with the guidance included in IAS 28 (r2000) and IAS 36.

20.10 Accounting for associates in consolidated financial statements

The general rule is to account for an investment in an associate in consolidated financial statements using the equity method. (IAS 28 (r2000).8) Since management of the investor exerts significant influence over the associate, the equity method of accounting is appropriate as it illustrates the stewardship of management in carrying out its responsibilities related to the associate more clearly than the cost method would.

However, there are two situations when accounting for an investment in an associate under the equity method is not appropriate in consolidated financial statements:

(a) when the investment was acquired and is held exclusively with a view to its disposal in the near future. (IAS 28 (r2000).8) Thus, deciding to hold an existing investment in an associate for sale is not enough, the investment must have been purchased for that purpose as well; and

(b) when the investment operates under severe long-term restrictions that significantly impair its ability to transfer funds to the investor. (IAS 28 (r2000).8)

Such investments should be accounted for in accordance with IAS 39 (r2000) *Financial Instruments: Recognition and Measurement* (see Chapters **10** and **12**).

Change in circumstances
In situations where an investor is applying the equity method and it:

(a) ceases to have significant influence due to a sale of some of its investment or other reasons; or
(b) becomes inappropriate to use the equity method because the associate now operates under severe long-term restrictions that significantly impair its ability to transfer funds to the investor,

the use of the equity method ceases. The carrying amount of the investment under the equity method at that date becomes its deemed cost. (IAS 28 (r2000).11)

Such an investment would thereafter be accounted for in accordance with IAS 39 (r2000) *Financial Instruments: Recognition and Measurement* (see Chapters **10** and **12**).

Disposal of an associate
When an associate is to be sold, the equity method is applied up to the date of disposal. However, if there are indicators of an impairment, an impairment test may need to be performed as discussed in **20.8** and the carrying amount adjusted accordingly.

20.10.1 Comparison with UK GAAP

As under IAS 28 (r2000), under FRS 9 *Associates and Joint Ventures*, the general rule is to account for associates using the equity method. The exclusion included in IAS 28 (r2000) relating to an investment acquired and held exclusively with a view to its disposal in the near future is consistent with FRS 9 although FRS 9 is more prescriptive in that an investment is not considered an associate (and thus accounted for under the equity method) only if the investment is reasonably expected to be disposed of within one year from its date of acquisition or the investment was acquired as a result of the enforcement of a security and the enterprise does not intend for it to become part of the continuing activities of the group. The exemption in IAS 28 (r2000) relating to the ability of an investee to transfer funds to the investor may or may not apply under FRS 9 depending on the circumstances. If this restriction indicates that the investor no longer retains significant influence over the enterprise, then under FRS 9, the investment would not be considered an associate and therefore would not be accounted for under the equity method. However, if the investor does retain significant influence over the enterprise despite the restrictions, under FRS 9, the investment would still be considered an associate and thus would still be accounted for under the equity method.

FRS 9 requires investment funds, such as those in the venture capital and investment trust industry, to include all investments that are held as part of their investment portfolio at cost or at market value, even those over which the investor has significant influence or joint control. No such exemption exists in IAS 28 (r2000).

20.10.2 Comparison with US GAAP

As under IAS 28 (r2000), under APB 18 *The Equity Method of Accounting for Investments in Common Stock* the general rule is to account for associates using the equity method. However, under US GAAP, when the exercise of significant influence is temporary, the use of the equity method is not appropriate. Although temporary control is not defined, it appears to be consistent with the exclusion in IAS 28 (r2000) for investments acquired and held exclusively with a view to their disposal in the near future. It is unclear whether or not this exclusion in US GAAP encompasses similar provisions to those included in IAS 28 (r2000) relating to restrictions on the ability of a subsidiary to transfer funds to the parent.

APB 18 does not prescribe a particular method of accounting when its exceptions apply. However, SFAS 115 *Accounting for Certain Investments in Debt and Equity Securities* requires that investments in equity shares that are not accounted for by the equity method be measured at market value if the market value is readily available. In summary, under US GAAP, the use of the cost method for accounting for investments in equity shares is very restricted.

20.11 Accounting for associates in separate financial statements of the investor

An investor in an associate may or may not prepare consolidated financial statements. For example, an investor may not prepare consolidated financial statements if it does not have any investments in subsidiaries or it meets the exemption requirements in IAS 27 (see Chapter **19**). Each situation is discussed below.

20.11.1 Investor prepares consolidated financial statements

When an investor prepares consolidated financial statements, its investment in an associate that is not held exclusively with a view to its disposal in the near future in its separate financial statements is required to be either:

(a) carried at cost;
(b) accounted for using the equity method; or
(c) accounted for as an available-for-sale financial asset in accordance with IAS 39 (r2000) (see Chapter 12).

(IAS 28 (r2000).12)

When an investment in an associate is held exclusively with a view to its subsequent disposal the use of equity method is inappropriate. (IAS 28 (r2000)) The implementation guidance on IAS 39 (r2000), contained in a series of published Questions & Answers, makes it clear that such investments should be accounted for in accordance with IAS 39 (r2000) as the scope exclusions of IAS 39 (r2000) do not apply (see Chapter **12**).

20.11.2 Investor does not prepare consolidated financial statements

When an investor does not prepare consolidated financial statements, its investment in an associate in its separate financial statements is required to be either:

(a) carried at cost;
(b) accounted for using the equity method if the equity method would be appropriate for the associate if the investor issued consolidated financial statements; or
(c) accounted for as an available-for-sale financial asset or a financial asset held for trading in accordance with IAS 39 (r2000) (see Chapter **12**).

(IAS 28 (r2000).14)

However, when an enterprise accounts for an investment in an associate under a method other than the equity method in its separate financial statements, and the equity method would be the appropriate accounting method for the associate if the investor issued consolidated financial statements, the investor is required to disclose what would have been the effect had the equity method been applied. Thus, an enterprise may not avoid disclosing information which may be useful to a financial statement user by choosing not to use the equity method. (IAS 28 (r2000).15)

20.11.3 Comparison with UK GAAP

Consistent with the permitted treatments in IAS 28 (r2000), under FRS 9 *Associates and Joint Ventures* investments in associates in separate financial statements are accounted for at cost or revaluation with any dividends received being accounted for as investment income. If an enterprise is exempt from the requirement to prepare group accounts, it must disclose the information provided by the equity method either by preparing a separate balance sheet and income statement using the equity method or by making relevant disclosures in the notes to the financial statements.

20.11.4 Comparison with US GAAP

As noted in the previous chapter, under US GAAP, consolidated financial statements are the only generally accepted financial statements.

20.12 Disclosure

When an enterprise holds investments in associates, the following disclosures are required:

> (a) 'an appropriate listing and description of significant associates including the proportion of ownership interest and, if different, the proportion of voting power held; and
> (b) the methods used to account for such investments.'
>
> (IAS 28 (r2000).27)

IAS 1 (r1997) requires separate disclosure of amounts payable to or receivable from associates. (IAS 1 (r1997).72)

As discussed in **20.11**, when an investor accounts for an investment in an associate in its separate financial statements at cost or at fair value in accordance with IAS 39 (r2000), and the equity method would have been the appropriate accounting method for the associate if the investor issued consolidated financial statements, the investor is required to disclose what would have been the effect had the equity method been applied.

20.12.1 Comparison with UK GAAP

Under FRS 9 *Associates and Joint Ventures*, where investments in associates in aggregate exceed a 15 per cent threshold or individual associates a 25 per cent threshold of certain key indicators, certain information is required to be disclosed. When the aggregate of the investor's share in its associates exceeds a 15 per cent threshold with respect to the investor group, disclosure of the aggregate of the investor's share in all of its associates for the following items is required:

(a) turnover;
(b) fixed assets;
(c) current assets;
(d) liabilities due within one year;
(e) liabilities due after one year or more.

(FRS 9.58(a))

When the investor's share in any individual associate exceeds a 25 per cent threshold with respect to the investor group, disclosure of the name of that associate and the investor's share of the following items is required:

(a) turnover;
(b) profit before tax;
(c) taxation;
(d) profit after tax;
(e) fixed assets;
(f) current assets;
(g) liabilities due within one year; and
(h) liabilities due after one year or more.

(FRS 9.58(c))

The following disclosures which are not required by IAS 28 (r2000) are required by FRS 9:

- the accounting period or date of the financial statements used in applying the equity method if it differs from those of the investing group;
- the investor's share of contingent liabilities and capital commitments of its associates;
- the extent of any restrictions on the ability of an associate to distribute its reserves to the investor;
- the justification for the rebuttal of the assumption that a 20 per cent interest allows an enterprise to exercise significant influence; and
- UK GAAP has similar requirements to IAS 28 (r2000) in respect of disclosure of the names of each principal associate and the percentage of ownership held by the investor.

20.12.2 Comparison with US GAAP

US GAAP contains extensive disclosure requirements about investments in associates that IAS 28 (r2000) does not. Such additional disclosure requirements include:

- for those investments in common shares for which a quoted market price is available, the aggregate value of each investment;
- when investments in common shares of investments accounted for under the equity method are, in the aggregate, material in relation to the financial position or results of operations of an investor, summarised information as to assets, liabilities and results of operations, either individually or in groups, as appropriate; and
- material effects of possible conversions, exercises or contingent issuances of common shares of the investee.

20.13 Examples from published financial statements

Note that the excerpts given do not always comply in full with all aspects of IAS and as such are not necessarily examples of best practice but merely of current practice.

Example 20.2

1B Accounting policies – Consolidation (excerpt)

Significant companies in which the Group exercises material influence are included in the financial statements on an equity basis, while joint ventures are consolidated on a proportional basis.

11. Investment in companies at equity

(In millions of French Francs)	*1999*	*1998*	*1997*
Teksid	1,217	–	–
Irisbus	64	–	–
Mals	225	374	391
Sofasa	(1)	17	64
Societe de Transmissions de Boutheon	90	91	–
Other	340	287	257
Total	**1,935**	**769**	**712**

Following Renault's agreement with Teksid to merge foundry activities, Renault acquired a 33.5% stake in Teksid. This investment is included in Group consolidated financial statements by the equity method from January 1, 1999.

Changes in this item were as follows:

(In millions of French Francs)	*1999*	*1998*	*1997*
Balance at January 1	**769**	**712**	**757**
Change in scope of consolidation	1,358	95	(364)
Change in translation adjustment and other changes	(65)	(11)	247
Dividend distribution	(8)	(22)	(13)
Increase in capital	50	83	15
Income	(169)	(88)	70
Balance at December 31	**1,935**	**769**	**712**

Key aggregated figures for all companies accounted for by the equity method are shown below:

(In millions of French Francs)	*Automobile Division*			*Commercial Vehicles Division*		
	1999	*1998*	*1997*	*1999*	*1998*	*1997*
Revenues	16,506	7,033	7,425	1,646	1,662	1,452
Net income/(loss)	(386)	(267)	36	(13)	14	(18)
Shareholders' equity	4,863	1,044	1,320	394	404	130
Balance sheet total	**15,418**	**3,762**	**3,325**	**975**	**443**	**717**

Renault Group
France
31 December 1999
International Accounting Standards (with exception of IAS 9 in relation to capitalisation of development costs)

Example 20.3

Equity in unconsolidated affiliates

Companies in which Thomson-CSF exercises a significant influence, directly or indirectly, but which it does not control (excluding joint ventures), are carried under the equity method.

The share of Thomson-CSF in the equity and income of these companies, after consolidation adjustments, is summarized below:

(In millions of French francs)	*% owned at year-end*			*Investment at year-end*			*Equity income*		
	1999	*1998*	*1997*	*1999*	*1998*	*1997*	*1999*	*1998*	*1997*
Alcatel Space	49	49	–	169.5	211.6	–	(4.9)	(7.0)(a)	–
Amber Programmes	49	49	49	5.8	4.4	4.1	2.0	0.3	1.1
Avimo	25	–	–	15.7	–	–	–(b)	–	–
Elettronica	33	33	33	5.5	4.6	43	0.8	0.3	(3.8)
FT2CI (SGS-Thomson)	–	–	–	–	–	–	–	–	26
Indra Sistemas	11	25	25	10.7	22.4	17.8	2.9	5.5	3.4
TCI Compensation	40	40	40	1.7	0.3	(2.7)	1.4	(9.1)	(10.1)
Stesa	49	49	49	2.0	(3.5)	0.3	(4.1)	(6.3)	(0.5)
Other	–	–	–	2.1	7.9	8.5	0.4	–	(0.3)
Total				**213**	**248**	**32**	**(1.5)**	**(16.3)**	**16**

(a) Thomson-CSF's interest in Alcatel Space amounts to 49%, of which 2.7% is held through its subsidiary Sextant Avionique. In 1998, as the contributions were made as of June 22, only restated income for the second half of 1998 is consolidated in the financial statements of the Group.

The equity income for 1999 and the last six months of 1998 can be determined as follows:

	1999	*1998* (last six months)
Alcatel space net income	23.0	17.0
Consolidation restatements specific to Thomson-CSF*	<33.0>	<31.0>
Net income/(loss) applied by Thomson-CSF	<10.0>	<14.0>
i.e., for its share	<4.9>	<7.0>

* These reclassifications are primarily made up of capital gains and share of the profit from dilution offset against goodwill.
(b) As this investment was acquired at the end of 1999, net income for the period is excluded from Thomson-CFS's financial statements.
(c) Income for the first half of 1997. This investment was sold during the second half of the year.

Thomson-CSF
France
31 December 1999
International Accounting Standards (with exception of presentation of certain elements of cash flows)

Example 20.4

Basis of consolidation (excerpt)

(ii) Associates are companies, not being subsidiaries, over which the Group exercises significant influence. Associates are included on the equity basis of accounting.

7. **Associates**	*2000* *US$m*	*1999* *US$m*
Listed investments in The Oriental Hotel (Thailand) PCL	**48.4**	48.1
Unlisted investments in other associates	**129.5**	84.2
Group share of attributable net assets of associates	**177.9**	132.3
Market value of listed investment in The Oriental Hotel (Thailand) PCL	**29.5**	36.7

The Group's share of attributable net assets of unlisted associates at 31st December 2000 includes goodwill of US$3.0 million (1999: Nil), net of accumulated amortisation of US$0.1 million (1999: Nil). The Group's share of operating results of associates includes US$0.1 million (1999: Nil) of amortisation of goodwill in respect of associates acquired in the year.

The Directors are satisfied that there is no permanent diminution in the carrying value of the listed investment notwithstanding the lower stock market valuation at the year end.

The land and buildings owned by associates were revalued at 31st December 1998 by independent valuers on an open market basis. The Directors have reviewed the carrying values of all operating properties at 31st December 1999 and 2000 in consultation with the Group's independent valuers. The Group's share of the underlying net revaluation deficit has been dealt with in capital reserves to the extent of US$20.1 million (1999: Nil) and in the profit and loss account to the extent of US$3.8 million (1999: Nil).

Mandarin Oriental International Limited
Hong Kong
31 December 2000
International Accounting Standards

CHAPTER 21

Consolidated financial statements: joint ventures

21.1 Sources

IAS 1 (r1997)	*Presentation of Financial Statements.*
IAS 18 (r1993)	*Revenue.*
IAS 31 (r2000)	*Financial Reporting of Interests in Joint Ventures.*
IAS 39 (r2000)	*Financial Instruments: Recognition and Measurement* (effective 1 January 2001).
SIC-13	*Jointly Controlled Entities – Non-monetary Contributions by Venturers.*

21.2 Development of the requirements

IAS 31 was issued in December 1990. It was reformatted in 1994 in order to bring it into line with the presentation adopted for International Accounting Standards from 1991 onwards. No substantive changes were made to the original approved text.

In April 1998 the IASC approved IAS 36 *Impairment of Assets*, which sets out guidelines for measuring impairment, including the impairment of investments in joint ventures. In July 1998 IAS 31 was revised to be consistent with IAS 36.

In October 2000 IAS 31 was again revised to reflect the introduction of IAS 39 (r2000) *Financial Instruments: Recognition and Measurement.*

In June 1998, the SIC adopted SIC-13 that deals with accounting for non-monetary contributions to jointly controlled entities.

In October 1999 IASC published a Special Report prepared by the former G4+1 group of standard setters (where IASC participated as an observer) titled *Reporting Interests in Joint Ventures and Similar Arrangements.* This paper reviews accounting for joint ventures in the jurisdictions of G4+1 members and recommends a common approach to the conceptual definition, accounting for and disclosure of investments in joint ventures and similar arrangements. The IASB has assigned joint ventures to phase 2 of its Business Combinations project, which the IASB will address in conjunction with its national standard setting partners.

21.3 Brief summary of the requirements

A joint venture is a contractual arrangement whereby two or more parties undertake an economic activity which is subject to joint control. IAS 31 (r2000) identifies three types of joint ventures: jointly controlled operations, jointly controlled assets and jointly controlled entities. Depending on the type of joint venture, a venturer may account for its own assets and liabilities and its share of those of the joint venture or account for its interest using proportionate consolidation or the equity method.

21.4 Joint ventures and joint control

> 'A joint venture is a contractual arrangement whereby two or more parties undertake an economic activity which is subject to joint control.'
>
> (IAS 31 (r2000).2)

> 'Joint control is the contractually agreed sharing of control over an economic activity.'
>
> (IAS 31 (r2000).2)

Thus a joint venture is based on the notion of contractually agreed joint control. Without such a contractual arrangement, there is no joint control and thus, an activity is not a joint venture. 'The contractual arrangement may be evidenced in a number of ways, for example by a contract between the venturers or minutes of discussions between the venturers. In some cases, the arrangement is incorporated in the articles or other by-laws of the joint venture. Whatever its form, the contractual arrangement is usually in writing and deals with such matters as:

(a) the activity, duration and reporting obligations of the joint venture;
(b) the appointment of the board of directors or equivalent governing body of the joint venture and the voting rights of the venturers;
(c) capital contributions by the venturers;
(d) the sharing by the venturers of the output, income, expenses or results of the joint venture' (IAS 31 (r2000).5); and
(e) 'identification of those decisions in areas essential to the goals of the joint venture which require the consent of all the venturers and those

decisions which may require the consent of a specified majority of the venturers.' (IAS 31 (r2000).6)

Joint control ensures that no single venturer is in a position to control unilaterally the activity of the joint venture. On the surface, the concepts of joint control and significant influence, as described in Chapter **20**, appear similar, and indeed they share some of the same characteristics. However, the existence of a contractual arrangement among a small number of venturers which establishes joint control differentiates a joint venture from an investment in an associate, where influence is usually achieved primarily as a result of the size of the ownership interest.

In practice, it is not uncommon for one of the venturers to be appointed as operator or manager of the day to day activities of the economic activity. As long as this operator does not have the power to control the financial and operating policies but is merely carrying out the managerial tasks delegated to it by the other venturers, the operator is not exercising control, and it accounts for any managerial fees received as revenue rather than as a return on its investment in the joint venture. However, if the operator is determining the financial and operating policies of the economic activity, in essence, it controls the economic activity, and as such, accounts for its interest as an investment in a subsidiary rather than as a joint venture. (IAS 31 (r2000).7)

21.4.1 Comparison with UK GAAP

Although FRS 9 *Associates and Joint Ventures* includes a similar definition of a joint venture to that found in IAS 31 (r2000) in that both definitions depend on the existence of contractually agreed joint control, the definition in FRS 9 additionally requires that a joint venture is a separate entity. However, FRS 9 also defines a joint arrangement that is not an entity. Such an arrangement is contractual in nature but is not an entity because the joint arrangement is not carrying on a trade or business of its own with all significant matters of operating and financial policy predetermined by the contractual agreement. Thus, jointly controlled assets and operations under IAS 31 (r2000) are likely to be 'joint arrangements not an entity' ('JANE') under FRS 9; and jointly controlled entities under IAS 31 (r2000) are likely to be joint ventures under FRS 9. A difference arises where a JANE under FRS 9 is structured as a legal entity which would be classified as a jointly controlled entity under IAS 31(r2000).

Additionally, differences between the two Standards appear to be in the following areas:

(a) FRS 9 requires active participation by joint venturers, while IAS 31 (r2000) only requires the existence of the contractual agreement that gives the parties joint control. IAS 31 (r2000) defines control as the *power* to govern the policies of an economic activity, whether it is being actively exercised or not;

(b) FRS 9 requires that the reporting entity hold a joint venture interest 'on a long-term basis'. IAS 31 (r2000) does not appear to have such a restriction. However, as discussed in **21.8.2,** if an investment in a jointly controlled entity is acquired with a view of subsequent resale, IAS 31 (r2000) requires a different accounting basis to be used than if it is held on a long-term basis.

Another area of difference is the treatment of venture capital companies. IAS does not specify any special accounting treatment for these types of companies. Therefore under IAS, venture capital companies are accounted for as either subsidiaries, associates, investments or joint ventures, depending on the nature of their relationship with the parent. In the UK, however, this used to be the treatment before the introduction of FRS 9.

The publication of FRS 9, however, heralded a u-turn by the ASB in relation to associates and joint ventures. In FRS 9 the ASB states that:

> 'Investment funds, such as those in the venture capital and investment trust industry, should include all investments that are held as part of their investment portfolio in the same way (i.e., at cost or market value), even those over which the investor has significant influence or joint control.'
>
> (FRS 9(49))

The ASB explains that:

> 'Investments are held as part of an investment portfolio if their value to the investor is through their marketable value as part of a basket of investments rather than as media through which the investor carries out its business.'

In FRS 9, the ASB explains that the investor's relationship to its investment tends to be that of portfolio investor and, for consistency, the investment should therefore be accounted for in the same way as the other investments in the portfolio. (FRS 9(50)) Where venture capital funds and investment trusts hold investments outside their portfolio that qualify as associates or joint ventures, FRS 9 requires them to be accounted for using the equity or gross equity method as appropriate. (FRS 9(50))

21.4.2 Comparison with US GAAP

Under US GAAP, APB 18 ***The Equity Method of Accounting for Investments in Common Stock***, defines a corporate joint venture in similar terms to that of a joint venture in IAS 31 (r2000) in that both definitions depend on joint control. However, under US GAAP, a contractual arrangement is not required as it is under IAS 31 (r2000).

21.5 Forms of joint venture

Although acknowledging that joint venture arrangements take many different forms both legally and in substance, IAS 31 (r2000) recognises three broad categories of joint ventures: jointly controlled operations, jointly controlled assets and jointly controlled enterprises. As described in the following sections, the accounting treatment prescribed for each category is different.

21.6 Jointly controlled operations

21.6.1 Description

Jointly controlled operations are normally established to take advantage of the operations, resources and expertise of the individual venturers in order to manufacture, market or distribute jointly a particular product. (IAS 31 (r2000).9) As such, these types of joint ventures generally do not involve the purchase of joint assets or the establishment of a separate legal entity. For example, a joint venture may be formed in order to construct an aircraft. One venturer may manufacture the engine while another may manufacture the frame and a third may furbish the interior.

In jointly controlled operations, each venturer:

(a) uses its own property, plant and equipment;
(b) carries its own inventories; and
(c) raises its own finance, which then represents its own obligation.

(IAS 31 (r2000).8)

Thus, it is not uncommon for work related to the joint venture to be carried out by the venturer's employees alongside the venturer's similar activities.

21.6.2 Accounting treatment

> 'In respect of its interests in jointly controlled operations, a venturer should recognise in its separate financial statements and consequently in its consolidated financial statements:
>
> (a) the assets that it controls and the liabilities that it incurs; and
> (b) the expenses that it incurs and its share of the income that it earns from the sale of goods or services by the joint venture.'
>
> (IAS 31 (r2000).10)

In essence, since the jointly controlled operation is not purchasing assets or raising finance in its own right, the assets and liabilities used in the activities of the joint venture are those of the venturers. As such, they are accounted for in the financial statements of the venturer to which they belong. Similarly, the income and expenses incurred by a venturer related to a jointly controlled operation are recorded by the venturer in its own financial statements. Since the underlying assets, liabilities, income and expenses are recorded in the books of the individual venturers, no additional entries are required on consolidation. However, adjustments in the separate financial statements of the enterprise, and thus in the consolidated financial statements, may be required in order to eliminate the transactions between the venturer and the joint venture (see **21.9**).

Since they are not separate legal entities, separate financial statements are not generally required for jointly controlled operations. However, the venturers may wish to have such financial statements prepared for management purposes.

21.6.3 Comparison to UK GAAP

As discussed in **21.4.1**, for a joint arrangement to meet the definition of a joint venture included in FRS 9 *Associates and Joint Ventures* it must be an entity. A jointly controlled operation as discussed in IAS 31 (r2000) is not an entity and thus would not be considered a joint venture under FRS 9 but would be considered a joint arrangement that is not an entity. However, this distinction is merely one of definition, as the treatment of jointly controlled operations is the same under IAS 31 (r2000) and FRS 9. Under both standards, a venturer recognises directly in its own financial statements the assets that it controls and the liabilities that it incurs as well as its share of the income and expenses of the jointly controlled operation.

21.6.4 Comparison to US GAAP

US GAAP does not specifically address jointly controlled operations. However, Accounting Interpretation 2 *Investments in Partnerships and Ventures* of Opinion 18 discusses the accounting for partnerships and unincorporated joint ventures and notes that a venturer may account in its financial statements for its proportionate share of the assets, liabilities, revenues, and expenses of the venture when this is in accordance with industry practice (such as in some oil and gas venture accounting). Thus, the accounting treatments may be the same in some cases.

21.7 Jointly controlled assets

21.7.1 Description

Jointly controlled assets involve the joint control, and often the joint ownership, of one or more assets contributed to or purchased by a joint venture and dedicated to the purpose of the joint venture. The assets are used to obtain benefits for the venturers. Each venturer may take a share of the output from the assets and each bears an agreed share of the expenses incurred. (IAS 31 (r2000).13) For example, enterprises in the oil production industry may jointly control and operate an oil pipeline. Each venturer uses the pipeline to transport its own product in return for which it bears an agreed proportion of the expenses of operating the pipeline.

These types of joint ventures do not involve the establishment of a separate entity, partnership or corporation. Each venturer shares in the economic benefits through its share of the jointly controlled assets.

21.7.2 Accounting treatment

In respect of its interest in jointly controlled assets, a venturer is required to recognise in its separate financial statements and consequently in its consolidated financial statements:

(a) its share of the jointly controlled assets, classified according to the nature of the assets. For example, a venturer's share of a jointly controlled building it occupied would be recognised as property, plant and equipment;
(b) any liabilities which it has incurred, for example, to finance its investment in the jointly controlled asset;
(c) its share of any liabilities incurred jointly with the other venturers in relation to the joint venture;
(d) any income from the sale or use of its share of the output of the joint venture, together with its share of any expenses incurred by the joint venture; and
(e) any expenses which it has incurred in respect of its interest in the joint venture, for example financing expenses related to its interest in the joint venture.

(IAS 31 (r2000).16 and 17)

Similar to jointly controlled operations, the underlying assets and liabilities of a venturer are recognised in its own separate financial statements. As such, no further adjustments are required on consolidation. However, adjustments in the separate financial statements of the enterprise may be warranted due to transactions between the venturer and the joint venture (see **21.9**).

Since they are not separate legal entities, separate financial statements are not generally required for jointly controlled assets. However, the venturers may wish to have such financial statements prepared for management purposes.

21.7.3 Comparison with UK GAAP

As discussed in **21.4.1**, for a joint arrangement to meet the definition of a joint venture included in FRS 9 *Associates and Joint Ventures* it must be an entity. A jointly controlled asset as discussed in IAS 31 (r2000) is not an entity and thus would not be considered a joint venture under FRS 9 but would be considered a joint arrangement that is not an entity. However, this distinction is merely one of definition, as the treatment of jointly controlled assets is the same under IAS 31 (r2000) and FRS 9. Under both standards, a venturer recognises directly in its own financial statements the assets that it controls and the liabilities that it incurs as well as its share of any jointly controlled assets and its share of any joint liabilities.

21.7.4 Comparison with US GAAP

US GAAP does not specifically address jointly controlled assets. However, they may be similar to the US notion of undivided interests.[1] The guidance provided in AICPA Accounting Interpretation 2 *Investments in Partnerships and Ventures* of Opinion 18 describes accounting procedures similar to those of IAS 31 (r2000) in industries which have established those procedures. However, in other circumstances, proportionate consolidation is appropriate. Accounting Interpretation 2 of Opinion 18 discusses the accounting for unincorporated joint ventures and notes that a venturer may account in its financial statements for its proportionate share of the assets, liabilities, revenues, and expenses of the venture when this is in accordance with industry practice (such as in some oil and gas venture accounting). Thus, the accounting treatments may be the same in some cases.

21.8 Jointly controlled entities

21.8.1 Description

> 'A jointly controlled entity is a joint venture which involves the establishment of a corporation, partnership or other entity in which each venturer has an interest. The entity operates in the same way as other enterprises, except that a contractual arrangement between the venturers establishes joint control over the economic activity of the entity.'
>
> (IAS 31 (r2000).19)

A jointly controlled entity acts as any other enterprise in that it controls the assets of the joint venture, incurs liabilities and expenses and earns income. It may enter into contracts in its own name and raise finance for the purposes of the joint venture activity.

> 'A common example of a jointly controlled entity is when two enterprises combine their activities in a particular line of business by transferring the relevant assets and liabilities into a jointly controlled entity. Another example arises when

[1] The IASC US Comparison Project: A Report on the Similarities and Differences between IASC Standards and US GAAP (Second Edition), p. 370, para 3.

an enterprise commences a business in a foreign country in conjunction with the government or other agency in that country, by establishing a separate entity which is jointly controlled by the enterprise and the government or agency.'
(IAS 31 (r2000).21)

In substance, many jointly controlled entities are similar to jointly controlled operations or jointly controlled assets and in fact, a joint venture may change classification after it is established. For example, the venturers may transfer a jointly controlled asset, such as an oil pipeline, into a jointly controlled entity, for tax or other reasons. Similarly, the venturers may contribute into a jointly controlled entity assets which will be operated jointly.

Since a jointly controlled entity is a separate enterprise, it maintains its own accounting records and prepares and presents financial statements in the same way as other enterprises in conformity with IASs.

21.8.2 Accounting treatment

When establishing a jointly controlled entity, 'Each venturer usually contributes cash or other resources to the jointly controlled entity. These contributions are included in the accounting records of the venturer and recognised in its separate financial statements as an investment in the jointly controlled entity.' (IAS 31 (r2000).24)

While the recognition and measurement of a contribution of cash or other monetary items by a venturer is relatively straightforward, recognition and measurement of non-monetary asset contributions are more complicated and are discussed in **21.9.1**.

An entity has a free choice when accounting for a jointly controlled entity in its consolidated financial statements between proportionate consolidation, the benchmark treatment, and the equity method, the allowed alternative treatment.

However, if an interest in a jointly controlled entity is acquired and held exclusively with a view to its subsequent disposal in the near future or the jointly controlled entity operates under severe long-term restrictions that significantly impair its ability to transfer funds to the venturer, the use of either proportionate consolidation or the equity method is inappropriate. Such an interest is accounted for in accordance with IAS 39 (r2000). See Chapters **10** and **12**. (IAS 31 (r2000).35)

An investor accounts for any deferred tax assets or liabilities arising from investments in joint ventures in accordance with IAS 12 (r2000) *Income Taxes*, as described in Chapter **23**.

Proportionate consolidation – benchmark treatment

> 'The application of proportionate consolidation means that the consolidated balance sheet of the venturer includes its share of the assets that it controls jointly and its share of the liabilities for which it is jointly responsible. The consolidated income statement of the venturer includes its share of the income and expenses of the jointly controlled entity. Many of the procedures appropriate for the application of proportionate consolidation are similar to the procedures for the consolidation of investments in subsidiaries.'
>
> (IAS 31 (r2000).27)

Such procedures include making adjustments to fair value the assets and liabilities at the date of acquisition, calculating goodwill or negative goodwill arising on acquisition, and eliminating proportionally transactions between the venturer and the jointly controlled entity (see Chapter **19**). However, under proportional consolidation, since only the venturer's proportion of the assets and liabilities is consolidated, the share of the net assets held by other venturers is not presented as minority interest.

IAS 31 (r2000) offers a choice of presentation when an enterprise adopts proportionate consolidation. The effect of each method on the net assets and net profit of the venturer is the same. The difference is merely presentational.

The first method is the line-by-line method of proportionate consolidation. This method is similar to the method used when consolidating a subsidiary. The venturer combines its share of each of the assets, liabilities, income and expenses of the jointly controlled entity with similar items in its consolidated financial statements on a line-by-line basis. Some argue that this method is inappropriate because it results in financial statement line items which are comprised of some items which are controlled by the enterprise and a proportion of other items which are jointly controlled. Therefore, IAS 31 (r2000) allows another method of presentation.

The second method of presentation is the separate line item method of presentation. Under this method, separate line items are presented for the venturer's share of the assets, liabilities, income and expenses of the jointly controlled entity. For example, on the face of the balance sheet, a separate line item may be included for the venturer's proportionate share of the current assets of a jointly controlled entity or for the venturer's proportionate share of the property, plant and equipment of a jointly controlled entity.

Consistent with IAS 1 (r1997), it is inappropriate for an investor to set-off its proportionate share of the assets and liabilities or income and the related expenses of a jointly controlled entity unless a legal right of set-off exists and the offsetting represents the expectation as to the realisation of the assets or settlement of the liability. (IAS 31 (r2000).29)

A venturer ceases use of the proportionate method of consolidation from the date on which it ceases to have joint control over a jointly controlled entity. (IAS 31 (r2000).30) From the date on which a venturer obtains control over a previously jointly controlled entity, its interest is considered an investment in a subsidiary and is accounted for as described in Chapter **19**.

The equity method – allowed alternative treatment

An enterprise may account for its interest in a jointly controlled entity under the equity method of accounting as described in Chapter **20**. However, IAS 31 (r2000) recommends use of the benchmark treatment. (IAS 31 (r2000).33)

A venturer ceases use of the equity method of consolidation from the date on which it ceases to have joint control over, or significant influence in, a jointly controlled entity. (IAS 31 (r2000).34) See Chapter **20** for a discussion of significant influence.

From the date on which a venturer obtains control over a previously jointly controlled entity, its interest is considered an investment in a subsidiary and is accounted for as described in Chapter **19**.

21.8.3 Comparison with UK GAAP

As discussed in **21.4.1**, for a joint arrangement to meet the definition of a joint venture included in FRS 9 *Associates and Joint Ventures* it must be an entity. IAS 31 (r2000).22 makes reference to many jointly controlled entities being 'similar in substance to jointly controlled operations or jointly controlled assets' and, therefore, where this is the case, the arrangement may not meet the FRS 9 definition of a joint venture, and will instead be treated as joint arrangement that is not an entity.

However, even where a joint entity as described in IAS 31 (r2000) meets the definition of a joint venture included in FRS 9, the accounting treatments prescribed by the two standards differ. Under FRS 9, a venturer accounts for its interest in a joint venture using the gross equity method. The amounts recognised in the financial statements under the equity method and the gross equity method are the same. However, the gross equity method requires disclosure on the face of the income statement of the venturer's share of the turnover of the joint venture and on the face of the balance sheet of the venturer's share of the gross assets and liabilities of the joint venture. As discussed above, IAS 31 (r2000) allows the equity method as an allowed alternative treatment and proportionate consolidation as the benchmark treatment.

21.8.4 Comparison with US GAAP

Under US GAAP, corporate joint ventures, which may be considered to be one type of jointly controlled entity, are accounted for using the allowed alternative treatment of IAS 31 (r2000), the equity method of accounting.

21.9 Transactions between a venturer and a joint venture

21.9.1 Sales and contributions of assets to a joint venture

> 'When a venturer contributes or sells assets to a joint venture, recognition of any portion of a gain or loss from the transaction should reflect the substance of the transaction. While the assets are retained by the joint venture and provided the venturer has transferred the significant risks and rewards of ownership, the venturer should recognise only that portion of the gain or loss which is attributable to the interests of the other venturers. The venturer should recognise the full amount of any loss when the contribution or sale provides evidence of a reduction in the net realisable value of current assets or an impairment loss.'
>
> (IAS 31 (r2000).39)

A venturer may sell assets to the joint venture in the normal course of the venturer's operations. These assets could include inventory items such as raw materials or finished goods, long-term tangible and intangible assets and other. When these assets are sold for an amount exceeding the carrying value of the assets in the financial statements of the venturer, the resultant gain is recognised in the income statement of the venturer to the extent of the equity interests of other joint venturers and investors in the joint venture. The remaining portion of the gain is not recognised at the date of the sale since the venturer retains the interest in the assets to the extent of its interest in the assets of the joint venture. This remaining portion of the gain is recognised when it is eventually realised. This happens, for example, when the assets are subsequently sold to a third party or depreciated to reflect their usage by the joint venture.

Example 21.1

Company A sets up a joint venture with a local partner to manufacture and sell its products in a foreign market. Both venturers hold 50 per cent interest in the joint venture. Subsequent to setting up of the joint venture, company A sells to the joint venture some items of plant and equipment in exchange for £2 million of cash. The carrying value of the plant and equipment in company A's financial statements at the date of sale is £1.5 million. In this case, the substance of the transaction is that of a sale, and in accordance with the requirements above, company A should recognise only that portion of the gain that is attributable to the interests of the other venturer. In this scenario, the portion of the gain attributable to the other venturer is equal to:

50% × (£2m − £1.5m) = £250,000

Depending on whether the proportionate consolidation or the equity method is chosen to account for investments in joint ventures in company A's *consolidated* financial statements, the *effect* of this transaction will be recorded as follows:

(a) proportionate consolidation

DR Cash	£1,000,000
CR Property, plant and equipment	£750,000
CR P/L account, gain on sale of tangible assets	£250,000

The effect of the entries being equivalent to recording a sale of 50% of the plant and equipment to a third party for 50% of the actual consideration received.

(b) equity method

DR Cash	£2,000,000
CR Property, plant and equipment	£1,500,000
CR Investment in associate	£250,000
CR P/L account, gain on sale of tangible assets	£250,000

In practice, whatever method is used to account for interests in joint venture in the consolidated financial statements of company A, the effect of the above entries is achieved by eliminating unrealised profit equal to company's A share of the gain as a consolidation adjustment.

Non-monetary contributions by a venturer to a jointly controlled entity

SIC-13 applies the general principle set out above to situations when a venturer transfers a non-monetary asset to a jointly controlled entity in exchange for an interest in that entity. Such contributions may take various forms and may be made simultaneously by the venturers upon establishing the jointly controlled entity or subsequently.

In respect of such contributions a venturer is required to recognise in the income statement the gain or loss that is attributable to the portion of the asset sold to third parties, i.e., the venturer recognises an amount equal to the total gain multiplied by the proportion of the jointly controlled entity not owned by the venturer, except when:

(a) the significant risks and rewards of ownership of the contributed non-monetary asset(s) have not been transferred to the jointly controlled entity (several examples of situations in which the enterprise may retain the significant risks and rewards of ownership are provided in IAS 18 (r2000).16 – see discussion in Chapter **6**);

Additionally, if, for example, at the end of the life of the jointly controlled entity, a contributed asset reverts to its contributor, it may be the case that a transfer of the risks and rewards of ownership has not occurred, and therefore, recognition of any gain or loss on the contribution would be inappropriate. Another common feature of such contributions is that the assets transferred are restricted in their type or amount of use by the jointly controlled entity. In such cases, it is again doubtful that the risks and rewards of ownership have passed, and thus recognition of any gain or loss on the transfer by a venturer may be inappropriate.

(b) the gain or loss on the non-monetary contribution cannot be measured reliably; or

(c) the non-monetary assets contributed are similar to those contributed by the other venturers. Non-monetary assets are similar to those contributed by other venturers when they have a similar nature, a similar use in the same line of business and a similar fair value. A contribution meets the similarity test only if all of the significant component assets thereof are similar to those contributed by the other venturers.

The logic here is that an exchange of a non-monetary item for a similar non-monetary item does not complete the earnings process. This principle is included in IAS 16 (r1998) *Property, Plant and Equipment* for items of property, plant and equipment and IAS 38 *Intangible Assets* for intangible assets.

(SIC-13.5)

When any of the exceptions above apply, the gain or loss would be considered unrealised and would not be recognised in the income statement. (SIC-13.5)

> 'Unrealised gains and losses on non-monetary assets contributed to jointly controlled entities should be eliminated against the underlying assets under the proportionate consolidation method or against the investment under the equity method. Such unrealised gains or losses should not be presented as deferred gains or losses in the venturer's consolidated balance sheet.'
>
> (SIC-13.7)

Example 21.2

A television production company contributes an intangible asset, the product rights to its television cartoon characters, in exchange for a 50 per cent interest in a jointly controlled entity. The other venturer is a toy manufacturer which contributes cash. If, even on winding up, the television production company is not entitled to any of the cash provided by the manufacturer and only participates in a return on the intangible asset it contributed once the characters have been turned into a design for children's dolls, produced and sold to a third party, in substance, the contribution of the asset by the television production company is not a transaction which completes the earnings process. The earnings process will only be complete, and thus revenue recognised, when the product rights have generated revenue, that is when the dolls are sold to a third party. In other words, the television production company retains the risks and rewards of ownership of the product rights despite the contribution.

The accounting treatment in this case will be as follows. Suppose that contribution of product rights is valued by the venturers at £2.5 million. The other party to the joint venture contributes £2.5 million of cash. The carrying value of the production rights in the television production company is £1m.

In its own financial statements the jointly controlled entity may record contributions by the venturers as £2.5m of cash and £2.5m of intangible assets. On recording its interest in the jointly controlled entity in the consolidated financial statements, the TV production company must eliminate the full amount of the resulting gain of £1.5 (equal to the difference between the carrying amount of the contributed production rights before the transaction and 50 per cent of the net assets of the jointly controlled entity).

Depending on whether the proportionate consolidation or the equity method is chosen to account for investments in joint ventures in the consolidated financial statements, on consolidation the gain will be eliminated as follows:

(a) proportionate consolidation

	50% of JV assets	*Adjustments*	*Amounts consolidated*
Intangible assets	£1,250,000	£(250,000)	£1,000,000
Cash	£1,250,000	£(1,250,000)	£NIL

(b) equity method

	50% of net assets in JV	*Adjustments*	*Amount included in consolidated FS*
Investment in JV	£2,500,000	£(1,500,000)	£1,000,000

However, if, in addition to receiving an equity interest in the jointly controlled entity, a venturer receives monetary or non-monetary assets dissimilar to those it contributed (for instance, cash), an appropriate portion of gain or loss on the transaction is always required to be recognised by the venturer in the income statement. (SIC-13.6)

Consistent with SIC-13.5(b) it is suggested that where a venturer sells an asset to a jointly controlled entity in exchange for a non-monetary asset, no gain is recognised if the value of the non-monetary asset received cannot be measured reliably.

Example 21.3

Suppose that subsequently to setting up the joint venture in *Example 21.2* above, the TV production company transfers to the joint venture product rights for other cartoon characters. In exchange it receives consideration that comprises two parts: a further 10 per cent equity interest in the joint venture and a cash portion. The gain attributable to the cash element is recognised to the extent of the other venturer's equity interest (now 40 per cent). The remaining gain is subject to the same test described in *Example 21.2*.

Once it has been established that the risks and rewards of ownership have passed (and the two other exemptions listed above do not apply) when a non-monetary contribution is made, the gain or loss on contribution is calculated. As noted above, for as long as the jointly controlled entity retains the assets, any such gain or loss is recognised only to the extent of the interests of the other venturers. However, the appropriate basis on which to calculate the gain or loss is not addressed. Therefore, a gain or loss could be calculated based on the fair value of the asset at the date of contribution or at the fair value of the interest in the jointly controlled entity received in exchange for the contribution. IAS 18 (r1993).12 addresses gains or losses on non-monetary transactions and states that when *dissimilar* items are exchanged, revenue is measured at the fair value of the item received unless the fair value of the item given up is more evident. Applying this logic to contributions to jointly controlled entities, it would appear that the fair value of the dissimilar asset given up will generally be more evident than an interest in a jointly controlled entity. Where this is the case, any gain or loss arising on such a transaction is calculated as the difference between the fair value of the asset contributed at the date of the contribution and its carrying value.

21.9.2 Purchases of assets from a joint venture

> 'When a venturer purchases assets from a joint venture, the venturer should not recognise its share of the profits of the joint venture from the transaction until it resells the assets to an independent party. A venturer should recognise its share of the losses resulting from these transactions in the same way as profits except that losses should be recognised immediately when they represent a reduction in the net realisable value of current assets or an impairment loss.'
>
> (IAS 31 (r2000).40)

To assess whether a transaction between a venturer and a joint venture provides evidence of impairment of an asset, the venturer determines the recoverable amount of the asset in accordance with IAS 36 *Impairment of Assets*.

In determining value in use, future cash flows from the asset are estimated based on continuing use of the asset and its ultimate disposal by the joint venture. (IAS 31 (r2000).41) See **10.12** for a discussion of requirements of IAS 36.

21.10 Separate financial statements of a venturer

Given the variety of reasons for which separate financial statements are prepared in different countries, IAS 31 (r2000) does not prescribe a method of accounting for jointly controlled entities in such financial statements. Thus, an enterprise has a choice when accounting for such an investment in its separate financial statements of cost, fair value (as permitted by IAS 39 (r2000)), the equity method or proportionate consolidation.

21.10.1 Comparison to UK GAAP

Under FRS 9 *Associates and Joint Ventures*, an interest in a joint venture is accounted for in the separate financial statements of a venturer as a long term investment and carried at either cost or a revalued amount. See **21.4.1** for a discussion of the treatment of joint arrangements that are not entities.

21.10.2 Comparison to US GAAP

As noted in Chapter **19**, under US GAAP, consolidated financial statements are the only generally accepted financial statements.

21.11 Reporting interests in joint ventures in the financial statements of an investor

When an investor does not have joint control over a joint venture, it reports its interest in a joint venture in its consolidated financial statements at either cost or in accordance with IAS 39 (r2000) as described in Chapter **12**. However, if the investor has significant influence over the joint venture, it accounts for its interest using the equity method as described in Chapter **20** in accordance with IAS 28 (r2000) *Accounting for Investments in Associates*. In the separate financial statements of an investor that issues consolidated financial statements, it may alternatively record the investment at cost.

21.12 Disclosure

> 'A venturer should disclose a listing and description of interests in significant joint ventures and the proportion of ownership interest held in jointly controlled entities. A venturer which reports its interests in jointly controlled entities using

the line-by-line reporting format for proportionate consolidation or the equity method should disclose the aggregate amount of each of current assets, long-term assets, current liabilities, long-term liabilities, income and expenses related to its interests in joint ventures.'

(IAS 31 (r2000).47)

A venturer is required to disclose the aggregate amount of the following contingencies, unless the probability of loss is remote, separately from the amount of other contingencies:

'(a) any contingencies that the venturer has incurred in relation to its interests in joint ventures and its share in each of the contingencies which have been incurred jointly with other venturers;
(b) its share of the contingencies of the joint ventures themselves for which it is contingently liable; and
(c) those contingencies that arise because the venturer is contingently liable for the liabilities of the other venturers of a joint venture.'

(IAS 31 (r2000).45)

Consistent with IAS 1 (r1997), a venturer is required to disclose the aggregate amount of the following commitments in respect of its interests in joint ventures separately from other commitments:

'(a) any capital commitments of the venturer in relation to its interests in joint ventures and its share in the capital commitments that have been incurred jointly with other venturers; and
(b) its share of the capital commitments of the joint ventures themselves.'

(IAS 31 (r2000).46)

An enterprise which does not issue consolidated financial statements is nevertheless required to provide the disclosures required by the above three paragraphs. (IAS 31.48)

21.12.1 Comparison with UK GAAP

FRS 9 *Associates and Joint Ventures* requires additional disclosures where joint ventures in aggregate exceed a 15 per cent threshold or individual joint ventures exceed a 25 per cent threshold of certain key indicators. When the aggregate of the venturer's share in joint ventures exceeds a 15 per cent threshold with respect to the venturer group, disclosure of the aggregate of the venturer's share in all of its joint ventures for the following items is required:

(a) fixed assets;
(b) current assets;
(c) liabilities due within one year;
(d) liabilities due after one year or more.

(FRS 9.58(b))

When the venturer's share in any individual joint venture exceeds a 25 per cent threshold with respect to the venturer group, disclosure of the name of that joint venture and the venturer's share of the following items is required:

(a) turnover;
(b) profit before tax;
(c) taxation;
(d) profit after tax;
(e) fixed assets;
(f) current assets;
(g) liabilities due within one year; and
(h) liabilities due after one year or more.

(FRS 9.58(c))

UK GAAP has similar requirements to IAS 31 (r2000) in respect of disclosure of the name of each principal joint venture and the percentage of ownership held by the venturer. It also has similar requirements in respect of disclosure of contingent liabilities in respect of joint ventures.

21.12.2 Comparison with US GAAP

The disclosures under US GAAP are similar but fewer. Similar to IAS 31 (r2000), APB 18 *The Equity Method of Accounting for Investments in Common Stock* requires disclosure of the names of each significant joint venture and the percentage of ownership held by the investor. Additionally, APB 18 says that where investments in joint ventures and other investments accounted for under the equity method are, in the aggregate, material to the financial position or results of operations of the investor it may be necessary to disclose summarised financial information of the investees (individually or in groups) in the notes to financial statements or in separate statements. As discussed above, IAS 31 (r2000) requires disclosure of the aggregate amount of each of current assets, long-term assets, current liabilities, long-term liabilities, income and expenses related to its interests in joint ventures.

21.13 Examples from published financial statements

Note that the excerpts given do not always comply in full with all aspects of IAS and as such are not necessarily examples of best practice but merely of current practice.

Example 21.4

Accounting Policies

Associates and joint ventures

Associates are companies, not being subsidiaries, over which the Group exercises significant influence.

Joint ventures are companies where the Group has a contractual arrangement with third parties to undertake an economic activity which is subject to joint control.

Associates and joint ventures are included on the equity basis of accounting. The results of associates and joint ventures are included or excluded from their effective dates of acquisition or disposal respectively, and are based on their latest financial statements.

Hongkong Land Holdings Limited
Hong Kong
31 December 2000
International Accounting Standards (with certain exceptions)

Example 21.5

Consolidation principles (excerpt)

Joint ventures are entities which the Group jointly controls with one or more other venturers. Joint ventures are included on the equity basis of accounting.

Note 10 Associates and joint ventures

	2000	*1999*
	US$m	*US$m*
Listed investment in The Oriental Hotel (Thailand) PCL	48.4	48.1
Unlisted investments in other associates	129.5	84.2
	177.9	132.3
Joint Ventures (see below)	51.3	35.6
	229.2	167.9
Market value of listed investment in The Oriental Hotel (Thailand) PCL	29.5	36.7

The Group's share of assets and liabilities and results of joint ventures is summarised below:

	2000	*1999*
	US$m	*US$m*
Non-current assets	55.1	39.4
Current assets	3.0	4.8
Current liabilities	(3.5)	(5.3)
Non-current liabilities	(3.3)	(3.3)
	51.3	35.6
Revenue	10.9	8.9
Profit before tax	1.2	1.7
Profit after tax	1.2	1.7
Net profit	1.2	1.7
Capital commitments	–	0.3
Contingent liabilities		–

The Group's share of attributable net assets of unlisted associates at 31st December 2000 includes goodwill of US$3.0 million (1999: Nil), net of accumulated amortisation of US$0.1 million (1999: Nil). The Group's share of operating results of associates includes US$0.1 million (1999: Nil) of amortisation of goodwill in respect of associates acquired in the year. The Directors are satisfied that there is no permanent diminution in the carrying value of the listed investment notwithstanding the lower stock market valuation at the year end. The land and buildings owned by associates and joint ventures were revalued at 31st December 1998 by independent valuers on an open market basis. The Directors have reviewed the carrying values of all operating properties at 31st December 1999 and 2000 in consultation with the Group's independent valuers. The Group's share of the net underlying net revaluation surplus has been dealt with in capital reserves to the extent of US$20.1 million (1999: Nil) and in the profit and loss account to the extent of US$3.8 million (1999: Nil).

Mandarin Oriental International Limited
Hong Kong
31 December 2000
International Accounting Standards

CHAPTER 22

Foreign currency

22.1 Sources

IAS 21 (r1993)	*The Effects of Changes in Foreign Exchange Rates.*
IAS 39 (r2000)	*Financial Instruments: Recognition and Measurement.*
SIC-7	*Introduction of the Euro.*
SIC-11	*Foreign Exchange – Capitalisation of Losses Resulting from Severe Currency Devaluations.*
SIC-19	*Reporting Currency – Measurement and Presentation of Financial Statements under IAS 21 and IAS 29.*

22.2 Brief summary of the requirements

An enterprise normally presents its financial statements using an appropriate measurement currency. Measurement currency is the currency of the economic environment in which the enterprise operates and is usually the currency of the country in which the enterprise has its business. Transactions in currencies other than the measurement currency are foreign currency transactions which fall within the scope of IAS 21 (r1993).

When an enterprise carries out transactions in foreign currencies, they are recorded by translating the foreign currency amount at the exchange rate at the date of the transaction. An approximation to the actual rate, such as an average for the week or month, may be used. In preparing financial statements, monetary items in the balance sheet are re-translated, using the closing rate at the period-end. Non-monetary items are generally not re-translated, but remain at the exchange rate at the date of the transaction. The only exception to this is non-monetary items carried at a fair value which was determined prior to the balance sheet date. Such items are re-translated at the date at which the fair value was determined.

Exchange differences are recognised as income or expenses in the period in which they arise, with two exceptions: where there is a monetary item that forms part of the enterprise's net investment in a foreign entity and where there is a foreign currency liability accounted for as a hedge of an enterprise's net investment in a foreign entity. In these two cases, the exchange differences are classified as equity until the disposal of the net investment.

Where there is a foreign operation which requires incorporation into the financial statements of the reporting enterprise or the group consolidated financial statements, there are two possible ways of translating its transactions and year-end balances:

- if the operation is integral to the operations of the reporting enterprise, the requirements set out above are followed, so that transactions are reflected as though the reporting enterprise carried them out itself; or
- if the operation operates independently of the reporting enterprise, its assets and liabilities are translated at the closing rate of exchange, while its income and expenses are translated at the rate ruling at the date of the transactions. In this case exchange differences are classified as equity until the disposal of the entity, at which time they are recognised as income or expense.

IAS 21 (r1993) requires a number of disclosures, principally the amount of exchange differences included in the net profit or loss for the period and the amount of exchange differences classified as equity.

22.3 Development of the requirements

First approved in 1983, IAS 21 was revised as part of the Improvements project when five changes were made which dealt with:

- the recognition of foreign exchange gains and losses on long-term monetary items;
- the recognition of foreign exchange losses on the acquisition of an asset that result from a severe devaluation against which there is no practical means of hedging;
- the exchange rates for use in the translation of the income statement of a foreign entity and the treatment of the differences on income statement items translated at other than closing rates;
- subsidiaries reporting in the currency of a hyper-inflationary economy; and
- the procedures that should be applied in the translation of the financial statements of a foreign operation that is integral to the operations of the parent.

(*Insight*, July, 1992, p.15)

During the revision of IAS 21, the Board was also considering a new IAS on Financial Instruments. To ensure that the revised IAS 21 did not conflict with any new Standard arising from the Financial Instruments project, the Board decided to remove from IAS 21 the guidance and standards relating to hedge accounting (except for the treatment of exchange differences arising on a foreign currency liability which hedges a net investment in a foreign entity) and leave them to be dealt with in the Financial Instruments project. This was subsequently issued as IAS 39 *Financial Instruments: Recognition and Measurement*.

In 1998, the SIC issued SIC-7 to cover the introduction of the Euro (see **22.10**). Also in 1998, the SIC reached consensus around some issues relating to the capitalisation of losses resulting from a severe devaluation of currency (see **22.6.7** for a discussion of consensus in SIC-11).

SIC-19, published in November 2000 and effective for periods beginning on or after 1 January 2001, establishes the principles involved in identification of the measurement currency and presentation of financial statements in a currency other than the measurement currency.

22.4 Scope

IAS 21 (r1993) sets out the methods to be adopted in:

- accounting for transactions which are carried out in foreign currencies; and
- translating the financial statements of foreign operations which are included in the financial statements of an enterprise through consolidation, proportional consolidation or the equity method. A foreign operation could be a subsidiary, associate, joint venture or branch of the reporting enterprise.

It does not address hedge accounting, except for the treatment of exchange differences arising on a foreign currency liability which hedges a net investment in a foreign entity. Hedge accounting is dealt with in IAS 39 (r2000) (see Chapter **12**).

IAS 21 (r1993) does not specify the currency in which an enterprise should present its financial statements, although it notes that this is usually the currency of the country in which it is domiciled. It also does not address how to restate an enterprise's financial statements into another currency. SIC-19 provides further guidance on the determination of the currency in which an enterprise should *measure* its transactions, and also places some restrictions on the choice of a method used to restate the financial statements from the measurement currency to another currency for presentation purposes.

Lastly, IAS 21 (r1993) does not deal with the implications for cash flow statements of foreign currency transactions and the consolidation of foreign operations. These matters are addressed in IAS 7 (r1992) *Cash Flow Statements* (see Chapter **13**).

22.5 Definitions

A reporting currency is the currency that an enterprise uses to present its financial statements. (IAS 21 (r1993).7) SIC-19 subdivides the term reporting currency into two parts: a currency for measuring items in the financial statements (the 'measurement currency') and a currency, other than the measurement currency, for presenting the financial statements (the 'presentation currency'). 'The measurement currency should provide information about the enterprise that is useful and reflects the economic substance of the underlying events and circumstances relevant to that enterprise.' (SIC-19.5) Normally the measurement currency is the currency of the country in which the enterprise is domiciled. However, this is not always the case. For example, a multi-national business domiciled in the UK may have only very limited UK operations and a substantial volume of business conducted in US dollars. To use US dollars as a measurement currency would reflect the economic substance of the underlying events and circumstances relevant to this business. Businesses in oil and insurance industries may often find the US dollar to be the appropriate measurement currency.

In a group situation, the measurement currency will often be the measurement currency of the parent. However, this may not be the case if significant operations of the group as a whole are conducted in another currency.

A foreign currency, as far as an enterprise is concerned, is any currency other than its measurement currency. (IAS 21 (r1993).7, SIC 19)

The closing rate is the spot rate (that is, the rate of exchange ruling) at the balance sheet date. (IAS 21(r1993).7)

A foreign operation is a subsidiary, associate, joint venture or branch of the reporting enterprise, the activities of which are based or conducted in a different country from that of the reporting enterprise. (IAS 21 (r1993).7)

A foreign entity is a foreign operation, the activities of which are not an integral part of those of the reporting enterprise. (IAS 21 (r1993).7)

22.6 Foreign currency transactions

Foreign currency transactions include:

- buying or selling goods or services, the price of which is denominated in a foreign currency;

- borrowing or lending funds when the amounts payable or receivable are denominated in a foreign currency;
- becoming a party to an unperformed foreign exchange contract; and
- acquiring or disposing of assets and incurring or settling liabilities denominated in a foreign currency. (IAS 21 (r1993).8)

22.6.1 *Initial recognition*

Where an enterprise carries out a transaction in a foreign currency, it is initially recorded in the reporting currency of that enterprise, by translating the foreign currency amount at the exchange rate at the date of the transaction (known as the 'spot rate'). An approximation to the spot rate may be used, such as an average for a week or a month, where a number of transactions have occurred and it is not practical to use the spot rate for every transaction.

If an approximation is used, it is applied to all transactions in each foreign currency during that period. (IAS 21 (r1993).10)

This may be interpreted as applying to all transactions *of a given type*. For example, it may be appropriate to record all inventory purchases in a particular currency at an average rate for a month where such purchases occur evenly throughout the period, while a large one-off transaction in the same currency, such as the purchase of an item of property, plant and equipment, is recorded using actual rates, since the use of an average rate in this case is unlikely to be a sufficiently close approximation to the actual rate.

Average rates are unlikely to be appropriate:

- where exchange rates fluctuate significantly over time; or
- where there are a small number of irregular transactions, rather than a steady stream of transactions of roughly equal value;

since in either of these cases an average rate may not be an adequate approximation of the rates at which transactions actually occurred.

In general, if an approximation such as an average rate is used, care needs to be taken that the carrying value of non-monetary assets (including inventory and property) is not materially different from what it would have been if actual rates had been used.

22.6.2 *Reporting at the balance sheet date*

In preparing the balance sheet for inclusion in the financial statements, different items are translated at different rates for presentation in the reporting currency. These are set out below (IAS 21 (r1993).11):

Type of balance sheet item	***Rate to be used in presenting the balance sheet***
Monetary items.	Closing rate.
Non-monetary items carried at historical cost (e.g., the cost and accumulated depreciation of items of property, plant and equipment, inventory, equity financial instruments).	Exchange rate at the date of the transaction with no subsequent retranslation.
Non-monetary items carried at fair value denominated in a foreign currency.	Exchange rate at the date the latest fair value was determined.

Monetary items are defined as cash held and assets and liabilities to be received or paid in fixed or determinable amounts of money (for example, debtors and creditors). (IAS 21 (r1993).7)

Fair value is 'the amount for which an asset could be exchanged, or a liability settled, between knowledgeable, willing parties in an arm's length transaction'. (IAS 21 (r1993).7)

Applying the rule to non-monetary items carried at fair value denominated in a foreign currency means that:

- a property located in a foreign country, which is revalued in a foreign currency, is re-translated at a rate ruling at the date of the revaluation;
- investments which are carried at market value are translated at the closing rate;
- investments in foreign enterprises, which have been written down, are translated at the rate at the date of the write down; and
- items carried at net realisable value (such as inventory) and intended to be sold in a foreign currency are translated at the closing rate, since that is the exchange rate at the date that the net realisable value was determined. This is illustrated in the example below.

Example 22.1

A Company whose measurement currency is X buys inventory in another currency. The transaction is recorded at the rate ruling at the date of the purchase. At the year end the inventory is written down to net realisable value. There are two possible scenarios.

If the inventory is to be sold in currency X, the net realisable value will be determined in currency X and no retranslation is necessary.

If the inventory is to be sold in a currency other than X, the net realisable value is determined in that currency and translated into X at the closing rate of exchange.

22.6.3 Recognition of exchange differences

In the case of monetary items, the exchange rate may change between the date of the transaction and the date of settlement. This leads to exchange differences arising:

- where the transaction is settled within the same period as that in which it occurred;
- between the date at which the transaction was initially recorded and the balance sheet date, where it is still unsettled at the period-end; and
- between the amount at which the transaction was recorded in the previous financial statements and the date of settlement or a new period-end.

All these exchange differences are recognised as income or expenses in the period in which they arise. (IAS 21 (r1993).15)

The IAS does not comment specifically on where in the income statement these exchange differences are recorded, however they will be included in operating or financing income or expenses as appropriate.

Example 22.2

Company X based in the UK buys inventory at a price of $50,000 in the US on 1 December 20x1 when the exchange rate is £1=$1.68. The inventory and creditor are recorded at £29,762. At the year-end, 31 December 20x1, the creditor has not been paid and the exchange rate has moved to £1=$1.71, such that the amount now required to pay the $50,000 is £29,240. For the year-end financial statements, the creditor is included at the closing rate (£29,240), while the inventory remains at the historic rate (£29,762) and an exchange difference of £522 is recognised as income. The creditor is settled on 1 March 20x2, at which date the exchange rate is £1=$1.63, hence the cost of settling the debt in pounds sterling is £30,675, resulting in a further exchange difference of £1,435 (£30,675 – £29,240) which is recognised as an expense in the year to 31 December 20x2.

22.6.4 *Exceptions to the rule in 22.6.3*

There are two exceptions to the general rule that exchange differences are recognised as income or expenses in the period in which they arise:

- where there is a monetary item that, in substance, forms part of the enterprise's net investment in a foreign entity (see **22.6.5**); and
- where there is a foreign currency liability which is accounted for as a hedge of an enterprise's net investment in a foreign entity (see **22.6.6**).

The exchange differences in these two cases are classified as equity in the financial statements of the enterprise, until the disposal of the net investment. In other words, the exchange differences are credited or debited directly to a translation reserve in equity, rather than being recognised as income or expenses for the period. This will normally be a separate reserve. Under IAS 1 (r1997) *Presentation of Financial Statements*, items recognised directly in equity, such as certain foreign exchange gains or losses, are disclosed in a statement showing movements in equity. Both IAS 1 (r1997) and IAS 21 (r1993).42 (b) require a reconciliation of the opening and closing balance of the translation reserve.

In either case, when disposal of the net investment takes place, the accumulated exchange differences which have been included in equity are recognised as income or expense in the period in which the gain or loss on the disposal is recognised. This is covered further in **22.7.12**.

22.6.5 *Determining the amount of the net investment in a foreign entity*

IAS 21 (r1993) defines the net investment in a foreign entity as the reporting enterprise's share in the net assets of the entity. (IAS 21 (r1993).7) Normally this will principally consist of an investment in the share capital of the foreign entity. However, monetary items that, in substance, form part of the enterprise's net investment in a foreign entity may also be included. Amounts receivable from or amounts payable to a foreign entity are deemed to be part of the enterprise's net investment provided that settlement is neither planned, nor likely to occur in the foreseeable future. (IAS 21 (r1993).18)

For example, a reporting enterprise may often make a long term loan to a subsidiary, rather than purchasing additional shares, but in substance, if the reporting enterprise has no intention of asking for the settlement of the loan, the intention of the investing enterprise is the same, and both a purchase of share capital and a loan may therefore be viewed as part of the enterprise's net investment in the foreign entity. However, trade receivables and trade payables are specifically excluded from being treated as part of the net investment in a foreign entity, since settlement is foreseeable.

Clearly there will be difficulties in determining the classification of individual balances. In practice there may be no loan agreements specifying dates for repayment, and hence theoretically loans will be repayable on demand. However, if it is clear that the intention of the reporting enterprise is to provide long term finance, the loan may be deemed part of the net investment. If, on the other hand, there is a loan agreement which specifies that repayment is due within a relatively short time-frame, it will be extremely difficult to override the legal form and argue that the reporting enterprise intends this loan, in substance, to be long term finance for which settlement is neither planned nor likely to occur in the foreseeable future.

Similar considerations to those set out above for amounts receivable *from* a foreign entity attach to liabilities due *to* a foreign entity. Liabilities, which are long term and are not likely to be settled in the foreseeable future, reduce the reporting enterprise's net investment in a foreign entity.

As discussed in **22.6.3**, any exchange differences arising on such a monetary item that forms part of the net investment should be classified as equity until the disposal of the net investment, at which time they should be recognised as income or expense. (IAS 21 (r1993).17)

22.6.6 Liabilities hedging a net investment in a foreign entity

As protection against the foreign exchange losses which may arise when retranslating an investment in a foreign entity, the reporting enterprise may take out a loan in the currency of the foreign entity to hedge its balance sheet exposure. The requirements set out in **22.6.2** (IAS 21 (r1993).11) would result in the loan being translated at closing rate and the net investment being carried at the historic rate (i.e., translated at the rate ruling at the date the investment was acquired). Exchange differences on the retranslation of the loan would then be charged or credited to income. Since this would not fairly represent the nature of the loan, which was taken out to protect the reporting enterprise against unfavourable foreign exchange differences on its investment, IAS 21 (r1993).19 requires the exchange differences on the loan to be classified as equity, i.e., deferred, until the disposal of the investment, at which time they will be recognised as income or expense.

IAS 39 (r2000) amplifies this requirement in three respects:

1. It extends the range of hedging instruments from foreign currency liabilities (IAS 21 (r1993).19) to any financial instrument which meets the criteria for an effective hedge. (IAS 39 (r2000).164)
2. It places the hedging of a net investment in a foreign entity within the framework of cash flow hedges, and thus within the scope of its requirements. This means that:

- the portion of a gain or loss on the hedging instrument that is determined to be an effective hedge is to be recognised directly in equity and reported through the statement of changes in equity; and
- the ineffective portion is to be reported: (i) immediately in net profit or loss if the hedging instrument is a derivative; or (ii) in equity until disposal of the net investment, in the limited circumstances in which the hedging instrument is not a derivative. (IAS 39 (r2000).164)

3. It provides criteria to determine whether a hedge is effective. The criteria are dealt with in detail in Chapter **12**. In summary, the criteria are:
    - at the inception of the hedge there is formal documentation to support classification as a hedge;
    - the hedge is expected to be highly effective;
    - a forecasted transaction which is the subject of the hedge must be highly probable;
    - the effectiveness of the hedge can be reliably measured; and
    - the hedge was assessed on a ongoing basis and determined actually to have been highly effective throughout the financial reporting period. (IAS 39.142)

The criteria above should be applied for the classification of hedges under IAS 21 (r1993).19.

22.6.7 Allowed alternative treatment

Whilst the treatment set out in **22.6.3** above is the most desirable treatment, IAS 21 (r1993) notes that an alternative treatment is allowable in the rare cases where:

(a) exchange differences result from a severe devaluation or depreciation of a currency;
(b) against which there is no practical means of hedging; and
(c) that affects liabilities which cannot be settled and which arise directly on the recent acquisition of an asset invoiced in a foreign currency.

When an enterprise adopts the allowed alternative treatment, the exchange differences are included in the initial carrying amount of the related asset, provided that this does not cause the carrying amount to exceed the lower of replacement cost and the amount recoverable from the sale or use of the asset. The logic behind this is that, in the very unusual circumstance where an enterprise cannot settle or hedge a liability which has arisen on the recent acquisition of an asset, the exchange difference is part of the directly attributable costs of acquiring the asset. This may happen, for example, where exchange controls are introduced, causing a delay in obtaining the foreign currency required to settle the debt.

The definition in IAS 21 (r1993).21 sets very strict criteria for the use of this alternative treatment. Areas which create difficulty in interpretation are:

- what constitutes 'a severe devaluation'? This may be deemed to occur when there is a major downwards adjustment to the value of a currency which is not expected to reverse in the near future, rather than a temporary fluctuation;
- when is a liability incurred 'directly' on an acquisition? Clearly the cost of the asset itself, or a loan taken out to finance the purchase, is such a liability. Legal fees on conveyancing would also be deemed to be direct cost as would a normal level of costs incurred in transporting the asset to its site of eventual use. Chapter **10** contains a discussion of what may be included in 'direct' costs (see **10.3.5, 10.4, 10.8.6** and **10.9.6**).

In addition SIC-11 addresses two further areas of difficulty:

- in which period the conditions that the liability 'cannot be settled' and that there is 'no practical means of hedging' should be applied; and
- when the acquisition of an asset is 'recent'.

'Cannot be settled' and 'no practical means of hedging'

SIC-11 argues that the Allowed Alternative Treatment is intended to allow capitalisation of exchange losses that are an unavoidable consequence of buying the asset. Therefore, SIC set two criteria for capitalisation of exchange losses on liabilities:

- the liability could not have been settled before the severe devaluation. It should be demonstrated that foreign currency was not available, for example, due to exchange control restrictions imposed by a government or central bank; and
- it was impracticable to hedge the exchange risk before the severe devaluation. It should be demonstrated that hedging instruments, for example, forward contracts, options or other financial instruments, were not available.

SIC does not appear to permit an argument that the cost of hedging instruments was prohibitively high. (SIC-11.3,4)

'Recent acquisition'

This is interpreted by the SIC as meaning acquisitions within twelve months prior to the severe devaluation or depreciation of the reporting currency. (SIC-11.6) This period relates to the date of acquisition only, and does not restrict the period of capitalisation of subsequent exchange losses provided that all conditions for capitalisation continue to be met. (SIC-11.5)

The SIC guideline appears to apply regardless of the normal period for settling debts. For example, for inventory this might be 30–60 days; for items of property, plant and equipment, the normal credit period may be a number of months. It is assumed that SIC-11 has adopted a fixed period which is reasonable for the circumstances of payment for an acquisition. However, adoption of a shorter period may be considered more appropriate in specific cases.

IAS 29 *Financial Reporting in Hyperinflationary Economies* places a further limitation on the use of the Allowed Alternative Treatment by banning it where the financial statements of the reporting enterprise are prepared in the currency of a hyperinflationary economy. (IAS 29.23)

22.6.8 Interaction between IAS 21 and IAS 39

Provisions in IAS 21 (r1993) and IAS 39 (r2000) partly overlap and the order in which IAS 21 (r1993) and IAS 39 (r2000) are applied can affect the measurement of assets and liabilities and the amounts reported in the income statement and equity.

Neither IAS 21 (r1993) nor IAS 39 (r2000) give a direct answer to this question. The answer is found in IAS 39 Implementation Guidance Question Other-5:

> 'generally, the measurement of a financial asset or financial liability at fair value, cost, or amortised cost is first determined in the foreign currency in which the item is denominated in accordance with IAS 39. Then, the foreign currency amount is reported in the reporting currency using the closing rate or a historical rate in accordance with IAS 21.'

Monetary financial assets and liabilities are first measured at cost, amortised cost or fair value in accordance with IAS 39 (r2000) in the currency of their denomination. Then, the foreign currency amount is reported using the closing rate of exchange under the rules of IAS 21 (r1993). Non-monetary assets are translated at closing rate if they are carried at fair value, and at a historic rate if they are not carried at fair value because their fair value cannot be reliably determined. However, if a non-monetary financial asset or financial liability is designated as a hedged item in a fair value hedge of the exposure to changes in foreign currency rates under IAS 39 (r2000), the hedged item is remeasured for changes in foreign currency rates as required by IAS 39 (r2000).153 and the foreign currency amount is reported using the closing rate even if it would otherwise have been reported using a historical rate under IAS 21 (r1993).

Unless a monetary item is designated as a cash flow hedge of an unrecognised firm commitment or forecasted transaction in foreign currency (see

Chapter **12**), any exchange differences are reported in net profit or loss in accordance with IAS 21 (r1993). (IAS 39 (r2000).78 and 94) IAS Implementation Guidance Question Other-5 further suggests that all differences relating to foreign currency movements should be accounted for in a similar manner to achieve consistency, with all other changes in the balance sheet measurement of a monetary item to be reported in net profit or loss or in equity in accordance with IAS 39 (r2000). The portion of the change in carrying value reported in equity and the portion reported in the net profit or loss cannot be offset even where, for example, the fair value of a financial asset has increased in foreign currency and decreased in the reporting currency.

Any change in the carrying value of a non-monetary item is:

- accounted for in accordance with normal rules in respect of held for trading financial instruments and available-for-sale financial assets in IAS 39 (r2000).103, if the non-monetary item is not part of hedging relationship; or

(IAS 39 (r2000).78 and 94)

- accounted for in accordance with the rules in IAS 39 (r2000).158 in respect of reporting gains and losses on cash flow hedges, if the non-monetary item is designated as a cash flow hedge of an unrecognised firm commitment or forecasted transaction in foreign currency.

Interaction of IAS 21 (r1993) and IAS 39 (r2000) in respect of accounting for financial instruments held by a foreign entity for the purposes of consolidation is discussed in **22.7.6** below.

22.7 Financial statements of foreign operations

22.7.1 Introduction

Once a foreign operation's own financial statements have been prepared in its local currency, they must then be translated into the reporting currency of the reporting enterprise or group before they can be incorporated into the reporting enterprise's separate financial statements or the group's consolidated financial statements.

There are two possible translation methods, the correct one to apply depends upon the way in which the foreign operation is financed and operates. A distinction is therefore made between:

- foreign operations that are integral to the operations of the reporting enterprise ('foreign operations'); and

- foreign entities, the activities of which are not an integral part of the activities of the reporting enterprise ('foreign entities'). (IAS 21 (r1993).23-25)

22.7.2 *Foreign operations that are integral to the operations of the reporting enterprise*

This type of operation functions as an extension of the operations of the reporting enterprise. The example given in IAS 21 (r1993).24 is where a foreign operation is solely concerned with selling goods which it has imported from the reporting enterprise and remits the proceeds to the latter. Another example is where components are manufactured in one or more countries and assembled or sold in a third country. Any change in the exchange rate will impact on the cash flow of the reporting enterprise almost immediately and consequently, as far as the reporting enterprise is concerned, individual monetary items flowing into and out of it are affected, and not just its net investment in the foreign operation.

22.7.3 *Foreign entities that are not integral to the operations of the reporting enterprise*

Foreign entities essentially operate independently of the reporting enterprise. They generate income and incur expenses independently and may even have their own local borrowing arrangements. In this situation, the reporting enterprise has invested in the net worth of the foreign entity, rather than in its individual assets and liabilities, and therefore it is the net worth which is affected by change in the exchange rate. The cash flows of the reporting enterprise and, indeed, the foreign entity, are not directly affected by such changes. Note that an operation, such as a subsidiary, may be ultimately *controlled* by the reporting enterprise but still exercise considerable autonomy in carrying out its activities. The question of control determines whether or not it is appropriate to consolidate an entity (see Chapter **19**) and is not relevant here.

22.7.4 *Factors to consider in classifying the foreign operation*

The table below sets out some of the areas to consider in determining whether any particular foreign operation is integral to the operations of the reporting enterprise. It is based on the guidance in IAS 21 (r1993).26.

Foreign operation	*Foreign entity*
The operation acts as an extension of the reporting enterprise's business.	The entity exercises significant autonomy in carrying out its activities.

A high proportion of the operation's activities are transactions with the reporting enterprise.	Transactions with the reporting enterprise form only a moderate part of the entity's activities.
The operation is financed principally by the reporting enterprise.	The entity is financed principally by its own operations or local borrowings.
The direct costs incurred by the operation in producing goods and services are primarily paid in the reporting currency.	The direct costs incurred by the entity are primarily paid in local currency.
Sales made by the operation are mainly in the reporting currency.	Sales made by the entity are mainly in foreign currencies.
The cash flows of the reporting enterprise are directly affected by the activities of the foreign operation.	The reporting enterprise is not directly affected on a day-to-day basis by the cash flows of the entity.

IAS 21 (r1993) indicates that whilst the classification is normally apparent from the facts of a situation, there are occasions when judgement is required. For example, in any particular situation it is unlikely that each of the factors listed in the table above will point to the same conclusion. No preference is indicated in IAS 21 (r1993) for either classification where there is uncertainty involved, but following IAS 21 (r1993).24-25 the main consideration is the extent to which the cash flows of the reporting enterprise are affected by the activities of the foreign operation: if there is a change in the exchange rate, does the reporting enterprise feel the effects immediately on its own cash flows, or is only its net investment affected?

Another factor to consider is to what extent the foreign operation is obliged to remit cash to the reporting enterprise by way of dividends. Those operations which are continually drained of cash and are not permitted to reinvest it are more likely to be 'integral' to the operations of the reporting enterprise. Conversely, an operation which relies on financial support from its parent is not automatically assumed to be 'integral'; it may simply be that the parent has access to finance and can provide it more cheaply than a third party. However, the frequency and nature of the cash injections need to be assessed: frequent short term loans (or the deferment of intercompany debts) to make good a temporary shortfall in working capital expose the parent to direct exchange gains or losses when that financing is repaid, while long term loans or capital injections affect only the parent's net investment in the foreign entity.

In arriving at a decision on the classification of the operation, it is important to look at how the operation *actually* conducts its business, rather than at any contractual arrangements it may have; substance is more important than legal form.

22.7.5 *Translating the financial statements of foreign operations*

Since a foreign operation which is integral to the operations of the reporting enterprise is effectively an extension of the latter's business, IAS 21 (r1993) requires its financial statements to be translated using the rules set out in **22.6** in respect of foreign currency transactions. That is to say, its transactions and year-end balances are incorporated into the financial statements of the reporting enterprise in the same way as if the reporting enterprise had carried out the transactions itself.

IAS 21 (r1993).28 makes it clear that adjustments may be required to reduce the carrying value of assets in the financial statements of the reporting enterprise to their recoverable amount even though no adjustment may be necessary in the financial statements of the foreign operation. On the other hand, a foreign operation may have made an adjustment to write down an asset which then needs to be reversed in the financial statements of the reporting enterprise on consolidation.

Example 22.3

A French subsidiary of a UK company acquires inventory for FF100 when the exchange rate is £1=FF10. At the period-end the subsidiary writes down the inventory to net realisable value which it determines as FF90, causing a loss to be recognised for the year. However, at the balance sheet date the exchange rate is £1=FF9, hence to the reporting enterprise there is no loss: the inventory was acquired for £10 and is still worth £10. The loss in the subsidiary's books needs to be reversed in the financial statements of the reporting enterprise such that no loss is shown in the consolidated income statement.

22.7.6 *Translating the financial statements of foreign entities*

In the case of foreign entities that are not integral to the operations of the reporting enterprise, the latter has invested in the net worth of the foreign entity, rather than in its individual assets and liabilities. The aim of translation is therefore to show the value of the net investment in the foreign entity and this is achieved by using the following rules (IAS 21 (r1993).30):

All assets and liabilities.	Translate at closing rate.
All income and expenses.	Translate at the rate ruling at the date of the transactions (an average rate may be used as an approximation). However, if the foreign entity reports in the currency of a hyper-inflationary economy, remeasure in terms of measurement unit current at the balance sheet date and translate at closing rate (see Chapter **28**).

Exchange differences arise due to:

- income and expenses being translated using the rate at the date of the transactions, while the balance sheet, including retained earnings, is translated at the closing rate;
- the difference between the value of the opening net investment in the foreign entity when translated at the closing rate at last period-end and its value when translated at the closing rate at this period-end;
- other changes to equity in the foreign entity. For example, if there has been a capital injection during the year a difference will arise between the injection translated at closing rate and the injection translated at the exchange rate ruling at the date of the transaction. Likewise, if there has been a capital reduction by a subsidiary, this will reduce the parent's net investment and exchange differences will arise from two sources:
  - the difference between the opening net investment translated at the closing rate at last period-end and the opening net investment translated at the exchange rate ruling on the date of the capital reduction; and
  - the difference between the remaining investment translated at the rate on the date of the capital reduction and that same remaining investment translated at the closing rate.

These exchange differences are to be classified as equity until the disposal of the entity. (IAS 21 (r1993).30(c)) It is not appropriate to recognise them as income or expenses of the period, as the change in the exchange rates does not directly affect the cash flows of either the reporting enterprise or the foreign entity (as explained in **22.7.4**).

Example 22.4

A German subsidiary of a US company has opening net assets of DM100 and makes a profit for the period of DM30. At the beginning of the period the exchange rate is \$1=DM2; at the end of the period it is \$1=DM3. The average exchange rate for the period which fairly approximates to the actual exchange rate is \$1=DM2.5. The total exchange difference is calculated as:

			$	$
Opening net assets @ opening rate	DM100 @ 2	=	50	
Opening net assets @ closing rate	DM100 @ 3	=	33	
Exchange difference				17
Profit for the period @ average rate	DM30 @ 2.5	=	12	
Profit for the period @ closing rate	DM30 @ 3	=	10	
Exchange difference				2
Total exchange difference taken to equity				19

Example 22.5

An Australian subsidiary of a UK parent is set up with opening net assets of A$100 and receives a capital injection of A$10 during the period but has no other transactions. At the beginning of the period the exchange rate is £1=A$2; at the time of the capital injection it is £1=A$2.5; at the end of the period it is £1=A$3. The total exchange difference is calculated as:

			£	£
Opening net assets @ opening rate	A$100 @ 2	=	50	
Opening net assets @ closing rate	A$100 @ 3	=	33	
Exchange difference				17
Capital injection @ actual rate	A$10 @ 2.5	=	4	
Capital injection @ closing rate	A$10 @ 3	=	3	
Exchange difference				1
Total exchange difference taken to equity				18

This can be proved as the parent has in its own balance sheet an investment of A$100 carried at historic cost (£50) plus a capital injection carried at historic cost (£4) – a total of £54. This can be compared with closing net assets in the subsidiary of A$110 which are translated for inclusion in the consolidated financial statements at the closing rate, giving £36. The difference is the exchange rate movement of £18 as calculated above.

IAS 39 (r2000) requires that changes in fair value of financial assets held for trading be reported in net profit or loss and allows an enterprise to adopt a policy of reporting changes in fair value of available for sale financial assets in net profit or loss. Additionally, IAS 39 (r2000) requires certain gains and losses resulting from changes in the carrying value of financial instruments to be recognised in net profit or loss if these financial instruments are part of a hedging relationship. IAS 21 (r1993).30, on the other hand, states that all exchange differences resulting from translating the financial statements of a foreign entity should be classified as equity until disposal of the net investment. IAS 39 Implementation Guidance (Question Other – 3) resolves this apparent contradiction by saying that enterprises should first apply the requirements of IAS 39 (r2000) in accounting for financial instruments in the financial statements of a foreign entity and then apply IAS 21 (r1993) to translate these financial statements for the purpose of incorporating them into the financial statements of the reporting enterprise.

22.7.7 Minority interest

Where there is a minority interest in a consolidated foreign entity, the accumulated exchange differences attributable to the minority interests are reported as part of the minority interest in the consolidated balance sheet. (IAS 21 (r1993).32)

22.7.8 Goodwill and fair value adjustments

Where goodwill and fair value adjustments have arisen on the acquisition of a foreign entity (see Chapter **18**) there is a choice of treatment (IAS 21 (r1993).33):

- either they are treated as assets and liabilities of the foreign entity, in which case they will be translated at the closing rate as in **22.7.6**; or
- they may be treated as assets and liabilities of the reporting enterprise, in which case either:
  - they are already expressed in the reporting currency, in which case no retranslation is required; or
  - they are non-monetary foreign currency items and hence reported using the exchange rate at the date of the transaction and not subsequently retranslated (as set out in **22.6.2**).

For goodwill this means that, having been capitalised in the balance sheet in line with IAS 22 (r1998), *Business Combinations* (see Chapter **18**) it may either be re-translated at the closing rate at each period-end (taking into account the amount of amortisation), or it may remain at historic rate.

The treatment adopted should reflect the way in which the goodwill is viewed: if the reporting enterprise considers it has invested in an asset which is measured at a certain point in time and valid only at that point in time in the circumstances then prevailing, i.e., invested in goodwill as part of the initial investment in a foreign entity, goodwill remains at the historic rate; if the reporting enterprise views goodwill as an asset which resides in the foreign entity's business and generates a foreign income stream, goodwill is retranslated at the closing rate. The choice of treatment may be linked to the method of funding the net investment: where a foreign currency loan is taken out to hedge the full cost of the acquisition, then treatment of goodwill as a foreign currency asset will generate exchange differences on the entire purchase price which will match differences on the related loan; where a foreign currency loan covers only the fair value of underlying net assets of the net investment (excluding goodwill), then treatment of goodwill as an asset of the reporting entity will be more appropriate.

For fair value adjustments the implication is that either they are notionally added to the carrying value of the assets and liabilities in the books of the acquired entity where they are translated together at the closing rate, or the adjustments are treated as isolated assets and liabilities in their own right and carried at historic rate while the underlying assets and liabilities in the acquired entity, whose value they are adjusting, are re-translated at the closing rate at each period-end.

IAS 21 (r1993) does not demonstrate a preference for either of these treatments, even though the decision may have a marked impact on the carrying value of goodwill, assets and liabilities in the balance sheet. However since the choice of treatment represents an accounting policy, once the decision is made it must be applied consistently to all acquisitions and from period to period.

22.7.9 Consolidation

Once the financial statements of the foreign entity have been translated, they are consolidated into the group accounts following the normal procedures as described in Chapter **19**. Intra-group balances will need to be eliminated. Since these intra-group balances expose the reporting enterprise to a gain or loss as a result of currency fluctuations, exchange differences arising are not eliminated and are recognised as income or an expense in the consolidated financial statements. (IAS 21 (r1993).34) The entity in which these differences are recorded depends upon the currency in which the balance is legally fixed.

Example 22.6

A Dutch parent lends its French subsidiary Dfl 100, denominated in Dutch guilders, when the exchange rate is Dfl 1 = FF 3. At the year-end, the exchange rate is Dfl 1 = FF 2.8. The French subsidiary initially recorded an amount payable of FF 300. When its financial statements are drawn up at the year-end, it only needs to show an amount payable of FF 280; the balance of FF 20 is credited to income. The FF 280 will then be retranslated at the closing rate for inclusion in the consolidation, giving an amount of Dfl 100. Meanwhile, the parent still shows a receivable of Dfl 100 in its books, consequently the intercompany balances agree, but the group has FF 20 of exchange differences credited to income.

The only exception to this is where the intra-group balance forms part of the reporting enterprise's net investment in the foreign entity. In this case, the exchange difference will be classified as equity until the disposal of the entity.

22.7.10 Liabilities hedging a net investment in a foreign entity

IAS 21 (r1993).17–19 and IAS 39 (r2000).164 consider liabilities used to hedge a foreign entity investment. (This was discussed in section **22.6.6**).

22.7.11 Different reporting dates

There may be occasions when a foreign entity has a different reporting date from that of the reporting enterprise. In this case, the entity often draws up an additional set of financial statements to the same date as the reporting enterprise specifically for the purpose of incorporation into the financial statements of the latter. (IAS 21 (r1993).35)

However, when it is 'impracticable' for the foreign entity to prepare such an additional set of financial statements, it is permissible to use financial statements drawn up to a different reporting date, providing that date is no more than three months different from the reporting date of the reporting enterprise.

Where this is the case, the assets and liabilities of the foreign entity are translated at the exchange rate ruling at its own balance sheet date, and not that at the balance sheet date of the reporting enterprise. However, adjustments are made for any significant movements in exchange rates up to the reporting date of the reporting enterprise.

22.7.12 Disposal of a foreign entity

When an enterprise disposes of its interest in a foreign entity, whether through sale, liquidation, abandonment or other means, the cumulative amount of the exchange differences relating to it which have previously been recognised in equity (i.e., deferred) are required to be recognised as income or expense in the period in which the gain or loss on disposal is recognised. (IAS 21 (r1993).37)

Where there is a partial disposal, the relevant proportion of the cumulative amount of exchange differences is included in the gain or loss. The payment of a dividend is not generally considered to be a partial disposal unless it constitutes a return of the investment. This would normally only be the case where payment of the dividend results in the distributable reserves of the foreign entity being reduced below their level at the date of acquisition (i.e., the dividend is paid from pre-acquisition reserves).

If the reporting enterprise makes a write-down in the carrying amount of a foreign entity, this is not to be interpreted as a disposal and no accounting adjustment is required to the deferred foreign exchange gain or loss.

22.7.13 Change in classification of a foreign operation or entity

The relationship between a reporting enterprise and an associated foreign operation may change, such that the latter is financed or operates in a different manner. In that case the classification may change and the way in which the entity is accounted for is altered henceforth. No retrospective adjustments are made. In the absence of a change in relationship, the classification remains the same, to ensure consistency of reporting from one year to the next. The only exception to this rule is where the previous classification is deemed to have been made in error, making the financial statements of prior periods no longer reliable (a 'fundamental error'). In that case the rules in IAS 8 (r1993) *Net Profit or Loss for the Period, Fundamental Errors and Changes in Accounting Policies* are applied (see Chapter **5**).

Where there is a change in relationship, exchange differences are to be dealt with as follows.

Initial classification		**New classification**
Foreign operation	➔	Foreign entity
Monetary items are treated the same for each type of classification: they are always translated at closing rate, hence the change of classification has no impact. However, for a foreign operation, non-monetary assets are translated at historic rate (or the rate ruling at the date of determination of fair value), whereas for a foreign entity they are translated at closing rate. Consequently, when the classification changes, non-monetary items need to be re-translated using the rate at the actual date of the change in relationship. Exchange differences arising on this re-translation are classified as equity, i.e., they are recognised not in the income statement but directly in equity. (IAS 21 (r1993).40)		

Initial classification		**New classification**
Foreign entity	➔	Foreign operation
Again, monetary items do not cause a problem, since they are carried at closing rate regardless of the classification of the operation. However, as regards non-monetary items, the translated amount at which they are carried at the date of the reclassification will thereafter be treated as the historical cost of those items both in the period of change and in subsequent periods and hence, no further re-translation will be required unless the items are restated at fair value in the accounts. Exchange differences which arose in the past on consolidation of the foreign entity will have been included in shareholders' equity and will remain there. They are not recognised as income or expenses until the disposal of the operation. (IAS 21 (r1993).40)		

22.8 Tax effects of exchange differences

The tax effect of gains and losses on exchange differences are to be accounted for in accordance with IAS 12 (r2000) *Income Taxes* (see Chapter **23**).

IAS 21 (r1993) does not deal with accounting for financial instruments such as forward exchange contracts and hedge accounting for foreign currency items (other than items that hedge a net investment in a foreign entity as discussed in **22.7.10**). IAS 39 (r2000) deals with this (see Chapter **12**).

22.9 Introduction of the Euro

From 1 January 1999, the euro became a currency in its own right and the conversion rates between the euro and participating national currencies were irrevocably fixed, i.e., the risk of subsequent exchange differences related to these currencies was eliminated from this date. Ahead of this date, the SIC considered a number of issues:

- whether the future fixing of exchange rates represented an adjusting post-balance sheet event for financial statements prepared for periods ending prior to 1 January 1999;
- whether anticipatory hedges of transactions or commitments after 1 January 1999 should cease to be deferred and matched to periods after 1 January 1999;
- whether the fixing of exchange rates represented a disposal event requiring immediate recognition as income or expense of cumulative exchange differences taken direct to equity; and
- whether currencies participating in the euro could give rise to an exchange difference which would qualify for inclusion in the carrying value of an asset.

Although the resulting interpretation SIC-7 deals primarily with financial statements prepared for periods ending prior to 1 January 1999, its principles would apply equally to the fixing of exchange rates when countries join the euro at later stages. (SIC-7.3) SIC-7 became effective on 1 June 1998.

22.9.1 Effect of future fixing of rates on monetary items

Foreign currency monetary items are required to be reported using the closing rate (IAS 21 (r1993).11(a)), and any exchange difference recognised as income or expense (IAS 21 (r1993).15). The fact that exchange rates would be fixed on 1 January 1999 raised the question whether, in any balance sheet prepared before that date, the known future rates should be used.

SIC concluded that the future fixing of exchange rates should not be applied in a balance sheet before 1 January 1999. Therefore, foreign currency monetary items should continue to be translated at actual closing rates, and resultant exchange differences reported in the period when rates changed. (SIC-7.4(a))

22.9.2 Effect on anticipatory hedges

Where an entity applied an accounting policy to defer an exchange gain or loss to a future period in order to match a future transaction or commitment as part of a hedging strategy, the question arose whether exchange gains and losses should continue to be deferred beyond 1 January 1999.

The SIC concluded that the introduction of the euro does not affect the economic rationale of such hedges (even though the economic impact between currencies entering the euro is eliminated from 1 January 1999). Therefore, no change to the accounting policy is required, and outstanding transactions should continue to be deferred and recognised in accordance with the established accounting policy. (SIC-7.4(a))

22.9.3 Effect on cumulative differences taken to equity

Cumulative exchange differences relating to the translation of the financial statements of a foreign entity which have been deferred in equity in accordance with IAS 21 (r1993).17, 19 or 30(c) are required to be recognised as income or expense in the same period in which the gain or loss on disposal of the foreign entity is recognised. The question arose whether the fixing of currencies entering the euro represented an event which required cumulative difference to be recognised as income or expense similar to the disposal of the foreign entity which gave rise to the differences. (IAS 21 (r1993).37)

The SIC concluded that the wording of IAS 21 (r1993).37 clearly identifies the events which would qualify as a disposal, and that fixing of exchange rates would not qualify as a disposal event. Therefore, cumulative differences should continue to be carried in equity, and recognised in income or expense only on the disposal of the net investment in the related foreign entity. (SIC-7.4(b))

22.9.4 Availability of the alternative treatment

Under the allowed alternative treatment of IAS 21 (r1993).21, exchange differences resulting from severe devaluations of currencies are included in the carrying amount of the related assets in certain limited circumstances. The question arose whether changes to currency rates to align with the fixed rates on entering the euro could be classified as severe devaluations for the purpose described.

SIC concluded that currencies entering the euro were part of established currency markets which did not meet the criteria intended by paragraph 21. The fixing of currencies entering the euro was to achieve stability of participating currencies, and that this was incompatible with classification as a severe devaluation. Therefore, exchange differences resulting from the translation of liabilities denominated in participating currencies should not be included in the carrying amount of assets. (SIC-7.4(c))

22.10 Presenting financial statements in a currency other than the measurement currency

Although an enterprise normally presents its financial statements using the currency of the country in which it is domiciled, which is also usually its measurement currency, it may choose to present them in a different currency. The choice of the *presentation currency* is not restricted by IAS, neither is the method of translating the financial statements from the *measurement currency* to the presentation currency. However, SIC-19 requires that the method used should not lead to reporting in a manner that is inconsistent with the measurement of items in the financial statements. (SIC-19.9)

SIC-D30 suggests that the requirements should be applied as follows:

- assets and liabilities should be translated at the closing rate at the date of each balance sheet presented, except when an enterprise's measurement currency is the currency of a hyperinflationary economy, in which case assets and liabilities should be translated at the closing rate existing at the date of the most recent balance sheet presented;
- income and expense items should be translated at the exchange rates existing at the dates of the transactions or a rate that approximates the actual exchange rates, except when an enterprise's measurement currency is the currency of a hyperinflationary economy, in which case income and expense items for all periods presented should be translated at the closing rate existing at the end of the most recent period presented; and
- all resulting exchange differences should be reported directly in equity.

SIC-D30 also addresses 'convenience translation' – what information should be disclosed when additional information not required by International Accounting Standards is displayed in a currency, other than the currency used in presenting its financial statements, as a convenience to certain users. The SIC agreed that in this circumstance an enterprise should:

- clearly identify the information as supplementary information to distinguish it from the information required by International Accounting Standards; and
- disclose the method of translation used as a basis for presenting the information.

22.11 Disclosure requirements

IAS 1 (r1997) requires the reporting currency to be prominently displayed and repeated as necessary for a proper understanding of the information presented. (IAS 1(r1997).46) This may be achieved by disclosing the reporting currency on every page of the financial statements in which numbers are presented.

A number of disclosures is required in the financial statements of the reporting enterprise.

(1) The amount of exchange differences included in the net profit or loss for the period should be disclosed. (IAS 21(r1993).42(a))
(2) Where exchange differences have been classified as equity, their net amount should be disclosed as a separate component of equity. A reconciliation should be provided between the opening and closing exchange differences. (IAS 21(r1993).42(b))
(3) Where exchange differences have been included in the carrying amount of an asset under the special circumstances set out in **22.6.7**, the amount of these should be disclosed. (IAS 21(r1993).42(c))
(4) If the reporting currency is different from the currency of the country in which the reporting enterprise is domiciled, the reason for this should be disclosed. (IAS 21(r1993).43)
(5) The reason for any change in the reporting currency should be disclosed. (IAS 21(r1993).43)
(6) If the classification of a significant foreign operation changes (from 'foreign operation' to 'foreign entity' or vice versa) it is necessary to disclose:
   - the nature of the change;
   - the reason for the change;
   - the impact of the change on shareholders' equity; and
   - what the effect would have been on the profit or loss for each prior period presented, if the change had occurred at the beginning of the earliest period presented.

   (IAS 21(r1993).44)
(7) The method used to translate goodwill and fair value adjustments arising on the acquisition of a foreign entity (see **22.7.8**) should be disclosed. (IAS 21(r1993).45)
(8) If there is a change in exchange rates occurring after the balance sheet date which is of such importance that non-disclosure would affect the ability of users of the financial statements to make proper evaluations and decisions, then the effect of that change on foreign currency monetary items or on the financial statements of a foreign operation should be disclosed. (IAS 21(r1993).46)

SIC-19.10 adds the following requirements for disclosure:

(9) The reason for using a measurement currency that is different from the currency of the country in which the enterprise operates.
(10) The reason for any change in the measurement currency or presentation currency.
(11) Where the presentation currency is different from the measurement currency, the measurement currency, the reason for using a different currency for presentation and the description of the method used in the translation process.

22.12 Transitional provisions

Where an enterprise applies this Standard for the first time, the only requirement is that the cumulative exchange differences classified as equity at the start of the accounting period are required to be separately classified and disclosed.

22.13 Comparison with UK GAAP

There are a number of areas where UK GAAP, principally embodied in SSAP 20 *Foreign Currency Translation* differs from IAS 21 (r1993).

(1) SSAP 20 does not make a distinction, as in **22.6.2**, between assets carried at historical cost and assets carried at fair value, but specifies that all non-monetary assets are to be translated at the exchange rate in operation on the day on which the transaction occurred. However, in practice the same approach is applied as that set out in IAS 21 (r1993);
(2) In the specific circumstance where foreign currency borrowings are used to finance, or provide a hedge against, a foreign equity investment, and certain conditions are met, SSAP 20 permits the investment as well as the loan to be retranslated at the closing rate of exchange at the balance sheet date and the exchange differences to be taken to reserves, where they will offset each other. (SSAP 20.51) IAS 21 (r1993).19 requires the exchange differences on the loan only, to be classified as equity.
(3) In rare circumstances, IAS 21 (r1993) allows exchange differences to be included in the initial carrying amount of an asset. This is where exchange differences result from 'a severe devaluation or depreciation of a currency against which there is no practical means of hedging and that affects liabilities which cannot be settled and which arise directly on the recent acquisition of an asset invoiced in a foreign currency' (see **22.6.7**). SSAP 20 does not provide for a different treatment to be adopted in these circumstances.

(4) On disposal of a foreign entity, UK GAAP does not recognise the cumulative foreign exchange differences as income or expense; they remain classified as equity;

(5) While SSAP 20 makes a similar distinction to IAS 21 (r1993) between 'foreign operations' and 'foreign entities', it also permits a choice in translating the profit and loss account of a foreign entity: it may either be translated at the rate of exchange ruling at the balance sheet date (the closing rate), or at an average rate. The average rate to be used is calculated by the method considered most appropriate for the circumstances of the foreign enterprise (SSAP 20.54). Under IAS 21(r1993), only the average rate is permitted.

22.14 Comparison with US GAAP

US GAAP is principally set out in SFAS 52 *Foreign Currency Translation*. The major differences from IAS 21 (r1993) are set out below.

(1) Accounting for forward exchange contracts and hedging are excluded from the scope of IAS 21 (r1993), but are covered in IAS 39 (r2000) effective for periods beginning on or after 1 January 2001. In the US, SFAS 133 *Accounting for Derivative Instruments and Hedging Activities*, and SFAS 138 *Accounting for Certain Derivative Instruments and Hedging Activities an amendment of FASB Statement No. 133*, have requirements for accounting for forward exchange contracts and hedging of foreign currency risk, and are effective for periods beginning after 15 June 2000.

(2) As set out in **22.12** and **22.6.7**, IAS 21 (r1993) allows exchange differences to be included in the initial carrying amount of an asset in certain rare circumstances. This is not permitted by SFAS 52.

(3) Where goodwill and fair value adjustments have arisen on the acquisition of a foreign entity, SFAS 52 specifies that the closing exchange rate should be used to translate these at each period-end. IAS 21 (r1993) permits use of either the closing rate of exchange or the historical rate with no subsequent re-translation.

(4) Where there is a foreign entity which reports in the currency of a hyperinflationary economy, and which is to be incorporated into the financial statements of the reporting enterprise, there are differences of treatment between IAS 21 (r1993) and SFAS 52 (see Chapter **28**).

SFAS 52 does not deal with a change in the reporting currency. SEC regulation S-X Rule 3-20 states that if the financial statements are stated in a currency that is different from that used in financial statements previously filed with the Commission, the issuer should recast its financial statements as if the newly adopted currency had been used since at least the earliest period presented in the filing. Additionally, the decision to change and the reason for the change in the reporting currency should be disclosed in a note to the financial statements in the period in which the change occurs. It is possible that some sort of convenience translation may be permitted if the change in reporting currency was necessitated by a change in the functional currency of the parent. However, accounting treatment for SEC registrants is also recommended for non-SEC registrants when changing reporting currency.

22.15 Examples from published financial statements

Examples of accounting policy notes relate to foreign currency translations that pre-date effective dates of IAS 39 (r2000) and SIC-19 (note that the excerpts given do not always comply in full with all aspects of IAS and as such are not necessarily examples of best practice but merely of current practice):

Example 22.7

Foreign currency translation

Most foreign currency receivables and payables of the consolidated companies are hedged, and are translated at the hedged rates in their financial statements. The remaining foreign currency receivables and payables are translated at closing rates.

The majority of foreign consolidated companies are to be regarded as foreign entities since they are financially, economically and organisationally autonomous. Their functional currencies according to IAS 21 (*The Effects of Changes in Foreign Exchange Rates*) are thus the respective local currencies. The assets and liabilities of these companies are therefore translated at closing rates, income and expense items at average rates for the year.

Where the operations of a foreign company are integral to those of Bayer AG, the functional currency is the euro. A temporal translation method is therefore used that is recognised in income.

Property, plant and equipment, intangible assets, investments in affiliated companies and other securities included in investments are translated at the average exchange rates in the year of addition, along with the relevant amortisation, depreciation and write-downs. All other balance sheet items are translated at closing rates. Income and expense items (except amortisation, depreciation and write-downs) are translated at average rates for the year.

Companies operating in hyperinflationary economies prepare their statements in hard currency and thus, in effect, by the temporal method described above.

Exchange differences arising from the translation of foreign companies' balance sheets are shown in a separate stockholders' equity item. In case of divestiture, the respective exchange differences are reversed and recognised in income.

The exchange rates for major currencies against the euro varied as follows:

€ 1		*Closing rate*		*Average rate*	
		2000	*1999*	*2000*	*1999*
USA	US$	0.93	1.00	0.93	1.07
UK	GB£	0.62	0.62	0.61	0.66
Japan	JPY	106.92	102.73	99.74	121.05
Canada	CAD	1.40	1.46	1.37	1.59
Switzerland	CHF	1.52	1.61	1.56	1.60

Bayer AG
Germany
31 December 2000
International Accounting Standards

Example 22.8

D. Translation of the financial statements of foreign subsidiaries

(a) In general, the financial statements of foreign subsidiaries are translated as follows:
- Balance sheet items other than shareholders' equity are translated at the year-end rate of exchange.
- Income statement items are translated at the average exchange rate for the year.
- The translation adjustment is included in consolidated shareholders' equity and has no impact on net income.

(b) The financial statements of foreign subsidiaries with autonomous activities operating in high-inflation economies (i.e., where total inflation over three years exceeded 100%) are translated as follows:
- Balance sheet items are translated into French francs at the year-end rate used for the transfer of dividends after adjusting non-monetary items for local inflation.
- After adjustment of monetary items for inflation, income statement items are translated using the same year-end rate as for the balance sheet.
- The translation adjustment is included in consolidated shareholders' equity and has no effect on net income.

(c) For foreign companies whose activities are an extension of the parent company's business, the historical-rate method is applied for non-monetary balance-sheet and income statement items and the translation adjustment is included in net income.

E. Translation of foreign currency transactions

At year-end, monetary balances denominated in foreign currencies that have not been hedged are translated at the year-end rate. The resulting foreign exchange differences, together with the exchange gains and losses on transactions in foreign currencies for the year, are recognised in the income statement. Hedged foreign currency operations are translated using the hedged rate.

Renault
France
31 December 1999
International Accounting Standards

CHAPTER 23

Taxes

23.1 Sources

IAS 12 (r2000)	*Income Taxes* (effective 1 January 2001).
IAS 16 (r1998)	*Property, Plant and Equipment.*
SIC-21	*Income Taxes – Recovery of Revalued Non-Depreciable Asset.*
SIC-25	*Income Taxes – Changes in the Tax Status of an Enterprise or its Shareholders.*

23.2 Brief summary of requirements

IAS 12 (r2000) sets out how to account for both current and deferred tax.

IAS 1 (r1997) *Presentation of Financial Statements* requires the current tax expense to be disclosed on the face of the income statement. (IAS 1 (r1997).75) Unpaid portions of current tax for the current and prior periods should be recognised in the balance sheet as a liability. Any excess paid over the amount due for those periods should be recognised as an asset.

In respect of deferred tax, the IAS advocates (with limited exceptions) a full provision basis, including a requirement to set up deferred tax on revaluation surpluses and on fair value adjustments.

Rather than applying an income statement liability method or a deferral method, the IAS takes a balance sheet approach under which the carrying amounts of assets and liabilities in the balance sheet are compared with their tax bases. The resulting difference, if any, is multiplied by the applicable tax rate. With limited exceptions, all such deferred tax liabilities must be recognised in the balance sheet whereas, again subject to limited exceptions, deferred tax assets are recognised in the balance sheet only to the extent that it is probable that there will be sufficient taxable profits in the future to enable the asset to be recovered.

The IAS requires the tax to be charged or credited wherever the underlying transaction has been recognised, namely, the income statement, equity, or, in the case of fair value adjustments, goodwill.

23.3 Development of the requirements

Originally approved in 1979, IAS 12 *Accounting for Taxes on Income*, was reformatted in 1994 to bring its presentation into line with the revised format adopted for IASs from 1991 onwards. The reformatting exercise did not result in any substantive changes. The Standard required deferred tax to be accounted for using either the deferral method or a liability method known as the 'income statement liability method'.

After two exposure drafts, the IASC approved the revised Standard, Income Taxes, in October 1996. The revised IAS eliminates many of the options permitted in the original Standard and requires the use of a liability method known as the 'balance sheet liability method'. This Standard is effective for periods beginning on or after 1 January 1998.

In October 2000, the IASC approved amendments to IAS 12. These limited revisions specify the accounting treatment for the income tax consequences of dividends. IAS 12 (r2000) is effective for financial statements covering periods beginning on or after 1 January 2001. Disclosure should be made of earlier adoption, which is encouraged.

SIC interpretation No.21, *Income Taxes – Recovery of Revalued Non-Depreciable Assets* is effective for periods beginning on or after 15 July 2000. The consensus, dated August 1999, is that the deferred tax liability or asset that arises from the revaluation of a non-depreciable asset should be measured based on the tax consequences that would follow from recovery of the carrying amount of that asset through sale, regardless of the basis of measuring the carrying amount of that asset.

SIC interpretation No.25, *Changes in the Tax Status of an Enterprise or its Shareholders*, is also effective for periods beginning on or after 15 July 2000. The consensus, dated August 1999, is that a change in the tax status of an enterprise or its shareholders does not give rise to increases or decreases in amounts recognised directly in equity. The tax consequences of a change in tax status should be recognised in the net profit or loss for the period unless those consequences relate to transactions or events that result, in the same or a different period, in a direct credit or charge to the recognised amount of equity.

23.4 Definitions

The following definitions are taken from the Standard. Other terms will be defined the first time they are used in the Chapter.

> '*Accounting profit* is net profit or loss for a period before deducting tax expense'.
>
> '*Tax expense (tax income)* is the aggregate amount included in the determination of net profit or loss for the period in respect of current tax and deferred tax'.
>
> '*Taxable profit (tax loss)* is the profit (loss) for a period, determined in accordance with the rules established by the taxation authorities, upon which income taxes are payable (recoverable)'.
>
> (IAS 12 (r2000).5)

23.5 Current tax

Current tax (which is defined in IAS 12 (r2000).5 as 'the amount of income taxes payable (recoverable) in respect of the taxable profit (tax loss) for a period') is the tax that an enterprise expects to pay (recover) in respect of the year. The Standard requires the amount to be calculated using the tax rules (including rates of tax) that have been 'enacted or substantively enacted by the balance sheet date'. (See step two: calculating deferred tax in **23.6.2** above for a discussion on 'enacted or substantively enacted by the balance sheet date'). (IAS 12 (r2000).46)

As with deferred tax, the current tax is recognised wherever the transaction or event that gave rise to the tax is recognised, with the income statement being the fallback. Thus current tax should be recognised in the income statement unless it arises from:

(i) a transaction or event which, in any accounting period, is recognised directly in equity, in which case the tax is also recognised directly in equity; or
(ii) a business combination that is accounted for as an acquisition, in which case the tax alters the amount of goodwill arising on acquisition.

(IAS 12 (r2000).58, 61, 66)

For example, if tax is charged on an exchange gain and that exchange gain is recognised directly in equity, the tax on the gain is also recognised directly in equity.

To the extent that the tax for the current and earlier periods is unpaid it is included in the balance sheet as a liability. (IAS 12 (r2000).12) Conversely any recoverable overpayment is included as an asset. (IAS 12 (r2000).12) An asset is similarly recognised when a tax loss can be carried back to recover the tax of an earlier period. (IAS 12 (r2000).13) The rules regarding presentation in the balance sheet and income statement are set out in step five: presentation in the balance sheet and income statement in **23.6.2** below.

If an enterprise has a tax loss in one year, say, 2000, and this is carried back and used to recover tax of an earlier period, say, 1999, the benefit of the recovery is recognised in the income statement in the year that the loss arises, namely 2000. (IAS 12 (r2000).14)

23.6 Deferred tax

23.6.1 Overview

The Standard requires a full provision approach to deferred tax which is based on 'temporary differences', being differences between the carrying value of an asset or liability and the amount attributed to it for tax purposes.

The IASC's starting point is the balance sheet; it argues that in recognising an asset or liability in the balance sheet at a particular amount, the enterprise expects either to recover the asset or to settle the liability for that amount. For example, if an asset of £20,000 in the balance sheet represents accrued interest receivable the enterprise expects to receive interest income of £20,000. Similarly where an item of property, plant or equipment is carried in the balance sheet at £100,000 the enterprise expects to generate economic benefits of £100,000 by selling the asset, by using the asset in its business and generating sales or by a combination of the two; if this were not true, the asset would be written down to its recoverable amount.

Having started with this premise, the IASC's approach requires an enterprise to consider whether the recovery of its assets and the settlement of its liabilities is taxable or tax deductible. Where any are taxable or tax deductible but in a different accounting period or over a different number of accounting periods to the one or ones in which the asset or liability will be recognised in the income statement or equity, the IAS requires, with limited exceptions, deferred tax to be recognised.

As a consequence, deferred tax is recognised when assets acquired in a business combination accounted for as an acquisition are recorded at fair value unless the tax authorities make a similar adjustment for tax purposes.

In reality, an enterprise will often generate economic benefits in excess of the carrying amount of its net assets. For example, a fixed asset may have a market value exceeding its carrying value. IAS 12 (r2000) does not require preparers to estimate the expected recoveries. Instead, deferred tax is calculated on the assumption that recoveries equal carrying value. In other words, the Standard requires tax to be accounted for only on the entries already recorded in the financial statements.

23.6.2 Calculation, recognition, measurement and presentation of deferred tax

Summary

- Step one in the calculation, recognition, measurement and presentation of deferred tax is to calculate the temporary difference (if any) for each asset and liability in the balance sheet.
- Step two is to calculate the deferred tax by multiplying the temporary difference by the tax rate that is expected to apply in the period when the asset is realised or the liability is settled. The calculation is based on tax rates and laws that have been enacted or substantively enacted by the balance sheet date. The tax rate used should reflect the way in which the enterprise expects to recover or settle the asset or liability. The deferred tax cannot be calculated on a discounted basis.
- Step three is to recognise in the balance sheet the deferred tax assets and liabilities meeting the recognition criteria laid down in the Standard.
- Step four is to recognise, in the income statement, equity or goodwill, the movement between the deferred tax balance in the opening and closing balance sheet.
- Finally, it is necessary to ensure that deferred tax assets and liabilities meeting the offset criteria are netted against one another and that the presentation of deferred tax in the balance sheet complies with the Standard's rules.

Step 1: calculating temporary differences

IAS 12 (r2000).5 states that:

> 'Temporary differences are differences between the carrying amount of an asset or liability in the balance sheet and its tax base. Temporary differences may be either:
>
> (a) taxable temporary differences, which are temporary differences that will result in taxable amounts in determining taxable profit (tax loss) of future periods when the carrying amount of the asset or liability is recovered or settled; or
>
> (b) deductible temporary differences, which are temporary differences that will result in amounts that are deductible in determining taxable profit (tax loss) of future periods when the carrying amount of the asset or liability is recovered or settled.'

In addition, the Standard defines the tax base of an asset or liability as 'the amount attributed to that asset or liability for tax purposes'. (IAS 12 (r2000).5)

Thus *temporary differences* are the difference between the *carrying amount* of a balance sheet asset or liability and its *tax base* (value for tax purposes).

IAS 12 (r2000).7 to 11 gives general guidance on how the tax base of assets and liabilities can be determined. The following table repeats this guidance and gives examples of how the tax base, and the resulting temporary difference, are calculated in various scenarios. The general rules for determining tax bases are in bold and the examples are included in italics.

Balance sheet item	*Tax base and the resulting temporary difference*
Asset giving rise to economic benefits that will be taxable in future periods	**The amount that will be deductible for tax purposes against the taxable economic benefits**
Example 1 – Interest receivable of £500 that will be taxed when it is received in cash.	*Example 1 – The tax base of the interest receivable is nil because when the interest is received in cash the entire £500 is taxed. A tax base of nil gives a temporary difference of £500.*
Example 2 – An item of plant which cost £500,000 and has accumulated depreciation to date of £100,000 (being two years at £50,000 p.a.). Revenue generated by the asset is taxable and a profit (loss) on disposal of the asset is taxable (tax deductible). The asset is deductible for tax purposes on a straight line basis over five years, thus £200,000 has been deducted in tax computations to date and £300,000 is still to be deducted either as the asset is used or as a deduction on disposal.	*Example 2 – The tax base is £300,000, being the tax allowances still to be deducted in future tax computations. This gives a temporary difference of £100,000 (being the carrying amount of £400,000 less the tax base of £300,000).*
Example 3 – As in example 2, but on the balance sheet date the asset is revalued from its historical cost net book value of £400,000 to its fair value of £700,000. The tax authorities base tax deductibility on the original cost figures and make no changes for tax purposes when assets are revalued in the financial statements.	*Example 3 – As in example 2 the tax base is £300,000. The temporary difference is therefore £400,000.*
Example 4 – Inventory is in the balance sheet at a cost of £10,000. The sale of the inventory will generate taxable	*Example 4 – The tax base of the inventory is £10,000, giving rise to a temporary difference of nil.*

income and the cost of the inventory will be deductible from the taxable income in the year the sale is made (being the year in which the cost of the inventory is charged in the income statement).	
Asset giving rise to economic benefits that will not be taxable *Example – Interest receivable of £100 in the financial statements that is not subject to tax either as it accrues or when it is received because it arises on a tax exempt bond held by a US subsidiary.*	**Carrying amount of the asset** *Example – The tax base is £100 giving rise to a temporary difference of nil.*
Asset that was taxed in an earlier period, being the same period in which it was accrued in the financial statements *Example – A trade receivable of £200,000 where tax arose on the sale when it was made and this is the same accounting period in which the sale was recognised in the financial statements.*	**Carrying amount of the asset** *Example – The tax base is £200,000 giving rise to a temporary difference of nil.*
Prepaid expenses deducted in a tax computation of an earlier period *Example – Rent of £1,000 paid in respect of the next accounting period and deducted against taxable income when it was paid.*	**Carrying amount less how much of that was deducted in an earlier period for tax purposes** *Example – The tax base is nil giving rise to a temporary difference of £1,000.*
Liability *Example 1 – Accrued rental expense of £40,000 which will be deducted for tax purposes when it is paid.* *Example 2 – Trade payable of £100,000 for purchases of goods for resale.*	**Carrying amount less amount that will be deductible for tax purposes in respect of the liability in future years** *Example 1 – The full amount will be deductible for tax in future, so the tax base is nil giving rise to a temporary difference of £40,000.* *Example 2 – The tax base is £100,000 giving rise to a temporary difference of nil. Although part of the £100,000 might have already been deducted in a tax computation (representing the*

	cost of goods sold during the period) and part will be deductible against future taxable income (being inventory to be sold in a future period) the settlement of the liability itself is not the event that gives rise to the tax deduction. When the goods are bought, the other side of the entry is to increase inventory, and it is the inventory that gives rise to income that will be taxable. Accordingly the tax base of the trade payable is the carrying amount giving a temporary difference of nil.
Example 3 – A loan of £100,000 repayable in five years' time. The repayment of the loan is not deductible for tax purposes.	*Example 3 – The tax base is £100,000 giving a temporary difference of nil.*
Example 4 – A loan of £100,000 taken out on the first day of the accounting period and repayable in five years. Commission costs of £10,000 were set against the loan in the balance sheet on day one. By the balance sheet date, £2,000 of the issue costs had been amortised, giving a carrying value in the balance sheet of £92,000. The repayment of the loan is not deductible for tax purposes, but the issue costs were tax deductible when paid.	*Example 4 – If the guidance for liabilities in IAS 12 (r2000), and set out above in bold, is strictly interpreted, the tax base would appear to be £92,000 (being carrying amount of £92,000 less any amount that is deductible for tax in the future). A tax base of £92,000 would give rise to a temporary difference of nil. However, since £10,000 was deducted for tax purposes in year 1 and the £10,000 is being expensed in the income statement over five years there should be a deferred tax entry in the income statement in each of the five years. Since, at the balance sheet date, £8,000 of the £10,000 is still to be recognised as an expense, deferred tax on the £8,000 should be set up.* *To achieve this it is necessary to view the £92,000 carrying amount as a liability of £100,000 and an asset of £8,000. Using the guidance for liabilities the tax base is £100,000 and the temporary difference is nil. Using the guidance above in respect of 'prepaid expenses deducted in a tax computation of an earlier period', the tax base of the issue costs is nil (being*

	a carrying amount of £8,000 less how much of that has been deducted in an earlier tax computation, i.e., £8,000) giving rise to a temporary difference of £8,000.
Revenue received in advance and deferred income *Example 1 – Sales revenue of £500,000 received in advance and recognised in the balance sheet as a liability. The revenue will be taxed when it is recognised in the income statement.* *Example 2 – A government grant of £100,000 is received towards the cost of an asset. The grant is recognised in the balance sheet as deferred income. It is to be amortised to the income statement over the life of the asset. The enterprise will not be taxed on the receipt or amortisation of the grant and receives a tax deduction on the full cost (i.e., with no deduction for the grant received) of the asset.*	**Carrying amount less any amount of the revenue that will not be taxable in future periods** *Example 1 – The tax base is £500,000, giving rise to a temporary difference of nil.* *Example 2 – The tax base of the government grant is nil since no element of the grant will be taxable in the future. This gives rise to a temporary difference of £100,000. However, this is an example of where the initial recognition of an asset or liability affects neither accounting nor taxable profit and thus, although there is a temporary difference (in balance sheet terms), deferred tax should not be recognised – see step three below.*
No balance sheet item, but the tax effect is in a future accounting period *Example – Expenses of £100,000 recognised in the income statement in the year they are paid, but which are not tax deductible until a future period.*	**The amount that is taxable or tax deductible in a future accounting period** *Example – The tax base will be £100,000 and so the temporary difference is also £100,000.*

In some jurisdictions an enterprise may be entitled to rollover relief when it disposes of an asset for a profit. Since this merely postpones, rather than eliminates, the payment of tax, IAS 12 (r2000) does *not* permit this relief to preclude the calculation of the temporary difference.

As discussed in the next step, the deferred tax asset or liability is established by multiplying the temporary difference (being carrying value less tax base) by the appropriate tax rate. Accordingly the IASC has stated that if ever the tax base is not obvious 'it is helpful to consider the fundamental principle upon which this Standard is based: that an enterprise should, with certain limited exceptions, recognise a deferred tax liability (asset) whenever recovery or settlement of the carrying amount of an asset or liability would make future tax payments larger (smaller) than they would be if such recovery or settlement were to have no tax consequences'. (IAS 12 (r2000).10)

Both the definition of temporary differences and the extract quoted in the paragraph above refer to *future* tax computations. For the Standard to operate effectively, it is necessary to set up deferred tax whenever the tax consequences of something are in a different accounting period, whether earlier or later, to the accounting consequences. It may not always be immediately obvious how this is achieved given the Standard's reference to 'future'. This can be illustrated with the example above of prepaid expenses being deducted in a tax computation of an earlier accounting period. The prepaid expenses were deducted in a tax computation of an earlier period and so it might be thought that, at the balance sheet date, the tax of a future period is not affected by the expenses; there will be no further tax deduction. However, the IAS takes the stance that the prepayment, on its own or in combination with other assets, will generate future revenue. The expense cannot be set against this future revenue for tax purposes. Thus under the Standard a future tax computation is affected by the asset and deferred tax should be set up. The practical effect of the Standard is that deferred tax is set up whenever the tax and accounting consequences of a transaction are in different accounting periods.

Where an enterprise is preparing consolidated financial statements, temporary differences are calculated using:

- carrying amounts taken from the consolidated balance sheet; and
- tax bases being whatever the tax authorities use – if the tax authorities calculate tax by reference to each individual company in the group, the tax bases will be taken from the individual companies' tax computations, but where the tax authorities calculate tax using consolidated figures, the tax bases will be taken from the consolidated tax figures.

(IAS 12 (r2000).11)

Step two: calculating deferred tax

IAS 12 (r2000). 47 requires deferred tax to be computed by multiplying the temporary difference by the tax rate that is expected to apply in the period when the asset is realised or the liability is settled, based on tax rates and laws that have been enacted or substantively enacted by the balance sheet date. Although the deferred tax so calculated will generally be paid in the future, the Standard precludes the tax from being calculated on a discounted basis. (IAS 12 (r2000).53)

The rate that is expected to apply to the period when the asset is realised or the liability is settled means the rate that will apply when the tax is paid or reduced.

Example 23.1

A company has interest receivable of £1,000 in its balance sheet as at 31 December 2001. The interest will be taxed when it is received, which will be during the year ending 31 December 2002. On 31 December 2001 the tax rate, which has remained unchanged for several years, is 30 per cent. On 1 February 2002 it is announced that the tax rate for the year ending 31 December 2002 will be increased to 35 per cent, and this change is enacted on 31 March 2002. The company finalises its financial statements for the year ended 31 December 2001 on 30 April 2002.

The temporary difference is £1,000.

Deferred tax of £300 will be included in the financial statements for the year ended 31 December 2001 in respect of the interest receivable. Although the company knows by the time that it finalises its financial statements that the tax rate applying to the interest income when it is received will be 35 per cent, the Standard precludes using the 35 per cent to calculate the deferred tax since this rate was neither enacted nor substantively enacted by 31 December 2001. In accordance with IAS 10 (r1999), *Events After the Balance Sheet Date*, the company would nevertheless include note disclosure of the change in tax rate.

Whether or not something has been enacted by the balance sheet date will be clear. Problems, however, are likely to be encountered in interpreting the phrase 'substantively enacted'. In some jurisdictions the announcement of new tax rates and tax laws by the government may have the substantive effect of enactment, even if formal enactment takes place some months later. In other countries it may be necessary for virtually all the legal stages towards enactment to have been completed before the rates can be considered 'substantively enacted'. Accordingly equal rate changes announced simultaneously in different countries may result in provision for taxes at different rates dependent upon how 'substantively enacted' is interpreted in the individual countries.

Where the amount of tax payable or receivable depends upon how the enterprise recovers the asset or settles the liability, the rate used to calculate the deferred tax should reflect the way in which the enterprise expects to recover or settle the asset or liability. (IAS 12 (r2000).51)

Example 23.2

A company is carrying an item of plant in its balance sheet at a net book value of £400,000 (cost of £500,000 less accumulated depreciation of £100,000). The asset's tax written down value is £300,000 (tax depreciation of £200,000 having been taken with £300,000 still to be taken).

Income generated by the asset is taxed at 25 per cent and thus the tax depreciation is deducted from income that is taxable at 25 per cent. If the asset is sold for an amount equal to or less than cost, the tax depreciation not previously taken is set against the sale proceeds and the excess taxed at 25 per cent. If the asset is sold for more than cost, any tax depreciation taken to the date of sale is included in taxable income and taxed at 25 per cent and any proceeds in excess of cost are taxed at 30 per cent.

The temporary difference is £100,000. If the company intends using the asset in its business and generating taxable income the deferred tax is £25,000 (£100,000 at 25 per cent). If, instead, the company intends to sell the asset for its carrying value of £400,000, the deferred tax is also £25,000 (being £100,000 tax depreciation written back at 25 per cent).

Example 23.3

Consider the same details as in *Example 23.2*, but on the balance sheet date the company revalues the asset to £700,000. The tax authorities make no adjustment for tax purposes, thus tax depreciation of only £300,000 is deductible against future income.

The temporary difference is £400,000 (being the carrying value of £700,000 less the tax written down value of £300,000).

If the company intends using the asset in its business and generating taxable income the deferred tax is £100,000 (£400,000 at 25 per cent).

If, instead, the company intends to sell the asset for its carrying value of £700,000 the deferred tax will be £110,000. The deferred tax is calculated as follows:

	Temporary difference		*Deferred tax*
	£'000		*£'000*
Proceeds in excess of cost	200	@ 30%	60
Tax depreciation written back	200	@ 25%	50
Total	400		110

Example 23.4

Consider the same details as in *Example 23.3*, but at the date of valuation the company intends to use the asset for a further five years and then sell it. The company expects to sell the asset for its book value in five years' time of £350,000.

At the date of valuation the temporary difference would still be £400,000.

A carrying value of £700,000 and expected sales proceeds of £350,000 means that the company expects to generate taxable income from using the asset over the next five years of £350,000; this will be taxed at 25 per cent. In addition the company expects to generate sales proceeds of £350,000; this is less than cost and so will also be taxed at 25 per cent. In addition the remaining tax depreciation of £300,000 will be deductible against the taxable income. The appropriate tax rate for the income and the deductions is 25 per cent.

Accordingly the deferred tax arising is £100,000 (being £400,000 at 25 per cent).

As seen above, the deferred tax reflects the manner in which an enterprise expects to recover an asset or settle a liability. The IAS provides that, in order to achieve this, not only does the tax rate reflect the particular circumstances, but the tax base (and thus the temporary difference) similarly reflect the particular means of recovery or settlement. (IAS 12 (r2000).52)

Example 23.5

Consider the same details as in example 23.3 except that any sale proceeds in excess of a base amount are taxed at 30 per cent. The base amount is cost uplifted by RPI. Assuming the RPI for the period since the plant was purchased is 8 per cent, the base amount if the asset is sold will be £540,000 (being the cost of £500,000 multiplied by 1.08).

If the company intends using the asset in its business and generating taxable income, the temporary difference is £400,000 and the deferred tax is £100,000 (£400,000 at 25 per cent).

If, instead, the company intends to sell the asset for its carrying value of £700,000, a different tax base, reflecting the intended manner of recovery of the asset, is calculated.

With an RPI uplift of 8 per cent, the deferred tax will be £98,000. The deferred tax is calculated as follows:

	Temporary difference		*Deferred tax*
	£'000		*£'000*
Proceeds in excess of cost uplifted by RPI (700 – 540)	160	@ 30%	48
Tax depreciation written back	200	@ 25%	50
Total	360		98

In this instance the tax base is £340,000, being cost of £500,000 uplifted by RPI (to give £540,000) less the tax depreciation taken to date that will be included in taxable income (£200,000). Another way of calculating the tax base is to take the carrying amount (£700,000) and deduct from it the temporary difference as calculated above (£360,000).

The consensus in SIC-21 *Income Taxes – Recovery of Revalued Non-Depreciable Assets* is that the deferred tax liability or asset that arises from the revaluation of a non-depreciable asset under IAS 16 (r1998) *Property, Plant and Equipment* should be measured based on the tax consequences that would follow from recovery of the carrying amount of that asset through sale, regardless of the basis of measuring the carrying amount of that asset.

As already indicated, tax law may specify a rate applicable to the taxable amount derived from the sale of an asset different from the tax rate applicable to the taxable amount derived from using the asset. In the case of a non-depreciable asset, the carrying value will be recovered through the eventual sale of the asset, irrespective of the fact that the asset is being used by the business and there are no intentions to sell it. Deferred tax should be recognised at the tax rate applicable to the taxable amount derived from sale at the carrying value. In many cases the carrying value of such an asset would be derived from a current use valuation. This may differ very significantly from the value at which the asset might eventually be sold. Irrespective of this, the tax rate applicable to taxable amounts derived from sale of the asset at its current carrying amount should be applied in calculating the deferred tax.

Example 23.6

A company is carrying land at a value of £900,000, being the current market value for its existing use. The land originally cost £500,000 and is used for the storage of the company's raw materials. The tax rate applicable to income is 25%, but any proceeds in excess of cost of fixed assets are taxed at 30%. The company has been advised that the land is suitable for development and that it could be sold for £3m for such purposes.

At the current use carrying value, the temporary difference is £400,000. Although the asset is being used by the company in the generation of taxable income, the value of the land is not being recovered this way. It will only be recovered through its eventual sale and therefore the applicable tax rate is 30%, the deferred tax arising being £120,000.

The potential value of the land is not relevant to the calculation.

SIC-21 specifically includes within its scope investment properties which are revalued in terms of IAS 25.23(b), but which would be non-depreciable if they were to be accounted for in terms of IAS 16 (r1998). Since IAS 25 *Accounting for Investments* has been superseded by IAS 40 *Investment Properties*, the scope now presumably includes investment properties which are revalued in terms of IAS 40.27. Only assets with an infinite life are non-depreciable in terms of IAS 16 (r1998) and hence the interpretation appears only to apply to land.

The scope effectively excludes and therefore leaves open the question of the appropriate rate to apply to revalued investment properties with finite lives, such as buildings, where the owner of those properties intends to use those properties. One possibility is that since the recovery of the value of the buildings through use is not reflected by a depreciation charge in the income statement, the deferred tax consequences should be measured at the tax rate applicable to a recovery through sale. Our preferred alternative is that, following the owner's intention to use the property, deferred tax should be measured at the rate applicable to the sale of the property.

Where the rate of tax varies with the amount of taxable income, the deferred tax is calculated using the average rate that is expected to be levied in the year of reversal. (IAS 12 (r2000).49)

Example 23.7

A company has interest receivable of £1,000 in its balance sheet as at 31 December 2001. The interest will be taxed when it is received, which will be during the year ending 31 December 2002. During the year ended 31 December 2001 the tax rate for the year ending 31 December 2002 is enacted; the rate will be 20 per cent for income up to £100,000, 25 per cent for income above this and up to £250,000 and 30 per cent for all other income.

The company estimates that its total taxable income for 2002 will be £750,000. Thus its estimated effective rate of tax is 27.67 per cent (being tax of £207,500 (£100,000 @ 20%, £150,000 @ 25% and £500,000 @ 30%) divided by the taxable income of £750,000). The temporary difference in respect of the interest receivable is £1,000.

A deferred tax liability of £277 will be included in the financial statements for the year ended 31 December 2001 in respect of the interest receivable.

Until its revision in 2000, IAS 12 did not specify when or how an enterprise should account for the tax consequences of dividends and other distributions by the reporting enterprise. In some jurisdictions, income taxes are payable at a higher or lower rate if all or part of the net profit or retained earnings is paid out as a dividend to shareholders. In some other jurisdictions, income taxes may be refundable or payable if part or all of the net profit or retained earnings is paid out as a dividend to shareholders. IAS 12 (r2000).52A requires current and deferred tax to be measured at the tax rates applicable to undistributed profits.

Following on from this, the income tax consequences of dividends are recognised when a liability to pay the dividend is recognised. These consequences should be recognised in the net profit or loss for the period except to the extent that the consequences arise from transactions or events recognised directly in equity or from a business combination that is an acquisition. (IAS 12 (r2000).52B)

Example 23.8

A company is in a jurisdiction where income taxes are payable at a higher rate on distributed profits. The tax rate on undistributed profits is 30%, and 40% on distributed profits.

For the year ended 31 December 2001 the company has taxable income of 300,000 and has proposed a dividend of 40,000.

The company recognises a current tax liability and current tax expense of 94,000 (300,000 @ 30% plus 40,000 @ 10%, being the additional tax payable on the amount distributed). Its deferred tax balances are recognised at a rate of 30%, being the rate applicable to undistributed profits.

In the year ended 31 December 2002 the company's taxable income is only 25,000, but its proposed dividend for the year is held at 40,000.

The company will recognise a current tax liability and current tax expense of 11,500 (25,000 @ 30% plus 40,000 @10%, being the additional tax payable on the amount distributed). The whole of this tax charge will be recognised as a current item, despite the distribution including amounts retained in prior periods, since the liability to pay the distribution was recognised in this period.

When an enterprise pays dividends to its shareholders, it may be required to pay a portion of the dividends to taxation authorities on behalf of the shareholders. This is frequently termed withholding tax. Such an amount paid or payable to the taxation authorities is charged to equity as part of the dividends. (IAS 12 (r2000).65A)

Step three: recognition in the balance sheet

The application of prudence results in different recognition rules for deferred tax assets and liabilities. Subject to certain exceptions, *all* deferred tax liabilities must be recognised in the balance sheet. A deferred tax asset, on the other hand, should be recognised in the balance sheet, again subject to certain exceptions, only to the extent that it is probable that there will be sufficient taxable profits in the future to enable the asset to be recovered. Where an enterprise has a deferred tax asset that has not been recognised because it failed this recovery test, the enterprise reassesses the position at each subsequent balance sheet date to see whether the test is subsequently met. Where the test is subsequently met, the asset is recognised at that later date. Similarly, where a deferred tax asset has been recognised in the balance sheet, its carrying amount should be reviewed at each subsequent balance sheet date and reduced to the extent that it is no longer probable that sufficient taxable profit will be available to recover it. (IAS 12 (r2000).15,24,37,56)

When can a deferred tax asset be recognised?

A deferred tax asset represents a future tax deduction. It is therefore valuable only if the enterprise will have future taxable profits which the deduction may reduce. Accordingly, as indicated above, the IAS permits a deferred tax asset to be recognised only when it is probable that the enterprise will have sufficient taxable profits in the future to enable the deferred tax assets to be recovered. (IAS 12 (r2000).24)

The important question to answer therefore is *when* is it probable that an enterprise will have sufficient taxable profits in the future to enable the deferred tax asset to be recovered? The IAS answers the question as follows:

- when there are sufficient deferred tax liabilities relating to the *same taxation authority and the same taxable enterprise* which either are expected to reverse in the same period as the deferred tax asset is expected to reverse or are expected to reverse in a period into which tax losses (arising from the deferred tax asset reversing) can be carried back or forward; (IAS 12 (r2000).28)
- when it is probable that the enterprise will have sufficient taxable profits (from sources other than deferred tax liabilities) relating to the *same taxation authority and the same taxable enterprise* in the same period as the deferred tax asset is expected to reverse or a period into which tax losses (arising from the deferred tax asset reversing) can be carried back or forward; (IAS 12 (r2000).29(a)) or
- when tax planning opportunities which will create taxable profits in appropriate periods are available to the enterprise. (IAS 12 (r2000).29(b))

Examples of tax planning opportunities include:

(a) being able to elect to have an income source taxed at an earlier point, e.g., electing to have interest income taxed on a receivable, rather than received, basis; and
(b) being able to defer to a future period the claim for certain tax deductible items, e.g., waiving a claim to first year allowances on an item of plant and instead taking writing down allowances on the full amount in future periods.

The references above to the *same taxation authority and the same taxable enterprise* acknowledges that although consolidated financial statements are prepared as if the group were a single enterprise, the taxation position nevertheless involves different enterprises and might also involve different tax jurisdictions. The taxation calculation, including deferred tax, for the group must reflect the relevant rules and cannot ignore the geographical boundaries.

In estimating whether there will be sufficient taxable profits for the purposes of the second bullet point above, deferred tax assets originating in future periods are ignored.

In the second bullet point above the IAS has used the same phrase that it was trying to explain. Clearly, whether it is probable that an enterprise will have sufficient taxable profits in future periods is a judgemental area, and firm rules cannot be laid down. The estimate of future taxable profits must be realistic and supportable.

Example 23.9

In 2001 a company has deferred tax assets arising of £4,500,000 and is determining whether it can recognise the entire £4,500,000 as an asset. The items giving rise to the 'asset' will result in deductions in the tax computation in 2002 and any losses arising therefrom will be available for carry forward only up to and including the year 2004.

Deferred tax liabilities of £1,000,000 also arise in 2001 and will be available in the appropriate group enterprises in appropriate future periods to enable £1,000,000 of the assets to be recoverable.

If in the past the enterprise has generated taxable profits, including the reversal of deferred tax liabilities, of approximately £3,000,000 per annum, it would be reasonable to recognise the full £4,500,000 as an asset in 2001's financial statements providing there is evidence to suggest that the past level of taxable profits will continue at least until the year 2004. Such evidence might be realistic budgets for the future periods together with evidence that variances from past budgets have not been material.

On the other hand, in the past the enterprise might have averaged taxable profits, including the reversal of deferred tax liabilities, of only £1,000,000. On the face of it, this would suggest that the asset cannot be recognised. However, the taxable profits might have been low in the past because a distinct division of the enterprise was loss making. If the losses averaged, say, £2,000,000 per annum, but will not be incurred going forward because in 2000 the enterprise closed down the division it might be reasonable to recognise the asset of £4,500,000 in 2001 notwithstanding that past tax figures would on the face of it suggest that the full £4,500,000 would not be recovered in the appropriate time frame. To recognise the deferred tax asset in these circumstances the enterprise would have to be satisfied that losses of approximately £2,000,000 had really gone away. If the enterprise had closed down the division but retained some of the expenses that were in the previous division, it would not have eliminated the entire £2,000,000. In this case it would need to evaluate very carefully how much, if any, of the deferred tax asset it could recognise.

Where an enterprise has incurred losses in recent years, greater caution is required before a deferred tax asset can be recognised. In such instances, IAS 12 (r2000) requires preparers to have regard to the guidance on whether a deferred tax asset can be recognised for the carry forward of unused tax losses and unused tax credits, on which there is a specific section in the IAS. The general principle set out in this section is, however, identical to that for the recognition of any deferred tax asset. The section does point out that unused tax losses provide 'strong evidence that future taxable profit may not be available'. It goes on to say that if there are insufficient deferred tax liabilities reversing in appropriate periods and enterprises, there must be 'convincing other evidence' that there will be sufficient taxable profits. It appears that this is no more stringent a test than for other deferred tax assets. Additional disclosure is required in such instances but this of itself does not make the test more stringent. Specifically in the area of tax losses, the Standard points out that preparers need to consider whether unused tax losses result from identifiable causes that are unlikely to recur. Where the losses are likely to recur, it is unlikely that a deferred tax asset can be recognised.

Where tax planning opportunities bring forward taxable profits to an earlier period, the Standard states that the utilisation of a tax loss or tax credit carry forward still depends on the existence of future taxable profit from sources other than future originating temporary differences.

Example 23.10

In 2001 a company has tax losses brought forward of £4,000,000. Under the tax law of the country in which the company operates these can be carried forward for three years only. The company expects taxable profits to be approximately £1,000,000 per annum for the next three years. However, tax planning opportunities should enable the company to bring forward a further £500,000 of taxable profit from later years into the three year period.

Subject to there being suitable evidence to support this level of future profitability, the company can therefore recognise an asset of £3,500,000.

Example 23.11

At the end of 2001 a company has tax losses carried forward of £500,000. If these are not utilised in 2002 they will be lost. The company expects a loss for tax purposes in 2002 of approximately £100,000. In reaching this estimate, however, the company assumed that it would claim capital allowances on plant of £900,000. Tax planning opportunities should enable the company to defer some of the capital allowances to 2003, thus enabling it to utilise the tax losses.

However, if the company cannot gain any benefit from its deferral of capital allowances because it anticipates further tax losses in 2003 and all subsequent years that the deferred capital allowances can be carried forward into, then it may not recognise an asset in 2001 in respect of the tax losses of £500,000. This is because the company will pay no tax in 2002 and 2003 (and any other year the capital allowances can be carried forward into) whether or not the allowances are carried forward and the losses utilised.

What are the exceptions to the requirement to provide for deferred tax?
The exceptions to the requirement to provide for deferred tax referred to above are deferred tax assets and liabilities arising from:

(i) positive goodwill for which amortisation is not deductible for tax purposes;
(ii) negative goodwill;
(iii) the initial recognition, other than in the case of a business combination, of an asset or liability which at the time of the transaction affects neither accounting profit/loss nor taxable profit/loss; and
(iv) certain differences associated with investments in subsidiaries, branches and associates and interests in joint ventures.

(IAS 12 (r2000).15, 24)

In short, no deferred tax is provided on the first three items and a modified approach is taken with the last. These four items are discussed in the following paragraphs:

(i) Positive goodwill for which amortisation is not deductible for tax purposes
The IAS states that it precludes recognising deferred tax on goodwill for which there is no tax deduction. The deductibility of goodwill varies by jurisdiction and, for example, it is deductible in the US.

Where goodwill is not deductible against taxable income, the Standard's rules nevertheless result in a temporary difference; this is because the asset goodwill is expected to generate benefits in the future that are taxable. Its tax base will be nil (nothing has been or will be tax deductible) and so the temporary difference equals the carrying value of the goodwill. However, deferred tax is not recognised on this temporary difference.

The Standard points out that if deferred tax were set up on the goodwill as part of the fair value exercise, the tax would itself increase the amount of goodwill, since goodwill is always the balancing figure in the fair value exercise.

The IAS argues that if the amortisation of goodwill is not tax deductible, it is likely that the goodwill will not be deductible if the subsidiary sold the underlying business. Nevertheless, even if the goodwill would be deductible on ultimate disposal, the rule in the IAS precludes setting up deferred tax on the goodwill whilst it is not tax deductible as it is amortised; this is for the same reason outlined above – if goodwill is a residual it should not be grossed up into two components.

Where goodwill is tax deductible as it is amortised, no temporary difference will arise on acquisition. The tax base will equal the carrying amount of the goodwill, thus giving rise to no temporary difference. In future periods, if the amortisation rates for tax and book purposes differ, temporary differences will arise.

(ii) Negative goodwill
Similarly, a deferred tax asset cannot be recognised if it arises as a result of negative goodwill treated in accordance with IAS 22 (r1998) *Business Combinations.* The arguments advanced are, as with positive goodwill, that of not grossing up a residual.

(iii) The initial recognition, other than in the case of a business combination, of an asset or liability which at the time of the transaction affects neither accounting profit/loss nor taxable profit/loss
We have seen above that where an asset or liability affects taxable profits in the same period as accounting profits are impacted or where an asset or liability has no impact on taxable profits no temporary difference arises. Consequently there is no deferred tax balance to recognise. However, sometimes an asset or liability gives rise to a temporary difference but the IAS nevertheless requires no deferred tax to be recognised in the financial statements; this is when an asset or liability is recognised that affects neither accounting profit/loss nor taxable profit/loss. Such circumstances exclude assets and liabilities, including positive and negative goodwill, recognised in a business combination. In practice such circumstances are likely to be rare.

One example given in the IAS is that of an asset for which the enterprise gets no deduction against taxable profits as it depreciates the asset and for which any capital gain or loss on disposal would not be taxable or tax deductible. At first glance this might suggest that there is no temporary difference. However, because the enterprise does not intend to sell the asset, but instead intends to use it in its business and generate, directly or indirectly, economic benefits that are taxable, a temporary difference does arise for balance sheet purposes. The IASC does not permit deferred tax to be set up in such instances; it argues that if deferred tax were set up on this asset it would have to be added to the asset's carrying value in the balance sheet and this would make the financial statements less transparent.

The Standard explains that the temporary difference in respect of an item of property, plant or equipment arises on the difference between the taxable income generated by the asset and the tax deductions available in respect of the asset. However, the guidance and examples in IAS 12 (r2000) assume that, for the purposes of calculating deferred tax, the taxable income generated by an asset is exactly equal to its carrying amount. Applying this to an item of plant, property and equipment results in the deferred tax recognised in the income statement in a year being the difference between the accounting depreciation (i.e., the movement between the opening and closing balance sheet carrying amount) and the tax depreciation (i.e., the difference between the opening and closing tax value). If there is no deduction for the asset's cost available against taxable profits in income statement terms, there is no difference that reverses (even though under the IAS's rules a 'temporary difference' is calculated). The IAS's rules result in a temporary difference because the balance sheet difference (being the difference between the carrying amount and nil) reverses as the asset is depreciated (the carrying amount itself ends up being nil). However there are equal and opposite entries in the income statement in each year, giving a net overall impact of nil; this is because there is no income statement difference that reverses.

A second example given in the Standard is that of the receipt of a non-taxable government grant.

Both examples given appear to be examples of items that, in traditional terms, represent permanent differences in the income statement, but for which application of the Standard's rules nevertheless result in a 'temporary difference' being calculated.

A literal interpretation of the initial recognition exemption has peculiar consequences in circumstances where an equal asset and liability are recognised as part of the same transaction, but both items have no tax base. For example, an asset which is capitalised under a finance lease may, in some jurisdictions, have a nil tax base because the lessee is not the legal owner of the asset and is therefore not able to claim tax deductions in respect of the asset. The lease liability may also have a nil tax base because the full amount of the lease payments (that is, both the capital and interest element) will be deductible for tax in future. A similar situation arises in the case of a provision for environmental rehabilitation where the rehabilitation costs will only be tax deductible when paid and the amount capitalised to the asset in terms of IAS 16 (r1998).15(e) will not be deductible for tax purposes.

In these cases, equal and opposite temporary differences arise on the initial recognition of the asset and liability and, because there is no immediate impact on accounting or taxable income, these temporary differences are excluded for the purposes of providing deferred tax. Although the net initial impact is nil, the unrecognised deferred tax may be significant in future periods because the asset and liability are amortised on different bases. This outcome does not appear to be consistent with the objective of the standard and the rationale for the initial recognition exclusion set out in IAS 12 (r2000).22(c), namely 'if the transaction is not a business combination, and affects neither accounting profit nor taxable profit, an enterprise would, in the absence of the exemption provided by paragraphs 15 and 24, recognise the resulting deferred tax liability or asset and adjust the carrying amount of the asset or liability by the same amount. Such adjustments would make the financial statements less transparent'. As a result, it may be appropriate to interpret the standard such that the type of temporary differences described in this paragraph are not excluded in terms of IAS 12 (r2000).15.

Under the Standard's rules, however, a deferred tax balance would have to be set up for any asset or liability in consolidated financial statements if the asset or liability were in a business that was acquired by another. The goodwill figure, which would have been increased by the amount of the deferred tax, would also be amortised to the income statement. The two amortisation periods (one for the deferred tax and one for the goodwill) may not necessarily coincide, thus the impact on the income statement may not be equal and opposite in any one year.

The deferred tax on an asset acquired as part of a business combination (which must be recognised) may be significantly different from the deferred tax on an asset acquired on its own (which should not be recognised on initial recognition). This may require judgement to be applied in certain circumstances to the question of the whether an acquisition constitutes a business combination or merely the acquisition of an asset.

Under IAS 32 (r1998) *Financial Instruments: Disclosure and Presentation* a compound financial instrument might be recognised in the balance sheet in two parts: a liability component and an equity component. In such an instance in some jurisdictions, the tax base of the liability might be the sum of the two parts. If so, under the Standard's rules a 'temporary difference' would arise. Using the above analysis it might be thought to be a permanent difference and thus no deferred tax recognised. However, the Standard specifically requires the deferred tax to be recognised in these instances and charged directly against the carrying amount of the equity component. Any change to the deferred tax in subsequent years would be required to be recognised in the income statement. (IAS 12 (r2000).23 and App 1.9)

(iv) Differences associated with investments in subsidiaries, branches and associates and interests in joint ventures

All deferred tax liabilities in respect of investments in subsidiaries, branches and associates and in respect of interests in joint ventures should be recognised except to the extent that:

- the parent, investor or venturer is able to control the timing of the reversal of the temporary difference; and
- it is probable that the temporary difference will not reverse in the foreseeable future. (IAS 12 (r2000).39)

Deferred tax assets in respect of investments in subsidiaries, branches and associates and in respect of interests in joint ventures should be recognised only to the extent that:

- the temporary difference will reverse in the foreseeable future; and
- taxable profit will be available against which the temporary difference can be utilised. (IAS 12 (r2000).44)

A parent/subsidiary relationship involves the parent controlling its subsidiary, including the subsidiary's dividend policy. Accordingly the Standard provides that when a parent has stipulated that undistributed profits in a subsidiary or branch will not be distributed for the foreseeable future, the parent does not recognise deferred tax on those undistributed profits. In practical terms, evidence would be required to support management's intentions in respect of dividend policy. This might include documented resolutions by the management of the parent and subsidiary, formal communication to minority shareholders and approval of budgets and projections for both entities on the basis that undistributed profits in the subsidiary will remain so for the foreseeable future. The same considerations apply to investments in branches. Conversely an investor/associate relationship does not involve the investor controlling its associate. Thus with an associate, an investor recognises deferred tax arising on undistributed profits unless there is an agreement requiring that profits will not be distributed in the foreseeable future. Where deferred tax has to be set up but the investor cannot calculate an accurate estimate, the minimum amount is provided.

With an interest in a joint venture, if the investor can control the sharing of profits and it is probable that the profits will not be distributed in the foreseeable future, a deferred tax liability is not recognised.

The Standard does not define what it means by 'foreseeable future'.

Step four: recognition of the movement between the opening and closing balance sheets

The movement between the deferred tax in the opening and closing balance sheets should be recognised in the income statement in arriving at the net profit or loss for the period, except for tax arising from:

- a transaction or event which is recognised, in any accounting period, directly in equity, in which case the movement in deferred tax should be accounted for directly in equity; or
- a business combination that is accounted for as an acquisition, in which case the movement in deferred tax is included in the resulting goodwill figure.

(IAS 12 (r2000).58, 61 & 66)

In this way the tax effect of a transaction is accounted for in the same place as the original transaction.

Example 23.12

A company, with a 31 December year end, purchased an asset on 1 January 2000 for £100,000. The asset's expected useful life is 10 years and depreciation of £10,000 per annum is charged in each of the 10 years.

For tax purposes, the asset's cost is depreciated over 8 years.

Date	*Carrying value*	*Tax base (= tax wd v)*	*Temporary difference*	*Deferred tax liability @ 30%*	*Movement in year*
	£	£	£	£	£
31.12.00	90,000	87,500	2,500	750	750
31.12.01	80,000	75,000	5,000	1,500	750
31.12.02	70,000	62,500	7,500	2,250	750
31.12.03	60,000	50,000	10,000	3,000	750
31.12.04	50,000	37,500	12,500	3,750	750
31.12.05	40,000	25,000	15,000	4,500	750
31.12.06	30,000	12,500	17,500	5,250	750
31.12.07	20,000	–	20,000	6,000	750
31.12.08	10,000	–	10,000	3,000	(3,000)
31.12.09	–	–	–	–	(3,000)
Total					–

The movement in deferred tax in each of the years would be recognised in the income statement.

Example 23.13

Consider the same details as in *Example 23.12* above except that on 31 December 2003 the company revalued the asset to £90,000. Depreciation of £15,000 per annum is charged thereafter.

For tax purposes, the asset's cost continues to be depreciated over 8 years; no uplift in value is made for tax deduction purposes.

First, we will look at the first four years.

Date	*Carrying value*	*Tax base (= tax wd v)*	*Temporary difference*	*Deferred tax liability @ 30%*	*Movement in year*
	£	£	£	£	£
31.12.00	90,000	87,500	2,500	750	750
31.12.01	80,000	75,000	5,000	1,500	750
31.12.02	70,000	62,500	7,500	2,250	750
31.12.03	90,000	50,000	40,000	12,000	9,750

The movement in deferred tax in each of the first three years (£750 per annum) would be recognised in the income statement.

In 2003 the total movement is £9,750. £750 (being 30 per cent of the difference between tax and accounting depreciation) would be recognised in the income statement and £9,000 (being 30 per cent of the revaluation surplus of £30,000) would be recognised in equity (to the revaluation reserve) to match against the revaluation surplus being credited to equity.

The entry in the income statement in respect of deferred tax in each of these four years is a debit entry.

Assume no further revaluations over the remainder of the asset's life.

Now we will look at the next four years.

Date	*Carrying value*	*Tax base (= tax wd v)*	*Temporary difference*	*Deferred tax liability @ 30%*	*Movement in year*
	£	£	£	£	£
31.12.04	75,000	37,500	37,500	11,250	(750)
31.12.05	60,000	25,000	35,000	10,500	(750)
31.12.06	45,000	12,500	32,500	9,750	(750)
31.12.07	30,000	–	30,000	9,000	(750)

The movement in the balance sheet values in these four years will also be £750 per annum, but now they are in the opposite direction to the first four years. These will be credits in the income statement.

In these years depreciation of £15,000 is charged in the income statement. If, as this is done, the company transfers from the revaluation reserve to retained earnings the difference between the actual depreciation charge and the charge that would have arisen had the asset not been revalued, namely, £5,000 per annum, the Standard requires it to make the transfer out of the revaluation reserve net of the deferred tax on the £5,000, giving a net annual transfer of £3,500. IAS 12 (r2000).64 points out that IAS 16 (1998) does not require but permits a transfer from the revaluation reserve to retained earnings as depreciation is recognised (see **10.3.9**).

If this is done, by 31.12.07 £6,000 of the £9,000 deferred tax originally debited to the revaluation reserve will have been credited to revaluation reserve and debited to retained earnings.

Now consider the final two years.

Date	*Carrying value*	*Tax base (= tax wd v)*	*Temporary difference*	*Deferred tax liability @ 30%*	*Movement in year*
	£	£	£	£	£
31.12.08	15,000	–	15,000	4,500	(4,500)
31.12.09	–	–	–	–	(4,500)

The movement in deferred tax in the two years (£4,500 in each year) is credited to the income statement.

As with the previous four years, the depreciation in excess of that charged on the historical cost basis net of the deferred tax thereon is transferred out of the revaluation reserve. This means that over the two years the final £3,000 deferred tax is credited to the revaluation reserve leaving a nil balance in that reserve.

The Standard establishes how the movements should be recognised in certain circumstances:

Uncertainty regarding amount to be recognised directly in equity
Where an enterprise is unable to determine the exact amount of deferred tax that is charged or credited directly to equity, the Standard allows the enterprise to base the amount on a reasonable pro rata allocation or some other method achieving a more appropriate allocation. (IAS 12 (r2000).63)

Revaluation for tax purposes
If an asset is revalued for tax purposes and this is linked to a past or future revaluation for accounting purposes, the resulting changes in deferred tax from the accounting revaluation and tax revaluation are taken directly to equity in whichever period they occur. Where there is a revaluation for tax purposes but there has not been, and is not to be, an accounting revaluation, the tax effect is recognised in the income statement. (IAS 12 (r2000).65)

The main example of a revaluation for tax, but not accounting, purposes is when tax authorities calculate any gain on disposal over and above a base cost that represents the original cost of the asset uplifted by an allowance to reflect the increase in inflation over the period of ownership.

Other changes in the carrying amount of a deferred tax asset or liability
Where the carrying amount of a deferred tax asset or liability changes for a reason other than because the temporary difference itself has changed, the Standard states that the change in deferred tax is to be recognised in the income statement unless the underlying item giving rise to the deferred tax was itself recognised in equity. Such changes might arise as a result of:

- a change in tax rates or laws;
- re-assessment of the recoverability of deferred tax assets; or
- a change in the expected manner of recovery of an asset.

(IAS 12 (r2000).60)

Changes in the tax status of an enterprise or its shareholders
A change in the tax status of an enterprise or of its shareholders may have consequences for an enterprise by increasing or decreasing its tax assets or liabilities. This may occur, for example, upon the public listing of an enterprise's equity investments, or upon a controlling shareholder's move to a foreign country. As a result of such an event, an enterprise may be taxed differently, which may have an immediate effect on the current and deferred tax assets and liabilities. The consensus in SIC-25 *Income Taxes – Changes in the Tax Status of an Enterprise or its Shareholders* establishes the accounting treatment for such changes.

SIC-25 requires the current and deferred tax consequences of a change in tax status to be included in the net profit or loss for the period, unless those consequences relate to transactions and events that result, in the same or a different period, in a direct credit or charge to the recognised amount of equity. Those tax consequences that relate to changes in the recognised amount of equity, in the same or a different period, should be charged or credited directly to equity.

Post acquisition adjustments to the carrying value of deferred tax
Where deferred tax is set up as part of a business combination, it is included in the resulting goodwill figure. Under the guidance set out above, subsequent changes in that deferred tax are taken to the income statement. However, if there is a change in assigned fair values, IAS 22 (r1998) *Business Combinations* would require the change in deferred tax to be reflected in the goodwill figure providing the change is included in the financial statements for the first full accounting period after the date of acquisition and the change is clearly not as a result of a post-acquisition event. It would seem that the rule in IAS 22 (r1998) prevails over this aspect of IAS 12 (r2000).

Example 23.14

Company X buys the shares in Company Y on 1 July 2001. Company X's accounting period ends on 31 December each year. The acquisition of Y was included in X's consolidated financial statements for the year to 31 December 2001; included in the fair value of net assets acquired was a deferred tax asset of £450,000, being temporary differences of £1,500,000 at 30 per cent. During the preparation of the financial statements for the year to 31 December 2002 management revises its estimate of the recoverability of the asset and now believes that differences of only £1,000,000 will be recoverable and so an asset of only £300,000 should be recognised. Providing the change in estimate is not as a result of a post-acquisition event, the change of £150,000 in deferred tax is taken to goodwill rather than to the income statement.

If the change in estimate of recoverability is because of revised estimates of future taxable profits but the revised estimates have not been prompted by a specific event (other than the 2002 results and there is no specific event that resulted in these being lower than anticipated at the end of the previous year) the change should be taken to goodwill. If, instead, the revised estimate has been prompted by a specific event, such as in 2002 another company started up in direct competition to companies X and Y and thus caused management to revise downwards its estimates of future accounting and taxable profits, the change should be taken to the income statement.

Had the revised estimate arisen during the preparation of the 2003, not 2002, financial statements, the change would have had to be taken to the income statement since it is outside the hindsight period stipulated in IAS 22 (r1998) (see **18.6.5** above).

Example 23.15

Company X buys the shares in Company Y on 1 July 2001. Company X's accounting period ends on 31 December each year. The acquisition of Y was included in X's consolidated financial statements for the year to 31 December 2001; included in the fair value of net assets acquired was a deferred tax liability of £450,000, being temporary differences of £1,500,000 at 30 per cent. On 1 May 2002 the tax rate applying to company profits for accounting periods beginning on or after 1 January 2003 increases to 33 per cent. By 31 December 2002 £1,000,000 of the temporary differences had reversed. The remaining £500,000 must now be accrued at 33 per cent, giving £165,000, not at 30 per cent, giving £150,000. The increase of £15,000 must be charged in the income statement. It cannot be taken to goodwill since the change results from a post-acquisition event.

A further example involving a post-acquisition adjustment to the carrying value of deferred tax is where a deferred tax asset exists in an acquiree at the date of the business combination, but is not recognised as one of the identifiable net assets arising on acquisition because, at the time, the management does not believe that it is probable that there will be sufficient taxable profits in the future for the asset to be recovered but subsequent events cause management in a later year to believe that the asset can after all be recovered. The Standard contains guidance on this specific example:

- the asset is recognised in the consolidated balance sheet of the acquirer in that later year;
- the deferred tax is credited in the income statement; and
- subject to neither creating nor increasing negative goodwill, the gross carrying amount of the goodwill and the amortisation thereof to date are adjusted to reflect the amounts that would be recorded had the deferred tax asset been recognised at the date of acquisition, with the movement in the net goodwill figure being expensed in the income statement.

(IAS 12 (r2000).68)

The following example is taken from IAS 12 (r2000) and illustrates the above point.

Example 23.16

An enterprise acquired a subsidiary which had deductible temporary differences of 300. The tax rate at the time of the acquisition was 30 per cent. The resulting deferred tax asset of 90 was not recognised as an identifiable asset in determining the goodwill of 500 resulting from the acquisition. The goodwill is amortised over 20 years. Two years after the acquisition, the enterprise assessed that future taxable profit would probably be sufficient for the enterprise to recover the benefit of all the deductible temporary differences.

The enterprise recognises a deferred tax asset of 90 (300 at 30 per cent) and, in the income statement, deferred tax income of 90. It also reduces the cost of the goodwill by 90 and the accumulated amortisation by 9 (representing 2 years' amortisation). The balance of 81 is recognised as an expense in the income statement. Consequently, the cost of the goodwill, and the related accumulated amortisation, are reduced to the amounts (410 and 41) that would have been recorded if a deferred tax asset of 90 had been recognised as an identifiable asset at the date of the business combination.

If the tax rate has increased to 40 per cent, the enterprise recognises a deferred tax asset of 120 (300 at 40 per cent) and, in the income statement, deferred tax income of 120. If the tax rate has decreased to 20 per cent, the enterprise recognises a deferred tax asset of 60 (300 at 20%) and deferred tax income of 60. In both cases, the enterprise also reduces the cost of the goodwill by 90 and the accumulated amortisation by 9 and recognises the balance of 81 as an expense in the income statement.

IAS 22's (r1998) hindsight period for making adjustments to identifiable net assets through goodwill is specifically varied for the situation where a deferred tax asset was not recognised on acquisition but is subsequently recognised (see **18.6.5** above).

If as a result of making an acquisition an enterprise believes that its previously unrecognised deferred tax asset can be recognised, the Standard requires the enterprise to include the recognition of its own deferred tax asset in the calculation of goodwill arising on the acquisition. This might arise if, for example, the acquirer has tax losses that can be used to relieve taxable profits in the acquiree. (IAS 12 (r2000).67)

Step five: presentation in the balance sheet and income statement

In a similar approach to that taken in IAS 1 (r1997) *Presentation of Financial Statements* and IAS 32 (r1998) *Financial Instruments: Disclosure and Presentation*, the Standard takes a strong line on the question of whether tax assets and liabilities can be offset against one another to present only a net figure in the balance sheet.

The rules laid down in the Standard regarding presentation of both current and deferred tax in the balance sheet are:

- tax assets and liabilities may not be combined with other assets and liabilities but must be shown separately on the balance sheet;
- deferred tax items must be presented separately from current tax items;
- deferred tax may not be classified as either a current asset or a current liability;
- current tax assets and current tax liabilities should be offset only where the enterprise has a legally enforceable right to set off the amounts and the enterprise intends either to settle on a net basis or to realise the asset and liability simultaneously; and
- deferred tax assets and deferred tax liabilities should be offset only where the enterprise has a legally enforceable right to set off current tax assets against current tax liabilities and the deferred tax assets and liabilities relate to taxes levied by the same taxation authority on either the same taxable enterprise or group enterprises meeting certain conditions (see below). (IAS 12 (r2000).69,70,71,74)

The Standard explains that an enterprise will normally have a legally enforceable right to set off current tax assets against current tax liabilities when they relate to taxes levied by the same taxation authority and that authority permits the enterprise to make or receive a single net payment. (IAS 12 (r2000).72) For example, if a British company is receiving group relief from another British company in the same group it would appear to qualify under the Standard to be offset against the company's tax liability.

Where an enterprise is preparing consolidated financial statements, it does not set off current tax assets and liabilities in different group enterprises unless the two enterprises have a legally enforceable right to make or receive a single net payment and the enterprises intend either to do this or to recover the asset and settle the liability simultaneously. (IAS 12 (r2000).73)

When preparing consolidated financial statements, a deferred tax asset in one group enterprise can be set against a deferred tax liability arising in a different group enterprise only if the above conditions have been met and the enterprises intend either to settle current tax assets and liabilities on a net basis or the recover the assets and settle the liabilities simultaneously in each future period in which significant amounts of the deferred tax is expected to be settled or recovered.

The only rule stipulated in respect of the income statement is that the tax expense or income related to the profit or loss from ordinary activities should be presented on the face of the income statement. This item can include foreign exchange differences arising on the deferred tax balances. (IAS 12 (r2000).77,78)

23.6.3 Disclosure requirements

The Standard has extensive disclosure requirements. These are set out below.

First, the major components of the tax charge or credit in the income statement should be disclosed separately. (IAS 12 (r2000).79) The components of tax expense or income may include:

- current tax expense or income;
- adjustments recognised in the current period in respect of earlier periods' current tax;
- deferred tax expense or income relating to the origination and reversal of temporary differences;
- adjustments to deferred tax resulting from changes in tax rates or the imposition of new taxes;
- the amount of the benefit resulting from a previously unrecognised tax loss, tax credit or temporary difference of a prior period that is used to reduce current tax expense;
- the amount of the benefit resulting from a previously unrecognised tax loss, tax credit or temporary difference of a prior period that is used to reduce deferred tax expense;
- deferred tax expense arising from the write-down, or income arising from the reversal of a previous write-down, of a deferred tax asset following the annual review of the carrying value of the asset; and
- the amount of tax expense or income relating to those changes in accounting policies and fundamental errors which are included in the determination of net profit or loss for the period in accordance with the allowed alternative treatment in IAS 8 (r1993) *Net Profit or Loss for the Period, Fundamental Errors and Changes in Accounting Policies.*

(IAS 12 (r2000).80)

The following are also required to be disclosed separately:

(a) the aggregate current and deferred tax relating to items that are charged or credited to equity;

(b) the tax relating to extraordinary items recognised during the period, if possible, giving the amount for each item;

(c) an explanation of the relationship between the tax charge or credit in the income statement and the accounting profit; the explanation should be in either or both of the following forms:

   (i) a numerical reconciliation between the tax charge or credit and the product of accounting profit multiplied by the applicable tax rate(s), disclosing also the basis on which the applicable tax rate(s) is (are) computed; or

   (ii) a numerical reconciliation between the average effective tax rate (being the tax expense or income divided by the accounting profit) and the applicable tax rate, disclosing also the basis on which the applicable tax rate is computed;

(d) an explanation of changes in the applicable tax rate(s) compared to the previous accounting period;

(e) the amount (and expiry date, if any) of deductible temporary differences, unused tax losses, and unused tax credits for which no deferred tax asset is recognised in the balance sheet;

(f) the aggregate amount of temporary differences associated with investments in subsidiaries, branches and associates and interests in joint ventures, for which deferred tax liabilities have not been recognised; in addition, the IASC recommends the amount of unrecognised deferred tax liabilities are disclosed where this is practicable;

(g) in respect of each type of temporary difference, and in respect of each type of unused tax losses and unused tax credits:
   (i) the amount of the deferred tax assets and liabilities recognised in the balance sheet for each period presented;
   (ii) the amount of the deferred tax income or expense recognised in the income statement, if this is not apparent from the changes in the amounts recognised in the balance sheet;

(h) in respect of discontinued operations, the tax expense relating to:
   (i) the gain or loss on discontinuance; and
   (ii) the profit or loss from the ordinary activities of the discontinued operation for the period, together with the corresponding amounts for each prior period presented;

(i) the amount of income tax consequences of dividends to shareholders of the enterprise that were proposed or declared before the financial statements were authorised for issue, but are not recognised in the financial statements;

(j) the amount of a deferred tax asset and the nature of the evidence supporting its recognition when the utilisation of the deferred tax asset is dependent on future taxable profits in excess of the profits arising from the reversal of existing taxable temporary differences and the enterprise has suffered a loss in either the current or preceding period in the tax jurisdiction to which the deferred tax asset relates;

(k) in circumstances where income taxes are paid at higher or lower rates if part or all of the net profit or retained earnings is paid out as a dividend to shareholders, an enterprise should disclose the nature of the potential income tax consequences that would result from the payment of dividends to its shareholders. In addition, the enterprise should disclose the amounts of potential income tax consequences practicably determinable and whether there are any potential income tax consequences not practicably determinable.

(IAS 12 (r2000).81,82,82A)

In making the disclosure under (c) above an enterprise should use the applicable tax rate that gives the most meaningful information. This might be the rate applying in the reporting enterprise's home country, alternatively it might be a weighted average of the rates applying in each country in which the enterprise operates. The Standard specifically permits an enterprise to satisfy the disclosure requirement by preparing a reconciliation for each jurisdiction in which it operates (using the tax rate applicable in each jurisdiction) and to aggregate the separate reconciliations.

23.7 Comparison with UK GAAP

UK GAAP in this area is primarily laid down in FRS 16, *Current tax*, and, for periods ending on or after 23 January 2002, FRS 19 *Deferred tax*. FRS 19 supersedes SSAP 15 *Accounting for deferred tax*.

There are very few rules for calculating current tax in UK GAAP, although in practice the calculation will be largely similar to that under IAS 12 (r2000). FRS 16 does not go into the detail of calculating current tax, but it does, however, clarify the treatment of withholding taxes and the effect they have on the income statement.

FRS 19 *Deferred Tax*, which has replaced SSAP 15, adopts a full provision approach based on timing differences. It requires a deferred tax provision or asset to be set up on all timing differences when the resulting deferred tax can be justified as representing an asset or liability in its own right.

Timing differences are defined by FRS 19 as:

> 'Differences between an entity's taxable profits and its results as stated in the financial statements that arise from the inclusion of gains and losses in tax assessments in periods different from those in which they are recognised in the financial statements. Timing differences originate in one period and are capable of reversal in one or more subsequent periods.'

This contrasts with the emphasis in IAS 12 (r2000) on temporary differences, which are differences between the carrying amount of an asset or liability in the balance sheet and its tax base. The ASB in the UK took the view that a standard based on timing differences was preferable to IAS 12 (r2000) which is based on temporary differences but permits exceptions for temporary differences that are not timing differences. Appendix V to FRS 19 sets out the ASB's reasoning in more detail.

Significant features of FRS 19 and differences between it and IAS 12 (r2000) are given below.

The general principle in FRS 19 *Deferred Tax*, is that deferred tax should be recognised in full in respect of transactions or events that have taken place by the balance sheet date and which give the entity an obligation to pay more or less tax in future. This is a form of full provision accounting which has been termed the incremental liability approach. (SSAP 15 took a very different approach, requiring partial, not full, provision to be made; thus deferred tax was provided only to the extent that it was probable that a liability or asset would crystallise.)

FRS 19 requires deferred tax to be calculated using enacted or substantially enacted rates at the balance sheet date. This is consistent with IAS 12 (r2000), although in the UK a rate is not considered substantively enacted until the Bill to introduce it has passed through all parliamentary procedures bar the House of Lords and Royal Assent.

Under FRS 19 deferred tax is only recognised on revaluations when there is a binding commitment to sell the asset at the balance sheet date, and the resulting gain/loss on disposal has been recognised in the financial statements. Even if these strict conditions are met, if the company thinks it is 'more likely than not' to obtain rollover relief, thereby postponing the tax on the gain until the disposal of the replacement asset at an unknown future date, then no deferred tax balance is recognised. If the tax on the gain is subject to holdover relief, deferred tax should be recognised on the gain as this form of relief simply delays the payment of the tax. However if, during the holdover relief period, the gain is rolled over into a qualifying replacement asset, thereby securing rollover relief, the deferred tax should cease to be recognised at that time. IAS 12 (r2000) does not consider rollover relief when calculating deferred tax balances and generally would require recognition of deferred tax on revaluations.

An exception to the FRS 19 rule above of not providing deferred tax on revaluations is on timing differences arising when an asset is continuously revalued to fair value with changes in fair value being recognised in the profit and loss account. This applies where entities, particularly financial institutions, value their current asset investments at market value, as opposed to the lower of cost and net realisable value – an approach known as 'marking to market'. FRS 19 and IAS 12 (r2000) would both require deferred tax on such revaluations.

The criteria for recognition of deferred tax assets under FRS 19 are very similar to those under IAS 12 (r2000), although there is a difference in the wording. FRS 19 uses the phrase 'more likely than not that there will be suitable taxable profits available', whereas IAS 12 (r2000) uses 'probable that the enterprise will have sufficient taxable profit'. The difference between 'more likely than not' and 'probable' is open to debate and it remains to be seen whether the FRS 19 recognition 'test' will be regarded as the more strict. Under SSAP 15 a deferred tax asset could only be recognised if its recovery was expected in the next accounting period.

FRS 19 requires deferred tax to be provided on the future remittance of past earnings of subsidiaries, associates or joint ventures to the extent that dividends have been accrued, or there is a binding agreement to distribute the earnings in the future. Under IAS 12 (r2000), when a company cannot control the timing of the future remittance of past earnings, then a provision should be made. This normally means that deferred tax will not be provided for subsidiaries and branches (and possibly joint ventures if control exists), but will normally be provided for associates.

The exposure draft that preceded FRS 19 proposed that long term deferred tax balances should be discounted. This provision was retained, but as an optional treatment in FRS 19. IAS 12 (r2000) does not permit discounting.

Therefore although both UK GAAP and IAS 12 (r2000) are now based on a full provision basis, UK GAAP applies an income statement liability method, as opposed to the balance sheet liability method currently used by IAS 12 (r2000). As a result differences, which will often be material, will still exist in the amounts included as deferred tax.

The provision for deferred tax does not have to be shown separately on the face of the balance sheet under UK GAAP. The disclosure can be in the notes to the financial statements, although separate disclosure is required if misinterpretation could arise without this. This separate disclosure may be in the notes or on the face of the balance sheet as appropriate. IAS 12 (r2000), on the other hand, requires the deferred tax to be shown separately on the face of the balance sheet.

On a business combination accounted for as an acquisition, FRS 7 *Fair values in acquisition accounting* requires the deferred tax position of the acquired enterprise to be considered in the group context and so it might be possible to recognise a deferred tax asset for losses in the acquiree where prior to acquisition an asset could not be recognised (say, because the losses can be used to offset profits in another group company). However, unlike IAS 12 (r2000), if the losses are in the acquirer (and the profits in the acquiree) the resulting deferred tax asset cannot be credited to goodwill under UK GAAP.

The recognition of deferred tax balances in the fair value process should be in accordance with FRS 19. The fair value adjustment is treated as if it were a timing difference in the acquired entity. Only if FRS 19 requires provision in respect of such a difference should deferred tax be recognised on the adjustment. For example, a deferred tax liability should only be recognised in respect of a revaluation if there is a binding sale agreement and the profit has been recognised before acquisition. This contrasts with IAS 12 (r2000).19.

23.8 Comparison with US GAAP

SFAS 109 *Accounting for income taxes*, which is the primary source for this topic under US GAAP, is very similar to IAS 12 (r2000) for both current and deferred taxes. Like the international approach, the US Standard requires full provision for deferred tax based on temporary differences.

One difference is that having calculated temporary differences, an enterprise adopting US GAAP is required to calculate the deferred tax using tax rates and laws enacted at the balance sheet date. IAS 12 (r2000), on the other hand, requires the tax to be calculated using tax rates and laws enacted *or substantively enacted* by the balance sheet date.

Under US GAAP, deferred tax assets are recognised unless it is more likely than not that they will not be realised. SFAS 109 states that 'more likely than not' is a likelihood of more than 50 per cent. IAS 12 (r2000) does not define 'probable' (its recognition test) and so it is difficult to know to what extent the US and international guidance differs. Some may argue that 'probable' is a higher hurdle than 'more likely than not'. In particular, in the US 'probable' is generally understood to mean closer to 75 per cent than 50 per cent, although there is no formal definition giving quantification. On the other hand, in other jurisdictions some might argue that, although the terminology differs the effect in practice is the same. Since IAS 12 (r2000) does not define probable, it is unclear whether the IASC intended a distinction between the terms.

Under SFAS 109, the tax base of an asset or liability is the amount attributed to it for tax purposes regardless of whether that amount can be deducted in subsequent determinations of taxable income. This differs to the IAS 12 (r2000) treatment as, if the cost of an asset cannot be deducted, the tax base is deemed to be zero. Therefore, some temporary differences arise under IAS 12 (r2000) which do not arise under SFAS 109. However, the impact of this difference may be insignificant as IAS 12 (r2000) provides an exception in that it prohibits the recognition of a deferred tax liability in these situations.

IAS 12 (r2000) requires and SFAS 109 prohibits allocation to equity of current year deferred tax related to items recognised in equity in prior years.

In relation to goodwill, if subsequent to the related acquisition, previously unrecognised, deferred tax assets are recognised, both Standards require the goodwill balance to be reduced. However under IAS 12 (r2000), if the goodwill is completely eliminated, the remaining balance increases earnings. Under SFAS 109, the balance is used to eliminate any other intangible assets related to the acquisition before increasing income.

SFAS 109 requires deferred tax liabilities and assets to be classified in the balance sheet as current or non-current according to the classification of the related asset or liability. Where a deferred tax liability or asset is not related to an asset or liability, it should be classified according to the expected reversal date of the temporary difference. On the other hand, IAS 12 (r2000) precludes deferred tax liabilities and assets from being classified as current liabilities and assets.

Another difference between IAS 12 (r2000) and SFAS 109 is the types of temporary difference for which no deferred tax need be provided. In simple terms, they are:

	Provision required?	
	SFAS 109	**IAS 12 (r2000)**
Goodwill for which amortisation is non-deductible	X	X
Investments in subsidiaries (regarded as permanently invested)	X (except earnings that arise in domestic subsidiaries in fiscal years beginning after 15 Dec 1992)	X (assuming can control dividend policy)
Investments in joint ventures (regarded as permanently invested)	X (except earnings that arise in domestic joint ventures in fiscal years beginning after 15 Dec 1992)	√ (unless can control dividend policy)
Investments in associated undertakings (regarded as permanently invested)	√	√ (unless can control dividend policy)
Temporary differences arising on initial recognition of asset or liability	√	X

Temporary differences arising when an overseas subsidiary is consolidated under the temporal method	X	√
Sundry industry exemptions (paragraphs 31 and 32 of SFAS 109)	X	√
Temporary differences arising on government grants and investment credits	√	X

There are also various differences in disclosure requirements

Additionally, there are differences in the way US GAAP addresses various aspects of accounting for income taxes. US GAAP goes into considerably more detail than IAS 12 (r2000).

23.9 Examples from published financial statements

Note that the excerpts given do not always comply in full with all aspects of IAS, and, as such, are not necessarily examples of best practice but merely of current practice.

Example 23.17

Note 11 – Income taxes

Income Tax Expenses

The amounts charged in the income statements are as follows:

	2000	*1999*
Current income taxes	2,913	1,103
Deferred income taxes	(641)	799
Total charge for income taxes	2,272	1,902

The Group's parent company, Roche Holding Limited, and several of the Group's operating companies are domiciled in Switzerland. The maximum effective rate of all income taxes on companies domiciled in Basel, Switzerland, is 8% for holding companies and 25% for operating companies (1998: 8% and 25%).

Since the Group operates across the world, it is subject to income taxes in many different tax jurisdictions. The Group calculates its average expected tax rate as a weighted average of the tax rates in the tax jurisdictions in which the Group operates.

The Group's effective tax rate differs from the Group's expected tax rate as follows:

	2000	*1999*
Group's average expected tax rate	20%	20%
Tax effect of		
– Income not taxable	(3%)	(2%)
– Expenses not deductible for tax purposes	3%	3%
– Benefit of prior year tax losses not previously recognised	–	–
– Other differences	(3%)	(3%)
– Gain from sales of Genentech shares	8%	(2%)
– Gain from sales of LabCorp shares	2%	–
– Impairment of long-term assets	(3%)	–
– Vitamin case	–	6%
– Genentech legal settlements	–	(1%)
Group's effective tax rate	24%	25%

Income tax assets and liabilities

Amounts recognised in the balance sheet for income taxes are as follows:

	2000	*1999*
Current income tax		
Current income tax assets	435	408
Current income tax liabilities	(882)	(728)
Net current income tax asset (liability) in the balance sheet	(447)	(320)
Deferred income taxes		
Deferred income tax assets	460	1,170
Deferred income tax liabilities	(2,535)	(3,895)
Net deferred income tax asset (liability) in the balance sheet	(2,075)	(2,075)

Amounts recognised in the balance sheet for deferred taxes are reported as long-term assets and non-current liabilities, of which approximately 50% and 15% respectively is current.

Deferred income tax assets are recognised for tax loss carry forwards only to the extent that realisation of the related tax benefit is probable. The Group has no significant unrecognised tax losses. Deferred income tax liabilities have not been established for the withholding tax and other taxes that would be payable on the unremitted earnings of certain foreign subsidiaries, as such amounts are currently regarded as permanently reinvested. These unremitted earnings totalled 24.8 billion Swiss francs at 31 December 2000 (1999: 19.2 billion Swiss francs).

The deferred income tax assets and liabilities and the deferred income tax charges (credits) are attributable to the following items:

	Property, plant and equipment, and intangible assets	*Restructuring provisions*	*Other temporary differences*	*Total*
2000				
Net deferred income tax asset (liability) at the beginning of the year	(3,128)	302	101	2,725
Adjustment from changes in accounting policies	49	–	–	49
On issue of debt instruments	–	–	(128)	(128)
(Charged) credited to the income statement	312	(144)	473	641
Changes in Group organisation and Givandan spin-off	(54)	(8)	(55)	(117)
Currency translation effects and other	(521)	(4)	730	205
Net deferred income tax asset (liability) at end of year	(3,342)	146	1,121	(2,075)

Comparatives for 1999 were also given.

Roche
Switzerland
31 December 2000
International Accounting Standards

Example 23.18

Notes

9. Tax

DKK million	*Group* 1998/99	1999/00
Current tax on the profit for the year	364	603
Change in deferred tax on the profit for the year	91	75
Other taxes, exchange adjustment, etc.	−5	3
Adjustment concerning previous years	−26	12
Tax in undertaking not subject to tax pooling	–	–
Total	**424**	**693**
The tax breaks down as follows:		
Tax on profit on ordinary activities	512	681
Adjustment of deferred tax for previous years due to change in Danish corporation tax rate	−62	–
Adjustment of tax for previous years	−26	12
Total	**424**	**693**
Applicable tax rate		
Danish corporation tax rate	32%	32%
Effect of difference in tax rate compared with 32%	1%	1%
Non-taxable income and non-deductible expenses	1%	−1%
Utilisation of non-capitalised tax losses	1%	−1%
Effect of change in Danish corporation tax rate	−4%	–
Other, incl. adjustment concerning previous years	−3%	1%
Effective tax rate before deductible amortisation of goodwill	26%	33%
Non-deductible amortisation of goodwill	5%	11%
Effective tax rate	**31%**	**44%**

17. Provisions for deferred tax

DKK million	*Group* 30 April 1999	30 April 2000
Deferred tax at 1 May	1,548	1,558
Adjustment for deferred tax 1 May	−52	33
Adjusted deferred tax 1 May	**1,496**	**1,591**
Tax concerning new/sold undertakings and other adjustments	−29	−206
Adjustment due to change in Danish corporation tax rate	−62	–
Effect of write down of fixed assets	–	−120
Change in deferred tax concerning the profit for the year	153	75
Balance at 30 April 2000	**1,558**	**1,340**

	Deferred tax assets	*Deferred tax liabilities*	*Deferred tax, net*
Specification of deferred tax 30 April 2000			
Intangible fixed assets	50	60	10
Tangible fixed assets	198	1,302	1,104
Financial fixed assets	–	45	45
Current assets	95	152	57
Amounts falling due within one year	152	228	76
Amounts falling due after more than one year	216	159	−57
Tax losses carried forward, net	128	–	−128
Non-capitalised tax assets in balance sheet items	−233	–	233
Tax assets/liabilities	606	1,946	1,340
Offset between legal entities and jurisdictions	−438	−438	–
Deferred tax at 30 April 2000	**168**	**1,508**	**1,340**
Deferred tax at 30 April 1999 amounted to	**45**	**1,603**	**1,558**

The tax base of non-capitalised tax losses carried forward amounts to DKK 458 million (1998/99 DKK 190 million). Around 70 per cent of this will be either used or lost within the next five years. Deferred tax on investments in subsidiaries not recorded as a liability amounts to DKK 75 million (1998/99 DKK 108 million).

Danisco
Denmark
30 April 2000
International Accounting Standards

CHAPTER 24

Accounting for leases

24.1 Sources

IAS 17 (r1997) *Leases.*
SIC-15 *Operating Leases – Incentives.*

24.2 Brief summary of the requirements

IAS 17 (r1997) differentiates two types of lease: finance leases where the lessee acquires rights and obligations that are similar to those acquired by an outright purchase of the legal title to an asset; and operating leases where the majority of such rights and obligations are not acquired by the lessee.

For finance leases, the substance and legal form of the transaction are not the same. IAS 17 (r1997) requires finance leases to be accounted for on the basis of substance:

- the lessee records an asset, being the capitalised value of rights in the asset, which is subject to depreciation, and a liability to make payments to the lessor; rentals paid are allocated between a capital element which reduces the outstanding liability and interest expense on the liability;
- the lessor does not record a physical asset, but rather a debtor for rentals receivable; rentals received are allocated between a capital element which reduces the debtor and interest income.

For operating leases, IAS 17 (r1997) similarly requires accounting on the basis of the underlying substance of the rental agreement, which equates with the legal form:

- the lessee records rentals payable as an expense;
- the lessor records its ownership interest in the physical asset which is subject to depreciation; rentals should be recognised as income on a straight line basis over the term of the lease unless another systematic basis is more appropriate.

Incentives provided by the lessor to the lessee to enter into an operating lease should be recognised over the lease term by both the lessor and lessee. (SIC-15.4 and 5)

The primary accounting issues relate to:

- the classification of finance and operating leases;
- the method of allocating finance lease rentals between capital and interest; and
- disclosure of commitments under both finance and operating leases.

24.3 Development of the requirements

Historically, transactions are reflected in financial statements on the basis of their legal form. For assets, this means legal ownership. In the first part of the twentieth century, this basis was considered appropriate since legal form generally portrayed the economic substance of transactions. The growth in lease and similar forms of finance in the latter part of the twentieth century led to this assumption being questioned. If lease transactions were accounted for on the basis of legal form, the lessor would account for its legal ownership interest in the physical assets that are the subject of a lease; the lessee would account only for lease rentals as expenses, but not the underlying physical asset.

The Framework for the Preparation and Presentation of Financial Statements recognises that there may be circumstances where the substance and legal form of a transaction are not the same. In such instances, precedence should be given to substance. IAS 17, first introduced in March 1982, applies this principle to leases. It identifies certain types of leases which are similar to an outright purchase by the lessee; these leases are called finance leases. Other leases are called operating leases. The distinction is based on whether the lease results in a transfer of substantially all of the risks and rewards related to ownership of the asset to the lessee.

IAS 17 was reformatted in 1994 but without substantive change to the original text. A revision in December 1997 (IAS 17 (r1997)), effective for periods beginning on or after 1 January 1999, removed one of the two methods previously allowed for lessors to allocate rentals between capital and income, and introduced a requirement for enhanced disclosures by both lessors and lessees.

Since finance leases are restricted to those where 'substantially all' of the risks and rewards of ownership are transferred to the lessee, there will be instances where the level of risks and rewards transferred is significant, but is insufficient to require classification as a finance lease under IAS 17 (r1997). The existence of significant lessee rights and obligations under operating leases would appear to meet the definition of assets and liabilities under the Framework.

In response, the IASC participated in research to determine an appropriate solution to this apparent anomaly. The G4+1 working group has issued two discussion papers. The first, in 1996, outlined the ideas and the second, in 1999, outlined a more developed framework.

The central proposal of the discussion paper is that accounting for leases should be approached in accordance with the normal principles of asset and liability recognition as set out in the Framework.

Lessees, the paper proposes, should recognise assets and liabilities in relation to the rights and obligations conveyed by a lease when the lessor has substantially performed its obligation to provide the lessee with access to the leased property for the lease term. The asset and corresponding liability would be recorded at the present value of the minimum payments required by the lease plus the fair value of any residual value guarantee. Rentals paid would then be allocated between the repayment of the liability and the interest charge so as to produce a constant periodic rate of charge on the remaining obligation. The paper includes recommendations in respect of various additional features of leases, for example residual value guarantees, contingent rentals and options.

The basic recommendation for lessors is that, on initial recording of the lease two components would be recorded – a financial asset being the rentals receivable, and a non-financial asset representing an interest in the residual asset at the end of the lease. Gains by a lessor at the inception of a lease should not be recognised except in the case of a manufacturer or dealer where there is evidence of an increase in the value of the assets as a result of the lease and the increase can be reliably measured. This would also be extended to allow a gain to be recognised in other cases if the carrying amount of the property subject to the lease is demonstrably lower than its fair value (e.g., a property which had been held for a number of years at historic cost).

The G4+1 working group was disbanded in early 2001 immediately prior to the convening of the IASB. This topic has been identified by the IASB as a leadership project to be taken forward in the medium term. This may, in due course, result in a reform of IAS 17 (r1997) along the lines of the proposals in the G4+1 paper.

In 2000, IAS 40 *Investment Property* amended certain paragraphs of IAS 17 (r1997), as did IAS 41 *Agriculture* in January 2001. These amendments are effective for periods beginning on or after 1 January 2001 and 2003 respectively.

24.4 Scope

IAS 17 (r1997) applies to all leases except for certain specialised types of leases where more specific industry guidance is generally applied. The exceptions are:

- lease agreements to explore for or use minerals, oil, natural gas and similar non-regenerative resources; and
- licensing agreements for such items as motion picture films, video recordings, plays, manuscripts, patents and copyrights.

In addition, IAS 17 (r1997) should not be applied to the measurement by:

- lessees of investment property held under finance leases (IAS 40 *Investment Property* (see Chapter **10**));
- lessors of investment property leased out under operating leases (IAS 40 *Investment Property* (see Chapter **10**));
- lessees of biological assets held under finance leases; or
- lessors of biological assets leased out under operating leases.

(IAS 17 (r1997).1)

IAS 17 (r1997) applies to contracts that transfer the right to use assets even though substantial services by the lessor are required in connection with the operation or maintenance of such assets. (IAS 17 (r1997).2)

Examples would include the supply of motor vehicles and photocopiers. A contract that includes both an asset and services should be separated where two or more identifiable streams operate independently of each other, for example, payments increase in response to different factors, parts of the contract run for different periods or can be terminated or renegotiated separately. In such cases, IAS 17 (r1997) should be applied to the part relating to asset provision or use.

Conversely, IAS 17 (r1997) does not apply to agreements that are contracts for services that do not transfer the right to use assets from one contracting party to the other. (IAS 17 (r1997).2)

Employment contracts generally fall into this category. It follows that it does not apply to the separable service component of contracts that include both asset and services. Examples would include the maintenance element of property and motor vehicle contracts.

24.5 Definitions

IAS 17 (r1997) contains 18 separate definitions. The majority relate to terms which appear in other definitions, or in the accounting or disclosure requirements.

> 'A ***lease*** is an agreement whereby the lessor conveys to the lessee in return for a payment or series of payments the right to use an asset for an agreed period of time.'
>
> (IAS 17 (r1997).3)

This definition includes contracts for the hire of an asset which contain a provision giving the hirer an option to acquire title to the asset upon the fulfilment of agreed conditions (IAS 17 (r1997).4), for example, the payment of a nominal amount. Such contracts are sometimes known as hire purchase contracts.

Two further definitions are crucial:

- 'A ***finance lease*** is a lease that transfers substantially all the risks and rewards incident to ownership of an asset. Title may or may not eventually be transferred.' This definition is explored in **24.6** below.
- 'An ***operating lease*** is a lease other than a finance lease.'

(IAS 17 (r1997).3)

The remaining 15 supporting definitions are as follows:

'A **non-cancellable lease** is a lease that is cancellable only:

(a) upon the occurrence of some remote contingency;
(b) with the permission of the lessor;
(c) if the lessee enters into a new lease for the same or an equivalent asset with the same lessor; or
(d) upon payment by the lessee of an additional amount such that, at inception, continuation of the lease is reasonably certain.'

The **inception of the lease** is the earlier of the date of the lease agreement or of a commitment by the parties to the principal provisions of the lease.

The **lease term** is the non-cancellable period for which the lessee has contracted to lease the asset together with any further terms for which the lessee has the option to continue to lease the asset, with or without further payment, which option at the inception of the lease it is reasonably certain that the lessee will exercise.

Minimum lease payments are the payments over the lease term that the lessee is, or can be required, to make excluding contingent rent, costs for services and taxes to be paid by and reimbursed to the lessor, together with:

(a) in the case of the lessee, any amounts guaranteed by the lessee or by a party related to the lessee; or
(b) in the case of the lessor, any residual value guaranteed to the lessor by either:
   (i) the lessee;
   (ii) a party related to the lessee; or
   (iii) an independent third party financially capable of meeting this guarantee.

However, if the lessee has an option to purchase the asset at a price which is expected to be sufficiently lower than the fair value at the date the option becomes exercisable that, at the inception of the lease, is reasonably certain to be exercised, the minimum lease payments comprise the minimum payments payable over the lease term and the payment required to exercise this purchase option.

Fair value is the amount for which an asset could be exchanged or a liability settled, between knowledgeable, willing parties in an arm's length transaction.

Economic life is either:

(a) the period over which an asset is expected to be economically usable by one or more users; or
(b) the number of production or similar units expected to be obtained from the asset by one or more users.

Useful life is the estimated remaining period, from the beginning of the lease term, without limitation by the lease term, over which the economic benefits embodied in the asset are expected to be consumed by the enterprise.

Guaranteed residual value is:

(a) in the case of the lessee, that part of the residual value which is guaranteed by the lessee or by a party related to the lessee (the amount of the guarantee being the maximum amount that could, in any event, become payable); and
(b) in the case of the lessor, that part of the residual value which is guaranteed by the lessee or by a third party unrelated to the lessor who is financially capable of discharging the obligations under the guarantee.

Unguaranteed residual value is that portion of the residual value of the leased asset, the realisation of which by the lessor is not assured or is guaranteed solely by a party related to the lessor.

Gross investment in the lease is the aggregate of the minimum lease payments under a finance lease from the standpoint of the lessor and any unguaranteed residual value accruing to the lessor.

Unearned finance income is the difference between:

(a) the aggregate of the minimum lease payments under a finance lease from the standpoint of the lessor and any unguaranteed residual value accruing to the lessor; and
(b) the present value of (a) above, at the interest rate implicit in the lease.

Net investment in the lease is the gross investment in the lease less unearned finance income.

The **interest rate implicit in the lease** is the discount rate that, at the inception of the lease, causes the aggregate present value of:

(a) the minimum lease payments; and
(b) the unguaranteed residual value to be equal to the fair value of the lease asset.

The **lessee's incremental borrowing rate of interest** is the rate of interest the lessee would have to pay on a similar lease or, if that is not determinable, the rate that, at the inception of the lease, the lessee would incur to borrow over a similar term, and with a similar security, the funds necessary to purchase the asset.

Contingent rent is that portion of the lease payments that is not fixed in amount but is based on a factor other than just the passage of time (e.g., percentage of sales, amount of usage, price indices, market rates of interest).'
(IAS 17 (r1997).3)

24.6 Classification of leases

The classification of leases is based on the definitions of finance leases and operating leases (see **24.5** above). These focus on the extent to which risks and rewards incident to ownership of an asset are transferred.

- No quantifiable tests are included within the definition, for example, in respect of the present value of minimum rentals, or the lease term as a proportion of the asset's life. It is intended that classification should not be based on a narrow numerical test, but rather take all features into consideration and thus reflect the substance of all aspects of the lease.
- Risks include the possibilities of losses from idle capacity or technological obsolescence and of variations in return due to changing economic conditions. (IAS 17 (r1997).5)
- Rewards may be represented by the expectation of profitable operation over the asset's economic life and of gain from appreciation in value or realisation of a residual value. (IAS 17 (r1997).5)

- Since the transaction between a lessor and a lessee is based on a lease agreement common to both parties, it is appropriate to use consistent definitions. (IAS 17 (r1997).7) While it follows that lessor and lessee may be expected to reach consistent classifications from the same information, this may not always happen in practice. Differences in classification may be due to differing circumstances affecting the two parties, the differing definitions of minimum lease payments or the result of judgement applied in 'close-call' situations.
- Changes to the provisions of a lease after inception, other than by renewing the lease, which would have resulted in a different classification of the lease had the changed terms been in effect at the inception of lease, should be considered at the inception of a revised agreement over the remaining term. (IAS 17 (r1997).10)

24.6.1 Finance leases

'A lease is classified as a finance lease if it transfers substantially all the risks and rewards incident to ownership' (IAS 17 (r1997).6) from lessor to lessee.

The classification is based on the substance of the whole transaction rather than the legal form. This means that greater weight will be given to those features which have a commercial effect in practice.

While not giving specific quantitative guidance on when transfer is deemed to have occurred, IAS 17 (r1997) gives eight indicators of situations which individually or in a combination could indicate that transfer has occurred.

(a) The lease transfers ownership of the asset to the lessee by the end of the lease term. (IAS 17 (r1997).8(a))

This condition would hold where transfer of legal title, and thus continued ownership risk and reward, is automatic either within the agreement or within a side agreement which forms part of the overall transaction. This condition will be met, in substance, where the lessor has a put option requiring the lessee to acquire legal title, and it is likely that such an option will be exercised by the lessor.

(b) The lessee has the option to purchase the asset at a price which is expected to be sufficiently lower than the fair value at the date the option becomes exercisable such that, at the inception of the lease, it is reasonably certain that the option will be exercised. (IAS 17 (r1997).8(b))

This condition extends condition (a) above to a lessee call option at a price which makes its exercise commercially likely to occur. An option at a nominal amount or at a price that is anticipated to be less than market value at the time it would be exercised would be examples of such options.

(c) The lease term is for the major part of the economic life of the asset even if title is not transferred. (IAS 17 (r1997).8(c))

This situation is one where substantially all the risks and rewards arise during the lease term for which the lessee controls the asset. No guidance on the proportion of the lease term is included in IAS 17 (r1997). A guideline of 75 per cent is outlined in terms of US GAAP.

(d) At the inception of the lease the present value of the minimum lease payments amounts to at least substantially all of the fair value of the leased asset. (IAS 17 (r1997).8(d)) The discount factor is the interest rate implicit in the lease, if this is practicable to determine; if not the lessee's incremental borrowing rate reflecting the risk inherent in the specific asset should be used. (IAS 17 (r1997).12) This condition tests whether the lessor receives a full return on their initial investment. The terms 'inception of the lease', 'minimum lease payments', and 'fair value' are defined in **24.5.**

In some countries, this test is included as the principal test of risk and reward transfer, and 'substantially all' is given a specific numerical meaning – usually 90 per cent. However, neither of these features are present in IAS 17 (r1997) with the effect that:

- a test based on the present value of minimum lease payments should only be considered as one of a number of tests which together provide evidence of the substance of the transaction;
- application of a rigid numerical limit (for example, 90 per cent of fair value) is not consistent with the objective of classification on the basis of substance.

More specific guidance on determining the present value of the minimum lease payments and unguaranteed residual value is provided below.

Interest rate implicit in a lease

IAS 17 (r1997) provides the following guidance in respect of accounting for finance leases by lessees:

> 'Lessees should recognise finance leases as assets and liabilities in their balance sheets at amounts equal at the inception of the lease to the fair value of the leased property or, if lower, at the present value of the minimum lease payments. In calculating the present value of the minimum lease payments the discount factor is the interest rate implicit in the lease, if this is practicable to determine; if not, the lessee's incremental borrowing rate should be used.'

The interest rate implicit in the lease is defined as:

> 'The discount rate that, at the inception of the lease, causes the aggregate present value of:
>
> (a) the minimum lease payments; and
> (b) the unguaranteed residual value to be equal to the fair value of the leased asset.'
>
> (IAS 17 (r1997).3))

Unguaranteed residual value is defined in IAS 17 (r1997) as 'that portion of the residual value of the leased asset, the realisation of which by the lessor is not assured or is guaranteed solely by a party related to the lessor.'

IAS 17 (r1997) does not define 'residual value'. IAS 16 (r1998), *Property, Plant and Equipment*, defines residual value as 'the net amount which the enterprise expects to obtain for an asset at the end of its useful life after deducting the expected costs of disposal'. IAS 16 (r1998) further notes that '[t]he estimate [of residual value] is based on the residual value prevailing at the date of the estimate for similar assets which have reached the end of their useful lives and which have operated under conditions similar to those in which the asset will be used'.

The unguaranteed residual value should therefore be determined using information relevant to the specific market at the time of inception of the lease. FAS 13 *Accounting for Leases*, provides guidance with regard to the estimation of the residual value. FAS 13 defines residual value as the estimated fair value of the leased property at the end of the lease term.

The minimum lease payments and the unguaranteed residual value, determined in accordance with the guidance above, should be added together and a calculation should be performed to determine the interest rate which amortises the sum of these two items to zero at the end of the lease. This is the implicit interest rate that is inherent in the lease. The minimum lease payments should then be discounted using the implicit rate and the present value thereof compared to the fair value of the asset to determine whether it amounts to substantially all of the fair value of the asset.

Irrespective of intention of use, the residual value should be determined based on the current market value of similar assets of an age equal to the lease term.

Minimum lease payments

Minimum lease payments are defined as :

> 'the payments over the lease term that the lessee is, or can be required, to make excluding contingent rent, costs for services and taxes to be paid by and reimbursed to the lessor, together with:

(a) in the case of the lessee, any amounts guaranteed by the lessee or by a party related to the lessee; or
(b) in the case of the lessor, any residual value guaranteed to the lessor by either:
   (i) the lessee;
   (ii) a party related to the lessee; or
   (iii) an independent third party financially capable of meeting this guarantee.

However, if the lessee has an option to purchase the asset at a price which is expected to be sufficiently lower than the fair value at the date the option becomes exercisable that, at the inception of the lease, is reasonably certain to be exercised, the minimum lease payments comprise the minimum payments payable over the lease term and the payment required to exercise this purchase option.'

(IAS 17 (r1997).3))

Guaranteed residual value is defined as:

'(a) in the case of the lessee, that part of the residual value which is guaranteed by the lessee or by a party related to the lessee (the amount of the guarantee being the maximum amount that could, in any event, become payable); and
(b) in the case of the lessor, that part of the residual value which is guaranteed by the lessee or by a third party unrelated to the lessor who is financially capable of discharging the obligations under the guarantee.'

(IAS 17 (r1997).3))

It is evident from the above that the minimum lease payments are not necessarily the payments outlined in the lease agreement and may include option payments and guaranteed residual values.

(e) The leased assets are of a specialised nature such that only the lessee can use them without modifications being made. (IAS 17 (r1997).8(e))

Where this condition is met, it is likely that the asset will have been constructed to the lessee's specification such that its market value is limited. It follows that the lessor will seek to recover their initial investment from the primary lease term. Examples of specialised assets include:

- assets that are located underground for mining purposes and are unable to be moved above ground to be used by competitors;
- certain intangible assets, for example, trade marks;
- assets in a location where it is unlikely that any other entities would consider moving to.

(f) If the lessee can cancel the lease, any losses associated with the cancellation are borne by the lessee. (IAS 17 (r1997).9(a))

Where the possibility of cancellation is relied on to reduce minimum lease payments, the likelihood of cancellation occurring in practice must be considered, and the consequences of a lessee decision to terminate must be evaluated. Evidence that the lessee suffers a financial penalty for cancelling the lease suggests that the original intention of the parties is that cancellation is not expected to occur. Conversely, arrangements for termination that are unlikely to be applicable in practice, for example following insolvency of the lessee or failure to pay rentals when due, will be less relevant.

(g) Gains or losses from the fluctuation in the fair value of the residual fall to the lessee (for example in the form of a rent rebate equalling most of the sales proceeds at the end of the lease). (IAS 17 (r1997).9(b))

Where the lessee does not acquire legal title, they may nevertheless bear the risk of variation in residual values of the asset through payment of a substantial fixed final rental ('balloon rental') followed by a repayment equal to all or substantially all of the sales proceeds.

(h) The lessee has the ability to continue the lease for a secondary period at a rent which is substantially lower than market rent. (IAS 17 (r1997).9(c))

Rental in a secondary period which is either a nominal amount or substantially below market rates suggests both that the lessor has received the required return of their initial investment, and that the lessee is likely to choose to enter into such a secondary period, thereby extending the lease term.

24.6.2 Operating leases

> 'A lease is classified as an operating lease if it does not transfer substantially all the risks and rewards incident to ownership'.
>
> (IAS 17 (r1997).6)

This classification will follow where the definition of a finance lease is not met.

24.7 Accounting by lessees

24.7.1 Finance leases

Lessees should recognise finance leases as both assets and liabilities in their balance sheets:

- the asset represents the capitalised value of rights to use the asset over the lease term;
- the liability represents the lessees obligation to pay rentals.

At the inception of the lease, the amount recognised for both asset and liability will be the lower of:

- the fair value of the leased property; and
- the present value of the minimum lease payments.

(IAS 17 (r1997).12)

Where minimum lease payments are used, the discount factor is the interest rate implicit in the lease, if this is practicable to determine; if not the lessee's incremental borrowing rate reflecting the risk inherent in the specific asset should be used.

Subsequent to the inception of the lease, the asset and liability amounts are unlikely to be the same. The asset amount will depend on the policy for depreciation (see below), while the liability will depend on the method used to allocate finance charges within rentals (see below).

Assets arising under finance leases are treated in the same way as other assets which are owned by the lessee. Consequently, depreciation expense should be provided and calculated on the basis set out in IAS 16 (r1998) *Property, Plant and Equipment* and IAS 38 *Intangible Assets* (see **10.3.9** and **10.7.12**). The depreciation policy for depreciable leased assets should be consistent with that for depreciable assets which are owned. Where there is reasonable certainty that the lessee will obtain ownership by the end of the lease term, the asset should be depreciated over the period that the lessee expects to own and use the asset. In other cases, the asset should be fully depreciated over the shorter of the lease term or its useful life. (IAS 17 (r1997).19) Assets are subject to the requirements of IAS 36 *Impairment of Assets*, which sets out the requirements for how an enterprise should perform an impairment review of its assets, including assets held under finance leases, and when it should recognise, or reverse, an impairment loss (see **10.7**).

Lease payments should be apportioned between:

- a finance charge, calculated so as to arrive at a constant periodic rate of interest on the outstanding balance of the liability for each period, and charged as a finance expense; and
- a balance which represents a reduction in the outstanding liability. (IAS 17 (r1997).17)

The total finance charge over the lease term is the difference between the total minimum lease payments, and the amount initially recorded as the balance sheet liability. The method of allocating this total to periods which produces the required 'constant period rate of interest on the remaining balance of the liability' is sometimes called the actuarial before tax method, and can be generated on spreadsheets. A method which provides an approximation to this method which is used in practice is the 'rule of 78', also known as the 'sum of digits' method. Note however that this method will only provide an acceptable basis if the results are not materially different from those obtained under a constant rate of interest. The degree of approximation will diverge when there are fewer payments and correspondingly fewer digits.

Example 24.1

Example of 'rule of 78' method

An asset is leased under a finance lease for a three year period, with 12 quarterly rental payments; the total finance charge amounts to Fr10,000.

(i) If rentals are paid quarterly in arrears

The digit assigned for the first period will be 12 (being the total number of payments, that is, 4 payments each for 3 years) and for the last period, one.

Period	*Quarter*	*Digit*	*Finance Charge allocation*	*Fr*
Year 1	1	12	Fr10,000 x 12/78	1,539
	2	11	Fr10,000 x 11/78	1,410
	3	10	Fr10,000 x 10/78	1,282
	4	9	Fr10,000 x 9/78	1,154
Year 2	1	8	Fr10,000 x 8/78	1,026
	2	7	Fr10,000 x 7/78	897
	3	6	Fr10,000 x 6/78	769
	4	5	Fr10,000 x 5/78	641
Year 3	1	4	Fr10,000 x 4/78	513
	2	3	Fr10,000 x 3/78	385
	3	2	Fr10,000 x 2/78	256
	4	1	Fr10,000 x 1/78	128
		78		10,000

Total finance charge for year 1 is the sum of the four quarters, that is Fr 1,539 + 1,410 + 1,282 + 1,154 = Fr 5,385.

(ii) If rentals are paid in advance

Since there is no capital outstanding during the final quarter of the last year, there is no finance charge allocation to that quarter. Consequently, the digit for the last period will be zero; and for the first period, eleven. The sum of the digits becomes 66.

The amount included in the balance sheet in respect of the outstanding liability will be the present value of finance lease liabilities. This may be reconciled as follows:

Gross minimum lease payments payable in the future	x
Less: Finance charges allocated to future periods	(x)
Net present value of lease liabilities	x

This net present value can be further classified into amounts due within one year, due in one to five years, and after five years, by classifying the gross minimum lease payments, and the finance charges allocated to future periods.

Lease liabilities should be disclosed within liabilities, and not deducted from the related assets. (IAS 17 (r1997).15)

24.7.2 Operating leases

For operating leases, lease payments (excluding costs for services such as insurance and maintenance) are recognised as an expense in the income statement on a straight line basis over the lease term unless another systematic basis is representative of the time pattern of the user's benefit, even if payments are not made on that basis. (IAS 17 (r1997).25 and 26)

Some operating leases, give rise to two situations where the basis of rental payments differs from the time pattern of the user's benefit. These are:

- incentives on entry to a lease such as rental holidays and reverse premiums; and
- vacancy.

Lease incentives

SIC-15 deals with the recognition of incentives in an operating lease by both the lessee and the lessor. A lessor may provide incentives to a lessee in negotiating a new or renewed operating lease. Such incentives may involve up-front cash payments, the reimbursement or assumption by the lessor of costs of the lessee (e.g., re-location costs, leasehold improvements and costs associated with a pre-existing lease commitment of the lessee), or initial periods being rent free or at a reduced rent. All incentives for the agreement of a new or renewed lease should be recognised as an integral part of the net consideration agreed for the use of the leased asset, irrespective of the incentive's nature or form or the timing of payments. (SIC-15.3) The lessee should recognise the aggregate benefit of incentives as a reduction of rental expense over the lease term, on a straight line basis, unless another systematic basis is representative of the time pattern of the lessee's benefits from the user of the leased asset. (SIC-15.5)

This will usually require the use of a straight-line basis over the lease term (commencing with the date of occupation) or, if shorter than the full lease term, to the date on which rentals are first adjusted to market rates.

Costs incurred by the lessee, including costs in connection with pre-existing leases (e.g., termination costs, relocation costs or cost of leasehold improvements), should be accounted for by the lessee in accordance with the applicable IAS irrespective of whether they are reimbursed through an incentive scheme. (SIC-15.6 and 11)

In many cases this will lead to such costs being expensed in the period incurred. It is not appropriate for such costs to be netted in the financial statements against the associated recoverable lease incentive, which will be realised as a reduction of rental expense over the lease term or a shorter period as discussed above.

Vacancy

Vacancy is not addressed in IAS 17 (r1997), but is covered by the guidance on onerous contracts in IAS 37 *Provisions, Contingent Liabilities and Contingent Assets*. When a lessee vacates a property before the end of the lease term, the user's benefit will cease unless a sub-tenant occupies the property and pays a sub-lease rental. Such a situation may give rise to an onerous contract under IAS 37 (see **11.9**). Where a property is vacant, a provision may be necessary to cover the legal obligation to make rental payments during the estimated period of vacancy. Where a sub-lease produces a rental which is less than the rental paid, a provision may be necessary for the shortfall for the duration of the sub-lease. Whilst a property is vacant or sub-let the lessee will continue to pay lease rentals as previously, but these, less any sub-rental income, will be offset against a vacant premise provision to the extent that one has been recognised.

24.8 Accounting by lessors

24.8.1 Finance leases

Under a finance lease substantially all the risks and rewards incident to ownership are transferred from the lessor to the lessee. The substance of the transaction is thus that the lessor has disposed of the rights associated with ownership in return for a stream of lease payment receipts. Accordingly, lessors should recognise assets held under a finance lease in their balance sheets as a receivable at an amount equal to the net investment in the lease. (IAS 17 (r1997).28)

Lease payments receivable are allocated by the lessor as part repayment of the investment (which reduces the carrying amount of the net investment) and part finance income. The recognition of finance income should be based on a pattern reflecting a constant periodic rate of return on the lessor's net investment outstanding in respect of the finance lease. (IAS 17 (r1997).30)

This method is called the net investment method, or actuarial before tax method. For many lessors, finance lease income is a significant part of overall income, and other simpler methods which produce an approximation are often used. This is acceptable provided the method is tested and does actually result in an amount which reasonably approximates the result using the effective interest rate method. Following the revision to IAS 17 in 1997, the net cash investment method (also known as the actuarial after tax method) is no longer permitted. It follows that any tax effects are dealt with in accordance with IAS 12 (r2000) *Income Taxes*.

At each balance sheet date, the investment in the lease may be reconciled as follows:

Gross rentals receivable in the future	x
Plus: Guaranteed residual value	x
Plus: Unguaranteed residual value	x
Gross investment in the lease	x
Less: Finance income allocated to future periods	(x)
Net investment in leases	x

This net investment should be further classified into amounts due within one year, and due in more than one year, by classifying the gross rentals receivable, and the finance income allocated to future periods.

Further guidance is provided on:

- Estimated unguaranteed residual values used in the lessor's gross investment in a lease, which should be reviewed regularly. Where there is a reduction, the income allocation over the lease term is revised and any reduction in respect of amounts already accrued is recognised immediately. (IAS 17 (r1997).32)
- Initial direct costs, such as commissions and legal fees, are often incurred by lessors in negotiating and arranging a lease. They may either be recognised immediately as expenses, or allocated against finance income over the lease term. The latter may be achieved by recognising, as an expense, the cost as incurred and recognising as income in the same period a portion of the unearned finance income equal to the initial direct costs. (IAS 17 (r1997).33)

24.8.2 Operating leases

Under an operating lease, the risks and rewards incident to ownership of an asset remain with the lessor. Therefore, the asset is treated as an asset by the lessor, and presented in the balance sheet according to the nature of the asset. (IAS 17 (r1997). 41)

Depreciation of depreciable leased assets should be provided on a basis consistent with the lessor's normal depreciation policy for similar assets. The charge should be calculated in accordance with IAS 16 (r1998) *Property, Plant and Equipment* and IAS 38 *Intangible Assets* (see Chapter **10**). The provisions of IAS 36 *Impairment of Assets* will be relevant. (IAS 17 (r1997).45-46) (See also **10.12**.)

Lease income (excluding receipts for services such as insurance and maintenance) should be recognised on a straight line basis over the lease term, even if the receipts are not on such a basis, unless another systematic basis is more representative of the time pattern in which useful benefit derived from the leased asset is diminished, for example, where rentals are based on usage.

Initial direct costs, such as direct costs for administration, advertising and consulting or legal fees, incurred specifically to earn revenues from an operating lease may either be deferred and allocated over the lease term in proportion to the recognition of rent income, or recognised as an expense in the period they are incurred. Other costs, including depreciation, incurred in earning the lease income are recognised as an expense. (IAS 17 (r1997).43-44; SIC-15.10)

The aggregate cost of incentives provided for the lessee in negotiating a new or renewed operating lease should be recognised as a reduction in rental income over the lease term, on a straight line basis, unless another systematic basis is representative of the time pattern over which the benefit of the leased asset is diminished. Such costs are, in substance, related to the consideration for the use of the leased asset and do not form part of the initial direct costs discussed above. (SIC-15.4 and 10)

24.8.3 Manufacturers and dealers

Where a manufacturer or dealer offers leasing terms as an option to normal selling terms (termed in the US, a 'sales-type lease'), an immediate selling profit may arise on leased assets when there has, in substance, been a disposal of that asset. This will occur when the lease is a finance lease.

Under a finance lease, the manufacturer or dealer gains two forms of income: the finance income over the lease term and an initial selling profit or loss equivalent to that on an outright sale, at normal selling prices, reflecting any applicable volume or trade discounts. The sales revenue recorded will be the fair value of the asset or, if lower, the present value of minimum lease payments accruing to the lessor computed using a commercial rate of interest. The cost of sale is the cost of the leased property (or carrying amount if different) less the present value of the unguaranteed residual value. The resulting profit or loss should be recognised in accordance with the policy followed by the enterprise for outright sales. (IAS 17 (r1997).34–36)

If artificially low rates of interest are quoted to customers, the selling profit should be restricted to that which would apply if a commercial rate of interest were charged. Initial direct costs should be charged as an expense in the period of sale because they are mainly related to earning the selling profit. (IAS 17 (r1997).34,37–38)

At inception of the lease the lessor's gross investment may be analysed as follows (assuming a commercial rate of interest and fair value of the asset equivalent to the present value of the minimum lease payments):

Income statement		
Revenue: PV of minimum lease payments		x
– Carrying value of asset	x	
– Less: PV of unguaranteed residual	(x)	
Cost of sales		(x)
Selling profit		x
Balance sheet		
PV of minimum lease payments		x
Plus: PV of unguaranteed residual		x
Net investment in the lease (recognised in balance sheet)		x
Reconciliation to gross investment:		
Plus: unearned finance income		x
Gross investment in the lease		x

For operating leases, the manufacturer or dealer has retained the asset with a view to using it to generate rental income. Consequently, no selling profit should be recognised and the asset should be included in the balance sheet initially at its purchase price or production cost. (IAS 17 (r1997).47)

24.9 Sale or lease and leaseback

A sale and leaseback transaction is a linked arrangement whereby the owner of an asset sells that asset and immediately leases it back from the purchaser. The accounting treatment of a sale and leaseback transaction depends upon the classification of the lease involved.

24.9.1 Classification of leaseback

The classification criteria for the leaseback are those set out in **24.6** above. The following points are relevant:

- Where the leaseback is a finance lease, it follows that substantially all risks and rewards incident to ownership of an asset remain with the seller. Conversely, where the leaseback is an operating lease, it follows that there has been a transfer of risks and rewards to the purchaser.
- A long lease involving property at a substantially fixed annual rental, or a rental adjusted by reference to changes in interest rates, is more likely to be a finance lease since it provides the lessor with a financier's return. Similarly, where the sale transaction is at a value substantially different to the fair value of the asset, the purchaser/lessor has not paid an arm's length

value for the risks and rewards incident to ownership of the asset; consequently, it is more likely that the terms of the leaseback will meet the definition of a finance lease.

Similar considerations apply to 'lease and leaseback' transactions. Lease and leaseback transactions are currently the subject of a SIC draft interpretation, SIC-D27 *Transactions in the Legal Form of a Lease and Leaseback* (see Appendix I). This draft interpretation considers whether a transaction that takes the legal form of a lease of assets from an enterprise and a lease of the same assets back to the same enterprise is a lease under IAS 17 (r1997). It also considers the treatment by an enterprise of balances arising and fees receivable under such arrangements where such a transaction is not considered to be a lease under IAS 17 (r1997). The draft consensus is that the accounting should reflect the substance of the transaction. All aspects of a transaction should be evaluated to determine its substance. A series of transactions linked in such a way that the effect cannot be understood without reference to the series of transactions as a whole should be accounted for as one transaction. When the investor/lessee does not, in substance, receive the right to use the underlying asset for an agreed period of time, the transaction is not a lease under IAS 17 (r1997), and other International Accounting Standards should be applied. The SIC agreed that the following would demonstrate that a lease does not, in substance, exist where:

- an enterprise retains all the risks and rewards incidental to ownership of the leased asset, and that it enjoys the same rights to use that it had before the arrangement; and
- an option is included on terms that make it highly likely that it will be exercised.

The SIC also addressed when fees associated with these types of agreements should be recognised. For these the SIC referred to IAS 18 (r1993) *Revenue*. Any fee payable by the investor/lessee as part of the arrangements (e.g., where the investor/lessee derives a taxation benefit from the arrangement and passes some of this to the enterprise as a fee), should be accounted for by the enterprise according to the features of the lease. Factors such as whether the investor/lessee has continuing involvement with the assets, the terms of any guarantees and the circumstances under which the fee could be repayable should be considered in determining the appropriate accounting treatment. The SIC discussed this draft Interpretation at its August 2001 meeting in London, and will submit a revised draft Interpretation to the IASB for approval.

24.9.2 Finance leaseback

If the leaseback is a finance lease, the transaction is a means whereby the lessor provides finance to the lessee, with the asset as security. For this reason it is not appropriate to regard an excess of sales proceeds over the carrying amount as income. Such excess, if recognised, is deferred and amortised over the lease term. (IAS 17 (r1997).50)

In practice, the most straightforward treatment is to leave the carrying value of the asset at its previous carrying amount and continue to account for the asset as if the sale and leaseback transaction had not occurred. This reflects that the sale and leaseback transaction has not resulted in any change to the seller's interest in the risks and rewards incident to ownership. Consequently, there is unlikely to be any change to the asset's useful life or residual value so far as the seller is concerned. Nevertheless, consideration should be given as to whether the transaction has resulted in an impairment in value, in which case the carrying amount is reduced to recoverable amount in accordance with IAS 36 *Impairment of Assets*. The proceeds from the 'sale' should not be recognised as income by the lessee, but should be deferred and amortised over the term of the lease.

24.9.3 Operating leaseback

If the leaseback is an operating lease, the asset will cease to be recognised. To determine how any gain or loss is treated, it is necessary to establish whether the sale price and the lease payments are established at fair value, above fair value, or below fair value.

- If the lease payments and the sale price are established at fair value, there has in effect been a normal sale transaction and any profit or loss is recognised immediately. (IAS 17 (r1997).53)
- If the sale price is above fair value:
  - the difference between fair value and carrying amount may be recognised immediately; but
  - the excess of proceeds over fair value should be deferred and amortised over the period for which the asset is expected to be used (IAS 17 (r1997).52) since the gain is compensated by future lease payments at above market price.
- If the sale price is below fair value:
  - the difference between sale price and carrying value should be recognised immediately except that, if the loss is compensated by future lease payments at below market price, it should be deferred and amortised in proportion to the lease payments over the period for which the asset is expected to be used. (IAS 17 (r1997).52)

Additionally if the fair value at the time of the transaction is less than the carrying amount of the asset, a loss equal to the amount of the difference between the carrying amount and fair value should be recognised immediately. (IAS 17 (r1997).54)

The difference between the sale proceeds and the reduced carrying value (i.e., fair value) would then be accounted for as noted above.

The following table illustrates the application of the above requirements in respect of operating leasebacks. A more detailed summary is given in the appendix to IAS 17 (r1997).

	Lease payments below market price	**Lease payments at market price**	**Lease payments above market price**
Sale price below fair value	Defer and amortise loss	Recognise profit or loss immediately	Not applicable
Sale price at fair value	Not applicable	Recognise profit or loss immediately	Not applicable
Sale price above fair value	Not applicable	Not applicable	Defer and amortise excess of sale price over fair value

24.10 Disclosures

IAS 17 (r1997) includes separate paragraphs dealing with disclosures by:

- Lessees with finance leases (IAS 17 (r1997).23)
- Lessees with operating leases (IAS 17 (r1997).27)
- Lessors with finance leases (IAS 17 (r1997).39)
- Lessors with operating leases (IAS 17 (r1997).48).

These are in addition to the disclosures required by:

- IAS 16 (r1998) *Property, Plant and Equipment* (see Chapter **10**), in respect of assets held under finance leases.
- IAS 32 (r1998) *Financial Instruments: Disclosure and Presentation* (see Chapter **12**) in respect of finance leases and individual amounts due and payable under operating leases (i.e., excluding amounts not due at the balance sheet date in respect of operating leases). Such items fall within financial instruments under IAS 32. (IAS 32.Appendix.6)
- IAS 39 (r2000) *Financial Instruments: Recognition and Measurement* (see Chapter **12**) in respect of lease receivables subject to the de-recognition provisions of IAS 39 and derivatives embedded in leases. (IAS 39.1(b))

Although there is a significant degree of duplication between the four paragraphs, the full text of each is reproduced below.

24.10.1 Lessees with finance leases (IAS 17 (r1997).23 & 24)

Lessees should make the following disclosures for finance leases:

(a) for each class of asset, the net carrying amount at the balance sheet date;

(b) a reconciliation between the total of minimum lease payments at the balance sheet date, and their present value. In addition, an enterprise should disclose the total of minimum lease payments at the balance sheet date, and their present value, for each of the following periods:
    (i) not later than one year;
    (ii) later than one year and not later than five years; and
    (iii) later than five years;
(c) contingent rents recognised in income for the period;
(d) the total of future minimum sublease payments expected to be received under non-cancellable subleases at the balance sheet date; and
(e) a general description of the lessee's significant leasing arrangements including, but not limited to, the following:
    (i) the basis on which contingent rent payments are determined;
    (ii) the existence and terms of renewal or purchase options and escalation clauses; and
    (iii) restrictions imposed by lease arrangements, such as those concerning dividends, additional debt, and further leasing.

In addition, the requirements on disclosure in IAS 16 (r1998) *Property, Plant and Equipment*, IAS 36 *Impairment of Assets*, IAS 38 *Intangible Assets*, IAS 40 *Investment Property* and IAS 41 *Agriculture*, apply to the amounts of leased assets under finance leases that are accounted for by the lessee as acquisitions of assets.

24.10.2 Lessees with operating leases (IAS 17 (r1997).27)

Lessees should make the following disclosures for operating leases:

(a) the total of future minimum lease payments under non-cancellable operating leases for each of the following periods:
    (i) not later than one year;
    (ii) later than one year and not later than five years;
    (iii) later than five years;
(b) the total of future minimum sublease payments expected to be received under non-cancellable subleases at the balance sheet date;
(c) lease and sublease payments recognised in income for the period, with separate amounts for minimum lease payments, contingent rents, and sublease payments;
(d) a general description of the lessee's significant leasing arrangements including, but not limited to, the following:
    (i) the basis on which contingent rent payments are determined;
    (ii) the existence and terms of renewal or purchase options and escalation clauses; and
    (iii) restrictions imposed by lease agreements, such as those concerning dividends, additional debt, and further leasing.

24.10.3 Lessors with finance leases (IAS 17 (r1997).39)

Lessors should make the following disclosures for finance leases:

(a) a reconciliation between the total gross investment in the lease at the balance sheet date, and the present value of minimum lease payments receivable at the balance sheet date. In addition, an enterprise should disclose the total gross investment in the lease and the present value of minimum lease payments receivable at the balance sheet date, for each of the following periods:
  (i) not later than one year;
  (ii) later than one year and not later than five years;
  (iii) later than five years;
(b) unearned finance income;
(c) the unguaranteed residual values accruing to the benefit of the lessor;
(d) the accumulated allowance for uncollectable minimum lease payments receivable;
(e) contingent rents recognised in income; and
(f) a general description of the lessor's significant leasing arrangements.

24.10.4 Lessors with operating leases (IAS 17 (r1997).48, 48A)

Lessors should make the following disclosures for operating leases:

(a) the future minimum lease payments under non-cancellable operating leases in the aggregate and for each of the following periods:
  (i) not later than one year;
  (ii) later than one year and not later than five years;
  (iii) later than five years;
(b) total contingent rents recognised in income; and
(c) a general description of the lessor's significant leasing arrangements.

In addition, the requirements on disclosure under IAS 16 (r1998) *Property, Plant and Equipment*, IAS 36 *Impairment of Assets*, IAS 38 *Intangible Assets*, IAS 40 *Investment Property* and IAS 41 *Agriculture*, apply to assets leased out under operating leases.

24.11 Comparison with UK GAAP

UK GAAP is principally set out in SSAP 21 *Accounting for Leases*, and supported by FRS 5 *Reporting the substance of transactions*, and UITF 28 *Lease Incentives*. The basic approaches are similar, but there are differences of detail. The principal areas of difference are:

- **Definition of a finance lease**. Although the definition is based on the transfer of substantially all the risks and rewards of ownership to the lessee, the UK standard adds a rebuttable presumption that this is assumed to have occurred if the present value of minimum lease payments amounts to 90 per cent or more of the fair value of the leased asset. In practice, whilst significant weight is placed on this numerical threshold, the type of factors listed in IAS 17 (r1997) are looked to in order to determine the substance of the lease in borderline cases. Where a lease forms one part of a more complex transaction, then FRS 5 would be applied and would require the substance of the series of linked transactions to be portrayed.

- **Lessor recognition of income**. The UK standard requires lessor's to allocate rentals receivable such that income is recognised on the net cash investment method. This is a post-tax method which results in income representing a constant percentage of the cash invested in the lease, including tax and other cash flows. The method is strongly supported by the UK lessor industry for whom the tax impact of leases is very material, but was removed from IAS 17 in the 1997 revision in favour of the pre-tax net investment method. The net investment method is only permitted in the UK for lessors where it is a reasonable approximation to the required method. It is acceptable to allocate an amount out of gross earnings equal to the lessor's estimated cost of finance, with the balance being recognised on a systematic basis.
- UITF 28, *Lease Incentives*, addresses the accounting for lease incentives from both the lessee and lessor perspectives and replaces UITF 12 *Lessee Accounting for Reverse Premiums and Similar Incentives.* UK GAAP is now consistent with IAS 17 (r1997) in respect of such incentives.
- In December 1999 the ASB issued a discussion paper *Leases: Implementation of a New Approach.* This was the G4+1 paper referred to in **24.3**. The ASB intends to proceed with a revision of SSAP 21 on the basis of this paper although some concerns have been expressed, in particular potential inconsistencies with FRS 5 *Reporting the Substance of Transactions.* The treatment of investment properties which are currently viewed as operating leases is an area of considerable debate as the general proposals of the discussion paper would lead such lessors to record a financial asset and a residual interest. In view of these concerns and the uncertain timing for the progression of the proposals by the IASB, the UK will not proceed until it is known where the IASB is going in this respect. It is, therefore, likely to be some time before an exposure draft of a revised UK standard is issued.

24.12 Comparison with US GAAP

US GAAP is principally set out in SFAS 13 *Leases.* As with UK GAAP, the basic approaches are similar, but there are differences of detail. The principal areas of difference are:

- **Terminology**. The US refer to a finance lease as a capital lease. Also, for a lessor, further sub-divisions of capital leases deal with specific circumstances: sales-type lease, direct financing lease, and leveraged lease.
- **Definition of a capital (finance) lease**. The US definition of a capital lease is not based on the transfer of substantially all risks and rewards of ownership. Rather it is met if any one of four specific tests are met. These relate to: transfer of ownership, bargain purchase options, lease term as a proportion (75 per cent) of the asset's life, and present value of minimum lease payments as a proportion (90 per cent) of the asset's fair value.
- **Lessor recognition of income**. The net investment method used in IAS 17 (r1997) is used, but further complex calculations arise where a finance lease involves third party financing (leveraged leases).
- **Manufacturer or dealer lessor**. Discount rate to be used is the interest rate implicit in the lease.
- **Sale and leaseback transactions**. General requirement to defer and amortise gains and losses, but immediate recognition required in defined circumstances involving property.

24.13 Examples from published financial statements

Note that the excerpts given do not always comply in full with all aspects of IAS and as such are not necessarily examples of best practice but merely of current practice.

Example 24.2

Leasing

Leases are classified as finance leases whenever the terms of the lease transfer substantially all the risks and rewards of ownership to the lessee. All other leases are classified as operating leases.

The group as lessor

Amounts due from lessees under finance leases are recorded as receivables at the amount of the group's net investment in the leases. Finance income is allocated to accounting periods so as to reflect a constant periodic rate of return on the group's net investment outstanding in respect of the leases.

Rental income from operating leases is recognised on a straight-line basis over the term of the relevant lease.

The group as lessee

Assets held under finance leases are recognised as assets of the group at their fair value at the date of acquisition. The corresponding liability to the lessor is disclosed as a finance lease obligation. Finance costs represent the difference between the total leasing commitments and the fair value of the assets acquired. They are charged to the income statement over the term of the relevant lease and at interest rates applicable to the lease on the remaining balance of the obligation for each accounting period.

Changes in accounting policy

Leases: IAS 17 (1997)

The accounting policy in respect of accounting for leases has been altered to comply with IAS 17 (revised 1997). A number of assets leased by Barloworld's leasing company to other group companies were previously not capitalised, although the assets were included in group receivables. As a result of adopting IAS 17 there has been a reallocation of these assets from receivables to property, plant and equipment. There is also a difference between amounts previously expensed as lease charges and the amounts are now charged to depreciation and finance costs.

Another consequence of adopting IAS 17 from a lessor perspective has been an increase in the amount disclosed as an investment in finance leases and finance income.

Barloworld Limited
South Africa
30 September 2000
International Accounting Standards

Example 24.3

Tangible fixed assets (extract)

Assets held under leasing agreements which may be considered as asset purchases in economic terms (finance leases) are capitalised as tangible fixed assets at the estimated present value of the underlying lease payments and depreciated over their useful service lives or the shorter lease period. Leasing commitments are shown under financial liabilities.

In the case of sale-and-leaseback transactions resulting in a finance lease, any profit or loss from the sale is deferred and amortised over the lease period. The associated lease finance costs are distributed over the lease period in such a way as to present a true and fair view of the actual costs incurred in each accounting period.

In the case of sale-and-leaseback transactions resulting in an operating lease, any profit from the sale is taken straight to the profit and loss account. Any loss whose market value is likely to be compensated for by reduced future leasing payments is capitalised and depreciated over the length of the leasing period; any other loss is recorded in the profit and loss account for the period concerned.

Leasing liabilities on leased assets defined as operating leases and thus having a rental character are expensed via the profit and loss account over the lease period.

SAirGroup
Switzerland
31 December 2000
International Accounting Standards

CHAPTER 25

Employee benefits

25.1 Sources

IAS 1 (r1997)	*Presentation of Financial Statements.*
IAS 2 (r1993)	*Inventories.*
IAS 8 (r1993)	*Net Profit or Loss for the Period, Fundamental Errors and Changes in Accounting Policies.*
IAS 16 (r1998)	*Property, Plant and Equipment.*
IAS 19 (r2000)	*Employee Benefits* (effective 1 January 2001).
IAS 22 (r1998)	*Business Combinations.*
IAS 24	*Related Party Disclosures.*
IAS 37	*Provisions, Contingent Liabilities and Contingent Assets.*
IAS 39 (r2000)	*Financial Instruments: Recognition and Measurement* (effective 1 January 2001).

25.2 Brief summary of the requirements

IAS 19 (r2000) addresses:

- short-term employee benefits, such as wages, salaries and social security contributions, paid annual leave and paid sick leave, profit sharing and bonuses (payable within 12 months of the year end), and non-monetary benefits for current employees;
- post-employment benefits (e.g., pensions, other retirement benefits, post-employment life insurance and post employment medical care);
- other long-term employee benefits (e.g., long-service leave);
- termination benefits; and
- equity compensation benefits.

(IAS 19 (r2000).4)

IAS 19 (r2000) deals with when the costs should be recognised and the amount that should be recognised. It also sets disclosure requirements. The following table summarises the accounting requirements.

Type of benefit	Accounting treatment
Short-term employee benefits: (see **25.6**)	Recognise costs when the employee has rendered service in exchange for those costs.
Post-employment benefits – defined contribution plans (see **25.8**)	Recognise contributions as employee renders service in exchange for them.
Post-employment benefits – defined benefit plans (see **25.9**)	• Recognise current service cost as an expense. • Measure plan assets at fair value. • Measure plan liabilities using the projected unit credit method and a discount rate by reference to high quality corporate bonds. • Amortise net cumulative unrecognised actuarial gains and losses beyond a 10 per cent corridor over the estimated average remaining service lives of participating employees. • Recognise past service cost on a straight line basis over the average period until they vest. • Recognise gains or losses on a curtailment or settlement when the curtailment or settlement occurs.
Other long-term employee benefits (see **25.14**)	Simplified version of defined benefit plans with actuarial gains and losses and all past service costs recognised immediately.
Termination benefits (see **25.15**)	Recognise when, and only when, the enterprise is demonstrably committed to terminate employment or to provide benefits as a result of an offer to encourage voluntary redundancy.
Equity compensation benefits (see **25.16**)	No recognition or measurement requirements given. Disclosure only.

25.3 Development of the requirements

The revision of IAS 19 in 1998 introduced a fundamental change in the requirements that had gone before.

Firstly the scope of the Standard was significantly expanded. Previously it had only dealt with retirement benefit costs; following the 1998 revision it also addressed accounting for short-term employment benefits (e.g., wages and salaries), other long-term employee benefits (e.g., long service leave) and termination benefits; and included disclosures in respect of equity compensation benefits.

Secondly the accounting for defined benefit plans was fundamentally amended with requirements introduced as to the balance sheet accounting; and a process adopted that follows more closely the requirements of the US

SFAS 87 *Employers Accounting for Pensions,* (e.g., plan assets fair valued, use of a 10 per cent corridor before actuarial gains or losses are spread).

A further revision to IAS 19 was made in 2000 to address certain pension fund arrangements which did not meet the previous definition of 'plan assets' in IAS 19 (r1998). The problem arose because in certain countries (e.g., Sweden and Germany) the employer retains an obligation to pay the benefits directly due to certain legal requirements. The third requirement of the definition of plan assets in IAS 19 (r1998) was that 'to the extent that sufficient assets are in the fund, the enterprise will have no legal or constructive obligation to pay the related employee benefits directly.' IAS 19 (r2000) changes the definition of plan assets to address this and introduces recognition, measurement and disclosure requirements for reimbursements (see **25.9.6**).

The title of IAS 19 was changed from *Retirement Benefit Costs* (IAS 19 (r1998)) to *Employee Benefits* (IAS 19 (r2000)), the new title more fully reflecting the scope of the Standard.

In 2000, the G4+1 issued a discussion paper on 'Share-based payments'. The paper discusses the accounting treatment of transactions where an entity purchases goods or services from other parties, such as suppliers or employees, by issuing them shares or share options. It focuses on accounting for employee share schemes. It proposes that share-based payment transactions should be recognised in the company's financial statements, measured at the fair value of the shares or share options at vesting date. In most cases, an option pricing model should be used to measure the fair value of an option. The paper also proposes that an estimate of the transaction amount should be accrued over the performance period and finalised on vesting date. Share-based payments has been identified by the IASB as a priority matter. IAS 19 (r2000) only addresses the disclosure of equity compensation benefits and does not deal with recognition or measurement issues. The IASB has put this topic on its official agenda as one of the first leadership projects it will take on (see Chapter **2**).

25.4 Scope

IAS 19 (r2000) applies to all employee benefits (i.e., forms of consideration given by an enterprise in exchange for services rendered by employees). Thus it applies to employee benefits under:

- formal plans and agreements between an enterprise and its employees (individually and on a group basis) or the representatives of its employees;

- national, state, industry or multi-employer plans where the employer is required to contribute pursuant to law or industry arrangements; and
- informal practices that give rise to a constructive obligation.

(IAS 19 (r2000).3)

> 'Employee benefits include benefits provided to either employees or their dependants and may be settled by payments (or the provision of goods or services) made either directly to the employees, to their spouses, children or other dependants or to others, such as insurance companies.'

(IAS 19 (r2000).5)

An employee may provide services to an enterprise on a full time, part time, permanent, casual or temporary basis. For the purpose of IAS 19 (r2000), employees include directors and other management personnel.

(IAS 19 (r2000).6)

25.5 Definitions

IAS 19 (r2000) includes 22 separate definitions. Those immediately below define the five forms of employee benefit covered by the Standard. The other definitions, which are used in explaining the accounting and disclosure requirements, are addressed below within the sections dealing with the requirements for each employee benefit in turn.

> '**Employee benefits** are all forms of consideration given by an enterprise in exchange for service rendered by employees.'
>
> '**Short-term employee benefits** are employee benefits (other than termination benefits and equity compensation benefits) which fall due wholly within twelve months after the end of the period in which the employees render the related service.'
>
> '**Post-employment benefits** are employee benefits (other than termination benefits and equity compensation benefits) which are payable after the completion of employment.'
>
> '**Other long-term employee benefits** are employee benefits (other than post-employment benefits, termination benefits and equity compensation benefits) which do not fall due wholly within twelve months after the end of the period in which the employees render the related service.'
>
> '**Termination benefits** are employee benefits payable as a result of either:
>
> (a) an enterprise's decision to terminate an employee's employment before the normal retirement date; or
>
> (b) an employee's decision to accept voluntary redundancy in exchange for those benefits.'
>
> '**Equity compensation benefits** are employee benefits under which either:
>
> (a) employees are entitled to receive equity financial instruments issued by the enterprise (or its parent); or

(b) the amount of the enterprise's obligation to employees depends on the future price of equity financial instruments issued by the enterprise.'

(IAS 19 (r2000).7)

25.6 Short-term employee benefits

Short-term employee benefits includes items such as:

- wages, salaries and social security contributions;
- short-term compensated absences (e.g., vacation or annual leave, sickness and short-term disability, maternity or paternity leave, jury service and military service – see **25.6.3**);
- profit sharing and bonus payments (see **25.6.4**) and
- non-monetary benefits.

(IAS 19 (r2000).8)

Applying the definition (see **25.5**), the above items should 'fall due wholly within twelve months after the end of the period in which the employees render the related service'. So, for example, the short-term compensated absences should be expected to occur, and bonuses be payable, within 12 months of the end of the period in which employees render the related service.

25.6.1 Recognition and measurement

The Standard is very specific as regards the entries in the income statement and balance sheet. An enterprise should recognise the undiscounted amount of short-term employee benefits expected to be paid in exchange for services rendered by an employee in an accounting period:

- in the income statement as an expense, unless another IAS requires or permits inclusion of the cost of the benefits in the cost of an asset; and
- in the balance sheet, as a liability (accrued expense), after deducting any amounts already paid; as an asset (prepaid expense), if the amount already paid exceeds the undiscounted amount of the benefits to the extent that the prepayment will be recoverable, for example by a reduction in future payments or a cash refund.

(IAS 19 (r2000).10)

The cost of all short-term employee benefits should be recognised as noted above. No actuarial assumptions are required (hence there are no actuarial gains and losses to address) and (due to their short-term nature) obligations are dealt with on an undiscounted basis. (IAS 19 (r2000).9) The Standard provides guidance on the application of the general recognition requirement to short-term compensated absences and profit sharing and bonus plans as noted below (see **25.6.3** and **25.6.4**).

25.6.2 *Disclosures*

No specific disclosures are required by IAS 19 (r2000) regarding short-term employee benefits although it notes that other standards may require disclosure (e.g., IAS 1 (r1997) and IAS 24) (see Chapters **14** and **17**). (IAS 19 (r2000).23)

25.6.3 *Short-term compensated absences*

Short-term compensated absences may be classified as accumulating or non-accumulating. Accumulating compensated absences are those that are carried forward and can be used in future accounting periods if the current period's entitlement is not used in full. Accumulating compensated absences may be further sub-divided as vesting (where employees are entitled to a cash payment for unused entitlement on leaving the enterprise) and non-vesting (where no entitlement arises). (IAS 19 (r2000).13)

Non-accumulating compensated absences are not capable of being carried forward; that is any unused entitlement is lost at the end of the current period and the employee is not entitled to a cash payment for unused entitlement on leaving the enterprise. (IAS 19 (r2000).16)

In applying the general rule in **25.6.1** to the expected cost of short-term compensated absences:

- for accumulating absences, the expense should be recognised when the employees render service that increases their entitlement to future compensated absences based on the additional amount that the enterprise expects to pay as a result of the unused entitlement accumulated at the balance sheet date; and
- for non-accumulating compensated absences the expense should be recognised as the absences occur.

(IAS 19 (r2000).11 & 14)

For accumulating absences the difference between vesting and non-vesting does not affect whether an obligation exists and should be recognised, but does effect the measurement, as there is a possibility that employees may leave before they use an accumulating non-vesting entitlement. (IAS 19 (r2000).13)

Example 25.1

An enterprise has 200 employees, who are each entitled to 10 working days of paid leave each year. Paid leave is first taken out of the current year's entitlement and then out of the balance brought forward from the previous year (a LIFO basis). Unused leave cannot be carried forward more than one year. At 31 December 20X0 the average unused entitlement was 3 days per employee (i.e., 600 days in total). The enterprise expects, based on past experience which is expected to continue, that 175 employees will take no more than their annual entitlement in 20X1 and that the remaining 25 employees will, in total, use 70 days of the entitlement brought forward from 20X0.

The enterprise recognises a liability and an expense at 31 December 20X0 of 70 days.

Had the employees been able to carry forward holiday indefinitely, and were entitled to a cash payment for unused holiday entitlement on leaving the enterprise (i.e., a vested entitlement), then the full 600 days would be accrued at 31 December 20X0.

25.6.4 Profit sharing and bonus plans

In applying the general rule at **25.6.1** to the expected cost of profit sharing and bonus plans, an enterprise should recognise the expected cost when and only when:

- it has a present legal or constructive obligation to make such payments as a result of past events; and
- a reliable estimate can be made.

In this context a present obligation exists when and only when the enterprise has no realistic alternative but to make the payments.

(IAS 19 (r2000).17)

The requirements above follow closely those relating to the recognition of provisions generally under IAS 37 (see Chapter **11**).

The Standard (IAS 19 (r2000).18) notes that an employee's entitlement to a profit share may depend on them staying with the enterprise for a specified period. In such circumstances, the plan creates a constructive obligation and the fact that employees may leave without receiving payments is reflected in the measurement of the constructive obligation.

The example illustrating IAS 19 (r2000).18 has the same accounting period end date, profit period end date and required service period end date and does not make clear what happens if the requirement for continued service extends beyond the end date of the accounting period.

In such a case, returning to the requirement of IAS 19 (r2000).10 (see **25.6.1**), the enterprise should recognise the amount of benefit to be paid in exchange for the employees service which implies the bonus is pro-rated between the accounting periods. Paragraph 18 supports this approach by noting that a constructive obligation arises 'as employees render service' so that the uncertainty that some employees may leave before becoming entitled to a profit share or bonus is reflected in making the estimate rather than in deferring recognition of the obligation until the employee completes the entitlement period.

Example 25.2

A profit sharing plan requires an enterprise to pay a specified proportion of its net profit for the financial year to 30 June 2002 to employees who serve throughout the calendar year 2002. If no employees leave during the year, the total profit sharing payments for the year will be 3 per cent of net profit. The enterprise estimates that staff turnover will reduce the payments to 2.5 per cent of net profit.

The enterprise recognises a liability and an expense of 2.5 per cent of 50 per cent of the net profit at 30 June 2002 in proportion to the part of the entitlement period for which the employees have rendered service that falls into the accounting period. If the plan had been in existence in the calendar year 2001, the financial year to 30 June 2002 would also be charged in respect of the last six months of the entitlement period for 2001. That amount would be fixed as it would have been paid at 30 June 2002 or the actual staff turnover for 2001 would have been known.

25.7 Post-employment benefits

'**Post-employment benefit plans** are formal or informal arrangements under which an enterprise provides post-employment benefits for one or more employees.'

(IAS 19 (r2000).7)

The above definition of post-employment benefits captures retirement benefits (e.g., pensions) and other post retirement benefits (e.g., post-employment life insurance or medical care). If an enterprise provides such benefits, the requirements of IAS 19 (r2000) apply irrespective of whether a separate entity is established to receive contributions and to pay benefits.

(IAS 19 (r2000).24)

25.7.1 Types of post-employment benefit plans

IAS 19 (r2000) classifies post-employment benefit plans into two main types:

- **defined contribution plans** – under which an enterprise's legal or constructive obligation is limited to the amount that it agrees to contribute to the fund. The actuarial and investment risk fall on the employee. The amounts to be paid as retirement benefits are determined by reference to contributions to a fund together with investment earnings thereon (see **25.8**).

- **defined benefit plans** – under which an enterprise's obligation is to provide agreed benefits to current and former employees. The actuarial and investment risk fall substantively on the enterprise. The amounts received by employees as retirement benefits are determined by reference to a formula usually based on employee's remuneration and/or years of service (see **25.9**).

(IAS 19 (r2000).25 to 27)

The definitions below are reproduced from paragraph 7 of IAS 19 (r2000).

'**Defined contribution plans** are post-employment benefit plans under which an enterprise pays fixed contributions into a separate entity (a fund) and will have no legal or constructive obligation to pay further contributions if the fund does not hold sufficient assets to pay all employee benefits relating to employee service in the current and prior periods.'

'**Defined benefit plans** are post-employment benefit plans other than defined contribution plans.'

The accounting treatment and required disclosures depend upon which of the above two categories the plan falls within. In addition to addressing defined contribution and defined benefit plans generally the Standard also gives guidance on how the requirements should be applied to insured benefits, multi-employer plans and state plans. These are discussed in **25.11** to **25.13**.

25.8 Defined contribution plans

The revision of IAS 19 in 1998 did not lead to any major change in the fundamentals of accounting for defined contribution plans but did make mention of the balance sheet treatment. The balance sheet should reflect any prepayment or accrual of the pension contribution, and contributions should be discounted if due more than 12 months after the end of the period to which the related employee service relates.

25.8.1 Recognition and measurement

The Standard is very specific as regards the entries in the income statement and balance sheet. An enterprise should recognise the contributions payable to a defined contribution plan in exchange for services rendered by an employee in an accounting period:

- in the income statement as an expense, unless another IAS requires or permits inclusion of the contribution in the cost of an asset (e.g., IAS 2 (r1993), *Inventories* and IAS 16 (r1998), *Property, Plant and Equipment*); and
- in the balance sheet, as a:
  - liability (accrued expense), after deducting any contribution already paid (to the extent that not all the contributions due for service before the balance sheet date have been paid at that date); or as an
  - asset (prepaid expense), if the amount already paid exceeds the contributions due for service before the balance sheet date, to the extent that the prepayment will be recoverable, for example by a reduction in future payments or a cash refund.

(IAS 19 (r2000).44)

Where contributions to a defined contribution plan do not fall due wholly within twelve months after the end of the period in which the employees render the related service, they should be discounted using the discount rate specified by the Standard for post-employment benefit obligations (see **25.9.3**) (i.e., determined by reference to market yields at the balance sheet date on high quality corporate bonds).

(IAS 19 (r2000).45)

25.8.2 Disclosure

The only disclosure specified by the Standard is the amount recognised as an expense for defined contribution plans.

(IAS 19 (r2000).46)

In addition enterprises may find it helpful to the users of their financial statements to disclose:

- a general description of the plan;
- any other significant matters relating to retirement benefits that effect comparability with the previous period.

Other standards may require additional disclosures, for example IAS 24, *Related Party Disclosures*, in respect of contributions in respect of key management personnel.

25.9 Defined benefit plans

Accounting for defined benefit plans is much more complex than the requirement for defined contribution plans. It requires actuarial techniques and assumptions to be used to measure the obligation and expense, the obligations being measured on a discounted basis. The possibility of actuarial gains and losses also arises, as assumptions used will usually differ from actual outcomes.

Defined benefit plans may be funded or unfunded. They may be funded by the employer and, sometimes, the employees, making payments into an entity or fund that is legally separate from the reporting entity. Even in the latter case the employer will be underwriting the risk that the separate fund may be unable to pay benefits as they fall due and hence the expense recognised is not limited to the contribution due for the period. (IAS 19 (r2000).49)

An enterprise should consider both its legal and constructive obligations when accounting for a defined benefit plan. A constructive obligation arises when an enterprise has no realistic alternative but to pay employee benefits, for example where a change in the enterprise's informal practices would cause unacceptable damage to its relationship with employees. An example cited by the Standard is where the formal terms of the plan permit the employer enterprise to terminate its obligations. In practice such a course of action would be difficult if employees are to be retained so that, unless there is evidence to the contrary, it will be assumed that the enterprise will continue to provide benefits over the remaining working lives of employees. (IAS 19 (r2000).52 and 53)

The revision of IAS 19 in 1998 brought about a major change in the fundamentals of accounting for defined benefit plans. The Standard requires:

- a single specified actuarial valuation method;
- use of a discount rate tied to high quality corporate bonds; and
- plan assets to be market valued.

25.9.1 Recognition and measurement

Balance sheet
The defined benefit liability recognised in the balance sheet is the net total of:

- the present value of the defined benefit obligation at the balance sheet date (i.e., the gross obligation before deducting the fair value of plan assets) (see **25.9.2**);
- plus actuarial gains, less actuarial losses, not recognised in the income statement (see **25.9.4**);
- less any past service cost not yet recognised in the income statement (see **25.9.5**);
- less the fair value at the balance sheet date of plan assets out of which the obligations are to be settled directly (see **25.9.6**);
- less the unrecognised part of the transitional liability (see **25.9.9**).

If the above amount is negative the resulting asset recognised in the balance sheet should be the lower of:

- the net total calculated above; and
- the net total of:
  - any actuarial losses and past service costs not recognised as an expense; and
  - the present value (using the discount rate specified in the Standard – see **25.9.3**) of any economic benefits available in the form of refunds from the plan or reductions in future contributions to the plan.

(IAS 19 (r2000).58)

Disclosure is required of the amount not recognised as an asset because of the above limits (see **25.9.10**).

The restriction above seeks to ensure that any asset recognised does not exceed the future economic benefit that it represents for the enterprise. Application of the restriction does not over-ride the delayed recognition requirements in respect of actuarial losses (see **25.9.5**) and past service costs (see **25.9.4**) but does override the transitional provisions (see **25.9.9**).

(IAS 19 (r2000).60)

Income statement

The enterprise should recognise the net total of the following amounts as expense or income:

- current service cost (see **25.9.2**);
- interest cost (see **25.9.3**);
- expected return on plan assets and on any reimbursement rights (see **25.9.6**);
- actuarial gains and losses to the extent recognised (see **25.9.4**);
- past service cost (see **25.9.5**), to the extent recognised; and
- effect of curtailments and settlements (see **25.9.7**)
- less the transitional liability to the extent recognised (see **25.9.9**).

(IAS 19 (r2000).61)

The initial interpretation of the above requirement is that a single net figure is recognised in the income statement. The example disclosure in Appendix B of the Standard supports this approach as it shows the net cost as being included within 'Staff costs'. However, paragraph 120 of the Standard requires disclosure of 'the line item(s) of the income statement' in which the above components are included. This would appear to allow the components to be allocated to different categories of the income statement (e.g., cost of goods sold, selling expenses or administration.) Interest cost and expected return on plan assets may be included in finance costs after the results of operating activities.

Where part of the cost above is permitted or required to be included in the cost of an asset by another IAS (See IAS 2 (r1993) and IAS 16 (r1998), Chapter **10**) it will include the appropriate proportion of the above items. (IAS 19 (r2000).62) For example, the cost of inventory may include the employment cost, including retirement benefits, related to the production workers.

If the net total above is an item of income it will be limited by the restriction on the size of the asset (see **Balance sheet** section above).

The table below illustrates the relationships between the entries in the income statement and the movement in the balance sheet figure.

	Income statement	Plan Assets	PV of plan Obligation	Unamortised actuarial gain/loss	Unamortised past service cost	Unamortised transitional expense
B/f		X	X	X	X	X
Contributions		X				
Benefits paid		(X)	(X)			
Current service cost	X		X			
Interest cost on obligation	X		X			
Expected return on plan assets	(X)	X				
Actuarial gain/loss on plan assets		X		X		
Actuarial gain/loss on obligation			X	X		
Amortisation of actuarial gain/loss	X			(X)		
Past service cost			X		X	
Amortisation of past service cost	X				(X)	
Amortisation of transitional expense	X					(X)
Curtailments/ settlements	X	X	X	X	X	(X)
Income/Expense	X					
C/f		X	X	X	X	X

25.9.2 *Defined benefit obligation and current service cost*

'The present value of a **defined benefit obligation** is the present value, without deducting any plan assets, of expected future payments required to settle the obligation resulting from employee service in the current and prior periods.'

'**Current service cost** is the increase in the present value of the defined benefit obligation resulting from employee service in the current period.'

(IAS 19 (r2000).7)

The final cost of a defined benefit plan is influenced by many factors. The use of actuarial techniques to value and allocate an obligation to accounting periods allows an enterprise to measure an obligation with sufficient reliability to justify recognition of a liability. (IAS 19 (r2000).68) The whole of the obligation is discounted, even if part of it falls due within 12 months of the balance sheet date. (IAS 19 (r2000).66)

A number of steps are required in order to measure the present value of a defined benefit obligation, as defined above, and the associated current service cost. These steps are:

- apply an actuarial valuation method;
- attribute benefit to the employees' periods of service; and
- make actuarial assumptions.

These steps are considered immediately below.

Actuarial valuation method

The projected unit credit method should be used to determine the present value of an enterprise's defined benefit obligation, the related current service cost and, where applicable, past service cost. (IAS 19 (r2000).64) The projected unit credit method (also known as the projected unit method) is an accrued benefits valuation method. IAS 19, since its revision in 1998, does not, unlike earlier versions of the Standard, permit the use of an alternative projected benefit valuation method.

Attributing benefits to periods of service

An enterprise should attribute benefits to periods of service under the plan's benefit structure when determining the present value of the defined benefit obligation, current service cost and past service cost.

An exception to the foregoing is made where the benefit levels are skewed to the later years of an employee's service. In such a case, benefits should be attributed on a straight line basis from the date that service first leads to benefits being earned under the plan (whether or not they are conditional on further service); until the date that further service yields no further material benefits other than from salary increases. This reflects the fact that entitlement to benefits at the higher level is earned by the employee's service throughout the period. (IAS 19 (r2000).67 and 70)

Example 25.3

From IAS 19 (r2000)

A post-employment medical plan reimburses 10 per cent of an employee's post-employment medical costs if the employee leaves after more than ten and less than twenty years of service and 50 per cent of those costs if the employee leaves after twenty or more years of service.

Service in later years will lead to a materially higher level of benefit than in earlier years. Therefore, for employees expected to leave after twenty or more years, the enterprise attributes benefit on a straight-line basis (as required by IAS 19 (r2000).68). Service beyond 20 years will lead to no material amount of further benefits. Therefore, the benefit attributed to each of the first 20 years is 2.5 per cent of the present value of the expected medical costs (50 per cent divided by 20).

For employees expected to leave between ten and twenty years, the benefit attributed to each of the first ten years is 1 per cent of the present value of the expected medical costs. For these employees, no benefit is attributed to service between the end of the tenth year and the estimated date of leaving.

For employees expected to leave within ten years, no benefit is attributed.

By attributing benefit to periods of service (as required by the projected unit credit method) it is possible to determine current service period cost, past service period costs (where applicable) and the defined benefit obligation. Even where the benefits have not vested, as they are conditional on future service, a constructive obligation arises in respect of current and past service. In such cases the probability that some employees might not reach the vesting criteria is reflected in the measurement of the obligation rather than its existence. Similarly, certain post retirement benefits (e.g., medical benefits) are only payable if a certain event occurs once the employee is no longer employed. Nonetheless, the obligation arises as services are rendered that provide entitlement to the benefit and the probability of the occurrence of the event leading to a payment affects the measurement of the obligation not its existence. (IAS 19 (r2000).68 and 69).

Actuarial assumptions

The actuarial assumptions should be unbiased and mutually compatible. (IAS 19 (r2000).72) Actuarial assumptions are an enterprise's best estimates of the variables that will determine the ultimate cost of providing post-employment benefits. They should be neither imprudent nor excessively conservative (unbiased) and should reflect the economic relationships between factors such as inflation, rates of salary increase, return on plan assets and discount rates (mutually compatible). (IAS 19 (r2000).74 and 75)

Actuarial assumptions comprise:

- demographic assumptions about the future characteristics of current and former employees (and their dependants) who are eligible for benefits. Demographic assumptions deal with matters such as:
  - rates of employee turnover, disability and early retirement;
  - the proportion of plan members with dependants who will be eligible for benefits; and
  - claim rates under medical plans; and
- financial assumptions, dealing with items such as:
  - the discount rate (see **25.9.3**);
  - future salary and benefit levels (see below);
  - in the case of medical benefits, future medical costs, including, where material, the cost of administering claims and benefit payments (see below); and
  - the expected rate of return on plan assets (see **25.9.6**).

(IAS 19 (r2000).73)

Financial assumptions should be based on market assumptions at the balance sheet date for the period over which the post-employment benefit obligations will be settled. Assumptions should be determined in actual, as opposed to 'real' (inflation-adjusted), terms. They should not be adjusted to real terms unless such measures are more reliable (e.g., in a hyper-inflationary economy – see Chapter **28**). (IAS 19 (r2000).76 and 77)

When considering **future salary increases** account should be taken of inflation, seniority, promotion and any other relevant factors (both internal and external), such as the scarcity or surplus of potential employees with the required skills. (IAS 19 (r2000).83 and 84)

The post-employment benefit obligation should reflect plan terms relating to **benefit levels** and any constructive obligation that extends those terms, at the balance sheet date. This would include an obligation to increase benefits to mitigate the effects of inflation (either as required by the terms of the plan or in line with the enterprise's past history of increasing benefits, i.e., a constructive obligation). Similarly it would include benefit improvements (required by the plan terms, legislation or established practice of the enterprise) arising from an actuarial gain that has already been recognised in the financial statements. (IAS 19 (r2000).83 and 85)

Certain post-employment benefits are linked to levels of state provided benefits, such as state provided retirement benefits and medical care. In such cases the post-employment benefit obligation should reflect estimated future changes in those state benefits if, and only if, the changes to the state benefits were enacted before the balance sheet date or past history and other reliable experience indicate the state benefits will change in a predictable manner (for example, in line with general salary or price levels). (IAS 19 (r2000).83 and 87)

Benefit changes that are not included in the actuarial assumption as they do not arise from the formal terms of the plan or from a constructive obligation would result in past service costs to the extent they have a retrospective impact; and current service costs to the extent that they change benefits for service after the change. (IAS 19 (r2000).86)

When measuring the obligation arising in respect of **post-employment medical benefits** additional assumptions are required. They include general inflation and specific changes in future medical costs, level and frequency of claims, technological advances, changes in the health status of participants in the plan and changes in the utilisation and delivery of health care. In making these assumptions reference may be made to historical data from the enterprise's own records and external data from other enterprises, insurers, medical providers and other sources. It is important that such assumptions are adjusted where the population providing the historical data differs from that for which the obligation arises. For example the level and frequency of claims may be sensitive to age, sex and current health status of those benefiting under the plan. The estimate of future medical costs should take account of contributions due from beneficiaries towards medical cost, based upon the terms of the plan, or additional constructive obligations, at the balance sheet date and also any cost that may be met by the state or other medical providers. (IAS 19 (r2000).88 to 91)

Frequency of actuarial valuation

The Standard does not specify the frequency of valuations, either to measure the plan assets or the present value of the defined benefit obligation. It requires that the valuations be performed 'with sufficient regularity that the amounts recognised in the financial statements do not differ materially from the amounts that would be determined at the balance sheet date.' (IAS 19 (r2000).56)

The Standard does not require the involvement of a qualified actuary (IAS 19 (r2000).57) but in practice it will be difficult to value defined benefit obligations without actuarial involvement.

An enterprise is not precluded from using a detailed valuation of the obligation at a date prior to the balance sheet date provided it is updated for any material transactions or other changes in the period up to the balance sheet date. (IAS 19 (r2000).57)

Although local legislation may not require a full plan valuation every year it may be necessary, to meet the requirement of paragraph 56 of the Standard (see above), for some aspects of the valuation to be reviewed at each balance sheet date. For example the fair value of plan assets and financial assumptions such as the discount rate and the rate of salary increase. Demographic assumptions, such as mortality rates and rate of employee turnover, may not need to be reviewed annually.

25.9.3 Interest cost and discount rate

'**Interest cost** is the increase during a period in the present value of a defined benefit obligation which arises because the benefits are one period closer to settlement.' (IAS 19 (r2000).7)

The interest cost is determined as:

Discount rate determined at start of period	×	Present value of the defined benefit obligation throughout that period

Note that the interest cost is calculated on the defined benefit obligation (i.e., the gross obligation before deducting the fair value of plan assets) not the balance sheet liability. Since it is the obligation 'throughout the period' the calculation should reflect material changes in the obligation. (IAS 19 (r2000).82)

The discount rate used **should not** reflect risk specific to the enterprise, the risk that actual experience may differ from assumptions, or the actuarial or investment risk. It **should** reflect the time value of money. The Standard requires that 'The rate used to discount post-employment benefit obligations (both funded and unfunded) should be determined by reference to market yields at the balance sheet date on high quality corporate bonds. In countries where there is no deep market in such bonds, the market yields (at the balance sheet date) on government bonds should be used. The currency and term of the corporate bonds or government bonds should be consistent with the currency and estimated term of the post-employment benefit obligations.' (IAS 19 (r2000).78 and 79).

The use of an AA corporate bond rate (as required by FRS 17 in the UK – see **25.17**) would be appropriate.

The requirement for the term of the bonds to be consistent with the term of the obligations means they should reflect the estimated timing of the benefit payments. The Standard notes that in practice this may be achieved by 'applying a single weighted average discount rate that reflects the estimated timing and amount of benefit payments and the currency in which the benefits are to be paid'. (IAS 19 (r2000).80)

If there is no deep market for bonds of a sufficiently long maturity date to match that of all the obligation payments, the enterprise may extrapolate current market rates for a shorter period along the yield curve. (IAS 19 (r2000).81)

25.9.4 *Actuarial gains and losses*

> '**Actuarial gains and losses** comprise:
>
> (a) experience adjustments (the effects of differences between the previous actuarial assumptions and what has actually occurred); and
>
> (b) the effects of changes in actuarial assumptions.'
>
> (IAS 19 (r2000).7)

Actuarial gains and losses can arise from changes in the present value of the defined benefit obligation or the fair value of the related plan assets. They arise because actual outcomes or current forecasts differ from the forecasts of earlier periods. For example, actual return on plan assets differs from the expected return, actual rate of employee turnover differs from the expected rate, or changes occur in forecast salary increases. (IAS 19 (r2000).94)

The Standard takes the view that, in the long term, actuarial gains and losses may offset each other and so adopts a range (commonly referred to as a 'corridor') around the best estimate of the post-employment benefit obligation. The minimum requirement of IAS 19 (r2000) is that to the extent the unrecognised gains and losses exceed a corridor of 10 per cent, then that excess is recognised in the income statement over a specified time span. Gains and losses falling within the 10 per cent corridor can remain unrecognised in the income statement indefinitely. The unrecognised cumulative actuarial gains and losses will form part of the net deferred benefit liability or asset (see **25.9.1**). The unrecognised cumulative actuarial gains and losses will comprise both those within the 10 per cent corridor that are being deferred indefinitely and that portion outside the corridor that has not been recognised in the income statement at the balance sheet date. Alternatively, a faster method of recognising the actuarial gain or loss is allowed provided certain criteria are met (see below). (IAS 19 (r2000).95)

In the news release that accompanied IAS 19 (r1998) the Board noted that 'In particular, the IASC Board does not wish to discourage a consistent policy of recognising all actuarial gains and losses immediately'. Further, in the Basis for Conclusions section in paragraph 41 of appendix C to the Standard, it is noted that 'The Board found the immediate recognition approach attractive. However, the Board believes that it is not feasible to use this approach for actuarial gains and losses until the Board resolves substantial issues about performance reporting. When the Board makes further progress with those issues, it may decide to revisit the treatment of actuarial gains and losses.' Therefore, the Board allows the corridor approach but could be seen to prefer immediate recognition, which is not precluded by the Standard.

Minimum recognition requirement – '10 per cent corridor' approach

The steps to be applied in applying the minimum recognition requirement are as follows:

1. Consider each defined benefit plan separately.
2. Calculate the excess amount falling outside the 'corridor' as:

   Net cumulative unrecognised actuarial gain or loss **at the end of the previous accounting period** *less* 10 per cent of the greater of:

   - the present value of the defined benefit obligation at that date (before deducting plan assets); and
   - fair value of the plan assets at that date.

3. Recognise in the income statement an amount equal to:

   - excess (as in 2 above) ***divided*** by the expected remaining working lives of the employees participating in the scheme.

4. The unrecognised cumulative actuarial gains and losses, which comprise both those within the 10 per cent corridor that are being deferred indefinitely and that portion outside the corridor that has not been recognised in the income statement at the balance sheet date, will form part of the net deferred benefit liability or asset.

Example 25.4

At the 31 December 20X0 a plan had a net cumulative unrecognised actuarial loss of 1,200. At the same date the present value of the defined benefit obligation was 10,200 and the fair value of the associated plan assets was 9,500. The expected remaining working lives of the employees participating in the scheme was 9 years.

In the income statement for the 12 months to 31 December 20X1 an amount of 20 will be recognised in respect of the actuarial loss. This is calculated as follows:

Net cumulative unrecognised actuarial loss	1,200
Less the greater of:	
10% of 10,200; and	
10% of 9,500	1,020
Excess	180
Average remaining working life	9
Actuarial loss to be recognised	20

Faster recognition of actuarial gains and losses

As an alternative to the minimum recognition requirement discussed above an enterprise may adopt any systematic method that results in faster recognition of actuarial gains and losses (including immediate recognition of the full amount), provided that:

- the same basis is applied to both gains and losses; and
- the basis is applied consistently from period to period.

An enterprise may apply such systematic methods to actuarial gains and losses even if they fall within the 10 per cent corridor described above. (IAS 19 (r2000).92 and 93)

Changes in the basis of systematically recognising actuarial gains and losses should be accounted for in terms of the provisions of IAS 8 (r1993) *Net Profit or Loss for the Period, Fundamental Errors and Changes in Accounting Policies.* If a company chooses to change its policy from one of full recognition of gains and losses to a system of writing off over a period of time, such a change should be treated as an accounting policy. Policies that write off gains and losses over the employees' remaining working lives, and therefore fluctuate year on year as the average remaining working life changes, should be treated as changes in estimates.

25.9.5 Past service cost

> '**Past service cost** is the increase in the present value of the defined benefit obligation for employee service in prior periods, resulting in the current period from the introduction of, or changes to, post-employment benefits or other long-term employee benefits. Past service cost may be either positive (where benefits are introduced or improved) or negative (where existing benefits are reduced).'
>
> (IAS 19 (r2000).7)

Past service cost may arise on the introduction of a defined benefit plan or on the amendment of benefits paid under an existing plan. Although the benefits relate to employee service rendered in past periods, the Standard requires that the cost be recognised in the income statement as an expense on a straight-line basis over the period until the benefits vest. To the extent that the benefits vest immediately then the cost should similarly be recognised immediately. Therefore, an increase in benefits for former employees who have retired would be recognised in full immediately. The amount of the past service cost is measured as the change in the present value of the defined benefit obligation. Any past service cost unrecognised in the income statement will form part of the net deferred benefit liability or asset (see **25.9.1**). Having established the amortisation schedule for past service costs when the benefits are introduced or established; it is only amended if there is a curtailment or settlement. (IAS 19 (r2000).96, 97 and 99)

Since 'past service costs' includes both positive (debits) and negative (credit) amounts (see definition above) and paragraph 96 of the Standard requires the past service cost to be recognised as an expense; any negative past service cost is also recognised over the average period until the reduced portion of the benefits vests (i.e., immediately to the extent that the reduction in benefits vests immediately) within expenses in the income statement. (IAS 19 (r2000).7, 96 and 100)

Past service cost is dealt with on a net basis where under the same plan and, for the same employees, certain benefits are reduced and, at the same time, other benefits increased. (IAS 19 (r2000).101)

Past service cost arises due to changes in post-employment benefits or other long-term employee benefits. It does not include differences between actuarial assumptions and actual performance, or curtailments. Thus it excludes:

- differences between the actual and previously assumed salary increases, and discretionary pension increases (where there is a constructive obligation to grant the latter); as these increases will have been allowed for in the actuarial assumptions (see **Actuarial assumptions** in **25.9.2**);
- an increase in vested benefits due to employees completing vesting requirements (rather than new or improved benefits being introduced) as the cost of the benefits now vesting will have been recognised as the employee service was rendered within the current service cost;
- estimates of benefit improvement (required by the plan terms, legislation or established practice of the enterprise) arising from an actuarial gain that has already been recognised in the financial statements (see **Actuarial assumptions** in **25.9.2**); and
- the effect of a curtailment that reduces benefits for **future** service (see **25.9.7**).

(IAS 19 (r2000).98)

25.9.6 Plan assets

Plan assets, at fair value (see definitions immediately below), are deducted in arriving at the net defined benefit liability (asset) in the balance sheet (see **Balance sheet** in **25.9.1**). An estimate will need to be made of the fair value of an asset if no market price is available. One method would be to discount expected future cash flows from the asset at a rate reflecting the risk associated with the asset and its expected maturity or disposal date. If the assets do not have a maturity date, reference should be made to the settlement date of the related obligation. (IAS 19 (r2000).102) Further guidance on estimation techniques is given in IAS 39 (r2000), paragraphs 100 and 101.

> 'Plan assets comprise:
>
> (a) assets held by a long-term employee benefit fund; and
> (b) qualifying insurance policies.'

Assets held by a long-term employee benefit fund are assets (other than non-transferable financial instruments issued by the reporting enterprise) that:

(a) are held by an entity (a fund) that is legally separate from the reporting enterprise and exists solely to pay or fund employee benefits; and

(b) are available to be used only to pay or fund employee benefits, and are not available to the reporting enterprise's own creditors (even in bankruptcy), and cannot be returned to the reporting enterprise, unless either:
   (i) the remaining assets of the fund are sufficient to meet all the related employee benefit obligations of the plan or the reporting enterprise; or
   (ii) the assets are returned to the reporting enterprise to reimburse it for employee benefits already paid.

A qualifying insurance policy is an insurance policy issued by an insurer that is not a related party (as defined in IAS 24) of the reporting enterprise, if the proceeds of the policy:

(a) can be used only to pay or fund employee benefits under a defined benefit plan;
(b) are not available to the reporting enterprise's own creditors (even in bankruptcy) and cannot be paid to the reporting enterprise, unless either:
   (i) the proceeds represent surplus assets that are not needed for the policy to meet all the related employee benefit obligations; or
   (ii) the proceeds are returned to the reporting enterprise to reimburse it for employee benefits already paid.

Fair value is the amount for which an asset could be exchanged or a liability settled between knowledgeable, willing parties in an arm's length transaction. (IAS 19 (r2000).7)

These definitions were revised in 2000 because employers in some countries retain the legal obligation to pay benefits directly, even when fully funded from insurance policies, and such arrangements would not meet the previous definition of plan assets. The previous definition of plan assets required the condition 'to the extent that sufficient assets are in the fund the enterprise will have no legal or constructive obligation to pay the related employee benefits directly' to be satisfied. (See also **Reimbursements** below.)

Where the plan's assets in qualifying insurance policies exactly match the amount and timing of part or all of the benefits payable under the plan, the fair value of those insurance policies is deemed to be the present value of the related obligations. The fair value of the policies is reduced if the amounts receivable under them are not recoverable in full. (See also **25.11**.) (IAS 19 (r2000).104)

Plan assets do not include unpaid contributions due from the reporting enterprise to the fund. Plan assets are reduced by any liabilities of the fund that do not relate to employee benefits, for example trade and other payables. (IAS 19 (r2000).103)

See **Frequency of actuarial valuation** in **25.9.2** as regards frequency of valuations.

Reimbursements

The revision of IAS 19 in 2000 addresses the situation where another party will reimburse some or all of the expenditure required to settle a defined benefit obligation. When, and only when, it is virtually certain that such reimbursement will be made, the enterprise should recognise its right to reimbursement as a separate asset, measured at fair value. In all other respects the enterprise should treat that asset as a plan asset. The expense related to a defined benefit plan in the income statement may be presented net of the amount recognised for reimbursement. (IAS 19 (r2000).104A)

This treatment as a separate asset does not apply where part or all of the expenditure required to settle a defined benefit obligation is met by a *qualifying insurance policy* (as defined above). Qualifying insurance policies are plan assets and should be accounted for as for all other plan assets and IAS 19 (r2000).104A does not apply. (IAS 19 (r2000).104B)

If an insurance policy is ***not*** a ***qualifying insurance policy***, it is not a plan asset and should be treated in accordance with paragraph 104A. The right to reimbursement is recognised as a separate asset and not deducted in determining the defined benefit liability. However, in all other respects it is treated as a plan asset. In particular any unrecognised net cumulative actuarial gains or losses on the reimbursement right are reflected in the defined benefit liability recognised under IAS 19 (r2000).54. The enterprise is required by IAS 19 (r2000).120(c)(vii) to disclose a brief description of the link between the reimbursement right and the related obligation. (IAS 19 (r2000).104C)

The following example from IAS 19 (r2000) illustrates the requirements in respect of reimbursements.

Example 25.5

Present value of obligation	1,241
Unrecognised actuarial gains	17
Liability recognised in balance sheet	1,258
Rights under insurance policies that exactly match the amount and timing of some of the benefits payable under the plan. Those benefits have a present value of 1,092.	1,092

The unrecognised actuarial gains of 17 are the net cumulative actuarial gains on the obligation and on the reimbursement rights.

Return on plan assets

The movement in plan assets may be expressed as:

Fair value carried forward	=	Fair value brought forward	+	Contributions received	–	benefits paid	+	actual return on plan assets.

> '**The return on plan assets** is interest, dividends and other revenue derived from the plan assets, together with realised and unrealised gains or losses on the plan assets, less any costs of administering the plan and less any tax payable by the plan itself.'
>
> (IAS 19 (r2000).7)

There are two measures of return on plan assets – expected and actual. The difference between the expected and actual return on plan assets is included within the net actuarial gains and losses (see **25.9.4**).

The expected return on plan assets reflects market expectations, at the start of the accounting period, of the returns over the life of the related obligation and changes in the fair value of plan assets as a result of contributions paid into the plan and benefits paid from it. The expected return on plan assets is one part of the net income or expense recognised in the income statement (see **Income statement** in **25.9.1**).

The actual and expected return on plan assets is measured net of any administrative expenses that have not otherwise been included within the actuarial assumptions used to measure the obligation.

Example 25.6

At 1 January 20X0 plan assets had a fair value of 6,550. On 30 June 20X0 the plan both paid benefits of 1,400 and received contributions of 3,400. At 31 December 20X0 the plan had a net cumulative unrecognised actuarial loss of 1,200, the present value of the defined benefit obligation was 10,200 and the fair value of the associated plan assets was 9,500.

At 1 January 20X0, the reporting enterprise had made the following estimates based upon market values at that date:

Interest and dividend income, after tax payable by the fund	9.25%
Realised and unrealised gains on plan assets (after tax)	2.00%
Administration costs not included in actuarial assumptions for pension obligation	(1.00)%
Expected rate of return	10.25%

For 20X0 the actual and expected return on plan assets are as follows:

Actual return:	
Fair value of plan assets at 31 December 20X0	9,500
Less fair value of plan assets at 1 January 20X0	(6,550)
Less contributions received in period	(3,400)
Plus benefits paid on period	1,400
Actual return on plan assets	950
Expected return:	
On plan assets at 1 January 20X0 – 6,550 for 12 months at 10.25%	671
On contributions received less benefits paid in the period – (3,400 – 1,400) for 6 months at 5% (equivalent to 10.25% annually, compounded every 6 months)	100
On plan assets for 20X0	771
Actuarial gain/(loss) on plan assets – [actual return less expected return]	179

The 179 gain on plan assets is included within the net cumulative unrecognised actuarial loss of 1,200 at 31 December 20X0. *Example 25.4* (see **25.9.4**) continues this example in 20X1 to illustrate the recognition of part of this actuarial loss in that period.

25.9.7 Curtailments and settlements

In calculating the present value of a defined benefit obligation, demographic assumptions (e.g., mortality rates during employment, rate of employee turnover, etc.) and financial asumptions (e.g., future salary and benefit levels) will assume the continuance of the plan in its current form and of the enterprise and it operations as a going concern (see **Actuarial assumptions** in **25.9.2**). Such assumptions do not allow for curtailments or settlements which crystallise in full or part the assets and obligations of the plan.

A settlement occurs when an enterprise eliminates **all** of its legal or constructive obligations for part or all of the defined benefits under a plan. For example by purchasing an annuity for, or making a lump sum payment to, plan participants in exchange for their rights to receive specified post-employment benefits. It should be noted that a settlement does not require the discontinuance of a plan or preclude the plan participants receiving the settlement from earning further benefits under the plan. (IAS 19 (r2000).112)

A curtailment occurs when, instead of settling an existing obligation, the enterprise restricts a new obligation being incurred by:

- becoming demonstrably committed to making a material reduction in the number of employees covered by a plan; or

- amending the terms of a defined benefit plan so that a material part of future service by current employees will only qualify for reduced benefits, or indeed will no longer qualify.

(IAS 19 (r2000).111)

A gain or loss arising on the curtailment or settlement of a defined benefit plan should be recognised immediately, when the curtailment or settlement occurs. Such a gain or loss will comprise the aggregate of:

- resulting changes in the present value of the defined pension obligation (i.e., the gross obligation before deducting the fair value of plan assets);
- resulting changes in the fair value of plan assets; and
- related actuarial gains and losses and past service costs that have not previously been recognised in the income statement.

IAS 19 (r2000).115 indicates that an appropriate amount of the unrecognised increase in the obligation deferred under the transitional provision may crystallise following a curtailment or settlement.

The pension obligation, and related plan assets, should be remeasured using current actuarial assumptions (e.g., current interest rate), before determining the 'resulting changes' arising from the curtailment or settlement.

(IAS 19 (r2000).109, 110 and 115)

Where a curtailment relates to only some of the members covered by a plan (e.g., where there is a material reduction in the workforce following a reorganisation) or where the obligation is only partly settled, then the gain or loss arising on the curtailment or settlement will incorporate a proportion of the previously unrecognised past service costs, actuarial gains and losses and the amount remaining unrecognised under the transitional provisions (see **25.9.9**). The proportion will be based on the present value of the obligation before and after the curtailment or settlement unless a more rational basis is appropriate. (IAS 19 (r2000).115)

A curtailment will be combined with a settlement when a plan is terminated and the outstanding obligation settled such that the plan ceases to exist. However, where the plan is to be replaced by a new plan offering substantially equal benefits it should not be considered as a settlement or curtailment and, consequently, no gain or loss recognised.

The acquisition of an insurance policy to fund some or all of the employee benefits relating to employee service in the current and prior periods is not a settlement if the enterprise retains a legal or constructive obligation to pay further amounts if the insurer does not pay the employee benefits specified in the policy. (IAS 19 (r2000).113)

25.9.8 Business combinations

IAS 22 (r1998) (see Chapter **18**) requires that, in accounting for a business combination that is an acquisition, an enterprise recognises 'net employee benefit assets or liabilities for defined benefit plans at the present value of the defined benefit obligation less the fair value of any plan assets'. (IAS 22 (r1998).39(h)) The present value of the defined benefit obligation would include all of the following even if they have not been recognised at the date of acquisition in the acquired enterprise's income statement:

- actuarial gains and losses arising prior to the date of acquisition (irrespective of the **10** per cent corridor);
- past service costs arising before the date of acquisition; and
- amounts deferred by the acquiree under the transitional arrangements (see **25.9.9**).

(IAS 19 (r2000).108)

The amount of an asset will be restricted by reference to any economic benefits available in the form of refunds from the plan or reductions in future contributions to the plan. (IAS 22 (r1998).39(h))

25.9.9 Transitional provisions

When it firsts implements IAS 19 (r2000) for a defined benefit plan, an enterprise will need to compute its transitional liability as:

- the present value of the defined benefit obligation (see **25.9.2**) at the date of adoption (i.e., the gross obligation before deducting the fair value of plan assets);
- less the fair value at the date of adoption of plan assets out of which the obligations are to be settled directly (see **25.9.6**);
- less any past service cost that, under the Standard, would not have been recognised at the date of adoption (see **25.9.5**).

(IAS 19 (r2000).154)

Although the Standard only refers to a transitional liability the formula above could result in an asset (i.e., a net negative figure) being produced. In the next few paragraphs the transitional provisions have been interpreted so as to address the situation whereby a transitional asset is introduced. Any such asset will be subject to the recoverability limits being the net total of:

- any actuarial losses and past service costs not recognised as an expense; and
- the present value (using the discount rate specified in the Standard – see **25.9.5**) of any economic benefits available in the form of refunds from the plan or reductions in future contributions to the plan.

(IAS 19 (r2000).58, 154 and 155)

Where the transitional liability calculated above is less than that which would have been recognised at the same date under the enterprise's previous accounting policy (or if negative the transitional asset is greater) then the gain should be recognised immediately under IAS 8 (r1993) (see Chapter **5**). (IAS 19 (r2000).155)

Where the transitional liability calculated above is more than that which would have been recognised at the same date under the enterprise's previous accounting policy (or if negative the transitional asset is less) then the loss may either be:

- charged immediately as a change in accounting policy under IAS 8 (r1993) (see Chapter **5**); or
- recognised as an expense on a straight line basis over a period up to five years from the date of adoption of the Standard.

The Standard emphasises that the choice between the above two treatments of the loss is irrevocable. (IAS 19 (r2000).155)

It should be noted that where the expense is spread under the second option above:

- additional disclosure requirements apply (see **25.9.10**).
- the related part of the unrecognised transitional liability should be included in determining any subsequent gain or loss on settlement or curtailment (see **25.9.7**).
- the recognition of any subsequent actuarial gains (but not negative past service costs) should be restricted 'to the extent that the net cumulative unrecognised actuarial gains (before recognition of that actuarial gain) exceed the unrecognised part of the transitional liability' (IAS 19 (r2000).155(b)(iii)).

Example 25.7

From IAS 19(r2000), illustrating the transitional provisions (paragraphs 154 to 156)

At 31 December 1998, an enterprise's balance sheet includes a pension liability of 100. The enterprise adopts the Standard as of 1 January 1999, when the present value of the obligation under the Standard is 1,300 and the fair value of plan assets is 1,000. On 1 January 1993, the enterprise had improved pensions (cost for non-vested benefits: 160; and average remaining period at that date until vesting: 10 years).

The transitional effect is as follows:	
Present value of the obligation	1,300
Fair value of plan assets	(1,000)
Less: past service cost to be recognised in later periods (160 × 4/10)	(64)
Transitional liability	236
Liability already recognised	100
Increase in liability	136

The enterprise may choose to recognise the increase of 136 either immediately or over up to 5 years. The choice is irrevocable.

At 31 December 1999, the present value of the obligation under the Standard is 1,400 and the fair value of plan assets is 1,050. Net cumulative unrecognised actuarial gains since the date of adopting the Standard are 120. The expected average remaining working life of the employees participating in the plan was eight years. The enterprise has adopted a policy of recognising all actuarial gains and losses immediately as permitted by paragraph 93.

The effect of the limit in paragraph 155(b)(iii) *(of IAS 19 (r2000))* is as follows. ***(In practice, this limit will rarely have a material effect).***

Net cumulative unrecognised actuarial gains	120
Unrecognised part of transitional liability (136 × 4/5)	(109)
Maximum gain to be recognised	11

The Standard does not explicitly address the question of how the unrecognised part of the transitional liability should be dealt with in the balance sheet or income statement. The most sensible approach would be to include this unrecognised balance in arriving at the defined benefit liability or asset. This would be consistent with the treatment required by paragraph 54 of the Standard in respect of unrecognised actuarial gains or losses and unrecognised past service cost (see **Balance sheet** in **25.9.1**). Such an approach to the transitional liability is reflected in the example in the Standard that illustrates paragraph 60. Similarly the charge to the income statement would be included within the net total (see **Income statement 25.9.1**).

All actuarial gains and losses that arose in earlier periods are included in calculating the effect of the change in accounting policy on first implementing the Standard. There is no allowance for an initial 10 per cent corridor. In the above example the full 136 uplift in the liability is recognised either immediately or over a period up to five years. (IAS 19 (r2000).156)

25.9.10 Disclosure

Considerable disclosure is required in respect of defined sbenefit plans ranging from the accounting policy for recognised gains and losses, through a reconciliation of the various categories discussed in **25.9.1** to the net totals in the balance sheet and income statement, any investment by the plan in the enterprise and principal actuarial assumptions.

Where an enterprise has a number of defined benefit plans, it is permitted to make the disclosure in aggregate subject to certain provisos as to the offset of surpluses and obligations (see **25.10**).

The disclosures required in respect of defined benefit plans are:

- accounting policy for recognising actuarial gains and losses;
- a general description of the type of plan (e.g., distinguishing flat salary plans, final salary plans and post-employment medical plans);
- a reconciliation of the assets and liabilities recognised in the balance sheet. The Standard specifies a minimum level of disclosure as follows:
  - the present value at the balance sheet date of defined benefit obligations that are wholly unfunded;
  - the present value (before deducting the fair value of plan assets) at the balance sheet date of defined benefit obligations that are wholly or partly funded;
  - the fair value of any plan assets at the balance sheet date;
  - the net actuarial gains or losses not recognised in the balance sheet;
  - the past service cost not yet recognised in the balance sheet ;
  - any amount not recognised as an asset, because of the limit thereon (see **Balance sheet** in **25.9.1**);
  - the fair value at the balance sheet date of any reimbursement right recognised as an asset under paragraph 104A and a brief description of the link between the reimbursement right and the related obligation; and
  - the other amounts recognised in the balance sheet.
- in respect of plan assets, any investment in each category of the reporting enterprise's own financial instruments or any property occupied by, or assets used by, the reporting enterprise;
- a reconciliation showing the movement in the period in the net liability or asset recognised in the balance sheet;
- the total expense recognised in respect of each of the constituent income statement items (see below) and the line items of the income statement in which they are included:
  - current service cost;
  - interest cost;
  - expected return on plan assets;
  - expected return on any reimbursement right recognised as an asset under paragraph 104A;
  - actuarial gains and losses;
  - past service cost; and

  - the effect of any curtailment or settlement;
- actual return on plan assets, as well as the actual return on any reimbursement rights recognised as an asset under paragraph 104A;
- the principal actuarial assumptions in absolute terms not as a margin between different percentage or other variables including discount rates, expected rates of return on plan assets and reimbursement rights; expected rate of salary increase; changes to any index to which plan benefits are linked; medical cost trend rates.

(IAS 19 (r2000).120)

If the enterprise is spreading the transitional expense (see **25.9.9**) it should disclose:

- the amount unrecognised at the balance sheet date; and
- the amount recognised in the period

(IAS 19 (r2000).155(b)(ii))

Other Standards may require additional disclosures, for example IAS 24 in respect of contributions in respect of key management personnel or related party transactions with post-employment benefit plans and IAS 37 in respect of contingencies arising from post-employment benefit obligations. (IAS 19 (r2000).124 and 125)

25.10 Enterprises with multiple plans

An employer may operate a number of plans, both defined contribution and defined benefit. Whilst the disclosures of defined contribution plans and defined benefit plans should be kept separate, the IAS permits disclosures to be made on a total basis for plans of a particular type, separately for each plan or in such groupings as are considered most useful. (IAS 19 (r2000). 46 and 122) This is subject to the proviso that for defined benefit plans an asset relating to one plan should not be offset against a liability relating to another plan unless the enterprise:

- has a legally enforceable right to use that surplus to settle the obligation; and
- intends to settle on a net basis or to realise the surplus and settle the obligation simultaneously.

(IAS 19 (r2000).116)

While there is no explicit guidance in the Standard regarding the offset of assets and liabilities in respect of defined contribution plans, they should not be offset unless 'offsetting is required or permitted by another International Accounting Standard'. (IAS 1(r1997).33). In accordance with IAS 32 (r1998) 'A financial asset and a financial liability should be offset and the net amount reported in the balance sheet when an enterprise:

- has a legally enforceable right to set off the recognised amounts; and
- intends either to settle on a net basis, or to realise the asset and settle the liability simultaneously.

(IAS 32(r1998).33)

25.11 Insured benefits

A post-employment retirement plan that is funded by insurance premiums will be treated as a defined benefit plan if the reporting enterprise will have a legal or constructive obligation to either:

- pay the employee benefits directly when they fall due; or
- pay further amounts if the insurer does not pay all future employee benefit relating to service in the current or prior periods.

An obligation as discussed above may be direct or indirect; through the plan, through the mechanism for setting future premiums or through a related party relationship between the reporting enterprise and the insurer. (IAS 19 (r2000).39 and 41)

In the absence of such a legal or constructive obligation, the plan will be treated as a defined contribution plan. (IAS 19 (r2000).39)

Thus insured plans are subject to the same distinction as other plans. If payment of the insurance premium is in substance the settlement of the obligation for a specified plan participant or group of participants, as opposed to an investment to meet the obligation, then the enterprise should treat such premiums as payments to a defined contribution plan as it no longer has an asset or liability. Where the enterprise retains a legal or constructive obligation (as discussed above), it will recognise qualifying insurance policies as plan assets, other insurance policies as reimbursement rights and the obligation (see **25.9.6** as regards the valuation of such policies). (IAS 19 (r2000). 41 and 42)

25.12 Multi-employer plans

'**Multi-employer plans** are defined contribution plans (other than state plans) or defined benefit plans (other than state plans) that:

(a) pool the assets contributed by various enterprises that are not under common control; and

(b) use those assets to provide benefits to employees of more than one enterprise, on the basis that contribution and benefit levels are determined without regard to the identity of the enterprise that employs the employees concerned.'

(IAS 19 (r2000).7)

Multi-employer plans should be classified as defined contribution or defined benefit and accounted for, and the relevant disclosures made, as appropriate. If classified as a defined benefit plan, it will be necessary to account for the proportionate share of the plan assets, obligation and costs as for any other defined benefit plan.

The Standard does not offer any guidance on the bases that might be appropriate to determine an enterprise's 'proportionate share' but does note that an enterprise 'may not be able to identify its share of the underlying financial position and performance of the plan with sufficient reliability for accounting purposes. This may occur if:

(a) the enterprise does not have access to information about the plan that satisfies the requirements of this Standard; or
(b) the plan exposes the participating enterprises to actuarial risks associated with the current and former employees of other enterprises, with the result that there is no consistent and reliable basis for allocating the obligation, plan assets and cost to individual enterprises participating in the plan.' (IAS 19 (r2000).32)

The above definition of a multi-employer plan includes the requirement that the 'basis that contribution and benefit levels are determined without regard to the identity of the enterprise that employs the employees concerned'. It thus seems inevitable that the participating enterprises will be exposed to actuarial risks associated with the current and former employees of other enterprises in the plan. Whether there is a consistent and reliable basis for allocating the components will depend on many factors including the frequency of enterprises leaving or joining the plan, the treatment of variations arising and the similarity of actuarial risks across the participating enterprises.

If an enterprise participates in a multi-employer plan that is a defined benefit plan, but there is not sufficient information available to use defined benefit accounting, the enterprise should:

- account for the plan as if it were a defined contribution plan (see **25.8**);
- disclose the fact that the plan is a defined benefit plan; and the reason why sufficient information is not available to account for the plan as a defined benefit plan; and
- to the extent that a surplus or deficit in the plan may affect the amount

of future contributions, disclose any available information about that surplus or deficit; the basis used to determine that surplus or deficit; and any implications for the enterprise.

(IAS 19 (r2000).30)

Multi-employer plans may be differentiated from group administration plans (also known as common investment funds). Group administration plans allow participating employers to pool their assets for investment purposes thus reducing administration and investment management costs. The claims of the different participating employers on the assets are segregated for the sole benefit of their employees and other beneficiaries of their plans so that there is no particular accounting problem in obtaining the information relating to a particular employer. Each participating employer is not exposed to the actuarial risks attaching to the obligations of the other participating employers. An enterprise should classify such plans as a defined contribution plan or defined benefit in the normal way. (IAS 19 (r2000).33)

25.13 State plans

Normally state plans will be defined contribution plans. A participating employer's liability will be restricted to contributions payable in a period, the plan, being funded on a pay-as-you-go basis. If the enterprise ceases to employ members of the state plan, it will no longer be liable for further payments even if the benefits of employees for prior periods under the state plan require additional funding. The Standard requires that state plans should be treated in the same way as for a multi-employer plan (see **25.12**). (IAS 19 (r2000).36 to 38)

25.14 Other long-term employee benefits

Other long term employee benefits (see **25.5**) includes items such as:

- compensated long-service or sabbatical leave;
- jubilee or other long-service benefits;
- profit sharing and bonus payments payable 12 months or more after the employee renders the related service; and
- deferred compensation paid 12 months or more after the period in which it is earned.

(IAS 19 (r2000).126)

Applying the definition (see **25.5**), the above items should fall due twelve months or more after the end of the period in which the employees render the related service. So, for example, the long term compensated absences should be expected to occur, and bonuses be payable, at least 12 months after the end of the period in which employees render the related service. (IAS 19 (r2000).126)

25.14.1 Recognition and measurement

The Standard's requirements relating to other long-term employment benefits is a simplified version of that applied to post-employment benefits. All past service cost and actuarial gains and losses are recognised immediately and there is no application of a corridor. In addition there is no provision permitting spreading of transitional cost (see **25.9.9**).

Balance sheet
The liability recognised in the balance sheet for other long-term employee benefits is the net total of:

- the present value of the defined benefit obligation at the balance sheet date (i.e., the gross obligation before deducting the fair value of plan assets) (see **25.9.6**);
- less the fair value at the balance sheet date of any plan assets and reimbursement rights out of which the obligations are to be settled directly (see **25.9.2**).

(IAS 19 (r2000).128)

Income statement
The income or expense recognised in the income statement for other long term employee benefits is the net total of:

- current service cost;
- interest cost;
- expected return on any plan assets and on any reimbursement rights recognised as an asset;
- actuarial gains and losses (which should all be recognised immediately);
- past service cost (which should all be recognised immediately); and
- effect of curtailments and settlements.

(IAS 19 (r2000).129)

If the net total above is an item of income it will be limited by the restriction on the size of the asset (See **Balance sheet** section in **25.9.1** above).

An example of a long-term employee benefit discussed in the Standard is long-term disability service. If such a benefit is independent of years of service, then a cost is not recognised until an event occurs that causes a long-term disability. If the benefit is dependant on years of service then an obligation should be recognised as the service is rendered based upon the probability and timing of payments expected to be made. (IAS 19 (r2000).130)

25.14.2 Disclosures

No specific disclosures are required by IAS 19 (r2000) regarding other long-term employee benefits although it notes that other Standards may require disclosure (e.g., IAS 8 (r1993) and IAS 24). (IAS 19 (r2000).131)

25.15 Termination benefits

Termination payments (or redundancy payments) by their very nature differ from other employee benefits as they arise not from the rendering of service by an employee but by the termination of that service. Consequently, they do not provide any further benefits and should be recognised as an expense immediately. Situations that give rise to termination benefits may also impact other employee benefits or give rise to a curtailment of retirement benefits (see **25.9.7**). (IAS 19 (r2000).132, 137 and 138)

Termination benefits (see **25.5** for definition) include:

- lump sum payments;
- enhanced retirement benefits or other post-employment benefits (provided directly or though an employee benefit plan); and
- salary paid until the end of a specified notice period even though the employee renders no service that provides economic benefits to the enterprise in that period.

(IAS 19 (r2000).135)

Employee benefits that are payable irrespective of the reason for an employee's departure (subject to any vesting or minimum service requirements) are post-employment benefits rather than termination payments and should be dealt with as a post-employment benefit in accordance with the requirements of **25.7** to **25.9**. In some cases, a higher benefit may be payable in the event of an involuntary termination, at the request of the enterprise, than is paid for a voluntary termination, at the request of the employee; such an additional benefit payable on involuntary termination would be a termination benefit. (IAS 19 (r2000).136)

Termination benefits are recognised if, and only if, the enterprise is demonstrably committed to either:

- terminating the employment of an employee or group of employees before their normal retirement date; or
- providing termination benefits as a result of an offer made to encourage voluntary redundancy.

(IAS 19 (r2000).132 and 133)

The approach outlined above is consistent with that taken by IAS 37 related to reorganisation provisions, in that by being demonstrably committed the enterprise is creating a legal (by legislation or contractual) or constructive (based on business practice, custom or a desire to act equitably) obligation.

Although not explicitly stated in IAS 19 (r2000), for a termination benefit to be recognised, the enterprise should be demonstrably committed to the termination at the balance sheet date.

In order to be demonstrably committed an enterprise must have a detailed formal plan from which it cannot realistically withdraw, a similar situation to that applying to restructuring provisions in IAS 37 (see Chapter **11**). IAS 19 (r2000) requires that as a minimum the detailed plan for the termination should include:

- the location, function, and approximate number of employees whose services are to be terminated;
- the termination benefits for each job classification or function; and
- the time at which the plan will be implemented. Implementation should begin as soon as possible and the period of time to complete implementation should be such that material changes to the plan are not likely.

(IAS 19 (r2000).134)

25.15.1 Recognition and measurement

An enterprise should recognise a termination payment as a provision and an expense immediately, when it becomes demonstrably committed to the termination as noted above. If the benefits fall due more than 12 months after the balance sheet date, they should be discounted using the discount rate noted in **25.9.3**. (IAS 19 (r2000).133, 137 and 139)

If the payment relates to a voluntary redundancy, the provision should reflect the number of employees expected to accept the offer. (IAS 19 (r2000).140)

25.15.2 Disclosures

There are no specific disclosure requirements required by IAS 19 (r2000) but disclosures may be required by other standards. For example:

- IAS 37, where there is uncertainty as to the number of employees accepting an offer of termination benefits;
- IAS 8 (r1993), if the termination benefit is of such size, nature or incidence that disclosure is required to explain performance for the period; or
- IAS 24 where termination benefits relate to key management personnel.

(IAS 19 (r2000).141 to 143)

25.16 Equity compensation benefits

Equity compensation benefits (see **25.5** for definition) include benefits in such forms as:

- shares, share options, and other equity instruments, issued to employees at less than the fair value at which those instruments would be issued to a third party; and
- cash payments, the amount of which will depend on the future market price of the reporting enterprise's shares.

IAS 19 (r2000) only addresses the disclosure of such items. It does not deal with recognition or measurement issues.

The disclosures required by IAS 19 (r 2000) in respect of equity compensation plans are:

- the nature and terms (including any vesting provisions);
- the accounting policy;
- the amounts recognised in the financial statements;
- the number and terms (including, where applicable, dividend and voting rights, conversion rights, exercise dates, exercise prices and expiry dates) of the enterprise's own equity financial instruments which are held by equity compensation plans (and, in the case of share options, by employees) at the beginning and end of the period. The extent to which employees' entitlements to those instruments are vested at the beginning and end of the period should be specified;
- the number and terms (including, where applicable, dividend and voting rights, conversion rights, exercise dates, exercise prices and expiry dates) of equity financial instruments issued by the enterprise to equity compensation plans or to employees (or of the enterprise's own equity financial instruments distributed by equity compensation plans to employees) during the period and the fair value of any consideration received from the equity compensation plans or the employees;
- the number, exercise dates and exercise prices of share options exercised under equity compensation plans during the period;
- the number of share options held by equity compensation plans, or held by employees under such plans, that lapsed during the period;
- the amount, and principal terms, of any loans or guarantees granted by the reporting enterprise to, or on behalf of, equity compensation plans;
- the fair value, at the beginning and end of the period, of the enterprise's own equity financial instruments (other than share options) held by equity compensation plans; and
- the fair value, at the date of issue, of the enterprise's own equity financial instruments (other than share options) issued by the enterprise to equity

compensation plans or to employees, or by equity compensation plans to employees, during the period.

If it is not practicable to determine the fair value of the equity financial instruments (other than share options), that fact should be disclosed. (IAS 19 (r2000).147 and 148)

If an enterprise has more than one equity compensation plan, the disclosure may be made in total, separately for each plan or, where it is useful to assessing the enterprise's obligations and changes in obligations, by grouping plans together. In the latter case disclosures will be on a weighted basis or within relatively narrow ranges. (IAS 19 (r2000).149)

In 2000, the G4+1 issued a discussion paper 'Share-based payments'. The paper discussed the accounting treatment of transactions where an entity purchases goods or services from other parties, such as suppliers or employees by issuing them shares or share options. It focused on accounting for employee share schemes. It proposed that share-based payment transactions should be recognised in the company's financial statements, measured at the fair value of the shares or share options at vesting date. In most cases, an option pricing model should be used to measure the fair value of an option. The paper also proposed that an estimate of the transaction amount should be accrued over the performance period and finalised on vesting date.

Share-based payments has been identified by the IASB as one of the first projects the new board will address. The IASB is planning on taking a leadership role amoung standardsetters in the field of reporting share-based payments (see Chapter **2**).

25.17 Comparison with UK GAAP

There are no UK standards that specifically address short-term employee benefits, other long-term employee benefits or termination benefits as addressed by IAS 19 (r2000). However, the requirements of IAS 19 (r2000) in these respects are not inconsistent with the more general UK standard FRS 12 *Provisions, Contingent Liabilities and Contingent Assets* (see **11.9.22**) which contains all the requirements of IAS 37 with no differences of substance between the common requirements. FRS 12 includes a similar exemption to IAS 37 as regards executory contracts (see **11.9.4**).

In November 2000 a new UK standard, FRS 17 *Retirement Benefits* was issued, replacing SSAP 24 *Accounting for Pension Costs.* FRS 17 has a lengthy transitional period, during which increasing amounts of disclosure are required by way of notes to the financial statements, until becoming mandatory for periods ending on or after 22 June 2003. FRS 17 also replaces UITF 6, which applied the principles of SSAP 24 to the measurement and disclosure of post retirement benefits other than pensions.

The accounting treatment and disclosures required by IAS 19 (r2000) in respect of defined contribution schemes are similar to those required by FRS 17. FRS 17 additionally requires disclosure of any outstanding or prepaid contributions at the balance sheet date. The accounting policy in respect of pension costs is disclosable in accordance with FRS 18 *Accounting Policies.*

The approach and requirements of SSAP 24 in respect of defined benefit schemes were very different from IAS 19 (r2000) (bearing a similarity to the 1993 revision of IAS 19). The requirements of FRS 17, however, are consistent with IAS 19 (r2000) in most respects, the only major difference being in the recognition of actuarial gains and losses. FRS 17 requires these to be recognised immediately (so there is no '10 per cent corridor' and no gradual recognition as under IAS 19 (r2000)). The actuarial gain or loss goes through the statement of total recognised gains and losses – a second performance statement additional to the profit and loss account. This immediate recognition is the approach the IASC found attractive at the time IAS 19 was revised in 1998, but they are unable to adopt it until such time as there are further developments in the reporting of financial performance. FRS 17 applies to all retirement benefits, but does not cover other employee benefits.

Under UK GAAP equity compensation benefits are currently addressed by UITF Abstract 17 *Employee Share Schemes.* In accordance with UITF 17, the charge to the profit and loss account is based on the difference between the fair value of the shares at the date of the award and the amount of any consideration to be paid by the participants. Frequently the price to be paid at the date of exercising the options is the share price at the date the options were issued, and accordingly no profit and loss account charge arises. The ASB has issued the G4+1 paper referred to above as a discussion paper. Under these proposals charges to the profit and loss account would be higher, being based on fair value of the shares or options at the vesting date, as opposed to the grant date. UK developments in this area are likely to mirror those of the IASB Share-Based Payments project.

25.18 Comparison with US GAAP

In 1999 FASB published an updated report comparing IASC Standards and US GAAP.[1]

1 2nd edition The IASC – US Comparison Project – A Report on the Similarities and Differences between IASC Standards and US GAAP.

This noted the US standards addressing the topics dealt with in IAS 19 (r2000) as follows:

Type of benefit	*US GAAP*
Short-term employee benefits	SFAS 43 *Accounting for compensated absences*
Post-employment benefits	SFAS 87 *Employers accounting for pensions* SFAS 88 *Employers accounting for settlements and curtailments of defined benefit pension plans and for termination benefits* SFAS 106 *Employers accounting for post retirement benefits other than pensions* SFAS 132 *Employers disclosures about pensions and other post employment benefits* SFAS 112 *Employers accounting for post-retirement benefits*
Other long-term employee benefits	APB 12 *Deferred compensation contracts* SFAS 112 *Employers accounting for post-retirement benefits*
Termination benefits	EITF 94-3 *Liability recognition for certain employee termination benefits and other costs to exit an activity (including certain costs incurred in a restructuring)* SFAS 88 *Employers accounting for settlements and curtailments of defined benefit pension plans and for termination benefits* SFAS 106 *Employers accounting for post retirement benefits other than pensions*
Equity compensation benefits	APB 25 *Accounting for stock issued to employees* SFAS 123 *Accounting for stock based compensation*

While the revision of IAS 19 (to produce IAS 19 (r1998)) has removed many of the differences previously noted between US GAAP and IAS the survey notes that 'several potentially significant differences remain'. These are discussed below. The survey notes that 'the ability under IAS 19 to anticipate changes in future benefits due to expectations about changes in law (see **25.18.5** below) and the absence of recognition and measurement guidance for equity compensation benefits (see **25.18.6** below) in IAS 19 (r2000) are the two most significant differences in comparability between IAS 19 (r2000) and US GAAP.'

25.18.1 Definition of defined contribution plans

The IAS definition concentrates on the contributions made by the sponsor as a whole (see **25.12**) but US GAAP looks at the contributions to be made to individual plans (SFAS 87). In addition US GAAP defines a defined benefit plan whereas IAS 19 (r2000) merely says that any plan that is not a defined contribution plan is a defined benefit plan. Thus there is potential for the same plan being categorised differently.

25.18.2 Multi-employer plans

IAS 19 (r2000) requires the accounting to follow the underlying nature of the plan (see **25.7.1**). US GAAP requires defined contribution accounting for all multi-employer plans.

25.18.3 Plan amendments that affect retirees

Under US GAAP prior service costs related to retirees are amortised over the average remaining service period of active plan participants or the average remaining life expectancy of retirees (depending on whether plan participants are mainly active employees or mainly retirees). IAS 19 (r2000) requires past service costs to be expensed over the period to vesting or immediately if they vest immediately (see **25.9.5**). In most cases past service cost relating to retirees will vest immediately and should therefore be charged immediately. It should be noted that IAS 19 (r2000) excludes from past service costs discretionary pension increases (where there is a constructive obligation to grant such increases) as they will have been allowed for in the actuarial assumptions.

25.18.4 Minimum liability provision in SFAS 87

As a minimum US GAAP requires recognition of the unfunded accumulated pension benefit obligation in the balance sheet. IAS 19 (r2000) has no such provision and so, in the early years of application when there may be an unrecognised transitional liability (see **25.9.9**) there may be significant differences.

25.18.5 Anticipation of changes in future benefits

IAS 19 (r2000) requires the post employment benefit obligation to reflect the estimated future changes in the level of state benefits that affect the benefits payable under the plan (see **Actuarial assumptions** in **25.9.2**). The standard says the changes in state benefits should be reflected, 'if and only if, either:

- (i) those changes were enacted before the balance sheet date; or
- (ii) past history, or other reliable evidence, indicates that those state benefits will change in some predictable manner, for example in line with future changes in general price levels or general salary levels.' (IAS19 (r2000). 83)

Thus future changes in law could be reflected where 'past history, or other reliable evidence' indicates that they law will change in a predictable manner.

However, SFAS 106 specifically states that that future changes in laws concerning medical costs covered by government programs should not be anticipated.

25.18.6 Treatment of equity compensation benefits

IAS 19 (r2000) does not give guidance on the recognition or measurement of the cost of such benefits restricting itself to disclosures only (see **25.16**). US GAAP requires recognition of an expense for compensatory plans. SFAS 123 defines a fair value method of accounting for equity-based employee compensation plans. However current guidance also allows an entity to account for those plans using the intrinsic value method (APB 25). The intrinsic value method of accounting for an equity-based employee compensation plan can result in no compensation expense to the entity. SFAS 123 is the preferred method of accounting by the FASB. An entity cannot change its method of accounting from the fair value method after adoption. In addition US GAAP includes extensive disclosure requirements which includes the method and assumptions used to estimate the fair value of options (SFAS 123). IAS 19 (r2000) does not require disclosure of the fair value of options. (IAS 19 (r2000). 148(a))

25.19 Examples from published financial statements

Illustrative disclosures are given in Appendix 2 of the Standard. Note that the excerpts given below do not always comply in full with all aspects of IAS, and, as such, are not necessarily examples of best practice but merely of current practice.

Example 25.8

Extracts from accounting policies notes

Employee benefits

Wages, salaries, social security contributions, paid annual leave and sick leave, bonuses, options and non-monetary benefits are accrued in the year in which associated services are rendered by employees of the Group. Where the Group provides long-term employee benefits the cost is accrued to match the rendering of the services by the employees concerned.

The Group operates a number of defined benefit and defined contribution plans throughout the world. The cost for the year for defined benefit plans is determined using the projected unit credit method. This reflects service rendered by employees to the dates of valuation and incorporates actuarial assumptions primarily regarding discount rates used in determining the present value of benefits, projected rates of remuneration growth, and long-term expected rates of return for plan assets. Discount rates are based on the market yields of high-quality corporate bonds in the country concerned. Differences between assumptions and actual experiences and effects of changes in actuarial assumptions are allocated over the estimated average remaining working lives of employees, where these differences exceed a defined corridor. Past service costs are allocated over the average period until the benefits become vested. Pension assets and liabilities in different defined benefit schemes are not offset unless the Group has a legally enforceable right to use the surplus in one plan to settle obligations in the other plan.

The Group's contributions to the defined contribution plans are charged to the income statement in the year to which they relate.

Note 8

Employee benefits	*2000*	*1999*
Amounts recognised in arriving at operating profit are as follows:		
Wages and salaries	6,156	5,613
Social security costs	746	719
Post-employment benefits: defined benefit plans	298	322
Post-employment benefits: defined contribution plans	58	41
Other employee benefits	325	236
Total employees' remuneration	7,583	6,931

The number of employees at the year-end was 64,758 (1999: 67,695).

Post-employment benefits

Most employees are covered by retirement benefit plans sponsored by Group companies. The nature of such plans varies according to legal regulations, fiscal requirements and economic conditions of the countries in which the employees are employed. Other post-employment benefits consist mostly of post-retirement healthcare and life insurance schemes, principally in the USA. Plans are usually funded by payments from the Group and by employees to trusts independent of the Group's finances. Where a plan is unfunded, a liability for the whole obligation is recorded in the Group's balance sheet.

The amounts recognised in arriving at operating profit for post-employment defined benefit plans are as follows:

	2000	*1999*
Current service cost	333	311
Interest cost	675	677
Expected return on plan assets	(714)	(645)
Net actuarial (gains) losses recognised	2	–
Past service cost	3	7
(Gains) losses on curtailment	(1)	(28)
Total included in employees remuneration	298	322

The actual return on plan assets was 1,175 million Swiss francs (1999: 932 million Swiss francs).

The movements in the net asset (liability) recognised in the balance sheet for post-employment defined benefit plans are as follows:

	2000	*1999*
At the beginning of the year as previously reported	(2,078)	(2,107)
Effect of implementing the revised International Accounting Standard for Employee Benefits in 1999		39
as restated	(2,078)	(2,068)
Changes in Group organisation and Givaudan spin-off	84	(4)
Total expenses included in employees' remuneration (as above)	(298)	(322)
Contributions paid	174	165
Benefits paid (unfunded plans)	135	125
Currency translation effects and other	134	26
At end of year (as below)	(1,849)	(2,078)

Amounts recognised in the balance sheet for post-employment defined benefit plans are as follows:

Unfunded plans	*2000*	*1999*
Recognised asset (liability) for actuarial present value of unfunded obligations due to past and present employees	(2,423)	(2,648)
Funded plans		
Actuarial present value of future obligations due to past and present employees	(9,034)	(9,028)
Plans asset held in trusts at fair value	10,448	10,046
Plan assets in excess of actuarial present value of funded obligations	1,414	1,018
Less		
unrecognised actuarial (gains) losses	(862)	(467)
unrecognised past service costs	22	19
Recognised asset (liability) for funded obligations due to past and present employees	574	570
Asset (liability) recognised		
Deficit recognised as part of liabilities for post employment benefits	(2,502)	(2,764)
Surplus recognised as part of other long-term assets	653	686
Total net asset (liability) recognised	(1,849)	

The above amounts include non-pension post-employment benefits schemes, principally medical plans, with an actuarial present value of obligations of 690 Swiss francs (1999: 703 million Swiss francs) and plan assets of 649 million Swiss francs (1999: 576 million Swiss francs). The related net liability recognised is 147 million Swiss francs (1999: 190 million Swiss francs). Actuarial gains of 106 million Swiss francs (1999: 63 million Swiss francs) were unrecognised.

Amounts recognised in the balance sheet for post-employment defined benefit plans are predominantly non-current and are reported as long-term assets and non-current liabilities.

Included within the fair value of the assets of the funded plans are 30 (1999: 1,700) of the Group's non-voting equity securities with a fair value of 0.5 million Swiss francs (1999: 32 million Swiss francs).

The Group operates defined benefit schemes in many countries and the actuarial assumptions vary based upon local economic and social conditions. The range of assumptions used in the actuarial valuations of the most significant defined benefit plans, which are in countries which stable currencies and interest rates, is as follows:

Discount rates	3 to 8%	(1999: 3 to 8%)
Projected rates of remuneration growth	2 to 9%	(1999: 2.5 to 9%)
Expected rates of return on plan assets	3 to 10%	(1999: 3.5 to 10%)
Healthcare cost trend rate	4 to 10%	(1999: 4 to 9%)

Roche Group
Switzerland
31 December 2000
International Accounting Standards

Example 25.9

Extracts from accounting policy notes

2.13 Retirement benefit costs

Payments to defined contribution retirement benefit plans are charged as an expense as they fall due. Payments made to industry-managed retirement benefits schemes are dealt with as defined contribution plans where the group's obligations under the schemes are equivalent to those arising in a defined contribution retirement benefit plan.

For defined benefit plans the cost of providing the benefits is determined using the projected unit credit method. Actuarial valuations are conducted on a triennial basis with interim valuations also performed on an annual basis on a date which does not coincide with the balance sheet date. Consideration is given to any event that could impact the funds up to balance sheet date.

Actuarial gains and losses which exceed 10% of the greater of the present value of the group's pension obligations and the fair value of plan assets are amortised over the expected average remaining working lives of the participating employees. Past-service cost is recognised immediately to the extent that the benefits are already vested, and otherwise is amortised on a straight-line basis over the average period until the amended benefits become vested.

The amount recognised in the balance sheet represents the present value of the defined benefit obligation as adjusted for unrecognised actuarial gains and losses and unrecognised past-service cost, and reduced by the fair value of plans assets. Any asset is limited to unrecognised actuarial losses, plus the present value of available refunds and reductions in future contributions to the plan.

To the extent that there is uncertainty as to the entitlement to the surplus, no asset is recorded.

Retirement benefit information

It is the policy of the group to encourage, facilitate and contribute to the provision of retirement benefits for all permanent employees. To this end the group's permanent employees are usually required to be members of either a pension or provident fund, depending on their preference and local legal requirements.

69% of employees belong to 16 defined benefit and 36 defined contribution retirement funds in which group employment is a prerequisite for membership. Of these, 13 defined benefit and 20 defined contribution funds are located outside of South Africa and accordingly are not subject to the provisions of the Pensions Funds Act of 1956. A further 23% of employees belong to defined contribution funds associated with industries or employees organisations.

Defined contribution plans

The total cost charged to income of R137 million (1999: R115 million) represents contributions payable to these schemes by the group at rates specified in the rules of the schemes.

Defined benefit plans

Principal assumptions express as weighted averages at 30 September 2000 were as follows:

	South Africa		*UK and Europe*	
	2000	*1999*	*2000*	*1999*
	%	%	%	%
Discount rate	12.0	5.0	6.5	8.0
Expected after-tax returns on fund assets	15.0	16.0	7.5	9.0
Future general and merit related salary increases	11.5	14.0	4.5	6.0

Funded status

The funded status of the defined benefit funds at 20 September 2000 were as follows:

		Group
	2000	*1999*
	R'm	*R'm*
Fair value of plan assets	5,623	4,929
Present value of funded obligation	(4,702)	(4,426)
	921	503
Unrecognised actuarial losses	(138)	(15)
Past service cost not recognised	(231)	
Net asset	552	488
Surplus not recognised	(419)	(374)
Net asset per balance sheet	133	114

In Spain, accrued employees' retirement benefits remain a direct liability of Finanzauto SA. This company has made a provision of R170 million (1999: R166 million), to provide for this estimated liability at 30 September 2000. In all other instances, the accrued value of retirement benefits is represented by assets held in separate funds administered by trustees.

The pension plan assets consist primarily of equity (local and offshore), interest-bearing stock and property.

The actuarial return on the plan assets at 30 September 2000 amounted to R596 million (1999: R527 million).

32.3 Employee benefits: IAS 19 (1999)

IAS 19 (revised 1998) dealing with employee benefits has been adopted for the first time during the current financial year. This has resulted in an adjustment to the leave pay provision in some operations where it was not fully provided. A further consequence of adopting this standard has resulted in the surplus on defined benefit plans being brought on balance sheet. The income statement charge has also been adjusted to meet the requirements of IAS 19.

Barloworld Limited
South Africa
30 September 2000
International Accounting Standards and South African GAAP

CHAPTER 26

Government grants

26.1 Sources

IAS 1 (r1997)	*Presentation of Financial Statements.*
IAS 18 (r1993)	*Revenue.*
IAS 20	*Accounting for Government Grants and Disclosure of Government Assistance.*
IAS 41	*Agriculture.*
SIC-10	*Government Assistance – no specific relation to operating activities.*

26.2 Brief summary of the requirements

There are two IAS standards that address government grants: IAS 20 *Accounting for Government Grants and Disclosure of Government Assistance*; and IAS 41 *Agriculture* (see Appendix II). IAS 20 sets out the accounting and disclosure requirements for government grants and other forms of government assistance while IAS 41 deals with government grants relating to agricultural activities only. Government grants include grants related to assets, grants related to income, and certain other forms of assistance from which the reporting enterprise has directly benefited.

A government grant is recognised when there is reasonable assurance that the enterprise will comply with any conditions attaching to it and that the grant will be received. Government grants are recognised as income over the periods necessary to match them with the costs they are intended to compensate.

IAS 20 does not cover:

(a) special problems arising from accounting for the effects of changing prices;
(b) government assistance in the form of benefits which affect the income tax liability of the enterprise;
(c) government participation in the ownership of the enterprise; or

(d) government grants relating to agricultural activities covered by IAS 41. (IAS 20.2)

26.3 Development of the requirements

IAS 20 was originally approved in November 1982. The Standard was reformatted in 1994 in order to bring it into line with the presentation adopted for International Accounting Standards from 1991 onwards. It was amended in December 2000 with the adoption of IAS 41 *Agriculture*.

IAS 41 *Agriculture* was approved by the Board in December 2000. Refer to Appendix II for a summary of IAS 41.

26.4 Scope

Certain forms of assistance and situations are specifically scoped out of the Standard. They are:

- the special problems arising in accounting for government grants in financial statements reflecting the effects of changing prices or in supplementary information of a similar nature;
- government assistance that is provided for an enterprise in the form of benefits that are available in determining taxable income or are determined or limited on the basis of income tax liability (such as income tax holidays, investment tax credits, accelerated depreciation allowances and reduced income tax rates); and
- government participation in the ownership of the enterprise.

(IAS 20.2)

Otherwise the Standard should be applied in accounting for government grants (defined in **26.5**) and in the disclosure of government grants and other forms of government assistance (defined in **26.5**).

26.5 Definitions

For the purposes of IAS 20, **government** refers to 'government, government agencies and similar bodies whether local, national or international.' (IAS 20.3) This is clearly a broad definition. For example, in the UK context it covers a wide range of bodies from district and borough councils at the local level to the European Commission and its agencies at the international level. Government bodies probably include so-called QUANGOs (quasi-autonomous non-government organisations), such as Training and Enterprise

Councils, which may give assistance to enterprises which is ultimately funded by local or central government.

Government assistance is 'action by government designed to provide an economic benefit specific to an enterprise or range of enterprises qualifying under certain criteria.' (IAS 20.3) This does not include benefits provided indirectly by government, such as the provision of infrastructure in development areas or measures designed to protect domestic enterprises from foreign competition. (IAS 20.3 and .38)

Government grants are 'assistance by government in the form of transfers of resources to an enterprise in return for past or future compliance with certain conditions relating to the operating activities of the enterprise.' (IAS 20.3) Implicit within this definition is the notion that a grant may not be given or may be withdrawn or may be required by government to be repaid in the event of failure to comply with the relevant conditions. The award of a government grant therefore means that the enterprise receiving it may have a contingent liability which requires disclosure (see **26.10**). A forgivable loan from government should be treated as a government grant when there is reasonable assurance that the enterprise will meet the terms for forgiveness of the loan. (IAS 20.10) Forms of government assistance that are not classified as government grants are those that cannot have a value placed upon them (such as free technical or marketing advice and guarantees) and transactions with government that are indistinguishable from the normal trading transactions of the enterprise. (IAS 20.3 and .34)

SIC-10 states that 'Government assistance to enterprises meets the definition of government grants in IAS 20, even if there are no conditions specifically relating to the operating activities of the enterprise other than the requirement to operate in certain regions or industry sectors.' Changes in accounting policy occurring on the adoption of SIC-10 should be accounted for according to the transition requirements of IAS 8 (r1993).46 (see Chapter **5**).

Government grants fall into two categories:

- **grants related to assets** 'are government grants whose primary condition is that the enterprise qualifying for them should purchase, construct or otherwise acquire long-term assets.' (IAS 20.3) There may also be subsidiary conditions restricting the type or location of the assets or the periods during which they are to be acquired or held.
- **grants related to income** are defined simply as 'government grants other than those related to assets.' (IAS 20.3) Generally these refer to financial assistance relating directly to revenue items, such as crop subsidies to farm enterprises.

It is worth noting that grants represent a particular form of government assistance involving awards given in return for the fulfilment of conditions. There are, however, many forms of assistance which may vary in their nature and in the conditions attached. In certain cases, it is not possible to place a value on the assistance given, for example free technical or marketing advice or export credit guarantees. Government assistance may also be given through transactions which cannot be distinguished from the normal trading transactions of the enterprise, such as a government procurement policy which is responsible for a significant part of the enterprise's sales. These forms of assistance are explicitly excluded from the definition of government grants. (IAS 20.3 and .34) Although the benefit resulting from such forms of assistance may not be measurable, if it is significant for the enterprise, it must be disclosed in order that the financial statements are not misleading (see **26.10**).

26.6 Recognition of government grants

A government grant is not recognised until there is reasonable assurance that the enterprise will comply with the conditions attaching to it and that the grant will be received. (IAS 20.7-8) Receipt of a grant is not of itself conclusive evidence that the conditions attaching to the grant have been or will be fulfilled.

IAS 20 does not define 'reasonable assurance'. However, one of the recognition criteria included in the Framework (which was developed after IAS 20) is that it must be probable that any future economic benefit associated with an item will flow to or from an enterprise. When IAS 18 *Revenue* was subsequently revised, this criterion was included in the Standard. It would therefore be consistent with the Framework and IAS 18 (r1993) to interpret 'reasonable assurance' in the present context as meaning that both compliance with the conditions attaching to a grant and its receipt are probable.

Government grants are recognised as income over the periods necessary to match them with the costs which they are intended to compensate. They are not credited directly to shareholders' interests on the balance sheet. (IAS 20.12) Thus IAS 20 clearly rules out what is referred to as the 'capital approach' to the accounting treatment of government grants, in favour of the 'income approach'. The arguments in support of the income approach are as follows:

- government grants are receipts from a source other than shareholders, and therefore ought to be recognised as income in appropriate periods;
- they are rarely given free of obligations, but are earned by the enterprise through compliance with the conditions attached, and therefore ought to be recognised as income and matched with the associated costs; and

- just as income and other taxes are charges against income, it is logical to treat government grants, which are an extension of fiscal policies, as a credit to the income statement. (IAS 20.15)

Consistent with IAS 1 (r1997), the income approach requires application of the accruals concept by recognising government grants as income over the periods necessary to match them with the related costs. In other words, grants are not recognised on receipt unless no rational basis exists for allocating a grant to a period other than the one in which it was received.

In most cases, it is not difficult to identify the periods over which expenditure relating to a government grant is recognised. For example, grants related to depreciable assets are usually recognised as income over the periods in which depreciation on the assets is charged, corresponding to the useful lives of the assets. Grants related to non-depreciable assets may have certain conditions attached, and thus are recognised over the periods in which the costs of meeting those conditions are incurred.

In some instances, a government grant may be receivable by an enterprise as compensation for expenses or losses already incurred in a previous accounting period. Alternatively, a grant may be receivable for the purpose of giving immediate financial support to the enterprise with no future related costs. In such cases, the grant is recognised as income in the period in which it becomes receivable, and if appropriate as an extraordinary item (see Chapter 5). (IAS 20.20)

On a note of caution, it should be mentioned that since the issue of IAS 20, the Standard relating to extraordinary items, IAS 8, has been revised. It is now extremely rare for a transaction to qualify as an extraordinary item. It is more likely that such government grants will come within the category of items which are of such size, nature or incidence that their separate disclosure in the financial statements is required. Such items are included within net profit or loss from ordinary activities.

26.7 Measurement of non-monetary government grants

If the government grant takes the form of a non-monetary asset, such as land or other resources, it is usual to account for the grant and the asset at fair value. This is consistent with the requirement in IAS 18(r1993) that revenue is measured at the fair value of the consideration received or receivable. Fair value is defined by IAS 20 as 'the amount for which an asset could be exchanged between a knowledgeable, willing buyer and a knowledgeable, willing seller in an arm's length transaction.' (IAS 20.3) As an alternative course, the grant and the asset are sometimes recorded at a nominal amount. (IAS 20.23)

26.8 Presentation

26.8.1 Grants related to assets

IAS 20 permits two methods of presentation in the financial statements of government grants related to assets:

(a) presenting the grant as deferred income which is recognised as income on a systematic and rational basis over the useful life of the asset; or

(b) deducting the grant in arriving at the carrying amount of the asset, in which case the grant is recognised as income over the life of the asset by way of a reduced depreciation charge.

(IAS 20.24)

While IAS 20 permits netting off government grants against the carrying value of related assets, it goes on to note that such transactions can have a significant impact on the cash flow of an enterprise. For this reason, and also to show the gross investment in assets, the cash flow statement often discloses as separate items the purchase of assets and the receipt of related grants regardless of whether or not the grant is deducted from the asset in the balance sheet presentation. (IAS 20.28) A further argument in favour of separate presentation is that when IAS 7 (r1992), *Cash Flow Statements*, was revised, subsequent to the issue of IAS 20, government grants and related capital expenditure were not included as items which could be presented on a net cash basis.

Example 26.1

Enterprise A invests £1,000,000 in an item of plant, which has an anticipated useful life of five years. Depreciation is charged on the straight-line basis, with a full year's charge being made in the year of acquisition. During the year of acquisition the enterprise receives a government grant of £250,000 towards purchase of the plant, which is conditional on certain employment targets being achieved within the next two years. Under the two methods of presentation, the disclosure is as follows:

Method A: Grant shown as deferred income

Year 1:	Credit to deferred income – grant received	£250,000
	Less: transfer to income statement (£250,000/5 years)	(50,000)
	Deferred income balance at year end	£200,000
	Cost of plant	£1,000,000
	Depreciation charge (£1,000,000/5 years)	(200,000)
	Carrying value of plant at year end	£800,000
Years 2–5:	Transfer of deferred income	£50,000
	Depreciation charge	(200,000)
	Net charge to income statement (£750,000/5 years)	(150,000)

Note that the condition requiring certain employment targets to be met within two years is not relevant for determining the period over which deferred income is credited to the income statement. The condition requires disclosure, however, as a contingency.

Method B: Grant deducted from cost of asset

Year 1:	Cost of plant	£1,000,000
	Less: grant received	(250,000)
	Net cost of plant	750,000
	Depreciation charge (£750,000/5 years)	(150,000)
	Carrying value of plant at year end	600,000
Years 2–5:	Depreciation charge	(150,000)

It is evident from the above example that while the net impact of the two methods on the reported result for the year is identical, the presentation in each case is very different. Method A clearly separates the asset from the deferred income, and also shows the crediting of the grant separately as income while charging depreciation in full. Method B nets off the asset and the liability, while showing only the depreciation charge, reduced by the amount which would otherwise have been credited for the grant, in the income statement.

In both of the above cases a deductible temporary difference arises if the grant is non-taxable. In Method A this arises as the difference between the carrying value of the deferred income and its tax base of nil. In Method B it is the difference between the carrying amount of the assets and its tax base. IAS 12 (r2000).33 prohibits recognition of a deferred tax asset under either scenario (see Chapter **23**).

26.8.2 Grants related to income

IAS 20 permits two methods of presentation in the financial statements of grants related to income:

- directly as a credit to the income statement, either separately or under a general heading such as 'other income'; or
- as a deduction in reporting the related expense.

(IAS 20.29)

Again, the Standard demonstrates its flexibility in permitting, as equally acceptable, alternative methods of presentation of government grants. Essentially, IAS 20 has sought to accommodate two rather differing views on the treatment of income related grants, namely those who oppose netting off income and expense items and prefer to keep disclosure of the grant separate for purposes of comparison; and those who argue that since the enterprise might not have incurred the expense if the grant had not been available, it would be misleading to show the expense without offsetting the grant. (IAS 20.30)

IAS 20 goes on to add that disclosure of the grant may be necessary for a proper understanding of the financial statements. (IAS 20.31) Presumably this means disclosure of the full amount of the grant by way of a note, regardless of whether or not the grant has been offset against the related expense. The Standard also states that disclosure is usually appropriate of the effect of the grant on any item of income or expenditure which is required to be shown separately.

26.8.3 Agricultural government grants

IAS 41 *Agriculture* prescribes a different treatment for government grants received for biological assets. IAS 41 requires that biological assets owned by an enterprise engaging in agricultural activities should be accounted for at fair value less estimated point-of-sale costs. The standard requires that unconditional government grants relating to biological assets that are measured at fair value less estimated point-of-sale costs should be recognised as income only when the government grant becomes unconditionally receivable.

If the grant is conditional, an enterprise should only include the grant as income when all the conditions attached to it have been met. Such conditions include, for example, requiring an enterprise not to engage in a specific activity, or to reduce livestock sizes. Conditions which have a fixed term attached, for example, to refrain from farming a certain crop for five years, should not be recognised until the five years have lapsed. If, however, the grant allows for a portion to be retained based on the passage of time that has passed, then the grant should be recognised in income as time passes.

Where a biological asset cannot be valued at fair value less estimated point-of-sale costs, IAS 41 requires that the asset should be accounted for at cost less accumulated depreciation and any impairments. Government grants relating to these assets should be accounted for under IAS 20, and not in terms of IAS 41.

IAS 41 is only effective for years beginning on or after 1 January 2003, but earlier adoption is encouraged in the standard. If an enterprise chooses not to adopt IAS 41 early, agricultural grants should be accounted for under IAS 20 as detailed above until the effective date. Refer to Appendix II for IAS 41.

26.9 Repayment of government grants

IAS 20 states: 'A government grant that becomes repayable should be accounted for as a revision to an accounting estimate.' (IAS 20.32) Thus, even if the grant has been recognised as income in prior periods, its repayment does not represent a fundamental error. As described in Chapter **5**, a change in estimate is accounted for in the period of change if the change affects the period only or the period of change and future periods, if the change affects both.

IAS 20 then proceeds to set out the accounting treatment of the repayment of a government grant, as follows:

- 'Repayment of a grant related to income should be applied first against any unamortised deferred credit set up in respect of the grant. To the extent that repayment exceeds any such deferred credit, or where no such deferred credit exists, repayment should be recognised immediately as an expense.'
- 'Repayment of a grant related to an asset should be recorded by increasing the carrying amount of the asset or reducing the deferred income balance by the amount repayable. The cumulative additional depreciation that would have been recognised to date as an expense in the absence of the grant should be recognised immediately as an expense.'

(IAS 20.32)

Example 26.2

With reference to *Example 26.1*, suppose that at the end of Year 3 it is evident that Enterprise A has failed to fulfil the employment conditions attached to the receipt of the asset-related grant. The grant therefore becomes repayable. Under the two methods of presentation of the grant, treatment of the repayment is as follows:

Method A: Grant shown as deferred income

Grant received, credited in Year 1 to deferred income		£250,000
Transfers to income statement Years 1–3	(3 × £50,000)	(150,000)
Deferred income balance at end of Year 3, before repayment of grant		100,000
Total repayment of grant	£250,000	
Repayment debited to deferred income balance	(100,000)	(100,000)
Balance of repayment charged to income statement		150,000 (see note 3 below)

Note that under this method, repayment of the grant has no effect on the carrying value of the plant or on the depreciation charge.

Method B: Grant deducted from cost of asset

Cost of plant	£1,000,000
Less: grant received in Year 1	(250,000)
Net cost of plant	750,000
Depreciation charges Years 1–3 (3 × £150,000)	(450,000)
Carrying value of plant at end of Year 3, before repayment of grant	300,000
Add back grant repayable	250,000
	550,000
Charge to income statement for cumulative additional depreciation for Years 1–3 (3 × £50,000) (see notes 1 and 3 below)	(150,000)
Carrying value of plant at end of Year 3, after repayment of grant (see note 2 below)	400,000

Notes

1 The additional annual depreciation charge is calculated as the amount of grant repayable/useful life of the asset (£250,000/5 years). The depreciation charge in each of years 4 and 5 will be £200,000 (1,000,000/5 years).

2 The carrying value is original cost less three years' depreciation based on original cost (1,000,000 − (3 × 200,000)).

3 Note that the charge to the income statement, due to the repayment of the grant, under both methods is the same at £150,000, but under Method A it is presented as the repayment of the grant, whereas under Method B it is presented as an additional depreciation charge.

IAS 20 concludes by observing that the circumstances surrounding the repayment of a government grant may require consideration to be given to the possible impairment of the new carrying value of the asset. (IAS 20.33) This could occur, for example, if the repayment of the grant resulted from failure to comply with government regulations or conditions attached to receipt of the grant, which in turn reflected adverse change in the operating environment of the enterprise. Reference should be made to IAS 36 as regards impairment of assets (see Chapter **10.12**).

26.10 Disclosure

IAS 20 requires the following disclosures in respect of government grants:

- 'the accounting policy adopted for government grants, including the methods of presentation adopted in the financial statements;
- the nature and extent of government grants recognised in the financial statements and an indication of other forms of government assistance from which the enterprise has directly benefited; and
- unfulfilled conditions and other contingencies attaching to government assistance that has been recognised.'

(IAS 20.39)

It is worth noting that the Standard states that it may be necessary to disclose forms of government assistance other than grants, such as free technical or marketing advice, guarantees, or loans at nil or low interest rates, where such assistance is significant. Even though such assistance is not recognised as income in the financial statements, it may benefit the enterprise to an extent that disclosure of the nature, extent and duration of the assistance is necessary for the financial statements not to be misleading. (IAS 20.34 to 38)

With respect to loans from government at nil or low interest rates, there is a distinction to be drawn between the treatment set out in IAS 20 and the interest revenue recognition criteria in IAS 18 (r1993). IAS 20.37 states that the benefit to an enterprise from government loans at nil or low interest rates is not quantified by the imputation of interest. By contrast, IAS 18 (r1993) indicates that in situations where interest-free credit is given or financing is provided at below market interest rates, the fair value of the transaction is determined by using an imputed rate of interest. (IAS 18 (r1993).11)

Also worth noting is that IAS 20 requires disclosure of any conditions attaching to receipt of a government grant which have not yet been fulfilled at the balance sheet date, non-fulfilment of which could result in repayment of the grant. This clearly represents a contingent liability to the enterprise, and together with any other grant-related contingencies is required to be disclosed in accordance with IAS 10 (r1999), *Events After the Balance Sheet Date* (see Chapter **11**). (IAS 20.11)

Under IAS 41, government grants relating to biological assets measured at fair value less estimated point-of-sale costs require the following disclosure:

(a) nature and extent of government grants recognised;
(b) unfulfilled conditions and other contingencies attaching to the grant; and
(c) significant decreases expected in the level of government grants.

26.11 Comparison with UK GAAP

There is a broad similarity of approach between IAS 20 and its UK equivalent SSAP 4 *Accounting for Government Grants.* There is little difference between the definitions and recognition criteria used in the IAS and UK standard, although IAS 20 contains definitions of certain terms – such as 'government assistance' and 'fair value' – which are not included in SSAP 4.

The most striking difference between IAS 20 and UK GAAP arises not so much from SSAP 4, as from the requirements of the Companies Act 1985. As has already been discussed, IAS 20 permits two methods of presentation for asset-related grants, which may be either treated as deferred income and recognised as income over the useful life of the asset or deducted from cost in arriving at the carrying value of the asset. SSAP 4 also considers both treatments to be acceptable and capable of giving a true and fair view, and therefore, in principle, permits deduction of the grant from the cost of the asset.

On the basis of legal opinion obtained by the (old) Accounting Standards Committee, however, SSAP 4 excludes in practice the deduction method for UK companies (although it would be acceptable for other entities) since it is in contravention of paragraphs 17 and 26 of Schedule 4 to the Companies Act 1985 which require a fixed asset to be shown at purchase price or production cost. This is in accordance with the general accounting principle set out in Schedule 4, that each individual asset and liability must be disclosed separately, that is, assets and liabilities must not be netted off against each other.

Certain other points of comparison between IAS 20 and SSAP 4 may also be noted:

- IAS 20 stipulates that a forgivable loan from government is treated as a grant when there is reasonable assurance that the terms for forgiveness will be met. (IAS 20.10) SSAP 4 is silent on this matter.
- There are differences between the disclosure requirements of IAS 20 and

SSAP 4. Specifically, IAS 20 stipulates the following disclosures not mentioned in SSAP 4: the nature and extent of government grants recognised in the financial statements; an indication of other forms of government assistance from which the enterprise has directly benefited; and unfulfilled conditions and other contingencies attaching to recognised grants. (IAS 20.39) Conversely, SSAP 4 stipulates the following disclosures not covered by IAS 20: the effects of government grants on the results for the period and/or the financial position of the enterprise; and the nature and effects of government assistance other than grants, including if possible an estimate of the effects. (SSAP 4.28)

There is no UK equivalent to IAS 41 *Agriculture*. Therefore government grants received by agricultural enterprises would follow the accounting treatment stipulated by SSAP 4.

26.12 Comparison with US GAAP

There is no pronouncement in US GAAP which specifically covers government grants to enterprises. Instead there are a number of pronouncements which deal with aspects of the issue, but taken together they do not cover the topic of government grants as widely or as explicitly as IAS 20.

The following points of comparison may be noted[1]:

- Unlike IAS 20, US GAAP stipulates no general disclosure requirements for government grants or other forms of government assistance.
- US GAAP contains little guidance on the treatment of income-related government grants. The main discussion is contained in ARB 43, chapter 11A, 'Government Contracts – Cost-Plus Fixed-Fee Contracts', and ARB 45 *Long-Term Construction-Type Contracts.* These recommend the credit of grant to revenue, whereas IAS 20 permits a choice between crediting to revenue or deducting from the relevant expense. Otherwise, US GAAP makes few stipulations regarding income-related grants, which may be treated as revenues, as reductions of expense, as reductions of asset costs, or as credits to shareholders' equity.
- With respect to asset-related grants, IAS 20 requires a grant to be recognised either by setting up the grant as deferred income, or by deducting it from the carrying amount of the asset. In either case, the grant is effectively recognised in the income statement over the useful life of the asset through the release of deferred income or the reduction of the depreciation charge on the related asset. Under US GAAP, however, recognition

[1] See *The IASC-U.S. Comparison Project: A Report on the Similarities and Differences between IASC Standards and U.S. GAAP*, chapter 18.

of the grant could occur earlier than under IAS 20, since US GAAP permits an enterprise to recognise revenue when the costs of purchase or construction are incurred, rather than over the life of the asset. On the other hand, if an enterprise adopts the alternative of accounting for the grant by reducing the carrying value of the asset, the treatment under US GAAP is the same as under IAS 20.

- For non-monetary grants related to assets, IAS 20 permits such grants to be shown at a nominal amount or at fair value. Where the grant is treated as a reduction in the cost of the asset, this may result in non-recognition of the asset if asset value and grant net off to zero. US GAAP, as set out in APB 29 *Accounting for Nonmonetary Transactions* requires measurement of the asset received at fair value, but is otherwise silent on the question of asset recognition.
- SFAS 109.45 requires disclosure of the significant components of income tax expense attributable to continuing operations and notes that those components would include government grants (to the extent recognised as a reduction of income tax expense). Government assistance in the form of benefits which affect the income tax liability of the enterprise are specifically excluded from the scope of IAS 20 (see **26.4**). (IAS 20.2) However, IAS 12 (r2000), *Income Taxes*, para.79 requires major components of tax expense or income to be separately disclosed. Whilst government assistance that is provided for an enterprise in the form of benefits that are available in determining taxable income or are determined or limited on the basis of income tax liability are not explicitly referred to in IAS 12 (r2000) they should, if material, be included within this disclosure.

26.13 Examples from published financial statements

Note that the excerpts given do not always comply in full with all aspects of IAS and as such are not necessarily examples of best practice but merely of current practice.

Example 26.3

2. Accounting Policies

Government grants

Government grants are deferred and recognized in the income statement over the period necessary to match them with the related costs which they are intended to compensate for.

Novartis Group
Switzerland
31 December 2000
International Accounting Standards

Example 26.4

Accounting Policies

Government loans and grants

Forgivable State development loans are recognised as income in the income statement as the research and development costs relating to the project are incurred provided that these costs are recognised as an expense in the income statement. In the event of repayment, the repayments including interest are charged as an expense in the income statement as the related income is recognised as income.

If the related development costs are capitalised in the balance sheet, the development loan will be shown in the balance sheet and recognised as income as the development costs are written off.

Lundbeck
Denmark
31 December 2000
International Accounting Standards

CHAPTER 27

Construction contracts

27.1 Source

IAS 11 (r1993) *Construction Contracts.*

27.2 Brief summary of the requirements

Construction contracts are accounted for using the percentage of completion method when an enterprise is able to estimate reliably the outcome of a contract. Under the percentage of completion method, contract revenue and expenses are recognised as work progresses rather than when the work is complete. However, if an enterprise estimates that a contract will result in a loss, the total estimated loss related to a contract is recognised immediately. When an enterprise is unable to estimate reliably the outcome of a contract, it recognises contract revenue only to the extent of contract costs incurred for which is believes it will be reimbursed.

As discussed in Chapter 6, when the outcome of a transaction involving the rendering of services can be estimated reliably, revenue related to the transaction is recognised using the percentage of completion method. Due to the scope limitations of IAS 18 (r1993), *Revenue*, it only discusses the recognition of revenue rather than both revenue and expenses. As such, IAS 18 (r1993) notes that the requirements of IAS 11 (r1993) are generally applicable to the recognition of revenue and the associated expenses for a transaction involving the rendering of services.

27.3 Development of the requirements

Originally issued in 1979, IAS 11 was revised as part of the Improvements project and the option of using the completed contract method was removed.

27.4 Definition and types of construction contracts

> 'A construction contract is a contract specifically negotiated for the construction of an asset or a combination of assets that are closely interrelated or interdependent in terms of their design, technology and function or their ultimate purpose or use.'
>
> (IAS 11 (r1993).3)

In the context of IAS 11 (r1993), construction contracts include:

(a) contracts for the rendering of services which are directly related to the construction of the asset, for example, those for the services of project managers and architects; and

(b) contracts for the destruction or restoration of assets, and the restoration of the environment following the demolition of assets.

(IAS 11 (r1993).5)

The compensation element of construction contracts may be negotiated in a number of ways. IAS 11 (r1993) classifies contracts according to their compensation element as either being fixed price contracts or cost plus contracts.

> 'A fixed price contract is a construction contract in which the contractor agrees to a fixed contract price, or a fixed rate per unit of output, which in some cases is subject to cost escalation clauses.'
>
> (IAS 11 (r1993).3)

> 'A cost plus contract is a construction contract in which the contractor is reimbursed for allowable or otherwise defined costs, plus a percentage of these costs or a fixed fee.'
>
> (IAS 11 (r1993).3)

Generally, commercial contracts are negotiated on a fixed price basis while, in the UK, cost plus contracts arise more frequently on government contracts.

27.5 Combining and segmenting construction contracts

In most cases, each construction contract is accounted for as one contract. However, in some circumstances, it may be appropriate to treat several related contracts as forming one contract or conversely, to treat one contract as comprising several separate contracts. The main factor in making such a determination is the manner in which the contract was negotiated. However, the IAS sets out several other factors which are to be considered as discussed below.

The requirements of the IAS around the combining or segmenting of contracts are aimed at reflecting the substance of the transaction(s) rather than their legal or contractual form. In other words, did the contractor negotiate the contract and related margin independently of other related contracts or was the deal negotiated as a package, although legally segmented into several contracts. As with most IAS, the substance takes precedence over the legal form.

Often one construction contract covers the construction of more than one asset. When this is the case, such contracts are required to be treated as separate contracts when:

'(a) separate proposals have been submitted for each asset;
(b) each asset has been subject to separate negotiation and the contractor and customer have been able to accept or reject that part of the contract relating to each asset; and
(c) the costs and revenues of each asset can be identified.'

(IAS 11 (r1993).8)

Example 27.1

A contractor submits two separate bids for the construction of a 10 mile section of motorway and a bridge included in the 10 mile stretch. The government has structured the tender process such that the contract for the motorway construction will be awarded separately from the contract for the bridge construction.

Since separate proposals have been submitted for the motorway and bridge, even if one contractor wins the work in relation to both pieces and the contract with the government for both pieces is included in one legal contract, each piece, the bridge and the motorway, will be accounted for separately under IAS 11 (r1993), and the contractor will need to have a cost system in place to allow segregation of costs between the two parts of the project.

In other circumstances, a group of contracts may be required to be treated as a single contract, despite the fact that the contracts may be with different parties when:

'(a) the group of contracts is negotiated as a single package;
(b) the contracts are so closely interrelated that they are, in effect, part of a single project with an overall profit margin; and
(c) the contracts are performed concurrently or in a continuous sequence.'

(IAS 11 (r1993).9)

Example 27.2

A contractor submits *one* bid for the construction of a 10 mile section of motorway and a bridge which is at one end of the 10 mile stretch. The bridge is in a different county from the motorway and therefore, although only one bid is submitted because the two counties have agreed to work together on the construction of the road, when the contracts are drawn up a separate contract exists for the bridge and the highway since the third party (the respective county government) differs in each case.

Since *one* proposal has been submitted for the motorway and bridge, even if two separate contracts are eventually signed, the contracts have been negotiated as a single package and, since the bid was submitted on the basis that one piece would not be awarded without the other piece, the contractor must have worked out the expected gross margin he was prepared to accept on both pieces together. Therefore, the two separate contracts will be accounted for as one contract under IAS 11 (r1993).

A construction contract may provide an option for the construction of an additional asset or the customer may amend the contract to include the construction of an additional asset. In such cases, the construction of an additional asset is required to be treated as a separate construction contract when:

'(a) the asset differs significantly in design, technology or function from the asset or assets covered by the original contract; or
(b) the price of the asset is negotiated without regard to the original contract price.'

(IAS 11 (r1993).10)

Example 27.3

A contractor is nearing completion of a 10 mile stretch of motorway under a contract with the government. Under the contract, the contractor is paid £10 million per mile. If the government and customer amend the contract to cover 13 miles of motorway at the same rate of £10 million per mile, the amendment is considered part of the original contract since the price of the amendment is the same as originally negotiated, and the asset (motorway) does not differ significantly from the asset (motorway) covered by the original contract.

27.6 Contract revenue

In order to apply the percentage of completion method to construction contracts, an enterprise must be able to estimate contract revenue and costs. This section deals with the components of contract revenue.

As one would expect, contract revenue comprises the initial amount of agreed revenue included in the construction contract. However, it also includes variations, claims and incentive payments to the extent that it is probable that they will result in revenue and that they are capable of being reliably measured. (IAS 11 (r1993).11)

Therefore, the revenue recognition criteria for variations, claims and incentive payments are the same as for other types of revenue. The additional criteria discussed below are included in the guidance paragraphs of the standard and are intended to reflect the Board's interpretation of how the revenue recognition criteria should be applied to variations, claims and incentive payments.

'A variation is an instruction by the customer for a change in the scope of the work to be performed under the contract.' (IAS 11 (r1993).13) Depending on the circumstances, variations may lead to increases or decreases in contract revenue. For example, once a project has been negotiated, a customer may finalise the design of the item to be constructed, and the changes in design have implications on the amount of work required by the contractor. These changes are referred to as variations. In practice, problems arise when assessing the likelihood of recovery of variations and thus whether or not they should be included in contract revenue. IAS 11 (r1993) suggests that a variation be included in contract revenue when:

> '(a) it is probable that the customer will approve the variation and the amount of revenue arising from the variation; and
> (b) the amount of revenue can be reliably measured.'
>
> (IAS 11 (r1993).13)

However, as discussed above, it is a matter of judgement whether or not a variation will be approved by the customer and, due to the fact that their recovery is often based on a negotiation process, the amount included in contract revenue related to variations is also usually an estimate.

'A claim is an amount that the contractor seeks to collect from the customer or another party as reimbursement for costs not included in the contract price.' (IAS 11 (r1993).14) A claim in this context does not usually imply that a legal claim has been filed in a court of law. Claims may arise from customer caused delays, errors in specifications or design, or disputed variations in contract work. Since claims are initiated by the contractor, their recoverability may be even more uncertain than that of variations. Since the recoverability of claims is unknown, the amount included in contract revenue with respect to claims is an estimate based on management's judgement. Similar to variations, claims are also often settled at the end of the contract as a result of a negotiation. IAS 11 (r1993) suggests that claims only be included in contract revenue when:

'(a) negotiations have reached an advanced stage such that it is probable that the customer will accept the claim; and
(b) the amount that it is probable will be accepted by the customer can be measured reliably.'

(IAS 11 (r1993).14)

As the name implies, incentive payments are additional amounts paid to the contractor if specified performance standards are met or exceeded. Commonly such incentive payments relate to completion dates where the earlier the work is completed, the more contract revenue will be receivable. IAS 11 (r1993) suggests that incentive payments be included in contract revenue when:

'(a) the contract is sufficiently advanced that it is probable that the specified performance standards will be met or exceeded; and
(b) the amount of the incentive payment can be measured reliably.'

(IAS 11 (r1993).15)

27.7 Contract costs

In order to apply the percentage of completion method to construction contracts, an enterprise must be able to estimate contract revenue and costs. This section deals with the components of contract costs.

Contract costs include:

(a) costs that relate directly to the specific contract such as:
  '(i) site labour costs, including site preparation;
  (ii) costs of materials used in construction;
  (iii) depreciation of plant and equipment used on the contract;
  (iv) costs of moving plant, equipment and materials to and from the contract site;
  (v) costs of hiring plant and equipment;
  (vi) costs of design and technical assistance that is directly related to the contract;
  (vii) the estimated costs of rectification and guarantee work, including expected warranty costs; and
  (viii) claims from third parties.'

(IAS 11 (r1993).17);

(b) costs that are attributable to contract activity in general and can be allocated on a systematic and rational basis to the contract such as insurance, costs of design and technical assistance that is not directly related to a specific contract and construction overheads; and
(c) such other costs as are specifically chargeable to the customer under the terms of the contract such as general and administrative costs and development costs for which reimbursement is specified in the terms of the contract.

Incidental income, such as income from the sale of surplus materials or the disposal of plant and equipment at the end of the contract, is not considered contract revenue and is offset against contract costs. (IAS 11 (r1993).17)

The SIC issued a draft interpretation in February 2000 on incidental operations. The draft SIC stated that before an asset that is being constructed or developed is ready for its intended use, income earned and expenses incurred can result from these incidential operations undertaken by an enterprise. The draft SIC proposed that the results of such operations should be recognised in profit and loss for the period.

At the IAS Board meeting in April 2001, the board did not approve the SIC interpretation, but concluded that the issue should be addressed in the Improvements Project (see Chapter **2**).

Offsetting is generally not permitted under IAS 1 (r1997), *Presentation of Financial Statements*, unless it is immaterial or another IAS permits or requires it. Paragraph 17 of IAS 11 (r1993) permits gains on disposal of plant and equipment to be offset against contract costs. If these gains are material, although not specifically required, it would be considered best practice to disclose them separately in the notes to the financial statements.

When costs cannot be allocated or attributed to a particular contract, they are not included in contract costs. IAS 11 (r1993) identifies the following costs which are unlikely to be includable in contract costs:

> '(a) general administration costs for which reimbursement is not specified in the contract;
> (b) selling costs;
> (c) research and development costs for which reimbursement is not specified in the contract; and
> (d) depreciation of idle plant and equipment that is not used on a particular contract.'
>
> (IAS 11 (r1993).20)

IAS 11 (r1993) allows a choice when dealing with costs associated with securing a contract. Such costs may be included in the cost of the contract if they can be separately identified and measured reliably and it is probable that a contract will be obtained. However, if an enterprise expenses such costs as they are incurred and subsequently receives a contract, it may not reinstate such costs as an asset. (IAS 11 (r1993).21)

An interesting question arises when costs associated with securing a contract have been incurred but the contract has not been received at the year end. The guidance clearly states that if the amounts are expensed, they may not be reinstated if subsequently the contract is received. However, the

Framework definition of an asset states that it is a resource controlled by the enterprise as a result of a past events and from which future economic benefits are expected to flow to the enterprise. It would be difficult to argue that the resource or potential asset of deferred acquisition costs is controlled and is the result of a past event since the contract has not been awarded. Therefore, generally such costs should not be capitalised over a period end unless immaterial.

27.8 Percentage of completion method

Construction contracts are accounted for using the percentage of completion method. Under this method, at the balance sheet date, an entity estimates the outcome, or total profit or loss, which will be made on a contract. As part of this estimation process, it estimates the stage or percentage of completion of the contract. When the enterprise is able to make a reliable estimate of the outcome of the contract, it applies the estimated percentage of completion to the total revenue and costs expected related to the contract to determine the amount of revenue and cost to be recognised in the period. If an enterprise expects that a loss will be made on a contract, it is recognised immediately. In summary, under this method, contract revenue is matched with the contract costs incurred in reaching the stage of completion at the balance sheet date, resulting in the reporting of revenue, expense and profit which can be attributed to the proportion of work completed.

It is *not* acceptable under IAS 11 (r1993) to recognise all of the revenue and costs related to a contract at the end of the contract. This method is sometimes referred to as the completed contract method. The only exceptions to this rule are if a contract begins and ends in the same period or if the contract and the aggregate of all similar contracts is immaterial since IASs do not apply to immaterial items.

27.8.1 Estimating the outcome of a contract

In order to make a reliable estimate of the outcome of a contract, an enterprise will need to make reference to the contract which sets out each party's enforceable rights regarding the asset to be constructed, the consideration to be exchanged, the manner of settlement, etc.

IAS 11 (r1993) sets out different criteria which must be met in order to estimate reliably the outcome of a contract for cost plus and fixed price contracts. In reality, if a contractor is unable to meet these criteria, it is unlikely that the contractor would have been able to complete the tender process in the first place.

When an enterprise enters into a cost plus contract, in order to estimate reliably the outcome of the contract, the following conditions must be satisfied:

- 'it is probable that the economic benefits associated with the contract will flow to the enterprise; and
- the contract costs attributable to the contract, whether or not specifically reimbursable, can be clearly identified and measured reliably.'

(IAS 11 (r1993).24)

Thus, when an enterprise enters into a cost plus contract, in order to estimate reliably the outcome of the contract, it must be able to identify contract costs attributable to the contract, whether or not they are specifically reimbursable. Unlike a fixed price contract, the amount of revenue related to a cost plus contract is generally unknown but can be calculated based on the terms of the contract and the estimated costs of the contract. In addition, in order to use the percentage of completion method, it must be probable that the economic benefits will flow to the enterprise.

When an enterprise enters into a fixed price contract, in order to estimate the outcome of the contract, the following conditions must be satisfied:

- 'total contract revenue can be measured reliably;
- it is probable that the economic benefits associated with the contract will flow to the enterprise;
- both the contract costs to complete the contract and the stage of contract completion at the balance sheet date can be measured reliably; and
- the contract costs attributable to the contract can be clearly identified and measured reliably so that actual contract costs incurred can be compared with prior estimates.'

(IAS 11 (r1993).23)

There are three tests to overcome in the four conditions set out above. First, an enterprise must be able to estimate reliably the outcome (profit or loss) of a fixed price contract, by estimating total contract revenue and costs to complete the contract. Second, in order to use the percentage of completion method, it must be probable that the economic benefits associated with the contract will flow to the enterprise. Third, an enterprise must be able to estimate the stage of completion of the contract. In order to make reliable estimations of costs incurred to date and to be incurred, the enterprise must have a cost system which is capable of identifying and measuring costs attributable to the contract.

In practice, progress payments or advances received from a customer are normally not reliable indicators of the percentage of completion of a contract since they are usually intended to fund the activities of the contractor rather than reimburse for work performed to date. There are several ways of estimating the percentage of completion including:

(a) using the proportion that contract costs incurred for work performed to date bear to the estimated total contract cots;
(b) surveys of work performed; or
(c) completion of a physical proportion of the contract work.

(IAS 11 (r1993).30)

When method (a) is chosen, only those contract costs that reflect work performed are included in costs incurred to date. For example contract costs that relate to future activity on the contract, such as costs of materials that have been purchased but not yet used, or payments made to subcontractors in advance of work being performed, would be excluded from costs incurred to date. However, if materials have been made specifically for the contract, they are included in contract costs even if they have not yet been used on the basis that it is unlikely that they would be suitable for use on other contracts.

Example 27.4

A contractor undertakes a three year contract. At the end of year 1, management estimates:

	£
Revenue	1,000
Costs incurred to date	(300)
Est. costs to complete	(600)
Est. gross profit	100

However, during year 1, the contractor purchased materials to be used in year 2 of £50. Therefore, when calculating the percentage of completion of this contract based on the proportion of costs incurred to date to total costs of the contract:

	£
Costs incurred to date	300
Less: materials purchased for future years	(50)
Cost incurred related to work performed to date	250
total estimated costs	900
Percentage of completion at end of year 1	28%

At a minimum, at each balance sheet date, an enterprise reviews its estimates relating to the outcome of a contract and makes revisions as appropriate. Since the percentage of completion method is applied to each contract on a cumulative basis, revisions are treated as changes in estimates and are used in estimating the percentage of completion and the outcome of the contract in the period of change and in future periods. As such, prior periods are not adjusted. In practice, most contractors review progress and expected outcomes much more frequently than each balance sheet date in order to maintain control over the project.

For a discussion of the accounting treatment when a reliable estimate of the outcome of a contract cannot be made, see **27.8.5**.

Example 27.5

Same facts as in *Example 27.4*.

In year 2, costs of £300 are incurred.

Management estimates that costs of £350 will be incurred in year 3.

Costs incurred in year 1 relating to work performed to date	250
Costs incurred in year 1 relating to materials used in year 2	50
Other costs incurred in year 2	300
Costs incurred to date	600
Estimated costs to complete	350
Total estimated costs	950
Estimated revenue	1,000
Estimated gross profit	50

A prior period adjustment is not made to the revenue and expenses recognised in year 1 due to the change in estimate in year 2. The change will be reflected in years 2 and year 3 which is consistent with IAS 8 (r1993), *Net Profit or Loss for the Period, Fundamental Errors and Changes in Accounting Policies.*

27.8.2 Recognition of contract losses

When an enterprise estimates that the outcome of a contract will be a loss, the expected loss is required to be recognised as an expense immediately. (IAS 11 (r1993).36) The amount of the loss expensed is the expected loss on the entire contract and thus is determined without reference to:

(a) whether or not work has commenced on the contract;
(b) the stage of completion of contract activity; or
(c) the amount of profits expected to arise on other contracts which are not treated as a single construction contract as described in **27.5**.

Example 27.6

Same facts as in *Example 27.5* but in year 2, the estimated costs to complete the contract in year are £500.

	£
Costs incurred to date	600
Estimated costs to complete	500
Total estimated costs	1100
Estimated revenue	1000
Estimated loss	(100)

Since management now estimates a loss on the contract, the £100 loss is recognised immediately as an expense in year 2 when the estimate is made. In addition, any profit recognised in year 1 is reversed in the current period.

Losses recognised on construction contracts should be credited to the work in progress account. Where there is no balance on the work in progress account, a provision for the loss should be created in the same way as a provision for losses under an onerous contract would be provided for under IAS 37 *Provisions, Contingent Liabilities and Contingent Assets* (see **11.9**). Even though IAS 37 scopes out construction contracts accounted for under IAS 11 (r1993), the treatment of onerous contracts would be the same for IAS 11 (r1993) provisions as IAS 11 (r1993) does not prescribe an accounting treatment for such provisions.

27.8.3 Recognition of contract revenue

In order to recognise the revenue earned to date on a contract, it must be probable that associated future economic benefits will flow to the enterprise and that their amount can be estimated reliably. In general, the amount of future economic benefits can be estimated reliably when it is possible to estimate reliably the outcome of a contract as described above. If it becomes apparent subsequent to recognition in the income statement, that revenue related to a contract will not be collectible, the uncollectible amount is recognised as a bad debt expense rather than as an adjustment of contract revenue.

The amount of revenue recognised in a period is determined by applying the estimated percentage of completion at the balance sheet date to total contract revenue.

Example 27.7

Same facts as in *Example 27.4.*

In year 1, management estimated that the contract was 28% complete.

Therefore the amount of revenue recognised at the end of year 1 is calculated as:

28% * £1000 = £280	Revenue recognised in year 1
250	Expenses recognised in year 1
30	Gross profit recognised in year 1

27.8.4 Recognition of contract costs

When the proportion of contract costs incurred for work performed to date to total contract costs is used to estimate the percentage of completion, this generally results in contract costs being expensed in the period incurred. However, if costs have been incurred which relate to future activity on the contract, they may be carried forward provided it is probable they will be recovered under the contract. As discussed above such costs may relate to, but are not limited to, materials purchased for future use or advance payments to subcontractors. However, if other methods are used to estimate the percentage of completion on a contract, this may result in contract costs being recognised in the balance sheet and recognised in future periods in the income statement.

Example 27.8

Same facts as in *Examples 27.4* and *27.7* except that rather than using the proportion that contract costs incurred for work performed to date bear to estimated total contract costs to estimate the percentage of completion, management uses surveys of work performed.

The surveys indicate that the work is 20% complete at the end of year 1.

Therefore revenue and expenses recognised in year 1 related to the contract are:

	£	
Revenue recognised in year 1	200	(£1000 * 20%)
Expenses recognised in year 1	180	(£900 * 20%)
Gross profit recognised in year 1	20	

Since expenses of £250 were incurred in year 1, not all of the costs incurred related to work performed on the contract has been expensed at the end of year 1. Thus, £70 being the difference between costs incurred and expenses recognised is recognised as an asset in the balance sheet at the end of year 1.

When contract costs are not probable of being recovered, they are recognised as an expense immediately. IAS 11 (r1993) gives the following examples of construction contracts where the recoverability of contract costs incurred may not be probable and in which contract costs may need to be recognised as an expense immediately; contracts:

> '(a) which are not fully enforceable, that is, their validity is seriously in question;
> (b) the completion of which is subject to the outcome of pending litigation or legislation;
> (c) relating to properties that are likely to be condemned or expropriated;
> (d) where the customer is unable to meet its obligations; or
> (e) where the contractor is unable to complete the contract or otherwise meet its obligations under the contract.'
>
> (IAS 11 (r1993).34)

27.8.5 When the outcome of a contract cannot be estimated reliably

When the outcome of a contract cannot be estimated reliably as described in **27.8.1**:

> '(a) revenue should be recognised only to the extent of contract costs incurred that it is probable will be recovered; and
> (b) contract costs should be recognised as an expense in the period in which they are incurred.'
>
> (IAS 11 (r1993).32)

When the outcome of a contract cannot be estimated, in order to be prudent, no profit is recognised on the contract. This is achieved by only recognising revenue to the extent of costs incurred and all costs being recognised as expenses as incurred. This method is often referred to as the zero profit method. The outcome of a contract often cannot be estimated during the early stages of a contract when it may not be possible to estimate the outcome of the entire contract but it is probable that contract costs will be covered. As discussed in section **27.8.2**, if it becomes apparent that a loss will be made on the contract, the full amount of the loss is expensed immediately.

Example 27.9

Same facts as *Example 27.7* except that management is unable to estimate reliably the costs which will be incurred in order to complete the contract. Therefore, revenue is only recognised to the extent of expenses incurred. Thus £250 of revenue is recognised and £250 of expense is recognised resulting in no gross profit being recognised in the period.

When the uncertainties which prevented reliable estimation of the outcome of a construction contract no longer exist, contract revenue and expenses are recognised using the percentage of completion method.

IAS 11 (r1993) does not address the disclosure in the period in which this occurs. Presumably, in the first period in which the percentage of completion method is applied, the profit on the contract which has not been recognised in previous periods will be recognised. This recognition would lead to a distortion of the profit figure included in the accounts related to a particular contract. Although not required, it would be good practice to disclose the reason for such distortion, if material.

27.8.6 Recognition of amounts in the balance sheet

At each balance sheet date, for all contracts in progress for which costs incurred plus recognised profits (less recognised losses) exceeds progress billings, a gross amount due from customers for contract work is recognised as an asset in the balance sheet. This amount is calculated as:

> *costs incurred plus recognised profits – the sum of recognised losses and progress billings*

Similarly, at each balance sheet date, for all contracts in progress for which progress billings exceed costs incurred plus recognised profits (less recognised losses), a gross amount due to customers for contract work is recognised as a liability in the balance sheet. This amount is calculated using the same formula as above. When the result of the formula is positive, an asset is recognised; when the result is negative, a liability is recognised.

The wording used in IAS 11 (r1993) of gross amount due from customers and gross amount due to customers is a bit misleading in that actual trade amounts receivable or payable which are outstanding with customers are not taken into account in this computation (only total progress billings). These are recognised as separate assets and liabilities in the balance sheet. In order to avoid confusion, an enterprise may present the amount under another more descriptive heading such as costs and estimated profits in excess of progress billings on uncompleted contracts or progress billings in excess of costs and estimated profits on uncompleted contracts.

Example 27.10

An enterprise enters into a 3 year contract.

Estimated revenues = £10,000.

Estimated total cost = £8,000.

However, during year 2, management revises its estimate of total costs incurred and thus the outcome of the contract. As a result, during year 2, a loss is recognised on the contract for the year, even though the contract will still be profitable overall.

	Year 1	*Year 2*	*Year 3*
Estimated revenue	10,000	10,000	10,000
Estimated total cost	8,000	9,000	9,000
Estimated total profit	2,000	1,000	1,000
Costs incurred to date	4,000	6,750	9,000
Percentage of completion	50%	75%	100%
Recognised profit/(loss) in year	1,000	(250)	250
Cumulative recognised profit	1,000	750	1,000

Progress billings of £4,000, £4,000 and £1,000 are made on the last day of each year and are received in the first month of the following year. The balance sheet asset at the end of each year is:

	Year 1	*Year 2*	*Year 3*
	£	£	£
Costs incurred	4,000	6,750	9,000
Recognised profits	1,000	1,000	1,250
(recognised losses)	–	(250)	(250)
(progress billings)	(4,000)	(8,000)	(9,000)
Amount recognised as an asset/(liability)	1,000	(500)	1,000

In addition, at each year end, the enterprise recognises a separate trade debtor for the amount outstanding at the end of the year of £4,000, £4,000 and £1,000.

27.9 Disclosure

'An enterprise should disclose:

(a) the amount of contract revenue recognised as revenue in the period;
(b) the methods used to determine the contract revenue recognised in the period; and
(c) the methods used to determine the stage of completion of contracts in progress.'

(IAS 11 (r1993).39)

> 'An enterprise should disclose each of the following for contracts in progress at the balance sheet date:
> (a) the aggregate amount of costs incurred and recognised profits (less recognised losses) to date;
> (b) the amount of advances received; and
> (c) the amount of retentions.'
>
> (IAS 11 (r1993).40)

'Advances are amounts received by the contractor before the related work is performed.' (IAS 11 (r1993).41) Advances are commonly made in order to fund the purchase of materials by a contractor before the related work on a contract begins. Advances are recognised as liabilities until the related revenue is earned. 'Retentions are amounts of progress billings which are not paid until the satisfaction of conditions specified in the contract for the payment of such amounts or until defects have been rectified.' (IAS 11 (r1993).41) In practice, retentions are recognised as receivables in the balance sheet of a contractor.

IAS 11 (r1993) contains a reminder that an enterprise discloses any contingent liabilities or assets such as warranty costs, claims, penalties or possible losses, in accordance with IAS 10 (r1999), *Events After the Balance Sheet Date* (see Chapter **15**).

27.10 Comparison to UK GAAP

The main source of authoritative literature on construction contracts in UK GAAP is SSAP 9 *Stocks and long-term contracts.* The requirements of SSAP 9 and IAS 11 (r1993) are very similar. However, in certain situations, IAS 11 (r1993) requires the combination or segmentation of contracts. This is not required under SSAP 9.

UK Company Law does not permit the inclusion of profit within the balance sheet classification of 'Stocks and work-in-progress'. Thus the value of work done is recognised in revenue and classified as a debtor, with a corresponding release of the relevant portion of the cost of work-in-progress to cost of sales. Progress payments are therefore regarded as a reduction of debtors.

27.11 Comparison to US GAAP

The main sources of authoritative literature on construction contracts in US GAAP are ARB No. 45 *Long-Term Construction-Type Contracts* and AICPA Statement of Position 81-1 *Accounting for Performance of Construction-Type and Certain Production-Type Contracts.*

Under US GAAP, use of the percentage of completion method is required unless an enterprise cannot determine contract revenues or costs, estimated costs to complete or the stage of completion. When an enterprise cannot estimate one of these items, use of the completed contract is required. However, if it is impractical to estimate the final outcome of a contract except to assure that no loss will be incurred, the zero per cent method may be applied. Under IAS 11 (r1993), use of the completed contract method is prohibited. In similar circumstances, under IAS 11 (r1993), use of the zero per cent method would be appropriate.

Under US GAAP, the combination or segregation of contracts is permitted in certain circumstances but not required. In contrast, in an attempt to curb profit manipulation through inconsistent combination or segregation of contracts, IAS 11 (r1993) requires segregation or combination when specific criteria are met.

27.12 Examples from published financial statements

Note that the excerpts given do not always comply in full with all aspects of IAS and as such are not necessarily examples of best practice but merely of current practice.

Example 27.11

Note 4, Revenue recognition

Revenues from construction contracts are recognized according to the percentage-of-completion method. Depending on the type of business, the stage of completion is determined by delivery events, by units of delivery or by a survey of work performed.

Note 9, Other Current Assets

(US$ in millions)	*1998*	*1997*
Non-trade receivables	1,688	1,625
Prepaid expenses/accrued income	937	887
Advances to suppliers	511	552
Advances to contractors	50	31
Sales in excess of invoicing	1,277	1,188
Total	**4,463**	**4,283**

Sales recognised in excess of invoicing originate from application of the percentage of completion method for construction contracts and are reported net of related advances spent, as follows:

Sales in excess of invoicing (gross)	3,241	2,808
Advances spent see Note 14	−1,964	−1,620
Sales in excess of invoicing (net)	1,277	1,188

Note 14, Advances from Customers

(US$ in millions)	*1998*	*1997*
Advances (gross)	5,704	5,740
Advances spent relating to sales in excess of invoicing	1,964	1,620
Advances spent relating to work in progress	−1,094	−1,508
Advances (net)	**2,646**	**2,612**

Advances (gross) represent the total of down and progress payments received for orders or parts of orders not yet invoiced.

Advances spent represent the part of gross advances consumed on work performed for orders not yet invoiced.

ABB AseaBrown Boveri Limited
Switzerland
31 December 1998
International Accounting Standards

Example 27.12

Balance Sheet

(All amounts in millions of Rands)	*2000*	*1999*
Current Assets		
Contracts in progress and contracts receivable	731,1	676,2

Accounting Policies

Contracts in progress and contract receivables

The valuation of contracts in progress and contract receivables takes account of all direct expenditure and related indirect expenditure on contracts and includes a proportion of profit determined with reference to the stage of completion and the nature of each contract. Payments on account and anticipated losses to completion are deducted.

Revenue

Revenue is the aggregate of the turnover of subsidiaries and the Group's share of joint ventures. Contracting turnover included therein comprises the value of work executed on contracts during the year.

Note 6, Contracts in progress and contract receivables

(All amounts in millions of Rands)	*2000*	*1999*
Amounts due on contracts	536,0	500,2
Retention receivable	195,1	176,0
	731,1	676,2

Murray & Roberts
South Africa
30 June 2000
South African Generally Accepted Accounting Standards

CHAPTER 28

Hyperinflationary economies

28.1 Sources

IAS 21 (r1993)	*The Effects of Changes in Foreign Exchange Rates.*
IAS 29	*Financial Reporting in Hyperinflationary Economies.*
SIC-19	*Reporting Currency – Measurement and Presentation of Financial Statements under IAS 21 and IAS 29.*

28.2 Brief summary of the requirements

IAS 29 requires any enterprise which is *reporting* in the currency of a hyperinflationary economy to prepare its financial statements in terms of the measuring unit current at the balance sheet date. This applies to figures for the current period and to comparative information. SIC-19 introduces the term *measurement currency,* establishing criteria for determining the measurement currency of an enterprise and clarifies that restatement under IAS 29 is always required where the measurement currency is a currency in a hyperinflationary economy. This applies whether the financial statements are published on their own or included in the financial statements of another enterprise under the requirements of IAS 21 (r1993) in respect of foreign entities.

28.3 Development of the requirements

This Standard was first approved in 1989 and 'reformatted' in 1994. This means that the layout and presentation were changed, as well as some of the terminology. However the content itself is otherwise unaltered.

SIC-19 was published in November 2000 and is effective for periods beginning on or after 1 January 2001.

In September 2001, the SIC issued SIC-D30 for comment.

28.4 Scope

IAS 29 addresses the issues associated with financial reporting when the reporting currency is that of a hyperinflationary economy. It does not apply in situations where an enterprise operates in a hyperinflationary economy, but reports in a more stable currency, such as US dollars. However, it would only be appropriate to report in a more stable currency if that currency is an appropriate measurement currency as defined by SIC-19 (see **28.6**).

IAS 29 applies to the financial statements of an individual enterprise and to consolidated financial statements. The premise for IAS 29 is that, since money rapidly loses its purchasing power in a hyperinflationary economy, to report an enterprise's operating results and financial position in a currency of that economy without restatement would be meaningless to a user of the accounts. Comparative information would have no value, and even the profits of a single financial period would be distorted. For example, the cost at which inventory is acquired and the price at which it is sold do not only reflect a normal trading profit margin, but also include a price change which is beyond the control of the enterprise.

IAS 29 applies equally to financial statements based on historical cost accounting and those based on current cost accounting. In either case they should be 'stated in terms of the measuring unit current at the balance sheet date.' (IAS 29.8)

28.5 Definitions

IAS 29 does not attempt to define precisely at what point hyperinflation is deemed to arise but stresses that this is a matter of judgement. One guideline that is suggested is an economic environment in which the cumulative rate of inflation over a three year period is in the region of 100 per cent or more. This is generally understood to be a compounded rate, although IAS 29 is not specific on this issue. Other suggested characteristics of hyperinflation are:

- people prefer to hold non-monetary assets, rather than cash, as the value of cash is quickly eroded. For the same reason, people prefer to have net monetary liabilities in the local currency, rather than net monetary assets as this increases their purchasing power;
- prices are quoted in a different, more stable currency;
- credit transactions are carried out at prices which compensate for the expected loss in purchasing power during the credit period; and
- interest rates, wages and prices are linked to a price index. (IAS 29.3)

In recent times a number of Asian, South American, African and Eastern European countries have suffered from hyperinflation. These include Brazil, Mexico, Turkey, Venezuela, Nigeria, Russia, Romania and Zimbabwe.

The general price index to be used is one that reflects changes in general purchasing power. (IAS 29.37) No further guidance is given in this area. IAS 29 states that it is desirable that all enterprises reporting in the currency of any particular hyperinflationary economy use the same index to achieve comparability between the financial statements of different entities. Any reporting enterprise implementing IAS 29 should therefore first consider which price index is used by other local reporting enterprises, particularly those in the same industry, and apply that index, provided it is believed to be an indicator of changes in general purchasing power. The statement notes that where a general price index is not available for the period, the inflation rate may be estimated by means of considering the depreciation of the exchange rate of the hyperinflationary currency against a relatively stable foreign currency. Although the statement does not specifically indicate this, it is submitted that a similar estimate should be used where the available general price index is unreliable.

Monetary items are defined as 'money held and items to be received or paid in money.' (IAS 29.12) This includes cash at bank and in hand, receivables and payables (trade and other), accrued expenses and loans.

An enterprise's net monetary position is the difference between its monetary assets and monetary liabilities.

28.6 Measurement currency

IAS 21 (r1993) uses the term *reporting currency* both to define foreign currency as any currency other the reporting currency and to refer to the currency used in presentation of the financial statements. This, in turn, has implications on the accounting for the foreign currency transactions under IAS 21 (r1993) (see **22.5**) and the requirements of hyperinflation restatement under IAS 29. To clarify this situation SIC-19 distinguishes between the *measurement currency* and the *presentation currency* as reflecting two aspects of the broader term – the reporting currency.

Prior to the issue of SIC-19, many companies chose to use a more stable currency, such as the US dollar, as their reporting currency, thus avoiding a complex, time consuming and expensive process of restating their financial statements under IAS 29. SIC-19 removes that option by requiring restatement in terms of IAS 29 for all enterprises whose *measurement currency* is a currency of a hyperinflationary economy. Having restated its financial statements under IAS 29, an enterprise may then decide to use a different currency for presentation of its financial statements. This is discussed in **22.11** above.

As discussed in **22.5** above, SIC-19 makes it clear that the determination of measurement currency is based on the facts and circumstances of each enterprise and is not a matter of choice. Measurement currency is normally the currency in which most of the company's transactions are denominated and settled.

However, if the currency of a country that does not have a hyperinflationary economy is determined to be an appropriate measurement currency, the enterprise is not required to restate its financial statements under IAS 29.

Although an enterprise that is domiciled in a hyperinflationary economy normally presents its financial statements using the currency of the country in which it is domiciled which is also usually its measurement currency, it may choose to present them in a different currency.

As discussed in **22.11** above, one possible way of restating financial statements prepared using the measurement currency into another currency for presentation purposes is to use the method prescribed by IAS 21 (r1993).30 in translating the financial statements of a foreign entity for incorporation in the consolidated financial statements of the investor (the 'net investment' method). If this method is used and the measurement currency of the enterprise is that of a hyperinflationary economy, further questions are whether the comparative amounts from the prior period restated under IAS 29 should be updated to the measurement unit current at the balance sheet date of the most recent period presented and whether they are translated using the closing rate of exchange for the prior period or the most recent period presented. See **28.8.5** for a discussion of the possible views on this matter.

28.7 Implementation

Where hyperinflation occurs, IAS 29 is applied to the primary financial statements of any enterprise reporting in that currency from the *beginning* of the period in which the existence of hyperinflation is identified. (IAS 29.4) Ideally IAS 29 will be applied to all enterprises reporting in the currency of that hyperinflationary economy from the same date, in order to achieve consistency in financial reporting between enterprises. However, clearly this will not always be the case in practice. (IAS 29.4)

In order to close down two possible areas of abuse IAS 29.7 states specifically that:

- it is not desirable to present separately a set of financial statements prepared under the normal rules; and
- it is not permitted under any circumstances to prepare primary financial statements under normal rules and simply append financial statements prepared in accordance with IAS 29.

The effect of this is that financial statements prepared in accordance with IAS 29 are to be presented as the definitive accounts of the enterprise. Where a set of financial statements prepared under normal rules is appended or otherwise shown separately (although this is discouraged), it will need to be made clear that their status is subordinate to the IAS 29 financial statements.

Regardless of whether financial statements are based on historical cost accounting or on current cost accounting, they are to be 'stated in terms of the measuring unit current at the balance sheet date.' (IAS 29.8) The cash flow statement is specifically included in this requirement. (IAS 29.33)

Any comparative information for earlier periods is stated in terms of the *same* measuring unit, and not the measurement units relating to the earlier periods. (IAS 29.34)

In practical terms this requirement means multiplying all comparative amounts by the conversion factor which reflects the change in the general price index from the previous balance sheet date to the current year balance sheet date, provided comparative amounts were prepared in accordance with IAS 29.

28.8 Historical cost financial statements

28.8.1 Balance Sheet

IAS 29 sets out the following treatments for balance sheet items.

	Balance Sheet Item	*Treatment*	*Examples*
1	Assets and liabilities having a pre-defined link to price changes.	Adjust in accordance with the particular agreements in place. (IAS 29.13)	Index linked bonds and loans.
2	Other monetary items.	These do not require restatement, since they are already expressed in terms of the measuring unit current at the balance sheet date. (IAS 29.12)	Cash, receivables and payables (see definition of monetary items given in **28.5**).
3	Non-monetary assets carried at a valuation which is current at the balance sheet date.	These do not require restatement, since they are already expressed in terms of the measuring unit current at the balance sheet date. (IAS 29.14)	Inventory carried at net realisable value; investment properties carried at revalued amounts at the balance sheet date.

4	Non-monetary assets carried at a valuation which is not current at the balance sheet date.	Restatement is required from the date of the valuation to the balance sheet date. (IAS 29.18)	Property revalued at a date other than the balance sheet date.
5	Other balance sheet amounts, i.e., items carried at cost, or cost less depreciation.	These are restated in terms of the measuring unit current at the balance sheet date by applying a general price index. (IAS 29.15) (See below.)	When carried at cost: property, plant and equipment, investments, inventories, goodwill and intangible assets. Also prepaid expenses and deferred income.

Therefore, the only substantive issues relate to the application of IAS 29 to items in categories 4 and 5 in the table above.

For category 4 items, the change in a general price index, from the date of the last valuation of the item to the balance sheet date, is applied to the revalued amount.

For category 5 items, the change in a general price index from the date of acquisition of the item (or date of payment if materially later) to the balance sheet date is applied to the historical cost (and, where relevant, accumulated depreciation).

Inventories are an area for particular consideration:

- raw materials are to be restated by applying the change in the general price index from the date of acquisition to the balance sheet date;
- work-in-progress and finished goods consist of a number of components and the dates at which the costs were incurred (for components, labour and depreciation where applicable) will need to be considered separately for the purpose of applying a general price index. This will often be a relatively complex exercise, particularly where products take a long period to manufacture.

Example 28.1

An enterprise operating in a hyperinflationary economy is preparing financial statements at its period end, 31 December. Assume labour overheads are utilised evenly over a period, and the following changes in the general price index apply:

31 August	100
30 September	105
31 October	110
30 November	115
31 December	120

		Historic cost at balance sheet date	*Indexing adjustment*	*31 December Adjusted balance*
Raw materials	Purchased 31 October.	250	120/110	273
	Purchased 30 November.	250	120/115	261
Work-in-progress	Use of raw materials purchased 30 September.	500	120/105	571
	Labour/overheads incurred from 31 October to 31 December.	500	120/115	522
Finished goods	Use of raw materials purchased 31 August.	500	120/100	600
	Labour/overheads incurred from 30 September to 31 December.	500	120/112.5	533
Total		**2,500**		**2,760**

The treatment of items of property, plant and equipment which have been depreciated may often also be complex.

- Cost is restated by adjusting the purchase price by the change in the index between the date of acquisition and the balance sheet date.
- Depreciation arises over time and hence the balance of accumulated depreciation brought forward at the start of each period must be adjusted by the change in the index between the start and end of the period, while the depreciation charge for each period is calculated based on the index-adjusted cost at the end of the period. Another way to arrive at the same answer is to apply the depreciation rate to the historic cost and apply the index from the date of acquisition of the asset to the balance sheet date.

Example 28.2

An enterprise acquires an item of property, plant and equipment on 31 December 20X0 for 1,000, when the general price index is 100. At 31 December 20X1, the index is 110 and the asset has been depreciated by 10%. At 31 December 20X2 the index is 120 and the asset has been depreciated at 10% for a second year.

	Balance brought forward	*Indexing adjustment*	*Calculation of Accumulated Depreciation*	*Adjusted balance*
Cost	1,000	110/100		1,100
Accumulated depreciation	Nil		(1,100 × 10%)	(110)
Balance at 31 Dec 20X1				**990**
Cost	1,100	120/110		1,200
Accumulated depreciation	110		(110 × 120/110) + (1,200 × 10%)	(240)
Balance at 31 Dec 20X2				**960**

Note: the depreciation charge for the period 1 January 20X2 to 31 December 20X2 can also be expressed as 1,000 × 10% × 120/100.

IAS 29 does not specifically address the restatement of deferred tax for hyperinflation. Paragraph A18 of Appendix 1 to IAS 12 (r2000) *Income Taxes* indicates, however, that deferred tax should be restated by comparing the restated assets and liabilities to their tax bases and recognising deferred tax on the resultant temporary differences. The appropriate deferred tax balance is therefore not derived by merely applying a general price index to the deferred tax balance before restatement. This is so because temporary differences are a function of carrying values, which are adjusted by the general price index, and tax bases, which generally remain unchanged in a hyperinflationary environment.

A similar problem arises in respect of the restatement of the comparative figure for deferred tax in accordance with IAS 29.8. Because the restatement of the comparative balance sheet, using a general price index, changes the temporary differences in respect of the comparative balance sheet, the comparative deferred tax may be restated to reflect tax on these restated temporary differences. This would result in an adjustment to the comparative deferred tax expense in addition to the restatement of that expense in accordance with the change in the general price index. Alternatively, the comparative deferred tax figure may be restated by the application of a general price index to the figure, in which case the current year deferred tax charge will include the additional adjustment referred to in the first treatment. Whichever treatment is adopted should be applied consistently.

Where a balance has been restated, the restated amount is compared with the item's 'recoverable amount' that is, the amount recoverable from its future use, including any amount receivable on sale or eventual disposal. (IAS 29.19) When the restated amount exceeds the recoverable amount, an impairment loss is recognised with the effect that:

- inventories will be written down to net realisable value in line with IAS 2 (r1993) *Inventories* (see Chapter **10**);
- items of property, plant and equipment and intangible assets will be reduced to their recoverable amount in accordance with IAS 36 *Impairment of Assets* (see Chapter **10**); and
- financial assets carried at amortised cost are written down to their recoverable amount in accordance with IAS 39 (r2000) *Financial Instruments: Recognition and Measurement* (see Chapters **10** and **12**).

IAS 36 defines recoverable amount as the higher of an asset's net selling price and its value in use which differs slightly from the description of recoverable amount included in IAS 29.19. Presumably this is because IAS 29.19 applies to a wider range of assets, being all assets held by an enterprise operating in a hyperinflationary economy, including inventories, and financial and other assets, which are outside the scope of IAS 36. However, in practice, the answer will be the same as the answer if the guidance in IAS 36 were applied, when evaluating items of property, plant and equipment and intangible assets to determine whether an impairment loss should be recognised and follow its rules on measurement.

28.8.2 Practical considerations

(1) IAS 29.10 notes that the overriding rule in applying this Standard is consistency from period to period in applying the procedures and making the judgement calls required. In other words, precise accuracy of amounts is less important than consistency of treatment. Since the aim is to provide meaningful financial statements, whatever approach is adopted it must be applied consistently, to achieve comparability between the results of different accounting periods.

(2) If detailed records of the acquisition dates of non-monetary assets are not available and cannot be estimated (IAS 29 mentions items of property, plant and equipment in particular), then in the first period in which IAS 29 is applied, it may be necessary for the items concerned to be valued by an independent professional. (IAS 29.16)

(3) If a general price index is not available for the period since acquisition, an estimate may be used. IAS 29 suggests deriving an estimate from movements in the exchange rate between the reporting currency and a relatively stable foreign currency. Items of property, plant and equipment are specifically mentioned in the Standard as they are the most likely to pre-date the existence of a suitable price index – an enterprise may have held land and buildings for many years, for which there are no statistics available. However the principle could also be applied to other non-current assets.

(4) IAS 29.21 addresses borrowing costs. In practice, in a hyperinflationary economy, loans may either be negotiated at an interest rate that will compensate for the loss in purchasing power of the money being loaned, or the loan agreement may provide for repayment of capital adjusted by a pre-defined index, with interest being charged at a 'normal' rate. IAS 23 (r1993) *Borrowing Costs*, allows the capitalisation of borrowing costs for certain qualifying assets (see Chapter **10**). However when an enterprise operates in a hyperinflationary economy, it is inappropriate to capitalise that part of the borrowing costs that compensates for inflation: this portion should be expensed as incurred. In other words, the portion of costs incurred over the 'normal' rate is not eligible for capitalisation.

(5) IAS 29.22 states that where assets are acquired and payment is not required immediately, where there is no explicit interest charge and it is impracticable to impute an amount of interest, assets are restated from the payment date and not the date of purchase.

The logic for this is as follows. Normally if resources flow out of the enterprise at the later date without any additional cost, the net monetary position can only be affected from that date. However, in practice, in a hyperinflationary economy, credit is only likely to be given if the cost of the asset is increased to compensate the seller for the loss in purchasing power of the cash during the credit period. Hence it should be possible to impute an interest rate to the transaction and therefore capitalise the asset at a lower amount. The interest itself will be charged against income and the asset will be restated from the date of purchase. If no amount of interest can be imputed, then a reasonable approximation to this technically 'correct' position may be achieved by putting the asset in the accounts at the value actually paid and applying the index from the payment date.

28.8.3 Equity

On implementation of IAS 29 the components of owner's equity at the *beginning* of the period are adjusted as follows (IAS 29.24 and 25):

Component	*Treatment*
Revaluation surpluses.	Eliminate, i.e., the revaluation surplus is absorbed in adjusted retained earnings.
Retained earnings.	Derive a restated figure: the opening figure for retained earnings is simply the balancing figure after all adjustments have been made to all other components of the balance sheet.
All other components of owners' equity (i.e., equity, share premium and any other existing reserves).	Restate by applying a general price index from the dates the components were contributed or arose.

After initial implementation, at the end of each period in which IAS 29 is adopted (including the first period), the components of equity are again restated, this time by applying a general price index from the beginning of the period or the date of contribution, whichever is the later.

28.8.4 Investments accounted for under the equity method

Where a reporting enterprise holds an investment in an entity which is accounted for under the equity method and that entity reports in the currency of a hyperinflationary economy, the following steps are followed (IAS 29.20):

(1) Restate the balance sheet and income statement of the investee in accordance with IAS 29.

(2) Translate the financial statements of the investee at the closing rate of

exchange. If the comparative figures of the investee are not restated in terms of the measuring unit current at the balance sheet date because the reporting currency of the investor is not hyperinflationary (see the discussion in **28.8.5** below), exchange differences will arise as part of this process. These exchange differences are a result of the opening equity of the investee being translated at the rates at which it was previously reported, while the closing net assets are translated at the closing exchange rate. These exchange differences should be recognised directly in equity in accordance with IAS 21.30(c).

(3) Calculate the investor's share of the net assets and results of operations of the entity in accordance with IAS 28 (r2000) *Accounting for Investments in Associates*, or IAS 31 (r2000) *Financial Reporting of Interests in Joint Ventures* (see Chapters **20** and **21**).

Where the reporting enterprise and investee use the same reporting currency, step 2 will not be required.

Where the investor and investee have different reporting dates, and it is impracticable for the investee to prepare financial statements to the same date as the investor, difficulties will arise. IAS 28 (r2000) says that where reporting dates differ, adjustments are made for the effects of any significant events that occur between the date of the associate's financial statements and the date of the investor's financial statements (IAS 28 (r2000).19). A hyperinflationary movement in the general purchasing power of the currency in which the investee reports will be one such event. Therefore, the financial statements of the investee need to be fully restated in accordance with IAS 29: all items in the financial statements of the investee, monetary and non-monetary, will need to be restated in terms of the measuring unit current at the balance sheet date of the reporting enterprise. This applies whether or not the reporting enterprise and investee use the same reporting currency.

28.8.5 Investments in subsidiaries

In consolidated financial statements, if there are foreign subsidiaries within the group for which the appropriate measurement currency (see **28.6** above) is a currency of a hyperinflationary economy, their financial statements will need to be restated by applying a general price index pertaining to that economy, before they can be translated and included in the consolidated financial statements. (IAS 21(r1993).36 and SIC-19.7) Translation of the financial statements of such subsidiaries is performed using closing rates of exchange. As noted above in respect of investments accounted for under the equity method, if comparative figures are not restated, this translation process will result in exchange differences which should be recognised in equity.

Similar procedures are performed if the reporting currency of the consolidated financial statements is itself a hyperinflationary currency. (IAS 29.35) It should be noted that in such circumstances, no exchange differences arise on translation of the subsidiary's financial statements into the group reporting currency because the comparative amounts of the subsidiary will have been restated to the closing exchange rate of the most recent period presented.

Again, difficulties will arise where the reporting enterprise and the subsidiary have different reporting dates. IAS 29.36 states that in this case all items, monetary and non-monetary, need to be restated into the measuring unit current at the date of the consolidated financial statements and only then translated at closing rate into the reporting currency.

Following IAS 27, subsidiaries would normally draw up an additional set of financial statements to the same date as the reporting enterprise specifically for the purpose of incorporation into the financial statements of the latter. However, when it is 'impracticable' for the foreign entity to prepare such an additional set of financial statements, it is permissible to use financial statements drawn up to a different reporting date, providing that date is no more than three months from the reporting date of the reporting enterprise.

Generally, where this exception is applied, the assets and liabilities of the foreign subsidiary are translated at the exchange rate ruling at its own balance sheet date, and not that at the balance sheet date of the reporting enterprise. However, IAS 27 acknowledges that adjustments should be made for any significant events up to the reporting date of the reporting enterprise. This would clearly include hyperinflationary movements in exchange rates. Consequently the financial statements of subsidiaries with a different year-end from that of the reporting enterprise should be restated using the current measurement unit at the date of the consolidated financial statements *and* translated using the exchange rate at the same date.

A further difficulty arises in interpreting the requirement in IAS 29.8 to restate comparative figures from the previous periods 'in terms of the measuring unit current at the balance sheet date' when applying it to the financial statements of a subsidiary included in the consolidated financial statements of a reporting enterprise which reports in the currency of a non-hyperinflationary economy. One view is that although IAS 21 (r1993).36 requires the application of IAS 29 in restating the financial statements of a subsidiary which reports in the currency of a hyperinflationary economy before they are included in consolidation, the requirement to restate comparative figures using the measuring unit current at the balance sheet date only applies to financial statements of the reporting enterprise presented on a stand-alone basis. As a result, comparative figures of the subsidiary are not restated and the prior year figures of the consolidated financial statements are presented as comparatives without adjustment.

An opposing view would require an enterprise to restate comparative figures of its subsidiary using the measurement unit current at the balance sheet date of the most recent period presented, i.e., to adjust comparative figures of the consolidated financial statements by translating the subsidiary's balances using the closing rate at the most recent balance sheet date. This method is likely to be impracticable because it will require continual restatement of prior period results of groups which have a non-hyperinflationary reporting currency if they have subsidiaries with reporting currencies of a hyperinflationary economy. This method also has the peculiar consequence of recognising in earnings the effect of the portion of exchange differences arising from inflation in the non-hyperinflationary economy. The draft interpretation recently issued by SIC (SIC-D30) confirms the latter view. Whatever method is chosen, it should be applied consistently. The proposals in SIC-D30 are covered in **22.10**.

28.8.6 Income statement

As in the balance sheet, all items in the income statement should be expressed in terms of the measuring unit current at the balance sheet date. Again, this is achieved by applying the change in a general price index from the dates when the income and expenses were first recorded. (IAS 29.26) Since there may be a large number of transactions in the income statement, some estimation may be necessary. Furthermore, the general price index selected may not be published daily. Clearly if prices are rising at a reasonably steady rate, and if the transactions being adjusted arise evenly, it might be an adequate approximation to use an average movement in the general price index over a period. However judgement is necessary as to whether an average will result in a fair approximation. For example, if there are large, irregular transactions, an average rate will be unsuitable and actual rates should be used.

The method of calculating the charge for depreciation is outlined in **28.8.1**. A further consideration is the calculation of the cost of goods sold for inclusion in the income statement.

Example 28.3

An enterprise has inventory of 200 at the beginning of the period, when the general price index is at 100. Purchases of 1,200 are made at an even rate throughout the year and closing inventory is 200. The closing inventory was acquired in two tranches in the last two months of the year, when the index was 120 and 122 respectively. At the balance sheet date, the general price index is 124, and inflation rose steadily all year, giving an average rate of 112.

		Unadjusted balances	*Indexing adjustment*	*Adjusted balances*
Opening inventory		200	124/100	248
Purchases		1,200	124/112	1,344
Closing inventory	100		124/120	
	100		124/122	
		(200)		(205)
		1,200		1,387

The restatement of the taxation charge arising from the movement in deferred taxation is not adequately addressed by IAS 29. The charge should be calculated as the difference between the opening deferred tax balance (that is, the comparative figure adjusted for the change in the general price index in the current period) and the closing deferred tax balance, restated as described in **28.8.1** above. It is submitted that, in terms of IAS 12 (r2000).79, that portion of the deferred tax which is attributable to the restatement of the balance sheet for hyperinflation should be disclosed.

In many hyperinflationary jurisdictions, the current tax charge is determined based upon historic cost results of operations. The current tax charge may be restated by applying a general price index to the tax charge from the dates at which the income and expenses to which the taxation relates. This treatment should maintain a similar rate of tax in respect of hyperinflation-adjusted earnings, excluding the gain or loss on net monetary position, to the rate of tax on historic cost earnings. However, since the current tax liability (asset) is a monetary item, determined at the year end in accordance with historic cost results, this treatment may result in a current tax charge which is significantly different from the current tax liability. Because IAS 29 is silent on this matter, an alternative treatment whereby the current tax charge is not restated, may also be applied. Effectively, this treatment considers tax as a charge which is incurred at the period end and is therefore current at the period end.

28.8.7 Gain or loss arising on net monetary position

The gain or loss arising on the net monetary position (see **28.5**) as a result of all the adjustments to items in the balance sheet is included in net income and separately disclosed. (IAS 29.9) IAS 29.27 suggests that the gain or loss may be estimated by applying the change in a general price index to the weighted average for the period of the difference between monetary assets and monetary liabilities. However it is more accurately calculated as the difference arising from:

- the restatement of non-monetary assets, owners' equity and income statement items; and
- the adjustment of index linked assets and liabilities (where these exist), such as index-linked bonds and loans.

(IAS 29.27)

IAS 29.28 appears to suggest separate but linked disclosure in the income statement of:

(a) the net effect of restating non-monetary assets, owners' equity and items in the income statement;
(b) the net effect of adjusting any index-linked assets and/or liabilities;
(c) interest income and expense; and
(d) foreign exchange differences relating to invested and/or borrowed funds.

Example 28.4

An enterprise has a loan linked to an index which was 100 at the start of the period and at the period end is 125. In preparing its financial statements the enterprise uses a different index, which, at the start of the period, was 100 and at the end of the period is 120. Inflation is assumed to have occurred at an even rate throughout the period. The unadjusted depreciation charge for the period relates to assets acquired (on average) when the index stood at 80.

	Unadjusted balances	*Indexing adjustment*	*Adjusted balances*	*Gain/Loss*	
Non-monetary assets	1,000	120/100	1,200		200
Monetary assets	500		500		
Index-linked loan	(100)	125/100	(125)	(25)	
Monetary liabilities	(100)		(100)		
	1,300		1,475		
Capital	500	120/100	600		(100)
Retained earnings b/f	600	120/100	720		(120)
Profit for the period:					
– before depreciation	250	120/110	273		(23)
– less depreciation	(50)	120/80	(75)		25
Profit after depreciation	200		198		
Net monetary and index loss			(43)	(25)	(18)
Retained earnings c/f	800		875		
	1,300		1,475		

Note: the loss of 25 on the index-linked loan has been shown separately in the column on the right to make it clear that separate disclosure appears to be required by IAS 29.28.

28.9 Current cost financial statements

As is clear from **28.8** items in the balance sheet already carried at current cost do not require restatement, since they are already expressed in terms of the measuring unit current at the balance sheet date. Hence items of property, plant and equipment, investments and inventories, which will have been restated to current cost, do not require further adjustment. Items linked to changes in prices will be adjusted in accordance with the relevant agreements and other monetary items will again require no adjustment.

Other items in the balance sheet will, however, need to be restated. (IAS 29.29) This includes goodwill, deferred credits and components of owners' equity. The guidance outlined above for items in a historical cost balance sheet should be applied.

As with historical cost accounts, all amounts in the income statement need to be restated in the measuring unit current at the balance sheet date by applying a general price index (IAS 29.30)

The gain or loss on the net monetary position is accounted for as set out above for historical cost financial statements. However, in current cost financial statements there may already be an adjustment taking items from a historical cost basis to a current cost basis. Such adjustments are treated as part of the gain or loss on the net monetary position, and the two amounts will be treated as one for the purpose of disclosure. (IAS 29.31)

28.10 Economies ceasing to be hyperinflationary

There are two simple rules to be applied when the economy ceases to be hyperinflationary (IAS 29.38):

(1) the enterprise will cease to prepare its financial statements in accordance with IAS 29; and
(2) the carrying value of assets and liabilities in the enterprise's previous set of financial statements, which are the opening balances for the period in which the economy ceases to be hyperinflationary, will henceforth be treated as the basis for the carrying amounts in its subsequent financial statements. No adjustment is required to any balances in the financial statements.

28.11 Disclosure requirements

Very few disclosures are required by IAS 29. These are set out in IAS 29.39:

(1) the fact that the financial statements and corresponding figures have been restated for changes in the general purchasing power of the reporting currency and consequently are stated in terms of the measuring unit current at the balance sheet date;
(2) whether the financial statements are based on a historical cost approach or a current cost approach. The two approaches result in different values for certain assets and liabilities, particularly property and investments.
(3) the price index which has been used, its level at the balance sheet date and the movement in the index during the current and previous reporting period.

IAS 29 does not further specify what is meant by 'movement during the period'; however simple disclosure of the level of the index at the start of the current and previous period may not be sufficient; an indication should also be given of the extent of fluctuations during the period where these are material.

28.12 Comparison with UK GAAP

UK GAAP contains very little guidance on accounting where hyperinflationary economies are involved. SSAP 20 *Foreign Currency Translation* recognises that, where a foreign enterprise operates in a country in which there is a very high rate of inflation, the local currency financial statements should be adjusted, where possible, to reflect current price levels before the translation process is undertaken. (SSAP 20.26) However it does not give guidance on how this requirement should be applied in practice.

UITF 9 *Accounting for Operations in Hyperinflationary Economies* attempts to fill this gap. The UITF refers to IAS 29 rather than attempting to give its own definition of hyperinflation. It requires adjustments to be made where the distortions caused by hyperinflation are such as to affect the true and fair view given by the group financial statements, and, in any event, where the cumulative inflation rate over three years is approaching, or exceeds 100 per cent, and the operations in the hyperinflationary economies are material.

Two acceptable methods of eliminating the distortions are given in UITF 9:

- adjust the local currency financial statements to reflect current price levels before the translation process is undertaken, as suggested in SSAP 20. This involves taking any gain or loss on the net monetary position through the profit and loss account. This is the method suggested by IAS 29 as set out above; or
- use a relatively stable currency as the functional currency for the relevant foreign operations, such as US dollar or UK sterling. Under the UITF, the stable currency would then be considered the 'local currency' for the purposes of translating the financial statements of the enterprise for inclusion in the consolidated group accounts. The transactions of the enterprise would either be initially recorded in the stable currency or would be translated into it by applying the temporal method. The effect is that the movement between the original currency and the stable currency is used as a proxy for an inflation index. (SIC-19 allows this possibility only where the stable currency is determined to be the appropriate measurement currency for an entity based in a hyperinflationary economy, in which case it will record all of the transactions in that measurement currency.)

If neither of the methods set out above is considered appropriate for operations which are material to the group, alternative methods may be used, but the reasons for not adopting one of the suggested methods should be disclosed.

28.13 Comparison with US GAAP

According to SFAS 89 *Financial Reporting and Changing Prices*, 'A business enterprise that prepares its financial statements in U.S. dollars and in accordance with U.S. generally accepted accounting principles is encouraged, but not required, to disclose supplementary information on the effects of changing prices.' The Appendix to SFAS 89 gives guidance on measurement and presentation of this supplementary information. However, such an enterprise may not prepare financial statements adjusted for inflation as its primary financial statements.

Where a reporting enterprise has foreign operations (for example a subsidiary, branch, division or joint venture) based in a highly inflationary economy and consolidated financial statements are prepared, the financial statements of the foreign entity shall be remeasured into the reporting currency before they are included in the consolidation in accordance with SFAS 52 *Foreign Currency Translation*. This differs from IAS 29, which requires the financial statements of the foreign entity to be restated in terms of the measurement unit current at the balance sheet date, and then translated into the reporting currency at the closing rate of exchange.

The SEC requires domestic US registrants to apply the SFAS 52 procedures for reporting the financial statements of a foreign entity operating in a highly inflationary economy. However, as a result of the issuing of FRR 43, the SEC permits foreign issuers to adopt an alternative translation methodology for their foreign entities operating in a highly inflationary economy, provided that methodology is consistently applied in all periods. The alternative methodology requires the historical cost amounts of such entities to be restated in terms of the measuring unit current at the balance sheet date (the historical cost/constant currency method) prior to translation into the reporting currency. The methodology should comply with the relevant requirements of IAS 21 and IAS 29. However, only the historical cost method of restatement described in IAS 29 is permitted; the current cost method is not permitted.

The definition of a highly inflationary economy is similar to that in IAS 29: it is 'one that has cumulative inflation of approximately 100 per cent or more over a 3-year period'. (SFAS 52.11)

Nevertheless, foreign enterprises based in highly inflationary economies may prepare financial statements adjusted for inflation following paragraph 26 of

APB Statement 3 *Financial Statements Restated for General Price-Level Changes*, if the financial statements are intended for readers in the United States and to the extent that it is not inconsistent with guidance in SFAS 89 regarding historical cost/constant purchase power accounting.

28.14 Example from published financial statements

Note that the excerpts given do not always comply in full with all aspects of IAS and as such are not necessarily examples of best practice but merely of current practice.

Example 28.5

3. Basis of Presentation (extract)

The adjustments and reclassifications made to the statutory accounts for the purpose of IAS reporting include the restatement for changes in the general purchasing power of the Rouble in accordance with IAS 29 *Financial Reporting in Hyperinflationary Economies* (IAS 29). IAS 29 requires that financial statements prepared in the currency of a hyperinflationary economy be stated in terms of the measuring unit current at the balance sheet date. The restatement was calculated from the conversion factors derived from the Russian Federation Consumer Price Index, published by the Russian State Committee on Statistics ('Goscomstat'), and from indices obtained from other published sources for years prior to 1992.

The indices used to restate the consolidated financial statements, based on 1988 prices (1988=100) for the five years ended 31 December 1999, and the respective conversion factors used are:

Year	*Index*	*Conversion Factor*
1995	487,575	3.4
1996	594,110	2.8
1997	659,403	2.5
1998	1,216,400	1.4
1999	1,661,481	1.0

The significant guidelines followed in restating the consolidated financial statements are:

- all amounts are stated in terms of the measuring unit current at 31 December 1999;
- monetary assets and liabilities are not restated because they are already expressed in terms of the monetary unit current at 31 December 1999;
- non-monetary assets and liabilities (items which are not expressed in terms of the monetary unit current at 31 December 1999) and shareholders' equity, including the share capital, are restated by applying the relevant conversion factors;

- all items in the consolidated statements of operations and of cash flows are restated by applying appropriate conversion factors;
- the effect of inflation on the Group's net monetary position is included in the consolidated statement of operations as a net monetary gain or loss; and
- comparative amounts for 1998 are restated using the conversion factor 1.3659 in order to state them in terms of the measuring unit current at 31 December 1999.

The consolidated statement of operations includes a net monetary gain of RR 51,243 and RR 85,944 for the years ended 31 December 1999 and 1998, respectively, because on average the Group had net monetary liabilities in both years.

OAO GAZPROM
Russian Federation
31 December 1999
International Accounting Standards

CHAPTER 29

Interim financial reporting

29.1 Sources

IAS 34	*Interim Financial Reporting.*
IAS 1 (r1997)	*Presentation of Financial Statements.*

29.2 Brief summary of the requirements

IAS 34 does not specify which enterprises should publish interim financial reports, how frequently, or how soon after the end of an interim period. However, if an enterprise wishes to publish an interim report in accordance with IAS, it must follow IAS 34. IAS 34 defines the minimum content, including disclosures, of an interim report and identifies the accounting recognition and measurement principles that should be applied in an interim report. The minimum content of an interim financial report is a condensed balance sheet, condensed income statement, condensed cash flow statement, and condensed statement showing changes in equity, and selected explanatory notes.

An enterprise applies the same accounting policies in its interim financial report as are applied in its annual financial statements, except for accounting policy changes made after the date of the most recent annual financial statements that will be reflected in the next annual financial statements. Measurement for interim reporting purposes is made on a year-to-date basis.

29.3 Development of the requirements

IAS 34 was approved by the IASC Board in February 1998 and became effective for financial statements covering periods beginning on or after 1 January 1999.

29.4 Scope

IAS 34 applies if an enterprise is required or elects to publish an interim financial report in accordance with IAS. However, enterprises who prepare annual financial statements in accordance with IAS are not precluded from preparing interim financial statements which do *not* comply with IAS, as long as the interims do not state that they are IAS compliant. (IAS 34.1-2)

29.5 Frequency

IAS 34 does not specify which enterprises are required to publish interim financial reports, how frequently, or how soon after the end of an interim period. The Standard notes that governments, securities regulators, stock exchanges, and accountancy bodies often require enterprises with publicly traded debt or equity to publish interim financial reports and those regulations generally specify the above requirements. However, IAS 34 *encourages* publicly traded enterprises to:

- provide interim financial reports at least as of the end of the first half of their financial year; and
- make their interim financial reports available no later than 60 days after the end of the interim period.

(IAS 34.1)

29.6 Content of an interim financial report

IAS 34 includes the minimum requirements, discussed below, for inclusion in an interim financial report. However, IAS 34 does not discourage or prohibit enterprises from producing a full set of financial statements for inclusion in its interim report. If an enterprise does choose this route, the form and content of the financial statements must conform with the requirements of IAS 1 (r1997). (IAS 34.7 and 9)

29.6.1 Minimum requirements

IAS 34 requires that, at a minimum, the following items be included in an interim financial report:

(a) condensed balance sheet;
(b) condensed income statement, including basic and diluted earnings per share on the face;
(c) condensed statement showing, in a manner consistent with the annual financial statements, either:

   (i) all changes in equity; or
   (ii) all changes in equity other than those arising from capital transactions with owners and distributions to owners;

(d) condensed cash flow statement; and
(e) selected explanatory notes (see **29.6.2**).

(IAS 34.8, 11, 13)

'Condensed' means that the statement should include, at a minimum, each of the headings and subtotals that were included in its most recent annual financial statements plus the selected explanatory notes required by IAS 34. Additional line items or notes are required if their omission would make the condensed interim financials misleading. (IAS 34.10)

29.6.2 Selected explanatory notes

IAS 34 works on the principle that anyone reading the interim report will have access to the annual financial statements. Therefore, all of the notes in the annual financial statements are not required since they would be repetitive. IAS 34 specifically requires, as a minimum, the following information to be disclosed on a year-to-date basis, in the notes (if material (see **29.7**)) unless these are disclosed elsewhere in the interim financial report:

(a) an explanation of events and transactions that are significant to an understanding of the changes in financial position and performance of the enterprise since the last annual reporting date;
(b) a statement that the same accounting policies and methods of computation are followed in the interim financial statements as in the most recent annual financial statements or, if those policies or methods have been changed, a description of the nature and effect of the change;
(c) explanatory comments about the seasonality or cyclicality of interim operations;
(d) the nature and amount of changes in estimates of amounts reported in prior interim periods of the current financial year or changes in estimates of amounts reported in prior financial years;
(e) issuances, repurchases, and repayments of debt and equity securities;
(f) dividends paid (aggregate and per share) separately for ordinary shares and other shares;
(g) if an enterprise is required to present segment information under IAS 14 (r1997) *Segment Reporting* (see Chapter **16**), segment revenue and segment result for the enterprise's primary basis of segment reporting (i.e., business or geographical);
(h) material events subsequent to the end of the interim period that have not been reflected in the financial statements for the interim period;
(i) the effect of changes in the composition of the enterprise during the interim period, including business combinations, acquisition or disposal

of subsidiaries and long-term investments, restructurings, and discontinuing operations;

(j) changes in contingent liabilities or contingent assets since the last annual balance sheet date (IAS 34.16);

(k) a statement of the fact that the interim financial report is in compliance with IAS 34. However, an interim financial report should not be described as complying with IASs unless it complies with all of the requirements of each applicable IAS and SIC Interpretation. (IAS 34.19)

IAS 34 provides the following examples of the kinds of disclosure required by the paragraph above:

(a) 'the write-down of inventories to net realisable value and the reversal of such a write-down;
(b) recognition of a loss from the impairment of property, plant, and equipment, intangible assets, or other assets, and the reversal of such an impairment loss;
(c) the reversal of any provisions for the costs of restructuring;
(d) acquisitions and disposals of items of property, plant, and equipment;
(e) commitments for the purchase of property, plant, and equipment;
(f) litigation settlements;
(g) corrections of fundamental errors in previously reported financial data;
(h) extraordinary items;
(i) any debt default or any breach of a debt covenant that has not been corrected subsequently; and
(j) related party transactions.'

(IAS 34.17)

IAS 34 clarifies that where other IASs call for disclosures in financial statements, in that context, it means complete sets of financial statements of the type normally included in an annual financial report. These types of disclosures are not required if the interim financial report includes only condensed financial statements and selected explanatory notes. (IAS 34.18)

IAS 35 *Discontinuing Operations*, para. 47 also requires that the notes to the interim financial report describe any significant activities or events since the end of the most recent annual reporting period relating to a discontinuing operation and any significant changes in the amount or timing of cash flows relating to the assets and liabilities to be disposed of or settled. This is to allow the users of the accounts to see how the sale or discontinuance has progressed since the annual accounts.

29.6.3 Consolidated vs parent's separate financial statements

If the most recent annual financial statements of an enterprise were prepared on a consolidated basis, the interim report is also prepared on a consolidated basis since parent only statements would not provide comparable information. If the annual financial statements included parent only information, IAS 34 neither requires nor prohibits the inclusion of such information in the interim financial report. (IAS 34.14)

29.6.4 Periods required to be presented

Interim reports are required by IAS 34.20 to include interim financial statements (condensed or complete) for the following periods:

Statement	**Current**	**Comparative**
Balance sheet	End of current interim period	End of immediately preceding financial year
Income statement	Current interim period and year-to-date	Same interim period and year-to-date of immediately preceding financial year
Statement showing changes in equity	Year-to-date	Year-to-date of immediately preceding financial year
Cash flow statement	Year-to-date	Year-to-date of immediately preceding financial year

Enterprises are not precluded from providing additional information. For example, enterprises whose business is highly cyclical may wish to disclose financial information related to the twelve month period ended on the interim date and comparative information on the same basis. (IAS 34.21)

Example 29.1

The following tables illustrate the periods required when an enterprise with a 31 December 2002 year end reports half-yearly and quarterly, respectively.

Half-yearly at 30 June 2001

	Current	**Comparative**
Balance sheet at	30 June 2002	31 December 2001
Income statement 6 months ended	30 June 2002	30 June 2001
Cash flow statement 6 months ended	30 June 2002	30 June 2001
Statement of changes in equity 6 months ended	30 June 2002	30 June 2001
Quarterly at 30 June 2002		
Balance sheet at	30 June 2002	31 December 2001
Income statement 6 months ended *and* 3 months ended	30 June 2002 30 June 2002	30 June 2001 30 June 2001
Cash flow statement 6 months ended	30 June 2002	30 June 2001
Statement of changes in equity 6 months ended	30 June 2002	30 June 2001

29.7 Materiality

IAS 34.28 states:

> 'In deciding how to recognise, measure, classify, or disclose an item for interim financial reporting purposes, materiality should be assessed in relation to the interim period financial data. In making assessments of materiality, it should be recognised that interim measurements may rely on estimates to a greater extent than measurements of annual financial data.'

Whilst materiality judgements are always subjective, the overriding concern here is to ensure that an interim financial report includes all information that is relevant to understanding the financial position and performance of an enterprise during the financial period. Therefore, it is inappropriate to base quantitative estimates of materiality on projected annual figures.

29.8 Recognition and measurement

29.8.1 Consistent accounting policies with annual statements

> 'An enterprise should apply the same accounting policies in its interim financial statements as are applied in its annual financial statements, except for accounting policy changes made after the date of the most recent annual financial statements that are to be reflected in the next annual financial statements. However, the frequency of an enterprise's reporting (annual, half-yearly, or quarterly) should not affect the measurement of its annual results. To achieve that objective, measurements for interim reporting purposes should be made on a year-to-date basis.'
>
> (IAS 34.28)

In one sense, the above paragraph seems to suggest that each interim period is treated as a stand alone period. Whilst in most ways this is true, the reference to the fact that the frequency of interim reporting should not affect annual results draws attention to the fact that interim results are prepared with reference to items in previous interim periods such as changes in estimates. The three examples below illustrate the principle.

Change in estimate
The rules for recognising and measuring losses from inventory write-downs, restructurings or impairments in an interim period are the same as those for an annual period. However, if such items are recognised and measured in, say, the first quarter of a financial year and in the second quarter, the estimate changes, the original estimate is changed in the second quarter either by accrual of an additional amount or by reversal of the previously recognised amount. (IAS 34.30(a))

If changes in estimates have been necessary, the interim financial report is not retrospectively adjusted. However, the nature and amount of any significant changes in estimates must be disclosed *either*:

(1) in the annual report if there has been no subsequent interim period financial report that has disclosed the change in estimate; or
(2) in the following interim period financial report of the same year; and
(3) in the following year's corresponding interim period report so that the comparative figures (which are not restated) will not be misleading.

(IAS 34.16(d), 26, 35 and 36)

Appendix 3 of IAS 34 includes 9 examples of the types of estimates which are frequently made as part of the interim reporting process.

Deferral of costs at an interim date

A cost that does not meet the definition of an asset at the end of an interim period is *not* deferred on the balance sheet either to await future information as to whether it has met the definition of an asset or to smooth earnings over interim periods within a financial year. (IAS 34.30(b)) Thus, when preparing interim financial statements, the reference to other interim periods does not override the normal recognition and measurement practices. For example, if costs are incurred during the first interim period related to the creation of an intangible asset, but at the end of this first interim period, the recognition criteria in IAS 38 *Intangible Assets* are not met, the costs are expensed. Only costs incurred *after* the specific point in time at which the criteria are met are capitalised. Deferral of costs as assets in an interim balance sheet in the hope that the criteria will be met before the year end is prohibited. (IAS 34.Appendix 2.8)

Tax estimates

The above two examples are relatively straightforward. However, when preparing the tax estimate to be included in an interim period, the tax expense is based on the best estimate of the weighted average *annual* income tax rate expected for the full financial year. Therefore, following the change in estimate example above, amounts accrued for income tax expense in one interim period may have to be adjusted in a subsequent interim period if the estimate of the *annual* income tax rate changes. (IAS 34.30(c))

29.8.2 Seasonal, cyclical or occasional revenues

Following on from the principle that the same accounting policies are used at interim and financial year ends, revenues that are received seasonally, cyclically or occasionally within a financial year may not be anticipated or deferred as of an interim date if anticipation or deferral would not be appropriate at the end of the financial year. Thus, a retailer does not divide its forecasted revenue by two to arrive at its half year revenue figures. Instead it reports its actual results for the 6 month period. If it would like to indicate that its revenues are seasonal, it may include the previous 12 month figures as comparative figures.

29.8.3 Uneven costs

The rule on revenues also applies to costs. 'Costs that are incurred unevenly during an enterprise's financial year should be anticipated or deferred for interim reporting purposes if, and only if, it is also appropriate to anticipate or defer that type of cost at the end of the financial year.' (IAS 34.39) This is expected to be rare.

29.8.4 Additional examples

Appendix 2 of IAS 34 contains 22 examples which illustrate the application of the recognition and measurement principles above.

29.9 Restatement of previously reported interim periods

A change in accounting policy, other than one for which the transitional provisions are specified by a new IAS, should be reflected by:

(a) restating the financial statements of prior interim periods of the current financial year and the comparable interim periods of prior financial years, if the enterprise follows the benchmark treatment in IAS 8 (r1993) *Net Profit or Loss for the Period, Fundamental Errors and Changes in Accounting Policies* (see Chapter **5**);
(b) restating the financial statements of prior interim periods of only the current financial year, if the enterprise follows the allowed alternative treatment under IAS 8 (r1993) (see Chapter **5**). Comparable interim periods of prior financial years are not restated.

(IAS 34.43)

29.10 Comparison with UK GAAP

Whilst in the UK there is no legal requirement for companies to prepare interim financial reports, a company which is listed on the London Stock Exchange or Alternative Investment Market must prepare a half-yearly report on a consolidated basis. This report must be published within four months of the end of the period to which it relates. The half yearly report should consist of figures and an explanatory statement relating to the group's activities and profit or loss during the relevant period. The figures to be presented are:

(1) net turnover;
(2) profit or loss before taxation and extraordinary items;
(3) taxation on profits (UK taxation and, if material, overseas and share of associated undertakings' taxation to be shown separately);
(4) minority interests;
(5) profit or loss attributable to shareholders, before extraordinary items;
(6) extraordinary items (net of taxation);
(7) profit or loss attributable to shareholders;
(8) rates of dividend(s) paid and proposed and amount absorbed thereby; and
(9) earnings per share expressed as pence per share.

Comparative figures in respect of the above items for the corresponding period in the preceding financial year should be given.

However, best practice in the UK has advanced beyond the requirements of the Listing Rules of the Financial Services Authority. The ASB's Statement on Interim Reports now sets out best practice but compliance is voluntary. The Statement encourages companies to make their interims available within 60 days after the interim period end. It is recommended that an interim report should include a narrative commentary, summarised profit and loss account, statement of total recognised gains and losses where relevant, summarised balance sheet and summarised cash flow statement. The interim accounts should be prepared on a consistent and comparable basis with the annual accounts.

The recommended minimum headings are:

For the profit and loss account:

- Turnover.
- Operating profit or loss.
- Interest payable less interest receivable (net).
- Profit or loss on ordinary activities before tax.
- Tax on profit or loss on ordinary activities.
- Profit or loss on ordinary activities after tax.
- Minority interests.
- Profit or loss for the period.
- Dividends paid and proposed.

For the balance sheet:

- Fixed assets.
- Current assets.
- Stocks.
- Debtors.
- Cash at bank and in hand.
- Other current assets.
- Creditors: amounts falling due within one year.
- Net current assets/liabilities.
- Total assets less current liabilities.
- Creditors: amounts falling due after more than one year.
- Provisions for liabilities and charges.
- Capital and reserves.
- Minority interests.

For the cash flow statement:

- headings required by FRS 1 (Revised 1996) *Cash Flow Statements.*
- reconciliation of operating profit to operating cash flow and reconciliation of the movement of cash in the period with the movement in net debt.

Other detailed recommendations are as follows:

- the commentary should be sufficient to enable users to appreciate the main factors influencing the company's performance during the period and its position at the period end. The focus should be on areas of change and key issues normally referred to in the Operating and Financial Review should be considered;
- acquisitions and discontinued operations should be disclosed separately on the face of the profit and loss account in accordance with FRS 3 *Reporting Financial Performance*;
- segmental analysis of turnover and profit/loss before interest should be provided in a manner similar to that disclosed in the annual report;
- exceptional items should be recognised and disclosed in the profit and loss account of the interim period in which they occur;
- earnings per share, both basic and any additional where provided in the annual financial statements, should be derived from the results for the interim period;
- recognition of the value changes of assets held at valuation will depend upon the nature of the assets and the difficulty of obtaining valuations;
- comparative figures for the profit and loss account and cash flow statement should be provided for both the corresponding interim period and the previous financial year;
- comparative figures for the balance sheet should be provided for the previous financial year.

The Statement suggests that disclosures required by FRSs and SSAPs but not specifically mentioned in the Statement could be omitted. Some additional disclosures will, however, be required:

- the period covered by the report;
- the date on which it is approved by the directors; and
- the extent to which the information it contains has been audited or reviewed.

Similar to IAS 34, the Statement recommends the discrete approach to measuring most financial statement items. In other words, each period is considered on its own. However, like IAS 34, the Statement includes some exceptions like tax, which is estimated using the estimated annual effective tax rate, and expenses/income which are recognised on an annual basis (i.e., contractual supplier volume discount should be calculated as a proportion of the expected annual discount).

29.11 Comparison with US GAAP

Like IAS 34, APB 28 *Interim Financial Reporting* provides guidance for the application of accounting policies to financial information reported for a period shorter than a fiscal year, whether the information presented is condensed or a complete set of financial statements. Like IAS 34, APB 28 requires use of accounting policies which are adopted in the annual financial statements in the interim financials with certain noted exceptions. Both standards include guidance on accounting for income taxes and LIFO liquidations. However, APB 28 also requires modifications that (1) defer purchase price variances and volume or corporate cost variances that are expected to be absorbed by year-end; (2) accrue or defer costs that clearly benefit two or more periods; and (3) do not require recognition of inventory losses from market declines that reasonably can be expected to be restored within the fiscal year. IAS 34 does not permit these same modifications.

APB 28 requires disclosure of income statement data and encourages publication of a balance sheet and cash flow data, whilst IAS 34 requires publication of all the primary financial statements. However, companies with publicly traded debt or equity in the US fall under the regulations of the SEC. The SEC rules detail presentation requirements for a public enterprise that issues condensed interim financial statements in Form 10-Q (a US quarterly filing). In general, the presentation and disclosure requirements of the SEC are similar to those of IAS 34.

APPENDIX I

Summary of SIC Exposure Drafts

Summaries of the following SIC Exposure Drafts are included in this Chapter:

SIC-D26	*Property, Plant and Equipment – Results of Incidental Operations.*
SIC-D27	*Transactions in the Legal Form of a Lease and Leaseback.*
SIC-D28	*Business Combinations – Measurement of Shares Issued as Purchase Consideration.*
SIC-D29	*Disclosure – Service Concession Arrangements.*
SIC-D30	*Reporting Currency – Translation from Measurement Currency to Presentation Currency.*
SIC-D31	*Revenue – Barter Transactions Involving Advertising Services.*
SIC-D32	*Intangible Assets – Web Site Costs.*

For progress on the exposure drafts, and for an updated list of exposure drafts issued after 31 July 2001, refer to www.iasplus.com.

SIC-D26 *Property, Plant and Equipment – Results of Incidental Operations*

SIC-D26 addresses the treatment of the results from operations, when the income recognition criteria have been met, that are incidental to the construction or development of property, plant and equipment. For example, income may be earned from a building site that is used as a car park until construction commences. SIC-D26 proposes that the results of incidental operations should be recognised in the net profit or loss for the period. They should not be recognised as an adjustment of the cost of the related property, plant, or equipment asset.

The draft interpretation was issued for public comment on 27 September 2000. The comment deadline was 30 November 2000.

At its meeting in February 2001, following its review of the comments received on SIC-D26, the SIC approved a final interpretation without any substantive changes to the proposed consensus. A final interpretation was submitted to the IASB for approval. However, at its April 2001 meeting, the IASB did not approve the proposed interpretation, concluding that the issue should, instead, be addressed in the Improvements Project. Consequently, the SIC is not pursuing a final interpretation at this time, but it has not withdrawn SIC-D26.

SIC-D27 *Transactions in the Legal Form of a Lease and Leaseback*

SIC-D27 addresses whether a transaction that takes the legal form of a lease of assets from an enterprise and a lease of the same assets back to the same enterprise is a lease under IAS 17, *Leases.*

The draft interpretation establishes the principle that the accounting should reflect the substance of the transaction. All aspects of a transaction should be evaluated to determine its substance, and whether a series of transactions are linked in such a way that the effect cannot be understood without reference to the series of transactions as a whole and should be accounted for as one transaction. The draft interpretation identifies the following as examples of indications that the transaction is not a lease:

- the lease/leaseback transactions are linked together such that, in substance, during the sublease period the enterprise retains control of the underlying asset and enjoys substantially the same rights to its use as before the arrangement; or
- the transaction has been arranged predominantly for a particular purpose other than leasing (for instance, solely to generate tax benefits that can be shared or to increase off balance sheet borrowings).

Most of these transactions involve a fee, and the draft interpretation proposes guidance on whether to recognise fee income when execution of the 'lease' agreement is finalised or to defer all or a portion of it to future periods. There is also guidance on determining whether separate investment account and the sublease payment obligations should be recognised.

The draft interpretation was issued for public comment on 20 October 2000. The comment deadline was 20 December 2000.

At its meeting in April 2001, IASB concluded that SIC should not issue the proposed interpretation in its current form. The SIC discussed the matter at its May 2001 meeting and will continue that discussion at its August 2001 meeting.

SIC-D28 *Business Combinations – Measurement of Shares Issued as Purchase Consideration*

SIC-D28 addresses when the date of exchange occurs in a purchase business combination in which shares are issued as the purchase consideration. If an acquisition is achieved in a single exchange transaction, the date of exchange is the date on which the acquirer obtains control over the net assets and operations of the acquiree. If an acquisition is achieved in stages by successive share purchases, the fair value of the shares issued as purchase consideration should be determined at the date that each exchange is recognised.

SIC-D28 also addresses when it is appropriate to use a price other than a published price at the date of exchange when determining the fair value of an acquirer's shares that are quoted in an active market. SIC-D28 proposes that the published price of a share in an active market at the date of exchange should be considered the best evidence of the share's fair value. Another price should be used only if it can be demonstrated that a price fluctuation is undue and the other price provides a more reliable measure of the share's fair value.

The draft interpretation was issued for public comment on 9 July 2001. The comment deadline was 10 September 2001.

SIC-D29 *Disclosure – Service Concession Arrangements*

SIC-D29 considers the information that should be disclosed in the notes to the financial statements by both parties to a service concession arrangement.

A service concession arrangement exists when an enterprise (the Concession Operator) agrees with another enterprise (the Concession Provider) to provide services that are normally considered public services. Examples of service concession arrangements involve water treatment and supply facilities, motorways, car parks, tunnels, bridges, airports and telecommunication networks. Examples of arrangements that are not service concession arrangements include an enterprise outsourcing the operations of its internal services (e.g., employee cafeteria and accounting or information technology functions).

The following should be disclosed in each period:

- description of the arrangement;
- significant terms such as the period of the concession, contractual repricing dates, and the basis upon which repricing or renegotiation is determined;

- the nature and extent (quantity, time period, or amount as appropriate) of the following:
  - transferred rights to use specified assets;
  - obligations to provide or rights to expect provision of services;
  - obligations to acquire or build items of property, plant and equipment;
  - obligations to deliver or rights to receive specified assets at the end of the concession period;
  - renewal options;
  - other rights and obligations (e.g., major overhauls); and
- changes in the arrangement occurring during the period.

The draft interpretation was issued for public comment on 9 July 2001. The comment deadline was 10 September 2001.

SIC-D30 *Reporting Currency – Translation from Measurement Currency to Presentation Currency*

SIC-D30 addresses how an enterprise should translate its financial statements from a currency used for measuring items in its financial statements (measurement currency) to another currency for presentation purposes (presentation currency). SIC-19, *Reporting Currency – Measurement and Presentation of Financial Statements Under IAS 21 and IAS 29*, requires that the translation method used does not lead to reporting in a manner that is inconsistent with the measurement of items in the financial statements.

The requirements of SIC-19.9 should be applied as follows:

- assets and liabilities should be translated at the closing rate at the date of each balance sheet presented, except when an enterprise's measurement currency is the currency of a hyperinflationary economy, in which case assets and liabilities should be translated at the closing rate existing at the date of the most recent balance sheet presented;
- income and expense items should be translated at the exchange rates existing at the dates of the transactions or a rate that approximates the actual exchange rates, except when an enterprise's measurement currency is the currency of a hyperinflationary economy, in which case income and expense items for all periods presented should be translated at the closing rate existing at the end of the most recent period presented; and
- all resulting exchange differences should be reported directly in equity.

SIC-D30 also addresses 'convenience translations': what information should be disclosed when additional information not required by International Accounting Standards is displayed in a currency other than the currency used in presenting its financial statements, as a convenience to certain users. The SIC agreed that in these circumstances an enterprise should:

- clearly identify the information as supplementary information to distinguish it from the information required by International Accounting Standards; and
- disclose the method of translation used as a basis for presenting the information.

The draft interpretation was issued for public comment on 9 July 2001. The comment deadline was 10 September 2001.

SIC-D31 *Revenue – Barter Transactions Involving Advertising Services*

SIC-D31 addresses how revenue from a barter transaction involving advertising should be measured, and the circumstances when the fair value of advertising services received or provided in a barter transaction be reliably measured.

The SIC agreed that:

- an enterprise providing advertising should measure revenue from a barter transaction based on the fair value of the advertising services it receives from its customer unless it is impracticable to measure reliably, in which case the enterprise should use the fair value of the advertising services it provides to the customer. If the fair value of the advertising services of both enterprises is not reliably measurable, the seller should recognise revenue only to the extent of the carrying amount of assets given up;
- the fair value of advertising services received or provided in a barter transaction can be reliably measured only by reference to non-barter transactions that:
  - involve advertising similar to the advertising in the barter transaction;
  - occur frequently;
  - are expected to continue occurring after the barter transaction;
  - represent a predominant source of revenue from advertising similar to the advertising in the barter transaction;
  - involve cash and/or another form of consideration (e.g., marketable securities, non-monetary assets and other services) that has a reliably measurable fair value; and
  - do not involve the same counterparty as in the barter transaction.

The draft interpretation was issued for public comment on 9 July 2001. The comment deadline was 10 September 2001.

SIC-D32 *Intangible Assets – Web Site Costs*

SIC-D32 addresses the accounting for an internal expenditure to develop, enhance and maintain a website by an enterprise for its own use. Specifically, it addresses the application of IAS 38, *Intangible Assets*, to website development costs.

SIC-D32 identifies the following stages of website development:

- planning;
- application and infrastructure development ;
- graphical design and content development; and
- operating.

SIC-D32 proposes that:

- A website developed by an enterprise for its own use is an internally generated intangible asset that is subject to the requirements of IAS 38.
- The planning stage of website development is similar in nature to the research phase described in IAS 38.42–44 and, therefore, expenditure incurred in this stage should be recognised as an expense when it is incurred.
- The application and infrastructure development stage and the graphical design and content development stage of website development are similar in nature to the development phase in IAS 38.45–52. Therefore, expenditure incurred in these stages is eligible for recognition as an intangible asset if, firstly, it meets the general requirements of IAS 38 for recognition and initial measurement of an intangible asset and, secondly, the enterprise can demonstrate that the conditions in IAS 38.45 are met. In addition:
  - an enterprise may be able to demonstrate how its website will generate probable future economic benefits under IAS 38.45(d) by using the principles in IAS 36, *Impairment of Assets*. This includes situations where the website is developed solely or primarily for promoting and advertising an enterprise's own products and services; and
  - an enterprise may incur expenditure to enable use of content, which had been purchased or created for another purpose, on its website (e.g., acquiring a licence to reproduce information) or may purchase or create content specifically for use on its website prior to the website becoming available for use. In such circumstances, an enterprise should determine whether a separate asset is identifiable with respect to such content (e.g., copyrights and licences), and if a separate asset is not identifiable, then the expenditure should be included in the cost of developing the website when the expenditure meets the conditions in IAS 38.54.

- The operating stage commences once the website is available for use, and therefore expenditure to maintain or enhance the website after development has been completed should be recognised as an expense when it is incurred unless it meets the criteria in IAS 38.60.

The draft interpretation was issued for public comment on 9 July 2001. The comment deadline was 10 September 2001.

APPENDIX II

Industry Specific Standards

Given the specialised nature of the standards listed below, and the limited number of enterprises to which they apply, a summary of their requirements has been presented in this Appendix since further discussion of these standards is beyond the scope of this book. The standards included are:

- IAS 26, *Accounting and Reporting by Retirement Benefit Plans*;
- IAS 30, *Disclosures in the Financial Statements of Banks and Similar Financial Institutions*; and
- IAS 41, *Agriculture*.

Retirement benefit plans, summary of IAS 26

Scope

- IAS 26, *Accounting and Reporting by Retirement Benefit Plans* applies to the reports of retirement benefit plans where such reports are prepared.
- All other IASs apply to the reports of retirement benefit plans to the extent that they are not superseded by IAS 26.
- Accounting for retirement benefits by the enterprises contributing to the funds is covered by IAS 19 (r2000), *Employee Benefits*. Refer to Chapter **25**.

Definitions

'Retirement benefit plans are arrangements whereby an enterprise provides benefits for its employees on or after termination of service (either in the form of an annual income or as a lump sum) when such benefits, or the employer's contributions towards them, can be determined or estimated in advance of retirement from the provisions of a document or from the enterprise's practices.'

(IAS 26.8)

'Net assets available for benefits are the assets of a plan less liabilities other than the actuarial present value of promised retirement benefits.'

(IAS 26.8)

'Actuarial present value of promised retirement benefits is the present value of the expected payments by a retirement benefit plan to existing and past employees, attributable to the service already rendered.'

(IAS 26.8)

Defined contribution plans

'Defined contribution plans are retirement benefit plans under which amounts to be paid as retirement benefits are determined by contributions to a fund together with investment earnings thereon.'

(IAS 26.8)

The report of a defined contribution plan is required to contain a statement of net assets available for benefits and a description of the funding policy.

The objective of reporting by a defined contribution plan is to provide periodically information about the plan and the performance of its investments. IAS 26 suggests that this objective is usually achieved by providing a report including:

- a description of significant activities for the period and the effect of any changes relating to the plan, and its membership, terms and conditions;
- statements reporting on the transactions and investment performance for the period and the financial position of the plan at the end of the period; and
- a description of the investment policies.

Defined benefit plans

'Defined benefit plans are retirement benefit plans under which amounts to be paid as retirement benefits are determined by reference to a formula usually based on employees' earnings and/or years of service.'

(IAS 26.8)

The objective of reporting by a defined benefit plan is to provide periodically information about the financial resources and activities of the plan that is useful in assessing the relationships between the accumulation of resources and plan benefits over time. IAS 26 suggests that this objective is usually achieved by providing a report including the following:

- a description of significant activities for the period and the effect of any changes relating to the plan, and its membership, terms and conditions;
- statements reporting on the transactions and investment performance for the period and the financial position of the plan at the end of the period;
- actuarial information either as part of the statements or by way of a separate report; and
- a description of investment policies.

IAS 26 permits three formats for reports of defined benefit plans. All three require a statement of net assets available for benefits and a statement of changes in net assets available for benefits. However, the disclosure of the actuarial present value of promised retirement benefits varies among the three.

- Under the first method, it is disclosed in the report along with the net assets available for benefits and the resulting excess or deficit. In addition, a statement of changes in the actuarial present value of promised retirement benefits is included.
- Under the second method, it is disclosed in the notes to the statements. The report may also include a report from an actuary supporting the actuarial present value of promised retirement benefits.
- Under the third method, it is contained in a separate actuarial report which accompanies the financial statements and is specifically referred to those statements.

If an actuarial report has not been prepared at the date of the report, the most recent valuation should be used as a base and the date of the valuation disclosed.

The actuarial present value of promised retirement benefits is based on the benefits promised under the terms of the plan on service rendered to date using either current salary levels or projected salary levels with disclosure of the basis used.

The effect of any changes in actuarial assumptions that have had a significant effect on the actuarial present value of promised retirement benefits should also be disclosed.

Valuation of plan assets (all plans)

Retirement benefit plan investments are required to be carried at fair value. In the case of marketable securities, fair value is market value. Where plan investments are held for which an estimate of fair value is not possible, disclosure is required as to the reason why fair value is not used.

Disclosure

In addition to the statements and disclosures described above, the report of a retirement benefit plan is required to contain the following information:

- a statement of changes in net assets available for benefits;
- a summary of significant accounting policies; and
- a description of the plan and the effect of any changes in the plan during the period.

The guidance in IAS 26 outlines information included in the statement of net assets available for benefits, the statement of changes in net assets available for benefits and other disclosures.

A statement of net assets available for benefits includes, as appropriate:

- assets at the end of the period suitably classified;
- the basis of valuation of assets;
- details of any single investment exceeding either 5 per cent of the net assets available for benefits or 5 per cent of any class or type of security;
- details of any investment in the employer; and
- liabilities other than the actuarial present value of promised retirement benefits.

A statement of changes in net assets available for benefits includes, as appropriate:

- employer contributions;
- employee contributions;
- investment income such as interest and dividends;
- other income;
- benefits paid or payable (analysed, for example, as retirement, death and disability benefits, and lump sum payments);
- administrative expenses;
- other expenses;
- taxes on income;
- profits and losses on disposal of investments and changes in value of investments; and
- transfers from and to other plans.

Other disclosures generally included in the report of a retirement benefit plan include:

- a description of the funding policy;
- for defined benefit plans, the actuarial present value of promised retirement benefits (which may distinguish between vested benefits and non-vested benefits) based on the benefits promised under the terms of the plan, on service rendered to date and using either current salary levels or projected salary levels; this information may be included in an accompanying actuarial report to be read in conjunction with the related financial information;
- for defined benefit plans, a description of the significant actuarial assumptions made and the method used to calculate the actuarial present value of promised retirement benefits; and
- the following, including any changes to these items during the period covered by the report:

- a description of the plan;
- the names of the employers and the employee groups covered;
- the number of participants receiving benefits and the number of other participants, classified as appropriate;
- the type of plan, i.e., defined contribution or defined benefit;
- a note as to whether participants contribute to the plan;
- a description of the retirement benefits promised to participants; and
- a description of any plan termination terms.

Banks and similar institutions, summary of IAS 30

Scope

- IAS 30, *Disclosures in the Financial Statements of Banks and Similar Financial Institutions*, applies to the financial statements of banks and similar financial institutions (subsequently referred to as 'banks').
- For purposes of IAS 30, 'bank' includes all financial institutions, one of whose principal activities is to take deposits and borrow with the objective of lending and investing and which are within the scope of banking or similar legislation. (IAS 30.2)
- IAS 30 supplements the requirements of other IASs unless banks are specifically exempted from the requirements of a particular IAS. (IAS 30.4)
- IAS 30 applies to the separate financial statements and the consolidated financial statements of a bank. (IAS 30.5)
- Recognition and measurement principles related to items included in the financial statements of banks are beyond the scope of IAS 30. However, many of the items are covered in IAS 39 (r2000), *Financial Instruments: Recognition and Measurement.*

Income statement

A bank is required to present an income statement which groups income and expenses by nature and discloses the amounts of the principal types of income and expenses. (IAS 30.9)

In addition to the disclosures required by other IASs including IAS 1 (r1997), *Presentation of Financial Statements*, an enterprise is required to present either on the face of the income statement or in the notes to the financial statements:

- interest and similar income;
- interest expense and similar charges;
- dividend income;
- fee and commission income;
- fee and commission expense;

- gains less losses arising from dealing securities;
- gains less losses arising from investment securities;
- gains less losses arising from dealing in foreign currencies;
- other operating income;
- losses on loans and advances;
- general administrative expenses; and
- other operating expenses.

(IAS 30.10)

Items of income and expense should not be offset except for those relating to hedges and to assets and liabilities for which a legal right of set-off exists and the offsetting represents the expectation as to the realisation or settlement of the asset or liability. (IAS 30.13)

However, gains and losses arising from each of the following are normally reported on a net basis:

- disposals and changes in the carrying amount of dealing securities;
- disposals of investment securities; and
- dealings in foreign currencies.

(IAS 30.15)

Balance sheet

A bank is required to present a balance sheet that groups assets and liabilities by nature and lists them in an order that reflects their relative liquidity. (IAS 30.19)

In addition to the disclosures required by other IASs including IAS 1 (r1997), an enterprise is required to present either on the face of the balance sheet or in the notes to the financial statements:

- Assets:
  - cash and balances with the central bank;
  - treasury bills and other bills eligible for rediscounting with the central bank;
  - government and other securities held for dealing purposes;
  - placements with, and loans and advances to, other banks;
  - other money market placements;
  - loans and advances to customers; and
  - investment securities.
- Liabilities:
  - deposits from other banks;
  - other money market deposits;
  - amounts owed to other depositors;

- certificates of deposits;
- promissory notes and other liabilities evidenced by paper; and
- other borrowed funds.

(IAS 30.19)

Current and non-current items are not presented separately because most assets and liabilities of a bank can be realised or settled in the near future. (IAS 30.20)

Offsetting of assets and liabilities is not permitted unless a legal right of set-off exists and the offsetting represents the expectation as to the realisation or settlement of the asset or liability. (IAS 30.23)

A bank should disclose the fair values of each class of its financial assets and liabilities as required by IAS 32 (r1998), *Financial Instruments: Disclosure and Presentation*, and IAS 39 (r2000), *Financial Instruments: Recognition and Measurement*. (IAS 30.24)

Accounting policies

Since IAS 30 does not prescribe recognition and measurement requirements for items included in the financial statements of a bank, disclosure of the accounting policies adopted is particularly important. In order to comply with IAS 1 (r1997), an enterprise may need to disclose its accounting policies dealing with the following:

- the recognition of the principal types of income;
- the valuation of investment and dealing securities;
- the distinction between those transactions and other events that result in the recognition of assets and liabilities on the balance sheet and those transactions and other events that give rise to contingencies and commitments;
- the basis for the determination of losses on loans and advances and for writing off uncollectable loans and advances; and
- the basis for the determination of charges for general banking risks and the accounting treatments of such charges.

(IAS 30.8)

Contingencies and commitments

A bank is required to disclose the following contingent liabilities and commitments required by IAS 10 (r1999), *Events After the Balance Sheet Date*, and IAS 37, *Provisions, Contingent Liabilities and Contingent Assets*:

- the nature and amount of commitments to extend credit that are irrevocable because they cannot be withdrawn at the discretion of the bank without the risk of incurring significant penalty or expense; and

- the nature and amount of contingent liabilities and commitments arising from off balance sheet items including those related to:
  - direct credit substitutes including general guarantees of indebtedness, bank acceptance guarantees and standby letters of credit serving as financial guarantees for loans and securities;
  - certain transaction-related contingent liabilities including performance bonds, bid bonds, warranties and standby letters of credit relating to particular transactions;
  - short-term, self-liquidating, trade-related contingent liabilities arising from the movement of goods, such as documentary credits where the underlying shipment is used as security;
  - those sale and repurchase agreements not recognised in the balance sheet;
  - interest and foreign exchange rate related items including swaps, options and futures; and
  - other commitments, note issuance facilities and revolving underwriting facilities.

(IAS 30.26)

Maturities of assets and liabilities

A bank is required to disclose an analysis of assets and liabilities into relevant maturity groupings based on the remaining period at the balance sheet date to the contractual maturity date. While IAS 30 does not prescribe specific maturity periods which must be disclosed, the maturity periods adopted need to be the same for assets and liabilities.

(IAS 30.30)

Concentrations of assets, liabilities and off balance sheet items

A bank is required to disclose any significant concentrations of its assets, liabilities and off balance sheet items. Such disclosures should be made in terms of geographical areas, customer or industry groups or other concentrations of risk. A bank is also required to disclose the amount of significant net foreign currency exposures. These disclosures are in addition to the segment disclosures required by IAS 14 (r1997), *Segment Reporting*.

(IAS 30.40)

Losses on loans and advances

A bank is required to disclose the following:

- the accounting policy which describes the basis on which uncollectable loans and advances are recognised as an expense and written off;

- details of the movements in the provision for losses on loans and advances during the period. It should disclose separately the amount recognised as an expense in the period for losses on uncollectable loans and advances, the amount charged in the period for loans and advances written off, and the amount credited in the period for loans and advances previously written off that have been recovered;
- the aggregate amount of the provision for losses on loans and advances at the balance sheet date; and
- the aggregate amount included in the balance sheet for loans and advances on which interest is not being accrued and the basis used to determine the carrying amount of such loans and advances.

(IAS 30.43)

Any amounts set aside in respect of losses on loans and advances in addition to those losses that have been specifically identified or potential losses which experience indicates are present in the portfolio of loans and advances are required to be accounted for as appropriations of retained earnings. Any credits resulting from the reduction of such amounts result in an increase in retained earnings and are not included in the determination of net profit or loss for the period.

(IAS 30.44)

Similarly, any amounts set aside for general banking risks, including future losses and other unforeseeable risks or contingencies are required to be separately disclosed as appropriations of retained earnings. Any credits resulting from the reduction of such amounts results in an increase in retained earnings and are not included in the determination of net profit or loss for the period.

(IAS 30.50)

Assets pledged as security

A bank is required to disclose the aggregate amount of secured liabilities and the nature and carrying amount of the assets pledged as security.

(IAS 30.53)

Future developments

In July 1999 the Board added to its agenda a project to consider the need to revise the presentation and disclosure requirements of IAS 30. This was in response to developments in the industry and the issuance of IAS 1 (r1997), *Presentation of Financial Statements*, and IAS 39 (r2000), *Financial Instruments: Recognition and Measurement*. A steering committee was appointed in June 2000.

The new IASB has adopted a project – Activities of Financial Institutions: Disclosures and Presentation. This project will address the issues raised by the steering committee considering the changes to IAS 30. This project aims to update existing disclosure requirements relating to the business activities of banks, and extend the scope of the new/revised standard to include other institutions whose business is to take deposits, grant credits or provide other financing or investment services. Both the Basle Committee and various financial institutions are supporting this project. The steering committee will continue its work and draft an exposure draft for the board.

Agriculture, summary of IAS 41

Scope

IAS 41, *Agriculture* should be used when accounting for biological assets, agricultural produce which is at the point of harvest, and government grants when they relate to agricultural activities.

It does not cover the accounting treatment for land on which agricultural activities are conducted nor the intangible assets relating to these activities. These are covered by IAS 16 (r1998), *Property, Plant and Equipment* and IAS 38, *Intangible Assets* respectively.

It should be borne in mind that the Standard only treats the biological assets to the point of harvest, and not any further transformations it may undergo thereafter. The assets are accounted for under IAS 2 (r1993), *Inventories* after harvest is completed.

Definitions

The following terms are defined in the standard:

> 'An active market is a market where all the following conditions exist:
> a. the items traded within the market are homogeneous;
> b. willing buyers and sellers can normally be found at any time; and
> c. prices are available to the public.'
>
> (IAS 41.8)

> 'Carrying amount is the amount at which an asset is recognised in the balance sheet.'
>
> (IAS 41.8)

> 'Fair value is the amount for which an asset could be exchanged, or a liability settled, between knowledgeable, willing parties in an arm's length transaction.'
> (IAS 41.8)

> 'Government grants are assistance by government in the form of transfers of resources to an enterprise in return for past or future compliance with certain conditions relating to the operating activities of the enterprise. They exclude

those forms of government assistance which cannot reasonably have a value placed upon them and transactions with government which cannot be distinguished from the normal trading transactions of the enterprise.'

(IAS 20.3)

Recognition and measurement

'An enterprise should recognise a biological asset or agricultural produce when, and only when:

a. the enterprise controls the asset as a result of past events;
b. it is probable that future economic benefits associated with the asset will flow to the enterprise; and
c. the fair value or cost of the asset can be measured reliably.'

(IAS 41.10)

Biological assets are initially recognised at fair value, and subsequently at fair value less point-of-sale costs at each balance sheet date.

Agricultural produce harvested is initially measured at fair value less estimated point-of-sale expenses at the point of harvest. Subsequently IAS 2 (r1993), *Inventory* will apply.

Point-of-sale costs include brokers' and dealers' commissions, levies, taxes and other duties. They exclude transportation and other costs of getting the product to market.

In determining the fair value of assets covered by IAS 41, assets or produce may be grouped by attribute, for example by age or quality. These attributes should correspond to the attributes used in the market as a basis for pricing.

Rates used in contracts selling the produce at a later date are not used as fair value rates as these do not represent the current market conditions. Fair values are also not adjusted due to the existence of such contracts.

If there is no active market, the following can be used in determining the fair value:

- the most recent market transaction price adjusted for any change in economic circumstances;
- market prices for similar assets adjusted to reflect any differences; and
- sector benchmarks.

If no determinable market price can be established, the enterprise should use the present value of the expected net cash flows discounted at a current market-determined pretax rate. No adjustments are made for any transformation that the asset or produce may undergo in the future that results in an increase in value. Cash flows from financing, taxation or re-establishment of biological assets are excluded.

As variations in cash flows would be included in determining the fair value in the market, such variations should also be taken into consideration when determining the expected cash flows or the discount rate, or a combination of the two.

Cost can be an approximate fair value when little biological transformation has taken place, for example, seedlings planted close to balance sheet date, or the transformation that has taken place in the period is not deemed to be material, for example the initial growth stage in a 30-year plantation.

Where land and the biological assets are attached, the values of the total package is usually more than the individual assets, for example a tree plantation. In this scenario the separate values of the assets may be ignored and the fair value of the entire package used to determine the value of the separate components. For example, the fair value of the land may be deducted from the fair value of the entire plantation in order to calculate the value of the biological assets.

Gains and losses

> 'A gain or loss arising on initial recognition of a biological asset at fair value less estimated point-of-sale costs and from a change in fair value less estimated point-of-sale costs of biological asset should be included in the profit and loss for the period in which it arises.'
>
> (IAS 41.26)

Gains and losses may arise on initial recognition of a biological asset. A loss may arise when point-of-sale costs are deducted in determining the fair value, or a gain on initial recognition, for example, of a calf being born.

> 'A gain or loss arising on initial recognition of agricultural produce at fair value less estimated point-of-sale costs should be included in net profit or loss for the period in which it arises.'
>
> (IAS 41.28)

Gains and losses may arise on initial recognition of produce as a result of harvesting.

Inability to measure fair value reliably

There is a presumption that fair value can be measured reliably for assets covered by IAS 41. The presumption is rebuttable on initial recognition where the market-determined fair value of a biological asset is not available, and alternative estimates are unreliable. In these cases the standard allows for the assets to be recorded at cost less any accumulated depreciation or impairment losses. The enterprise should account for the assets at fair value less point-of-sale costs once this amount becomes determinable.

Enterprises that have previously recorded biological assets at fair value less estimated point-of-sale costs should continue to do so until disposal.

In all cases, agricultural produce at the point of harvest is accounted for at fair value less estimated point-of-sale costs.

In determining cost, accumulated depreciation and impairment, an enterprise should look to IAS 2 (r1993), *Inventories*, IAS 16 (r1998), *Property, Plant and Equipment* and IAS 38, *Impairment of Assets.*

Government grants

Unconditional grants relating to biological assets that are measured at fair value less estimated point-of-sale costs should be recognised as income when the grant becomes receivable.

If the grant is conditional, it should be recognised as income when the conditions attached to the grant are met. This includes grants where enterprises are required not to engage in a specified activity.

Where an asset cannot be fair valued, it is recorded at cost less accumulated depreciation and impairments as detailed above. Government grants relating to these assets are accounted for under IAS 20, *Accounting for Government Grants and Disclosure of Government Assistance* (See Chapter **26**).

Presentation and disclosure

Biological assets should be carried separately on the face of the balance sheet.

Gains and losses on initial recognition and subsequent fair value adjustments should be disclosed for all biological assets.

A description of each group of biological asset should be given in a narrative or quantified description. Enterprises are encouraged to distinguish between consumable and bearer biological assets or between mature and immature biological assets.

The following should be disclosed:

- the nature of its activities involving each group of biological assets; and
- non-financial measures or estimates of the physical quantities of:
  - each group of the enterprise's biological assets at the end of the period; and
  - output of agricultural produce during the period.

Methods and assumptions used in determining fair value should be disclosed.

The fair value less estimated point-of-sale costs of produce harvested during the year, determined at the point of harvest, should be disclosed.

The existence and carrying amounts of assets whose title is restricted, or assets pledged as security should be disclosed.

Commitments for development or acquisition of biological assets should be disclosed.

The enterprise's financial risk management strategies in relation to their agricultural activities should be disclosed.

A reconciliation of the opening and closing balances of biological assets is required, without comparatives, which includes:

- gains and losses arising from changes in fair values;
- increases from purchases;
- decreases from sales;
- decreases due to harvest;
- increases from business combinations;
- net exchange differences arising from the translation of financial statements of foreign entities; and
- any other changes.

When an enterprise has a production cycle of more than one year, disclosure of physical and price changes is useful in evaluating current performance and future prospects.

Agricultural enterprises are often exposed to natural risks such as disease and adverse weather. The nature and amounts of income and expenditure related to these events should be disclosed in accordance with IAS 8 (r1993), *Net Profit or Loss for the Period, Fundamental Errors and Changes in Accounting Policies.*

If biological assets are measured at cost less accumulated depreciation and impairments, the following disclosure is required:

- description of the assets;
- explanation why fair value cannot be reliably determined;
- range of estimated fair values, if possible;
- depreciation method;
- useful lives or depreciation rate used; and
- gross carrying amount and accumulated depreciation and impairments at the beginning and end of the period.

In addition to the reconciliation described for biological assets above, enterprises that account for biological assets at cost should disclose the gains and losses on sale of these assets separately. In addition, the reconciliation should disclose impairment losses, reversals of impairments and depreciation charged to net income during the period.

Where an enterprise moves from a cost basis to a fair value basis during the year, it should disclose a description of the affected biological assets, an explanation of why the fair value can now be measured reliably, and the effects of the change.

Government grants in relation to agricultural activity require the following disclosure:

- nature and extent of government grants recognised;
- unfulfilled conditions and other contingencies attaching to the grant; and
- significant decreases expected in the level of government grants.

Effective date

The standard is effective for periods beginning on or after 1 January 2003. Earlier application is encouraged. Disclosure of early adoption is required.

APPENDIX III

Model Financial Statements

International GAAP Holdings Ltd

The model financial statements of International GAAP Holdings Limited are intended to address the presentation and disclosure requirements of IAS. They also contain additional disclosures which are considered to be best practice, particularly where such disclosures are included in illustrative examples provided with a specific Standard.

These model financial statements have been presented without regard to local laws or regulation. Preparers of financial statements will need to ensure that the options selected under IAS do not conflict with such sources of regulation (e.g., the revaluation of assets is not permitted within certain regimes – but these financial statements illustrate the presentation where the alternative treatment under IAS 16(r1998), *Property, Plant and Equipment*, is adopted). In addition, local laws or securities' regulations may specify disclosures in addition to those required by IAS (e.g., in relation to directors' remuneration). Preparers of financial statements will consequently need to adapt the model financial statements to comply with such additional local requirements.

Suggested disclosures are cross-referenced to the relevant requirements in the Presentation and Disclosure Checklist (see Appendix **IV**). References are also provided to the underlying requirements in the texts of the relevant Standards. References are made by IAS number, followed by the paragraph number e.g., 27.26 refers to paragraph 26 of IAS 27. For those Standards revised since their original issue, the year of the most recent revision is also noted e.g., 14(r1997).55 refers to paragraph 55 of IAS 14 (Revised 1997).

For the purposes of presenting the income statement, statement of changes in equity and cash flow statement – the various alternatives allowed by IAS for those primary statements have been illustrated. Preparers should select the alternatives most appropriate to their circumstances.

MODEL FINANCIAL STATEMENTS
INTERNATIONAL GAAP HOLDINGS LIMITED

for the year ended 31 December 2001

Source	Checklist	INTERNATIONAL GAAP HOLDINGS LIMITED	

CONTENTS

Source	Checklist	INTERNATIONAL GAAP HOLDINGS LIMITED			
1(r1997).7(b)	2001,2018	CONSOLIDATED INCOME STATEMENT			
1(r1997).46(b),(c)	2019(b),(c)	FOR THE YEAR ENDED 31 DECEMBER 2001			[Alt 1]
1(r1997).92	8003		NOTES	Year ended	Year ended
1(r1997).46(d),(e)	2019(d),(e)			31/12/01 CU'000	31/12/00 CU'000
1(r1997).75(a)	3002(a)	Revenue	4	1,224,098	869,453
1(r1997).77	3006	Other operating income		10,150	6,745
1(r1997).77	3006	Changes in inventories of finished goods and work in progress		5,446	7,329
1(r1997).77	3006	Raw materials and consumables used		(769,541)	(557,328)
1(r1997).77	3006	Staff costs		(247,901)	(223,537)
1(r1997).77	3006	Depreciation and amortisation expense		(32,594)	(20,135)
1(r1997).77	3006	Other operating expenses		(33,200)	(22,965)
8(r1993).16	8055	Restructuring costs	6	(18,300)	–
1(r1997).75(b)	3002(b)	Profit from operations	7	138,158	59,562
1(r1997).75(c)	3002(c)	Finance costs	8	(36,680)	(32,995)
28(r2000).28	3005	Income from associates		12,763	983
1(r1997).75	3003	Income from investments	9	2,938	673
35.39	3004	Profit on disposal of discontinuing operations	10	8,493	–
		Profit before tax		125,672	28,223
12(r2000).77	3002(e)	Income tax expense	11	(19,606)	(4,370)
		Profit after tax		106,066	23,853
1(r1997).75(h)	3002(h)	Minority interest		(609)	(97)
1(r1997).75(i)	3002(i)	Net profit for the year		105,457	23,756
		Earnings per share	13		
		Including discontinuing operations:			
33.47	3008	Basic		70.3 cents	15.8 cents
33.47	3008	Diluted		55.4 cents	N/A
		Excluding discontinuing operations:			
33.51	3010	Basic		63.2 cents	13.1 cents
33.51	3010	Diluted		49.9 cents	N/A

Note: The format outlined above aggregates expenses according to their nature.

Source	Checklist	INTERNATIONAL GAAP HOLDINGS LIMITED			
1(r1997).7(b) 1(r1997).46(b),(c)	2001,2018 2019(b),(c)	CONSOLIDATED INCOME STATEMENT FOR THE YEAR ENDED 31 DECEMBER 2001			[Alt 2]
1(r1997).92 1(r1997).46(d),(e)	8003 2019(d),(e)		NOTES	Year ended 31/12/01 CU'000	Year ended 31/12/00 CU'000
1(r1997).75(a)	3002(a)	Revenue	4	1,224,098	869,453
1(r1997).77	3006	Cost of sales		(797,027)	(661,851)
		Gross profit		427,071	207,602
1(r1997).77	3006	Other operating income		10,150	6,745
1(r1997).77	3006	Distribution costs		(108,298)	(52,688)
1(r1997).77	3006	Administrative expenses		(149,065)	(84,373)
1(r1997).77	3006	Other operating expenses		(23,400)	(17,724)
8(r1993).16	8055	Restructuring costs	6	(18,300)	–
1(r1997).75(b)	3002(b)	Profit from operations	7	138,158	59,562
1(r1997).75(c)	3002(c)	Finance costs	8	(36,680)	(32,995)
28(r2000).28	3005	Income from associates		12,763	983
1(r1997).75	3003	Income from investments	9	2,938	673
35.39	3004	Profit on disposal of discontinuing operations	10	8,493	–
		Profit before tax		125,672	28,223
12(r2000).77	3002(e)	Income tax expense	11	(19,606)	(4,370)
		Profit after tax		106,066	23,853
1(r1997).75(h)	3002(h)	Minority interest		(609)	(97)
1(r1997).75(i)	3002(i)	Net profit for the year		105,457	23,756
		Earnings per share	13		
		Including discontinuing operations:			
33.47	3008	Basic		70.3 cents	15.8 cents
33.47	3008	Diluted		55.4 cents	N/A
		Excluding discontinuing operations:			
33.51	3010	Basic		63.2 cents	13.1 cents
33.51	3010	Diluted		49.9 cents	N/A

Note: The format outlined above aggregates expenses according to their function.

Source	Checklist	INTERNATIONAL GAAP HOLDINGS LIMITED			
1(r1997).7(b)	2001,2018	CONSOLIDATED BALANCE SHEET			
1(r1997).46(b),(c)	2019(b),(c)	AT 31 DECEMBER 2001			
1(r1997).92	8003		NOTES	2001	2000
1(r1997).46(d),(e)	2019(d),(e)			CU'000	CU'000
		ASSETS			
1(r1997).53	4006	**Non-current assets**			
1(r1997).66(a)	4001(a)	Property, plant and equipment	14	659,603	566,842
1(r1997).67	4002	Investment property	15	12,000	11,409
1(r1997).67	4002	Goodwill	16	1,205	2,538
1(r1997).67	4002	Negative goodwill	17	(773)	(2,455)
1(r1997).66(b)	4001(b)	Intangible assets	18	26,985	21,294
28(r2000).28	4004	Investments in associates	20	45,060	12,274
1(r1997).66(c)	4001(c)	Investments in securities	22	23,373	20,000
1(r1997).67	4002	Finance lease receivables	24	114,937	104,489
12(r2000).69,70	8125	Deferred tax assets	35	2,661	3,400
				885,051	739,791
1(r1997).53	4006	**Current assets**			
1(r1997).66(e)	4001(e)	Inventories	23	118,065	108,698
1(r1997).67	4002	Finance lease receivables	24	54,713	49,674
1(r1997).66(f)	4001(f)	Trade and other receivables	25	134,194	129,950
1(r1997).66(c)	4001(c)	Investments in securities	22	37,243	29,730
1(r1997).66(g)	4001(g)	Bank balances and cash	25	5,609	1,175
				349,824	319,227
		Total assets		1,234,875	1,059,018

Source	Checklist	INTERNATIONAL GAAP HOLDINGS LIMITED			
		CONSOLIDATED BALANCE SHEET AT 31 DECEMBER 2001 – continued			
			NOTES	2001 CU'000	2000 CU'000
		EQUITY AND LIABILITIES			
1(r1997).66(m)	4001(m)	**Capital and reserves**			
		Share capital	27	120,000	120,000
		Capital reserves	28	32,934	32,098
		Revaluation reserves	29	95,241	29,159
		Hedging and translation reserves	30	(11,708)	338
		Accumulated profits	31	259,740	159,493
				496,207	341,088
1(r1997).66(l), 27.26	4001(l), 4005	**Minority interest**		3,185	2,576
1(r1997).53	4006	**Non-current liabilities**			
1(r1997).66(k)	4001(k)	Bank loans – due after one year	32	388,729	474,902
		Convertible loan notes	33	24,327	–
1(r1997).67	4002	Retirement benefit obligation	46	30,196	34,001
12(r2000).69,70	8125	Deferred tax liabilities	35	15,447	6,372
1(r1997).67	4002	Obligations under finance leases – due after one year	36	923	1,244
				459,622	516,519
1(r1997).53	4006	**Current liabilities**			
1(r1997).66(h)	4001(h)	Trade and other payables	37	141,949	86,291
1(r1997).67	4002	Retirement benefit obligation	46	3,732	4,473
12(r2000).69	8125	Tax liabilities		8,229	1,986
1(r1997).67	4002	Obligations under finance leases – due within one year	36	1,470	1,483
1(r1997).66(k)	4001(k)	Bank overdrafts and loans – due within one year	32	111,931	102,537
1(r1997).66(j)	4001(j)	Provisions	38	8,550	2,065
				275,861	198,835
		Total equity and liabilities		1,234,875	1,059,018

Source	Checklist	
10(r1999).16	8190	The financial statements on pages 3 to 64 were approved by the board of directors and authorised for issue on 15 March 2002 and are signed on its behalf by:

A J SMITH — F R JONES

DIRECTOR — DIRECTOR

Source	Checklist	INTERNATIONAL GAAP HOLDINGS LIMITED		
1(r1997).7(c)(ii) 1(r1997).46(b),(c)	2001,2018 2019(b),(c)	CONSOLIDATED STATEMENT OF RECOGNISED GAINS AND LOSSES FOR THE YEAR ENDED 31 DECEMBER 2001		[Alt 1]
1(r1997).46(d),(e)	2019(d),(e)		Year ended 31/12/01 CU'000	Year ended 31/12/00 CU'000
1(r1997).86(b)	5001(b)	Revaluation increase/(decrease) on land and buildings	64,709	(4,049)
1(r1997).86(b)	5001(b)	Deferred tax liability arising on revaluation of properties	(3,699)	–
1(r1997).86(b)	5001(b)	Increase in fair value of hedging derivatives	510	–
1(r1997).86(b)	5001(b)	Increase in fair value of available-for-sale investments	251	–
1(r1997).86(b)	5001(b)	Exchange differences arising on translation of overseas operations	(13,446)	2,706
1(r1997).86(b)	5001(b)	Net gains/(losses) not recognised in the income statement	48,325	(1,343)
1(r1997).86(a)	5001(a)	Net profit for the year	105,457	23,756
		Total recognised gains and losses	153,782	22,413
1(r1997).86(c)	5001(c)	Prior period adjustments (see note 2)		
		(Decrease)/increase in accumulated profits	(170)	253
		Decrease in investment properties revaluation reserve	–	(253)
		Increase in investments revaluation reserve	5,432	–
		Increase in hedging reserve	890	–
			6,152	–

Note: IAS 1(r1997) requires that the financial statements should include a statement showing either all changes in equity, or changes in equity other than those arising from capital transactions with owners and distributions to owners.

The above illustrates an approach which presents those changes in equity that represent gains and losses in a separate component of the financial statements. If this method of presentation is adopted, a reconciliation of the opening and closing balances of share capital, reserves and accumulated profits is required to be provided in the explanatory notes (see notes 27 to 31). An alternative method of presenting changes in equity is illustrated on the next page.

Source	Checklist	INTERNATIONAL GAAP HOLDINGS LIMITED						
1(r1997).7(c)(i) 1(r1997).46(b),(c)	2001,2018 2019(b),(c)	CONSOLIDATED STATEMENT OF CHANGES IN EQUITY FOR THE YEAR ENDED 31 DECEMBER 2001						[Alt 2]
1(r1997).74(b) 1(r1997).46(d),(e) 1(r1997).86(e),(f) 16(r1998).64(f)	8118 2019(d),(e) 5002(b),(c) 5003(c)		Share capital CU'000	Capital reserves CU'000	Revaluation reserves CU'000	Hedging and translation reserves CU'000	Accumulated profits CU'000	Total CU'000
		Balance at 1 January 2000						
		– as originally stated	120,000	32,098	33,461	(2,368)	143,524	326,715
1(r1997).86(c)	5001(c)	– prior period adjustments (note 2)	–	–	(253)	–	253	–
		– as restated	120,000	32,098	33,208	(2,368)	143,777	326,715
16(r1998).64(f)	5003(c)	Revaluation decrease on land and buildings	–	–	(4,049)	–	–	(4,049)
21(r1993).42(b)	5003(f)	Exchange differences arising on translation of overseas operations	–	–	–	2,706	–	2,706
1(r1997).86(b)	5001(b)	Net gains/(losses) not recognised in the income statement	–	–	(4,049)	2,706	–	(1,343)
1(r1997).86(a)	5001(a)	Net profit for the year	–	–	–	–	23,756	23,756
1(r1997).86(d)	5002(a)	Dividends	–	–	–	–	(8,040)	(8,040)
		Balance at 1 January 2001	120,000	32,098	29,159	338	159,493	341,088
1(r1997).86(c)	5001(c)	– prior period adjustments (note 2)	–	–	5,432	890	(170)	6,152
		– as restated	120,000	32,098	34,591	1,228	159,323	347,240
16(r1998).64(f)	5003(c)	Revaluation increase on land and buildings	–	–	64,709	–	–	64,709
12(r2000).81(a)	5003(b)	Deferred tax liability arising on revaluation of properties	–	–	(3,699)	–	–	(3,699)
39(r2000).169(c)	8148(a)	Increase in fair value of hedging derivatives	–	–	–	510	–	510
39(r2000).170(a)	5003(e)	Increase in fair value of available-for-sale investments	–	–	251	–	–	251
21(r1993).42(b)	5003(f)	Exchange differences arising on translation of overseas operations	–	–	–	(13,446)	–	(13,446)
1(r1997).86(b)	5001(b)	Net gains/(losses) not recognised in the income statement	–	–	61,261	(12,936)	–	48,325
1(r1997).86(f)	5002(c)	Equity component of convertible loan notes	–	836	–	–	–	836
39(r2000).170(a)	5003(e)	Released on disposal of available-for-sale investments	–	–	(611)	–	–	(611)
1(r1997).86(a)	5001(a)	Net profit for the year	–	–	–	–	105,457	105,457
1(r1997).86(d)	5002(a)	Dividends	–	–	–	–	(5,040)	(5,040)
		Balance at 31 December 2001	120,000	32,934	95,241	(11,708)	259,740	496,207

Note: See previous page for alternative method of presenting changes in equity.

The above layout combines reserves of a similar nature for ease of presentation. However, IAS 1(r1997) requires a reconciliation of the opening and closing position on each reserve separately. Therefore, if such a combined presentation is adopted for the purposes of the statement of changes in equity, further details should be presented in the notes to the financial statements (see notes 27 to 31).

Source	Checklist	INTERNATIONAL GAAP HOLDINGS LIMITED			
1(r1997).7(d) 1(r1997).46(b),(c)	2001,2018 2019(b),(c)	CONSOLIDATED CASH FLOW STATEMENT FOR THE YEAR ENDED 31 DECEMBER 2001			[Alt 1]
1(r1997).92	8003		NOTES	Year ended	Year ended
1(r1997).46(d),(e)	2019(d),(e)			31/12/01 CU'000	31/12/00 CU'000
7(r1992).10	6002	OPERATING ACTIVITIES			
7(r1992).18(a)	6003(a)				
		Cash receipts from customers	39	1,229,374	835,187
		Cash paid to suppliers and employees		(1,042,076)	(816,963)
		Cash generated by operations		187,298	18,224
7(r1992).35	6008	Income taxes paid		(7,407)	(2,129)
7(r1992).31	6006	Interest paid		(42,209)	(32,995)
		NET CASH FROM/(USED IN) OPERATING ACTIVITIES		137,682	(16,900)
7(r1992).10	6002	INVESTING ACTIVITIES			
7(r1992).31	6006	Interest received		1,202	368
7(r1992).31	6006	Dividends received from associate		11,777	2,725
7(r1992).31	6006	Dividends received from trading investments		2,299	349
		Proceeds on disposal of trading investments		25,230	–
		Proceeds on disposal of available-for-sale investments		2,416	–
7(r1992).39	6010	Disposal of subsidiary	40	6,517	–
		Proceeds on disposal of property, plant and equipment		4,983	4,500
		Purchases of property, plant and equipment		(58,675)	(28,198)
		Acquisition of investment in an associate		(31,800)	–
		Purchases of trading investments		(34,023)	(15,328)
		Purchases of patents and trademarks		(3,835)	(18,617)
		Expenditure on product development		(3,600)	–
7(r1992).39	6010	Acquisition of subsidiary	41	(3,670)	–
		NET CASH USED IN INVESTING ACTIVITIES		(81,179)	(54,201)

Source	Checklist	INTERNATIONAL GAAP HOLDINGS LIMITED			
		CONSOLIDATED CASH FLOW STATEMENT FOR THE YEAR ENDED 31 DECEMBER 2001 – continued [Alt 1]			
			NOTES	Year ended 31/12/01 CU'000	Year ended 31/12/00 CU'000
7(r1992).10	6002	FINANCING ACTIVITIES			
7(r1992).31	6006	Dividends paid		(5,040)	(8,040)
		Repayments of borrowings		(86,777)	–
		Repayments of obligations under finance leases		(1,897)	–
		Proceeds on issue of convertible loan notes		25,000	–
		New bank loans raised		–	72,265
		Increase in bank overdrafts		16,396	5,482
		NET CASH (USED IN)/FROM FINANCING ACTIVITIES		(52,318)	69,707
		NET INCREASE/(DECREASE) IN CASH AND CASH EQUIVALENTS		4,185	(1,394)
		CASH AND CASH EQUIVALENTS AT BEGINNING OF YEAR		1,175	1,907
		Effect of foreign exchange rate changes		249	662
		CASH AND CASH EQUIVALENTS AT END OF YEAR			
7(r1992).45	6014	Bank balances and cash		5,609	1,175

Note: *The above illustrates the direct method of reporting cash flows from operating activities.*

Source	Checklist	INTERNATIONAL GAAP HOLDINGS LIMITED			
1(r1997).7(d) 1(r1997).46(b),(c)	2001,2018 2019(b),(c)	CONSOLIDATED CASH FLOW STATEMENT FOR THE YEAR ENDED 31 DECEMBER 2001			[Alt 2]
1(r1997).92	8003		NOTES	Year ended	Year ended
1(r1997).46(d),(e)	2019(d),(e)			31/12/01 CU'000	31/12/00 CU'000
7(r1992).10	6002	OPERATING ACTIVITIES			
7(r1992).18(b)	6003(b)	Cash generated from operations	39	187,298	18,224
7(r1992).35	6008	Income taxes paid		(7,407)	(2,129)
7(r1992).31	6006	Interest paid		(42,209)	(32,995)
		NET CASH FROM/(USED IN) OPERATING ACTIVITIES		137,682	(16,900)
7(r1992).10	6002	INVESTING ACTIVITIES			
7(r1992).31	6006	Interest received		1,202	368
7(r1992).31	6006	Dividends received from associates		11,777	2,725
7(r1992).31	6006	Dividends received from trading investments		2,299	349
		Proceeds on disposal of trading investments		25,230	–
		Proceeds on disposal of available-for-sale investments		2,416	–
7(r1992).39	6010	Disposal of subsidiary	40	6,517	–
		Proceeds on disposal of property, plant and equipment		4,983	4,500
		Purchases of property, plant and equipment		(58,675)	(28,198)
		Acquisition of investment in an associate		(31,800)	–
		Purchases of trading investments		(34,023)	(15,328)
		Purchases of patents and trademarks		(3,835)	(18,617)
		Expenditure on product development		(3,600)	–
7(r1992).39	6010	Acquisition of subsidiary	41	(3,670)	–
		NET CASH USED IN INVESTING ACTIVITIES		(81,179)	(54,201)

Source	Checklist	INTERNATIONAL GAAP HOLDINGS LIMITED			
		CONSOLIDATED CASH FLOW STATEMENT FOR THE YEAR ENDED 31 DECEMBER 2001 – continued			[Alt 2]
			NOTES	Year ended 31/12/01 CU'000	Year ended 31/12/00 CU'000
7(r1992).10	6002	FINANCING ACTIVITIES			
7(r1992).31	6006	Dividends paid		(5,040)	(8,040)
		Repayments of borrowings		(86,777)	–
		Repayments of obligations under finance leases		(1,897)	–
		Proceeds on issue of convertible loan notes		25,000	–
		New bank loans raised		–	72,265
		Increase in bank overdrafts		16,396	5,482
		NET CASH (USED IN)/FROM FINANCING ACTIVITIES		(52,318)	69,707
		NET INCREASE/(DECREASE) IN CASH AND CASH EQUIVALENTS		4,185	(1,394)
		CASH AND CASH EQUIVALENTS AT BEGINNING OF YEAR		1,175	1,907
		Effect of foreign exchange rate changes		249	662
7(r1992).45	6014	CASH AND CASH EQUIVALENTS AT END OF YEAR			
		Bank balances and cash		5,609	1,175

Note: The above illustrates the indirect method of reporting cash flows from operating activities.

Source	Checklist	
		INTERNATIONAL GAAP HOLDINGS LIMITED
		NOTES TO THE CONSOLIDATED FINANCIAL STATEMENTS FOR THE YEAR ENDED 31 DECEMBER 2001
		1. PRESENTATION OF FINANCIAL STATEMENTS
1(r1997).11	2003	The financial statements have been prepared in accordance with International Accounting Standards (IAS).
21(r1993).43 SIC19.10(c)	8004	These financial statements are presented in Currency Units (CU) since that is the currency in which the majority of the Group's transactions are denominated.
		2. ADOPTION OF INTERNATIONAL ACCOUNTING STANDARDS
8(r1993).53	7004	In the current year, the Group has adopted the following International Accounting Standards for the first time:

IAS 39 Financial Instruments: Recognition and Measurement

IAS 40 Investment Property

Revisions to a number of other IAS also took effect in 2001. Those revisions concerned matters of detailed application which have no significant effect on amounts reported for the current or prior accounting periods.

IAS 39 has introduced a comprehensive framework for accounting for all financial instruments. The Group's detailed accounting policies in respect of such instruments are set out below. The principal effects of the adoption of IAS 39 have been that the majority of the Group's investments in securities are now carried at fair value, and that derivative financial instruments have been brought on-balance sheet. The effects of the remeasurement of investments to fair value and bringing the derivative financial instruments on-balance sheet at fair value have been recognised with effect from 1 January 2001. The effects can be summarised as follows:

	Accumulated profits	Investments revaluation reserve	Hedging reserve
	CU'000	CU'000	CU'000
Excess of fair value of available-for-sale investments over cost	–	5,432	–
Net fair value of derivatives designated as hedging instruments	–	–	890
Net fair value of derivatives not designated as hedging instruments	(170)	–	–
Adjustment at 1 January 2001	(170)	5,432	890

Source	Checklist	INTERNATIONAL GAAP HOLDINGS LIMITED

NOTES TO THE CONSOLIDATED FINANCIAL STATEMENTS
FOR THE YEAR ENDED 31 DECEMBER 2001 – continued

These changes in policy have resulted in a decrease in profits reported in 2001 of CU0.1 million, an increase in the investments revaluation reserve for the year of CU0.25 million and an increase in the hedging reserve for the year of CU0.51 million.

The hedge accounting policies that the Group has followed in prior years are appropriate under IAS 39.

Under IAS 40, the Group's investment property continues to be accounted for at fair value. However, following the adoption of IAS 40, gains and losses arising from changes in the fair value of investment property are included in net profit or loss for the period in which they arise, rather than in equity. This change in policy has been applied retrospectively. The effect of this change in policy has been to increase accumulated profits and decrease the investment property revaluation reserve at 1 January 2000 by CU0.25 million. The profit for the year ended 31 December 2000 has been decreased by CU0.05 million and for the year ended 31 December 2001, increased by CU0.59 million.

1(r1997).91(a) 7001
1(r1997).97 7002

3. SUMMARY OF SIGNIFICANT ACCOUNTING POLICIES

The financial statements have been prepared on the historical cost basis, except for the revaluation of land and buildings and certain financial instruments. The principal accounting policies adopted are set out below.

Basis of consolidation

The consolidated financial statements incorporate the financial statements of the Company and enterprises controlled by the Company (its subsidiaries) made up to 31 December each year. Control is achieved where the Company has the power to govern the financial and operating policies of an investee enterprise so as to obtain benefits from its activities.

On acquisition, the assets and liabilities of a subsidiary are measured at their fair values at the date of acquisition. The interest of minority shareholders is stated at the minority's proportion of the fair values of the assets and liabilities recognised.

The results of subsidiaries acquired or disposed of during the year are included in the consolidated income statement from the effective date of acquisition or up to the effective date of disposal, as appropriate.

Where necessary, adjustments are made to the financial statements of subsidiaries to bring the accounting policies used into line with those used by other members of the Group.

All significant intercompany transactions and balances between group enterprises are eliminated on consolidation.

Source	Checklist	INTERNATIONAL GAAP HOLDINGS LIMITED
		NOTES TO THE CONSOLIDATED FINANCIAL STATEMENTS FOR THE YEAR ENDED 31 DECEMBER 2001 – continued
28(r2000).27(b)	7003(b)	**Investments in associates**

An associate is an enterprise over which the Group is in a position to exercise significant influence, through participation in the financial and operating policy decisions of the investee.

The results and assets and liabilities of associates are incorporated in these financial statements using the equity method of accounting. The carrying amount of such investments is reduced to recognise any impairment in the value of individual investments.

Where a group enterprise transacts with an associate of the Group, unrealised profits and losses are eliminated to the extent of the Group's interest in the relevant associate, except where unrealised losses provide evidence of an impairment of the asset transferred.

Interests in joint ventures

A joint venture is a contractual arrangement whereby the Group and other parties undertake an economic activity which is subject to joint control.

Where a group company undertakes its activities under joint venture arrangements directly, the Group's share of jointly controlled assets and any liabilities incurred jointly with other venturers are recognised in the financial statements of the relevant company and classified according to their nature. Liabilities and expenses incurred directly in respect of interests in jointly controlled assets are accounted for on an accrual basis. Income from the sale or use of the Group's share of the output of jointly controlled assets, and its share of joint venture expenses, are recognised when it is probable that the economic benefits associated with the transactions will flow to/from the Group and their amount can be measured reliably.

Joint venture arrangements which involve the establishment of a separate entity in which each venturer has an interest are referred to as jointly controlled entities. The Group reports its interests in jointly controlled entities using proportionate consolidation – the Group's share of the assets, liabilities, income and expenses of jointly controlled entities are combined with the equivalent items in the consolidated financial statements on a line-by-line basis.

Where the Group transacts with its jointly controlled entities, unrealised profits and losses are eliminated to the extent of the Group's interest in the joint venture, except where unrealised losses provide evidence of an impairment of the asset transferred.

Source	Checklist	INTERNATIONAL GAAP HOLDINGS LIMITED

NOTES TO THE CONSOLIDATED FINANCIAL STATEMENTS
FOR THE YEAR ENDED 31 DECEMBER 2001 – continued

Goodwill

Goodwill arising on consolidation represents the excess of the cost of acquisition over the Group's interest in the fair value of the identifiable assets and liabilities of a subsidiary, associate or jointly controlled entity at the date of acquisition. Goodwill is recognised as an asset and amortised on a straight-line basis following an assessment of its useful life.

Goodwill arising on the acquisition of an associate is included within the carrying amount of the associate. Goodwill arising on the acquisition of subsidiaries and jointly controlled entities is presented separately in the balance sheet.

On disposal of a subsidiary, associate or jointly controlled entity, the attributable amount of unamortised goodwill is included in the determination of the profit or loss on disposal.

Negative goodwill

Negative goodwill represents the excess of the Group's interest in the fair value of the identifiable assets and liabilities of a subsidiary, associate or jointly controlled entity at the date of acquisition over the cost of acquisition. Negative goodwill is released to income based on an analysis of the circumstances from which the balance resulted. To the extent that the negative goodwill is attributable to losses or expenses anticipated at the date of acquisition, it is released to income in the period in which those losses or expenses arise. The remaining negative goodwill is recognised as income on a straight-line basis over the remaining average useful life of the identifiable acquired depreciable assets. To the extent that such negative goodwill exceeds the aggregate fair value of the acquired identifiable non-monetary assets, it is recognised in income immediately.

Negative goodwill arising on the acquisition of an associate is deducted from the carrying value of that associate. Negative goodwill arising on the acquisition of subsidiaries or jointly controlled entities is presented separately in the balance sheet as a deduction from assets.

18(r1993).35(a) | 7003(f) | **Revenue recognition**

Sales of goods are recognised when goods are delivered and title has passed.

Interest income is accrued on a time basis, by reference to the principal outstanding and at the interest rate applicable.

Dividend income from investments is recognised when the shareholders' rights to receive payment have been established.

Source	Checklist	INTERNATIONAL GAAP HOLDINGS LIMITED
		NOTES TO THE CONSOLIDATED FINANCIAL STATEMENTS FOR THE YEAR ENDED 31 DECEMBER 2001 – continued
11(r1993).39) (b),(c)	7003(g)	**Construction contracts**

Where the outcome of a construction contract can be estimated reliably, revenue and costs are recognised by reference to the stage of completion of the contract activity at the balance sheet date, as measured by the proportion that contract costs incurred for work performed to date bear to the estimated total contract costs. Variations in contract work, claims and incentive payments are included to the extent that they have been agreed with the customer.

Where the outcome of a construction contract cannot be estimated reliably, contract revenue is recognised to the extent of contract costs incurred that it is probable will be recoverable. Contract costs are recognised as expenses in the period in which they are incurred.

When it is probable that total contract costs will exceed total contract revenue, the expected loss is recognised as an expense immediately.

Leasing

Leases are classified as finance leases whenever the terms of the lease transfer substantially all the risks and rewards of ownership to the lessee. All other leases are classified as operating leases.

The Group as lessor

Amounts due from lessees under finance leases are recorded as receivables at the amount of the Group's net investment in the leases. Finance lease income is allocated to accounting periods so as to reflect a constant periodic rate of return on the Group's net investment outstanding in respect of the leases.

Rental income from operating leases is recognised on a straight-line basis over the term of the relevant lease.

The Group as lessee

Assets held under finance leases are recognised as assets of the Group at their fair value at the date of acquisition. The corresponding liability to the lessor is included in the balance sheet as a finance lease obligation. Finance costs, which represent the difference between the total leasing commitments and the fair value of the assets acquired, are charged to the income statement over the term of the relevant lease so as to produce a constant periodic rate of charge on the remaining balance of the obligations for each accounting period.

Rentals payable under operating leases are charged to income on a straight-line basis over the term of the relevant lease.

Source	Checklist	INTERNATIONAL GAAP HOLDINGS LIMITED
		NOTES TO THE CONSOLIDATED FINANCIAL STATEMENTS FOR THE YEAR ENDED 31 DECEMBER 2001 – continued
		Foreign currencies
		Transactions in currencies other than Currency Units are initially recorded at the rates of exchange prevailing on the dates of the transactions. Monetary assets and liabilities denominated in such currencies are retranslated at the rates prevailing on the balance sheet date. Profits and losses arising on exchange are included in net profit or loss for the period.
		In order to hedge its exposure to certain foreign exchange risks, the Group enters into forward contracts and options (see below for details of the Group's accounting policies in respect of such derivative financial instruments).
		On consolidation, the assets and liabilities of the Group's overseas operations are translated at exchange rates prevailing on the balance sheet date. Income and expense items are translated at the average exchange rates for the period. Exchange differences arising, if any, are classified as equity and transferred to the Group's translation reserve. Such translation differences are recognised as income or as expenses in the period in which the operation is disposed of.
		The financial statements of foreign subsidiaries and associates that report in the currency of a hyperinflationary economy are restated in terms of the measuring unit current at the balance sheet date before they are translated into Currency Units.
21(r1993).45	7003(e)	Goodwill and fair value adjustments arising on the acquisition of a foreign entity are treated as assets and liabilities of the foreign entity and translated at the closing rate.
23(r1993).29(a)	7003(h)	**Borrowing costs**
		Borrowing costs directly attributable to the acquisition, construction or production of qualifying assets, which are assets that necessarily take a substantial period of time to get ready for their intended use or sale, are added to the cost of those assets, until such time as the assets are substantially ready for their intended use or sale. Investment income earned on the temporary investment of specific borrowings pending their expenditure on qualifying assets is deducted from the cost of those assets.
		All other borrowing costs are recognised in net profit or loss in the period in which they are incurred.
20.39(a)	7003(i)	**Government grants**
		Government grants towards staff re-training costs are recognised as income over the periods necessary to match them with the related costs and are deducted in reporting the related expense.

Source	Checklist	INTERNATIONAL GAAP HOLDINGS LIMITED

NOTES TO THE CONSOLIDATED FINANCIAL STATEMENTS
FOR THE YEAR ENDED 31 DECEMBER 2001 – continued

Retirement benefit costs

Payments to defined contribution retirement benefit plans are charged as an expense as they fall due. Payments made to state-managed retirement benefit schemes are dealt with as payments to defined contribution plans where the Group's obligations under the schemes are equivalent to those arising in a defined contribution retirement benefit plan.

19(r2000).120(a) 7003(j) For defined benefit retirement benefit plans, the cost of providing benefits is determined using the projected unit credit method, with actuarial valuations being carried out at each balance sheet date. Actuarial gains and losses which exceed 10 per cent of the greater of the present value of the Group's pension obligations and the fair value of plan assets are amortised over the expected average remaining working lives of the participating employees. Past service cost is recognised immediately to the extent that the benefits are already vested, and otherwise is amortised on a straight-line basis over the average period until the amended benefits become vested.

The amount recognised in the balance sheet represents the present value of the defined benefit obligation as adjusted for unrecognised actuarial gains and losses and unrecognised past service cost, and reduced by the fair value of plan assets. Any asset resulting from this calculation is limited to unrecognised actuarial losses and past service cost, plus the present value of available refunds and reductions in future contributions to the plan.

Taxation

The charge for current tax is based on the results for the year as adjusted for items which are non-assessable or disallowed. It is calculated using tax rates that have been enacted or substantively enacted by the balance sheet date.

Deferred tax is accounted for using the balance sheet liability method in respect of temporary differences arising from differences between the carrying amount of assets and liabilities in the financial statements and the corresponding tax basis used in the computation of taxable profit. In principle, deferred tax liabilities are recognised for all taxable temporary differences and deferred tax assets are recognised to the extent that it is probable that taxable profits will be available against which deductible temporary differences can be utilised. Such assets and liabilities are not recognised if the temporary difference arises from goodwill (or negative goodwill) or from the initial recognition (other than in a business combination) of other assets and liabilities in a transaction which affects neither the tax profit nor the accounting profit.

Deferred tax liabilities are recognised for taxable temporary differences arising on investments in subsidiaries and associates, and interests in joint ventures, except where the Group is able to control the reversal of the temporary difference and it is probable that the temporary difference will not reverse in the foreseeable future.

Source	Checklist	INTERNATIONAL GAAP HOLDINGS LIMITED

NOTES TO THE CONSOLIDATED FINANCIAL STATEMENTS
FOR THE YEAR ENDED 31 DECEMBER 2001 – continued

Deferred tax is calculated at the tax rates that are expected to apply to the period when the asset is realised or the liability is settled. Deferred tax is charged or credited in the income statement, except when it relates to items credited or charged directly to equity, in which case the deferred tax is also dealt with in equity.

Deferred tax assets and liabilities are offset when they relate to income taxes levied by the same taxation authority and the Group intends to settle its current tax assets and liabilities on a net basis.

16(r1998).60 (a),(b),(c) 7003(l) **Property, plant and equipment**

Land and buildings held for use in the production or supply of goods or services, or for administrative purposes, are stated in the balance sheet at their revalued amounts, being the fair value on the basis of their existing use at the date of revaluation, less any subsequent accumulated depreciation. Revaluations are performed with sufficient regularity such that the carrying amount does not differ materially for that which would be determined using fair values at the balance sheet date.

Any revaluation increase arising on the revaluation of such land and buildings is credited to the properties revaluation reserve, except to the extent that it reverses a revaluation decrease for the same asset previously recognised as an expense, in which case the increase is credited to the income statement to the extent of the decrease previously charged. A decrease in carrying amount arising on the revaluation of land and buildings is charged as an expense to the extent that it exceeds the balance, if any, held in the properties revaluation reserve relating to a previous revaluation of that asset.

On the subsequent sale or retirement of a revalued property, the attributable revaluation surplus remaining in the revaluation reserve is transferred to accumulated profits.

Properties in the course of construction for production, rental or administrative purposes, or for purposes not yet determined, are carried at cost, less any identified impairment loss. Cost includes professional fees and, for qualifying assets, borrowing costs capitalised in accordance with the Group's accounting policy. Depreciation of these assets, on the same basis as other property assets, commences when the assets are ready for their intended use.

Fixtures and equipment are stated at cost less accumulated depreciation.

Depreciation is charged so as to write off the cost or valuation of assets, other than land and properties under construction, over their estimated useful lives, using the straight-line method, on the following bases:

Buildings	4%
Fixtures and equipment	10%–30%

Source	Checklist	INTERNATIONAL GAAP HOLDINGS LIMITED

NOTES TO THE CONSOLIDATED FINANCIAL STATEMENTS
FOR THE YEAR ENDED 31 DECEMBER 2001 – continued

Assets held under finance leases are depreciated over their expected useful lives on the same basis as owned assets or, where shorter, the term of the relevant lease.

The gain or loss arising on the disposal or retirement of an asset is determined as the difference between the sales proceeds and the carrying amount of the asset and is recognised in income.

Investment property

Investment property, which is property held to earn rentals and/or for capital appreciation, is stated at its fair value at the balance sheet date. Gains or losses arising from changes in the fair value of investment property are included in net profit or loss for the period in which they arise.

38.107 | 7003(n) | **Internally-generated intangible assets – research and development expenditure**

Expenditure on research activities is recognised as an expense in the period in which it is incurred.

An internally-generated intangible asset arising from the Group's e-business development is recognised only if all of the following conditions are met:

- an asset is created that can be identified (such as software and new processes);
- it is probable that the asset created will generate future economic benefits; and
- the development cost of the asset can be measured reliably.

Where no internally-generated intangible asset can be recognised, development expenditure is recognised as an expense in the period in which it is incurred. Internally-generated intangible assets are amortised on a straight-line basis over their useful lives, which is usually no more than 5 years.

38.107 | 7003(n) | **Patents and trademarks**

Patents and trademarks are measured initially at purchase cost and amortised on a straight-line basis over their estimated useful lives, which is on average 10 years.

Source	Checklist	INTERNATIONAL GAAP HOLDINGS LIMITED
		NOTES TO THE CONSOLIDATED FINANCIAL STATEMENTS FOR THE YEAR ENDED 31 DECEMBER 2001 – continued
		Impairment
		At each balance sheet date, the Group reviews the carrying amounts of its tangible and intangible assets to determine whether there is any indication that those assets have suffered an impairment loss. If any such indication exists, the recoverable amount of the asset is estimated in order to determine the extent of the impairment loss (if any). Where it is not possible to estimate the recoverable amount of an individual asset, the Group estimates the recoverable amount of the cash-generating unit to which the asset belongs.
		If the recoverable amount of an asset (or cash-generating unit) is estimated to be less than its carrying amount, the carrying amount of the asset (cash-generating unit) is reduced to its recoverable amount. Impairment losses are recognised as an expense immediately, unless the relevant asset is land or buildings at a revalued amount, in which case the impairment loss is treated as a revaluation decrease.
		Where an impairment loss subsequently reverses, the carrying amount of the asset (cash-generating unit) is increased to the revised estimate of its recoverable amount, but so that the increased carrying amount does not exceed the carrying amount that would have been determined had no impairment loss been recognised for the asset (cash-generating unit) in prior years. A reversal of an impairment loss is recognised as income immediately, unless the relevant asset is carried at a revalued amount, in which case the reversal of the impairment loss is treated as a revaluation increase.
2(r1993).34(a)	7003(o)	**Inventories**
		Inventories are stated at the lower of cost and net realisable value. Cost comprises direct materials and, where applicable, direct labour costs and those overheads that have been incurred in bringing the inventories to their present location and condition. Cost is calculated using the weighted average method. Net realisable value represents the estimated selling price less all estimated costs to completion and costs to be incurred in marketing, selling and distribution.
32(r1998).47(b)	7003(p)	**Financial instruments**
		Financial assets and financial liabilities are recognised on the Group's balance sheet when the Group has become a party to the contractual provisions of the instrument.
		Trade receivables
		Trade receivables are stated at their nominal value as reduced by appropriate allowances for estimated irrecoverable amounts.
		Investments in securities
		Investments in securities are recognised on a trade-date basis and are initially measured at cost.

Source	Checklist	INTERNATIONAL GAAP HOLDINGS LIMITED

NOTES TO THE CONSOLIDATED FINANCIAL STATEMENTS
FOR THE YEAR ENDED 31 DECEMBER 2001 – continued

At subsequent reporting dates, debt securities that the Group has the expressed intention and ability to hold to maturity (held-to-maturity debt securities) are measured at amortised cost, less any impairment loss recognised to reflect irrecoverable amounts. The annual amortisation of any discount or premium on the acquisition of a held-to-maturity security is aggregated with other investment income receivable over the term of the instrument so that the revenue recognised in each period represents a constant yield on the investment.

39(r2000).167(b) 7003(p) Investments other than held-to-maturity debt securities are classified as either held for trading or available-for-sale and are measured at subsequent reporting dates at fair value. Where securities are held for trading purposes, unrealised gains and losses are included in net profit or loss for the period. For available-for-sale investments, unrealised gains and losses are recognised directly in equity, until the security is disposed of or is determined to be impaired, at which time the cumulative gain or loss previously recognised in equity is included in the net profit or loss for the period.

Bank borrowings

Interest-bearing bank loans and overdrafts are recorded at the proceeds received, net of direct issue costs. Finance charges, including premiums payable on settlement or redemption, are accounted for on an accrual basis and are added to the carrying amount of the instrument to the extent that they are not settled in the period in which they arise.

Convertible loan notes

Convertible loan notes are regarded as compound instruments, consisting of a liability component and an equity component. At the date of issue, the fair value of the liability component is estimated using the prevailing market interest rate for similar non-convertible debt. The difference between the proceeds of issue of the convertible loan notes and the fair value assigned to the liability component, representing the embedded option to convert the liability into equity of the Group, is included in capital reserves (equity).

The interest expense on the liability component is calculated by applying the prevailing market interest rate for similar non-convertible debt to the instrument. The difference between this amount and the interest paid is added to the carrying value of the convertible loan note.

Trade payables

Trade payables are stated at their nominal value.

Equity instruments

Equity instruments are recorded at the proceeds received, net of direct issue costs.

Source	Checklist	INTERNATIONAL GAAP HOLDINGS LIMITED

NOTES TO THE CONSOLIDATED FINANCIAL STATEMENTS
FOR THE YEAR ENDED 31 DECEMBER 2001 – continued

Derivative financial instruments

Derivative financial instruments are initially recorded at cost and are remeasured to fair value at subsequent reporting dates.

Changes in the fair value of derivative financial instruments that are designated and effective as cash flow hedges are recognised directly in equity. Amounts deferred in equity are recognised in the income statement in the same period in which the hedged firm commitment or forecasted transaction affects net profit or loss.

Changes in the fair value of derivative financial instruments that do not qualify for hedge accounting are recognised in the income statement as they arise.

Provisions

Provisions are recognised when the Group has a present obligation as a result of a past event which it is probable will result in an outflow of economic benefits that can be reasonably estimated.

Provisions for restructuring costs are recognised when the Group has a detailed formal plan for the restructuring which has been notified to affected parties.

4. REVENUE

18(r1993).35(b) | 8028(a) | An analysis of the Group's revenue is as follows:

Source	Checklist		Year ended 31/12/01 CU'000	Year ended 31/12/00 CU'000
		Continuing operations:		
		Sales of electronic goods	743,127	504,633
11(r1993).39(a)	8029	Revenue from construction contracts	304,073	209,562
		Equipment leasing income	16,858	13,492
40.66(d)(i)	8041(a)	Property rental income	602	563
			1,064,660	728,250
		Discontinuing operations:		
		Sales of toys	159,438	141,203
			1,224,098	869,453

Source	Checklist	
		INTERNATIONAL GAAP HOLDINGS LIMITED
		NOTES TO THE CONSOLIDATED FINANCIAL STATEMENTS FOR THE YEAR ENDED 31 DECEMBER 2001 – continued

5. BUSINESS AND GEOGRAPHICAL SEGMENTS

Note: The following analysis by business and geographical segment is required by IAS 14(r1997) ***Segment Reporting*** *to be presented by enterprises whose equity or debt securities are publicly traded or that are in the process of issuing equity or debt securities in public securities markets. If an enterprise whose securities are not publicly traded chooses to disclose segment information voluntarily in financial statements that comply with IAS, that enterprise should comply fully with the requirements of IAS 14(r1997).*

14(r1997).81 | 8024(a) | **Business segments**

1(r1997).102(b) | 8001(b) | For management purposes, the Group is currently organised into three operating divisions – electronic goods, construction and leasing. These divisions are the basis on which the Group reports its primary segment information.

Principal activities are as follows:

Electronic goods	–	manufacture and distribution of electronic consumer goods.
Construction	–	construction of properties on a contract basis.
Leasing	–	leasing of electronic equipment and property rental.

In prior years, the Group was also involved in the manufacture and sale of toys. That operation was discontinued from 30 November 2001 (see note 10).

Source	Checklist	
		INTERNATIONAL GAAP HOLDINGS LIMITED
		NOTES TO THE CONSOLIDATED FINANCIAL STATEMENTS FOR THE YEAR ENDED 31 DECEMBER 2001 – continued
		Segment information about these businesses is presented below.

Source	Checklist	2001	Electronic goods Year ended 31/12/01 CU'000	Construction Year ended 31/12/01 CU'000	Leasing Year ended 31/12/01 CU'000	Toys Year ended 31/12/01 CU'000	Eliminations Year ended 31/12/01 CU'000	Consolidated Year ended 31/12/01 CU'000
14(r1997).51	8013(a)	**REVENUE**						
		External sales	743,127	304,073	17,460	159,438	–	1,224,098
		Inter-segment sales	10,020	–	–	–	(10,020)	–
14(r1997).67	8015(a)	Total revenue	753,147	304,073	17,460	159,438	(10,020)	1,224,098
14(r1997).75	8021(b)	Inter-segment sales are charged at prevailing market rates.						
		RESULT						
14(r1997).52	8013(b)	Segment result	95,292	34,879	16,699	4,493	(3,005)	148,358
		Unallocated corporate expenses						(10,200)
14(r1997).67	8015(b)	Profit from operations						138,158
		Finance costs						(36,680)
14(r1997).64	8013(h)	Income from associates	10,392	2,371				12,763
		Income from investments						2,938
		Profit on disposal of discontinuing operations						8,493
		Profit before tax						125,672
		Income tax expense						(19,606)
14(r1997).67	8015(b)	Profit after tax						106,066

Source	Checklist	**OTHER INFORMATION**	Electronic goods CU'000	Construction CU'000	Leasing CU'000	Toys CU'000	Other CU'000	Consolidated CU'000
14(r1997).57	8013(e)	Capital additions	64,748	–	1,525	–	2,781	69,054
14(r1997).58	8013(f)	Depreciation and amortisation	21,603	6,120	192	1,420	3,259	32,594
36.116	8014	Impairment losses recognised in income	–	–	–	4,130	–	4,130

Source	Checklist	**BALANCE SHEET**	31/12/01 CU'000	31/12/01 CU'000	31/12/01 CU'000	31/12/01 CU'000	31/12/01 CU'000
		ASSETS					
14(r1997).55	8013(c)	Segment assets	673,160	149,890	208,798	–	1,031,848
14(r1996).66	8013(i)	Investments in associates	33,071	11,989	–	–	45,060
		Unallocated corporate assets					157,967
14(r1997).67	8015(c)	Consolidated total assets					1,234,875
		LIABILITIES					
14(r1997).56	8013(d)	Segment liabilities	397,330	90,467	153,178	6,058	647,033
		Unallocated corporate liabilities					88,450
14(r1997).67	8015(d)	Consolidated total liabilities					735,483

Source	Checklist	INTERNATIONAL GAAP HOLDINGS LIMITED

NOTES TO THE CONSOLIDATED FINANCIAL STATEMENTS
FOR THE YEAR ENDED 31 DECEMBER 2001 – continued

Source	Checklist	**2000**	Electronic goods Year ended 31/12/00 CU'000	Construction Year ended 31/12/00 CU'000	Leasing Year ended 31/12/00 CU'000	Toys Year ended 31/12/00 CU'000	Eliminations Year ended 31/12/00 CU'000	Consolidated Year ended 31/12/00 CU'000
14(r1997).51	8013(a)	**REVENUE**						
		External sales	504,633	209,562	14,055	141,203	–	869,453
		Inter-segment sales	9,370	–	–	–	(9,370)	–
14(r1997).67	8015(a)	Total revenue	514,003	209,562	14,055	141,203	(9,370)	869,453
14(r1997).75	8021(b)	Inter-segment sales are charged at prevailing market rates.						
		RESULT						
14(r1997).52	8013(b)	Segment result	33,993	15,930	9,929	5,390	(1,902)	63,340
		Unallocated corporate expenses						(3,778)
14(r1997).67	8015(b)	Profit from operations						59,562
		Finance costs						(32,995)
14(r1997).64	8013(h)	Income from associates		983				983
		Income from investments						673
		Profit before tax						28,223
		Income tax expense						(4,370)
14(r1997).67	8015(b)	Profit after tax						23,853

Source	Checklist	**OTHER INFORMATION**	Electronic goods CU'000	Construction CU'000	Leasing CU'000	Toys CU'000	Other CU'000	Consolidated CU'000
14(r1997).57	8013(e)	Capital additions	39,856	–	2,277	–	4,682	46,815
14(r1997).58	8013(f)	Depreciation and amortisation	10,122	4,944	158	2,897	2,014	20,135

Source	Checklist	**BALANCE SHEET**	31/12/00 CU'000	31/12/00 CU'000	31/12/00 CU'000	31/12/00 CU'000	31/12/00 CU'000
		ASSETS					
14(r1997).55	8013(c)	Segment assets	572,546	105,002	189,021	36,062	902,631
14(r1997).66	8013(i)	Investments in associates	–	12,274	–	–	12,274
		Unallocated corporate assets					144,113
14(r1997).67	8015(c)	Consolidated total assets					1,059,018
		LIABILITIES					
14(r1997).56	8013(d)	Segment liabilities	425,931	38,114	145,519	12,300	621,864
		Unallocated corporate liabilities					93,490
14(r1997).67	8015(d)	Consolidated total liabilities					715,354

Source	Checklist	INTERNATIONAL GAAP HOLDINGS LIMITED
		NOTES TO THE CONSOLIDATED FINANCIAL STATEMENTS FOR THE YEAR ENDED 31 DECEMBER 2001 – continued

The average number of employees for the year for each of the Group's principal divisions was as follows:

Source	Checklist		Year ended 31/12/01	Year ended 31/12/00
		Electronic goods	2,182	2,483
		Construction	619	473
		Leasing	76	68
		Toys	345	430
		Head office and administration	278	248
1(r1997).102(d)	8001(d)		3,500	3,702

Geographical segments

14(r1997).81 8024(b) The Group's operations are located in A Land, B Land, C Land and D Land. The Group's construction and leasing divisions are located in A Land. Manufacturing of electronic goods is carried out in B Land, C Land and D Land. As discussed in note 19, the financial statements of the Group's subsidiary in C Land have not been consolidated due to restrictions on the Group's ability to exercise control.

14(r1997).69(a) 8016(a) The following table provides an analysis of the Group's sales by geographical market, irrespective of the origin of the goods/services:

	Sales revenue by geographical market	
	Year ended 31/12/01	Year ended 31/12/00
	CU'000	CU'000
P Land	822,699	584,347
A Land	171,486	121,803
B Land	52,701	37,432
Q Land	137,892	97,942
Other	39,320	27,929
	1,224,098	869,453

35.27(b) 8030(b) Revenue from the Group's discontinuing operations was derived principally from P Land (2001: CU81.4 million, 2000: CU103.3 million) and A Land (2001: CU75.5 million, 2000: CU35.8 million).

Source	Checklist	INTERNATIONAL GAAP HOLDINGS LIMITED

NOTES TO THE CONSOLIDATED FINANCIAL STATEMENTS
FOR THE YEAR ENDED 31 DECEMBER 2001 – continued

14(1997).69(b),(c) 8016(b),(c)

The following is an analysis of the carrying amount of segment assets, and additions to property, plant and equipment and intangible assets, analysed by the geographical area in which the assets are located:

	Carrying amount of segment assets		Additions to property, plant and equipment and intangible assets	
	Year ended 31/12/01	Year ended 31/12/00	Year ended 31/12/01	Year ended 31/12/00
	CU'000	CU'000	CU'000	CU'000
A Land	521,709	436,508	33,402	21,399
B Land	363,310	415,654	16,398	17,502
D Land	349,856	206,856	19,254	7,914
	1,234,875	1,059,018	69,054	46,815

8(r1993).16 8055

6. RESTRUCTURING COSTS

In November 2001, the Group disposed of Subsix Limited (see note 10). Certain of the non-core assets of the toy division were retained by the Group. In addition, the shipping and distribution operations of the toy division were segregated from the manufacturing operations and retained by the Group. The assets retained were scrapped, and an impairment loss recognised in the amount of their previous carrying amount. To the extent that workers in the shipping and distribution operations could not be redeployed, termination terms were agreed.

Source	Checklist		Year ended 31/12/01 CU'000
36.113(a)	8109(a)	Loss on impairment of assets	4,130
		Redundancy costs	14,170
			18,300

In addition, redundancy costs of CU1.42 million (2000: CU1.95 million) were incurred following the acquisition of Sub A Limited. This charge was offset by the release of negative goodwill of the same amount (see note 17).

Source	Checklist	INTERNATIONAL GAAP HOLDINGS LIMITED		
		NOTES TO THE CONSOLIDATED FINANCIAL STATEMENTS FOR THE YEAR ENDED 31 DECEMBER 2001 – continued		
		7. PROFIT FROM OPERATIONS		
		Profit from operations has been arrived at after charging (crediting):		
			Year ended 31/12/01 CU'000	Period ended 31/12/00 CU'000
21(r1993).42(a)	8043(a)	Net foreign exchange losses/(gains)	1,278	(731)
38.115	8042	Research and development costs	4,800	6,560
20.39(b)	8185(a)	Government grants towards training costs	(398)	(473)
		Amortisation		
22(r1998).88(d)	7003(c)	– goodwill (included in [depreciation and amortisation expense/other operating expenses])	463	247
38.107(d)	7003(n)	– intangible assets (included in [depreciation and amortisation expense/ other operating expenses])	2,614	846
			3,077	1,093
22(r1998).91(c)	7003(d)	Release of negative goodwill to income		
		– included in other operating income	(258)	(257)
		– offset against restructuring costs	(1,424)	(1,953)
			(1,682)	(2,210)
1(r1997).83	3007	Total staff costs incurred during the period amounted to CU247.9 million (2000: CU223.5 million) and total depreciation amounted to CU29.5 million (2000: CU19 million).		
		Note: Separate disclosure of staff costs and depreciation is required where the expenses presented in the income statement are analysed by function (see Income Statement – Alt 2)		

Source	Checklist	
		INTERNATIONAL GAAP HOLDINGS LIMITED
		NOTES TO THE CONSOLIDATED FINANCIAL STATEMENTS FOR THE YEAR ENDED 31 DECEMBER 2001 – continued

8. FINANCE COSTS

Source	Checklist		Year ended 31/12/01 CU'000	Year ended 31/12/00 CU'000
		Interest on bank overdrafts and loans	40,923	32,762
		Interest on convertible loan notes (note 33)	1,260	–
		Interest on obligations under finance leases	348	233
		Total borrowing costs	42,531	32,995
23(r1993).29(b)	8046(a)	Less: amounts included in the cost of qualifying assets	(5,951)	–
			36,580	32,995
39(r2000).170(c)	8152	Loss arising on derivatives trading	100	–
			36,680	32,995

23(r1993).29(c) — 8046(b) — Borrowing costs included in the cost of qualifying assets during the year arose on the general borrowing pool and are calculated by applying a capitalisation rate of 7 per cent to expenditure on such assets.

9. INCOME FROM INVESTMENTS

18(r1993).35(b) 8028(a)
39(r2000).170(c) 8152

Source	Checklist		Year ended 31/12/01 CU'000	Year ended 31/12/00 CU'000
		Interest on bank deposits	1,202	368
		Dividends from trading investments	2,299	349
39(r2000).170 (c)(iii)	8152	Loss on disposal of trading investments	(892)	–
		Unrealised loss on trading investments	(388)	(44)
		Profit on disposal of available-for-sale investments	717	–
			2,938	673

Source | Checklist | INTERNATIONAL GAAP HOLDINGS LIMITED

NOTES TO THE CONSOLIDATED FINANCIAL STATEMENTS
FOR THE YEAR ENDED 31 DECEMBER 2001 – continued

10. DISCONTINUING OPERATIONS

35.27(c) 8030(c) On 14 May 2001, the Group entered into a sale agreement to dispose
35.27(a),(b) 8030(a),(b) of Subsix Limited, which carried out all of the Group's toy
manufacturing operations. The disposal was effected in order to
35.27(d) 8030(d) generate cash flow for the expansion of the Group's other businesses.
The disposal was completed on 30 November 2001, on which date
control of Subsix Limited passed to the acquirer.

35.27(f) 8030(f) The results of the toy manufacturing operations for the period from
35.45 8040 1 January 2001 to 30 November 2001, which have been included in
the consolidated financial statements, were as follows:

	Period ended 30/11/01 CU'000	Year ended 31/12/00 CU'000
Revenue	159,438	141,203
Operating costs	(136,645)	(135,813)
Restructuring costs	(18,300)	–
Finance costs	(493)	(830)
Profit before tax	4,000	4,560
Income tax expense	(1,817)	(389)
Profit from ordinary activities after tax	2,183	4,171

Details of the restructuring costs arising following the disposal of Subsix Limited are set out in note 6.

35.27(g) 8030(g) During the year, Subsix Limited contributed CU4.8 million (2000:
35.45 8040 CU4.25 million) to the Group's net operating cash flows, paid
CU1.37 million (2000: CU2.89 million) in respect of investing
activities and paid CU0.9 million (2000: CU3.71 million) in
respect of financing activities.

The carrying amounts of the assets and liabilities of Subsix Limited at the date of disposal are disclosed in note 40.

35.31(a) 8032(a) A profit of CU8.5 million arose on the disposal of Subsix Limited,
being the proceeds of disposal less the carrying amount of the
subsidiary's net assets and attributable goodwill (see note 40). No tax
charge or credit arose from the transaction.

Source	Checklist	INTERNATIONAL GAAP HOLDINGS LIMITED

NOTES TO THE CONSOLIDATED FINANCIAL STATEMENTS
FOR THE YEAR ENDED 31 DECEMBER 2001 – continued

11. INCOME TAX EXPENSE

Source	Checklist		Year ended 31/12/01 CU'000	Year ended 31/12/00 CU'000
12(r2000).79	8048	Current tax:		
		Domestic	5,408	1,994
		Foreign	7,972	1,426
			13,380	3,420
		Deferred tax (note 35):		
		Current year	6,046	838
		Attributable to a reduction in the rate of domestic income tax	(90)	–
			5,956	838
		Taxation attributable to the Company and its subsidiaries	19,336	4,258
		Share of taxation attributable to associates	270	112
			19,606	4,370

12(r2000).81(d) 8050(a)

Domestic income tax is calculated at 16 per cent (2000: 16.5 per cent) of the estimated assessable profit for the year. The rate of tax has been amended with effect from the 2001/02 year of assessment.

Taxation for other jurisdictions is calculated at the rates prevailing in the respective jurisdictions.

12(r2000).81(h) 8050(b)(ii)

Of the charge to domestic income tax, approximately CU1.8 million (2000: CU0.4 million) related to profits arising in the toy division, which was disposed of during the year. No tax charge or credit arose on the disposal of the relevant subsidiary.

Source	Checklist	INTERNATIONAL GAAP HOLDINGS LIMITED
		NOTES TO THE CONSOLIDATED FINANCIAL STATEMENTS FOR THE YEAR ENDED 31 DECEMBER 2001 – continued

12(r2000).81(c) | 8049

The charge for the year can be reconciled to the profit per the income statement as follows:

	Year ended 31/12/01 CU'000	%	Year ended 31/12/00 CU'000	%
Profit before tax	125,672		28,223	
Tax at the domestic income tax rate of 16% (2000: 16.5%)	20,108	16.0	4,657	16.5
Tax effect of expenses that are not deductible in determining taxable profit	301	0.2	23	0.1
Tax effect of utilisation of tax losses not previously recognised	(1,185)	(0.9)	(392)	(1.4)
Decrease in opening deferred tax liability resulting from a reduction in tax rates	(90)	(0.1)	–	–
Effect of different tax rates of subsidiaries operating in other jurisdictions	472	0.4	82	0.3
Tax expense and effective tax rate for the year	19,606	15.6	4,370	15.5

12(r2000).81(a) | 5003(b)

In addition to the amount charged to the income statement, deferred tax relating to the revaluation of the Group's properties amounting to CU3.7 million and to the equity component of convertible bonds issued amounting to CU0.16 million has been charged directly to equity (see note 35).

12. DIVIDENDS

1(r1997).85 | 8056

On 23 May 2001, a dividend of 4.2 cents (2000: 6.7 cents) per share was paid to shareholders.

1(r1997).74(c) | 8057

In respect of the current year, the directors propose that a dividend of 9.8 cents per share will be paid to shareholders on 25 May 2002. This dividend is subject to approval by shareholders at the Annual General Meeting and has not been included as a liability in these financial statements.

Source | Checklist | INTERNATIONAL GAAP HOLDINGS LIMITED

NOTES TO THE CONSOLIDATED FINANCIAL STATEMENTS
FOR THE YEAR ENDED 31 DECEMBER 2001 – continued

The proposed dividend for 2001 is payable to all shareholders on the Register of Members on 21 April 2002. The total estimated dividend to be paid is CU14.7 million.

13. EARNINGS PER SHARE

Note: IAS 33 ***Earnings Per Share*** *requires that Earnings Per Share (EPS) information be presented by enterprises whose ordinary shares or potential ordinary shares are publicly traded and by enterprises that are in the process of issuing ordinary shares or potential ordinary shares in public securities markets. If other enterprises choose to disclose EPS information in financial statements that comply with IAS, they should comply fully with the requirements of IAS 33.*

Including discontinuing operations

The calculation of the basic and diluted earnings per share is based on the following data:

Source	Checklist	INTERNATIONAL GAAP HOLDINGS LIMITED
		NOTES TO THE CONSOLIDATED FINANCIAL STATEMENTS FOR THE YEAR ENDED 31 DECEMBER 2001 – continued

33.49(a) | 3009(a)

Earnings

	Year ended 31/12/01 CU'000	Year ended 31/12/00 CU'000
Earnings for the purposes of basic earnings per share (net profit for the year)	105,457	23,756
Effect of dilutive potential ordinary shares: Interest on convertible loan notes (net of tax)	1,058	
Earnings for the purposes of diluted earnings per share	106,515	

33.49(b) | 3009(b)

Number of shares

	Year ended 31/12/01 '000	Year ended 31/12/00 '000
Weighted average number of ordinary shares for the purposes of basic earnings per share	150,000	150,000
Effect of dilutive potential ordinary shares: Convertible loan notes	42,188	
Weighted average number of ordinary shares for the purposes of diluted earnings per share	192,188	

33.43 | 3011(c)

The denominators for the purposes of calculating both basic and diluted earnings per share have been adjusted to reflect the capitalisation issue in February 2002 (see note 27).

Excluding discontinuing operations

The additional basic and diluted earnings per share present earnings data after elimination of the effects of operations discontinued in the period.

Source	Checklist	INTERNATIONAL GAAP HOLDINGS LIMITED

NOTES TO THE CONSOLIDATED FINANCIAL STATEMENTS
FOR THE YEAR ENDED 31 DECEMBER 2001 – continued

33.51 3010 Earnings figures are calculated as follows:

	Year ended 31/12/01 CU'000	Year ended 31/12/00 CU'000
Net profit for the year	105,457	23,756
Adjustments for:		
Profit after tax from discontinuing operations	(2,183)	(4,171)
Profit on disposal of discontinuing operations	(8,493)	–
Earnings for the purposes of basic earnings per share excluding discontinuing operations	94,781	19,585
Interest on convertible loan notes (net of tax)	1,058	
Earnings for the purposes of diluted earnings per share excluding discontinuing operations	95,839	

The denominators used are the same as those detailed above for both basic and diluted earnings per share.

Source	Checklist	

INTERNATIONAL GAAP HOLDINGS LIMITED

NOTES TO THE CONSOLIDATED FINANCIAL STATEMENTS
FOR THE YEAR ENDED 31 DECEMBER 2001 – continued

14. PROPERTY, PLANT AND EQUIPMENT

Source	Checklist		Land and buildings CU'000	Properties under construction CU'000	Fixtures and equipment CU'000	Total CU'000
16(r1998).60(d),(e)	8061(b),(c)	COST OR VALUATION				
		At 1 January 2001	442,099	77,700	103,870	623,669
16(r1998).61(c)	8062(b)	Additions	–	17,260	44,359	61,619
		Acquired on acquisition of a subsidiary	–	–	8,907	8,907
		Exchange differences	2,103	–	972	3,075
		Disposed of on disposal of a subsidiary	–	–	(22,402)	(22,402)
		Disposals	–	–	(6,413)	(6,413)
		Revaluation increase	41,586	–	–	41,586
		At 31 December 2001	485,788	94,960	129,293	710,041
16(r1998).60(a)	8061(a)	Comprising:				
		At cost	–	94,960	129,293	224,253
		At valuation 2001	485,788	–	–	485,788
			485,788	94,960	129,293	710,041
		ACCUMULATED DEPRECIATION				
		At 1 January 2001	9,900	–	46,927	56,827
		Charge for the year	13,172	–	16,345	29,517
36.113	8109	Impairment loss	–	–	4,130	4,130
		Exchange differences	51	–	927	978
		Eliminated on disposals	–	–	(5,614)	(5,614)
		Eliminated on disposal of a subsidiary	–	–	(12,277)	(12,277)
		Eliminated on revaluation	(23,123)	–	–	(23,123)
		At 31 December 2001	–	–	50,438	50,438
		CARRYING AMOUNT				
		At 31 December 2001	485,788	94,960	78,855	659,603
		At 31 December 2000	432,199	77,700	56,943	566,842

The impairment loss on fixtures and equipment arose in connection with the restructuring following the disposal of Subsix Limited (see note 6).

17(r1997).23(a) | 8131(a) | The carrying amount of the Group's fixtures and equipment includes an amount of CU2.55 million (2000: CU1.40 million) in respect of assets held under finance leases.

Source	Checklist	INTERNATIONAL GAAP HOLDINGS LIMITED
		NOTES TO THE CONSOLIDATED FINANCIAL STATEMENTS FOR THE YEAR ENDED 31 DECEMBER 2001 – continued
16(r1998).61(a)	8062(a)	The Group has pledged land and buildings having a carrying amount of approximately CU370 million (2000: CU320 million) to secure banking facilities granted to the Group.
16(r1998).64 (a),(b),(c)	8063(a), (b),(c)	Land and buildings were revalued at 31 December 2001 by Messrs. Lacey & King, Chartered Surveyors, on an open market existing use basis. Messrs. Lacey & King are not connected with the Group.
16(r1998).64(e)	8063(e)	At 31 December 2001, had the land and buildings of the Group been carried at historical cost less accumulated depreciation, their carrying amount would have been approximately CU390 million (2000: CU410 million).

15. INVESTMENT PROPERTY

Source	Checklist		2001 CU'000
40.67	8068	FAIR VALUE	
		At 1 January 2001	11,409
		Increase in fair value during the year	591
		At 31 December 2001	12,000

Source	Checklist	
40.66(b),(c)	8066	The fair value of the Group's investment property at 31 December 2001 has been arrived at on the basis of a valuation carried out at that date by Messrs R P Trent, Chartered Surveyors, on an open market value basis. The valuation was arrived at by reference to market evidence of transaction prices for similar properties.
40.66(e)	8067	The Group has pledged all of its investment property to secure general banking facilities granted to the Group.
40.66(d)	8041	The property rental income earned by the Group from its investment property, all of which is leased out under operating leases, amounted to CU0.6 million (2000: CU0.56 million). Direct operating expenses arising on the investment property in the period amounted to CU0.16 million (2000: CU0.23 million).

Source	Checklist	INTERNATIONAL GAAP HOLDINGS LIMITED	
		NOTES TO THE CONSOLIDATED FINANCIAL STATEMENTS FOR THE YEAR ENDED 31 DECEMBER 2001 – continued	
		16. GOODWILL	
			2001 CU'000
22(r1998).88(e)	8074	COST	
		At 1 January 2001	8,624
		Exchange differences	194
		Arising on acquisition of a subsidiary	2,043
		Eliminated on disposal of a subsidiary	(6,503)
		At 31 December 2001	4,358
		AMORTISATION	
		At 1 January 2001	6,086
		Exchange differences	149
		Eliminated on disposal of a subsidiary	(3,545)
		Charge for the year	463
		At 31 December 2001	3,153
		CARRYING AMOUNT	
		At 31 December 2001	1,205
		At 31 December 2000	2,538
22(r1998).88(a)	7003(c)	Goodwill is amortised over its estimated useful life. The foreseeable life of the goodwill arising on past acquisitions ranges from 12 to 20 years.	

Source	Checklist	INTERNATIONAL GAAP HOLDINGS LIMITED
		NOTES TO THE CONSOLIDATED FINANCIAL STATEMENTS FOR THE YEAR ENDED 31 DECEMBER 2001 – continued

17. NEGATIVE GOODWILL

Source	Checklist		2001 CU'000
22(r1998).91(d)	8077	GROSS AMOUNT	
		At 1 January and 31 December 2001	4,665
		RELEASED TO INCOME	
		At 1 January 2001	2,210
		Release in the year	1,682
		At 31 December 2001	3,892
		CARRYING AMOUNT	
		At 31 December 2001	773
		At 31 December 2000	2,455

22(r1998).91(b) 7003(d)
22(r1998).91(a) 8076

The negative goodwill arose on the Group's acquisition of Sub A Limited in February 2000. At date of acquisition, CU3.37 million of the negative goodwill was identified as relating to anticipated redundancy costs, expected to be incurred during 2000 and 2001. In 2000, redundancy costs of CU1.95 million were incurred and an equivalent portion of the negative goodwill was released to income. In 2001, final settlements in respect of redundancies amounted to CU1.42 million, and the remaining balance of negative goodwill attributable to such expenses was released to income.

The remaining negative goodwill of CU1.3 million is released to income on a straight-line basis over the remaining weighted average useful life of the depreciable assets acquired of five years.

Source	Checklist	INTERNATIONAL GAAP HOLDINGS LIMITED
		NOTES TO THE CONSOLIDATED FINANCIAL STATEMENTS FOR THE YEAR ENDED 31 DECEMBER 2001 – continued

18. INTANGIBLE ASSETS

38.107(c),(e) 8078

	Development costs	Patents and trademarks	Total
	CU'000	CU'000	CU'000
COST			
At 1 January 2001	–	31,617	31,617
Additions	3,600	3,835	7,435
Acquired on acquisition of a subsidiary	–	870	870
At 31 December 2001	3,600	36,322	39,922
AMORTISATION			
At 1 January 2001	–	10,323	10,323
Charge for the year	360	2,254	2,614
At 31 December 2001	360	12,577	12,937
CARRYING AMOUNT			
At 31 December 2001	3,240	23,745	26,985
At 31 December 2000	–	21,294	21,294

Source	Checklist	
		INTERNATIONAL GAAP HOLDINGS LIMITED
		NOTES TO THE CONSOLIDATED FINANCIAL STATEMENTS FOR THE YEAR ENDED 31 DECEMBER 2001 – continued

19. SUBSIDIARIES

27.32(a) 8085 Details of the Company's subsidiaries at 31 December 2001 are as follows:

Name of subsidiary	Place of incorporation (or registration) and operation	Proportion of ownership interest %	Proportion of voting power held %	Principal activity
Subone Limited	A Land	100	100	Property investment and construction
Subtwo Limited	A Land	70	55	Equipment leasing
Subthree Limited	B Land	100	100	Manufacture of electronic equipment
Subfour Limited	C Land	70	70	Manufacture of electronic equipment
Subfive Limited	D Land	100	100	Manufacture of electronic equipment

27.32(b)(i) 8087(a) The financial statements of Subfour Limited are not consolidated in the Group financial statements. As previously reported, the assets and liabilities of Subfour Limited were placed under court administration during 1998 pending investigation of allegations of misconduct by the minority shareholder and general manager. Consequently, the Group's ability to exercise control has been restricted. As the directors considered that the Group was unlikely to recover any of its investment, the resulting impairment loss was recognised in previous years.

Subsequent to the balance sheet date, the administration proceedings were completed and an application was made to wind-up Subfour Limited (see note 47).

20. INVESTMENTS IN ASSOCIATES

	2001 CU'000	2000 CU'000
Cost of investment	32,920	1,120
Share of post-acquisition profit, net of dividends received	12,140	11,154
	45,060	12,274

Source	Checklist	INTERNATIONAL GAAP HOLDINGS LIMITED
		NOTES TO THE CONSOLIDATED FINANCIAL STATEMENTS FOR THE YEAR ENDED 31 DECEMBER 2001 – continued
28(r2000).27(a)	8102(a)	Details of the Group's associates at 31 December 2001 are as follows:

Name of Associate	Place of incorporation and operation	Proportion of ownership interest	Proportion of voting power held	Principal activity
Aplus Limited	A Land	30%	30%	Manufacture of electronic equipment
Bplus Limited	D Land	45%	40%	Construction

21. JOINT VENTURES

31(r2000).47 | 8104

The Group had the following significant interests in joint ventures:

(a) a 25 per cent share in the ownership of a property located in Central District, City A. The Group is entitled to a proportionate share of the rental income received and bears a proportionate share of the outgoings.

(b) a 33.5 per cent equity shareholding with equivalent voting power, in JV Electronics Limited, a joint venture established in D Land.

31(r1998).47 | 8105

The following amounts are included in the Group's financial statements as a result of the proportionate consolidation of JV Electronics Limited:

	2001 CU'000	2000 CU'000
Current assets	33,129	46,382
Long-term assets	15,302	38,577
Current liabilities	17,639	15,278
Long-term liabilities	29,214	24,730
Income	8,329	47,923
Expenses	51,702	46,378

Source	Checklist	INTERNATIONAL GAAP HOLDINGS LIMITED

NOTES TO THE CONSOLIDATED FINANCIAL STATEMENTS
FOR THE YEAR ENDED 31 DECEMBER 2001 – continued

22. INVESTMENTS IN SECURITIES

Available-for-sale investments

	2001 CU'000
At 1 January 2001	
– as originally stated (cost)	20,000
– prior period adjustment to reflect adoption of IAS 39 (see note 2)	5,432
– as restated (fair value at 1 January 2001)	25,432
Disposed of in the year	(2,310)
Increase in fair value	251
Fair value at 31 December 2001	23,373

Trading investments

	2001 CU'000	2000 CU'000
Fair value at 31 December	37,243	29,730

32(r1998).47(a) 8140
32(r1998).77 8143

The investments in securities included above represent investments in listed equity securities which present the Group with opportunity for return through dividend income and trading gains. The fair values of these securities are based on quoted market prices.

2(r1993).34(b) 8113(a)

23. INVENTORIES

	2001 CU'000	2000 CU'000
Raw materials	84,425	80,504
Work-in-progress	2,578	1,893
Finished goods	31,062	26,301
	118,065	108,698

Source	Checklist	INTERNATIONAL GAAP HOLDINGS LIMITED NOTES TO THE CONSOLIDATED FINANCIAL STATEMENTS FOR THE YEAR ENDED 31 DECEMBER 2001 – continued				
2(r1993).34(c)	8113(b)	Included above are raw materials of CU1.2 million (2000: CU0.8 million) and work-in-progress of CU0.3 million (2000: Nil) carried at net realisable value.				
2(r1993).34(f)	8113(e)	Inventories with a carrying amount of CU26 million (2000: CU19.3 million) have been pledged as security for certain of the Group's bank overdrafts.				
		24. FINANCE LEASE RECEIVABLES				
			Minimum lease payments		Present value of minimum lease payments	
			2001	2000	2001	2000
			CU'000	CU'000	CU'000	CU'000
17(r1997).39(a)	8106(a),(b)	Amounts receivable under finance leases:				
		Within one year	72,526	65,948	54,713	49,674
		In the second to fifth years inclusive	120,875	109,913	114,937	104,489
			193,401	175,861	169,650	154,163
17(r1997).39(b)	8106(c)	Less: unearned finance income	(23,751)	(21,698)	N/A	N/A
		Present value of minimum lease payments receivable	169,650	154,163	169,650	154,163
1(r1997).54	4014	Analysed as:				
		Non-current finance lease receivables (recoverable after 12 months)			114,937	104,489
		Current finance lease receivables (recoverable within 12 months)			54,713	49,674
					169,650	154,163
17(r1997).39(f) 32(r1998).47(a)	8106(g) 8140	The Group enters into finance leasing arrangements for certain of its electronic equipment. The average term of finance leases entered into is 4 years.				
17(r1997).39(c)	8106(d)	Unguaranteed residual values of assets leased under finance leases are estimated at CU0.37 million (2000: CU0.25 million).				

Source	Checklist	INTERNATIONAL GAAP HOLDINGS LIMITED
		NOTES TO THE CONSOLIDATED FINANCIAL STATEMENTS FOR THE YEAR ENDED 31 DECEMBER 2001 – continued
32(r1998).56	8141	The interest rate inherent in the leases is fixed at the contract date for all of the lease term. The weighted average interest rate on finance lease receivables at 31 December 2001 was 11.9 per cent (2000: 12.5 per cent).
32(r1998).77	8143	The fair value of the Group's finance lease receivables at 31 December 2001 is estimated at CU182 million (2000: CU163 million).
		25. OTHER FINANCIAL ASSETS
32(r1998).47(a)	8140	**Trade and other receivables** comprise amounts receivable from the sale of goods of CU83 million (2000: CU112 million), amounts due from construction contract customers of CU25 million (2000: CU17 million), deferred consideration for the disposal of Subsix Limited of CU24 million (see note 40), and currency and interest rate derivatives with a fair value of CU1.4 million (see note 34).
		The average credit period taken on sale of goods is 35 days. An allowance has been made for estimated irrecoverable amounts from the sale of goods of CU3.24 million (2000: CU4.39 million). This allowance has been determined by reference to past default experience.
32(r1998).77	8143	The directors consider that the carrying amount of trade and other receivables approximates their fair value.
32(r1998).47(a) 32(r1998).77	8140 8143	**Bank balances and cash** comprise cash and short-term deposits held by the group treasury function. The carrying amount of these assets approximates their fair value.
32(r1998).66	8142	**Credit risk**
		The Group's credit risk is primarily attributable to its trade and finance lease receivables. The amounts presented in the balance sheet are net of allowances for doubtful receivables, estimated by the Group's management based on prior experience and the current economic environment.
		The credit risk on liquid funds and derivative financial instruments is limited because the counterparties are banks with high credit-ratings assigned by international credit-rating agencies.
		The Group has no significant concentration of credit risk, with exposure spread over a large number of counterparties and customers.

Source	Checklist	INTERNATIONAL GAAP HOLDINGS LIMITED		
		NOTES TO THE CONSOLIDATED FINANCIAL STATEMENTS FOR THE YEAR ENDED 31 DECEMBER 2001 – continued		
		26. CONSTRUCTION CONTRACTS		
			2001 CU'000	2000 CU'000
		Contracts in progress at balance sheet date:		
11(r1993).42(a)	8116(a)	Amounts due from contract customers included in trade and other receivables	24,930	17,302
11(r1993).42(b)	8116(b)	Amounts due to contract customers included in accounts payable	(3,587)	(3,904)
			21,343	13,398
11(r1993).40(a)	8115(a)	Contract costs incurred plus recognised profits less recognised losses to date	59,039	33,829
		Less: progress billings	(37,696)	(20,431)
			21,343	13,398
11(r1993).40 (b),(c)	8115(b),(c)	At 31 December 2001, retentions held by customers for contract work amounted to CU2.3 million (2000: CU1.8 million). Advances received from customers for contract work amounted to CU0.85 million (2000: Nil).		
1(r1997).54	4014	At 31 December 2001, amounts of CU4.3 million (2000: CU2.1 million) included in trade and other receivables and arising from construction contracts are due for settlement after more than 12 months.		
1(r1997).74(a)	8117	**27. SHARE CAPITAL**		
			2001 CU'000	2000 CU'000
		Authorised: Ordinary shares of CU1 each	200,000	200,000
		Issued and fully paid: Ordinary shares of CU1 each	120,000	120,000
		There were no movements in the share capital of the Company in either the 2001 or 2000 reporting periods.		
		The Company has one class of ordinary shares which carry no right to fixed income.		

Source	Checklist	INTERNATIONAL GAAP HOLDINGS LIMITED

NOTES TO THE CONSOLIDATED FINANCIAL STATEMENTS
FOR THE YEAR ENDED 31 DECEMBER 2001 – continued

On 14 February 2002, a capitalisation issue of 1 bonus share for every four shares in issue resulted in an increase in issued share capital of CU30 million, and an equivalent reduction in the share premium account.

1(r1997).74(b) 8118
1(r1997).86 5002

28. CAPITAL RESERVES

	Share premium CU'000	Equity reserve CU'000	Total CU'000
Balance at 1 January and 31 December 2000	32,098	–	32,098
Equity component of convertible loan notes issued (see note 33)	–	836	836
Balance at 31 December 2001	32,098	836	32,934

Source	Checklist	INTERNATIONAL GAAP HOLDINGS LIMITED
		NOTES TO THE CONSOLIDATED FINANCIAL STATEMENTS FOR THE YEAR ENDED 31 DECEMBER 2001 – continued
1(r1997).74(b) 1(r1997).86	8118 5002	**29. REVALUATION RESERVES**

Source	Checklist		Investment property revaluation reserve CU'000	Other properties revaluation reserve CU'000	Investments revaluation reserve CU'000	Total CU'000
		Balance at 1 January 2000				
		– as originally stated	253	33,208	–	33,461
		– prior period adjustment (see note 2)	(253)	–	–	(253)
		– as restated	–	33,208	–	33,208
		Revaluation decrease on land and buildings	–	(4,049)	–	(4,049)
		Balance at 1 January 2001	–	29,159	–	29,159
		– prior period adjustment (see note 2)	–	–	5,432	5,432
		– as restated	–	29,159	5,432	34,591
16(r1998).64(f)	5003(c)	Revaluation increase on land and buildings	–	64,709	–	64,709
12(r2000).81(a)	5003(b)	Deferred tax liability on revaluation of land and buildings	–	(3,699)	–	(3,699)
39(r2000).170(a)	5003(e)	Released on disposal of available-for-sale investments	– –		(611)	(611)
39(r2000).170(a)	5003(e)	Increase in fair value of available-for-sale investments	–	–	251	251
		Balance at 31 December 2001	–	90,169	5,072	95,241

Source	Checklist	INTERNATIONAL GAAP HOLDINGS LIMITED

NOTES TO THE CONSOLIDATED FINANCIAL STATEMENTS
FOR THE YEAR ENDED 31 DECEMBER 2001 – continued

1(r1997).74(b) | 8118
1(r1997).86 | 5002

30. HEDGING AND TRANSLATION RESERVES

Source	Checklist		Hedging reserve CU'000	Translation reserve CU'000	Total CU'000
		Balance at 1 January 2000	–	(2,368)	(2,368)
21(r1993).42(b)	5003(f)	Exchange differences on overseas operations	–	2,706	2,706
		Balance at 1 January 2001			
		– as originally stated	–	338	338
		– prior period adjustment (see note 2)	890	–	890
		– as restated	890	338	1,228
21(r1993).42(b)	5003(f)	Exchange differences on overseas operations	–	(13,446)	(13,446)
39(r2000).169(c)	8148(a)	Fair value gains in the period	510	–	510
		Balance at 31 December 2001	1,400	(13,108)	(11,708)

Source	Checklist	INTERNATIONAL GAAP HOLDINGS LIMITED
		NOTES TO THE CONSOLIDATED FINANCIAL STATEMENTS FOR THE YEAR ENDED 31 DECEMBER 2001 – continued
1(r1997).74(b) 1(r1997).86	8118 5002	**31. ACCUMULATED PROFITS**

	CU'000
Balance at 1 January 2000	
– as originally stated	143,524
– prior period adjustment (see note 2)	253
– as restated	143,777
Dividends paid	(8,040)
Net profit for the year	23,756
Balance at 1 January 2001	159,493
– prior period adjustment (see note 2)	(170)
– as restated	159,323
Dividends paid	(5,040)
Net profit for the year	105,457
Balance at 31 December 2001	259,740

Source	Checklist	
		INTERNATIONAL GAAP HOLDINGS LIMITED
		NOTES TO THE CONSOLIDATED FINANCIAL STATEMENTS FOR THE YEAR ENDED 31 DECEMBER 2001 – continued
32(r1998).47(a)	8140	**32. BANK OVERDRAFTS AND LOANS**
32(r1998).56	8141	

	2001 CU'000	2000 CU'000
Bank overdrafts	51,907	41,909
Bank loans	448,753	535,530
	500,660	577,439

The borrowings are repayable as follows:

	2001 CU'000	2000 CU'000
On demand or within one year	111,931	102,537
In the second year	46,727	71,728
In the third to fifth years inclusive	81,076	134,112
After five years	260,926	269,062
	500,660	577,439
Less: Amount due for settlement within 12 months (shown under current liabilities)	(111,931)	(102,537)
Amount due for settlement after 12 months	388,729	474,902

Analysis of borrowings by currency:

2001	Currency Units CU'000	A Currency CU'000	B Currency CU'000	C Currency CU'000
Bank overdrafts	15,182	11,288	18,530	6,907
Bank loans	340,315	108,438	–	–
	355,497	119,726	18,530	6,907

2000	Currency Units CU'000	A Currency CU'000	B Currency CU'000	C Currency CU'000
Bank overdrafts	3,434	14,282	14,842	9,351
Bank loans	360,791	174,739	–	–
	364,225	189,021	14,842	9,351

Source	Checklist	INTERNATIONAL GAAP HOLDINGS LIMITED

NOTES TO THE CONSOLIDATED FINANCIAL STATEMENTS
FOR THE YEAR ENDED 31 DECEMBER 2001 – continued

The average interest rates paid were as follows:

	2001	2000
Bank overdrafts	8.7%	9.2%
Bank loans	7.8%	8.1%

Bank loans of CU108 million (2000: CU175 million) were arranged at fixed interest rates. Other borrowings are arranged at floating rates.

32(r1998).77 8143 The directors estimate the fair value of the Group's borrowings as follows:

	2001 CU'000	2000 CU'000
Bank overdrafts	51,907	41,909
Bank loans	463,000	540,000

The other principal features of the Group's borrowings are as follows:

(i) Bank overdrafts are repayable on demand. Overdrafts of CU20.9 million (2000: CU15.4 million) have been secured by a charge over the Group's inventories.

(ii) The Group has two principal bank loans:

(a) a 20 year loan of CU340 million (2000: CU361 million) repayable by equal monthly instalments commencing 1 May 2000 and secured by a charge over certain of the Group's properties dated 3 March 2000.

1(r1997).63 4012 (b) a loan of CU108 million (2000: 175 million) secured on certain current and non-current assets of the Group. This loan was advanced on 1 July 1999 and was originally due for repayment in full on 30 June 2002. Subsequent to the balance sheet date, the bank has agreed to reschedule the loan repayments so that they are now payable by instalments through to 3 January 2004. On the basis of the post-year end agreement to reschedule the repayments, the relevant portions of the loan continue to be treated as long-term.

Source | Checklist | INTERNATIONAL GAAP HOLDINGS LIMITED

NOTES TO THE CONSOLIDATED FINANCIAL STATEMENTS
FOR THE YEAR ENDED 31 DECEMBER 2001 – continued

33. CONVERTIBLE LOAN NOTES

32(r1998).47(a) 8140
32(r1998).56 8141

The convertible loan notes were issued on 1 April 2001, and are secured by a personal guarantee of a director. The notes are convertible into ordinary shares of the Company at any time between the date of issue of the notes and their settlement date. On issue, the loan notes were convertible at 18 shares per CU10 loan note. The conversion rate has been adjusted to 22.5 shares per CU10 loan note following the capitalisation issue of shares on 14 February 2002.

If the notes have not been converted, they will be redeemed on 1 April 2003 at par. Interest of 5 per cent will be paid annually up until that settlement date.

The proceeds received from the issue of the convertible loan notes have been split between the liability element and an equity component, representing the fair value of the embedded option to convert the liability into equity of the Group.

	2001 CU'000
Nominal value of convertible loan notes issued	25,000
Equity component (net of deferred tax)	(836)
Deferred tax liability	(159)
Liability component at date of issue	24,005
Interest charged	1,260
Interest paid	(938)
Liability component at 31 December 2001	24,327

32(r1998).77 8143

The directors estimate the fair value of the convertible loan notes to be approximately CU23.7 million.

32(r1998).47(a) 8140
32(r1998).56 8141
32(r1998).77 8143

34. DERIVATIVE FINANCIAL INSTRUMENTS

Currency derivatives

The Group utilises currency derivatives to hedge future transactions and cash flows. The Group is party to a variety of foreign currency forward contracts and options in the management of its exchange rate exposures. The instruments purchased are primarily denominated in the currencies of the Group's principal markets.

Source	Checklist	INTERNATIONAL GAAP HOLDINGS LIMITED

NOTES TO THE CONSOLIDATED FINANCIAL STATEMENTS
FOR THE YEAR ENDED 31 DECEMBER 2001 – continued

At the balance sheet date, the Group had contracted to sell the following amounts under forward contracts.

	2001	2000
	CU'000	CU'000
Currency of P Land	497,233	354,782
Others	49,807	48,791
	547,040	403,573

In addition, the Group had options to purchase currency of D Land equivalent to an amount of approximately CU50 million as a hedge against future exchange losses on purchases of goods.

These arrangements are designed to address significant exchange exposures for the first half of 2002, and will be renewed on a revolving basis as required.

At 31 December 2001, the fair value of the Group's currency derivatives is estimated to be approximately CU0.74 million (1 January 2001: CU0.46 million). These amounts are based on market values of equivalent instruments at the balance sheet date, comprising CU1.01 million assets included in trade and other receivables and CU0.27 million liabilities included in trade and other payables. The fair value of currency derivatives that are designated and effective as cash flow hedges amounting to CU1.10 million (1 January 2001: CU0.63 million) has been deferred in equity. Changes in the fair value of non-hedging currency derivatives amounting to CU0.1 million have been charged to income in the year (1 January 2001: CU0.17 million charged against accumulated profits).

Interest rate swaps

The Group uses interest rates swaps to manage its exposure to interest rate movements on its bank borrowings. Contracts with nominal values of CU20 million fix interest payments at an average rate of 7 per cent for periods up until 2005.

The fair value of swaps entered into at 31 December 2001 is estimated at CU0.39 million (1 January 2001: CU0.26 million). These amounts are based on market values of equivalent instruments at the balance sheet date. All of these interest rate swaps are designated and effective as cash flow hedges and the fair value thereof has been deferred in equity.

Source	Checklist	
		INTERNATIONAL GAAP HOLDINGS LIMITED

NOTES TO THE CONSOLIDATED FINANCIAL STATEMENTS
FOR THE YEAR ENDED 31 DECEMBER 2001 – continued

35. DEFERRED TAX

	2001 CU'000	2000 CU'000
Analysis for financial reporting purposes		
Deferred tax liabilities	15,447	6,372
Deferred tax assets	(2,661)	(3,400)
Net position at 31 December	12,786	2,972

The movement for the year in the Group's net deferred tax position was as follows:

	Year ended 31/12/01 CU'000	Year ended 31/12/00 CU'000
At 1 January	2,972	2,172
Charge to income for the year	6,046	838
Charge to equity for the year	3,858	–
Net liability disposed of on disposal of subsidiary	(189)	–
Net asset acquired on acquisition of subsidiary	(201)	–
Exchange differences	390	(38)
Effect of change in tax rate	(90)	–
At 31 December	12,786	2,972

12(r2000).81(g) 8128(c) The following are the major deferred tax liabilities and assets recognised by the Group and movements thereon during the period:

Deferred tax liabilities

	Accelerated tax depreciation CU'000	Deferred development costs CU'000	Revaluation of properties CU'000	Convertible bond-equity component CU'000	Total
At 1 January 2001	4,696	–	1,676	–	6,372
Charge to income for the year	4,748	547	–	(52)	5,243
Charge to equity for the year	–	–	3,699	159	3,858
Acquisitions/disposals	(140)	–	–	–	(140)
Exchange differences	317	–	8	–	325
Effect of change in tax rate	(127)	–	(84)	–	(211)
At 31 December 2001	9,494	547	5,299	107	15,447

Source	Checklist	INTERNATIONAL GAAP HOLDINGS LIMITED
		NOTES TO THE CONSOLIDATED FINANCIAL STATEMENTS FOR THE YEAR ENDED 31 DECEMBER 2001 – continued
12(r2000).81(g)	8128(c)	**Deferred tax assets**

	Retirement benefit obligations CU'000	Tax losses CU'000	Total CU'000
At 1 January 2001	(2,561)	(839)	(3,400)
Charge to income for the year	214	589	803
Acquisitions/disposals	141	(391)	(250)
Exchange differences	65	–	65
Effect of change in tax rate	97	24	121
At 31 December 2001	(2,044)	(617)	(2,661)

Source	Checklist	
12(r2000).81(e)	8128(a)	At the balance sheet date, the Group has unused tax losses of CU11.23 million (2000: CU16.53 million) available for offset against future profits. A deferred tax asset has been recognised in respect of CU3.86 million (2000: CU5.08 million) of such losses. No deferred tax asset has been recognised in respect of the remaining CU7.37 million (2000: CU11.45 million) due to the unpredictability of future profit streams. Included in unrecognised tax losses are losses of CU2.38 million (2000: CU3.29 million) which will expire in 2004. Other losses may be carried forward indefinitely.
12(r2000).81(f)	8128(b)	At the balance sheet date, the aggregate amount of temporary differences associated with undistributed earnings of subsidiaries for which deferred tax liabilities have not been recognised was CU7.9 million (2000: CU6.3 million). No liability has been recognised in respect of these differences because the Group is in a position to control the timing of the reversal of the temporary differences and it is probable that such differences will not reverse in the foreseeable future.
12(r2000).81(f)	8128(b)	Temporary differences arising in connection with interests in associates and joint ventures are insignificant.

Source	Checklist	INTERNATIONAL GAAP HOLDINGS LIMITED

NOTES TO THE CONSOLIDATED FINANCIAL STATEMENTS
FOR THE YEAR ENDED 31 DECEMBER 2001 – continued

36. OBLIGATIONS UNDER FINANCE LEASES

Source	Checklist		Minimum lease payments 2001 CU'000	Minimum lease payments 2000 CU'000	Present value of minimum lease payments 2001 CU'000	Present value of minimum lease payments 2000 CU'000
17(r1997).23(b)	8131(b),(c)	**Amounts payable under finance leases**				
		Within one year	1,655	2,245	1,470	1,483
		In the second to fifth years inclusive	1,014	1,365	923	1,244
			2,669	3,610	2,393	2,727
		Less: future finance charges	(276)	(883)	N/A	N/A
		Present value of lease obligations	2,393	2,727	2,393	2,727
		Less: Amount due for settlement with 12 months (shown under current liabilities)			(1,470)	(1,483)
1(r1997).54	4014	Amount due for settlement after 12 months			923	1,244

17(r1997).23(e) 8131(f)
32(r1998).47(a) 8140
32(r1998).56 8141

It is the Group's policy to lease certain of its fixtures and equipment under finance leases. The average lease term is 3–4 years. For the year ended 31 December 2001, the average effective borrowing rate was 8.5 per cent. Interest rates are fixed at the contract date. All leases are on a fixed repayment basis and no arrangements have been entered into for contingent rental payments.

All lease obligations are denominated in Currency Units.

The fair value of the Group's lease obligations approximates their carrying amount.

The Group's obligations under finance leases are secured by the lessor's charge over the leased assets.

37. OTHER FINANCIAL LIABILITIES

32(r1998).47(a) 8140

Trade and other payables principally comprise amounts outstanding for trade purchases and ongoing costs. The average credit period taken for trade purchases is 45 days.

Source	Checklist	

INTERNATIONAL GAAP HOLDINGS LIMITED

NOTES TO THE CONSOLIDATED FINANCIAL STATEMENTS
FOR THE YEAR ENDED 31 DECEMBER 2001 – continued

32(r1998).77 | 8143

The directors consider that the carrying amount of trade payables approximates to their fair value.

In addition, trade and other payables include currency derivative liabilities with a fair value of CU0.27 million (see note 34).

38. PROVISIONS

37.84 | 8170

	Warranty provision CU'000	Restructuring provision CU'000	Other CU'000	Total CU'000
At 1 January 2001	1,572	–	493	2,065
Additional provision in the year	946	14,170	58	15,174
Utilisation of provision	(298)	(8,112)	(279)	(8,689)
At 31 December 2001	2,220	6,058	272	8,550

37.85 | 8171

The warranty provision represents management's best estimate of the Group's liability under 12 month warranties granted on electrical products, based on past experience and industry averages for defective products.

37.85 | 8171

The restructuring provision relates to redundancy costs incurred on the disposal of Subsix Limited (see note 6). As at 31 December 2001, approximately 50 per cent of the workers had left the Group's employment, with the remainder departing in January 2002.

Source	Checklist	INTERNATIONAL GAAP HOLDINGS LIMITED

NOTES TO THE CONSOLIDATED FINANCIAL STATEMENTS
FOR THE YEAR ENDED 31 DECEMBER 2001 – continued

7(r1992).18(b) 6003(b)

39. RECONCILIATION OF PROFIT FROM OPERATIONS TO NET CASH FROM/(USED IN) OPERATING ACTIVITIES

	Year ended 31/12/01 CU'000	Year ended 31/12/00 CU'000
Profit from operations	138,158	59,562
Adjustments for:		
Depreciation of property, plant and equipment	29,517	19,042
Impairment loss on equipment	4,130	–
Amortisation of goodwill	463	247
Amortisation of intangible assets	2,614	846
Negative goodwill released to income	(1,682)	(2,210)
Revaluation (increase)/decrease in investment properties	(591)	49
Gain on disposal of property, plant and equipment	(4,184)	(500)
Increase/(decrease) in provisions	6,485	(2,000)
Operating cash flows before movements in working capital	174,910	75,036
Increase in inventories	(21,697)	(28,960)
Decrease/(increase) in receivables	5,276	(31,993)
Increase in payables	28,809	4,141
Cash generated from operations	187,298	18,224

Note: The above reconciliation is only required where the indirect method of presenting operating cash flows is adopted (see pages 1125 and 1126).

Source	Checklist	INTERNATIONAL GAAP HOLDINGS LIMITED		
		NOTES TO THE CONSOLIDATED FINANCIAL STATEMENTS FOR THE YEAR ENDED 31 DECEMBER 2001 – continued		
		40. DISPOSAL OF SUBSIDIARY		
		As referred to in note 10, on 30 November 2001 the Group discontinued its toy operations at the time of the disposal of its subsidiary Subsix Limited.		
7(r1992).40(d) 35.31(b) 35.45	6011(d) 8032(b)(iii) 8040	The net assets of Subsix Limited at the date of disposal and at 31 December 2000 were as follows:		
			30/11/01 CU'000	31/12/00 CU'000
		Property, plant and equipment	10,125	7,293
		Inventories	11,976	14,247
7(r1992).40(c)	6011(c)	Trade receivables	12,264	11,685
		Bank balances and cash	4,382	1,946
		Retirement benefit obligation	(4,932)	(5,107)
		Deferred tax liability	(189)	–
		Income tax liability	(1,854)	(37)
		Trade payables	(2,387)	(2,104)
		Bank overdraft	(6,398)	(7,200)
		Attributable goodwill	2,958	3,039
			25,945	23,762
		Gain on disposal	8,493	
7(r1992).40(a) 35.31(b)	6011(a) 8032(b)(i)	Total consideration	34,438	
		Satisfied by:		
7(r1992).40(b)	6011(b)	Cash	10,899	
		Deferred consideration	23,539	
			34,438	
		Net cash inflow arising on disposal:		
		Cash consideration	10,899	
		Bank balances and cash disposed of	(4,382)	
			6,517	
35.31(b)	8032(b)(ii)	The deferred consideration will be settled in cash by the purchaser on or before 30 May 2002.		
27.32(b)(iv)	8087(d)	The impact of Subsix Limited on the Group's results in the current and prior periods is disclosed in note 10.		

Source	Checklist	
		INTERNATIONAL GAAP HOLDINGS LIMITED

NOTES TO THE CONSOLIDATED FINANCIAL STATEMENTS
FOR THE YEAR ENDED 31 DECEMBER 2001 – continued

41. ACQUISITION OF SUBSIDIARY

22(r1998).86 8090
22(r1998).87 8091
On 1 August 2001, the Group acquired 100 per cent of the issued share capital of Subfive limited for cash consideration of CU7.9 million. This transaction has been accounted for by the purchase method of accounting.

7(r1992).40(d) 6011(d) Net assets acquired:

Source	Checklist		2001 CU'000
		Property, plant and equipment	8,907
		Trade marks	870
		Deferred tax asset	201
		Inventories	2,854
		Trade receivables	12,520
7(r1992).40(c)	6011(c)	Bank and cash balances	4,272
		Retirement benefit obligation	(2,436)
		Warranty provision	(289)
		Trade payables	(21,000)
			5,899
		Goodwill	2,043
7(r1992).40(a)	6011(a)	Total consideration	7,942
7(r1992).40(b)	6011(b)	Satisfied by cash	7,942
		Net cash outflow arising on acquisition:	
		Cash consideration	(7,942)
		Bank balances and cash acquired	4,272
			(3,670)

27.32(b)(iv) 8087(d) Subfive Limited contributed CU15.3 million of revenue and CU1.2 million of profit before tax for the period between the date of acquisition and the balance sheet date.

7(r1992).43 6013

42. NON-CASH TRANSACTIONS

Additions to fixtures and equipment during the year amounting to CU1.563 million were financed by new finance leases.

Source	Checklist	INTERNATIONAL GAAP HOLDINGS LIMITED
		NOTES TO THE CONSOLIDATED FINANCIAL STATEMENTS FOR THE YEAR ENDED 31 DECEMBER 2001 – continued

37.86 | 8173

43. CONTINGENT LIABILITIES

During the reporting period, a customer of the Group instigated proceedings against it for alleged defects in an electronic product which, it is claimed, was the cause of a major fire in their premises in February 2001. Total losses to the customer have been estimated at CU29.8 million and this amount is being claimed from the Group.

The Group's lawyers have advised that they do not consider that the suit has merit, and they have recommended that it be contested. No provision has been made in these financial statements as the Group's management do not consider that there is any probable loss.

31(r2000).45 | 8180

Contingent liabilities arising from interests in joint ventures

	2001 CU'000	2000 CU'000
Guarantees given to banks in respect of bank facilities utilised by jointly controlled entities	22,981	23,023
Share of contingent liabilities of jointly controlled entities arising from bills of exchange discounted with recourse	7,720	5,029
Guarantees given to banks in respect of bank facilities utilised by joint venture partners	5,371	8,209
	36,072	36,261

44. CAPITAL COMMITMENTS

Source	Checklist		2001 CU'000	2000 CU'000
16(r1998).61(d)	8181	Commitments for the acquisition of property, plant and equipment	9,965	20,066

40.66(f) | 8182 | In addition, the Group has entered into a contract for the maintenance of its investment property for the next 5 years, which will give rise to an annual charge of CU0.12 million.

31(r2000).46 | 8184 | The Group's share of capital commitments of joint ventures at the balance sheet date amounted to CU1.47 million (2000: CU0.38 million).

Source	Checklist	
		INTERNATIONAL GAAP HOLDINGS LIMITED
		NOTES TO THE CONSOLIDATED FINANCIAL STATEMENTS FOR THE YEAR ENDED 31 DECEMBER 2001 – continued

45. OPERATING LEASE ARRANGEMENTS

The Group as lessee

Source	Checklist		Year ended 31/12/01 CU'000	Year ended 31/12/00 CU'000
17(r1997).27(c)	8132(c)	Minimum lease payments under operating leases recognised in income for the period	297	283

17(r1997).27(a) | 8132(a) — At the balance sheet date, the Group had outstanding commitments under non-cancellable operating leases, which fall due as follows:

	2001 CU'000	2000 CU'000
Within one year	309	297
In the second to fifth years inclusive	1,420	1,439
After five years	692	930
	2,421	2,666

17(r1997).27(d) | 8132(d) — Operating lease payments represent rentals payable by the Group for certain of its office properties. Leases are negotiated for an average term of seven years and rentals are fixed for an average of three years.

17(r1997).48(c), (d) | 8107(b),(c) — **The Group as lessor**

Property rental income earned during the year was CU0.6 million (2000: CU0.6 million). Certain of the Group's properties held for rental purposes, with a carrying amount of CU3.89 million, have been disposed of since the balance sheet date. The remaining properties are expected to generate rental yields of 10 per cent on an ongoing basis. All of the properties held have committed tenants for the next seven years.

17(r1997).48(b) | 8107(a) — At the balance sheet date, the Group had contracted with tenants for the following future minimum lease payments:

	2001 CU'000	2000 CU'000
Within one year	810	602
In the second to fifth years inclusive	3,179	3,240
After five years	1,539	2,288
	5,528	6,130

Source	Checklist	INTERNATIONAL GAAP HOLDINGS LIMITED

NOTES TO THE CONSOLIDATED FINANCIAL STATEMENTS FOR THE YEAR ENDED 31 DECEMBER 2001 – continued

46. RETIREMENT BENEFITS PLANS

Defined contribution plans

The Group operates defined contribution retirement benefit plans for all qualifying employees of its construction and leasing divisions in A Land. The assets of the schemes are held separately from those of the Group in funds under the control of trustees. Where there are employees who leave the scheme prior to vesting fully in the contributions, the contributions payable by the Group are reduced by the amount of forfeited contributions.

The employees of the Group's subsidiary in B Land are members of a state-managed retirement benefit scheme operated by the government of B Land. The subsidiary is required to contribute a specified percentage of their payroll costs to the retirement benefit scheme to fund the benefits. The only obligation of the Group with respect to the retirement benefit scheme is to make the specified contributions.

19(r2000).46 8158 The total cost charged to income of CU9.8 million (2000: CU7.3 million) represents contributions payable to these schemes by the Group at rates specified in the rules of the schemes. As at 31 December 2001, contributions of CU0.7 million (2000: CU0.8 million) due in respect of the current reporting period had not been paid over to the schemes.

Defined benefit plan

19(r2000).120(b) 8161(a) The Group operates a defined benefit plan for qualifying employees of its subsidiaries in D Land, and previously for the employees of Subsix Limited. Under the schemes, the employees are entitled to retirement benefits varying between 40 and 65 per cent of final salary on attainment of a retirement age of 60. No other post-retirement benefits are provided.

19(r2000).120(f) 8159 Amounts recognised in income in respect of that scheme are as follows:

	Year ended 31/12/01 CU'000	Year ended 31/12/00 CU'000
Current service cost	16,449	12,297
Interest costs	9,021	7,057
Expected return on plan assets	(10,675)	(9,503)
Net actuarial losses	232	1,309
Past service cost	1,652	1,888
	16,679	13,048

Source	Checklist	INTERNATIONAL GAAP HOLDINGS LIMITED

NOTES TO THE CONSOLIDATED FINANCIAL STATEMENTS
FOR THE YEAR ENDED 31 DECEMBER 2001 – continued

19(r2000).120(f) | 8159

The charge for the year has been included in staff costs. *[Where analysis of expenditure in the income statement is by nature]*

OR

Of the charge for the year, CU12.83 million (2000: CU10.03 million) has been included in cost of sales and CU3.85 million (2000: CU3.02 million) has been included in administrative expenses. *[Where analysis of expenditure in the income statement is by function]*

19(r2000).120(g) | 8161(e)

The actual return on plan assets was CU10.32 million (2000: CU9.7 million).

19(r2000).120(c) | 8161(b)

The amount included in the balance sheet arising from the Group's obligation in respect of defined benefit retirement benefit plans is as follows:

	2001 CU'000	2000 CU'000
Present value of funded obligations	160,512	177,395
Unrecognised actuarial losses	(17,310)	(15,372)
Unrecognised past service cost	(4,181)	(4,721)
Fair value of plan assets	(105,093)	(118,788)
	33,928	38,514

19(r2000).120(e) | 8161(d)

Movements in the net liability in the current period were as follows:

	2001 CU'000	2000 CU'000
At 1 January	38,474	39,438
Exchange differences	438	(721)
Net liability transferred on disposal of subsidiary	(4,932)	–
Net liability acquired on acquisition of a subsidiary	2,436	–
Amounts charged to income	16,679	13,048
Contributions	(19,167)	(13,291)
At 31 December	33,928	38,474

Source	Checklist	INTERNATIONAL GAAP HOLDINGS LIMITED
		NOTES TO THE CONSOLIDATED FINANCIAL STATEMENTS FOR THE YEAR ENDED 31 DECEMBER 2001 – continued

1(r1997).54 | 4014 — Analysis for financial reporting purposes:

	2001 CU'000	2000 CU'000
Current liabilities	3,732	4,473
Non-current liabilities	30,196	34,001
	33,928	38,474

19(r2000).120(h) | 8161(f) — Key assumptions used:

	2001	2000
Discount rate	7%	7%
Expected return on plan assets	8%	9%
Expected rate of salary increases	5%	5%
Future pension increases	4%	4%

10(r1999).20 | 8193

47. SUBSEQUENT EVENTS

Subsequent to 31 December 2001, the court administration proceedings relating to Subfour Limited (see note 19) were completed and an application was made to wind-up the company. No further distributions to the Group are anticipated. The Group has no obligation to meet the outstanding liabilities of Subfour Limited.

On 14 February 2002, the Company made a bonus issue of shares (see note 27).

24.22 | 8187

48. RELATED PARTY TRANSACTIONS

24.20 | 8186
1(r1997).102(c) | 8001(c)

The holding company and ultimate holding company respectively of the Group are X Holdings Limited (incorporated in M Land) and Y Holdings Limited (incorporated in N Land).

Trading transactions

1(r1997).72 | 8189

During the year, group companies entered into the following transactions with related parties who are not members of the Group:

Source	Checklist	

INTERNATIONAL GAAP HOLDINGS LIMITED

NOTES TO THE CONSOLIDATED FINANCIAL STATEMENTS
FOR THE YEAR ENDED 31 DECEMBER 2001 – continued

	Sales of goods		Purchases of goods		Amounts owed by related parties		Amounts owed to related parties	
	Year ended 31/12/01	Year ended 31/12/00	Year ended 31/12/01	Year ended 31/12/00	31/12/01	31/12/00	31/12/01	31/12/00
	CU'000	CU'000	CU'000	CU'000	CU'000	CU'000	CU'000	CU'000
X Holdings Ltd.	693	582	439	427	209	197	231	139
Subsidiaries of Y Holdings Ltd.	1,289	981	897	883	398	293	149	78
Associates and joint ventures	398	291	-	-	29	142	-	-

Sales of goods to related parties were made at the Group's usual list prices, less average discounts of 5 per cent. Purchases were made at market price discounted to reflect the quantity of goods purchased and the relationships between the parties.

Directors' and executives' remuneration

Remuneration paid to directors and other members of key management during the year was as follows:

	Year ended 31/12/01	Year ended 31/12/00
	CU'000	CU'000
Salaries	10,681	9,270
Discretionary bonuses	4,153	2,769
Benefits in kind	949	863
	15,783	12,902

The remuneration of directors and key executives is decided by the remuneration committee having regard to comparable market statistics.

Note: IAS 24 does not specifically require the disclosure of the remuneration of directors and key management. The Standard acknowledges that disclosures will generally be specified by local laws or stock exchange regulations. However, if there are no such local requirements, the payment of such remuneration constitutes a transaction between the enterprise and a related party and, as such, is prima facie disclosable.

In addition to the above, X Holdings Limited performed certain administrative services for the Company, for which a management fee of CU0.18 million (2000: CU0.16 million) was charged, being an appropriate allocation of costs incurred by relevant administrative departments.

The convertible loan notes issued during the period are secured by a personal guarantee of one of the directors. No charge has been made for this guarantee.

Source	Checklist	INTERNATIONAL GAAP HOLDINGS LIMITED

REPORT OF THE AUDITORS

(APPROPRIATE ADDRESSEE)

We have audited the accompanying balance sheet of International GAAP Holdings Limited as of 31 December 2001 and the related statements of income, cash flows and changes in equity for the year then ended. These financial statements are the responsibility of the Group's management. Our responsibility is to express an opinion on these financial statements based on our audit.

We conducted our audit in accordance with International Standards on Auditing. Those Standards require that we plan and perform the audit to obtain reasonable assurance about whether the financial statements are free of material misstatement. An audit includes examining, on a test basis, evidence supporting the amounts and disclosures in the financial statements. An audit also includes assessing the accounting principles used and significant estimates made by the management, as well as evaluating the overall financial statement presentation. We believe that our audit provides a reasonable basis for our opinion.

In our opinion, the financial statements present fairly, in all material respects, the financial position of the Group as of 31 December 2001 and the results of its operations and its cash flows for the year then ended, in accordance with International Accounting Standards.

Deloitte Touche Tohmatsu
15 March 2002

Note: The audit of the financial statements may be conducted in accordance with International Standards on Auditing (ISA) or applicable local standards. Where appropriate, reference should be made to local laws or regulations requiring financial statements to show a true and fair view. The format of the report above is as specified by ISA 700 ***The Auditor's Report on Financial Statements****. Alternatively, a format specified by the equivalent local auditing standard may be used.*

APPENDIX IV

International Accounting Standards Presentation and Disclosure Checklist

Instructions for completion of this checklist

This checklist is intended to aid the user in determining if the presentation and disclosure requirements of International Accounting Standards (IAS) have been met. It does not address the requirements of IAS as regards recognition and measurement. [References are made by IAS number, followed by the paragraph number, e.g., 8.53 refers to paragraph 53 of IAS 8. For those Standards revised since their original issue, the year of the most recent revision is also noted, e.g., 14(r1997).55 refers to paragraph 55 of IAS 14 (Revised 1997).]

The checklist addresses the presentation and disclosure requirements of IAS in issue at 31 July 2001.

All items in Parts 1 to 8 of the checklist are of general application. Sections 9 to 12 address additional disclosures in general purpose financial statements for banks and similar financial institutions, enterprises reporting the effects of changing prices, enterprises reporting in the currency of a hyperinflationary economy, and enterprises engaging in agricultural activity, and should be completed where applicable.

The checklist does not include the presentation and disclosure requirements of IAS 34 *Interim Financial Reporting* or IAS 26 *Accounting and Reporting by Retirement Benefit Plans.*

Contents

Section 1 Information accompanying financial statements

Ref.	Presentation/Disclosure Requirement	Source	Y, N or N/A	W/P Ref.
	The requirements of International Accounting Standards are confined to matters dealt with in the financial statements.	1(r1997).8,9		
	However, IAS 1(r1997) encourages enterprises to present, outside the financial statements, a financial review by management which describes and explains the main features of the enterprise's financial performance and financial position, and the principal uncertainties it faces.			
	Such a report might include a review of:			
	(a) the main factors and influences determining performance, including changes in the environment in which the enterprise operates, the enterprise's response to those changes and their effect, and the enterprise's policy for investment to maintain and enhance performance, including its dividend policy;			
	(b) the enterprise's sources of funding, its policy on gearing and its risk management policies; and			
	(c) the strengths and resources of the enterprise whose value is not reflected in the balance sheet under International Accounting Standards.			
	Enterprises are also encouraged to present additional statements outside the financial statements, such as environmental reports and value added statements, if management believes they will assist users in making economic decisions.			
	Where the enterprise has significant dealings in financial instruments, IAS 32 *Financial Instruments: Disclosure and Presentation* suggests that a discussion of management's policies for controlling the risks associated with such instruments would be helpful. Matters to be addressed might include policies on matters such as hedging of risk exposure, avoidance of undue concentrations of risk and requirements for collateral to mitigate credit risks.	32(r1998).42		

Section 2 General principles of presentation

Ref.	Presentation/Disclosure Requirement	Source	Y, N or N/A	W/P Ref.
	COMPONENTS OF FINANCIAL STATEMENTS			
2001	The financial statements should include the following components: (a) balance sheet; (b) income statement; (c) a statement showing either: (i) all changes in equity; or (ii) changes in equity other than those arising from capital transactions with owners and distributions to owners; (d) cash flow statement; and (e) accounting policies and explanatory notes.	1(r1997).7		
	FAIR PRESENTATION AND COMPLIANCE WITH IAS			
2002	The financial statements should present fairly the financial position, financial performance and cash flows of the enterprise.	1(r1997).10		
2003	The financial statements should disclose the fact that they comply with International Accounting Standards. *Notes:* 1. *Financial statements should not be described as complying with IAS unless they comply with all of the requirements of each applicable Standard and each applicable Interpretation of the Standing Interpretations Committee.* 2. *A particular exemption is permitted in respect of IAS 15* ***Information Reflecting the Effects of Changing Prices****. Arising from the failure to reach international consensus on the disclosure of information reflecting the effects of changing prices, the IASC has determined that enterprises need not disclose the information required by IAS 15 in order that their financial statements conform with IAS.* 3. *First-time application of IAS:* *In the period when IAS are applied in full for the first time as the primary accounting basis, the*	1(r1997).11		

Ref.	Presentation/Disclosure Requirement	Source	Y, N or N/A	W/P Ref.
	financial statements of an enterprise should be prepared and presented as if the financial statements had always been prepared in accordance with the Standards and Interpretations effective for the period of first-time application. Therefore, the Standards and Interpretations effective for the period of first-time application should be applied retrospectively, except when: *(a) individual Standards or Interpretations require or permit a different transitional treatment; or* *(b) the amount of the adjustment relating to prior periods cannot be reasonably determined.* *Comparative information should be prepared and presented in accordance with IAS.* *Any adjustment resulting from the transition to IAS should be treated as an adjustment to the opening balance of retained earnings of the earliest period presented in accordance with IAS.* *When IAS are applied in full as the primary accounting basis for the first time, an enterprise should apply the transitional provisions of the effective Standards and Interpretations only for periods ending on the date prescribed in the respective Standards and Interpretations.* ***[SIC-8]***			
2004	In the period when IAS are applied in full for the first time as the primary accounting basis, the enterprise should disclose: (a) where the amount of the adjustment to the opening balance of retained earnings cannot be reasonably determined, that fact; (b) where it is impracticable to provide comparative information, that fact; and (c) for each IAS that permits a choice of transitional accounting policies, the policy selected.	SIC-8.7		

Ref.	Presentation/Disclosure Requirement	Source	Y, N or N/A	W/P Ref.
	Note: ***Enterprises are also encouraged to disclose, in connection with the disclosures required by item 2003 above, the fact that IAS are being applied in full for the first time. [SIC-8.8]***			
2005	In the extremely rare circumstances where management concludes that compliance with a Standard would be misleading, and therefore that departure is necessary to achieve a fair presentation, the following information should be disclosed: (a) the fact that management has concluded that the financial statements fairly present the enterprise's financial position, financial performance and cash flows; (b) that applicable Standards have been complied with in all material respects, except for a departure from a Standard in order to achieve a fair presentation; (i) the Standard from which the enterprise has departed; (ii) the nature of the departure (including the treatment that the Standard would require); (iii) the reason why that treatment would be misleading in the circumstances; and (iv) the treatment adopted; and (d) the financial impact of the departure on the enterprise's net profit or loss, assets, liabilities, equity and cash flows for each period presented.	1(r1997).13		
2006	When, in accordance with the specific requirements in that Standard, an IAS is applied before its effective date, that fact should be disclosed.	1(r1997).19		
	GOING CONCERN			
2007	When management is aware, in making its assessment of the enterprise's ability to continue as a going concern, of any material uncertainties related to events or conditions which may cast significant doubt upon the enterprise's ability to continue as a going concern, those uncertainties should be disclosed.	1(r1997).23		

Ref.	Presentation/Disclosure Requirement	Source	Y, N or N/A	W/P Ref.
2008	When the financial statements are not prepared on a going concern basis, that fact should be disclosed, together with the basis on which the financial statements are prepared and the reason why the enterprise is not considered to be a going concern.	1(r1997).23		
	CONSISTENCY OF PRESENTATION			
2009	The presentation and classification of items in the financial statements should be retained from one period to the next, unless: (a) a significant change in the nature of the operations of the enterprise or a review of its financial statements presentation demonstrates that the change will result in a more appropriate presentation of events or transactions; or (b) a change in presentation is required by an IAS or by an Interpretation of the Standing Interpretations Committee.	1(r1997).27		
	MATERIALITY, AGGREGATION AND OFFSETTING			
2010	Each material item should be presented separately in the financial statements.	1(r1997).29		
2011	Immaterial items should be aggregated with amounts of a similar nature or function and need not be presented separately.	1(r1997).29		
2012	Assets and liabilities should not be offset except when offsetting is required or permitted by another IAS.	1(r1997).33		
2013	Items of income and expense should be offset when, and only when: (a) an IAS requires or permits it; or (b) immaterial gains, losses and related expenses arising from the same or similar transactions and events are aggregated.	1(r1997).34		

Ref.	Presentation/Disclosure Requirement	Source	Y, N or N/A	W/P Ref.
	COMPARATIVE INFORMATION			
2014	Unless an IAS permits or requires otherwise, comparative information should be disclosed in respect of the previous period for all numerical information in the financial statements.	1(r1997).38		
2015	Comparative information should be included for narrative and descriptive information when it is relevant to an understanding of the current year's financial statements.	1(r1997).38		
2016	When the presentation or classification of items in the financial statements is amended: (a) comparative amounts should be reclassified, unless it is impracticable to do so; (b) the nature, amount of, and reason for, any reclassification should be disclosed; and (c) when it is not practicable to reclassify comparative amounts, the enterprise should disclose the reason for not doing so, as well as the nature of the changes that would have been made if amounts were reclassified.	1(r1997).40		
	STRUCTURE AND CONTENT			
2017	The financial statements should be clearly identified and distinguished from other information in the same published document.	1(r1997).44		
2018	Each component of the financial statements should be clearly identified.	1(r1997).46		
2019	The following information should be prominently displayed, and repeated when it is necessary for a proper understanding of the information presented: (a) the name of the reporting enterprise or other means of identification; (b) whether the financial statements cover the individual enterprise or a group of enterprises; (c) the balance sheet date or the period covered by the financial statements, whichever is appropriate to the related component of the financial statements; (d) the reporting currency; and	1(r1997).46		

Ref.	Presentation/Disclosure Requirement	Source	Y, N or N/A	W/P Ref.
	(e) the level of precision used in the presentation of figures (e.g., in thousands or millions of units of the reporting currency).			
2020	When, in exceptional circumstances, the balance sheet date changes and annual financial statements are presented for a period longer or shorter than one year, the enterprise should disclose: (a) the period covered by the financial statements; (b) the reason for a period other than one year being used; and (c) the fact that comparative amounts for the income statement, changes in equity, cash flows and related notes are not comparable.	1(r1997).49		

Section 3 Income statement

Ref.	Presentation/Disclosure Requirement	Source	Y, N or N/A	W/P Ref.
	CONTENTS – GENERAL			
3001	All items of income and expense recognised in the period should be included in the determination of the net profit and loss for the period, unless an IAS requires or permits otherwise.	8(r1993).7		
3002	As a minimum, the face of the income statement should include line items which present the following amounts: (a) revenue; (b) the results of operating activities; (c) finance costs; (d) share of profits and losses of associates and joint ventures accounted for using the equity method; (e) tax expense/income tax related to profit or loss from ordinary activities; (f) profit or loss from ordinary activities; (g) extraordinary items; (h) minority interest; and (i) net profit or loss for the period.	1(r1997).75 8(r1993).10 12(r2000).77 27.26		
3003	Additional line items, headings and subtotals should be presented on the face of the income statement when required by an IAS, or when such presentation is necessary to present fairly the enterprise's financial performance.	1(r1997).75		
3004	In respect of discontinuing operations, the amount of the pre-tax gain or loss recognised on the disposal of assets or settlement of liabilities attributable to a discontinuing operation should be disclosed on the face of the income statement.	35.39		
3005	The investor's share of the profits or losses of associates accounted for using the equity method should be disclosed as a separate item in the income statement.	28(r2000).28		
	ANALYSIS OF EXPENSES			
3006	The financial statements should present, either on the face of the income statement or in the notes to	1(r1997).77		

Ref.	Presentation/Disclosure Requirement	Source	Y, N or N/A	W/P Ref.
	the income statement, an analysis of expenses using a classification based on either the nature of the expenses (staff costs, depreciation, etc.) or their function within the enterprise (cost of sales, distribution costs, administrative expenses, etc.).			
3007	When expenses are classified by function, additional information should be disclosed on the nature of expenses, including depreciation and amortisation expense and staff costs.	1(r1997).83		
	EARNINGS PER SHARE			
	Note: IAS 33 *Earnings Per Share* applies to enterprises whose ordinary shares or potential ordinary shares are publicly traded, to enterprises in the process of issuing ordinary shares or potential ordinary shares in public securities markets, and to any other enterprise which discloses earnings per share. When both parent and consolidated financial statements are presented, earnings per share information need be presented only on the basis of consolidated information.			
3008	Basic and diluted earnings/(loss) per share should be presented on the face of the income statement (with equal prominence for all periods presented) for each class of ordinary shares that has a different right to share in the net profit for the period.	33.47,48		
3009	The enterprise should disclose the following: (a) the amounts used as the numerators in calculating basic and diluted earnings per share, and a reconciliation of those amounts to the net profit or loss for the period; and (b) the weighted average number of ordinary shares used as the denominator in calculating basic and diluted earnings per share, and a reconciliation of those denominators to each other.	33.49		
3010	If additional per share amounts are presented: (a) where a reported component of net profit other than net profit or loss for the period	33.51		

Ref.	Presentation/Disclosure Requirement	Source	Y, N or N/A	W/P Ref.
	attributable to ordinary shareholders is used as the numerator, the per share amounts should be calculated using the weighted average number of ordinary shares determined in accordance with IAS 33; (b) where the numerator is a component of net profit which is not reported as a line item in the income statement, a reconciliation should be provided between the component used and a line item which is reported in the income statement; and (c) basic and diluted per share amounts should be presented with equal prominence.			
3011	The calculation of the basic and diluted earnings per share for all periods presented should be adjusted retrospectively for: (a) any increases in the number of shares or potential ordinary shares outstanding during the period as a result of a capitalisation or bonus issue or share split; (b) any decreases in the number of shares or potential ordinary shares outstanding during the period as a result of a reverse share split; (c) any such increases or decreases which occur after the balance sheet date but before the issue of the financial statements; (d) the effects of fundamental errors reported by adjusting the opening balance of retained earnings; (e) any adjustments resulting from changes in accounting policies which have been applied retrospectively; and (f) the effects of a business combination which is a uniting of interests.	33.43		
3012	Where applicable, the fact should be disclosed that per share calculations have been adjusted retrospectively to reflect increases/decreases in the number of ordinary or potential ordinary shares outstanding arising from capitalisation issues or share splits/reverse share splits.	33.43		

Section 4 Balance sheet

Ref.	Presentation/Disclosure Requirement	Source	Y, N or N/A	W/P Ref.
	CONTENTS – GENERAL			
4001	As a minimum, the face of the balance sheet should include line items which present the following amounts: (a) property, plant and equipment; (b) intangible assets; (c) financial assets (excluding amounts under (d), (f) and (g)); (d) investments accounted for using the equity method; (e) inventories; (f) trade and other receivables; (g) cash and cash equivalents; (h) trade and other payables; (i) tax liabilities/assets as required by IAS 12 (r2000) *Income Taxes*; (j) provisions; (k) non-current interest-bearing liabilities; (l) minority interest; and (m) issued capital and reserves.	1(r1997).66		
4002	Additional line items, headings and subtotals should be presented on the face of the balance sheet where an IAS requires it, or when such presentation is necessary to present fairly the enterprise's financial position.	1(r1997).67		
4003	An enterprise should disclose, either on the face of the balance sheet or in the notes, further sub-classifications of the line items presented, classified by the nature of the items, in a manner appropriate to the enterprise's operations.	1(r1997).72		
4004	Investments in associates accounted for using the equity method should be classified as long-term assets and disclosed as a separate item in the balance sheet.	28(r2000).28		
4005	Minority interests should be presented in the consolidated balance sheet separately from liabilities and the parent shareholders' equity.	27.26		

Ref.	Presentation/Disclosure Requirement	Source	Y, N or N/A	W/P Ref.
	CURRENT/NON-CURRENT DISTINCTION			
4006	Each enterprise should determine, based on the nature of its operations, whether or not to present current and non-current assets, and current and non-current liabilities as separate classifications on the face of the balance sheet.	1(r1997).53		
4007	Where current and non-current assets, and current and non-current liabilities, are not presented as separate classifications on the face of the balance sheet, assets and liabilities should be presented broadly in order of their liquidity.	1(r1997).53		
4008	An asset should be classified as a current asset when: (a) it is expected to be realised in, or is held for sale or consumption in, the normal course of the enterprise's operating cycle; or (b) it is held primarily for trading purposes or for the short-term, and is expected to be realised within 12 months of the balance sheet date; or (c) it is cash or a cash equivalent asset which is not restricted in its use.	1(r1997).57		
4009	All assets, other than those meeting one of the criteria outlined in 4008 above, should be classified as non-current assets.	1(r1997).57		
4010	A liability should be classified as a current liability when: (a) it is expected to be settled in the normal course of the enterprise's operating cycle; or (b) it is due to be settled within 12 months of the balance sheet date.	1(r1997).60		
4011	All liabilities, other than those meeting one of the criteria outlined in 4010 above, should be classified as non-current liabilities.	1(r1997).60		
4012	An enterprise should continue to classify its long-term interest-bearing liabilities as non-current, even when they are due to be settled within 12 months of the balance sheet date, if: (a) the original term was for a period of more than 12 months;	1(r1997).63		

Ref.	Presentation/Disclosure Requirement	Source	Y, N or N/A	W/P Ref.
	(b) it is intended to refinance the obligation on a long-term basis; and (c) that intention is supported by an agreement to refinance, or to reschedule payments, which is completed before the financial statements are authorised for issue.			
4013	The amount of any liability that has been excluded from current liabilities in accordance with item 4012 above should be disclosed in the notes to the financial statements, together with information in support of this presentation.	1(r1997).63		
4014	Irrespective of whether the enterprise presents current and non-current assets and current and non-current liabilities separately, for each asset and liability item that combines amounts expected to be recovered or settled both before and after 12 months, the enterprise should disclose the amount expected to be recovered or settled after more than 12 months.	1(r1997).54		

Section 5 Statement of changes in equity

Ref.	Presentation/Disclosure Requirement	Source	Y, N or N/A	W/P Ref.
	Note: IAS 1(r1997) acknowledges that the requirement to present a statement of changes in equity may be met in a number of ways. The approach adopted in many jurisdictions follows a columnar format which reconciles between the opening and closing balances of each element within shareholders' equity, encompassing all of the items listed at 5001 and 5002 below. An alternative is to present a separate component of the financial statements which presents only the items specified by 5001 below. Under this approach, the items described in 5002 are shown in the notes to the financial statements. Both approaches are illustrated in the appendix to IAS 1(r1997). Whichever approach is adopted, a subtotal of the items specified by 5001(b) is required, in order to enable users to derive the total gains and losses arising from the enterprise's activities during the period.			
5001	An enterprise should present, as a separate component of the financial statements, a statement showing: (a) the net profit or loss for the period; (b) each item of income and expense, gain or loss which, as required by other Standards, is recognised directly in equity, and the total of those items; and (c) the cumulative effect of changes in accounting policy and the correction of fundamental errors dealt with under the benchmark treatments of IAS 8.	1(r1997).86		
5002	The following items should be presented, either within the statement referred to in item 5001, or in the notes to the financial statements: (a) capital transactions with owners and distributions to owners; (b) the balance of accumulated profit or loss at the beginning of the period and at the balance sheet date, and movements for the period; and (c) a reconciliation between the carrying amount of each class of equity capital, share premium and each reserve at the beginning and end of	1(r1997).86		

Ref.	Presentation/Disclosure Requirement	Source	Y, N or N/A	W/P Ref.
	the period, separately disclosing each movement.			
5003	The following amounts charged or credited directly to equity should be separately disclosed (as required by specific Standards):			
	(a) the aggregate current tax relating to items that are charged or credited to equity;	12(r2000).81(a)		
	(b) the aggregate deferred tax relating to items that are charged or credited to equity;	12(r2000).81(a)		
	(c) the revaluation surplus arising on property, plant and equipment, indicating the movement for the period and any restrictions on the distribution of the balance to shareholders;	16(r1998).64(f)		
	(d) the amount of the revaluation surplus that relates to intangible assets at the beginning and end of the period, indicating the changes during the period and any restrictions on the distribution of the balance to shareholders;	38.113(b)		
	(e) the amount recognised in equity in the period for gains/losses from remeasuring available-for-sale financial assets to fair value, and the amount that was removed from equity and reported in net profit or loss for the period;	39(r2000).170		
	(f) the net exchange difference classified as equity, and a reconciliation of the amount of such exchange differences at the beginning and end of the period;	21(r1993).42(b)		
	(g) the amount of reductions to equity for treasury shares held; and	SIC-16.6		
	(h) the amount of transaction costs accounted for as a deduction from equity in the period.	SIC-17.9		

Section 6 Cash flow statement

Ref.	Presentation/Disclosure Requirement	Source	Y, N or N/A	W/P Ref.
6001	A cash flow statement should be presented as an integral part of the financial statements for each period for which financial statements are presented.	7(r1992).1		
	CLASSIFICATION OF CASH FLOWS			
6002	The cash flow statement should report cash flows during the period classified by operating, investing and financing activities.	7(r1992).10		
6003	The enterprise should report cash flows from operating activities using either: (a) the direct method, whereby major classes of gross cash receipts and gross cash payments are disclosed; or (b) the indirect method, whereby net profit or loss is adjusted for the effects of transactions of a non-cash nature, any deferrals or accruals of past or future operating cash receipts or payments, and items of income or expense associated with investing or financing cash flows.	7(r1992).18		
6004	Major classes of gross cash receipts and gross cash payments arising from investing and financing activities should be separately reported, except to the extent that they are specifically permitted by the Standard to be presented on a net basis. *Note:* The following classes of cash flow may be reported on a net basis: (a) cash flows arising from the following operating, investing or financing activities: (i) cash receipts and payments on behalf of customers when the cash flows reflect the activities of the customer rather than those of the enterprise; and (ii) receipts and payments for items in which the turnover is quick, the amounts are large, and the maturities are short; and (b) cash flows arising from each of the following activities of a financial institution:	7(r1992).21,22,24		

Ref.	Presentation/Disclosure Requirement	Source	Y, N or N/A	W/P Ref.
	(i) cash receipts and payments for the acceptance and repayment of deposits with a fixed maturity date; (ii) the placement of deposits with and withdrawal of deposits from other financial institutions; and (iii) cash advances and loans made to customers and the repayment of those advances and loans.			
	EXTRAORDINARY ITEMS			
6005	The cash flows associated with extraordinary items should be classified as arising from operating, investing or financing activities as appropriate and separately disclosed.	7(r1992).29		
	INTEREST AND DIVIDENDS			
6006	Cash flows from interest and dividends received and paid should each be disclosed separately.	7(r1992).31		
6007	Cash flows from interest and dividends received and paid should each be classified in a consistent manner from period to period as either operating, investing or financing activities.	7(r1992).31		
	TAXES ON INCOME			
6008	Cash flows arising from taxes on income should be separately disclosed.	7(r1992).35		
6009	Cash flows arising from taxes on income should be classified as cash flows from operating activities unless they can be specifically identified with financing or investing activities.	7(r1992).35		
	ACQUISITIONS AND DISPOSALS OF SUBSIDIARIES AND OTHER BUSINESS UNITS			
6010	The aggregate cash flows arising from acquisitions and from disposals of subsidiaries or other business units should be presented separately and classified as investing activities.	7(r1992).39		

Ref.	Presentation/Disclosure Requirement	Source	Y, N or N/A	W/P Ref.
6011	The following information should be disclosed, in aggregate, in respect of both acquisitions and disposals of subsidiaries or other business units during the period: (a) the total purchase or disposal consideration; (b) the portion of the purchase or disposal consideration discharged by means of cash and cash equivalents; (c) the amount of cash and cash equivalents in the subsidiary or business unit acquired or disposed of; and (d) the amount of the assets and liabilities other than cash or cash equivalents in the subsidiary or business unit acquired or disposed of, summarised by each major category.	7(r1992).40		
	NON-CASH TRANSACTIONS			
6012	Investing and financing transactions that do not require the use of cash or cash equivalents should be excluded from the cash flow statement.	7(r1992).43		
6013	Investing and financing transactions that do not require the use of cash or cash equivalents should be disclosed elsewhere in the financial statements in a manner that provides all of the relevant information about these investing and financing activities.	7(r1992).43		
	OTHER DISCLOSURES			
6014	The components of cash and cash equivalents should be disclosed.	7(r1992).45		
6015	A reconciliation should be presented of the amounts of the components of cash and cash equivalents in the cash flow statement with the equivalent items reported in the balance sheet.	7(r1992).45		
6016	The enterprise should disclose the amount of significant cash and cash equivalent balances held by the enterprise that are not available for use by the group, together with a commentary by management.	7(r1992).48		

Section 7 Accounting policies

Ref.	Presentation/Disclosure Requirement	Source	Y, N or N/A	W/P Ref.
	GENERAL REQUIREMENTS			
7001	The notes to the financial statements should present information about the basis of preparation of the financial statements and the specific accounting policies selected and applied for significant transactions and events.	1(r1997).91(a)		
7002	The accounting policies section of the notes should describe:	1(r1997).97		
	(a) the measurement bases used in preparing the financial statements; and			
	(b) each specific accounting policy that is necessary for a proper understanding of the financial statements.			
	POLICIES REQUIRED TO BE DISCLOSED BY SPECIFIC STANDARDS			
7003	The following accounting policies should be disclosed, as required by specific Standards:			
	(a) Subsidiaries			
	– in the parent's separate financial statements, the method used to account for subsidiaries.	27.32(c)		
	(b) Associates			
	– the methods used to account for investments in associates.	28(r2000).27(b)		
	(c) Goodwill			
	– the amortisation period adopted;	22(r1998).88(a)		
	– if goodwill is amortised over more than 20 years:	22(r1998).88(b)		
	(i) the justification for rebuttal of the presumption that the useful life of goodwill will not exceed 20 years from initial recognition; and			
	(ii) a description of the factor(s) that played a significant role in determining the life of goodwill;			
	– if goodwill is not amortised on a straight-line basis, the basis used and the reason why that basis is more appropriate than the straight-line basis; and	22(r1998).88(c)		
	– the line item(s) of the income statement in which the amortisation of goodwill is included.	22(r1998).88(d)		

Ref.	Presentation/Disclosure Requirement	Source	Y, N or N/A	W/P Ref.
	(d) Negative goodwill			
	– the period(s) over which negative goodwill is recognised as income; and	22(r1998).91(b)		
	– the line item(s) of the income statement in which negative goodwill is recognised as income.	22(r1998).91(c)		
	(e) Goodwill and fair value adjustments			
	– the method selected in accordance with IAS 21 (paragraph 33) (see below) to translate goodwill and fair value adjustments arising on the acquisition of a foreign entity.	21(r1993).45		
	Note: IAS 21(r1993).33 states that goodwill and fair value adjustments to the carrying amounts of assets and liabilities are treated either: (i) as assets and liabilities of the foreign entity and translated at the closing rate in accordance with IAS 21(r1993).30; or (ii) as assets and liabilities of the reporting entity which either are already expressed in the reporting currency or are non-monetary foreign currency items reported using the exchange rate at the transaction date in accordance with IAS 21(r1993).11(b).			
	(f) Revenue			
	– the accounting policies adopted for the recognition of revenue, including the methods adopted to determine the stage of completion of transactions involving the rendering of services.	18(r1993).35(a)		
	(g) Construction contracts			
	– the methods used to determine the contract revenue recognised in the period; and	11(r1993).39(b)		
	– the methods used to determine the stage of completion of contracts in progress.	11(r1993).39(c)		
	(h) Borrowing costs			
	– the accounting policy adopted for borrowing costs.	23(r1993).29(a)		
	(i) Government grants			
	– the accounting policy adopted for government grants, including the methods of presentation adopted in the financial statements.	20.39(a)		
	(j) Retirement benefit costs			
	– for defined benefit plans, the enterprise's accounting policy for recognising actuarial gains and losses.	19(r2000).120(a)		

Ref.	Presentation/Disclosure Requirement	Source	Y, N or N/A	W/P Ref.
	(k) Equity compensation plans			
	– the accounting policy for equity compensation plans.	19(r2000).147(b)		
	(l) Property, plant and equipment – for each class of asset			
	– the measurement basis used for determining the gross carrying amount;	16(r1998).60(a)		
	– the depreciation methods used;	16(r1998).60(b)		
	– the useful lives or the depreciation rates used; and	16(r1998).60(c)		
	– the accounting policy for the estimated costs of restoring the site of items of property, plant and equipment.	16(r1998).61(b)		
	(m) Investment property carried at cost less accumulated depreciation			
	– the depreciation methods used; and	40.69(a)		
	– the useful lives or the depreciation rates used.	40.69(b)		
	(n) Intangible assets – for each class of asset, distinguishing between internally-generated intangible assets and other intangible assets			
	– the useful lives or the amortisation rates used;	38.107(a)		
	– the amortisation methods used;	38.107(b)		
	– the line item(s) of the income statement in which the amortisation of intangible assets is included;	38.107(d)		
	– if an intangible asset is amortised over more than 20 years: (i) the justification for rebuttal of the presumption that the useful life of an intangible asset will not exceed 20 years from the date when the asset is available for use; and (ii) a description of the factor(s) that played a significant role in determining the useful life of the asset; and	38.111(a)		
	– for intangible assets acquired by way of a government grant and initially recognised at fair value, whether they are carried under the benchmark or the allowed alternative treatment for subsequent measurement.	38.111(c)(iii)		
	(o) Inventories			
	– the accounting policies adopted in measuring inventories, including the cost formula used.	2(r1993).34(a)		
	(p) Financial instruments			
	– the accounting policies and methods adopted for each class of financial asset, financial liability and equity instrument, both recognised and unrecognised,	32(r1998).47(b)		

Ref.	Presentation/Disclosure Requirement	Source	Y, N or N/A	W/P Ref.
	including the criteria for recognition and the basis of measurement applied;			
	– the methods and significant assumptions (separately for each significant class of financial assets) applied in estimating fair values for the financial assets and financial liabilities that are carried at fair value;	39(r2000).167(a)		
	– whether gains and losses arising from changes in the fair value of available-for-sale financial assets carried at fair value are included in net income for the period or are recognised directly in equity until the financial asset is disposed of; and	39(r2000).167(b)		
	– for each category of financial assets defined in IAS 39, whether 'regular way' purchases and sales of financial assets are accounted for at trade date or settlement date.	39(r2000).167(c)		
	CHANGES IN ACCOUNTING POLICIES			
7004	Where the benchmark treatment is adopted for changes in accounting policies, and the change in accounting policy has a material effect on the current period or any prior period presented, or may have a material effect in subsequent periods, the following should be disclosed: (a) the reasons for the change; (b) the amount of the adjustment for the current period and for each period presented; (c) the amount of the adjustment relating to periods prior to those included in the comparative information; and (d) the fact that comparative information has been restated or that it is impracticable to do so.	8(r1993).53		
7005	Where the allowed alternative treatment is adopted for changes in accounting policies, and the change in accounting policy has a material effect on the current period or any prior period presented, or may have a material effect in subsequent periods, the following should be disclosed: (a) the reasons for the change; (b) the amount of the adjustment recognised in net profit or loss in the current period;	8(r1993).54,57		

Ref.	Presentation/Disclosure Requirement	Source	Y, N or N/A	W/P Ref.
	(c) additional pro forma information prepared in accordance with the benchmark treatment; (d) the amount of the adjustment included in each period for which pro forma information is presented and the amount of the adjustment relating to periods prior to those included in the financial statements; and (e) where it is impracticable to present pro forma information, a statement of that fact.			

Section 8 Explanatory notes

Ref.	Presentation/Disclosure Requirement	Source	Y, N or N/A	W/P Ref.
	GENERAL			
8001	The following details should be disclosed in the financial statements, if they are not disclosed elsewhere in information published with the financial statements: (a) the domicile and legal form of the enterprise, its country of incorporation and registered office address (or principal place of business, if different from the registered office); (b) a description of the nature of the enterprise's operations and its principal activities; (c) the name of the parent enterprise and the ultimate parent enterprise of the group; and (d) either the number of employees at the end of the period, or the average for the period.	1(r1997).102		
8002	The notes to the financial statements should: (a) disclose the information required by IAS that is not presented elsewhere in the financial statements; and (b) provide additional information which is not presented on the face of the financial statements, but which is necessary for a fair presentation.	1(r1997).91(b),(c)		
8003	The notes to the financial statements should be presented in a systematic manner, with each item on the face of the balance sheet, income statement and cash flow statement cross-referenced to any related information in the notes.	1(r1997).92		
8004	When the measurement currency used for the purposes of preparing the financial statements is different from the currency of the country in which the enterprise is domiciled, the reason for using a different currency should be disclosed.	21(r1993).43 SIC-19.10(a)		
8005	When the financial statements are presented in a currency different from the enterprise's measurement currency, the following should be disclosed: (a) the measurement currency; (b) the reason for using a different presentation currency; and	SIC-19.10(c)		

Ref.	Presentation/Disclosure Requirement	Source	Y, N or N/A	W/P Ref.
	(c) a description of the method used in the translation process.			
8006	The reason for any change in the measurement currency or the presentation currency should be disclosed.	21(r1993).43 SIC19.10(a)		
	FUNDAMENTAL ERRORS			
8007	Where the benchmark treatment is adopted for fundamental errors, the following should be disclosed: (a) the nature of the fundamental error; (b) the amount of the correction for the current period and for each prior period presented; (c) the amount of the correction relating to periods prior to those included in the comparative information; and (d) the fact that comparative information has been restated or that it is impracticable to do so.	8(r1993).37		
8008	Where the allowed alternative treatment is adopted for fundamental errors, the following should be disclosed: (a) the nature of the fundamental error; (b) the amount of the correction recognised in net profit or loss for the current period; (c) additional pro forma information prepared in accordance with the benchmark treatment; (d) unless it is impracticable to do so, the amount of the correction included in each period for which pro forma information is presented and the amount of the correction relating to periods prior to those included in the pro forma information; and (e) where it is impracticable to present pro forma information, a statement of that fact.	8(r1993).38,40		
	CHANGES IN ACCOUNTING ESTIMATES			
8009	The effect of a change in an accounting estimate should be included in the same income statement classification as was used previously for the estimate.	8(r1993).28		

Ref.	Presentation/Disclosure Requirement	Source	Y, N or N/A	W/P Ref.
8010	The nature and, unless it is impracticable to do so, the amount of a change in accounting estimate that has a material effect in the current period, or which is expected to have a material effect in subsequent periods, should be disclosed.	8(r1993).30		
8011	If it is impracticable to quantify the amount of a change in accounting estimate that has a material effect in the current period, or which is expected to have a material effect in subsequent periods, that fact should be disclosed.	8(r1993).30		
8012	If an estimate of an amount reported in an interim period is changed significantly during the final interim period of the financial year, but a separate financial report is not issued for that final interim period, the nature and amount of that change in estimate should be disclosed in a note to the annual financial statements for that financial year.	34.26		
	SEGMENT REPORTING			
	Notes: 1. *IAS 14(r1997)* ***Segment Reporting*** *applies to enterprises whose equity or debt securities are publicly traded and to enterprises that are in the process of issuing equity or debt securities in public securities markets, and to any other enterprise which voluntarily discloses segment information.* 2. *When both parent and consolidated financial statements are presented, segment information need be presented only on the basis of the consolidated financial statements. When separate financial statements of an equity method associate or joint venture are included in the financial report of the investing enterprise, segment information need be presented only on the basis of the investing enterprise's financial statements. If any subsidiary or equity method associate or joint venture is itself an enterprise whose securities are publicly traded, it should present segment information in its own financial report.*			
8013	The following disclosures should be made for each reportable segment based on the enterprise's primary reporting format:	14(r1997).50		

Ref.	Presentation/Disclosure Requirement	Source	Y, N or N/A	W/P Ref.
	(a) segment revenue, separately distinguishing segment revenue from sales to external customers and segment revenue from transactions with other segments;	14(r1997).51		
	(b) segment result;	14(r1997).52		
	(c) total carrying amount of segment assets;	14(r1997).55		
	(d) segment liabilities;	14(r1997).56		
	(e) total cost incurred during the period to acquire segment assets that are expected to be used during more than one period (property, plant, equipment and intangible assets); *Note:* *This information should be presented on an accrual basis, not a cash basis.*	14(r1997).57		
	(f) total amount of expense included in segment results for depreciation and amortisation of segment assets for the period;	14(r1997).58		
	(g) total amount of significant non-cash expenses, other than depreciation and amortisation, that are included in segment expense and, therefore, deducted in measuring segment result;	14(r1997).61		
	(h) the aggregate of the enterprise's share of the net profit or loss of associates, joint ventures, or other investments accounted for under the equity method if substantially all of those operations are within that single segment; and	14(r1997).64		
	(i) where the group's share of results of associates and joint ventures is disclosed under (h) above, the aggregate investments in those associates and joint ventures.	14(r1997).66		
	Notes: *1. Enterprises are encouraged, but not required, to disclose the nature and amount of any items of segment revenue and segment expense that are of such size, nature or incidence that their disclosure is relevant to explain the performance of each reportable segment for the period.*	14(r1997).59		
	2. An enterprise that provides the segment cash flow disclosures that are encouraged by IAS 7 (r1992) need not also disclose depreciation and amortisation expenses or non-cash expenses pursuant to (f) and (g) above.	14(r1997).63		
8014	The enterprise should disclose the following for each reportable segment based on its primary format:	36.116		

Ref.	Presentation/Disclosure Requirement	Source	Y, N or N/A	W/P Ref.
	(a) the amount of impairment losses recognised in the income statement and directly in equity during the period; and (b) the amount of reversals of impairment losses recognised in the income statement and directly in equity during the period.			
8015	The enterprise should present a reconciliation between the information disclosed for reportable segments and the aggregated information in the consolidated or enterprise financial statements, including: (a) segment revenue reconciled to enterprise revenue from external customers (including disclosure of the amount of enterprise revenue from external customers not included in any segment's revenue); (b) segment result reconciled to a comparable measure of enterprise operating profit or loss as well as to enterprise net profit or loss; (c) segment assets reconciled to enterprise assets; and (d) segment liabilities reconciled to enterprise liabilities.	14(r1997).67		
8016	If the enterprise's primary format for reporting segment information is business segments, it should also report the following information: (a) segment revenue from external customers, by geographical area, based on the geographical location of its customers, for each geographical segment whose revenue from sales to external customers is 10 per cent or more of total enterprise revenue from sales to all external customers; (b) the total carrying amount of segment assets, by geographical location of assets, for each geographical segment whose segment assets are 10 per cent or more of the total assets of all geographical segments; and (c) the total cost incurred during the period to acquire segment assets that are expected to be used during more than one period (property, plant, equipment and intangible assets), by geographical location of assets, for each geographical segment whose segment assets are	14(r1997).69		

Ref.	Presentation/Disclosure Requirement	Source	Y, N or N/A	W/P Ref.
	10 per cent or more of the total assets of all geographical segments.			
8017	If the enterprise's primary format for reporting segment information is geographical segments (whether based on location of assets or location of customers), it should also report the following segment information for each business segment whose revenue from sales to external customers is 10 per cent or more of total enterprise revenue from sales to all external customers or whose segment assets are 10 per cent or more of the total assets of all business segments: (a) segment revenue from external customers; (b) the total carrying amount of segment assets; and (c) the total cost incurred during the period to acquire segment assets that are expected to be used during more than one period (property, plant, equipment, and intangible assets).	14(r1997).70		
8018	If the enterprise's primary format for reporting segment information is geographical segments that are based on location of assets, and if the location of its customers is different from the location of its assets, then it should also report revenue from sales to external customers for each customer-based geographical segment whose revenue from sales to external customers is 10 per cent or more of total enterprise revenue from sales to all external customers.	14(r1997).71		
8019	If the enterprise's primary format for reporting segment information is geographical segments that are based on location of customers, and if the enterprise's assets are located in different geographical areas from its customers, then it should also report the following segment information for each asset-based geographical segment whose revenue from sales to external customers or segment assets are 10 per cent or more of related consolidated or total enterprise amounts: (a) the total carrying amount of segment assets by geographical location of the assets; and (b) the total cost incurred during the period to acquire segment assets that are expected to be	14(r1997).72		

Ref.	Presentation/Disclosure Requirement	Source	Y,N or N/A	W/P Ref.
	used during more than one period (property, plant, equipment and intangible assets) by location of the assets.			
8020	If a business segment or geographical segment for which information is reported to the board of directors and chief executive officer is not a reportable segment because it earns a majority of its revenue from sales to other segments, but nonetheless its revenue from sales to external customers is 10 per cent or more of total enterprise revenue from sales to all external customers, the enterprise should disclose: (a) the fact that these circumstances exist; (b) the amount of revenue from sales to external customers; and (c) the amount of revenue from internal sales to other segments.	14(r1997).74		
8021	For inter-segment transfers: (a) segment revenue from transactions with other segments should be measured and reported on the basis actually used to price those transfers; and (b) the basis of pricing inter-segment transfers and any change therein should be disclosed.	14(r1997).75		
8022	Where changes in accounting policies are adopted for segment reporting that have a material effect on segment information: (a) prior period segment information presented for comparative purposes should be restated unless it is impracticable to do so; and (b) details of the change should be disclosed, including: (i) a description of the nature of the change; (ii) the reasons for the change; (iii) the fact that comparative information has been restated or that it is impracticable to do so; and (iv) the financial effect of the change, if it is reasonably determinable.	14(r1997).76		
8023	If the enterprise changes the identification of its segments and it does not restate prior period	14(r1997).76		

Ref.	Presentation/Disclosure Requirement	Source	Y, N or N/A	W/P Ref.
	segment information on the new basis because it is impracticable to do so then, for the purpose of comparison, the enterprise should report segment data for both the old and the new bases of segmentation in the year in which it changes the identification of its segments.			
8024	If not otherwise disclosed in the financial statements or elsewhere in the financial report, the enterprise should indicate, for both primary and secondary segments: (a) the types of products and services included in each reported business segment; and (b) the composition of each reported geographical segment.	14(r1997).81		
8025	If the enterprise applies IAS 14(r1997) for an accounting period commencing before 1 July 1998 (its effective date), that fact should be disclosed.	14(r1997).84		
8026	If the financial statements include comparative information for periods prior to the effective date or earlier voluntary adoption of IAS 14(r1997), the comparative segment data should be restated to conform to the requirements of IAS 14(r1997), unless it is not practicable to do so.	14(r1997).84		
8027	Where it is not practicable to restate comparative segment data as required under item 8026, that fact should be disclosed.	14(r1997).84		
	REVENUE			
8028	The following items should be disclosed:			
	(a) the amount of each significant category of revenue recognised during the period including revenue arising from: (i) the sale of goods; (ii) the rendering of services; (iii) interest; (iv) royalties; and (v) dividends;	18(r1993).35(b)		
	(b) the amount of revenue arising from exchanges of goods or services in each significant category of revenue.	18(r1993).35(c)		

Ref.	Presentation/Disclosure Requirement	Source	Y, N or N/A	W/P Ref.
8029	The enterprise should disclose the amount of revenue arising on construction contracts recognised as revenue in the period.	11(r1993).39(a)		
	DISCONTINUING OPERATIONS			
8030	The following information should be disclosed relating to a discontinuing operation, beginning with the financial statements for the period in which the initial disclosure event occurs: (a) a description of the discontinuing operation; (b) the business or geographical segment(s) in which it is reported in accordance with IAS 14 (r1997) *Segment Reporting*; (c) the date and nature of the initial disclosure event; (d) if known or determinable, the date or period in which the discontinuance is expected to be completed; (e) the carrying amounts, as of the balance sheet date, of the total assets and the total liabilities to be disposed of; (f) the amounts of revenue, expenses and pre-tax profit or loss from ordinary activities attributable to the discontinuing operation during the current financial reporting period, and the income tax expense relating thereto; and (g) the amounts of net cash flows attributable to the operating, investing and financing activities of the discontinuing operation during the current financial reporting period.	35.27		
8031	Where an initial disclosure event has occurred after the end of the enterprise's financial reporting period, but before the financial statements for that period are authorised for issue, the financial statements should include the disclosures specified in item 8030 above for the period covered by those financial statements.	35.29		
8032	If the enterprise has disposed of assets or settled liabilities attributable to a discontinuing operation or entered into binding agreements for the sale of such assets or the settlement of such liabilities, the following information should be included in the financial statements when the events occur:	35.31		

Ref.	Presentation/Disclosure Requirement	Source	Y, N or N/A	W/P Ref.
	(a) for any gain or loss that is recognised on the disposal of assets or settlement of liabilities attributable to the discontinuing operation: (i) the amount of the pre-tax gain or loss; and (ii) the income tax expense relating to the gain or loss; and (b) for those net assets for which the enterprise has entered into one or more binding sale agreements: (i) the net selling price or range of prices (which is after deducting the expected disposal costs); (ii) the expected timing of receipt of those cash flows; and (iii) the carrying amount of those net assets.			
8033	In addition to the disclosures specified in items 8030 and 8032, the enterprise should include in its financial statements, for periods subsequent to the one in which the initial disclosure event occurs, a description of any significant changes in the amount or timing of cash flows relating to the assets and liabilities to be disposed of or settled and the events causing those changes.	35.33		
8034	The disclosures required by items 8030 to 8033 should be continued in financial statements for periods up to and including the period in which the discontinuance is completed.	35.35		
8035	Where the enterprise abandons or withdraws from a plan that was previously reported as a discontinuing operation, that fact and its effect should be disclosed.	35.36		
8036	The specified disclosures should be presented separately for each discontinuing operation.	35.38		
8037	The disclosures specified in respect of discontinuing operations should be presented either in the notes to the financial statements or on the face of the financial statements [other than item 8032(a)(i) above, which is required to be presented on the face of the income statement].	35.39		
8038	Any income or expense relating to a discontinuing operation should be presented within ordinary activities and not as an extraordinary item.	35.41		

Ref.	Presentation/Disclosure Requirement	Source	Y, N or N/A	W/P Ref.
8039	The use of the term 'discontinuing operation' should be restricted to restructurings, transactions and events that meet the definition of a discontinuing operation under IAS 35.	35.43		
8040	Comparative information for prior periods that is presented in financial statements prepared after the initial disclosure event, should be restated to segregate continuing and discontinuing assets, liabilities, income, expenses and cash flows.	35.45		
	INCOME FROM INVESTMENT PROPERTY			
8041	The enterprise should disclose amounts included in the income statement for: (a) rental income from investment property; (b) direct operating expenses (including repairs and maintenance) arising from investment property that generated rental income during the period; and (c) direct operating expenses (including repairs and maintenance) arising from investment property that did not generate rental income during the period.	40.66(d)		
	OTHER ITEMS OF INCOME AND EXPENDITURE			
	Research and development costs			
8042	The financial statements should disclose the aggregate amount of research and development expenditure recognised as an expense during the period.	38.115		
	Exchange differences			
8043	The following should be disclosed: (a) the amount of exchange differences included in the net profit or loss for the period; and (b) the amount of exchange differences arising during the period that are included in the carrying amount of an asset in accordance with the allowed alternative treatment permitted under IAS 21(r1993).21.	21(r1993).42(a),(c)		

Ref.	Presentation/Disclosure Requirement	Source	Y, N or N/A	W/P Ref.
8044	On the first occasion that an enterprise applies IAS 21 (r1993), except where the amount is not reasonably determinable, the enterprise should classify separately and disclose the cumulative balance, at the beginning of the period, of exchange differences deferred and classified as equity in previous periods.	21(r1993).48		
	Costs of inventories			
8045	The financial statements should disclose either: (a) the cost of inventories recognised as an expense during the period; or (b) the operating costs, applicable to revenues, recognised as an expense during the period, classified by their nature.	2(r1993).37		
	Borrowing costs			
8046	The following should be disclosed: (a) the amount of borrowing costs added to the cost of qualifying assets during the period; and (b) the rate used to determine the amount of borrowing costs eligible for such treatment.	23(r1993).29(b),(c)		
	Compensation received			
8047	Monetary or non-monetary compensation received for the impairment or loss of items of property, plant and equipment should be disclosed separately.	SIC-14.5		
	TAXATION			
8048	The major components of tax expense/income should be separately disclosed.	12(r2000).79		
8049	An explanation should be provided of the relationship between the tax expense/income and the accounting profit in either or both of the following forms: (a) a numerical reconciliation between the tax expense/income and the product of accounting profit multiplied by the applicable tax rate, disclosing also the basis on which the applicable tax rate is computed; and/or (b) a numerical reconciliation between the average effective tax rate and the applicable tax rate, disclosing also the basis on which the applicable tax rate is computed.	12(r2000).81(c)		

Ref.	Presentation/Disclosure Requirement	Source	Y, N or N/A	W/P Ref.
8050	The following should be disclosed:			
	(a) an explanation of changes in the applicable tax rate compared to the previous accounting period; and	12(r2000).81(d)		
	(b) in respect of discontinuing operations, the tax expense relating to: (i) the gain or loss on discontinuance; and (ii) the profit or loss from the ordinary activities of the discontinuing operation for the period, together with the corresponding amounts for each prior period presented.	12(r2000).81(h)		
8051	For each type of temporary difference, and each type of unused tax losses and unused tax credits, the enterprise should disclose the amount of the deferred tax income or expense recognised in the income statement, where not readily apparent from the changes in the amounts recognised in the balance sheet.	12(r2000).81(g)		
8052	If IAS 12(r1996) *Income Taxes* is applied for financial statements covering periods beginning before 1 January 1998 (its effective date), that fact should be disclosed.	12(r2000).89		
8053	Specific amendments to IAS 12 become operative for annual financial statements covering periods beginning on or after 1 January 2001. If earlier adoption of these amendments affects the financial statements, that fact should be disclosed.	12(r2000).91		
	EXTRAORDINARY ITEMS			
8054	The following should be disclosed separately for extraordinary items:			
	(a) the nature and amount of each item; and	8(r1993).11		
	(b) the tax expense/income relating to extraordinary items recognised during the period.	12(r2000).81(b)		

Ref.	Presentation/Disclosure Requirement	Source	Y, N or N/A	W/P Ref.
	OTHER UNUSUAL ITEMS			
8055	Where items of income and expense within profit or loss from ordinary activities are of such size, nature or incidence that their disclosure is relevant to explain the performance of the enterprise for the period, the nature and amount of such items should be disclosed separately.	8(r1993).16		
	DIVIDENDS			
8056	The enterprise should disclose, either on the face of the income statement or in the notes, the amount of dividends per share, declared or proposed, for the period covered by the financial statements.	1(r1997).85		
8057	The enterprise should disclose the amount of dividends that were proposed or declared after the balance sheet date but before the financial statements were authorised for issue.	1(r1997).74(c)		
8058	The enterprise should disclose the amount of the income tax consequences of dividends to shareholders of the enterprise that were proposed or declared before the financial statements were authorised for issue, but are not recognised as a liability in the financial statements.	12(r2000).81(i)		
8059	The enterprise should disclose the amount of any cumulative preference dividends not recognised.	1(r1997).74(d)		
	PROPERTY, PLANT AND EQUIPMENT			
8060	Items classified as property, plant and equipment in the financial statements should be limited to tangible assets that are both: (a) held by an enterprise for use in the production or supply of goods or services, for rental to others, or for administrative purposes; and (b) expected to be used during more than one period.	16(r1998).6		
8061	The following information should be disclosed for each class of property, plant and equipment:			

Ref.	Presentation/Disclosure Requirement	Source	Y, N or N/A	W/P Ref.
	(a) when more than one measurement basis has been used, the gross carrying amount included for each measurement basis in each category;	16(r1998).60(a)		
	(b) the gross carrying amount and the accumulated depreciation (aggregated with accumulated impairment losses) at the beginning and end of the period; and	16(r1998).60(d)		
	(c) a reconciliation of the carrying amount at the beginning and end of the period showing: (i) additions; (ii) disposals; (iii) acquisitions through business combinations; (iv) increases or decreases during the period resulting from revaluations and from impairment losses recognised or reversed directly in equity (if any); (v) impairment losses recognised in the income statement during the period (if any); (vi) impairment losses reversed in the income statement during the period (if any); (vii) depreciation; (viii) the net exchange differences arising on the translation of the financial statements of a foreign entity; and (ix) other movements.	16(r1998).60(e)		
	Note: ***Comparative information is not required for the reconciliation required by item 8061(c).***			
8062	The financial statements should also disclose the following information:			
	(a) the existence and amounts of restrictions on title, and property, plant and equipment pledged as security for liabilities; and	16(r1998).61(a)		
	(b) the amount of expenditure on account of property, plant and equipment in the course of construction.	16(r1998).61(c)		
8063	When items of property, plant and equipment are stated at revalued amounts, the following additional information should be disclosed:	16(r1998).64		
	(a) the basis used to revalue the assets; (b) the effective date of the revaluation;			

Ref.	Presentation/Disclosure Requirement	Source	Y, N or N/A	W/P Ref.
	(c) whether an independent valuer was involved; (d) the nature of any indices used to determine replacement cost; and (e) the carrying amount of each class of property, plant and equipment that would have been included in the financial statements had the assets been carried under the benchmark treatment.			
	INVESTMENT PROPERTY			
8064	Assets classified as investment property in the financial statements should be limited to property held to earn rentals, or for capital appreciation, or both, rather than for: (a) use in the production or supply of goods or services or for administrative purposes; or (b) sale in the ordinary course of business.	40.4		
	Note: *The disclosures set out below are in addition to those in IAS 17(r1997). Under IAS 17(r1997), the owner of an investment property gives a lessor's disclosures about operating leases. Under IAS 17(r1997), an enterprise that holds an investment property under a finance lease gives a lessee's disclosures about that finance lease and a lessor's disclosure about any operating leases that the enterprise has granted*	40.65		
	Disclosures for all investment property			
8065	When the determination of the appropriate classification for property is difficult, the financial statements should disclose the criteria developed by the enterprise to distinguish investment property from owner-occupied property and property held for sale in the ordinary course of business.	40.66(a)		
8066	(a) The enterprise should disclose the methods and significant assumptions applied in determining the fair value of investment property.	40.66(b)		
	(b) The disclosures under 8066(a) should include a statement as to whether the determination of fair value was supported by market evidence or was more heavily based on other factors (which the enterprise should disclose) because of the	40.66(b)		

Ref.	Presentation/Disclosure Requirement	Source	Y, N or N/A	W/P Ref.
	nature of the property and lack of comparable market data.			
	(c) The extent to which the fair value of investment property (as disclosed in the financial statements) is based on a valuation by an independent valuer who holds a recognised qualification and who has recent experience in the location and category of the investment property being valued.	40.66(c)		
	(d) If there has been no valuation by an independent valuer, as described in the previous paragraph that fact should be disclosed.	40.66(c)		
8067	The enterprise should disclose the existence and amount of restrictions on the realisability of investment property or the remittance of income and proceeds of disposal.	40.66(e)		
	Fair value model			
8068	In addition to the disclosure required by items 8065 to 8067 above, an enterprise that applies the fair value model in accounting for its investment property should also disclose a reconciliation of the carrying amount of investment property at the beginning and end of the period showing the following: (a) additions, disclosing separately those additions resulting from acquisitions and those resulting from capitalised subsequent expenditure; (b) additions resulting from acquisitions through business combinations; (c) disposals; (d) net gains or losses from fair value adjustments; (e) the net exchange differences arising on the translation of the financial statements of a foreign entity; (f) transfers to and from inventories and owner-occupied property; and (g) other movements. *Note:* *Comparative information need not be provided for the reconciliation specified in item 8068.*	40.67		
8069	(a) In the exceptional circumstances when an enterprise measures investment property using the benchmark treatment in IAS 16 *Property,*	40.68		

Ref.	Presentation/Disclosure Requirement	Source	Y, N or N/A	W/P Ref.
	Plant and Equipment (because of the lack of a reliable fair value) the reconciliation required by item 8068 above should disclose amounts relating to that investment property separately from amounts relating to other investment property.			
	(b) In addition, the enterprise should disclose: (i) a description of the investment property; (ii) an explanation of why fair value cannot be reliably measured; (iii) if possible, the range of estimates within which fair value is highly likely to lie; and (iv) on disposal of investment property not carried of fair value: – the fact that the enterprise has disposed of investment property not carried at fair value; – the carrying amount of that investment property at the time of sale; and – the amount of the gain or loss recognised.	40.68		
	Cost model			
8070	In addition to the disclosure required by items 8065 to 8067 above, an enterprise that applies the cost model in accounting for its investment property should also disclose: (a) the gross carrying amount and the accumulated depreciation (aggregated with accumulated impairment losses) at the beginning and end of the period; and (b) a reconciliation of the carrying amount of investment property at the beginning and end of the period showing the following: (i) additions, disclosing separately those additions resulting from acquisitions and those resulting from capitalised subsequent expenditure; (ii) additions resulting from acquisitions through business combinations; (iii) disposals; (iv) depreciation; (v) the amount of impairment losses recognised, and the amount of impairment losses reversed, during the	40.69		

Ref.	Presentation/Disclosure Requirement	Source	Y, N or N/A	W/P Ref.
	period under IAS 36 *Impairment of Assets*; (vi) the net exchange differences arising on the translation of the financial statements of a foreign entity; (vii) transfers to and from inventories and owner-occupied property; and (viii) other movements. *Note:* ***Comparative information need not be provided for the reconciliation specified in item 8070(b).***			
8071	Enterprises using the cost model should disclose the fair value of investment property. In the exceptional circumstances when an enterprise cannot determine the fair value of the investment property reliably, the enterprise should disclose: (a) a description of the investment property; (b) an explanation of why fair value cannot be determined reliably; and (c) if possible, the range of estimates within which fair value is highly likely to lie.	40.69(e)		
	Transitional provision			
8072	Under the fair value model, an enterprise should report the effect of adopting IAS 40 on its effective date (or earlier) as an adjustment to the opening balance of retained earnings for the period in which IAS 40 is first adopted. In addition: (a) if the enterprise has previously disclosed publicly (in financial statements or otherwise) the fair value of its investment property in earlier periods (determined on a basis that satisfies the definition of fair value in IAS 40.4 and the guidance in IAS 40.29 to 46), the enterprise is encouraged, but not required, to: (i) adjust the opening balance of retained earnings for the earliest period presented for which such fair value was disclosed publicly; and (ii) restate comparative information for those periods; and (b) if the enterprise has not previously disclosed publicly the information described in item 8072(a), the enterprise should not restate	40.70		

Ref.	Presentation/Disclosure Requirement	Source	Y, N or N/A	W/P Ref.
	comparative information and should disclose that fact.			
	Effective date			
8073	Where IAS 40 is applied for periods beginning before 1 January 2001, its effective date, that fact should be disclosed.	40.74		
	GOODWILL			
8074	The financial statements should provide a reconciliation of the carrying amount of goodwill at the beginning and end of the period showing: (a) the gross amount and the accumulated amortisation (aggregated with accumulated impairment losses) at the beginning of the period; (b) any additional goodwill recognised during the period; (c) any adjustments resulting from subsequent identification or changes in value of identifiable assets and liabilities; (d) any goodwill derecognised on the disposal of all or part of the business to which it relates during the period; (e) amortisation recognised during the period; (f) impairment losses recognised during the period under IAS 36 *Impairment of Assets* (if any); (g) impairment losses reversed during the period under IAS 36 *Impairment of Assets* (if any); (h) other changes in the carrying amount of goodwill during the period (if any); and (i) the gross amount and the accumulated amortisation (aggregated with accumulated impairment losses), at the end of the period.	22(r1998).88(e)		
	Note: *Comparative information need not be provided for the reconciliation specified in item 8074.*			
	NEGATIVE GOODWILL			
8075	Negative goodwill should be presented as a deduction from the assets of the reporting enterprise, in the same balance sheet classification as goodwill.	22(r1998).64		

Ref.	Presentation/Disclosure Requirement	Source	Y, N or N/A	W/P Ref.
8076	To the extent that negative goodwill is accounted for under IAS 22(r1998).61 (i.e., associated with anticipated losses and expenses), the enterprise should disclose a description, the amount and the timing of the expected future losses and expenses.	22(r1998).91(a)		
8077	The financial statements should disclose a reconciliation of the carrying amount of negative goodwill at the beginning and end of the period showing: (a) the gross amount of negative goodwill and the accumulated amount of negative goodwill already recognised as income, at the beginning of the period; (b) any additional negative goodwill recognised during the period; (c) any adjustments resulting from subsequent identification or changes in value of identifiable assets and liabilities; (d) any negative goodwill derecognised on the disposal of all or part of the business to which it relates during the period; (e) negative goodwill recognised as income during the period, showing separately the portion of negative goodwill recognised as income under IAS 22(r1998).61 (if any); (f) other changes in the carrying amount during the period (if any); and (g) the gross amount of negative goodwill and the accumulated amount of negative goodwill already recognised as income, at the end of the period. *Note:* *Comparative information need not be provided for the reconciliation specified in item 8077.*	22(r1998).91(d)		
	INTANGIBLE ASSETS			
8078	The financial statements should disclose the following for each class of intangible assets, distinguishing between internally generated intangible assets and other intangible assets:			

Ref.	Presentation/Disclosure Requirement	Source	Y, N or N/A	W/P Ref.
	(a) the gross carrying amount and the accumulated amortisation (aggregated with accumulated impairment losses) at the beginning and end of the period; and	38.107(c)		
	(b) (a reconciliation of the carrying amount at the beginning and end of the period showing: (i) additions, indicating separately those from internal development and through business combinations; (ii) retirements and disposals; (iii) increases or decreases during the period resulting from revaluations and from impairment losses recognised or reversed directly in equity (if any); (iv) impairment losses recognised in the income statement during the period (if any); (v) impairment losses reversed in the income statement during the period (if any); (vi) amortisation recognised during the period; (vii) net exchange differences arising on the translation of the financial statements of a foreign entity; and (viii) other changes in the carrying amount during the period.	38.107(e)		
	Note: ***Comparative information is not required for the reconciliation specified under item 8078(b).***			
8079	The financial statements should also disclose a description, the carrying amount and remaining amortisation period of any individual intangible asset that is material to the financial statements of the enterprise as a whole.	38.111(b)		
8080	For intangible assets acquired by way of government grant and initially recognised at fair value, the enterprise should disclose: (a) the fair value initially recognised for those assets; and (b) their carrying amount.	38.111(c)		
8081	The financial statements should disclose the existence and carrying amounts of:	38.111(d)		

Ref.	Presentation/Disclosure Requirement	Source	Y, N or N/A	W/P Ref.
	(a) intangible assets whose title is restricted; and (b) intangible assets pledged as security for liabilities.			
8082	If intangible assets are carried at revalued amounts, the following details should also be disclosed by class of intangible assets: (a) the effective date of the revaluation; (b) the carrying amount of revalued intangible assets; and (c) the carrying amount that would have been included in the financial statements had the revalued intangible assets been carried under the benchmark treatment.	38.113(a)		
8083	In the first annual financial statements issued under IAS 38, the enterprise should disclose the transitional provisions adopted where transitional provisions under the Standard permit a choice.	38.121		
8084	Where IAS 38 is applied for annual financial statements covering periods before 1 July 1999 (its effective date), the enterprise should: (a) disclose that fact; and (b) adopt IAS 22(r1998) *Business Combinations* and IAS 36 *Impairment of Assets* at the same time.	38.122		
	SUBSIDIARIES			
8085	The consolidated financial statements should include a listing of significant subsidiaries with disclosure of the name, country of incorporation or residence, proportion of ownership interest and, if different, the proportion of voting power held.	27.32(a)		
8086	Where a parent does not prepare consolidated financial statements because it is a wholly-owned or a virtually wholly-owned subsidiary, the following disclosures should be made: (a) the reasons why consolidated financial statements have not been presented together with the bases on which subsidiaries are accounted for in the parent's separate financial statements; and	27.8		

Ref.	Presentation/Disclosure Requirement	Source	Y, N or N/A	W/P Ref.
	(b) the name and registered office of its parent that publishes consolidated financial statements.			
8087	The consolidated financial statements should disclose, where applicable: (a) the reasons for not consolidating a subsidiary; (b) the nature of the relationship between the parent and a subsidiary in which the parent does not own, directly or indirectly through subsidiaries, more than half of the voting power; (c) the name of any enterprise in which more than half of the voting power is owned, directly or indirectly through subsidiaries, but which, because of the absence of control, is not a subsidiary; and (d) the effect of the acquisition and disposal of subsidiaries on the financial position at the reporting date, the results for the reporting period and on the corresponding amounts for the preceding period.	27.32(b)		
8088	Where it is not practicable to use uniform accounting policies for the purposes of consolidated financial statements, that fact should be disclosed, together with the proportions of the items in the consolidated financial statements to which the different accounting policies have been applied.	27.21		
8089	When there is a change in the classification of a significant foreign operation, the following matters should be disclosed: (a) the nature of the change in classification; (b) the reason for the change; (c) the impact of the change in classification on shareholders' equity; and (d) the impact on net profit or loss for each prior period presented had the change in classification occurred at the beginning of the earliest period presented.	21(r1993).44		
	BUSINESS COMBINATIONS			
8090	For all business combinations, the following disclosures should be made in the financial statements	22(r1998).86		

Ref.	Presentation/Disclosure Requirement	Source	Y, N or N/A	W/P Ref.
	for the period during which the combination takes place: (a) the names and descriptions of the combining enterprises; (b) the method of accounting for the combination; (c) the effective date of the combination for accounting purposes; and (d) any operations resulting from the business combination which the enterprise has decided to dispose of.			
8091	For a business combination which is an acquisition, the following disclosures should be made in the financial statements for the period during which the acquisition takes place: (a) the percentage of voting shares acquired; and (b) the cost of acquisition and a description of the purchase consideration paid or contingently payable.	22(r1998).87		
8092	The disclosure requirements of IAS 37 *Provisions, Contingent Liabilities and Contingent Assets* should be applied to provisions for terminating or reducing the activities of an acquiree, recognised under IAS 22(r1998).31.	22(r1998).92		
8093	Provisions for terminating or reducing activities as described in item 8092 above should be dealt with as a separate class of provisions for the purposes of disclosure under IAS 37.	22(r1998).92		
8094	The aggregate carrying amount of such provisions under IAS 22(r1998).31 should be disclosed for each individual business combination.	22(r1998).92		
8095	In an acquisition, if the fair values of the identifiable assets and liabilities or the purchase consideration can only be determined on a provisional basis at the end of the period in which the acquisition took place, this should be stated and reasons given.	22(r1998).93		
8096	When there are subsequent adjustments to the provisional fair values described at item 8095, those adjustments should be disclosed and explained in the financial statements of the period concerned, with separate disclosure of the amount of the adjustment that relates to prior and comparative periods.	22(r1998).93 SIC22.8		

Ref.	Presentation/Disclosure Requirement	Source	Y, N or N/A	W/P Ref.
8097	For a business combination which is a uniting of interests, the following additional disclosures should be made in the financial statements for the period during which the uniting of interests takes place: (a) a description and the number of shares issued, together with the percentage of each enterprise's voting shares exchanged to effect the uniting of interests; (b) the amounts of assets and liabilities contributed by each enterprise; and (c) the sales revenue, other operating revenues, extraordinary items and net profit or loss of each enterprise prior to the date of the combination that are included in the net profit or loss shown by the combined enterprise's financial statements.	22(r1998).94		
8098	For business combinations effected after the balance sheet date, the information required by items 8090 to 8097 should be disclosed.	22(r1998).96		
8099	If it is impracticable to disclose any of the information required by item 8098, this fact should be disclosed.	22(r1998).96		
8100	In the first annual financial statements issued under IAS 22(r1998), the enterprise should disclose the transitional provisions adopted where transitional provisions under the Standard permit a choice.	22(r1998).101		
8101	If IAS 22(r1998) is applied for annual financial statements covering periods beginning before 1 July 1999 (its effective date), the enterprise should: (a) disclose that fact; and (b) adopt IAS 36 *Impairment of Assets*, IAS 37 *Provisions, Contingent Liabilities and Contingent Assets* and IAS 38 *Intangible Assets* at the same time.	22(r1998).102		
	INVESTMENTS IN ASSOCIATES			
8102	The following disclosures should be made in relation to investments in associates:			
	(a) an appropriate listing and description of significant associates, including the proportion	28(r2000).27(a)		

Ref.	Presentation/Disclosure Requirement	Source	Y, N or N/A	W/P Ref.
	of ownership interest and, if different, the proportion of voting power held; and (b) the investor's share of any extraordinary or prior period items, separately disclosed.	28(r2000).28		
8103	If the investor discontinues recognition of its share of losses of an investee (generally where the share of losses equals or exceeds the carrying amount of its investment), the investor should disclose in its financial statements the amount of its unrecognised share of losses of the investee, both during the period and cumulatively.	SIC-20.10		
	INTERESTS IN JOINT VENTURES			
	Note: ***The disclosures listed below are required for all venturers, including those that do not issue consolidated financial statements because they do not have subsidiaries.***			
8104	The venturer should disclose a listing and description of interests in significant joint ventures and the proportion of ownership interest held in jointly controlled entities.	31(r2000).47,48		
8105	Where the venturer reports its interests in jointly controlled entities using the line-by-line reporting format for proportionate consolidation or the equity method, it should disclose the aggregate amount of each of current assets, long-term assets, current liabilities, long-term liabilities, income and expenses related to its interests in joint ventures.	31(r2000).47,48		
	ACCOUNTING FOR LEASES BY LESSORS			
8106	The following disclosures should be made in the financial statements for finance leases: (a) a reconciliation between the total gross investment in the lease at the balance sheet date, and the present value of minimum lease payments receivable at the balance sheet date; (b) the total gross investment in the lease and the present value of minimum lease payments receivable at the balance sheet date, for each of	17(r1997).39		

Ref.	Presentation/Disclosure Requirement	Source	Y, N or N/A	W/P Ref.
	the periods not later than one year, later than one year and not later than five years, and later than five years;			
	(c) unearned finance income;			
	(d) the unguaranteed residual values accruing to the benefit of the lessor;			
	(e) the accumulated allowance for uncollectible minimum lease payments receivable;			
	(f) contingent rents recognised in income; and			
	(g) a general description of the lessor's significant leasing arrangements.			
8107	The following disclosures should be made in the financial statements for operating leases:			
	(a) the future minimum lease payments under non-cancellable operating leases, in aggregate and for each of the periods not later than one year, later than one year and not later than five years, and later than five years;	17(r1997).48(b)		
	(b) total contingent rents recognised in income; and	17(r1997).48(c)		
	(c) a general description of the lessor's significant leasing arrangements.	17(r1997).48(d)		
	Notes:			
	1. The disclosures specified in items 8106 and 8107 are in addition to the requirements of IAS 32 ***Financial Instruments: Disclosure and Presentation****.*	17(r1997).48		
	2. In addition to the requirements set out at item 8107, the requirements on disclosure under IAS 16 ***Property, Plant and Equipment****, IAS 36* ***Impairment of Assets****, IAS 38* ***Intangible Assets****, IAS 40* ***Investment Property*** *and IAS 41* ***Agriculture*** *apply to assets leased out under operating leases.*	17(r1997).48A		
8108	Where the enterprise applies IAS 17(r1997) for an accounting period beginning before 1 January 1999 (its effective date), that fact should be disclosed.	17(r1997).59		
	IMPAIRMENT OF ASSETS			
	Note: *IAS 36 should be applied in accounting for the impairment of all assets, except inventories (IAS 2), construction contracts (IAS 11), deferred tax assets*			

Ref.	Presentation/Disclosure Requirement	Source	Y, N or N/A	W/P Ref.
	(IAS 12), assets arising from employee benefits (IAS 19), financial assets falling within the scope of IAS 32 and investment property that is measured at fair value (IAS 40).			
8109	For each class of assets, the financial statements should disclose:			
	(a) the amount of impairment losses recognised in the income statement during the period and the line item(s) of the income statement in which those impairment losses are included;	36.113(a)		
	(b) the amount of reversals of impairment losses recognised in the income statement during the period and the line item(s) of the income statement in which those impairment losses are reversed;	36.113(b)		
	(c) the amount of impairment losses recognised directly in equity during the period; and	36.113(c)		
	(d) the amount of reversals of impairment losses recognised directly in equity during the period.	36.113(d)		
8110	If an impairment loss for an individual asset or a cash-generating unit is recognised or reversed during the period and is material to the financial statements of the reporting enterprise as a whole, the enterprise should disclose:	36.117		
	(a) the events and circumstances that led to the recognition or reversal of the impairment loss;			
	(b) the amount of the impairment loss recognised or reversed;			
	(c) for an individual asset: (i) the nature of the asset; and (ii) if the enterprise applies IAS 14(r1997) *Segment Reporting*, the reportable segment to which the asset belongs, based on the enterprise's primary format;			
	(d) for a cash-generating unit: (i) a description of the cash-generating unit (such as whether it is a product line, a plant, a business operation, a geographical area, a reportable segment as defined in IAS 14(r1997) *Segment Reporting* or other); (ii) the amount of the impairment loss recognised or reversed by class of assets and, if the enterprise applies			

Ref.	Presentation/Disclosure Requirement	Source	Y, N or N/A	W/P Ref.
	IAS 14(r1997) *Segment Reporting*, by reportable segment based on the enterprise's primary format; and (iii) if the aggregation of assets for identifying the cash-generating unit has changed since the previous estimate of the cash-generating unit's recoverable amount (if any), the enterprise should describe the current and former ways of aggregating assets and the reasons for changing the way the cash-generating unit is identified; (e) whether the recoverable amount of the asset (cash-generating unit) is its net selling price or its value in use; (f) if recoverable amount is net selling price, the basis used to determine net selling price (such as whether selling price was determined by reference to an active market or in some other way); and (g) if recoverable amount is value in use, the discount rate(s) used in the current estimate and previous estimate (if any) of value in use.			
8111	If impairment losses recognised (reversed) during the period are material in aggregate to the financial statements of the reporting enterprise as a whole, the enterprise should disclose a brief description of the following: (a) the main classes of assets affected by impairment losses (reversals of impairment losses) for which no information is disclosed under item 8110; and (b) the main events and circumstances that led to the recognition (reversal) of these impairment losses for which no information is disclosed under item 8110.	36.118		
8112	If the enterprise applies IAS 36 for an accounting period beginning before 1 July 1999 (its effective date), that fact should be disclosed.	36.122		
	Inventories			
8113	The following items should be disclosed in the financial statements: (a) the total carrying amount of inventories and the carrying amount in classifications appropriate to the enterprise;	2(r1993).34		

Ref.	Presentation/Disclosure Requirement	Source	Y, N or N/A	W/P Ref.
	(b) the carrying amount of inventories carried at net realisable value; (c) the amount of any reversal of any write-down that is recognised as income in the period; (d) the circumstances or events that led to the reversal of a write-down of inventories; and (e) the carrying amount of inventories pledged as security for liabilities.			
8114	When the cost of inventories is determined using the LIFO formula in accordance with the allowed alternative treatment under IAS 2(r1993), the financial statements should disclose the difference between the amount of inventories as shown in the balance sheet and either: (a) the lower of the amount arrived at in accordance with the FIFO or weighted average cost formulas and net realisable value; or (b) the lower of current cost at the balance sheet date and net realisable value.	2(r1993).36		
	Construction Contracts			
8115	The enterprise should disclose each of the following for contracts in progress at the balance sheet date: (a) the aggregate amount of costs incurred and recognised profits (less recognised losses) to date; (b) the amount of advances received; and (c) the amount of retentions.	11(r1993).40		
8116	The enterprise should present: (a) the gross amount due from customers for contract work as an asset; and (b) the gross amount due to customers for contract work as a liability.	11(r1993).42		
	Shareholders' Equity			
8117	For each class of share capital, the following information should be disclosed, either on the face of the balance sheet or in the notes: (a) the number of shares authorised; (b) the number of shares issued and fully paid, and issued but not fully paid;	1(r1997).74(a)		

Ref.	Presentation/Disclosure Requirement	Source	Y, N or N/A	W/P Ref.
	(c) par value per share, or that the shares have no par value; (d) a reconciliation of the number of shares outstanding at the beginning and at the end of the year; (e) the rights, preferences and restrictions attaching to that class, including restrictions on the distribution of dividends and the repayment of capital; (f) shares in the enterprise held by the enterprise itself or by subsidiaries or associates of the enterprise; and (g) shares reserved for issuance under options and sales contracts, including the terms and amounts.			
8118	The financial statements should include a description of the nature and purpose of each reserve within owners' equity, either on the face of the balance sheet or in the notes.	1(r1997).74(b)		
8119	An enterprise without share capital (e.g., a partnership), should disclose information equivalent to that required by items 8117 and 8118, showing movements during the period in each category of equity interest and the rights, preferences and restrictions attaching to each category of equity interest.	1(r1997).74		
	Treasury Shares			
8120	Treasury shares should be presented in the balance sheet as a deduction from equity.	SIC-16.4		
8121	The acquisition of treasury shares should be presented in the financial statements as a change in equity.	SIC-16.4		
8122	Consideration received on the sale issuance or cancellation of treasury shares should be presented in the financial statements as a change in equity.	SIC-16.5		
8123	The amounts of reductions to equity for treasury shares held should be disclosed separately either on the face of the balance sheet or in the notes.	SIC-16.6		
8124	Where the enterprise, or any of its subsidiaries (including special purpose entities) reacquires its own shares from parties able to control or exercise	SIC-16.7		

Ref.	Presentation/Disclosure Requirement	Source	Y, N or N/A	W/P Ref.
	significant influence over the enterprise, this should be disclosed as a related party transaction in accordance with IAS 24.22 (see item 8187 below).			
	Note: *The acquisition cost of treasury shares held by the enterprise (and, in a consolidated balance sheet, by its subsidiaries) should be presented in one of the following ways:*	SIC-16.10		
	(a) total cost is shown as a one-line adjustment of equity; or			
	(b) the par value, if any, is shown as a deduction from share capital, with adjustment of premiums or discounts against other categories of equity; or			
	(c) each category of equity is adjusted.			
	Tax Assets and Liabilities			
8125	The following principles should be applied in the presentation of tax assets and liabilities:			
	(a) tax assets and tax liabilities should be presented separately from other assets and liabilities in the balance sheet;	12(r2000).69		
	(b) current tax assets and liabilities should be distinguished from deferred tax assets and liabilities; and	12(r2000).69		
	(c) when the enterprise distinguishes between current and non-current assets and liabilities in its financial statements, deferred tax assets (liabilities) should not be treated as current assets (liabilities).	12(r2000).70		
8126	Current tax assets and current tax liabilities should be offset if, and only if, both of the following conditions are satisfied:	12(r2000).71		
	(a) there is a legally enforceable right to set off the recognised amounts; and			
	(b) it is intended either to settle on a net basis, or to realise the asset and settle the liability simultaneously.			
8127	Deferred tax assets and deferred tax liabilities should be offset if, and only if, both of the following conditions are satisfied:	12(r2000).74		

Ref.	Presentation/Disclosure Requirement	Source	Y, N or N/A	W/P Ref.
	(a) there is a legally enforceable right to set off current tax assets against current tax liabilities; and (b) the deferred tax assets and the deferred tax liabilities relate to income taxes levied by the same taxation authority on either: (i) the same taxable entity; or (ii) different taxable entities which intend either to settle current tax liabilities and assets on a net basis, or to realise the assets and settle the liabilities simultaneously, in each future period in which significant amounts of deferred tax liabilities or assets are expected to be settled or recovered.			
8128	The following should be disclosed:			
	(a) the amount (and expiry date, if any) of deductible temporary differences, unused tax losses and unused tax credits for which no deferred tax asset is recognised in the balance sheet;	12(r2000).81(e)		
	(b) the aggregate amount of temporary differences associated with investments in subsidiaries, branches and associates, and interests in joint ventures, for which deferred tax liabilities are not recognised; and	12(r2000).81(f)		
	(c) the amount of the deferred tax assets and liabilities recognised in the balance sheet for each period presented in respect of each type of temporary difference, and in respect of each type of unused tax losses and unused tax credits.	12(r2000).81(g)		
8129	When the utilisation of a deferred tax asset is dependent on future taxable profits in excess of the profits arising from the reversal of existing taxable temporary differences, and the enterprise has suffered a loss in either the current or the preceding period in the tax jurisdiction to which the deferred tax asset relates, the amount of such asset and the nature of the evidence supporting its recognition should be disclosed.	12(r2000).82		
8130	Where current and deferred tax assets and liabilities are measured at the tax rate applicable to undistributed profits, but the net income taxes payable will be affected if part of the retained	12(r2000).82A		

Ref.	Presentation/Disclosure Requirement	Source	Y, N or N/A	W/P Ref.
	earnings is paid out as a dividend to shareholders, the enterprise should disclose: (a) the nature of the potential income tax consequences that would result from the payment of dividends to its shareholders; (b) the amounts of the potential income tax consequences that are practicably determinable; and (c) whether there are any potential income tax consequences that are not practicably determinable.			
	Accounting for Leases by Lessees			
8131	The following disclosures should be made in the financial statements for finance leases: (a) for each class of asset, the net carrying amount at the balance sheet date; (b) a reconciliation between the total of minimum lease payments at the balance sheet date and their present value; (c) the total of minimum lease payments at the balance sheet date for each of the periods not later than one year, later than one year and not later than five years, and later than five years, and their present value; (d) contingent rents recognised in income in the period; (e) the total of future minimum sublease payments expected to be received under non-cancellable subleases at the balance sheet date; and (f) a general description of the lessee's significant leasing arrangements including, but not limited to, the basis on which contingent rents are determined; the existence and terms of renewal or purchase options and escalation clauses; and restrictions imposed by lease arrangements (such as those concerning dividends, additional debt and further leasing).	17(r1997).23		
	Note: *In addition to the requirements set out at item 8131, the requirements on disclosure under IAS 16 **Property, Plant and Equipment**, IAS 36 **Impairment of Assets**, IAS 38 **Intangible Assets**, IAS 40 **Investment Property** and IAS 41 **Agriculture** apply to the amounts of leased assets held under finance leases that are accounted for by the lessee as acquisitions of assets.*	17(r1997).24		

Ref.	Presentation/Disclosure Requirement	Source	Y, N or N/A	W/P Ref.
8132	The following disclosures should be made in the financial statements for operating leases: (a) the total of future minimum lease payments under non-cancellable operating leases for each of the periods not later than one year, later than one year and not later than five years, and later than five years; (b) the total of future minimum sublease payments expected to be received under non-cancellable subleases at the balance sheet date; (c) lease and sublease payments recognised in income for the period, with separate amounts for minimum lease payments, contingent rents, and sublease payments; and (d) a general description of the lessee's significant leasing arrangements including, but not limited to, the basis on which contingent rents are determined; the existence and terms of renewal or purchase options and escalation clauses; and restrictions imposed by lease arrangements (such as those concerning dividends, additional debt and further leasing).	17(r1997).27		
	Note: *The disclosure specified in items 8131 and 8132 are in addition to the requirements of IAS 32* ***Financial Instruments: Disclosure and Presentation****.*	17(r1997).23, 27		
8133	Where the enterprise applies IAS 17(r1997) for an accounting period beginning before 1 January 1999 (its effective date), that fact should be disclosed.	17(r1997).59		
	Financial Instruments: Disclosure and Presentation			
8134	The issuer of a financial instrument should classify the instrument (or its component parts), as either a liability or as equity, in accordance with the substance of the contractual arrangement on initial recognition and by reference to the definitions of a financial liability and an equity instrument.	32(r1998).18		
	Note: *Where the rights and obligations regarding the manner of settlement of a financial instrument depend on the occurrence or non-occurrence of uncertain future events or on the outcome of uncertain circumstances that are beyond the control of both the issuer and holder, the financial instrument*			

Ref.	Presentation/Disclosure Requirement	Source	Y, N or N/A	W/P Ref.
	should be classified as a liability except where the possibility of the issuer being required to settle in cash or another financial asset is remote at the time of issuance, when the contingent settlement provision should be ignored and the instrument should be classified as equity.			
	[SIC-5.5 and 6]			
8135	The issuer of a financial instrument that contains both a liability and an equity element, should classify the component parts separately in accordance with item 8134 above.	32(r1998).23		
8136	Interest, dividends, losses and gains relating to a financial instrument, or a component part, which is classified as a financial liability, should be reported in the income statement as expense or income.	32(r1998).30		
8137	Distributions to holders of financial instruments which are classified as equity instruments should be debited directly to equity.	32(r1998).30		
8138	A financial asset and a financial liability should be offset, and the net amount reported in the balance sheet if, but only if, both of the following conditions are met: (a) the enterprise has a legally enforceable right to set off the recognised amounts; and (b) the enterprise intends either to settle on a net basis, or to realise the asset and settle the liability simultaneously.	32(r1998).33		
8139	The enterprise should describe its financial risk management objectives and policies, including its policy for hedging each major type of forecasted transaction for which hedge accounting is used.	32(r1998).43A		
8140	For each class of financial asset, financial liability and equity instrument, both recognised and unrecognised, the enterprise should disclose information about the extent and nature of the financial instruments, including significant terms and conditions that may affect the amount, timing and certainty of future cash flows.	32(r1998).47(a)		

Ref.	Presentation/Disclosure Requirement	Source	Y, N or N/A	W/P Ref.
8141	For each class of financial asset and financial liability, both recognised and unrecognised, the enterprise should disclose information about its exposure to interest rate risk, including: (a) contractual repricing or maturity dates, whichever dates are earlier; and (b) effective interest rates, when applicable.	32(r1998).56		
8142	For each class of financial asset, both recognised and unrecognised, the enterprise should disclose information about its exposure to credit risk, including: (a) the amount that best represents its maximum credit risk exposure at the balance sheet date, without taking account of the fair value of any collateral, in the event that other parties fail to perform their obligations under financial instruments; and (b) significant concentrations of credit risk.	32(r1998).66		
8143	For each class of financial asset and financial liability, both recognised and unrecognised, the enterprise should disclose information about fair value, unless it is impracticable to do so.	32(r1998).77		
8144	When it is not practicable to disclose such fair value information, within given constraints of timeliness or cost, that fact should be disclosed, together with information about the principal characteristics of the underlying financial instrument that are pertinent to its fair value.	32(r1998).77		
8145	Where an enterprise carries one or more financial assets at an amount in excess of their fair value, it should disclose both: (a) the carrying amount and the fair value of either the individual assets or appropriate groupings of those individual assets; and (b) the reasons for not reducing the carrying amount, including the nature of the evidence that provides the basis for management's belief that the carrying amount will be recovered.	32(r1998).88		
	Note: ***The requirements of items 8142 to 8145 above do not apply to those financial assets and financial liabilities carried at fair value.***	39(r2000).166		

Ref.	Presentation/Disclosure Requirement	Source	Y, N or N/A	W/P Ref.
8146	The enterprise should disclose a description of its financial risk management objectives and policies, including its policy for hedging each major type of forecasted transaction.	39(r2000).169(a)		
8147	The financial statements should disclose the following (separately for designated fair value hedges, cash flow hedges and hedges of a net investment in a foreign entity): (a) a description of the hedge; (b) a description of the financial instruments designated as hedging instruments for the hedge and their fair values at the balance sheet date; (c) the nature of the risks being hedged; and (d) for hedges of forecasted transactions, the periods in which the forecasted transactions are expected to occur, when they are expected to enter into the determination of net profit or loss, and a description of any forecasted transaction for which hedge accounting had previously been used but that is no longer expected to occur.	39(r2000).169(b)		
8148	If a gain or loss on derivative and non-derivative financial assets and liabilities designated as hedging instruments in cash flow hedges has been recognised directly in equity, the following should be disclosed: (a) the amount that was so recognised in equity during the current period; (b) the amount that was removed from equity and reported in net profit or loss for the period; and (c) the amount that was removed from equity and added to the initial measurement of the acquisition cost or other carrying amount of the asset or liability in a hedged forecasted transaction during the current period (see IAS 39(r2000).160).	39(r2000).169(c)		
8149	If a gain or loss from remeasuring available-for-sale financial assets to fair value (other than assets relating to hedges) has been recognised directly in equity, the financial statements should disclose: (a) the amount that was so recognised in equity during the current period; and	39(r2000).170(a)		

Ref.	Presentation/Disclosure Requirement	Source	Y, N or N/A	W/P Ref.
	(b) the amount that was removed from equity and reported in net profit or loss for the period.			
8150	If the presumption that fair value can be reliably measured for all financial assets that are available-for-sale or held for trading has been overcome and the enterprise is, therefore, measuring any such financial assets at amortised cost, that fact should be disclosed, together with a description of the financial assets, their carrying amount, an explanation of why fair value cannot be reliably measured, and, if possible, the range of estimates within which fair value is highly likely to lie.	39(r2000).170(b)		
8151	If financial assets whose fair value previously could not be measured reliably are sold, that fact should be disclosed as well as the carrying amount of such financial assets at the time of sale, and the amount of gain or loss recognised.	39(r2000).170(b)		
8152	The financial statements should disclose significant items of income, expense, and gains and losses resulting from financial assets and financial liabilities, whether included in net profit or loss or as a separate component of equity. *Notes:* 1. *For the purpose of item 8152, total interest income and total interest expense should be disclosed separately.* 2. *For the purpose of item 8152, with respect to available-for-sale financial assets that are adjusted to fair value after initial acquisition, total gains and losses from derecognition of such financial assets and included in net profit or loss for the period should be reported separately from total gains and losses from fair value adjustments of recognised assets and liabilities included in net profit or loss for the period. A similar split of 'realised' versus 'unrealised' gains and losses with respect to financial assets and liabilities held for trading is not required.* 3. *For the purpose of item 8152, the enterprise should disclose the amount of interest income that has been accrued on impaired loans pursuant to IAS 39(r2000).116 and that has not yet been received in cash.*	39(r2000).170(c)		

Ref.	Presentation/Disclosure Requirement	Source	Y, N or N/A	W/P Ref.
8153	If the enterprise has entered into a securitisation or repurchase agreement, it should disclose, separately for such transactions occurring in the current financial reporting period and for remaining retained interests from transactions occurring in prior financial reporting periods: (a) the nature and extent of such transactions, including a description of any collateral, and quantitative information about the key assumptions used in calculating the fair values of new and retained interests; and (b) whether the financial assets have been derecognised.	39(r2000).170(d)		
8154	If the enterprise has reclassified a financial asset as one required to be reported at amortised cost rather than at fair value, the reason for that reclassification should be disclosed.	39(r2000).170(e)		
8155	Disclosure should be made of the nature and amount of any impairment loss or reversal of an impairment loss recognised for a financial asset, separately for each significant class of financial asset.	39(r2000).170(f)		
8156	A borrower should disclose the carrying amount of financial assets pledged as collateral for liabilities and any significant terms and conditions relating to pledged assets.	39(r2000).170(g)		
8157	A lender should disclose: (a) the fair value of collateral (both financial and non-financial assets) that it has accepted and that it is permitted to sell or repledge in the absence of default; (b) the fair value of collateral that is sold or repledged; and (c) any significant terms and conditions associated with its use of collateral.	39(r2000).170(h)		
	EMPLOYEE BENEFITS			
8158	For defined contribution plans, the enterprise should disclose the amount recognised as an expense in the period.	19(r2000).46		

Ref.	Presentation/Disclosure Requirement	Source	Y, N or N/A	W/P Ref.
8159	For defined benefit plans, the enterprise should disclose the total expense recognised in the income statement for each of the following, and the line item(s) of the income statement in which they are included:	19(r2000).120(f)		
	(a) current service cost; (b) interest cost; (c) expected return on plan assets; (d) expected return on any reimbursement right recognised as an asset under IAS 19(r2000).104A; (e) actuarial gains and losses; (f) past service cost; and (g) the effect of any curtailment or settlement.			
8160	An asset relating to one retirement benefit plan should be offset against a liability relating to another plan when, and only when, the following conditions are satisfied:	19(r2000).116		
	(a) the enterprise has a legally enforceable right to use a surplus in one plan to settle obligations under the other plan; and (b) the enterprise intends either to settle the obligations on a net basis, or to realise the surplus on one plan and settle its obligations under the other plan simultaneously.			
8161	The following information should be disclosed about defined benefit plans:			
	(a) a general description of the type of plan;	19(r2000).120(b)		
	(b) a reconciliation of the assets and liabilities recognised in the balance sheet, showing at least: (i) the present value at the balance sheet date of defined benefit obligations that are wholly unfunded; (ii) the present value (before deducting the fair value of plan assets) at the balance sheet date of defined benefit obligations that are wholly or partly funded; (iii) the fair value of any plan assets at the balance sheet date; (iv) the net actuarial gains or losses not recognised in the balance sheet; (v) the past service cost not yet recognised in the balance sheet; (vi) any amount not recognised as an asset,	19(r2000).120(c)		

Ref.	Presentation/Disclosure Requirement	Source	Y, N or N/A	W/P Ref.
	because of the limit restrictions imposed by IAS 19(r2000).58(b); (vii) the fair value at the balance sheet date of any reimbursement right recognised as an asset under IAS 19(r2000).104A (with a brief description of the link between the reimbursement right and the related obligation; and (viii) the other amounts recognised in the balance sheet;			
	(c) the amounts included in the fair value of plan assets for: (i) each category of the reporting enterprise's own financial instruments; and (ii) any property occupied by, or other assets used by, the reporting enterprise;	19(r2000).120(d)		
	(d) a reconciliation showing the movements during the period in the net liability (or asset) recognised in the balance sheet;	19(r2000).120(e)		
	(e) the actual return on plan assets, as well as the actual return on any reimbursement right recognised as an asset under IAS 19(r2000).104A and;	19(r2000).120(g)		
	(f) the principal actuarial assumptions used as at the balance sheet date, including, where applicable: (i) the discount rates; (ii) the expected rates of return on any plan assets for the periods presented in the financial statements; (iii) the expected rates of return for the periods presented in the financial statements on any reimbursement right recognised as an asset under IAS 19 (r2000).104A; (iv) the expected rates of salary increases (and of changes in an index or other variable specified in the formal or constructive terms of a plan as the basis for future benefit increases); (v) medical cost trend rates; and (vi) any other material actuarial assumptions used. *Note:* ***The enterprise should disclose each actuarial assumption in absolute terms (for example as an absolute percentage) and not just as a margin between different percentages or other variables.***	19(r2000).120(h)		

Ref.	Presentation/Disclosure Requirement	Source	Y, N or N/A	W/P Ref.
8162	Where a multi-employer plan is accounted for as a defined benefit plan, the enterprise should disclose the information specified in item 8161.	19(r2000).29		
8163	Where a multi-employer plan is a defined benefit plan, but is accounted for as a defined contribution plan because sufficient information is not available to use defined-benefit accounting, the enterprise should disclose: (a) the fact that the plan is a defined benefit plan; (b) the reason why sufficient information is not available to enable the enterprise to account for the plan as a defined benefit plan; and (c) to the extent that a surplus or deficit in the plan may affect the amount of future contributions: (i) any available information about that surplus or deficit; (ii) the basis used to determine that surplus or deficit; and (iii) the implication, if any, for the enterprise.	19(r2000).30		
8164	In respect of equity compensation benefits, the following should be disclosed: (a) the nature and terms (including any vesting rules) of equity compensation plans; (b) the amounts recognised in the financial statements for equity compensation plans; (c) the number and terms (including, where applicable, dividend and voting rights, conversion rights, exercise dates, exercise prices and expiry dates) of the enterprise's own equity financial instruments which are held by equity compensation plans (and, in the case of share options, by employees) at the beginning and end of the period, and the extent to which employees' entitlements to those instruments are vested at the beginning and end of the period; (d) the number and terms (including, where applicable, dividend and voting rights, conversion rights, exercise dates, exercise prices and expiry dates) of equity financial instruments issued by the enterprise to equity compensation plans or to employees (or of the enterprise's own equity financial instruments	19(r2000).147		

Ref.	Presentation/Disclosure Requirement	Source	Y, N or N/A	W/P Ref.
	distributed by equity compensation plans to employees) during the period and the fair value of any consideration received from the equity compensation plans or the employees; (e) the number, exercise dates and exercise prices of share options exercised under equity compensation plans during the period; (f) the number of share options held by equity compensation plans, or held by employees under such plans, that lapsed during the period; and (g) the amount, and principal terms, of any loans or guarantees granted by the reporting enterprise to, or on behalf of, equity compensation plans.			
8165	Unless it is impracticable to do so, the following additional items should be disclosed: (a) the fair value, at the beginning and end of the period, of the enterprise's own equity financial instruments (other than share options) held by equity compensation plans; and (b) the fair value, at the date of issue, of the enterprise's own equity financial instruments (other than share options) issued by the enterprise to equity compensation plans or to employees during the period.	19(r2000).148		
8166	If it is not practicable to determine the fair value of the equity financial instruments specified for disclosure under item 8165, that fact should be disclosed.	19(r2000).148		
8167	On implementation of IAS 19(r2000), the enterprise should determine its transitional liability in accordance with IAS 19(r2000).154. Where the enterprise elects to recognise any excess of the transitional liability over the liability that would have been arrived at under its previous accounting policy over a period of up to five years, rather than immediately, it should disclose at each balance sheet date: (a) the amount of the excess that remains unrecognised; and (b) the amount recognised in the current period.	19(r2000).155(b)		

Ref.	Presentation/Disclosure Requirement	Source	Y, N or N/A	W/P Ref.
8168	Where the enterprise applies IAS 19(r1998) for an accounting period beginning before 1 January 1999 (its effective date), that fact should be disclosed.	19(r2000).157		
8169	Specific amendments to IAS 19 become operative for annual financial statements beginning on or after 1 January 2001. If earlier adoption of these amendments affects the financial statements, that fact should be disclosed.	19(r2000).159		
	Provisions, contingent liabilities and contingent assets			
8170	For each class of provision, the enterprise should disclose: (a) the carrying amount at the beginning and end of the period; (b) additional provisions made in the period, including increases to existing provisions; (c) amounts used (i.e., incurred and charged against the provision) during the period; (d) unused amounts reversed during the period; and (e) the increase during the period in the discounted amount arising from the passage of time and the effect of any change in the discount rate. *Note:* *Comparative information is not required for the disclosures specified in item 8170.*	37.84		
8171	The enterprise should disclose the following for each class of provision: (a) a brief description of the nature of the obligation and the expected timing of any resulting outflows of economic benefits; (b) an indication of the uncertainties about the amount or timing of those outflows including, where necessary to provide adequate information, the major assumptions made concerning future events; and (c) the amount of any expected reimbursement, stating the amount of any asset that has been recognised for that expected reimbursement.	37.85		

Ref.	Presentation/Disclosure Requirement	Source	Y, N or N/A	W/P Ref.
8172	Unless the possibility of any outflow in settlement is remote, the enterprise should disclose, for each class of contingent liability at the balance sheet date, a brief description of the nature of the contingent liability.	37.86		
8173	Where practicable, the following information should also be disclosed in respect of contingent liabilities: (a) an estimate of the financial effect of the contingent liability, under the measurement rules specified in IAS 37.36 to 52; (b) an indication of the uncertainties relating to the amount or timing of any outflow; and (c) the possibility of any reimbursement.	37.86		
8174	Where an inflow of economic benefits is probable, the enterprise should disclose a brief description of the nature of the contingent assets at the balance sheet date.	37.89		
8175	Where practicable, the enterprise should also disclose an estimate of the financial effect of contingent assets, measured using the principles specified in IAS 37.36 to 52.	37.89		
8176	Where any of the information required by items 8172 to 8175 is not disclosed, because it is not practicable to do so, that fact should be stated.	37.91		
8177	In the extremely rare case where information is not disclosed because disclosure of some or all of the information required by items 8170 to 8175 could be expected to prejudice seriously the position of the enterprise in a dispute with other parties on the subject matter of the provision, contingent liability or contingent asset, the enterprise should disclose the general nature of the dispute, together with the fact that, and the reason why, the information has not been disclosed.	37.92		
8178	On implementation of IAS 37, if comparative information is not restated, that fact should be disclosed.	37.93		
8179	If the enterprise applies IAS 37 for periods beginning before 1 July 1999 (its effective date), that fact should be disclosed.	37.95		

Ref.	Presentation/Disclosure Requirement	Source	Y, N or N/A	W/P Ref.
8180	A venturer should disclose the aggregate amount of the following contingent liabilities (unless the probability of loss is remote) separately from the amount of other contingent liabilities: (a) any contingent liabilities that the venturer has incurred in relation to its interests in joint ventures and its share in each of the contingent liabilities which have been incurred jointly with other venturers; (b) its share of the contingent liabilities of the joint ventures themselves for which it is contingently liable; and (c) those contingent liabilities that arise because the venturer is contingently liable for the liabilities of the other venturers in a joint venture.	31(r2000).45,48		
	COMMITMENTS			
8181	The financial statements should disclose the amount of commitments for the acquisition of property, plant and equipment.	16(r1998).61(d)		
8182	The financial statements should disclose material contractual obligations to purchase, construct or develop investment property, or for repairs, maintenance or enhancements.	40.66(f)		
8183	The financial statements should disclose the amount of commitments for the acquisition of intangible assets.	38.111(e)		
8184	A venturer should disclose the aggregate amount of the following commitments in respect of its interests in joint ventures separately from the amount of other commitments: (a) any capital commitments that the venturer has incurred in relation to its interests in joint ventures and its share in each of the capital commitments that have been incurred jointly with other venturers; and (b) its share of the capital commitments of the joint ventures themselves.	31(r2000).46,48		

Ref.	Presentation/Disclosure Requirement	Source	Y, N or N/A	W/P Ref.
	Government Grants			
8185	The following information should be disclosed in the financial statements:			
	(a) the nature and extent of government grants recognised in the financial statements and an indication of other forms of government assistance from which the company has directly benefited; and	20.39(b)		
	(b) unfulfilled conditions and other contingencies attaching to government assistance that has been recognised.	20.39(c)		
	Related Party Disclosures			
8186	Related party relationships where control exists should be disclosed in the financial statements, irrespective of whether there have been transactions between the related parties.	24.20		
8187	If there have been transactions between related parties, the enterprise should disclose the nature of the related party relationships, as well as the types of transactions and the elements of the transactions necessary for an understanding of the financial statements.	24.22		
8188	Items of a similar nature should only be aggregated when such aggregation is appropriate on the basis that separate disclosure is not necessary for an understanding of the effects of related party transactions on the financial statements.	24.24		
8189	Separate disclosure should be made of amounts payable to and receivable from:	1(r1997).72		
	(a) the parent enterprise; (b) fellow subsidiaries and associates; and (c) other related parties.			
	EVENTS AFTER THE BALANCE SHEET DATE			
8190	The enterprise should disclose the date when the financial statements were authorised for issue.	10(r1999).16		

Ref.	Presentation/Disclosure Requirement	Source	Y, N or N/A	W/P Ref.
8191	If the enterprise's owners or others have the power to amend the financial statements after issuance, the enterprise should disclose that fact.	10(r1999).16		
8192	If the enterprise receives information after the balance sheet date about conditions that existed at the balance sheet date, the enterprise should update disclosures that relate to these conditions, in the light of the new information.	10(r1999).18		
8193	Where non-adjusting events after the balance sheet date are of such importance that non-disclosure would affect the ability of the users of financial statements to make proper evaluations and decisions, the enterprise should disclose the following information for each significant category of non-adjusting event after the balance sheet date: (a) the nature of the event; and (b) an estimate of its financial effect, or a statement that such an estimate cannot be made.	10(r1999).20		

Section 9 Additional disclosure requirements – banks and similar financial institutions (IAS 30)

Ref.	Presentation/Disclosure Requirement	Source	Y, N or N/A	W/P Ref.
	INCOME STATEMENT – GENERAL			
9001	The income statement should group income and expenses by nature and disclose the amounts of the principal types of income and expenses.	30.9		
9002	In addition to the requirements of other IAS, the following items of income and expense should be disclosed in the income statement or in the notes to the financial statements: (a) interest and similar income; (b) interest expense and similar charges; (c) dividend income; (d) fee and commission income; (e) fee and commission expense; (f) gains less losses arising from dealing securities; (g) gains less losses arising from investment securities; (h) gains less losses arising from dealing in foreign currencies; (i) other operating income; (j) losses on loans and advances; (k) general administrative expenses; and (l) other operating expenses.	30.10		
9003	Items of income and expense should be offset only when they are related to hedges or to assets and liabilities that have been offset in compliance with item 9006 below.	30.13		
	BALANCE SHEET – GENERAL			
9004	The balance sheet should group assets and liabilities by nature and list them in an order that reflects their relative liquidity.	30.18		
9005	In addition to the requirements of other IAS, the following assets and liabilities should be disclosed in the balance sheet or in the notes to the financial statements:	30.19		

Ref.	Presentation/Disclosure Requirement	Source	Y, N or N/A	W/P Ref.
	Assets (a) Cash and balances with the central bank; (b) treasury bills and other bills eligible for rediscounting with the central bank; (c) government and other securities held for dealing purposes; (d) placements with, and loans and advances to, other banks; (e) other money market placements; (f) loans and advances to customers; and (g) investment securities. ***Liabilities*** (a) Deposits from other banks; (b) other money market deposits; (c) amounts owed to other depositors; (d) certificates of deposit; (e) promissory notes and other liabilities evidenced by paper; and (f) other borrowed funds.			
9006	Assets and liabilities should be offset only when a legal right of set-off exists and the offsetting represents the expectation as to the realisation of the asset or settlement of the liability.	30.23		
9007	The bank should disclose the fair value of each class of its financial assets and liabilities as required by IAS 32 *Financial Instruments: Disclosure and Presentation* and IAS 39 *Financial Instruments: Recognition and Measurement*.	30.24		
	CONTINGENT LIABILITIES AND COMMITMENTS (INCLUDING OFF-BALANCE SHEET ITEMS)			
9008	The bank should disclose the following contingent liabilities and commitments: (a) the nature and amount of commitments to extend credit that are irrevocable because they cannot be withdrawn at the discretion of the bank without the risk of incurring significant penalty or expense; and (b) the nature and amount of contingent liabilities and commitments arising from off-balance sheet items, including those relating to:	30.26		

Ref.	Presentation/Disclosure Requirement	Source	Y, N or N/A	W/P Ref.
	(i) direct credit substitutes, including general guarantees of indebtedness, bank acceptance guarantees and standby letters of credit serving as financial guarantees for loans and securities; (ii) certain transaction-related contingent liabilities, including performance bonds, bid bonds, warranties and standby letters of credit related to particular transactions; (iii) short-term, self-liquidating, trade-related contingent liabilities arising from the movement of goods, such as documentary credits where the underlying shipment is used as security; (iv) any sale and repurchase agreements not recognised in the balance sheet; (v) interest and foreign exchange rate-related items, including swaps, options and futures; and (vi) other commitments, note issuance facilities and revolving underwriting facilities.			
	MATURITIES OF ASSETS AND LIABILITIES			
9009	The bank should provide an analysis of assets and liabilities into relevant maturity groupings based on the remaining period from the balance sheet date to the contractual maturity date.	30.30		
	CONCENTRATIONS OF ASSETS AND LIABILITIES			
9010	The bank's financial statements should disclose: (a) any significant concentrations of its assets, liabilities and off-balance sheet items, in terms of geographical areas, customer or industry groups or other concentrations of risk; and (b) the amount of significant net foreign currency exposures.	30.40		

Ref.	Presentation/Disclosure Requirement	Source	Y, N or N/A	W/P Ref.
	LOSSES ON LOANS AND ADVANCES			
9011	The bank should disclose the following: (a) the accounting policy that describes the basis on which uncollectible loans and advances are recognised as an expense and written off; (b) details of the movements in the provision for losses on loans and advances during the period, disclosing separately: (i) the amount charged to income in the period for losses on uncollectible loans and advances; (ii) the amount charged in the period for loans and advances written off; and (iii) the amount credited in the period for loans and advances previously written off that have been recovered; (c) the aggregate amount of the provision for losses on loans and advances at the balance sheet date; and (d) the aggregate amount included in the balance sheet for loans and advances on which interest is not being accrued and the basis used to determine the carrying amount of such loans and advances.	30.43		
9012	Any amounts that have been set aside in respect of losses on loans and advances (in addition to those losses that have been specifically identified or potential losses that experience indicates are inherent in any portfolio of loans and advances) should be accounted for as appropriations of retained earnings.	30.44		
9013	Any credits resulting from the reduction of the amounts referred to in item 9012 should be excluded from the determination of net income and credited to retained earnings.	30.44		
	GENERAL BANKING RISKS			
9014	Any amounts that have been set aside for general banking risks (including those covering future losses and other unforeseeable risks or contingencies) should be separately disclosed as appropriations of retained earnings.	30.50		

Ref.	Presentation/Disclosure Requirement	Source	Y, N or N/A	W/P Ref.
9015	Any credits resulting from the reduction of the amounts referred to in item 9014 should be excluded from the determination of net profit or loss for the period and should be credited to retained earnings.	30.50		
	ASSETS PLEDGED AS SECURITY			
9016	The bank should disclose: (a) the aggregate amount of secured liabilities; and (b) the nature and carrying amount of the assets pledged as security.	30.53		

Section 10 Disclosure of information reflecting the effects of changing prices (IAS 15)

Ref.	Presentation/Disclosure Requirement	Source	Y, N or N/A	W/P Ref.
	Notes: *1. The IASC has granted a particular exemption in relation to IAS 15. Arising from the failure to reach international consensus on the disclosure of information reflecting the effects of changing prices, the IASC has determined that enterprises need not disclose the information required by IAS 15 in order that their financial statements conform with International Accounting Standards. However, enterprises are encouraged to disclose information reflecting the effects of changing prices and, where they do so, to disclose the items required by IAS 15.* *2. IAS 15 applies to enterprises whose levels of revenues, profit, assets or employment are significant in the economic environment in which they operate. When both parent company and consolidated financial statements are presented, the information called for by this section need be presented only on the basis of consolidated information.* *The information is not required for a subsidiary operating in the country of domicile of its parent if consolidated information on this basis is presented by the parent. For subsidiaries operating in a country other than the country of domicile of the parent, the information specified is required only when it is accepted practice for similar information to be presented by enterprises of economic significance in that country.* *3. Presentation of information reflecting the effects of changing prices is encouraged for other entities in the interest of promoting more informative financial reporting.*			
10001	The following items should be disclosed using an accounting method reflecting the effects of changing prices:	15.8		
	(a) the amount of the adjustment to or the adjusted amount of depreciation of property, plant and equipment;	15.21(a)		
	(b) the amount of the adjustment to or the adjusted amount of cost of sales;	15.21(b)		

Ref.	Presentation/Disclosure Requirement	Source	Y, N or N/A	W/P Ref.
	(c) the adjustments relating to monetary items, the effect of borrowing, or equity interests when such adjustments have been taken into account in determining income under the accounting method adopted;	15.21(c)		
	(d) the overall effect of the adjustments described in (a) and (b) and, where appropriate, (c), as well as any other items reflecting the effects of changing prices that are reported under the accounting method adopted;	15.21(d)		
	(e) if a current cost method is adopted, the current cost of property, plant and equipment, and of inventories; and	15.22		
	(f) a description of the methods adopted to compute the information specified by (a) to (e) above, including the nature of any indices used.	15.23		
10002	If the information specified above has not been presented in the primary financial statements, it should be provided on a supplementary basis.	15.24		

Section 11 Disclosures for enterprises reporting in the currency of a hyperinflationary economy (IAS 29)

Ref.	Presentation/Disclosure Requirement	Source	Y, N or N/A	W/P Ref.
	Note: *This section applies to the primary financial statements, including the consolidated financial statements, of any enterprise that reports in the currency of a hyperinflationary economy.*			
11001	The financial statements of an enterprise that reports in the currency of a hyperinflationary economy (whether based on a historical cost approach or a current cost approach) should be stated in terms of the measuring unit current at the balance sheet date.	29.8		
11002	The corresponding figures for the previous period, and any information in respect of earlier periods, should be stated in terms of the measuring unit current at the balance sheet date.	29.8		
11003	The gain or loss on the net monetary position should be included in net income and separately disclosed.	29.9		
11004	The financial statements should disclose the following information: (a) the fact that the financial statements and the corresponding figures for previous periods have been restated for the changes in the general purchasing power of the reporting currency and, as a result, are stated in terms of the measuring unit current at the balance sheet date; (b) whether the financial statements are based on a historical cost or current cost approach; and (c) the identity and level of the price index at the balance sheet date and the movement in the index during the current and the previous reporting period.	29.39		
11005	When the economy has ceased to be hyperinflationary, and the enterprise has discontinued the preparation and presentation of financial statements prepared in accordance with IAS 29, the enterprise should treat the amounts expressed in the measuring unit current at the end of the previous reporting period as the basis for the carrying amounts in its subsequent financial statements.	29.38		

Section 12 Disclosures for enterprises engaged in agricultural activity (IAS 41)

Ref.	Presentation/Disclosure Requirement	Source	Y, N or N/A	W/P Ref.
	Note: *IAS 41* ***Agriculture*** *is effective for annual financial statements covering periods beginning on or after 1 January 2003. Earlier adoption is encouraged.*			
12001	The enterprise should present the carrying amount of its biological assets separately on the face of its balance sheet.	41.39		
	GENERAL DISCLOSURES			
12002	The enterprise should disclose the aggregate gain or loss arising during the current period on initial recognition of biological assets and agricultural produce and from the change in fair value less estimated point-of-sale costs of biological assets.	41.40		
12003	The enterprise should provide a description of each group of biological assets, either in narrative form or as a quantified description.	41.41		
12004	If not disclosed elsewhere in information published with the financial statements, the enterprise should describe: (a) the nature of its activities involving each group of biological assets; and (b) non-financial measures or estimates of the physical quantities of: (i) each group of the enterprise's biological assets at the end of the period; and (ii) output of agricultural produce during the period.	41.46		
12005	The enterprise should disclose the methods and significant assumptions applied in determining the fair value of each group of agricultural produce at the point of harvest and each group of biological assets.	41.47		
12006	The enterprise should disclose the fair value less estimated point-of-sale costs of agricultural produce harvested during the period, determined at the point of harvest.	41.48		

Ref.	Presentation/Disclosure Requirement	Source	Y, N or N/A	W/P Ref.
12007	The enterprise should disclose: (a) the existence and carrying amounts of biological assets whose title is restricted, and the carrying amounts of biological assets pledged as security for liabilities; (b) the amount of commitments for the development or acquisition of biological assets; and (c) financial risk management strategies related to agricultural activity.	41.49		
12008	The enterprise should present a reconciliation of changes in the carrying amount of biological assets between the beginning and the end of the current period, including: (a) the gain or loss arising from changes in fair value less estimated point-of-sale costs; (b) increases due to purchases; (c) decreases due to sales; (d) decreases due to harvest; (e) increases resulting from business combinations; (f) net exchange differences arising on the translation of financial statements of a foreign entity; and (g) other changes. *Note:* *Comparative information is not required for the reconciliation specified in item 12008.*	41.50		
	ADDITIONAL DISCLOSURES FOR BIOLOGICAL ASSETS WHERE FAIR VALUE CANNOT BE MEASURED RELIABLY			
12009	If an enterprise measures biological assets at their cost less any accumulated depreciation and any accumulated impairment losses at the end of the period, the enterprise should disclose for such biological assets: (a) a description of the biological assets; (b) an explanation of why fair value cannot be measured reliably; (c) if possible, the range of estimates within which fair value is highly likely to lie;	41.54		

Ref.	Presentation/Disclosure Requirement	Source	Y, N or N/A	W/P Ref.
	(d) the depreciation method used; (e) the useful lives or the depreciation rates used; and (f) the gross carrying amount and the accumulated depreciation (aggregated with accumulated impairment losses) at the beginning and end of the period.			
12010	If, during the current period, an enterprise measures biological assets at their cost less any accumulated depreciation and any accumulated impairment losses, the enterprise should disclose any gain or loss recognised on disposal of such biological assets and the reconciliation required under item 12008 above should disclose amounts related to such biological assets separately.	41.55		
12011	In the circumstances described at item 12010, the reconciliation should also include the following amounts included in net profit or loss related to those biological assets: (a) impairment losses; (b) reversals of impairment losses; and (c) depreciation.			
12012	If the fair value of biological assets previously measured at their cost less any accumulated depreciation and any accumulated impairment losses becomes reliably measurable during the current period, the enterprise should disclose for those biological assets: (a) a description of the biological assets; (b) an explanation of why fair value has become reliably measurable; and (c) the effect of the change.	41.56		
	GOVERNMENT GRANTS			
12013	The enterprise should disclose the following related to agricultural activity covered by IAS 41: (a) the nature and extent of government grants recognised in the financial statements; (b) unfulfilled conditions and other contingencies attaching to government grants; and	41.57		

Ref.	Presentation/Disclosure Requirement	Source	Y, N or N/A	W/P Ref.
	(c) significant decreases expected in the level of government grants.			
	TRANSITION			
12014	If the enterprise applies IAS 41 for periods beginning before 1 January 2003 (its effective date), that fact should be disclosed.	41.58		

Index

References are to paragraph number.

Examples and Appendices in the text are indicated by italic type. The abbreviation App indicates references to the Appendices